T0183140

Lecture Notes in Computer Science 9878

Commenced Publication in 1973
Founding and Former Series Editors:
Gerhard Goos, Juris Hartmanis, and Jan van Leeuwen

More information about this series at http://www.springer.com/series/7410

Ioannis Askoxylakis · Sotiris Ioannidis
Sokratis Katsikas · Catherine Meadows (Eds.)

Computer Security – ESORICS 2016

21st European Symposium on Research in Computer Security
Heraklion, Greece, September 26–30, 2016
Proceedings, Part I

 Springer

Editors

Ioannis Askoxylakis
Institute of Computer Science
Foundation for Research and
  Technology - Hellas
Heraklion
Greece

Sotiris Ioannidis
Institute of Computer Science
Foundation for Research and
  Technology - Hellas
Heraklion
Greece

Sokratis Katsikas
Norwegian University of Science and
  Technology
Gjøvik
Norway

Catherine Meadows
Naval Research Laboratory
Washington, DC
USA

ISSN 0302-9743   ISSN 1611-3349 (electronic)
Lecture Notes in Computer Science
ISBN 978-3-319-45743-7   ISBN 978-3-319-45744-4 (eBook)
DOI 10.1007/978-3-319-45744-4

Library of Congress Control Number: 2016949626

LNCS Sublibrary: SL4 – Security and Cryptology

Printed on acid-free paper

This Springer imprint is published by Springer Nature
The registered company is Springer International Publishing AG Switzerland

Preface

This volume contains papers selected for presentation and publication at the 21st European Symposium on Research in Computer Security, ESORICS, held September 26–30, in Heraklion, Greece.

Out of 285 submissions from 40 countries, the conference accepted 60 papers, resulting in an acceptance rate of 21 %. These papers cover a wide range of topics in security and privacy, including data protection, systems security, network security, access control, authentication, and security in such emerging areas as cloud computing, cyber-physical systems, and the Internet of Things. The papers were reviewed and then discussed online by a 105-member Program Committee, along with 313 external reviewers.

ESORICS 2016 would not have been possible without the contributions of the many volunteers who devoted their time and energy to make this happen. We would like to thank the Program Committee and the external reviewers for their hard work in evaluating the papers. We would also like to thank the ESORICS Steering Committee and its Chair Pierangela Samarati; the Publicity Chairs, Manolis Stamatogiannakis and Youki Kadobayashi; the Local Arrangement Committee, Nikolaos Petroulakis, Andreas Miaoudakis, and Panos Chatziadam, for arranging the beautiful location in Crete; the workshop chair, Javier Lopez, and all workshop co-chairs, who organized workshops co-located with ESORICS. We also give thanks to the many institutions for their support of ESORICS: the Horizon 2020 projects SHARCS and Virtuwind, the Hellenic Authority for Communication Security and Privacy (ADAE), the European Agency for Network and Information Security (ENISA), Huawei Technologies Co., Bournemouth University, and the CIPSEC project.

Finally, we would like to give our thanks to the authors who submitted their papers to ESORICS. They, more than anyone else, are what makes this conference possible. Welcome to ESORICS 2016!

July 2016

Ioannis Askoxylakis
Sotiris Ioannidis
Sokratis Katsikas
Catherine Meadows

Organization

General Chairs

Ioannis Askoxylakis   Hellenic Authority for Communication Security
and Privacy (ADAE) & FORTH, Greece
Sotiris Ioannidis   FORTH, Greece

Program Chairs

Sokratis K. Katsikas   Norwegian University of Science and Technology,
Norway
Catherine Meadows   Naval Research Laboratory, USA

Workshops Chair

Javier Lopez   University of Malaga, Spain

Program Committee

Gail-Joon Ahn   Arizona State University, USA
Magnus Almgren   Chalmers University of Technology, Sweden
Manos Antonakakis   Georgia Institute of Technology, USA
Alessandro Armando   DIBRIS - University of Genoa, Italy
Michael Backes   Saarland University and Max Planck Institute
for Software Systems, Germany
Giampaolo Bella   Università degli studi di Catania, Italy
Carlo Blundo   Università degli Studi di Salerno, Italy
Stefan Brunthaler   SBA Research, Austria
Rainer Böhme   University of Innsbruck, Austria
Christian Cachin   IBM Research - Zurich, Switzerland
Liqun Chen   Hewlett Packard Labs, UK
Tom Chothia   University of Birmingham, UK
Sherman S.M. Chow   Chinese University of Hong Kong, Hong Kong
Cas Cremers   University of Oxford, UK
Frédéric Cuppens   Telecom Bretagne, France
Nora Cuppens-Boulahia   Telecom Bretagne, France
Mads Dam   KTH, Sweden
Sabrina De Capitani   Università degli Studi di Milano, Italy
di Vimercati
Hervé Debar   Télécom SudParis, France
Roberto Di Pietro   Bell Labs, France

Additional Reviewers

Ahmed, Tahmina
Akand, Mamun
Ali, Mohammed
Aliberti, Giulio
Aminanto, Muhamad Erza
Anagnostopoulos, Marios
Anand, S. Abhishek
Asghari, Hadi
Asif, Hafiz
Axelsson, Stefan
Bacis, Enrico
Balliu, Musard
Bardas, Alexandru G.
Batten, Ian
Baumann, Christoph
Bayou, Lyes
Bello, Luciano
Berrang, Pascal
Bhatt, Sandeep
Biswas, Bhaskar
Blanco-Justicia, Alberto
Bruni, Alessandro
Bugiel, Sven
Calzavara, Stefano
Carbone, Roberto
Carmichael, Peter
Cha, Sang Gil
Chang, Bing
Chen, Ping
Chen, Rongmao
Cheng, Yuan
Choi, Rakyong
Chu, Cheng Kang
Chu, Cheng-Kang
Ciampi, Michele
Cianfriglia, Marco
Clarke, Dylan
Cohn-Gordon, Katriel
Coletta, Alessio
Costa, Gabriele
Costantino, Gianpiero
Cuvelier, Edouard

Dai, Ting
Davies, Philip
De Gaspari, Fabio
De Meo, Federico
Dehnel-Wild, Martin
Denzel, Michael
Dimitriadis, Antonios
Djoko, Judicael
Dreier, Jannik
Drogkaris, Prokopios
Drosatos, George
Elkhiyaoui, Kaoutar
Emms, Martin
Engelke, Toralf
Espes, David
Fahl, Sascha
Farràs, Oriol
Fett, Daniel
Fuchs, Ludwig
Garratt, Luke
Garrison, William
Gay, Richard
Geneiatakis, Dimitris
Georgiopoulou,
    Zafeiroula
Giannetsos, Thanassis
Giustolisi, Rosario
Gottschlich, Wolfram
Grohmann, Bjoern
Guan, Le
Guanciale, Roberto
Guarnieri, Marco
Gupta, Maanak
Gyftopoulos, Sotirios
Hallberg, Sven M.
Hallgren, Per
Han, Jinguang
Hassan, Sabri
Haupert, Vincent
He, Yongzhong
Hedin, Daniel
Henricksen, Matt

Hitaj, Briland
Horst, Matthias
Hu, Wenhui
Huang, Heqing
Huang, Qiong
Hummer, Matthias
Iliadis, John
Imran-Daud, Malik
Iovino, Vincenzo
Iwaya Horn, Leonardo
Jackson, Dennis
Jager, Tibor
Jarecki, Stanislaw
Jasser, Stefanie
Jiang, Hemin
Journault, Anthony
Kamm, Liina
Kandias, Miltos
Karegar, Farzaneh
Karopoulos, George
Koshutanski, Hristo
Koutsiamanis,
    Remous Aris
Krishnan, Ram
Kuchta, Veronika
Kunz, Michael
Kywe, Su Mon
Köhler, Olaf Markus
Lai, Russell W.F.
Lancrenon, Jean
Laube, Stefan
Lauer, Sebastian
Leichter, Carl
Lerman, Liran
Li, Depeng
Li, Yan
Li, Yuping
Lim, Hoon Wei
Lindemann, Jens
Lindner, Andreas
Liu, Jianghua
Liu, Naiwei

Liu, Ximing
Liu, Xing
Luhn, Sebastian
Lyvas, Christos
Ma, Jinhua
Magkos, Emmanouil
Magri, Bernardo
Manoharan, Praveen
Manulis, Mark
Marktscheffel, Tobias
Martinovic, Ivan
Marwah, Manish
Marx, Matthias
McCorry, Patrick
Mehrnezhad, Maryam
Meng, Weizhi
Merlo, Alessio
Meyer, Maxime
Min, Byungho
Moataz, Tarik
Mogire, Nancy
Mohamed, Manar
Mohammadi, Esfandiar
Montoya, Lorena
Moore, Nicholas
Mowbray, Miranda
Mueller, Johannes
Mykoniati, Maria
Mylonas, Alexios
Möser, Malte
Müller, Tilo
Müller, Tobias
Nelson, Mark
Nemati, Hamed
Neupane, Ajaya
Nguyen, Binh
Nuñez, David
Ntantogian, Christoforos
Önen, Melek
Pagnin, Elena
Palmieri, Paolo
Panico, Agostino
Pankova, Alisa
Park, Jaehong
Parra Rodriguez, Juan D.
Parra-Arnau, Javier

Peroli, Michele
Peters, Thomas
Petrovic, Slobodan
Pham, Vinh
Pitropakis, Nikolaos
Pridöhl, Henning
Puchta, Alexander
Pulls, Tobias
Quaglia, Elizabeth
Radomirovic, Sasa
Rafnsson, Willard
Ranise, Silvio
Rao, Prasad
Reif, Sebastian
Reinecke, Philipp
Rekleitis, Evangelos
Ren, Chuangang
Reuben, Jenni
Rial, Alfredo
Ribeiro De Mello,
    Emerson
Ribes-González, Jordi
Ricci, Sara
Richthammer, Hartmut
Rios, Ruben
Rizomiliotis, Panagiotis
Rocchetto, Marco
Rochet, Florentin
Roenne, Peter
Roth, Christian
Rothstein Morris, Eric
Ruan, Na
Salas, Julián
Saracino, Andrea
Schmitz, Guido
Schranz, Oliver
Schreckling, Daniel
Schöttle, Pascal
Seidel, Peter-Michael
Sgandurra, Daniele
Shafienejad, Masoumeh
Shah, Ankit
Shahandashti, Siamak
Sharifian, Setareh
Sheikhalishahi, Mina
Shi, Jie

Shirvanian, Maliheh
Shojaie, Bahareh
Shrestha, Babins
Shrestha, Prakash
Shulman, Haya
Sideri, Maria
Siim, Sander
Sjösten, Alexander
Soria-Comas, Jordi
Sorniotti, Alessandro
Sprick, Barbara
Squarcina, Marco
Stamatelatos, Giorgos
Stamatiou, Yannis
Staudemeyer, Ralf C.
Stergiopoulos, George
Stüttgen, Johannes
Su, Dong
Sy, Erik
Sänger, Johannes
Taheri, Somayeh
Tasch, Markus
Tasidou, Aimilia
Teheri, Somayeh
Teixeira, André
Tempesta, Mauro
Thoma, Cory
Thompson, Matthew
Truderung, Tomasz
Tsalis, Nikolaos
Tsoumas, Bill
Tupakula, Udaya
Verderame, Luca
Virvilis, Nick
Vrakas, Nikos
Walter, Marie-Therese
Wang, Bolun
Wang, Gang
Wang, Guilin
Wang, Ruoyu
Weber, Alexandra
Weber, Michael
Wei, Zhuo
Williams, David
Wolff, Marcus
Wu, Shuang

Wu, Wei
Wundram, Martin
Wüchner, Tobias
Xiao, Gaoyao
Xing, Xinyu
Xu, Jia
Xu, Ke
Yahia, Muzamil
Yaich, Reda

Yang, Guomin
Yang, Weining
Yautsiukhin, Artsiom
Yerukhimovich, Arkady
Yfantopoulos, Nikos
Yu, Jiangshan
Yu, Xingjie
Yuen, Tsz Hon
Zang, Wanyu

Zavatteri, Matteo
Zerkane, Salaheddine
Zhang, Liang Feng
Zhang, Weiquan
Zhao, Yongjun
Zhou, Lan
Zimmer, Ephraim

Contents – Part I

Detection and Monitoring

Cryptography for Cloud Computing

Operating Systems Security

Information Flow

Software Security

Contents – Part II

E-voting and E-commerce

Security of the Internet of Things

Data Privacy

Security of Cyber-Physical Systems

Attacks

Attribute-Based Cryptography

Network and Web Security

Understanding Cross-Channel Abuse with SMS-Spam Support Infrastructure Attribution

Bharat Srinivasan[1]([✉]), Payas Gupta[2], Manos Antonakakis[1], and Mustaque Ahamad[1,2]

[1] Georgia Institute of Technology, Atlanta, USA
{bharat.srini,manos}@gatech.edu, mustaq@cc.gatech.edu
[2] New York University Abu Dhabi, Abu Dhabi, UAE
payasgupta@nyu.edu

Abstract. Recent convergence of telephony with the Internet offers malicious actors the ability to craft cross-channel attacks that leverage both telephony and Internet resources. Bulk messaging services can be used to send unsolicited SMS messages to phone numbers. While the long-term properties of email spam tactics have been extensively studied, such behavior for SMS spam is not well understood. In this paper, we discuss a novel SMS abuse attribution system called CHURN. The proposed system is able to collect data about large SMS abuse campaigns and analyze their passive DNS records and supporting website properties. We used CHURN to systematically conduct attribution around the domain names and IP addresses used in such SMS spam operations over a five year time period. Using CHURN, we were able to make the following observations about SMS spam campaigns: (1) only 1 % of SMS abuse domains ever appeared in public domain blacklists and more than 94 % of the blacklisted domain names did not appear in such public blacklists for several weeks or even months after they were first reported in abuse complaints, (2) more than 40 % of the SMS spam domains were active for over 100 days, and (3) the infrastructure that supports the abuse is surprisingly stable. That is, the same SMS spam domain names were used for several weeks and the IP infrastructure that supports these campaigns can be identified in a few networks and a small number of IPs, for several months of abusive activities. Through this study, we aim to increase the situational awareness around SMS spam abuse, by studying this phenomenon over a period of five years.

1 Introduction

The telephony channel has undergone radical changes in the recent past, including its *convergence with the Internet* via technologies such as smartphones and Voice over IP (VoIP). Although this convergence offers many benefits, it also provides malicious actors the ability to design new attack vectors that combine resources from both the telephony and Internet channels. For instance, text messages containing web links can be sent to phone numbers to direct unsuspecting users to malicious websites [19]. Attacks that exploit the telephony channel can

© Springer International Publishing Switzerland 2016
I. Askoxylakis et al. (Eds.): ESORICS 2016, Part I, LNCS 9878, pp. 3–26, 2016.
DOI: 10.1007/978-3-319-45744-4_1

potentially be more effective than traditional attacks over the Internet, as they can abuse the trust that has traditionally been associated with telephony. Similar to traditional email messaging, SMS [18] has become a popular abuse target, as past research efforts have shown [30,35,36,38].

While traditional email spamming activities have been extensively studied, long-term properties of SMS spam operations are not well understood by the community. SMS abuse data and long-term network traffic observation of such abuse are necessary to study the behavior of SMS spam operations. By using data that spans a period of close to five years, in this study we aim to present such a long-term analysis of SMS spam abuse. Our hope is that such analysis will provide better understanding of the network properties of SMS spam abuse which can be used to build more effective defenses against it.

We call SMS spam *cross-channel abuse* because it relies on and can be observed in both the telephony and Internet channels. In other words, such attacks involve both a telephony resource (e.g., a phone number) and a traditional Internet resource (i.e., a domain name and/or an IP address). To study cross channel abuse, we explore how SMS spam campaigns utilize the domain name system (DNS) and other Internet infrastructure. We build a SMS spam attribution system called CHURN, which is used to analyze abuse data from a period of five years. CHURN analyzes SMS-spam datasets from two different abuse reporting sources: passive DNS datasets from a large Internet Service Provider (ISP), and application layer web information around these SMS spam campaigns. CHURN's ultimate goal is the attribution of SMS spam campaigns with respect to the domain name infrastructure they employ in their abuse activities.

Our SMS spam attribution analysis reveals that cross channel abuse is highly effective and long lived. We found that the Internet IP infrastructure used by the spammers to support SMS spam campaigns is surprisingly stable. For example, abuse campaigns tend to use a handful of IPs in a few networks over several years to continue their activities. This shows current defenses are either unaware of the abuse infrastructure utilized by SMS spam campaigns or they are not effectively using such information to combat cross-channel abuse. We hope that our paper will demonstrate the value of situational awareness around this problem, which could be used to reduce the potential for social engineering and other attacks facilitated through such cross channel abuse. Summarizing, our paper makes the following contributions:

- We build and present a cross-channel attribution system to automate the collection and analysis of SMS spam abuse. Our system, namely CHURN, uses a hierarchical clustering technique that employs network level, application level, and popularity-based statistical features to cluster related SMS spam domain names into campaigns over time.
- Using CHURN, we conduct a five year study that yields attribution results for a plethora of real world SMS spam campaigns. We use (1) 8.32 million SMS abuse reports that consist of messages that directed users to scam websites, (2) more than 56 thousand DNS resource records related to the SMS

abuse reports since 2011, and (3) more than 67 thousand web pages reflecting the application layers of the SMS spam campaign. Our experiment helps us conclude the following:

- We show that a mere 1 % of SMS abuse domains appear on public Internet domain blacklists. Among the blacklisted domain names, 94 % appeared on blacklists weeks or even months after they were first seen in abuse reports.
- We show that the domains are long lived during the period of abuse with over 40 % of the SMS spam domains being active for over 100 days.
- We dive deep into the three largest and most long-lived case studies of SMS spam campaigns identified by CHURN. We show that (1) spammers were able to operate these campaigns for more than three years, (2) they consistently used a handful of IPs in a few abuse friendly networks, and (3) the average SMS spam domain name lifetime was in the order of two months, further emphasizing the lack of situational awareness around such cross-channel threats.

2 Background

Spammers have been evolving their operations for more than a decade. It comes as no surprise that as Internet defenses are bolstered, the telephony channel has become an attractive spam target. To better understand this, we aim to study the properties of unsolicited bulk SMS messaging (a.k.a. SMS spam) containing URLs with respect to the Internet infrastructure that supports this abuse. Since the attack relies on both telephony and Internet infrastructure (e.g., domains included in SMS spam URLs and associated IPs), we refer to this problem as "cross-channel abuse". In this section, we provide a high-level overview of the ecosystem that facilitates this cross channel abuse.

Delivering SMS Spam at Scale: To successfully "trick" users into scam operations, spammers need a way to reach potential victims. Because phone numbers come from a limited name space with a defined format, they can be auto-generated randomly or picked selectively. Armed with phone numbers, fraudsters can accomplish large scale distribution of SMS spam in several ways.

1. **Disposable SIMs:** Spammers can purchase disposable subscriber identification module (SIM) cards with gateways having slots to hold hundreds of them or use stolen cell phones and USB modems/Aircards [38] as an entry point into the cellular networks. They can then program these devices using off the shelf bulk SMS software or even Arduino [23] micro-controllers to send well crafted bulk SMS spam.
2. **Exploiting Cloud Telephony Services:** Legitimate cloud telephony Infrastructure as a Service (IaaS) providers such as Twilio [21] and Tropo [20], or even cellular ISPs [38], can be abused by spammers to deliver bulk SMS messages. This is achieved in one of three ways: (1) creating fraudulent

accounts on these platforms, (2) hijacking existing (legitimate) accounts, or (3) exploiting unprotected SMS application programming interfaces (APIs) that allow users to transmit a large volume of SMS messages in an automated fashion[1].

3. **Bulk SMS Services:** Spammers can exploit or collude with existing bulk SMS services to deliver messages. Sometimes, services offered by legitimate service providers enable bridging of the email and SMS mediums by allowing email to be sent as an SMS (or vice versa). This can be abused by spammers.

Monetization: After delivering the spam SMS messages, in order for monetization spammers lure victims into responding to, or interacting with, the message. Specially crafted messages with easy-to-click URLs provide an effective way to automate such response. On smartphone-like devices, victims can simply click these URLs and visit a traditional web site that will lure them into the scam. The key point here is that, while the attack vector clearly started as a telephony based communication (vis-à-vis, the SMS spam), these spammers will often try to social engineer the user into a scam using traditional Internet resources. There are multiple reasons to do this, from minimizing the forensic trail in the telephony network to re-utilizing already provisioned Internet infrastructure for abusive actions. Often the content of such illicit webpages can be tailored to the specific scam.

Observing Cross-Channel Abuse: Cross-channel abuse can be observed in both the telephony and Internet channels. Prior work in combating telephony abuse mainly relied on call detail records (CDRs) to identify and block phone numbers that originate spam SMS messages [35,38]. Cross-channel abuse also requires traditional Internet resources to direct victims to scam websites. This provides an opportunity to observe such communications by passively monitoring network traffic (i.e., the DNS resolutions). For example, when the recipient of an SMS message clicks an embedded link, it typically initiates a DNS resolution process. The end result of this resolution process is the mapping between the requested domain and the IP address hosting it. The client device typically requests the web page associated with the clicked link from the resolved IP address. The DNS visibility at the ISP (cellular or otherwise) recursive resolver level can serve as a great vantage point to study the SMS spam cross-channel abuse with respect to the Internet channel.

3   Cross-Channel Attribution Engine

In this section, we discuss the details of our Cross Channel Attribution Engine called CHURN. The goal of CHURN is to help understand SMS abuse by attributing domain names in SMS-spam campaigns. CHURN achieves this by clustering network (i.e., domain names and IPs) and application (i.e., HTML

---

[1] Although Twilio and others have a policy against such abuse [22], spammers often find ways to violate it [14].

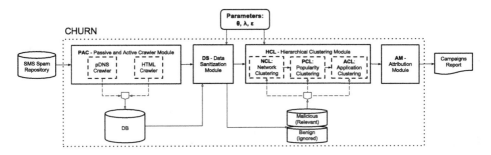

Fig. 1. The cross-channel attribution engine.

content) layer signals that facilitate a given spam campaign. CHURN starts with crowd sourced abuse complaints and produces attributed campaigns with associated network resources. To accomplish this, it performs four tasks serially, as can be seen in Fig. 1. Next, we describe in detail each of these four tasks.

3.1   Data Collection Module

Our data collection module takes as input external data source(s) of known SMS-spam. In our case, this dataset comes from two sources: (i) SMS-spam complaint reports filed by consumers to the Federal Trade Commission (FTC) [3], which were made available to participants in the Robocall Challenge [6], and (ii) publicly available SMS complaint reports from the online portal SMS watchdog [15][2]. While reports from SMS watchdog were crawled between Jan 2011–Aug 2015, the FTC complaint records were limited to the period Jan 2011-Dec 2012 consisting of reports with anonymized destination numbers. Using SMS messages from user complaints as input, we extract the source (e.g., phone number), timestamp t_d, and URL from each SMS-spam report. Using the URLs, we actively crawl different public and private data sources, which provides information about both the website and the network hosting infrastructure facilitating the scam.

Passive DNS Crawler (Network Intelligence): Cross channel attacks, like users responding to SMS-spam messages, can be observed in the Internet when the recipient of the message clicks on the URL of a spam message. In this case, a DNS resolution request will be observable at the local recursive DNS servers. This forensic signal cannot be used to estimate the global abuse properties of a particular SMS-spam campaign, as it is non-trivial to obtain global visibility in the DNS recursive plane. However, given a large enough recursive DNS visibility, it could provide forensic evidence and lower bounds on the following three questions: (i) how long was the campaign active, (ii) what was the average lookup volume and a lower bound on the victims that were targeted by each SMS-spam

---

[2] smswatchdog.com was down when we last checked as on 02/18/2016 but snapshots of it can be found on the Wayback Machine [9].

message, and (iii) what was the domain name and IP network infrastructure that supported this cross channel abuse?

By gaining access to a large private passive DNS repository, we were able to "crawl" and collect datasets that could answer these three questions for every domain name contained in our SMS-spam abuse dataset. As we will discuss in Subsect. 3.3, the passive DNS (pDNS) dataset plays an important role in our effort to statistically describe the network properties of SMS-based abuse.

HTML Crawler (Application Intelligence): We implement both an active and a passive method to collect datasets that capture application layer properties of the SMS-spam websites. We download and store the full HTML source from the web page pointed to by each URL seen in SMS-spam reports. In many cases, however, the websites of interest were taken down before we could recover any useful intelligence. For such cases, we relied on the Wayback machine [9].

3.2   DS: Data Sanitization Module

The lifecycle of a spam domain involves multiple phases. In the first phase, when the threat is active, the domain will point to IP infrastructure that facilitates the spam operation. Once the spam operation is over, or the domain simply ceases to be used by the spammers, it will enter a phase when it is "parked" or is taken down by network defenders or eventually expires. From the threat analysis and attack attribution point of view, we care to analyze the network infrastructure when the domain is actively used by a spam campaign. The goal of the sanitization module is to weed out the benign infrastructure (in the form of legitimate IP addresses) and HTML sources (related to parked domains) while retaining the network and application information that can be used to analyze the campaigns. Next, we discuss in detail how we can achieve this sanitization of the datasets.

Filtering the pDNS Datasets: Among the domains included in the URLs received in the complaints, we first remove any records containing domains historically appearing in the Alexa [2] top 1 million ranks since 2011. We were able to remove 715 domains using this filter. Next, we use two heuristics to remove DNS information that is related to legitimate IP infrastructure from our datasets. The first heuristic aims to capture the *popularity* of the infrastructure supporting a domain. Parking IP address space is often used to host a relatively large number of domains, at least that is how "domaineers" operate. The number of resource records per IP is a good measure of this as it encapsulates both the diversity in the domains and the popularity in DNS lookup value to domains hosted on certain IPs. The second heuristic aims toward the characterization of the *name server* list supporting a domain. Some name servers (NS) are well known to be associated with parking activities, as they do not try to hide. We create a hard curated list of such name servers using publicly available information and prior work [8, 44].

More precisely, given a set of pDNS resource records denoted by RR, the sanitization module uses a filter method that uses parking IP threshold θ_p and a name server list, denoted by NS, to create a filtered set, $RR^{\theta_p, NS}$, which consists of all $rr \in RR$ s.t. (i) IP in rr is pointed to by $<\theta_p$ resource records, and (ii) the name server for the domain name d in the $rr \notin \{NS\}$. Figure 2 shows the cumulative distribution function (eCDF) of the number of resource records hosted per IP in our dataset and the cut-off threshold θ_p. In total we were able to identify

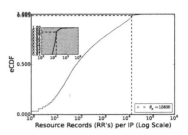

Fig. 2. CDF of resource records per IP with cut-off threshold θ_p.

$\sim 1\%$ (232 out of 23,269) IPs as parking and ignore records associated with them for the shown value of θ_p.

Filtering Application-level Data: To identify the full HTML sources relating to parked domains, we built a supervised binary classifier to identify if an HTML source file was related to a parked domain or not. To train our classifier, we used 20 features extracted from HTML sources. These features included number of links in the source, number of unique domains in the links, minimum, maximum and average link length, number of external links, ratio of internal to external links, website directory presence, source length, text to html ratio based on the number of characters, presence of Javascript redirect and meta refresh redirection mechanisms, boolean value for if the meta domain was external, number of frames and iframes and respective number of distinct frame and iframe domains and boolean values to indicate if any of the iframe or frame domains were external. We also counted the number of images present in the HTML source. Intuition behind these features can be found in the work by Vissers et al. [44].

We trained the SVM model [31] using the 10-fold cross validation technique on a set of 200 parking and 200 non-parking feature vectors extracted from webpages in our dataset. With a threshold of 0.5 we were able to achieve a reasonable TPR of 99.5% and FPR of 1.5%.

Table 1. Confusion matrix for the parking classifier.

	Predicted: NP	Predicted: P	Total
Actual: NP	197	3	200
Actual: P	1	199	200
Total	198	202	

Table 1 shows the confusion matrix using 10-fold cross validation related to this experiment, where NP denotes non-parking webpages and P denotes parking webpages. In total, the classifier was able to identify $\approx 10\%$ (7510/75,085) webpages as parking. These were discarded from further processing.

3.3   HCL: Hierarchical Clustering Module

To find clusters of related domain names associated with cross-channel abuse in a given epoch (time period, t), we follow a hierarchical clustering process. This process can be separated into three different levels. In the first level (NCL), we cluster together domain names based on the network infrastructure properties. In the second level (PCL), first level (NCL) clusters that satisfy a cardinality constraint (based on threshold λ) get further clustered according to the DNS volumetric popularity of the domains within it. In the third and final clustering step (ACL), second level (PCL) clusters that satisfy an entropy (flux) constraint (based on threshold ϵ) get further separated based on the web content of each domain within it. This way, the entire process produces clusters of high quality at different levels which are then labeled by the attribution module (Sect. 3.4).

   In order to execute these three different clustering steps, we employ the most common statistical features from the areas of DNS [25–27] and HTML [42] modeling. To be clear, we do not claim novelty about the use of these features. Rather, our goal is to show that already discussed features combined in this novel hierarchical clustering method can provide an efficient and effective attribution system for SMS-spam abuse. Next, we briefly discuss how we used these established statistical features in the context of the three modules of our system.

Network-Based Clustering (NCL): To compute network layer features in a given time epoch t, for each domain d in the domain set $\mathcal{D}$ under consideration, we compute two sets: (i) RHIP(d) which is a set of all IPs that have historically mapped to domain d, and (ii) RHDN(IP) which is the set of domains that have historically been linked with the IP in the RHIP set. This could also include domains that are not in $\mathcal{D}$. Using the collection of all domains $\mathcal{D}$, the $pDNS$ dataset and a specified epoch t, the network feature-based clustering submodule generates a matrix $A_{m \times n}$ where $m = |\mathcal{D}|$ represents the total number of domains and $n = |\underset{i}{\cup} RHIP(d_i)|$ represents the total number of IPs historically associated with all domains in $\mathcal{D}$ during an epoch t. The matrix A is computed as follows,

$$A_{i,j} = \begin{cases} \frac{H(d_i)}{|RHDN(ip_j)|} & \text{if } ip_j \in RHIP(d_i) \\ 0 & \text{otherwise} \end{cases} \tag{1}$$

where $i \in \{0, 1, \ldots |\mathcal{D}| - 1\}$ and $j \in \{0, 1, \ldots | \underset{i}{\cup} RHIP(d_i)| - 1\}$. Also, $H(d) = -\sum_{k \in C(d)} p_k * log_2(p_k)$, where $C(d)$ represents the unique set of characters in domain name d and p_k represents the probability of the occurrence of a given character in the domain name. Thus, $H(d)$ gives us the entropy of the name of domain d based on relative character frequencies. The inclusion of the entropy factor in the numerator increases the confidence of producing high quality clusters given the frequent use of DGAs [28, 46] by adversaries.

   Finally, we use Singular Value Decomposition (SVD) [45] to reduce the dimensionality of the sparse matrix $A_{m \times n}$ to $A_{m \times \tilde{n}}$ where $\tilde{n} < n$. The network clustering module then uses the X-Means clustering algorithm [40] to cluster domains having similar network-level properties.

Popularity-Based Clustering (PCL): Sometimes, network level properties may be insufficient to distinguish between unrelated domains, leading to the formation of large clusters. We will see this in Sect. 4.2. Popularity based clustering uses features extracted from observing the popularity of domain names as measured by the number of the successful DNS resolutions to it within the epoch t. This in turn gives us a lower bound on the number of visits potentially made to the domain name via clicking on a URL embedded in an SMS message. It is computed using the information gathered in the passive DNS dataset. Let Lookup (d, dt) be a function that returns the number of lookups (or in other words, successful DNS resolutions) for domain d on a given date dt. And let C be the set of clusters produced by NCL. Using the pDNS data collection and a specified epoch t, the popularity cluster submodule builds matrices $B_{p \times q}(c_r)$ $\forall c_r \in C$ s.t. $|c_r| \geq \lambda$, $r \in \{0, 1, \ldots |C| - 1\}$ where λ is a provided threshold and $|C|$ is the number of clusters produced by NCL. Here, $p = |c_r|$, the number of domains in a cluster from NCL and q are the total dates in a given epoch. The matrix B is computed as follows, $B_{i,j}(c_r) = Lookup(d_i, dt_j)$ where d_i is a domain name and dt_j is a date in epoch t and c_r is a NCL cluster. The intuition behind this matrix follows from the work by Antonakakis et al. [26] which aims to measure the volumetric DNS request patterns to domain names over time, within a NCL cluster (in our case).

Similar to the NCL module, each matrix is dimensionally reduced using SVD followed by X-Means clustering algorithm to cluster domains having similar popularity levels. Therefore, at the end of PCL, we have: (i) smaller clusters from NCL that had sufficient network level information ($|c_r| < \lambda$), and (ii) PCL (sub)-clusters from the larger NCL clusters that required the additional popularity information for further refinement.

Application-Based Clustering (ACL): To further refine and resolve any remaining confusion between domain names after PCL, we proceed to a final clustering step that aims to group together domain names with similar domain structure and web content. To cluster similar domains based on their structure, we compute the standard deviation σ of the entropy of domain names in a cluster produced after the PCL module. Let T represent the set of domains in a PCL cluster and $H(T)$ be the set of entropies associated with domain names in T. If $\sigma(H(T)) \geq \epsilon$, i.e., the standard deviation in the entropy of the domain names in the cluster is greater than the threshold ϵ, we apply application based clustering to a PCL cluster. Again, the motivation behind using entropy as a metric to assess the quality of clusters is similar to its purpose during NCL.

Once the clusters requiring application based clustering are identified, we use features extracted from the full HTML source of the web pages associated with domains. Note that there could be multiple and different sources of web pages associated with a certain domain. We use the timestamp of the complaint associated with domains to identify relevant HTML sources in a given epoch. Once we have the domains and their corresponding HTML content, we compute TF-IDF statistical vector on the bag of words on each cluster c [42]. Since the matrix is expected to be quite sparse, the application cluster submodule performs dimensionality reduction using SVD. Once we have the reduced application based feature vectors representing corresponding domains, this module uses the X-Means clustering algorithm to cluster domains hosting similar content.

3.4   AM: Cluster Attribution Module

The cluster attribution module is used to label clusters with keywords that are representative of a campaign's theme. To do this, we leverage the observation that a majority of the domain names involved with cross-channel abuse, despite being auto-generated using domain generation algorithms (DGAs) [28,46], have certain keywords in the domain name itself that are relevant to the theme of a campaign. In other words, the domain names are not completely random. The aim is to lure the victim into visiting these domains via their smartphones and a well designed domain name increases the odds of clicking the URL. For example, domain names `yourfastcashsystem[dot]com`, `24hrpaysite[dot]com`, `target.com.ctarg[dot]com`, have keywords cash, pay and target respectively that give us useful clues to what the domain might pertain to.

Using this observation, we use the Viterbi algorithm [33] to filter the domain names in a given cluster to a sequence of words such as [`your`, `fast`, `cash`, `system`] in the case of `yourfastcashsystem[dot]com` and [`24`, `hr`, `pay`, `site`] in the case of `24hrpaysite[dot]com`. More formally, let C be a cluster produced after the entire clustering process and let D be the set of domains in the cluster. For each domain $d \in D$, we create a set $U(d)$ that consists of all the parts of the domain name d except the effective top level domain (eTLD) (e.g. U('abc.example.com') = {abc, example}). Next, we compute the set of words $W(U(d))$ using the Viterbi algorithm. Therefore, W(U('abc.example.com')) = {example} since 'abc' is not a valid English word. Using W, we increment the frequency counter for the word 'example' in a cluster specific dictionary. In this manner, after iterating over all domains in the cluster, we get a keyword to frequency mapping from which we pick the top most frequent word(s) to attribute the cluster.

4   Results

In this section, we begin by describing the data collected and used in CHURN for SMS-spam attribution. We then dive deeper into both CHURN's clustering results and the attribution accuracy of the system.

4.1   Datasets

CHURN starts with an SMS-spam repository we developed from the sources mentioned in Sect. 3. It had ≈8.32 million SMS-spam reports. The data collection module used the domain names found in these reports to collect surrounding pDNS, HTML and domain blacklist information using passive and active crawling methods. All these datasets were continuously gathered over a period of four

Table 2. Summary of collected datasets.

Epoch	RRs (Domain, IP) tuples	Domains (FQDN)	IPs (Hosts)	HTML sources	Complaints
Jan–Dec 2011	17,291	6,159	10,537	16,492	30,973
Jan–Dec 2012	17,316	7,846	8,218	16,321	125,960
Jan–Dec 2013	18,374	7,682	8,793	15,553	2,504,836
Jan–Dec 2014	22,426	7,438	8,858	15,334	3,286,988
Jan–Aug 2015	10,165	5,067	5,627	3,875	2,371,417
Total:	56,940	17,528	23,037	67,575	8,320,174

years and eight months, starting in January 2011 and ending in August 2015, ensuring an overlapping time period.

The pDNS crawler was able to observe and record DNS Resource Records (RRs), which gives us a temporal mark between a domain name and an IP address when the SMS-spam was active. We collected 17,528 unique fully qualified domain names, 23,037 distinct IP addresses and 56,940 unique RRs related to the cross-channel abuse. Regarding the HTML datasets around this SMS spam abuse, we were able to download 67,575 distinct pages with the corresponding HTML source code. We summarize all this information across different epochs in Table 2.

Temporal Characteristics of Cross-Channel SMS-Spam. Figure 3(a) shows the number of daily SMS complaint reports retrieved and analyzed by our system. Although there are fluctuations in the number of daily complaints, the overall volume of such complaints steadily increased over time. We suspect that the sudden surge in the number of complaints received in early 2013 is due to both a proactive effort by both FTC (and other regulatory parties) to encourage people to report such spam and also an increase in the awareness among consumers of the available reporting tools. The period between mid-2013 to mid-2015 shows a relatively steady volume of SMS-spam reports with only marginal increase in the number of daily complaints. This signals that the more

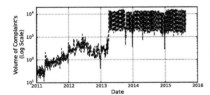 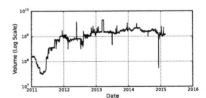

(a) Number of daily complaints from both smswatchdog.com and FTC complaints.

(b) Daily aggregated passive DNS lookup volume trend for cross-channel spam domains.

Fig. 3. Temporal characteristics of collected datasets.

dominant spam campaigns had stabilized during this time period. In addition, it is also possible that the number of consumers willing to report such spam had reached a saturation point. Finally, Fig. 3(b) shows the daily aggregated DNS lookup volume to SMS-spam domains based on data collected from a large passive DNS repository. We clearly see an uptake and a steady DNS lookup volume over time, showing that the cross-channel SMS based abuse is a persisting phenomenon.

Lifetime of SMS-Spam Domains. Figure 4 shows the empirical cumulative distribution function (eCDF) of the lifetime of all domains seen in the campaigns. The lifetime of a domain is derived by using the timestamp of the first and last seen DNS resolution to a particular domain. We observe that ≈30 % of the domains had a lifetime of less than 10 days, close to ≈30 % of domains had a lifetime between 10 and 100 days and the remaining ≈40 % had a lifetime between 100 and 480 days. This indicates that cross-channel spam domains are alive for much longer periods compared to traditional spam abuse, and

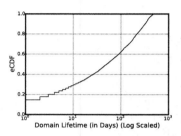

Fig. 4. The eCDF of the lifetime of all domains showing long-lived SMS-spam domains.

even certain type of agile botnet abuse such as fast-flux networks [39]. To better study the evolution of SMS-spam abuse, in the remainder of the paper we break and analyze the datasets into yearly epochs.

Reputation Properties of SMS-Spam Infrastructure. Using domains from public blacklists (PBL), namely 'Malware Domains List' [12], 'sans' [17], 'Spamhaus Blacklist' [16], 'itmate' [10], 'sagadc' [13], 'hphosts' [7], 'abuse.ch' [1] and 'MalcOde' Database [11], we verify if and when an SMS-spam domain appeared in any of the PBLs. These PBLs typically include phishing domains, botnet domains, malware sites and other unsafe domains serving malicious content. Given that the cross-channel domains are alive for a long time and the cross-channel spamming is relatively newer, it was not clear whether the traditional blacklists are keeping pace with SMS-spam domains. Indeed, our finding shows that SMS-spam abuse is practically unknown to the PBLs. In total, we had only 177 out of the 17,528, a mere 1 %, fully qualified domain names (FQDNs) listed in PBLs. Out of this, 170 domains were listed in a single list while seven domains were listed in two different lists. Moreover, when we checked all the effective second level domain names (e2LD) against the same lists, we only found 15 out of 17,502 (a minuscule 0.08 %) e2LDs listed in one or more of the lists — with 11 e2TLDs being listed in a single list while four eTLDs were listed in two different lists. This provides clear evidence that traditional reputation feeds are failing to identify the cross-channel domains even in a postmortem way.

Diving a bit deeper in the blacklisted domains, we wanted to measure the timeliness of the blacklist updates. To achieve this, we computed two metrics Δ_1 and Δ_2. For a blacklisted SMS-spam domain d, $\Delta_1(d)$ measures the difference in

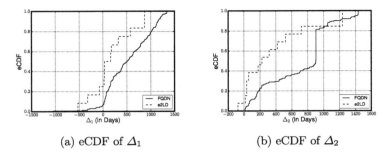

(a) eCDF of Δ_1 (b) eCDF of Δ_2

Fig. 5. Timeliness of blacklists

days between the earliest date the SMS-spam domain was seen on a blacklist and the earliest date the domain was seen in an SMS-spam message in our complaint repository. $\Delta_2(d)$ measures the difference in days between the earliest date the domain was seen in a blacklist and the earliest date it was looked up, according to the passive DNS visibility we obtained.

Figure 5(a) shows the empirical cumulative distribution (eCDF) of Δ_1 over all blacklisted domains. We show two plots, one for the FQDNs and the other for the e2LDs. A positive value for Δ_1 means that the blacklisting happened after the earliest complaint was received, whereas a negative value implies that the blacklisting happened before the earliest complaint was received. From the eCDF of FQDNs, it is clear that around 94 % of the blacklisted FQDNs were blacklisted after the complaint was received ranging from zero to 1,393 days. It is clear that the blacklists are rather slow in incorporating the domains. In some cases, about 6 % FQDNs were blacklisted even before a complaint was received, indicating that sometimes either the SMS-spam is not reported on time or existing abuse domains related to traditional spam are being reused to cater to cross-channel spam. We observed a similar pattern in the case of e2LD.

Figure 5(b) shows the eCDF for Δ_2 for FQDNs and e2LDs. A positive value for Δ_2 means that the blacklisting happened after the earliest pDNS lookup as seen by our sensors, whereas a negative value implies that the blacklisting happened before the earliest pDNS lookup as seen in the pDNS database. In majority of the cases we observed a huge lag in the timeliness of the blacklist update. The lag ranged from 13 to 1433 days in the case of FQDNs and from −78 to 1506 days (only one negative value was seen) in the case of e2LDs. Although these findings are for a relatively small number of domains (those that ever appeared in a blacklist), it is clear that the blacklists appear to be lagging in discovering SMS-spam domains.

4.2 Clustering Results

Given a time period or an epoch and a set of domains, CHURN processes them in the hierarchical way as described in Sect. 3.3. We discuss the clustering results at various levels next.

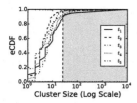
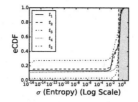
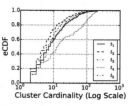

(a) eCDF of the cardinality of the clusters produced in the NCL module. Clusters with cardinality $\geqslant \lambda = 25$ (shown as vertical line $x = 25$) are processed further.

(b) eCDF of the standard deviation (σ) of entropy of domain names for clusters after the PCL module. Clusters with $\sigma \geqslant \epsilon = 0.2$ (shown as vertical line $x = 0.2$) are processed further.

(c) eCDF of the cardinality of all the clusters produced after all modules (NCL, PCL and ACL) for five different epochs.

Fig. 6. HCL thresholds

Clustering Network and Application Level Information. Figure 6(a) shows the empirical cumulative distribution of the cardinality (size) of the clusters produced after the network based clustering (NCL) step. Most of the clusters at this level contain few domains, but there exist some clusters that are quite large. We observed that up to 10 % of the clusters produced during network level clustering had a cardinality ≥ 25, with one cluster being as large as almost half the number of domains under consideration. For these large clusters we leverage the domain popularity information to further break them down during the popularity based clustering (PCL) phase. By setting $\lambda = 25$, we were able to identify clusters to be processed by the popularity clustering submodule.

Once we have clusters from the NCL and PCL phases, the resulting clusters with disparate domain names are further refined using application level clustering (ACL). This is necessitated for some large clusters produced in the PCL module. Figure 6(b) shows the eCDF of the standard deviation (σ) in entropy of domain names for all clusters thus produced, differentiated based on epoch. Selecting as threshold $\epsilon = 0.2$, we were able to mark up to 60 % of the clusters for further processing by the ACL module. Note that both the parameters λ (used in PCL) and ϵ (used in ACL) could be set according to the operator's needs. The application level clustering module gave us fine-grained clusters of very good quality with the largest cluster consisting of 201 domains across all epochs. Figure 6(c) shows the eCDF from the distribution of final cardinalities of all the clusters produced after all modules (NCL, PCL and ACL).

AM Results. The attribution module (AM) is used to label the clusters with keywords based on the domain name patterns. For illustration, Table 3 shows a sample output from this module. It can be seen that domains from certain campaigns can be attributed immediately after the NCL module. Some, however, are attributed after the PCL module and others after the ACL module. This indicates

Table 3. Representative sample of attributed clusters at various levels of the clustering hierarchy. Apart from the above and the case studies, we discovered campaigns related to selling drugs, adult content, free cruises, fake deals and many more.

Cluster level	Domain-(FQDN)	Label(s)	Epoch	Sample domains
3	8	Wire, deposit	2011	wire600.com, deposit1500.com
1	23	Buy, best	2012	bestbuy.com.bexy.biz, bestbuy.com.bwty.biz
2	20	Phone	2012	mobiletestandkeep.com, iphone5tryout.com
3	58	Cash	2013	startcreatingcash.com, trackingyoursuccess.com
1	4	News	2014	cnbcnews29.com, cnbcnews34.com
3	129	Loans, day, pay	2015	instanteasyloans.co.uk, checkonlinepaydayloans.com

that some campaigns can be identified just by using network features, while others require a combination of network, popularity and application features.

Evaluation. To evaluate the output of CHURN and validate our results, we created ground truth data by labeling domains with group labels. Each group label represents a campaign. We made the judgement of assigning a specific group label to a domain based on looking at the domain names and loading up their associated webpages in a browser. Our experiment consisted of six group labels corresponding to the Bestbuy, Target, Walmart, Financial Freedom, Payday and News campaigns depicted as Group 1–6 in that order. We were able to label 653 (3.7 %) domains in total to help us validate our results.

Table 4 shows how the results from CHURN measured up against the labeled data. System parameters λ and ϵ are varied to show the different cases. When λ is set to a relatively large value (i.e., 10,000), the output from the HCL module of CHURN is reduced to just the output of the NCL module since condition for PCL processing is never satisfied. The fourth threshold configuration shows that 427 out of the 653 domains were correctly attributed by CHURN using this setting. In the case when λ is set to a relatively small value (i.e., 2) and ϵ is set to a relatively large value (i.e., 2), the output from the HCL module of CHURN is reduced to output produced from applying the NCL and PCL modules sequentially but skipping the ACL module altogether. The third configuration shows that we attributed 504 out of 653 domains correctly using this setting.

Next is the case where λ and ϵ both are relatively small (i.e., 2 and 10^{-12} respectively). Such a setting results in all the modules NCL, PCL and ACL being serially applied to all clusters and domains without exception. This second configuration

Table 4. CHURN evaluation based on ground truth with different system parameter settings across all epochs.

		Group1	Group2	Group3	Group4	Group5	Group6	Total	Parameter setting
1.	✓	77	65	14	277	205	12	650	$\lambda = 25$ & $\epsilon = 0.2$
	✗	0	0	0	0	2	1	3	
2.	✓	76	57	14	257	192	12	609	$\lambda = 2$ & $\epsilon = 10^{-12}$
	✗	1	8	0	20	15	1	44	
3.	✓	67	54	10	208	155	10	504	$\lambda = 2$ & $\epsilon = 2$
	✗	10	11	4	69	52	3	149	
4.	✓	64	35	8	188	125	7	427	$\lambda = 10000$ & $\epsilon = N/A$
	✗	13	30	6	89	82	6	226	
Total		77	65	14	277	207	13	653	

run shows that the number of correctly attributed domains increases from 609 to 653 domains. Finally, when λ and ϵ are set to 25 and 0.2 respectively, based on the justification presented in Sect. 4.2, NCL, PCL and ACL are applied to domains and clusters depending on the condition(s) being satisfied. This resulted in a marked improvement with 650 out of 653 domains being correctly attributed. The first configuration shows the results using this setting.

5   Case Studies

After CHURN's attribution module generates labels for clusters, these clusters and their associated labels are used to identify and group domains that are part of the same scam campaign. We present case studies for three of the most prominent campaigns that are known SMS scams. As a general takeaway across all three case studies, we observed that the domains supporting the scams were hosted in diverse but few IP locations and for a long period of time. While the distributed infrastructure ensures reliability, the long term activity behind the domain names suggests the relative ineffectiveness of defenses against these social engineering cross-channel attacks compared to similar attacks via the internet channel.

Financial Freedom: Upon landing on the Financial Freedom web page an embedded video explains the purported benefits of enrolling into the program. The victim is asked to provide her personal information for 'Free Instant Access' to the program. The scam targeted consumers who are financially weak and looking for a solution to credit card debt problems. In our dataset, this scam consisted of 277 FQDNs (e.g. `morefreedomforall[dot]com`) and 187 IPs belonging to 49 distinct/24 subnetworks. None of the domains in this scam were seen in domain blacklists and the domains ended up being clustered in the ACL module. Figure 7(g) shows that the campaign used dedicated infrastructure to operate in a stealthy mode thus surviving for a long time, as can be seen in Fig. 7(a), (d). Legal proceedings of a law suit initiated against the perpetrators of this scam can be found here [4].

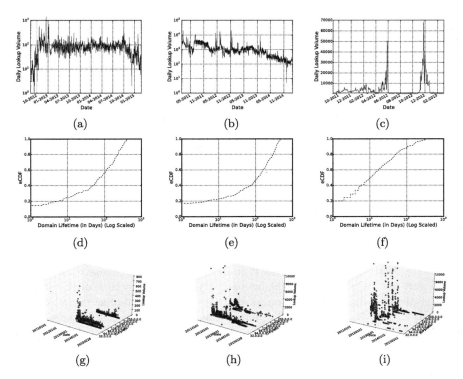

Fig. 7. Three campaigns: financial freedom, payday and gift Card. For each we show (7(a)–(c)) daily lookup volumes according to our pDNS database, (7(d)–(f)) eCDF of the lifetime of the domains seen and (7(g)–(i)) 3D view of campaigns based on time, popularity and network infrastructure (IPs binned by/24 prefix).

Payday: Payday loan is a short term, high interest cash advance that has been banned in many states in the United States, and the Federal Trade Commission (FTC) has issued warnings regarding it [5]. For example, in one instance the defendants' online contract stated that a $300 loan would cost $390 to repay, but the defendants then charged consumers $975 to repay the loan. This is a case of obscuring the 'Terms of service' specified on the site, which make it hard for the victim to realize they are being scammed. The scam works by sending a victim a SMS message with a URL. Upon clicking the URL, the victim is asked to enter personal information, phone number, and loan amount to proceed further.

A particular online payday loan campaign was clustered in our SMS spam dataset consisting of 207 unique domains; hosted in 212 unique IP addresses; belonging to 142 distinct/24 subnetworks. 68 out of 207 such domains were part of the .co.uk TLD. Eight domains in this scam were seen in PBL and they were mainly clustered by the ACL module. Figure 7(b), (e) shows that despite the warnings by consumer protection authorities (especially in the USA), this scam has survived and continues to victimize consumers. In addition to this, Fig. 7(h) shows the stability behind the network infrastructure used to support the scam domains.

Giftcard: In this case study, the scam works by sending the victim a SMS message with a URL and a code. Upon clicking the URL, the victim is asked to enter his/her personal details including phone number followed by entering the code in order to receive a fake free gift card from the associated brand (e.g., Target, Bestbuy, Walmart etc.). Thereafter, victims were told to sign up for more than a dozen risky trial offers, none of which were free, to qualify for the promised 'free' gift card. In many cases, the correct code confirmed to the gift card scam operators that the mobile number is indeed active and they use this entry as a pretense to falsely subscribe the victim's mobile number to premium rate services.

The giftcard campaign consisted of 207 domains and 215 IPs belonging to 85 distinct/24 subnetworks. Four domains under this scam were seen in PBL and the domains were mostly clustered in the NCL module. This campaign was mostly active during two distinct time periods in 2012 and 2013, as can be seen in Fig. 7(c). The resurgence of the campaign the second time coincides with the shopping/holiday season between November 2012 and January 2013 where a lucrative deal for a gift card is more likely to catch the victim's attention. Figure 7(f) shows that $\approx$45 % of the domains had a lifetime of less than 10 days, $\approx$45 % were active between 10–100 days and the remaining $\approx$10 % of the domains were relatively long lived. We found that out of 207 domains, many of them were well crafted 4LDs (4th level domains), named after specific brands such as BestBuy (114), Target (77) or Walmart (16) e.g. `target.com.tthg[dot]biz`. We also noticed that the domains hosting these web pages have very similar layout, structure and content. The majority of the Giftcard scam domains had a relatively shorter lifetime and were more agile in using their network resources.

The FTC pressed charges against the perpetrators of the Gift Card campaign for illegally sending $\approx$42.5 million text messages to consumers containing bogus offers for 'free' Gift Cards. These charges were publicly reported to be settled in September 2013 [19]. This is reflected in Fig. 7(c), where we see very few to no lookups during the second half of 2013.

6   Related Work

Although there has been work in both SMS spam detection [35, 38] and discovering SMS spam campaigns [30], our focus on and characterization of the network infrastructure used by SMS spam campaigns provides new insights that are not available from past research. Jiang et al. [35] use the concept of 'grey' phone numbers, which are phone numbers associated with data-only devices such as laptop data cards and electricity meters, as honeypot end points to capture SMS-spam. They then apply statistical models on the collected data to identify the source phone numbers generating spam. Murynets and Jover [38] conducted an empirical analysis of SMS-spam collected from fraudulent accounts in a large cellular provider to uncover spamming sources and their strategies. Our work differs from these works because of our focus on characterization of the network infrastructure rather than source phone numbers of spam. Moreover, while their analysis is based on call detail records (CDR's) generated on the telephony channel, we explore the cross-channel nature of such abuse by attributing the Internet infrastructure that facilitates SMS abuse by using crowd-sourced complaint and passive DNS and application datasets.

Boggs et al. [30] propose a method to discover emergent malicious campaigns in cellular networks by using graph clustering methods with mutual contact graphs that capture interactions between nodes which represent phone numbers or domain names. In addition to discovering SMS spam campaigns, we explore the properties of the infrastructure that supports such campaigns using both passive DNS data and the application level information available from webpages to which users are directed when they click on URLs contained in SMS messages. Our results show that some of the assumptions made in earlier work do not actually hold. For example, [30] assumes that Internet public blacklists can be helpful in detecting and stopping malicious SMS messages but we show that little overlap exists between domains in SMS messages and these public blacklists.

There have been numerous studies that cluster spam infrastructure and campaigns based on URL [43], IP infrastructure [25,29] and content [24,32]. Although we do not claim novelty around the individual features used in clustering SMS-spam infrastructure, our contribution lies in observing that it is most effective to use features from different layers of the network stack in a hierarchical manner so as to capture the diverse types of SMS-spam campaigns. Prior work has shown the ineffectiveness of traditional blacklists in protecting services such as instant messaging (IM) [41], and social media [34,43]. Our demonstration of the poor blacklist coverage of SMS-spam domains is similar. The significant gap in blacklist coverage and longevity of SMS-spam domains shows the limits of using email and malware abuse intelligence to fight cross channel abuse. Lever et al. [37] analyzed malicious cellular DNS traffic generated by mobile applications to conclude that mobile app-level protection (eg. app-market security) suffices to curtail mobile attacks. Our work shows that the emergent cross-channel abuse strategy bypasses this and is a more serious threat to mobile users.

Key Differences: In summary, much of the past work in SMS abuse has focused on the analysis of call detail records to identify spam source phone numbers rather than on the characterization of the network infrastructure that facilitates the abuse. Such network characterization has helped us demonstrate that current publicly available Internet threat intelligence largely fails to identify this infrastructure to stop long-lived SMS spam campaigns. Our work differs in both the long-term analysis of the problem, but also the new methods we propose to cluster and attribute SMS spam messages over time.

7   Limitations

Data collected and analyzed by CHURN, which includes consumer complaints and passive DNS data, is primarily US-centric, making it difficult to generalize the findings to other parts of the world. Indeed, cross-channel spam trends could be different in Europe or Asia as compared to the US. However, our attribution system, CHURN is designed to be easily deployable elsewhere, without much change. In future work, we hope to be able to use CHURN with data from other countries and provide insights on cross-channel abuse from around the world. CHURN's evaluation is based on a limited set of labeled data/ground truth. Although, we consciously made an effort to label data that is representative of all the spam domains under consideration, by randomizing the selection process for manually inspecting the domains, we recognize the need to scale this experiment and plan to do it in the future while adding more capabilities to our system.

8 Conclusion

In cross-channel abuse, SMS-spammers are able to exploit the ubiquity of mobile devices and trust in the telephony channel to craft attacks that could be more successful than spam on the Internet channel alone. Such illicit activities have become a serious problem, with several reported scams that have lasted for several years. Using data from multiple sources, we seek to attribute cross-channel abuse to the Internet infrastructure that facilitates it. Our research results confirm that SMS-spam is not well defended against, as such campaigns are able to run for long periods of time. Although there is some agility in the network resources used by them, very few of the domains used, appear on traditional domain blacklists.

Acknowledgements. This work was supported in part by National Science Foundation grants CNS-1318167 and CNS-1514035. Any opinions, findings, and conclusions or recommendations expressed in this material are those of the author(s) and do not necessarily reflect the views of the National Science Foundation.

A   Appendix

A.1   Prominent Campaigns Snapshots

Figure 8 shows the snapshots of the three campaigns discussed in this paper.

| (a) | (b) | (c) |

Fig. 8. Three campaigns: financial freedom, payday and gift Card. For each we show (8(a)–(c)) web pages rendered on a mobile browser.

A.2   Hierarchical Clustering Module Dendogram

Figure 9 graphically depicts all the attributed clusters in our study at different levels for epoch t_2 (2012) as a radial dendogram plot. The center represents all the domains under consideration and the concentric circles represent the cluster labels at each level starting from NCL (level 1), to PCL (level 2) and ACL (level 3), as we move outward radially.

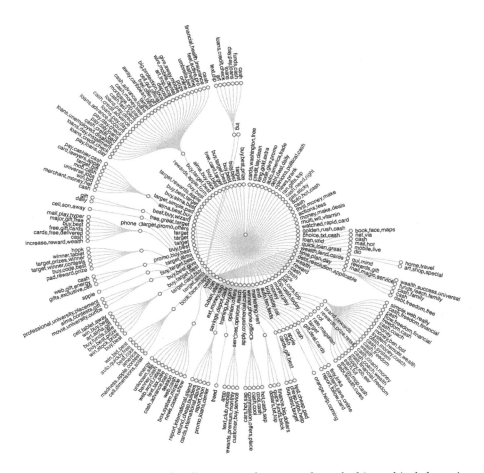

Fig. 9. A radial dendrogram plot illustrating the output from the hierarchical clustering module for a single epoch.

References

1. Abuse.ch - the swiss security blog. https://www.abuse.ch/
2. Alexa top sites. http://www.alexa.com/topsites

3. Federal trade commission FTC complaint assistant. https://www.ftccomplaintassistant.gov/#crnt&panel1-1
4. FTC on financial freedom. https://www.ftc.gov/enforcement/cases-proceedings/092-3056/financial-freedom-processing-inc-formerly-known-financial
5. FTC on payday lending. https://www.ftc.gov/news-events/media-resources/consumer-finance/payday-lending
6. FTC robocall challenge. https://robocall.devpost.com/
7. hphosts. http://www.hosts-file.net/
8. Identifying parking IP infrastructure: understanding malware evolution and the implications on data modeling. https://www.damballa.com/identifying-parking-ip-infrastructure-understanding-malware-evolution-and-the-implications-on-data-modeling/
9. Internet archive: wayback machine. https://archive.org/web/
10. I.T. mate product support. http://support.it-mate.co.uk/
11. Malc0de database. http://malc0de.com/database/
12. Malware domain list. http://www.malwaredomainlist.com/
13. SagaDC summary. http://dns-bh.sagadc.org/
14. SMS phishers exploit twilio and ow.ly to steal mobile account logins. http://blog.cloudmark.com/2014/02/13/sms-phishers-exploit-twilio-and-owly-to-steal-mobile-account-logins/
15. SMSWatchDog. http://www.smswatchdog.com
16. SPAMHaus Blocklist. https://www.spamhaus.org/lookup/
17. Suspicious domains - SANS internet storm center. https://isc.sans.edu/suspicious_domains.html
18. Technical realization of the short message service (SMS), 3Gpp. TS 23.040, v13.0.0. http://www.3gpp.org/dynareport/23040.htm
19. Text spammers settle FTC charges they illegally sent consumers bogus offers for 'free' gift cards. https://www.ftc.gov/news-events/press-releases/2013/09/text-spammers-settle-ftc-charges-they-illegally-sent-consumers
20. Tropo. https://www.tropo.com
21. Twilio. http://www.twilio.com
22. What kind of SMS messages are not allowed to be sent using Twilio? https://www.twilio.com/help/faq/sms/what-kind-of-sms-messages-are-not-allowed-to-be-sent-using-twilio
23. Your very own SMS internet gateway with arduino. http://x-ian.net/2012/10/09/your-very-own-sms-internet-gateway-with-arduino/
24. Anderson, D.S., Fleizach, C., Savage, S., Voelker, G.M., Spamscatter: characterizing internet scam hosting infrastructure. Ph.D. thesis, University of California, San Diego (2007)
25. Antonakakis, M., Perdisci, R., Dagon, D., Lee, W., Feamster, N.: Building a dynamic reputation system for DNS. In: 19th USENIX Security Symposium, 11–13 August 2010, Washington, DC, USA, Proceedings, pp. 273–290. USENIX Association (2010)
26. Antonakakis, M., Perdisci, R., Lee, W., Vasiloglou, N., Dagon, D.: Detecting malware domains in the upper DNS hierarchy. In: The Proceedings of 20th USENIX Security Symposium (USENIX Security 2011) (2011)
27. Antonakakis, M., Perdisci, R., Nadji, Y., Vasiloglou, N., Abu-Nimeh, S., Lee, W., Dagon, D.: From throw-away traffic to bots: detecting the rise of DGA-based malware. In: The Proceedings of 21th USENIX Security Symposium (USENIX Security 2012) (2012)

28. Antonakakis, M., Perdisci, R., Nadji, Y., Vasiloglou, N., Abu-Nimeh, S., Lee, W., Dagon, D.: From throw-away traffic to bots: detecting the rise of DGA-based malware. In: Presented as part of the 21st USENIX Security Symposium (USENIX Security 2012), Bellevue, pp. 491–506. USENIX (2012)
29. Bilge, L., Kirda, E., Kruegel, C., Balduzzi, M.: EXPOSURE: finding malicious domains using passive DNS analysis. In: Proceedings of the Network and Distributed System Security Symposium (NDSS 2011), 6th February - 9th, San Diego, California, USA. The Internet Society, February 2011
30. Boggs, N., Wang, W., Mathur, S., Coskun, B., Pincock, C.: Discovery of emergent malicious campaigns in cellular networks. In: Proceedings of the 29th Annual Computer Security Applications Conference (ACSAC 2013), New York, NY, USA, pp. 29–38. ACM (2013)
31. Burges, C.J.: A tutorial on support vector machines for pattern recognition. Data Mining Knowl. Discov. **2**(2), 121–167 (1998)
32. Der, M.F., Saul, L.K., Savage, S., Voelker, G.M.: Knock it off: profiling the online storefronts of counterfeit merchandise. In: The 20th ACM SIGKDD International Conference on Knowledge Discovery and Data Mining (KDD 2014), 24–27 August 2014, New York, NY, USA, pp. 1759–1768 (2014)
33. Forney Jr., G.D.: The Viterbi algorithm. Proc. IEEE **61**(3), 268–278 (1973)
34. Grier, C., Thomas, K., Paxson, V., Zhang, M.: @spam: the underground on 140 characters or less. In: Proceedings of the 17th ACM Conference on Computer and Communications Security (CCS 2010), New York, NY, USA, pp. 27–37. ACM (2010)
35. Jiang, N., Jin, Y., Skudlark, A., Zhang, Z.-L.: Greystar: fast and accurate detection of SMS spam numbers in large cellular networks using grey phone space. In: Proceedings of the 22Nd USENIX Conference on Security (SEC 2013), Berkeley, CA, USA, pp. 1–16. USENIX Association (2013)
36. Jiang, N., Jin, Y., Skudlark, A., Zhang, Z.-L.: Understanding SMS spam in a large cellular network: characteristics, strategies and defenses. In: Stolfo, S.J., Stavrou, A., Wright, C.V. (eds.) RAID 2013. LNCS, vol. 8145, pp. 328–347. Springer, Heidelberg (2013)
37. Lever, C., Antonakakis, M., Reaves, B., Traynor, P., Lee, W.: The core of the matter: analyzing malicious traffic in cellular carriers. In: 20th Annual Network and Distributed System Security Symposium (NDSS 2013), 24–27 February 2013, San Diego, California, USA. The Internet Society (2013)
38. Murynets, I., Jover, R.P.: Crime scene investigation: SMS spam data analysis. In: Byers, J.W., Kurose, J., Mahajan, R., Snoeren, A.C., (eds.) Proceedings of the 12th ACM SIGCOMM Conference on Internet Measurement (IMC 2012), 14–16 November 2012, Boston, MA, USA, pp. 441–452. ACM (2012)
39. Nazario, J., Holz, T.: As the net churns: fast-flux botnet observations. In: 3rd International Conference on Malicious and Unwanted Software (MALWARE 2008), 7–8 October 2008, Alexandria, Virginia, USA, pp. 24–31 (2008)
40. Pelleg, D., Moore, A.W., et al.: X-means: extending k-means with efficient estimation of the number of clusters. In: ICML, pp. 727–734 (2000)

41. Polakis, I., Petsas, T., Markatos, E.P., Antonatos, S.: A systematic characterization of IM threats using honeypots. In: Proceedings of the Network and Distributed System Security Symposium (NDSS 2010), 28th February - 3rd, San Diego, California, USA, March 2010
42. Salton, G., McGill, M.J.: Introduction to Modern Information Retrieval. McGraw-Hill Inc., New York (1986)
43. Thomas, K., Grier, C., Ma, J., Paxson, V., Song, D.: Design and evaluation of a real-time URL spam filtering service. In: 32nd IEEE Symposium on Security and Privacy (S&P 2011), 22–25 May 2011, Berkeley, California, USA, pp. 447–462. IEEE Computer Society (2011)
44. Vissers, T., Joosen, W., Nikiforakis, N.: Parking sensors: analyzing and detecting parked domains. In: 22nd Annual Network and Distributed System Security Symposium (NDSS 2015), 8–11 February 2014, San Diego, California, USA (2015)
45. Wall, M.E., Rechtsteiner, A., Rocha, L.M.: Singular value decomposition and principal component analysis. In: Berrar, D.P., Dubitzky, W., Granzow, M. (eds.) A Practical Approach to Microarray Data Analysis, pp. 91–109. Springer, Heidelberg (2003)
46. Yadav, S., Reddy, A.K.K., Reddy, A., Ranjan, S.: Detecting algorithmically generated malicious domain names. In: Proceedings of the 10th ACM SIGCOMM Conference on Internet Measurement, pp. 48–61. ACM (2010)

Toward an Efficient Website Fingerprinting Defense

Marc Juarez[1]([✉]), Mohsen Imani[2], Mike Perry[3],
Claudia Diaz[1], and Matthew Wright[2]

[1] KU Leuven, ESAT/COSIC and iMinds, Leuven, Belgium
{marc.juarez,claudia.diaz}@esat.kuleuven.be
[2] The University of Texas at Arlington, Arlington, TX, USA
mohsen.imani@mavs.uta.edu, mwright@cse.uta.edu
[3] The Tor Project, 217 1st Avenue South #4903, Seattle, WA 98194, USA
mikeperry@torproject.org
https://torproject.org

Abstract. Website Fingerprinting attacks enable a passive eavesdropper to recover the user's otherwise anonymized web browsing activity by matching the observed traffic with prerecorded web traffic templates. The defenses that have been proposed to counter these attacks are impractical for deployment in real-world systems due to their high cost in terms of added delay and bandwidth overhead. Further, these defenses have been designed to counter attacks that, despite their high success rates, have been criticized for assuming unrealistic attack conditions in the evaluation setting. In this paper, we propose a novel, lightweight defense based on Adaptive Padding that provides a sufficient level of security against website fingerprinting, particularly in realistic evaluation conditions. In a closed-world setting, this defense reduces the accuracy of the state-of-the-art attack from 91 % to 20 %, while introducing zero latency overhead and less than 60 % bandwidth overhead. In an open-world, the attack precision is just 1 % and drops further as the number of sites grows.

Keywords: Privacy · Anonymous communications · Website Fingerprinting

1 Introduction

Website Fingerprinting (WF) is a type of traffic analysis attack that allows an attacker to recover the browsing history of a client. The attacker collects a database of web traffic templates and matches the client's traffic with one of the templates. WF has been shown to be effective in a wide variety of scenarios ranging from HTTPS connections [15], SSH tunnels [9], one-hop proxies [10], VPNs [19] and even anonymous communication systems such as Tor [5].

The success of WF against Tor, one of the largest deployed systems for anonymously browsing the Web [20], is particularly problematic. Tor offers stronger

© Springer International Publishing Switzerland 2016
I. Askoxylakis et al. (Eds.): ESORICS 2016, Part I, LNCS 9878, pp. 27–46, 2016.
DOI: 10.1007/978-3-319-45744-4_2

security than one-hop proxies and it is meant to protect against attacks like WF that require only a local eavesdropper or a compromised guard node. However, recent WF attacks achieve more than 90 % accuracy against Tor [5,23,24], thus breaking the anonymity properties that it aims to provide.

To counter these attacks, a broad range of defenses has been proposed. The key building block of most of these defenses is *link padding*. Link padding adds varying amounts of delays and dummy messages to the packet flows to conceal patterns in network traffic. Given that bandwidth and latency increases come at a cost to usability and deployability, these defenses must strive for a trade-off between security and performance overheads. Unfortunately, the state-of-the-art link-padding defenses are not acceptable for use in Tor: they increase latency, delaying page loads between *two* and *four* times and impose bandwidth overheads between 40 % [4] and 350 % [8] on average.

We note that any delays introduced by a defense are a concern for low-latency systems, as they have a direct impact on the usability of the system in interactive applications. Moderate bandwidth overheads may also impact the user experience but the load factor needs to increase substantially before being noticeable by users. Moreover, the Tor network has spare bandwidth on the ingress edge of the network, making it possible to afford a client-side defense that consumes a moderate amount of bandwidth. In this work, we thus explore the design space of effective link-padding defenses with minimal latency overhead and modest bandwidth overhead.

The contributions of the following sections are:

An analysis of the suitability of WF defenses for deployment in Tor. In Sect. 2, we define the threat model and give a background of existing attacks and defenses. Based on this literature review, we discuss the suitability of these defenses for an implementation in Tor.

A lightweight defense against WF attacks. We have adapted Adaptive Padding to combat WF in Tor and dubbed this new defense *Website Traffic Fingerprinting Protection with Adaptive Defense* (WTF-PAD). Section 3 gives its specification, and Sect. 4 presents an evaluation and a comparison of WTF-PAD with the existing WF defenses. We find that WTF-PAD is effective and has reasonable overheads for a system like Tor.

An evaluation of the defense in realistic scenarios. Prior work has shown that the accuracy of the WF attack decreases significantly when certain assumptions about the setting or user behavior do not hold [11], but to the best of our knowledge this is the first study that evaluates the effectiveness of a WF defense in these scenarios. In Sect. 5, we show the results for two realistic scenarios: (i) *open-world*, in which the attacker monitors a small set of web pages and, (ii) *multi-tab*, where the users browse the pages using multiple tabs. We show that for these scenarios, the defense substantially reduces the accuracy of the state-of-the-art WF attack.

2   Website Fingerprinting (WF)

Tor is an overlay network that routes connections through three-hop circuits using *onion routing* [7]. The onion routers encrypt the messages in layers so that neither the relays nor localized network eavesdroppers can know both the origin and the destination of a connection.

In this paper, we assume that the client connects to Tor through a *bridge*, a volunteer-run proxy to the Tor network (see Fig. 1). The adversary has access to the communication at a point between the client and the bridge. The adversary is *local*, meaning that he is unable to observe other parts of the network, and *passive*: he can observe and record packets but cannot modify, delay, drop or inject new packets. We also assume that the adversary cannot learn anything about packet payloads due to the use of layered encryption.

Defensive padding is performed end-to-end between trusted endpoints, with the adversary only having access to the padded traces. For this research, we assume the bridge is trusted. This allows to implement the defense as a *Pluggable Transport* (PT) [21], avoiding modifications in the Tor source code. Note this model is equivalent for a client connecting to the trusted entry guard without a bridge, but in that case the defense would need to be implemented at the guard.

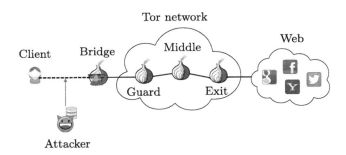

Fig. 1. The WF adversary model considering Tor bridges.

The objective of the WF adversary is to determine what pages the user downloads over Tor by looking at the network traces. Early works on this problem [10,19] assumed a user model that could only access a small set of pages—an assumption that is unlikely to be met in practice. This assumption is known as the *closed-world assumption*, and it overly simplifies the problem to the point of being irrelevant to most real-world settings. In contrast, the more realistic *open-world* allows the user to visit *any* page and the attacker's goal is to determine whether the user downloads one of a small set of *monitored* pages. We have evaluated both scenarios: the closed world favors the attacker and gives a lower bound of the defense effectiveness, but our objective is to measure the performance of the defense in realistic conditions.

WF attacks are a serious threat to Tor's security: the adversary only needs the ability to eavesdrop on the client's link to the network, which can be achieved with moderate resources. With the continuous improvement in WF classifier accuracy over the past few years, this is a pressing concern. The first attack against Tor obtained 3 % accuracy with a Naive Bayes classifier [9] in a closed world and without any WF countermeasures. However, the attack has been revisited with more refined feature sets [17], and state-of-the-art attacks attain over 90 % accuracy [5, 16, 23, 24].

2.1   Defenses

Most of the defenses in the literature are theoretical designs without a specification for an implementation. Only a few have been evaluated for anonymous communications, and the only one that is currently implemented in Tor does not work as expected. In this section, we review WF defenses proposed in the literature and discuss their suitability for implementation in Tor.

Application-level defenses. These defenses work at the application layer. *HTTPOS* modifies HTTP headers and injects HTTP requests strategically [13], while *Randomized Pipelining*, a WF countermeasure currently implemented in the Tor Browser, randomizes the pipeline of HTTP requests. Both defenses have been shown to be ineffective in several evaluations [5, 11, 23, 24].

Supersequences and traffic morphing. Recent works have proposed defenses based on generalizing web traffic traces [3, 23]. They create anonymity sets by clustering pages and morphing them to look like the centroid of their cluster. This approach aims to optimally reduce the amount of padding needed to confound the attacker's classifier. These defenses, as well as traffic morphing techniques [12, 25], have the shortcoming that require a database of webpage templates that needs to be frequently updated and would be costly to maintain [11].

Constant-rate padding defenses. Dyer et al. evaluated the impact of padding individual packets [8], finding that this is not sufficient to hide coarse-grained features such as *bursts* in traffic or the total size and load time of the page. Dyer et al. simulated a proof-of-concept countermeasure called *BuFLO*, which used constant-rate traffic with fixed-size packets. The authors report excessive bandwidth overheads in return for moderate security. The condition to stop the padding after the transmission ends is critical to adjust the trade-off between overheads and security. BuFLO stops when a page has finished loading and a minimum amount of time has passed, not covering the size of a page that lasts longer than the minimum time.

  Tamaraw [4] and *CS-BuFLO* [2,5], both attempt to optimize the original design of BuFLO. Instead of setting a minimum duration of padding, Tamaraw stops padding when the total number of transmitted bytes is a multiple of a certain parameter. This approach groups webpages in anonymity sets, with the amount of padding generated being dependent on the webpage's total size. Given the asymmetry of web browsing traffic, Cai et al. also suggest treating incoming and outgoing traffic independently, using different packet sizes and padding at different rates. Furthermore, the authors sketched CS-BuFLO as a practical version of BuFLO, extended with congestion sensitivity and rate adaptation.

Following Tamaraw's grouping in anonymity sets by page size, they propose either padding up to a power of two, or to a multiple of the amount of transmitted application data.

We question the viability of the BuFLO-based defenses for Tor. Their latency overheads are very high, such as two-to-three times longer than without defense, and the bandwidth overheads for BuFLO and CS-BuFLO are over 100 %. In addition, due to the popularity of dynamic web content, it is challenging to determine when a page load completes, as needed in Tamaraw and CS-BuFLO. Nevertheless, in this paper, we compare our system against these defenses because they are the closest to meeting the deployment constraints of Tor.

3 Adaptive Padding

Adaptive Padding (AP) was proposed by Shmatikov and Wang to defend against end-to-end traffic analysis [18]. Even though WF attacks are significantly different from these end-to-end attacks, AP can be adapted to protecting against WF due to its generality and flexibility. AP has the defender examine the outgoing traffic pattern and generate dummy messages in a targeted manner to disrupt distinctive features of the patterns—"statistically unlikely" delays between packets. Shmatikov and Wang showed that with 50 % bandwidth overhead, the accuracy of end-to-end timing-based traffic analysis is significantly degraded [18].

In the BuFLO family of defenses, the inter-arrival time between packets is fixed and application data is delayed, if needed, to fit the rigid schedule of constant packet timings. This adds delays in the common case that multiple real cells are sent all at once, making this family of defenses ill-suited for a system like Tor, as it would significantly harm user experience. By contrast, Adaptive Padding (AP) does not delay application data; rather, it sends it immediately. This minimal latency overhead makes AP a good candidate for Tor.

In the rest of this section, we describe AP and explain how we adapt it to defend against WF attacks in Tor.

3.1 Design Overview

To clarify the notation adopted in this paper, we use *outgoing* to refer to the direction from the PT instance running at the client to the PT at the bridge, and conversely, *incoming* is the direction from the PT server to the client.

The basic idea of AP is to match the gaps between data packets with a distribution of generic web traffic. If an unusually large gap is found in the current stream, AP adds padding in that gap to prevent long gaps from being a distinguishing feature. Shmatikov and Wang recognized the importance of bursts in web traffic and thus developed a dual-mode algorithm. In *burst mode*, the algorithm essentially assumes there is a burst of real data and consequently waits for a longer period before sending any padding. In *gap mode*, the algorithm assumes there is a gap between bursts and consequently aims to add a fake burst of padding with short delays between packets. In this paper, we follow Shmatikov and Wang and define a burst in terms of bandwidth: a burst is a sequence of packets that has been sent in a short time period. Conversely, a gap is a sequence of packets that are spread over a long timespan.

AP algorithm. The AP algorithm is defined by two histograms of delays that we call H_B (used in burst mode) and H_G (used in gap mode). The histograms have a set of bins that spans over the range of possible inter-arrival times. Each bin contains a number of *tokens*, which can be interpreted as the probability of selecting an inter-arrival time within the range of delays represented by that bin. The last bin, which we dub the "infinity bin", includes all possible values greater than the second-to-last bin. For more details on how these histograms are defined in WTF-PAD we refer the reader to Appendix A.

AP implements the state machine shown in Fig. 2 in each defense endpoint, i.e. both PT client and server. For simplicity, let us consider just the client's state machine in the following explanation. The operation of the server is symmetrical.

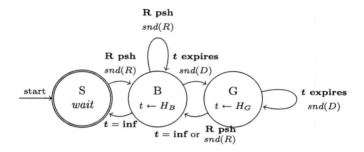

Fig. 2. AP algorithm as a finite state machine as implemented in the PT client. The events are in bold and the actions in italics. The action $(snd(\cdot))$ refers to sending messages, either *real* (R) or *dummy* (D). The **psh** event means a message pushed from the application (Tor browser) to the PT client.

Burst mode. As depicted in the diagram, AP starts idle (state S) until the packet with the HTTP request is pushed from the browser (R). This causes it to enter burst mode (state B), drawing a delay t from the H_B histogram. Then it starts to count down until either new data is pushed or t expires. In the first case, the data is immediately forwarded, a new delay is sampled and the process is repeated again, i.e. it remains in burst mode. Otherwise, a dummy message (D) is sent to the other end and AP switches to state G (gap mode). The H_B histogram is built using a large dataset of web traffic, out of which we sample the times between the end of a burst and the beginning of the following burst (see Sect. 3.3). Therefore, while we are in a burst, the delays we sample from H_B will not expire until we find an inter-arrival time that is longer than typical within a burst, which will make the delay expire and trigger the G state.

Gap mode. While AP is in state G, it samples from histogram H_G and sends dummy messages when the times it samples expire. The histogram for gap mode,

H_G, is built from a sample of inter-arrival times *within* a burst in traffic collected for a large sample of sites. That is, by sending packets with inter-arrival times drawn from H_G, we are able to generate fake bursts that follow the timing distribution of an average burst. A transition from G back to B occurs upon either sampling a token from the infinity bin or receiving a real packet. Similarly, a transition from B to S happens when we sample a token from the infinity bin.

Note that AP immediately forwards all application data. Since sending a real packet means that the timeout expired, AP has to correct the distribution by returning the token to its bin and removing a token from the bin representing the actual delay. This prevents the combined distribution of padding and real traffic from skewing towards short values and allows AP to adapt to the current transmission rate [18]. If a bin runs out of tokens, to minimize its effect on the resulting distribution of inter-arrival times, we remove tokens from the next non-empty greater bin [18]. In case all bins are empty, we refill the histogram with the initial sample.

3.2   WTF-PAD

We propose a generalization of AP called *Website Traffic Fingerprinting Protection with Adaptive Defense (WTF-PAD)*. WTF-PAD includes implementation techniques for use in Tor and a number of link-padding primitives that enable more sophisticated padding strategies than the basic AP described above. These features include:

Receive histograms. A key feature to make padding realistic is to send padding messages as a response to messages received from the other end. In WTF-PAD, we implement this by keeping another AP state machine that reacts to messages received from the other PT endpoint: the PT client has a *rcv* event when it gets a packet from the PT server. This allows us to encode dependencies between incoming and outgoing bursts and to simulate request-response HTTP transactions with the web server. Padding introduced by the *rcv* event further distorts features on bursts, as just one packet in the outgoing direction might split an incoming burst as considered by the attacks in the literature.

Control messages. WTF-PAD implements control messages to command the PT server padding from the PT client. Using control messages, the client can send the distribution of the histograms to be used by the PT server. This way, the PT client is in full control of the padding scheme. It can do accounting on received padding traffic and alert the user if relays in its circuits are sending unscheduled padding.

Beginning of transmission. Control messages can also be used to signal the beginning of the transmission. If we are in state S and a new page is requested, we will need to flag the server to start padding. Otherwise, the transmission from the first request to the following response is uncovered and reveals the size of the `index.html` page.

Soft stopping condition. In contrast to Tamaraw and CS-BuFLO, WTF-PAD does not require an explicit mechanism to conceal the total time of the transmission. At the end of the transmission, the padding is interrupted when we hit the infinity bin in the gap state and then the infinity bin in the burst state. See the Appendix A for further discussion on how to set the tokens in the infinity bins. The lack of a firm stop condition represents an advantage over existing link-padding-based defenses, which require a mechanism to flag the boundaries of the transmission. The probability of stopping will depend on the shape of the histograms at the end of the transmission.

3.3   Inter-arrival Time Distributions

Shmatikov and Wang did not specify in the original AP paper how to build and use the distribution of inter-arrival times in the AP histograms. In their simulations, they sampled the inter-arrival times for both real and padding traffic from the same distribution. To build the histograms, we have sampled the times from a crawl of the top 35 K pages in the Alexa list. First, we uniformly selected a sample of approximately 4,000 pages and studied the distribution of inter-arrival times within their traces.

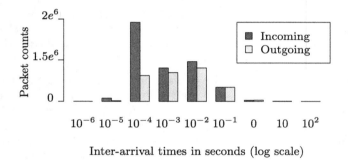

Fig. 3. Histogram of the inter-arrival times in a large sample of the top 35 K Alexa.

In order to implement WTF-PAD without revealing distinguishing features between real and fake messages, we need to send dummies in time intervals that follow the same distribution as real messages. In Fig. 3, we observe that times for incoming and outgoing traffic have different distributions. The asymmetric bit rates in the connection we used to conduct the crawl account for this difference. Since WTF-PAD has different histograms in the client and the bridge we can simulate traffic that follows different distributions depending on the direction.

Next, we explain how to find the bursts and the gaps in the inter-arrival time distribution and build the histograms H_B and H_G. Intuitively, the burst-mode histogram H_B should consist of larger delays covering the duration of typical bursts, while the gap-mode histogram H_G should consist of smaller delays that can be used to mimic a burst. To split inter-arrival times into the two histograms, we calculate the instantaneous bandwidth at the time of each inter-arrival time to determine if it is part of a burst or not. Then, we set a threshold on the bandwidth to draw the line between bursts and gaps.

We estimate the instantaneous bandwidth using a sliding window over a sequence of consecutive packets. We have experimented with different window lengths and threshold values. The best results against the state-of-the-art WF attack are achieved for a window of two consecutive packets and a threshold set to the total average bandwidth for the whole sample of traces.

3.4 Tuning Mechanism

AP can hide inter-arrival times that are longer than the average, but it does not hide times that are shorter than the average. To effectively hide these times we need to either add delays to exceptionally long traces or add more padding over all traces to level them off and make them less distinctive. We focus on the latter approach because our objective is to minimize delay. WTF-PAD provides a mechanism to tune the trade-off between bandwidth overhead and security: one can modify the parameters of the distributions used to build the histograms to add more padding and react to shorter inter-arrival times.

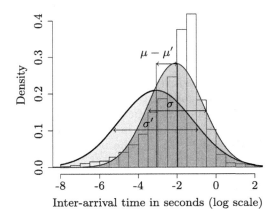

Fig. 4. Histogram of times between consecutive bursts for incoming traffic. In dark gray we superpose the PDF of our log-normal fit. In light gray, we show the PDF of a shifted log-normal distribution that we use to build the H_B histogram.

To illustrate this, we show in Fig. 4 the H_B histogram as sampled from our dataset. We observe that the distribution of the logarithm of these times can be approximated with a normal distribution $\mathcal{N}(\mu, \sigma^2)$. That is, the inter-arrival times follow a log-normal distribution. We can modify its mean and variance to obtain another normal distribution $\mathcal{N}(\mu', \sigma'^2)$ that we will use to sample the inter-arrival times of H_B. By using $\mathcal{N}(\mu', \sigma'^2)$ we are shifting the average distribution of inter-arrival times toward shorter values. This results in a greater amount of short times being covered by padding, which increases the bandwidth overhead but causes the pages become less distinguishable and thereby reduces the attacker's accuracy.

We created a statistical model of the underlying distributions of inter-arrival times from the samples we extracted from our dataset. We experimented with multiple positively skewed distributions to build the model and test the goodness of fit with the Kolmogorov-Smirnov test. We estimated the parameters of the distributions using maximum likelihood estimation. Even though Pareto and Beta distributions seemed to fit best, we decided for simplicity to use normal and log-normal distributions, given that the error was not significantly greater than that observed in the other distributions.

To calibrate the possible shifts, we set μ' and σ' according to the percentile of the real data we want to include. For instance, assuming a normal distribution, if we adjust μ' to the 50th percentile, we obtain $\mu' = \mu$ and $\sigma' = \sigma$. If we set μ' to the value of the Probability Density Function (PDF) at the 10th percentile, we then derive the σ' using the formula of the PDF of the normal distribution.

4   Evaluation

In this section we discuss how we evaluated WTF-PAD, present our findings and compare them with the results we obtained for existing defenses.

4.1   Data

Unlike most previous defense evaluations, which used simulated data, we have used web traffic that has been collected over Tor. We used a dataset that had been collected for a study about a realistic evaluation of WF attacks [11]. This dataset consists of 40 instances, collected in ten batches of four visits, for each *homepage* in top-100 Alexa sites [1]. For the open-world, the dataset also has one instance for each website in the Alexa 35,000 most popular websites.

4.2   Methodology

To evaluate the improvements in performance offered by the defense, we applied the attack's classifier on both the original traffic traces and traces that have been protected by applying the defense. The difference in bandwidth and latency between the original and protected traces provides us with an estimate of the overheads. We applied the state-of-the-art attack on the set of protected traces to evaluate the effectiveness of the defense. The average accuracy over multiple runs determines the security provided by the defense.

In the closed world, we measure the accuracy as the True Positive Rate (TPR), or *Recall*. We also measure the False Positive Rate (FPR), the Positive Predictive Value (PPV)—also called *Precision*, and the harmonic mean of precision and recall (*F1-Score*), as they play an important role on evaluating the effectiveness of the attack in the open-world.

The state-of-the-art attack is based on a k-NN model [23]. k-NN is a supervised learning algorithm that selects the k closest instances (the *neighbors*), and outputs the class of the majority of the neighbors. Wang et al. determined that the number of neighbors that optimizes the trade-off between TPR and FPR is $k = 5$. The distance defined by Wang et al. for use in k-NN is a weighted sum of a set of features. This feature set is the most extensive in the WF literature with more than 4,000 features and including features that extensively exploit bursts.

In order to have a comprehensive evaluation of WTF-PAD, we also evaluated it with other existing WF attacks that take into account features that are not included in k-NN.

4.3 Results

To evaluate the trade-off between bandwidth overhead and accuracy provided by WTF-PAD, we applied the attack on protected traces with different percentile values, ranging from 0.5 (low protection) to 0.01 (high protection) percentiles.

In Fig. 5, we show the trade-off curves for both normal and log-normal fits. We observe a steeper decrease in accuracy for the normal model with respect to the log-normal one. Remarkably, beyond a certain point (around 0.1 percentile), the tuning mechanism saturates to 15 % accuracy for both models: percentiles lower than that point do not further reduce accuracy and only increase bandwidth overhead. The trend we observe is the cost in bandwidth exponentially growing with the protection level that the defense attempts to provide

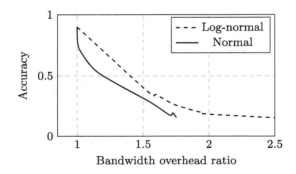

Fig. 5. Average accuracy versus median bandwidth overhead ratio.

Table 1 summarizes the security versus overhead trade-off obtained for different attacks (i.e., k-NN, NB, SVM, DL) and defenses BuFLO, Tamaraw, CS-BuFLO and WTF-PAD. As we see, WTF-PAD is the only defense to provide zero latency overhead. The other defenses we tested produce between 145–200% additional average delay to fetch a webpage. WTF-PAD also offers moderate bandwidth overhead. For our datasets, we observed that the bandwidth overhead was always below 60 % while attaining decreases in the accuracy of the attack that are comparable with the other defenses.

Table 1. Performance and security comparison among link-padding defenses in a closed world.

Defense	Parameters	Accuracy (%)				Overhead (%)	
		kNN	Pa-SVM [17]	DL-SVM [24]	VNG++ [8]	Latency	Bandwidth
BuFLO [8]	$\tau = 10\,\mathrm{s}$, $\rho = 20\,\mathrm{ms}$, $d = 1500\,\mathrm{B}$	14.9	14.1	18.75	N/A	145	348
CS-BuFLO [2]	$\rho = [20, 200]\,\mathrm{ms}$, $d = 1500\,\mathrm{B}$, CPSP	N/A	30.6	40.5	22.5	173	130
Tamaraw [23]	$\rho_{out} = 0.053$, $\rho_{in} = 0.138$, $d = 1500\,\mathrm{B}$	13.6	10.59	18.60	12.1	200	38
WTF-PAD	Normal fit, $p = 0.4$, $d = 1500\,\mathrm{B}$	17.25	15.33	23	26	0	54

ROC curve. To study the impact of WTF-PAD on the performance of k-NN, we also plotted the ROC curve with and without protection. The ROC curve represents the performance of the classifier when its discrimination parameter changes. The standard k-NN is not a parametric algorithm, meaning that there is no explicit parameter that one can use to set the threshold and tune the trade-off. We have defined more or less restrictive classifications of k-NN by setting a minimum number of votes required to classify a page. We used 10-fold cross-validation to average the ROC curve for $k = 5$ neighbors in a closed world of 100 pages. To plot the ROC graph we had to *binarize* the classification: we divided the set of pages into two halves, 50 monitored and 50 non-monitored, and considered the monitored as the positive class and the non-monitored as the negative one. Then, all the positive (monitored) observations that are classified as a page in the positive class are counted as true positives, even if the instances were classified as a *different* monitored page. This is a more advantageous scenario for a surveillance-type of attacker that only tries to identify whether the page is monitored or not.

In Fig. 6, we compare the ROC curves for the data before and after applying the defense with respect to random guessing. We notice a significant reduction in the performance of the classifier. Compared to unprotected data with an AUC of 0.95 (close to perfect classification), WTF-PAD has an AUC of 0.66, which is substantially closer to random guessing.

5   Realistic Scenarios

In this section, we present the results of the evaluation of the defense in two realistic scenarios: the open world and the use of multi-tab browsing.

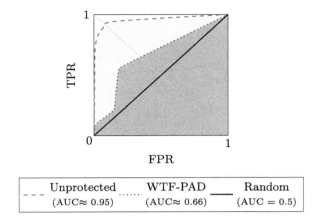

Fig. 6. 10-fold cross-validated ROC curves of k-NN with five neighbors and using a strict consensus threshold.

5.1 Open-World Evaluation

We now evaluate the performance of the defense against the k-NN algorithm in the open-world scenario. Our definition of the open-world is similar to the ones described in prior work. We have evaluated the k-NN with the evaluation method used by Wang et al. and incorporating the changes suggested by Wang [22], so that we can compare our results with the ones they obtained [23]

In Wang's open-world classification, they consider one class for each of the monitored pages and one single class for all the non-monitored pages. Then, the attacker aims to identify the exact monitored pages the user visits and to classify all the visits to non-monitored pages into the non-monitored class regardless of the actual page.

We observe that even though the accuracy initially increases as the world grows and saturates to 95 % at the maximum considered world size, the F1-Score decreases and levels off to 50 %. This is because even though the FPR rapidly drops to zero, the TPR decreases below 40 %. The accuracy is so high because the classifier reaches almost perfect classification for the non-monitored class. This high accuracy is due to the stringent threshold used in the k-NN which requires all neighbors to vote to the same class and reduces the FPR.

We observe that the TPR and FPR after applying the defense are dramatically lower than the rates shown in Fig. 7. However, due to the skew between the positive and the negative classes, the ROC curves of the k-NN are biased towards the negative class and do not reflect well the performance of the classifier. For imbalanced datasets, it is recommended to use the Precision-Recall ROC (P-ROC) instead of the ROC [6]. Similarly to the standard ROC, P-ROC represents the interaction of TPR (recall) and PPV (precision), instead of FPR, with respect to variations on the discriminant of the classifier. Precision in the open-world scenario conveys the fraction of monitored pages that were correctly

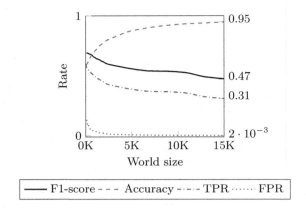

Fig. 7. Performance metrics for the classification of a k-NN classifier with $k = 4$ neighbors for an open world up to 15 K pages [22].

detected by the k-NN. Precision is invariant to the size of the negative class and thus gives a more accurate estimation of the classifier's performance in the open-world.

In the P-ROC graph, the perfect classifier has a curve that coincides with the top-right corner and the random classifier is calculated as the number of positives divided by the total number of instances, i.e., the probability of selecting a positive instance uniformly at random. This random curve is used as a baseline because no classifier can have lower precision than it. As in the standard ROC, classifiers can be bench-marked by comparing their area under the curve (AUC).

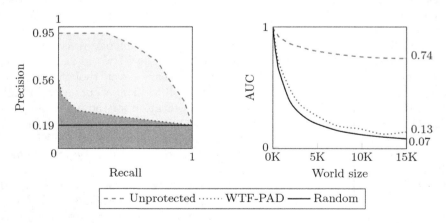

Fig. 8. The figure on the left shows the P-ROC curves for the k-NN attack on the protected and unprotected datasets for 5,000 pages. On the right, a comparison of P-ROC AUC with respect to the world size.

Figure 8 (left) shows the P-ROC curve of the k-NN when applied on the set of traces before and after WTF-PAD. Again, we observe that the AUC for the unprotected case is reduced significantly (from 0.79 to 0.27) and is close to random. However, this graph is a snapshot of the performance of the classifier for a fixed world size (5,000 pages). In order to evaluate how the size of the world affects the attack for the unprotected and protected data, we plot in Fig. 8 (right) the AUC estimates while varying the size of the world. The first data point represents a closed world where all pages are monitored and, as expected, all classifiers perform as in perfect classification (AUC = 1). However, as we increase the size of the world, the baseline classification tends to zero because a random guess is less likely to succeed. The k-NN levels off to AUC 0.74, which means that it is not heavily affected by the size of the world. Notably, when we apply the defense on the traces, all AUC values are close to random even for the largest world size that we have considered (15 K pages). WTF-PAD steadily decreases the attack's success at the same rate as the random classifier does.

5.2   Multi-tab Evaluation

The objective of the experiments in this section is to evaluate the efficacy of the WTF-PAD defense when the user is browsing with multiple tabs open. For this evaluation, we considered two scenarios and in both, the goal of the attacker is to identify one of the pages that compose the traffic trace.

Table 2. TPR for protected and unprotected traces in Scenarios 1 and 2.

	TPR	
	Unprotected	WTF-PAD
Scenario 1	14 %	8 %
Scenario 2	68 %	22 %

In Scenario 1, we trained the k-NN attack on a single-tab dataset and tested on a mixed dataset of single tab traces and multi-tab traces generated by a crawl with two simultaneous tabs. The first tab was loaded following the Alexa top 100 sequentially. The second tab was open with a delay from 0.5 to 5 seconds and was chosen uniformly at random from the same list. Table 2 shows the result of Scenario 1 for traces with and without the protection offered by WTF-PAD.

Since the accuracy of the k-NN is already low when training on single-tab and testing on multi-tab (Scenario 1 in Table 2), the defense does not impact significantly the TPR of the classifier.

In Scenario 2, we trained and tested k-NN on a dataset that includes multi-tab and single-tab traces. In this scenario, the attack achieves 68 % TPR on unprotected multi-tab traces, much higher than the 14 % found in Scenario 1. However, the success rate on protected traces drops to 22 %.

Table 3. TPR with respect to each traffic type. Each cell shows the number of background pages (the first tab) detected among truly detected multi-tab traces.

	Scenario 1 (TP/Total)			Scenario 2 (TP/Total)		
	Single	Multi	First	Single	Multi	First
Unprotected	233/300	901/8100	544/901	263/300	482/810	449/482
WTF-PAD	95/300	598/8100	333/598	108/300	137/810	103/137

In Table 3 we group the detection rates by traffic type (single or multi tab) as used to build the test set. k-NN can successfully classify unprotected single-tab traces with an accuracy of 87 %, which is close to the accuracy rate of k-NN in the closed-world setting. The accuracy decreases to just 36 % when we protect the traces with WTF-PAD.

6   Discussion and Future Work

WF attacks fall within the Tor threat model [7], as it only requires one point of observation between the client and the bridge or guard, and the attack potentially de-anonymizes users by linking them with their browsing activity. Even with the challenges of open-world and multi-tab browsing [11], some websites may exhibit especially unique traffic patterns and be prone to high-confidence attacks. Attacks may observe visits to the same site over multiple sessions and gain confidence in a result.

Protecting Tor users from WF attacks, however, must be done while maintaining the usability of Tor and limiting costs to Tor relay operators. Delay is already an issue in Tor, so adding additional delay would harm usability significantly. The BuFLO family of defenses add between 145–200 % additional delay to the average website download, i.e. up to *three times as long* to get a webpage, which makes them very unlikely to be adopted in Tor.

The main overhead in WTF-PAD is bandwidth, which was under 60 % overhead in all scenarios we tested. We do not know the exact percentage that is acceptable for use in Tor, but we note the following points. First, approximately 40 % of Tor traffic is bulk downloads (from 2008, the last data we know of) [14]. To the extent that this holds today, only the remaining 60 % of traffic needs to be covered by this defense. Second, the bottleneck in Tor bandwidth today is exit nodes. WF defenses do not need to extend to exit nodes, stopping at the bridge (in our framework) or at the guard or middle node when fully implemented. Thus, the bandwidth overhead only extends to one or two relays in a circuit and crucially not to the most loaded relay, making the overhead cost much less in practice. Third, given our findings for the open-world setting, it may be possible to tune WTF-PAD further to lower the bandwidth and maintain useful security gains in realistic use cases.

The construction of the histograms H_B and H_G is critical for the correct performance of the defense. First, since these distributions depend on the client's connection, we cannot estimate them a priori and ship them with WTF-PAD. A solution is to consider groups of clients with similar connections and have a precomputed configuration for each group. Then, the clients will estimate the properties of their network and only download the configuration that best matches their connection. Future work in developing WTF-PAD could explore the use of genetic algorithms to find the optimal histogram for each specific situation. A genetic algorithm could optimize a fitness function composed by the bandwidth overhead and the accuracy of the WF attack. Under mild assumptions on the distribution, histograms can be represented efficiently to reduce the search space.

7   Conclusion

In this paper, we described the design of WTF-PAD, a probabilistic link-padding defense based on Adaptive Padding. We studied the effectiveness and overheads of WTF-PAD, and compared it to existing link-padding-based defenses, showing that it offers reasonable protection with lower overhead costs. In particular, our results show that WTF-PAD does not introduce any delay in the communication while introducing moderate bandwidth overheads, which makes it especially suitable for low-latency communications such as Tor. Additionally, we have evaluated the effectiveness of WTF-AP in open-world and multi-tab scenarios. The results show that the defense reduces the performance of the classifier to random guessing.

Acknowledgments. A special acknowledgement to Gunes Acar, Ero Balsa, Filipe Beato and Stijpan Picek for reviewing the draft version of the paper. We appreciate the interesting discussions with Yawning Angel, Rishab Nithyanand, Jamie Hayes, Giovanni Cherubin, Tao Wang, Oscar Reparaz and Iraklis Symeonidis that helped developing this paper. This material is based upon work supported by the National Science Foundation under Grants No. CNS-1423163 and CNS-0954133 and the European Commission through H2020-DS-2014-653497 PANORAMIX and H2020-ICT-2014-644371 WITDOM. Marc Juarez is funded by a PhD fellowship of the Fund for Scientific Research - Flanders (FWO).

A   WTF-PAD Histograms

A histogram is defined as a disjoint partition of the support of the inter-arrival time distribution $[0, +\infty)$. Each sub-interval, that we call *bin*, is a half-closed interval $I_i = [a_i, b_i)$ with $0 \leq a_i, b_i \leq +\infty$ for all $i = 1, \ldots, n$, where $n \geq 2$ is the total number of bins in the partition. The bin lengths used in the AP histogram increase exponentially with the bin index, namely, the intermediate bins have the following endpoints:

$$a_i = \frac{M}{2^{n-i}}, b_i = \frac{M}{2^{n-i-1}},$$

for $i = 2, \ldots, n - 1$. $M > 0$ is the maximum inter-arrival time considered in practice. The first bin is $I_1 = [0, \frac{M}{2^{n-2}})$ and the last bin is $I_n = [M, +\infty)$.

An exponential scale for the bins provides more resolution for values in a neighborhood of zero, which is convenient to represent distributions with heavy positive skew, such as the distribution of inter-arrival times in network traffic.

When we sample from a bin, AP returns a value sampled uniformly from $[a_i, b_i)$, except for the last bin $[M, +\infty)$, in which case AP returns "∞".

In Fig. 9, we show a simplified version of the histograms we used in the WTF-PAD instance at the client. The histograms that we use have 20 bins.

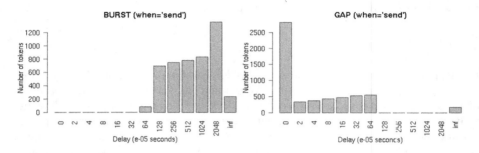

Fig. 9. Example of WTF-PAD histograms at the client. The histogram on the top is the H_B and the one at the bottom is H_G.

Each bin contains a number of tokens k_i. We denote K the sum of tokens in all the bins except the infinity bin, i.e.:

$$K := \sum_{i=1}^{n-1} k_i.$$

If we assume the probability of selecting a token is uniform over the total number of tokens, then the probability of sampling a delay from that bin can be estimated as:

$$P_i := \frac{k_i}{K + k_n}. \tag{1}$$

We assume that all the bins I_i for $i < n$ are already filled as explained in Sect. 3.3. In the following we describe how to set the number of tokens in I_n, the infinity bin, for both histograms, H_B and H_G.

Infinity bin in H_B. According to the notation introduced above, P_n in H_B is the probability of falling into the infinity bin and thus defines the probability of not sending padding (and not starting a fake burst) when we draw a sample from it. To express k_n in terms of the probability of sampling from I_n and the current sum of tokens in the histogram, we clear Eq. 1 for k_n:

$$k_n = \frac{P_n}{1 - P_n} K.$$

For instance, if we decide on setting the probability of generating a fake burst to 0.9, then we need to set $P_n = 0.1$. Assuming $K = 300$ tokens, using the equation above we obtain $k_n \approx 34$.

Infinity bin in H_G. The number of tokens we will sample from H_G until we hit the infinity bin is the number of dummy messages we will send within a fake burst. Since the probability of drawing a token is uniform, we can think the histogram as one single bucket that contains tokens from I_n and tokens from the other bins. Then, the expected number of draws without replacement, L, until we draw the first token from the infinity bin is a known result one can find in any probability textbook:

$$E[L] = \frac{K + k_n + 1}{k_n + 1}.$$

We know the expected value of the length of a burst from our estimations on a large dataset of web traffic. Let μ_L be the mean burst length. In order to make sure fake bursts have the same mean length as real bursts, we must impose the expected number of tokens we sample until we hit the infinity bin to be: $E[L] = \mu_L$. Then, we only need to clear k_n from the equation:

$$k_n = \frac{K - \mu_L + 1}{\mu_L - 1}.$$

This equation is well defined because, typically, the mean length of a burst is small: $K >> \mu_L$.

References

1. Alexa. Alexa Top 500 Global Site (2015). http://www.alexa.com/topsites
2. Cai, X., Nithyanand, R., Johnson, R.-B.: A congestion sensitive website fingerprinting defense. In: Workshop on Privacy in the Electronic Society (WPES), pp. 121–130. ACM (2014)
3. Cai, X., Nithyanand, R., Johnson, R.: Glove: A bespoke website fingerprinting defense. In: Workshop on Privacy in the Electronic Society (WPES), pp. 131–134. ACM (2014)
4. Cai, X., Nithyanand, R., Wang, T., Johnson, R., Goldberg, I.: A systematic approach to developing and evaluating website fingerprinting defenses. In: ACM Conference on Computer and Communications Security (CCS), pp. 227–238. ACM (2014)
5. Cai, X., Zhang, X.C., Joshi, B., Johnson, R.: Touching from a distance: website fingerprinting attacks and defenses. In: ACM Conference on Computer and Communications Security (CCS), pp. 605–616 (2012)
6. Davis, J., Goadrich, M.: The relationship between precision-recall and ROC curves. In: Proceedings of the 23rd international conference on Machine learning, pp. 233–240. ACM (2006)
7. Dingledine, R., Mathewson, N., Syverson, P.: Tor: the second-generation onion router. In: USENIX Security Symposium. USENIX Association (2004)

8. Dyer, K.P., Coull, S.E., Ristenpart, T., Shrimpton, T.: Peek-a-boo still see you i: why efficient traffic analysis countermeasures fail. In: IEEE Symposium on Security and Privacy (S&P), pp. 332–346. IEEE (2012)

9. Herrmann, D., Wendolsky, R., Federrath, H.: Website fingerprinting: attacking popular privacy enhancing technologies with the multinomial Naïve-Bayes classifier. In: ACM Workshop on Cloud Computing Security, pp. 31–42. ACM (2009)

10. Hintz, A.: Fingerprinting websites using traffic analysis. In: Dingledine, R., Syverson, P.F. (eds.) PET 2002. LNCS, vol. 2482, pp. 171–178. Springer, Heidelberg (2003)

11. Juarez, M., Afroz, S., Acar, G., Diaz, C., Greenstadt, R.: A critical analysis of website fingerprinting attacks. In: ACM Conference on Computer and Communications Security (CCS), pp. 263–274. ACM (2014)

12. Lu, L., Chang, E.-C., Chan, M.C.: Website fingerprinting and identification using ordered feature sequences. In: Gritzalis, D., Preneel, B., Theoharidou, M. (eds.) ESORICS 2010. LNCS, vol. 6345, pp. 199–214. Springer, Heidelberg (2010)

13. Luo, X., Zhou, P., Chan, E., Lee, W.: Sealing information leaks with browser-side obfuscation of encrypted flows. In: Network & Distributed System Security Symposium (NDSS). IEEE Computer Society (2011)

14. McCoy, D., Bauer, K., Grunwald, D., Kohno, T., Sicker, D.C.: Shining light in dark places: understanding the Tor network. In: Borisov, N., Goldberg, I. (eds.) PETS 2008. LNCS, vol. 5134, pp. 63–76. Springer, Heidelberg (2008)

15. Miller, B., Huang, L., Joseph, A.D., Tygar, J.D.: I know why you went to the clinic: risks and realization of HTTPS traffic analysis. In: De Cristofaro, E., Murdoch, S.J. (eds.) PETS 2014. LNCS, vol. 8555, pp. 143–163. Springer, Heidelberg (2014)

16. Panchenko, A., Lanze, F., Zinnen, A., Henze, M., Pennekamp, J., Wehrle, K., Engel, T.: Website fingerprinting at internet scale. In: Network & Distributed System Security Symposium (NDSS). IEEE Computer Society (2016)

17. Panchenko, A., Niessen, L., Zinnen, A., Engel, T.: Website fingerprinting in onion routing based anonymization networks. In: ACM Workshop on Privacy in the Electronic Society (WPES), pp. 103–114. ACM (2011)

18. Wang, M.-H.: Timing analysis in low-latency mix networks: attacks and defenses. In: Gollmann, D., Meier, J., Sabelfeld, A. (eds.) ESORICS 2006. LNCS, vol. 4189, pp. 18–33. Springer, Heidelberg (2006)

19. Sun, Q., Simon, D. R., Wang, Y.M.: Statistical identification of encrypted web browsing traffic. In: IEEE Symposium on Security and Privacy (S&P), pp. 19–30. IEEE (2002)

20. The Tor project. Users statistics. https://metrics.torproject.org/users.html. Accessed 20 July 2015

21. The Tor project. Pluggable Transports (2012). Tor spec: https://gitweb.torproject. org/torspec.git/tree/pt-spec.txt. Accessed 15 December 2015

22. Wang, T.: Website fingerprinting: attacks and defenses. PhD thesis University of Waterloo (2016)

23. Wang, T., Cai, X., Nithyanand, R., Johnson, R., Goldberg, I.: Effective attacks and provable defenses for website fingerprinting. In: USENIX Security Symposium, pp. 143–157. USENIX Association (2014)

24. Wang, T., Goldberg, I.: Improved website fingerprinting on Tor. In: ACM Workshop on Privacy in the Electronic Society (WPES), pp. 201–212. ACM (2013)

25. Wright, C.V., Coull, S.E., Monrose, F.: Traffic morphing: An efficient defense against statistical traffic analysis. In: Network & Distributed System Security Symposium (NDSS) (2009)

Proactive Verification of Security Compliance for Clouds Through Pre-computation: Application to OpenStack

Suryadipta Majumdar[1(✉)], Yosr Jarraya[2], Taous Madi[1],
Amir Alimohammadifar[1], Makan Pourzandi[2], Lingyu Wang[1],
and Mourad Debbabi[1]

[1] CIISE, Concordia University, Montreal, QC, Canada
{su_majum,t_madi,ami_alim,wang,debbabi}@encs.concordia.ca
[2] Ericsson Security Research, Ericsson Canada, Montreal, QC, Canada
{yosr.jarraya,makan.pourzandi}@ericsson.com

Abstract. The verification of security compliance with respect to security standards and policies is desirable to both cloud providers and users. However, the sheer size of a cloud implies a major challenge to be scalability and in particular response time. Most existing approaches are either after the fact or incur prohibitive delay in processing user requests. In this paper, we propose a scalable approach that can reduce the response time of online security compliance verification in large clouds to a practical level. The main idea is to start preparing for the costly verification proactively, as soon as the system is a few steps ahead of potential operations causing violations. We present detailed models and algorithms, and report real-life experiences and challenges faced while implementing our solution in OpenStack. We also conduct experiments whose results confirm the efficiency and scalability of our approach.

Keywords: Proactive compliance verification · Cloud security · Auditing · OpenStack

1 Introduction

The widespread adoption of cloud computing as the replacement of traditional IT solutions is still being hindered by various security concerns [5]. In particular, the multi-tenant and self-service nature of clouds usually implies significant operational complexity, which may prepare the floor for misconfigurations and vulnerabilities leading to violations of security compliance. Therefore, the security compliance verification w.r.t. security standards, policies, and properties, is desirable to both cloud providers and users. Evidently, the Cloud Security Alliance (CSA) has recently introduced the Security, Trust & Assurance Registry (STAR) for security assurance in clouds, which defines three levels of certifications (self-auditing, third-party auditing, and continuous, near real-time verification of security compliance) [7].

© Springer International Publishing Switzerland 2016
I. Askoxylakis et al. (Eds.): ESORICS 2016, Part I, LNCS 9878, pp. 47–66, 2016.
DOI: 10.1007/978-3-319-45744-4_3

However, the sheer size of clouds (e.g., a *decent-size* cloud is said to have around 1,000 tenants and 100,000 users [23]) implies one of the main challenges in verifying security compliance, specifically the scalability and response time. To that end, existing approaches can be roughly divided into three categories (a more detailed review of related work will be given in Sect. 6). First, the *retroactive approaches* (e.g., [17,18]) catch compliance violations after the fact, which means they cannot prevent security breaches from propagating or causing potentially irreversible damages (e.g., leaks of confidential information or denial of service). Second, the *intercept-and-check* approaches (e.g., [3,21]) verify the compliance of each user request before either granting or denying it, which may lead to a substantial delay to users' requests, as will be further illustrated later in this section. Third, the *proactive approaches* in [3,21] verify user requests in advance, which, however, assume the sequence of such requests is known beforehand.

In this paper, we propose a scalable approach for proactive verification of security compliance in large clouds, by avoiding the limitations of the last two approaches mentioned above (i.e., *intercept-and-check* and *proactive*). Specifically, unlike both existing approaches, we start to prepare for the costly verification proactively, as soon as the system is N-step (N is an integer) ahead of the operations causing compliance violations (namely, *critical operations*), such that the actual verification of critical operations is reduced to a simple search in a pre-computed table (namely, *watchlist*), causing negligible delay.

To illustrate the idea, Fig. 1 compares how user requests are processed under a typical *intercept-and-check* approach and under our solution, respectively. In the upper timeline, an intercept-and-check approach intercepts and then verifies the *update port* user request against the desired security property[1]. The state of the art, as reported in [3], would take over four minutes for checking the current cloud (medium-size) state to determine whether the request should be granted or denied. Extrapolating such a result to a larger cloud would result in hours of delay, which is clearly infeasible. On the other hand, as depicted in the lower timeline, our approach works very differently. It proactively conducts a set of pre-computations distributed among N-steps ahead of the actual occurrence of the critical operation (*update port*). These pre-computations incrementally prepare the needed information for efficiently verifying the critical operation later on, and consequently the actual verification only takes six milliseconds, instead of four minutes [3], as shown in the timeline.

The main contributions of our paper are as follows:

- To the best of our knowledge, the proposed proactive verification approach is the first solution that can reduce the response-time of online security compliance verification in large clouds to a practical level (e.g., the response time is about 8.5 ms for a large cloud with 100,000 virtual ports).
- We devise dependency models to capture the relationships between various management operations and related security properties, for both the identity

---

[1] Here we consider the "no bypass" security property for the anti-spoofing mechanisms in the cloud, which can be violated by real world vulnerabilities (e.g., OpenStack vulnerability [20]).

and access management service and the virtualized infrastructure in clouds, which serve as the foundation of our approach.

- We provide detailed methodology and algorithms. We also report real-life experiences and challenges faced while implementing our solution in Open-Stack [22].
- We conduct experiments to evaluate the performance of our solution, and the results confirm the efficiency and scalability to be practical for large clouds.
- Finally, our solution goes inline with the continuous monitoring-based certi-fication, which is the most demanding level specified by CSA [7].

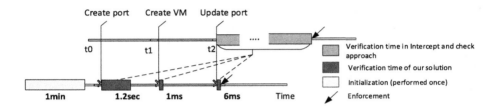

Fig. 1. Comparison of the execution time of our solution with the *intercept-and-check*.

The paper is organized as follows. Section 2 describes the threat model fol-lowed by our running example and the dependency models for the virtualized infrastructure, and for the access control management service. Section 3 details our methodology. Section 4 provides the implementation details and experimen-tal results. Section 5 discusses different aspects of our approach. Section 6 sum-marizes related works and compares them with our approach. Section 7 concludes the paper providing future research directions.

2 Models

Here, we give the threat model and present the dependency models.

2.1 Threat Model

We assume that the cloud infrastructure management systems (a) may be trusted for the integrity of the API calls, event notifications, and database records (exist-ing techniques on trusted computing may be applied to establish a chain of trust from TPM chips embedded inside the cloud hardware, e.g., [1]), and (b) may have implementation flaws, misconfigurations and vulnerabilities that can be potentially exploited by malicious entities to violate security properties specified by the cloud tenants. The cloud users including cloud operators and agents (on behalf of a human) may be malicious.

Though our framework may catch violations of specified security properties due to either misconfigurations or exploits of vulnerabilities, our focus is not to detect specific attacks or intrusions. We assume that, before our proactive approach is launched, an initial auditing is performed and potential violations are resolved. However, if our solution is added from the commencement of a cloud, obviously no prior security verification is required. This work focuses on attacks directed through the cloud management interfaces and more specifically cloud management operations (e.g., create/delete/update tenant, user, VM, etc.). Any violation bypassing the cloud management interface is beyond the scope of this work. To make our discussions more concrete, the following shows an example of in-scope threats based on a real vulnerability.

Running Example. Real world vulnerabilities such as the one in Open-Stack [20][2], can be exploited to bypass anti-spoofing mechanisms. These mechanisms are implemented in OpenStack using firewall rules enforcing tenants' layer 3 network isolation. Figure 2 shows the attack scenario to exploit this vulnerability. The exploit consists in changing the device owner (step 3 in Fig. 2) of an instance's port to a string starting with the word `network`, right after the instance is created (steps 1 & 2) and just before security group gets attached to it (race condition). As a result, the firewall rules of the compute node are not applied to that port, since it is treated as a network owned port. Consequently, a malicious tenant can launch IP, MAC, and DHCP spoofing attacks (step 4).

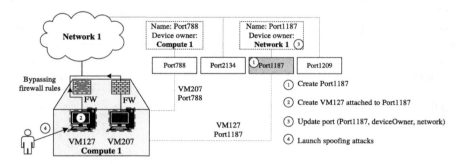

Fig. 2. An exploit of a vulnerability in OpenStack [20], leading to bypassing the anti-spoofing mechanism.

2.2   Dependency Models

Figure 3 illustrates the two dependency models that we derive for an OpenStack-managed cloud covering virtual infrastructure (Fig. 3(a)) and user access control (Fig. 3(b)). Each dependency model can be used for proactively auditing multiple security properties. We validate these dependency models based on extensive study of OpenStack APIs from different related OpenStack services (e.g., Neutron, Nova, and Keystone) and Open vSwitch. For the user access control model,

---

[2] OpenStack [22] is an open-source cloud infrastructure management platform.

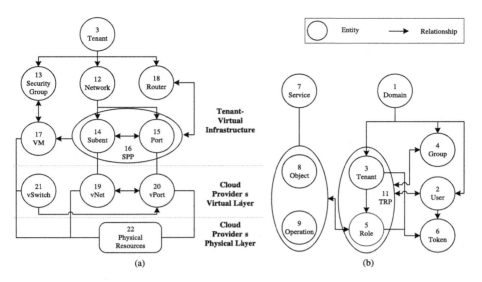

Fig. 3. Dependency models: (a) cloud infrastructure and (b) access control management.

we are inspired by the OSAC model by Tang et al. [32]. To better explain the usefulness of these models, we start by providing an example on how the cloud infrastructure dependency model (see Fig. 3(a)) allows us to relate actual management operations/events happening in the cloud to the "no bypass" security property presented in Sect. 2.1.

Example 1. *According to the attack scenario presented in Fig. 2, the critical management operation that leads to the violation of the "no bypass" security property is* update port. *The model in Fig. 3(a) includes* port *(vertex 15) and* VM *(vertex 17). The* vertex 16 *is a specific vertex grouping a port and a subnet pair. The* update port *operation is related to the entity* port *(vertex 15 in Fig. 3(a)). As it can be seen in Fig. 3(a),* update port *depends on other operations such as* create port *(edge (12,15)) and* create VM *(edge 16, 17). More precisely,* create VM *attaches a port (vertex 15) on a subnet (vertex 14) to a VM (vertex 17).*

As the create port *and* create VM *operations are closely related to the actual critical operation (*update port*), our model captures this dependency relationship and aids to avoid the security violation by starting preparation from the* create port *operation. Furthermore, these operations in turn depend on the existence/creation of a subnet, a network and a tenant. This induces a chain of dependencies between a set of events that could be related to this security property.*

Formally, the dependency model is a graph $G = (V, E)$, where vertices V_i are individual cloud entities (e.g., user, role, tenant, port, VM, etc.) or groups of entities (e.g., (port, subnet) pair) and edges E_{ij} are dependency relationships between connected vertices. These relationships are activated by events/operations in the cloud (e.g., create/delete port, attach VM to a (port, subnet) pair, etc.). We use edges' attributes to store information on which security property are associated with the events that are related to the edge and on the type of this event per property. We define four kinds of relationships. We use different types of edges (unidirectional, bidirectional, or non-directional) to differentiate the following relationships based on their semantics.

- *Precedence* relation, represented by a unidirectional edge, such that $E_{ij} = (V_i, V_j)$ denotes that the entity V_i must exist before being able to create entity V_j within V_i.
- *Association* relation, represented by a bidirectional edge, such that $E_{ij} = (V_i, V_j)$ denotes that entities V_i and V_j should both exist (i.e., created) to be able to make any association between them.
- *Mapping* relation, represented by a non-directional edge, such that $E_{ij} = \{V_i, V_j\}$ denotes a correspondence relationship between entities V_i and V_j existing in different layers in the cloud.
- *Reflexive* relation (not represented in the graph), representing a relation from a node to itself such as updating attributes of the node.

We leverage the knowledge captured by these dependencies to appropriately identify the intercepted events, relate them to the security property, identify their roles in the context of proactive compliance verification, and determine the distance to a critical state. More details are provided in Sect. 3. It is worth noting that these models are static and do not depend on the execution context of the cloud. They consist of a relatively small set of entities and relationships. For example, for Neutron, Nova, and Keystone services, we enumerated only 86 different entities and about 400 events that are relevant to configuration changes and management.

Table 1 enlists an excerpt of the security properties supported by the cloud infrastructure dependency model. Here, we categorize events mainly into two types: critical event (CE) and watchlist event (WE). A CE (e.g., `update port`) potentially leads to the violation of the associated property. A WE corresponds to an event that impacts the content of the watchlist associated with the security property (e.g., `create port` and `create VM`). The third type of event is the trigger event (TE), which is neither critical nor watchlist-related, however is useful to determine the distance to a critical state. Note that an event may have multiple types considering different security properties. For example, `create VM` is a WE event for the *no bypass* property, but it is of type CE for the *no co-residency* property.

3 Proactive Verification of Security Compliance (PVSC)

In this section, we detail our solution to proactively verify security violation and enforce compliance in the cloud.

3.1   Overview

We devise a novel approach, namely Proactive Verification of Security Compliance (*PVSC*), that proactively conducts a set of pre-computations distributed along *N-step* ahead of the occurrence of a critical operation, where N is a parameter tailored for each considered security property and defined as the expected minimal distance to a critical state, which corresponds to the minimal number of operations from the current state. Note that this distance is called minimal as operations related to security properties may be interleaved with unrelated operations. In PVSC, the pre-computations incrementally prepare the needed conditions to preserve security compliance, and are stored in *watchlists*. These *watchlists* are used to detect violations of security properties when critical operations are about to occur. To measure *N-step* and avoid state explosion, we leverage abstract dependency models described in Sect. 2.2.

An overview of this solution is depicted in Fig. 4. Initially, data from the dependency models and the initialized watchlists (generated with the watchlist contents mentioned in Table 1 for each security property) are pre-computed and stored in databases. PVSC uses this data to efficiently intercept and identify relevant operations (*Interceptor & Matcher*) but only blocks the critical ones. This data would be also used together with cloud context information to estimate the minimal distance towards the violation (*N-step Evaluator*). By identifying the type of intercepted operations and their impact on security properties, we elaborate different watchlists that are progressively updated (*Watchlist Updater*). These watchlists are consulted to evaluate the impact of a critical operation (*Violation Detector*). According to the later decision, the critical operation can be realized or blocked to preserve security compliance.

Table 1. An excerpt of the security properties supported by the cloud infrastructure model with their corresponding critical and watchlist events, and the watchlist contents.

Property	Critical event (CE)	Watchlist event (WE)	Watchlist per tenant
No bypass [6]	update port (15,15)	create VM (16,17) create port (12,15)	Ports except VM ports
Port consistency [6,12]	create vPort (21,20)	create port (12,15)	Ports at tenant layer
No abuse of resources [6]	create VM (16,17), create vNet (14,19)	create VM (16,17), create vNet (14,19)	Counters for VM/vNet
		delete VM (16,17), delete vNet (14,19)	
Common port ownership [6]	attach port to a router (16,18)	create router (3,18)	Router-tenant pair
Port isolation [6,12]	add vPort to vNet (19,20)	create vNet (14,19)	vNets in a subnet
No co-residency[a] [6,12]	create VM (16,17), migrate VM (17,22)	create VM (16,17) migrate VM (17,22)	Hosts with no conflicting VMs

[a]This property requires tenant-specific policy additionally

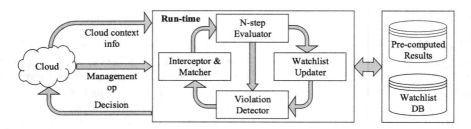

Fig. 4. An overview of our proactive solution.

3.2   Methodology

PVSC consists of two phases: an initialization phase that is performed offline only once and a run-time verification phase, which is performed online but proactively.

Figure 5 depicts a detailed overview of PVSC. The initialization phase is mainly meant to pre-process data from different sources. Once the initialization phase is completed, the run-time detection phase serves at intercepting cloud operations, proactively finding out whether considered security properties are about to be compromised, determining the distance N (where N is the number of steps) towards critical states, and acting on re-enforcement towards preserving security compliance. In the following, we describe each phase and other related components of our approach in more details.

Initialization Phase. This phase collects initial data from the cloud infrastructure and pre-processes the data in order to prepare the ground for the run-time phase. For each security property, all dependency models are to obtain: (i) the involved cloud entities, (ii) the related abstract-events with their types, and (iii) all possible values of N. Pre-computing all needed information from the dependency models at the initialization phase avoids tracing the models at run-time, which fosters better efficiency. Following we describe different tables we leverage during the initialization phase.

- **Property-WL:** specifying the content of watchlist for each security property to aid watchlist initialization.
- **Event-operation:** mapping events to different operations in different cloud environment to easily integrate different cloud implementations and used as input to the initialization phase.
- **Property-N-thresholds:** mapping the specified security properties and their associated thresholds (denoted as $N\text{-}th$), where thresholds are security property specific and inputs from the administrators.
- **Model-event:** relating each security property with the elements of the dependency models including the events with their types.
- **Model-N-property:** storing all possible values of N (denoted as $N\text{-}cp$) for each property.

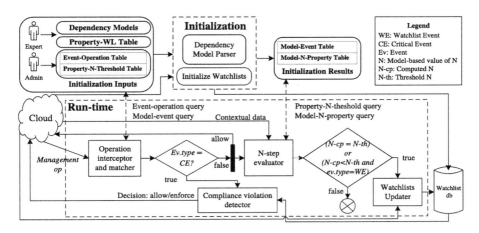

Fig. 5. A detailed overview of PVSC composed of an one-time initialization phase and a run-time verification phase.

Example 2. *Figure 6 shows the outcome of the initialization phase for the no bypass property. The traversal of the dependency model using the identified property and searching in the attributes of the corresponding edges allow identifying that, for the considered property,* create port *and* create VM *are of type WE and* update port *is of type CE. This information is stored in the* Model-event *table. Other events of type TE such as* create network, create subnet *are not shown for brevity. The* Event-operation *table shows that the* create port *event corresponds to the* neutron port-create *operation in OpenStack. The minimal distance from the critical event at which our solution should react is (N-th = 3), as shown in the* Property-N-thresholds *table. The* Model-N-property *table stores all possible computed values of N taking into account the security property and the dependency model. Finally, the watchlist is initialized for the no bypass property based on data collected from the cloud.*

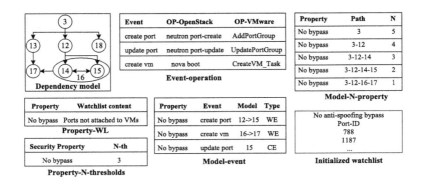

Fig. 6. The result of the initialization phase for the *no bypass* property.

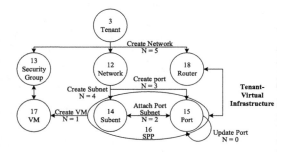

Fig. 7. A part of the cloud infrastructure dependency model annotated with all possible values of N that is relevant to the *no bypass* property.

For each tenant, the watchlist is populated with the list of virtual ports that are not attached to a VM as in the `Property-WL` *table.*

Precomputation of N consists in traversing the dependency graph for each security property from the edge corresponding to its critical event backward until reaching the root node of the graph, finding out all dependent events and entities and storing precomputed values of N for each possible configuration in the `Model-N-property` table. A configuration is an abstract state that allows to determine whether the entities that the security properties depend on, actually exist. The minimal distance to the critical event from the root node is the total number of events that the critical event depends on. This distance represents $N\text{-}max$, the maximal value of N from which we can apply our proactive approach for this property. The minimum value of N is 1 and it corresponds to the configuration where the next event to be observed is possibly the critical event.

Example 3. *For the no bypass property, the* `Model-N-property` *table stores five entries that cover all possible values of N and the associated configuration (See Fig. 7). For instance, if only a tenant already exists (vertex 3) without yet any network, subnet, ports, and VMs, we need to observe at least 5 events before being able to intercept the critical event* `update port`*. If we observe an event for the creation of network within this tenant (i.e., edge $(3, 12)$) without yet any subnet, ports, and VMs, the minimal distance to see the* `update port` *event would be $N = 4$. The event preceding* `update port` *is the* `create VM` *(i.e., edge $(16, 17)$) event, and the minimal distance is 1.*

Run-Time Computation. At run-time, our system intercepts all operation performed in the cloud, but only blocks those which are matched with the critical events. Matching operation with an event consists in querying the `Event-operation` table. For those critical events, the corresponding operations are halted only during compliance verification, which consists in searching a set of values (e.g., values of the operation's parameters) in the corresponding watchlist. The verification decision is either to allow the operation to continue

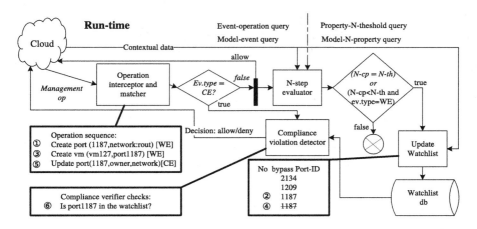

Fig. 8. An excerpt of runtime verification of the *no bypass* property.

or apply the planned enforcement approach as specified by the administrator. Being able to intercept all operations, including the non-critical ones as soon as they are executed allows progressively updating watchlists, without impacting the performance of the cloud. At each matched non-critical events (WE or TE), our system updates the estimated current minimal distance to violation, namely $N\text{-}cp$, for the related property using the `N-step evaluator`. The latter collects contextual data from the cloud and uses it to query the table of precomputed values of N, namely `Model-N-property`. When the value of the estimated current distance to violation becomes equal to the threshold value, the watchlist corresponding to the security property is updated using data from the cloud regardless of the event type to ensure that its content is up-to-date, hence allowing appropriate detection. For $N\text{-}cp < N\text{-}th$, whenever a WE-type operation is encountered, the watchlist is directly updated using the values of the parameters of the intercepted operations.

The `N-step evaluator` evaluates at run-time the value of N, whenever a non-critical event concerning a given security property has been matched with the intercepted operation. First, the related context data is then gathered from the cloud to determine whether the status of the dependent entities. The evaluator uses this information and the security property in focus to make a specific query to the `Model-N-property` table, to collect the value of N corresponding to the current context.

Example 4. *Figure 8 illustrates the run-time workflow for the no bypass property assuming that a tenant, a network and a subnet already exist.*

To rectify the situation described in the running example, our solution incrementally builds a watchlist with ports that are not attached to VMs, and verifies the `update port` *operation with this watchlist. Firstly, we intercept the* `create port 1187` *operation, identifies the event type (which is WE), and measure the value of N (= 3) respectively from the* `Model-event` *and* `Property-N-threshold` *tables. Since the* `create port` *event is a WE event for the no bypass property and evaluating N results in N-cp = N-th = 3, we add* `port1187` *to the watchlist without blocking it. Secondly, we intercept* `create VM127 attached to port1187` *operation and measure N similarly. Then,* `port1187` *is removed from the watchlist, as it is now attached to* `VM127`*. Finally, after intercepting the* `update port(port1187, deviceOwner, network)` *operation and measuring N, we identify that this is a CE event. Therefore, we verify with the watchlist with blocking the operation, find that* `port1187` *is not in the watchlist, and hence PVSC recommends denial of this operation to preserve the no bypass property.*

4   Proof of Concept in OpenStack

This section describes how we integrate PVSC into OpenStack and presents our experimental results.

4.1   Implementation

We detail the implementations of both the initialization and the runtime detection phases.

Background. OpenStack [22] is an open-source cloud infrastructure management platform that is being used almost in half of private clouds and significant portions of the public clouds (see [8] for detailed statistics). Keystone [22] is the OpenStack identity service for authentication and authorization. Keystone implements the RBAC model [28]. Neutron [22] provides tenants with capabilities to build networking topologies through the exposed APIs. Nova [22] is the OpenStack project designed to provide on-demand access to compute resources, and relies on VMs.

Initialization Phase. Firstly, we map all operations in OpenStack API [25] corresponding to the events that are relevant to the monitored security properties. During this phase, we store our pre-computated results and tenant-specific watchlists in a MySQL database; which allows us to efficiently query OpenStack cloud data, which is also stored in databases. Our Python scripts derive the association between the model provided in Fig. 3 and the security properties, and populate our database by adding the dependency information and the values of the precomputed N. Additionally, we capture the current state of the OpenStack cloud by collecting data from the Keystone, Neutron and Nova databases.

Run-Time Phase. Firstly, the Interceptor module, which is implemented in Python, intercepts operations based on the existing intercepting methods (e.g., audit middleware [24]) supported in OpenStack. Events are primarily created via the notification system in OpenStack; Nova, Neutron, etc. emits notifications in a JSON format. Here, we leverage the audit middleware in Keystone, which was previously supported by pyCADF [4], to intercept Keystone, Neutron and Nova events by enabling the audit middleware and configuring filters. After intercepting an operation, its details (e.g., name and parameters) are processed by our Matcher module to determine the criticality of the current operation, and later forwarded to our MySQL stored procedures (e.g., N-step evaluator, Watchlist updater and Violation detector). The N-step evaluator measures the distance from any possible violation. Based on the outcome of both the Matcher and N-step evaluator modules, any of the following is processed: (i) the Watchlist updater adds the parameter(s) of the current operation to the watchlist database, (ii) the Violation detector searches the current values of the parameter(s) in the corresponding watchlist, and (iii) forward the decision (e.g., allow or deny) to the cloud based on the enforcement options.

4.2   Experimental Results

In this section, we discuss time and memory requirements of PVSC.

Experiment Settings. All experiments are conducted on the OpenStack setup inside a lab environment. Our OpenStack version is Liberty with Keystone API version v3 and Neutron API version v2. There are one controller node and three compute nodes, each having Intel i7 dual core CPU and 2 GB memory with the Ubuntu 14.04 server. Based on a recent survey [23] on OpenStack, we simulated an environment with maximum 100,000 users, 10,000 tenants, 500 domains, 100,000 VMs, 40,000 subnets, 20,000 routers and 100,000 ports. We conduct the experiment for 10 different datasets varying the most important factor and fixing others to the largest value, e.g., for the *no bypass* property, both the number of ports (from 10,000 to 100,000 with the gap of 10,000) and the number of tenants (from 1,000 to 10,000 with the gap of 1,000) are varied, as the content of the watchlist is tenant-specific and a list of ports. For the *common ownership*[3] property, the number of tenants is varied from 1,000 to 10,000 with the gap of 1,000 having 5 roles in each tenant. We repeat each experiment 100 times.

Results. The objective of the first set of experiment is to demonstrate the time efficiency of our proactive solution. Intercepting operations to identify the type of operation, which is the minimum time we need to black for all operations (CE and WE, and all others), is taking constant time (0.266 ms) (INT in Fig. 9(a)). Moreover, calculating N-step (NSE in Fig. 9(a)) completes in constant time (0.133 ms for the largest datasets) for the *no bypass* (NB) property, and in quasi constant time (varying from 0.773 ms to 0.794 ms) for the *common ownership* (CO) property. Violation detector blocks only critical operation for a maximum extra delay of 8.2 ms (VD in Fig. 9(b)) for the largest dataset. Figure 10(a) shows the required execution time to pre-compute the watchlists for the *no bypass* and *common ownership* properties are 5,000 ms and 5,400 ms respectively, for our largest dataset. As expected, the watchlist pre-computation step, which involves access to the cloud databases, requires comparatively longer time. However, this step is performed only during the

---

[3] This property allows users to hold only the roles that are defined within their domains [6, 12].

initialization phase. Any later update of the watchlist is performed incrementally, and takes few milliseconds. Figure 10(a) depicts the execution time for the largest dataset (10,000 tenants and 100,000 ports), and shows that preparing watchlist is comparatively time consuming and beneficial to perform proactively, as we spend about 5,400 ms in preparing watchlist during initialization though the subsequent enforcement takes only 8 ms per critical operation call at run-time.

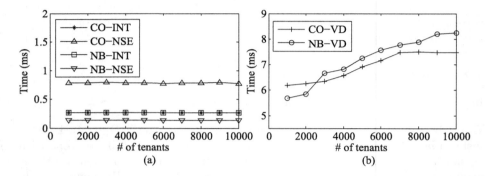

Fig. 9. Time duration (in ms) for different modules (INT: Interceptor, NSE: N-step evaluator, VD: Violation detector) of PVSC for the *common ownership* (CO) and *no bypass* (NB) properties by varying the number of tenants. The number of ports is also varied from 10,000 to 100,000, and each tenant contains 5 roles. Time required for the steps: (a) intercepting operations, evaluating N-step, and (b) detecting violations.

In the second part of the experiment, we measure the memory cost for the watchlists. Figure 10(b) depicts that the memory requirement increases quasi linearly with the dataset size. We are able to restrict the watchlist size in few

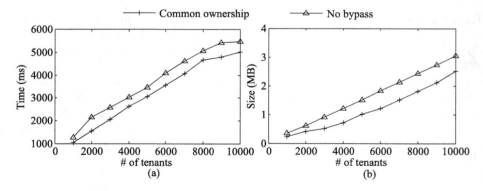

Fig. 10. (a) Time required (in ms) for preparing watchlist for different properties varying the number of tenants at the initialization step. (b) Memory requirement (in MB) for watchlists processing for different properties by varying the number of tenants. Number of ports is also varied from 10,000 to 100,000, and each tenant contains 5 roles.

Table 2. Comparing execution time (in ms) between PVSC and our alternative implementation of *intercept-and-check* for the *no bypass* property.

Number of ports	10,000	20,000	30,000	40,000	50,000	60,000	70,000	80,000	90,000	100,000
Intercept-and-check	60,200	107,209	184,230	237,245	317,252	357,261	407,268	437,271	455,276	480,277
PVSC	5.928	6.09	6.916	7.016	7.496	7.815	8.024	8.14	8.453	8.501

MBs by choosing the content of the watchlist carefully. Therefore, we show that our approach improves the execution time without excessive memory costs. We store roles and corresponding tenants for the common ownership property, and only ports for the no bypass property.

Table 2 compares the execution time of PVSC and our alternative implementation of *intercept-and-check*, in which after detecting a critical event we collect data from the cloud and start verifying security properties using a SAT solver (e.g., Sugar [31]). We observe that verifying with the *intercept-and-check* approach including data collection takes 15 seconds (for common ownership) to 8 min (for no bypass) for our largest dataset. Therefore, each critical operation would experience long response time. Contrarily, PVSC experiences maximum response time of 8.5 ms. Our solution only permits allowed actions, hence any further accuracy evaluation is irrelevant.

5   Discussions

As our experiment results shown in the Sect. 4.2, PVSC can verify security properties for large size cloud in only few seconds at run time. There could be some cases when the pre-computed information used at run-time needs to be updated. The cases are when a change in the cloud dependency or in the cloud management API specifications occurs, or when extending verification to new security properties. In these cases, the PVSC initialization must be repeated. Even though the initialization can take several minutes, this task can be executed in parallel with run time verification and the pre-computed information updated instantly to minimize the impact on verifications at run time. Note that there are few cases where the pre-computation needs to be repeated and those cases regarding management API changes in the cloud are by nature not frequent.

Our PVSC algorithm needs only few seconds for run time verifications, this response time is satisfactory when the management operations are manually done by the administrators. But in the case of batch execution for management operations as described in [3], when these operations are executed in short intervals and if the subsequent operations impact the same watchlists, then it could imply the need for updating the same watchlists between two operations. Figure 11 depicts how events occur before the watchlist is prepared. This watchlist update takes some time and then increases the response time for PVSC at run time. However, the worst case response time for watchlist preparation is less than 6 s for the largest dataset according to our experiments. Comparing this

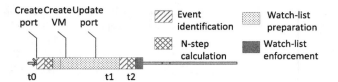

Fig. 11. Our proactive analysis approach with a batch of user requests.

time with the *intercept-and-check* naive approach (requiring few minutes) and Weatherman [3] (requiring few hours), we consider the costs of our approach to be reasonable even for large data centers. As future work, to address this use case we consider maintaining a scheduler including an event queue with different threads for different tasks in order to prepare concurrently watchlists and therefore reduce the response time in this case.

In this work, we cover structural properties involving cloud management operations (e.g., creating a tenant, granting a role, assignment of instances to physical hosts and the proper configuration of virtualization mechanisms). The properties involving session/context specific data are not yet considered. In our running example, if the malicious tenant can somehow successfully bypass the firewall rules and launch a spoofing attack, our solution cannot yet detect such spoofing attacks. As our solution relies on the information reported through the management interface, any verification by extracting the information from the actual infrastructure components (e.g., virtual or hardware) is not covered in this paper and considered as a potential future work.

6   Related Work

Auditing security compliance in the cloud has recently been explored. For instance, Solonas et al. [30] detect illegal activities in the cloud only based on collected billing data in order to preserve privacy. In [17,18], formal auditing approaches are proposed for security compliance checking in the cloud. Unlike our work, those approaches can detect violations only after they occur, which may expose the system to high risks.

VeriFlow [14] and NetPlumber [13] monitor network events and check network properties and policies at runtime to capture bugs before or as soon as they occur. They rely on incremental calculations to achieve the runtime verification. These works focus on operational network properties (e.g., black holes and forwarding loops) in traditional networks, whereas our effort is oriented toward preserving compliance with structural security properties that impact isolation in cloud virtualized infrastructures.

Various mechanisms and concepts for designing security service-level-agreement-based cloud monitoring services have been discussed in [27]. Cloud-Sec [11] and CloudMonatt [33] propose VM security monitoring. Our work covers a larger spectrum of properties (beyond the scope of VMs) that require collecting data from various sources. In addition, unlike intercepting security measurements, we intercept multiple kinds of events and assess their impact on the cloud system before applying them. In [26], a host-based secure active monitoring mechanism, where protected hooks into untrusted VMs are installed to intercept malicious events, is proposed. Once a malicious action is intercepted, the control is transferred to security tools running on a trusted VM. They detect unwanted operations initiated by malicious softwares; whereas, our contribution is at a higher level covering events initiated by potentially untrusted users.

Proactive security analysis has been explored for software security enforcement through monitoring programs' behaviors and taking specific actions (e.g., warning) in case security policies are violated. Many state-based formal models are proposed for those program monitors over the last two decades. First, Schneider [29] modelled program monitors using an infinite-state-automata model to enforce safety properties. Those automata recognize invalid behaviors and halt the target application before the violation occurs. Ligatti [15] builds on Schneider's model and defines a more general program monitors model based on the so called edit/security automata. Rather than just recognizing executions, edit automata-based monitors are able to suppress bad and/or insert new actions, transforming hence invalid executions into valid ones. Mandatory Result Automata (MRA) is another model proposed by Ligatti et al. [9,16] that can transform both actions and results. Narain [19] proactively generates correct network configurations using the model finder Alloy.

Our work further expands the proactive monitoring approach into cloud environments differing in scope and approach.

Weatherman [3] is the most closely related work to ours. Aiming at mitigating misconfigurations and enforcing security policies in a virtualized infrastructure, Weatherman has both online and offline approaches. Their online approach intercepts management operations for analysis, and relays them to the management hosts only if Weatherman confirms no security violation caused by those operations. Otherwise, they are rejected with an error signal to the requester.

The work defines a realization model, that captures the virtualized infrastructure configuration and topology in a graph-based model. The latter is synchronized with the actual infrastructure using the approach in [2]. Two major limitations of this proposition are: (i) the model capturing the whole infrastructure causes a scalability issue for the solution, and (ii) the time consuming operation-checking that should be performed on the emergence of each event, makes security enforcement not feasible for large size data centers. Our work overcomes these limitations using dependency models, which are not context-dependent, and the pre-computation steps, which considerably reduce the response-time.

Congress [21] is an OpenStack project offering both online and offline policy enforcement approaches. The offline approach requires submitting a future change plan to Congress, so that the changes can be simulated and the impacts of those changes can be verified against specific properties. In the online approach, Congress first applies the operation to the cloud, then checks its impacts. In case of a violation, the operation is reverted. However, the time elapsed before reverting the operation can be critical to perform some illicit actions, for instance, transferring sensitive files before loosing the assigned role. Foley et al. [10] provide an algebra to assess the effect of security policies replacement and composition in OpenStack. Their solution can be considered as a proactive approach for checking operational properties violations, whereas our work targets the runtime verification of structural security property violations.

7   Conclusion

The near-real-time and scalable verification of security compliance with respect to security standards and policies is important to both cloud providers and users. In this paper, we proposed a scalable proactive approach that can significantly reduce the response-time of online security compliance verification in large clouds. To this end, we devised dependency models to capture the relationships between different virtual infrastructure and management operations based on related security properties. We use this dependency model for incrementally pre-compute the needed information for efficiently verify the management operations. We provided a proof of concept in OpenStack, one of the most popular cloud management platforms. Our experiment results show our proactive approach can be used for security compliance verification in large data centers with short response time. We believe this approach based on dependency models usage at verification time can be extended to other security properties and provide basis for new ways of handling proactive security compliance verification.

As future directions, we intend to deal with concurrent critical management operations; which may require a parallel or distributed approach. We will also investigate the feasibility of our solution for all security properties such as those related to network forwarding functionality with access control lists and routing policies.

Acknowledgements. The authors thank the anonymous reviewers for their valuable comments. This work is partially supported by the Natural Sciences and Engineering Research Council of Canada and Ericsson Canada under CRD Grant N01566.

References

1. Bellare, M., Yee, B.: Forward integrity for secure audit logs. Technical report, Citeseer (1997)
2. Bleikertz, S., Vogel, C., Groß, T.: Cloud radar: near real-time detection of security failures in dynamic virtualized infrastructures. In: Proceedings of the 30th Annual Computer Security Applications Conference, ACSAC 2014 (2014)
3. Bleikertz, S., Vogel, C., Groß, T., Mödersheim, S.: Proactive security analysis of changes in virtualized infrastructure. In: Proceedings of the 31st Annual Computer Security Applications Conference, ACSAC 2015 (2015)
4. Cloud Auditing Data Federation: pyCADF: A Python-based CADF library (2015). https://pypi.python.org/pypi/pycadf
5. Cloud Security Alliance: Security guidance for critical areas of focus in cloud computing v3.0 (2011)

6. Cloud Security Alliance: Cloud control matrix CCM v3.0.1. https://cloudsecurityalliance.org/research/ccm/
7. Cloud Security Alliance: CSA STAR program and open certification framework in 2016 and beyond (2016). https://downloads.cloudsecurityalliance.org/star/csa-star-program-cert-prep.pdf
8. Data Center Knowledge: Survey one-third of cloud users' clouds are private, heavily OpenStack (2015). http://www.datacenterknowledge.com/archives/2015/01/30/survey-half-of-private-clouds-are-openstack-clouds
9. Dolzhenko, E., Ligatti, J., Reddy, S.: Modeling runtime enforcement with mandatory results automata. Int. J. Inf. Secur. (2014)
10. Foley, S.N., Neville, U.: A firewall algebra for openstack. In: IEEE Conference on Communications and Network Security (CNS) (2015)
11. Ibrahim, A.S., Hamlyn-Harris, J., Grundy, J., Almorsy, M.: CloudSec: a security monitoring appliance for virtual machines in the IaaS cloud model. In: 5th International Conference on Network and System Security (NSS) (2011)
12. ISO Std IEC. ISO 27017: Information technology - Security techniques - Code of practice for information security controls based on ISO/IEC 27002 for cloud services (DRAFT) (2012). http://www.iso27001security.com/html/27017.html
13. Kazemian, P., Chang, M., Zeng, H., Varghese, G., McKeown, N., Whyte, S.: Real time network policy checking using header space analysis. In: Proceedings of the 10th USENIX Symposium on Networked Systems Design and Implementation (NSDI 2013) (2013)
14. Khurshid, A., Zou, X., Zhou, W., Caesar, M., Godfrey, P.B.: VeriFlow: verifying network-wide invariants in real time. In: Proceedings of the 10th USENIX Symposium on Networked Systems Design and Implementation (NSDI 2013) (2013)
15. Ligatti, J., Bauer, L., Walker, D.: Run-time enforcement of nonsafety policies. ACM Trans Inf. Syst. Secur. (TISSEC) **12**, 19 (2009)
16. Ligatti, J., Reddy, S.: A theory of runtime enforcement, with results. In: Gritzalis, D., Preneel, B., Theoharidou, M. (eds.) ESORICS 2010. LNCS, vol. 6345, pp. 87–100. Springer, Heidelberg (2010)
17. Madi, T., Majumdar, S., Wang, Y., Jarraya, Y., Pourzandi, M., Wang, L.: Auditing security compliance of the virtualized infrastructure in the cloud: application to OpenStack. In: Proceedings of the Sixth ACM on Conference on Data and Application Security and Privacy (CODASPY) (2016)
18. Majumdar, S., Madi, T., Wang, Y., Jarraya, Y., Pourzandi, M., Wang, L., Debbabi, M.: Security compliance auditing of identity and access management in the cloud: application to OpenStack. In: IEEE 7th International Conference on Cloud Computing Technology and Science (CloudCom) (2015)
19. Narain, S.: Network configuration management via model finding. In: Proceedings of the 19th Conference on Large Installation System Administration Conference, LISA 2005 (2005)
20. OpenStack: Neutron firewall rules bypass through port update. https://security.openstack.org/ossa/OSSA-2015-018.html
21. OpenStack: OpenStack Congress. https://wiki.openstack.org/wiki/Congress
22. OpenStack: OpenStack open source cloud computing software. http://www.openstack.org
23. OpenStack: OpenStack user survey. https://www.openstack.org/assets/survey/Public-User-Survey-Report.pdf
24. OpenStack: OpenStack audit middleware. http://docs.openstack.org/developer/keystonemiddleware/audit.html

25. OpenStack: OpenStack command list. http://docs.openstack.org/developer/python-openstackclient/command-list.html
26. Payne, B.D., Carbone, M., Sharif, M., Lee, W.: Lares: an architecture for secure active monitoring using virtualization. In: IEEE Symposium on Security and Privacy (SP 2008) (2008)
27. Petcu, D., Craciun, C.: Towards a security SLA-based cloud monitoring service. In: Proceedings of the 4th International Conference on Cloud Computing and Services Science (2014)
28. Sandhu, R., Coyne, E.J., Feinstein, H.L., Youman, C.E.: Role-based access control models. IEEE Comput. **29**, 38–47 (1996)
29. Schneider, F.B.: Enforceable security policies. ACM Trans. Inf. Syst. Secur. (TISSEC) **3**, 30–50 (2000)
30. Solanas, M., Hernandez-Castro, J., Dutta, D.: Detecting fraudulent activity in a cloud using privacy-friendly data aggregates. Technical report, arXiv preprint (2014)
31. Tamura, N., Banbara, M.: Sugar: a CSP to SAT translator based on order encoding. In: Proceedings of the Second International CSP Solver Competition (2008)
32. Tang, B., Sandhu, R.: Extending OpenStack access control with domain trust. In: Au, M.H., Carminati, B., Kuo, C.-C.J. (eds.) NSS 2014. LNCS, vol. 8792, pp. 54–69. Springer, Heidelberg (2014)
33. Zhang, T., Lee, R.B.: Cloudmonatt: an architecture for security health monitoring and attestation of virtual machines in cloud computing. In: ACM/IEEE 42nd Annual International Symposium on Computer Architecture (ISCA) (2015)

Authentication

Comparing Password Ranking Algorithms on Real-World Password Datasets

Weining Yang[1], Ninghui Li[1(✉)], Ian M. Molloy[2], Youngja Park[2], and Suresh N. Chari[2]

[1] Purdue University, West Lafayette, IN, USA
{yang469,ninghui}@purdue.edu
[2] IBM T. J. Watson Research Center, Yorktown Heights, NY, USA
{molloyim,young_park,schari}@us.ibm.com

Abstract. Password-based authentication is the most widely used authentication mechanism. One major weakness of password-based authentication is that users generally choose predictable and weak passwords. In this paper, we address the question: How to best check weak passwords? We model different password strength checking methods as Password Ranking Algorithms (PRAs), and introduce two methods for comparing different PRAs: the β-Residual Strength Graph (β-RSG) and the Normalized β-Residual Strength Graph (β-NRSG). In our experiments, we find some password datasets that have been widely used in password research contain many problematic passwords that are not naturally created. We develop techniques to cleanse password datasets by removing these problematic accounts. We then apply the two metrics on cleansed datasets and show that several PRAs, including the dictionary-based PRA, the Markov Models with and without backoff, have similar performances. If the size of PRAs are limited in order to be able to be transmitted over the internet, a hybrid method combining a small dictionary of weak passwords and a Markov model with backoff with a limited size can provide the most accurate strength measurement.

1 Introduction

Password-based authentication is the most widely used authentication mechanism. Despite countless attempts at designing mechanisms to replace it, password-based authentication appears more widely used and firmly entrenched than ever [6,7,21]. One major weakness of password-based authentication is the inherent tension between the security and usability of passwords [4,28]. More precisely, secure passwords tend to be difficult to memorize (i.e., less usable) whereas passwords that are memorable tend to be predictable. Generally individuals side with usability of passwords by choosing predictable and weak passwords [4,18,20,23,30].

To deal with this, the most common approach is to forbid the use of weak passwords, or give warnings for passwords that are "somewhat weak". This approach requires an effective way to identify weak passwords. One way is to use

© Springer International Publishing Switzerland 2016
I. Askoxylakis et al. (Eds.): ESORICS 2016, Part I, LNCS 9878, pp. 69–90, 2016.
DOI: 10.1007/978-3-319-45744-4_4

password composition policies, i.e., requiring passwords to satisfy some syntactical properties, e.g., minimum length and/or categories of characters. An alternative is to use proactive password checkers that are based on a weak password dictionary [5, 27, 32]. More recently, probabilistic password models, which work by assigning a probability to each password, were introduced [13, 26, 29, 37].

How to best check weak passwords is still an open question. A study in 2014 [14] examined several password meters in use at popular websites and found highly inconsistent strength estimates for the same passwords using different meters. The report did not answer the question of which meter is the best, nor what methods should be used to compare them. Designing an effective password meter requires solving two problems: (1) How to accurately assess the strength of passwords chosen by the users; and (2) How to communicate the strength information to and interact with the users to encourage them to choose strong passwords. These two problems are largely orthogonal. In this paper we focus on solving the first problem.

We model different password strength assessing methods (including composition policies) as Password Ranking Algorithms (PRAs), which assign a rank to every password. One state-of-the-art method for comparing PRAs is the Guess Number Graph (GNG), which plots the number of guesses vs. the percentage of passwords cracked in the test dataset. However, GNG measures only the total density of the uncracked passwords, but not their distribution, which is critical in assessing the effectiveness to defend against guessing attacks after deploying the PRA. To address this limitation of GNG, we propose the β-Residual Strength Graph (β-RSG), which measures the strength of the β most common passwords in the test dataset, after forbidding the weakest passwords identified by a PRA. When a PRA forbids a large number of passwords that users are extremely unlikely to use, it performs poorly under β-RSG. To limit the influence of these passwords, we also propose Normalized β-Residual Strength Graph (β-NRSG), which ignores how passwords that do not appear in the testing dataset are ranked. β-NRSG also has the advantage that we can use it to evaluate blackbox password strength services for which one can query the strength of specific passwords, but cannot obtain all weak passwords.

Surprisingly, we observed that all PRAs perform significantly worse on password datasets from Chinese websites than on datasets from English websites, because some of the most frequent passwords in the testing dataset are not recognized as weak passwords by all the PRAs. Further investigation revealed that these passwords are in all likelihood due to "fake accounts", possibly created by site administrators to artificially boost the number of registered users. The evidences for this include that the user IDs associated with such passwords look suspicious. These suspicious IDs fall in two categories: appending a counter to a fixed prefix; and a large number of fixed-length strings that apparently look random. While these datasets have been used in previous papers, we are the first to report such fake accounts. We developed a data cleansing technique to identify and remove such "fake" accounts in order to obtain a more accurate evaluation.

Our evaluation is based on the cleansed password datasets. We have compared the Probabilistic Context-Free Grammar (PCFG) [37] method, Markov models with and without backoff [13,26,29], blacklists based on training datasets, the Combined method proposed by Ur et al. [34], password composition policies, as well as two versions of *zxcvbn* [38]. We also how GNG, β-RSG, and β-NRSG differ. We found that when one places no limit on the mode size, several methods including the blacklist approach, Markov Models, and the Combined method have similar performance. When one wants to check the strength of passwords on the client side, without sending passwords over the network, the model size must be limited. We found that a blacklist with a limited size still provide the most accurate strength measurement for the most popular passwords. However, only a limited number of passwords are covered.

We then propose a new client-end PRA that uses a hybrid method; it uses a small blacklist to assess the strength of most popular passwords, and evaluate the other passwords based on a limited size Markov model with backoff. We show that the hybrid method inherits the advantages of both methods, and consistently outperform the other client-end PRAs.

The rest of this paper is organized as follows. We discuss related work in Sect. 2. We propose metrics evaluate password ranking algorithms (PRAs) in Sect. 3. The observation of suspicious accounts and the corresponding data cleansing are described in Sect. 4 and the evaluation is reported in Sect. 5. Finally, we conclude in Sect. 6.

2   Related Work

The quality of passwords has traditionally been measured using a combination of standard password cracking tools, such as John the Ripper (JTR) [3], and ad hoc approaches for estimating the information entropy of a set of passwords.

In 1990, Klein et al. [23] proposed the concept of a proactive password checker, which checks the strength of newly created passwords and prevents users from choosing weak passwords. Since then, multiple blacklist-based proactive password checkers were proposed. Spafford et al. [32] and Bergadano et al. [5] developed methods for filtering passwords based on efficiently stored password dictionaries. Manber et al. [27] described an approach that refused not only exact words in dictionaries but also passwords that are a single insertion, deletion, or substitution from a dictionary word. Yan et al. [39] suggested that besides dictionary checking, password checker should consider length and character types of passwords as well.

In terms of entropy estimation, Florencio and Herley [18], Forget et al. [19], and Egelman et al. [16] use the formula where the bit strength of a password is considered to be $\log_2\left(|\varSigma|^{len}\right)$ for alphabet $\varSigma$. A more sophisticated approach, known as the NIST guidelines [11], calculates password entropy using several factors, including how many numbers, symbols, and uppercase letters are used and where they appear.

The effect of different password composition policies was studied by Komanduri et al. [25] and Kelley et al. [22] using probability model-based cracking tools. They both suggested that passwords generated under the policy "Password must have at least 16 characters" provides the best security.

In 2010, Weir et al. [36] measured the strength of password creation policies by using large-scale real-world datasets and showed that entropy values would not tell the defender anything about how vulnerable a policy would be to an online password cracking attack. They also showed that many rule-based policies perform poorly for ensuring a desirable level of security. Instead, they suggest measuring the strength of user-chosen passwords by password models and rejecting passwords with high probabilities. Schechter et al. [31] also suggested allowing users to choose any password they want, so long as it is not already too popular with other users.

Probabilistic models of passwords work by assigning a probability to each string. Some models divide a password into several segments, often by grouping consecutive characters of the same category (e.g., lower-case letters, digits, etc.) into one segment, and then generate the probability for each segment independently. Examples include the model in [29], and the Probabilistic Context Free Grammar (PCFG)-based approach developed in [37]. The PCFG approach was later improved in [22,35]. A whole-string model, on the other hand, does not divide a password into segments, e.g., the Markov chain model in [12,13]. Ma et al. [26] showed that Markov chain model with backoff smoothing outperforms PCFG models.

Dell'Amico and Filippone [15] proposed a method to estimate the number of guesses needed to find a password using modern attacks and probabilistic models. Given a probabilistic model, the strength of a passwords is estimated by sampling from the model, i.e., generating random passwords according to the probabilities assigned by the model. This motivates our work to find a way to compare password models, as a better probabilistic model will produce a more accurate estimation.

Recently, Ur et al. [34] compared cracking approaches used by researchers with real-world cracking by professionals. They found that semi-automated cracking by professionals outperforms popular fully automated approaches, but can be approximated by combining multiple approaches and assuming the rank of a password is its highest rank among the approaches examined.

Egelman et al. [16] examined the impact of password meters on password selection and reported that the presence of meters yielded significantly stronger passwords in a laboratory experiment. However, the meters made no observable difference in a field study when creating passwords for unimportant accounts. Ur et al. [33] also showed that scoring passwords stringently results in stronger passwords in general. Komanduri et al. [24] showed that Telepathwords, which makes realtime predictions for the next character that user will type, can help users choosing stronger passwords.

In 2014, de Carné de Carnavalet and Mannan [14] examined several password meters in use at selected popular websites, and revealed how the meters work. They found gross inconsistencies, with the same password resulting in very different strength across different meters.

In [38], *zxcvbn*, which is an open-source meter designed to run entirely in clients' browser, is proposed. *zxcvbn* decomposes a given password into patterns, and then assigns each pattern an estimated "entropy". The final password entropy is calculated as the sum of its constituent patterns' entropy estimates. The algorithm detects multiple ways of decomposing a password, but keeps only the lowest of all possible summations as an underestimate.

3   How to Compare PRAs

At the core of any password strength meter is a Password Ranking Algorithm (PRA), which is a function that sorts passwords from weak (common) to strong (rare).

Definition 1 (Password Ranking Algorithm (PRA)). *Let $\mathcal{P}$ denote the set of all allowed passwords. A Password Ranking Algorithm $r : \mathcal{P} \rightarrow$ Rnk is a function that maps each password to a ranking in Rnk, where Rnk = $\{1, \ldots, |\mathcal{P}|\} \cup \{\infty\}$.*

Intuitively, a password with rank 1 means that it is considered to be one of the weakest password(s); and a password with rank ∞ means that it is considered to be strong enough to not need a ranking. The above definition accommodates PRAs that rank only a subset of all passwords as well as PRAs that rank some passwords to be of equal strength. A password composition policy can be modeled as a PRA that assigns a rank of 1 to passwords that do not satisfy the policy, and ∞ otherwise. Probabilistic password models that assign a probability to each password can be converted into a PRA by sorting, in decreasing order, the passwords based on their probabilities in the model. Arguably, this captures the essential information for determining the strengths of passwords, since both cracking passwords and choosing which passwords to forbid should be done based on the ranking.

3.1   Guess Number Graph (GNG)

The state-of-the-art method for comparing PRAs is the Guess Number Graph (GNG), which plots the number of guesses vs. the percentage of passwords cracked in the dataset. A point (x, y) on a curve means that y percent of passwords are included in the first x guesses. When evaluating PRAs for their effectiveness in cracking passwords, GNG is an ideal choice. For the same x value, a PRA that has a higher y value is better. However, one limitation of GNG is that it does not convey information regarding the distribution of uncracked passwords. For example, suppose that two PRAs r_1 and r_2 both cover 40 % of passwords after making 10^6 guesses. Under r_1 there remain uncovered 5 passwords each appearing 200 times and a large number of passwords that appear just once. And under r_2 there remain 500 passwords each appearing 2 times together with a similarly large number of passwords that appear just once. In this case, if we decide to forbid the first 10^6 passwords that are considered weak and an adversary is limited to 5 guess attempts per account (e.g., because of rate limiting), the adversary can successfully break into 1,000 accounts based on r_1, but only 10 accounts based on r_2. Obviously, r_1 is worse than r_2, even though they look the same under the GNG. Therefore, GNG is not appropriate for the effectiveness of using a PRA for identifying and forbidding the usage of weak passwords, especially since the primary objective of checking password strength is to defend against online guessing attacks, as offline attacks are best defended against by improving site security and by using salted, slow cryptographic hash functions when storing password hashes.

3.2   The β-Residual Strength Graph (β-RSG)

To deal with the limitation of GNG, we propose to use the β-Residual Strength Graph. Each PRA r corresponds to a curve, such that a point (x, y) on the curve means that after forbidding what r considers to be the x weakest passwords, the strength of the remaining passwords is y. For the choice of y, we use the effective key-length metric corresponding to the β-success-rate, proposed by Boztaş [8] and Bonneau [6], to measure the strength of the probabilities of the remaining passwords, which we call the residual distribution.

More specifically, given a password dataset D, we use $p_D(w)$ to denote a password w's frequency in D, i.e., $p_D(w) = \frac{\text{number of times } w \text{ occurs in } D}{|D|}$. Given a PRA r and a number x, let w_i be the ith most frequent password in D that is not among the x weakest passwords according to r. Then the β-Residual Strength is computed as:

$$y = \lg \left(\frac{\beta}{\sum_{i=1}^{\beta} p_D(w_i)} \right),$$

Intuitively, β-RSG provides a measure of the strength of the remaining weakest passwords after a certain number of weak passwords according to r are forbidden. It translates the total frequencies of the β unremoved weakest passwords into a bit-based security metric, which can be viewed as finding the entropy of a uniform distribution where the probability of each element equals that of the average of these β passwords.

We need to choose appropriate values for β. In [6], $\tilde{\lambda}_{10}$ is used, which corresponds to an online attack setting where 10 guesses are allowed, which was recommended by usability studies [9]. We adapt the setting.

3.3   The Normalized β-Residual Strength Graph (β-NRSG)

Password composition policies (such as the ones that require mixing letters with digits and special symbols), when viewed as PRAs, tend to perform poorly under the RSG, because they rule out a large number of passwords, e.g., all passwords that consist of only letters. This demonstrates that one weakness of password composition policies is that they prevent some strong passwords (such as unpredictable passwords consisting of only letters) from being used. However, one may argue that this is not completely fair to them. The cost of forbidding a strong (i.e., rarely used) password is that users who naturally want to use such a password cannot do so, and have to choose a different password, which they may have more trouble remembering. However, if users are extremely unlikely to choose the password anyway, then there is very little cost to forbid it.

We thus propose a variation of RSG, which "normalizes" a RSG curve by considering only passwords that actually appear in the testing dataset D. More specifically, a point (x, y) on the curve for a PRA r means that after choosing a threshold such that x passwords that appear in D are forbidden, the residual strength is y. We call this the Normalized β-Residual Strength Graph (β-NRSG). A NRSG curve can be obtained from a corresponding RSG curve by shrinking the x axis; however, different PRAs may have different shrinking effects, depending on how many passwords that are considered weak by the PRAs do not appear in the testing dataset. Under β-NRSG, PRAs are not penalized for rejecting passwords that do not appear in the testing dataset. A PRA would perform well if it considers the weak (i.e., frequent) passwords in the dataset to be weaker than the passwords that appear very few times in it. β-NRSG also has the advantage that we can use it to evaluate blackbox password strength services for which one can query the strength of specific passwords, but cannot obtain all weak passwords. We suggest using both RSGs and NRSGs when comparing PRAs.

3.4   Client Versus Server PRAs

A PRA can be deployed either at the server end, where a password is sent to a server and has its strength checked, or at the client end, where the strength checking is written in JavaScript and executed in the client side inside a browser. PRAs deployed at the server end are less limited by the size of the model. On the other hand, deploying PRAs on the client side increases confidence in using them, especially when password strength checking tools are provided by a third party. Thus it is also of interest to compare the PRAs that have a relatively small model size, and therefore can be deployed at the client end. We say a PRA is a Client-end PRA if the model size is less than 1 MB, and a Server-end PRA otherwise.

Table 1. Server-end PRAs and Client-end PRAs. X_c means reduced-size version of model X in order to be deployed at the client side.

Server-end	Markov Model [13], Markov Model with backoff [26], Probabilistic Context-free Grammar [37], Google API, Blacklist, Combined [34]
Client-end	$zxcvbn_1$ [38], $zxcvbn_2$ [38], Blacklist$_c$, Markov Model$_c$, Markov Model with backoff$_c$, Hybrid

3.5   PRAs We Consider

The PRAs that are considered in this paper are listed in Table 1. In Client-end PRAs, the size of $zxcvbn_1$, $zxcvbn_2$ are 698 KB and 821 KB correspondingly. For password models whose model sizes are adjustable, we make the model size to be approximately 800 KB to have a fair comparison.

PCFG. In the PCFG approach [37], one divides a password into several segments by grouping consecutive characters of the same category (e.g., letters, digits, special symbols) into one segment. Each password thus follows a pattern, for example, L_7D_3 denotes a password consisting of a sequence of 7 letters followed by 3 digits. The distribution of different patterns as well as the distribution of digits and symbols are learned from a training dataset. PCFG chooses words to instantiate segments consisting of letters from a dictionary where all words in the dictionary are assumed to be of the same probability. The probability of a password is calculated by multiplying the probability of the pattern by the probabilities of the particular ways the segments are instantiated.

Markov Model. N-gram models, i.e., Markov chains, have been applied to passwords [13]. A Markov chain of order d, where d is a positive integer, is a process that satisfies

$$P(x_i|x_{i-1}, x_{i-2}, \ldots, x_1) = P(x_i|x_{i-1}, \ldots, x_{i-d})$$

where d is finite and $x_1, x_2, x_3, \ldots$ is a sequence of random variables. A Markov chain with order d corresponds to an n-gram model with $n = d + 1$.

We evaluate 5-gram Markov Model (MC_5), as recommended in [26], within Server-end PRAs setting. In order to fit the Markov Model into a Client-end PRA, if we store the frequency of each sequence in a trie structure, the leaf level contains 95^n nodes, where 95 is the total number of printable characters. To limit the size of Markov model to be no larger than 1 MB, n should be less than 4. We use 3-order Markov Model MC_3 in our evaluation.

Markov Model with Backoff. Ma et al. [26] proposed to use the Markov Model with backoff to model passwords. The intuition is that if a history appears frequently, then we would want to use that to estimate the probability of the next character. In this model, one chooses a threshold and stores all substrings whose counts are above the threshold, and use the frequency of these substrings to compute the probability. Therefore, the model size of a Markov Model with backoff depends on the frequency threshold selected. In this paper, we consider two sizes of Markov Model with backoff by varying frequency threshold. We first pick a relatively small threshold 25 (MCB_{25}), as suggested in [26], to construct a Server-end PRA.

For Client-end PRAs, similar to the Markov model, we record the model in a trie structure, where each node contains a character and the corresponding count of the sequence starting from the root node to the current node. We measure the size of data after serializing the trie into JSON format. Table 3 shows the size of the models trained on *Rockyou* and *Duduniu* dataset with different frequency thresholds. The size of the Markov Models with backoff when trained on *Duduniu* dataset is significantly smaller than that of models trained on the *Rockyou* dataset. This is primarily due to the difference in character distribution between English and Chinese users. English users are more likely to use letters while Chinese users are more likely to use digits. As a result, the most frequent sequences in *Rockyou* are mainly constructed by letters while those in *Duduniu* are mainly constructed by digits. The difference in the size of the models comes from the different search space in letters and digits. In order to approximate the size of the model to that of *zxcvbn*, we choose MCB_{1500} for English datasets and MCB_{500} for Chinese datasets.

Dictionary-Based Blacklist. Dictionary-based blacklists for filtering weak passwords have been studied for decades, e.g., [5,27,32]. Some popular websites, such as Pinterest and Twitter, embed small weak password dictionaries, consisting of 13 and 401 passwords respectively, on their registration pages. We use a training dataset to generate the blacklist dictionary. The order of the passwords follows the frequency of passwords in the training dataset in a reversed order. Assuming each password contains 8 characters on average, a dictionary with 100,000 passwords is approximately 900KB. Such blacklist ($Blacklist_c$) is used in Client-end PRAs settings.

Combined Method. Ur et al. [34] proposed Min_{auto} metric, which is the minimum guess number for a given password across multiple automated cracking approaches. We implement a password generator which outputs passwords in the order of their corresponding Min_{auto}. Passwords with smaller Min_{auto} are generated earlier. In the Combined PRA, the rank of a password is the order of the passwords generated. In this paper, Min_{auto} is calculated by combining 4 well-studied approaches: Blacklist, PCFG, Markov, and Markov with backoff.

Google Password Strength API. Google measures the strength of passwords by assigning an integer score ranging from 1 to 4 when registering on their website. We found that the score is queried via an AJAX call and the API is publicly available[1]. We use this service to assess the strength of passwords. We are not able to generate passwords and get the exact ranking as the underlying algorithm has not been revealed.

Zxcvbn Version 1. Zxcvbn is an open-source password strength meter developed by Wheeler [38]. It decomposes a given password into chunks, and then assigns each chunk an estimated "entropy". The entropy of each chunk is estimated depending on the pattern of the chunk. The candidate patterns are "dictionary", "sequence", "spatial", "year", "date", "repeat" and "bruteforce". For example, if a chunk is within the pattern "dictionary", the entropy is estimated as the log of the rank of word in the dictionary. Additional entropy is added if uppercase letters are used or some letters are converted into digits or sequences (e.g. a⇒@). There are 5 embedded frequency-ordered dictionaries:

---

[1] https://accounts.google.com/RatePassword.

7140 passwords from the Top 10000 password dictionary; and three dictionaries for common names from the 2000 US Census. After chunking, a password's entropy is calculated as the sum of its constituent chunks' entropy estimates.

$$\text{entropy}(pwd) = \sum \text{entropy}(chunk_i)$$

A password may be divided into chunks in different ways, Zxcvbn finds the way that yields the minimal entropy and uses that.

Zxcvbn Version 2. In October 2015, a new version of *zxcvbn* was published. Zxcvbn$_2$ also divides a password into chunks, and computes a password's strength as the "minimal guess" of it under any way of dividing it into chunks. A password's "guess" after being divided into chunks under a specific way is:

$$l! \times \prod_{i=1}^{l} (chunk_i.guesses) + 10000^{l-1}$$

where l is the number of the chunks. The factorial term is the number of ways to order l patterns. The $10000^{(l-1)}$ term captures the intuition that a password that has more chunks are considered stronger. Another change in the new version is that if a password is decomposed into multiple chunks, the estimated guess number for each chunk is the larger one between the chunks' original estimated guess number and a *min_guess_number*, which is 10 if the chunk contains only one character or 50 otherwise. While these changes are heuristic, our experimental results show these changes cause significant improvements under our methods of comparison.

Hybrid Method. Observing the promising performance of dictionary methods and the limited number of passwords covered (see Sect. 5.2 for details), we propose a hybrid PRA which combines a blacklist PRA with a backoff model. In the hybrid PRA, we reject passwords belonging to a blacklist dictionary or with low scores using the backoff model. To make the size of the PRAs consistent, we further limit the size for both dictionary and backoff model. We chose to use a dictionary containing 30 000 words, which takes less than 300KB. In order to keep the total size of the model consistent, we used MCB_{2000} and MCB_{1000} for English datasets and Chinese datasets, respectively.

4   Data Cleansing

Poor Performance of PRAs on Chinese Datasets. In our evaluation comparing PRAs, we observe that almost all PRAs perform poorly on some Chinese dataset.

Figure 1 shows the results of an β-Residual Strength Graph(β-RSG) evaluation on *Xato* (an English dataset) and *178* (a Chinese dataset). A point (x, y) on a curve means if we want to reject top x passwords from a PRA, the residual strength is y. It is clear that the residual strength for *178* is much lower than that

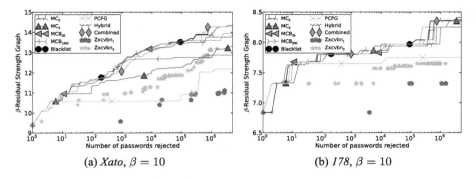

(a) *Xato*, $\beta = 10$ (b) *178*, $\beta = 10$

Fig. 1. β-Residual Strength Graph(β-RSG) on original *Xato* and *178* datasets. A point (x, y) on a curve means if we want to reject top x passwords from a PRA, the strength of the remaining passwords is y.

of *Xato*. In *178*, even if 1 million passwords are rejected, the residual strength is around or lower than 8 for all PRAs we examined, which means the average of the remaining top 10 passwords's probability is as high as $\frac{1}{2^8} \approx 0.39\%$. We found that 12 out of the top 20 passwords in *178* were not among the first million weakest passwords for any PRA. This led us to investigate why this occurs.

Evidences of Suspicious IDs. We found that the dataset contains a lot of suspicious account IDs which mostly fall in to two patterns: (1) *Counter*: a common prefix appended by a counter; (2) *Random*: a random string with a fixed length. Table 2 lists some suspicious accounts sampled from the *178* dataset, which we believe were created either by a single user in order to benefit from the bonus for new accounts, or by the system administrator, in order to artificially boost the number users on the sites. Either way, such passwords are not representative of actual password choices and should be removed.

Table 2. Examples of IDs in *178* Dataset.

Password	*Counter* IDs (sampled)	*Random* Ids (sampled)
zz12369	badu1; badu2; ...; badu50	vetfg34t; gf8hgoid; vkjjhb49; 5t893yt8; 9y4tjreo; 09rtoivj; kdznjvhb
qiulaobai	qiujie0001; qiujie0002; ...; qiujie0345	j3s1b901; ul2c6shx; a3bft0b8; wzjcxytp; 7fmjwzg2; 0ypvjqvo
123456	1180ma1; 1180ma2; ...; 1180ma49	x2e03w5suedtu; 7kjwddqujornc; inrrgjhm2dh8r; 3u2lnalg91u9i;

Suspicious Account Detection. We detect and remove suspicious passwords (accounts) using the user IDs and email addresses. *Yahoo* and *Duduniu* datasets only have email address available. We first remove the email provider, i.e., the postfix starting from @, and then, treat the prefix of email addresses as account IDs.

Table 3. Model size of Markov Model with backoff using different frequency threshold.

Train	Frequency Threshold					
	25	200	500	1000	1500	2000
RockYou	18 M	3.4 M	1.7 M	1 M	712 K	556 K
Duduniu	7.8 M	1.5 M	604 K	368 K	268 K	200 K

Table 4. Number of accounts removed.

Dataset	Yahoo	Xato	Duduniu	CSDN	178
Removed	232	9577	9796	69317	1639868
Total	434131	9148094	7304316	6367411	8434340

Rockyou and *Phpbb* datasets are excluded in the following analysis, as we do not have access to user IDs/emails.

We identify *Counter* IDs utilizing Density-based Spatial Clustering of Applications with Noise (DBSCAN) [17]. DBSCAN is a density-based clustering algorithm. It groups together points that are closely packed together (a brief overview of DBSCAN is provided in Appendix A). In our case, each ID is viewed as a point, and the distance between two IDs are measured by the Levenshtein distance, which measures the minimum number of single-character edits. Given a password, we first extract all the corresponding IDs in the dataset, and then generate groups of IDs, where the IDs in the same group share a common prefix with length at least 3. The grouping is introduced to reduce the number of points to be clustered, as calculating pairwise distance of a large number of data points is slow. Next, we apply DBSCAN with $\epsilon = 1$ and $minPts = 5$ to each group. Finally, we label all IDs in clusters with size at least 5 as suspicious.

Random. IDs are identified based on probabilities of IDs, which are calculated utilizing a Markov Model. Intuitively, *Random* IDs are ids whose probabilities are "unreasonably small". Observing that *Random* IDs are generally with the same length and the probabilities of IDs can be approximated by lognormal distribution (see Appendix B), we perform "fake" account removal for IDs with the same length based on $-\log p$, where p is probabilities of IDs. Note that in a normal distribution, nearly all values are within three standard deviations of the mean (three-sigma rule of thumb), we therefore believe $\mu + 3\sigma$ is a reasonable upper-bound for "real" IDs, where μ and σ are mean and standard deviation of $-\log p$, respectively.

In addition, if most of the IDs corresponding to a high-frequency password P in dataset D are detected as suspicious, and P does not appear in password datasets other than D, we remove all accounts associated with the P.

Table 5. Top 5 Passwords with Most Accounts Removed. $pwd_{r/o}$ means the original count of pwd in the dataset is o, and r accounts are removed.

Rank	Yahoo	Xato	Duduniu	Csdn	178
1	1a1a1a1b$_{131/131}$	klaster$_{1705/1705}$	aaaaaa$_{3103/10838}$	dearbook$_{44636/44636}$	qiulaobai$_{57963/57963}$
2	welcome$_{101/437}$	iwantu$_{885/885}$	111111$_{1203/21763}$	xiazhili$_{3649/3649}$	wmsxie123$_{48258/49162}$
3	-	1232323q$_{450/450}$	123456$_{1076/93259}$	12345678$_{2222/212743}$	123456$_{47536/261692}$
4	-	galore$_{393/393}$	9958123$_{461/3981}$	123456789$_{1482/234997}$	w2w2w2$_{35762/35762}$
5	-	wrinkle1$_{243/243}$	a5633168$_{457/457}$	11111111$_{1301/76340}$	wolf8637$_{31909/31909}$

Results of Cleansing. Table 4 lists the number of suspicious accounts removed. In general, the suspicious accounts count for a small portion in English and *Duduniu* datasets. However, the number of suspicious accounts detected in *CSDN* and *178* datasets are significantly larger. In *178* dataset, about one fifth accounts are suspicious. Table 5 lists the top 5 passwords with most accounts removed in each dataset. Despite the accounts correspond to uncommon passwords, a significant number of accounts with popular passwords, such as 123456, are removed as well. Evidences suggest that some datasets contain many waves of creation of suspicious accounts, some using common passwords such as 123456, as illustrated in Table 2.

5   Experimental Results

5.1   Experimental Datasets and Settings

We evaluate PRAs on seven real-world password datasets, including four datasets from English users, *Rockyou* [1], *Phpbb* [1], *Yahoo* [1], and *Xato* [10], and three datasets from Chinese users, CSDN [2], *Duduniu*, and *178*.

Some PRAs require a training dataset for preprocessing. For English passwords, we train on *Rockyou* and evaluate on (1) *Yahoo* + *Phpbb*; (2) *Xato*, as *Rockyou* is the largest password dataset available. We combine *Yahoo* and *Phpbb* datasets because the size of them are relatively small. For Chinese passwords, the evaluation was conducted on any pair of datasets. For each pair, we trained PRAs on one dataset and tested on the other. Because of the page limit, we only present results of using *Duduniu* as the training dataset.

Probabilistic Password Models. For all probabilistic password models we evaluate, we generate 10^8 passwords following the descending order of probabilities. The order of the password generated is essentially the ranking of the password in the corresponding PRA.

Blacklist PRAs. We directly use the training dataset as blacklist. Namely, in the PRA, the ranking of a password is the order of its frequency in the training dataset. We vary the size of blacklist by removing the lowest-rank passwords in order to adjust the number of passwords rejected.

Zxcvbn. *Zxcvbn* was designed to evaluate entropy for passwords from English speaking users only. When applied to Chinese datasets, we modify it by adding a new dictionary of Chinese words. In addition, we implemented a password generator which generate passwords in the order of entropy measured by the model. The implementation details are in Appendix C.

5.2   Experimental Results

Figure 2 illustrates the Guess Number Graph (GNG), the β-Residual Strength Graph (β-RSG), and the Normalized β-Residual Strength Graph (β-NRSG) evaluated on *Xato* and *178* datasets. The corresponding training datasets are *Rockyou* and *Duduniu*, respectively. The evaluation on the other datasets leads to similar results.

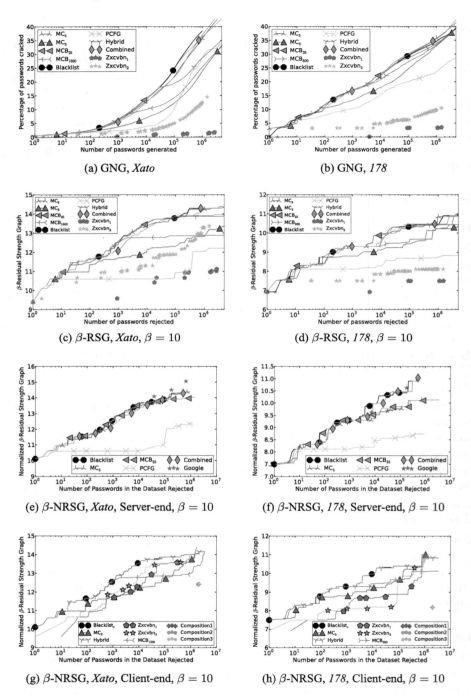

Fig. 2. The Guess Number Graph (GNG), the β-Residual Strength Graph (β-RSG), and the Normalized β-Residual Strength Graph (β-NRSG) evaluated on *Xato* and *178* datasets.

Figure 2(a) and (b) show the evaluation of the Guess Number Graph (GNG). Both Client-end and Server-end PRAs, except Google's password strength assessment from which we are not able to generate passwords, are measured. We do not plot the Blacklist PRA with limited size, as it overlaps with the regular Blacklist PRA. We plot scatter points for *zxcvbn* to avoid ambiguity, since it generates multiple passwords with the same entropy. A point (x, y) on a curve means that y percent of passwords in the test dataset are included in the first x guesses.

Figure 2(c) and (d) illustrate the β-Residual Strength Graph (β-RSG) for $\beta = 10$. In the evaluation, we vary the number of passwords rejected x in PRAs (i.e., passwords ranked as top x are not allowed). In the figures, a point (x, y) on a curve means if we want to reject top x passwords from a PRA, the residual strength is y. For a fixed x, a larger y indicates smaller portion of accounts will be compromised within β guesses after rejecting x passwords. Comparing Fig. 1(b) and Fig. 2(d), we can observe that the performance of PRAs on cleansed data significantly boost, which confirm the need of data cleansing.

The Normalized β-Residual Strength Graphs (β-NRSG) for Server-end PRAs are illustrated in Fig. 2(e) and (f), and the Client-end PRAs' evaluation is shown in Fig. 2(g) and (h). In addition to PRAs compared in GNG and β-RSG, we evaluate the effect of composition policies and Google's password strength API as well. Three commonly used composition rules are examined. Composition rule 1 is adapted by Ebay.com, which ask for at least two types of characters from digits, symbols and letter. Composition rule 2 is adapted by Live.com, which also ask for two types of characters, but it further split letters into uppercase and lowercase letters. Composition rule 3 is adapted by most of the online banking sites (e.g. BOA). At least one digit and one letter are required.

Server-end PRAs. In general, Server-end PRAs (Blacklist, MC_5, MCB_{25}, Combined) outperform Client-end PRAs (Hybrid, MC_3, MCB_{1500}/MCB_{500}), which confirms that a PRA's accuracy grows with the size of its model, and Server-end PRAs are recommended for websites where security is one of the most important factors, e.g., online banks.

The Google password strength API, which is only evaluated in β-NRSG (Fig. 2(e) and (f)) is the top performer on both English and Chinese datasets. The three points from left to right in each graph illustrate the effect of forbidding passwords whose score is no larger than 1, 2, and 3, respectively. In practice, all passwords with score 1 are forbidden. The high residual strength indicates that most of the high-frequency passwords are successfully identified.

For the other Server-end PRAs, the three metrics (Fig. 2(a)-(f)) all suggest that several PRAs including the Blacklist PRA, the Markov Model with backoff with a frequency threshold of 25 (MCB_{25}) [26], the 5-order Markov Model [26], and the Combined method [34] have similar performance, and they are almost always on the top of the graphs, which is consistent with the results in the previous works [15, 26, 34].

Client-end PRAs. From Fig. 2(g) and (h), it is clear that composition rules do not help prevent weak passwords, as the corresponding points are far below the other curves. In addition, the composition rules generally reject more than one tenth of passwords in the datasets, which might lead to difficulty and confusion in password generation, and is not appropriate.

Among the other Client-end PRAs, the Blacklist PRA outperform the others when the number of passwords rejected is small. However, because of the limited size, the small blacklist can only cover a small proportion of passwords (less than 10,000) in the testing dataset. The reduced-size Markov models (MC_3 and MCB_c) perform significantly worse than the corresponding Server-end models (MC_5 and MCB_{25}), especially when the number of passwords rejected is relatively large. The low order Markov models cannot capture most of the features in the real passwords distribution and the strength measurement is not accurate. MCB_c performs similar to the Blacklist PRA when x is small, as the frequencies of the most popular patterns are high enough to be preserved, with the cost of losing most of the other precise information. As a result, the performance of MC_3 is better than MCB_c with the growth of x.

A noticeable improvement of $zxcvbn_2$ over $zxcvbn_1$ can be observed in all the three metrics (Fig. 2(a)-(d), (g), and (h)). The figures also suggest that $zxcvbn$ is not optimized for passwords created by non-English speaking users, as the performance of the PRAs significantly drops in the evaluation on Chinese datasets.

The Hybrid Method. Observing the promising performance of Blacklist methods and the limited number passwords covered in the testing dataset, we propose a hybrid PRA which combines a blacklist PRA with a backoff model. In the Hybrid PRA, we first reject passwords based on the order in the Blacklist, and apply the backoff model after the Blacklist is exhausted. To make the size of the PRA consistent, we further limit the size for both the Blacklist and Markov Model with backoff. We set the frequency threshold to 2000 for the English password datasets and 1000 for the Chinese password datasets (see Table 3 for model sizes). We further reduce the size of the Blacklist to 30,000 words, resulting in a dictionary smaller than 300 KB. The total size of the hybrid model is less than 800KB. The figures (Fig. 2(a)-(d), (g), and (h)) show that the hybrid method inherits the advantage of Blacklist PRA and Markov Model with backoff. Hybrid method can accurately reject weak passwords, and can provide a relatively accurate strength assessment for any passwords. As a result, it is almost always on the top of all client-end PRAs, and is even comparable with Server-end PRAs in β-RSG and β-NRSG measurements.

Differences Among the Three Metrics. Table 6 lists the y values in GNG and β-RSG when $x = 10^4$ and $x = 10^6$. From the table, we can observe that although the percentage of passwords cracked by PRAs significantly increase from when rejecting ten thousand passwords to when rejecting one million passwords, the difference between y values in β-RSG is limited, especially for the top-performing PRAs, such as the blacklist method. The different behavior between GNG and β-RSG indicates that the percentage of passwords cracked, which is shown in GNG, cannot infer the residual strength, which is the observation from β-RSG. A high coverage and a low coverage in password cracking might result in similar residual strength, as the most frequent remaining passwords might

Table 6. y values of GNG and β-RSG when $x = 10^4$ and $x = 10^6$. $Y+P$ stands for *Yahoo + Phpbb*. $\beta = 10$

	English Datasets								Chinese Datasets							
	GNG				RSG				GNG				RSG			
Dataset	$Y+P$		$Xato$		$Y+P$		$Xato$		$CSDN$		178		$CSDN$		178	
x	10 K	1 M	10 K	1 M	10 K	1 M	10 K	1 M	10 K	1 M	10 K	1 M	10 K	1 M	10vK	1 M
MC_5	14 %	34 %	13 %	36 %	12.7	13.1	13.4	14.2	16 %	26 %	22 %	36 %	10.2	10.3	9.7	10.9
MC_3	7.3 %	21 %	6.9 %	24 %	11.5	12.4	12.1	12.8	13 %	23 %	18 %	33 %	9.7	9.9	9.1	10.2
MCB_{25}	16 %	35 %	14 %	36 %	12.8	13.2	13.5	13.9	17 %	27 %	23 %	36 %	10.3	10.4	9.9	10.4
MCB_c	11 %	22 %	10.0 %	25 %	12.6	12.7	12.8	12.9	16 %	25 %	21 %	33 %	10.1	10.3	9.3	10.2
zxcvbn	0.7 %	1.4 %	0.5 %	1.3 %	10.1	10.8	10.0	11.0	0.1 %	3.5 %	0.3 %	3.4 %	6.6	7.1	7.0	7.5
zxcvbn$_{v2}$	2.5 %	13 %	2.4 %	13 %	11.2	12.8	11.3	13.3	3.5 %	11 %	4.8 %	9.8 %	7.1	8.9	7.8	8.1
Blacklist	16 %	38 %	14 %	38 %	12.8	13.3	13.5	14.3	17 %	26 %	23 %	35 %	10.3	10.3	10.0	10.4
PCFG	2.2 %	22 %	3.9 %	29 %	10.2	11.9	10.6	12.0	16 %	21 %	15 %	24 %	9.7	9.8	8.3	8.7
Hybrid	16 %	27 %	14 %	29 %	12.8	13.0	13.5	13.9	17 %	25 %	23 %	34 %	10.3	10.3	10.0	10.4
Combined	13 %	36 %	13 %	37 %	12.8	13.2	13.2	14.3	17 %	27 %	22 %	36 %	10.3	10.3	9.5	10.5

be similar. The result from the table confirms that if the thread model is online guessing attacks in which the number of attempts allowed by an adversary is limited, GNG cannot accurately measure the crack-resistency of PRAs, and β-RSG is a more appropriate metrics in this use case. The low marginal effect in β-RSG also indicates that websites might not need to reject too many passwords if the major concern is online guessing attacks.

From Fig. 2, perhaps the most noticeable difference among the metrics is the relative order of the PCFG method, two versions of *zxcvbn*, and the Hybrid method, comparing with the other Client-end PRAs.

The PCFG method performs reasonably well in GNG, but poorly in β-RSG and β-NRSG. While PCFG can cover many passwords in the testing datasets, which leads to the low total density of passwords not cracked in GNG, some of the high-frequency passwords remain uncovered. As a result, the residual strength of PCFG is lower than most of the other PRAs.

On the other hand, the hybrid method and $zxcvbn_2$ perform much better in β-RSG and β-NRSG than in GNG. Although the high-ranking passwords in the PRAs only include a relative low number of unique passwords in the testing datasets, the popularly selected passwords are mostly covered. Therefore, after rejecting the top-ranking passwords from the PRAs, an adversary can only break into a limited number of accounts within a small number of guesses, which results in a high residual strength.

Another observation is that the performance of the two *zxcvbn* PRAs, especially $zxcvbn_2$ significantly boost in β-NRSG comparing with that in β-RSG. The residual strength resulted by $zxcvbn_2$ is even higher than the size-limited Markov Models (MC_3 and MCB_c). The observation indicates that the relative poor performance of *zxcvbn* in β-RSG is mainly due to the penalization from the large number of passwords, which are extremely not likely to be used, generated.

Overall, several Server-end PRAs including the Blacklist PRA, the Markov Models, and the Combined method result in similar performances. The hybrid method, which inherits the advantage of Blacklist PRAs and Markov Model with backoff, outperform the other Client-end PRAs.

6 Conclusion

In this paper, we model different password strength checking methods (including password strength meters) as Password Ranking Algorithms (PRAs), and we introduce two metrics: the β-Residual Strength Graph (β-RSG) and the Normalized β-Residual Strength Graph (β-NRSG), to compare them using real world password datasets. In our evaluation, we find unreasonably high frequency of some suspicious passwords. We remove the associated accounts by identifying suspicious account IDs. We then, apply the metrics on cleansed datasets, and show that dictionary-based PRA has similar performance with the sophisticated PRAs. If the size of PRAs are limited in order to be fit into a client, a hybrid method combining a small dictionary of weak passwords and a Markov Model with backoff with a limited size can provide the most accurate strength measurement.

Acknowledgement. This paper is based upon work supported in part by an IBM OCR grant from IBM Research.

A DBSCAN

DBSCAN [17] is a density-based clustering algorithm. It groups together points that are closely packed together. DBSCAN requires two parameters: ϵ and the minimum number of points required to form a dense region $minPts$. It starts with an arbitrary starting point that has not been visited. This point's $\epsilon-$neighborhood is retrieved, and if it contains sufficiently many points, a cluster is started. Otherwise, the point is labeled as noise. Note that this point might later be found in a sufficiently sized $\epsilon-$environment of a different point and hence be made part of a cluster. If a point is found to be a dense part of a cluster, its $\epsilon-$neighborhood is also part of that cluster. Hence, all points that are found within the $\epsilon-$neighborhood are added, as is their own $\epsilon-$neighborhood when they are also dense. This process continues until the density-connected cluster is completely found. Then, a new unvisited point is retrieved and processed, leading to the discovery of a further cluster or noise. Please refer to [17] for more details.

B Lognormal Distribution in Entropy of IDs

Figure 3 shows CDF of $-\log_{10} p$ of all IDs with length 10, which is the most frequently chosen ID length, from the 5 datasets containing IDs. For each dataset,

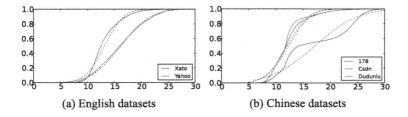

(a) English datasets   (b) Chinese datasets

Fig. 3. CDF of $-\log_{10} p$. The dashed lines are CDF of normal distribution with the same mean and standard deviation

we calculate probabilities of IDs utilizing 5-order Markov Model trained on itself. The dashed lines in the graph illustrate CDF of normal distribution with the same mean and standard deviation as the corresponding distribution. The figures show that except *178* dataset, the distributions fits relatively well, especially for English datasets. The difference between the distribution from Chinese datasets, *178* in particular, and the corresponding normal distribution is larger, we believe the distribution is biased by the problematic IDs.

C   Zxcvbn Password Generation and Modification

Password Generation. *Zxcvbn* was designed to evaluate password strength only. We implemented a password generator following the logic, which takes an input as the maximum entropy, and generate all passwords whose entropy is less than that value. The password generation is a recursive depth-first search process. We start from an empty string. In each iteration, we append a chunk to the current string. If the current entropy is less than the maximum entropy allowed, we record the password, and continue the recursion process. Note that we might duplicated generate passwords as each password might have multiple ways to be decomposed into patterns. Therefore, after the password generation, we conduct a further post-processing step. If a password appears multiple times, we keep the one with the lowest entropy, and then sort all the unique passwords based on entropy.

In practice, an integer score from 0 to 4 is calculated from entropy and each value is assigned with a description (e.g., Weak, Medium, Strong). Passwords with entropy less than 20 are assigned with a score is 0, and are usually rejected. We first tried to create all passwords within 20-bits of entropy. However, after 1 billion attempts, we still have not finished generating passwords start from "mary", which is the first word in female names dictionary. The number of passwords considered as weak by *zxcvbn* is much larger than any of the known weak password dictionary. Alternatively, we generated 10,478,853 unique passwords with entropy less than 4 for $zxcvbn_1$, and 1,834,980 unique passwords with entropy less than 12 for $zxcvbn_2$.

Adapting Zxcvbn to Chinese Datasets. *Zxcvbn* is originally designed for English speaking users, as it supports English words only [38]. In order to adapt the method for evaluating Chinese passwords, we create another dictionary for evaluating Chinese passwords. We construct such a Chinese dictionary using the *Duduniu* dataset. For each password in *Duduniu*, we first split the word into chunks based on character types, e.g. letters, digits, and symbols. We then, count the frequency of letter chunks after turning all letters into lower cases. Finally, we generate the dictionary by outputting all the letter chunks that contains at least three characters and with frequencies of at least 100 in the descending order of their frequency. There are 5,553 words in the dictionary.

Table 7. Top 20 words in the new dictionary for *zxcvbn*.

Rank	Words									
1–10	asd	woaini	wang	abc	zhang	liu	qwe	love	qaz	yang
11–20	chen	zxc	aaa	wei	www	long	lin	xiao	aaaaaa	huang

Table 7 lists the first 20 words in order. Most of the common words used are the syllables of last names in Chinese, e.g. wang, zhang, liu, etc. The rest of them are either keyboard patterns or letter sequences. Not many English words appears in the dictionary. There are many three letter combinations in the dictionary, such as wjq, ljh, zjh. We believe these are initials of the syllables in Chinese names. There is no need to construct separate name dictionaries as the most common names are already covered.

We were able to generate 9,316,973 passwords with entropy less than 3 for $zxcvbn_1$, and 1,913,061 unique passwords with entropy less than 12 for $zxcvbn_2$.

References

1. Passwords (2009). http://wiki.skullsecurity.org/Passwords
2. CSDN cleartext passwords (2011). http://dazzlepod.com/csdn/
3. John the ripper password cracker (2014). http://www.openwall.com/john/
4. Adams, A., Sasse, M.A.: Users are not the enemy. Commun. ACM **42**(12), 40–46 (1999)
5. Bergadano, F., Crispo, B., Ruffo, G.: Proactive password checking with decision trees. In: Proceedings of the 4th ACM Conference on Computer and Communications Security, pp. 67–77 (1997)
6. Bonneau, J.: The science of guessing: analyzing an anonymized corpus of 70 million passwords. In: Proceedings of the IEEE Symposium on Security and Privacy, pp. 538–552 (2012)
7. Bonneau, J., Herley, C., van Oorschot, P.C., Stajano, F.: Passwords and the evolution of imperfect authentication. Commun. ACM **58**(7), 78–87 (2015)
8. Boztas, S.: Entropies, guessing, and cryptography. Technical report 6, Department of Mathematics, Royal Melbourne Institute of Technology (1999)
9. Brostoff, S., Sasse, M.A.: "Ten strikes and you're out": increasing the number of login attempts can improve password usability. In: Proceedings of the Human-computer Interaction Security Workshop (2003)

10. Burnett, M.: Today I am releasing ten million passwords (2015). https://xato.net/passwords/ten-million-passwords/
11. Burr, W.E., Dodson, D.F., Polk, W.T.: Electronic authentication guideline. US Department of Commerce, Technology Administration, National Institute of Standards and Technology (2004)
12. Castelluccia, C., Chaabane, A., Dürmuth, M., Perito, D.: When privacy meets security: Leveraging personal information for password cracking. arXiv preprint arXiv:1304.6584 (2013)
13. Castelluccia, C., Dürmuth, M., Perito, D.: Adaptive password-strength meters from Markov models. In: Proceedings of the Network and Distributed System Security Symposium (2012)
14. de Carné de Carnavalet, X., Mannan, M.: From very weak to very strong: analyzing password-strength meters. In: Proceedings of the Network and Distributed System Security Symposium (2014)
15. Dell'Amico, M., Filippone, M.: Monte carlo strength evaluation: fast and reliable password checking. In: Proceedings of the 22nd ACM Conference on Computer and Communications Security, pp. 158–169 (2015)
16. Egelman, S., Sotirakopoulos, A., Muslukhov, I., Beznosov, K., Herley, C.: Does my password go up to eleven?: the impact of password meters on password selection. In: Proceedings of the SIGCHI Conference on Human Factors in Computing Systems, pp. 2379–2388 (2013)
17. Ester, M., Kriegel, H.-P., Sander, J., Xu, X.: A density-based algorithm for discovering clusters in large spatial databases with noise. In: Proceedings of the 2nd ACM Conference on Knowledge Discovery and Data Mining, vol. 96, pp. 226–231 (1996)
18. Florêncio, D., Herley, C.: A large-scale study of web password habits. In: Proceedings of the 16th International Conference on World Wide Web, pp. 657–666 (2007)
19. Forget, A., Chiasson, S., van Oorschot, P.C., Biddle, R.: Improving text passwords through persuasion. In: Proceedings of the 4th Symposium on Usable Privacy and Security, pp. 1–12 (2008)
20. Grampp, F.T., Morris, R.H.: The unix system: unix operating system security. AT&T Bell Laboratories Tech. J. **63**(8), 1649–1672 (1984)
21. Herley, C., van Oorschot, P.C.: A research agenda acknowledging the persistence of passwords. IEEE Secur. Priv. **10**(1), 28–36 (2012)
22. Kelley, P.G., Komanduri, S., Mazurek, M.L., Shay, R., Vidas, T., Bauer, L., Christin, N., Cranor, L.F., Lopez, J.: Guess again (and again and again): measuring password strength by simulating password-cracking algorithms. In: Proceedings of the IEEE Symposium on Security and Privacy, pp. 523–537(2012)
23. Klein, D.V.: Foiling the cracker: a survey of, and improvements to, password security. In: Proceedings of the 2nd USENIX Security Workshop, pp. 5–14 (1990)
24. Komanduri, S., Shay, R., Cranor, L.F., Herley, C., Schechter, S.: Telepathwords: preventing weak passwords by reading users' minds. In: Proceedings of the 23rd USENIX Security Symposium, pp. 591–606 (2014)
25. Komanduri, S., Shay, R., Kelley, P.G., Mazurek, M.L., Bauer, L., Christin, N., Cranor, L.F., Egelman, S.: Of passwords and people: measuring the effect of password-composition policies. In: Proceedings of the SIGCHI Conference on Human Factors in Computing Systems, pp. 2595–2604 (2011)
26. Ma, J., Yang, W., Luo, M., Li, N.: A study of probabilistic password models. In: IEEE Symposium on Security and Privacy (SP), pp. 689–704. IEEE (2014)

27. Manber, U., Wu, S.: An algorithm for approximate membership checking with application to password security. Inf. Process. Lett. **50**(4), 191–197 (1994)
28. Morris, R., Thompson, K.: Password security: a case history. Commun. ACM **22**(11), 594–597 (1979)
29. Narayanan, A., Shmatikov, V.: Fast dictionary attacks on passwords using time-space tradeoff. In Proceedings of the 12th ACM Conference on Computer and Communications Security, pp. 364–372 (2005)
30. Riley, S.: Password security: What users know and what they actually do. In: Chaparro, B.S. (ed.) Usability News, vol. 8 of 1, Software Usability Research Laboratory (SURL) at Wichita State University (2006)
31. Schechter, S., Herley, C., Mitzenmacher, M.: Popularity is everything: a new approach to protecting passwords from statistical-guessing attacks. In: Proceedings of the 5th USENIX Conference on Hot Topics in Security, pp. 1–8 (2010)
32. Spafford, E.H.: OPUS: preventing weak password choices. Comput. Secur. **11**(3), 273–278 (1992)
33. Ur, B., Kelley, P.G., Komanduri, S., Lee, J., Maass, M., Mazurek, M., Passaro, T., Shay, R., Vidas, T., Bauer, L., et al.: How does your password measure up? The effect of strength meters on password creation. In: Proceedings of the 21st USENIX Security Symposium, pp. 65–80 (2012)
34. Ur, B., Segreti, S.M., Bauer, L., Christin, N., Cranor, L.F., Komanduri, S., Kurilova, D., Mazurek, M.L., Melicher, W., Shay, R.: Measuring real-world accuracies and biases in modeling password guessability. In: Proceeding of the 24th USENIX Security Symposium, pp. 463–481 (2015)
35. Veras, R., Collins, C., Thorpe, J.: On the semantic patterns of passwords and their security impact. In: Proceedings of the Network and Distributed System Security Symposium (2014)
36. Weir, M., Aggarwal, S., Collins, M., Stern, H.: Testing metrics for password creation policies by attacking large sets of revealed passwords. In: Proceedings of the 17th ACM Conference on Computer and Communications Security, pp. 162–175 (2010)
37. Weir, M., Aggarwal, S., de Medeiros, B., Glodek, B.: Password cracking using probabilistic context-free grammars. In: Proceedings of the IEEE Symposium on Security and Privacy, pp. 391–405 (2009)
38. Wheeler, D.: zxcvbn: realistic password strength estimation. Dropbox blog article (2012)
39. Yan, J.J.: A note on proactive password checking. In: Proceedings of the 2001 Workshop on New Security Paradigms, pp. 127–135 (2001)

Scalable Two-Factor Authentication
Using Historical Data

Aldar C.-F. Chan$^{1(\boxtimes)}$, Jun Wen Wong^2, Jianying Zhou^2, and Joseph Teo^3

^{1} Hong Kong R&D Centre for LSCM Enabling Technologies, Hong Kong, China
aldar@graduate.hku.hk
^{2} Institute for Infocomm Research, A*STAR, Singapore, Singapore
{jwwong,jyzhou}@i2r.a-star.edu.sg
^{3} CSIT, Singapore, Singapore
josephteo2003@gmail.com

Abstract. Two-factor authentication is increasingly demanded in the Internet of Things (IoT), especially those deployed in the critical infrastructure. However, resource and operational constraints of typical IoT devices are the key impediment, especially when the IoT device acts as a verifier. This paper proposes a novel authentication factor (namely, historical data) which, when combined with the conventional first authentication factor (a secret key), results in a scalable, lightweight two-factor entity authentication protocol for use in the IoT. In the new authentication factor, the data exchanged between a verifier and a prover is used as the secret information for the verifier to prove his identity to the verifier. Practically, the verifier needs all the historical data to prove his identity. Yet, through an innovative use of the proof of retrievability, the verifier only needs a constant storage regardless of the size of the historical data. Leveraging on the data retrieval and searching capability of contemporary big data technologies, the proposed authentication factor can achieve realtime, fault-tolerant verification. The use of historical data as an authentication factor has a very interesting leakage-resilience property. Besides, the proposed scheme demonstrates a tradeoff between security and computational overhead, and such scalability particularly suits the IoT, with devices of diverse capabilities.

1 Introduction

Two-factor authentication, which corroborates the identities of legitimate users based on two sources of secret information (called factors), generally provides a better security guarantee than its one-factor counterpart and is widely used in Internet services [1,6,7,9,12,15–17,23,24,26,32–34], such as Google's 2-step authentication [14]. Although entity authentication in the Internet of Things

This work was supported in part by the National Research Foundation (NRF), Prime Ministers Office, Singapore, under its National Cybersecurity R&D Programme (Award No. NRF2014NCR-NCR001-31) and administered by the National Cybersecurity R&D Directorate.

© Springer International Publishing Switzerland 2016
I. Askoxylakis et al. (Eds.): ESORICS 2016, Part I, LNCS 9878, pp. 91–110, 2016.
DOI: 10.1007/978-3-319-45744-4_5

(IoT) is still largely achieved by one-factor authentication with a pre-shared secret key or password [30] as limited by resource and operational constraints, two-factor authentication is increasingly demanded in the IoT, especially those deployed in the critical infrastructure. This paper proposes a novel authentication factor based on historical data and explores its use in the IoT. It not only provides a more leakage-resilient alternative to passwords/secret keys, but also extends the use of two-factor authentication to the challenging area of the IoT with resource-constrained devices. While it is feasible to use historical data as the primary factor, this paper basically focuses on its use as the secondary factor.

There has been an ever-increasing need to improve the security of the IoT with two-factor authentication. On one hand, many of these systems are deployed for safety-critical applications, thus demanding a higher level of security in general to match up with the high cost of failures. For instance, modern mass transportation systems usually consist of resource-constrained devices — be they in the legacy sub-systems or in their contemporary counterparts — but are relatively intolerant to breaches. The deployment of two-factor authentication is usually inevitable to achieve the needed security assurance. On the other hand, a single level of security is usually insufficient to satisfactorily capture all the requirements of the variety of operations and functions in a typical IoT system. To implement multi-level security, it is necessary to deploy two-factor authentication for more sensitive operations, such as firmware update and configuration change, wherein one-factor authentication is deemed as insufficient.

As an example, EPRI (Electric Power Research Institute) has identified about 100 representative failure scenarios in the smart grid [19,21,22], out of which about 30 % are attributed to the use of weak or one-factor authentication in security-sensitive operations. These EPRI reports also recommend multi-factor authentication as a mitigation to these scenarios. Most interesting is the case of meter disconnection or firmware update for smart meters [19], wherein entity authentication based on an established secret key between a meter and the utility company is deemed as insufficient because the secret key can be leaked out in one shot during routine operations through a contractor or disgruntled former employee. In fact, since the same secret key is typically used to establish a secure session for normal message exchange between the meter and the utility (to key the encryption and message authentication algorithms), there are various vectors through which this secret key can be leaked out [11,13]; assuming perfect security of a secret key is unrealistic. In particular, there is plenty of economic incentive for a firmware modification attack, say, to report a lower consumption. There is consensus that a second authentication factor which is more leakage-resilient should be sought.

The key impediment to the adoption of two-factor authentication in the IoT is resource constraints of typical devices (as driven by the low-cost requirement). Direct application of existing mechanisms originally designed for online services [1,6,7,9,12,15–17,23,24,26,32–34] to the IoT is practically infeasible. Adding to the complexity is that a resource-constrained IoT device has to act as the verifier of authentication, whereas, existing schemes mostly assume a powerful machine as the verifier, for instance, banks' backend servers. Despite the existence of a handful of proposals using a physical token [10,31] for sensor network authentication, it is fair to say two-factor authentication for resource-constrained IoT devices remains largely an open problem. To fill this gap, we propose to leverage on the "big data" notion [35] and technologies to implement a novel, scalable authentication factor, namely, historical data, for IoT devices. A big data application is basically characterized by a large *volume* of data of a great *variety* generated at a great *velocity* [35].

1.1 Overview of Our Technique

The basic idea of the new authentication protocol is to use the whole history of the data exchanged between an IoT device V (the verifier) and a server P (the prover) as the second authentication factor, in addition to the conventional first factor of a shared secret key. In order to pass the verification by the IoT device, the server must has full access to all the historical data sent from the IoT device. The secret key and the historical data are both needed to generate a correct response for a given challenge issued by the IoT device in a typical challenge-response protocol [4].

Roughly speaking (in the big data context), we can view the second factor as a very big piece of secret key which an attacker would need significantly greater effort to fully compromise. The adversary has to eavesdrop the communication between the IoT device and the server over an extended period of time and break the encryption (if one is used), or to steal a considerable amount of data from the server, in order to have a good chance to pass the verification. Besides, such actions could make the attacker more susceptible to detection. This model resembles the underlying assumption of the *bounded storage model* [2,13] and the *bounded retrieval model* [11]: the secret information has a considerably high entropy that leakage is only gradual (i.e. bounded) in practice. In addition, as data are constantly generated by the IoT device and sent to the server, it becomes increasingly difficult for an adversary to gain full knowledge of the growing dataset. This also improves the resilience of the second authentication factor as an adversary having captured a fixed amount of historical data, say, through a lunchtime attack [3], will only find himself holding a diminishing portion of the second authentication factor as time goes by. As a result, the security requirements on the storage for this authentication factor is significantly relaxed, compared to the conventional secret key. In fact, we assume no extra protection is needed for storing the historical data.

We consider the second authentication factor as a big dataset. In general, retrieving selected pieces of data from such a large amount of data (for generating the proof) usually encounters unreasonably long latency. Nevertheless, with the use of big data platforms such as Hadoop over parallel clusters, the searching and retrieving of the data could be achieved with close-to-constant time [5], which makes the proposed authentication protocol practical. Besides, despite its huge volume, corruption of historical data is generally not an issue for conventional big data platforms like Hadoop. HDFS (Hadoop File System) is considered highly fault-tolerant [5,25]. It should be noted that the proposed authentication based on historical data is scalable in the sense that a huge data set is not a prerequisite for the protocol to operate correctly. While a larger historical dataset implies better security, only a small number of data pieces (say, 5) would be sufficient to bootstrap the protocol, and these data could be readily provided by the set of pre-set configuration data of the IoT device.

The idea of using historical data as an authentication factor is not entirely new. For instance, the "life questions" used to reset a password or when a token is lost in online banking is one embodiment. However, all such schemes require the verifier to keep a synchronized record of all historical data, the volume of which seems overwhelming to a typical IoT device. Relying on a small, selected set of historical data (as in the online banking scenario), though practically achievable, may not provide sufficient security. Intuitively, storing the whole dataset at the IoT device is necessary for verifying the validity of any response generated from a subset of it. However, through the use of the proof of retrievability protocol [27] in a different manner, we achieve a security protocol which can utilize all the historical data for authentication, while maintaining a constant storage at the IoT device (verifier), more precisely, 512 bits of secret keys for 256-bit security.[1] *A proof-of-retrievability protocol is conventionally used for a user to verify whether a cloud storage provider keeps all his data. This paper presents a novel and non-trivial application of it to a very different context to achieve a very different, but commonly sought, security objective, namely, entity authentication.*

1.2   Comparison with the Trivial Scheme Using Two Keys

The proposed scheme differs from the trivial extension running two instances of the one-factor authentication protocol using two distinct secret keys in at least two ways.

First, although the historical dataset as an authentication factor can be seen as a large secret key, the way to compromise it is rendered considerably different due to its much larger size than a typical secret key (256 bits). While an adversary, after gaining access to a system, can easily steal/copy a 256-bit key unnoticeably, it takes significantly more time (and operations by the system) to copy just a small portion of a big data set of a few hundred GB. In order to pass the authentication with a reasonably high probability, an attacker has to capture most of the historical dataset. It is thus reasonable to assume that the amount of information of the second authentication factor leaked out in any single (undetected) incident could be insignificant to help the adversary to pass

---

[1] The protocol also stores the last historical data index L at the IoT device.

the subsequent authentication. In other words, the historical data as an authentication factor exhibits some form of leakage-resilience property which cannot be found in a typical secret key. For the same reason, confidentiality requirements for the storage of the historical data as an authentication factor are considerably relaxed, compared to that for a secret key (which usually requires storage in a tamper-resistant token). In fact, we assume the data (but not the tags) can be shared in the proposed scheme.

Second, to achieve the same level of leakage-resilience for the authentication factor, a trivial composition requires a linear storage complexity at the IoT device (verifier), whereas, only a constant storage is needed in the proposed scheme.

1.3 Our Contributions

The key contribution of this paper is a novel authentication factor based on historical data, which is leakage-resilient, thereby lowering the confidentiality requirements on its storage and management. It is fair to say this is the first scheme in the literature to demonstrate the potential of the big data for the purpose of entity authentication. A lightweight two-factor authentication scheme suitable for the IoT is achieved as a result, which only requires a constant storage at the IoT device as the verifier. The proposed construction is also highly scalable in the sense that a tradeoff between the computation overhead and attainable security level is inherent in the protocol design — a much needed property for the IoT (with diverse devices). By increasing the number of elements in the authentication challenge, the difficulty for an adversary increases exponentially while the computation overhead increases linearly.

The organization of the paper is as follows. Next section presents related work, and Sect. 3 discusses the problem setting including the security model. Section 4 gives the protocol design details. The security and performance of the protocol is discussed in Sects. 5 and 6 respectively. Section 7 illustrates a mechanism to strength the first authentication factor's security. Finally, the conclusion is given in Sect. 8.

2 Related Work

Multi-factor authentication has been widely studied [1,6,7,9,12,15–17,23,24,26, 32–34] in the literature. In general, there are three common types of authentication factor, namely, "what you know," "what you have," and "what you are" [6]. A fourth type of authentication factor, such as "whom you know" [6] and "where you are" [9,20], has been proposed. This paper proposes another novel form of authentication factor — "what have been discussed" — which can be seen as a parallel effort.

A two-factor authentication scheme using a physical token for sensor networks is proposed in [10], and subsequently corrected by [31]. Since the same token is used over all the sensor nodes [10,31], these schemes are not resilient to node compromise. In contrast, the historical datasets for different devices are inherently different in our scheme. Biometrics [1,16,17] is a common form of the "what you are" factor, but is ruled out for use in IoT devices, given their resource constraints. The "what you have" factor is most popular and has a variety of forms, from a physical token [7,10,23,24], a dedicated physical channel [20,29,33], to a separate logical channel [12]. The need of multiple channels could be over-demanding for IoT devices. Indeed, the desirable property of using a single channel for authentication has been sought [17]. Historical data as an authentication factor can also be considered as a kind of the "what you have" factor. While a physical token stores a secret key for authentication, in our scheme, the secret information needed for authentication is embedded as part of a large body of historical data, which is too big for an adversary to collect beforehand.

This paper proposes using the past history of payload data between the verifier and prover as a new form of authentication factor. In [32], email messages are used as the second authentication factor. While email messages can be seen as a form of historical data, the email message transmission is initiated only after the verification of the first factor succeeds, as an extra confirmation. More precisely, [32] should be seen as using a dedicated channel instead. Besides, only one email message is used in [32], in contrast to random samples from the whole of historical dataset proposed in this paper. The closest existing proposal to this paper is [28] which uses continuous dynamic data generated by a smart phone owner as an authentication factor. The phone has to store the whole set of data for verification, whereas, this paper only requires the tag generation key to be stored at the IoT device for verification. Some schemes [26,34] are dedicated to combining two authentication factors, addressing a different, orthogonal perspective of the multi-factor authentication problem.

The security mechanism to use historical data as an authentication factor in this paper resembles those in the proof of receipt [8] and proof of retrievability protocols [27]. In fact, regardless of efficiency, it is possible to convert any proof of retrievability protocol into an authentication protocol using historical data. This paper extends the underlying mechanism for use in a different application to achieve a different but more popular security objective, namely, entity authentication. Unlike [27], which has to handle the data corruption issue through erasure code, this paper assumes that the issue has been adequately addressed by most big data platforms which are highly fault-tolerant by design. This paper achieves the leakage resilience property of the second authentication factor through the realization of the bounded-storage model [2,13] or bounded-retrieval model [11] using historical data in the big data context.

3   Background and Model

3.1   Protocol Syntax

A two-factor authentication scheme involves two parties, a prover P and a verifier V. P is a server and V is an IoT device corroborating P's identity. Corresponding to the two authentication factors are two secret keys, sk_1, sk_2, but sk_2 is not directly used. Instead, V generates the historical dataset $\mathcal{D}$ and processes it with sk_2 (by tagging each $d_i \in \mathcal{D}$) to form $\mathcal{D}^*$ that P uses as the second authentication factor. The scheme defines four algorithms Init, Tag, Auth$_P$, Auth$_V$, and a two-party interactive protocol:

Init(1^λ). This randomized algorithm generates a pair (sk_1, sk_2) where sk_1 is the secret key used as the first authentication factor shared between P and V, and sk_2 is the secret key used by V to tag the historical data $\mathcal{D}$ to generate the second authentication factor $\mathcal{D}^*$ for P. While both P and V keep a copy of sk_1, the key sk_2 is known to nobody except V. Concretely, $sk_1 = mk$ and $sk_2 = (K, K')$ in this paper.

Tag(sk_2, d_i). This data tagging algorithm is used by V with input sk_2 to mark each piece of data $d_i \in \mathcal{D}$ to generate a tag t_i. (d_i, t_i) is sent to P and forms part of $\mathcal{D}^*$.

(Auth$_P(sk_1, \mathcal{D}^*)$, **Auth**$_V(sk_1, sk_2))$. The randomized proving and verifying algorithms define a protocol for proving P's identity to V. During protocol execution, P takes as input the two authentication factors — sk_1 and $\mathcal{D}^*$ — and V uses (sk_1, sk_2) to verify. More specifically, V selects some random challenges and a set I of indices corresponding to t pieces of historical data in $\mathcal{D}$ to request P to generate a response to prove his identity. P uses sk_1 and the specified data tuples $\{(d_i, t_i) \in \mathcal{D}^* : i \in I\}$ to generate the response. Finally, Auth$_V$ outputs a bit b where $b = 1$ corresponds to a success of the authentication instance and $b = 0$ corresponds to a failure. We can denote a run of two machines executing the algorithms as: $\{0, 1\} \leftarrow (\mathsf{Auth}_V(sk_1, sk_2) \rightleftharpoons \mathsf{Auth}_P(sk_1, \mathcal{D}^*))$.

The correctness requirement is that for all λ and some data set $\mathcal{D}$, if $(sk_1, sk_2) \leftarrow \mathsf{Init}(1^\lambda)$, and $\mathcal{D}^* = \{(d_i, t_i) : d_i \in \mathcal{D}\}$ where $t_i \leftarrow \mathsf{Tag}(sk_2, d_i), \forall d_i \in \mathcal{D}$, then the output b of the protocol $(\mathsf{Auth}_V(sk_1, sk_2) \rightleftharpoons \mathsf{Auth}_P(sk_1, \mathcal{D}^*))$, with all messages delivered correctly between P and V, will be 1 except for negligible probability.

3.2   Adversarial Model

The goal of the adversary Adv is to carry out an authentication attack to impersonate P to V. A two-factor authentication scheme based on historical data is sound if any cheating prover P' which convinces the verifier V (running Auth$_V$) that he is the prover P actually possesses sk_1 and $\mathcal{D}^*$. That is, anyone passing the authentication must possess sk_1 and $\mathcal{D}^*$ (or sk_2 which only V knows and P does not). We assume that Adv does not corrupt V to obtain (sk_1, sk_2); if V is corrupted, there is no need for Adv to carry out an authentication attack to prove his identity to V. Similarly, if P is fully compromised, there is no need for Adv to impersonate P.

We assume that Adv, without all the authentication factors, has a full control of the communication channel through eavesdropping, injecting, modifying and deleting messages exchanged between P and V, including initiating authentication sessions. Adv is also able to obtain some tuples of historical data $(d_i, t_i) \in \mathcal{D}^*$

through eavesdropping, temporarily breaking into P alike the lunchtime attack [3], or other insider threats. However, we assume as in the bounded-storage model [2,13] that $\mathcal{D}^*$ is sufficiently large that Adv is not able to compromise all data in $\mathcal{D}^*$. This assumption is reasonable because, taking the smart meter scenario as an example, a former employee or contractor of the utility company could capture, over a *finite* period of time, the smart meter data during normal operations — which allows him to obtain a portion but not all of the historical dataset — but extensive data capture would be susceptible to detection. In addition, the data are usually sent over a secure channel in encrypted forms, meaning eavesdropping alone might not capture a significant fraction of the historical dataset. The proposed authentication factor ensures that, unless a significant percentage of the historical data has been compromised, these captured data would not give the adversary any significant advantage to successfully pass subsequent authentication sessions.

We consider the following authentication game denoted by $\mathsf{Auth}_{2FA}^{Adv}$, which takes a tuple $(\lambda, t, q_T, q_E, q_V, q_P)$ as input and executes between Adv and an environment:

1. The environment runs $\mathsf{Init}(1^\lambda)$ to generate the key pair (sk_1, sk_2) for the two authentication factors. It randomly picks L pieces of data to form the historical dataset $\mathcal{D} = \{d_1, d_2, \ldots, d_L\}$, and runs Tag with sk_2 to tag d_i's to form $\mathcal{D}^* = \{(d_1, t_1), (d_2, t_2), \ldots, (d_L, t_L)\}$. The two authentication factors are sk_1 and $\mathcal{D}^*$.

2. Adv can choose none or one of the two authentication factors — sk_1, $\mathcal{D}^*$ — to compromise. The environment gives the selected factor to Adv. For the second authentication factor, the environment also gives sk_2 to Adv.

3. If Adv has not chosen the second authentication factor $\mathcal{D}^*$ to compromise, it can make at most $q_T < L$ queries to obtain q_T pairs of $(d_i, t_i) \in \mathcal{D}^*$ at his choice.

4. Adv can observe the execution of q_E instances of the authentication protocol, that is, $\mathsf{Auth}_V(sk_1, sk_2) \rightleftharpoons \mathsf{Auth}_P(sk_1, \mathcal{D}^*)$ and obtain the transcripts for them.

5. Adv can execute the authentication protocol as the verifier by interacting with q_P instances of Auth_P, that is, $Adv \rightleftharpoons \mathsf{Auth}_P(sk_1, \mathcal{D}^*)$.

6. Adv can execute the authentication protocol as the prover by interacting with q_V instances of Auth_V, that is, $\mathsf{Auth}_V(sk_1, sk_2) \rightleftharpoons Adv$.

7. Finally, Adv is challenged to authenticate himself to a *new* instance of Auth_V, and no more queries can be made. Adv succeeds if this instance $\mathsf{Auth}_V(sk_1, sk_2) \rightleftharpoons Adv$ outputs $b = 1$. Such an event is denoted by $Succ_{Adv}$.

Definition 1 (Authentication Attack Resistance). *A two-factor authentication scheme based on historical data is $(\delta_{12}, \delta_i, \delta_2)$-sound for parameters $(\lambda, t, q_T, q_E, q_V, q_P)$, where q_T, q_E, q_V, q_P are polynomial in λ, if for any algorithm Adv whose running time is bounded, the following holds for random execution of an authentication game $\mathsf{Auth}_{2FA}^{Adv}(\lambda, t, q_T, q_E, q_V, q_P)$:*

1. $Pr[Succ_{Adv}] \leq \delta_{12}$ *if Adv does not compromise any authentication factor.*
2. $Pr[Succ_{Adv}] \leq \delta_1$ *if Adv only compromises the second authentication factor* $\mathcal{D}^*$ *but not the first authentication factor.*
3. $Pr[Succ_{Adv}] \leq \delta_2$ *if Adv only compromises the first authentication factor* sk_1 *but not the second authentication factor.*

We assume that (d_i, t_i)-tuples are leaked out in *all* queries, not just in Tag queries, especially when sk_1 has been compromised. Note that the need to authenticate to a new Auth_V instance in the challenge step prevents *Adv* from using concurrently running query instances of $\mathsf{Auth}_P(sk_1, \mathcal{D}^*)$ to win the challenge.

4   Two-Factor Authentication Using Historical Data

For the sake of generality, we present the scheme assuming all the arithmetic is done in a certain finite field $\mathbb{F}$ without discussing its parameters or using special notations. To help understand the design, one can simply understand all the arithmetic in $\mathbb{Z}_p$ (integers mod p) for a large prime p of length λ bits. There is flexibility in choosing the finite field arithmetic used for the protocol: $\mathbb{Z}_p$ or $GF(2^\lambda)$ (the binary extension field of length λ bits). In the implementation in Sect. 6, we used $GF(2^{256})$. It should be noted that *addition in any finite field achieves perfect secrecy as one-time pad does if the key is truly random, even though the operation is not exclusive-OR.* In fact, for a binary extension field (which is used in this paper), an addition is simply an exclusive-OR.

The design is a typical 2-step challenge-response protocol to prove the possession of sk_1 and $\mathcal{D}^*$. The key building blocks include two pseudorandom functions (PRFs) f, E (instantiated by SHA256-HMAC in Sect. 6). More precisely, E is a pseudorandom permutation. A cryptographic hash function h is used simply for mapping an arbitrary data piece $d_i \in \{0,1\}^*$ to an element in the finite field (which is an λ-bit string for $GF(2^\lambda)$).

For the sake of clarity, we assume all data are tagged.[2] Then L is cardinality of the historical dataset $\mathcal{D}$. The design uses an adjustable security parameter t, which is size of the set I of indices of the selected samples from $\mathcal{D}^*$ needed to generate the response.

The two factor authentication protocol using big data runs as follows.

---

[2] In practice, the set I of challenge indices could be generated by some random number generator with a seed s chosen by V or just indices spaced equally. For the latter case, $I = \{i + w : i \bmod a = 0; 0 \leq i < L; w \in [0, a-1]\}$ where a is the space between two consecutive indices in I and w is a random number. Suppose, t indices are needed in the challenge, then a could be determined as $\lceil \frac{L}{t} \rceil$.

Two-factor Authentication Protocol using Historical Data

In the following, all the arithmetic is done in a certain *finite field* $\mathbb{F}$ (which can be $\mathbb{Z}_p$ or $GF(2^\lambda)$).
For a security parameter λ, $f : \{0,1\}^\lambda \times \{0,1\}^* \to \mathbb{F}$ is a pseudorandom function which takes a λ-bit key and an arbitrary-length string to output an element in $\mathbb{F}$.
$E : \{0,1\}^\lambda \times \{0,1\}^\lambda \to \{0,1\}^\lambda$ is another pseudorandom function with equal input and output length; that is, E is a pseudorandom permutation.
$h : \{0,1\}^* \to \mathbb{F}$ is a cryptographic hash function mapping an arbitrary-length message to an element in $\mathbb{F}$.

Initialization $\mathsf{Init}(1^\lambda)$:
For a security parameter λ,

1. Randomly choose a secret key $mk \in \{0,1\}^\lambda$. Set $sk_1 = mk$
2. Randomly choose two secret keys $K \in \mathbb{F}^*$, $K' \in \{0,1\}^*$. Set $sk_2 = (K, K')$
3. Load $sk_1 = mk$ to P and $(sk_1, sk_2) = (mk, K, K')$ to V.

Tag Generation $\mathsf{Tag}((K, K'), d_i)$:
For a new piece of data d_i with index i (selected for tagging),

1. V retrieves (K, K');
2. V generates a new segment key k_i for i by computing $k_i = f_{K'}(i)$ and compute the tag $t_i = K \cdot h(d_i) + k_i$;
3. V increases L by 1 and sends (i, d_i, t_i) to P.
4. P stores (d_i, t_i) to $\mathcal{D}^*$ and increases L by 1.

Authentication Protocol $\mathsf{Auth} = (\mathsf{Auth}_V(mk, (K, K')) \rightleftharpoons \mathsf{Auth}_P(mk, \mathcal{D}^*))$:

1. Auth_V: Suppose P attempts to authenticate to V. V randomly chooses a set I of t indices from $[1, L]$, and then picks a random bit-string $r \in \{0,1\}^\lambda$. The challenge $\mathcal{C}$ is (I, r). V sends $\mathcal{C}$ to P.
2. Auth_P: Upon receiving the challenge $\mathcal{C}$, P computes the response $\mathcal{R}$ using the two factors $sk_1, \mathcal{D}^*$ as follows:
   (a) On r, use mk to compute $r' = E_{mk}(r)$.
   (b) On I, for each $i \in I$, retrieve $(d_i, t_i) \in \mathcal{D}^*$ and compute
   $$X = \sum_{i \in I} f_{r'}(i) \cdot h(d_i),$$
   $$Y = \sum_{i \in I} f_{r'}(i) \cdot t_i.$$
   (c) P sends the response $\mathcal{R}(\mathcal{C}) = (X, Y)$ to V.
3. Auth_V: Given a response $\mathcal{R}' = (X', Y')$ and a challenge $\mathcal{C} = (I, r)$, V uses $sk_1 = mk$, $sk_2 = (K, K')$ to verify as follows:
   (a) Use mk to compute $r' = E_{mk}(r)$.
   (b) Compute $K_I = \sum_{i \in I} f_{K'}(i) \cdot f_{r'}(i)$.
   (c) Check
   $$Y' \stackrel{?}{=} K_I + K \cdot X'.$$
   If yes, return 1, otherwise, return 0.

4.1   Correctness

The correctness of the proposed protocol can be shown easily as follows. For the first authentication factor, both P and V carry out the same computation: $r' = E_{mk}(r)$. Based on the correctness of the pseudorandom permutation E, if P and V use the same mk and r, the results of r' computed at P and V respectively should be identical. Given the same value of r', the correctness of the second authentication factor can be easily shown as follows by substituting $t_i = K \cdot h(d_i) + f_{K'}(i)$ into Y:

$$Y = \sum_{i \in I} f_{r'}(i) \cdot t_i = \sum_{i \in I} f_{r'}(i) \cdot (K \cdot h(d_i) + f_{K'}(i)) = K \cdot X + K_I.$$

Note that the last step results from substituting $X = \sum_{i \in I} f_{r'}(i) \cdot h(d_i)$ and $K_I = \sum_{i \in I} f_{K'}(i) \cdot f_{r'}(i)$ into the equation.

5   Security Analysis

Intuitively, for the first authentication factor sk_1, without knowledge of sk_1, it would be difficult to get the same value of $r' = E_{sk_i}(r)$ as computed by V, since the security property of PRF guarantees that, for anyone not knowing the key, the output of E is computationally indistinguishable from a truly random λ-bit string. For the second authentication factor $\mathcal{D}^*$, it can be shown, as in [27], that either knowledge of $sk_2 = (K, K')$ or knowledge of all tuples of $(d_i, t_i) \in \mathcal{D}^*$ with $i \in I$ is necessary to pass the authentication by V with non-negligible probability of success.

Although there are many pairs of (X, Y) which allow Adv to pass the authentication, the probability of finding these pairs is negligibly small in the security parameter λ. Let the number of elements in the underlying finite field $\mathbb{F}$ be q. Note that $q \sim O(2^\lambda)$. For $\mathbb{F} = \mathbb{Z}_p$, $q = p$ where p is λ bits. An adversary, without knowledge of $\mathcal{D}^*$, has to find a pair (X, Y) such that $Y = K_I + K \cdot X$ in order to pass the verification check by V. This pair is not unique for any given K_I and K. There are q possible (X, Y) pairs which satisfy this constraint. However, Adv has to find these q correct pairs out of all q^2 possible combinations of X, Y. In other words, the probability of passing P's verification (say, by random guess) is about $\frac{1}{q} \sim O(\frac{1}{2^\lambda})$ which is still negligible in λ. The security of the proposed authentication scheme is summarized as follows.

Theorem 1 (First Authentication Factor Security). *If E is a secure PRF, then the proposed two-factor authentication protocol remains sound against an adversary Adv which compromises $\mathcal{D}^*$ and sk_2 only.*

Proof. We prove by contradiction. Suppose E is a secure PRF with the advantage (to distinguish its output from a random number) bounded by ϵ_E. Assume there exists a PPT adversary Adv_{2FA} which can break the soundness of the two-factor authentication (2FA) after compromising the second factor. That is, Adv_{2FA}

can win the $\mathsf{Auth}_{2FA}^{Adv}$ game with non-negligible probability of success p_{2FA}. We can then construct another adversary Adv_E to break the indistinguishability property of the PRF E as follows:

Pick K, K' for the second authentication factor. Generate $\mathcal{D}$ and $\mathcal{D}^*$ accordingly. Given $\mathcal{D}^*$ and (K, K') to Adv_{2FA}, since he chooses to compromise the second authentication factor. Since Adv_{2FA} has compromised $\mathcal{D}^*$, there is no need to answer any Tag queries. For the other three types of queries, Adv_E can make PRF queries and use the results to answer the execution, prover and verifier queries from Adv_{2FA}. In the challenge phase, Adv_E picks a random $r \in \{0,1\}^*$ and sends it to the PRF challenger to receive a challenge r'. Adv_E has to decide whether $r' = E_k(r)$ for unknown key k or r' is a random string. To respond, Adv_E picks a challenge set I for Adv_{2FA} and sends (r, I) as a challenge for Adv_{2FA}, which outputs (X, Y). Adv_E uses K', r' (the challenge received from the PRF challenger) and $i \in I$ to compute K_I. Adv_E checks if $Y = K_I + K \cdot X$. If yes, it returns 1 to its challenger to indicate that $r' = E_k(r)$; otherwise, it outputs 1.

The advantage of Adv_E is then p_{2FA} (a contradiction). Hence, p_{2FA} must be negligible. In fact, $p_{2FA} < \epsilon_E$, much smaller than the probability of a random guess: $\frac{1}{2^\lambda}$.

Theorem 2 (Second Authentication Factor Security). *If h is a collision resistant hash function and f is a secure PRF, then the proposed two-factor authentication protocol remains secure against an adversary Adv which compromises sk_1 only.*

Proof. We prove Theorem 2 through a sequence of games, starting with Game 0 being the adversary game defined for the soundness property of the two-factor authentication in Sect. 3.2. In Game 0, we assume the adversary Adv has compromised the first authentication factor sk_1. In the following, we introduce one minor modification between successive games and interleave analyses between games.

Game 1. Game 1 is the same as Game 0 with only one difference: the tagging algorithm uses truly random numbers instead of PRF outputs to tag d_i's. The challenger remembers all these random numbers in a table to compute K_I for verification later on.

Analysis. If there is a difference in the adversary's probability of success between Game 0 and Game 1, we can use the adversary to break the security of the PRF f. Such a reduction implies that, in subsequent analyses, we can treat $t_i = K \cdot h(D_i) + f_{K'}(i)$ for any $d_i \in \mathcal{D}$ as a truly random λ-bit string t'_i, and $K_I = \sum_{i \in I} f_{K'}(i) \cdot f_{r'}(i)$ also as a truly random λ-bit string. As a result, Y is also a random number.

Game 2. In Game 2, the challenger handles the tagging and authentication execution differently. It keeps a copy of all tuples of $(d_i, t_i) \in \mathcal{D}$. To check the validity of a pair (X', Y'), it computes (X, Y) directly from its copy of (d_i, t_i)-tuples. The challenger accepts (X', Y') only if $(X, Y) = (X', Y')$. That is, it may be possible that $Y' = K_I + K \cdot X'$ for the given (r, I) but $(X', Y') \neq (X, Y)$, and this case is rejected.

Analysis. To satisfy the second authentication factor, Auth_S checks if $Y' = K_I + K \cdot X'$. Note that K_I cannot be distinguished from a truly random value and is not known to the adversary. They therefore look like independent in each instance of execution. Since we assume d_i's are publicly known, X is known to the adversary. The only possibility for the adversary to guess Y and K_I correctly to satisfy the relation without knowing K is that the challenge set I is covered by the union of (d_i, t_i)-tuples leaked out from the execution, tagging and prover queries, plus the probability of a correct random guess. The total number of distinct tuples leaked out is $< q_T + (q_P + q_E) \cdot t$. The corresponding probability of success for the adversary is therefore approximately $(\frac{q_T + (q_P + q_E) \cdot t}{L})^t$. The probability for a correct random guess is $\frac{1}{2^\lambda}$. Alternatively, another possibility is that the challenge set is the same as a previous one, which is negligibly small. The total probability of success for the adversary is therefore $\frac{1}{2^\lambda} + (\frac{q_T + (q_P + q_E) \cdot t}{L})^t$.

Overall, the security of the two-factor authentication using historical data is summarized by the following theorem, the proof of which follows directly from Theorems 1 and 2. The reason why δ_{12} is much smaller compared to δ_2 is that when sk_1 is in the adversary's hand, execution and prover queries would leak out the (d_i, t_i)-tuples involved.

Theorem 3. *If f and E are secure PRFs, the two-factor authentication using historical data is $(\delta_{12}, \delta_1, \delta_2)$-sound, with $\delta_{12} = (\frac{1}{2^{2\lambda}} + \frac{1}{2^\lambda} \cdot (\frac{q_T}{L})^t)$, $\delta_1 = 1/2^\lambda$ and $\delta_2 = \frac{1}{2^\lambda} + (\frac{q_T + (q_P + q_E) \cdot t}{L})^t$, where λ is the security parameter of the PRFs and $L = |\mathcal{D}^*|$ and q_T, q_E, q_P are respectively the number of tagging, execution and prover queries made by the adversary, and t is number of indices in the challenge set I.*

5.1 Resilience to Leakage of Historical Data

This section studies the resilience of the proposed two-factor authentication scheme to leakage of the historical dataset $\mathcal{D}^*$. Suppose the first authentication factor sk_1 has been compromised, and all $d_i's$ are public and the adversary has obtained a set $A \subset \mathcal{D}^*$ which contains S distinct tuples of $(d_i, t_i) \in \mathcal{D}^*$, equivalent to a p fraction of the L pieces of t_i's. That is, $S/L = p$. Recall that t is the number of indices chosen in the challenge set I by design. The probability of success for the adversary is then given by:

$$p_{success} = \frac{\binom{S}{t}}{\binom{L}{t}} = \frac{\binom{\lceil pL \rceil}{t}}{\binom{L}{t}} = \frac{\lceil pL \rceil \cdot (\lceil pL \rceil - 1) \cdot (\lceil pL \rceil - 2) \cdot \ldots \cdot (\lceil pL \rceil - t + 1)}{L \cdot (L - 1) \cdot (L - 2) \cdot \ldots \cdot (L - t + 1)}.$$

For $pL \gg t$, $p_{success} \approx p^t$. Since $0 < p < 1$, $p_{success}$ drops considerably as t increases. As an example, suppose $p = 0.8$ (that is, the adversary has compromised 80% of the tuples) and $L = 10,000$; for $t = 1$, $p_{success} = 0.8$; $p_{success}$

drops to approximately 0.107 for $t = 10$. As can be seen, the proposed protocol is scalable because there is a clear tradeoff between the security level and the computational overhead by adjusting the design parameter t.

Figures 1 and 2 plot the actual values (not the approximation) of $p_{success}$ for the adversary (to break the proposed authentication scheme) against different values of the design parameter $t = |I|$, to illustrate the resilience of the proposed authentication scheme with respect to the cardinality of the tagged historical dataset $\mathcal{D}^*$ and the fraction of data compromised by the adversary. As shown in Figs. 1 and 2, the probability of success $p_{success}$ for an adversary having compromised p fraction of the L tuples of $\mathcal{D}^*$ drops considerably as t increases. We will see in the next section, the computational overhead for verifying a response is linearly proportionate to the parameter t. As the IoT is constituted with a variety of devices with vastly different resources and capabilities, the proposed two-factor authentication scheme exhibits a practically interesting and desirable property, namely, the security and computation tradeoff is tunable by adjusting the parameter t. Roughly, in practice, $t \approx 5$ seems sufficient to cover most scenarios, as suggested by Fig. 1. In typical operating scenarios, it should be rare for an attacker to be able to successfully compromise half of all the data tuples in $\mathcal{D}^*$ (without being detected and dealt with). Note that t_i is not necessarily shared. For $p < 0.5$, $t = 5$ seems sufficient to achieve a reasonably small $p_{success}$.

Besides, as can be seen from Fig. 2, p_{succes} seems largely (or solely) determined by the fraction of compromised tuples p, regardless of the size L of the historical dataset $\mathcal{D}^*$. That is, $p_{success}$ could be mono-variate in p. This interesting property means that, as data are continuously generated by the IoT device V and exchanged with P, an adversary has to compromise an *continuously increasing* number of historical data tuples accordingly in order to maintain the same level of advantage in terms of $p_{success}$ to break the two-factor authentication based on historical data. In other words, the overall security improve substantially as $\mathcal{D}^*$ gets larger.

This property is mainly because as the set of historical data enlarges, it becomes less likely that the challenge set I would be a subset of the dataset A held by the adversary, if $|A|$ does not increase at the same time. That is, unless the adversary could keep up with the growth of the historical dataset $\mathcal{D}^*$, it becomes increasingly difficult for the adversary to break the protocol using the same set A. In order for the adversary to keep up with a growing $\mathcal{D}^*$ while maintaining a constant p, he needs to capture more data tuples proportionately, which usually would translates to increased duration for eavesdropping or break-in to P for the adversary, thus making his task more difficult. In fact, V could generate dummy data at random interval to grow $\mathcal{D}^*$ if necessary to increase the difficulty to break the authentication.

5.2   Practical Considerations and Limitation

The security of the proposed authentication factor is wholly based on the *bounded retrieval model* [11], assuming that the adversary cannot obtain a significant fraction (say, >50 %) of the historical dataset in the GB range containing months

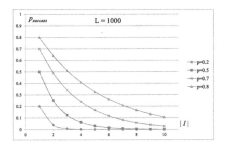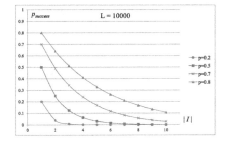

(a) Size of the historical dataset, L = 1000   (b) Size of the historical dataset, L = 10000

Fig. 1. Resilience of the proposed authentication with respect to different sizes L of the historical dataset: $p_{success}$ for the attacker to break the scheme against different sizes of the challenge set I for different sizes of the historical dataset ($L = 1000$ and $L = 10000$).

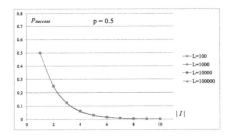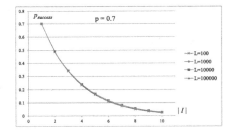

(a) Fraction of compromised data: p = 0.5   (b) Fraction of compromised data: p = 0.7

Fig. 2. Resilience of the proposed authentication with respect to different fraction p of the data being compromised: $p_{success}$ for the attacker to break the scheme against different sizes of the challenge set I after the attacker has compromised $p = 0.5$ and $p = 0.7$ of the historical dataset.

or years of data. If this is violated, the scheme will become insecure. Nevertheless, this assumption can be reasonably fulfilled in practice. For instance, the (d_i, t_i)-tuples are usually transmitted over a secured channel between V and P (which can be established through the master key of the first authentication factor or other means); hence, an adversary eavesdropping and logging the communication between V and P might not be able to obtain these tuples. As discussed in Sect. 1, despite the established secure channel, a second authentication factor is still required for security-critical or sensitive usages. In general, the (d_i, t_i)-tuples would be leaked out in normal communication or authentication execution only when the adversary has compromised the secure channel. Even so, the secret of the second authentication factor would only be leaked out gradually through the (d_i, t_i)-tuples; it takes time for an eavesdropper to compromise the old tuples already stored at P. While an adversary could possibly obtain tuples through a lunchtime attack at P, compromising a significant fraction of the historical dataset without being detected is still challenging as this paper considers tens of GB of data stored in protected servers in a big data cluster. Besides, it is not mandatory to store d_i's and t_i's together. In particular, t_i's have no information value other than authentication, and hence can be stored offline when not used, to add extra protection. Similarly, it is not necessary to store the two authentication factors in the same server. The design goal of the two-factor authentication is to allow V to authenticate P. It is therefore outside the scope of this paper to consider attacks based on a compromised server P. After all, P normally has more resources to defend against the adversary, compared to V.

Finally, to bootstrap the second authentication factor initially, the initial configuration settings of the IoT device V can be used as the first few pieces of historical data d_i. This is possible since the protocol is designed to accept data of different formats and types. It is also practically reasonable to assume that these first few data tuples of (d_i, t_i) can be transported to P in proximity prior deployment via a very secure channel. Roughly, 5 pieces of initial data suffice. If necessary, dummy data can also generated by V and transported to P in the pre-deployment setup stage. Hence, initial bootstrapping of the protocol safely should not be an issue.

6   Implementation and Performance

6.1   Parameter Selection

This section discusses the components of the proposed protocol and the considerations for choosing their parameters. First, the parameters of the underlying finite field $\mathbb{F}$ should be fixed according to the security parameter λ. Then all the components can be selected accordingly. Both integers mod p and binary extension fields can be used. In our implementation, we use $GF(2^{256})$, the 256-bit binary extension field (i.e. $\lambda = 256$), defined by a low-weight irreducible polynomial: $x^{256} + x^{10} + x^5 + x^2 + 1 \in \mathbb{F}_2[x]$. Parameter selection for the components are as follows:

1. A collision-resistant, length-matching hash function $h()$ is used to map d_i (an arbitrary-length string) to an element of the underlying finite field, which has a wide range of choices. In our implementation, the arithmetic is in $GF(2^{256})$. Hence, SHA-256 is used to implement h.
2. The main core of the proposed protocol includes two PRFs: E, f (more precisely, E is a pseudorandom permutation). The key size for E, f should be λ. E is to map a random challenge r to a key r' to key the PRF f. Hence, the output of E should be λ. SHA-HMAC [18], AES-OMAC, or any block ciphers in general, can be used to realize E. All these are standard primitives. The other PRF f is to map an arbitrary-length string to an element in $\mathbb{F}$. Ideally, f should be selected such that its output matches the element size of $\mathbb{F}$. But in practice, truncation of the output of f is acceptable. Like E, there are many possible conjectured PRFs to instantiate f.

For our case, $\lambda = 256$. Therefore, the key is 256 bits long and the arithmetic is in $GF(2^{256})$. For the sake of simplicity, we use SHA256-HMAC ($\{0,1\}^{256} \times \{0,1\}^* \rightarrow \{0,1\}^{256}$) to instantiate both E and f. Note that the output of SHA256-HMAC is an element in $GF(2^{256})$ as well as a 256-bit binary string. Besides, the same implementation of SHA256 is used to instantiate h. While this implementation may not be optimized in computation resources, it minimizes the code size. For devices with a hardware implementation of AES, a more efficient implementation is attainable using AES-OMAC.

6.2   Performance

The two-factor authentication scheme is implemented in Java using JDK 7u07. A finite field defined by the irreducible polynomial $x^{256} + x^{10} + x^5 + x^2 + 1 \in \mathbb{F}_2[x]$ is used. In the experiment, an Intel core 2 Quad 2.4 GHz processor with 3 GB RAM is used for the prover P, and a BeagleBone-Black board with an ARM Cortex-A8 processor for the lightweight verifier V. Table 1 depicts the computational performance of the novel authentication factor. In Table 1, the bit complexity of one invocation of the cryptographic hash function h is denoted by l_h, and the bit complexity of generating a λ-bit random number by $O(\lambda)$. For λ-bit security, the finite field $\mathbb{F}$ used consists of λ-bit elements, implying that the complexity for multiplication and addition in $\mathbb{F}$ are $O(\lambda^2)$ and $O(\lambda)$ respectively. Finally, $O(l_D)$ denotes the complexity for searching and retrieving random items over a big data set, dependent on the platform being used.

Figure 3 explicitly shows the experimental results for the computational time needed for proof generation (in μs) and verification (in ms) on the two platforms (P and V) respectively for different challenge difficulty t (also denoted as $|I|$, i.e. the number of d_i's needed to generate the response). The running time of both the proof generation and proof verification has a linear relationship with t.

Regarding the bandwidth used, each tag t_i is λ bits long. For SHA-256, $\lambda = 256$ bits or 32 bytes, which seems practically reasonable. Depending on the tagging frequency, the actual communication overhead for the tags could be adjusted. As shown in Sect. 5.1, the proposed scheme is relatively resilient even with a small data set $\mathcal{D}^*$, implying that a relatively low tagging frequency may suffice in practice. For an authentication session, the challenge size is 2λ plus

Table 1. Computational performance of the authentication factor using historical data

	Bit complexity	Execution time
Key generation by P	$O(\lambda)$	9.88 μs
Key generation by V	$O(\lambda)$	45.88 ms
Tag generation by V	$O(l_h) + O(\lambda^2)$	88 ms
Challenge generation by V	$t \cdot O(\lambda)$	45.86 ms
Proof generation by P ($t = 10$)	$O(l_D) + t \cdot (O(l_h) + O(\lambda^2))$	542.50 μs
Proof verification by V ($t = 10$)	$t \cdot (O(l_h) + O(\lambda^2))$	937 ms

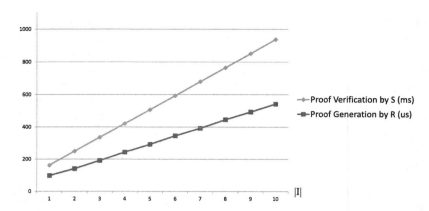

Fig. 3. Computation time for proof generation by P (in μs) and proof verification by V (in ms) as the design parameter $t = |I|$ (no. of indices in the challenge set I) varies.

the data size needed to specify I (which depends on how the elements of I are specified) and the response size is 3λ. For SHA-256, the challenge and response are 64 bytes and 96 bytes respectively. If I is specified as a set of equally spaced integers, then the data size needed could be quite small.

7   Prover Delegation

In order to accommodate the usual operations, say, in the power grid, which have risks in leaking out the first authentication factor mk, a secure prover delegation mechanism can be constructed to allow the server P to delegate its prover capability to a user U (which can be an employee or a contractor). The basic idea is that, instead of using the master secret key mk directly in executing the protocol, mk is used to derive a user key k_U, say, with a PRF by computing $k_U = PRF_{mk}(id_U)$ where id_U is a bit string representing U's identity. In the protocol, k_U is used in place of mk for the first authentication factor. A secure (i.e. private and authenticated) channel between P and U is assumed. The security assurance of the second authentication factor is reduced to that of the first authentication factor. Yet, there is still considerably advantage over the case which concurrently executes the challenge-response protocol twice with distinct secret keys. First, P has more resources as the verifier than V to implement more sophisticated authentication methods, such as biometrics. Second, the leakage resilience property of the second authentication factor is inherent in the modification.

8   Conclusion

This paper addresses the problem of two-factor authentication for resource-constrained IoT devices, which is largely an open problem, especially when a resource-limited device is used as a verifier. A novel authentication factor, using historical data as facilitated by big data platforms, is proposed, to complement the conventional authentication factor, in the form of a pre-shared secret key, to achieve a reasonably lightweight scheme for the IoT. Inherent in the new authentication factor is the much needed *leakage resilience* property, making it robust to compromise or leakage of secret authentication information. Besides, only a constant storage is required in the verifier, regardless of the size of the historical data. Another interesting property is that, as the volume of the historical data increases, the security of the protocol is improved proportionately. With the new authentication factor, a lightweight two-factor authentication protocol is designed and implemented. The design is scalable in the sense that, a tradeoff between the computational overhead and the security level of the two-factor authentication protocol can be varied by adjusting the challenge set size t, thus allowing the protocol to be tuned for different IoT scenarios with devices of vastly different capabilities.

References

1. Adams, N.P., Sibley, R.P., Davis, D.L.M., Singh, R.: Simplified multi-factor authentication, US Patent 8370640 (2013)
2. Aumann, Y., Yan, Z.D., Rabin, M.O.: Everlasting security in the bounded storage model. IEEE Trans. Inf. Theory **48**(6), 1668–1680 (2002)
3. Bellare, M., Desai, A., Pointcheval, D., Rogaway, P.: Relations among notions of security for public-key encryption schemes. In: Krawczyk, H. (ed.) CRYPTO 1998. LNCS, vol. 1462, pp. 26–45. Springer, Heidelberg (1998)
4. Bishop, M.: The Art and Science of Computer Security. Addison-Wesley, Boston (2002)
5. Borthakur, D.: HDFS architecture guide, r.1.2.1. https://hadoop.apache.org/docs/r1.2.1/hdfs_design.html
6. Brainard, J., Juels, A., Rivest, R., Szydlo, M., Yung, M.: Fourth factor authentication: somebody you know. In: ACM CCS 2006, pp. 168–178 (2006)
7. Buer, M.: Multi-factor authentication using a smartcard, US Patent 8245292 (2012)
8. Chan, A.C.-F.: Efficient defence against misbehaving TCP receiver DoS attacks. Comput. Netw. **55**(17), 3904–3914 (2011)
9. Choi, S., Zage, D.: Addressing insider threat using "where you are" as fourth factor authentication. In: ICCST 2012 (2012)
10. Das, M.L.: Two-factor user authentication in wireless sensor networks. IEEE Trans. Wirel. Commun. **8**(3), 1086–1090 (2009)
11. Di Crescenzo, G., Lipton, R.J., Walfish, S.: Perfectly secure password protocols in the bounded retrieval model. In: Halevi, S., Rabin, T. (eds.) TCC 2006. LNCS, vol. 3876, pp. 225–244. Springer, Heidelberg (2006)
12. Dispensa, S.T.: Multi factor authentication, US Patent 8365258 (2013)
13. Dziembowski, S.: Intrusion-resilience via the bounded-storage model. In: Halevi, S., Rabin, T. (eds.) TCC 2006. LNCS, vol. 3876, pp. 207–224. Springer, Heidelberg (2006)
14. Google. Google authenticator for two-step verification. https://www.google.com/landing/2step/

15. Grim, E.T.: Two-factor authentication systems and methods, US Patent 8578454 (2013)
16. Headley, P.: Multi-channel multi-factor autentication, US Patent 8516562 (2013)
17. Headley, P., Collins, K.: Single-channel multi-factor authentication, US Patent 8536976 (2013)
18. Krawczyk, H., Bellare, M., Canetti, R.: HMAC: keyed-hashing for message authentication. RFC 2104 (Informational), February 1997
19. Lee, A.: Integrating electricity subsector failure scenarios into a risk assessment methodology. Technical Report 3002001181, EPRI, December 2013
20. Marforio, C., Karapanos, N., Soriente, C., Kostiainen, K., Capkun, S.: Smartphones as practical and secure location verification tokens for payments. In: NDSS 2014 (2014)
21. National Electric Sector Cybersecurity Organization Resource (NESCOR). Analysis of selected electric sector high risk failure scenarios, ver. 1.0. Technical report, EPRI, September 2013
22. National Electric Sector Cybersecurity Organization Resource (NESCOR). Electric sector failure scenarios and impact analyses, ver. 1.0. Technical report, EPRI, September 2013
23. Noe, F., Hoomaert, F., Marien, D., Fort, N.: Two-factor USB authentication token, US Patent 8214888 (2012)
24. Pan, W., Liu, G.: Two-factor authentication of a remote administrator, US Patent 7971238 (2011)
25. Sammer, E.: Hadoop Operations: A Guide for Developers and Administrators. O'Reilly Media, Sebastopol (2012)
26. Samuelsson, J., Camaisa, A.: System and method for second factor authentication services, US Patent 8533791 (2013)
27. Shacham, H., Waters, B.: Compact proofs of retrievability. J. Cryptol. **26**(3), 442–483 (2013)
28. Shirook, A.A., Labrador, C., Warden, J., Wilson, K.S.: Method and apparatus for providing continuous authentication based on dynamic personal information, PCT Patent WO 2012017326 A1 (2012)
29. Shirvanian, M., Jarecki, S., Saxena, N., Nathan, N.: Two-factor authentication resilient to server compromise using mix-bandwidth devices. In: NDSS 2014 (2014)
30. Bluetooth SIG. Bluetooth core specifications v4.2, December 2014
31. Vaidya, B., Makrakia, D., Mouftah, H.T.: Improved two-factor user authentication in wireless sensor networks. In: International Workshop on Network Assurance and Security Services in Ubiquitous Environments (2010)
32. Weber, F.: Multi-factor authentication, US Patent 7770002 (2010)
33. William, O.N., Shoemaker, E.: Multi-factor authentication system, US Patent 7373515 (2008)
34. Zhang, L.: Enhanced multi-factor authentication, US Patent 8286227 (2012)
35. Zikopoulos, P., Deroos, D., Parasuraman, K., Deutsch, T., Corrigan, D., Giles, J.: Harness the power of big data (2012)

On the Implications of Zipf's Law in Passwords

Ding Wang[1] and Ping Wang[1,2(✉)]

[1] School of EECS, Peking University, Beijing 100871, China
{wangdingg,pwang}@pku.edu.cn
[2] School of Software and Microelectronics, Peking University, Beijing 100260, China

Abstract. Textual passwords are perhaps the most prevalent mechanism for access control over the Internet. Despite the fact that human-beings generally select passwords in a highly skewed way, it has long been assumed in the password research literature that users choose passwords randomly and uniformly. This is partly because it is easy to derive concrete (numerical) security results under the uniform assumption, and partly because we do *not* know what's the exact distribution of passwords if we do not make a uniform assumption. Fortunately, researchers recently reveal that user-chosen passwords generally follow the Zipf's law, a distribution which is vastly different from the uniform one.

In this work, we explore a number of foundational security implications of the Zipf-distribution assumption about passwords. Firstly, we how the attacker's advantages against password-based cryptographic protocols (e.g., authentication, encryption, signature and secret share) can be 2–4 orders of magnitude more accurately captured (formulated) than existing formulation results. As password protocols are the most widely used cryptographic protocols, our new formulation is of practical significance. Secondly, we provide new insights into popularity-based password creation policies and point out that, under the current, widely recommended security parameters, usability will be largely impaired. Thirdly, we show that the well-known password strength metric α-guesswork, which was believed to be parametric, is actually non-parametric in two of four cases under the Zipf assumption. Particularly, nine large-scale, real-world password datasets are employed to establish the practicality of our findings.

Keywords: User authentication · Zipf's law · Password-based protocol · Password creation policy · Password strength metric

1 Introduction

With so much of our lives digital and online, it is essential that our digital assets are well-protected from unauthorized access. Since passwords are easy to use, low-cost to implement and convenient to change, almost every web service today authenticates its users by passwords, ranging from low value news portals and technical forums, moderate value e-commerce and email to highly sensitive financial transactions and genomic data protection [21]. Although its security

© Springer International Publishing Switzerland 2016
I. Askoxylakis et al. (Eds.): ESORICS 2016, Part I, LNCS 9878, pp. 111–131, 2016.
DOI: 10.1007/978-3-319-45744-4_6

weaknesses (e.g., vulnerable to guessing attacks [29]) and usability issues (e.g., typo and memorability [17,39]) have been constantly articulated, and a variety of alternative authentication methods (e.g., multi-factor authentication and graphical passwords) have also been successively proposed, password-based authentication firmly remains the most prevalent mechanism for access control and reproduces in nearly every new service and system. As no alternative schemes can provide all the benefits that passwords offer [9], and further due to inertia and economic reasons [19], passwords are likely to continue to be the dominant authentication mechanism in the foreseeable future.

Since system-assigned passwords are of poor usability, in most cases users are allowed to select passwords by themselves. It is well-known, however, that users tend to choose weak passwords for convenience (e.g., passwords based on dictionary words, meaningful phrases and personal information [28,39]) and to reuse or slightly modify existing passwords for saving efforts [35]. Thus, it has been widely recognised (see [8,30]) that user-chosen passwords are *unlikely* to be uniformly randomly distributed. For a concrete grasp of the distribution of passwords, we exemplify two large-scale real-world password lists in Fig. 1. Our other datasets also exhibit similar distributions but cannot be shown here only due to space constraints. Clearly, they are all far from a uniform distribution. Now a critical question naturally arises: *if human-chosen passwords do not follow a uniform distribution, then what is their exact distribution?*

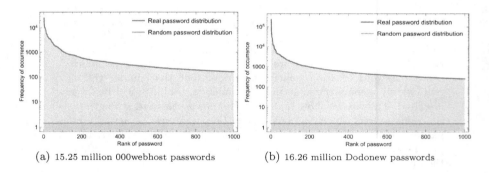

(a) 15.25 million 000webhost passwords   (b) 16.26 million Dodonew passwords

Fig. 1. Frequency distribution of two large-scale real-word password datasets.

This question has remained as an open problem for decades, which is partly due to the scarcity of real-world password datasets (because real-life passwords are sensitive and difficult to gather) and partly due to the fact that resolving this problem involves some recent advancements in the inter-discipline knowledge, such as computational statistics and natural language processing (NLP). As a result, among these password-related works that *must* rely on an explicit assumption about the distribution of passwords, most ones (e.g., password-based cryptographic protocols such as authentication [1], encryption [5], signature [18] and secret sharing [40]), *reluctantly*, make the unrealistic assumption that user-chosen passwords are uniformly randomly distributed, while the few remaining ones *wittingly* make various assumptions about the password distribution just for convenience of security analysis (e.g., the binomial distribution in [13] and min-entropy model in [2,27]). As for these works that do *not* have to rely on an explicit assumption about the distribution of passwords, they (e.g., password creation policies [34] and strength metrics for password datasets [8]) generally simply *avoid involving* an assumption about the password distribution.

As we will demonstrate in this work, the above unrealistic assumptions about the distribution of passwords often give rise to serious security and usability issues (e.g., there are, as shown in Sect. 3, *two to four orders of magnitude underestimation* in the attacker's online guessing advantages between a uniform assumption made in [1,5,18,23,25] and the reality. For these works (e.g., [8,34]) that avoid involving an assumption about the password distribution, many important properties or goals that actually rely on an assumption are left undiscussed. For instance, if the password creation policy proposed in [34] is imposed by a web service, what fraction of users will be potentially annoyed? This kind of prediction is important yet virtually impossible if one makes no assumption about the password distribution.

Fortunately, with the help of 14 large-scale datasets and by introducing a number of statistical and NLP techniques, researchers recently reveal that human-chosen passwords generally follow a Zipf distribution [36]. This theory has already been successfully adopted into the "GenoGuard" genome cryptosystem [21] and "CASH" password hash scheme [7]. It implies that the frequency of passwords decreases polynomially with the increase of their rank, and this behavior is distinct from that of a uniform distribution. In this work, we give an improved version (named CDF-Zipf) of the PDF-Zipf model in [36], and show that most of the above-mentioned issues can be well addressed. Specifically, we show how the attacker's advantages in password-based protocols (e.g., [1,5,25,40]) can be 2–4 orders of magnitude more accurately captured, predict what fraction of users will be annoyed under the popularity-based policy [34] when given a specific threshold, and reveal an important property for the well-known α-guesswork in [8].

Our contributions. The key contributions of this work are as follows:

(1) First, we propose to use the formulation $C' \cdot Q(k)^{s'}$ to capture an attacker's advantages in making at most $Q(k)$ on-line guesses against password-based cryptographic protocols, superseding the traditional ones (i.e., $Q(k)/|\mathcal{D}|$ [1,25] and $Q(k)/2^m$ [2,27]), where k is the system security parameter, $\mathcal{D}$ is the password space, C' and s' are the CDF-Zipf regression parameters of $\mathcal{D}$, and m denotes the min-entropy of $\mathcal{D}$. Experiments on 9 large-scale password datasets show the superiority of our new formulation over existing ones. Given a target system, the values of C' and s' can be approximated by leaked datasets from sites with a similar service, language (and policy). For instance, if the protocol is to be deployed in a Chinese e-commerce site, one can set $C' = 0.019429$ and $s' = 0.211921$, which come from the leaked Dodonew site.
(2) Second, based on the Zipf assumption of passwords, we propose a series of prediction models to facilitate the choices of parameters for the promising

popularity-based password creation policy in [34]. Our models provide new insights and highlight that, usability will be largely impaired if the threshold parameter $\mathcal{T}$ is improperly chosen. For instance, when setting $\mathcal{T} = 1/10^6$ (which is widely recommended [17,34]) for Internet-scale sites, our model predicts that an average of 38.73 % of users will be potentially annoyed. Our theory well accords with the extensive experiments.

(3) Third, we, for the first time, reveal that the widely used password strength metric α-guesswork [8], which was believed to be parametric, is actually non-parametric in two of four cases under the Zipf assumption of passwords. As passwords are generally Zipf-distributed, this result makes α-guesswork much simpler to use — now we only need a single value of the advantage α instead of "all values of α" [8] to inform decisions.

2   Preliminaries

In this section, we first describe the nine datasets used. Then, we briefly review the Zipf model [36], and finally present an improved fitting methodology.

2.1   Descriptions of Real-World Password Datasets

We employ nine large-scale password datasets, a total of 111.94 million real-world passwords, to enable a comprehensive evaluation of the revealed implications. The basic info about these datasets is summarized in Table 1. Some of them have been widely used in password studies [29,35,36]. They were somehow breached by hackers or leaked by insiders, and then publicly disclosed over the Internet. Most of these breaches have been confirmed by the victim sites [31,32]. Our datasets range from low-value gaming and programmer forums, moderate-value social networks, to relatively sensitive email, e-commerce and web hosting service. They have a time span of 10 years, and come from four countries located in three distant continents. They are in four different languages, including two most-spoken ones (i.e., English and Chinese) in the world. To the best of knowledge, our corpus is amongst the largest and most diversified ones ever used for password-related studies. We refer the readers to [29,35,36] for a grasp of user-chosen passwords and learn what might impact users' password choices: language, service type, password policy, culture, faith among others.

2.2   Review of the PDF-Zipf Model

It has long been an open problem as to what is the distribution that user-chosen passwords follow. It is well-known that user-spoken words follow a Zipf's law, whether user-chosen passwords follow the same law? In 2012, Bonnneau [8] and Malone-Maher [30] separately studied this question, and both works plot the probability density function (PDF) of password datasets with the x-axis variable being the rank r of passwords and y-axis variable being the frequency f_r of the

Table 1. Basic info about the nine real-world password datasets

Dataset	Web service	Location	Language	When leaked	Unique PWs	$TotalPWs$
Rockyou	Social forum	USA	English	Dec. 2009	14,326,970	$32,581,870$
000webhost	Web hosting	USA	English	**Oct. 2015**	10,583,709	$15,251,073$
Battlefield	Gaming site	USA	English	June 2011	417,453	$542,386$
Tianya	Social forum	China	Chinese	Dec. 2011	12,898,437	$30,901,241$
Dodonew	Game&Ecommerce	China	Chinese	Dec. 2011	10,135,260	$16,258,891$
CSDN	Programmer forum	China	Chinese	Dec. 2011	4,037,605	$6,428,277$
Mail.ru	Email	Russia	Russian	Sep. 2014	2,954,907	$4,932,688$
Gmail.ru	Email	Russia	Russian	Sep. 2014	3,132,028	$4,929,090$
Flirtlife.de	Dating site	Germany	German	**May 2006**	115,589	$343,064$

password with rank r. They use a Zipf model to approximate the PDF graphs, yet the Kolmogorov-Smirnov (KS) tests suggest a negative answer.

In 2014, Wang et al. [36] made a further attempt. Different from these two studies [8,30] that fit all passwords in a dataset into the Zipf model, the work in [36] first eliminates the least frequent (LF) passwords (e.g., $LF < 4$) from datasets, and then use a Zipf model to approximate the PDF graphs of the remaining passwords. More specifically, Wang et al. found:

$$f_r = \frac{C}{r^s}, \tag{1}$$

where C and s are constants depending on the password dataset and can be calculated using methods like least squares or maximum likelihood estimation (MLE). We denote this Zipf model as the PDF-Zipf model. The KS tests (with samples of size 500K) accept most of the PDF-Zipf fittings. Equation 1 is better illustrated to show the nature of a Zipf's law in a log-log plot (see the green dotted lines in Figs. 2(a) and (b)), where $\log(f_r)$ is linear with $\log(r)$:

$$\log f_r = \log C - s \cdot \log r. \tag{2}$$

This means that, on a log-log plot the PDF regression line will be a straight line.

2.3   Our CDF-Zipf Model

As shown in Figs. 2(a) and (b) and also in [36], one undesirable feature of the PDF-Zipf model is that, it can not well capture the distribution of the first few most popular passwords (e.g., passwords with rank less than 1000).[1] We have tried various means to adjust the PDF-Zipf parameters to accommodate these most popular passwords, yet we are always caught in a dilemma: if they are well captured, the overall fitting cannot be accepted by KS tests; if they are not considered, the overall fitting will be acceptable.

---

[1] Note that the least frequent passwords are inherently difficult to be captured by a theoretic model due to the law of large numbers, and see more discussions in [36].

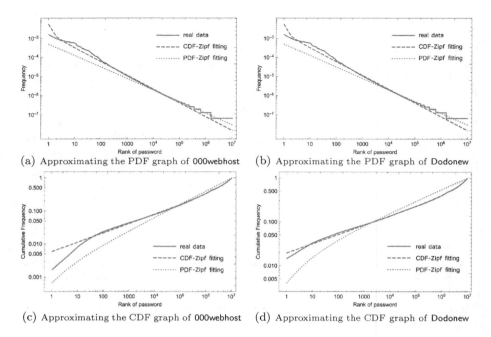

(a) Approximating the PDF graph of 000webhost   (b) Approximating the PDF graph of Dodonew

(c) Approximating the CDF graph of 000webhost   (d) Approximating the CDF graph of Dodonew

Fig. 2. A grasp of effectiveness of the PDF-Zipf approach and CDF-Zipf approach (Color figure online).

Essentially, the KS test quantifies the distance between the cumulative distribution function (CDF) $F_n(x)$ of an empirical distribution and the CDF $F(x)$ of the theoretic distribution (e.g., obtained by fitting):

$$D = \sup_x |F_n(x) - F(x)|,$$

where n is the sample size and $\sup_x$ is the supremum of the set of distances. This statistic $D \in [0, 1]$ is essentially the max gap between the two CDF curves $F_n(x)$ and $F(x)$, the smaller the better. It is used to conduct KS tests (see [36]). As the PDF and the CDF of a distribution can be converted to each other, whether we can directly model the CDF of a password distribution? Interestingly, we find the Zipf model well fits to the CDF graphs of *entire* datasets (see the dashed blue lines in Figs. 2(c) and (d)). We call this model the CDF-Zipf model:

$$F_r = C' \cdot r^{s'}, \tag{3}$$

where F_r is the cumulative frequency of passwords up to rank r, C' and s' are constants depending on the password dataset and can be calculated by linear regression. $F_r(\cdot)$ is a step function, because $r = 1, 2, 3, \cdots$. Thus, we have

$$f_r = F_r - F_{r-1} = C' \cdot r^{s'} - C' \cdot (r-1)^{s'}. \tag{4}$$

Table 2. Comparison of our CDF-Zipf model with the PDF-Zipf model [36]. All the timings use second as the unit.

Dataset	PDF-Zipf model [36]				Our CDF-Zipf model			
	Timing	Statistic D^a	C	s	Timing	Statistic D	C'	s'
Rockyou	23.41	0.193567	0.025464	0.913760	52917.74	**0.045874**	0.037433	0.187227
000webhost	13.23	0.111546	0.000512	0.603784	30236.77	0.006170	0.005858	0.281557
Battlefield	0.35	0.225527	0.003522	0.692898	973.79	0.010557	0.010298	0.294932
Tianya	22.95	0.161718	0.018684	0.895411	44702.48	0.022798	0.062239	0.155478
Dodonew	12.08	0.164640	0.002566	0.740560	29526.20	**0.004926**	0.019429	0.211921
CSDN	3.61	**0.268982**	0.008176	0.853028	10954.37	0.022319	0.058799	0.148573
Mail.ru	3.61	0.168754	0.006142	0.768912	8274.22	0.020773	0.025211	0.218212
Gmail	3.63	0.217463	0.007013	0.793667	8743.09	0.020543	0.020963	0.225653
Flirtlife.de	0.13	**0.062585**	0.016824	0.745634	159.26	0.036448	0.034577	0.291596

[a] The statistic Ds obtained by the CDF-Zipf model are always smaller than the PDF-Zipf model, indicating the former is better. Hereafter we only use parameters fitted from the CDF-Zipf model.

Note that, f_r can be approximated by using the derivative of F_r when seeing F_r as a continuous function: $f_r \approx d(F_r)/dr = C' \cdot s' \cdot r^{s'-1}$, implying a Zipf's law.

We fit the CDF-Zipf model to our nine datasets (see Fig. 3), and always obtain better fittings than the PDF-Zipf model in terms of the KS statistic D (i.e., the max gap between the CDF curves of a fitted model and the real data). Our CDF-Zipf parameters are calculated by linear regression using the well-known golden-section-search method on an Intel i7-4790 3.60 GHz PC. As summarized in Table 2, the *largest* D from fittings under our CDF-Zipf model is *smaller* than the smallest D of the PDF-Zipf model (set `least frequency` = 4). This means that the max CDF gap under the CDF-Zipf model is always smaller than those of the PDF-Zipf model. This suggests the superiority of our CDF-Zipf model.

Table 3 shows that our CDF-Zipf model is stable: the parameters fitted from subsets of a dataset remain largely the same with the parameters fitted from the entire dataset. For instance, the parameters (i.e., $C' = 0.019440$ and $s' = 0.211843$) fitted from *1/4* of Dodonew are almost the same with those (i.e., $C' = 0.019429$ and $s' = 0.211921$, see Table 2) fit-

Table 3. The CDF-Zipf model is stable.

Dataset	CDF-Zipf C'	CDF-Zipf s'	Max-CDF-gap[a]
1/4 Rockyou	0.031065	0.205094	0.034697
1/4 000webhost	0.005407	0.287458	0.003948
1/4 Battlefield	0.008033	0.323953	0.007699
1/4 Tianya	0.056322	0.164992	0.019645
1/4 Dodonew	0.019440	0.211843	0.004901
1/4 CSDN	0.059822	0.142107	0.023216
1/4 Mail.ru	0.019689	0.240814	0.011068
1/4 Gmail	0.016879	0.247743	0.013908
1/4 Flirtlife.de	0.026715	0.327783	0.023809

[a] "Max-CDF-gap" measures the largest distance between the CDF curve of each *entire* dataset and that of the CDF-Zipf model fitted with *1/4* dataset.

ted from the *entire* Dodonew. All the Max-CDF-gap$s$ are <0.035 (avg. 0.015). However, as shown in [36], this feature does not hold in the PDF-Zipf model.

Summary. Our CDF-Zipf model is superior to the PDF-Zipf model [36] in four-fold: (1) its fitted parameters more accurately approximate the real distribution (data); (2) it does *not* need to eliminate the unpopular passwords (e.g., with $f_r < 4$) when performing a Zipf fitting; (3) the most popular passwords can be

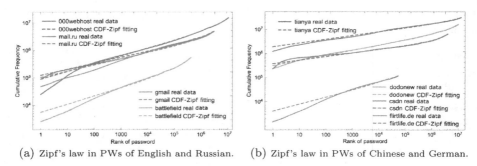

(a) Zipf's law in PWs of English and Russian.   (b) Zipf's law in PWs of Chinese and German.

Fig. 3. Zipf's law in nine real-life password datasets from four different populations, using our CDF-Zipf fitting approach. For detailed CDF-Zipf parameters, see Table 2.

well captured; and (4) it is stable. Note that, our CDF-Zipf model achieves these superiority at the cost of about 3000–4000 times higher fitting timings. Still, all our CDF-Zipf fittings can be completed in one day on a common PC.

3   Implication for Password-Based Cryptographic Protocols

In this section, we mainly use the most common password-based cryptographic protocol, i.e. password-based authentication, as a case study to show the implication, and then show its generality to other kinds of password-based protocols.

3.1   Implication for Password-Based Authentication Protocols

It is expected that, the most foundational implication of the discovery of Zipf's law in passwords is for *hundreds* of existing provably secure authentication protocols that involve passwords. According to whether additional authentication factors are involved, password authentication protocols can be classified into password-based single-factor schemes (e.g., two-party [25] and multi-party [15]) and password-based multi-factor schemes (e.g., two-factor [38] and three-factor [20]). Here we first show the implication for password-based single-factor schemes (also called PAKE protocols) and then for multi-factor schemes.

Uniform-based security formulation. In most of the provably secure PAKE protocols (e.g., [1,3,15,24] in the random oracle model and [25,26,40] in the standard model), it is typically assumed that "password pw_U (for each client U) is chosen independently and *uniformly at random* from a dictionary $\mathcal{D}$ of size $|\mathcal{D}|$, where $|\mathcal{D}|$ is a fixed constant independent of the security parameter k" [25], then a security model is described, and finally a "standard" definition of security as the one in [25] is given:

> "··· ··· Protocol $\mathcal{P}$ is a secure protocol for password-only authenticated key-exchange if, for all [password] dictionary sizes $|\mathcal{D}|$ and for all

ppt[probabilistic polynomial time] adversaries $\mathcal{A}$ making at most $Q(k)$ on-line attacks, there exists a negligible function $\epsilon(\cdot)$ such that:

$$\text{Adv}_{\mathcal{A},\mathcal{P}}(k) \leq Q(k)/|\mathcal{D}| + \epsilon(k), \tag{5}$$

where $\text{Adv}_{\mathcal{A},\mathcal{P}}(k)$ is the advantage of $\mathcal{A}$ in attacking $\mathcal{P}$."

Generally, user-generated passwords offer about 20–21 bits [8] of actual security against an optimal offline dictionary attack, which means the effective password space $\mathcal{D}$ is of size about 2^{20}–2^{21}. This indicates that a system which employs a PAKE protocol achieving the security goal of Eq. 5 can assure that one online guessing attempt will attain a success rate no larger than $1/2^{20}$–$1/2^{21}$. This is not the case in reality, and actually it may convey an overly optimistic sense of security to common users and security engineers.

As shown in Table 4, within 10^3 online guesses, the real attacker's advantages against most of the real-world sites are *three to four orders of magnitude higher* than that of a uniform-modelled attacker. For instance, the actual advantages of the real attacker against the gaming&e-commerce site www.dodonew.com reach 1.45 % when $Q(k) = 3$, 3.28 % when $Q(k) = 10$ and 5.60 % when $Q(k) = 100$. They are far beyond the theoretic results (see the last row in Table 4) given by Eq. 5.

Table 4. The cumulative percentages of top-x most popular passwords of each real-life password dataset ("Uni. dist." stands for uniform distribution).

Datasets	Top 1	Top 3	Top 10	Top 10^2	Top 10^3	Top 10^4	Top $\frac{1}{10}$	Top $\frac{1}{10^2}$	Top $\frac{1}{10^3}$	Top $\frac{1}{10^4}$
Tianya	3.98 %	5.59 %	7.43 %	11.50 %	16.04 %	25.78 %	58.21 %	41.19 %	27.45 %	16.70 %
Dodonew	1.45 %	2.15 %	3.28 %	5.60 %	8.59 %	13.62 %	39.97 %	22.72 %	13.66 %	8.61 %
CSDN	3.66 %	8.15 %	10.44 %	13.26 %	16.54 %	23.91 %	42.66 %	28.46 %	20.62 %	14.97 %
Rockyou	0.89 %	1.37 %	2.05 %	4.55 %	11.30 %	22.31 %	57.28 %	39.30 %	24.24 %	12.84 %
000webhost	0.16 %	0.34 %	0.79 %	2.32 %	4.30 %	7.71 %	34.09 %	15.17 %	7.83 %	4.36 %
Battlefield	0.48 %	0.71 %	1.14 %	3.21 %	8.13 %	17.91 %	30.57 %	13.49 %	5.78 %	2.16 %
Mail.ru	1.82 %	3.06 %	4.05 %	6.37 %	9.94 %	17.40 %	43.88 %	24.92 %	12.46 %	7.81 %
Gmail.ru	0.97 %	1.43 %	2.08 %	3.88 %	8.66 %	17.77 %	41.65 %	23.79 %	12.63 %	5.76 %
Flirtlife.de	1.30 %	2.00 %	3.47 %	10.83 %	28.51 %	58.01 %	48.73 %	22.52 %	7.92 %	2.55 %
Avg. above	**1.63 %**	**2.76 %**	**3.86 %**	**6.84 %**	**12.45 %**	22.71 %	44.11 %	25.73 %	14.73 %	8.42 %
Uni. dist	0.01‰	0.03‰	0.1‰	1‰	0.10 %	1.00 %	10.00 %	1.00 %	0.10 %	0.01 %

As a prudent side note, some PAKE studies (e.g., [25,26]) complement that the assumption of a uniform distribution of passwords with a constant-size dictionary is made for simplicity only, and their security proofs can be extended to handle more complex cases where passwords do not distribute uniformly, different distributions exist for different clients, or the password dictionary size depends on the security parameter. However, such a complement only serves to obscure their security statements and undermine the readers' understanding of *to exactly what extent they can have confidence in the authentication protocol used to protect systems, because no one knows what the security guarantees would be if "user-chosen passwords do not distribute uniformly"*. This defeats the purpose of constructing provably secure protocols which "explicitly capture the inherently *quantitative* nature of security, via a concrete or exact treatment of security" and "offer *quantitative* security guarantee" [4] in the first place.

Our Zipf-based security formulations. According to the Zipf theory, now it is fundamentally unnecessary to make the uniform assumption of password distribution. Since system-assigned random passwords are hardly usable [39], most services allow users to generate their own passwords. This would generally lead to the passwords complying with the Zipf's law as we have shown in Sect. 2.3. Therefore, it is more desirable to make the Zipf assumption about password distributions. Under the PDF-Zipf model in [36], it is natural to reach that:

$$\mathrm{Adv}_{\mathcal{A},\mathcal{P}}(k) = \frac{C/1^s}{\sum_{i=1}^{|\mathcal{D}|}\frac{C}{i^s}} + \frac{C/2^s}{\sum_{i=1}^{|\mathcal{D}|}\frac{C}{i^s}} + \cdots + \frac{C/Q(k)^s}{\sum_{i=1}^{|\mathcal{D}|}\frac{C}{i^s}} = \frac{\sum_{j=1}^{Q(k)}\frac{1}{j^s}}{\sum_{i=1}^{|\mathcal{D}|}\frac{1}{i^s}} + \epsilon(k), \quad (6)$$

Under our CDF-Zipf model (see Eq. 3), it is natural to reach that:

$$\mathrm{Adv}_{\mathcal{A},\mathcal{P}}(k) = C' \cdot Q(k)^{s'} + \epsilon(k), \tag{7}$$

where the parameters C, C', s and s' are referred to Eqs. 1 and 3 in Sect. 2.3.

   Figure 4 shows that $\mathcal{A}$'s advantage is more accurately captured by Eq. 7 than by Eq. 6. This is expected according to the results in Sect. 2.3.

Our popularity-policy-based formulation. Figure 4 (as well as Figs. 2(c) and (d)) shows that, an attacker who only tries a rather small number (e.g., $Q(k) = 100$) of the most popular passwords can crack a non-negligible proportion of user accounts. In other words, even if the authentication protocol implemented is provably secure, secure user identification still cannot be reached if the passwords of the system obey Zipf's law. Countermeasures like the popularity-based password policy [34] can be taken. In this case, the skewed Zipf distribution seems hardly possible to be mathematically characterized, we are stuck in a conundrum to formulate $\mathrm{Adv}_{\mathcal{A},\mathcal{P}}(k)$. Inspired by the essential notion of security that a secure PAKE protocol can provide – only online impersonation attacks are helpful to the adversary in breaking the security of the protocol [2,25], we manage to get out of the problem by giving up the idea of firstly characterizing the exact distribution of passwords and then formulating the definition of security. And instead, whenever a policy like [34] is in place, we provide a tight upper bound for the adversary's advantage. More specifically, Eq. 5 now is amended as follows:

$$\mathrm{Adv}_{\mathcal{A},\mathcal{P}}(k) \leq F_1 \cdot Q(k)/|\mathcal{DS}| + \epsilon(k), \tag{8}$$

where F_1, as said earlier, is the frequency of the most popular password in the dataset $\mathcal{DS}$, $|\mathcal{DS}|$ is the (expected) number of user accounts of the target authentication system, and the other notations are the same with those of Eq. 5. Note that, dictionary $\mathcal{D}$ is *the password sample space* and it is a *set*, while dataset $\mathcal{DS}$ is *a (specific) password sample* and it is a *multiset*. Therefore, the value of $F_1/|\mathcal{DS}|$ is exactly the threshold probability $\mathcal{T}$ (e.g., $\mathcal{T} = 1/16384$) that the underlying password policy (see [34]) maintains. For a system to reach a Level 1 certification [10], the success chance of an online guessing attacker should be no larger than 1 in 1024, which indicates $F_1/|\mathcal{DS}| \leq 1/1024$; Similarly, for a Level 2 certification, the system shall ensure $F_1/|\mathcal{DS}| \leq 1/16384$. For example, for the gaming and e-commerce website www.dodonew.com to achieve a Level 2 security, F_1 should have been no larger than $991 (\approx 16231271/16384)$. Also note that, Eq. 5 is actually a special case of Eq. 8, where $F_1 = 1$ and $|\mathcal{DS}| = |\mathcal{D}|$.

Min-entropy-based security formulation. In 2015, Abdalla et al. [2] proposed a provably secure PAKE protocol that does not employ the traditional security formulation like Eq. 5, but uses a different one:

$$\text{Adv}_{\mathcal{A},\mathcal{P}}(k) \leq Q(k)/2^m + \epsilon(k), \tag{9}$$

where m is the *min-entropy* [8] of a password dataset.[2] Actually, it is not difficult to see that Abdalla et al.'s this formulation is in essential the same with Eq. 8, because one can derive that $m = -\log_2(F_1/|\mathcal{DS}|)$. However, no rationale or justification for preferring Eq. 9 rather than Eq. 5 has been given in [2]. In comparison, our formulation Eq. 8 is more concrete and easily understood than Eq. 9 from the prospective of password policy.

In addition, as with our Eq. 8, Abdalla et al.'s Eq. 9 (i.e., the min-entropy model) is *only* effective when a popularity-based password policy like [34] is in place, resulting in that the password distribution does not follow the Zipf's law. However, without such a policy in place, passwords are likely to follow the Zipf's law, and thus both Eqs. 8 and 9 will be useless. This has not been pointed out in [2]. Recent studies [12,37] and our exploration of 120 top sites show that, such a policy has not been adopted into leading web services or password managers.

Also note that, if m is defined to be the *entropy* of passwords, then Eq. 9 is virtually equal to Eq. 5 and it provides a *mean* value for the online guessing difficulty, for one can derive that $m = \sum_{r=1}^{|\mathcal{D}|} -p_i\log_2 p_i$, where p_i is the probability of the ith most frequent password in $\mathcal{D}$ (e.g., $p_1 = F_1/|\mathcal{DS}|$). This well explicates why Benhamouda et al. (see Sect. 6.1 of [6]) stated that "equivalently the advantage of any adversary can be bounded" by either Eqs. 5 or 9. However, as we have shown, if m is defined as the *min-entropy* of passwords, Eqs. 5 and 9 (or equally, Eq. 8) will be significantly different from each other.

Comparison and summary. We show in Fig. 4 how the existing two PAKE security formulations (i.e., Eqs. 5 and 9) and the two Zipf-based formulations (i.e., Eqs. 6 and 7) approximate the real attacker (using 000webhost and Dodonew for example). Since online guessing attacks are generally prevented by lockout, rate-limiting techniques or suspicious login detection [16], the attackers cannot make a large number of login attempts, and thus the guess number is often small (generally, $Q(k) \leq 10^4$). One can see that, *our CDF-Zipf*

---

[2] We note that, in Sects. 5.2–5.4 of [2], m is re-defined to be the *entropy* of passwords. This inconsistence would lead to great differences in security guarantees. We conjecture typos have occurred there.

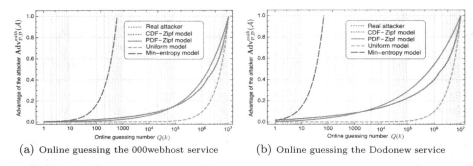

(a) Online guessing the 000webhost service   (b) Online guessing the Dodonew service

Fig. 4. With $Q(k)$ online guessing attempts, the advantages of the real attacker, the uniform-modeled attacker [1, 24, 26], min-entropy-modeled attacker [2, 27], PDF-Zipf-modeled attacker [36] and our CDF-Zipf-modeled attacker. Our model almost *overlaps* with the real attacker.

model well approximates the real attacker — its advantage curve almost over-laps with that of the real attacker, substantially outperforming the three other models. For instance, the actual advantages of $\mathcal{A}$ against Dodonew reach 5.60 % when $Q(k) = 10^2$ and 8.59 % when $Q(k) = 10^3$. They are far beyond 0.00098 % and 0.0098 % given by Eq. 5 [1, 24, 26], and far less than 100 % and 100 % given by Eq. 9 [2, 27], respectively. Fortunately, our CDF-Zipf model (i.e., Eq. 7) predicts a 5.15 % when $Q(k) = 10^2$ and a 8.40 % when $Q(k) = 10^3$, respectively. In all, CDF-Zipf model performs the best and yields results well accord with the real attacker's guessing advantages.

3.2 Implication for Multi-factor Authentication Protocols

Without loss of generality, here we use the most widely used smart-card-based password authentication protocols as an example. The major goal of designing two-factor schemes is to achieve "truly two-factor security" [38] which means that only an entity who knows *both* the password and the smart card can login to the server. This means an attacker who knows either the password factor or the smart card factor shall be unable to login.

The crux of designing a protocol with "truly two-factor security" lies in how to resist offline password guessing attack, in case the smart card has been stolen and extracted by the attacker [38]. This means now the protocol security only relies on the password. The attacker $\mathcal{A}$ can use the stolen smart card and tries to login with the guessed passwords $pw_1, pw_2, \cdots$, until the server locks out the account. Since such an online guessing is always unavoidable, the best security that a two-factor protocol $\mathcal{P}$ can achieve is to ensure that: such an online guessing attack is the best that $\mathcal{A}$ can do. Accordingly, protocol $\mathcal{P}$ is said secure only if

$$\text{Adv}^{\text{2fa}}_{\mathcal{A},\mathcal{P}}(k) \leq Q(k)/|\mathcal{D}| + \epsilon(k), \tag{10}$$

where $\text{Adv}^{\text{2fa}}_{\mathcal{A},\mathcal{P}}(k)$ is $\mathcal{A}$'s advantage in attacking $\mathcal{P}$ with $Q(k)$ online guesses.

Essentially the same security formulation like Eq. 10 are made in most of the provably secure two-factor schemes (e.g., see Sect. 2.2.1 of [11], Definition 1 of [24]). As discussed in Sect. 3.1, our Zipf theory invalidates such, at best unrealistic and at worst misleading (i.e., convey a false sense of security guarantees), forms of formulation. A formulation like our proposed Eq. 7 is much more accurate and desirable (see Fig. 4):

$$\text{Adv}_{\mathcal{A},\mathcal{P}}^{\text{2fa}}(k) = C' \cdot Q(k)^{s'} + \epsilon(k), \tag{11}$$

where $\text{Adv}_{\mathcal{A},\mathcal{P}}(k)$ is the advantage of $\mathcal{A}$ in attacking $\mathcal{P}$ with $Q(k)$ online guesses, and C' and s' are the parameters calculated using the CDF-Zipf model.

3.3 Implication for Other Kinds of Password-Based Protocols

Without loss of generality, here we mainly use typical examples to show the applicability of our formulation Eq. 7 to password-protected secret sharing [23], password-based signatures [18] and password-based encryption [5].

In 2016, Jarecki et al. [23] proposed an efficient and composable password-protected secret sharing (PPSS) protocol. In Definition 2 of [23], it is assumed that "$pw \leftarrow_R \mathcal{D}$", which means password pw are drawn uniformly at random from password space $\mathcal{D}$. Further, they defined the protocol security to be $\text{Adv}_{\mathcal{A}}^{\text{pss}}(k) = (q_S + q_U)/|\mathcal{D}| + \epsilon$. According to the CDF-Zipf theory, a formulation like our proposed Eq. 7 is much more accurate and desirable:

$$\text{Adv}_{\mathcal{A}}^{\text{pss}}(k) = C' \cdot Q(k)^{s'} + \epsilon(k), \tag{12}$$

Similarly, for password-based signatures (PBS, e.g. [18]), when defining "Blindness" it generally involves an explicit assumption of the distribution of passwords. Most of related works assume "$pw \leftarrow_R \text{PW}$" [18]. For password-based encryption (PBE) schemes, most related works assume "$pw \leftarrow_\$ A_1(\lambda)$" (see Fig. 7 of [5]) which means passwords are drawn uniformly. All such password- related protocols can be readily designed with the Zipf assumption of password distribution, and give more realistic security formulations like Eq. 7.

Summary. To the best of our knowledge, we, for the first time, pay attention to the joint between passwords and password-based authentication protocols. With the knowledge of the exact distribution of passwords, we manage to develop a more accurate and realistic formulation (i.e., $\text{Adv}_{\mathcal{A},\mathcal{P}}(k) = C' \cdot Q(k)^{s'} + \epsilon(k)$) to characterize the formal security results for password-based authentication protocols. Given a target system, the values of C' and s' can be predicted (approximated) by leaked datasets from sites with a similar service, language and policy. For instance, if the protocol is to be deployed in a English gaming site, one can set $C' = 0.010298$ and $s' = 0.294932$, which come from the leaked Battlefiled site. As a rule of thumb, high-value sites can prefer C' and s' from Dodonew/000webhost; medium-value sites prefer those of Gmail/Battlefield; low-value sites prefer those of Tianya/Rockyou. *This enables an accurate, quantitative and practical assessment of the security provisions of a password system about which we have no password data.*

Here we have mainly taken password-based authentication as a case study. As we have sketched in Sect. 3.3, the results revealed herein can also be readily applied to other kinds of password-based cryptographic protocols whose security formulation essentially relies on the *explicit* assumption of the distribution of user-chosen passwords, such as PBE [5], PBS [18] and PPSS [3,23].

4   Implications for Password Creation Policies

Recently, it has been popular (e.g., [17,34]) to advocate a password policy that disallows users from choosing undesirably popular passwords (e.g., `123456` and `letmein`) that are more frequently chosen than a predefined threshold $\mathcal{T}$ (e.g., $\mathcal{T} = 1/10^6$). The motivation underlying such a policy is that some users prefer dangerously popular passwords, and as shown in Eq. 7 of Sect. 3.2, such passwords would make $\mathcal{A}$'s advantage $\mathrm{Adv}_{\mathcal{A},\mathcal{P}}(k) = C' \cdot Q(k)^{s'} + \epsilon(k)$ extremely high with even a small guess number $Q(k)$.

However, under the PDF-Zipf model, Wang et al. [36] suggested a number of prediction models, and pointed out that this popularity-based policy would largely impair usability. For example, given a threshold $\mathcal{T} = 1/10^6$, 60 % of users in most Internet-scale sites will be *potentially* annoyed to abandon their old, popular password and select a new one. As such theoretical predictions is important, and now a natural question arise: how to obtain more accurate prediction models under our CDF-Zipf model?

4.1   Our Prediction Models

In Sect. 2.3, our CDF-Zipf model reveals that in reality, users choose passwords far from uniform and the CDF of passwords follows a Zipfian distribution. More specifically, this means that *the rank r of a password* and *the cumulative frequency F_r of passwords up to r* obey the equation $F_r = \frac{C'}{r^{s'}}$, where C' and s' are constants calculated from the CDF-Zipf regression. In other words,

$$P(rank \leq r) = C' \cdot r^{s'}, \tag{13}$$

Generally, there is finite number (say N) of distinct passwords. Thus, we have:

$$P(rank \leq N) = C' \cdot N^{s'} = 1 \quad \Rightarrow \quad N = (\frac{1}{C'})^{1/s'}. \tag{14}$$

Consequently, the number of these top η (e.g., $\eta = 1\,\%$) of passwords is $\eta \cdot N$. Then, the cumulative frequency of these top $\eta \cdot N$ passwords will be:

$$P(rank \leq \eta \cdot N) = C' \cdot (\eta \cdot N)^{s'} = C' \cdot (\eta \cdot (1/C')^{1/s'})^{s'} = C' \cdot \eta^{s'} \cdot (1/C') = \eta^{s'}. \tag{15}$$

This indicates that $W_p(\eta) = P(rank \leq \eta \cdot N) = \eta^{s'}$ of passwords will be potentially affected. For better illustration, assume the frequency f_r of a password with rank r is a continuous real variable. Thus, the frequency of a password with rank r is

$$f_r = \frac{d(F_r)}{dr} = \frac{d(C' \cdot r^{s'})}{dr} = C' \cdot s' \cdot r^{s'-1}. \tag{16}$$

Now we can obtain the relationship between the top fraction η and the popularity threshold $\mathcal{T}$. Assume the rank of the password with frequency equals $\mathcal{T}$ to be $r_{\mathcal{T}}$. On the one hand, Eq. 16 suggests that: $\mathcal{T} = C' \cdot s' \cdot r_{\mathcal{T}}^{s'-1}$; On the other hand, $\eta = r_{\mathcal{T}}/N$. Further according to Eq. 14, we get

$$\eta = \frac{r_{\mathcal{T}}}{N} = (\frac{\mathcal{T}}{C' \cdot s'})^{\frac{1}{s'-1}} \cdot \frac{1}{N} = (\frac{\mathcal{T}}{C' \cdot s'})^{\frac{1}{s'-1}} \cdot (C')^{\frac{1}{s'}}. \tag{17}$$

Equation 17 suggests that the frequency of a password with rank $\eta \cdot N$ will be $C' \cdot s' \cdot (\eta \cdot N)^{s'-1}$. Therefore, among these $W_p(\eta)$ of passwords that are *potentially* affected, the fraction of users that *actually* will *not* be affected is $C' \cdot s' \cdot (\eta \cdot N)^{s'-1} \cdot \eta \cdot N = s' \cdot \eta^{s'}$. Thus, the fraction will be actually affected is:

$$W_a(\eta) = W_p(\eta) - s' \cdot \eta^{s'} = (1 - s') \cdot \eta^{s'}. \tag{18}$$

There is a subtlety to be noted. $W_p(\eta)$ and $W_a(\eta)$ are indeed two independent and useful indicators to measure the extent to which usability will be affected. For instance, suppose an Internet-scale English social-network site www.example. com wants to enforce a popularity-based policy with $\mathcal{T} = 1/10^6$, then we can predict (by using CDF-Zipf parameters of Rockyou) that there will be $W_p(\eta) = 36.08\%$ accounts with passwords more popular than $\mathcal{T} = 1/10^6$. This means each of these 36.08% accounts has *an equal potential* to be required to change a new password. However, there will only be $W_a(\eta) = 29.32\%$ accounts that are *actually* required to choose a different password for the reason that, after $W_a(\eta) = 29.32\%$ accounts have already been changed, the remaining $W_p(\eta) - W_a(\eta) = 6.76\%$ accounts will be with passwords less popular than $\mathcal{T} = 1/10^6$ and comply with the policy.

4.2 Our Empirical Results

In Fig. 5 we depict the form of the curves of $W_p(\eta)$ and $W_a(\eta)$ against η for various values of s' as listed in Table 2. The rapid increase of W_p and W_a at the top-10% of their curves (see Fig. 5) clearly reveals that, a significant fraction of users will be annoyed despite that only a marginal fraction of popular passwords are prohibited. Since $W_p(\eta) = \eta^{s'}$, an average of $W_a = 38.73\%$ (Max $= 51.72\%$, Min $= 19.46\%$) of users in the 7 million-size sites (see Table 1) will be potentially inconvenienced when $\mathcal{T} = 1/10^6$. To see whether our theory accords with the reality, we also summarize the statistical results from 9 real-life password datasets in Table 5. Generally, when $\mathcal{T} < 1/16384$ the theoretical W_a is *lower* than the empirical W_a by a factor < 1, much smaller than that of [36]. The means that our predictions would serve as conservative indicators of usability degradations.

Summary. Our above prediction models (i.e., η, $W_p(\eta)$ and $W_a(\eta)$) indicate that $\mathcal{T} = 1/10^6$ might be too restrictive for Internet-scale sites in terms of usability. In contrast, less than 17% of users in most systems will be potentially annoyed

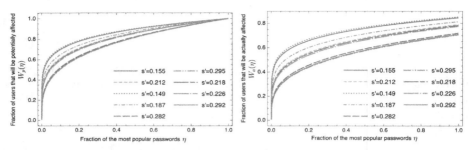

(a) Users *potentially* affected with top fraction η (b) Users *actually* affected with top fraction η

Fig. 5. The fraction of users that will be potentially/actually affected by a popularity-based policy, when passwords follow a Zipf law with s' as listed in Table 2.

Table 5. Effects of policy threshold $\mathcal{T}$ on the proportion (i.e., η) of undesirable popular passwords and on the proportion (i.e., W_a) of users that will be actually annoyed.

Password dataset	$\mathcal{T}=1/1024$		$\mathcal{T}=1/10000$		$\mathcal{T}=1/16384$		$\mathcal{T}=1/1000000$	
	η	W_a	η	W_a	η	W_a	η	W_a
Rockyou	0.0000 %	1.22 %	0.0020 %	4.13 %	0.0040 %	5.70 %	0.4863 %	27.30 %
000webhost	0.0000 %	0.07 %	0.0007 %	1.36 %	0.0106 %	3.31 %	0.2668 %	7.45 %
Battlefield	0.0007 %	0.42 %	0.0393 %	2.34 %	1.0698 %	9.69 %	100.0000 %	100.00 %
Tianya	0.0001 %	6.61 %	0.0014 %	10.76 %	0.0022 %	11.64 %	0.4394 %	30.92 %
Dodonew	0.0001 %	2.30 %	0.0011 %	4.61 %	0.0020 %	5.19 %	0.3962 %	14.71 %
CSDN	0.0002 %	9.46 %	0.0029 %	12.28 %	0.0049 %	12.87 %	0.8441 %	24.69 %
Mail.ru	0.0003 %	3.08 %	0.0043 %	5.40 %	0.0879 %	9.54 %	2.8439 %	26.26 %
Gmail.ru	0.0002 %	1.24 %	0.0049 %	2.94 %	0.1339 %	9.66 %	2.4732 %	23.34 %
Flirtlife.de	0.0594 %	3.02 %	1.9939 %	19.06 %	3.3126 %	24.19 %	100.0000 %	100.00 %

when we set $\mathcal{T} = 1/16384$ which complies with a Level 2 certification [10]. We suggest that $\mathcal{T} = 1/16384$ would be more acceptable for most Internet-scale sites, especially those care for user experience, such as e-commerce and gaming.

5   Implications for the α-guesswork Metric

Now we show that the password strength metric α-guesswork [8], which previously was deemed as fully parametric and has been widely used (e.g., [14,22]), is actually non-parametric in two of four cases when measuring passwords. This inherent property would make α-guesswork much simpler to use.

5.1   Review of the α-guesswork Metric

For ease of understanding, here the notations follow [8]. $\mathcal{X}$ stands for the password distribution, and each password x_i is randomly drawn from $\mathcal{X}$ with a probability p_i, where $\sum p_i = 1$. Without loss of generality, suppose $p_1 \geq p_2 \geq \cdots \geq p_{\mathcal{N}}$, where $\mathcal{N}$ is the total number of possible individual passwords in $\mathcal{X}$.

Before we present α-guesswork $G_\alpha(\mathcal{X})$, two other statistic-based metrics (i.e., β-success-rate $\lambda_\beta(\mathcal{X})$ and α-work-factor $\mu_\alpha(\mathcal{X})$) are reviewed:

$$\lambda_\beta(\mathcal{X}) = \sum_{i=1}^{\beta} p_i, \tag{19}$$

which measures the expected advantages of $\mathcal{A}$ restricted to β guesses per account.

$$\mu_\alpha(\mathcal{X}) = min\{j| \sum_{i=1}^{j} p_i \geq \alpha\}, \tag{20}$$

where $0<\alpha\leq 1$. $\mu_\alpha(\mathcal{X})$ denotes the least number of fixed guesses per account when $\mathcal{A}$ aims to guess no less than a fraction α of total accounts. Therefore, λ_{μ_α} stands for $\mathcal{A}$'s actual advantages when given μ_α guesses per account and $\lambda_{\mu_\alpha} \geq \alpha$. With the above two definitions, α-guesswork is specified as:

$$G_\alpha(\mathcal{X}) = (1 - \lambda_{\mu_\alpha}) \cdot \mu_\alpha + \sum_{i=1}^{\mu_\alpha} p_i \cdot i, \tag{21}$$

The rationales behind Eq. 21 are referred to [8].

5.2   Defect in the α-guesswork Metric

The α-guesswork metric has been widely employed in recent studies (e.g., [14,22]), and the related paper also won the "NSA 2013 annual Best Scientific Cybersecurity Paper Award" [33]. However, it is subject to a defect — it is non-deterministic. More specifically, it is always parameterized on the success rate α (e.g., a relationship of $G_{0.51}(\mathcal{X}_A) > G_{0.51}(\mathcal{X}_B)$ can never guarantee that $G_{0.52}(\mathcal{X}_A) \geq G_{0.52}(\mathcal{X}_B)$), as admitted in [8] that "we can't rely on any single value of α, each value provides information about a fundamentally different attack scenario." Thus, for a fair comparison, entire curves (i.e., with α ranging from 0 to 1) of $G_\alpha(\mathcal{X}_A)$ and $G_\alpha(\mathcal{X}_B)$ have to be drawn. This makes it quite cumbersome to use. This defect is inherently due to the fact that α-guesswork does not employ the knowledge of the explicit distribution of passwords.

5.3   Our New Observations

Interestingly, we observe that, based on the Zipf assumption of passwords (which is generally the case in reality), G_α can be shown to be no longer parameterized in two of four cases. Note that, λ_β stands for the success rate by β guesses under the *optimal* attack. This means the curve of λ_β is essentially the same the CDF curve of distribution $\mathcal{X}$. The latter, as shown in Sect. 2.3 can be well approximated by our CDF-Zipf model. Therefore, we have

$$\lambda_\beta = \sum_{i=1}^{\beta} p_i \approx F_\beta = C' \cdot \beta^{s'}. \tag{22}$$

where β is the number of online guesses in an optimal order.

Theorem 1. *For two password distributions $\mathcal{X}_A$ and $\mathcal{X}_B$, suppose $C'_A \leq C'_B$, $s'_A \leq s'_B$. Then*

$$G_\alpha(\mathcal{X}_A) \geq G_\alpha(\mathcal{X}_B),$$

where $0 \leq \alpha \leq 1$. If either inequalities of the above two conditions is strict, then $G_\alpha(\mathcal{X}_A) > G_\alpha(\mathcal{X}_B)$, where $0 < \alpha \leq 1$.

Proof. Firstly, since $C'_A \leq C'_B$ and $s'_A \leq s'_B$, we can get that $\lambda_\beta(\mathcal{X}_A) \leq \lambda_\beta(\mathcal{X}_B)$:

$$\lambda_\beta(\mathcal{X}_A) = \sum_{i=1}^{\beta} p_i^A \approx F_\beta(\mathcal{X}_A) = C'_A \cdot \beta^{s'_A} \leq C'_B \cdot \beta^{s'_B} = F_\beta(\mathcal{X}_B) \approx \sum_{i=1}^{\beta} p_i^B = \lambda_\beta(\mathcal{X}_B), \quad (23)$$

where $1 \leq \beta \leq \max\{|\mathcal{X}_A|, |\mathcal{X}_B|\}$. Secondly, with Eq. 20 and $\lambda_\beta(\mathcal{X}_A) \leq \lambda_\beta(\mathcal{X}_B)$ (i.e., Eq. 23), it is natural to get $\mu_\alpha(\mathcal{X}_A) \geq \mu_\alpha(\mathcal{X}_A)$. Thirdly, we can derive

$$
\begin{aligned}
G_\alpha &= (1 - \lambda_{\mu_\alpha}) \cdot \mu_\alpha + \sum_{i=1}^{\mu_\alpha} p_i \cdot i = \sum_{i=1}^{\mu_\alpha} \sum_{j=1}^{i} p_i + (1 - \lambda_{\mu_\alpha}) \cdot \mu_\alpha \\
&= \sum_{j=1}^{\mu_\alpha} \sum_{i=j}^{\mu_\alpha} p_i + \sum_{j=1}^{\mu_\alpha} (1 - \lambda_{\mu_\alpha}) = \sum_{j=1}^{\mu_\alpha} (1 - \lambda_{\mu_\alpha} + \sum_{i=j}^{\mu_\alpha} p_i) \\
&= \sum_{j=1}^{\mu_\alpha} (1 - \lambda_{j-1}).
\end{aligned}
$$

Since $\mu_\alpha(\mathcal{X}_A) \geq \mu_\alpha(\mathcal{X}_B)$ and $\lambda_j(\mathcal{X}_A) \leq \lambda_j(\mathcal{X}_B)$, we get

$$G_\alpha(\mathcal{X}_A) \geq G_\alpha(\mathcal{X}_B).$$

If either of the two conditions in Theorem 1 is strict, then it holds that $G_\alpha(\mathcal{X}_A) > G_\alpha(\mathcal{X}_B)$, where $0 < \alpha \leq 1$.

Corollary 1. *Suppose $C'_A \geq C'_B, s'_A \geq s'_B$. Then*

$$G_\alpha(\mathcal{X}_A) \leq G_\alpha(\mathcal{X}_B),$$

This corollary holds due to the evident fact that it is exactly the converse-negative proposition of Theorem 1.

The above theorem and corollary indicate that, given two password datasets A and B, we can first use liner regression to obtain their fitting lines (i.e., C'_A, s'_A, C'_B and s'_B), and then compare C'_A with C'_B and s'_A with s'_A, respectively. This gives rise to four cases, among which are the two cases (i.e., $\{C'_A \geq C'_B, s'_A \geq s'_B\}$ and $\{C'_A \leq C'_B, s'_A \leq s'_B\}$) where we can show α-guesswork [8] is deterministic. This makes it much simpler to use in these two cases.

6   Conclusion

In this paper, we have revealed three important implications of the Zipf's law in passwords. While most password-related cryptographic protocols, security policies and metrics either are based on the uniform assumption of password distribution or simply avoid making an explicit assumption of password distribution, it is of great importance to study the implications when user-chosen passwords actually follow the Zipf's law, a distribution far from uniform. We have provided more accurate security formulations for provably secure password protocols, suggested policy parameters with better security and usability tradeoff, and proved a new, inherent property for the metric α-guesswork. Particularly, extensive experiments on 9 large-scale password datasets, which consist of 112 million real-world passwords and cover various popular Internet services and diversified user bases, demonstrate the validity of our proposed implications. Besides, Zipf's law can be useful for other situations, e.g., to evaluate the goodness/validity of algorithms/studies (such as honeywords generation, password hash and user studies) in which a human password distribution needs to be reproduced.

Acknowledgment. We are grateful to the anonymous reviewers for their invaluable comments. Ping Wang is the corresponding author. This research was supported by the National Natural Science Foundation of China (NSFC) under Grant No. 61472016.

References

1. Abdalla, M., Benhamouda, F., MacKenzie, P.: Security of the J-PAKE password-authenticated key exchange protocol. In: Proceedings of IEEE S&P 2015, pp. 571–587 (2015)
2. Abdalla, M., Benhamouda, F., Pointcheval, D.: Public-key encryption indistinguishable under plaintext-checkable attacks. In: Katz, J. (ed.) PKC 2015. LNCS, vol. 9020, pp. 332–352. Springer, Heidelberg (2015)
3. Bagherzandi, A., Jarecki, S., Saxena, N., Lu, Y.: Password-protected secret sharing. In: Proceedings of ACM CCS 2011, pp. 433–444 (2011)
4. Bellare, M.: Practice-oriented provable-security. In: Proceedings of ISC 1997, pp. 221–231 (1997)
5. Bellare, M., Hoang, V.T.: Adaptive witness encryption and asymmetric password-based cryptography. In: Katz, J. (ed.) PKC 2015. LNCS, vol. 9020, pp. 308–331. Springer, Heidelberg (2015)
6. Benhamouda, F., Blazy, O., Chevalier, C., Pointcheval, D., Vergnaud, D.: New techniques for SPHFs and efficient one-round PAKE protocols. In: Canetti, R., Garay, J.A. (eds.) CRYPTO 2013, Part I. LNCS, vol. 8042, pp. 449–475. Springer, Heidelberg (2013)
7. Blocki, J., Datta, A.: CASH: a cost asymmetric secure hash algorithm for optimal password protection. In: IEEE CSF 2016 (2016). arxiv.org/pdf/1509.00239v1.pdf
8. Bonneau, J.: The science of guessing: analyzing an anonymized corpus of 70 million passwords. In: Proceedings of IEEE S&P 2012, pp. 538–552 (2012)
9. Bonneau, J., Herley, C., Oorschot, P., Stajano, F.: The quest to replace passwords: a framework for comparative evaluation of web authentication schemes. In: Proceedings of IEEE S&P 2012, pp. 553–567 (2012)

10. Burr, W., Dodson, D., Perlner, R., Gupta, S., Nabbus, E.: NIST SP800-63-2: electronic authentication guideline. Technical report, National Institute of Standards and Technology, Reston, VA, August 2013

11. Byun, J.W.: Privacy preserving smartcard-based authentication system with provable security. Secur. Commun. Netw. **8**(17), 3028–3044 (2015)

12. Carnavalet, X., Mannan, M.: A large-scale evaluation of high-impact password strength meters. ACM Trans. Inform. Syst. Secur. **18**(1), 1–32 (2015)

13. Castelluccia, C., Dürmuth, M., Perito, D.: Adaptive password-strength meters from markov models. In: Proceedings of NDSS 2012, pp. 1–15 (2012)

14. Chatterjee, R., Bonneau, J., Juels, A., Ristenpart, T.: Cracking-resistant password vaults using natural language encoders. In: Proceedings of IEEE S&P 2015, pp. 481–498 (2015)

15. Chen, L., Lim, H.W., Yang, G.: Cross-domain password-based authenticated key exchange revisited. ACM Trans. Inform. Syst. Secur. **16**(4), 1–37 (2014)

16. Dürmuth, M., Freeman, D., Biggio, B.: Who are you? A statistical approach to measuring user authenticity. In: NDSS 2016, pp. 1–15 (2016)

17. Florêncio, D., Herley, C., van Oorschot, P.: An administrators guide to internet password research. In: Proceedings of USENIX LISA 2014, pp. 44–61 (2014)

18. Gjøsteen, K., Thuen, Ø.: Password-based signatures. In: Petkova-Nikova, S., Pashalidis, A., Pernul, G. (eds.) EuroPKI 2011. LNCS, vol. 7163, pp. 17–33. Springer, Heidelberg (2012)

19. Herley, C., Van Oorschot, P.: A research agenda acknowledging the persistence of passwords. IEEE Secur. Priv. **10**(1), 28–36 (2012)

20. Huang, X., Xiang, Y., Bertino, E., Zhou, J., Xu, L.: Robust multi-factor authentication for fragile communications. IEEE Trans. Depend. Secur. Comput. **11**(6), 568–581 (2014)

21. Huang, Z., Ayday, E., Hubaux, J., Juels, A.: Genoguard: protecting genomic data against brute-force attacks. In: Proceedings of IEEE S&P 2015, pp. 447–462 (2015)

22. Huh, J.H., Oh, S., Kim, H., et al.: Surpass: system-initiated user-replaceable passwords. In: Proceedings of CCS 2015, pp. 170–181 (2015)

23. Jarecki, S., Kiayias, A., Krawczyk, H., Xu, J.: Highly-efficient and composable password-protected secret sharing. In: Proceedings of IEEE EuroS&P 2016, pp. 276–291 (2016)

24. Jarecki, S., Krawczyk, H., Shirvanian, M., Saxena, N.: Device-enhanced password protocols with optimal online-offline protection. In: ASIACCS 2016, pp. 177–188 (2016)

25. Katz, J., Ostrovsky, R., Yung, M.: Efficient and secure authenticated key exchange using weak passwords. J. ACM **57**(1), 1–41 (2009)

26. Katz, J., Vaikuntanathan, V.: Round-optimal password-based authenticated key exchange. J. Crypt. **26**(4), 714–743 (2013)

27. Kiefer, F., Manulis, M.: Zero-knowledge password policy checks and verifier-based PAKE. In: Kutyłowski, M., Vaidya, J. (eds.) ESORICS 2014, Part II. LNCS, vol. 8713, pp. 295–312. Springer, Heidelberg (2014)

28. Li, Y., Wang, H., Sun, K.: A study of personal information in human-chosen passwords and its security implications. In: Proceedings of INFOCOM 2016, pp. 1–9 (2016)

29. Ma, J., Yang, W., Luo, M., Li, N.: A study of probabilistic password models. In: Proceedings of IEEE S&P 2014, pp. 689–704 (2014)

30. Malone, D., Maher, K.: Investigating the distribution of password choices. In: Proceedings of WWW 2012, pp. 301–310 (2012)

31. Martin, R.: Amid Widespread Data Breaches in China, December 2011. http://www.techinasia.com/alipay-hack/
32. Mick, J.: Russian Hackers Compile List of 10M+ Stolen Gmail. Yandex, Mailru, September 2014. http://t.cn/R4tmJE3
33. 1st NSA Annual Best Scientific Cybersecurity Paper Competition, July 2013. http://cps-vo.org/group/sos/papercompetition2012
34. Schechter, S., Herley, C., Mitzenmacher, M.: Popularity is everything: a new approach to protecting passwords from statistical-guessing attacks. In: Proceedings of HotSec 2010, pp. 1–8 (2010)
35. Wang, D., He, D., Cheng, H., Wang, P.: fuzzyPSM: a new password strength meter using fuzzy probabilistic context-free grammars. In: Proceedings of DSN 2016, pp. 595–606 (2016)
36. Wang, D., Jian, G., Huang, X., Wang, P.: Zipf's law in passwords. IEEE Trans. Inform. Foren. Secur. (2016, in press). http://t.cn/RqT51U8
37. Wang, D., Wang, P.: The emperor's new password creation policies: an evaluation of leading web services and the effect of role in resisting against online guessing. In: Proceedings of ESORICS 2015, pp. 456–477 (2015)
38. Wang, Y.: Password protected smart card and memory stick authentication against off-line dictionary attacks. In: Gritzalis, D., Furnell, S., Theoharidou, M. (eds.) SEC 2012. IFIP AICT, vol. 376, pp. 489–500. Springer, Heidelberg (2012)
39. Yan, J., Blackwell, A.F., Anderson, R.J., Grant, A.: Password memorability and security: empirical results. IEEE Secur. Priv. **2**(5), 25–31 (2004)
40. Yi, X., Hao, F., Chen, L., Liu, J.K.: Practical threshold password-authenticated secret sharing protocol. In: Pernul, G., Ryan, P.Y.A., Weippl, E. (eds.) ESORICS. LNCS, vol. 9326, pp. 347–365. Springer, Heidelberg (2015). doi:10.1007/978-3-319-24174-6_18

Encrypted Search

PPOPM: More Efficient Privacy Preserving Outsourced Pattern Matching

Jun Zhou, Zhenfu Cao$^{(\boxtimes)}$, and Xiaolei Dong$^{(\boxtimes)}$

Shanghai Key Lab for Trustworthy Computing, East China Normal University, Shanghai 200062, China
{jzhou,zfcao,dongxiaolei}@sei.ecnu.edu.cn

Abstract. Secure outsourced pattern matching permits both the sender and receiver with resource-constrained mobile devices to respectively delegate text T and pattern P to the cloud for the computationally-intensive task of pattern matching. Unfortunately, outsourcing both the computation and storage to the semi-trusted or malicious cloud has brought a series of security and privacy issues. Most of the state-of-the-art exploited the technique of computationally-intensive public key (fully) homomorphic encryption (FHE) as primitives which is inappropriate for resource-constrained devices and the work not depending on FHE cannot well guarantee either text privacy or pattern privacy. To well address this problem, a more efficient privacy preserving outsourced pattern matching PPOPM is proposed in this paper. As a building block, a privacy preserving outsourced discrete fourier transform protocol OFFT is firstly devised to allow the cloud perform OFFT in the encrypted domain, without disclosing either the coefficient privacy or the input privacy. Based on OFFT, we propose an efficient secure outsourced polynomial multiplication protocol OPMUL which is further exploited in designing the final efficient outsourced pattern matching protocol PPOPM. Without exploiting public key FHE, the proposed PPOPM achieves secure outsourced pattern matching with well protected text privacy and pattern privacy against the collusion between the cloud and the receiver or the sender, by performing any one-way trapdoor permutation only once. Finally, the universal composable (UC) technique is adopted to formally prove the security of our proposed PPOPM under the semi-honest environment. The extensive evaluations demonstrate the efficiency and practicability of our proposed PPOPM.

Keywords: Outsourced pattern matching · Privacy preserving · Discrete fourier transform · Efficiency · Universal composable security

1 Introduction

The problem of securely outsourcing computation to semi-trusted or malicious servers has been increasingly becoming significant with the fast development of wireless communication where the resource-constrained mobile devices cannot

© Springer International Publishing Switzerland 2016
I. Askoxylakis et al. (Eds.): ESORICS 2016, Part I, LNCS 9878, pp. 135–153, 2016.
DOI: 10.1007/978-3-319-45744-4_7

afford the computationally intensive tasks [1]. In outsourced computing, clients can take advantage of abundant computational resources in the "pay-per-use" manner instead of depending on their own infrastructure. While it has brought about considerable benefit to efficiency enhancement, the security and privacy issues have significantly impeded its wide adoption. It is well known that the cloud is generally assumed to work under the semi-honest or malicious environment: the former of which refers to the cloud would faithfully execute the protocol but try to extract the secret information from the interactions between the clients and itself; while the latter means the cloud can perform arbitrarily to destroy the protocol run. Therefore, a series of cryptographic techniques have been devised to address the issue of secure outsourced computation [2,3].

Outsourced pattern matching, as a kind of valuable outsourced computation, generally refers to delegating the task of finding all the positions where the receiver's pattern P of size m matches the sender's text T of size n to the cloud and it is required to run in the encrypted domain to guarantee user privacy. Therefore, in addition to the traditional security requirements such as data confidentiality and authentication, there exist a series of unique security and privacy requirements for outsourced pattern matching: (1) pattern privacy means the pattern queried by the receiver should be well protected against the collusion between the cloud and the malicious sender; (2) text privacy denotes that the text held by the sender should be well protected against the collusion between the cloud and the malicious receiver. Consider the e-healthcare cloud computing systems, secure outsourced genome fragment matching allows to judge the probability of one person to suffer from specific diseases and take effective preventive measures to avoid its deterioration without exposing both the template (specific genome fragment inferring the disease) and the text (the person's genome sequence). The physicians can also seek the best clinic decisions, by outsourced searching other patients with the same genome fragments associated to the specific disease and analyzing the effect of their prescriptions. In searchable encryption, secure outsourced pattern matching enables to query the encrypted files embracing substring of particular keywords without revealing both the substring (pattern privacy) and the keyword (text privacy).

Vergnaud proposed a secure generalized pattern matching protocol by exploiting ElGamal's homomorphic encryption [15]. However, the high computational complexity cannot be tolerated by resource-constrained mobile devices and directly performing ElGamal's public key homomorphic encryption [34] on data deviates the principle of hybrid encryption that public key encryption is adopted to encrypt short symmetric data encryption key which is further used to encrypt the data themselves. The technique of fully homomorphic encryption (FHE) can be straightforwardly applied to solve secure outsourced computation [5–20, 26–33, 35, 36]. Unfortunately, Lauter et al. pointed that regardless of great effort on designing lightweight FHE, its high complexity can still not well adapt to computationally-weak mobile devices [4]. More seriously, the fact that public key FHE is required to be performed on each character of both text and pattern (i.e. the complexity is $O(n + m)$) even made the outsourced pattern matching impractical owing to the intolerably high computational overhead on resource-constrained users' ends. Recently, Faust et al. proposed an outsourced pattern matching protocol simulation-based secure in the presence of semi-honest and malicious environment under the random oracle model [5]. It was achieved not by exploiting the traditional technique of FHE, but based on an instance of subset sum problem that is solvable in polynomial time. Unfortunately, this protocol was constructed under the assumption that private channels were well established since it cannot resist the collusion attack against pattern privacy launched between the cloud knowing the exact matching positions and the sender who holds the text and the size of the pattern.

Based on the observations presented above, we briefly sketch the key motivations and solutions of our proposed more efficient privacy-preserving outsourced pattern matching protocol PPOPM, to save the computational cost from the following three aspects: the first is to replace public key FHE by a newly-devised lightweight integration of any one-way trapdoor permutation $f(\cdot)$ to encode a private key and a keyed symmetric fully homomorphic mapping on data m_i in $\mathbb{Z}_N (N = pq)$ as $h_{fhom,U}(m_i) = q^{-1}qm_{i,p}^p + p^{-1}pm_{i,q}^q$, where $m_i \in \mathbb{Z}_N, m_{i,l} \equiv m_i \bmod l$ $(l \in \{p, q\})$ and p, q are big primes of 512-bits. This design also satisfies the principle of hybrid encryption. Another critical intuition for efficiency enhancement is that although the complexity of public key encryption (i.e. we mean any public key encryption based on specific one-way trapdoor permutation used in our construction) can be hardly reduced, we can still reduce the computational cost of secure outsourced pattern matching in a whole, by reducing the usage times of the associated public key encryption to only once in the optimized case. Last but not least, the secret key sk_f and the randomnesses $r, r"$ privately kept by the authorized receivers permit they are the only entities who can successfully decipher and deblind the authentic matching positions, and the pattern privacy would be well protected. In this paper, we proposed a more efficient privacy-preserving outsourced pattern matching protocol PPOPM without exploiting the technique of public key (fully) homomorphic encryption. The main contributions are described as follows.

Firstly, without adopting public key (fully) homomorphic encryption, a secure outsourced discrete fourier transform OFFT is proposed by exploiting any one-way trapdoor permutation only once, where both the input privacy and coefficient privacy are well protected. It is the building block of a new secure outsourced polynomial multiplication protocol OPMUL which is further used to design our final construction PPOPM.

Then, a more efficient privacy preserving outsourced pattern matching protocol PPOPM is designed through polynomial multiplication OPMUL realized by our newly-devised OFFT. Pattern privacy is guaranteed against the collusion attack launched between the sender and the cloud; while text privacy is well protected against the collusion attack between the receiver and the cloud.

Finally, the proposed PPOPM is formally proved secure under the universal composable (UC) model in the presence of semi-honest environment in the random oracle model. The time complexity on the cloud and the resource-constrained user's (both sender and receiver) ends are respectively $O(nlogm)$ and $O(1)$. Extensive performance evaluations demonstrate the efficiency advantage of our proposed PPOPM over the state-of-the-art in both computational and communication cost.

The remainder of this paper is organized as follows. The problem statement and the formal security model are presented in Sect. 2. A secure outsourced discrete fourier transform OFFT and more efficient privacy preserving outsourced pattern matching PPOPM are respectively proposed in Sects. 3 and 4. Section 5 gives the formal security proof, followed by the performance evaluation in Sect. 6. Finally, we conclude our paper in Sect. 7.

2   Problem Statement and Security Model

2.1   Problem Statement

The problem of pattern matching sets the goal to find all the positions where the pattern P of size m matches the text T of size n. Both the text T and pattern P are sequences of characters in a finite character set U. It can be further categorized into two classes, namely pattern matching with perfect precision and pattern matching with wildcards. In the first case, the problem is to find all occurrences of a pattern $P \in U^m$ in a text $T \in U^n$; while in the latter case, it is aimed to find all occurrences of a pattern $P \in (U \bigcup \{*\})^m$ in a text $T \in (U \bigcup \{*\})^n$ where a wildcard character $* \notin U$ can match any character in U.

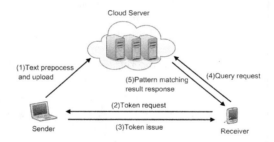

Fig. 1. Network architecture of outsourced pattern matching

Outsourced pattern matching problem is delegated to the cloud since both the sender holding text T and the receiver holding pattern P are assumed to be resource-constrained in wireless mobile communications such as E-health systems, VANETs and cannot afford this computationally-intensive task of pattern matching. To protect both the text and pattern privacy, the cloud is required to perform the pattern matching operation in the encrypted domain. Figure 1 demonstrates the network architecture of privacy preserving outsourced pattern matching. It is observed that there exist three entities, namely the sender, the cloud and the receiver. The process of outsourced pattern matching can be described as following steps: In step (1), the sender (i.e. we use sender and owner exchangeably in the following) partitions, encrypts and outsources the preprocessed text T to the cloud; in steps (2) and (3), the receiver resorts to the sender for a query token TOK permitting him to launch a pattern matching operation w.r.t. text T; in steps (4) and (5), the receiver appropriately encrypts the pattern by exploiting the token TOK issued by the sender, and outsources it to the cloud. Finally, the cloud performs the outsourced pattern matching in the encrypted domain and returns the result to the receiver. The preprocessing step is required to run only once, the complexity of which is apportioned among multiple receivers querying the text with different patterns.

2.2   Definitions and Security Model

In this section, we mainly focus on the honest-but-curious (semi-trusted) security model. Specifically, the goal of the receiver is to know the positions where pattern P matches in the text without disclosing anything about the pattern to even the collusion between the cloud and the sender. On the other hand, the text T is also required to be well protected against even the collusion between the cloud and the receiver.

We formalize the security of our proposed PPOPM through the universal composable (UC) model using the ideal/real paradigm. The functionality of F_{PPOPM} implemented via three two-party protocols $PTL = (PTL_{Pre}, PTL_{Qry}, PTL_{Opm})$ is described as follows.

Functionality(F_{PPOPM}): Let $n, m, \lambda \in \mathbb{Z}_N$. The functionality F_{PPOPM} initially sets an empty table Tab and perform the following operations. It interacts with the sender, receiver, server and adversary Sim.

(i) Upon receiving a message (Txt, T, m) from the sender, it sends $(Pre, |T|, m)$ to the cloud and Sim, and records (Txt, T), where $|T|$ means the size of text T;

(ii) Upon receiving a message (Qry, P_i) from the receiver where $i \in [1, poly(\lambda)]$ (i.e. the receiver is allowed to launch multiple times of query which is a polynomial of security parameter λ), it firstly checks whether message $(Txt, \cdot)$ has been recorded and $|P_i| = m$ where $|P_i|$ means the size of pattern P_i. If passed, it further checks whether there exists an entry of $(P_i, \cdot)$ in table Tab. If it is not the case, it picks a new identifier $ID \in \{0, 1\}^*$ and adds the entry (P_i, ID) into table Tab. Then, it sends (Qry, Rec) to the sender and Sim.

(iii-a) Upon receiving message (Apr, Rec) from the sender, it reads the entry (P_i, ID) from Tab and sends message $(Qry, Rec, (Cov_{1,u}^{Enc}, Cov_{2,u}^{Enc}, Cov_{3,u}^{Enc}), ID)$ to the cloud, where $u \in [0, n - m])$ refers to $n - m + 1$ possible positions that pattern P_i occurs in text T. Otherwise, it sends $\perp$ to the receiver and abort.

(iii-b) Upon receiving message (Apr, Rec) from Sim, it reads the entry (P_i, ID) from Tab and sends message $(Qry, P_i, (Cov_{1,u}^{Enc}, Cov_{2,u}^{Enc}, Cov_{3,u}^{Enc}), ID)$ to the receiver. Otherwise, it sends $\perp$ to the receiver.

It is noted that distinguishing from the existing work [5], even the server is corrupted, the positions the pattern occurs in the text can still not be disclosed, since only $(Cov_{1,u}^{Enc}, Cov_{2,u}^{Enc}, Cov_{3,u}^{Enc})$ inferring the encrypted matching positions are obtained by the cloud which can only be successfully deciphered by the authorized receivers. Therefore, both text privacy and pattern privacy can be well protected against collusion attacks. Formally, if we define $\mathbf{IDEAL}_{F_{PPOPM}, Sim(z)}$ $(\lambda, p, (T, (P_1, \cdots, P_{poly(\lambda)})))$ $(\mathbf{REAL}_{PTL, Adv(z)}(\lambda, p, (T, (P_1, \cdots, P_{poly(\lambda)}))))$ as the output of an ideal adversary Sim (adversary Adv), the cloud, the sender and the receiver in the ideal execution of F_{PPOPM} (the real execution of protocol $PTL = (PTL_{Pre}, PTL_{Qry}, PTL_{Opm})$) upon the inputs $(\lambda, p, (T, (P_1, \cdots, P_{poly(\lambda)})))$ and the auxiliary input z for $Sim(Adv)$, we can derive the following security definition of our proposed privacy preserving outsourced pattern matching protocol PPOPM.

Definition 1. We say protocol $PTL = (PTL_{Pre}, PTL_{Qry}, PTL_{Opm})$ securely implements the functionality F_{PPOPM}, if and only if for any probabilistic polynomial time (PPT) real adversary Adv, there exists a probabilistic polynomial time ideal adversary (simulator) Sim such that for any inputs $(\lambda, T, (P_1, \cdots, P_{poly(\lambda)}))$ and auxiliary input z, we have

$$\{\mathbf{IDEAL}_{F_{PPOPM}, Sim(z)}(\lambda, (T, (P_1, \cdots, P_{poly(\lambda)})))\}_{\lambda \in \mathbb{N}}$$
$$\approx_c \{\mathbf{REAL}_{PTL, Adv(z)}(\lambda, (T, (P_1, \cdots, P_{poly(\lambda)})))\}_{\lambda \in \mathbb{N}},$$

where $\approx_c$ denotes computationally indistinguishability. The proposed PPOPM implements ideal functionality F_{PPOPM} in the random oracle model. Functions H_0, H_1 behaving as truly random functions are public and can be queried by all parts polynomial times to security parameter λ.

3   Efficient Privacy-Preserving Outsourced Discrete Fourier Transform OFFT

In this section, an efficient privacy preserving outsourced discrete fourier transform protocol OFFT without exploiting FHE is proposed to protect both the input privacy and the coefficient privacy. Discrete fourier transform refers to the following mapping between two vectors

$$\boldsymbol{a} = (a_0, a_1, \cdots, a_{n-1}) \rightarrow \hat{\boldsymbol{a}} = (\hat{a}_0, \hat{a}_1, \cdots, \hat{a}_{n-1}) \tag{1}$$

such that $\hat{a}_l = \sum_{i=0}^{n-1} a_i w_n^{il} (l = 0, 1, \cdots, n-1)$. The proposed OFFT is mainly composed of the following four algorithms: **Setup, Encrypt, Evaluation** and **Decrypt**, which are detailed as follows.

Setup(1^λ): On input 1^λ where λ is the security parameter, it runs a trapdoor permutation generator denoted as a probabilistic polynomial time (PPT) algorithm $\mathcal{G}$ and outputs a tuple of permutations $(f, f^{-1}) : \{0, 1\}^{2\lambda} \rightarrow \{0, 1\}^{2\lambda}$ with a pair of corresponding keys (pk_f, sk_f). It also outputs two hash functions

$H_0, H_1 : \{0,1\}^* \rightarrow \{0,1\}^{2\lambda}$. The public parameters are $PPR = (pk_f, H_0, H_1)$ and the secret key is sk_f assigned to the receiver.

Encrypt$(pk_f, w_n, m_i(i = 0, 1, \cdots, n-1))$: Let w_n be an n-th complex root of 1, that is $w_n = e^{j\frac{2\pi}{n}}$ where $j^2 = -1$. $m_i = m_{i,1} + jm_{i,2}$ where $m_i = (m_{i,1}, m_{i,2}) \in (\{0,1\}^{2\lambda})^2 (i = 0, 1, \cdots, n-1)$ are the inputs and $w_n = w_{n,1} + jw_{n,2}$ where $w_n = (w_{n,1}, w_{n,2}) \in (\{0,1\}^{2\lambda})^2$ is the coefficient for the discrete fourier transform. It is noted that for cryptography usage convenience, both $w_{n,1}, w_{n,2}$ here have been enlarged by an appropriate scaling factor so that they can be located in $\{0,1\}^{2\lambda}$ (i.e. the methods for choosing a proper scaling factor and the corresponding result recovery can refer [20]). The data owner randomly selects two big primes p, q of $|p| = |q| = \lambda$ which are kept secret by the owner, and computes $N = pq$ which is publicized for the receiver. Then, the owner randomly selects $r' \in_R \{0,1\}^{\lambda}$ and computes $C_{1,1} = f(p \parallel r')$ where $\parallel$ means the random padding operation of p to the length of 2λ. For each m_i and w_n, it computes $m_{i,p} \equiv m_i \bmod p, m_{i,q} \equiv m_i \bmod q, w_{n,p} \equiv w_n \bmod p, w_{n,q} \equiv w_n \bmod q$. It is noted that the modular operation for complex numbers is defined as the modular operations respectively on the real part and the imaginary part. Then, it randomly selects $U_i^{mul}, U_k^{mul} \in_R \mathbb{Z}_N (k = 0, 1, \cdots, il; l = 0, 1, \cdots, n-1)$ and computes

$$C_{2,i} = (q^{-1}qm_{i,p}^p + p^{-1}pm_{i,q}^q)U_i^{mul} \bmod N,$$
$$C_{3,k} = (q^{-1}qw_{n,p}^p + p^{-1}pw_{n,q}^q)U_k^{mul} \bmod N, \qquad (2)$$

where q^{-1}, p^{-1} respectively denote the inverses of $q \ (mod p)$ and $p \ (mod q)$. Finally, the owner publicizes $U_{i,T}^{mul} = U_i^{mul} \prod_{k=0}^{il} U_k^{mul}$, computes $C_{ram}^{mul} = H_0(p \parallel \bigcup_{i=0}^{n-1} C_{2,i} \parallel \bigcup_{k=0}^{il} C_{3,k})$ and sends $C_{u,i} = (C_{1,1}, C_{2,i}, C_{3,k}, C_{ram}^{mul})$ to the cloud.

Evaluate$(C_{2,i}, C_{3,k}(i, l = 0, 1, \cdots, n-1; k = 0, 1, \cdots, il), C_{ram}^{mul})$: The cloud evaluates the discrete fourier transform in the encrypted domain Firstly, the cloud performs the addition and multiplication aggregation operations

$$C_{i,T}^{mul} = C_{2,i} \prod_{k=0}^{il} C_{3,k}(U_{i,T}^{mul})^{-1} \bmod N$$
$$= (q^{-1}qm_{i,p}^p + p^{-1}pm_{i,q}^q)(q^{-1}qw_{n,p}^p + p^{-1}pw_{n,q}^q)^{il} \bmod N$$
$$= q^{-1}q(m_{i,p}w_{n,p}^{il})^p + p^{-1}p(m_{i,q}w_{n,q}^{il})^q \bmod N,$$

$$C_{\hat{a}_l} = \sum_{i=0}^{n-1} C_{i,T}^{mul} \bmod N$$
$$= q^{-1}q\sum_{i=0}^{n-1}(m_{i,p}w_{n,p}^{il})^p + p^{-1}p\sum_{i=0}^{n-1}(m_{i,q}w_{n,q}^{il})^q \bmod N$$
$$= q^{-1}q(\sum_{i=0}^{n-1}m_{i,p}w_{n,p}^{il})^p + p^{-1}p(\sum_{i=0}^{n-1}m_{i,q}w_{n,q}^{il})^q \bmod N$$
$$C_3 = H_1(C_{\hat{a}_l} \parallel C_{ram}^{mul}) \qquad (3)$$

and sends $C_A = (C_{1,1}, C_{2,i}, C_{3,k}, C_{\hat{a}_l}, C_{ram}^{mul}, C_3)$ to the receiver.

Decrypt$(sk_f, C_{1,1}, C_{\hat{a}_l}, C_{ram}^{mul}, C_3)$: The receiver firstly computes $p \parallel r' = f^{-1}(C_{1,1})$ by using her/his secret key sk_f, derives p by removing the last λ bits for random padding, and checks whether both $C_{ram}^{mul} = H_0(p \parallel \bigcup_{i=0}^{n-1} C_{2,i} \parallel \bigcup_{k=0}^{il} C_{3,k})$ and $C_3 = H_1(C_{\hat{a}_l} \parallel C_{ram}^{mul})$ hold. If not, this algorithm outputs $\perp$; otherwise, the receiver continues to compute $q = Np^{-1}$ and

$$C_{\hat{a}_l} \bmod p = q^{-1}q\left(\sum_{i=0}^{n-1} m_{i,p}w_{n,p}^{il}\right)^p + p^{-1}p\left(\sum_{i=0}^{n-1} m_{i,q}w_{n,q}^{il}\right)^q \bmod p$$

$$= q^{-1}q\left(\sum_{i=0}^{n-1} m_{i,p}w_{n,p}^{il}\right)^p \bmod p = M_{T,p} \bmod p,$$

$$C_{\hat{a}_l} \bmod q = q^{-1}q\left(\sum_{i=0}^{n-1} m_{i,p}w_{n,p}^{il}\right)^p + p^{-1}p\left(\sum_{i=0}^{n-1} m_{i,q}w_{n,q}^{il}\right)^q \bmod q$$

$$= p^{-1}p\left(\sum_{i=0}^{n-1} m_{i,q}w_{n,q}^{il}\right)^q \bmod q = M_{T,q} \bmod q. \tag{4}$$

where

$$M_{T,p} = \sum_{i=0}^{n-1} m_{i,p}w_{n,p}^{il} \bmod p, M_{T,q} = \sum_{i=0}^{n-1} m_{i,q}w_{n,q}^{il} \bmod q. \tag{5}$$

It is noted that the fully homomorphic property is preserved on both operations with modulus p and q as presented above. Then, the receiver can recover the fully homomorphic results M_T, namely the result of discrete fourier transform $\hat{a}_l$ by exploiting the Chinese Remainder Theorem (CRM) on Eq. (5) as follows,

$$\hat{a}_l = M_T = M_p'qM_{T,p} + M_q'pM_{T,q} \bmod N \tag{6}$$

where M_p', M_q' respectively satisfies $M_p'q \equiv 1 \bmod p, M_q'p \equiv 1 \bmod q$, that can be efficiently computed since the greatest common divisor of p and q namely $(p, q) = 1$.

4   The Proposed PPOPM

4.1   Efficient Privacy Preserving Outsourced Polynomial Multiplication

An efficient privacy preserving outsourced polynomial multiplication scheme OPMUL based on our newly-devised OFFT is proposed, serving the cornerstone of our secure outsourced pattern matching. Both the inputs and the coefficients of the polynomial are well protected against the cloud, and only the authorized receiver can successfully decipher the multiplication result. Without loss of generality, it is assumed that there exist two polynomials $P(x), Q(x) \in \mathbb{Z}_N[x]$ of the degree $n - 1$, where n is assumed as a power of 2,

$$P(x) = a_{n-1}x^{n-1} + \cdots + a_1 x + a_0, Q(x) = b_{n-1}x^{n-1} + \cdots + b_1 x + b_0. \tag{7}$$

Note that it can be easily achieved since if not the case, the higher order terms with zero coefficients can be added as $a_k = b_k = 0(k = n, n+1, \cdots, 2^{\lceil log_2 n \rceil} - 1)$ where $\lceil x \rceil$ denotes the minimum integer not smaller than x. The goal is to compute $MUL(x) = P(x)Q(x) = c_{2n-2}x^{2n-2} + \cdots + c_1 x + c_0$. The details are presented as follows.

Setup. The setup algorithm is the same as **OFFT.Setup**.

Encrypt. The Encrypt algorithm is the same as **OFFT.Encrypt** with the exception that $l = 0, 1, \cdots, 2n - 1$ and m_i is replaced by the coefficients of polynomials $P(x), Q(x) \in \mathbb{Z}_N[x]$, namely $\boldsymbol{a} = (a_0, \cdots, a_{n-1})$ and $\boldsymbol{b} = (b_0, \cdots, b_{n-1})$. It is also noted that for polynomial evaluation and multiplication applications, only a special case of our newly-designed privacy-preserving outsourced discrete fourier transform is exploited where we only focus the real part of m_i.

Evaluate. The data owner securely outsources the evaluation of polynomials $P(x)$ and $Q(x)$ at $2n$ points $w_{2n}^0, w_{2n}^1, \cdots, w_{2n}^{2n-1}$ by exploiting the algorithm **OFFT.Evaluate**, where w_{2n} is a $2n$-th complex root of 1, namely $w_{2n} = e^{j \frac{\pi}{n}}$ and $j^2 = -1$. We use polynomial $P(x)$ for example to briefly describe how to efficiently evaluate polynomials in the encrypted domain and the case of $Q(x)$ is the same. It is noted that the polynomial evaluation on the corresponding encrypted points of $w_{2n}^l (l = 0, 1, \cdots, 2n - 1)$ can be performed by using the algorithm **OFFT.Evaluate** in our newly-designed privacy preserving outsourced discrete fourier transformation OFFT in Sec. 3 for $\hat{a}_l = \sum_{i=0}^{n-1} a_i w_{2n}^{il}$ with the only exception that $l = 0, 1, \cdots, 2n - 1$.

On the other hand, it is observed that polynomial $P(x)$ can be divided into two polynomials $P_0(x)$ and $P_1(x)$ of the same degree $\frac{n}{2} - 1$,

$$P_0(x) = a_{n-2}x^{\frac{n}{2}-1} + \cdots + a_2 x + a_0, P_1(x) = a_{n-1}x^{\frac{n}{2}-1} + \cdots + a_3 x + a_1. \quad (8)$$

such that $P(x) = P_0(x^2) + xP_1(x^2)$. Therefore, the problem of $P(x)$ evaluation can be divided into two steps: firstly evaluate $P_0(x)$ and $P_1(x)$ at $(w_{2n}^0)^2, (w_{2n}^1)^2, \cdots, (w_{2n}^{2n-1})^2$ and then integrate the final result accordingly. Note that $(w_{2n}^0)^2, (w_{2n}^1)^2, \cdots, (w_{2n}^{2n-1})^2$ only comprise n complex roots of unity, namely $w_{2n}^0, w_{2n}^2, \cdots, w_{2n}^{2n-2}$, therefore the subproblems of privacy preserving outsourced computing $P_0(x)$ and $P_1(x)$ possess exactly the same form of the original problem of evaluating $P(x)$ with the half size and we can solve it by recursively exploiting our newly-designed privacy preserving outsourced discrete fourier transform OFFT in Sect. 3 described in Algorithm 1.

Then, the cloud can obtain the encrypted results of polynomial $Q(x)$ evaluation at these $2n$ points $w_{2n}^0, w_{2n}^1, \cdots, w_{2n}^{2n-1}$ in the same way. Let $C_{\hat{a}_l}^s (l \in \{0, 1, \cdots, 2n - 1\}; s \in \{P, Q\})$ be the encrypted results of polynomials $P(x)$ and $Q(x)$ at points w_{2n}^l, the cloud can also evaluate the encrypted product of $MUL(x) = P(x)Q(x)$ at these points through pairwise multiplication

$$\boldsymbol{C_{\hat{a}}}^{PQ} = C_{\hat{a}_l}^{PQ} = C_{\hat{a}_l}^P C_{\hat{a}_l}^Q (l = 0, 1, \cdots, 2n - 1). \quad (9)$$

Finally, the cloud interpolates polynomial $MUL(x)$ at the encrypted product values by exploiting inverse fourier transform to obtain the encrypted

---

Algorithm 1. Privacy Preserving Outsourced Polynomial Evaluation: $Recursive\ OFFT(\boldsymbol{a} = (a_0, a_1, \cdots, a_{n-1}), 2n)$

    Begin
1: **if** n=1 **then**
2:    return
    $\boldsymbol{a}^{Enc} \leftarrow (OFFT.Encrypt(a_0), OFFT.Encrypt(a_1), \cdots, OFFT.Encrypt(a_{n-1}))$
3: **end if**
4: $OFFT.Encrypt(w_{2n}) \leftarrow OFFT.Encrypt(w_{2n,1} + jw_{2n,2})$,
    $OFFT.Encrypt(w) \leftarrow OFFT.Encrypt(1)$
5: $\boldsymbol{a}_0^{Enc} \leftarrow (OFFT.Encrypt(a_0), OFFT.Encrypt(a_2), \cdots, OFFT.Encrypt(a_{n-2}))$
6: $\boldsymbol{a}_1^{Enc} \leftarrow (OFFT.Encrypt(a_1), OFFT.Encrypt(a_3), \cdots, OFFT.Encrypt(a_{n-1}))$
7: $C_{\hat{a}_0} \leftarrow Recursive\ OFFT(\boldsymbol{a}_0, n)$, $C_{\hat{a}_1} \leftarrow Recursive\ OFFT(\boldsymbol{a}_1, n)$
8: **for** $j = 0$ to $n-1$ **do**
9:    $C_{\hat{a}_j} \leftarrow C_{\hat{a}_{0,j}} + OFFT.Encrypt(w)C_{\hat{a}_{1,j}}$
10:   $C_{\hat{a}_{j+n}} \leftarrow C_{\hat{a}_{0,j}} - OFFT.Encrypt(w)C_{\hat{a}_{1,j}}$
11:   $OFFT.Encrypt(w) \leftarrow OFFT.Encrypt(w)OFFT.Encrypt(w_{2n})$
12: **end for**
13: return $(C_{\hat{a}_0}, C_{\hat{a}_1}, \cdots, C_{\hat{a}_{2n-1}})$
    End

---

coefficients $\boldsymbol{c}^{Enc} = (OFFT.Encrypt(c_0), OFFT.Encrypt(c_1), \cdots, OFFT.Encrypt(c_{2n-1}))$. Specifically,

$$\boldsymbol{c}^{Enc} = (V_{2n}^{Enc})^{-1} \boldsymbol{C}_{\hat{a}_l}^{PQ}, \tag{10}$$

where the matrix V_{2n}^{Enc} is presented in Eq. (11).

Decrypt. The Decrypt algorithm is the same as **OFFT.Decrypt** with the exception that

$$V_{2n}^{Enc} = \begin{pmatrix} OFFT.Enc(1) & OFFT.Enc(1) & OFFT.Enc(1) & \cdots & OFFT.Enc(1) \\ OFFT.Enc(1) & OFFT.Enc(w_{2n}) & OFFT.Enc(w_{2n}^2) & \cdots & OFFT.Enc(w_{2n}^{2n-1}) \\ \vdots & \vdots & \vdots & \vdots & \vdots \\ OFFT.Enc(1) & OFFT.Enc(w_{2n}^{2n-1}) & OFFT.Enc(w_{2n}^{2(2n-1)}) & \cdots & OFFT.Enc(w_{2n}^{(2n-1)^2}) \end{pmatrix}. \tag{11}$$

$C_{\hat{a}_l}$ is replaced by each element $OFFT.Encrypt(c_l)(l = 0, 1, \cdots, 2n-1)$ of $\boldsymbol{c}^{Enc}$.

4.2 Efficient Privacy Preserving Outsourced Pattern Matching

In this subsection, an efficient privacy-preserving outsourced pattern matching protocol PPOPM is proposed based on the proposed OPMUL. It is observed that the pattern matching problem can be reduced to computing the sum of square differences between text T of size n and the pattern P of size m for each possible alignment. Specifically, in the case of no-wildcards, there exists an exact match if and only if for each position $u \in [0, n-m]$, the following judging equation

$$f_{nw} = \Sigma_{v=0}^{m-1}(p_v - t_{u+v-1})^2 = \Sigma_{v=0}^{m-1}(p_v^2 - 2p_v t_{u+v-1} + t_{u+v-1}^2) = 0 \tag{12}$$

holds; while in the case of wildcards, the judging equation is replaced by

$$f_w = \Sigma_{v=0}^{m-1} p_v t_{u+v-1}(p_v - t_{u+v-1})^2 = \Sigma_{v=0}^{m-1}(p_v^3 t_{u+v-1} - 2p_v^2 t_{u+v-1}^2 + p_v t_{u+v-1}^3) = 0, \tag{13}$$

filling wildcard characters with "0"s instead. Therefore, the cloud is respectively required to calculate one convolution and two aligned multiplication for no-wildcard case, and three convolutions for wildcard case in the encrypted domain if one of the vectors is re-aligned in its reversed order, by exploiting our proposed privacy-preserving outsourced polynomial multiplication OPMUL, according to the convolution theorem. Moreover, to achieve the pattern privacy against the collusion between the sender and the cloud, it is required for the receiver to hide the authentic pattern by the randomnesses $r, r"$ in respective cases, which results in that the sender cannot correctly decipher the sum of aligned multiplications and convolutions to judge whether there exists a precise matching at position $u \in [0, n - m]$ and derive the receiver's queried pattern. The details of the proposed PPOPM are described as follows.

Setup. The **Setup** algorithm is invoked between the sender and the cloud, which is the same as **OPMUL.Setup** with the following exceptions. Given the text T and integer m, the sender firstly partitions text T into $\frac{n}{m}$ overlapping substrings of size $2m$. The first substring starts at the beginning of the text and each subsequent substring has an overlap of size m with the previous one. The processed text T' can be represented as

$$T' = (B_1, \cdots, B_s) = ((t_0, \cdots, t_{2m-1}), (t_m, \cdots, t_{3m-1}), \cdots, (t_{(s-1)m}, \cdots, t_{n-1})), \tag{14}$$

where $s = \lceil \frac{n}{m} \rceil - 1$ and the following privacy-preserving outsourced pattern matching is performed on each block $B_d(d = 1, \cdots, s)$. Then, the sender encrypts each element $t_u(u \in [(d-1)m, (d+1)m - 1])$ for the first $s - 1$ blocks and $t_u(u \in [(s-1)m, n-1])$ for the last block to generate $T'^{,Enc}$ by exploiting the algorithm **OPMUL.Encrypt**, with the only exception that the ciphertext $C_{1,1}$ is delayed to be computed and delivered as the token in the **Query** phase.

Query. In the query phase, the sender is required to transmit a query token $TOK = f(p \parallel r')$ for all the authorized receivers holding pattern P. Note that the one-way trapdoor permutation f can be flexibly implemented by identity-based encryption or attribute-based encryption according to different security and privacy requirements. Then, the authorized receiver performs decryption on TOK using secret key sk_f, and obtains the private key p that is used to encrypt the queried pattern P afterwards by moving the last λ bits as random padding.

Outsourced Pattern Matching. Firstly, the receiver randomly selects $r \in_R \mathbb{Z}_N$, computes $p_v' = rp_v(v \in [0, m - 1])$ and encrypts p_v' by exploiting **OPMUL.Encrypt**.

In the case of no-wildcards, for each position $u \in [(d-1)m, (d+1)m - 1]$ in block B_d (i.e. without loss of generality, we take the first $s - 1$ blocks to explain the outsourced pattern matching process, the case of the last block B_s is the same), the cloud computes

$$Cov_{1,u} = \sum_{v=0}^{m-1} r^2 p_v^2, Cov_{2,u} = \sum_{v=0}^{m-1} rp_v t_{u+v}, Cov_{3,u} = \sum_{v=0}^{m-1} t_{u+v}^2 \qquad (15)$$

in the encrypted domain by exploiting the algorithm **OPMUL.Evaluate**. Specifically, without loss of generality, we take the computation of Cov_2 for example. While re-arranging vector p_v in its reversed order, $Cov_{2,u}$ can be rewritten as its standard convolution representation of $Cov_{2,u}^{std} = \sum_{v=0}^{m-1} t_{u+v} p_{m-1-v}$ deriving the same value of each other. If we let $P(x) = t_{u+m-1}x^{u+m-1} + \cdots + t_{u+1}x^{u+1} + t_u x^u$ and $Q(x) = p_0 x^{m-1} + \cdots + p_{m-2}x + p_{m-1}$, the calculation of $Cov_{2,u}^{std}$ can be considered as computing the coefficient of item x^{u+m-1} in the polynomial multiplication of $P(x)$ and $Q(x)$. It is noted that for brief presentation, the problem equals to compute the coefficient of item x^{m-1} in the polynomial multiplication of $P'(x)$ and $Q(x)$ if we let $P'(x) = \frac{P(x)}{x^u} = t_{u+m-1}x^{m-1} + \cdots + t_{u+1}x + t_u$. The privacy preserving outsourced evaluation in the encrypted domain for $Cov_{1,u}$ and $Cov_{3,u}$ can be executed in the same way. Finally, the cloud sends the corresponding encrypted results $Cov_{1,u}^{Enc}, Cov_{2,u}^{Enc}, Cov_{3,u}^{Enc}$ to the receiver. The case of wildcards is the same with the exception of outsourcing the convolution computations

$$Cov_{1,u}' = \sum_{v=1}^{m-1} (r'')^3 p_v^3 t_{u+v}, Cov_{2,u}' = \sum_{v=1}^{m-1} (r'')^2 p_v^2 t_{u+v}^2, Cov_{3,u}' = \sum_{v=1}^{m-1} r'' p_v t_{u+v}^3$$

$$(16)$$

in the encrypted domain instead, where $r'' \in_R \mathbb{Z}_N$ is the blinding factor selected by the receiver.

After receiving the encrypted results from the cloud, the receiver performs the decryption by exploiting the algorithm **OPMUL.Decrypt**. In the case of no-wildcards, the receiver continues to obtain the authentic judging polynomial evaluation by de-blinding

$$f_{nw} = (r^{-1})^2 Cov_{1,u} - 2r^{-1} Cov_{2,u} + Cov_{3,u}. \qquad (17)$$

Finally, the receiver can judge whether an exact matching occurs at position $u \in [(d-1)m, (d+1)m - 1]$ in block B_d by checking whether $f_{nw} = 0$ (i.e. or $f_{nw} < k$ where k is a predefined threshold for approximate pattern matching). The case of wildcards is similar with the exception of judging whether $f_w = 0$ to decide an exact matching.

5   Security Proof

In this section, we give the formal security proof of our proposed privacy preserving outsourced pattern matching protocol PPOPM in the universal composable (UC) model.

Intuitively, the text privacy can be well protected against the collusion between the cloud and the receiver, since in the algorithm **Setup** of our proposed PPOPM, the sender encrypts each character t_u of text T by not only the knowledge of N-factoring namely the secret keys p and q, but also an multiplicative blinding factor U_u^{mul}. Therefore, the cloud and even the authorized receivers possessing the knowledge of N-factoring can still not obtain the original text T since the randomness U_u^{mul} is unavailable. Therefore, the text privacy can be well protected against the collusion between the cloud and the receiver.

On the other hand, the pattern privacy can also be well protected against the collusion between the cloud and the sender, since the sender nor the cloud can successfully obtain the exact matching positions. The reason is that even the sender possesses the knowledge of N-factoring, it is still not able to calculate the correct judging polynomial evaluations including pattern characters p_v, since each p_v is not only encrypted by the secret keys p and q derived from the token TOK, but also blinded by a randomness r selected by the receiver while being outsourced to the cloud in the algorithm of **Query** in our proposed PPOPM. Factually, the sender is only allowed to decipher $Cov_{1,u}, Cov_{2,u}, Cov_{3,u}$, but not the authentic polynomial evaluations of f_{nw} (or f_w) in Eq. (12) by successfully removing the randomness r (or r ").

Table 1. A summary of complex and security comparison (n, m respectively denotes the sizes of text T and pattern P)

Type	Entity	Faust et al.'s [5]	Vergnaud's [15]	Our PPOPM
		Server-aided	Peer-to-peer	Server-aided
Comp.	Sender	$O(n+m)$	$O(n+nlogm)$	$O(1)$
	Cloud	$O(nlogm)$	/	$O(nlogm)$
	Receiver	$O(m)$	$O(m+nlogm)$	$O(1)$
Comm.	Sender	$O(n+m)$	$O(n)$	$O(n)$
	Cloud	$O(n)$	/	$O(n+m)$
	Receiver	$O(m)$	$O(m)$	$O(m)$
Security	Text privacy	Yes	Yes	Yes
	Pattern privacy	No	Yes	Yes

Theorem 1. *Let $\lambda \in \mathbb{Z}_N$ be the security parameter. For integers n, m, we set $s = \lceil \frac{n}{m} \rceil - 1$ and assume $H_0, H_1 : \{0,1\}^* \to \{0,1\}^{2\lambda}$ are random oracle. $N = pq$ where $|p| = |q| = \lambda$ and $f : \{0,1\}^{2\lambda} \to \{0,1\}^{2\lambda}$ is a one-way trapdoor permutation. Then, the proposed protocol PTL (PPOPM) securely implements the functionality F_{PPOPM} in the presence of semi-honest adversaries, namely satisfying the security Definition 1.*

Proof. Due to the space limitation, we only give the proof sketch of our proposed PPOPM in the random oracle model here and please refer to the full version of our paper for the constructions secure in the standard model for the malicious setting with the full proof by exploiting the techniques of [21,24,25]. We firstly formally prove Theorem 1 that our proposed PPOPM achieves the security Definition 1 for each corruption setting of sender, server and receiver respectively. We take the case of corrupted server for example to explain our proof idea that Theorem 1 can be derived by the integration of Claims 1 and 2. We firstly define a hybrid distribution $\mathbf{HYB}_{PTL,Adv(z)}(\lambda,(T,(P_1,\cdots,P_{poly(\lambda)})))$ which can be defined as a real experiment $\mathbf{REAL}_{PTL,Adv(z)}(\lambda,(T,(P_1,\cdots,P_{poly(\lambda)})))$ with the exception that the encrypted text T^{Enc} is replaced by a random function f_λ instead and derive the following claim by the reduction to the security of our proposed primitive $OPMUL$.

Claim 1. Let $OPMUL$ exploited in $PPOPM$ be secure under the hardness of both N-factoring and inverting one-way trapdoor permutation without secret key sk_f, there exists a negligible function $negl(\cdot)$ such that for sufficiently large $\lambda \in \mathbb{Z}_N$, any tuple of inputs $(T,(P_1,\cdots,P_{poly(\lambda)}))$ and auxiliary input z, it holds that

$$\{\mathbf{REAL}_{PTL,Adv(z)}(\lambda,(T,(P_1,\cdots,P_{poly(\lambda)})))\}_{\lambda\in\mathbb{N}}$$
$$\approx_c \{\mathbf{HYB}_{PTL,Adv(z)}(\lambda,(T,(P_1,\cdots,P_{poly(\lambda)})))\}_{\lambda\in\mathbb{N}}.$$

By computing the negligible probability of Bad event we defined that occurs when Sim_R aborts in the ideal environment, we can derive the following claim.

Claim 2. For any input text T, patterns $P_1,\cdots,P_{poly(\lambda)}$, and the auxiliary input z, it holds that

$$\{\mathbf{IDEAL}_{F_{PPOPM},Sim(z)}(\lambda,(T,(P_1,\cdots,P_{poly(\lambda)})))\}_{\lambda\in\mathbb{N}}$$
$$\equiv_s \{\mathbf{HYB}_{PTL,Adv(z)}(\lambda,(T,(P_1,\cdots,P_{poly(\lambda)})))\}_{\lambda\in\mathbb{N}},$$

where $\equiv_s$ denotes statistically indistinguishability.

For the colluding case, it is required to show that the cloud and the receiver (i.e. or the sender) cannot obtain any additional information about the text (i.e. or the pattern) other than what is leaked from the queries (i.e. or the matching result response).

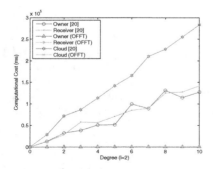
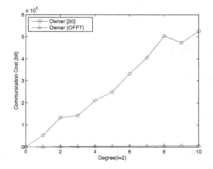

Fig. 2. Computational cost comparison of secure outsourced discrete fourier transform

Fig. 3. Communication cost comparison of secure outsourced discrete fourier transform

6   Performance Evaluation

In this section, we mainly evaluate the performance of our proposed privacy preserving outsourced discrete fourier transformation OFFT and outsourced pattern matching protocol PPOPM in the following aspects: the computational and communication cost comparison between the proposed OFFT/PPOPM and the existing work [5,15,20] exploiting the techniques of public key homomorphic encryptions. We also study the pattern matching probability comparison respectively in the plaintext domain and encrypted domain.

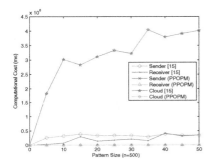

Fig. 4. Computational cost comparison of secure outsourced pattern matching

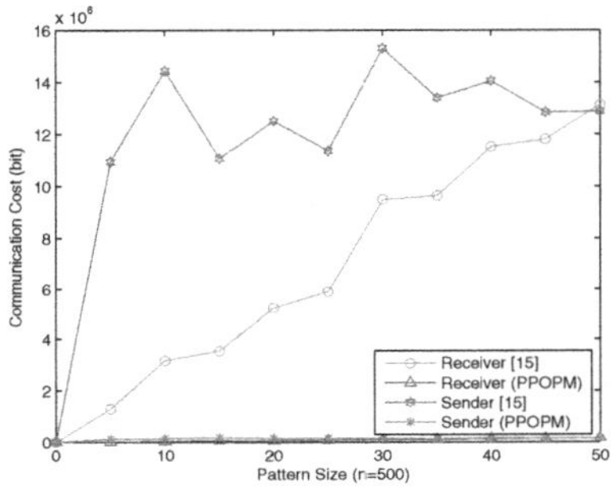

Fig. 5. Communication cost comparison of secure outsourced pattern matching

6.1   Complexity Analysis

Before delving into the experimental results, we firstly provide an overview of the complexity of our proposed PPOPM on all three participating entities. Table 1 summarizes the complexities and the security levels for Faust et al.'s protocol [5], Vergnaud's protocol [15] and our proposed PPOPM. The time complexity of Faust et al.'s [5] and our PPOPM in the outsourced model are both $O(nlogm)$, owing to the divide-and-conquer technique by dividing text T into $\frac{n}{m}$ overlapping substrings (blocks) of $2m$. However, for Vergnaud's protocol [15] in two-party secure computation model, both sender and receiver are required not only for pattern matching, but also performing ElGamal's encryption [34] on each text/pattern element, the time complexity are respectively $O(n + nlogm)$ and $O(m + nlogm)$.

Additionally, since it is required to process each possible pattern for each block in setup phase and the oblivious PRF is needed to achieve pattern privacy in query phase for Faust et al.'s [5] (i.e. it is also the reason for that the communication complexity of the sender in Faust et al.'s [5] is $O(n + m)$), the time complexity of the sender and receiver are respectively $O(n+m)$ and $O(m)$. While in our PPOPM, owing to the newly-devised primitive OPMUL based on recursive OFFT (i.e. Algorithm 1) and partition techniques, the time complexity

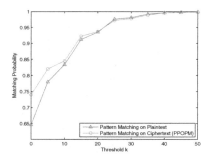

Fig. 6. Matching probability comparison

on the cloud end is $O(nlogm)$. The one-way trapdoor permutation is required to perform only once (obviously $O(1)$) at both the sender and receiver's ends for uploading the encrypted text T, pattern P and decipher the matching result. Therefore, it is observed that the efficiency complexity of the proposed PPOPM far outperforms Faust et al.'s [5] and Vergnaud's [15] while achieving both text privacy and pattern privacy.

6.2 Experimental Evaluation

We conduct the experiments by exploiting PBC and MIRACLE libraries [22,23] running on Linux platform with 2.93 GHz processor to study the operation costs. We mainly focus on the most computationally-intensive component, namely the one-way trapdoor permutations containing most modular exponentiation operations and most ciphertext expansions which considerably contribute to computational and communication cost. It is respectively implemented by the Paillier's additive homomorphic encryption [33] on $\mathbb{Z}_{N^2}$ in [20] and RSA on $\mathbb{Z}_N$ where $|N| = 1024$-bit long in our proposed OFFT. Figures 2 and 3 demonstrate the computational and communication cost comparison between our proposed OFFT and the existing work [20] adopting the technique of Paillier's cryptosystem [33]. Figure 2 shows us as the degree i in FFT increases while fixing subscript $l = 2$ (i.e. we recall the definition of discrete FFT as $\hat{a}_l = \sum_{i=0}^{n-1} a_i w_n^{il} (l = 0, 1, \cdots, n-1)$), both the computational cost of our proposed OFFT and [20] increase accordingly since there are more w_ns are required to be encrypted using Paillier's cryptosystem in [20] or blinded by the multiplicative factor $U_k^{mul} (k = 0, 1, \cdots, il)$. However, the computational cost of OFFT is approximately zero compared to [20] no matter at the owner, the receiver or the cloud's ends. The reason is that to securely outsource each item computation in the FFT of $\hat{a}_l$ as $ITM_i = a_i w_n^{il}$, it is required in [20] to execute Paillier's additive homomorphic encryption [33] il times; while in our proposed OFFT, the RSA is required to perform only once. Additionally, owing to the fact that Paillier's cryptosystem is located in $\mathbb{Z}_{N^2}$, both the computational cost of a single encryption and the ciphertext expansion are significantly heavier than RSA adopted in our OFFT. Therefore, the overall complexity of our OFFT is dramatically lower than [20]. Based on the same observation, Fig. 3 shows us the communication cost of our OFFT has also been significantly reduced in contrast to [20].

For comparison convenience, we firstly extend [15] to an outsourced setting and eliminate the comparison to [5] owing to the different security levels between [5] and our PPOPM. As is respectively shown in Figs. 4 and 5, as the pattern size increases while fixing the text length $n = 500$, both the computational and communication cost increase accordingly and the efficiency of our OFFT is optimized compared to [15]. The reason is that the outsourced pattern matching in OFFT and [20] are both achieved by securely computing three convolutions adopting secure discrete fourier transform as the cornerstone, and the advantages of our proposed OFFT is perfectly inherited. Figure 6 demonstrates that the matching probability of our proposed PPOPM on the ciphertext domain is comparable to the one on the plaintext domain.

7   Conclusion

In this paper, without exploiting public key (fully) homomorphic encryption, we firstly present an efficient privacy-preserving outsourced discrete fourier transform OFFT by exploiting any one-way trapdoor permutation only once, where both the input privacy and coefficient privacy are well protected. Based on OFFT, we propose a privacy preserving outsourced polynomial multiplication OPMUL as a new building block. Finally based on OPMUL, a more efficient privacy preserving outsourced pattern matching PPOPM is proposed where both text privacy and pattern privacy are well protected against the collusion between the cloud and malicious receiver or malicious senders. Finally, formal security proof and extensive evaluations demonstrate the practicability and efficiency of our proposed PPOPM.

Acknowledgments. This work was supported in part by the National Natural Science Foundation of China under Grant 61373154, 61371083, 61411146001, 6163000206 and 6160060473, in part by the Prioritized Development Projects through the Specialized Research Fund for the Doctoral Program of Higher Education of China under Grant 20130073130004, in part by Shanghai High-tech field project under Grant 16511101400, and in part by Natural Science Foundation of Shanghai under Grant 16ZR1409200.

References

1. Abrahamson, K.R.: Generalized string matching. SIAM J. Comput. **16**(6), 1039–1051 (1987)
2. Gennaro, R., Gentry, C., Parno, B.: Non-interactive verifiable computing: outsourcing computation to untrusted workers. In: Rabin, T. (ed.) CRYPTO 2010. LNCS, vol. 6223, pp. 465–482. Springer, Heidelberg (2010)
3. Benabbas, S., Gennaro, R., Vahlis, Y.: Verifiable delegation of computation over large datasets. In: Rogaway, P. (ed.) CRYPTO 2011. LNCS, vol. 6841, pp. 111–131. Springer, Heidelberg (2011)

4. Lauter, K., Naehrig, M., Vaikuntanathan, V.: Can homomorphic encryption be practical? In: ACM CCS (2011)
5. Faust, S., Hazay, C., Venturi, D.: Outsourced pattern matching. In: ICALP (2013)
6. Yao, A.: Protocols for secure computations. In: Proceedings of the 23rd Annual Symposium on Foundations of Computer Science, pp. 160–164 (1982)
7. Zhou, J., Cao, Z., Dong, X., Lin, X., Vasilakos, A.V.: Securing m-healthcare social networks: challenges, countermeasures and future directions. IEEE Wirel. Commun. **20**(4), 12–21 (2013)
8. Troncoso-Pastoriza, J.R., Katzenbeisser, S., Celik, M.: Privacy preserving error resilient DNA searching through oblivious automata. In: ACM CCS 2007, pp. 519–528. ACM Press, New York (2007)
9. Zhou, J., Dong, X., Cao, Z., Vasilakos, A.V.: Secure and privacy preserving protocol for cloud-based vehicular DTNs. IEEE Trans. Inf. Forensics Secur. **10**(6), 1299–1314 (2015)
10. Knuth, D.E., Morris Jr., J.H., Pratt, V.R.: Fast pattern matching in strings. SIAM J. Comput. **6**(2), 323–350 (1977)
11. Hazay, C., Lindell, Y.: Efficient protocols for set intersection and pattern matching with security against malicious and covert adversaries. J. Cryptology **23**(3), 422–456 (2010)
12. Gennaro, R., Hazay, C., Sorensen, J.S.: Text search protocols with simulation based security. In: Nguyen, P.Q., Pointcheval, D. (eds.) PKC 2010. LNCS, vol. 6056, pp. 332–350. Springer, Heidelberg (2010)
13. Hazay, C., Toft, T.: Computationally secure pattern matching in the presence of malicious adversaries. In: Abe, M. (ed.) ASIACRYPT 2010. LNCS, vol. 6477, pp. 195–212. Springer, Heidelberg (2010)
14. Zhou, J., Cao, Z., Dong, X., Lin, X.: TR-MABE: white-box traceable and revocable multi-authority attribute-based encryption and its applications to multi-level privacy-preserving e-heathcare cloud computing systems. In: IEEE INFOCOM (2015)
15. Vergnaud, D.: Efficient and secure generalized pattern matching via fast fourier transform. In: Nitaj, A., Pointcheval, D. (eds.) AFRICACRYPT 2011. LNCS, vol. 6737, pp. 41–58. Springer, Heidelberg (2011)
16. Zhou, J., Lin, X., Dong, X., Cao, Z.: PSMPA: patient self-controllable and multi-level privacy-preserving cooperative authentication in distributed m-Healthcare cloud computing system. IEEE Trans. Parallel Distrib. Syst. **26**(6), 1693–1703 (2015)
17. Wang, D., Jia, X., Wang, C., Yang, K., Fu, S., Xu, M.: Generalized pattern matching string search on encrypted data in cloud systems. In: IEEE INFOCOM (2015)
18. Zhou, J., Cao, Z., Dong, X., Xiong, N., Vasilakos, A.V.: 4S: a secure and privacy-preserving key management scheme for cloud-assisted wireless body area network in m-healthcare social networks. Inf. Sci. **314**, 255–276 (2015)
19. Katz, J., Malka, L.: Secure text processing with applications to private DNA matching. In: ACM CCS (2010)
20. Bianchi, T., Piva, A., Barni, M.: On the implementation of the discrete fourier transformation in the encrypted domain. IEEE Trans. Forensics Secur. **4**(1), 86–97 (2009)
21. Cramer, R., Shoup, V.: A practical public key cryptosystem provably secure against adaptive chosen ciphertext attack. In: CRYPTO (1998)
22. PBC Library. http://crypto.stanford.edu/pbc/times.html
23. Multiprecision integer and rational arithmetic c/c++ library. http://www.shamus.ie/

24. Waters, B.: Efficient identity-based encryption without random oracles. In: Cramer, R. (ed.) EUROCRYPT 2005. LNCS, vol. 3494, pp. 114–127. Springer, Heidelberg (2005)

25. Lewko, A., Okamoto, T., Sahai, A., Takashima, K., Waters, B.: Encryption, fully secure functional: attribute-based encryption and (Hierarchical) inner product encryption. In: EUROCRYPT (2010)

26. Wang, X., Huang, Y., Zhao, Y., Tang, H., Wang, X., Bu, D.: Efficient genome-wide privacy-preserving similar patient query based on private edit distance. In: ACM CCS (2015)

27. Kamara, S., Mohassel, P., Raykova, M.: Outsourcing Multi-Party Computation. IACR Cryptology ePrint Archive 2011, 272 (2011)

28. Lopez-Alt, A., Tromer, E., Vaikuntanathan, V.: On-the-fly multiparty computation on the cloud via multikey fully homomorphic encryption. In: Proceedings of the Forty-Fourth Annual ACM Symposium on Theory of Computing, pp. 1219–1234. ACM (2012)

29. Kamara, S., Mohassel, P., Riva, B.: Salus: a system for server-aided secure function evaluation. In: ACM CCS (2012)

30. Choi, S.G., Katz, J., Kumaresan, R., Cid, C.: Multi-client non-interactive verifiable computation. In: Sahai, A. (ed.) TCC 2013. LNCS, vol. 7785, pp. 499–518. Springer, Heidelberg (2013)

31. Chung, K., Kalai, Y.T., Vadhan, S.P.: Improved delegation of computation using fully homomorphic encryption. In: CRYPO (2010)

32. Asharov, G., Jain, A., López-Alt, A., Tromer, E., Vaikuntanathan, V., Wichs, D.: Multiparty computation with low communication, computation and interaction via threshold FHE. In: Pointcheval, D., Johansson, T. (eds.) EUROCRYPT 2012. LNCS, vol. 7237, pp. 483–501. Springer, Heidelberg (2012)

33. Paillier, P.: Public-key cryptosystems based on composite degree residuosity class. In: EUROCRYPT (1999)

34. ElGamal, T.: A public-key cryptosystem and a signature scheme based on discrete logarithms. IEEE Trans. Inf. Theory $31(4)$, 469–472 (1985)

35. Wang, Q., Hu, S., Ren, K., He, M., Du, M., Wang, Z.: CloudBI: practical privacy-preserving outsourcing of biometric identification in the cloud. In: ESORICS (2015)

36. Cao, Z.: New trends of information security-how to change people's life style? Sci. China Inf. Sci. $59(5)$, 050106:1–050106:3 (2016)

An Efficient Non-interactive Multi-client Searchable Encryption with Support for Boolean Queries

Shi-Feng Sun[1], Joseph K. Liu[2(✉)], Amin Sakzad[2], Ron Steinfeld[2], and Tsz Hon Yuen[3]

[1] Shanghai Jiao Tong University, Shanghai, China
crypto99@sjtu.edu.cn
[2] Faculty of Information Technology, Monash University, Melbourne, Australia
{joseph.liu,amin.sakzad,ron.steinfeld}@monash.edu
[3] Huawei, Singapore, Singapore
YUEN.TSZ.HON@huawei.com

Abstract. Motivated by the recent searchable symmetric encryption protocol of Cash et al., we propose a new multi-client searchable encryption protocol in this work. By tactfully leveraging the RSA-function, our protocol avoids the per-query interaction between the data owner and the client, thus reducing the communication overhead significantly and eliminating the need of the data owner to provide the online services to clients at all times. Furthermore, our protocol manages to protect the query privacy of clients to some extent, meaning that our protocol hides the exact queries from the data owner. In terms of the leakage to server, it is exactly the same as Cash et al., thus achieving the same security against the adversarial server. In addition, by employing attribute-based encryption technique, our protocol also realizes the fine-grained access control on the stored data. To be compatible with our RSA-based approach, we also present a deterministic and memory-efficient 'keyword to prime' hash function, which may be of independent interest.

Keywords: Cloud storage · Searchable encryption · Non-interaction · Multi-client · RSA function

1 Introduction

Cloud technology is now a major industry trend that offers great benefits to users. Cloud storage (or data outsourcing) provides an excellent way to extend the capability to store large volume of data, to prepare for the high velocity of data generation, and to easily process the high variety of data (the "3V" of Big Data). In other words, cloud storage is well designed for the big data era. Meanwhile, data outsourcing raises confidentiality and privacy concerns [2,9,20–24]. Simple encryption technology can protect data confidentiality easily. However, it is not possible to search within the encrypted domain. In order to

© Springer International Publishing Switzerland 2016
I. Askoxylakis et al. (Eds.): ESORICS 2016, Part I, LNCS 9878, pp. 154–172, 2016.
DOI: 10.1007/978-3-319-45744-4_8

search for a particular keyword, user has to decrypt the data first, before starting the searching process. It is not practical especially when the volume of data
is large. Searchable encryption (SE) [5, 7, 8, 11, 32] is a cryptographic primitive
addressing encrypted search.

The architecture of SE can be classified into 4 types: single-writer/
single-reader, single-writer/multi-reader, multi-writer/single-reader and multi-
writer/multi-reader. The traditional single-writer/single-reader allows the data
owner to first use a special encryption algorithm which produces an encrypted
version of the database, including encrypted metadata, that is then stored on
an external server. Later, data owner can interact with the server to carry out a
search on the database and obtain the results (this is also called the symmetric
setting as there is only one writer to the database, the owner, who uses symmetric encryption.) Single-writer/multi-reader SE allows an arbitrary group of
parties other than the owner to submit search queries. The owner can control
the search access by granting and revoking searching privileges to other users.

In the setting of searching on public-key-encrypted data, users who encrypt
the data can be different from the owner of the decryption key. This creates
the model for multi-writer/single-reader SE. A more generalized model further
allows every user to write an encrypted document to the database as well as to
search within the encrypted domain, including those ciphertexts produced by
other users. This is the multi-reader/multi-writer setting.

In the rest of the paper, we focus on the single-writer/multi-reader setting. In
this framework, whenever a reader (or client) wants to search over the database,
she usually needs to perform a per-query interaction with the writer (or data
owner) and asks the data owner to produce and send back the necessary trapdoor
information to help her carry out the search, as shown in the representative
work [16]. Thus, the data owner is required to be online all the time. However,
the initial goal of the data owner is to outsource his storage and services to the
cloud server, so removing the per-query interaction between the data owner and
the client is a desired feature.

1.1 Our Contributions

In this work, we first present a deterministic and memory-efficient hash function,
which maps keywords to primes. With this function, we then propose an efficient
non-interactive multi-client searchable encryption in the single-writer/ multi -
reader setting, with support for boolean queries. Our construction enjoys the
following nice features:

1. Our construction is motivated by the searchable symmetric encryption (SSE)
   protocol of Cash et al. [7] (CASH). When compared to its multi-client version [16] (MULTI), we improve the communication overhead between the
   data owner and the client significantly. In fact, MULTI requires the client to
   interact with the data owner each time she wants to search on database. For
   each query, the data owner responds by generating a partial search token and

sending it back to the client. Then the client generates the full token and forwards it to the server to facilitate the searching process. In return, the server sends to the client an encrypted index (or document identifier), by decrypting which the client gets the plaintext document identifier. In our construction, we totally eliminate the interactive process, except at the beginning the client needs to obtain a search-authorized private key from the data owner for some permitted keywords. With the private key, the client can generate a search token for any boolean queries on those permitted keywords. In the return of the encrypted indices from the server, the client is also able to decrypt them without obtaining any assistance from the data owner.

2. We also note that there is a naive approach to turn MULTI into non-interactive setting. The data owner can pre-generate all possible search tokens for the client. The number of pre-generated tokens is of order $\mathcal{O}(M)$, where M is the number of possible queries the client is allowed to make. Our construction only requires the data owner to generate a search-authorized secret key to the client. The size of the secret key is of order $\mathcal{O}(1)$, which is actually just 3072 bits (with respect to 1024-bit RSA security) regardless of the number of permitted queries.

3. We deploy Attribute-Based Encryption (ABE) mechanism to allow the client to decrypt the encrypted indices given by the server without any assistance from the data owner. According to our framework, the data owner can also realize fine-grained access control on his data. In addition, the data owner in our protocol does not know which particular queries the client has generated or which documents the client has retrieved, provided that the data owner has authorized the client to search for a set of permitted keywords. In terms of information leakage to the server, we show that our construction is exactly the same as CASH, meaning the transcripts between the client and the server in real protocol can be properly simulated only with the same leakage profile as CASH. Regarding the expressiveness, our protocol is similar to CASH, which allows clients to perform arbitrary boolean queries efficiently.

1.2   Related Works

The first SE by Song et al. [32] is presented in the single-writer/single-reader setting. The first notion of security for SE was introduced by Goh [14]. Curtmola et al. [11] proposed the strong security notion of IND-CKA2. Kurosawa and Ohtaki [19] provided the IND-CKA2 security in the universal composability (UC) model. On the other hand, Boneh et al. [5] introduced the first public key encryption with keyword search, together with the security model in the multi-writer/single-reader architecture.

Kamara et al. [17,18] proposed dynamic SE schemes which allow efficient update of the database. Golle et al. [15] gave the first SE with conjunctive keyword searches, in the single-writer/single-reader setting, but its search time is linear in the number of keywords to search. Most recently, Cash et al. [7] proposed the first sublinear SE with support for boolean queries and efficiently implemented it in a large database [6].

In the single-writer/multi-reader architecture, Curtmola et al. [11] proposed a general construction based on broadcast encryption, which leads to a relatively inefficient implementation. The search time of the scheme by Raykova et al. [29] is linear in the number of documents. The scheme uses deterministic encryption and directly leaks the search pattern in addition to the access pattern. Recently, Jarecki et al. [16] extend the scheme by Cash et al. [7] to a single-writer/multi-reader setting, which preserves all nice features provided by the original scheme but requires a per-query interaction between the data owner and the client.

In the multi-writer/multi-reader setting, a number of schemes [1,3,12,33] were presented with a high level of security, but the search time is linear in the number of keywords per document. The scheme in [27] improved the search complexity by removing the need of TTP in previous schemes. In addition, a stronger model for access pattern privacy was proposed in [30]. However, all these schemes only support single keyword searches.

2   Preliminaries

In this section, we give a list of notations and terminologies (cf. Table 1) used through our work and a brief review of hardness assumptions and cryptographic primitives deployed in our construction.

2.1   Hardness Assumptions

Definition 1 (DDH problem). *Let $\mathbb{G}$ be a cyclic group of prime order p, the decisional Diffie-Hellman (DDH) problem is to distinguish the ensembles $\{(g, g^a, g^b, g^{ab})\}$ from $\{(g, g^a, g^b, g^z)\}$, where the elements $g \in \mathbb{G}$ and $a, b, z \in \mathbb{Z}_p$ are chosen uniformly at random. Formally, the advantage for any PPT distinguisher $\mathcal{D}$ is defined as:*

$$Adv_{\mathcal{D}, \mathbb{G}}^{DDH}(\kappa) = |\Pr[\mathcal{D}(g, g^a, g^b, g^{ab}) = 1] - \Pr[\mathcal{D}(g, g^a, g^b, g^z) = 1]|.$$

We say that the DDH assumption holds if for any PPT distinguisher $\mathcal{D}$, its advantage $Adv_{\mathcal{D}, \mathbb{G}}^{DDH}(\kappa)$ is negligible in κ.

Definition 2 (Strong RSA Problem) [10]. *Let $n = pq$, where p and q are two κ-bit prime numbers such that $p = 2p' + 1$ and $q = 2q' + 1$ for some primes p', q'. Let g be a random element in $\mathbb{Z}_n^*$. We say that an efficient algorithm $\mathcal{A}$ solves the strong RSA problem if it receives as input the tuple (n, g) and outputs two elements (z, e) such that $z^e = g \bmod n$.*

2.2   Pseudorandom Functions

Let $F : \{0,1\}^\kappa \times \mathcal{X} \to \mathcal{Y}$ be a function defined from $\{0,1\}^\kappa \times \mathcal{X}$ to $\mathcal{Y}$. We say F is a pseudorandom function (PRF) if for all efficient adversaries $\mathcal{A}$, its advantage $Adv_{F,\mathcal{A}}^{\mathrm{prf}}(\kappa) = |\Pr[\mathcal{A}^{F(K,\cdot)}(1^\kappa)] - \Pr[\mathcal{A}^{f(\cdot)}(1^\kappa)]| < negl(\kappa)$, where $K \xleftarrow{\$} \{0,1\}^\kappa$ and f is a random function from $\mathcal{X}$ to $\mathcal{Y}$.

Table 1. Notations and terminologies

Notation	Meaning
κ	A security parameter
id_i	The document identifier of the i-th document
W_{id_i}	A list of keywords contained in the i-th document
$DB = (id_i, W_{id_i})_{i=1}^d$	A database consisting of a list of document identifier and keyword-set pairs
$DB[w] = \{id : w \in W_{id}\}$	The set of identifiers of documents that contain keyword w
$W = \bigcup_{i=1}^d W_{id_i}$	The keyword set of the database
RDK	The retrieval decryption key array, used to retrieve the original documents
$\mathcal{U}$	The attribute universe of the system
$[T]$	The set of positive integers not larger than T, i.e., $\{1, 2, \ldots, T\}$
a$\|$b	The concatenation of a and b
$s \xleftarrow{\$} S$	The operation of uniformly sampling a random element s from a set S
sterm	The least frequent term among queried terms (or keywords) in a search query
xterm	Other queried terms in a search query (i.e., the queried terms excluding sterm)
PPT	The abbreviation of probabilistic polynomial time
$negl(\kappa)$	A negligible function in the security parameter κ

2.3   Non-interactive Multi-client Searchable Encryption

In our single-writer/multi-reader (we call it multi-client in the rest of this paper) setting, there are three parties: the data owner of the plaintext database, a service provider that stores the encrypted database, and the clients who want to perform search queries over the database. In more details, the data owner outsources his search service to a cloud server, and generates a search-authorized private key for each client in terms of her credentials. When a client performs a search query, she generates the search token by herself using her own private key and then forwards the token to the service provider. With the token, the server finally retrieves the encrypted identifier or documents for the client. Formally, the syntax of our non-interactive multi-client searchable encryption consists of the following algorithms:

- EDBSetup(1^κ, DB, RDK, $\mathcal{U}$): the data owner takes κ, DB, RDK and $\mathcal{U}$ as input and generates the system master key MK and public key PK, with which he processes the plaintext database DB and outsources the encrypted database EDB and XSet to the server.

- ClientKGen(MK, S, **w**): for a client with attribute set S, the data owner takes MK, S and a set **w** of permitted keywords as input and generates a search-authorized private key sk for the client. Note that **w** is authorized by the data owner according to the client's credentials.
- TokenGen(sk, Q): the client uses her private key sk to produce the search token st for the query Q she wants to perform.
- Search(st, EDB, XSet): with the search token st, the server carries out the search over the encrypted database EDB and XSet and returns the matching results R to the client.
- Retrieve(sk, R): the client uses her private key sk to decrypt the search result R (returned by the sever) and retrieves the original documents using the relevant document identifiers and decryption keys.

2.4 Security Definitions

In this section, we give security definitions of our searchable encryption. In the multi-client setting, we consider both securities with respect to (w.r.t.) the adversarial server and the clients. Similar to [7], we do not model the retrieval of encrypted documents in the security analysis and just focus on the storage and processing of the metadata.

First, let us consider the security w.r.t. the adversarial server, which can be extended straightforwardly from [7]. This security is parameterized by a leakage function $\mathcal{L}$, as described below, which captures information allowed to learn by an adversary from the interaction with a secure scheme. Loosely speaking, the security says that the server's view during an adaptive attack can be properly simulated given only the output of the leakage function $\mathcal{L}$. As in [7], the "adaptive" here means the server selects the database and queries. Moreover, it selects the authorized keywords for each client in our setting.

Let Π = (EDBSetup, ClientKGen, TokenGen, Search) be a searchable encryption scheme and $\mathcal{A}, \mathcal{S}$ be two efficient algorithms. The security is formally defined via a real experiment $\mathbf{Real}^{\Pi}_{\mathcal{A}}(\kappa)$ and an ideal experiment $\mathbf{Ideal}^{\Pi}_{\mathcal{A},\mathcal{S}}(\kappa)$ as follows:

$\mathbf{Real}^{\Pi}_{\mathcal{A}}(\kappa)$: $\mathcal{A}(1^{\kappa})$ chooses a database DB. Then the experiment runs the algorithm (MK, PK, EDB, XSet) $\leftarrow$ EDBSetup(1^{κ}, DB, RDK, $\mathcal{U}$) and returns (PK, EDB, XSet) to $\mathcal{A}$. After that, $\mathcal{A}$ selects a set **w** of authorized keywords for a client and then repeatedly chooses a search query q, where we assume the keywords associated with q are always within the authorized keyword set **w**. To respond, the experiment runs the remaining algorithms in Π (including ClientKGen, TokenGen and Search), and gives the transcript and client output to $\mathcal{A}$. Eventually, the experiment outputs the bit that $\mathcal{A}$ returns.

$\mathbf{Ideal}^{\Pi}_{\mathcal{A},\mathcal{S}}(\kappa)$: The game initializes an empty list **q** and a counter $i = 0$. $\mathcal{A}(1^{\kappa})$ chooses a DB. Then the experiment runs (PK, EDB, XSet) $\leftarrow$ $\mathcal{S}(\mathcal{L}(\text{DB}))$ and gives (PK, EDB, XSet) to $\mathcal{A}$. $\mathcal{A}$ then repeatedly chooses a search query q. To respond, the experiment records this query as **q**$[i]$, increments i and gives the output of $\mathcal{S}(\mathcal{L}(\text{DB}, \mathbf{q}))$ to $\mathcal{A}$, where **q** consists of all previous queries in addition to the latest query issued by $\mathcal{A}$. Eventually, the experiment outputs the bit that $\mathcal{A}$ returns.

Definition 3 (Security w.r.t. Server). *The scheme* Π *is called* $\mathcal{L}$-*semantically-secure against adaptive attacks if for all PPT adversaries* $\mathcal{A}$ *there exists an efficient simulator* $\mathcal{S}$ *such that* $|\Pr[\mathbf{Real}_{\mathcal{A}}^{\Pi}(\kappa) = 1] - \Pr[\mathbf{Ideal}_{\mathcal{A},\mathcal{S}}^{\Pi}(\kappa)]| \leq negl(\kappa)$.

Before going ahead, we first give the description of leakage function $\mathcal{L}$ used in our security analysis. We note that, for sake of simplicity, we only present the detailed security proof of our scheme for conjunctive queries, so we start by describing the leakage function for such a simple scenario. Actually, the scheme and security proof can be readily adapted to any search boolean queries, which will be further discussed later.

In the following, we represent a sequence of T conjunctive queries by $\mathbf{q} = (\mathbf{s}, \mathbf{x})$, where $\mathbf{s}[t]$ and $\mathbf{x}[t, \cdot]$ for $t \in [T]$ denote the sterm and xterms in the t-th query respectively, and each individual query is written as $\mathbf{q}[i] = (\mathbf{s}[i], \mathbf{x}[i, \cdot])$. With DB and $\mathbf{q}$ as input, the leakage function outputs the following leakage items:

- $N = \sum_{i=1}^{d} |W_{id_i}|$ is the number of keyword-document pairs, which is the size of EDB and XSet.
- $\bar{\mathbf{s}} \in \mathbb{N}^T$ is the equality pattern of the sterms $\mathbf{s}$, indicating which queries have the same sterms. It is calculated as an array of integers, such that each integer represents one sterm. For instance, if we have $\mathbf{s} = (a, b, c, a, a)$, then $\bar{\mathbf{s}} = (1, 2, 3, 1, 1)$.
- $SP[\sigma]$ is the size pattern of the queries, which is the number of matching results returned for each stag. Note that we index it by the values of $\bar{\mathbf{s}}$, i.e., $\sigma \in \bar{\mathbf{s}}$, instead of the query number t as in [7], so we have $SP[\bar{\mathbf{s}}[t]] = |DB[\mathbf{s}[t]]|$.
- $RP[t, \alpha] = DB[\mathbf{s}[t]] \cap DB[\mathbf{x}[t, \alpha]]$, where $\mathbf{s}[t] \neq \mathbf{x}[t, \alpha]$, reveals the intersection of the sterm with any other xterm in the same query.
- $SRP[t] = DB[\mathbf{s}[t]]$ is the search result pattern corresponding to the stag of the t-th query.
- $IP[t_1, t_2, \alpha, \beta] = \begin{cases} DB[\mathbf{s}[t_1]] \cap DB[\mathbf{s}[t_2]], & \text{if } \mathbf{s}[t_1] \neq \mathbf{s}[t_2] \text{ and } \mathbf{x}[t_1, \alpha] = \mathbf{x}[t_2, \beta] \\ \emptyset, & \text{otherwise} \end{cases}$
  is the conditional intersection pattern, which is a generalization of the IP structure in [7].
- $XT[t] = |\mathbf{x}[t, \cdot]|$ is the number of xterms in the t-th query.

The leakage function for our protocol is similar to [7], but a number of components have been generalized and some additional components are introduced. The generalization of SP is straightforward. RP has changed a lot. Within a query, it is possible to test the results from the stag against any other keyword, since a full xtoken is sent to the server. RP captures this as the intersection between the sterm and xterms. IP is also generalized, where any of the sterms for each conjunctive query is considered instead of only one xterm per query. Of the additional pieces of leakage, XT is straightforward. However, there is also a component SRP which represents the results corresponding to any sterm. This component overstates the true leakage but is required by the design of the proof.

Actually, RP and IP also overstate the leakage they represent, because the server in real protocol never has access to the unencrypted indices.

Next, we continue to consider the security w.r.t. adversarial clients. In our setting, whenever a legitimate client registers to the system, the data owner assigns a set of keywords and generates the associated private key for the client according to her attributes or credentials. Thus, each client is only permitted to perform search queries on the authorized keywords in our system. Loosely speaking, the security requires that it be impossible to forge a valid search token for a query containing some non-authorized keywords, even for an adaptive client (who can select the authorized keywords by herself). That is, the malicious client is not allowed to gain information beyond what she is authorized for. Formally, the security is defined via the following game $\mathbf{Exp}^{\mathrm{UF}}_{\mathcal{A},token}(\kappa)$ played between a challenger $\mathcal{C}$ and an adversary $\mathcal{A}$:

Initialization: the challenger runs the setup algorithm $(\mathrm{MK}, \mathrm{PK}, \mathrm{EDB}, \mathrm{XSet}) \leftarrow \mathrm{EDBSetup}(1^\kappa, \mathrm{DB}, \mathrm{RDK}, \mathcal{U})$ and returns the system public key PK to the adversary $\mathcal{A}$.
Client key extraction: when receiving a private key extraction request for keywords $\mathbf{w} = (w_1, \ldots, w_n)$, the challenger $\mathcal{C}$ runs the client key generation algorithm $sk \leftarrow \mathrm{ClientKGen}(\mathrm{MK}, S, \mathbf{w})$ and sends back sk to $\mathcal{A}$.
Output: Eventually, the adversary outputs a search token st for a new query containing some keyword $w' \notin \mathbf{w}$, and the challenger outputs 1 if st is valid.

Definition 4 (Security w.r.t. Client). *The search token in* Π *is said to be unforgeable against adaptive clients if for all PPT adversaries* $\mathcal{A}$ *its advantage* $\Pr[\mathbf{Exp}^{\mathrm{UF}}_{\mathcal{A},token}(\kappa) = 1] \leq negl(\kappa)$.

Note that in our syntax search tokens are produced by clients using their private keys, so if the generation of valid tokens is (almost) equivalent to that of the corresponding private key, then the security can be formulated in terms of forging a valid private key instead of a search token (i.e., the goal of the adversary in the game is to finally output a valid private key for some un-authorized keyword $w' \notin \mathbf{w}$). For the proof of our scheme, we will follow the latter equivalent way.

3 A Deterministic, Memory-Efficient Mapping from Keywords to Primes

Before presenting our multi-client SE protocol, we first give an efficient 'keyword to prime' hash function. In our work, we assume that the search index keywords have been mapped during the encrypted database setup to *prime* integers, in order to be compatible with our RSA-based token-derivation function, and that the token generation and search algorithms can re-compute the same correspond-ing primes for the keywords searched by the client. A straightforward approach to implement such a mapping would be to use a lookup table at the data owner and client, storing all keywords and their corresponding primes. While computationally efficient, this approach requires memory storage at the data owner proportional to the total number $|W|$ of keywords in the database index, and memory storage at the client proportional to the number of keywords n to be searched for by this client, which may be prohibitive and would eliminate the advantage of the compact (constant length independent of n) client tokens of our protocol.

In this section, we show how to avoid the storage overheads of the lookup table approach, by constructing a *deterministic* and *memory-efficient* collision-resistant hash function for mapping keywords to their corresponding primes. In this construction, the memory requirements at the data owner and client are constant, indpendent of the number of keywords $|W|$ in the index or the number of keywords n at the client.

Our construction of a 'keyword to prime' collision-resistant hash is a deterministic variant of the randomized 'strings to primes' hash function introduced by Gennaro, Halevi and Rabin [13].

Construction. The main idea is to use the randomized hash function introduced in [13] along with a primality test algorithm, derandomizing the result by using a pseudorandom function (PRF) and choosing the first prime in a psedurandom sequence of integers as the hash output. Our construction builds a collision-resistant 'keyword-to-prime' hash function family $\mathcal{H}$, where each function $h \in \mathcal{H}$ maps the keyword space W to the set $P_{2\kappa}$ of 2κ-bit prime integers. The construction uses the following ingredients:

- A collision-resistant hash family $\bar{\mathcal{H}}$, where each function $\bar{h} \in \bar{\mathcal{H}}$ maps W to the set of κ-bit strings $\{0,1\}^{\kappa}$.
- A PRF family $\mathcal{F}$, where each function $F_k \in \mathcal{F}$ maps $\{0,1\}^{\kappa}$ to $\{0,1\}^{\kappa}$.

We let Int denote the natural mapping from a binary string in $c \in \{0,1\}^{\kappa}$ to the integer $\mathsf{Int}(c)$ in $[0, 2^{\kappa} - 1]$ whose binary representation is c, and denote by Bin its inverse mapping from integers to binary strings. A hash function $h : W \to P_{2\kappa}$ from our family $\mathcal{H}$ is specified by randomly picking a function $\bar{h}$ from the collision-resistant family $\bar{\mathcal{H}}$ and a pseudorandom function F_k from the PRF family $\mathcal{F}$. The algorithm for evaluating the function h on a given keyword $x \in W$ using $(\bar{h}, F_k)$ to get a corresponding prime $w \in P_{2\kappa}$ is presented in Algorithm 1.

Lemma 1. (1) *The hash family $\mathcal{H}$ is collision-resistant if the hash family $\bar{\mathcal{H}}$ is collision-resistant.* (2) *Furthermore, if family $\mathcal{F}$ is a pseudorandom function family, and the density of primes in the intervals $[2^{\kappa} \cdot \bar{h}(x), 2^{\kappa} \cdot \bar{h}(x) + 2^{\kappa} - 1]$ is $\geq 1/\ln(2^{2\kappa})$ for each x (as heuristically expected from the Prime Number Theorem), then for each input $x \in W$ and $m \geq 1$, the number of iterations of the while loop in Algorithm 1 is $\leq 1.4 \cdot m \cdot \kappa$, except with probability negligibly larger than $\exp(-m)$.*

We now estimate the practical cost of evaluating our hash function h. The memory storage costs are constant (independent of the size of the keyword set W), namely the cost of storing the two keys for the functions $\bar{h}$ and the

Algorithm 1. h: Hashing from Keywords to Primes

Input: keyword $x \in W$, functions $\bar{h} : W \rightarrow \{0,1\}^\kappa \in \bar{\mathcal{H}}$, $F_k : \{0,1\}^\kappa \rightarrow \{0,1\}^\kappa \in \mathcal{F}$
Output: prime integer $w \in P_{2\kappa}$
1: foundprime $\leftarrow$ False
2: $r \leftarrow 0$.
3: **while** foundprime $=$ False **do**
4:      let $w \leftarrow 2^\kappa \cdot \mathsf{Int}(\bar{h}(x)) + \mathsf{Int}(F_k(\mathsf{Bin}(r)))$ // random int. with MS bits equal to $\bar{h}(x)$
5:      **if** w is prime **then**
6:          let foundprime $\leftarrow$ True
7:      **end if**
8:      let $r \leftarrow r + 1 \bmod 2^\kappa$
9: **end while**
10: **return** w.

PRF F_k. The main computation cost in Algorithm 1 is the cost of each primality check of the 2κ-bit integer w in the iterations of the while loop. According to Lemma 1 with $m = 3$, the number of such primality tests would be $L \leq 4.2 \cdot \kappa$, except with small probability ≈ 0.05. Let $T_{\exp}(2\kappa)$ denote the time needed to compute a full exponentiation modulo a 2κ-bit modulus. Assuming that we implement these primality checks using a Miller-Rabin probabilistic primality test [25,28], the expected cost [31, Chap. 10] of these L tests (at a $2^{-\kappa}$ false positive probability) would be at most $\kappa/2$ exponentiations modulo a 2κ-bit integer for the last while loop iteration, plus an expected ≤ 2 exponentiations modulo a 2κ-bit modulus for all other $L - 1$ iterations (which give composites), giving a total expected time of $T_h \leq (\kappa/2 + 2 \cdot L) \cdot T_{\exp}(2\kappa)$. Furthermore, using fast trial division by small primes up to (say) 101 before testing with Miller-Rabin, would reduce the number of dominant Miller-Rabin tests to $L_{\mathrm{MR}} \approx (\prod_{\mathrm{prime}\ p \leq 101} \frac{p-1}{p}) \cdot L \leq 0.11 \cdot L$. Thus, the overall expected time for evaluating our hash function would be

$$T_h \leq (\kappa/2 + 0.22 \cdot L) \cdot T_{\exp}(2\kappa) \approx 1.5\kappa \cdot T_{\exp}(2\kappa).$$

Thus, for a typical security parameter $\kappa = 100$, we estimate T_h to be equivalent to about $150 \cdot T_{\exp}(200)$ (i.e. 150 exponentiations with a 200-bit modulus). To put this into context with the rest of our protocol, the latter requires during each token generation to perform an exponentiation modulo a $\lambda \approx 2048$-bit modulus (to make sure the RSA problem has a $\approx 2^{100}$ secrity level) for each keyword w. Since the time $T_{\exp}(\kappa)$ for an exponentiation modulo a κ-bit modulus is, assuming classical arithmetic, at least quadratic in κ, we have $T_{\exp}(\lambda)/T_{\exp}(2\kappa) = T_{\exp}(2048)/T_{\exp}(200) \geq (2048/200)^2 \approx 104$, so the cost of evaluating our hash function for w is expected to be only $T_h \approx 150/104 \cdot T_{\exp}(2048) \approx 1.44 \cdot T_{\exp}(2048)$, i.e. equivalent to only 1.44 exponetiations with a 2048-bit modulus, thus adding only a reasonable overhead to the computation time of our protocol for typical security parameters (2.44 exponentiations instead of 1 exponentiation modulo 2048-bit per keyword).

4   Our Construction

In this section, we present our SE scheme which mainly consists of four algorithms Π = (EDBSetup, ClientKGen, TokenGen, Search). For completeness, we also give the description of a simple original document retrieval algorithm Retrieve, by which the client finally retrieves the desired documents from the cloud server. In our construction, we deploy CP-ABE as a primitive, which has been an effective and scalable access control mechanism for encrypted data and generally consists of four algorithms ABE = (ABE.Setup, ABE.KeyGen, ABE.Enc, ABE.Dec). For its formal syntax and semantic security, please refer to [4]. We always assume that the set $W = \bigcup_{i=1}^{d} W_{id_i}$ of keywords in DB = $(id_i, W_{id_i})_{i=1}^{d}$ consists of distinct primes, which are mapped from the real keywords by our 'keyword to prime' function given in Sect. 3, and that a specific policy $\mathbb{A}$ is implicitly specified for each document identifier id_i.

EDBSetup(1^κ, DB, RDK, $\mathcal{U}$): takes as input a security parameter κ, a database DB = $(id_i, W_i)_{i=1}^{d}$, a retrieval decryption key array RDK and an attribute universe $\mathcal{U}$, it chooses big primes p, q, random keys K_I, K_Z, K_X for a PRF F_p and K_S for a PRF F. Then it outputs the system master key MK = $(p, q, K_S, K_I, K_Z, K_X, g_1, g_2, g_3, msk)$ and the corresponding system public key PK = (n, g, mpk), where $(mpk, msk) \leftarrow$ ABE.Setup($1^\kappa, \mathcal{U}$), $n = pq$, $g \xleftarrow{\$} \mathbb{G}$ and $g_i \xleftarrow{\$} \mathbb{Z}_n^*$ for $i \in [3]$. Then it generates the encrypted database EDB and XSet with the system keys as the following Algorithm 2.

Algorithm 2. EDB Setup Algorithm

Input: MK, PK, DB, RDK
Output: EDB, XSet
 1: **function** EDBGEN(MK, PK, DB, RDK)
 2:     EDB $\leftarrow$ {}; XSet $\leftarrow \emptyset$
 3:     **for** $w \in W$ **do**
 4:         $c \leftarrow 1$; $\text{stag}_w \leftarrow F(K_S, g_1^{1/w} \bmod n)$
 5:         **for** $id \in$ DB[w] **do**
 6:             $\ell \leftarrow F(\text{stag}_w, c)$; $e \leftarrow$ ABE.Enc($mpk, id||k_{id}, \mathbb{A}$)
 7:             $\text{xind} \leftarrow F_p(K_I, id)$; $z \leftarrow F_p(K_Z, g_2^{1/w} \bmod n||c)$
 8:             $y \leftarrow \text{xind} \cdot z^{-1}$; $\text{xtag} \leftarrow g^{F_p(K_X, g_3^{1/w} \bmod n) \cdot \text{xind}}$
 9:             EDB[ℓ] = (e, y); XSet $\leftarrow$ XSet $\cup$ {xtag}
10:             $c \leftarrow c + 1$
11:         **end for**
12:     **end for**
13:     **return** EDB, XSet
14: **end function**

ClientKGen(MK, S, **w**): assuming that a legitimate client with attribute set S is permitted to perform searches over keywords **w** = $(w_1, w_2, \ldots, w_n)$, the data owner generates a corresponding private key $sk = (K_S, K_I, K_Z, K_X, sk_S, sk_\mathbf{w})$, where $sk_S \leftarrow$ ABE.KeyGen(msk, S) and $sk_\mathbf{w} = (sk_\mathbf{w}^{(1)}, sk_\mathbf{w}^{(2)}, sk_\mathbf{w}^{(3)})$ is computed as

---

Algorithm 3. Token Generation Algorithm

Input: sk, Q
Output: st
1: **function** TOKENGEN(sk, Q)
2:     $st, \mathsf{xtoken} \leftarrow \{\}; \ \bar{\mathbf{s}} \leftarrow \emptyset$
3:     $\bar{\mathbf{s}} \leftarrow \bar{\mathbf{s}} \cup \{w'_1\}$
4:     $\mathbf{x} \leftarrow \bar{\mathbf{w}} \setminus \bar{\mathbf{s}}$
5:     $\mathsf{stag} \leftarrow F\big(K_S, (sk_{\mathbf{w}}^{(1)})^{\prod_{w \in \mathbf{w} \setminus \{w'_1\}} w} \bmod n\big) = F(K_S, g_1^{1/w'_1} \bmod n)$
6:     **for** $c = 1, 2, \ldots$ until the server stops **do**
7:         **for** $i = 2, \ldots, m$ **do**
8:             $\mathsf{xtoken}[c, i] \leftarrow g^{F_p(K_Z, (sk_{\mathbf{w}}^{(2)})^{\prod_{w \in \mathbf{w} \setminus \{w'_1\}} w} \bmod n || c) \cdot F_p(K_X, (sk_{\mathbf{w}}^{(3)})^{\prod_{w \in \mathbf{w} \setminus \{w'_i\}} w} \bmod n)}$
              $= g^{F_p(K_Z, g_2^{1/w'_1} \bmod n || c) \cdot F_p(K_X, g_3^{1/w'_i} \bmod n)}$
9:         **end for**
10:     **end for**
11:     $st \leftarrow (\mathsf{stag}, \mathsf{xtoken})$
12:     **return** st
13: **end function**

$$sk_{\mathbf{w}}^{(i)} = \left(g_i^{1/\prod_{j=1}^{n} w_j} \bmod n\right) \text{ for } i \in [3].$$

At last, the data owner sends back sk together with $\mathbf{w}$ to the client, where we implicitly assume that the keyword appearance frequency satisfies $|w_1| < |w_2| < \cdots < |w_n|$.

TokenGen(sk, Q): whenever the client wants to search a boolean query Q on keywords $\bar{\mathbf{w}} \subseteq \mathbf{w}$, she first chooses sterms $\bar{\mathbf{s}} \subseteq \bar{\mathbf{w}}$ according to the query Q. For simplicity, we take the conjunctive query, $Q = w'_1 \wedge w'_2 \wedge \cdots \wedge w'_m$, as an example and assume that w'_1 is the chosen sterm, then the search token st (including stags and xtoken) for this query is computed as in Algorithm 3.

Search$(st, \mathsf{EDB}, \mathsf{XSet})$: takes the search token $st = (\mathsf{stag}, \mathsf{xtoken}[1], \mathsf{xtoken}[2], \cdots)$ for a query Q and $(\mathsf{EDB}, \mathsf{XSet})$, the server returns the search result R as in Algorithm 4.

Retrieve(sk, R): the client with private key sk_S decrypts the encrypted indices (search result R) and gets the matching document identifiers and retrieval decryption keys:

- For each $e \in \mathrm{R}$, recover $(id||k_{id}) \leftarrow \mathsf{ABE.Dec}(sk_S, e)$ if the client's attributes in S satisfy the access policy $\mathbb{A}$ assigned by the data owner to document identifier id.
- Send id to the server, get the encrypted document $ct = \mathsf{Enc}(k_{id}, doc)$, and retrieve the document $doc = \mathsf{Dec}(k_{id}, ct)$ with the corresponding symmetric key k_{id}.

Note that our protocol is derived from CASH and the RSA function, its correctness is easy to verify, which follows from the correctness of CASH and the underlying ABE. In addition, it is easy to observe that the plaintext identifiers

Algorithm 4. Search Algorithm
***
Input: $st = (\text{stag}, \text{xtoken}[1], \text{xtoken}[2], \cdots), \text{EDB}, \text{XSet}$
Output: R
 1: **function** SEARCH(st, EDB, XSet)
 2:     $R \leftarrow \{\}$
 3:     **for** stag $\in$ stags **do**
 4:         $c \leftarrow 1; \ell \leftarrow F(\text{stag}, c)$
 5:         **while** $\ell \in$ EDB **do**
 6:             $(e, y) \leftarrow \text{EDB}[\ell]$
 7:             **if** $\text{xtoken}[c, i]^y \in$ XSet for all i **then**
 8:                 $R \leftarrow R \cup \{e\}$
 9:             **end if**
10:             $c \leftarrow c + 1; \ell \leftarrow F(\text{stag}, c)$
11:         **end while**
12:     **end for**
13:     **return** R
14: **end function**
***

are leaked to the server during the second step of our Retrieve procedure, which in fact can be avoided by deploying e.g., blind storage in [26]. In this work, we are mainly concerned with search on encrypted indices, for more details about blind storage please refer to [26].

5   Security Analysis

In this section, we show the security of our protocol against the adaptive server and the client one after another. Similar to [7], we first give a proof of security against non-adaptive attacks w.r.t. server, and further discuss the proof of full security later. As to the security w.r.t. client, we use a slight variant of security definition where the goal of the adversarial client is to generate a new valid private key.

Theorem 1. *Our scheme* Π *is* $\mathcal{L}$*-semantically secure against non-adaptive attacks where* $\mathcal{L}$ *is the leakage function defined as before, assuming that the DDH assumption holds in* $\mathbb{G}$*, that* F *and* F_p *are secure PRFs and that* ABE *is a CPA secure attribute-based encryption.*

Theorem 2. *Our scheme* Π *is secure against malicious clients, i.e., search token in* Π *is unforgeable against adaptive attacks, assuming that the strong RSA assumption holds.*

Theorem 3. *Let* $\mathcal{L}$ *be the leakage function defined before, our scheme* Π *is* $\mathcal{L}$*-semantically secure against adaptive attacks, assuming that the DDH assumption holds in* $\mathbb{G}$*, that* F *and* F_p *are secure PRFs and that* ABE *is a CPA secure attribute-based encryption.*

We remark that for lack of space, we omit the detailed proofs here, which will be given in the full version.

6   Further Extension

For sake of simplicity, we only presented our protocol and its security analysis for the case of conjunctive queries. Similar to [7,16], our protocol can also be readily adapted to support such form of boolean queries "$w_1 \wedge \psi(w_2, \ldots, w_m)$", where ψ is a boolean formula over the keywords $(w_2, \ldots, w_m)$ and w_i belongs to the client's permitted keyword set $\mathbf{w}$. In this case, the client calculates the stag corresponding w_1 and the xtoken for the other keywords and forwards the search token (stag, xtoken) and the boolean formula ψ to the server. Then the server uses stag to retrieve the tuples (e, y) containing w_1. The only difference from the conjunctive case for the server is the way he determines which tuples match the sub-boolean query ψ. For the t-th tuple, instead of checking if $\mathsf{xtoken}[c, i]^y \in \mathsf{XSet}$ for all $2 \leq i \leq m$, the server will set a series of boolean variables $v_2, \ldots, v_m$ such that

$$v_i = \begin{cases} 1, & \mathsf{xtoken}[c, i]^y \in \mathsf{XSet} \\ 0, & \text{otherwise} \end{cases},$$

and evaluate the value of $\psi(v_2, \ldots, v_m)$. If it is true, meaning the tuple matches the query, the server returns the encrypted index e. Clearly, the search complexity for such boolean queries is still $\mathcal{O}(|\mathsf{DB}[w_1]|)$, the same as for conjunctive queries. For the same set of keywords, the leakage information to the server for boolean case is also the same as for the conjunctive case, except that the boolean formula ψ is exposed to the server too. Hence, the proof for this case can also be readily adapted. For the support of other boolean queries, please refer to the details of [7].

7   Security and Performance Comparison

In general, we focus on the privacy of data owner in (multi-client) searchable encryption settings. In some scenarios, however, the clients may not want the data owner to get the information about the search queries they made or hope that the data owner learns as little as possible about the queries performed by themselves.

To achieve the additional property mentioned above, Jarecki et al. [16] further augmented their multi-client SSE to the outsourced private information retrieval (OSPIR) setting. Same as the underlying protocol, the enhanced protocol OSPIR still requires the clients to interact with the data owner and to submit each boolean formula for each boolean query, although it enables to hide the exact queried values from data owner. Our initial goal is to avoid the interaction between the data owner and the clients, but we also succeed to protect the privacy of the clients to some extent. More precisely, the data owner in our multi-client SE only knows the queried values belong to the keyword set that is authorized by the data owner according to the client's credentials at the beginning, but he has no means to learn what kind of queries the client made. Moreover, he cannot learn the exact queried values of the search. Therefore, our multi-client SSE also enjoys some additional nice security features.

In contrast to previous works such as [7,16], we further enforce the security of documents by employing CP-ABE to encrypt the document identifiers and retrieval decryption keys, by which our protocol realizes the fine-grained access control on the documents at the same time. In this case, even though the client can retrieve many encrypted indices, she still cannot learn the matching document identifiers and retrieval keys if her attributes do not satisfy the access policy associated with the ciphertext (encrypted index). Regarding the leakage information learned by the server, it is easy to observe that our protocol is exactly the same as [7,16].

Both our protocol and MULTI [16] are based on the CASH [7], but they rely on different methods and have distinct features. Compared to MULTI, our protocol manages to avoid the interaction between the data owner and the client, except at the beginning the client gets a search-authorized private key for some permitted keyword set. Moreover, as discussed before, we achieve the fine-grained access control on the stored documents by leveraging the ABE technique. Identical to MULTI, our protocol also supports any boolean queries. All the functionality features are summarized in Table 2.

Table 2. Functionality analysis

Reference	Query-type	Multi-user	Interaction[a]	Access control
Cash et al. [7]	Boolean	No	-	No
Jarecki et al. [16]	Boolean	Yes	Yes	No
Our scheme	Boolean	Yes	No	Yes

[a]The interaction needed between the data owner and the clients whenever a client performs search queries.

In the above, we give a brief security and function analysis of our protocol and a comparison with the representative multi-client SSE in [16] (MULTI). Next, we continue to analyze the efficiency of our protocol. Due to the fact that both our protocol and the MULTI are under the framework of CASH, the communication overhead between the data owner and the server (mainly contributed by (EDB, XSet) during the setup phase) and that between the client and the server (mainly contributed by (stag, xtoken) during the search phase) are almost identical, except that in our protocol document identifiers are encrypted via ABE instead of symmetric encryption. Beside the storage overhead introduced by the ABE ciphertext, using ABE also brings some computational cost to the data owner in contrast to exploiting symmetric encryption. In addition, the data owner needs to compute one extra exponentiation (i.e., the RSA function) for each calculation of the PRF during the setup phase, totally introducing $(2\sum_{w\in W}|DB[w]| + |W|)$ exponentiation operations for the whole database. Fortunately, the encrypted database (EDB, XSet) are outsourced to the server once and forever, hence in this part we focus on analyzing the communication overhead between the data owner and the client as well as their computational cost introduced by the frequent search queries.

For a conjunctive query, e.g., $Q = (w_1 \land w_2 \land \cdots \land w_m)$ performed by a client, we assume that the associated keywords belong to the client's authorized keyword set $\mathbf{w}$, i.e., $w_i \in \mathbf{w}$ for $i \in [m]$. To perform such a search, the client in [16] has to interact with the data owner each time and gets the corresponding trapdoor information and authentication information, where the data owner needs to calculate $(m - 1)$ exponentiations and an authenticated encryption. In contrast, the client in our protocol only needs to get from the data owner some keyword-related (and attribute-related) secret information at the beginning, where the data owner needs to computes 3 exponentiations and generates an attribute-related secret key for each client, and then she can perform the following searches by herself at the cost of introducing $(m + 1)$ additional exponentiations to the generation of xtoken. Note that following our approach the client needs not to intact with the data owner ever after receiving her secret key because she can use the keyword-related part to generate the search tokens by herself only if she performs a query complying to the authorized keyword set. Therefore, once the data owner in our protocol outsourced his data to the server, he needs not to be online all the time. Precisely, the communication (comm.) overhead and the computational (comp.) cost w.r.t. the data owner and the client during each query are summarized in Table 3. We remark that in the table we only focus on the main comm. overhead and comp. cost contributed by the queried keywords, and omit the less contributed part, e.g., AuthEnc in [16] and ABE.KeyGen (which is only computed once for each client) in our protocol.

Table 3. Communication overhead between client and data owner & their computational cost

Conjunctive query $Q = (w_1 \land w_2 \land \cdots \land w_m)$, where $w_i \in \mathbf{w}$			
Reference	Comm. overhead	Data owner's comp. cost	Clients' comp. cost
Cash et al. [7]	-	$|DB[w_1]|(m - 1) \cdot \exp$	-
Jarecki et al. [16]	$(m - 1)|\mathbb{G}|$	$(m - 1) \cdot \exp$	$|DB[w_1]|(m - 1) \cdot \exp$
Our scheme	$3|\mathbb{Z}_n^*|$	$3 \cdot \exp$	$(|DB[w_1]|(m - 1) + (m + 1)) \cdot \exp$

exp: the exponentiation operation on the group; $|\cdot|$: the size of a finite set or group, e.g., $|\mathbb{G}|$; $\mathbf{w}$: the authorized keyword set for a client.

It is easy to see from this table the communication complexity of our protocol for each conjunctive query is $\mathcal{O}(1)$, even taking into account of all the other part of the private key, e.g., the attribute-related key sk_S, and that of Jarecki et al. [16] is $\mathcal{O}(m)$. Moreover, when the client performs k conjunctive queries, which are assumed comply to her authorized keyword set $\mathbf{w}$, the complexity of our protocol remains the same but that of [16] is $\mathcal{O}(k \cdot m)$, which increases linearly with the number of legitimate queries.

8   Conclusions

In this paper we present a new efficient multi-client searchable encryption protocol based on the RSA function. Our protocol avoids the per-query interaction between the data owner and the client, which decreases their communication overhead significantly. Meanwhile, our protocol can protect the privacy of the client to some extent. Precisely, the data owner in our protocol only knows the permitted search keyword set of the client, but has no means to learn the exact type of search queries or documents. Moreover, by employing attribute-based encryption, our protocol realizes fine-grained access control on the stored data. Support for searchability and access control simultaneously is actually a desirable feature in the practical data sharing scenarios. However, our current protocol only allows one data owner to share his data with many clients. We leave as an open problem to construct a system with the same advantages of ours while also support multi-data owner setting.

Acknowledgement. This work is supported by National Natural Science Foundation of China (61472083) and Australian Research Council (ARC), ARC Discovery Grant DP150100285.

References

1. Asghar, M.R., Russello, G., Crispo, B., Ion, M.: Supporting complex queries and access policies for multi-user encrypted databases. In: CCSW 2013, Berlin, Germany, 4 November, pp. 77–88 (2013)
2. Baek, J., Vu, Q.H., Liu, J.K., Huang, X., Xiang, Y.: A secure cloud computing based framework for big data information management of smart grid. IEEE Trans. Cloud Comput. **3**(2), 233–244 (2015)
3. Bao, F., Deng, R.H., Ding, X., Yang, Y.: Private query on encrypted data in multi-user settings. In: Chen, L., Mu, Y., Susilo, W. (eds.) ISPEC 2008. LNCS, vol. 4991, pp. 71–85. Springer, Heidelberg (2008)
4. Bethencourt, J., Sahai, A., Waters, B.: Ciphertext-policy attribute-based encryption. In: IEEE S&P 2007, Oakland, California, USA, 20–23 May 2007, pp. 321–334 (2007)
5. Boneh, D., Di Crescenzo, G., Ostrovsky, R., Persiano, G.: Public key encryption with keyword search. In: Cachin, C., Camenisch, J.L. (eds.) EUROCRYPT 2004. LNCS, vol. 3027, pp. 506–522. Springer, Heidelberg (2004)
6. Cash, D., Jaeger, J., Jarecki, S., Jutla, C., Krawczyk, H., Rosu, M., Steiner, M.: Dynamic searchable encryption in very-large databases: data structures and implementation. In: NDSS 2014, San Diego, California, USA, 23–26 February 2014
7. Cash, D., Jarecki, S., Jutla, C., Krawczyk, H., Roşu, M.-C., Steiner, M.: Highly-scalable searchable symmetric encryption with support for boolean queries. In: Canetti, R., Garay, J.A. (eds.) CRYPTO 2013, Part I. LNCS, vol. 8042, pp. 353–373. Springer, Heidelberg (2013)
8. Chase, M., Kamara, S.: Structured encryption and controlled disclosure. In: Abe, M. (ed.) ASIACRYPT 2010. LNCS, vol. 6477, pp. 577–594. Springer, Heidelberg (2010)

9. Chu, C., Zhu, W.T., Han, J., Liu, J.K., Xu, J., Zhou, J.: Security concerns in popular cloud storage services. IEEE Pervasive Comput. **12**(4), 50–57 (2013)

10. Cramer, R., Shoup, V.: Signature schemes based on the strong RSA assumption. In: ACM CCS 1999, Singapore, 1–4 November 1999, pp. 46–51 (1999)

11. Curtmola, R., Garay, J.A., Kamara, S., Ostrovsky, R.: Searchable symmetric encryption: improved definitions and efficient constructions. In: ACM CCS 2006, Alexandria, VA, USA, 30 October–3 November 2006, pp. 79–88 (2006)

12. Dong, C., Russello, G., Dulay, N.: Shared and searchable encrypted data for untrusted servers. In: Atluri, V. (ed.) DAS 2008. LNCS, vol. 5094, pp. 127–143. Springer, Heidelberg (2008)

13. Gennaro, R., Halevi, S., Rabin, T.: Secure hash-and-sign signatures without the random oracle. In: Stern, J. (ed.) EUROCRYPT 1999. LNCS, vol. 1592, pp. 123–139. Springer, Heidelberg (1999)

14. Goh, E.: Secure indexes. IACR Cryptology ePrint Archive, 2003:216 (2003)

15. Golle, P., Staddon, J., Waters, B.: Secure conjunctive keyword search over encrypted data. In: Jakobsson, M., Yung, M., Zhou, J. (eds.) ACNS 2004. LNCS, vol. 3089, pp. 31–45. Springer, Heidelberg (2004)

16. Jarecki, S., Jutla, C., Krawczyk, H., Rosu, M., Steiner, M.: Outsourced symmetric private information retrieval. In: ACM CCS 2013, pp. 875–888. ACM (2013)

17. Kamara, S., Papamanthou, C.: Parallel and dynamic searchable symmetric encryption. In: FC 2013, Okinawa, Japan, 1–5 April 2013, pp. 258–274 (2013)

18. Kamara, S., Papamanthou, C., Roeder, T.: Dynamic searchable symmetric encryption. In: ACM CCS 2012, Raleigh, NC, USA, 16–18 October 2012, pp. 965–976 (2012)

19. Kurosawa, K., Ohtaki, Y.: UC-secure searchable symmetric encryption. In: FC 2012, Kralendijk, Bonaire, 27 Februray–2 March 2012, pp. 285–298 (2012)

20. Liang, K., Au, M.H., Liu, J.K., Susilo, W., Wong, D.S., Yang, G., Phuong, T.V.X., Xie, Q.: A dfa-based functional proxy re-encryption scheme for secure public cloud data sharing. IEEE Trans. Inf. Forensics Secur. **9**(10), 1667–1680 (2014)

21. Liang, K., Liu, J.K., Wong, D.S., Susilo, W.: An efficient cloud-based revocable identity-based proxy re-encryption scheme for public clouds data sharing. In: Kutyłowski, M., Vaidya, J. (eds.) ICAIS 2014, Part I. LNCS, vol. 8712, pp. 257–272. Springer, Heidelberg (2014)

22. Liang, K., Susilo, W., Liu, J.K.: Privacy-preserving ciphertext multi-sharing control for big data storage. IEEE Trans. Inf. Forensics Secur. **10**(8), 1578–1589 (2015)

23. Liu, J., Huang, X., Liu, J.K.: Secure sharing of personal health records in cloud computing: ciphertext-policy attribute-based signcryption. Future Gener. Comp. Syst. **52**, 67–76 (2015)

24. Liu, J.K., Liang, K., Susilo, W., Liu, J., Xiang, Y.: Two-factor data security protection mechanism for cloud storage system. IEEE Trans. Comput. **65**(6), 1992–2004 (2016)

25. Miller, G.L.: Riemann's hypothesis and tests for primality. J. Comput. Syst. Sci. **13**(3), 300–317 (1976)

26. Naveed, M., Prabhakaran, M., Gunter, C.A.: Dynamic searchable encryption via blind storage. In: IEEE SP 2014, Berkeley, CA, USA, 18–21 May 2014, pp. 639–654 (2014)

27. Popa, R.A., Zeldovich, N.: Multi-key searchable encryption. IACR Cryptology ePrint Archive 2013:508 (2013)

28. Rabin, M.O.: Probabilistic algorithm for testing primality. J. Number Theor. **12**(1), 128–138 (1980)

29. Raykova, M., Vo, B., Bellovin, S.M., Malkin, T.: Secure anonymous database search. In: CCSW 2009, Chicago, IL, USA, 13 November 2009, pp. 115–126 (2009)

30. Van Rompay, C., Molva, R., Önen, M.: Multi-user searchable encryption in the cloud. In: López, J., Mitchell, C.J. (eds.) ISC 2015. LNCS, vol. 9290, pp. 299–316. Springer, Heidelberg (2015)

31. Shoup, V.: A Computational Introduction to Number Theory and Algebra. Cambridge University Press, New York (2008). Also available on the Internet

32. Song, D.X., Wagner, D., Perrig, A.: Practical techniques for searches on encrypted data. In: IEEE S&P 2000, Berkeley, California, USA, 14–17 May 2000, pp. 44–55 (2000)

33. Yang, Y., Lu, H., Weng, J.: Multi-user private keyword search for cloud computing. In: CloudCom 2011, Athens, Greece, 29 November–1 December 2011, pp. 264–271 (2011)

Efficient Encrypted Keyword Search for Multi-user Data Sharing

Aggelos Kiayias[1], Ozgur Oksuz[2(✉)], Alexander Russell[2], Qiang Tang[3], and Bing Wang[2]

[1] University of Edinburgh, Edinburgh, UK
`aggelos@cse.uconn.edu`
[2] University of Connecticut, Storrs, USA
{`ozgur.oksuz,bing`}`@engr.uconn.edu, acr@cse.uconn.edu`
[3] Cornell University/NJIT, Ithaca, USA
`qt44@cornell.edu`

Abstract. In this paper, we provide a secure and efficient encrypted keyword search scheme for multi-user data sharing. Specifically, a data owner outsources a set of encrypted files to an untrusted server, shares it with a set of users, and a user is allowed to search keywords in a subset of files that he is authorized to access. In the proposed scheme, (a) each user has a constant size secret key, (b) each user generates a constant size trapdoor for a keyword without getting any help from any party (e.g., data owner), independent of the number of files that he is authorized to search, and (c) for the keyword ciphertexts of a file, the network bandwidth usage (from the data owner to the server) and storage overhead at the server do not depend on the number of users that are authorized to access the file. We show that our scheme has data privacy and trapdoor privacy. While several recent studies are on secure keyword search for data sharing, we show that they either suffer from scalability issues or lack user privacy.

Keywords: Data sharing · Keyword search · Broadcast encryption

1 Introduction

Cloud computing has become a prevalent and economic platform for users to outsource and share data. For instance, through a file or picture sharing service (e.g., Dropbox, Flickr), users can conveniently upload files or pictures to the cloud to share them with their friends, family or colleagues. In a health information sharing system, a number of research institutes and hospitals may share medical data to facilitate collaboration and accelerate scientific discovery. In such data sharing applications, the sensitive nature of the data means that it is necessary for data owners to encrypt the data before outsourcing it

Research supported by H2020 Project Panoramix # 653497.

I. Askoxylakis et al. (Eds.): ESORICS 2016, Part I, LNCS 9878, pp. 173–195, 2016.
DOI: 10.1007/978-3-319-45744-4_9

to the cloud. On the other hand, useful functions, e.g., searching over the out-sourced encrypted data, should still be supported to preserve the utility of the data. Another complication in such data sharing applications is that data owners often selectively share data with others. For instance, Alice may want to share family pictures with her family members, while share work related files with her colleagues. As such, a user can only have access to a subset of the files that are permitted by the corresponding data owners. Since different users have access to different files, a natural way for encryption is that a data owner encrypts different files using different keys. After that, a data owner gives each user the encryption/decryption keys of all the files that the user is authorized to search. This trivial solution is clearly inefficient. First, the number of keys that the data owner needs to send to a user depends on the number of files. Secondly, the number of trapdoors (or tokens) that a user needs to submit when searching for a keyword also depends on the number of files.

In a recent study [25], Popa and Zeldovich solve the above problem by propos-ing a *multi-key searchable encryption* scheme that allows a user to provide a *single* search token to the server, while allowing the server to search for the (encrypted) keyword in documents encrypted with *different* keys. Their solution requires each data owner to send the server some public information (delta val-ues) for each user that is allowed to search a file. In general, suppose a data owner has m files, each file is shared with up to n users, and each file contains up to k keywords, the data owner needs to outsource $O(m(n + k))$ amount of data to the server to support keyword search, where $O(mn)$ and $O(mk)$ corre-spond to delta values and keyword ciphertexts, respectively. As a result, both the network bandwidth overhead (from the data owner to the server) and stor-age overhead (at the server) are $O(m(n + k))$. While the overhead associated with outsourcing keyword ciphertexts is unavoidable, it is desirable to reduce the overhead for outsourcing the delta values, which can dominate the overhead when $k \ll n$ (e.g., for a picture with a small number of keywords but shared with many users).

Our contributions. Our contributions are as follows:

- We give an efficient encrypted keyword search scheme for multi-user data sharing that overcomes the drawbacks in [25]. Specifically, in our scheme, when a data owner has m files, each file has up to k keywords, to support encrypted keyword search by up to n users, the data owner only needs to outsource $O(mk)$ amount of information to the cloud. Given that outsourcing keyword ciphertexts is unavoidable (which is $O(mk)$), our scheme is asymptotically optimal in network bandwidth usage and cloud storage. In addition, each user has constant size secret keys and generates constant size trapdoor for a keyword search in all the files that he is authorized to search by a data owner.
- Our scheme requires very different techniques to compress ciphertexts and succinctly represent the search/access policies that dictate which files a user can access. We model and analyze the security of our construction and provide detailed proofs for keyword, file and trapdoor privacy, respectively.

- We give an extension that allows a system with multiple trusted parties (e.g., managers, data owners) to generate distributively the public key for the system and secret keys for the users, thus eliminating the need of having a single trusted party.

Related Work. To the best of our knowledge, no existing study achieves efficiency comparable to ours in the setting that we study. Our work is related to searchable encryption in general. Single-user searchable encryption considers a single data owner and only the data owner is allowed to submit search queries. It has been studied extensively, with focus on symmetric-key settings [13,16,19,27], asymmetric-key settings [5,8], supporting complicated (conjunctive, subset, or boolean) queries [10,12], or dynamic settings [21]. Our work is in multi-user setting where a group of users can submit search queries.

Multi-user searchable encryption. While multi-user searchable encryption has been investigated in a number of studies, these studies differ from our study in important aspects. In [16], a user is allowed to search *all* the files owned by a data owner while in our study each user is allowed to search a different *subset* of the files. The study in [4] relies on a fully trusted user manager, which not only sets system public parameters but also generates secret keys of all parties. In addition, when a data owner outsources his data, he needs to interact with the semi-trusted server, and the keyword ciphertext size depends on the number of users. Similar to [4], the study in [17] also uses a fully trusted third party. In addition, their scheme does not provide an access control mechanism that specifies which users can access which files. A recent study [20] proposes multi-user searchable encryption that supports boolean queries. It does not provide an access control mechanism either. In addition, an authorized user needs to interact with the data owner to get a token. Then, he can generate a trapdoor based on the token for the query. The same limitations hold for [18], which extends [20] to support range, substring, wildcard and phrase queries.

In the above studies, the documents are encrypted with a single key. In other studies, the documents are encrypted with different keys. We have mentioned [25], which has motivated our study. Tang [28] improves the study of [25] by presenting a new security model for multiparty searchable encryption and proposing a scheme that authorizes users to share their files. Liu et al. [24] propose a data sharing scheme, which however has two major drawbacks. First, a user needs to interact with a honest-but-curious server to download some information in advance to generate a trapdoor. Secondly, the trapdoor size is linear in the number of files. Cui et al. [15] adapt the idea in [14] and propose a key-aggregate searchable encryption scheme. In their scheme, a data owner provides a single aggregated key that contains information about all files that a user is authorized to search. Each user is given a secret key (i.e., the aggregated key) and then a user generates constant size trapdoor to search a keyword from all files. Their scheme is, however, vulnerable to cross pairing attack, and hence has neither data privacy nor trapdoor privacy. Basically, an untrusted server can figure out the encrypted keyword from the ciphertext and recover the aggregate key of any user (see more details in Appendix A.1). Rompay et al. [29] propose a scheme that uses a proxy based architecture to achieve a stronger security model. Their scheme suffers from the same inefficiency problem as that in [25].

Other related primitives for encrypted keyword search. The study [8] introduces a scheme that transforms a given identity based encryption (IBE) to public key encryption with keyword search (PEKS). A later study [1] examines the relationships between these two primitives and points out that if one has an anonymous IBE scheme, then he achieves secure PEKS. Attrapadung et al. [2,3] introduce a new cryptographic primitive called *coupling*. It is a broadcast encryption that further has hierarchical identity based dimension. It combines user index with identity. They provide restricted anonymous identity based encryption. Their scheme does not have a concrete proof of security. Moreover, it cannot be applied to our setting since the transformation does not provide trapdoor privacy. Last, existing studies [23,30] investigate attribute based keyword search, which differ significantly from our study. In [30], the access control policy is based on keywords instead of files, while [23] does not allow a secret key holder to generate search token (trapdoor) individually. In [23], the trapdoor is generated by the collaboration between a secret key holder and the fully trusted PKG (private key generator). In addition, in both schemes, the keyword cliphertext, and trapdoor and secret key sizes depend on the total number of attributes that are involved in a data owner's access control policy.

2   Preliminaries

Bilinear Map: (1) $\mathbf{G}_1$, $\mathbf{G}_2$ and $\mathbf{G}'$ are three multiplicative cyclic groups of prime order p; (2) g_1 is a generator of $\mathbf{G}_1$, g_2 is a generator of $\mathbf{G}_2$. A bilinear map $e : \mathbf{G}_1 \times \mathbf{G}_2 \to \mathbf{G}'$ has the following properties: (1) for all $u \in \mathbf{G}_1, v \in \mathbf{G}_2$ and $a, b \in \mathbb{Z}_p$, we have $e\left(u^a, v^b\right) = e\left(u, v\right)^{ab}$; (2) the map is not degenerate, i.e., $e\left(g_1, g_2\right) \neq 1$. It is a symmetric bilinear map when $\mathbf{G}_1 = \mathbf{G}_2 = \mathbf{G}$.

2.1   Popa-Zeldovich Scheme [25]

We briefly summarize the construction in [25]. For simplicity, we only present the scenario where a single data owner has m files (each file is encrypted with a different key) and can search all the files with a single trapdoor (token).

Let $H : \{0,1\}^* \to \mathbf{G}_1$, $H_2 : \mathbf{G}' \times \mathbf{G}' \to \{0,1\}^*$ be hash functions that are modeled as random oracles. Let $e : \mathbf{G}_1 \times \mathbf{G}_2 \to \mathbf{G}'$ be a bilinear map. The multi-key searchable encryption (MKSE) scheme proposed in [25] is as follows.

- **MK.Setup(λ):** return params $(p, \mathbf{G}_1, \mathbf{G}_2, \mathbf{G}, e, g_1, g_2, g')$.
- **MK.KeyGen(params):** returns $uk, k_1, ..., k_m$, where uk is the user secret key, k_j is the encryption key of file j.
- **MK.Delta($uk, k_1, ..., k_m$):** returns $\Delta_j = g_2^{k_j/uk} \in \mathbf{G}_2$.
- **MK.Token(uk, w):** returns $tk_w = H(w)^{uk} \in \mathbf{G}_1$.
- **MK.Enc(k_j, w):** Draw $r \in \mathbf{G}'$, outputs $c_{j,w} = (r, h)$, where

$$h = H_2(r, e(H(w), g_2)^{k_j}).$$

- **MK.Adjust**(tk_w, Δ_j): returns $stk_{j,w} = e(tk_w, \Delta_j) = e(H(w)^{uk}, g_2^{k_j/uk})$.
- **MK.Match**$(stk_{j,w}, c_{j,w})$: parse $c_{j,w}$ as (r, h) and check if $H_2(r, stk_{j,w}) \stackrel{?}{=} h$. if so, outputs $b = 1$, otherwise $b = 0$.

In the above construction, to search T different keywords, a user only needs to provide $O(T + m)$ pieces of information to the server (T trapdoors and m delta values), much more efficient than that when using standard searchable encryption (which needs $O(Tm)$ pieces of information).

The authors show that the MKSE scheme has data hiding and token hiding properties. Data hiding (privacy) requires that the semi-honest adversary is not able to distinguish between ciphertexts of two values not matched by some token. Token hiding (privacy) requires that the adversary cannot learn the keyword that one searches for.

The MKSE scheme is inefficient since the data owner needs to provide a delta value for each user that is authorized to search a file. Hence the number of delta values for a file is linear in the number of users. This results a significant communication overhead between a data owner and the server when the data owner outsources the delta values, and significant storage overhead for the server to store these ciphertexts.

2.2 Complexity Assumptions

Decision Linear Assumption. Let $\mathbf{G}$ be a bilinear group of prime order p. The Decision Linear problem [7] in $\mathbf{G}$ is stated as follows: given a vector $(g, Z_1 = g^{z_1}, Z_2 = g^{z_2}, Z_{13} = g^{z_1 z_3}, Z_{24} = g^{z_2 z_4}, Z) \in \mathbf{G}^6$ as input, determine whether $Z = g^{z_3 + z_4}$ or a random value $R \in \mathbf{G}$. The advantage of an algorithm $\mathcal{B}$ in deciding the decision linear problem in $\mathbf{G}$ is

$$\left| \Pr\left[\mathcal{B}\left(g, g^{z_1}, g^{z_2}, g^{z_1 z_3}, g^{z_2 z_4}, g^{z_3 + z_4} \right) = 0 \right] \right.$$
$$\left. - \Pr\left[\mathcal{B}\left(g, g^{z_1}, g^{z_2}, g^{z_1 z_3}, g^{z_2 z_4}, R \right) = 0 \right] \right| \leq \epsilon.$$

ℓ-Bilinear Diffie-Hellman Exponentiation Assumption (ℓ-BDHE) [6]. Let $\mathbf{G}$ be a bilinear group of prime order p. The ℓ-BDHE problem in $\mathbf{G}$ is defined as follows: given a vector of $2\ell + 1$ elements $(h, g, g^\alpha, g^{\alpha^2}, ..., g^{\alpha^\ell}, g^{\alpha^{\ell+2}}, ..., g^{\alpha^{2\ell}})$ as input, output $e(g, h)^{\alpha^{\ell+1}}$. Once g and α are specified, we denote $g_i = g^{\alpha^i}$ as shorthand. An algorithm $\mathcal{A}$ has advantage ϵ in solving ℓ-BDHE in $\mathbf{G}$ if

$$\Pr\left[\mathcal{A}\left(h, g, g^\alpha, ..., g^{\alpha^\ell}, g^{\alpha^{\ell+2}}, ..., g^{\alpha^{2\ell}} \right) = e\left(g^{\alpha^{\ell+1}}, h \right) \right] \geq \epsilon,$$

where the probability is over the random choice of generators $g, h \in \mathbf{G}$, the random choice of $\alpha \in Z_p$ and random bits used by $\mathcal{B}$. The decisional version of the ℓ-BDHE problem in $\mathbf{G}$ is defined analogously. Let

$$\bar{\boldsymbol{y}}_{g,\alpha,\ell} = \left(g^\alpha, ..., g^{\alpha^\ell}, g^{\alpha^{\ell+2}}, ..., g^{\alpha^{2\ell}} \right).$$

An algorithm $\mathcal{B}$ that outputs $b \in \{0,1\}$ has advantage ϵ in solving decision ℓ-BDHE in $\mathbf{G}$ if

$$\left| \Pr\left[\mathcal{B}\left(g, h, \bar{\boldsymbol{y}}_{g,\alpha,\ell}, e\left(g_{\ell+1}, h\right)\right) = 0 \right] - \Pr\left[\mathcal{B}\left(g, h, \bar{\boldsymbol{y}}_{g,\alpha,\ell}, R\right) = 0\right] \right| \geq \epsilon,$$

where the probability is over the random choice of generators g, h in $\mathbf{G}$, the random choice of $\alpha \in Z_p$, the random choice of $R \in \mathbf{G}'$, and the random bits consumed by $\mathcal{B}$.

n-Decisional Diffie-Hellman Inverse Assumption (n-DDHI). Let $\mathbf{G}$ be a bilinear group of prime order p. The n-DDHI assumption in $\mathbf{G}$ is stated as follows: given a vector $g, \bar{\boldsymbol{y}}_{g,\alpha,n} = (g_1, \ldots, g_n, g_{n+2}, \ldots, g_{2n}), g^\gamma, h = g^z, Z \in \mathbf{G}^{2n+3}$ as input, determine whether $Z = h^{\gamma/\alpha^{n+1}}$ or a random value R in $\mathbf{G}$. The advantage of an algorithm $\mathcal{B}$ in deciding the n-DDHI in $\mathbf{G}$ is

$$\left| \Pr\left[\mathcal{B}\left(g, \bar{\boldsymbol{y}}_{g,\alpha,n}, g^\gamma, g^z, g^{z\gamma/\alpha^{n+1}} \right) = 0 \right] - \Pr\left[\mathcal{B}\left(g, \bar{\boldsymbol{y}}_{g,\alpha,n}, g^\gamma, g^z, R\right) = 0\right] \right| \leq \epsilon.$$

We provide security evidence of our hardness assumption (n-DDHI) by presenting bounds on the success probabilities of an adversary $\mathcal{A}$. We follow the theoretical generic group model (GGM) as presented in [26] and show the justification of it.

Theorem 1. *Let $\mathcal{A}$ be an algorithm that solves the n-DDHI problem in the generic group model, making a total of at most q queries to the oracles computing the group action in $\mathbf{G}, \mathbf{G}'$ and the oracle computing the bilinear pairing e. If $\alpha, \gamma, r, z \in Z_p^*$ and ξ, ξ' are chosen at random, then*

$$\Pr\left[\begin{array}{l} \mathcal{A}(p, \xi(1), \xi(z), \xi(\alpha), \ldots, \xi(\alpha^n), \\ \xi(\alpha^{n+2}), \ldots, \xi(\alpha^{2n}), \xi(\gamma), \xi(t_0), \xi(t_1)) = d : \\ \alpha, \gamma, z \leftarrow Z_p^*, d \leftarrow \{0,1\}, t_d \leftarrow \frac{z\gamma}{\alpha^{n+1}}, t_{1-d} \leftarrow r \end{array} \right] \leq \frac{1}{2} + \frac{16n(q+n+1)^2}{p}.$$

We provide security evidence for the hardness of the n-DDHI in Appendix A.2.

3   Secure and Efficient Multi-user Encrypted Keyword Search (SEMEKS)

In this section, we define the notion of secure and efficient multi-user encrypted keyword search (SEMEKS) for data sharing. The constructions are deferred to Sect. 4.

Definition 1. *In SEMEKS, there are n users, m documents (files) and a server. Let U denote the set of users and $D = \{M_1, \ldots, M_m\}$ denote the set of documents. Each document has a set of unique keywords. Let F_j denote the set of unique keywords in M_j. Let $S_j \subseteq U$ denote the set of users that can access file j. If user $i \in S_j$, then he is able to search any keyword in F_j and retrieve M_j.*

The server $\mathcal{S}$ stores all ciphertexts for keywords and documents. The server is **honest-but-curious**, *i.e., he does not change any data, and he gives the query results honestly, but he is curious in that he is trying to learn more information from the data and queries (for extracting keywords from ciphertexts and trapdoors). Our model does not allow the adversary (the server) to collude with any of the users. Otherwise, it leaks keywords.*

Definition 2. *A SEMEKS scheme consists of the following five algorithms.*

- **Setup**(n, λ): *a randomized algorithm that takes the number of users n, and the security parameter λ, as input. It outputs $(pk, \{sk_1, \ldots, sk_n\})$, where pk is the set of system public key and sk_i is the secret key of user i.*
- **Enc**(pk, F_k, S_k, M_k): *a randomized algorithm that takes file M_k, the set of unique keywords F_k, public key pk, and user set S_k as input. It outputs keyword ciphertext C_k and file ciphertext C_k''.*
- **Trap**(sk_i, w): *a randomized algorithm that takes secret key sk_i and keyword w as input. It outputs trapdoor $t_{i,w}$ for user i to query w.*
- **Test**$(pk, S_k, t_{i,w}, C_k)$: *a deterministic algorithm that takes keyword ciphertext C_k, trapdoor $t_{i,w}$, user set S_k, and public key pk as input. It outputs $b \in \{0, 1\}$, where $b = 1$ if $i \in S_k$ and C_k includes the ciphertext of w; otherwise, $b = 0$.*
- **Dec**(pk, sk_i, C_k'', S_k): *a deterministic algorithm. If $b = 1$, then the algorithm takes public key pk, secret key sk_i, file ciphertext C_k'' and user set S_k as input, and outputs the plaintext file M_k. Otherwise, it outputs $\perp$.*

We consider keyword privacy, file privacy, and trapdoor privacy. In addition, we refer to keyword and file privacy together as data privacy. The security definitions of keyword and trapdoor privacy are similar as those defined in [25] with some differences (our encryption scheme uses asymmetric key, and hence the adversary is able to encrypt keywords himself in our setting, which differs from that in [25]). File privacy is defined in our study while not in [25] since it does not consider file decryption functionality.

We define a semantically secure keyword privacy game. In the game, $\mathcal{A}$ is static that he outputs a keyword and a set pair that he wants to be challenged on. He observes encryption of keywords and trapdoors. However, he is not able to distinguish whether the challenge ciphertext is encoded by the challenge keyword or a random keyword.

Definition 3 (Keyword Privacy). *We define static semantic security for keyword privacy in SEMEKS by the following game between an adversary $\mathcal{A}$ and a challenger $\mathcal{C}$. Both $\mathcal{C}$ and $\mathcal{A}$ are given (n, λ) as input.*

- **Init:** *$\mathcal{A}$ takes security parameter λ and outputs a set S_0, a keyword w^* that he wants to be challenged on.*
- **Setup:** *$\mathcal{C}$ runs Setup(n, λ) algorithm to obtain system public key pk and a set of private keys, $sk_1, \ldots, sk_n$. It then gives the public key pk to $\mathcal{A}$.*
- **Query:** *$\mathcal{A}$ adaptively issues queries $q_1, \ldots, q_\lambda$, where query q_k is a trapdoor query (i, w). For such a query, $\mathcal{C}$ responds by running algorithm Trap(sk_i, w) to derive $t_{i,w}$, and sends it to $\mathcal{A}$.*

- **Guess:** C picks a random number $b \in \{0, 1\}$, computes (C_0, S_0) as the output of $Enc(pk, w_b, S_0)$, where $w_0 = w^*$, and w_1 is a random keyword (of the same length as w_0), returns the value (C_0, S_0) to A. A outputs its guess $b' \in \{0, 1\}$ for b and wins the game if $b = b'$.

Restriction: The adversary asks trapdoor queries only when $i \notin S_0$ and $w \neq w^*$.

A SEMKS scheme is keyword private if, for all PPT adversaries A, for all sufficiently large λ, $\Pr[\text{win}_A(\lambda, n)] < 1/2 + \text{negl}(\lambda, n)$, where $\text{win}_A(\lambda, n)$ is a random variable indicating whether the adversary wins the game for security parameter λ.

We define a file privacy game that is similar to a semantically secure broadcast encryption definition since a file is encrypted for a set of users. If a user is a member of the corresponding set, he can download the file ciphertext and retrieves the file using his decryption key. In file privacy game, A outputs two messages M_0, M_1 and a user set S_0 he wants to be challenged upon. He gets public parameters and user secret keys that are not in the target user set (S_0). However, he is not able to distinguish whether the given ciphertext is the ciphertext of M_0 or M_1.

Definition 4 (File Privacy). *We define static semantic security for file privacy in SEMEKS by the following game between a challenger C and an adversary A.*

- **Init:** A takes parameters (n, λ) and outputs a set S_0 and two messages M_0, M_1 that he wants to be challenged on.
- **Setup:** C runs $Setup(n, \lambda)$ algorithm to obtain system public key pk. It then gives the public key pk to A.
- **Query:** A adaptively issues private key queries of user $j \notin S_0$. C gives the secret keys, sk_j to A, where $j \notin S_0$.
- **Challenge:** C chooses a random $b \in \{0, 1\}$ and runs $Enc(S_0, pk, M_b)$ to obtain the ciphertext C'''^*, and gives it to A.
- **Guess:** A guesses $b' \in \{0, 1\}$ for b and wins the game if $b = b'$.

File privacy game is secure against CPA if for all attacks $|\Pr[b = b'] - 1/2| \leq \text{negl}(\lambda, n)$.

We define a static trapdoor privacy game that A outputs challenge user index and keyword pair at the beginning of the game to be challenged on. In the game, A can observe encryptions of keywords and the challenge trapdoor, but he is not able to distinguish the challenge keyword from a random keyword.

Definition 5 (Trapdoor Privacy). *The trapdoor privacy game is between a challenger C and an adversary A as follows:*

- **Init:** A takes parameters (n, λ) and outputs a user and keyword tuple (i^*, w^*) that he wants to be challenged on.
- **Setup:** C runs $Setup(n, \lambda)$ to obtain system public key pk and private keys $sk_1, ..., sk_n$. It gives pk to A.

- **Query:** $\mathcal{A}$ *adaptively issues queries* $q_1, ..., q_\lambda$, *where query* q_k *is a trapdoor query* (i, w). $\mathcal{C}$ *responds by running algorithm* $Trap(sk_i, w)$ *to derive* $t_{i,w}$, *and sends it to* $\mathcal{A}$.
- **Guess:** $\mathcal{C}$ *runs Trapdoor algorithm on input* (i^*, w_b^*) *for a random bit* b *to obtain* t_{i^*, w_b^*}, *where* $w_b^* = w^*$ *if* $b = 0$, *otherwise, it is a random keyword, and sends it to* $\mathcal{A}$. $\mathcal{A}$ *outputs its guess* $b' \in \{0, 1\}$ *for* b *and wins the game if* $b = b'$.

A SEMEKS scheme is trapdoor private if, for all PPT adversaries $\mathcal{A}$,

$$\Pr[\mathrm{win}_{\mathcal{A}}(\lambda, n)] < 1/2 + \mathrm{negl}(\lambda).$$

4 Constructions

In this section, we give two constructions. For simplicity, we present the constructions assuming there is a single data owner; the scenario where there are multiple data owner can be solved similarly. For ease of exposition, we start with assuming that a centralized trusted third party initializes the system public keys; in Sect. 6, we describe how to eliminate the need of this trusted party. The data owner generates the secret key for each user, and then distributes the secret key to the user.

We adapt the coupling primitive in [2,3] carefully to the setting of multi-user keyword search where the data owner encrypts each file with a different key; different users are allowed to search different subset of (encrypted) files. Specifically, we couple the broadcast dimension (user index; each user is assigned an index) and the keyword dimension (keyword searchability). When user i wants to retrieve the documents that contain keyword w, user i generates trapdoor $t_{i,w}$ that has two dimensions: index i and keyword w. It binds both dimensions (index, keyword) to let the server search w in all the files that user i is allowed to access, and then retrieve the corresponding files. Both constructions use two useful cryptographic primitives: broadcast encryption from [9] and anonymous identity-based encryption from [11]. The broadcast encryption primitive provides constant size keyword ciphertexts and user secret keys. Specifically, it uses an aggregation method for ciphertexts that results in constant size ciphertexts (i.e., ciphertext size does not depend on the number of users). The anonymous encryption primitive provides anonymity of the keyword that is being encrypted. It uses anonymous encryption that does not reveal keyword from the ciphertext. Specifically, it uses linear splitting method on the random exponent values, which does not allow the adversary to do guessing attack (cross pairing attack).

The first construction uses a single server. We show that it satisfies data privacy but does not satisfy trapdoor privacy. The second construction (i.e., the main construction) is developed to address the problem. It uses two servers that do not collude. We show that it satisfies both data privacy and trapdoor privacy. At the end, we describe how to eliminate the need of having a single trusted party in our constructions.

4.1 First Construction

Setup(n, λ): Let $\mathbf{G}$ be a bilinear group of prime order p. The algorithm first picks a random generator $g \in \mathbf{G}$ and a random value $\alpha \in Z_p$. It computes $g_i = g^{\alpha^i} \in \mathbf{G}$ for $i = 1, 2, \ldots, n, n+2, \ldots, 2n$ (these values are generated by the centralized trusted third party). Next, it picks at random $\gamma, \beta \in Z_p$ and sets $v = g^\gamma, v' = g^\beta \in \mathbf{G}$. It then picks random elements $h_{0,1}, h_{0,2}, h_{1,1}, h_{1,2} \in \mathbf{G}$ and $a_1, b_1, a_2, b_2 \in Z_p$ (these values are picked by the data owner (DO)). The public key is: $pk = (g, g_1, \ldots, g_n, g_{n+2}, \ldots, g_{2n}, v, v', h_{\ell,1}^{a_1}, h_{\ell,1}^{b_1}, h_{\ell,2}^{a_2}, h_{\ell,2}^{b_2})$, where $\ell = \{0, 1\}$. The secret key of the DO is $sk_{DO} = (\gamma, \beta, a_1, b_1, a_2, b_2)$. The algorithm outputs pk and sk_{DO}. For users' secret keys, the DO chooses random $\rho_{i1}, \rho_{i2}, \rho'_{i1}, \rho'_{i2}$ for user i and computes secret key for user i as follows:

$$d_{i,1} = g_i^\gamma, \qquad d_{i,2} = g^{a_1\rho_{i1}}, \qquad d_{i,3} = g^{a_1\rho'_{i1}},$$

$$d_{i,4} = g^{a_2\rho_{i2}}, \qquad d_{i,5} = g^{a_2\rho'_{i2}}, \qquad d_{i,6} = g^{b_1\rho_{i1}},$$

$$d_{i,7} = g^{b_1\rho'_{i1}}, \qquad d_{i,8} = g^{b_2\rho_{i2}}, \qquad d_{i,9} = g^{b_2\rho'_{i2}},$$

$$d_{i,10} = h_{0,1}^{a_1 b_1 \rho_{i1}} h_{0,2}^{a_2 b_2 \rho_{i2}}, \quad d_{i,11} = h_{0,1}^{a_1 b_1 \rho'_{i1}} h_{0,2}^{a_2 b_2 \rho'_{i2}}, \quad d_{i,12} = h_{1,1}^{a_1 b_1 \rho_{i1}} h_{1,2}^{a_2 b_2 \rho_{i2}},$$

$$d_{i,13} = h_{1,1}^{a_1 b_1 \rho'_{i1}} h_{1,2}^{a_2 b_2 \rho'_{i2}}, \quad d_{i,14} = g_i^\beta.$$

These values are given to user i via a secure channel. Specifically, $sk_i = (d_{i,1}, \ldots, d_{i,14})$.

Enc(pk, w, S_k, M_k): The DO picks random values $t, t', t_1, t_2 \in Z_p$ for keyword w from F_k, and computes the following:

$$K = e(g_{n+1}, g)^t, \qquad K' = e(g_{n+1}, g)^{t'}, \qquad hdr_{k,1} = (h_{0,1}^{a_1}(h_{1,1}^{a_1})^w)^{t_1},$$

$$hdr_{k,2} = (h_{0,1}^{b_1}(h_{1,1}^{b_1})^w)^{t-t_1}, \quad hdr_{k,3} = (h_{0,2}^{a_2}(h_{1,2}^{a_2})^w)^{t_2}, \qquad hdr_{k,4} = (h_{0,2}^{b_2}(h_{1,2}^{b_2})^w)^{t-t_2},$$

$$hdr_{k,5} = g^t, \qquad hdr_{k,6} = \left(v \prod_{j \in S_k} g_{n+1-j}\right)^t, \qquad hdr_{k,7} = K,$$

$$hdr_{k,8} = g^{t'}, \qquad hdr_{k,9} = \left(v' \prod_{j \in S_k} g_{n+1-j}\right)^{t'}, \quad hdr_{k,10} = K' M_k.$$

Let the first part of the ciphertext $C_k = (hdr_{k,1}, \ldots, hdr_{k,7})$. Let the second part of the ciphertext $C''_k = (hdr_{k,8}, hdr_{k,9}, hdr_{k,10})$

Trap$(d_{i,1}||\ldots||d_{i,13}, w)$: User i picks $r, r' \in Z_p$ and computes $t_{i,w}$ as

$$tr_1 = d_{i,1} d_{i,10}^r d_{i,11}^{r'} \left(d_{i,12}^r d_{i,13}^{r'}\right)^w, \qquad tr_2 = d_{i,2}^r d_{i,3}^{r'}, \qquad tr_3 = d_{i,4}^r d_{i,5}^{r'},$$

$$tr_4 = d_{i,6}^r d_{i,7}^{r'}, \qquad\qquad\qquad\qquad tr_5 = d_{i,8}^r d_{i,9}^{r'}.$$

Test$(pk, S_k, t_{i,w}, C_k)$: The server checks if

$$hdr_{k,7} \overset{?}{=} \frac{e(g_i, hdr_{k,6}) e(hdr_{k,1}, tr_4) T}{e(tr_1 \prod_{j \in S_k, i \neq j} g_{n+1-j+i}, hdr_{k,5})},$$

where $T = e(hdr_{k,3}, tr_5)e(hdr_{k,2}, tr_2)e(hdr_{k,4}, tr_3)$. If the equality holds, then the test result $b = 1$. Otherwise, $b = 0$.

Dec$(pk, d_{i,14}, C''_k, S_k)$: Once the server outputs $b = 1$ from the **Test** algorithm, he sends S_k, C''_k to user i (we call this process as *download*). Then, user i does the decryption in the same way as that in [9] to recover first K' then extracts M_k by computing $M_k = K'M_k/K'$.

It is easy to see that the keyword ciphertext does not reveal w by using cross pairing. The data privacy is achieved by using linear splitting method that is introduced in [11] for ciphertexts. The idea in [11] is to use different random blind values in ciphertexts. This scheme is correct as follows:
$(pk, sk_{DO}, sk_i = (d_{i,1}||\ldots||d_{i,14})_{i=1,\ldots n})) \leftarrow$ **Setup**(n, λ),
$(C_k, C''_k) = (hdr_{k,j})_{j=[1,10]} \leftarrow$ **Enc**(pk, w, S_k, M_k),
$t_{i,w} = (tr_l)_{l=[1,5]} \leftarrow$ **Trap**$(sk_i = (d_{i,1}||\ldots||d_{i,13}), w)$,
If $i \in S_k, b \leftarrow$ **Test**$(pk, t_{i,w}, C_k, S_k)$,
Otherwise, $\perp \leftarrow$ **Test**$(pk, t_{i,w}, C_k, S_k)$,
If $b = 1, M_k \leftarrow$ **Dec**$(pk, d_{i,14}, S_k, C''_k)$.

The first construction does not have trapdoor privacy. The first reason is that the adversary (i.e., the server) can extract the keyword from the generated trapdoor. The problem happens because user i does not blind his first part of the secret key $d_{i,1}$ when he generates the first part of the trapdoor tr_1. The attack basically occurs when given a trapdoor for a keyword w from user i, $t_{i,w} = (tr_1, tr_2, tr_3, tr_4, tr_5)$, the server picks a keyword w^* and checks if

$$\frac{e(tr_1, g)}{e(h_{0,1}^{b_1}, tr_2)e(h_{0,2}^{b_2}, tr_3)e(g_i, g^\gamma)} = e(h_{1,1}^{a_1}, tr_4)^{w^*} e(h_{1,2}^{a_2}, tr_5)^{w^*}.$$

If the above equality holds, the server concludes that $w = w^*$. The second reason is going to be explained in Sect. 5.2.

To counter the above attack, we need to blind the first part of the secret key of a user, which however breaks the BGW decryption process since it needs the first part of the secret key not to be blinded. We solve the above issue in the following construction by using two servers $\mathcal{S}_{main}$ and $\mathcal{S}_{aid}$. In our new model, $\mathcal{S}_{aid}$ is trusted while $\mathcal{S}_{main}$ is the semi-honest adversary. In trapdoor phase, a user chooses three random values r, r', r'' and generates the trapdoor using r, r', r''. The user uses r'' to blind the first part of secret key d_1 and uses r, r' to blinds other parts of the secret keys (d_j, where $j = 2, .., 13$). Then, the user sends a random value r_2 with trapdoor to $\mathcal{S}_{main}$ and another random value r_1 to $\mathcal{S}_{aid}$. Here, r'' can be thought as a function of r_1, r_2: $f(r_1, r_2) = r''$. In our construction, the function f simply takes r_1, r_2 and outputs $r'' = r_1 + r_2$. $\mathcal{S}_{aid}$ stores the values $C'_k = hdr_{k,5}, hdr_{k,6}, hdr_{k,7}, S_k$ while $\mathcal{S}_{main}$ stores $(C_k, C''_k) = (hdr_{k,1}, hdr_{k,2}, hdr_{k,3}, hdr_{k,4}, hdr_{k,5}, hdr_{k,6}, hdr_{k,7}, hdr_{k,8}, hdr_{k,9}, hdr_{k,10}, S_k)$ for file F_k. Once the user sends trapdoor and random values to the servers, $\mathcal{S}_{aid}$ first computes $f_1(r_1, C'_k)$ and sends it to $\mathcal{S}_{main}$. Then $\mathcal{S}_{main}$ internally checks if the keyword appears in the ciphertext by using $t_{i,w}, f_2(r_2, C_k), f_1(r_1, C'_k), C_k, S_k$. If so, $\mathcal{S}_{main}$ sends C''_k and S_k to the user. The user decrypts it and recovers the

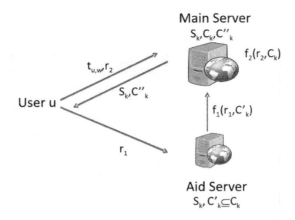

Fig. 1. Illustration of the secure and efficient construction.

plaintext file k where the keyword appears. We illustrate the query process in Fig. 1.

4.2   Main Construction

This construction has two servers. It is as follows (illustrated in Fig. 1).
Setup(n, λ): This algorithm is the same as that in the first construction in Sect. 4.1. It outputs system public key pk and user secret key sk_i for user $i = 1, \ldots, n$.
Enc(pk, w, S_k, M_k): This algorithm is the same as that in the first construction in Sect. 4.1 and outputs $hdr_{k,1} \ldots hdr_{k,10}$. Let the first part of the ciphertext $C_k = (hdr_{k,1}, \ldots, hdr_{k,7})$. Let the second part of the ciphertext $C''_k = (hdr_{k,8}, hdr_{k,9}, hdr_{k,10})$. In addition, let $C'_k = (hdr_{k,5}, hdr_{k,6}, hdr_{k,7})$. The main server $\mathcal{S}_{main}$ stores C_k, C''_k and S_k. The aid server $\mathcal{S}_{aid}$ stores C'_k and S_k.
Trap$(d_{i,1} || \ldots || d_{i,13}, w)$: User i picks $r, r', r'' \in Z_p$ and computes $t_{i,w}$ as

$$tr_1 = d_{i,1}^{r''} d_{i,10}^{r} d_{i,11}^{r'} \left(d_{i,12}^{r} d_{i,13}^{r'} \right)^w, \qquad tr_2 = d_{i,2}^{r} d_{i,3}^{r'}, \qquad tr_3 = d_{i,4}^{r} d_{i,5}^{r'},$$

$$tr_4 = d_{i,6}^{r} d_{i,7}^{r'}, \qquad\qquad tr_5 = d_{i,8}^{r} d_{i,9}^{r'}, \qquad tr_6 = g_{n+1+i}^{r''}.$$

He sends $t_{i,w} = (tr_1, \ldots, tr_6)$ and r_2 to $\mathcal{S}_{main}$, and sends r_1 to $\mathcal{S}_{aid}$.
Test$(pk, S_k, f_2(r_2, C_k), f_1(r_1, C'_k), t_{i,w}, C_k)$: Both servers compute

$$A_k = \frac{e\left(g_i, hdr_{k,6}\right)}{hdr_{k,7} e\left(\prod_{j \in S_k, i \neq j} g_{n+1-j+i}, hdr_{k,5}\right)}$$

for file k. The aid server sends $f_1(r_1, C'_k) = A_k^{r_1}$ to $\mathcal{S}_{main}$. $\mathcal{S}_{main}$ then computes $f_2(r_2, C_k) f_1(r_1, C'_k) = A_k^{r_2} A_k^{r_1} = A_k^{r}$ and checks if

$$\frac{e\left(tr_1, hdr_{k,5}\right)}{e\left(hdr_{k,1}, tr_4\right) T} = A_k^{r},$$

where $T = e(hdr_{k,3}, tr_5)e(hdr_{k,2}, tr_2)e(hdr_{k,4}, tr_3)$. If the equality holds, then the test result $b = 1$. Otherwise, $b = 0$.

Dec$(pk, d_{i,14}, C_k'', S_k)$: Once the server outputs $b = 1$ from the **Test** algorithm, he sends S_k, C_k'' to user i (we call this process as *download*). Then, user i does the decryption in the same way as that in [9] to recover first K' then extracts M_k by computing $M_k = K'M_k/K'$.

5   Security

5.1   Data Privacy

Proving Security: We prove security using a hybrid experiment as that in [11]. Let $[hdr_{0,1}, hdr_{0,2}, hdr_{0,3}, hdr_{0,4}, hdr_{0,5}, hdr_{0,6}, hdr_{0,7}]$ denote the challenge ciphertext for keyword w^* and user set S_0 that are given to the adversary during a real attack. Additionally, let R, R' be two random elements of $\mathbf{G}$. We define the following hybrid games which differ on what challenge ciphertext is given by a simulator $\mathcal{SIM}$ to the adversary:

Γ_0: The challenge ciphertext is

$$C_0 = [hdr_{0,1}, hdr_{0,2}, hdr_{0,3}, hdr_{0,4}, hdr_{0,5}, hdr_{0,6}, hdr_{0,7}].$$

Γ_1: The challenge ciphertext is

$$C_1 = [hdr_{0,1}, R, hdr_{0,3}, hdr_{0,4}, hdr_{0,5}, hdr_{0,6}, hdr_{0,7}].$$

Γ_2: The challenge ciphertext is

$$C_2 = [hdr_{0,1}, R, hdr_{0,3}, R', hdr_{0,5}, hdr_{0,6}, hdr_{0,7}].$$

We remark that the challenge ciphertext in Γ_2 leaks no information about the keyword since it is composed of seven random group elements, whereas in Γ_0 the challenge is well formed. We show that the transitions from Γ_0 to Γ_1 and Γ_1 to Γ_2 are all computationally indistinguishable.

Since we use two servers, we slightly change the definition of keyword privacy game in Sect. 3. During the game, the adversary makes encryption queries since S_{aid} is trusted and controlled by the simulator. The adversary is not able to upload any ciphertext that he wants. We restrict the adversary.

Theorem 2 (Keyword Privacy). *The main construction of the SEMEKS scheme has keyword privacy under Decision Linear Assumption.*

Proof. Suppose the existence of an adversary $\mathcal{A}$ that distinguishes between the two games (Γ_0 and Γ_1) with a non-negligible advantage ϵ. Then we construct $\mathcal{SIM}$ that wins the Decision Linear game as follows. $\mathcal{SIM}$ takes in a decision linear instance $g, g^{z_1}, g^{z_2}, g^{z_1 z_3}, g^{z_2 z_4}, Z$, where Z is either $g^{z_3 + z_4}$ or random in $\mathbf{G}$ with equal probability. For convenience, we rewrite this as $g, g^{z_1}, g^{z_2}, g^{z_1 z_3}, Y, g^t$ for t such that $g^t = Z$, and consider the task of deciding whether $Y = g^{z_2(t - z_3)}$. $\mathcal{SIM}$ plays the game in the following stages.

- **Init:** $\mathcal{A}$ gives $\mathcal{SIM}$ the challenge keyword w^* and the challenge set S_0.
- **Setup:** The simulator first chooses random exponents $\alpha, \gamma, \zeta, a_2, b_2$. It uses the same g as in the decision linear instance, and sets $g_1, \ldots, g_n, g_{n+2}, \ldots, g_{2n}$, v, where $g_i = g^{\alpha^i}$, $v = g^\gamma$, $h_{0,1} = g^{-w^*\zeta+\zeta}$, $h_{1,1} = g^\zeta$, $h_{0,2} = g^{z_2(-w^*\zeta)}g^\zeta$, $h_{1,2} = g^{z_2\zeta}$. Next the simulator sets $h_{0,1}^{a_1} \leftarrow (g^{z_1})^{-w^*\zeta+\zeta}$, $h_{1,1}^{a_1} \leftarrow (g^{z_1})^\zeta$, $h_{0,1}^{b_1} \leftarrow (g^{z_2})^{-w^*\zeta+\zeta}$, $h_{1,1}^{b_1} \leftarrow (g^{z_2})^\zeta$, $h_{0,2}^{a_2} \leftarrow g^{a_2 z_2(-w^*\zeta)}g^{a_2\zeta}$, $h_{1,2}^{a_2} \leftarrow g^{a_2 z_2\zeta}$, $h_{0,2}^{b_2} \leftarrow g^{b_2 z_2(-w^*\zeta)}g^{b_2\zeta}$, $h_{1,2}^{b_2} \leftarrow g^{b_2 z_2\zeta}$.
  The system public key is $pk = g, g_1, \ldots, g_n, g_{n+2}, \ldots, g_{2n}, v, h_{0,1}^{a_1}, h_{1,1}^{a_1}, h_{0,1}^{b_1}, h_{1,1}^{b_1}, h_{0,2}^{a_2}, h_{1,2}^{a_2}, h_{0,2}^{b_2}, h_{1,2}^{b_2}$ and $\mathcal{SIM}$ gives the public key to $\mathcal{A}$ and $\mathcal{S}_{aid}$.
- **Query(S_ℓ, w_ℓ):** To answer encryption query for (S_ℓ, w_ℓ) where $w_\ell \neq w^*$, the simulator picks ℓ, ℓ_1, ℓ_2, and computes $hdr_{k,1}, \ldots, hdr_{k,7}$ as

$$K = e(g_{n+1}, g)^\ell, \qquad\qquad hdr_{k,1} = (h_{0,1}^{a_1}(h_{1,1}^{a_1})^{w_\ell})^{\ell_1},$$

$$hdr_{k,2} = (h_{0,1}^{b_1}(h_{1,1}^{b_1})^{w_\ell})^{\ell-\ell_1}, \qquad hdr_{k,3} = (h_{0,2}^{a_2}(h_{1,2}^{a_2})^{w_\ell})^{\ell_2},$$

$$hdr_{k,4} = (h_{0,2}^{b_2}(h_{1,2}^{b_2})^{w_\ell})^{\ell-\ell_2}, \qquad hdr_{k,5} = g^\ell,$$

$$hdr_{k,6} = \left(v \prod_{j \in S_\ell} g_{n+1-j}\right)^\ell, \qquad hdr_{k,7} = K$$

and gives them to $\mathcal{A}$ ($\mathcal{S}_{main}$) and gives $hdr_{k,5}, hdr_{k,6}, hdr_{k,7}, S_\ell$ to $\mathcal{S}_{aid}$.
- **Query(i, w):** To answer trapdoor queries for (i, w) where $i \notin S_0$ and $w \neq w^*$, the simulator picks $\rho_{i1}, \rho_{i1}', \rho_{i2}, \rho_{i2}', r, r', r''$, and computes $t_{i,w} = (tr_1, \ldots, tr_6)$ as

$$tr_1 = g_i^{r''\gamma}(h_{0,2}h_{1,2}^w)^{a_2 b_2 Y}(g^{\frac{-z_1 X\zeta}{w-w^*}})(g^{-z_1 X\zeta}), \quad tr_2 = g^{z_1 X},$$

$$tr_3 = g^{z_2 X}, \qquad\qquad tr_4 = g^{a_2 Y}g^{\frac{-z_1 X}{b_2}}g^{\frac{-z_1 X}{b_2(w-w^*)}},$$

$$tr_5 = g^{b_2 Y}g^{\frac{-z_1 X}{a_2}}g^{\frac{-z_1 X}{a_2(w-w^*)}}, \qquad tr_6 = g_{n+1+i}^{r''},$$

where $X = \rho_{i1}r + \rho_{i1}'r'$, $Y = \rho_{i2}r + \rho_{i2}'r'$. Then, he gives $tr_1, tr_2, tr_3, tr_4, tr_5, tr_6, r_2$ to $\mathcal{A}$ and r_1 to $\mathcal{S}_{aid}$.
- **Guess:** The simulator responds with a challenge ciphertext for the keyword w^* and the set S_0. Assume $t_1 = z_3$. The simulator picks random $t_2 \in Z_p$. To proceed, the simulator outputs the ciphertext as

$$hdr_{0,1} = (g^\zeta)^{(t_1 z_1)}, \qquad hdr_{0,2} = Y^\zeta, \qquad hdr_{0,3} = (g^\zeta)^{(t_2 a_2)},$$

$$hdr_{0,4} = Z^{\zeta b_2}g^{-\zeta b_2 t_2}, \qquad hdr_{0,5} = Z = g^t, \qquad hdr_{0,6} = \left(v \prod_{j \in S_0} g_{n+1-j}\right)^t,$$

$$hdr_{0,7} = K = e(g_{n+1}, g)^t.$$

If $Y = g^{z_2(t-z_3)}$ so $Z = g^t$, then all parts of the challenge are well formed and the simulator simulates game Γ_0. If instead Y is independent of z_1, z_2, t, t_1, t_2, which happens when Z is random, then the simulator emulates the game Γ_1.

- **Output:** $\mathcal{A}$ outputs a bit b to guess which hybrid game the simulator has been playing. To conclude, the simulator forwards b as its own answer in the Decision Linear game.

Restriction: $\mathcal{S}_{aid}$ does not use the public key g_i that is asked in trapdoor query to compute function $f(r_1, C')$. The function should be independent of g_i since the index i does not appear in the set S_0.

Analysis: Since the challenge ciphertext is independent of w^*, the adversary's best success probability is $1/2$ when the adversary $\mathcal{A}$ gets Γ_1 as challenge ciphertext. The success probability is $\Pr[\text{win}_{\mathcal{A}}(\lambda, n)] < 1/2 + \epsilon$ when $\mathcal{A}$ gets Γ_0 as challenge ciphertext. So, $\mathcal{SIM}$ breaks the Decision Linear assumption with probability $|\Pr(\mathcal{A}(\Gamma_0) = 1) - \Pr(\mathcal{A}(\Gamma_1) = 1| = 1/2 + \epsilon - 1/2 = \epsilon$, which is non-negligible. □

Remark 1. The indistinguishability of the hybrid games Γ_1 and Γ_2 can be shown similarly by adjusting the parameters as $a_2 = z_1$, $b_2 = z_2$.

Theorem 3 (File Privacy). *The main construction of SEMEKS has file privacy under n-DBDHE assumption.*

Proof. The other parts of the (file) ciphertexts, $(g^{t'}, (v'(\prod_{j \in S_0} g_{n+1-j}))^{t'}, K'M_0)$ are just for downloading process (independent of the first part of the keyword ciphertext and other public key values that are formed by $a_1, a_2, b_1, b_2, \gamma$ and $h_{0,1}, h_{1,1}, h_{0,2}, h_{1,2}$) when the searched keyword matches the first part of the keyword ciphertexts. These parts, C_0'', can be simulated in the same way as in [9]. In the interests of space, we do not give concrete proof.

As a proof sketch, once $\mathcal{SIM}$ gets n-DBDHE parameters, he will set pk, $hdr_{0,8}$, $hdr_{0,9}$, v' and user secret keys $d_{j,14}$, where $j \notin S_0$, in the same way as in [9]. Then, he follows the same game steps (Challenge and Guess) as those in [9]. □

5.2 Trapdoor Privacy

Formalizing a security model for trapdoor privacy is challenging since an adversary can use the public resource and/or provided secret information (trapdoor) to verify if the given trapdoor is generated under a specific keyword. This is a serious problem if a scheme is built in a public key setting. It is because the adversary can encrypt any keyword, then he can verify if the encrypted keyword and the given trapdoor are generated under the same keyword. The solution for this is to restrict the adversary to avoid generating any ciphertext for a set of users to verify if the given trapdoor and the generated ciphertext match under the same keyword.

Our Solution: Since we use a two-server solution for trapdoor privacy, we change the definition of trapdoor privacy in Sect. 3. In the new model, we are going to have some query restrictions.

Restriction: For a challenge trapdoor (i^*, w^*) in the trapdoor privacy game, the restriction on $\mathcal{A}$ for encryption query $\text{Enc}(pk, w, S_j)$: if $i^* \in S_j$ or $w = w^*$, the simulator outputs $\bot$. It means that the adversary is not able to ask the challenger an encryption query where the challenge user index is in the given set S_j or the challenge keyword. One can think that the adversary can encrypt whatever he wants to encrypt since he has the system public key pk. However, in our model $\mathcal{S}_{aid}$ is trusted and is controlled by the simulator. So, the adversary is not able to upload any keyword ciphertext to $\mathcal{S}_{aid}$. But he can encrypt keywords on his will offline. It means that he can encrypt keywords and see the ciphertext but he is not able to use them in test algorithm since he needs $\mathcal{S}_{aid}$ to send partial trapdoor information. Another restriction is that $\mathcal{S}_{aid}$ does not use the public key of the challenge user (g_i) to compute function $f(r_1, C')$. The function should be independent of g_i.

Theorem 4 (Trapdoor Privacy). *The construction of SEMEKS is trapdoor private under n-DDHI assumption.*

In the interest of space, we leave the proof to Appendix A.3.

6   Eliminating Single Trusted Party

The two constructions above use a single trusted party to generate the public key pk. The single trusted party can be a manager or a DO. In either case, a DO generates secret keys for the users that are eligible to do keyword search on the DO's files and distributes the secret keys to the users. A user's secret key is hence known by the DO, which is not desirable since a user might want her secret key to be only known by herself. Furthermore, when there are multiple DOs and a user wants to search multiple DOs' data files, each DO needs to generate and send a secret key to the user, and the user needs to generate a trapdoor that is linear in the number of DOs. This results in a scalability problem. In addition, if there are multiple DOs, each setting her own public key which is of size $O(n)$, the system total public key size is going to be $O(n^2)$ for n DOs. This results in another scalability problem.

To address the above issues, we can use the recently proposed *distributed parameter generation protocol* [22]. In [22], n parties can jointly generate system public key and user secret keys that eliminates the need of having a single trusted authority. These n parties can be all DOs that share their data files with each other (group data sharing), or a single DO that share his files with $n - 1$ users. Since most parts of the system public key are in the from of n-*BDHE* parameters, they can be generated straightforwardly from [22]. The remaining part of the values $h_{0,1}^{a_1}, h_{1,1}^{a_1}, h_{0,1}^{b_1}, h_{1,1}^{b_1}, h_{0,2}^{a_2}, h_{1,2}^{a_2}, h_{0,2}^{b_2}, h_{1,2}^{b_2}$ can be distributively generated by applying $\mathcal{DKG}$ and $\mathcal{REC}$ a couple of times. The secret keys of the users can be distributively generated by applying $\mathcal{DKG}, \mathcal{REC}$ and $\mathcal{RECSQ}$ sub-protocols. Since these are straightforward, we do not provide the constructions explicitly.

7   Conclusion

We have proposed a secure and efficient encrypted keyword search (SEMEKS) scheme for multi-user data sharing. In the scheme, an authorized user uses a single trapdoor to search all files that he is authorized to search. In addition, for keyword ciphertexts of a file, the network bandwidth usage and the storage required at the server does not depend on the number of authorized users that can search that file. We have also performed rigorous security analysis to show that SEMEKS has trapdoor privacy and data privacy.

As future work, we will investigate how to use a single server to achieve secure and efficient keyword search for data sharing. In addition, we want to support boolean and not conjunctive keyword queries and update users set efficiently (adding or removing users from pre-defined authorized set).

A   Appendix

A.1   Vulnerability of the Scheme in [15]

Cui et al. [15] proposed a scheme that provides an aggregation method on files for a user. Basically, each user's secret key is mapped to an aggregated number of files. With this aggregation function, in their scheme, a file size does not depend on the number users. In addition, in their scheme, keyword ciphertext size is constant. We argue that their scheme is vulnerable to cross pairing attacks. Specifically, (1) the adversary (server) is able to extract keywords from the ciphertext, and (2) the adversary captures the secret key of any user so the adversary is able to build trapdoors to search any keyword as an authorized user. The first attack (cross-pairing or dictionary or guessing) is to the ciphertexts as follows. Since each file j is encrypted with a single encryption key t_j, the ciphertexts of the keywords are of the form

$$ C_{w_1} = \frac{e(H(w_1), g)^{t_j}}{e(g_n, g_1)^{t_j}}, \qquad C_{w_2} = \frac{e(H(w_2), g)^{t_j}}{e(g_n, g_1)^{t_j}} . $$

Given $C_{w_1}, C_{w_2}, C_1 = g^{t_j}$, $C_2 = (vg_j)^{t_j}$, the server (adversary) picks two keywords w_1^*, w_2^* and checks if $e(H(w_1^*), g)^{t_j}/C_{w_1} = e(g_n, g_1)^{t_j} = e(H(w_1^*), g)^{t_j}/C_{w_2}$. If so, the server concludes that $w_1^* = w_1, w_2^* = w_2$. Moreover, the adversary recovers $e(g_n, g_1)^{t_j}$ for file j.

Another weakness of the scheme in [15] happens in producing a trapdoor. Basically, the DO computes a secret key for a user by computing $k_{agg} = \prod_{j \in S} g_{n+1-j}^{\gamma}$, where $\gamma \in Z_p$ is the secret key of the DO, and any subset $S \subseteq \{1, .., n\}$ which contains the indices of documents that the user is authorized to search. Once the user gets the secret key, he makes a query for keyword w_1 by computing $Tr_1 = k_{agg} H(w_1)$. The user sends (Tr_1, S) to the could server. If the same user makes another query for keyword w_2, he sends $(Tr_2 = k_{agg} H(w_2), S)$ to the server. The problem is that the server can choose two keywords w^*, w^{**} and computes $H(w^*), H(w^{**})$. Then, the server checks if $Tr_1H(w^*) = Tr_2H(w^{**})$ or $Tr_1H(w^{**}) = Tr_2H(w^*)$. If the first equality holds, the server concludes $H(w_1) = H(w^{**})$ and $H(w_2) = H(w^*)$ while the second equality holds, the server concludes $H(w_1) = H(w^*)$ and $H(w_2) = H(w^{**})$. Either case, the server obtains secret key of the user k_{agg}. This is the very crucial information because the server makes query as if an authorized user.

A.2   Generic Security of n-DDHI Assumption

In the generic group model, elements of $\mathbf{G}$ and $\mathbf{G}'$ appear to be encoded as unique random strings, so that no property other than equality can be directly tested by the adversary $\mathcal{A}$. Three oracles are assumed to perform operations between group elements, such as computing the group action in each of the two groups $\mathbf{G}, \mathbf{G}'$ and the bilinear pairing $e : \mathbf{G} \times \mathbf{G} \to \mathbf{G}'$. The opaque encoding of the elements of $\mathbf{G}$ is modeled as injective functions ξ, ξ' that are chosen at random.

Let $\xi : Z_p \to \Xi$, where $\Xi \subset \{0,1\}^*$, which maps all $a \in Z_p$ to the string representation $\xi(g^a)$ of $g^a \in \mathbf{G}$. We similarly define $\xi' : Z_p \to \Xi'$ for $\mathbf{G}'$. The attacker $\mathcal{A}$ communicates with the oracles using the ξ-representations of the group elements only.

Let $\alpha, \gamma, z \in Z_p^*$, $T_0 \leftarrow g^{\frac{z\gamma}{\alpha^{n+1}}}$, where $h = g^z$, $T_1 \leftarrow g^r$, and $d \leftarrow \{0,1\}$. We show that no generic algorithm $\mathcal{A}$ that is given the encodings of $g, h = g^z, g_1, .., g_n, g_{n+2}, .., g_{2n}, g'$, where $g_i = g^{\alpha^i}$, $g' = g^\gamma$ and makes up to q oracle queries can guess the value of d with probability greater than $1/2 + \Omega(q^2 n^3/p)$.

Proof of Theorem 1. Consider an algorithm $\mathcal{B}$ that plays the following game with $\mathcal{A}$. $\mathcal{B}$ maintains two lists of pairs, $L_1 = \{(F_{1,i}, \xi_{1,i}) : i = 0, ..., \tau_1 - 1\}, L_T = \{(F_{T,i}, \xi'_{T,i}) : i = 0, ..., \tau_2 - 1\}$, under the invariant that, at step τ in the game, $\tau_1 + \tau_T = \tau + 2n + 2$. Here, the $F_{*,*} \in Z_p[A, \Gamma, Z, T_0, T_1]$ are polynomials in the indeterminates A, Γ, Z, T_0, T_1 with coefficients in Z_p. The $\xi'_{*,*} \in \{0,1\}^*$ are arbitrary distinct strings.

The lists are initialized at step $\tau = 0$ by initializing $\tau_1 \leftarrow 2n + 2, \tau_T \leftarrow 0$, and setting $F_{1,0} = 1$, $F_{1,1} = A$, $F_{1,2} = A^2$,..., $F_{1,n} = A^n$, $F_{1,(n+2)} = A^{n+2}$,..., $F_{1,2n} = A^{2n}$, $F_{1,2n+1} = \Gamma$, $F_{1,2n+2} = z$, $F_{1,2n+3} = T_0$, $F_{1,2n+4} = T_1$. The corresponding strings are set to arbitrary distinct strings in $\{0,1\}^*$ (Here, $F_{1,n+1}$ is skipped).

We may assume that $\mathcal{A}$ only makes oracle queries on strings previously obtained from $\mathcal{B}$, since $\mathcal{B}$ can make them arbitrarily hard to guess. We note that $\mathcal{B}$ can determine the index i of any given string $\xi_{1,i}$ in L_1 (resp. $\xi'_{T,i} \in L_T$), where ties between multiple matches are broken arbitrarily.

$\mathcal{B}$ starts the game by providing $\mathcal{A}$ with the encodings $\xi_{1,0}, \xi_{1,1}, \xi_{1,2}, \ldots, \xi_{1,n}$, $\xi_{1,(n+2)}, \ldots, \xi_{1,2n}, \xi_{1,(2n+1)}, \xi_{1,2n+2}, \xi_{1,2n+3}, \xi_{1,2n+4}$. The simulator $\mathcal{B}$ responds to algorithm $\mathcal{A}$'s queries as follows.

Group action. Given a multiply/divide selection bit and two operands $\xi_{1,i}$ and $\xi_{1,j}$ with $0 \le i, j < \tau_1$, compute $F_{1,\tau_1} \leftarrow F_{1,i} \mp F_{1,j}$ depending on whether a multiplication or a division is requested. If $F_{1,\tau_1} = F_{1,l}$ for some $l < \tau_1$, set $\xi_{1,\tau_1} \leftarrow \xi_{1,l}$; otherwise, set ξ_{1,τ_1} to a string in $\{0,1\}^*$ distinct from $\xi_{1,0}, ..., \xi_{1,\tau_1-1}$.

Add $(F_{1,\tau_1}, \xi_{1,\tau_1})$ to the list L_1 and give ξ_{1,τ_1} to $\mathcal{A}$, then increment τ_1 by one. Group action queries in $\mathbf{G}'$ are treated similarly.

Pairing. Given two operands $\xi_{1,i}$ and $\xi_{1,j}$ with $0 \leq i, j < \tau_1$, compute the product $F_{T,\tau_T} \leftarrow F_{T,i} F_{T,j}$. If $F_{T,\tau_T} = F_{T,l}$ for some $l < \tau_T$, set $\xi'_{T,\tau_T} \leftarrow \xi'_{T,l}$; otherwise, set ξ'_{T,τ_T} to a string in $\{0,1\}^* \setminus \{\xi'_{T,0}, ..., \xi'_{T,\tau_T-1}\}$. Add $(F_{T,\tau_T}, \xi'_{T,\tau_T})$ to the list L_T, and give ξ'_{T,τ_T} to $\mathcal{A}$, then increment τ_T by one.

Observe that at any time in the game, the total degree of any polynomial in each of the two lists is bounded as follows: $deg(F_{1,i}) \leq 2n$, $deg(F_{T,i}) \leq 4n$. After at most q queries, $\mathcal{A}$ terminates and returns a guess $d' \in \{0,1\}$. At this point $\mathcal{B}$ chooses random $\alpha, \gamma, z \leftarrow Z_p$. Consider $t_d \leftarrow \frac{z\gamma}{\alpha^{n+1}}$ and $t_{1-d} \leftarrow r$ for both choices of $d \in \{0,1\}$. The simulation provided by $\mathcal{B}$ is perfect and reveals nothing to $\mathcal{A}$ about d unless the chosen random values for the indeterminates give rise to a nontrivial equality relation (identical polynomial in any of the lists L_1, L_T) between the simulated group elements that was not revealed to $\mathcal{A}$, i.e., when we assign $A \leftarrow \alpha, \Gamma \leftarrow \gamma$, and either $T_0 \leftarrow \frac{z\gamma}{\alpha^{n+1}}, T_1 \leftarrow r$ or the converse $T_0 \leftarrow r, T_1 \leftarrow \frac{z\gamma}{\alpha^{n+1}}$. This happens only if for some i, j one of the following holds:

- $F_{1,i}(\alpha, .., \alpha^n, \alpha^{n+2}, \dots, \alpha^{2n}, \gamma, z, \frac{\gamma}{\alpha^{n+1}}, r) -$
  $F_{1,j}(\alpha, .., \alpha^n, \alpha^{n+2}, \dots, \alpha^{2n}, \gamma, z, \frac{\gamma}{\alpha^{n+1}}, r) = 0$, yet $F_{1,i} \neq F_{1,j}$,
- $F_{T,i}(\alpha, .., \alpha^n, \alpha^{n+2}, \dots, \alpha^{2n}, \gamma, z, \frac{\gamma}{\alpha^{n+1}}, r) -$
  $F_{T,j}(\alpha, .., \alpha^n, \alpha^{n+2}, \dots, \alpha^{2n}, \gamma, z, \frac{\gamma}{\alpha^{n+1}}, r) = 0$, yet $F_{T,i} \neq F_{T,j}$,
- any relation similar to the above in which $\frac{\gamma}{\alpha^{n+1}}$ and r have been exchanged.

We now determine the probability of a random occurrence of a non-trivial numeric cancellation. Since $F_{1,i} - F_{1,j}$ for fixed i and j is a polynomial of degree at most $2n$, it vanishes for random assignment of the indeterminates in Z_p with probability at most $2n/p$. Similarly, for fixed i and j, the second case occurs with probability $\leq 4n/p$. The same probabilities are found in the analogous cases where γ/α^{n+1} and r have been exchanged.

Now, absent of any of the above events, the distribution of the bit d in $\mathcal{A}$'s view is independent, and $\mathcal{A}$'s probability of making a correct guess is exactly $\frac{1}{2}$. Thus, by summing over all valid pairs i, j in each case, we find that $\mathcal{A}$ makes a correct guess with advantage

$$\leq 2 \left(\binom{\tau_1}{2} \frac{2n}{p} + \binom{\tau_T}{2} \frac{4n}{p} \right).$$

Since $\tau_1 + \tau_T \leq q + 2n + 2$, we have $\epsilon \leq 16n(q+n+1)^2/p$, as required.

A.3   Proof of Theorem 4

We will show trapdoor privacy that is the challenge keyword is indistinguishable from the same length random keyword. To show this we will present two games $\mathcal{G}_1, \mathcal{G}_2$. In $\mathcal{G}_1$ (*ideal* game), $\mathcal{SIM}$ chooses uniformly random r_1, r_2 values while in $\mathcal{G}_2$ (*real* game), $\mathcal{SIM}$ follows the protocol $r'' = r_1 + r_2$ and we show that these two games are indistinguishable.

Proof. We first consider $\mathcal{G}_1$. Suppose there exists an adversary $\mathcal{A}$ that distinguishes between challenge keyword w^* from random keyword with advantage ϵ. Then we construct a simulator $\mathcal{SIM}$ that wins the n-DDHI game as follows. Once $\mathcal{SIM}$ gets a n-DDHI instance $g, g_1, \ldots, g_n, g_{n+2}, \ldots, g_{2n}, g^\gamma, h, Z = h^{\frac{\gamma}{\alpha^{n+1}}}$, the game between $\mathcal{SIM}$ and $\mathcal{A}$ is as follows:

- **Init:** $\mathcal{A}$ gives $\mathcal{SIM}$ the challenge keyword w^*, user index i^* that he wants to be challenged on.
- **Setup:** $\mathcal{SIM}$ lets $g, g_1, \ldots, g_n, g_{n+2}, \ldots, g_{2n}$ in the simulation be as in the instance and picks $a_1, b_1, a_2, b_2, \zeta, \zeta', \theta, \theta'$ values from Z_p. He also sets $h_{0,1} \leftarrow g^{-w^*\zeta+\zeta'}$, $h_{1,1} \leftarrow g^\zeta$, $h_{0,2} \leftarrow g^{-w^*\theta+\theta'}$, $h_{1,2} \leftarrow g^\theta$, He computes public key parameters as $h_{0,1}^{a_1} = (g^{a_1})^{-w^*\zeta+\zeta'}$, $h_{1,1}^{a_1} = (g^{a_1})^\zeta$, $h_{0,1}^{b_1} = (g^{b_1})^{-w^*\zeta+\zeta'}$, $h_{1,1}^{b_1} = (g^{b_1})^\zeta$, $h_{0,2}^{a_2} = (g^{a_2})^{-w^*\theta+\theta'}$, $h_{1,2}^{a_2} = (g^{a_2})^\theta$, $h_{0,2}^{b_2} = (g^{b_2})^{-w^*\theta+\theta'}$, $h_{1,2}^{b_2} = (g^{b_2})^\theta$, $v = g^\gamma$ and gives them to both $\mathcal{A}$ and $\mathcal{S}_{aid}$. $\mathcal{SIM}$ generates user secret keys sk_i by running Setup algorithm. As a note that, the simulator does not know the values α, γ. Then, $\mathcal{SIM}$ gives public parameters to $\mathcal{A}$ and $\mathcal{S}_{aid}$.
- **Query:** $\mathcal{A}$ makes the following queries to $\mathcal{SIM}$ adaptively. For encryption query (S_ℓ, w_ℓ),
  If $w_\ell \neq w^* \wedge i^* \notin S_\ell$, the simulator picks k, k_1, k_2 encryption keys for file ℓ and gives the computed values,
  $hdr_{\ell,1} = g^{a_1(w_\ell-w^*)\zeta k_1} g^{a_1\zeta' k_1}$, $hdr_{\ell,2} = g^{(w_\ell-w^*)b_1\zeta(k-k_1)} g^{b_1\zeta'(k-k_1)}$, $hdr_{\ell,3} = g^{a_2(w_\ell-w^*)\theta k_2} g^{a_2\theta' k_2}$, $hdr_{\ell,4} = g^{(w_\ell-w^*)b_2\theta(k-k_2)} g^{b_2\theta'(k-k_1)}$, $hdr_{\ell,5} = g^k$,
  $hdr_{\ell,6} = \left(g^\gamma \prod_{j\in S_\ell} g_{n+1-j}\right)^k$, $hdr_{\ell,7} = e(g_{n+1}, g)^k, S_\ell$ and gives them to $\mathcal{A}$ and gives $hdr_{\ell,5}, hdr_{\ell,6}, hdr_{\ell,7}, S_\ell$ to $\mathcal{S}_{aid}$.
  if $i^* \in S_\ell \vee w^* = w_l$: The simulator outputs $\perp$.
- **Guess:** $\mathcal{SIM}$ assigns h is the form of $h = g_{n+1+i}^{r''}$ (r'' is unknown to $\mathcal{SIM}$). He picks random $\rho_{i1}, \rho_{i1}', \rho_{i2}, \rho_{i2}', r, r'$ then computes the trapdoor as $tr_1 = Z g^{a_1 b_1 \zeta' X} g^{a_2 b_2 \theta' Y}$, $tr_2 = g^{a_1 X}$, $tr_3 = g^{a_2 Y}$, $tr_4 = g^{b_1 X}$, $tr_5 = g^{b_2 Y}$, $tr_6 = h = g_{n+1+i}^{r''}$, where $X = \rho_{i1} r + \rho_{i1}' r'$, $Y = \rho_{i2} r + \rho_{i2}' r'$. Then, he gives $tr_1, tr_2, tr_3, tr_4, tr_5, tr_6, r_2$ to $\mathcal{A}$ and r_1 to $\mathcal{S}_{aid}$.
- **Output:** $\mathcal{A}$ outputs a bit b. To conclude, the simulator forwards b as its own answer in the n-DDHI game. If the n-DDHI instances are well formed, the adversary outputs $b = 0$ which is a random keyword, otherwise it outputs $b = 1$ which keyword is w^*.

Analysis: Under the restriction in the encryption phase, $\mathcal{S}_{aid}$ does not store keyword ciphertext that is formed by the challenge index (the public key of the challenge user g_{i^*}). Therefore, the challenge trapdoor and any keyword ciphertexts are not going to be compatible when $\mathcal{S}_{aid}$ computes function of r_1, C'. It means that the challenge trapdoor is independent of w^*, the adversary's best success probability is $1/2$ when $\mathcal{A}$ outputs $b = 0$ if the game is totally random. The success probability is $\Pr[\text{win}_\mathcal{A}(\lambda)] < 1/2 + \epsilon$ when $\mathcal{A}$ outputs $b = 1$ if the n-DDHI instances are well formed. So, $\mathcal{SIM}$ breaks n-DDHI assumption with probability $|\Pr(\mathcal{A}(b = 1) = 1) - \Pr(\mathcal{A}(b = 0) = 1| = 1/2 + \epsilon - 1/2 = \epsilon$, which is non-negligible. So

$$\left|\Pr\left[\mathcal{G}_1^\mathcal{A}\right]\right| \geq \epsilon$$

In $\mathcal{G}_2$, $\mathcal{SIM}$ follows real game, chooses r_1 and r_2 such that $r'' = r_1 + r_2$ and gives r_1 to $\mathcal{S}_{aid}$ and r_2 to $\mathcal{A}$. In the real game, $\mathcal{A}$ can not ask encryption queries that user index $i^* \in S_\ell$ or $w^* = w_l$. This results $\mathcal{A}$ is not able to test if the keyword is w^* or a random keyword. We argue that since $\mathcal{A}$ gets the function of r_1 and C' and he is not able to learn any non-trivial information about r_1 under the restriction of the game. The function of r_1 and C' is totally random to $\mathcal{A}$ for every r_1 since for each encryption of a keyword w the challenger chooses fresh (random) elements (k, k_1, k_2) from Z_p. Basically, the information (randomized ciphertext) given to $\mathcal{A}$ is semantically secure. Let ε is the advantage of $\mathcal{A}$ winning the semantic security encryption then we can say $\mathcal{SIM}$ breaks n-DDHI assumption with probability $|\Pr(\mathcal{A}(b = 1) = 1) - \Pr(\mathcal{A}(b = 0) = 1| = 1/2 + \epsilon - (1/2 + \varepsilon) = \epsilon - \varepsilon$. Then,

$$\left| \Pr\left[\mathcal{G}_2^{\mathcal{A}} \right] \right| \le \epsilon - \varepsilon$$

As a result,

$$\left| \Pr\left[\mathcal{G}_1^{\mathcal{A}} \right] \right| - \left| \Pr\left[\mathcal{G}_2^{\mathcal{A}} \right] \right| \le \varepsilon$$

This completes the proof. ☐

References

1. Abdalla, M., Bellare, M., Catalano, D., Kiltz, E., Kohno, T., Lange, T., Malone-Lee, J., Neven, G., Paillier, P., Shi, H.: Searchable encryption revisited: consistency properties, relation to anonymous IBE, and extensions. In: Shoup, V. (ed.) CRYPTO 2005. LNCS, vol. 3621, pp. 205–222. Springer, Heidelberg (2005)
2. Attrapadung, N.: Unified Frameworks for Practical Broadcast Encryption and Public Key Encryption with High Functionalities. Ph.D. thesis, University of Tokyo (2007)
3. Attrapadung, N., Furukawa, J., Imai, H.: Forward-secure and searchable broadcast encryption with short ciphertexts and private keys. In: Lai, X., Chen, K. (eds.) ASIACRYPT 2006. LNCS, vol. 4284, pp. 161–177. Springer, Heidelberg (2006)
4. Bao, F., Deng, R.H., Ding, X., Yang, Y.: Private query on encrypted data in multi-user settings. In: Chen, L., Mu, Y., Susilo, W. (eds.) ISPEC 2008. LNCS, vol. 4991, pp. 71–85. Springer, Heidelberg (2008)
5. Bellare, M., Boldyreva, A., O'Neill, A.: Deterministic and efficiently searchable encryption. In: Menezes, A. (ed.) CRYPTO 2007. LNCS, vol. 4622, pp. 535–552. Springer, Heidelberg (2007)
6. Boneh, D., Boyen, X., Goh, E.-J.: Hierarchical identity based encryption with constant size ciphertext. In: Cramer, R. (ed.) EUROCRYPT 2005. LNCS, vol. 3494, pp. 440–456. Springer, Heidelberg (2005)
7. Boneh, D., Boyen, X., Shacham, H.: Short group signatures. In: Franklin, M. (ed.) CRYPTO 2004. LNCS, vol. 3152, pp. 41–55. Springer, Heidelberg (2004)
8. Boneh, D., Di Crescenzo, G., Ostrovsky, R., Persiano, G.: Public key encryption with keyword search. In: Cachin, C., Camenisch, J.L. (eds.) EUROCRYPT 2004. LNCS, vol. 3027, pp. 506–522. Springer, Heidelberg (2004)
9. Boneh, D., Gentry, C., Waters, B.: Collusion resistant broadcast encryption with short ciphertexts and private keys. In: Shoup, V. (ed.) CRYPTO 2005. LNCS, vol. 3621, pp. 258–275. Springer, Heidelberg (2005)

10. Boneh, D., Waters, B.: Conjunctive, subset, and range queries on encrypted data. In: Vadhan, S.P. (ed.) TCC 2007. LNCS, vol. 4392, pp. 535–554. Springer, Heidelberg (2007)
11. Boyen, X., Waters, B.: Anonymous hierarchical identity-based encryption (without random oracles). In: Dwork, C. (ed.) CRYPTO 2006. LNCS, vol. 4117, pp. 290–307. Springer, Heidelberg (2006)
12. Cash, D., Jarecki, S., Jutla, C.S., Krawczyk, H., Roşu, M.-C., Steiner, M.: Highly-scalable searchable symmetric encryption with support for boolean queries. In: Canetti, R., Garay, J.A. (eds.) CRYPTO 2013, Part I. LNCS, vol. 8042, pp. 353–373. Springer, Heidelberg (2013)
13. Chang, Y.-C., Mitzenmacher, M.: Privacy preserving keyword searches on remote encrypted data. In: Ioannidis, J., Keromytis, A.D., Yung, M. (eds.) ACNS 2005. LNCS, vol. 3531, pp. 442–455. Springer, Heidelberg (2005)
14. Chu, C.-K., Chow, S.S.M., Tzeng, W.-G., Zhou, J., Deng, R.H.: Key-aggregate cryptosystem for scalable data sharing in cloud storage. IEEE Trans. Parallel Distrib. Syst. 25(2), 468–477 (2014)
15. Cui, B., Liu, Z., Wang, L.: Key-aggregate searchable encryption (KASE) for group data sharing via cloud storage. IEEE Trans. Comput. 65(8), 2374–2385 (2016)
16. Curtmola, R., Garay, J., Kamara, S., Ostrovsky, R.: Searchable symmetric encryption: improved definitions and efficient constructions. In: CCS (2006)
17. Dong, C., Russello, G., Dulay, N.: Shared and searchable encrypted data for untrusted servers. In: Proceedings of the 22nd Annual IFIP WG 11.3 Working Conference on Data and Applications Security (2008)
18. Faber, S., Jarecki, S., Krawczyk, H., Nguyen, Q., Rosu, M., Steiner, M.: Rich queries on encrypted data: beyond exact matches. In: Pernul, G., Ryan, P.Y.A., Weippl, E. (eds.) ESORICS. LNCS, vol. 9327, pp. 123–145. Springer, Heidelberg (2015). doi:10.1007/978-3-319-24177-7_7
19. Goh, E.-J.: Secure indexes. Cryptology eprint archive, report 2003/216 (2003)
20. Jarecki, S., Jutla, C.S., Krawczyk, H., Rosu, M., Steiner, M.: Outsourced symmetric private information retrieval. In: CCS (2013)
21. Kamara, S., Papamanthou, C., Roeder, T.: Dynamic searchable symmetric encryption. In: CCS (2012)
22. Kiayias, A., Oksuz, O., Tang, Q.: Distributed parameter generation for bilinear Diffie Hellman exponentiation and applications. In: López, J., Mitchell, C.J. (eds.) ISC 2015. LNCS, vol. 9290, pp. 548–567. Springer, Heidelberg (2015)
23. Liang, K., Susilo, W.: Searchable attribute-based mechanism with efficient data sharing for secure cloud storage. IEEE Trans. Inform. Forensics Secur. 10, 1981–1992 (2015)
24. Liu, Z., Li, J., Chen, X., Yang, J., Jia, C.: TMDS: thin-model data sharing scheme supporting keyword search in cloud storage. In: Susilo, W., Mu, Y. (eds.) ACISP 2014. LNCS, vol. 8544, pp. 115–130. Springer, Heidelberg (2014)
25. Popa, R.A., Zeldovich, N.: Multi Key Searchable Encryption (2013). https://people.csail.mit.edu/nickolai/papers/popa-multikey-eprint.pdf
26. Shoup, V.: Lower bounds for discrete logarithms and related problems. In: Fumy, W. (ed.) EUROCRYPT 1997. LNCS, vol. 1233, pp. 256–266. Springer, Heidelberg (1997)
27. Song, D.X., Wagner, D., Perrig, A.: Practical techniques for searches on encrypted data. In: IEEE Symposium on Security and Privacy (2000)

28. Tang, Q.: Nothing is for free: security in searching shared and encrypted data. IEEE Trans. Inform. Forensics Secur. **9**, 1943–1952 (2014)
29. Van Rompay, C., Molva, R., Önen, M.: Multi-user searchable encryption in the cloud. In: López, J., Mitchell, C.J. (eds.) ISC 2015. LNCS, vol. 9290, pp. 299–316. Springer, Heidelberg (2015)
30. Zheng, Q., Xu, S., Ateniese, G.: VABKS: verifiable attribute-based keyword search over outsourced encrypted data. In: INFOCOM (2014)

Detection and Monitoring

Membrane: A Posteriori Detection of Malicious Code Loading by Memory Paging Analysis

Gábor Pék[✉], Zsombor Lázár, Zoltán Várnagy, Márk Félegyházi,
and Levente Buttyán

CrySyS Lab, Budapest University of Technology and Economics, Budapest, Hungary
pek@crysys.hu

Abstract. In this paper, we design and implement Membrane, a memory forensics tool to detect code loading behavior by stealthy malware. Instead of trying to detect the code loading itself, we focus on the changes it causes on the memory paging of the Windows operating system. As our method focuses on the anomalies caused by code loading, we are able to detect a wide range of code loading techniques. Our results indicate that we can detect code loading malware behavior with 86–98 % success in most cases, including advanced targeted attacks. Our method is generic enough and hence could significantly raise the bar for attackers to remain stealthy and persist for an extended period of time.

Keywords: Code loading · Memory paging · Windows · Memory forensics

1 Introduction

Recent years' targeted attack have shown that even the most advanced systems can be compromised. Some of these targeted attacks used sophisticated intrusion techniques [3] and others were quite simple [1]. These malware attacks typically employed a sequence of steps to compromise a target system. A majority of these malware codes have information gathering and information stealing capabilities. Once they have access to their target, these malware codes typically perform a number of operations to cover their traces and remain undetected. Intuitively, the more the malware can persist in the target system, the more information it can collect. Often, the attacks persist for years in the target systems and the attackers get access to a substantial amount of confidential information (as reported for example in [11]). It is reasonable to assume that these long-term operations leave a noticeable trace, yet many examples show that the complexity and rich features of contemporary operating systems leaves ample space for the attackers to hide their operation.

Code loading is one of the key techniques that malware employs to achieve persistence. Code loading happens when the malware adds to or replaces the functionality of existing code to execute its own components. It is typically

© Springer International Publishing Switzerland 2016
I. Askoxylakis et al. (Eds.): ESORICS 2016, Part I, LNCS 9878, pp. 199–216, 2016.
DOI: 10.1007/978-3-319-45744-4_10

possible as, for example, the Windows operating systems provides various methods (e.g., legitimate API functions, registry entries) to support this. Thus, code loading usually exploits the conditions given by a legitimate process. That is why code loading is used to achieve evasion of detection or bypass restrictions enforced on a process level.

There has been efforts to develop various memory and disk forensics techniques to pinpoint system anomalies caused by such malware infections [5]. One of the biggest problem with current memory forensics techniques is that they only utilize memory locations that were actively used by the OS at the moment of acquisition. That is, important information about code loading can be lost if the malware or part of it was inactive when the memory was grabbed. Furthermore, the rich feature set of Windows allows miscreants to build unique code loading techniques (e.g., Flame's code loading mechanism) that evades signature-based protections.

In this paper, we explore the realm of Windows memory management, systematically identify key paging states and build upon the details of these paging states to detect malicious behavior after a successful system compromise. We design and implement *Membrane*, an anomaly-based memory forensics tool to detect code loading attacks by malicious software. Membrane is based on the popular memory forensics framework Volatility [18]. Membrane performs detection by analyzing the number of memory paging states. Our approach is different from approaches in related work because we focus on detecting anomalies (symptoms) concerning paging states of malware code loading behavior instead of the code loading actions themselves. While code loading actions can only be pinpointed by live analysis, our approach focuses on the consequences of these actions that may persist in the system for an extended period of time.

Our cardinality-based analysis is advantageous for several reasons: (i) it is generic, (ii) this technique is less researched and can provide new insights into malware detection, (iii) it can be used in combination with other detection techniques to maximize the confidence of detection, and (iv) arguably, evasion against this method is difficult (see Sect. 6). These characteristics allow us to provide a solution that can detect a wide variety of code loading attacks. This could significantly raise the bar for miscreants to implement memory-resident and stealthy malware attacks.

This paper is organized as follows. In Sect. 2, we give an overview of code loading techniques employed by malware and mitigation techniques designed against code loading attacks. Section 3 gives a short motivation and a high-level overview about our memory paging based approach to detect the traces of malware code loading after infection. In Sect. 4, we present Membrane and give details of our methodology including the implementation of Membrane. Section 5 shows the efficiency of Membrane to detect a posteriori code loading attacks. We discuss evasion techniques and other concerns in Sect. 6. Finally, Sect. 7 summarizes our work.

2   Background and Related Work

2.1   Code Loading Techniques and Types

Malware can use a wide range of means to take control over a system and hide its presence. Due to its versatility, code loading is commonly used by contemporary malware in spite of the effort that has been spent on developing defenses. Recent advanced targeted attacks, most prominently infostealers, still used this technique to surpass defenses and ensure an extended operation. To achieve this goal, the malware employs more complex code loading techniques that go beyond the simple use of operating system functions (e.g., the Flame malware described in Sect. 3.1).

First and quite surprisingly, Windows provides a wide range of user mode (e.g., `VirtualAllocEx`, `WriteProcessMemory`) and kernel mode functions (e.g., `KeAttachProcess`, `ZwAllocateVirtualMemory`) that can be used to inject code into processes. DLL loading can be achieved by using, for example `VirtualAllocEx` and `WriteProcessMemory` to allocate *private* memory in a target process and to store the name of the DLL to load. Then, `CreateRemoteThread` is called to start a new thread in the virtual address space of the target process which loads the corresponding DLL.

The *detours library* was implemented by Microsoft back in 1999 which provides a rich feature set to load DLL into running processes or program binaries. Miscreants can also insert various DLL paths into the *AppInit_DLLs* registry value, which forces newly created processes to load those DLLs. *DLL preloading* is another notorious technique, which enforces legitimate binaries to load illegitimate DLLs when the program starts. Another technique is called *process replacement* where the malware launches a legitimate process, but replaces its memory content when the image file is mapped into memory. For completeness, we mention *pure kernel rootkits* which load a new kernel driver or hijack an existing one. They operate without using any user-space component. Writing reliable kernel rootkits is challenging, however, as it is difficult to control simple functionalities from the kernel space such as network communication. Another challenge for malware writers is that the kernel is quite volatile and this requires that the kernel space malware is well-written. Additionally, recent Windows operating systems enforce code signing for kernel drivers, whose evasion requires an extra effort from attackers (e.g., Flame, Duqu [2]).

In this work, we focus on detecting code loading techniques in the user space. As discussed above, malware manipulating only the kernel functionality requires more substantial effort from attackers. We note, however, that our method does detect kernel-space malware with user-space components.

2.2   Mitigating Code Loading Attacks

Windows implements various protection mechanisms, for example, a private virtual address space for processes to mitigate code loading attacks. But, it also allows to use simple API functions to circumvent such protections. For instance

`WriteProcessMemory` can write into a target process when called with appropriate privileges. As `WriteProcessMemory` invokes kernel mode code in the context of the target process no address space restriction is violated. In this section, we present various techniques preventing and detecting code loading attacks and discuss their merits and limitations.

Prevention. Various preventive methods have been designed in recent years to thwart the loading of illegitimate codes. These techniques include the use of whitelisting, checksums or enforcing signed code loading. Unfortunately all of these techniques can be circumvented by determined attackers. An example for this is Flame, which created fake, but valid certificates for its component to deceit Windows.

Recent targeted attacks have demonstrated that preventive approaches might not be able to block attackers. Thus, we assume that attackers succeed in compromising the target system and focus on detecting their activity.

Detection. There are various approaches suggested over the years to detect the integrity violations of operating system structures [7,17] using either virtualization or a new architecture design [13]. In memory forensics, integrity protection of user-space code using cryptographic hashes has been proposed by White *et al.* [19] to detect in-memory code placed by malware. The proposed hashing algorithm matches the in-memory code with its binary counterpart. The problem with integrity checking is that dynamically allocated memory locations (e.g., heap) cannot be verified in this way due to its alternating nature. Srivastava and Giffin [17] design and develop a hypervisor-based system using virtual machine introspection, Pyrenée. This aggregates and correlates information from sensors at the network level, the network-to-host boundary, and the host level to identify the true origin of malicious behavior. While Pyrenée's host-based sensor checks code loading mechanisms from the perspective of processes, Membrane is a system-centric approach which makes our detection mechanism more generic. For this reason, Membrane includes the detection of widely-used code loading techniques such as AppInit_DLLs or DLL preloading previously overlooked by related work.

The Volatility memory forensics tool [18] offers the *malfind* plugin to find malicious or hidden code segments from memory dumps. Malfind crawls process VADs (see Sect. 3.2) and looks for entries with suspicious protection bits (i.e., RWX) and type. However, these permission bits can be manipulated by the malware at a later point of time, which may turn such solutions ineffective. In contrast to malfind which checks only VAD entries, Membrane tracks per process memory paging modifications from the perspective of the OS. Various free anti-rootkit tools are also available to hunt for hidden threads and processes. Unfortunately, *none* of the tested 33 anti-rootkit tools could detect hidden processes or threads in case of Flame [2]. Thus, we need another approach which tackles the problem of code loading from another aspect. We believe, that Membrane can be successfully used in combination with previous solutions to build more effective detectors.

3   Approach

3.1   Motivation: The Case Study of Flame

For motivation, we quickly show a case study about the Flame [2] targeted attack. Flame employs an entirely unique, but sophisticated thread injection method to hide its malicious activity via a chain of system processes. This unique technique *allows Flame to completely mimic the behavior of a normal Windows update process* by the runtime patching of `services.exe`, `explorer.exe` and `iexplore.exe`. As Flame uses `iexplore.exe` for network connection [3], it can evade many malware scanners by default.

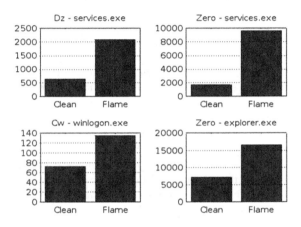

Fig. 1. Cardinality of different paging states in `services.exe`,`winlogon.exe` and `explorer.exe` on a clean and a Flame-infected 32-bit Windows 7 system.

For demonstration purposes, we infected a 32-bit Windows 7 machine with Flame malware to see what kind of page type modifications it causes. Surprisingly, the fine-grained process injection method it used to stay silent, entirely distorts the normal memory usage of system processes. Figure 1 shows that the number of certain page types (see Sect. 4.2 for more details) increases significantly when Flame is present.

This observation started us on a quest to use memory usage anomalies to detect code loading attacks.

3.2   Windows Memory Management

In order to understand, how different code loading attacks modify the state of memory, we introduce some important details about Windows' internal memory management. This will lead us to create our code loading detection technique in Sect. 4.

The virtual memory management unit of an operating system offers a transparent access method to physical addresses located in the host physical memory or the hard disk (e.g., in a pagefile). For Windows operating systems [16], this functionality is maintained by the hardware Memory Management Unit (i.e., *hardware MMU*) and a proprietary memory management kernel component which is called *memory manager* in [16]. In this work, we refer Windows' internal memory manager as the softwareMemory Management Unit (i.e., *software MMU*). The hardware MMU uses multi-level translation tables (i.e., page tables) to resolve virtual memory addresses pointing to pages which are loaded into the physical memory (i.e., valid pages). The software MMU, however, is used for invalid pages (e.g., memory is allocated, but never used), thus extra operation needs to be performed by the OS to, for example, bring them into the physical memory. In other words, Windows defers to build hardware page tables, until a page is first accessed by a thread. This approach of the OS is also called *demand paging.*

Hardware Supported Memory Management. When a virtual address points to a valid page, the hardware MMU uses multi-level translation tables, where the number of levels is influenced by the architecture. For the clarity of presentation, in this section we only discuss the 32-bit non-PAE case where each process owns a single page directory and multiple page tables. When a context switch occurs, the OS consults a kernel structure (i.e., KPROCESS) to retrieve the physical address of the process page directory. This address is loaded into a privileged CPU register called CR3, which allows the hardware MMU and software MMU to start the translation for process private virtual addresses. *Page directory entries (PDEs)* store the state and location of all the page tables belonging to a process. Due to Windows' lazy memory management, page-tables are built on demand, so only a small set of page tables are created in reality for processes. Similarly to page directories, page tables are built up from *page table entries (PTEs)* containing the location (i.e., page frame number) of the referenced page and certain flags which indicate the state and protection of the corresponding page [16]. We refer to the state of PTEs and PDEs as *paging entry types.*

Software Supported Memory Management. When the hardware MMU intends to access an invalid page, indicated by a status flag in the corresponding PTE, a page fault occurs which has to be handled by the OS. More precisely, when a hardware PTE is invalid it is referred as a *software* PTE, because the software MMU takes care of it by checking other PTE status flags to determine how to evaluate this software PTE. This evaluation process will be discussed later in Sect. 4.2. As Windows defers to build hardware PTEs until, for example, an allocated memory is first accessed, it has to record the allocation information internally. To achieve this, the software MMU maintains a self-balanced tree called *Virtual Address Descriptors (VAD)* tree [4] for each user-space process and stores the root of it (i.e., *VadRoot*) to help its traversal. Thus, whenever a memory is allocated, for example, by the NtVirtualAllocate native function, Windows adds a new VAD entry to the VAD tree of the allocator process.

Each VAD entry describes a virtually contiguous non-free virtual address range including protection information and the type of this range (e.g., copy-on-write, readable, writable). Windows makes a difference between (i) dynamically allocated memory and (ii) memory which contains data from files. The former is called *private memory* and reflects allocations on the heap or stack, the the latter one is called *file-backed or mapped memory* as it is associated with files, such as data files, executables, or page files, which can be mapped into the address space [20].

3.3 Root Cause Analysis

In order to understand why memory paging analysis can be a prominent method to detect malicious code loading, we explored the details of Windows internals by using various resources [14,16,20] as well as the static and dynamic analysis of the Windows 7 kernel. For dynamic analysis, we used WinDbg. In this way, we could understand how certain WinAPI, and thus, kernel functions influence per process paging entry types. Please see Table 1 for more details on the paging entry types.

A typical code loading attack first calls `VirtualAllocEx` to allocate a *private* memory in the target process to store the name of the DLL we intend to load into that process. It creates and initializes a single VAD entry with *RW* protection bits set, *zeroes out the PTE* (i.e., zero type software PTE is created) of the allocated memory range and sets up the page fault handler (#PF). The `NtProtectVirtualMemory` kernel function is also called after this, which sets software PTE protection bits, thus the software PTE is changed to be Demand Zero (Dz). When `WriteProcessMemory` tries to access the page, the page fault handler is invoked. At this point, the page fault is caught, hardware PTE is created and initialized (i.e., Valid and Write hardware PTE bits are set) using the previously created VAD entry as a template. This lazy memory allocation mechanism allows Windows to build page tables for only accessed pages. When #PF finished, the execution is handed to the `NtWriteVirtualMemory` kernel function, which writes the name of the malicious DLL to be loaded by the target process. As the allocated pages were accessed and modified, the hardware MMU now sets the accessed (A) and dirty (D) bits on the PTE, respectively. In the next step, `CreateRemoteThread` is called by setting the newly created thread's start address to the `LoadLibrary` WinAPI function.

At this point, `LoadLibrary` is invoked by the newly created thread with the name of the malicious DLL to be loaded. As `LoadLibrary` first invokes `NtOpenFile` to return a file handle, that is handed to `NtCreateSection` to create a *Section* object for the corresponding DLL. Due to the lazy memory management of Windows no hardware PTE is created at this point, however, only Prototype PTE kernel structures are initialized. This structure is used by the OS to handle shared memory between different processes. We emphasize here, that PPTEs are initialized with `EXECUTE_WRITECOPY` protection masks to enable Copy-On-Write operations. To support memory sharing the DLL is now mapped as view of the section object (i.e., file-backed-image is mapped) by the

`NtMapViewOfSection` kernel function, which also creates a VAD entry by using the Prototype PTEs and sets up the page fault handler to build hardware PTEs when the mapped DLL is first accessed. Finally the opened file handler was closed by `NtClose`.

If certain parts of the loaded DLL is not used currently, the OS swaps the corresponding pages and creates *Prototype PTE* entries which point to the original *Prototype PTEs*. In this way, the memory manager can quickly load back the page when it is referenced again, and uses the Prototype PTE as a template to set the protection masks to build a new hardware PTE. The presented code loading technique creates *Zero software PTEs* and *hardware PTEs with Valid, Writable, Accessed, Dirty and Copy-on-Write bits set*. This example shows fairly well, how some simple WinAPI functions influence the management of memory in Windows OSs. This rich behavior allows us to observe how different code loaders manipulate per process PTEs.

It is important to emphasize that not only the fact of code loading diverts memory paging states, but also do those *malicious functionalities* (e.g., data exfiltration, keylogging) that the loaded code executes.

3.4 Overview of Membrane

Membrane is a Volatility extension and works on virtual machine memory snapshots. Membrane detects all the active processes when the analyzed snapshot was taken and starts to dissect these processes to determine their memory paging states. By doing so, Membrane first restores a wide range of memory paging states as Table 1 shows it. To the best of our knowledge, we are the first, who restore memory paging states in that detail and use them for a posteriori malware detection as detailed in Sect. 4.2. Then, Membrane calculates different paging state cardinalities (e.g., the number of zeroed out pages present in the address space of a given process) and creates features from them. These feature candidates are accumulated into a feature set, and out of these candidates the prominent features are selected by a machine learning algorithm. These feature are later used for decision making as described in Sect. 4.3.

4   Implementation

First, we select key features of paging states and train a *random forest classifier* to detect code loading behavior. These candidate features are later evaluated and filtered to pick the most relevant ones suitable to detect code loading. In the testing phase, we repeat the training phase, but samples are classified (i.e., detected as malicious or not) only with the chosen features.

4.1   Collecting Samples

To train our system, we first collect samples for our benign and malicious datasets. Thus, we prepare our malware dataset with prudent practices [15] to have a ground truth consisting of malicious samples using malicious code loading. Considering malicious samples, we work with one dataset of generic malware and one dataset of targeted malware samples. We collect the *generic* dataset from a large set of generic malware samples retrieved from public and private malware data feeds. Our initial *generic* dataset comprised of 9905 samples, however, our thorough dataset preparation process (see Sect. 2.2 in [12] for details) resulted in a balanced dataset of 1095 binaries adequate to start and analyze their runtime behavior. Out of these, we have found 194 active malware samples that exhibited code loading. Similarly, we prepare goodware programs to have a balanced dataset for machine learning, we perform later. Then, we install and start multiple benign applications and a single malicious sample into a VM under analysis. Next, snapshots are retrieved from this running VM, which are handed to our tool, Membrane, for analysis. For testing *targeted* malware, we manually selected 7 malware samples from active targeted campaigns excluding malware whose C&C servers have been sinkholed or shut down.

4.2   Feature Creation

The observations in Fig. 1 strongly suggest that code loading attacks have a significant effect on the frequency of different paging states. Thus, we use the frequency of various paging state to set up detection *features*. We summarize all the paging states we handled during our feature creation process in Table 1.

Membrane internals. We carefully investigated Windows-specific page types and their corresponding translation process to restore our features from paging states. Albeit, most of these page types are documented with a certain level of granularity [8,16,20], some of them are still not well understood. Our implementation currently supports both x86 PAE enabled and x64 images. While we tested the former case on 32-bit Windows XP and 7 OSs, the latter was verified on 64-bit Windows 7 and 8.1 snapshots. As a result of our translation process we are capable of restoring 28 different paging states as shown in Table 1.

Our translation process works as follows. We first natively open the memory snapshot file (i.e., .vmsn) with Volatility. We then locate *VadRoot* values for running processes by iterating through the *EPROCESS* kernel structure. VadRoot stores the virtual address of the process VAD tree [4]. At this point, we traverse the VAD tree by locating VAD entries which describe all the valid virtual addresses belonging to the process virtual address space. From this point on, we need to resolve all these virtual addresses by slicing them into page-sized buffers.

As a next step, we modified Volatility's internal address translation process as follows. Whenever a new process virtual address is retrieved by Volatility, it starts to resolve the address by traversing the process page tables. Similarly to the hardware MMU, it returns the corresponding physical address if all the page table entries (e.g., PDE, PTE) were valid. If it encountered an invalid entry (e.g., Software PTE), it raises an exception or returns with zero values. Thus, we had to implement the software MMU here to retrieve exact paging entry types. To do

Table 1. Paging entries we restored for feature creation.

Name	Description
RESTORED FEATURES FOR NON-PAE 32-BIT WINDOWS XP	
Valid	The PTE points to a page residing in the physical memory
Zero PDE	The Page Directory Entry contains all zeroes
Zero PTE	The Page Table Entry contains all zeroes
Pagefile	The PTE points to a page which is swapped out
Large	The PDE maps a 4-MB large page (or 2MB on PAE systems)
Demand Zero	The memory manager needs to provide a zeroed out page
Valid Prototype	The *PPTE points to (directly or via VAD) a PPTE which points to a valid page
Invalid Prototype	The PPTE points to an unresolvable page
Pagefile Prototype	The *PPTE points to a PPTE which points into a pagefile
Demand Zero Prototype	The *PPTE points to a PPTE which translates to a zeroed out page
Mapped File	The PTE is Zero, thus we resolve it from VAD which points to the mapped file
Mapped File Prototype	The *PPTE points to a PPTE where the prototype bit is set and has *Subsection* type
Unknown Prototype	The same as Mapped File Prototype, but PPTE has no *Subsection* type
Writable	The PTE points to a writable page
Owner (Kernel mode)	The corresponding page can be accessed in user- or kernel mode
Cache Disabled	The PTE points to a page where CPU caching is disabled
Writethrough	The PTE points to a write-through or write combined page
Accessed	The PTE points to an accessed page
Dirty	The PTE points to a written page
Transition	A shared page is no longer referenced and moved to the transition list
Copy-on-write	The PTE points to a copy-on-write page
Global PDE	The address translation applies to all processes
Unknown	The PTE is not empty, but does not belong to any of the cases
ADDITIONAL FEATURES FOR PAE-ENABLED 32-BIT WINDOWS 7	
Non-executable	The PTE points to a non-executable page
VAD Prototype	The *PPTE points to a location described by the VAD tree
Modified-no-write	The requested page is in the physical memory and on the modified-no-write list
Zero PDPTE	The Page-directory Pointer Table Entry contains all zeroes
ADDITIONAL FEATURES FOR 64-BIT WINDOWS 7	
Zero PML4E	The Pagetable Level 4 Entry contains all zeroes

that, we resolve invalid entries using the VAD tree as Fig. 2 shows it. Furthermore, Table 1 details how we resolved different paging entry types and restored paging entry states from them.

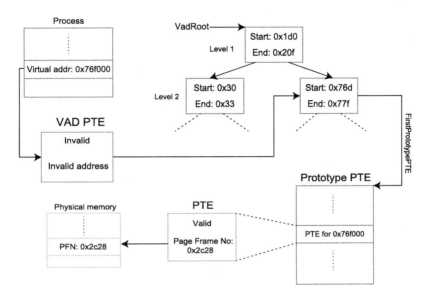

Fig. 2. Crawling VAD tree by Membrane to resolve invalid paging entries and restore the corresponding paging states.

4.3   Feature Selection and Classification

After evaluating possible paging states, we defined 28 different features under Windows 7 and 23 features under Windows XP as shown in Table 1. We selected these features to train our system. Thus, we had an X matrix with m rows and 28/23 columns, where m is associated with the number of different code loader malware samples. As our training set is relatively small, we used various methods for better evaluation. First, we used feature scaling to represent our features on the same scale (i.e., we used the interval of $[0-1]$). Then, we applied feature reduction to avoid overfitting by calculating the Gini index of our normalized features. The Gini index shows the inequality among the values of a frequency distribution. In our case, per process frequency distributions are defined by the cardinality of given per process paging states in n consecutive memory snapshots. The lower this index is, the more equal the values are in a frequency distribution.

For later classification, we selected features that had smaller index than the mean of all indexes. This resulted in using features *Zero PTE, Demand Zero, Valid Prototype, Mapped File Prototype* and *Copy-on-write* under Windows XP. The selected features under Windows 7 are *Zero PTE, Accessed, Demand Zero,*

Writable, Owner, Writethrough, Cache disabled, Pagefile, Valid Prototype, Valid, Dirty and *Mapped file.* The process noise under Windows 7 is higher than in Windows XP, thus we needed more features for classification.

4.4 Detecting Code Loading

After selecting the prominent features we used *random forest* classification to detect code loading. Random forest is a bag of randomly split decision trees. We can collect the trees with this method and the majority voting of the trees will classify a given sample.

Initially, we followed the hint obtained from the execution of the Flame malware shown in Fig. 1. We first took single snapshots of malware infected VMs to see if we detect some of the features we identified in Sect. 4.3.

We then created multiple snapshots periodically from the same infected VM to understand in detail how code loading attacks modify the number of paging states and how the OS manipulates them over time. There are various reasons to perform this measurement. First, single snapshots could miss the activation of execution-stalling malware which defer their parasitic behavior until a certain event occurs (e.g., no keyboard press for 5 min for Duqu). Second, malware could retrieve further components and load them into other system processes as well. This behavior can only be detected if we repeatedly take snapshots. Third, Windows OSs use various memory optimization methods, for example, to conserve physical memory. These optimization routines could also affect our features.

To measure the *accuracy (ACC)* of our classification process, we calculate the ratio of all the correctly classified machines per all the machines we tested. More precisely, $ACC = \frac{TP+TN}{P+N}$, where TP, TN refer to the number of successfully identified infected and clean VMs, and P, N indicates the number of infected and benign machines, respectively.

Furthermore, we calculate *true positive rates (TPR)* to denote the ratio of correctly classified infected machines compared to all the infected machines we tested (i.e., $TPR = \frac{TP}{P}$). Finally, the false positive rate ($FPR = \frac{FP}{N}$) is used to denote misclassification of benign machines, where FP means that an infected machine bypasses detection and is marked as clean.

5   Analysis

We now present our result detecting code loading behavior in contemporary malware. We then apply our code loading detection method for a dataset composed of generic malware samples as well as hand-picked samples from recent targeted attacks.

5.1 Analysis Setup

We built a dynamic execution environment for Membrane to systematically detect code loading by contemporary malware. We instrument virtual machines

(VMs) using VMware's ESXi to run malware samples with various operating system and network settings. Designing a containment policy for prudent malware experiments is essential and we used the guidelines of [9, 15] to design our containment policy.

We implemented our execution environment for Membrane on *two* identical physical machines with Intel Core i7-4770 CPUs, 32 GB of memory and VMware ESXi 5.5 OSs. Host machine (*ESX1*) runs our VMs and takes snapshots, and the other one (*ESX2*) is responsible to retrieve information from these snapshots and perform analysis by Membrane which enables detection. We used a controller VM (*CTRL*) to invoke VMware vSphere API via the *psphere* python module. This module is a native binding to control VMware ESXi environments. We executed our tests on multiple VMs with different OS configurations (*WinXP, Win7_1, Win7_2*) to test the robustness of our approach against system changes. While WinXP and Win7_1 are 32-bit Windows XP and 7 installations, Win7_2 is a 64-bit Windows 7 OS. Our exact system configuration is detailed in Table 2.

Table 2. Machine configurations we used in our malware detection and analysis system. Virtual machines WinXP, Win7_1 and Win7_2 are running on the ESX1 host machine and are used for snapshot based malware detection. Note that Win7_2 was configured with 1 and 4 GBs of memory for more complete evaluation. Note that the default setup comes with 1 GB of memory, so the other case is explicitly mentioned when used.

Type	Name	Memory size	OS
Host	ESX1	32 GB	ESXi 5.5 U1
	ESX2	32 GB	ESXi 5.5 U1
VM	CTRL	4 GB	64-bit Ubuntu 14.04
	WinXP	512 MB	32-bit Win XP SP3
	Win7_1	1 GB	32-bit Windows 7
	Win7_2	1/4 GB	64-bit Windows 7

We instrumented our experiments with two different network configurations to study the activation behavior of various malware samples. The two configurations are the following: (i) no Internet connection is enabled, (ii) real Internet connection is enabled with a carefully crafted containment policy following the suggestions of Rossow *et al.* [15]. When Internet connection was enabled, we used NAT with the following containment policy: (a) we enabled known C&C TCP ports (e.g., HTTP, HTTPS, DNS, IRC) (b) we redirected TCP ports with supposedly harmful traffic (e.g., SMTP, ports not registered by IANA) to our INetSim network simulator [6] we also configured, and (c) we set rate-limitation on analyzed VMs to mitigate DoS attacks.

5.2 Detecting Malware

First, we created a cross-validation dataset from generic malware samples to test our tool with the features selected in Sect. 4.3. To make sure that the feature

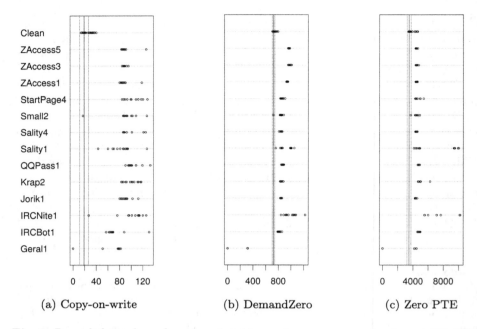

Fig. 3. Recorded number of paging states in `explorer.exe` running in our WinXP environment. Each dot on horizontal lines shows the number of paging state in a given snapshot. The vertical straight line corresponds to the median of clean executions, while the dashed lines depict the standard deviation.

selection is not biased towards our training dataset, we also compiled a test-only dataset from a mix of generic malware and confirmed targeted attack samples.

Birds-eye-view Analysis. We first created sample runs on our test machine WinXP VM with only legitimate applications installed (see Sect. 2.2 in [12]) as a benchmark. We also infected these systems with samples from selected malware families performing code loading.

We repeated our evaluation process 13 times in case of malware samples and 54 times for goodware. In this way, we estimated certain statistics (i.e., median, standard deviation) to see whether these features can be used to detect the of malware. Figure 3 shows how the cardinality of certain paging state changes in `explorer.exe` on Win XP for different generic malware executions.

Detailed Analysis. Then, we executed an extensive set of experiments with the two network containment configurations described in Sect. 5.1. Out of the 194 generic code injector malware, 128 samples targeted `explorer.exe` which turned to be the most popular injection target. That is why our classification algorithm works with these samples. Our evaluation process comprises three parts: (i) code loaders are evaluated on VMs with preinstalled and started benign applications with K-fold cross-validation in accordance with our methodology detailed in

Sect. 4, (ii) same as the previous point, but no benign processes are installed and started, (iii) the best performing random forest classificator is chosen from the cross-validation process to evaluate our test-only dataset.

In cases (i) and (ii), we infected our prepared Windows XP (i.e., WinXP) and Windows 7 (i.e., Win7_1) environments in each network containment configuration. After retrieving snapshots with Membrane, we run our classification algorithm to find malicious infections. Note that we put equal number of benign and infected snapshots into each cross-validation process. Table 3 summarizes our results and strengthens some of our key observations. According to our observations running processes raise the noise of certain system processes. This observation manifests in lower detection ratio as the (i) and (ii) versions of Win7_1 show it. Our next observation is that the execution environment also affects detection accuracy as the *TPR* of Win7_1 and WinXP setups show it.

While the detection rates are fairly good in case of Windows XP, the results are worse for Windows 7 snapshots due to the increased baseline memory paging of `explorer.exe` in Win7_1. Interested readers can read more about our measured baseline noises in Table 2.15 in [12]. We can increase the detection accuracy by stopping legitimate processes and thus offloading `explorer.exe`. We see this increase when the TPR in Table 3 increases from 75.92 % to 86 %.

Considering case (iii), we could detect all the *generic* samples in our test-only dataset in both environments by using the best classificator chosen by the cross-validation process. Note that we also detected all the *targeted* samples of our test-only dataset (i.e., Flame, Shale, Snake, Epic and Turlae where the latter four belongs to the Uroburos campaign revealed by G Data in 2014) on Win7_1, all injecting into `explorer.exe`.

Interestingly, however, the state of network connection slightly increased the detection accuracy on Win7_1 setups, and decreased it on WinXP. One of the explanations could be that injected payloads on Windows 7 downloaded extra components, which added extra process noise that was easier to detect.

While `explorer.exe` is the most popular target of code loading according to our dataset, there are many other system processes with lower noise (e.g., `services.exe` or `winlogon.exe`) that are known to be also preferred by miscreants.

A combined detection over several processes could further increase accuracy for malware that injects into multiple processes (e.g. Flame). We did not do this extensive study as it was not our focus.

6   Discussion

Systems Under Heavy Load. Our results showed that our experiments on the *WinXP* operating system were fairly accurate with a very low false positive rate. We noticed, however, that occasionally on *Win7* the baseline operation of the system was dependent on the realistic system load and the target process. This meant that heavy system use (e.g. watching Youtube videos, installing and starting of various applications or stress-testing the memory) caused a significant increase in the number of paging states (for example, the `explorer.exe`

Table 3. Detecting generic and targeted code loading malware on our WinXP and Win7_1 VMs with different network connections in `explorer.exe`. We used a $K = 5$ cross-validation iteration for the measurements. Note that the targeted samples of our test-only dataset were executed only under Win7_1.

CROSS-VALIDATION DATASET				
Internet	VM	ACC %	TPR %	FPR %
no	WinXP	98.67	98.82	1.18
	Win7_1	73.59	75.92	28.46
yes	WinXP	92.81	90.88	5.45
	Win7_1	79.45	82.69	23.59
CROSS-VALIDATION DATASET WITH NO ADDITIONAL PROCESSES				
no	Win7_1	77.16	86.00	34.73
TEST-ONLY DATASET				
no	WinXP	100	100	-
	Win7_1	100	100	-

process produced a high number of Copy-on-Write and Demand Zero paging states on a *Win7_1*). This somewhat reduced the efficiency of detection in these cases. As `explorer.exe` is taking care of the graphic shell, every newly spawned GUI application can raise process noise. That is a key observation especially for Windows 7 systems, where our detection ratio was lower.

Clearly this increase in the number of paging states only appeared when the system was under a heavy load. One can circumvent this anomaly by establishing baseline cardinality of paging states under normal system load (e.g., in a nightly operation). Assuming that the system is not under a permanent load, we can wait until it returns to normal load and perform the detection then.

Countering Evasion. Legitimate software sometimes uses code loading to achieve more functionalities [17]. For example, the Google toolbar uses DLL loading for legitimate purposes. Debuggers, such as the Microsoft Visual Studio Debugger also exhibit this behavior. Our tool detects the fact of code loading, but it cannot judge if it was for legitimate purposes. To filter out the false positives caused by legitimate applications, we can mark them and compile a whitelist. This whitelist can be constructed for example by using cryptographic hashes to user space memory allowing the identification of known code [19]. These legitimately injecting applications could then be excluded from analysis.

Unfortunately, this solution would open the door for malware to evade detection by loading code into the whitelisted applications. We can counter this option by applying our memory paging analysis on the application process instead of the system processes. We can first establish a baseline for a clean operating system running the code injecting legitimate application. Then, we proceed as follows. First, we run Membrane comparing the baseline behavior without code loading with the system behavior. If Membrane indicates an alarm, we check if any of the legitimate code loading mechanisms are running on the system. If such an application exists, then we run Membrane against the baseline behavior established earlier for this application. If Membrane still raises an alarm that is a good indicator that a malware infected the system, otherwise the previous alarm was a false alarm caused by the legitimate code injecting application.

Performance Issues. As snapshot creation can be a heavy-duty operation, we further designed and implemented a live monitoring version of Membrane called Membrane Live by extending a virtual machine introspection-based malware analysis tool called DRAKVUF [10]. This tool is used solely for evaluation purposes, and to compare the performance of snapshot and live monitoring-based approaches. More information about Membrane Live can be found in Sect 2.2 in [12].

7   Conclusion

In this paper, we present a memory forensics tool called Membrane to detect code loading behavior of malware programs. Instead of detecting various code loading actions, our tool focuses on identifying the cardinality of paging states caused by code loading. With this more generic technique, we are able to detect a wide range of malware code loading techniques. Our results show that we are able to identify 86–98 % of code loading malware samples on Windows machines, depending on the system load and the targeted process. In summary, we show that Membrane significantly raises the bar for miscreants to employ code loading attacks.

While for certain conditions (e.g., explorer.exe on Windows 7 under heavy load) our approach may seem less effective, we do emphasize that this condition is one of the worst cases according to our measurements. In future work, we will study how detection can be further improved. We will also investigate if Membrane can be extended to detect kernel-only code loading attacks. All in all, we believe that our approach tackles the problem of code loading from another, interesting aspect which can even be combined with existing methods effectively.

References

1. ALIENVAULT. Batchwiper: Just another wiping malware. https://www.alienvault.com/open-threat-exchange/blog/batchwiper-just-another-wiping-malware. Accessed 13 Nov 2014
2. Bencsáth, B., Pék, G., Buttyán, L., Felegyhazi, M.: The cousins of stuxnet: duqu, flame, and gauss. Future Internet **4**(4), 971–1003 (2012)
3. CERT.PL. More human than human - Flame's code injection techniques. http://www.cert.pl/news/5874/langswitch_lang/en. Accessed 13 Nov 2014
4. Hand, S., Lin, Z., Gu, G., Thuraisingham, B.: The vad tree: a process-eye view of physical memory. Digit. Invest. **4**, 62–64 (2007)

5. Idika, N., Mathur, A.P.: A survey of malware detection techniques. Technical report, Purdue University (2007)
6. INETSIM. http://www.inetsim.org/. Accessed 10 Nov 2014
7. Jiang, X., Wang, X., Xu, D.: Stealthy malware detection through vmm-based "out-of-the-box" semantic view reconstruction. In: Proceedings of the 14th ACM Conference on Computer and Communications Security, CCS 2007, pp. 128–138. ACM, New York (2007)
8. Kornblum, J.D.: Using every part of the buffalo in windows memory analysis. Digit. Invest. 4(1), 24–29 (2007)
9. Kreibich, C., Weaver, N., Kanich, C., Cui, W., Paxson, V.: Gq: practical containment for measuring modern malware systems. In: Proceedings of the 2011 ACM SIGCOMM Internet Measurement Conference (IMC), pp. 397–412. ACM (2011)
10. Lengyel, T.K., Maresca, S., Payne, B.D., Webster, G.D., Vogl, S., Kiayias, A.: Scalability, fidelity and stealth in the DRAKVUF dynamic malware analysis system. In: Proceedings of the 30th Annual Computer Security Applications Conference, December 2014 (to appear)
11. MANDIANT. APT1: Exposing One of China's Cyber Espionage Units (2013). http://intelreport.mandiant.com/
12. Pék, G.: New methods for detecting malware infections and new attacks against hardware virtualization. Ph.D. thesis, Budapest University of Technology and Economics (2015)
13. Petroni Jr., N.L., Fraser, T., Walters, A., Arbaugh, W.A.: An architecture for specification-based detection of semantic integrity violations in kernel dynamic data. In: Proceedings of the 15th Conference on USENIX Security Symposium, USENIX-SS 2006, vol. 15. USENIX Association, Berkeley (2006)
14. REACTOS. A free open source operating system based on the best design principles found in the Windows NT architecture. http://doxygen.reactos.org. Accessed 8 Nov 2014
15. Rossow, C., Dietrich, C.J., Grier, C., Kreibich, C., Paxson, V., Pohlmann, N., Bos, H., Van Steen, M.: Prudent practices for designing malware experiments: status quo and outlook. In: 2012 IEEE Symposium on Security and Privacy, pp. 65–79. IEEE (2012)
16. Russinovich, M., Solomon, D.A., Ionescu, A.: Windows Internals, 6th ed. Microsoft Press (2012)
17. Srivastava, A., Giffin, J.: Automatic discovery of parasitic malware. In: Jha, S., Sommer, R., Kreibich, C. (eds.) RAID 2010. LNCS, vol. 6307, pp. 97–117. Springer, Heidelberg (2010)
18. Volatility. The Volatility Framework. https://code.google.com/p/volatility/. Accessed 13 Nov 2014
19. White, A., Schatz, B., Foo, E.: Integrity verification of user space code. Digit. Invest. 10, 59–S68 (2013)
20. Willems, C.: Internals of windows memory management (not only) for malware analysis. Technical report, Ruhr Universität Bochum (2011)

Mobile Application Impersonation Detection Using Dynamic User Interface Extraction

Luka Malisa$^{(\boxtimes)}$, Kari Kostiainen, Michael Och, and Srdjan Capkun

Institute of Information Security, ETH Zurich, Zürich, Switzerland
{luka.malisa,kari.kostiainen,srdjan.capkun}@inf.ethz.ch,
michael.och@alumni.ethz.ch

Abstract. In this paper we present a novel approach for detection of mobile app impersonation attacks. Our system uses dynamic code analysis to extract user interfaces from mobile apps and analyzes the extracted screenshots to detect impersonation. As the detection is based on the visual appearance of the application, as seen by the user, our approach is robust towards the attack implementation technique and resilient to simple detection avoidance methods such as code obfuscation. We analyzed over 150,000 mobile apps and detected over 40,000 cases of impersonation. Our work demonstrates that impersonation detection through user interface extraction is effective and practical at large scale.

Keywords: Mobile · Visual · Repackaging · Phishing · Impersonation

1 Introduction

Mobile application *visual impersonation* is the case where one application intentionally misrepresents itself in the eyes of the user. Such applications impersonate either the whole, or only a small part of the user interface (Fig. 1). The most prominent example of whole UI impersonation is application repackaging; the process of republishing an app to the marketplace under a different author. It's a common occurrence [39] for an attacker to take a paid app and republish it to the marketplace for less than it's original price. In such cases, the repackaged application is stealing sales revenue from the original developers.

In the context of mobile malware, the attacker's goal is to distribute a malicious application to a wide user audience while minimizing the invested effort. Repackaging a popular app, and appending malicious code to it, has become a common malware deployment technique. Recent work [40] showed that 86 % of analyzed malware samples were repackaged versions of legitimate apps. As users trust the familiar look and feel of their favourite apps, such a strategy tricks the user into believing that she is installing, and interacting with, a known app.

Application fingerprinting [4,12,14–16,36–38,41] is a common approach to detect repackaging. All such works compare fingerprints extracted from some feature of the application, such as their code or runtime behaviour. However, an adversary that has an incentive to avoid detection can *easily modify* all such

© Springer International Publishing Switzerland 2016
I. Askoxylakis et al. (Eds.): ESORICS 2016, Part I, LNCS 9878, pp. 217–237, 2016.
DOI: 10.1007/978-3-319-45744-4_11

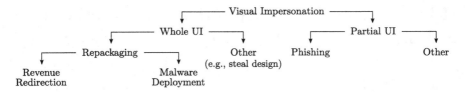

Fig. 1. Taxonomy of mobile app visual impersonation. Existing works primarily focused on detecting repackaging. Our goal is to detect all types of impersonation.

features without affecting the appearance of the app, as seen by the user. For example, an attacker can obfuscate the app by adding dummy instructions to the application code. Code comparison approaches would fail because the new fingerprint would be significantly different, and we demonstrate that such detection avoidance is both effective and simple to implement.

Instead of impersonating the whole UI, malicious apps can also impersonate only a small part of the UI by, e.g., creating a fake login screen in order to phish login credentials. Phishing apps that target mobile banking have become a recurring threat, with serious incidents already reported [26, 28]. Prior works on repackaging detection and common malware detection [4, 13, 24, 31, 32] are ill-suited for detecting such phishing cases as the malicious apps share little resources with the original, they don't exhibit specific system call patterns, nor do they require any special permissions—they only draw to the device screen.

Due to these inherent limitations of previous detection techniques, we propose a conceptually different approach. Our goal is to design an impersonation detection system that is resistant to common detection evasion techniques (e.g., obfuscation) and that can be configured to efficiently detect different types of impersonation; from repackaging (whole UI) to phishing (partial UI). We observe that, for visual impersonation to succeed, and irrespective of possible modifications introduced to the app, *the adversary must keep the runtime appearance of the impersonation app close to the original.* A recent study [19] showed that the more the visual appearance of a mobile app is changed, the more likely the user is to become alarmed. We propose a detection system that leverages this unavoidable property of impersonation.

Our system complements existing fingerprint-based approaches, runs on the marketplace and can analyze large amounts of Android apps using dynamic analysis and visual comparison, prior to their deployment onto the market. Our system runs the app inside an emulator for a specified time (e.g., 20 min), dynamically explores the mobile app user interface and extracts screenshots using GUI crawling techniques. If two apps have more than a threshold amount of screenshots in common (either exact or near matches), the apps are labeled as an instance of impersonation. In contrast to previous works, we do not base our detection on some easily modified feature of the app's resources, but rather on the final visual result of executing any app—the screenshot presented to the user. As a result, our system is robust towards attacker introduced perturbations to either application resources, or to the way the UI is created—*as long as the application looks the same at runtime, our system will detect the impersonation.* No prior detection schemes offer this property.

To realize a system that is able to analyze a large number of apps, we had to overcome technical challenges. The existing GUI crawling tools [2,20,22] require application-specific knowledge or manual user input, and are therefore not applicable to automated, large-scale analysis. To address those challenges, we developed novel GUI crawling techniques that force the analyzed app to draw its user interface. Our system requires no user input, no application-specific knowledge, it supports the analysis of native applications, and thus enables automated analysis of apps at the scale of modern application marketplaces. Our system uses locality-sensitive hashing (LSH) [10] for efficient screenshots retrieval.

To evaluate our system, we dynamically analyzed over 150,000 applications downloaded from Google Play and other mobile app markets. Our system extracted approximately 4.3 million screenshots and found over 40,000 cases of impersonation; predominantly repacks (whole UI) but also apps that impersonate only a single registration screen (partial UI). These experiments demonstrate that impersonation detection through dynamic user interface extraction is effective and practical, even in the scale of large mobile application marketplaces.

To summarize, our main contributions are:

- We demonstrate that existing impersonation detection techniques can be easily avoided.
- We propose a novel approach for impersonation detection based on dynamic analysis and user interface extraction that is robust towards the way the adversary implements impersonation.
- We built a detection system for large-scale analysis of mobile apps and as a part of the system we developed novel UI exploration techniques.
- We analyzed over 150,000 applications and found both whole and partial UI impersonation instances.

The rest of this paper is organized as follows. In Sect. 2 we explain the problem of app impersonation in detail. We describe our solution in Sect. 3 and evaluate it in Sect. 4. We present our results in Sect. 5, and security analysis in Sect. 6. We discuss deployments aspects in Sect. 7 and review related work in Sect. 8. We conclude in Sect. 9.

2   Motivation and Case Study

Whole UI impersonation. The first type of impersonation we consider is whole UI impersonation (Fig. 1). Since a typical repackaged app shares majority of its code and runtime behaviour with the original application, fingerprinting can be an effective way to detect such impersonation. Known techniques leverage static application features, such as code structure [12], imported packages [41] and dynamic features [4,13,24,31,32], such as system call [18] or network traffic patterns [25]. Using fingerprinting, large number of repacks have been detected

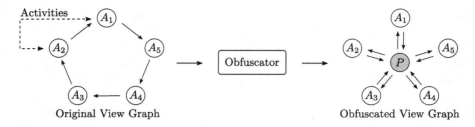

Fig. 2. We developed a small obfuscation tool that modifies the activity transition graphs of an app without affecting user experience. The obfuscation introduces additional proxy activities that mediate transitions between UI screens. In the original app, the user transitions (e.g., by clicking a button) $A_1 \rightarrow A_5$. Afterwards, the transition becomes $A_1 \rightarrow P \rightarrow A_5$. The transition occurs so fast that the user does not notice it.

from several Android application marketplaces [9]. The inherent limitation of fingerprinting approaches is that the adversary can easily modify the above listed (or any similar) features without affecting the runtime appearance of the application towards the user. In this section we demonstrate that such modifications are both easy to implement and effective in avoiding detection.

Case study. We present a case study on MassVet [9], a recent static analysis system that has demonstrated good results in detecting repackaging. MassVet extracts two types of static fingerprints from a mobile application: *m-cores* define application code flow graph and sequence of instructions and *v-cores* express UI state transitions from one activity to another. The rationale behind these fingerprints is that repackaged apps typically share majority of their functionality, as well as user interface structure.

We built a simple obfuscation tool (less than 200 lines of code) that modifies both extracted features (m-cores and v-cores). Our tool adds blocks of unused code, as well as proxy activities that modify activity transitions. Our modifications have no visible effect on the user experience (see Fig. 2). To evaluate the tool, we took 1259 apps from the Android Malware Genome project [1]. We ran those apps through the MassVet tool online interface[1] and 559 applications were identified as potentially malicious repackaged apps. We obfuscated all of these apps using our tool and rerun them on the MassVet system—92 % of the obfuscated apps were no longer detected. We argue that similar limitations apply to any fingerprinting solution and adoption of obfuscation introduces little to no cost to repackaging adversaries, as it merely implies running an automated tool. We demonstrated only one possible approach, and such obfuscation tools can be implemented for all prior fingerprinting approaches (both static and dynamic), in a similar manner and level of complexity.

Partial UI impersonation. The second type of visual impersonation are apps that only impersonate a small portion of the UI. Application phishing is an example of impersonation, where a malicious application constructs a single

---

[1] http://www.appomicsec.com/.

screen that visually resembles one of a another app, but otherwise shares no similarities (e.g., no shared code or resources) with the original app. For example, a malicious game asks the user to perform an in-app purchase, but instead of starting the legitimate banking app, the game presents a phishing screen that mimics the login screen of the bank. Distinguishing the phishing screen from the genuine login screen is difficult for the user, as modern mobile platforms do not enable the user to identify the application currently drawing on the screen.

Fingerprinting is not effective against such impersonation apps, as the malicious app does not share large parts of resources (e.g., code). Furthermore, traditional mobile malware detection schemes that, e.g., examine API call patterns [7] and permissions [6] are also ill-suited for the detection of phishing. Such applications differ from regular malware as they often require no special permissions, nor do they necessarily perform any suspicious actions. They only perform a single operation—*drawing on the device screen*.

Adversarial model. We consider a strong attacker that can implement impersonation in various ways. The attacker can create the UI by, e.g., using standard OS libraries, implement it in a custom manner, or show static images of the interface. On Android, the attacker could implement the app in Java, native code, or as a web app. For a more thorough introduction of the various ways of creating user interfaces in Android, we refer the reader to Appendix A. On top of that, the adversary can modify the application code or resource files in arbitrary ways (e.g., obfuscation). Such an adversary is both realistic and practical. The attacker can freely create the impersonated screens by any means allowed by the underlying Android system. Running an (off-the-shelf or custom) obfuscation tool comes at little to no cost to the adversary.

3   Visual Impersonation Detection System

As demonstrated in the previous section, the adversary has significant *implementation freedom* in performing an impersonation attack and, at the same time, the adversary has a clear incentive to keep the visual appearance of the app close to the original. A previous study [19] has shown that the more the adversary deviates from the appearance of the original mobile application user interfaces, the more likely the user is to become alarmed. We say that the adversary has limited *visual freedom* and our solution leverages this property.

Our goal is to develop a robust visual impersonation detection mechanism that is based on visual similarity—a feature the attacker cannot modify without affecting the success of the attack. More precisely, the system should: (i) detect both whole (e.g., repackaging) and partial UI impersonation (e.g., phishing), (ii) be robust towards the used impersonation implementation type and applied detection avoidance method (e.g., obfuscation), (iii) analyze large numbers of apps in an automated manner (e.g., on the scale of modern app stores).

Figure 3 shows an overview of our system that works in two main phases. In the first phase, the system extracts user interfaces from a large number of mobile apps in a distributed and fully autonomous manner. The system takes

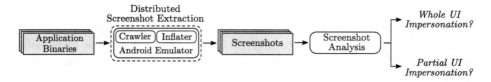

Fig. 3. An overview of the impersonation detection system that works in two phase. First, we extract user interfaces from a large number of applications. Then we analyze the extracted screenshots to detect repackaging and impersonation.

as input only the application binary, and requires no application-specific knowledge or manual user input. We run each analyzed app in an emulated Android environment, and explore its user interface through crawling. An attacker could develop a malicious app that detects emulated environments. However our system can be executed on real hardware as well (Sect. 7). In a best-effort manner, we extract as many screenshot as possible within a specified time limit. Full exploration coverage is difficult to achieve [5,30], and as our results in Sect. 4 show, not necessary for effective impersonation detection. During crawling, our system also automatically identifies reference screens (e.g., ones with login and registration functionality) that benefit from impersonation protection.

In the second phase, the system examines the extracted screenshots to find cases of impersonation. To detect whole UI impersonation, our system finds applications that share the majority of their screenshots with a queried app. To detect partial UI impersonation, our system finds applications that share a similar (e.g., login or user registration) screen with the reference app, but have otherwise different screenshots.

Our system can be deployed on the marketplace and used to detect impersonation, e.g., upon submitting the app to the market. We emphasize that our system can be combined with existing approaches to enhance impersonation detection. For example, only apps that are considered as benign by a fast fingerprint-based approach could be submitted to our, more costly analysis.

3.1   Design Challenges

To realize the system outlined above, we must overcome a number of technical challenges. First, the existing GUI crawling approaches were designed for development and testing, and a common assumption is that the test designers have access to application-specific knowledge, such as source code, software specifications or valid login credentials. Login screens are a prominent example of how crucial application-specific knowledge is in GUI exploration, as such tools need to know a valid username and password to explore beyond the login screens of apps. Another example are games where, in order to reach a certain GUI state, the game needs to be won. In such cases, the exploration tool needs to be instructed how to win the game. Previous crawling tools address these issues of reachability limitations using application-specific exploration rules [5,33] and pre-defined crawling actions [34]. As our system is designed to analyze a large number of mobile apps, similar strategies that require app-specific configuration are not possible. In Sect. 3.2 we describe a mobile app crawler that works fully autonomously, and in Sect. 3.3 we describe new user interface exploration techniques that increase its coverage.

Second, dynamic code analysis is significantly slower than static fingerprinting. In Sect. 3.2 we describe a distributed analysis architecture that enables us to analyze applications in a fully scalable manner. And third, many repackaged apps and known phishing malware samples [28] contain minor visual differences to their target apps. Our system must efficiently find screenshots that are exact or near matches, from a large set of screenshots. In Sect. 3.4 we describe a system that uses locality-sensitive hashing [10] for efficient screenshot analysis.

3.2   Automated Crawling

We designed and implemented a UI crawler as part of the Android core running inside an emulator (Fig. 3). The crawler uses the following basic strategy. For each new activity, and every time the view hierarchy (tree of UI elements) of the current activity changes, our crawler takes a screenshot. The crawler continues exploration in a depth-first manner [5], as long as there are clickable elements (views) in the user interface. To support autonomous user interface exploration, our crawler must determine which views are clickable without prior knowledge. We implemented the crawler as a part of the Android core, which gives it full access to the state of the analyzed app, and we examine the current state (i.e., traverse the view tree) to identify clickable elements. We observed that in many apps, activities alter their view hierarchy shortly after their creation. For example, an activity might offload a lengthy initialization process to a background thread, show a temporary UI layout first, and the final one later. To capture such layout changes, our crawler waits a short time period after every transition.

To increase the robustness of crawling, we made an additional modification to the Android core. If the crawled application creates an Intent that triggers another app to start, we immediately terminate it, and resume the execution of the analyzed app. In practice this approach turned out to be an efficient way to continue automated user interface exploration.

Reference screen identification. To enable partial UI impersonation detection, our system automatically identifies screens that benefit from impersonation protection. We have tailored our implementation to identify screens that contain login or registration functionality. While crawling an app, we traverse the view hierarchy tree of each screen and consider the screen a possible login or user registration screen, when the hierarchy contains at least one password field, one editable text field, and one clickable element or meets other heuristics, such as the name of the activity contain word "login" or "register". If such a screen is found, we save it as a *reference screen* for partial UI impersonation detection (Sect. 3.4). Reference screen identification is intended for benign apps that have no incentive to hide their UI structure, but we repeat the process for all crawled apps, since we do not know which apps are benign.

Distributed architecture. We built a distributed analysis architecture that leverages cloud platforms for analysis of multiple apps. Our architecture consists of a centralized server and an arbitrary number of analysis instances. The server has a database of apps, orchestrates the distributed analysis process, and collects the extracted user interfaces. Each analysis instance is a virtual machine that contains our dynamic analysis tools.

3.3   Coverage Improvements

In this section we describe techniques we implemented to increase the coverage of our user interface exploration.

Out-of-order execution. The crawler starts from the entry-point activity defined in the manifest file. For some apps only a small part of the user interface is reachable from the entry point without prior application-specific knowledge (e.g., a login screen requires valid credentials to proceed). To improve our crawling coverage, we additionally force the application to start all its activities out of order. This is a best-effort approach, as starting the execution from an arbitrary activity may crash the app without correct Intent or application state.

Layout file inflation. We implemented a tool that automatically renders (inflates) mobile app user interfaces based on XML layout files and web resources. As many apps customize the XML layouts in code, the final visual appearance cannot be extracted from the resource file alone. We perform resource file inflation from the context of the analyzed app which ensures that any possible customization will be applied to UI elements defined in the resource file. We implemented a dedicated enforcer activity and force each app to load it at startup. This activity iterates through the app's layout files, renders them one by one and takes a screenshot. We noticed that increasingly many mobile apps build their user interface using web technologies (e.g., HTML5). To improve the coverage of such apps, we perform similar inflation for all web resources. Our enforcer activity loads all local web resources of the application one by one.

Layout file inflation is conceptually different from, e.g., extracting fingerprints from resource files. The layout files can be modified by the attacker without affecting our analysis, as we take a screenshot of the final rendered layout.

User interface decomposition. Our crawling approach relies on the assumption that we can determine all clickable UI elements by analyzing the view hierarchy of the current activity. While this assumption holds for many apps, there are cases where clickable elements cannot be identified from the view tree, and therefore our crawler cannot proceed. For instance, mobile apps that implement their user interfaces in OpenGL (mostly games) and malicious apps that intentionally attempt to hide parts of their user interface from crawling.

We integrated a user interface decomposition outlined in [19] to our crawler to improve its coverage and attack resistance. Our experiments (Sect. 4.1) show that by using this extension we are able to crawl a number of mobile apps whose user interfaces we would not be able to crawl otherwise.

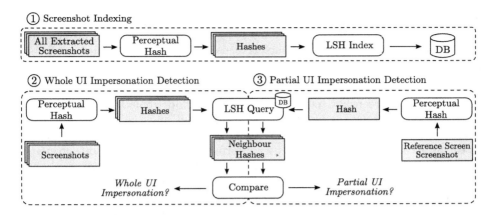

Fig. 4. Screenshot analysis system for impersonation detection. All extracted screenshots are indexed to a database using locality-sensitive hashing (LSH). To find impersonation applications from a large dataset, we first find nearest neighbor screenshots using the LSH database, and then perform an more expensive pairwise comparison.

3.4   Screenshot Analysis

Our initial experiments showed that many screenshots extracted from repackaged apps have minor visual differences in them. Some of the observed differences are caused by the application (e.g., different version, language or color scheme) while others are artifacts of our exploration approach (e.g., a blinking cursor visible in one screenshot but not in the other). Also the phishing screens seen in known malware samples contain minor visual differences to their target apps [28].

Our system handles visual differences in the extracted screenshots using *perceptual hashing*. The goal of a perceptual hash is to provide a compact representation of an image that maintains its main visual characteristics. In contrast to a cryptographic hash function, a small modification in the image produces a hash value that is close to the hash of the original image. Perceptual hashing algorithms reduce the size and the color range of an image, average color values and reduce their frequency. The perceptual hash algorithm we use [8] produces 256-bit hashes and the visual similarity of two images can be calculated as the Hamming distance between two hashes. To enable analysis of large number of screenshots, we leverage *locality-sensitive hashing* [11] (LSH). LSH algorithms are used to perform fast approximate nearest neighbour queries on large amounts of data.

Using these two techniques (perceptual hashing and LSH), we built a screenshot analysis system, as shown in Fig. 7. The system consists of three operations: (1) indexing, detection for (2) whole and (3) partial UI impersonation.

Indexing. In the indexing phase, a perceptual hash is created for each extracted screenshot and all hashes are fed to our LSH implementation. We use bit sampling for reducing the dimensionality of input items, as our perceptual hashing algorithm is based on the Hamming distance. We set the LSH parameters through manual experimentation (Sect. 4). To reduce false positives, we manually created a list of screenshots belonging to shared libraries (e.g., ad or game frameworks), and we removed all such screenshots from the database.

Whole UI impersonation detection. To detect impersonation, we use the intuitive metric of *containment* (C), i.e., how many screenshots of one app are included in the screenshot set of another app. To find whole UI impersonation apps, our system takes as input a queried app, and finds all apps whose user interface has high similarity to it. We note that, while our system is able to detect application pairs with high user interface similarity, it cannot automatically determine which of the apps in the relationship (if any) is the original one.

Our system analyzes one app at a time, and the first step in whole UI impersonation detection is to obtain the set of all screenshots (Q) of the current queried app. For every screenshot, we hash it and query the indexed LSH database. For each query, LSH returns a set of nearest neighbour screenshot hashes, their app identifiers and distances to the queried hash. For returning the nearest neighbours, we use the cutoff hamming distance $d = 10$, as explained in Sect. 4.

We sort this dataset based on the application identifiers to construct a list of candidate applications, where P_i is the set of their screenshots. For each candidate app we find the best screenshot match to the queried app. As a result, we get a set of matching screenshots for each candidate app. We consider the candidate app as a potential impersonation app when (1) the ratio (containment C) between the number of matched app and reference app screenshots is larger than a threshold T_w, and (2) the number of considered screenshots meets a minimum threshold T_s. Without loss of generality, we assume $|P_i| \leq |Q|$.

$$C = \frac{|P_i \cap Q|}{|P_i|} \geq T_w \tag{1}$$

$$|P_i| \geq T_s \tag{2}$$

In Sect. 4 we describe the experiments we used to set these thresholds (T_w, T_s). To find all potential repacks from a large dataset of applications, the same procedure is repeated for each application.

Partial UI impersonation detection. For partial UI impersonation, we no longer require a significant visual similarity between the two apps (target and malware). Only specific screens, such as login or registration screens, must be visually similar to perform a convincing impersonation attack of this kind. To scan our dataset for such applications, we adjusted the search criteria accordingly. Given our set of potential reference screens (Sect. 3.2) extracted during our dynamic analysis phase, we target applications that contain the same or a very similar screen but otherwise do not share a significant visual similarity in other aspects of the application. We only consider applications to be of interest if their containment with the queried application is less than a threshold $(C \leq T_p)$, as long as the app contains the queried login or registration screen.

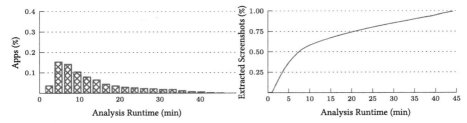

Fig. 5. The distribution of analysis time.

Fig. 6. Average number of screenshots extracted from an app, as a function of time.

4 Evaluation

In this section we evaluate the detection system. For evaluation we downloaded 158,449 apps from Google Play and other Android application repositories (see Table 1 in the Appendix). From Google Play we downloaded approximately 250 most popular apps per category. Our rationale was that popular apps would be likely impersonation targets. We also included several third-party markets to our dataset, as repacks are often distributed via third-party stores [9].

4.1 User Interface Extraction

Analysis time. We deployed our system on the Google Cloud Compute platform. The analysis time of a single application varies significantly, as apps have user interfaces of different size and complexity. While the majority of apps have less than 20 activities, few large apps have up to 100 activities. Furthermore, some applications (e.g., games) may dynamically create a large number of new user interface states and in such cases the dynamic user interface exploration is an open ended process. To address such cases, in our tests we set the maximum analysis time to generous 45 min. On the average, the analysis of one mobile app took only 7 min and we plot the distribution of analysis time in Fig. 5. Extracting screenshots is the most time-consuming part of our system. Once the screenshots are extracted, querying LSH and deciding if any impersonation exists is fast (few seconds per app).

On 1000 computing instances on the Google Cloud Compute platform the entire analysis of over 150,000 apps took 36 h. On the same rate and similar computing platform, the entire Google Play market (1.6 million apps) could be analyzed in approximately two weeks. We consider this a feasible one-time investment and the overall analysis time could be further reduced by limiting the maximum analysis time further (e.g., to 20 min as discussed below).

Analysis coverage. From the successfully analyzed 139,656 apps we extracted over 4.3 million screenshots after filtering our duplicates from the same application and low-entropy screenshots, e.g., single-color backgrounds that are not useful in impersonation detection. The majority of applications produced less than 50 screenshots, but we were able to extract up to 150 screenshots from some apps. Figure 6 plots the percentage of extracted screenshots as a function of analysis time. We extract approximately 75 % of all the screenshots during the first 20 min of analysis. The steeper curve during the first 7 min of the analysis is due to the fact that we run the inflater tool first and after that we start our crawler. The crawler tool extracted 58 % of the screenshots and the inflater contributed additional 42 %. Majority (97 %) of the extracted screenshots come from user interfaces implemented using standard Android user interface elements and a small share originates from user interfaces implemented using web techniques or as an OpenGL surface. Figure 10 summarizes the user interface extraction results.

We use *activity coverage* as a metric to compare the coverage of our crawler to previous solutions. Activity coverage is defined as the number of explored activities with respect to the total number of activities in an app [5]. While activity coverage does not account for all possible user interface implementation options, it gives a good indication of the extraction coverage when analyzing large number of apps. Our tool achieves 65 % activity coverage, and is comparable to previous solutions (e.g., 59 % in [5]). However, previous crawling tools that achieve similar coverage require application-specific configuration or manual interaction.

We separately tested our user interface decomposition extension on 200 apps (mostly games) that implement their UI using OpenGL surface. Without the decomposition extension, our crawler was only able to extract a single screenshot from each of the tested apps (the entry activity). With decomposition, we were able to extract several screenshots (e.g., 20) from 30 % of the tested apps. This experiment demonstrates that there is a class of mobile apps whose user interfaces can be crawled with better coverage using decomposition.

4.2 Screenshot Comparison

Perceptual hash design. We investigated two different perceptual hashing techniques, based on image moments [29] and DCT [8] (pHash). Preliminary analysis of the results from both hashing techniques revealed that the image moments based approach is not suitable for the hashing and comparing of user interface screenshots, as both very similar as well as very dissimilar pairs of screenshots resulted in almost equivalent distances. The *pHash* [35] based approach yielded promising results with a good correlation between visual similarity of user interface screenshots and the hamming distance between their respective hashes. Screenshots of user interfaces are quite different from typical natural images: clearly defined boundaries from UI elements, few color gradients, and a significant amount of text. To account for these characteristics and improve the performance of the hashing algorithm, we performed additional transformations (e.g., dilation) to the target images as well as the final hash computation.

To find a good cutoff hamming distance threshold below which we consider images to be visually similar, we randomly selected pairs of images and computed their distance until we had 100 pairs of screenshots for the first 40 distances.

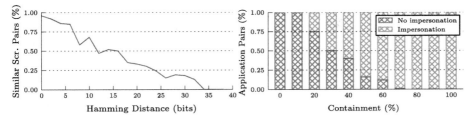

Fig. 7. Manual evaluation of hamming distances of screenshot hashes.

Fig. 8. Manual evaluation of false positives and false negatives.

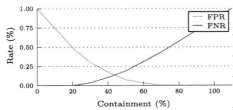

Number of successfully analyzed apps	**139,656**
Number of extracted screenshots	**4,302,413**
Extracted by the crawler	57.89%
Extracted by the inflater	42.11%
Originated from widget-based UI	96.95%
Originated from a HTML asset	2.17%
Originated from an OpenGL surface	0.88%

Fig. 9. False positive and false negative rates. Equal-error rate is at cont. 45 %.

Fig. 10. User interface extraction results.

We then manually investigated each distance bucket and counted the number of screenshot pairs we considered to be visually similar. The result are shown in Fig. 7, and we concluded that a distance $d = 10$ is a reasonable threshold.

Containment threshold. Similar to the distance threshold evaluation, we randomly selected pairs of apps from our dataset and computed their containments, creating 10 buckets for possible containment values between $[0, 100]$ percent, until we had 100 unique pairs of apps for all containment values. We then manually examined those apps and counted the number of application pairs which we consider to be whole UI impersonations, as shown in Fig. 8. The false negative and false positive rates are shown in Fig. 9, yielding $T_w = 0.45$ containment to be a reasonable threshold for whole UI impersonation detection, above which applications within a pair are considered impersonation cases of each other. To verify that our manually derived false negatives rates were representative, we performed an additional check outlined in Appendix B. To detect partial UI impersonation, in our experiments, we found that setting the containment threshold to $T_p = 0.10$ gave good results.

5   Detection Results

To demonstrate that our system is able to catch impersonation attacks, we analyzed each application in our dataset and we report the following results.

Whole UI impersonation. Using perceptual hash distance $d = 10$ and containment threshold $T_w = 0.45$, our system detected 43,904 impersonating apps out of 137,506 successfully analyzed apps. Such a high number of impersonation instances is due to the fact that a large part of our apps are from third-party markets. From the set of detected apps, our system does not automatically detect which apps are originals and which are impersonators.

At $T_w = 0.45$ our system has an estimated 15 % false negatives. We remind the reader that these false negatives refer to missed *application pairs*, and not missed repacks. To illustrate, let us consider a simple example where our system is deployed on a market, and 3 apps are submitted (the original Facebook app, and 2 apps that impersonate it). The first app will be added and no impersonation can be detected. On the second app, our system has a 15 % to miss the relation between the queried app and the one already in the store. However, the third app has approximately only $0.15^2 = 0.02$ chance of missing both relations and not being identified as impersonation with regards to the other two apps in the store. During our experiments, we found instances of clusters containing up to 200 apps, all repackaging the same original app.

Similarly, at $T_w = 0.45$ our system has also 15 % false positives, which is arguably high. However, due to the fact that apps are repacked over and over again, on a deployed system we can set the containment threshold to be higher (e.g., $T_w = 0.60$). At that value, our system has only 3 % false positives, and 31 % false negatives. However, if the app is repacked a modest number of 5 times, the chances of missing all impersonation relationships becomes less than half a percent $0.31^5 = 0.002$.

In the above examples, we assumed that the analysis of each app is an independent event. In reality, this may not be the case. For example, if one impersonation app is missed, a closely related impersonation app may be missed with higher probability (i.e., the events are not independent). However, the more apps impersonate an original app, the higher the chances of our system catching it.

Partial UI impersonation. Using the metric described in Sect. 3.4, and $T_p = 0.10$, we found approximately 1,000 application pairs that satisfy the query. We randomly selected and manually inspected 100 pairs of apps to understand their relationships. In most cases, we found repackaged applications with a large number of additional advertising libraries attached.

Among these results, we also found an interesting case of a highly suspicious impersonation application. In this sample, the impersonation target is a dating app. The registration screen of the impersonation app appears visually identical to original. However, manually inspecting the code reveals that a new payment URL has been added to the application, no longer pointing to the dating website, but instead to a different IP. We uploaded the sample to virustotal.com to confirm our suspicions, and the majority of scanners indicated maliciousness. The code similarity between the original and impersonating apps (according to Androguard) is only 22 %, largely due to added advertising libraries.

Our similarity metric allows us to find specialized kinds of impersonation attacks that deviate from the more primitive repackaging cases. Interesting user interfaces with certain characteristics (e.g. login behaviour) can be queried from a large data-set of analysed applications to find various kinds of impersonation, drastically reducing the necessary manual verification done by humans.

6 Security Analysis

Detection avoidance. Our user interface extraction system executes applications in an emulator environment. A repackaging adversary could try to fingerprint the execution environment and alter the behavior of the application accordingly (e.g., terminate execution if it detects emulator). The obvious countermeasure is to perform the user interface exploration on real devices. While the analysis of large number of apps would require a pool of many devices (potentially hard to organize), user interface exploration would be faster on real devices [21] compared to an emulator. Our user interface extraction system could be easily ported from the emulator environment to real Android devices.

A phishing adversary could construct the phishing screen in a way that complicates its extraction. To avoid the inflater, the adversary can implement the phishing screens without any resource files. To complicate extraction by crawling, the adversary could try to hide the phishing screen behind an OpenGL surface that is hard to decompose and therefore explore or make the appearance of the phishing screen conditional to an external event or state that does not necessarily manifest itself during the application analysis. Many such detection avoidance techniques reduce the likelihood that the phishing screen is actually seen by the user (a necessary precondition of any phishing attack). While our solution does not make impersonation impossible, it raises the bar for attack implementation and reduces the chances that users fall for the attack.

7 Discussion

Improvements. Our crawler could be extended to create randomized events and common touch screen gestures (e.g., swipes) for improved coverage. Our current out-of-order execution could be improved as well. Currently, startup of many activities fails due to missing arguments or incompatible application state. One could try to infer these from the application code through static analysis. Static code analysis could be also used to identify sections of application code that perform any drawing on the screen and the application could be attempted to force the execution of this code segment, e.g., leveraging symbolic execution. We consider such out-of-order execution a challenging problem.

Deployment. The primary deployment model we consider is one where a marketplace, mobile platform provider, anti-virus vendor or a similar entity wants to examine a large number of mobile apps to detect impersonation in the Android ecosystem. As shown in Sect. 4, the analysis of large number of apps requires significant resources, but is feasible for the types of entities we consider. Once the initial, one-time investment is done, detection for new applications is inexpensive. User interface extraction for a single application takes on the average

7 min and finding matching repacks or phishing apps can be done in the matter of seconds. As a comparison, the Google Bouncer system dynamically analyzes each uploaded app for approximately 5 min [23]. Our system streams screenshots to the central analysis server as they are extracted. The system can therefore stop further analysis if a decision can be made.

Post-detection actions. Once an application has been identified as a potential impersonation app, it should be examined further. Ad revenue stealing repacks could be confirmed by comparing the advertisements libraries and their configurations in two apps with matching user interfaces; sales revenue stealing repacks could be confirmed by comparing the publisher identities; repacks with malicious payload could be detected using analysis of API calls [3], comparison of code differences [9], known malware fingerprints or manual analysis; and phishing apps could be confirmed by examining the network address where passwords are sent. Many post-detection actions could be automated, but implementation of these tools is out of scope for this work.

8   Related Work

Repackaging detection. The previous work on repackaging detection is mostly based on static fingerprinting. EagleDroid [27] extracts fingerprints from Android application layout files. ViewDroid [36] and MassVet [9] statically analyze the UI code to extract a graph that expresses the user interface state and transitions. The rationale behind these works is that while applications code can be easily obfuscated, the user interface structure must remain largely unaffected. We have showed that detection based on static fingerprinting can be easily avoided (Sect. 2) and our solution provides more robust repackaging detection, at the cost of increased analysis time.

Phishing detection. The existing application phishing detection systems attempt to identify API call sequences that enable specific phishing attacks vectors (e.g., activation from the background when the target application is started [7]). While such schemes can be efficient to detect certain, known attacks, other attacks require no specific API calls. Our solution applies to many types of phishing attacks, also ones that leverages previously undiscovered attack vectors.

User interface exploration. The previous work on mobile application user interface exploration focuses on maximizing GUI coverage and providing means to reason about the sequence of actions required to reach a certain application state for testing purposes [2,5,17,33]. These approaches require instrumentation of the analysis environment with application-specific knowledge, customized companion applications, or even source code modifications to the target application. Our crawler works autonomously and achieves similar (or better) coverage.

9   Conclusions

In this paper we have proposed and demonstrated a novel approach for mobile app impersonation detection. Our system extracts user interfaces from mobile apps and finds applications with similar user interfaces. Using the system we found thousands of impersonation apps. In contrast to previous fingerprinting systems, our approach provides improved resistance to detection avoidance, such as obfuscation, as the detection relies on the final visual appearance of the examined application, as seen by the user. Another benefit of the system is that it can be fine-tuned for specialized cases, like the detection of phishing apps. The main drawback of our approach is the significantly increased analysis time compared to static analysis. However, our experiments show that impersonation detection at the scale of large application stores is practical. Finally, the novel user interface exploration techniques that we have developed as part of this work, may have numerous other applications besides impersonation detection.

Acknowledgements. This work was partially supported by the Zurich Information Security Center. It represents the views of the authors.

A   Android UI Background

In this section we provide a concise primer on Android application user interfaces. Android apps with graphical user interfaces are implemented using activity components. A typical app has multiple activities, one for every separate functionality. For example, a messaging app could have activities for reading a message, writing a message, and browsing received messages. Each activity provides a window to which the app can draw its user interface, that usually fills the entire device screen, but it may also be smaller and float on top of other windows. The Android system maintains the activities of recently active apps in a stack. The window surface from the top activity is shown to the user or if the window of the top activity does not cover the entire screen, the user sees also the window beneath it. The user interface within a window is constructed using views, where each view is either a visible user interface element (e.g., a button or an image) or a set of subviews. The views are organized in a tree hierarchy that defines the layout of the user interface.

The recommended way to define user interface layouts in Android is using XML resource files, but Android apps can also construct view hierarchies (UI element trees) programmatically. Furthermore, Android apps can construct their user interfaces using OpenGL surfaces and WebViews. The OpenGL user interfaces are primarily used by games, while WebView is popular with many cross-platform apps. Inside a WebView, the user interface is constructed using common HTML. All of the methods stated above can be implemented in Java, as well as native code.

Every Android application contains a manifest file that defines the application's activities. One activity is defined as the application entry point, but the execution of the application can be started from other activities as well. When an activity is started, the Android framework automatically renders (inflates) the layout files associated with the activity.

B   Containment Threshold Verification

To further verify our manual containment threshold evaluation performed in Sect. 4.2, we created a large ground truth of application pairs known to be trivial repacks of each other. We define a trivial repacks as any pair of applications where both applications have at least 90 % identical resource files as well as a code similarity (computed using Androguard) of 90 % or higher. For such pairs, we can be confident that the apps are indeed repacks. Over the course of several days, we compiled a list of 200,000 pairs to serve as a ground truth of known repacks. We then ran our system against every pair in this list, querying either app of the pair. If the system did not find the corresponding app, or if their containment is below the threshold value of 45 %, we consider this a false negative. We repeated this exercise for different threshold values and compared the results to the expected false negative rates, confirming that the pairs considered in our manual verification are indeed representative for our large data-set.

C   Application Dataset

Here we present the statistics of all the applications we used in our experiments.

Table 1. Application dataset.

Marketplace	Apps
play.google.com (US)	14,323
coolapk.com (CN)	5666
m.163.com (CN)	24,069
1mobile.com (CN)	24,173
mumayi.com (CN)	29,990
anzhi.com (CN)	36,202
slideme.org (US)	19,730
android.d.cn (CN)	4635
Total	**158,449**

References

1. Android malware genome project. http://www.malgenomeproject.org
2. Amalfitano, D., Fasolino, A.R., Tramontana, P., De Carmine, S., Memon, A.M.: Using gui ripping for automated testing of android applications. In: International Conference on Automated Software Engineering (ASE) (2012)
3. Arp, D., Spreitzenbarth, M., Hubner, M., Gascon, H., Rieck, K., Siemens, C.: Drebin: effective and explainable detection of android malware in your pocket. In: Network and Distributed System Security (NDSS)

4. Arzt, S., Rasthofer, S., Fritz, C., Bodden, E., Bartel, A., Klein, J., Le Traon, Y., Octeau, D., McDaniel, P.: Flowdroid: precise context, flow, field, object-sensitive and lifecycle-aware taint analysis for android apps. In: ACM SIGPLAN Notices, vol. 49, pp. 259–269. ACM (2014)
5. Azim, T., Neamtiu, I.: Targeted and depth-first exploration for systematic testing of android apps. In: ACM Conference on Object Oriented Programming Systems Languages and Applications (OOPSLA) (2013)
6. Barrera, D., Kayacik, H.G., van Oorschot, P.C., Somayaji, A.: A methodology for empirical analysis of permission-based security models and its application to android. In: Proceedings of the 17th ACM Conference on Computer and Communications Security, pp. 73–84. ACM (2010)
7. Bianchi, A., Corbetta, J., Invernizzi, L., Fratantonio, Y., Kruegel, C., Vigna, G.: What the app. is that? deception and countermeasures in the android user interface. In: Symposium on Security and Privacy (SP) (2015)
8. Buchner, J.: https://pypi.python.org/pypi/ImageHash
9. Chen, K., Wang, P., Lee, Y., Wang, X., Zhang, N., Huang, H., Zou, W., Liu, P.: Finding unknown malice in 10 seconds: mass vetting for new threats at the google-play scale. In: USENIX Security Symposium (2015)
10. Datar, M., Immorlica, N., Indyk, P., Mirrokni, V.S.: Locality-sensitive hashing scheme based on p-stable distributions. In: Annual symposium on Computational Geometry (CG) (2004)
11. Datar, M., Immorlica, N., Indyk, P., Mirrokni, V.S.: Locality-sensitive hashing scheme based on p-stable distributions. In: Proceedings of the Twentieth Annual Symposium on Computational Geometry, pp. 253–262. ACM (2004)
12. Feng, Y., Anand, S., Dillig, I., Aiken, A.: Apposcopy: semantics-based detection of android malware through static analysis. In: Proceedings of the 22nd ACM SIGSOFT International Symposium on Foundations of Software Engineering
13. Gilbert, P., Chun, B.-G., Cox, L.P., Jung, J.: Vision: automated security validation of mobile apps at app. markets. In: Proceedings of the Second International Workshop on Mobile Cloud Computing and Services, pp. 21–26. ACM (2011)
14. Grace, M., Zhou, Y., Zhang, Q., Zou, S., Jiang, X.: Riskranker: scalable and accurate zero-day android malware detection. In: Proceedings of the 10th International Conference on Mobile Systems, Applications, and Services
15. Griffin, K., Schneider, S., Hu, X., Chiueh, T.: Automatic generation of string signatures for malware detection. In: Kirda, E., Jha, S., Balzarotti, D. (eds.) RAID 2009. LNCS, vol. 5758, pp. 101–120. Springer, Heidelberg (2009)
16. Hanna, S., Huang, L., Wu, E., Li, S., Chen, C., Song, D.: Juxtapp: a scalable system for detecting code reuse among android applications. In: Flegel, U., Markatos, E., Robertson, W. (eds.) DIMVA 2012. LNCS, vol. 7591, pp. 62–81. Springer, Heidelberg (2013)
17. Kropp, M., Morales, P.: Automated gui testing on the android platform. In: International Conference on Testing Software and Systems (ICTSS) (2010)
18. Lin, Y.-D., Lai, Y.-C., Chen, C.-H., Tsai, H.-C.: Identifying android malicious repackaged applications by thread-grained system call sequences. Comput. Secur. **39**, 340–350 (2013)
19. Malisa, L., Kostiainen, K., Capkun, S.: Detecting mobile application spoofing attacks by leveraging user visual similarity perception. Cryptology ePrint Archive, Report 2015/709 (2015). http://eprint.iacr.org/
20. Memon, A., Banerjee, I., Nagarajan, A.: Gui ripping: reverse engineering of graphical user interfaces for testing. In: Working Conference on Reverse Engineering (WCRE) (2003)

21. Mutti, S., Fratantonio, Y., Bianchi, A., Invernizzi, L., Corbetta, J., Kirat, D., Kruegel, C., Vigna, G.: Baredroid: large-scale analysis of android apps on real devices. In: Proceedings of the 31st Annual Computer Security Applications Conference, pp. 71–80. ACM (2015)
22. Nguyen, B.N., Robbins, B., Banerjee, I., Memon, A.: Guitar an innovative tool for automated testing of gui-driven software. Autom. Softw. Eng. **21**(1), 65–105 (2014)
23. Oberheide, J., Miller, C.: Dissecting the android bouncer. In: SummerCon (2012)
24. Rastogi, V., Chen, Y., Enck, W.: Appsplayground: automatic security analysis of smartphone applications. In: Proceedings of the Third ACM Conference on Data and Application Security and Privacy, pp. 209–220. ACM (2013)
25. Shabtai, A., Kanonov, U., Elovici, Y., Glezer, C., Weiss, Y.: andromaly: a behavioral malware detection framework for android devices. J. Intell. Inf. Syst. **38**(1), 161–190 (2012)
26. Stefanko, L.: Android Banking Trojan, March 2016. http://www.welivesecurity.com/2016/03/09/android-trojan-targets-online-banking-users/
27. Sun, M., Li, M., Lui, J.: Droideagle: seamless detection of visually similar android apps. In: Conference on Security and Privacy in Wireless and Mobile Networks (Wisec) (2015)
28. Symantec. Will Your Next TV Manual Ask You to Run a Scan Instead of Adjusting the Antenna? April 2015. http://goo.gl/xh58UN
29. Tang, Z., Dai, Y., Zhang, X.: Perceptual hashing for color images using invariant moments. Appl. Math **6**(2S), 643S–650S (2012)
30. Tikir, M.M., Hollingsworth, J.K.: Efficient instrumentation for code coverage testing. In: ACM International Symposium on Software Testing and Analysis (ISSTA) (2002)
31. Vidas, T., Tan, J., Nahata, J., Tan, C.L., Christin, N., Tague, P.: A5: automated analysis of adversarial android applications. In: Proceedings of the 4th ACM Workshop on Security and Privacy in Smartphones & Mobile Devices
32. Yan, L.K., Yin, H.: Droidscope: seamlessly reconstructing the os and dalvik semantic views for dynamic android malware analysis. In: Presented as part of the 21st USENIX Security Symposium (USENIX Security 2012), pp. 569–584 (2012)
33. Yang, W., Prasad, M.R., Xie, T.: A grey-box approach for automated GUI-model generation of mobile applications. In: Cortellessa, V., Varró, D. (eds.) FASE 2013 (ETAPS 2013). LNCS, vol. 7793, pp. 250–265. Springer, Heidelberg (2013)
34. Zadgaonkar, H.: Robotium Automated Testing for Android. Packt Publishing, Birmingham (2013)
35. Zauner, C.: Implementation and benchmarking of perceptual image hash functions (2010)
36. Zhang, F., Huang, H., Zhu, S., Wu, D., Liu, P.: Viewdroid: towards obfuscation-resilient mobile application repackaging detection. In: ACM Conference on Security and Privacy in Wireless and Mobile Networks (Wisec) (2014)
37. Zhang, Q., Reeves, D.S.: Metaaware: identifying metamorphic malware. In: Twenty-Third Annual Computer Security Applications Conference, ACSAC 2007, pp. 411–420. IEEE (2007)
38. Zhou, W., Zhou, Y., Grace, M., Jiang, X., Zou, S.: Fast, scalable detection of piggybacked mobile applications. In: Proceedings of the Third ACM Conference on Data and Application Security and Privacy, pp. 185–196. ACM (2013)

39. Zhou, W., Zhou, Y., Jiang, X., Ning, P.: Detecting repackaged smartphone applications in third-party android marketplaces. In: Proceedings of the Second ACM Conference on Data and Application Security and Privacy
40. Zhou, Y., Jiang, X.: Dissecting android malware: characterization and evolution. In: IEEE Symposium on Security and Privacy (S&P), May 2012
41. Zhou, Y., Wang, Z., Zhou, W., Jiang, X.: Hey, you, get off of my market: detecting malicious apps in official and alternative android markets. In: NDSS (2012)

A Machine Learning Approach
for Detecting Third-Party Trackers on the Web

Qianru Wu[1(✉)], Qixu Liu[2], Yuqing Zhang[1], Peng Liu[3], and Guanxing Wen[4]

[1] National Computer Network Intrusion Protection Center,
University of Chinese Academy of Science, Beijing, China
wuqianru11@mails.ucas.ac.cn, zhangyq@ucas.ac.cn
[2] Institute of Information Engineering, Chinese Academy of Sciences, Beijing, China
liuqixu@iie.ac.cn
[3] College of Information Sciences and Technology, Pennsylvania State University,
University Park, PA, USA
[4] Team Pangu, Shanghai, China

Abstract. Nowadays, privacy violation caused by third-party tracking has become a serious problem and yet the most effective method to defend against third-party tracking is based on blacklists. Such method highly depends on the quality of the blacklist database, whose records need to be updated frequently. However, most records are curated manually and very difficult to maintain. To efficiently generate blacklists, we propose a system with high accuracy, named DMTrackerDetector, to detect third-party trackers automatically. Existing methods to detect online tracking have two shortcomings. Firstly, they treat first-party tracking and third-party tracking the same. Secondly, they always focus on a certain way of tracking and can only detect limited trackers. Since anti-tracking technology based on blacklists highly depends on the coverage of the blacklist database, these methods cannot generate high-quality blacklists. To solve these problems, we firstly use the structural hole theory to preserve first-party trackers, and only detect third-party trackers based on supervised machine learning by exploiting the fact that trackers and non-trackers always call different JavaScript APIs for different purposes. The results show that 97.8 % of the third-party trackers in our test set can be correctly detected. The blacklist generated by our system not only covers almost all records in the Ghostery list (one of the most popular anti-tracking tools), but also detects 35 unrevealed trackers.

1 Introduction

A website page (called first-party website) always embeds many unrelated websites belonging to different administrative entities (called third-party website) in the form of JavaScript, iframe, images or flash to gain functionality (such as advertisement, web analytic and social network). We call the websites who identify and collect private information (such as browser history) about users as trackers. First-party websites and third-party websites may both track users for different purposes. A first-party tracker usually tracks users for antifraud or

I. Askoxylakis et al. (Eds.): ESORICS 2016, Part I, LNCS 9878, pp. 238–258, 2016.
DOI: 10.1007/978-3-319-45744-4_12

paywalls [1]. If the web tracking was blocked, this first-party website may not work right or pose a threat to users' security. A third-party tracker can stealthily collect users' web browsing history for purposes such as targeted advertising or predicting trends, which generates enormous benefits at the expense of users' privacy [2].

Nowadays, privacy violation caused by third-party tracking has become a serious problem, and a considerable amount of effort has been made to protect users' privacy against online tracking. Anti-tracking technology based on black-lists is most effective [2–4]. Many commercial anti-tracking tools (Adblock [5], DoNotTrackMe [6], Ghostery [7]) are based on blacklists. They generate black-lists offline and block requests to the URLs in the blacklist online. This method highly depends on the records in the blacklist whereas a tracking company can adopt new domains to track users [8]. These known blacklists need to be updated regularly. However, these blacklists are usually manually curated and difficult to maintain.

To efficiently generate blacklists, several approaches have been proposed to detect trackers automatically [9–11]. However, these solutions are grossly inadequate. Firstly, existing methods to detect online tracking treat first-party track-ers and third-party trackers the same. Secondly, they always focus on a certain way of tracking and can only detect limited trackers. Since anti-tracking technol-ogy based on blacklists highly depends on the coverage of the blacklist database, these methods cannot generate high-quality blacklists.

In this paper, we propose an efficient and adaptive system with high accuracy, named DMTrackerDetector, to detect third-party trackers while preserving first-party trackers, which can make it easier to generate a blacklist and reduce human work. Firstly, since a first-party file only exists in this website while a third-party file exists in many websites, we use structural hole theory, which is always used in social networks to find the 'tie' among several communities, to filter out first-party trackers. Secondly, instead of focussing on a certain way of tracking, DMTrackerDetector detects third-party trackers based on supervised machine learning by exploiting the fact that trackers and non-trackers always call different JavaScript APIs for different purposes. To exploit this fact, DMTrack-erDetector takes all JavaScript APIs features to build a classifier. DMTrackerDe-tector can automatically generate the blacklist of third-party trackers based on the structural holes and the classifier.

The contributions of this paper can be summarised as follows:

1. We distinguish first-party trackers and third-party trackers in a straightfor-ward and effective way based on structural hole theory.
2. We propose an adaptive method to detect all JavaScript-based tracking tech-nologies based on supervised machine learning.
3. We provide not only the effective features to distinguish trackers and non-trackers but also the effective way to extract these features.
4. We evaluate the effectiveness of our system, and 97.8 % of the third-party JavaScript are classified correctly. We also compare our system with Ghostery (one of the most popular anti-tracking tools), and the results show that the

list generated by DMTrackerDetector not only covers almost all JavaScript-based trackers records in the Ghostery list, but also contains more trackers than Ghostery.
5. We make a detailed analysis about the correlation of JavaScript APIs which can help us better understand trackers. We distill the top 20 JavaScript APIs most correlated to the fact that a JavaScript file is a tracker and the top 20 JavaScript APIs most uncorrelated to this fact.

The rest of this paper is organised as follows. First, we introduce the background and related work in Sect. 2. Section 3 is the detailed description of the design and implementation of DMTrackerDetector. The experiment evaluation results are presented in Sect. 4. Next, we discuss the limitation of the proposed system in Sect. 5. Finally we conclude this paper in Sect. 6.

2   Background and Related Work

2.1   Background

Web tracking technologies can be divided into stateful tracking and stateless tracking according to whether or not there is a dependence on client-side information storage [4]. The most commonly used stateful tracking technique is HTTP cookies, which can store limited bytes and be deleted easily. Later on, Flash cookies and LocalStorage are used because of their larger storage and better concealment compared to HTTP Cookies [11–13]. However, stateful tracking can be deleted by users as they store on the client side, which motivates trackers to find new ways to link users to their browsing histories. Trackers learn properties about the browser that, taken together, form a unique or nearly unique identifier, which is called stateless (fingerprinting) tracking [4,9,14].

JavaScript is used mainly to dynamically manipulate a page's DOM, control the browser, and communicate asynchronously. In this paper, we refer to all JavaScript objects, properties and methods provided by browsers as JavaScript APIs. Most JavaScript-based behaviours are non-tracker behaviours, such as loading new page content, submitting data to the server without reloading the page, animation of page elements, interactive content, validating input values of a web form to make sure that they are acceptable before being submitted to the server, and so on.

JavaScript also plays an important role in web tracking, and we focus on detecting JavaScript-based third-party trackers in this paper. JavaScript can implement most tracking behaviours:

Stateful Tracking. JavaScript can set, read, modify and remove HTTP Cookies, LocalStorage and SessionStorage by calling APIs. What is more, trackers may pass pseudonymous IDs associated with a given user, typically stored in cookies, amongst each other via JavaScript execution in order to better facilitate targeting and real-time bidding [15].

Stateless Tracking. The privileged position inside the browser makes JavaScript a strong fingerprinting tool, which can access browser resources [11].

Information about the browser vendor, supported plugins, MIME types, operating system, display settings and installed fonts can all be gained by calling JavaScript APIs.

2.2   Related Work

Existing Anti-tracking Mechanisms. Although web tracking has garnered much attention, no effective defense system has been proposed. Roesner et al. [16] proposed a tool called ShareMeNot, but it can only defend against social media button tracking, a small subset of tracking practices. Disabling script execution [17] provides protection at the cost of pages failing to open or render properly [18]. Private browsing mode significantly affects user experience as users cannot consistently save anything on the client-side state and users can still be tracked before closing the browser. The Do Not Track (DNT) header and legislation require tracker compliance and cannot effectively protect users from tracking in reality [4,16]. Opting out of cookies [19,20] and disabling third-party cookies can be easily bypassed through non-cookie-based tracking approaches [12,13]. Moreover, as trackers can make regular information available in a typical HTTP request, disabling HTTP cookies or flash cookies [21] is useless. Rather, the most effective method to defend against third-party tracking is based on blacklists, and most commercial anti-tracking tools [2–4] are based on blacklists.

Existing Non-machine Learning-based Tracking Detection Mechanisms. Existing non-machine learning-based focussed on a certain way of tracking and cannot be used to generate blacklists alone. Nikiforakis et al. [9] studied three previously known fingerprinting companies and found 40 such sites among the top 10 K sites employing practices such as font probing and the use of Flash to circumvent proxy servers. Acar et al. [10] used behavioural analysis to detect fingerprinting scripts that employ font probing and found that 404 sites in the top million deployed JavaScript-based fingerprinting. In the followup study, Acar et al. [11] proposed three heuristics to estimate whether a canvas is being used to fingerprint.

Existing Machine Learning-based Tracking Detection Mechanisms. To efficiently generate blacklists, several machine learning-based approaches have been proposed to detect trackers automatically. Most of these approaches are used to detect advertisement-related web tracking since web tracking is usually used in advertising.

Kushmerick et al. [22] first suggested using machine learning to block online advertisements, utilising the C4.5 classification scheme to build an advertisement image blocker called AdEater, which only blocked advertisement images of static pages while many advertisements on the current Web are loaded dynamically via JavaScript or as flash objects. Orr et al. [23] trained a classifier for detecting advertisements loaded via JavaScript code with the features extracted through static program analysis. In this study, they manually labelled the advertisement-related JavaScript code and other JavaScript code of 339 websites by visiting each website and using the Firebug extension. Bhagavatula et al. [24] presented a technique for detecting advertisement resources utilising the k-nearest neighbours classification based on EasyList, which is the primary subscription of Adblock aimed at removing advertisements from web pages. Different from Orr, their basic idea was using the classification criteria of an older version of EasyList to train a classifier to accurately identify advertisements according to a much newer blacklist.

However, the machine learning-based approaches discussed above only focussed on detecting advertisement-related contents, including loading advertisement content (image or flash), which is not considered to be tracking behaviour in some studies because no privacy information is leaked in this situation.

We only focus on detecting tracking behaviours in this paper. Yamada et al. [25] had the same goal as us, and they proposed web tracker detection and blacklist generation based on a temporal link analysis. Their system classified suspicious sites by using machine-learning algorithms, and only 62 %–73 % blacklisted sites were detected. In our former work [2], we trained an incremental classifier to detect third-party trackers through static JavaScript analysis, and 93 % trackers in the test set can be classified correctly. However, that method had some shortcomings compared to this paper: (1) we made no distinction between first-party trackers and third-party trackers in the former work; (2) code obfuscation makes feature extraction hard through static analysis, which will introduce errors; (3) it is easy to bypass the detection by adding some useless JavaScript APIs. We have solved all these problems in this paper.

3   Design and Implementation

3.1   Basic Idea and System Overview

First-party websites and third-party websites may both track users by executing JavaScript, while our goal is to block third-party tracking while preserving first-party tracking. Therefore, we should filter out first-party files before any other action. The most intuitive and effective way to determine whether a file belongs to the first-party website or a third-party website is based on the file location. If the file is located in the first-party server, we consider it to be a first-party file. However, a first-party website may choose to cache files downloaded from third-party websites on its own server for performance or security issues. According to its location, we consider this kind of file to be first-party files in this paper.

Third-party trackers track users in two steps: (1) obtain the users' information and (2) generate an HTTP request with users' information to third-party servers. Take the third-party tracker google-analytics.com for example, as shown in Fig. 1. Case 1 and Case 2 demonstrate how it tracks users. The JavaScript code ga.js is acquired from google-analytics.com when a user visits the first-party website a.com (**Case 1**) or is downloaded from google-analytics.com and cached in first-party website b.com (**Case 2**). Then, an HTTP request with users' information, which is generated by executing the JavaScript code ga.js, is sent to the third-party server google-analytics.com.

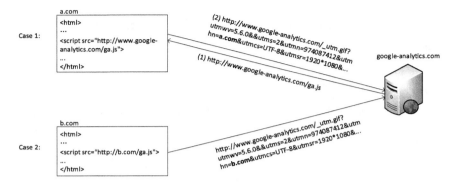

Fig. 1. Third-party tracking examples

The JavaScript ga.js is a tracking JavaScript file and the HTTP request _utm.gif is generated by executing ga.js. In case 1, we can block third-party tracking by blocking the tracking JavaScript (ga.js) or its generated request with users' information (_utm.gif). In case 2, since we remove all first-party JavaScript at first, it cannot block third-party tracking by blocking the tracking JavaScript. Therefore, we can block third-party tracking by blocking the HTTP request with users' information generated by executing the tracking JavaScript in case 2.

Different behaviours lead to different API sets being called, so JavaScript-based trackers and non-trackers call different API sets because of different purposes. Based on these facts, we can get the tracking JavaScript through machine learning. If the tracking JavaScript was blocked, its generated request would not be generated. To get the generated HTTP requests, we can compare the HTTP requests crawling when no JavaScript is blocked with the HTTP requests crawling when the tracking JavaScript is blocked. At last, we add both the tracking JavaScript and its generated HTTP request to the blacklist.

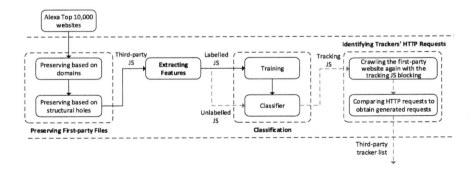

Fig. 2. System overview

As shown in Fig. 2, at a high level, the process includes four parts: preserving first-party files, extracting features, classification and identifying trackers' HTTP requests. We crawled the homepages of the Alexa top 10,000 websites. Firstly, we filter out all first-party files and only focus on third-party files. Secondly, we extracted features of third-party JavaScript files via Chromium browser with hooked JavaScript interface. Then, we labelled some JavaScript instances and built a classifier with the labelled third-party JavaScript instances in the classification part. With the classifier, the blacklist can be automatically generated as follows:

1. Unlabelled third-party JavaScript instances are classified by using the classifier to get third-party tracking JavaScript.
2. Crawl these first-party websites again by blocking the third-party tracking JavaScript. Compare the HTTP requests crawling when the tracking JavaScript is blocked with the HTTP requests crawling when no JavaScript is blocked in order to get the requests generated by the tracking JavaScript.
3. Add third-party tracking JavaScript and its generated requests to the blacklist.

3.2 Preserving First-Party Files

As introduced in Sect. 3.1, we consider a file to be a first-party file if it is located in the first-party server. First-party files and third-party files have one different feature: a first-party file only exists in this website, while a third-party file exists in many websites. Especially, if the url of a file has the same domain as the first-party website', it is a first-party file.

Therefore, we automatically preserved first-party files in two steps. Firstly, if a file has the same domain as the first-party website, it is considered to be a first-party file. This step is easy to determine by checking domain names. Secondly, if a file only exists in one first-party website, it is considered to be a first-party file. This step can be determined based on structural hole theory: if a file is not a structural hole of the relation graph, it is considered to be a first-party file. First-party files will be preserved.

Structural hole theory is always used in social networks to find the 'tie' among several communities. If a first-party website and all its HTTP requests can be regarded as a community, then a third-party file should be a structural hole since it exists in many first-party websites.

To be specific, we built a relation graph which consists of nodes and directed edges. All HTTP request URLs consist of nodes. If HTTP request b is sent when visiting the first-party website A, there is a directed edge from A to b as shown in Fig. 3. A first-party website (the big nodes) and all its HTTP requests (the small nodes) form a community. A first-party file (the small and white nodes) only exists in the first-party website. A third-party file (the black nodes) exists in several communities, and it becomes the tie between them. The structural holes in the relation graph have larger in-degree than other nodes, so we find structural holes via in-degree of the nodes.

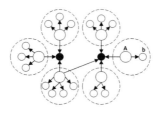

Fig. 3. The relation graph of websites

3.3 Feature Extraction

We have proved that it can successfully classify trackers and non-trackers by using JavaScript API sets [2]. In our former work, we extracted features via static analysis. However, code obfuscation, which is a common technique for JavaScript aimed at making the code difficult to read so that it can protect the code from theft and reuse, makes it hard to extract APIs precisely through static analysis. Moreover, it is easy for trackers to add some useless features to bypass the detection when extracting features based on static analysis.

Therefore, we extracted APIs through dynamic analysis. We modified parts of the WebKit source code, which is the rendering engine used by Chromium, to intercept and log the JavaScript APIs a JavaScript file invokes when executing. We preferred to work at the native code level instead of developing browser extensions or JavaScript patches for several reasons: to detect the origin of events more precisely and to defend against JavaScript attacks that block or circumvent extensions and getter methods[1].

We try to hook as many APIs as possible when modifying the WebKit source code, and a JavaScript file is encoded as a 505-dimensional binary vector through feature extraction: if an API is invoked by the JavaScript file it is set to be 1, or it is set to be 0. For example, as shown in Fig. 4, a.js, b.js and c.js are embedded in the same page. The JavaScript file b.js invokes the function track_by_fingerprint written in a.js, and c.js invokes itself and the function track_by_cookie written in b.js. Thus, a.js invokes no APIs; b.js invokes screen.width, screen.height, document.referrer, document.write etc.; and c.js invokes document.cookie, document.write etc. Then a.js is encoded as a 505-dimensional 0 vector, b.js is encoded as a 505-dimensional binary vector whose features screen.width, screen.height, document.referrer and document.wirte are set to be 1, and c.js is encoded as a 505-dimensional binary vector whose features document.cookie and document.write are set to be 1.

3.4 Classification

The training component has two subcomponents: labelling the dataset and training the classifier.

---

[1] http://code.google.com/p/chromium/issues/detail?id=55084.

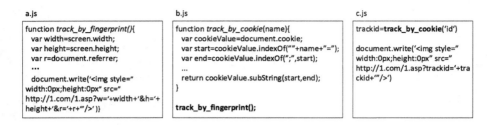

Fig. 4. The example code of function invocation

Labelling Dataset. Before we trained the classifier, we had to label the training set. According to the JavaScript invocation, we call the JavaScript which provides functions and is invoked by other JavaScript as *JavaScript Library*. As opposed to the JavaScript library, we call the JavaScript which invokes a JavaScript library or invokes itself as *JavaScript caller*. A JavaScript file may be both a library and a caller according to different invocation relation. For example, as shown in Fig. 4, b.js invokes the function written in a.js, so b.js is a JavaScript caller to a.js and a.js is a JavaScript library to b.js. C.js invokes the function written in b.js, so c.js is JavaScript caller to b.js and b.js is JavaScript library to c.js.

We only labelled tracking callers as tracking JavaScript. Because blocking tracking libraries or tracking callers can both block tracking, while tracking behaviours happen in tracking callers and through feature extraction a tracking library may be encoded as 0 vector which cannot be used to train the classifier. As shown in Fig. 4, a.js should be labelled as non-tracker since a.js only provides function and no features are extracted from a.js, b.js should be labelled as tracker since b.js invokes function track_by_fingerprint to track users by fingerprinting, and c.js should be labelled as tracker since c.js invokes function track_by_cookie and itself to track users via HTTP cookies.

Easy List[2], Easy Privacy[3] and Ghostery [7] are the most effective blacklists [26]. Unfortunately, third-party trackers and non-trackers cannot be labelled simply based on these lists, because these blacklists label third-party trackers without distinguishing tracking libraries and tracking callers, while we could not label tracking libraries as trackers when training the classifier. Therefore, to train the classifier, we labelled the training set firstly by using Ghostery, Easy List and Easy Privacy separately, then manually confirmed the JavaScript files determined as trackers by these lists and relabelled the JavaScript files determined as non-trackers by these lists according to our former experience [2].

Most obfuscation used by normal websites cannot conceal JavaScript APIs. We can understand the code with the help of deobfuscated tools. However, it is possible that some JavaScript code may be highly obfuscated, and we did not label the highly obfuscated JavaScript files because we could not understand them.

---

[2] https://easylist-downloads.adblockplus.org/easylist.txt.
[3] https://easylist-downloads.adblockplus.org/easyprivacy.txt.

Training Classifier. We trained the classifier by using the labelled instances. To determine what classification scheme fit our data best, we implemented several of the most common classifiers used for supervised learning with the help of WEKA [27], a statistical software package. We will discuss the choice of the classifiers in Sect. 4.3.

4   Evaluation

The experiment was conducted on a machine with 8-GB memory and Inter (R) Core (TM) 2 Quad 2.93-GHz processor. The classification was implemented with WEKA [27], a statistical software package. Other parts of the system are programmed in Python language.

Firstly, we evaluated the effectiveness of every single part of our system. Then we evaluated the overall effectiveness of DMTrackerDetector and compared the efficiency of DMTrackerDetector and Ghostery. For our experiments, we crawled the home pages of the Alexa top 10,000 websites. We built the relation graph used to preserve first-party files based on all HTTP requests of the crawled websites. We randomly selected 500 websites and spent less than 3 weeks (one person) to manually label all third-party JavaScript files to train the classifier, turning out 1,237 unique third-party non-tracker instances and 1,199 unique third-party tracker instances. We randomly selected another 100 websites to test the effectiveness of the classifier.

We did not use the dataset in our former work because at that time we labelled instances mainly based on Ghostery, whereas Ghostery labels third-party trackers without distinguishing tracking libraries and tracking callers. As introduced in Sect. 3.4, in this paper we could not label tracking libraries as trackers when training the classifier, so we had to label the training set manually. The dataset in our former work was too large to manually label. However, our training set in this paper is large enough to build a strong classifier, since high accuracy is obtained with the test set.

4.1   The Results of Preserving First-Party Files

As noted in Sect. 3.2, we preserved first-party files in two steps. Firstly, if a file has the same domain as the first-party website, it is considered to be a first-party file. This step is easy to determine by checking domain names.

Secondly, if a file only exists in one first-party website, it is considered to be a first-party file. This step can be determined based on structural hole theory. We made a relation graph based on all HTTP request URLs of the crawled 10,000 websites. Many files have fundamentally the same content but different URLs, such as http://s7.addthis.com/js/250/addthis_widget.js and http://s7.addthis.com/js/300/addthis_widget.js. Therefore, instead of URLs, we took domains as nodes. We chose the nodes whose in-degree is larger than 2 as structural holes (third-party domains) because: (1) Many websites have two domain names, e.g. renren.com and xiaonei.com are the same website; (2) A tracker existing in two websites tracks users only across the two first-party websites, and it will not bring severe privacy threat. The relation graph consists of 15,892 nodes. Among these, 1,999 nodes have larger than 2 in-degrees. So the 1,999 nodes are considered to be third-party domains. The domain google-analytics.com is the structural hole with the largest in-degrees of 4,317.

We tested the quality of the structural holes by manually checking nodes in the relation graph whose in-degree was 3. We determined a domain to be a third-party domain through search engine, whois and visiting websites directly. If a domain appears in more than one website under the control of different administrative entities, it is a third-party domain. There are 544 domains whose in-degree is 3 in our dataset, and 522 (95.96 %) of them are third-party domains. The errors occur in this situation: when an administrative entity has many domains, all domains belonging to the administrative entity may be considered to be third-party domains. For example, the domains aliexpress.com, alibaba.com and aliimg.com belong to the same administrative entity and interact with each other, so they will be considered to be third-party domains.

We do not test the quality of the structural holes whose in-degree is larger than 3, because domains with larger in-degrees are more likely to be third-party domains and we only need to check the worst situation. We can raise the quality of the structural holes by choosing nodes whose in-degree is larger than 3 as third-party domains, since a tracker existing in three websites tracks users only across the three first-party websites and it still will not bring severe privacy threats. However, we chose the nodes whose in-degree is larger than 2 as structural holes at last, because the quality of the structural holes whose in-degree is 3 is acceptable.

4.2   The Effectiveness of Features

To determine the effectiveness of features we used in the classification process, we evaluated which features contributed more to the classification at first by using χ^2 algorithm. The χ^2 of a feature represents the degree of correlation with classification. The feature with larger χ^2 can be considered that it contributes more to the classification. Table 1 lists the top 40 features ranked by χ^2.

Then, we looked at the correlation of the features in greater detail. We wanted to know which features are correlated to being a tracker. The correlation analysis we have adopted is based on the value of the Spearman's correlation coefficient. As shown in Fig. 5, after calculating the Spearman's correlation coefficient, we list the top 20 features which are the most correlated to the fact that a JavaScript file is a tracker, and the top 20 features which are the most uncorrelated to that fact. As shown in Table 1, the bold features are positively correlated to being a non-tracker. Not surprisingly, we can infer the following conclusions from Table 1 and Fig. 5:

1. According to the correlation of the features, trackers are chiefly concerned with the operations of getting information (such as screen information, location information, navigator information, referrer, plugin information, etc.)

Table 1. Top 40 features of the classification ranked by χ^2

Rank	Feature	χ^2	Rank	Feature	χ^2
1	Document::cookie	851.29	21	DOMPluginArray::length	74.25
2	Document::referrer	631.60	22	Navigator::javaEnabled	69.99
3	Document::setCookie	624.74	23	DOMPlugin::name	69.99
4	Screen::height	286.38	24	DOMPluginArray::pluginData	69.31
5	Screen::width	279.72	25	Document::domain	65.98
6	Location::url	274.24	26	Location::host	59.40
7	Location::hostname	234.70	27	**Document::createDocumentFragment**	57.47
8	Storage::getItem	231.44	28	**HTMLInputElement::value**	52.73
9	Document::title	140.92	29	**HTMLInputElement::maxLength**	52.51
10	Screen::colorDepth	138.28	30	**HTMLInputElement::setValue**	51.98
11	Location::protocol	128.56	31	Document::webkitHidden	51.71
12	Location::href	125.83	32	**HTMLElement::setInnerText**	50.60
13	Storage::setItem	124.46	33	DOMWindow::innerWidth	45.71
14	Navigator::language	117.30	34	**Element::hasAttribute**	42.61
15	Location::search	103.28	35	**Node::getElementsByName**	42.41
16	Navigator::cookieEnabled	100.76	36	**Document::defaultView**	41.81
17	HTMLImageElement::setHeight	98.92	37	Navigator::vendor	38.45
18	HTMLImageElement::setWidth	98.92	38	**Document::createComment**	36.69
19	DOMPluginArray::item	78.99	39	**Element::webkitMatchesSelector**	34.09
20	Location::hash	77.11	40	**HTMLTextAreaElement::value**	33.80

and manipulating HTTP cookies and LocalStorage (such as invoking Document::cookie, Document::setCookie, Document::domain, Storage::getItem, Storage::setItem, etc.) for the main goal of trackers is to get and record users' privacy information.

2. Stateful tracking may be more widely used than stateless tracking, because the APIs for HTTP cookies (such as Document::cookie, Document::setCookie, Location::url, etc.) have larger Spearman's coefficient value than the APIs for fingerprinting (such as class Screen, Navigator, DOMPlugin, DOMPluginArray, etc.).

3. Non-trackers tend to be used for the operations of HTML element (such as class HTMLElement, HTMLInputElement, Element, etc.) and DOM nodes (such as class Node) as the main goal of non-trackers is to enrich the user experiences.

4. As shown in Table 1, the features which are the most correlated to the fact that a JavaScript file is a tracker have larger χ^2 than the features which are the most correlated to the fact that a JavaScript file is a non-tracker. Therefore, the behaviours of trackers play a more important role than non-trackers in the classification.

4.3 The Classifier Results

As introduced in Sect. 3.3, a JavaScript file may be encoded as 0 vector. The 0 vector instances were considered to be non-trackers and we removed all 0 vector

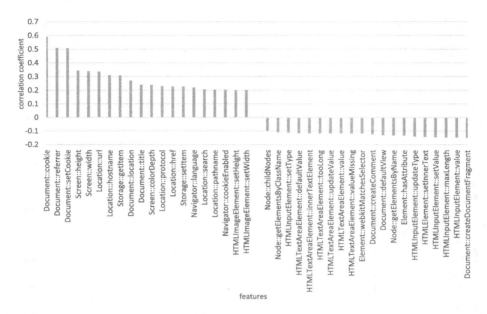

Fig. 5. Spearman's Correlation Coefficient between features and being a tracker in the classification

instances when training the classifier. The classifier is trained by using 2,436 third-party non-zero instances in 500 websites, which consists of 1,199 unique trackers and 1,237 unique non-trackers.

We employed Naive Bayes, Logistic Regression, SMO, Id3, ADTree, J48 and Random Forest classification models. Table 2 shows a comparison of the accuracy measures among different classifiers. Even though Id3 and Random Forest perform well in the case of the training set, both of them have low accuracy in the 10-fold cross validation. J48 shows high accuracy in the case of the training set and the best accuracy values in the 10-fold cross validation. As a result, we selected the J48 classification model to train our classifier.

Table 3 shows the results of our classifier obtained using the training set, and Table 4 shows the results of our classifier in 10-fold cross validation. To evaluate the classifier in real scenarios, we also manually labelled a test set. We randomly selected 100 websites and manually labelled all third-party JavaScript files, turning out 314 non-zero non-tracking instances and 388 non-zero tracking instances. Table 5 lists the confusion matrix on the test set, and 97.8 % instances are classified correctly.

4.4   The Results of Identifying Trackers' HTTP Requests

We compared the HTTP requests crawling when no JavaScript is blocked with the HTTP requests crawling when the tracking JavaScript is blocked in order to get the missing requests. In addition to the generated requests, the missing

Table 2. Comparison of classifier models

Classifier models	Accuracy obtained using training set(%)	Accuracy in 10-fold cross validation(%)
NaiveBayes	85.8	84.98
ADTree	93.56	93.06
Logistic	97.33	93.1
SMO	96.51	94.17
RandomForest	99.92	95.32
Id3	99.92	96.02
J48	98.72	96.31

Table 3. Results obtained using the training set

Accuracy(%)	TP rate	FP rate	Class
98.72	0.988	0.013	Non-tracker
	0.987	0.012	Tracker

Table 4. Results of the 10-fold cross validation

Accuracy(%)	TP rate	FP rate	Class
96.31	0.959	0.033	Non-tracker
	0.967	0.041	Tracker

Table 5. Confusion matrix on test set of the classifier

Truth \ Prediction	Non-tracker	Tracker
Non-tracker	311	3
Tracker	12	376

requests may contain HTTP requests for files (such as images, css, JavaScript files, etc.), which are randomly generated and different each time the website is visited. The HTTP requests generated by the third-party tracking JavaScript are always sent to third-party servers with some parameters in the URLs. Therefore, we get the trackers' HTTP requests in two steps: (1) Compare the HTTP requests crawled twice to get the missing requests. (2) Remove the requests sent to the first-party server and the requests whose URLs contain less than 2 parameters.

To test the effectiveness of the method above, we crawled the 500 websites again by blocking the manually labelled third-party tracking JavaScript, compared the HTTP requests crawled twice to get the missing requests, and removed the first-party requests and the requests whose URLs contain less than 2 parameters.

Only one unique normal HTTP request is determined by mistake, and less than 10 unique HTTP requests generated by executing third-party tracking JavaScript are determined by mistake because they contain only one parameter in the URLs. In conclusion, based on this method the trackers' HTTP requests can be almost completely correctly obtained when crawling the 500 websites. That is to say, **the overall effectiveness of DMTrackerDetector depends almost entirely on the effectiveness of the classifier**.

Since google-analytics.com is the third-party tracker which appears most frequently in our crawled websites, we also evaluated the situation where first-party websites cache the tracking JavaScript downloaded from google-analytics.com. We found that 62 websites in the 10,000 crawled websites had cached the tracking JavaScript downloaded from google-analytics.com in their own servers.

4.5   Comparison with the Ghostery List

Easy List, Easy Privacy and Ghostery [7] are the most effective blacklists [26]. Easy List is used for blocking advertisement-related tracking, including behaviours such as loading advertisement images, while such behaviours do not collect users' information [2]. Easy Privacy is used for blocking all kinds of tracking, though the number of trackers in Easy Privacy is fewer than Ghostery. In comparison, the Ghostery list covers most trackers, and we compared the efficiency of the list generated by DMTrackerDetector with the Ghostery list.

For the comparison, we firstly obtained the tracking JavaScript through the classifier using the test set in Sect. 4.3. Then, we obtained the HTTP requests generated by the third-party tracking JavaScript, and added all third-party tracking JavaScript and the trackers' generated HTTP requests to the blacklist. Then we labelled all HTTP requests in the 100 websites by using the Ghostery list.

As introduced in Sect. 3.4, Ghostery labels third-party trackers without distinguishing tracking JavaScript libraries and tracking callers, while DMTrackerDetector does not label JavaScript tracking libraries as trackers. Thus, we grouped trackers by domains to compare them. Ghostery labels 283 group trackers in the test set and 243 groups can also be identified by DMTrackerDetector. 40 groups are not considered to be trackers by DMTrackerDetector: 11 groups are used to present advertisements which do not have tracking behaviours; 2 groups are not JavaScript-based trackers which may get users' information such as IP address, city and country by executing background code and send this information to third-party websites via json files; 21 groups are 1*1 pixel images with fewer than two parameters in their URL parameters (15 of them are only images without any information); and only 6 groups are JavaScript-based trackers. Moreover, 35 unrevealed group trackers are detected by DMTrackerDetector, as listed in Table 6.

In conclusion, the results show that our list not only covers almost all JavaScript-based tracking records in the Ghostery list but also contains more trackers than Ghostery.

Table 6. The trackers detected by DMTrackerDetector

ID	The website which embed the tracker	Trackers
1	http://enter.ru	http://adforce.ru/rtcode/p2.php?rp=actionpay&uvid=5ed86fb1b0007c910ea39335&source=enter
2	http://enter.ru	http://ads.admized.com/rtb/usermatch.php?umid=37&dataid=0&userid=55417943288144%20293&redirecturl=http%3A%2F%2Feu-sonar.sociomantic..com%2Fimg%2F2010-07-01%2Faction%2Fmatch%3Faid%3Dadmized-eu%26fpc%3D55417%209432%208814420293%26id%3D%25userid%3D%25%26&call.type=redirect
3	http://fnac.es	http://ums.adtechjp.com/mapuser?providerid=1006;userid=80569223659%2043981727
4	http://szonline.net	http://jsonp.aid.alibaba.com/Umid/getDeviceInfo?_cbFunction=fn.qPPsje6I&tokenid=x1K6YmVvY0jbtleDiujejqGkV6O WQKDM&acookie=BmlfDxUpthECAXwQRha3xiwK&n=first
5	http://fnac.es	http://audienceinsights.net/cs/s?t=http%3A%2F%2Frtb-csync.smartadserver.com%2Fredir%2F%3Fpartnerid%3D53%26partneruserid%3D
6	http://komputronik.pl	http://prf.audiencemanager.de/log/profile/user-match?type=js&sec=7f2e41a3309071%202432b572a6eaf6b10b&advertiserId= 56c58220b1a43db6323c052&pid=56c58220b1a43db6323&r=295053053
7	http://fnac.es	http://adserving.avazudsp.net/dspJS.js
8	http://fnac.es	http://adserving.avazudsp.net/check.adv.php?r=0.762057748623%201923&runid=NTg2aWVyX2ZnKzQ=.0&advid= MTgxNG11X3QvNGIr&pid=0&gettype=0&httptype=1&pid=0&prunid=NTg2aWVyX2ZnKzQ=&k=&MastWeb=&loc= http%3A//www.fnac.es//&referer=&h=480&w=640
9	http://fnac.es	http://www.barilliance.net/data.js.php?a=pv&sid=46133&uid=3328725599&pid=&enc=utf-8&cfp=1&lvt=null&ut= 1457026759&ses=1&spv=1&1&ref=&br=Chrome&v=32&os=Linux&scw=640&sch=480&th=18&tdw=4&tdm=3&xtr1= %20&xtr2=%20&xtr3=%20&curl=http%3A%2F%2Fwww.fnac.es%2F%2F&pcm=1&pcm=0&abt=a&pt=U&pidu=1&attu [Member%20Status]=Non-Member&&attud[Member%20Status]=&&&kts=3226
9	http://theblaze.com	http://match.basebanner.com/match?excid=7&cijs=0
10	http://kenh14.vn	http://log1.channelvn.net/scripts/log.js?v=261115
10	http://kenh14.vn	http://log1.channelvn.net/_ltm.gif?utmu=12862171190&ltma=54548145.194480496.162368097&ltmb=54548145.194480496 &ltmc=54548145&ltmts=1457025349569&ltmk=192847022&ltmap=LA-54548145-1&ltmcs=UTF-8&ltmsr=640x480& ltmsc=8-bit&ltmul=en-us&ltmr=0&rf=http://kenh14.vn/
11	http://tv2.dk	https://go.ffx1.com/uid?anuid=2552025266156320933&t=&m=84&_rdnr=1
11	http://tv2.dk	https://go.ffx1.com/imp?id=6143&m=84&pl=39&pubid=TV2.dk&csiz=320x100&advid=Danske+Spil&plid= S%c3%a6rplacering&cpid=2016_DLO_Kontinuerlig_Performance+spor_uge+9-53&cid=EJP_Image_uge36&out= https://go.ffx1.com/empty?&rnd=64084
12	http://drudgereport.com	http://dtm.gap.com/dmm/contextweb/match?fpc=3132&pnid=14200&trid=2668032597339262205&fpctok=1

(Continued)

Table 6. (*Continued*)

ID	The website which embed the tracker	Trackers
13	http://povarenok.ru	http://idntfy.ru/token?e=base64&u=aHR0cDovL290Y2xpcY2stYWR2LnJlL2NvcmUuY29kZS5qcz9waWQ9NTg3Jn.Jp ZD01MjAwMTgmcmw9Jmxs PWh0dHA1M0EvL3d3d3w3Yy3wb3zhcmVub2suY2Z/TTyMCZvaD00NjAmc3c9NjQw JnNoPTQ4MCZwZ2D04JnZpZHN1dHHVwPTE=&p=idntfy&n=otclick
14	http://job.ru	http://imrk.net/services/nslookup?app=conv&referer-kw=poadcp+poadcp6116&setuid=1&f=1&test=1&random=8876190
		http://imrk.net/userbind?src=btw&pbf=1&gi=1
15	http://theblaze.com	http://sync.ipredictive.com/d/sync/cookie/generic?http://us-u.openx.net/w/1.0/sd?id=537073028&val=$ADELPHIC_CUID
16	http://bongda.com.vn	http://pub.lavanetwork.net/sites/bongda.com.vn/m.bongda.com.vn.js
17	http://mrporter.com	https://dc.ads.linkedin.com/collect/?pid=6883&opid=8868&fmt=gif&gtmcb=1663206603&ck=&3pc=true&an.user.id= 3247088782189976807
18	http://bonprix.de	https://tracking.m6r.eu/sync/adscaleSyncDone?userBuyeruid=c2482089cc8add393ae5721d56e49283&userId=adscale-user:9702114570275563663
		https://tracking.m6r.eu/pixel/container?pixelId=6ee465d6-190a-432b-8eac-d14a6d2771e8&pageType=view-home&userId= 193704509060411502 3&gender=&customerType=&shopCountry=DE
19	http://enter.ru	http://cm.marketgid.com/i.gif?dsp=actionpay&c=56d86fb1b0007c910ea39335
20	http://komputronik.pl	http://app.marketizator.com/mktzsave?event=view&uid=494076034114696932 2&session=ses19047461 68ion&id_website= 2823&page_url=http%3A%2F%2Fwww.komputronik.pl%2F&time=2016-03-3—18:46:15&svo=0&browser=Chrome%2032 &resolution=640x480&device_type=desktop&referer_type=direct&visitor_type=new&country=undefined&region=& city=&os=Linux
21	http://couriermail.com.au	http://tags.news.com.au/prod/utrack/utrack.js?cb=14570269227840.0329553757328540 1
		http://tags.news.com.au/prod/metrics/metrics.js
22	http://couriermail.com.au	http://pixel.newsdiscover.com.au/px1.gif?net_uid=d25dbaf8e951ebf16b279635498dd117&net_platform=web&net_site=tcm &pc_acclevel=none&pc_byref=none&pc_conttypegrant=none&pc_conttyperule=none&pc_memtype=anonymous&pc_pcsid= none&newskey_geo_network=unknown&cbd=11011&nk=d25dbaf8e951ebf16b279635498dd117&nk_src=generator.html &nk_ts=1457026871&nk_isnew=0&nk_chk=32466009-339818230131641103&nk_utl=1&l_nk_src=utrack.js&l_nk_ts= 1488562924&ad_krux_segs=&ad_krux_user=&app_pi_ts=1457026966090&app-pi_tz=1&bhgt=460&bwdth=620
23	http://postaffiliatepro.com	https://support.qualityunit.com/scripts/track_visit.php?t=Y&C=Track&B=joxpv41uhy67nfpm5m1qo0liq9xyz&S= 26olukdouf1azh3lkgmjwnoxbcokk&pt=Post%20Affiliate%20Pro%20-%20Affiliate%20Tracking%20%20%26%20Affiliate% 20Program%20Software&url=_S_www.postaffiliatepro.com%2F&ref=&sr=640x480&ud=%7B%7D&vn=Y&ci=
24	http://enter.ru	http://cdn.retailrocket.ru/content/javascript/tracking.js

(*Continued*)

Table 6. (*Continued*)

ID	The website which embed the tracker	Trackers
25	http://povarenok.ru	http://adcode.rontar.com/SspCookieySync.axd?dspId=5&userId=3015197682235478616
26	http://rurubu.travel	http://rt.rtoaster.jp/t/?a=RTA-bc4a-1bb923b71630&l=http%3A%2F%2Frurubu.travel%2F&r=&m=&p=&i=0.08605761686339974&c=Shift_JIS
27	http://komputronik.pl	http://app2.salesmanago.pl/static/sm.js
		http://app2.salesmanago.pl/api/r.gif?uri=%2F&location=www.komputronik.pl&uuid=1533d96eb8a-52e9673b9f07-7637696d-a333f81e-7b7d56dd-52e382ca8b0e&referrer=&smid=pazk8cw3on87gvmw&time=2016-03-03T17%3A46%3A54Z&title=Sklep%20komputerowy%20-%20Komputronik.pl&cp=1457027214224
28	http://carsales.com.au	http://ads.stickyadstv.com/user-registering?dataProviderId=183&userId=f7ee56d8-6ff7-4200-869d-3522ea667792
29	http://drudgereport.com	http://cs.tekblue.net/u/cejeiejcfebegdhddhbfbhff.gif?redir=http%3A%2F%2Fr.openx.net%2Fset%2Fpid%3D342e478d-4d67-267b-f081-0eff5f6bc080%26rtb%3D_TEKBLUE_UUID
30	http://shopclues.com	http://st.targetix.net/match?id=4&burl=http%3A%2F%2Fsync.audtd.com%2Fmatch%2Ftargetix%3Fuid%3D%24%7BVID%7D%26fpd%3Dgetintent
31	http://tvtoday.de	http://i.tfag.de/js-ng/tvt.tfm-container.js
		http://i.tfag.de/js-ng/js-gpt-tvt.js
32	http://mediamarkt.de	http://widgets.trustedshops.com/js/X850885BCC73A48D1B290F0459CA39921.js
33	http://shopclues.com	http://tracker.unbxdapi.com/v2/1p.jpg?data=%7B%22url%22%3A%22http%3A%2F%2Fwww.shopclues.com%2F%22%2C%22referrer%22%3A%22%22%2C%22%22%2C%22visit_type%22%3A%22first_time%22%2C%22ver%22%3A%222.11.8%22%7D&UnbxdKey=shopclues.dev-u1447936138700&action=visitor&uid=uid-1457025422905-73509&t=1457025422957|0.03593841101974249
34	http://clicksor.com	http://support.yesup.net/visitor/index.php?_m=livesupport&_a=htmlcode&departmentid=4,2,69&custom=YToyOntpOjA7czo4NzoiPGltZyBzcmM9M9Imh0dHA6Ly93d3cuY2xpY2tzb3IuY29tL2ltYWdlcy93Y3yBzcmM9M9Imh0dHA6Ly93d3cuY2xpY2tzb3IuY29tL2ltYWdlcy9jIGFsdD0iIiBpZD0iIiBjbGFzcz0iIiAvPg1VXHII1IGFsdD0iIiBpZD0iIiBjbGFzcz0iIiAvPg1VXHII1uY29tL2ltYWdlcy9jIGFsdD0iIiBpZD0iIiBjbGFzcz0iIiAvPg1VXHII:
35	http://mrporter.com	https://media.yoox.biz/newsl/rd/yorb.htm?yorbid=e254173b-26c0-4cc2-99b4-a137967d6ed7

5   Discussions

Firstly, since we labelled the training dataset manually, the training dataset may contain some bias. However, it is extremely challenging to obtain an ideal, unbiased dataset with perfect ground truth. To reduce possible data sampling bias, we labelled the training dataset by the popular blacklists first, then manually confirmed the JavaScript files labelled as trackers by these lists and manually relabelled the JavaScript files labelled as non-trackers by these lists. We believe that even though the effectiveness of classification in our work may vary a little bit when using different training sets, our major conclusions and insights will likely still hold.

Secondly, this work improves upon our former work in that the APIs correlated to being a tracker now play a key role in the classification, so it is difficult to evade our detection by adding or reducing irrelevant APIs in a tracking JavaScript file. However, it would be feasible to bypass the proposed detection mechanism if one can perform the splitting and merging of JavaScript files. If we split one tracking JavaScript file into different JavaScript files to weaken the impact of the APIs correlated to being a tracker, every JavaScript would likely call a similar API set to non-tracking JavaScript. Thus, trackers can evade our detection by merging pieces of users' fingerprint information in the server side to identify users. For example, a tracker can call screen.height in a.js, screen.width in b.js, location.hostname in c.js, document.title in d.js, etc., and also call some useless APIs in each files (such as document.createcommnet, etc.). The information the tracker obtains in each JavaScript can be used together to identify a user. However, we have not encountered such a situation so far.

Thirdly, another way for trackers to evade our detection is to generate the HTTP requests with some random strings in the URLs when executing the tracking JavaScript. In this way, it would be feasible to bypass the detection when the tracking JavaScript caches in the first-party server. To defend against third-party tracking in this situation, we can normalise the generated URLs to match the random string part; for example we can normalize the URLs by using regular expression. We will normalise the generated URLs to match the random string part in the future work.

6   Conclusion

Third-party tracking on the web has attracted much attention in recent years. The most effective method to defend against third-party tracking is based on blacklists. However, this method highly depends on the records in the database and these known blacklists need to be updated regularly. In this paper, we proposed an effective system named DMTrackerDetector, which can automatically detect third-party trackers offline and output a blacklist. Our system consists of preserving first-party files, extracting features, classification and identifying trackers' HTTP requests. To detect third-party trackers, the four parts work together, and high accuracy is obtained. We also compared the list generated by our system with the Ghostery list. The results showed that our list not only covers almost all JavaScript-based tracking records in the Ghostery list but also contains more trackers than Ghostery.

Acknowledgement. This work is supported in part by the National Natural Science Foundation of China (61272481, 61303239, 61572460), the National key research and development project (2016YFB0800703), the National Information Security Special Projects of National Development and Reform Commission of China [(2012)1424], open Project Program of the State Key Laboratory of Information Security(2015-MS-04). Peng Liu was supported by NSF SBE-1422215, ARO W911NF-13-1-0421 (MURI), and ARO W911NF-15-1-0576.

References

1. Nikiforakis, N., Kapravelos, A., Joosen, W., Kruegel, C., Piessens, F., Vigna, G.: On the workings and current practices of web-based device fingerprinting. Secur. Priv. IEEE **12**(3), 28–36 (2014)
2. Qianru, W., Liu, Q., Zhang, Y., Wen, G.: Trackerdetector: A system to detect third-party trackers through machine learning. Comput. Netw. **91**, 164–173 (2015)
3. Bau, J., Mayer, J., Paskov, H., Mitchell, J.C.: A promising direction for web tracking countermeasures. In: Web, vol. 2 (2013)
4. Mayer, J.R., Mitchell, J.C.: Third-party web tracking: Policy and technology. In: 2012 IEEE Symposium on Security and Privacy (SP), pp. 413–427. IEEE (2012)
5. Adblock plus (2016). https://addons.mozilla.org/zh-cn/firefox/addon/adblock-plus/
6. Donottrackme: Online privacy protection (2016). https://addons.mozilla.org/zh-cn/firefox/addon/donottrackplus/
7. Ghostery (2016). https://addons.mozilla.org/zh-cn/firefox/addon/ghostery/
8. Pan, X., Cao, Y., Chen, Y.: I do not know what you visited last summer: Protecting users from third-party web tracking with trackingfree browser (2015)
9. Nikiforakis, N., Kapravelos, A., Joosen, W., Kruegel, C., Piessens, F., Vigna, G.: Cookieless monster: Exploring the ecosystem of web-based devicefingerprinting. In: 2013 IEEE Symposium on Security and Privacy (SP), pp. 541–555. IEEE (2013)
10. Acar, G., Juarez, M., Nikiforakis, N., Diaz, C., Gürses, S., Piessens, F., Preneel, B.: Fpdetective: dusting the web for fingerprinters. In: Proceedings of the 2013 ACM SIGSAC Conference on Computer and Communications Security, pp. 1129–1140. ACM (2013)
11. Acar, G., Eubank, C., Englehardt, S., Juarez, M., Narayanan, A., Diaz, C.: The web never forgets: Persistent tracking mechanisms in the wild. In: Proceedings of the 2014 ACM SIGSAC Conference on Computer and Communications Security, pp. 674–689. ACM (2014)
12. Ayenson, M., Wambach, D.J., Soltani, A., Good, N., Hoofnagle, C.J.: Flash cookies and privacy ii: Now with html5 and etag respawning. Available at SSRN 1898390 (2011)
13. Soltani, A., Canty, S., Mayo, Q., Thomas, L., Hoofnagle, C.J.: Flash cookies and privacy. In: AAAI Spring Symposium: Intelligent Information Privacy Management (2010)
14. Eckersley, P.: How unique is your web browser? In: Atallah, M.J., Hopper, N.J. (eds.) PETS 2010. LNCS, vol. 6205, pp. 1–18. Springer, Heidelberg (2010)

15. Doubleclick ad exchange real-time bidding protocol: cookie matching. https://developers.google.com/ad-exchange/rtb/cookie-guide
16. Kohno, T., Roesner, F.: University of Washington David Wetherall. Detecting and defending against third-party tracking on the web. In: Proceedings of the 9th USENIX Conference on Networked Systems Design and Implementation (2012)
17. Noscript (2016). https://addons.mozilla.org/zh-cn/firefox/addon/noscript/
18. Krishnamurthy, B., Naryshkin, K., Wills, C.: Privacy leakage vs. protection measures: the growing disconnect. Proc. Web **2**, 1–10 (2011)
19. Keep-my-opt-outs   (2016).   https://chrome.google.com/webstore/detail/keep-my-opt-outs/hhnjdplhmcnkiecampfdgfjilccfpfoe
20. Targeted advertising cookie opt-out (2016). https://addons.mozilla.org/zh-cn/firefox/addon/targeted-advertising-cookie-op/
21. Betterprivacy   (2016).   https://addons.mozilla.org/zh-cn/firefox/addon/better privacy/
22. Kushmerick, N.: Learning to remove internet advertisements. In: Proceedings of the Third Annual Conference on Autonomous Agents, pp. 175–181. ACM (1999)
23. Orr, C.R., Chauhan, A., Gupta, M., Frisz, C.J., Dunn, C.W.: An approach for identifying javascript-loaded advertisements through static program analysis. In: Proceedings of the 2012 ACM Workshop on Privacy in the Electronic Society, pp. 1–12. ACM (2012)
24. Bhagavatula, S., Dunn, C., Kanich, C., Gupta, M., Ziebart, B.: Leveraging machine learning to improve unwanted resource filtering. In: Proceedings of the 2014 Workshop on Artificial Intelligent and Security Workshop, pp. 95–102. ACM (2014)
25. Yamada, A., Masanori, H., Miyake, Y.: Web tracking site detection based on temporal link analysis. In: 2010 IEEE 24th International Conference on Advanced Information Networking and Applications Workshops (WAINA), pp. 626–631. IEEE (2010)
26. Mayer, J.: Tracking the trackers: Self-help tools. http://cyberlaw.stanford.edu/blog/2011/09/tracking-trackers-self-help-tools, 9 2011
27. Witten, I.H., Frank, E., Trigg, L.E., Hall, M.A., Holmes, G., Cunningham, S.J., Weka: Practical machine learning tools and techniques with java implementations (1999)

Cryptography for Cloud Computing

Privately Outsourcing Exponentiation to a Single Server: Cryptanalysis and Optimal Constructions

Céline Chevalier[1], Fabien Laguillaumie[2], and Damien Vergnaud[3(✉)]

[1] CRED (U. Panthéon–Assas Paris II), Paris, France
[2] LIP (UCBL, U. Lyon, CNRS, ENS Lyon, INRIA), Lyon, France
[3] DI/ENS (ENS, CNRS, INRIA, PSL), Paris, France
damien.vergnaud@ens.fr

Abstract. We address the problem of speeding up group computations in cryptography using a single untrusted computational resource. We analyze the security of an efficient protocol for securely outsourcing multi-exponentiations proposed at ESORICS 2014. We show that this scheme does not achieve the claimed security guarantees and we present practical polynomial-time attacks on the delegation protocol which allow the untrusted helper to recover part (or the whole) of the device secret inputs. We then provide simple constructions for outsourcing group exponentiations in different settings (*e.g.* public/secret, fixed/variable bases and public/secret exponents). Finally, we prove that our attacks on the ESORICS 2014 protocol are unavoidable if one wants to use a single untrusted computational resource and to limit the computational cost of the limited device to a constant number of (generic) group operations. In particular, we show that our constructions are actually optimal in terms of operations in the underlying group.

1 Introduction

The problem of "outsourcing" computation has been considered in various settings since many years. The proliferation of mobile devices provides yet another venue in which a computationally weak device would like to be able to outsource a costly operation to a third party helper. Such devices do not usually have the computational or memory resources to perform complex cryptographic operations and it is natural to outsource these operations to some helper. However, in this scenario, this helper can, potentially, be operated by a malicious adversary and we usually need to ensure that it does not learn anything about what it is actually computing. The wild and successful deployment of cloud storage services make users outsource their data, for a personal or commercial purpose. These users actually have to trust their storage providers concerning the availability of their data, and indeed outages happen regularly. Cryptographic primitives are needed to convince customers that their platforms are reliable. Among such primitives, provable data possessions [1] and proofs of retrievability [16] allow

© Springer International Publishing Switzerland 2016
I. Askoxylakis et al. (Eds.): ESORICS 2016, Part I, LNCS 9878, pp. 261–278, 2016.
DOI: 10.1007/978-3-319-45744-4_13

the storage cloud to prove that a file uploaded by a client has not been deteriorated or that it can be entirely retrieved. The computation needed on the verification side by the client are highly *"exponentiation-consuming"*. Indeed, the core operation of these cryptosystems is group exponentiation, i.e., computing u^a from a group element u and an exponent a. The main goal of this paper is to analyze new and existing protocols outsourcing group exponentiation to a *single* untrusted helper.

Prior work. In 2005, Hohenberger and Lysyanskaya [14] provided a formal security definition for *securely* outsourcing computations from a computationally limited device to untrusted helpers and they presented two practical schemes. Their first scheme shows how to securely outsource group exponentiations to two, possibly dishonest, servers that are physically separated (and do not communicate). Their protocol achieves security as long as one of them is honest. In 2012, Chen, Li, Ma, Tang and Lou [8] presented a nice efficiency improvement to the protocol from [14], but the security of their scheme also relies on the assumption that the two servers cannot communicate.

Since this separation of the two servers is actually a strong assumption hard to be met in practice, at ESORICS 2014 [27], Wang, Wu, Wong, Qin, Chow, Liu and Tan proposed a protocol to outsource group exponentiations to a *single* untrusted server. Their generic algorithm is very efficient and allows to outsource multi-exponentiations with fixed or variable exponent and bases (that can be public or secret).

Contributions of the paper. Our contributions are both theoretical and practical. Our first result is a practical attack on the protocol for outsourcing multi-exponentiation proposed by Wang *et al.* [27]. Our attack allows to recover secret information in polynomial time using lattice reduction. It shows that their solution is completely insecure. We later show in Theorem 2 that what they expected to achieve (namely, to limit the computational cost of the limited device to a constant number of (generic) group operations) is actually theoretically impossible.

Our second contribution is the proposal of a taxonomy of exponentiation delegation protocols and the associated simple yet precise and formal models of protocols that allow a client $\mathcal{C}$ (or delegator) who wants to compute a multi-exponentiation (which is a computation of the form $\prod_{i=1}^{n} u_i{}^{a_i}$ for group elements u_i's and exponents a_i's) to delegate an intermediate exponentiation to a more powerful server $\mathcal{S}$ (or delegatee). The client's contribution in the computation is then only few multiplications of group elements and arithmetic operations modulo the underlying group order. We consider in this work only prime-order groups. Our taxonomy covers all the practical situations: the group elements can be secret or public, variable or fixed, the exponents can be secret or public, and the result of the multi-exponentiation can also be either public or secret. As an example, a BLS digital signature [4] is a group element $\sigma = h(m)^a$, where m is the signed message, h a hash function, and a the secret key. The signature computation can be delegated with our protocol for a public group element (the hashed value of the message), a secret exponent (the secret key), and a public output (the signature). During an ElGamal decryption of a ciphertext $(c_1, c_2) = (g^r, m \cdot y^r)$ (where m is the plaintext and $y = g^a$ is the public key), one may want to securely delegate the computation of $c_1{}^a$ (to recover m as $c_2/c_1{}^a$). Such an exponentiation can be delegated with our protocol for known group element (c_1), secret exponent (a) and secret result ($c_1{}^a$, in order to keep the plaintext m secret). We propose a delegation protocol for each of the previously mentioned scenarios. The latency of sending messages back and forth has been shown to often be the dominating factor in the running time of cryptographic protocols. Indeed, round complexity has been the subject of a great deal of research in cryptography. We thus focus on the problem of constructing one-round delegation protocols; i.e., where we authorize the client to call only once the server $\mathcal{S}$, and give him access to some pre-computations (consisting of pairs of the form (k, g^k)). We then consider their complexity, in terms of group operations needed by the client to eventually get the desired result securely.

Our third and main contribution is the computation of lower bounds on the number of group operations needed on the delegator's side to securely compute his exponentiation when it has access to a helper server. To give these lower bounds, we analyze the security of delegation protocols in the generic group model which considers that algorithms do not exploit any properties of the encodings of group elements. This model is usually used to rule out classes of attacks by an adversary trying to break a cryptographic assumption. We use it only to prove our lower bounds but we do not assume that an adversary against our protocols is limited to generic operations in the underlying group. As mentioned above, these lower bounds tell us that our protocols are optimal in terms of operations in the underlying group (in other words, they cannot be significantly improved).

A summary of our results for outsourcing protocols for single exponentiation is given in Table 1. For the ease of reference, all our results are collected in Table 2 given on page 16.

2 Preliminaries

Exponentiation Delegation: Definitions. The (multi-)exponentiations are computed in a group $\mathbb{G}$ whose description is provided by an algorithm GroupGen, which takes as input a security parameter λ. It provides a set *params* which contains the group description, its prime[1] order, say p, and one or many generators. Let n be an integer, we denote by $\mathbf{a}$ (*resp.* $\mathbf{u}$) a vector of n exponents $a_i \in \mathbb{Z}_p$ (*resp.* group elements $u_i \in \mathbb{G}$). The aim of the protocols that follow is to compute $\prod_{i=1}^{n} u_i^{a_i}$, denoted as $\mathbf{u}^{\mathbf{a}}$.

We consider a delegation of an exponentiation as a 2-party protocol between a client $\mathcal{C}$ and a server $\mathcal{S}$. We denote as $(y_{\mathcal{C}}, y_{\mathcal{S}}, tr) \leftarrow (\mathcal{C}(1^\lambda, params, (\mathbf{a}, \mathbf{u})), \mathcal{S}(1^\lambda))$ the protocol at the end of which $\mathcal{C}$ knows $y_{\mathcal{C}}$ and $\mathcal{S}$ learns $y_{\mathcal{S}}$ (usually an empty string). The string tr is the transcript of the interaction. In all our protocols, the

---

[1] In this paper, following prior works, we consider only prime order groups, but most of our results can be generalized to composite order groups.

Table 1. Results Summary: ℓ is the number of available pairs (k, g^k), $p = |\mathbb{G}|$ and Prot. means "Protocol" (p. 12). The given complexities are the number of operations in $\mathbb{G}$.

Outsourcing Fixed Base Exp.							Outsourcing Var. Base Exp.						
u	a	u^a	#delegations	Lower bound	Achieved Complexity	Optimality	u	a	u^a	# delegations	Lower bound	Achieved Complexity	Optimality
Pub.	Pub.	Pub.					Pub.	Pub.	Pub.				
Pub.	Pub.	Sec.					Pub.	Pub.	Sec.				
Pub.	Sec.	Pub.	1	0	0 (Prot. 2)	✓	Pub.	Sec.	Pub.	s	$\frac{\log p}{s+1}$	$\frac{\log p}{s+1}$ (Prot. 4&5)	✓
Pub.	Sec.	Sec.	1	1	1 (Prot. 3)	✓	Pub.	Sec.	Sec.	s	$\frac{\log p}{s+1}$	$\frac{\log p}{s+1}$ (Prot. 4&5)	✓
Sec.	Pub.	Pub.					Sec.	Pub.	Pub.				
Sec.	Pub.	Sec.	1	1	1 (Prot. 1)	✓	Sec.	Pub.	Sec.	1	$\frac{\log p}{\ell+3}$ *	$\frac{\log p}{\ell}$ (Prot. 8)	✗
										2	≤ 3	3 (Prot. 7)	✗
Sec.	Sec.	Pub.	1	0	0 (Prot. 2)	✓	Sec.	Sec.	Pub.	s	$\frac{\log p}{s+1}$	$\frac{\log p}{s}$ (Prot. 6)	✗
Sec.	Sec.	Sec.	1	1	1 (Prot. 1)	✓	Sec.	Sec.	Sec.	s	$\frac{\log p}{s+1}$	$\frac{\log p}{s}$ (Prot. 6)	✗

server will be very basic, since it will only perform exponentiations whose basis and exponent are sent to him by the client. In [7], Cavallo *et al.* emphasized the need for delegation of group inverses since almost all known protocols for delegated exponentiation do require inverse computations from the client. They presented an efficient and secure protocol for delegating group inverses. However, our protocols do not require such computations and our lower bounds hold even in groups in which inverse computation is efficient (and therefore does not need to be delegated, see Remark 4).

To model the security notions, and to simplify the exposition, we describe by a *computation code* β (which is a binary vector of length 4), the scenario of the computation. Indeed, according to the applications, some of the data on which the computations are performed may be either public or secret. In the computation of $\mathbf{u}^{\mathbf{a}}$, the vector of basis $\mathbf{u}$, the vector of exponents $\mathbf{a}$ or the result $\mathbf{u}^{\mathbf{a}}$ may be unknown (and especially to the adversary). The three first entries of the code describe the secrecy of respectively $\mathbf{u}$, $\mathbf{a}$ and $\mathbf{u}^{\mathbf{a}}$: a 0 means that the data is hidden to the adversary, and 1 means that the data is public. The last entry indicates whether the base if fixed (f) or variable (v). For instance, the code 101v means that $\mathbf{u}$ is public, the exponent $\mathbf{a}$ is secret, and the result $\mathbf{u}^{\mathbf{a}}$ is public, while the base is variable. Note that we consider the *whole* vectors (*i.e.*, all of its coordinates) to be either public or private, whereas we could imagine that, for a vector $\mathbf{u}$ of exponents for instance, some of these could be public, and others could be kept secret. The following notions should then be declined according to these scenarios.

- **Correctness.** This requirement means that when the server and the client follow honestly the protocol, the client's output is actually the expected (multi-)exponentiation.
- **One-wayness.** This natural security basically means that an attacker cannot compute any secret data involved during the computation.
- **Privacy.** This indistinguishability-based security notion [7] captures that given two secret inputs (even adversarially chosen), an "honest-but-curious" adversary cannot tell which input was used (with a probability significantly better than that of guessing).

We refer the reader to the paper full version [9] for formal definitions.

Remark 1. *As mentioned in [6, 10, 18], a delegation protocol that does not ensure verifiability may cause severe security problems. Even though our protocols are not verifiable, the computational lower bounds on the efficiency of private outsourcing exponentiation protocols we prove in Sect. 5 readily imply that these bounds also holds for verifiable protocols. In a forthcoming paper, we will show how our methods can be extended to propose verifiable delegation protocols and to improve corresponding efficiency lower bounds.*

Generic Group Model. The generic group model (see [24] for details) is an idealized cryptographic model where algorithms (generally adversaries) do not exploit any properties of the encodings of group elements. They can access group elements only via a random encoding algorithm that encodes group elements as random bit-strings. Proofs in the generic group model provide heuristic evidence of some problem hardness, but they do not necessarily say anything about the difficulty of a specific problem in a concrete group [12].

Computations of pairs (g^k, k)**.** To outsource the computation of an exponentiation in a group $\mathbb{G}$ of prime order p, (pseudo-)random pairs of the form $(g^k, k) \in \mathbb{G} \times \mathbb{Z}_p$ are sometimes used to hide sensitive information to the untrusted server. This looks like a "chicken-and-egg problem" but there exist several techniques to make it possible for a computationally limited device to have such pairs at its disposal, at a low cost. A trivial method is to load its memory with many genuine (generated by a trusted party) random and independent couples. In other settings, a mobile device with limited computing capabilities can precompute "offline" such pairs at low speed and power. If the device can do a little more computation, there exist other preprocessing techniques, that may depend whether the base or the exponent varies.

We only mention here the main technique to produce these pairs. The key ingredient is Boyko, Peinado and Venkatesan generator from [5]: the idea is to store a small number of precomputed pairs (g^{α_i}, α_i), and when a fresh pair is needed, the device outputs a product $g^k = \prod_{i \in S} g^{\alpha_i}$ with $k = \sum_{i \in S} \alpha_i$ for a random set S. It has then been improved by Nguyen, Shparlinski and Stern generator [20], that allows to re-use some α_i in the product. This generator is secure against adaptive adversaries and performs $O(\log \log(p)^2)$ group operations. For some parameters, the generator from [20] is proved to have an output distribution statistically close to the uniform distribution. Obviously, these generators are of practical interest only if the base g is fixed and used multiple times.

In the sequel we will assume that the delegator may have access to some *(pseudo-)random power generator* $\mathcal{B}(\cdot)$ that at invocation (with no input) outputs a single (pseudo)-random pair $(g^k, k) \in \mathbb{G} \times \mathbb{Z}_p$ where k is uniformly distributed in $\mathbb{Z}_p$ (or statistically close to the uniform distribution). If the generator $\mathcal{B}(\cdot)$ is invoked several times, we assume that the output pairs are independent. In order to evaluate the efficiency of delegation protocols, we consider explicitly the query complexity to the generator $\mathcal{B}(\cdot)$ (depending on the context, this can be interpreted as storage of precomputed values, offline computation or use of the generator from [20] and thus additional multiplications in $\mathbb{G}$).

3   Attack on Wang *et al.*'s Algorithm from ESORICS 2014

Wang *et al.* proposed a generic algorithm to outsource the computation of several multi-exponentiations with variable exponents and variable bases. Their algorithm, called GExp, takes as input a list of tuples $((\{a_{i,j}\}_{1 \leq j \leq s}; \{u_{i,j}\}_{1 \leq j \leq s}))_{1 \leq i \leq r}$ and computes the list of multi-exponentiations $(\prod_{j=1}^{r} u_{i,j}^{a_{i,j}})_{1 \leq i \leq s}$. It is claimed that this algorithm is secure in a strong model where the computation is outsourced to a single untrusted server [27, Theorem 1]. We will show that GExp can be broken in polynomial time using lattice reduction if two (simple) exponentiations are outsourced with the *same* exponent, which is the case in the scenario of proof of data possession presented in [27, Section 4]. This means that GExp does not achieve the claimed security.

Description of Wang *et al.*'s protocol. The setting of GExp is the following: $\mathbb{G}$ is a cyclic group of prime order p, and g is a generator. For $1 \leq i \leq r$ and $1 \leq j \leq s$, $a_{i,j}$ are uniform and independent elements of $\mathbb{Z}_p^*$, and $u_{i,j}$ are random elements from $\mathbb{G}$. They assume the $a_{i,j}$'s, the $u_{i,j}$'s and the result are secret (and the $u_{i,j}$ are variable, i.e. $\beta = 000v$ with our notations). The protocol is divided into three steps:

– **Step 1.** The delegator $\mathcal{C}$ generates four random pairs $(\alpha_k, \mu_k)_{1 \leq k \leq 4}$ where $\mu_k = g^{\alpha_k}$ (using a pseudo-random power generator). A Υ-bit element χ is randomly picked (for some parameter Υ). Then, for all $1 \leq i \leq r$ and $1 \leq j \leq s$, the elements $b_{i,j}$ are randomly picked in $\mathbb{Z}_p^*$. It sets[2]

$$c_{i,j} = a_{i,j} - b_{i,j}\chi \mod p \tag{1}$$

$$\theta_i = (\alpha_1 \sum_{j=1}^{s} b_{i,j} - \alpha_2) + (\alpha_3 \sum_{j=1}^{s} c_{i,j} - \alpha_4) \mod p. \tag{2}$$

and $w_{i,j} = u_{i,j}/\mu_1$ and $h_{i,j} = u_{i,j}/\mu_3$.

---

[2] Note that the protocol from [27] can also be described without inversion in the group $\mathbb{G}$ but to help the reader familiar with this paper, we use the same description.

- **Step 2.** The second step consists in invoking the (untrusted) delegatee S for some exponentiations. To do so, C generates (using a (pseudo-)random power generator) $r + 2$ random pairs $(g^{t_i}, t_i)_{1 \leq i \leq r+2}$ and queries (in random order) S on
  - $(g^{t_i}, \theta_i/t_i)$ to obtain $B_i = g^{\theta_i}$ for all $1 \leq i \leq r$,
  - $(g^{t_{r+1}}, \theta/t_{r+1})$ to obtain $A = g^{\theta}$ with $\theta = t_{r+2} - \sum_{i=1}^{r} \theta_i \mod p$,
  - $\begin{cases} (w_{i,j}, b_{i,j}) \text{ to get } C_{i,j} = (u_{i,j}/\mu_1)^{b_{i,j}} \\ (h_{i,j}, c_{i,j}) \text{ to get } D_{i,j} = (u_{i,j}/\mu_3)^{c_{i,j}} \end{cases}$ for $1 \leq i \leq r$ and $1 \leq j \leq s$.

- **Step 3.** It consists in combining the different values obtained from S to recover the desired multi-exponentiations. In particular, an exponentiation to the power χ is involved. The protocol to be efficient, needs χ not too large.

Simple attack. Suppose that a delegation of a single exponentiation u^a, for u and a secret, is performed using Wang *et al.*'s protocol. If a is a secret key, an element of the form h^a is likely to be known by the adversary, together with h (one can think of a public key in a scenario of delegation of BLS signatures [4], for instance)). In this case, as the attacker sees an element of the form $c = a - b\chi$ (see Eq. (1)) and knows b (cf. Step 2), he can compute h^c which is equal to $h^a \cdot (h^{\chi})^{-b}$, so that recovering χ can be done by computing the discrete logarithm of $(h^a/h^c)^{b^{-1}}$ in base h. Using a baby-step giant-step algorithm, this can be done in $2^{\Upsilon/2}$ operations, which contradicts [27, Theorem 1].

Main attack. The crucial weakness of this protocol is the use of this *small* element χ which hides the exponents. The authors suggest to take it of bit-size Υ, for $\Upsilon = 64$. We will show that it cannot be that small since it can be recovered in polynomial time if two exponentiations with the *same* exponent are outsourced to the server S. The scenario of our attack is the following: two exponentiations of the form $\mathsf{GExp}((a_{1,1}, \ldots, a_{1,s}); (u_{1,1}, \ldots, u_{1,s}))$ and $\mathsf{GExp}((a_{1,1}, \ldots, a_{1,s}); (u'_{1,1}, \ldots, u'_{1,s}))$ are queried to S. The exponentiations are computed with the *same* exponents. This is typically the case in the first application proposed in [27, Section 4.1] to securely offload Shacham and Waters's proofs of retrievability [23].

For the sake of clarity, it is sufficient to focus on the elements that mask the first exponent $a_{1,1}$. An attacker will obtain (see Step 2) $b_{1,1}$, $b'_{1,1}$, $c_{1,1}$ and $c'_{1,1}$ such that $c_{1,1} = a_{1,1} - b_{1,1}\chi \mod p$ and $c'_{1,1} = a_{1,1} - b'_{1,1}\chi' \mod p$. Subtracting these two equations gives a modular bi-variate linear equation:

$$b_{1,1}X - b'_{1,1}Y + c_{1,1} - c'_{1,1} = 0 \mod p \qquad (3)$$

which has χ and χ' as roots, satisfying $\chi \leq X$ and $\chi' \leq Y$, for some X and Y which will be larger that 2^{Υ}, say 2^{64}. We show that it is (heuristically) possible to recover in polynomial time any χ and χ' that are lower than $\sqrt{p}$.

Solving this bi-variate polynomial equation with small modular roots can be done using the well-known Coppersmith technique [11]. Finding small roots of modular bi-variate polynomials was studied in [17], but his method is very general, whereas we consider here only simple linear polynomials. The following lemma, inspired by Howgrave-Graham's lemma [15] suggests how to construct a particular lattice that will help to recover small modular roots of a linear polynomial in $\mathbb{Z}[x, y]$. We denote as $\| \cdot \|$ the Euclidean norm of polynomials.

Lemma 1. *Let $g(x, y) \in \mathbb{Z}[x, y]$ be a linear polynomial that satisfies*

- $g(x_0, y_0) = 0 \mod p$ *for some* $|x_0| < X$ *and* $|y_0| < Y$,
- $\|g(xX, yY)\| < p/\sqrt{3}$.

Then $g(x_0, y_0) = 0$ holds over the integers.

Let us write a bi-variate linear polynomial as $P(x, y) = x + by + c$, with $b, c \in \mathbb{Z}_p$, which has a root (x_0, y_0) modulo p satisfying $|x_0| < X$ and $|y_0| < Y$. It suffices to divide by $b_{1,1}$ the polynomial from Eq. (3) to make it unary in the first variable. Lemma 1 suggests to find a small-norm polynomial $h(x, y)$ that shares its root with the initial polynomial $P(x, y)$. To do so, we construct the matrix whose rows are formed by the coefficients of the polynomials p, pyY and $P(xX, yY)$ in the basis $(1, X, Y)$. Using the LLL algorithm [19], we can find a small linear combination of these polynomials that will satisfy Lemma 1. Indeed, this matrix has determinant p^2XY and an LLL reduction of the basis of the lattice spanned by the rows of M will output one vector of norm upper bounded by $2^{3/4}(\det(M))^{1/3}$. We expect the second vector to behave as the first, which is confirmed experimentally.

To obtain two polynomials which satisfy Lemma 1, we need the inequality $2^{3/4}(\det(M))^{1/3} < p/\sqrt{3}$, i.e. $XY < 3^{-3/2} \cdot 2^{-9/4}p$. If $g(x, y) = g_0 + g_1x + g_2y$ and $h(x, y) = h_0 + h_1x + h_2y$ are the polynomials corresponding to the shortest vectors output by LLL, we can recover (x_0, y_0) as

$$x_0 = \frac{X(h_0g_2 - g_0h_2)}{g_1h_2 - h_1g_2} \text{ and } y_0 = \frac{Y(h_0g_1 - h_1g_0)}{g_2h_1 - h_2g_1}.$$

As a consequence, this method makes it possible to recover in polynomial time any values χ and χ' that mask the secret value $a_{1,1}$ if they are both below $\sqrt{p}$. The complexity of Nguyen and Stehlé's LLL is quadratic [21], in our case it is $O(d^5 \log(3/2 \log(p))^2)$, with $d = 3$. Then $a_{1,1}$ can be computed as $a_{1,1} = c_{1,1} + b_{1,1}\chi \mod p$. The scheme from [27] is therefore completely insecure.

Remark 2. *One could fix this issue in Wang et al.'s protocol by using a larger Υ (such that the value χ is actually uniformly distributed over $\mathbb{Z}_p$). This would make the protocol not more efficient for the delegator than the actual computation of a single exponentiation. However, even this inefficient protocol would not achieve the privacy security notion as explained in the paper's full version [9, §C].*

4   Generic Constructions for Privately Outsourcing Exponentiation

We focus on protocols for outsourcing a single exponentiation $(u, a) \mapsto u^a$. Protocols for outsourcing multi-exponentiations are given in the full version of the paper [9]. As mentioned in the introduction, round complexity is the main bottleneck in improving the efficiency of secure protocols due to latency, and we consider only 1-round delegation protocols.

Protocols for fixed base exponentiation are probably folklore (e.g., see [18] for a verifiable variant of the protocol corresponding to the computation code $\beta = 001f$) but remain unpublished (to the best of our knowledge). Protocols for variable base exponentiation seem to be new and are inspired by Gallant, Lambert and Vanstone's decomposition algorithm [13] (see below).

We recall that each case is referred to as its computation code β (see Sect. 2). All these protocols are secure in the (indistinguishability) privacy notion defined in [9], in the information-theoretic sense.

Theorem 1 (see [9]). *Let* GroupGen *be a group generator, let λ be a security parameter and let $\mathbb{G}$ be a group of prime order p output by* GroupGen(λ). *Let $(\mathcal{C}, \mathcal{S})$ be one client-server protocol for the delegated computation of the exponentiation u^a described in Protocols 1 – 8 (for the corresponding computation code $\beta \in \{0,1\}^4$ given in their description). The protocol $(\mathcal{C}, \mathcal{S})$ is unconditionally $(\tau, 0)$-private against an honest-but-curious adversary for any time τ.*

Tools. In our protocols, we use two classical algorithms. The first one (Algorithm 1) computes the multi-exponentiation $\prod_{i=1}^{t} g_i^{x_i}$, for $g_1, \dots, g_t \in \mathbb{G}$ and $x_1, \dots, x_t \in \mathbb{N}$ by using the simultaneous 2^w-ary method introduced by Straus [26]. The minimal cost (which depends on w) is $\ell(1 + o(1))$ multiplications overall, where ℓ denotes the maximal bit-length of the x_i's. The method looks at w bits of each of the exponents for each evaluation stage group multiplication (where w is a small positive integer), (see [2] for details).

Algorithm 1. Multi-Exponentiation by Simultaneous 2^w-ary method

---

Input: $g_1, \dots, g_t \in \mathbb{G}$, $x_1, \dots, x_t \in \mathbb{N}$ with $\ell = \max_{i \in \{1,\dots,t\}} \lceil \log x_i \rceil$ and
$\quad x_j = \sum_{i=0}^{\lfloor \ell/w \rfloor - 1} e_{i,j} 2^{wi} \in \mathbb{N}$ and $e_{i,j} \in \{0, 2^w - 1\}$ for $i \in \{0, \dots, \lfloor \ell/w \rfloor - 1\}$ and
$\quad j \in \{1, \dots, t\}$
Output: $g_1^{x_1} \cdots g_t^{x_t} \in \mathbb{G}$
$\quad$**for** all non-zero t-tuples $E = (E_1, \dots, E_t) \in \{0, \dots, 2^w - 1\}^t$ **do**
$\quad\quad g_E \leftarrow \prod_{1 \leq i \leq t} g_i^{E_i}$ $\qquad\qquad\qquad\qquad\qquad$ ▷ Precomputation stage
$\quad$**end for**
$\quad h \leftarrow 1_{\mathbb{G}}$
$\quad$**for** i from $\lfloor \ell/w \rfloor - 1$ to 0 **do**
$\quad\quad h \leftarrow h^{2^w}$
$\quad\quad E \leftarrow (e_{i,1}, e_{i,2}, \dots, e_{i,t})$
$\quad\quad h \leftarrow h \cdot g_E$ $\qquad\qquad$ ▷ Multiply h by table entry $g_E = \prod_{1 \leq k \leq t} g_i^{e_{i,k}}$
$\quad$**end for**
$\quad$**return** h

Let p be a prime number and $a \in \mathbb{Z}_p$. Let $s \geq 1$ be an integer and $\boldsymbol{\rho} = (\rho_1, \dots, \rho_s) \in \mathbb{Z}_p^s$. An *s-dimensional decomposition of a with respect to $\boldsymbol{\rho}$* is an s-dimensional vector $\boldsymbol{\alpha} = (\alpha_1, \dots, \alpha_s) \in \mathbb{Z}_p^s$ such that

$$\langle \boldsymbol{\alpha}, \boldsymbol{\rho} \rangle := \alpha_1 \rho_1 + \cdots + \alpha_s \rho_s = a \bmod p.$$

It is well-known that if the scalars ρ_i for $i \in \{1, \dots, s\}$ have pairwise differences of absolute value at least $p^{1/s}$, then there exists a polynomial-time algorithm which on inputs a and $\boldsymbol{\rho}$ outputs an s-dimensional decomposition $\boldsymbol{\alpha} \in \mathbb{Z}_p^s$ of a with respect to $\boldsymbol{\rho}$ such that $0 \leq \alpha_i \leq C \cdot p^{1/s}$ for $i \in \{1, \dots, s\}$ (for some small constant $C > 0$). To find this "small decomposition" of a, the algorithm applies a lattice reduction algorithm (such as the LLL-algorithm) to produce a short basis of the $\mathbb{Z}$-lattice of dimension $s + 1$ spanned by the vectors $(p, 0, 0, \dots, 0)$, $(\rho_1, 1, 0, \dots, 0)$, $(\rho_2, 0, 1, \dots, 0)$, $\dots$, $(\rho_s, 0, 0, \dots, 1)$ and applies Babai rounding algorithm [3] to find a nearby vector in this lattice from $(a, 0, \dots, 0)$ (see [25] for details). In the following, we will refer to this second algorithm as the GLV Decomposition Algorithm (GLV-Dec for short) since the method was first introduced by Gallant, Lambert and Vanstone [13] to perform group exponentiations with endomorphism decomposition.

4.1   Constructions for Outsourcing Fixed Base Exponentiation

When the base u is fixed, one can assume that $\mathcal{C}$ can use a pseudo-random power generator for u. As described in Sect. 2, this generator $\mathcal{B}$ is invoked with no input and outputs a single (pseudo)-random pair $(u^k, k) \in \mathbb{G} \times \mathbb{Z}_p$ where k is uniformly distributed in $\mathbb{Z}_p$ (or statistically close to the uniform distribution). If the generator $\mathcal{B}(\cdot)$ is invoked several times, we assume that the output pairs are independent.

Trivial Cases. Obviously, the case $111f$ (everything public) is trivial (simply ask in clear to the delegatee $\mathcal{S}$ the computation of u^a as $\mathcal{S}(u, a)$) and the case $110f$ does not make sense (public inputs and private output), as well as the case $011f$ (secret base) in the prime order setting.

Cases where the Base is Secret $(0{*}{*}f)$**.** If everything is secret (case $000f$), it is easy to delegate the computation of u^a for any exponent a using Protocol 1. The delegator computation amounts to two invocations of the generator $\mathcal{B}$ and one multiplication in $\mathbb{G}$, with only one exponentiation delegated to $\mathcal{S}$.

Even if the exponent is public (case $010f$), Protocol 1 remains the best possible in terms of multiplications in $\mathbb{G}$ (with only one invocation to $\mathcal{S}$) since there is only one multiplication and it is needed to hide the private result.

If the result is public (case $001f$), one can propose the improved Protocol 2, which needs only one invocation of the pseudo-random power generator and no multiplication in $\mathbb{G}$, with only one exponentiation delegated to $\mathcal{S}$.

Cases where the Base is Public $(1{*}{*}f)$**.** If the result is public (case $101f$), Protocol 2 remains the best possible in terms of multiplications in $\mathbb{G}$ (with only one invocation to $\mathcal{S}$) since no multiplication is needed.

If the result is secret (case $100f$), Protocol 3 is the best possible in terms of multiplications in $\mathbb{G}$ since it only needs one invocation of the pseudo-random power generator and one multiplication in $\mathbb{G}$ (needed to hide the private result of the exponentiation), with only one exponentiation delegated to $\mathcal{S}$.

4.2   Constructions for Outsourcing Variable Base Exponentiation

We consider the case when $\mathcal{C}$ wants to delegate the computation of u^a but with a variable u. One cannot assume that $\mathcal{C}$ can use a pseudo-random power generator for u but we can still suppose that it can use a pseudo-random power generator for a fixed generator g that we still call $\mathcal{B}$ with the same properties as before.

Trivial Cases. As above, the case $111v$ (everything public) is trivial (simply ask in clear to the delegatee $\mathcal{S}$ the computation of u^a as $\mathcal{S}(u,a)$) and the case $110v$ does not make sense (public inputs and private output), as well as the case $011v$ (secret base) in the prime order setting.

Cases where the Base is Public $(1{*}{*}v)$. We first consider the case where the variable base u can be made public but not the exponent nor the result (case $100v$). We propose a family of protocols depending on a parameter s that perform the computation of u^a by delegating s exponentiations to a delegator and $\log(p)/(s+1)$ operations in $\mathbb{G}$.

This family of protocols is given in Protocol 5 and the specific case $s = 1$ is Protocol 4. Note that these protocols do not make use of the pseudo-random power generator for g. Unfortunately, the efficiency gain is only a factor s and if the number of delegated exponentiations is constant the delegator still has to perform $O(\log p)$ operations in $\mathbb{G}$.

These protocols are actually optimal in terms of operations in $\mathbb{G}$, as shown in Theorem 2. Obviously, we can also use these protocols if we allow the result u^a to be public (case $101v$) and the optimal result of Theorem 2 show that even in this easier setting, the protocol cannot be improved.

Cases where the Base is Private $(0{*}{*}v)$. We can use this protocol family to construct another delegation protocol for the corresponding cases where the base is kept secret ($000v$ and $001v$). We obtain Protocol 6 that makes two invocations of the pseudo-random generator for g and requires the delegation of one further exponentiation compared to Protocol 5 (and Protocol 4). We do not actually know if these protocols are optimal but the gap is rather tight (see Table 2).

Constructing an outsourcing protocol in these cases with only one exponentiation delegation (or proving it is impossible) is left as an open problem.

We can also use this protocol if we allow the exponent a to be public ($010v$). However, in this case one can improve it with Protocol 7 where the delegator performs only a constant number of group operations in $\mathbb{G}$. In this case, one can also improve it with Protocol 8 where the delegator makes only one call to the delegatee, but at the price of a $O(\log(p))$ number of group operations in $\mathbb{G}$.

Remark 3. *In [7], Cavallo et al. presented two other protocols for outsourcing private variable base and public exponent exponentiation. The first one [7, §4, p. 164], recalled in Protocol 9, achieves only the basic security requirement (i.e., in the sense of one-wayness instead of indistinguishability). It relies on a subset-sum in a group and in order to achieve a stronger privacy notion, the delegation scheme actually becomes less efficient for the delegator than performing* *the exponentiation on its own. The second scheme is much more efficient since the delegator computation is constant but it requires a stronger pseudo-random power generator $\mathcal{B}$ that outputs pseudo-random triples of the form (g^r, g^{ar}, r). In particular, this second protocol can only be used for fixed values of the public exponent a.*

_____ **Protocol 1:** $000f$ (and $010f$) _____

Input: $u \in \mathbb{G}$, $a \in \mathbb{Z}_p$
Output: $u^a \in \mathbb{G}$
  $(u^r, r) \leftarrow \mathcal{B}(\cdot)$ $(u^s, s) \leftarrow \mathcal{B}(\cdot)$
  $t \leftarrow (a - s)/r \bmod p$
  $h \leftarrow \mathcal{S}(u^r, t \bmod p)$
  return $h \cdot u^s$

_____ **Protocol 2:** $001f$ (and $101f$) _____

Input: $u \in \mathbb{G}$, $a \in \mathbb{Z}_p$
Output: $u^a \in \mathbb{G}$
  $(u^k, k) \leftarrow \mathcal{B}(\cdot)$
  $h \leftarrow \mathcal{S}(u^k, a/k \bmod p)$
  return h

_____ **Protocol 3:** $100f$ _____

Input: $u \in \mathbb{G}$, $a \in \mathbb{Z}_p$
Output: $u^a \in \mathbb{G}$
  $(u^k, k) \leftarrow \mathcal{B}(\cdot)$
  $h \leftarrow \mathcal{S}(u, a - k \bmod p)$
  return $h \cdot g^k$

_____ **Protocol 4:** $100v$ (and $101v$) _____

Input: $u \in \mathbb{G}$, $a \in \mathbb{Z}_p$
Output: $u^a \in \mathbb{G}$
  $T \leftarrow \lceil \sqrt{p} \rceil$
  $h \leftarrow \mathcal{S}(u, T)$
  $a_0 = a \bmod T$
  $a_1 = a \operatorname{div} T$ $\triangleright$ Euclidean division:
                                $a = a_1 \cdot T + a_0$
  return $u^{a_0} h^{a_1}$ $\triangleright$ using Alg. 1

_____ **Protocol 5:** $100v$ (and $101v$) _____

Input: $u \in \mathbb{G}$, $a \in \mathbb{Z}_p$
Output: $u^a \in \mathbb{G}$
  $T \leftarrow \lceil p^{1/s+1} \rceil$
  for i from 1 to s **do**
    $h_i \leftarrow \mathcal{S}(u, T^i)$
  end for
  $temp \leftarrow a$
  for i from s down to 0 **do**
    $a_i = temp \operatorname{div} T^i$
    $temp = temp - a_i \cdot T^i$
  end for
          $\triangleright$ $a = a_s \cdot T^s + \cdots + a_1 T + a_0$
  return $u^{a_0} \prod_{i=1}^{s} h_i^{a_i}$ $\triangleright$ using Alg. 1

_____ **Protocol 6:** $000v$ (and $001v$) _____

Input: $u \in \mathbb{G}$, $a \in \mathbb{Z}_p$
Output: $u^a \in \mathbb{G}$
  $(g^{k_1}, k_1) \leftarrow \mathcal{B}(\cdot)$; $(g^{k_2}, k_2) \leftarrow \mathcal{B}(\cdot)$
  $v \leftarrow u \cdot g^{k_1}$
  $h_1 \leftarrow v^a$ $\triangleright$ delegated with Prot. 5
  $h_2 \leftarrow \mathcal{S}(g, -ak_1 - k_2 \bmod p)$
  return $h_1 \cdot h_2 \cdot g^{k_2}$

_____ **Protocol 7:** $010v$ _____

Input: $u \in \mathbb{G}$, $a \in \mathbb{Z}_p$
Output: $u^a \in \mathbb{G}$
  $(g^r, r) \leftarrow \mathcal{B}(\cdot)$; $(g^s, s) \leftarrow \mathcal{B}(\cdot)$
  $(g^t, t) \leftarrow \mathcal{B}(\cdot)$
  $k \leftarrow (t - ra)/s \bmod p$
  $h_1 \leftarrow \mathcal{S}(u \cdot g^r, a)$; $h_2 \leftarrow \mathcal{S}(g^s, k)$
  return $h_1 h_2 g^t$

_____ **Protocol 8:** $010v$ _____

Input: $u \in \mathbb{G}$, $a \in \mathbb{Z}_p$
Output: $u^a \in \mathbb{G}$
  $(g^r, r) \leftarrow \mathcal{B}(\cdot)$
  for i from 1 to s **do**
    $(g^{t_i}, t_i) \leftarrow \mathcal{B}(\cdot)$
  end for
  $(k_0, k_1, \ldots, k_s) \leftarrow$
  GLV-Dec$(1, t_1, \ldots, t_s, -ra \bmod p)$
                    $\triangleright$ with $k_i \leq p^{1/(s+1)}$
  $h_1 \leftarrow \mathcal{S}(u \cdot g^r, a)$
  $h_2 \leftarrow g^{k_0} (g^{t_1})^{k_1} \ldots (g^{t_s})^{k_s}$ $\triangleright$ Alg.1
  return $h_1 h_2$

_____ **Protocol 9:** $010v$ from [7] _____

Input: $u \in \mathbb{G}$, $a \in \mathbb{Z}_p$
Output: $u^a \in \mathbb{G}$
  for i from 1 to s **do**
    $g_i \xleftarrow{R} \mathbb{G}$
  end for
  $\mathcal{I} \xleftarrow{R} \mathfrak{P}_m(\{1, \ldots, s\})$ $\triangleright$ random
                    subset of cardinal m of $\{1, \ldots, s\}$
  $g_{s+1} \leftarrow u \cdot \prod_{i \in \mathcal{I}} g_i$
  for i from 1 to s **do**
    $h_i \leftarrow \mathcal{S}(g_i, -a)$
  end for
  $h_{s+1} \leftarrow \mathcal{S}(g_{s+1}, a)$
  return $h_{s+1} \cdot \prod_{i \in \mathcal{I}} h_i$

5   Complexity Lower Bound for One-Round Protocols

We focus on studying protocols with minimal interaction, namely the delegator is allowed to delegate the computation of several group exponentiations but it must send all of them to the delegatee in only one communication round. Indeed, interactions over computer networks are usually the most time consuming operations (due to lagging or network congestion) and it is very important to study protocols which require the minimal number of rounds to complete. In the full version [9], we also present complexity lower bounds for multi-round protocols.

By "lower bounds", we mean that the number of calls to the delegatee oracle $\mathcal{S}$ and to the pseudo-random power generator $\mathcal{B}$ are fixed, and that we consider the number of group operations. Concerning the first part of Table 2, the bounds come from the protocols given in Sect. 4, since at least one call to the group oracle is mandatory when the result is private (the delegator $\mathcal{C}$ needs to do at least one computation after having received a public result from the delegatee oracle $\mathcal{S}$). The cases $101v$ and $100v$ are then dealt with in Theorem 2. For all these cases, the protocols proposed in Sect. 4 are thus actually optimal. As for Case $010v$, the lower bound for a unique call to $\mathcal{S}$ is proven in Theorem 3, whereas Protocol 7 gives a (constant) upper bound in case we allow a second call to $\mathcal{S}$. Finally, the lower bounds for Cases $001v$ and $000v$ come from the equivalent bounds for Cases $101v$ and $100v$, since the variable base is furthermore assumed to be secret.

In what follows, and as mentioned above, we use the generic group model to prove these lower bounds. We model the different operations as follows:

- The group oracle $\mathcal{G}$ takes as inputs two encodings $\sigma_1 = \sigma(h_1)$ and $\sigma_2 = \sigma(h_2)$ and outputs the encoding σ_3 such $\sigma_3 = \sigma(h_1 h_2)$ (see [24]).
- The pseudo-random power generator $\mathcal{B}$ outputs pairs $(t, \sigma(g^t))$ where the scalar t is picked uniformly at random in $\mathbb{Z}_p$ (independently for all queries).
- The delegatee oracle $\mathcal{S}$ takes as inputs an encoding $\sigma_0 = \sigma(h)$ and a scalar x and outputs the encoding $\sigma_0' = \sigma(h^x)$ (*i.e.* $\sigma^{-1}(\sigma_0') = \sigma^{-1}(\sigma_0)^x$).

In order to prove our complexity lower bounds, we make use of the following simple lemma (whose proof is provided in the paper full version [9]):

Lemma 2. *Let* GroupGen *be a group generator, let* $\mathbb{G}$ *be a group of prime order* p *output by* GroupGen *and let* $\mathcal{A}$ *be a generic algorithm in* $\mathbb{G}$. *If* $\mathcal{A}$ *is given as inputs encodings* $\sigma(g_1), \ldots, \sigma(g_n)$ *of groups elements* $g_1, \ldots, g_n \in \mathbb{G}$ *(for* $n \in \mathbb{N}$*) and outputs the encoding* $\sigma(h)$ *of a group element* $h \in \mathbb{G}$ *in time* τ, *then there exists positive integers* $\alpha_1, \ldots, \alpha_n$ *such that* $h = g_1^{\alpha_1} \ldots g_n^{\alpha_n}$ *and* $\max(\alpha_1, \ldots, \alpha_n) \leq 2^\tau$.

The following theorems assert that for the cases $101v$ and $100v$, the protocols proposed in Sect. 4 are actually optimal in terms of calls to $\mathcal{S}$ and $\mathcal{G}$.

Theorem 2. *Let* GroupGen *be a group generator and let* $(\mathcal{C}, \mathcal{S})$ *be one client-server protocol for the delegated computation of the exponentiation* u^a *for the corresponding computation code* $\beta = 101v$. *We assume that the delegator* $\mathcal{C}$ *is a generic group algorithm that uses*

– $c \log(p) + O(1)$ *generic group operations (for all groups* $\mathbb{G}$ *of primer order* p
  output by GroupGen(λ)*) for some constant* c,
– $\ell = O(1)$ *queries to the (private) pseudo-random power generator* $\mathcal{B}$
– *and only 1 delegated exponentiation to the delegatee* $\mathcal{S}$

If $c < 1/2$*, then* $(\mathcal{C}, \mathcal{S})$ *is not private: there exists an algorithm running in
polynomial-time such that* $\Pr[bit \leftarrow \mathbf{Exp}_{priv}(\mathcal{A}) : bit = 1] \geq 1 - \lambda^{O(1)}$.

Proof. For the ease of exposition, we present a proof for the simple case $s = 1$
where the delegator $\mathcal{C}$ outsources only one exponentiation to the delegatee $\mathcal{S}$.
The complete proof is given in the full version of the paper [9]. We assume that
$\mathcal{C}$ gets as input two encodings $\sigma(u)$, $\sigma(g)$ of *two* group elements u and g and
one scalar a in $\mathbb{Z}_p$ and outputs the encoding $\sigma(u^a)$ of the group element u^a by
making q queries to the group oracle $\mathcal{G}$, ℓ queries to the (private) pseudo-random
power generator $\mathcal{B}$ and 1 query to $\mathcal{S}$.

We assume that $q = c \log p + O(1)$ with $c < 1/2$ and we prove that it is not
possible for $\mathcal{C}$ to compute $\sigma(u^a)$ in such a way that the delegatee $\mathcal{S}$ learns no
information on a. More precisely, we construct a polynomial-time adversary $\mathcal{A}$
for the privacy security notion. The adversary chooses a group element u and two
scalars $(a_0, a_1) \in \mathbb{Z}_p^2$. For the sake of simplicity, we assume that the adversary
picks $(a_0, a_1) \in \mathbb{Z}_p^2$ uniformly at random among the scalars of bit-length $\log(p)$
and u uniformly at random in $\mathbb{G}$. The challenger picks uniformly at random a
bit $b \in \{0, 1\}$ and sets $a = a_b$. The delegator runs the delegation protocol with
inputs u and a and delegates one exponentiation to the adversary acting as the
delegatee. The adversary has to guess the bit b.

Let us denote $(t_1, \sigma(g^{t_1})), (t_2, \sigma(g^{t_2})), \dots, (t_\ell, \sigma(g^{t_\ell}))$ the pairs obtained from
the pseudo-random power generator $\mathcal{B}$ by the delegator $\mathcal{C}$. Since $\mathcal{B}$ takes no inputs
and outputs independent pairs, we can assume without loss of generality that the
delegator $\mathcal{C}$ makes the ℓ queries to $\mathcal{B}$ in a first phase of the delegation protocol.
We denote $(\sigma(h), x)$ the unique pair encoding of group element/scalar made
by $\mathcal{C}$ to the delegatee $\mathcal{S}$ (which is executed by the adversary $\mathcal{A}$ in an "honest-
but-curious" way). Using generic group operations, $\mathcal{C}$ can only construct the
corresponding group elements such that:

$$h = u^{\alpha'} \cdot g^{\kappa'} \cdot g^{t_1 \gamma_1'} \dots g^{t_\ell \gamma_\ell'} \tag{4}$$

for some scalars $(\alpha', \kappa', \gamma_1', \dots, \gamma_\ell')$. We denote $k = h^x$ the response of $\mathcal{S}$. Eventually, the delegator $\mathcal{C}$ outputs the encoding $\sigma(u^a)$ of the group element u^a. Again,
using generic group operations, it can only construct it as

$$u^a = u^\alpha g^\kappa \cdot g^{t_1 \gamma_1} \dots g^{t_\ell \gamma_\ell} k^\delta h^\varepsilon \tag{5}$$

for some scalars $(\alpha, \kappa, \gamma_1, \dots, \gamma_\ell, \delta, \varepsilon)$. If we assume that $q = c \log n + O(1)$ (and
in particular $q = o(\sqrt{p})$), the delegator $\mathcal{C}$ is not able to compute the discrete
logarithm of u in base g. This means that necessarily the exponent of g in
Eq. (5) cancels out. Recall that $k = h^x$, h being constructed as in Eq. (4). Thus,
taking only the discrete logarithms of powers of u in base u of this equation, we
obtain

$$a = \alpha + \varepsilon \alpha' + \delta \alpha' x \mod p \tag{6}$$

We denote τ_1 the number of group operations performed by $\mathcal{C}$ in the computation of h described in Eq. (4) and τ_2 the number of operations in the computation of u^a described in Eq. (5). By assumption, $\tau_1 + \tau_2 \leq c \log p + O(1)$. Furthermore, since $\mathcal{C}$ only used generic group operations, we have (by Lemma 2) $\alpha' \leq 2^{\tau_1}$, $\alpha \leq 2^{\tau_2}$, $\delta \leq 2^{\tau_2}$ and $\varepsilon \leq 2^{\tau_2}$. If we note $\rho_1 = \alpha + \varepsilon\alpha'$ and $\rho_2 = \delta\alpha'$, Eq. (6) becomes $a = \rho_1 + x\rho_2 \bmod p$, where x is known to the adversary, $\rho_2 = \delta\alpha' \leq 2^{\tau_1}2^{\tau_2} = 2^{\tau_1+\tau_2} \leq p^{c+o(1)}$ and $\rho_1 = \alpha + \varepsilon\alpha' \leq 2^{\tau_1} + 2^{\tau_1}2^{\tau_2} \leq p^{c+o(1)}$.

The adversary $\mathcal{A}$ can then try to decompose a_0 and a_1 as $a_i = \rho_{i,1} + x\rho_{i,2}$ $\bmod p$, with $\rho_{i,1}, \rho_{i,2} \leq p^{c+o(1)}$. For $a_b = a$, the decomposition algorithm provided in the paper full version [9] (which generalizes the main attack on Wang et al.'s protocol) will recover $\rho_{b,1}$ and $\rho_{b,2}$ in polynomial time. However, for a given x and a random a_{1-b} of bit-length $\log(p)$, there is only a negligible probability that such a decomposition exists (less than $p^{c+o(1)} \times p^{c+o(1)} = p^{2c+o(1)} = o(p)$) scalars can be written in this way). Thus, the adversary can simply run the decomposition algorithm mentioned above on (a_0, x) on one hand and on (a_1, x) on the other hand and returns the bit b for which the algorithm returns a "small decomposition" on input (a_b, x). By the previous analysis, its advantage is noticeable.

Remark 4. *It is worth mentioning that even in (generic) groups where division is significantly less expensive than multiplication (such as elliptic curves or class groups of imaginary quadratic number fields), this lower bound (as well as the following ones) still holds (see the paper full version [9] for details).*

Protocol 7 shows that it is possible to delegate a secret base, public exponent exponentiation with only a constant number of operations if the delegator can delegate at least two exponentiations. Theorem 3 asserts that if the delegator is only allowed to delegate one exponentiation then Protocol 8 is almost optimal in this setting. More precisely, we show that the delegator has to perform at least $O(\log(p))$ group operations if it delegates only one exponentiation and makes at most a constant number of queries to the pseudo-random power generator $\mathcal{B}$. Due to lack of space, the proof is provided in the full version of the paper [9].

Theorem 3. *Let* GroupGen *be a group generator and let* $(\mathcal{C}, \mathcal{S})$ *be one client-server protocol for the delegated computation of one exponentiation for the computation code* $\beta = 010v$. *We assume that the delegator* $\mathcal{C}$ *is a generic group algorithm that uses*

- $c \log(p) + O(1)$ *generic group operations (for groups* $\mathbb{G}$ *of order* p *output by* GroupGen(λ)*),*
- $\ell = O(1)$ *queries to the (private) pseudo-random power generator* $\mathcal{B}$
- *and only 1 delegated exponentiation to the delegatee* $\mathcal{S}$

If the constant c *satisfies* $c < 1/(\ell+2)$, *then* $(\mathcal{C}, \mathcal{S})$ *is not private: there exists an algorithm running in time* $O(p^{c/2+o(1)})$ *s.t.* $\Pr[bit \leftarrow \mathbf{Exp}_{priv}(\mathcal{A}) : bit = 1] = 1$.

Table 2. Outsourcing protocols for single exponentiation

Constructions for Outsourcing Fixed Base Exponentiation (with a pseudo-random power generator of pairs (k, u^k) available)

Code	u	a	u^a	Secure protocol*	Complexity	Resources	Complexity Lower Bound (for $\mathcal{G}$)		
							Lower Bound	Proof	Optimality
111f	Public	Public	Public	Trivial					
110f	Public	Public	Secret	Non-sense					
101f	Public	Secret	Public	Protocol 2	$1\,\mathcal{S} + 1\,\mathcal{B}$	$(1\,\mathcal{S}, \ell\,\mathcal{B})$	$0\,\mathcal{G}$	From Protocol 2	✓
100f	Public	Secret	Secret	Protocol 3	$1\,\mathcal{S} + 1\,\mathcal{G} + 1\,\mathcal{B}$	$(1\,\mathcal{S}, \ell\,\mathcal{B})$	$1\,\mathcal{G}$	From Protocol 3	✓
011f	Secret	Public	Public	Non-sense†					
010f	Secret	Public	Secret	Protocol 1	$1\,\mathcal{S} + 1\,\mathcal{G} + 2\,\mathcal{B}$	$(1\,\mathcal{S}, \ell\,\mathcal{B})$	$1\,\mathcal{G}$	From Protocol 1	✓
001f	Secret	Secret	Public	Protocol 2	$1\,\mathcal{S} + 1\,\mathcal{B}$	$(1\,\mathcal{S}, \ell\,\mathcal{B})$	$0\,\mathcal{G}$	From Protocol 2	✓
000f	Secret	Secret	Secret	Protocol 1	$1\,\mathcal{S} + 1\,\mathcal{G} + 2\,\mathcal{B}$	$(1\,\mathcal{S}, \ell\,\mathcal{B})$	$1\,\mathcal{G}$	From Case 010f	✓

Constructions for Outsourcing Variable Base Exponentiation (with a pseudo-random power generator of pairs (k, g^k) available)

Code	u	a	u^a	Secure protocol*	Complexity	Resources	Complexity Lower Bound (for $\mathcal{G}$)		
							Lower Bound	Proof	Optimality
111v	Public	Public	Public	Trivial					
110v	Public	Public	Secret	Non-sense					
101v	Public	Secret	Public	Protocol 4	$1\,\mathcal{S} + L_p/2\,\mathcal{G}$	$(1\,\mathcal{S}, \ell\,\mathcal{B})$	$L_p/2\,\mathcal{G}$	Theorem 2, Section 5	✓
				Protocol 5	$s\,\mathcal{S} + L_p/(s+1)\,\mathcal{G}$	$(s\,\mathcal{S}, \ell\,\mathcal{B})$	$L_p/(s+1)\,\mathcal{G}$	Theorem 2, Section 5	✓
100v	Public	Secret	Secret	Protocol 4	$1\,\mathcal{S} + L_p/2\,\mathcal{G}$	$(1\,\mathcal{S}, \ell\,\mathcal{B})$	$L_p/2\,\mathcal{G}$	Theorem 2, Section 5	✓
				Protocol 5	$s\,\mathcal{S} + L_p/(s+1)\,\mathcal{G}$	$(s\,\mathcal{S}, \ell\,\mathcal{B})$	$L_p/(s+1)\,\mathcal{G}$	Theorem 2, Section 5	✓
011v	Secret	Public	Public	Non-sense†					
010v	Secret	Public	Secret	Protocol 8	$1\,\mathcal{S} + L_p/\ell\,\mathcal{G} + \ell\,\mathcal{B}$	$(1\,\mathcal{S}, \ell\,\mathcal{B})$	$L_p/(\ell+3)\,\mathcal{G}$	Theorem 3, Section 5	✗
				Protocol 7	$2\,\mathcal{S} + 3\,\mathcal{G} + 3\,\mathcal{B}$	$(2\,\mathcal{S}, \ell\,\mathcal{B})$	$t^{\ddagger}\,\mathcal{G}$	From Protocol 7	✗
001v	Secret	Secret	Public	Protocol 6 (using 4)	$2\,\mathcal{S} + L_p/2\,\mathcal{G} + 2\,\mathcal{B}$	$(1\,\mathcal{S}, \ell\,\mathcal{B})$	$L_p/2\,\mathcal{G}$	From Case 101v	/
						$(2\,\mathcal{S}, \ell\,\mathcal{B})$	$L_p/3\,\mathcal{G}$	From Case 101v	✗
				Protocol 6 (using 5)	$s\,\mathcal{S} + L_p/s\,\mathcal{G} + 2\,\mathcal{B}$	$(s\,\mathcal{S}, \ell\,\mathcal{B})$	$L_p/(s+1)\,\mathcal{G}$	From Case 101v	✗
000v	Secret	Secret	Secret	Protocol 6 (using 4)	$2\,\mathcal{S} + L_p/2\,\mathcal{G} + 2\,\mathcal{B}$	$(1\,\mathcal{S}, \ell\,\mathcal{B})$	$L_p/2\,\mathcal{G}$	From Case 100v	/
						$(2\,\mathcal{S}, \ell\,\mathcal{B})$	$L_p/3\,\mathcal{G}$	From Case 100v	✗
				Protocol 6 (using 5)	$s\,\mathcal{S} + L_p/s\,\mathcal{G} + 2\,\mathcal{B}$	$(s\,\mathcal{S}, \ell\,\mathcal{B})$	$L_p/(s+1)\,\mathcal{G}$	From Case 100v	✗

Notations: $\ell = O(1)$ and $L_p = \log(p)$.   * refers to the protocols page 12   † Prime order setting.   ‡ With $t \in \{0, 1, 2, 3\}$.

6   Conclusion and Future Work

All our results on (one-round) secure delegation of group exponentation are collected in Table 2. In addition, we also provide protocols and lower-bounds for multi-exponentiations and lower bounds for multi-round delegation of exponentiation protocols in the paper full version [9]. As a future work, understanding the relationship between computational efficiency and memory usage is vital when implementing delegation protocols. In particular, it is interesting to propose efficient delegation protocols and to improve our lower bounds in settings where the memory complexity of the delegator is limited.

Acknowledgments. The authors are supported in part by the French ANR JCJC ROMAnTIC project (ANR-12-JS02-0004), the French ANR EnBid Project (ANR-14-CE28-0003) and by ERC Starting Grant ERC-2013-StG-335086-LATTAC. The authors thank Guillaume Hanrot and Damien Stehlé for helpful discussions, and Olivier Billet for his comments and for pointing out references.

References

1. Ateniese, G., Burns, R.C., Curtmola, R., Herring, J., Kissner, L., Peterson, Z.N.J., Song, D.X.: Provable data possession at untrusted stores. In: Ning et al. [22], pp. 598–609. http://doi.acm.org/10.1145/1315245.1315318
2. Avanzi, R.M.: The complexity of certain multi-exponentiation techniques in cryptography. J. Cryptology **18**(4), 357–373 (2005)
3. Babai, L.: On Lovász' lattice reduction and the nearest lattice point problem. Combinatorica **6**(1), 1–13 (1986)
4. Boneh, D., Lynn, B., Shacham, H.: Short signatures from the Weil pairing. J. Cryptology **17**(4), 297–319 (2004)
5. Boyko, V., Peinado, M., Venkatesan, R.: Speeding up discrete log and factoring based schemes via precomputations. In: Nyberg, K. (ed.) EUROCRYPT 1998. LNCS, vol. 1403, pp. 221–235. Springer, Heidelberg (1998)
6. Canard, S., Devigne, J., Sanders, O.: Delegating a pairing can be both secure and efficient. In: Boureanu, I., Owesarski, P., Vaudenay, S. (eds.) ACNS 2014. LNCS, vol. 8479, pp. 549–565. Springer, Heidelberg (2014)
7. Cavallo, B., Crescenzo, G.D., Kahrobaei, D., Shpilrain, V.: Efficient and secure delegation of group exponentiation to a single server. In: Mangard, S., Schaumont, P. (eds.) Radio Frequency Identification. LNCS, vol. 9440, pp. 156–173. Springer, Heidelberg (2015)
8. Chen, X., Li, J., Ma, J., Tang, Q., Lou, W.: New algorithms for secure outsourcing of modular exponentiations. In: Foresti, S., Yung, M., Martinelli, F. (eds.) ESORICS 2012. LNCS, vol. 7459, pp. 541–556. Springer, Heidelberg (2012)
9. Chevalier, C., Laguillaumie, F., Vergnaud, D.: Privately outsourcing exponentiation to a single server: Cryptanalysis and optimal constructions. Cryptology ePrint Archive, Report 2016/309 (2016). http://eprint.iacr.org/
10. Chevallier-Mames, B., Coron, J.-S., McCullagh, N., Naccache, D., Scott, M.: Secure delegation of elliptic-curve pairing. In: Gollmann, D., Lanet, J.-L., Iguchi-Cartigny, J. (eds.) CARDIS 2010. LNCS, vol. 6035, pp. 24–35. Springer, Heidelberg (2010)

11. Coppersmith, D.: Finding a small root of a univariate modular equation. In: Maurer, U.M. (ed.) EUROCRYPT 1996. LNCS, vol. 1070, pp. 155–165. Springer, Heidelberg (1996)

12. Dent, A.W.: Adapting the weaknesses of the random oracle model to the generic group model. In: Zheng, Y. (ed.) ASIACRYPT 2002. LNCS, vol. 2501, pp. 100–109. Springer, Heidelberg (2002)

13. Gallant, R.P., Lambert, R.J., Vanstone, S.A.: Faster point multiplication on elliptic curves with efficient endomorphisms. In: Kilian, J. (ed.) CRYPTO 2001. LNCS, vol. 2139, pp. 190–200. Springer, Heidelberg (2001)

14. Hohenberger, S., Lysyanskaya, A.: How to securely outsource cryptographic computations. In: Kilian, J. (ed.) TCC 2005. LNCS, vol. 3378, pp. 264–282. Springer, Heidelberg (2005)

15. Howgrave-Graham, N.: Finding small roots of univariate modular equations revisited. In: Darnell, M. (ed.) Crytography and Coding. LNCS, vol. 1355, pp. 131–142. Springer, Heidelberg (1997)

16. Juels, A., Kaliski Jr., B.S.: PORS: proofs of retrievability for large files. In: Ning et al. [22], pp. 584–597. http://doi.acm.org/10.1145/1315245.1315317

17. Jutla, C.S.: On finding small solutions of modular multivariate polynomial equations. In: Nyberg, K. (ed.) EUROCRYPT 1998. LNCS, vol. 1403, pp. 158–170. Springer, Heidelberg (1998)

18. Kiraz, M.S., Uzunkol, O.: Efficient and verifiable algorithms for secure outsourcing of cryptographic computations. Int. J. Inf. Secur, 1–19 (2015, to appear). doi:10.1007/s10207-015-0308-7

19. Lenstra, A.K., Lenstra, H.W.J., Lovász, L.: Factoring polynomials with rational coefficients. Math. Ann. **261**, 515–534 (1982)

20. Nguyen, P., Shparlinski, I., Stern, J.: Distribution of modular sums and the security of server aided exponentiation. Workshop Comp. Number Theor. Crypt. **20**, 1–16 (1999)

21. Nguyen, P.Q., Stehlé, D.: Floating-point LLL revisited. In: Cramer, R. (ed.) EUROCRYPT 2005. LNCS, vol. 3494, pp. 215–233. Springer, Heidelberg (2005)

22. Ning, P., di Vimercati, S.D.C., Syverson, P.F. (eds.): Proceedings of the 2007 ACM Conference on Computer and Communications Security, CCS 2007, Alexandria, Virginia, USA, October 28–31, 2007. ACM (2007)

23. Shacham, H., Waters, B.: Compact proofs of retrievability. In: Pieprzyk, J. (ed.) ASIACRYPT 2008. LNCS, vol. 5350, pp. 90–107. Springer, Heidelberg (2008)

24. Shoup, V.: Lower bounds for discrete logarithms and related problems. In: Fumy, W. (ed.) EUROCRYPT 1997. LNCS, vol. 1233, pp. 256–266. Springer, Heidelberg (1997)

25. Smith, B.: Easy scalar decompositions for efficient scalar multiplication on elliptic curves and genus 2 Jacobians. Contemp. Math. Ser. **637**, 15 (2015)

26. Straus, E.G.: Problems and solutions: Addition chains of vectors. Am. Math. Mon. **71**, 806–808 (1964)

27. Wang, Y., Wu, Q., Wong, D.S., Qin, B., Chow, S.S.M., Liu, Z., Tan, X.: Securely outsourcing exponentiations with single untrusted program for cloud storage. In: Kutyłowski, M., Vaidya, J. (eds.) ESORICS 2014, Part I. LNCS, vol. 8712, pp. 326–343. Springer, Heidelberg (2014)

Attribute-Based Signatures for Supporting Anonymous Certification

Nesrine Kaaniche[(✉)] and Maryline Laurent

SAMOVAR, Telecom SudParis, CNRS, University Paris-Saclay, Evry, France
{nesrine.kaaniche,maryline.laurent}@telecom-sudparis.eu

Abstract. This paper presents an anonymous certification (AC) scheme, built over an attribute based signature (ABS). After identifying properties and core building blocks of anonymous certification schemes, we identify ABS limitations to fulfill AC properties, and we propose a new system model along with a concrete mathematical construction based on standard assumptions and the random oracle model. Our solution has several advantages. First, it provides a data minimization cryptographic scheme, permitting the user to reveal only required information to any service provider. Second, it ensures unlinkability between the different authentication sessions, while preserving the anonymity of the user. Third, the derivation of certified attributes by the issuing authority relies on a non interactive protocol which provides an interesting communication overhead.

Keywords: User privacy · Anonymous certification · Attribute-based signatures

1 Introduction

Anonymous Credentials (AC) were first introduced by David Chaum [9] in 1982, and fully formalized by Camenisch and Lysyanskaya [4] in 2001. These schemes are considered to be an important building block in privacy-preserving identity management systems, as they permit users to prove ownership of credentials to service providers while not being traced in the system. That is, after he gets credentials over some of his attributes from some trusted issuing authorities, the user can derive proofs for successive presentations to service providers. The AC properties include that the service providers are not able to link a single received proof to another or to any information relative to the owner, even in case of collusion between providers and with the credential issuer.

Up to now, two main AC solutions emerged from industry, the Idemix scheme [15] from IBM based on the Camenish-Lysyanskaya (CL) signatures [4,5], which is a close variant of group signatures, and the U-Prove scheme [20] from Microsoft which relies on the Brands' blind signature [2].

N. Kaaniche and M. Laurent—Member of the Chair Values and Policies of Personal Information.

© Springer International Publishing Switzerland 2016
I. Askoxylakis et al. (Eds.): ESORICS 2016, Part I, LNCS 9878, pp. 279–300, 2016.
DOI: 10.1007/978-3-319-45744-4_14

Interest for AC comes from their ability to strictly support the data minimization principle [17], which expects that data collection should be proportional and not excessive compared to the purpose of the collection. This interest is today magnified as this principle is at the core of the future European General Data Protection Regulation [11] and also the U.S. National Strategy for Trusted Identities in Cyberspace (NSTIC) [14].

This paper proposes a new AC scheme based on the Attribute Based Signatures (ABS). Originally, the ABS is designed for the user to sign a message with fine grained control over identifying information, and it does not support the properties required for AC. As such, after a clear identification of missing properties, an abstract scheme $\mathcal{HABS}$ is presented followed by a concrete construction detailing how these access-policy based signatures can efficiently serve AC objectives. Our scheme has several advantages over industrial AC solutions. First, the issuance procedure is much more efficient, as there is no need for a heavy interactive protocol between the user and the issuer. The issuer can generate a credential based on the user's public key only, while Idemix and U-Prove schemes require the user to introduce a random part of the secret key each time a new credential is certified as they rely on group and blind signatures. Second, our scheme supports a flexible selective disclosure mechanism at no extra computation cost, which is inherited from the expressiveness of ABS for defining access policies.

PAPER ORGANIZATION – Section 2 introduces Anonymous Credential systems (AC) along with the actors, procedures and security requirements. Section 3 defines the Attribute based Signatures (ABS), and provides a generic analysis of ABS properties thus highlighting the missing properties for the ABS to align to the AC requirements. Section 5 presents a concrete construction of our novel AC system, and Sect. 6 gives a detailed security analysis with an extension of the scheme to support multiple issuers. Finally, theoretical comparisons with existing systems are discussed in Sect. 7 and conclusions are given in Sect. 8.

2 Anonymous Credentials

Anonymous Credentials (AC) also known as privacy preserving attribute credentials refer to some well identified entities and procedures and need to achieve some security requirements.

ENTITIES – An anonymous credential system involves several entities. Some entities, such as the *user*, the *verifier* and *issuer* are mandatory, while other entities, such as the *revocation authority* and the *inspector* are optional [3].

The *user* is the central entity, whose interest is to get privacy-preserving access to services, offered by service providers, known as *verifiers*. Each verifier enforces an access control policy to its resources and services based on the credentials owned by the users and the information selected and included in *presentation tokens*. For this purpose, each user has first to obtain credentials from the *issuer(s)*. Then, he selects the appropriate information from the credentials and shows the selected information to the requesting verifier, under a presentation token. Note that the verifier access control policy is referred to as *presentation policy*. Both the user and the verifier have to obtain the most recent revocation information from the *revocation authority* to generate, respectively verify, presentation tokens. The *revocation authority* has to revoke issued credentials and maintain the list of valid credentials in the system. When revoked, a credential can no longer be used to derive presentation tokens. The *inspector* is a trusted entity, which has the technical capabilities to remove the anonymity of a user when needed.

PROCEDURES – An AC system is defined by the following algorithms:

- SETUP: this algorithm takes as input a security parameter ξ (security level) and outputs the public parameters *params* and the public-private key pair of the issuer (pk_{is}, sk_{is}).
- USERKG: this algorithm takes as input $j \in \mathbb{N}$ and outputs the key pair (pk_u, sk_u) of the user j.
- OBTAIN ↔ ISSUE: the OBTAIN ↔ ISSUE presents the issuance procedure. The ISSUE algorithm performed by the issuer takes as input the public parameters *params*, the private key of the issuer pk_{is}, the public key of the user sk_u and the set of attributes $\{a_i\}_{i=1}^N$, where N is the number of attributes. The OBTAIN algorithm executed by the user takes as input the secret key of the user sk_u and the public key of the issuer pk_{is}. At the end of this phase, the user receives from the issuer a credential C.
- SHOW ↔ VERIFY: the SHOW ↔ VERIFY is the presentation procedure between the user and the verifier. With respect to the presentation policy, the SHOW algorithm takes as input the user's secret key sk_u, the issuer's public key pk_{is}, the set of required attributes $\{a_i\}_{i=1}^{N'}$ and a credential C, and it outputs a presentation token. VERIFY is a public algorithm performed by the verifier; it takes as input the public key of the issuer pk_{is}, the set of attributes $\{a_i\}_{i=1}^{N'}$, and the presentation token. At the end of this presentation phase, the VERIFY outputs a bit $b \in \{0, 1\}$ for success of failure of the verification.

SECURITY REQUIREMENTS – Anonymous credential systems have to fulfill the following security properties:

correctness – a honest user must always succeed in proving validity of proofs to the verifier in an anonymous way.

anonymity – the user must remain anonymous among a set of users during the presentation procedure to the verifier.

unforgeability – a user not owning an appropriate legitimate credential is not able to generate a valid presentation token.

unlinkability – this property is essential for user privacy support and is closely related to the anonymity property. Unlinkability is divided into two properties *issue-show unlinkability* and *multi-show unlinkability* as follows: (i) the issue-show unlinkability ensures that any information gathered during credential issuing cannot be used later to link the presentation token to the original credential, (ii) the multi-show unlinkability guarantees that several presentation tokens derived from the same credential and transmitted over several sessions can not be linked by the verifier.

Additionally, privacy preserving attribute based credentials have to ensure several functional features, namely revocation, inspection and *selective disclosure*. The selective disclosure property refers to the ability provided to the user to present to the verifier partial information extracted or derived from his credential, for instance, to prove he is older than 18 to purchase liquors, while not revealing his birth date.

3   Attribute Based Signatures for Anonymous Credentials

This section introduces Attribute based Signature schemes (ABS) with their associated algorithms and their security properties. Then, an analysis shows that ABS is missing some properties to serve as a building block for AC support.

3.1   Attribute-Based Signatures (ABS)

Attribute-based Signatures (ABS) [19] is a flexible primitive that enables a user to sign a message with fine grained control over identifying information. In ABS, the user possesses a set of attributes and one secret signing key per attribute which is obtained from a trusted authority. The user can sign a message with respect to a predicate satisfied by his attributes. In commonly known settings, the different parties include a Signature Trustee (ST), the Attribute Authority (AA), and potentially several signers and verifiers. The ST acts as a global entity that generates authentic global systems parameters, while the AA issues the signing keys for the set of attributes of the users (signers). The role of ST and AA can be merged into the same entity. ABS supports the following property which is fundamental for support of privacy. AA, although knowing the signing keys and the attributes of the users, is unable to identify which attributes have been used in a given valid signature, and thus he is unable to assign the signature to his originating user and/or to link several signatures as originating from the same user. In the last few years, multiple ABS schemes emerged in the cryptographic literature, considering different design directions. In a nutshell, (i) the attribute value can be a binary-bit string [13,18,19,21,22], or has a particular data structure [23], (ii) access structures may support threshold policies [13,18,22], monotonic policies [19,23] or non-monotonic policies [21], and (iii) the capacity of attributes' private keys issuance can be provided by a single authority [19,22,23], or a group of authorities [19,21].

Let us explain the general ABS signing procedure in the simple case with one single AA authority. First, the AA derives the private keys $\{sk_1, \cdots, sk_N\}$, with respect to the attribute set identifying the requesting signer, denoted by $\mathcal{S} = \{a_1, \cdots, a_N\}$, where N is the number of attributes. The private keys' generation procedure is performed using the AA's master key MK and some related public parameters, both generated during the setup phase. Then, for signing a message m sent by the verifier along with a signing predicate Υ, the user needs his private keys and a set of attributes satisfying the predicate Υ. Finally, the verifier is able to verify that some user who holds a set of attributes satisfying the signing predicate has signed the message. An ABS scheme is defined by the following algorithms:

- $\mathcal{ABS}$.setup – this algorithm is performed by (ST). It takes as input the security parameter ξ and outputs the global public parameters $params$, considered as an auxiliary input to all the following algorithms, and the master key MK of AA.
- $\mathcal{ABS}$.keygen – this algorithm executed by AA takes as input his master key MK and a set of attributes $\mathcal{S} \subset \mathbb{S}$ (where $\mathcal{S} = \{a_i\}_{i=1}^N$, N is the number of attributes and $\mathbb{S}$ is the attribute universe). It outputs a signing key $sk_{\mathcal{S}}$[1].
- $\mathcal{ABS}$.sign – this algorithm takes as input the private key $sk_{\mathcal{S}}$, a message m and a signing predicate Υ, such as $\Upsilon(\mathcal{S}) = 1$ ($\mathcal{S}$ satisfies Υ). This algorithm outputs a signature σ (or an error message $\perp$).
- $\mathcal{ABS}$.verif – this algorithm takes as input the received signature σ, the signing predicate Υ and the message m. It outputs a bit $b \in \{0, 1\}$, where 1 denotes $accept$; i.e., the verifier successfully checks the signature, with respect to the signing predicate. Otherwise, 0 means $reject$.

3.2 Security Properties of Attribute Based Signatures

First, an ABS scheme has to satisfy the correctness property (Definition 1)

Definition 1. *Correctness* – *An ABS scheme is correct, if for all ($params$, MK) $\leftarrow \mathcal{ABS}$.* setup(ξ), *all messages m, all attribute sets $\mathcal{S}$, all signing keys $sk_{\mathcal{S}} \leftarrow \mathcal{ABS}$.keygen($\mathcal{S}, MK$), all claiming predicates Υ such as $\Upsilon(\mathcal{S}) = 1$ and all signatures $\sigma \leftarrow \mathcal{ABS}$.sign($sk_{\mathcal{S}}, m, \Upsilon$), we have $\mathcal{ABS}$.verif(σ, m, Υ) = 1.*

In addition, based on Maji et al. work [19], we provide the two following formal definitions that capture security properties of ABS schemes.

Definition 2. *Perfect Privacy* – *An ABS scheme is perfectly private, if for all ($params, MK$) $\leftarrow \mathcal{ABS}$.setup(ξ), all attribute sets $\mathcal{S}_1$, $\mathcal{S}_2$, all secret signing keys $sk_1 \leftarrow \mathcal{ABS}$.keygen($\mathcal{S}_1, MK$), $sk_2 \leftarrow \mathcal{ABS}$.keygen($\mathcal{S}_2, MK$), all messages m and all claiming predicates Υ such as $\Upsilon(\mathcal{S}_1) = \Upsilon(\mathcal{S}_2) = 1$, the distributions $\mathcal{ABS}$.sign(sk_1, m, Υ) and $\mathcal{ABS}$.sign(sk_2, m, Υ) are indistiguishable.*

In a nutshell, if the perfect privacy property holds, then a signature does not leak which set of attributes or private signing key were originally used.

Definition 3. *Unforgeability* – *An ABS scheme is unforgeable if the adversary $\mathcal{A}$ can not win the following game:*

- *setup phase: the challenger $\mathcal{C}$ chooses a large security parameter ξ and runs* setup. *$\mathcal{C}$ keeps secret the master key MK and sends params generated from $\mathcal{ABS}$.setup to the adversary $\mathcal{A}$.*

---

[1] For ease of presentation, we denote the signing key as a monolithic entity, but, in many existing schemes, the signing key consists of separate elements for each single attribute in $\mathcal{S}$.

– *query phase: the adversary $\mathcal{A}$ can perform a polynomially bounded number of queries on $\mathcal{S}$ and (m, Υ) to first the private key generation oracle and second the signing oracle.*
– *forgery phase: $\mathcal{A}$ outputs a signature σ^* on messages m^* with respect to Υ^*.*

The adversary $\mathcal{A}$ wins the game if σ^* is a valid signature on messages m^* for a predicate Υ^*, the couple (m^*, Υ^*) has not been queried to the signing oracle and no attribute set $\mathcal{S}^*$ satisfying Υ^* has been submitted to the private key generation oracle.

This unforgeability property also includes the collusion among users trying to override their rights by combining their complementary attributes to generate a signature satisfying a given predicate Υ. It also covers the non-frameability case when a user also aims to override his rights but on his own.

3.3   Bridging the Gap Between ABS and AC

As far as we know, ABS is still considered as being incompatible with AC purpose of anonymity [21], mostly because ABS assumes that AAs are fully trusted authorities as they know the secret keys of each user. Moreover, in case of multiple AAs, as needed in AC systems, the issued credentials can be linked by the AAs as they are all based on the same public key.

Let us give a simple example to illustrate how ABS could be adapted to AC purpose. A student (acting as user) obtains a certified credential (i.e. student card) by the University (which plays the role of the issuer) over the set of his attributes $\mathcal{S} = \{a_1 := \texttt{Name}; a_2 := \texttt{Bob}, a_3 := \texttt{City}, a_4 := \texttt{Paris}, a_5 := \texttt{Studies}, a_6 := \texttt{InformationSecurity}\}$. The whole set of attributes is committed to a single value using the public key of the user, and it is signed with the private key of the issuer, to generate the resulting credential, denoted by C.

Later, the student can, for example, prove that he is student living in Paris, without revealing his name nor his studies' major. For this purpose, we consider the signing predicate $\Upsilon = (\texttt{Studies} \vee \texttt{Teaches}) \wedge (\texttt{City} \wedge (\texttt{Paris} \vee \texttt{Lille}))$. The user whose attributes satisfy the predicate can use his credential C to successfully extract the appropriate keys relative to the requested attributes a_3, a_4 and a_5. The student thus remains anonymous among the group of students living in Paris, and is able to prove the requested features because the signature of the University over the student's attributes is valid. This example brings first elements for adaptation of ABS to AC purpose, but additional work is necessary.

ADDITIONAL REQUIREMENTS FOR ABS – Let us analyse first the formal security model proposed in the litterature for ABS to satisfy the required AC properties of anonymity and unforgeability (Sect. 2). The first model is proposed by Shahandashti and Safavi-Naini [22], and gives main procedures and basic security properties, such as correctness, unforgeability and signer-attribute privacy. Later, Maji et al. [19] and El Kaafarani et al. [10] introduce and formalize the *perfect privacy* property which requires that a signature reveals neither the identity of the user nor the set of attributes used for the signing procedure. These models do not entirely match our needs for the design of secure AC scheme. More precisely, the following requirements need to be addressed:

- TRACEABILITY OF SIGNATURES: by essence, an ABS scheme supports the anonymity of the user. As a consequence, there is a need to introduce a new procedure INSPEC to remove anonymity, and identify the user originating an ABS signature. To prevent issuers to trace users, this algorithm should be carried out by a tracing authority, equipped with a secret key and referred to as inspector. Such a feature is important in settings where accountability and abuse prevention are required.
- UNLINKABILITY BETWEEN ISSUERS: in ABS schemes, when a user requests multiple authorities to issue credentials with respect to his attributes, these authorities can link issued credentials to one user through its public key. To satisfy the unlinkability property of AC schemes, a novel ABS issuance procedure has to be designed.
- REPLAYING SESSIONS: to counteract ABS signature replay attacks, the verifier has to generate for each authentication session, a new message which can might depend on the session data, such as the verifier's identity and the current time.

4   Our New Anonymous Certification Scheme

This section gives a high-level presentation of our new AC scheme based on ABS with an overview of the procedures and algorithms. Then the considered security model with formalized security properties are defined.

4.1   System Model

Our new privacy-preserving attribute based signature $\mathcal{HABS}$ relies on three procedures based on the following seven algorithms that might involve several users (i.e.; signers). The verification and inspection procedures involve only public data. In the following, we denote by $\mathcal{HABS}$ our new AC scheme and by $\mathcal{ABS}$ the ABS basic functions as defined in Sect. 3.

$\mathcal{HABS}$.SETUP – this algorithm runs the $\mathcal{ABS}$.setup algorithm. It takes as input the security parameter ξ and outputs the global public parameters $params$. This algorithm also derives a pair of public and private keys (pk_{ins}, sk_{ins}) for the tracing authority referred to as the inspector. In the following, public parameters $params$ are assumed to include the public key of the inspector, and all the algorithms have default input $params$.

$\mathcal{HABS}$.KEYGEN – this algorithm takes as input the global parameters $params$ and outputs the pair of public and private keys either for users and for the issuer. The public and private keys are noted respectively $(pk_u, sk_u)_j$ for user j and (pk_{is}, sk_{is}) for the issuer.

$\mathcal{HABS}$.OBTAIN $\leftrightarrow$ $\mathcal{HABS}$.ISSUE – the credential issuing procedure corresponds to the $\mathcal{ABS}$.keygen algorithm. The $\mathcal{HABS}$.ISSUE algorithm executed by the issuer takes as input the public key of the user pk_u, a set of attributes $\mathcal{S} \subset \mathbb{S}$

(where $\mathcal{S} = \{a_i\}_{i=1}^{N}$, N is the number of attributes and $\mathbb{S}$ is referred to as the attribute universe), the private key of the issuer sk_{is} and the public key of the inspector pk_{ins}. It outputs a signed commitment C over the set of attributes $\mathcal{S}$.

The $\mathcal{HABS}$.OBTAIN algorithm is executed by the user and corresponds to the collection of the certified credentials from the issuer. This is up to the user to verify the correctness of the received signed commitment over his attributes. In case of verification, the $\mathcal{HABS}$.OBTAIN algorithm takes as input the signed commitment C, the private key of the user sk_u, the public key of the issuer pk_{is} and eventually the public key of the inspector pk_{ins}. It outputs a bit $b \in \{0, 1\}$.

$\mathcal{HABS}$.SHOW $\leftrightarrow$ $\mathcal{HABS}$.VERIFY – the presentation procedure includes the $\mathcal{ABS}$.sign and $\mathcal{ABS}$.verif algorithms of the ABS signature. This procedure enables the verifier to check that a user has previously obtained credentials on some attributes from a certified (i.e.; authentic) issuer and that he is authorized to access a service with respect to some access policy. As such, the verifier has first to send a random value m (which corresponds to the message m in $\mathcal{ABS}$.sign) to the user. To counteract replay attacks (Sect. 3.3), each authentication session is personalized with this random value which can be for instance the verifier's identity concatenated with his clock value. Second, the user signs the received random value, based on his credential. In a nutshell, the user first selects the sub-set of his attributes that satisfies the signing predicate Υ ($\Upsilon(\mathcal{S}') = 1$) and he signs the received value m. Note that an attribute based signature can generally be considered as a non-interactive proof of knowledge based on the Fiat-Shamir heuristic [12]. That is, instead of sending his attributes to the verifier, the user only has to prove he gets from a certified issuer some attributes satisfying the access policy. The user finally sends his signature Σ to the verifier who checks the resulting signature by verifying whether $\mathcal{ABS}$.verif$(pk_{is}, \Sigma, \Upsilon, m) = 1$.

The $\mathcal{HABS}$.SHOW algorithm takes as input the randomized message m, a signing predicate Υ, the private key of the user sk_u, the credential C and a subset of his attributes $\mathcal{S}'$, such as $\Upsilon(\mathcal{S}') = 1$. This algorithm outputs a signature Σ (or an error message $\perp$).

The $\mathcal{HABS}$.VERIFY algorithm takes as input the received signature Σ, the public key of the issuer(s) pk_i, the signing predicate Υ and the message m. It outputs a bit $b \in \{0, 1\}$, where 1 denotes *accept* for a successful verification of the signature, and 0 means *reject*.

$\mathcal{HABS}$.INSPEC – our scheme supports the inspection procedure performed by a separate and trusted entity referred to as the inspector. It relies on two algorithms namely $\mathcal{HABS}$.trace and $\mathcal{HABS}$.judge needed to identify the user and give a proof of judgment.

The $\mathcal{HABS}$.trace algorithm takes as input the secret key of the inspector sk_{ins}, the issuer(s) public key(s) pk_{is} and the signature Σ. It outputs the index j of the user that has signed the message m with respect to the predicate Υ. It also outputs a proof ϖ.

The $\mathcal{HABS}$.judge algorithm takes as input the public key(s) of the issuer(s) pk_{is}, the signature Σ, the user index j and the proof ϖ. It outputs $b \in \{0, 1\}$, where 1 means that ϖ is a valid proof proving that user j originating the signature Σ.

4.2   Security Model

We consider two realistic threat models for proving security and privacy properties of our attribute based credential construction. We first point out the case of *honest but curious* verifiers and issuers. That is, both the verifiers and issuers are honest as they provide proper inputs or outputs, at each step of the protocol, properly performing any calculations expected from them, but they are curious in the sense that they attempt to gain extra information from the protocol. As such, we consider the honest but curious threat model against the privacy requirement with respect to the anonymity and unlinkability properties.

Second, we consider the case of malicious users trying to override their rights. That is, malicious users may attempt to deviate from the protocol or to provide invalid inputs. As such, we consider the malicious user security model mainly against the unforgeability requirement, as presented in Sect. 4.2.1.

4.2.1   Unforgeability

The unforgeability property means that unless the private key of the issuer (resp. the user) is known, it is not possible to forge a valid credential – in case of ISSUE (resp. the presentation token of the user – in case of SHOW). This property also covers non frameability and ensures that even if users collude, they cannot frame a user who did not generate a valid presentation token. We thus define unforgeability based on three security games between an adversary $\mathcal{A}$ and a challenger $\mathcal{C}$, that simulates the system procedures to interact with the adversary.

Definition 4. *Unforgeability* – *We say that $\mathcal{HABS}$ satisfies the unforgeability property, if for every PPT adversary $\mathcal{A}$, there exists a negligible function ϵ such that:*

$$Pr[\boldsymbol{Exp}_{\mathcal{A}}^{unforg}(1^{\xi}) = 1] \leq \epsilon(\xi)$$

where $\boldsymbol{Exp}_{\mathcal{A}}^{unforg}$ is the security experiment against the unforgeability property, with respect to MC-Game, MU-Game and Col-Game introduced hereafter.

On the one hand, *MC-Game*, formally defined hereafter, enables to capture the behaviour of malicious users trying to forge a valid credential. That is, during the first phase, **Phase I**, the challenger $\mathcal{C}$ runs the $\mathcal{HABS}$.SETUP algorithm, gives the public parameters *params* to the adversary $\mathcal{A}$ and proceeds as follows:

- *Keygen*: the challenger $\mathcal{C}$ runs the $\mathcal{HABS}$.KEYGEN algorithm, in order to get the key pairs of the issuer, the inspector, and a user (u). The key pair of the user (pk_u, sk_u) is sent to the adversary.
- *Issue-Query*: the adversary $\mathcal{A}$ can request $\mathcal{C}$, as many times as he wants, for getting the credential result C_i (for session i) obtained from the $\mathcal{HABS}$.ISSUE algorithm applied over the public key pk_u, and a set of attributes $\mathcal{S}_i$.

Then, in **Phase II**, $\mathcal{C}$ requests the adversary to provide a valid credential over a set of attributes $\mathcal{S}$ (such that $\mathcal{S}$ has not been output during the previous *Issue-Query* phase). Thus, $\mathcal{A}$ runs *ForgeCred* and tries to compute a valid credential C^*. The adversary $\mathcal{A}$ wins the game if he provides a valid credential. That is, the $\mathcal{HABS}$.OBTAIN(C^*, sk_u, pk_{is}) algorithm returns an *accept*.

On the other hand, *MU-Game* and *Col-Game* security games enable to capture the behaviour of a malicious user, trying a forgery of the presentation token, either on his own (i.e.; *MU-Game*) or by colluding with other legitimate users (i.e.; *Col-Game*).

First, the *MU-Game* is formally defined as follows: during **Phase I**, the challenger $\mathcal{C}$ runs the $\mathcal{HABS}$.SETUP algorithm, gives the public parameters *params* to the adversary $\mathcal{A}$ and proceeds as follows:

- *Keygen*: the challenger $\mathcal{C}$ runs the $\mathcal{HABS}$.KEYGEN algorithm, in order to get the key pairs of the issuer, the inspector, and a user (u). The key pair of the user (pk_u, sk_u) is sent to the adversary.
- *Issue*: the challenger $\mathcal{C}$ runs the $\mathcal{HABS}$.ISSUE algorithm over the public key pk_u, and a set of attributes $\mathcal{S}$. He sends to the adversary $\mathcal{A}$ the set of attributes $\mathcal{S}$, the credential C and a predicate Υ such that $\Upsilon(\mathcal{S}) = 1$.
- *Show-Query*: the adversary $\mathcal{A}$ can request as many times as he wants the $\mathcal{HABS}$.SHOW over the predicate Υ, the private key of the user sk_u, a randomly generated message m_i (for session i), and a sub-set of his attributes $\mathcal{S}'$ where $\Upsilon(\mathcal{S}') = 1$. Each request i results in a signature Σ_i.

Then, in **Phase II**, the challenger $\mathcal{C}$ requests the adversary to provide a valid signature over a randomized message m (such that m has not been output during the previous *Show-Query* phase). Thus, the adversary $\mathcal{A}$ executes *ForgeSig* and tries to compute a valid signature Σ^*.

Second, the *Col-Game*, considered as a sub-case of the *MU-Game*, is formally defined as follows: the challenger $\mathcal{C}$ first runs the $\mathcal{HABS}$.SETUP algorithm, gives the public parameters *params* to the adversary $\mathcal{A}$ and proceeds such as:

- *Keygen*: the challenger $\mathcal{C}$ runs the $\mathcal{HABS}$.KEYGEN algorithm, in order to get the key pairs of the issuer, the inspector, and two users u_1 and u_2. Both key pairs obtained (pk_{u_1}, sk_{u_1}) and (pk_{u_2}, sk_{u_2}) are sent to the adversary $\mathcal{A}$.
- *Issue*: $\mathcal{C}$ runs the $\mathcal{HABS}$.ISSUE algorithm over the public key pk_{u_k} ($k \in \{1, 2\}$), and a set of attributes $\mathcal{S}_k$ where $\mathcal{S}_1$ and $\mathcal{S}_2$ are disjoint and non empty. He sends to $\mathcal{A}$ the set of attributes $\mathcal{S}_k$, the obtained credential C_k, a random m and a predicate Υ for which $\Upsilon(\mathcal{S}_k) \neq 1$, but $\Upsilon(\mathcal{S}_1 \cup \mathcal{S}_2) = 1$.
- *Show-Query*: $\mathcal{A}$ can request as many times as he wants the $\mathcal{HABS}$.SHOW algorithm over the private key sk_{u_k}, the message m, a sub-set of his attributes $\mathcal{S}'_k$ and a predicate Υ_i where $\Upsilon_i(\mathcal{S}'_k) = 1$ to get back a signature Σ_{ik}.

During the second phase, $\mathcal{C}$ requests the adversary to provide a signature over message m and predicate Υ. As such, $\mathcal{A}$ tries to compute a valid signature σ^*.

We say that the AC scheme is unforgeable if the probability that the $\mathcal{HABS}$.VERIFY procedure in the *MU-Game* and *Col-Game* returns *accept* is negligible.

4.2.2   Privacy

The privacy property covers the anonymity, the issue-show and multi-show requirements, as defined in Sect. 2. In this section, we define three realistic privacy games – *PP-Game*, *MS-Game* and *IS-Game* – based on an adversary $\mathcal{A}$ and a challenger $\mathcal{C}$ where $\mathcal{A}$ has only access to public data, except in one game where he has access to credentials. Thus, $\mathcal{A}$ cannot run on his own the $\mathcal{HABS}$.OBTAIN $\leftrightarrow$ ISSUE, or $\mathcal{HABS}$.SHOW $\leftrightarrow$ VERIFY algorithms, but has to request the results of these algorithms to the challenger $\mathcal{C}$ which is responsible for simulating the system procedures.

Definition 5. *Privacy* – *We say that $\mathcal{HABS}$ satisfies the privacy property, if for every PPT adversary $\mathcal{A}$, there exists a negligible function ϵ such that:*

$$Pr[\boldsymbol{Exp}_{\mathcal{A}}^{priv}(1^{\xi}) = 1] = \frac{1}{2} \pm \epsilon(\xi)$$

where $\boldsymbol{Exp}_{\mathcal{A}}^{priv}$ is the security experiment against the privacy property, with respect to PP-Game, MS-Game and IS-Game introduced hereafter.

We formally define our three games as follows: during the first phase, **Phase I**, $\mathcal{C}$ runs the $\mathcal{HABS}$.SETUP algorithm, gives the global public parameters *params* to $\mathcal{A}$ and proceeds as follows:

- *Keygen*: the challenger $\mathcal{C}$ runs the $\mathcal{HABS}$.KEYGEN algorithm to get the pair of keys (pk_{is}, sk_{is}) and (pk_{u_j}, sk_{u_j}) (j is for user u_j, $j \in \{1,2\}$). $\mathcal{C}$ sends the public key of the issuer pk_{is} to the adversary $\mathcal{A}$.
- *Issue*: the challenger $\mathcal{C}$ runs the $\mathcal{HABS}$.ISSUE algorithm over the public key pk_{u_j} ($j \in \{1,2\}$), and a set of attributes $\mathcal{S}$ ($\mathcal{S}=\mathcal{S}_1=\mathcal{S}_2$). $\mathcal{C}$ gets the credential $\mathcal{C}_j$, and only sends the set of attributes $\mathcal{S}_j$ to $\mathcal{A}$.
- *Show-Query*: $\mathcal{A}$ can request $\mathcal{C}$ as many times as he wants, for getting the result of $\mathcal{HABS}$.SHOW algorithm applied on user u_j (only index j is given to $\mathcal{C}$), with respect to some message m_{jk}, predicate Υ_{jk} and set of attributes $\mathcal{S}'_{jk}$ selected by $\mathcal{A}$ (where $\mathcal{S}'_{jk} \subset \mathcal{S}_j$). $\mathcal{A}$ gets back the presentation token Σ_{jk}.

Afterwards, during **Phase II**, $\mathcal{A}$ can select one of the following games:

- *PP-Game* – for proving the anonymity property. $\mathcal{A}$ selects $j \in \{1,2\}$, and generates a message m, a predicate Υ and a subset of attributes $\mathcal{S}_{jk}$ ($k \in \{1,2\}$) such that $\mathcal{S}_{jk} \subset \mathcal{S}_j$, $\mathcal{S}_{j1} \neq \mathcal{S}_{j2}$, $\Upsilon(\mathcal{S}_{jk}) = 1$, and the triplet $(m, \Upsilon, \mathcal{S}_{jk})$ has never been output during the *Show-Query* phase. $\mathcal{A}$ then sends m, Υ and $\mathcal{S}_{jk}$ to $\mathcal{C}$ which chooses a random bit $b \in \{1,2\}$, runs $\mathcal{HABS}$.SHOW over m, Υ, attributes $\mathcal{S}_{jb}$, and sk_{u_j}. $\mathcal{C}$ sends back to $\mathcal{A}$ the obtained presentation token Σ_{jb}. The adversary $\mathcal{A}$ wins the game if he is able to guess the value of b, i.e. the set of attributes $\mathcal{S}_{jb}$ used to derive the presentation token.
- *MS-Game* – for proving the multi-show property. The adversary $\mathcal{A}$ selects $j \in \{1,2\}$ and generates a message m, a predicate Υ and a subset of attributes $\mathcal{S}'$, such that $\mathcal{S}' \subset \mathcal{S}$, $\Upsilon(\mathcal{S}') = 1$. Note that the triplet $(m, \Upsilon, \mathcal{S}')$ has never been output during the *Show-Query* phase. $\mathcal{A}$ then sends m, Υ, and $\mathcal{S}'$ to

the challenger $\mathcal{C}$ which chooses a random bit $b \in \{1,2\}$, runs $\mathcal{HABS}$.SHOW over (m, Υ), the attributes' set $\mathcal{S}'$ and private key sk_{u_b}. $\mathcal{C}$ sends back the presentation token Σ_b to $\mathcal{A}$. The adversary $\mathcal{A}$ wins the game if he is able to guess the value of b, i.e. the user u_b having generated the presentation token.

- *IS-Game* – for proving the issue-show property. The adversary $\mathcal{A}$ generates a message m, a predicate Υ such that $\Upsilon(\mathcal{S}) = 1$, such as the triplet $(m, \Upsilon, \mathcal{S})$ has never been output during the *Show-Query* phase. $\mathcal{A}$ then sends m, Υ and $\mathcal{S}$ to the challenger $\mathcal{C}$ which chooses a random bit $b \in \{1,2\}$, runs $\mathcal{HABS}$.SHOW for user u_b over m, Υ, $\mathcal{S}$, and sk_{u_b}. $\mathcal{C}$ sends back to $\mathcal{A}$ Σ_b and credentials C_1 and C_2. The adversary $\mathcal{A}$ wins the game if he is able to guess the value of b, i.e. to which credential C_b the presentation token refers to.

4.2.3   Anonymity Removal

Our $\mathcal{HABS}$ system should fulfill the inspection property meaning that the `trace` algorithm is able to return the right identity of the actual user, for each verified tuple $(m, \Upsilon, \Sigma, pk_{is})$. As the unforgeability Subsect. 4.2.1 already takes care of subcases of anonymity removal, this section focuses only on the *IA-Game* leading an adversary $\mathcal{A}$ to successfully pass the $\mathcal{HABS}$.SHOW $\leftrightarrow$ VERIFY procedure, while the inspector is unable to trace the identity of the signature originator.

The *IA-Game* is formally defined as follows: during the first phase, **Phase I**, the challenger $\mathcal{C}$ runs the $\mathcal{HABS}$.SETUP and $\mathcal{HABS}$.KEYGEN algorithms to get the key pairs of the issuer, the inspector and a user u_1 indexed as 1. It gives the public parameters $params$ and the key pair (pk_{u_1}, sk_{u_1}) to the adversary $\mathcal{A}$ with a predicate Υ, and a random message m.

- *Keygen*: the adversary $\mathcal{A}$ runs the $\mathcal{HABS}$.KEYGEN algorithm, in order to get the key pair (pk_{u_1}, sk_{u_1}).
- *Issue*: the adversary $\mathcal{A}$ requests $\mathcal{C}$ for getting the result of $\mathcal{HABS}$.ISSUE algorithm over the public key pk_{u_1} and a set of attributes $\mathcal{S}$ such as $\Upsilon(\mathcal{S}) = 1$. He gets back the credential C.
- *Show-Query*: $\mathcal{A}$ can request as many times as he wants the $\mathcal{HABS}$.SHOW over the predicate Υ, the private key sk_{u_1}, the message m, and a sub-set of his attributes $\mathcal{S}_i$ where $\Upsilon(\mathcal{S}_i) = 1$. Each request i results in a signature Σ_i.

Then, during **Phase II**, $\mathcal{C}$ requests the adversary to provide a valid but untraceable signature over message m and predicate Υ. As such, $\mathcal{A}$ runs *ForgeProof* and the adversary $\mathcal{A}$ tries to compute a signature Σ^*, such as $\mathcal{HABS}$.VERIFY $(m, \Upsilon, \Sigma, pk_{is}) = 1$ and $\mathcal{HABS}$.trace$(\Sigma, sk_{ins}) = \perp$ or k $(k \neq 1)$.

We say that the AC scheme is resistant to inspection abuse attack if the probability that the $\mathcal{HABS}$.INSPEC procedure in the *IA-Game* returns *accept* is negligible.

5   Concrete Construction

In this section, we give a concrete attribute based signature scheme that fulfills the features introduced in Sect. 3 and that can be used to design a secure anonymous credential system.

5.1   Mathematical Background

We first introduce the access structure in Sect. 5.1.1. Then, in Sect. 5.1.2, we present the bilinear maps. Finally, we introduce security assumptions.

5.1.1   Access Structures

Definition 6 *(Access Structure [1]). Let $\mathcal{P} = \{P_1, P_2, \cdots, P_n\}$ be a set of parties, and a collection $\mathbb{A} \subseteq 2^{\{P_1, P_2, \cdots, P_n\}}$ is called monotone if $\forall B, C \subseteq 2^{\{P_1, P_2, \cdots, P_n\}}$: if $B \in \mathbb{A}$ and $B \subseteq C$ then $C \in \mathbb{A}$. An access structure is a collection $\mathbb{A}$ of non-empty subsets of $\{P_1, P_2, \cdots, P_n\}$; i.e. $\mathbb{A} \subseteq 2^{\{P_1, P_2, \cdots, P_n\}} \setminus \{\emptyset\}$. The sets in $\mathbb{A}$ are called authorized sets, and the sets not in $\mathbb{A}$ are called unauthorized sets.*

We note that in recent ABS schemes, the parties are considered as the attributes.

Definition 7 *(Linear Secret Sharing Schemes (LSSS) [1]). A secret sharing scheme Π over a set $\mathcal{P} = \{P_1, P_2, \cdots, P_n\}$ is called linear (over $\mathbb{Z}_p$) if:*

1. *the share for each party forms a vector over $\mathbb{Z}_p$;*
2. *there exists a matrix M with l rows called the sharing generating matrix for Π. For each $i \in [1, l]$, we let the function ρ define the party labeling the row i of the matrix M as $\rho(i)$. When we consider the column vector $\boldsymbol{v} = (v_1, \cdots, v_k)^T$, where $v_1 = s \in \mathbb{Z}_p$ is the secret to be shared, and $v_t \in \mathbb{Z}_p$, where $t \in [2, k]$ are chosen randomly, then $M \cdot \boldsymbol{v}$ is the vector of l shares of s according to Π. The share $\lambda_i = (M \cdot v)_i$ belongs to the party $\rho(i)$.*

Suppose that Π is an LSSS for the access structure $\mathbb{A}$. Let S be an authorized set, such as $S \in \mathbb{A}$, and $I \subseteq \{1, 2, \cdot, l\}$ is defined as $I = \{i : \rho(i) \in S\}$. If $\{\lambda_i\}_{i \in I}$ are valid shares of a secret s according to Π, there exist constants $\{w_i \in \mathbb{Z}_p\}_{i \in I}$, that can be computed in a polynomial time, such as $\sum_{i \in I} \lambda_i w_i = s$ [1].

We note that any monotonic boolean formula can be converted into LSSS representation. Generally, boolean formulas are used to describe the access policy, and equivalent LSSS matrix is used to sign and verify the signature. We must note that the labeled matrix in Definition 7 is also called monotone span program [16].

Definition 8 *(Monotone Span Programs (MSP) [16,19]). A Monotone Span Program (MSP) is the tuple $(\mathbb{K}, M, \rho, \boldsymbol{t})$, where $\mathbb{K}$ is a field, M is a $l \times c$ matrix (l is the number of rows and c is the numbers of columns), $\rho : [l] \to [n]$ is the labeling function and $\boldsymbol{t}$ is the target vector. The size of the MSP is the number l of rows.*

As ρ is the function labeling each row i of M to a party $P_{\rho(i)}$, each party can be considered as associated to one or more rows. For any set of parties $S \subseteq \mathcal{P}$, the sub-matrix consisting of rows associated to parties in S is denoted M_S.

The span of a matrix M, denoted $span(M)$ is the subspace generated by the rows of M, i.e.; all vectors of the form $\boldsymbol{v} \cdot M$. An MSP is said to compute an access structure $\mathcal{A}$ if:

$$S \in \mathcal{A} \quad iff \quad t \in span(M_S)$$

In other words:

$$\mathcal{A}(S) = 1 \Longleftrightarrow \exists \boldsymbol{v} \in \mathbb{K}^{1 \times l} : \boldsymbol{v}M = \boldsymbol{t}$$

5.1.2 Bilinear Maps

Let $\mathbb{G}_1$, $\mathbb{G}_2$, and $\mathbb{G}_T$ be three cyclic groups of prime order p. Let g_1, g_2 be generators of respectively $\mathbb{G}_1$ and $\mathbb{G}_2$. A bilinear map $\hat{e}$ is a map $\hat{e} : \mathbb{G}_1 \times \mathbb{G}_2 \to \mathbb{G}_T$ satisfying the following properties: (i) bilinearity: for all $g_1 \in \mathbb{G}_1, g_2 \in \mathbb{G}_2$, (ii) non-degeneracy: $\hat{e}(g_1, g_2) \neq 1$ and (iii) there is an efficient algorithm to compute $\hat{e}(g_1, g_2)$ for any $g_1 \in \mathbb{G}_1$ and $g_2 \in \mathbb{G}_1$.

5.1.3 Complexity Assumptions

For our construction, we consider the following complexity assumptions:

- **q-Diffie Hellman Exponent Problem (q-DHE)** – Let $\mathbb{G}$ be a group of a prime order p, and g is a generator of $\mathbb{G}$. The q-DHE problem is, given a tuple of elements $(g, g_1, \cdots, g_q, g_{q+2}, \cdots, g_{2q})$, such that $g_i = g^{\alpha^i}$, where $i \in \{1, \cdots, q, q+2, \cdots, 2q\}$ and $\alpha \xleftarrow{R} \mathbb{Z}_p$, there is no efficient probabilistic algorithm $\mathcal{A}_{qDHE}$ that can compute the missing group element $g_{q+1} = g^{\alpha^{q+1}}$.
- **Computational Diffie Hellman Assumption (CDH)** – Let $\mathbb{G}$ be a group of a prime order p, and g is a generator of $\mathbb{G}$. The CDH problem is, given the tuple of elements (g, g^a, g^b), where $\{a, b\} \xleftarrow{R} \mathbb{Z}_p$, there is no efficient probabilistic algorithm $\mathcal{A}_{CDH}$ that computes g^{ab}.

5.2 Overview

In this section, we review the procedures and algorithms of $\mathcal{HABS}$. Our proposal is composed of seven algorithms defined as follows:

- SETUP: this algorithm takes as input the security parameter ξ and outputs the public parameters *params*. As presented in Sect. 4.1, we suppose that the public parameters includes the public key of the inspector and are considered as an auxiliary input to all $\mathcal{HABS}$ algorithms
  Global Public Parameters params – the SETUP algorithm first generates an asymmetric bilinear group environment such as $(p, \mathbb{G}_1, \mathbb{G}_2, \mathbb{G}_T, \hat{e})$ where $\hat{e}$ is an asymmetric pairing function such as $\hat{e} : \mathbb{G}_1 \times \mathbb{G}_2 \to \mathbb{G}_T$. Random generators $g_1, \{u_i\}_{i \in [1, U]} \in \mathbb{G}_1$ (i.e.; U is the maximum number of attributes supported by the span program) and $g_2 \in \mathbb{G}_2$ are also generated, together with $\alpha \in \mathbb{Z}_p$. Let $h_1 := g_1^{\alpha} \in \mathbb{G}_1$ and $h_2 := g_2^{-\alpha} \in \mathbb{G}_2$. Let $\mathcal{H}$ be a cryptographic hash function. The global parameters of our system are as follows:

$$params = \{\mathbb{G}_1, \mathbb{G}_2, \mathbb{G}_T, \hat{e}, p, g_1, \{u_i\}_{i \in [1, U]}, g_2, h_1, h_2, \mathcal{H}\}$$

We note that the secret key of the inspector is $sk_{ins} = \alpha$.

- KEYGEN – this algorithm outputs a pair of private and public keys for each participating entity. In our proposal, each entity (i.e.; issuer and user) has a pair of private and public keys. That is, the user has a pair of keys (sk_u, pk_u) where sk_u is randomly chosen in $\mathbb{Z}_p$ and pk_u is the couple $(X_u, Y_u) = (g_1^{sk_u}, \hat{e}(g_1, g_2)^{sk_u})$. The issuer has a pair of secret and public keys (sk_{is}, pk_{is}). The issuer secret key sk_{is} is the couple defined as $sk_{is} = (s_{is}, x_{is})$ where s_{is} is randomly chosen in $\mathbb{Z}_p$ and $x_{is} = g_1^{s_{is}}$. The issuer public key pk_{is} is the couple $(X_{is}, Y_{is}) = (\hat{e}(g_1, g_2)^{s_{is}}, h_2^{s_{is}})$.

- ISSUE: this algorithm is performed by the issuer in order to issue the credential to the user with respect to a pre-shared set of attributes $\mathcal{S} \subset \mathbb{S}$ ($\mathbb{S}$ is referred to as the attribute universe). The set of attributes $\mathcal{S}$ is defined as follows: $\mathcal{S} = \{a_1, a_2, \cdots, a_N\}$, where N is the number of attributes. The ISSUE algorithm takes as input the public key of the user pk_u, a set of attributes $\mathcal{S}$ and the private key of the issuer sk_{is}. It outputs the credential C defined as $C = (C_1, C_2, C_3, \{C_{4,i}\}_{i \in [1,N]}) = (x_{is} \cdot [X_u^{\mathcal{H}(\mathcal{S})^{-1}}] \cdot h_1^r, g_1^{-r}, g_2^r, \{u_i^r\}_{i \in [1,N]})$, where $\mathcal{H}(\mathcal{S}) = \mathcal{H}(a_1)\mathcal{H}(a_2)\cdots\mathcal{H}(a_N)$, r is an integer randomly selected by the issuer and u_i^r presents the secret key associated to the attribute a_i, where $i \in [1, N]$.

- OBTAIN: this algorithm is executed by the user. It takes as input the credential C, the public key of the user pk_u, the public key of the issuer pk_{is} and the set of attributes $\mathcal{S}$. The correctness of the obtained credential is given by Eq. 1, as follows:

$$\hat{e}(C_1, g_2) \overset{?}{=} X_{is} \cdot \hat{e}(X_u^{\mathcal{H}(\mathcal{S})^{-1}}, g_2) \cdot \hat{e}(h_1, C_3) \tag{1}$$

- SHOW: this algorithm is performed by the user, in order to authenticate with the verifier. That is, when the user wants to access a service, he sends a request to the verifier. As such, the verifier sends his presentation policy. The presentation policy is given by a randomized message m, a predicate Υ and the set of attributes that have to be revealed. The user has to sign the message m with respect to the predicate Υ satisfying a sub-set of his attributes $\mathcal{S}$. As presented in Sect. 3, the message m should be different for each authentication session.

  In the following, we denote by $\mathcal{S}_R$, the set of attributes revealed to the verifier, and $\mathcal{S}_H$ the set of non-revealed attributes, such as $\mathcal{S} = \mathcal{S}_R \cup \mathcal{S}_H$.

  Let the signing predicate Υ can be represented by an LSSS access structure (M, ρ), i,e; M is an $l \times k$ matrix, and ρ is an injective function that maps each row of the matrix M to an attribute. The SHOW algorithm takes in input the user secret key sk_u, the credential C, the attribute set $\mathcal{S}$, the message m and the predicate Υ such that $\Upsilon(\mathcal{S}) = 1$. The showing process is as follows:

  1. The user should first blind his credential C in the following way: the user first selects at random an integer $r' \in \mathbb{Z}_p$ and sets $C'_1 = C_1 \cdot h_1^{r'} = x_{is} \cdot X_u^{\mathcal{H}(\mathcal{S})^{-1}} \cdot h_1^r \cdot h_1^{r'} = x_{is} \cdot X_u^{\mathcal{H}(\mathcal{S})^{-1}} \cdot h_1^{r+r'}$, $C'_2 = C_2 \cdot g_1^{-r'} = g_1^{-(r+r')}$ and $C'_3 = C_3 \cdot g_2^{r'} = g_2^{r+r'}$.

     Then, the user blinds the secret value associated to each attribute required in the access policy such that: $\forall a_i \in \mathcal{S}, u'_i = u_i^r \cdot u_i^{r'} = u_i^{r+r'}$. Thus, the new blinded credential C' presents the tuple $(C_1', C_2', C_3', C_{4,i}') = (x_{is} \cdot X_u^{\mathcal{H}(\mathcal{S})^{-1}} \cdot h_1^{r+r'}, g_1^{-(r+r')}, g_2^{r+r'}, u_i^{r+r'})$.

2. As the user's attributes $\mathcal{S}$ satisfies Υ, the user can find a vector $\boldsymbol{v} = (v_1, \cdots, v_l)$ that satisfies $\boldsymbol{v}M = (1, 0, \cdots, 0)$ according to Definition 8.

3. For each attribute a_i, where $i \in [1, l]$, the user first computes $\omega_i = C_3'^{v_i}$. Then, he calculates $B = \prod_{i=1}^{l} (u_{\rho(i)}')^{v_i}$.

4. Afterwards, the user selects a random r_m and computes the couple $(\sigma_1, \sigma_2) = (C_1' \cdot B \cdot g_1^{r_m m}, g_1^{r_m})$.
   We note that the user may not have the secret value of each attribute mentioned in Υ. But, in this case, $v_i = 0$ and thus the value is not needed.

5. Finally, the user computes an accumulator on non-revealed attributes, using his secret key such as $A = g_2^{\frac{sk_u \mathcal{H}(\mathcal{S}_H)^{-1}}{r_m}}$. Then, he outputs a presentation token Σ, which mainly includes the signature of the message m with respect to the predicate Υ such that $\Sigma = (\Omega, \sigma_1, \sigma_2, C_1', C_2', A, \mathcal{S}_R)$. We note that $\Omega = \{\omega_1, \cdots, \omega_l\}$ is the set of committed elements' values of the vector $\boldsymbol{v}$, based on the credential's item C_3'.

- VERIFY: this algorithm is performed by the verifier. It takes as input the public key of the issuer pk_{is}, the presentation token Σ, the set of revealed attributes $\mathcal{S}_R$, the message m and the signing predicate Υ corresponding to $(M_{l \times k}, \rho)$. It outputs a bit $b \in \{0, 1\}$. The verifier proceeds as follows:
  First, the verifier checks the received set of revealed attributes $\mathcal{S}_R$, and computes an accumulator A_R such as $A_R = \sigma_2^{\mathcal{H}(\mathcal{S}_R)^{-1}}$.
  Then, the verifier chooses at random $k - 1$ values from $\mathbb{Z}_p$, denoted by $\mu_2, \cdots, \mu_k$ respectively and sets the vector $\boldsymbol{\mu} = (1, \mu_2, \cdots, \mu_k)$.
  Consequently, the verifier calculates $\tau_i = \sum_{j=1}^{k} \mu_j M_{i,j}$ where $M_{i,j}$ is an element of the matrix M. Finally, the verifier checks the correctness of the received presentation token (Eq. 2):

$$\hat{e}(\sigma_1, g_2) \stackrel{?}{=} X_{is} \hat{e}(A_R, A) \hat{e}(C_2', h_2) \prod_{i=1}^{l} \hat{e}(u_{\rho(i)} h_1^{\tau_i}, \omega_i) \hat{e}(\sigma_2, g_2^m) \qquad (2)$$

- INSPEC: this algorithm is performed by the inspector, the authority in possession of the secret sk_{ins}. The inspector can decrypt Elgamal ciphertext (C_1', C_2') to retrieve $\varpi^* = C_1' \cdot C_2'^{\alpha}$. Then, the inspector uses the issuer table in order to retrieve an entry $(u_j^*, pk_j, Y_{u_j}^{\mathcal{H}(\mathcal{S})^{-1}})$, such that $\hat{e}(\varpi^*, g_2) \cdot [X_{is}]^{-1} = \hat{e}(X_u^{\mathcal{H}(\mathcal{S})^{-1}}, g_2)$. The proof of validity of such an inspection procedure is done by proving that the decryption is correctly done, using the knowledge of sk_{ins} (Eq. 3).

$$\hat{e}(\varpi^*, g_2) \cdot X_{is}^{-1} \stackrel{?}{=} \hat{e}(X_u^{-\mathcal{H}(\mathcal{S})}, g_2) \qquad (3)$$

6   Security Analysis

In this section, we first prove that $\mathcal{HABS}$ provides the security requirements defined in Sect. 4.2. Then, we discuss an extension to support multiple issuers.

6.1   Security of the Main Scheme

The security of our main scheme $\mathcal{HABS}$ relies on the following Theorems:

Theorem 1. *Correctness* – $\mathcal{HABS}$ *is correct if for all (params)* $\leftarrow$ SETUP(ξ), *all pair of public and private keys* $\{(pk_{is}, sk_{is}), (pk_u, sk_u)\}$ $\leftarrow$ KEYGEN$(params)$, *all attribute sets* $\mathcal{S}$, *all credentials* $C \leftarrow$ ISSUE $(\mathcal{S}, sk_{is}, pk_u)$, *all claiming predicates* Υ *such as* $\Upsilon(\mathcal{S}) = 1$, *all presentation tokens* $\Sigma \leftarrow$ SHOW (C, sk_u, m, Υ) *and all proofs* $\varpi \leftarrow$ trace$(sk_{ins}, \sigma, pk_{is})$, *we have* OBTAIN $(C, sk_u, pk_{is}, \mathcal{S}) = 1$, VERIF $(\Sigma, m, \Upsilon, pk_{is}) = 1$ *and* judge$(\varpi) = 1$.

Theorem 2. *Unforgeability* – $\mathcal{HABS}$ *satisfies the unforgeability requirement, under the CDH, q-DHE and DLP assumptions.*

Theorem 3. *Privacy* – $\mathcal{HABS}$ *achieves the privacy requirement, with respect to the anonymity and unlinkability properties.*

Theorem 4. *Anonymity Removal* – *Our attribute based credential system* $\mathcal{HABS}$ *achieves the inspection feature, with respect to IA-Game.*

For detailed security proofs, please refer to http://www-public.tem-tsp.eu/ ~laurenm/ABS-AC/securityanalysis.pdf

6.2   Homomorphism to Support Multiple Issuers

As presented in Sect. 3.3, when a user requests multiple authorities to issue credentials with respect to his attributes, the different sessions are linked through the user's public key. To satisfy the unlinkability property of AC schemes between several issuance sessions, a novel ABS issuance procedure has to be designed, leading us to extend our proposal to support pseudonym systems and public key masking during the issuance procedure, presented hereafter. Also our construction is demonstrated to support an homomorphism property helpful for defining a new $\mathcal{HABS}$.agg algorithm, and a modified $\mathcal{HABS}$.VERIFY algorithm.

ASSUMPTIONS – Extra assumptions are requested for the support of multiple issuers: (i) all the issuing authorities AA_j share the same public parameters $params$, but have distinct key pairs (sk_{is_j}, pk_{is_j}), (ii) the public parameters $params$ include the secrets u_i relative to the attributes that might be certified by diverse issuers, (iii) the user is provided with one pseudonym nym_j per authority, and enables the user to authenticate to the issuers with different identities. For consistency among obtained credentials (i.e. C_1), each pseudonym nym_j should rely on the private key of the user and the related issuing authority AA_j and the $\mathcal{HABS}$.ISSUE should be extended with works of Chase and Chow [7] and Chase et al. [8] for masking the public key of the user.

HOMOMORPHISM CONSTRUCTION – For simplicity reasons, the reasoning next is limited to two issuers IS_i and IS_j, but it can be easily extended to n (different) issuer(s), where $n \geq 2$. Let us then assume that a user receives two signed sets of attributes from two different attribute authorities IS_i and IS_j.

The user receives $C_i = \mathcal{HABS}.\text{ISSUE}\ (sk_{is}{}^{(i)}, \mathcal{S}_i)$ and $C_j = \mathcal{HABS}.\text{ISSUE}$ $(sk_{is}{}^{(j)}, \mathcal{S}_j)$, from IS_i and IS_j, respectively. The sets of attributes are represented by $\mathcal{S}_i = \{a_{i,1}, \cdots, a_{i,n_i}\}$ and $\mathcal{S}_j = \{a_{j,1}, \cdots, a_{j,n_j}\}$, where n_k is the number of attributes in the set $\mathcal{S}_k$ and $k \in \{i, j\}$.

The idea is to aggregate credentials C_i and C_j to form a new C_R covering the attributes $\mathcal{S} = \mathcal{S}_i \cup \mathcal{S}_j$. We define the **agg** algorithm as follows:

agg – this algorithm takes as input two credentials C_i and C_j corresponding to the sets of attributes $\mathcal{S}_i$ and $\mathcal{S}_j$ respectively, and the public keys of issuers $pk_{is}{}^i$ and $pk_{is}{}^j$. It outputs a resulting signed commitment C_R, where C_R is a signature over the union of the two sets of attributes $\mathcal{S}_i$ and $\mathcal{S}_j$. We note that the **agg** algorithm has to fulfill the *correctness* and *homomorphism* properties.

Recall that the credential C_k, obtained from the issuer IS_k, is denoted by $C_k = (C_1, C_2, C_3, \{C_{l,4}\}_{l \in [1, n_l]})^{(k)} = (x_{is_k}[X_u{}^{\mathcal{H}(\mathcal{S}_k)^{-1}}]h_1{}^{r_k}, g_1{}^{-r_k}, g_2{}^{r_k}, \{u_l{}^{r_k}\}_{l \in [1, N]})$, where $k \in \{i, j\}$ and n_l is the number of certified attributes by the issuer IS_k.

Let us define the following theorem defining the aggregation algorithm:

Theorem 5. *Let us consider the algorithms* $\mathcal{HABS}.\text{ISSUE}$, $\mathcal{HABS}.\text{OBTAIN}$, $\mathcal{HABS}.\text{SHOW}$ *and* $\mathcal{HABS}.\text{VERIFY}$ *defined in Sect. 5.2. Let* $\mathcal{HABS}.\text{agg}$ *be the aggregation algorithm such as:*

$$\text{agg}(C^{(i)}, C^{(j)}, \mathcal{S}_i, \mathcal{S}_j, pk_{is}{}^i, pk_{is}{}^j) = \mathcal{HABS}.\text{ISSUE}(pk_u, \mathcal{S}_i \cup \mathcal{S}_j), a.sk_{is_i} + b.sk_{is_j}) \tag{4}$$

where a and b are two integers that might be computed by the user based on the union set $\mathcal{S}_i \cup \mathcal{S}_j$.

That theorem and homomorphism property come directly from the following Lemma 1 which expresses $\mathcal{H}(\mathcal{S}_i \cup \mathcal{S}_j)$ based on $\mathcal{H}(\mathcal{S}_i)$ and $\mathcal{H}(\mathcal{S}_j)$ in order to write $C_{\{1, \mathcal{S}_i \cup \mathcal{S}_j\}}$ with respect to $C_1{}^{(i)}$ and $C_1{}^{(j)}$.

Lemma 1. *Given the hash function* $\mathcal{H}$ *and for every sets of attributes* S_i *and* S_j, *there exist two integers a and b, such that* $\mathcal{H}(S_i \cup S_j)^{-1} = a\mathcal{H}(S_i)^{-1} + b\mathcal{H}(S_j)^{-1}$.

Proof. Referring to the Bezout's lemma, the gcd satisfies the following property:

$$gcd(\mathcal{H}(S_i), \mathcal{H}(S_j)) = b\mathcal{H}(S_i) + a\mathcal{H}(S_j) \tag{5}$$

where a and b are two non zero integers (a and b are called Bezout coefficients). In addition, the gcd and lcm satisfy Eq. 6 such that

$$gcd(\mathcal{H}(S_i), \mathcal{H}(S_j)) * lcm(\mathcal{H}(S_i), \mathcal{H}(S_j)) = \mathcal{H}(S_i)\mathcal{H}(S_j) \tag{6}$$

As such, using Eq. 6, we have:

$$lcm(\mathcal{H}(S_i), \mathcal{H}(S_j))^{-1} = \frac{gcd(\mathcal{H}(S_i), \mathcal{H}(S_j))}{\mathcal{H}(S_i)\mathcal{H}(S_j)} = \frac{b\mathcal{H}(S_i) + a\mathcal{H}(S_j)}{\mathcal{H}(S_i)\mathcal{H}(S_j)} = b\mathcal{H}(S_j)^{-1} + a\mathcal{H}(S_i)^{-1} \tag{7}$$

On the other side, we write $\mathcal{H}(S_i \cup S_j)$ as follows:

$$\mathcal{H}(S_i \cup S_j) = \prod_{a_k \in S_i \cup S_j} \mathcal{H}(a_k) = lcm(\prod_{a_k \in S_i} \mathcal{H}(a_k), \prod_{a_k \in S_j} \mathcal{H}(a_k)) = lcm(\mathcal{H}(S_i), \mathcal{H}(S_j)) \tag{8}$$

6.3 Proof of Homomorphism

In order to prove the homomorphism property with respect to the union operator, we first express $[C_1^{(i)}]^a \cdot [C_1^{(j)}]^b$, denoted by RS, as a function of $\mathcal{S}_i \cup \mathcal{S}_j$, sk_{is_i} and sk_{is_j}, as follows:

$$RS = [x_{is_i} \cdot [X_u^{\mathcal{H}(\mathcal{S}_i)^{-1}}] \cdot h_1^{r_i}]^a \cdot [x_{is_j} \cdot [X_u^{\mathcal{H}(\mathcal{S}_j)^{-1}}] \cdot h_1^{r_j}]^b$$
$$= g_1^{a.s_{is_i}+b.s_{is_j}} \cdot [X_u^{a\mathcal{H}(\mathcal{S}_i)^{-1}+b\mathcal{H}(\mathcal{S}_j)^{-1}}] \cdot h_1^{a.r_i+b.r_j}$$
$$= g_1^{a.s_{is_i}+b.s_{is_j}} \cdot [X_u^{\mathcal{H}(\mathcal{S}_i\cup\mathcal{S}_j)^{-1}}] \cdot h_1^{a.r_i+b.r_j}$$

Similarly, we can write the elements of the resulting credential C_R, such that $C_R = (C_{1,\mathcal{S}_i\cup\mathcal{S}_j}, C_{2,\mathcal{S}_i\cup\mathcal{S}_j}, C_{3,\mathcal{S}_i\cup\mathcal{S}_j}, \{C_{l,4,\mathcal{S}_i\cup\mathcal{S}_j}\}_{l\in[1,N]})$, where $C_{1,\mathcal{S}_i\cup\mathcal{S}_j} = [C_1^{(i)}]^a \cdot [C_1^{(j)}]^b = x_{is_i}^a \cdot x_{is_j}^b \cdot [X_u^{\mathcal{H}(\mathcal{S}_i\cup\mathcal{S}_j)}] \cdot h_1^{a.r_i+b.r_j}$, $C_{2,\mathcal{S}_i\cup\mathcal{S}_j} = [C_2^{(i)}]^a \cdot [C_2^{(j)}]^b = g_1^{-(a.r_i+b.r_j)}$ $C_{3,\mathcal{S}_i\cup\mathcal{S}_j} = [C_3^{(i)}]^a \cdot [C_3^{(j)}]^b = g_2^{a.r_i+b.r_j}$ and $\{C_{l,4,\mathcal{S}_i\cup\mathcal{S}_j}\}_{l\in[1,N]} = \{u_l^{a.r_i+b.r_j}\}_{l\in[1,N]}$, (i.e.; N is the maximum number of attributes).

The form of the aggregated credential $C_{1,\mathcal{S}_i\cup\mathcal{S}_j}, C_{2,\mathcal{S}_i\cup\mathcal{S}_j}, C_{3,\mathcal{S}_i\cup\mathcal{S}_j}$, $\{C_{l,4,\mathcal{S}_i\cup\mathcal{S}_j}\}_{l\in[1,N]}$ is similar to the individual credentials like C_i, thus leading to the aggregated presentation token Σ_R by applying exactly the same $\mathcal{HABS}$SHOW algorithm. The obtained Σ_R is as follows: $\Sigma_R = (\Omega_R, \sigma_{1,R}, \sigma_{2,R}, C'_{1,R}, C'_{2,R}, A, \mathcal{S}_R)$.

6.4 Proof of Correctness

We show how the verifier can rely on the aggregated presentation token Σ_R, to authenticate the user (u), with respect to his access policy Υ, such as $\Upsilon(\mathcal{S}_i \cup \mathcal{S}_j) = 1$, where $\mathcal{S}_k$ presents the set of attributes certified by the issuer IS_k, $k \in \{i,j\}$. Using the properties of the pairing function $\hat{e}$, we can easily prove the correctness of Eq. 9:

$$\hat{e}(\sigma_{1,R}, g_2) \stackrel{?}{=} X_{is_i}^a X_{is_j}^b \hat{e}(A_R, A)\hat{e}(C'_{2,R}, h_2) \prod_{i=1}^{l} \hat{e}(u_{\rho(i)}h_1^{\tau_i}, \omega_i)\hat{e}(\sigma_{2,R}, g_2^m) \tag{9}$$

where a and b are two integers as defined in Lemma 1.

By equivalence to Eq. 2, we can consider that $D = a.r_i + b.r_j + r'$ presents the quantity $R = r + r'$. Thus, for proving the correctness of Eq. 9, let us denote by ⑤ the quantity $\hat{e}(\sigma_{1,R}, g_2)$:

$$⑤ = \hat{e}(x_{is_i}^a x_{is_j}^b \cdot X_u^{\mathcal{H}(\mathcal{S}_i\cup\mathcal{S}_j)} \cdot h_1^D \cdot \prod_{i=1}^{l}(u_{\rho(i)})^{Dv_i} \cdot g_1^{r_m m}, g_2)$$

$$= \hat{e}(x_{is_i}, g_2)^a \cdot \hat{e}(x_{is_j}, g_2)^b \cdot \hat{e}(X_u^{\mathcal{H}(\mathcal{S}_i\cup\mathcal{S}_j)}, g_2) \cdot \hat{e}(h_1^D, g_2) \cdot \hat{e}(g_1^{r_m m}, g_2) \cdot \hat{e}(\prod_{i=1}^{l} u_{\rho(i)}^{Dv_i}, g_2)$$

$$= X_{is_i}^a \cdot X_{is_j}^b \cdot \hat{e}(g_1^{\mathcal{H}(\mathcal{S}_R)^{-1}}, [g_2^{sk_u}]^{\mathcal{H}(\mathcal{S}_H)^{-1}}) \cdot \hat{e}(C'_{2,R}, h_2) \cdot \hat{e}(\sigma_2, g_2^m) \cdot \prod_{i=1}^{l} \hat{e}(u_{\rho(i)}, \omega_i)$$

$$= X_{is_i}^a X_{is_j}^b \hat{e}(A_R, A)\hat{e}(C'_{2,R}, h_2) \prod_{i=1}^{l} \hat{e}(u_{\rho(i)}h_1^{\tau_i}, \omega_i)\hat{e}(\sigma_{2,R}, g_2^m)$$

Table 1. Comparisons between $\mathcal{HABS}$ and the related works

Scheme	Keys (N attributes per credential)			Issuance procedure		
	Groups	$params$	Credential size	User	Issuer	Bw
[15]	$\mathbb{Z}_n$: RSA: 1024	$\mathcal{O}(N)$	$\mathcal{O}(1)$	$\simeq 2600 + 1024$	$\mathcal{O}(N)$: $\mathbb{Z}_n$		
[20]	$p = 1024 : q = 128$	$\mathcal{O}(N)$	$\mathcal{O}(1)$	$3 \cdot |\mathbb{G}_q| + 128$	$\mathcal{O}(N)$: $\mathbb{G}_q$		$\mathcal{O}(1)$
[6]	$\mathbb{F}_p$: $|\mathbb{G}_1| \simeq 170$	$\mathcal{O}(1)$	$\mathcal{O}(N)$	$(2N+2) \cdot (|\mathbb{G}_1| + |\mathbb{Z}_p|)$	$\mathcal{O}(1)$	$\mathcal{O}(N)$: $\mathbb{G}_1$	
$\mathcal{HABS}$	$\mathbb{F}_p$: $|\mathbb{G}_1| \simeq 170$	$\mathcal{O}(N)$	$\mathcal{O}(N)$	$(N+3) \cdot |\mathbb{G}_1|$	$\mathcal{O}(1)$	$\mathcal{O}(N)$: $\mathbb{G}_1$	

	Presentation Procedure								
	User	Verifier	Bw.	User	Verifier	Bw.	User	Verifier	Bw.
	$single\text{-}use$			$single\text{-}use$		$l\text{-}out\text{-}of\text{-}N$ attributes	$K\text{-}use$	N attributes	
[15]	$\mathcal{O}(N)$: $\mathbb{Z}_n$		$\mathcal{O}(1)$	$\mathcal{O}(N)$		$\mathcal{O}(N-l)$	$\mathcal{O}(N)$: $\mathbb{Z}_n$		$\mathcal{O}(1)$
[20]	$\mathcal{O}(N)$		$\mathcal{O}(N)$	$\mathcal{O}(l)$		$\mathcal{O}(N)$	$\mathcal{O}(KN)$: $\mathbb{Z}_q$		$\mathcal{O}(KN)$
[6]	$\mathcal{O}(1)$	$2 \cdot \mathcal{O}(N)$	$\mathcal{O}(N)$	$\mathcal{O}(1)$	$2 \cdot \mathcal{O}(N)$	$\mathcal{O}(l)$	$\mathcal{O}(N)$	$2 \cdot \mathcal{O}(N)$	$\mathcal{O}(N)$
$\mathcal{HABS}$	$\mathcal{O}(k)^*$			$\mathcal{O}(k)^*$			$\mathcal{O}(k)^*$		

This proves the correctness of our $\mathcal{HABS}$.VERIFY, while considering a multi-issuers setting according to the **agg** algorithm.

7   Comparison

In this section, we give a quantitative comparison between related works and our anonymous credential system based on attribute based signatures $\mathcal{HABS}$. That is, we give in Table 1 several elements of comparison between our construction and most closely related anonymous credential systems, with respect to processing and communication overhead.

The first column underlines the algebraic structure for each AC system. It may be an RSA environment [15], $\mathbb{Z}_n$ with a subgroup of order q [20], or bilinear groups $\hat{e}(\mathbb{G}_1, \mathbb{G}_2)$ over a base field $\mathbb{F}_p$ [6].

We denote by N the maximum number of attributes issued by an authority into a single credential. The bandwidth, for issuing and showing protocols, presents the exchanged quantity of data during protocols' running.

The credential size presents the size of public keys or a certificate. The memory consumption for credentials is given with asymptotic complexity and some concrete size in bits. Table 1 also details the processing complexity at the issuer, user and verifier sides, while considering the number of operations in the underlying algebraic structures. As presented before, Table 1 shows that our $\mathcal{HABS}$ is a direct signature, and thus the issuance procedure is rather interesting, compared to IBM Identity Mixer [15] and U-Prove [20] solutions. The [6] construction presents also a direct sanitizable signature applications for anonymous credential systems. However, $\mathcal{HABS}$ presents an interesting overhead, for the showing protocol, compared to existing solutions. That is, the computation and communication overhead depends only on attributes required for satisfying the access policy of the verifier, referred to as k in Table 1, whereas we denote by K the set of attributes that have to be disclosed with respect to presentation policy of the verifier. In addition, our attribute-based construction $\mathcal{HABS}$ bring multiple-use credentials, likely as [6,15] with an interesting processing overhead, compared to the UProve's technology which is a single-use credentials' solution.

8   Conclusion

In this paper, we proposed a new way to design anonymous credential systems, based on the use of attribute based signatures. Our anonymous certification system $\mathcal{HABS}$ enables a user to anonymously authenticate with a verifier, while providing only required information for the service provider, with respect to its presentation policy. Indeed, $\mathcal{HABS}$ supports a flexible selective disclosure mechanism with no-extra processing cost, which is directly inherited from the expressiveness of attribute based signatures for defining access policies.

Additionally, our proposal is deliberately designed to ensure unlinkability between the different sessions while preserving the anonymity of the user. An extension of $\mathcal{HABS}$ is also detailed to preserve users' privacy with ensuring the unlinkability between multiple issuers. Finally, a quantitative comparison of $\mathcal{HABS}$ with most closely-related technologies shows the interesting processing and communication cost of our construction, especially due to the application of direct attribute based signatures for the issuing protocol.

References

1. Beimel, A.: Secret sharing and key distribution. In: Research Thesis (1996)
2. Brands, S.A.: Rethinking Public Key Infrastructures and Digital Certificates: Building in Privacy. MIT Press, Cambridge (2000)
3. Camenisch, J., Krenn, S., Lehmann, A., Mikkelsen, G.L., Neven, G., Pederson, M.O.: Scientific comparison of abc protocols: Part i - formal treatment of privacy-enhancing credential systems (2014)
4. Camenisch, J.L., Lysyanskaya, A.: An efficient system for non-transferable anonymous credentials with optional anonymity revocation. In: Pfitzmann, B. (ed.) EUROCRYPT 2001. LNCS, vol. 2045, pp. 93–118. Springer, Heidelberg (2001)
5. Camenisch, J.L., Lysyanskaya, A.: A signature scheme with efficient protocols. In: Cimato, S., Galdi, C., Persiano, G. (eds.) SCN 2002. LNCS, vol. 2576, pp. 268–289. Springer, Heidelberg (2003)
6. Canard, S., Lescuyer, R.: Protecting privacy by sanitizing personal data: a new approach to anonymous credentials. In: ASIA CCS 2013 (2013)
7. Chase, M., Chow, S.S.M.: Improving privacy and security in multi-authority attribute-based encryption. In: Proceedings of the 16th ACM Conference on Computer and Communications Security, pp. 121–130 (2009)
8. Chase, M., Kohlweiss, M., Meiklejohn, S., Lysyanskaya, A.: Malleable signatures: complex unary transformations and delegatable anonymous credentials (2013)
9. Chaum, D.: Blind signatures for untraceable payment. In: Advances in Cryptology: Proceedings of Crypto 1982 (1982)

10. El Kaafarani, A., Ghadafi, E., Khader, D.: Decentralized traceable attribute-based signatures. In: Benaloh, J. (ed.) CT-RSA 2014. LNCS, vol. 8366, pp. 327–348. Springer, Heidelberg (2014)
11. Europe, C.: Proposal for a regulation of the european parliament and of the council on the protection of individuals with regard to the processing of personal data and on the free movement of such data. In: General Data Protection Regulation, January 2016
12. Fiat, A., Shamir, A.: How to prove yourself: practical solutions to identification and signature problems. In: Odlyzko, A.M. (ed.) CRYPTO 1986. LNCS, vol. 263, pp. 186–194. Springer, Heidelberg (1987)
13. Herranz, J., Laguillaumie, F., Libert, B., Ràfols, C.: Short attribute-based signatures for threshold predicates. In: Dunkelman, O. (ed.) CT-RSA 2012. LNCS, vol. 7178, pp. 51–67. Springer, Heidelberg (2012)
14. House, W.: Enhancing online choice, efficiency, security, and privacy. In: National Strategy for Trusted Identities in Cyberspace, April 2011
15. IBM: Ibm identity mixer, idemix (2012)
16. Karchmer, M., Wigderson, A.: On span programs. In: Proceedings of the 8th IEEE Structure in Complexity Theory (1993)
17. Langheinrich, M.: Privacy by design - principles of privacy-aware ubiquitous systems. In: Abowd, G.D., et al. (eds.) UbiComp 2001. LNCS, vol. 2201, pp. 273–291. Springer, Heidelberg (2001)
18. Li, J., Au, M.H., Susilo, W., Xie, D., Ren, K.: Attribute-based signature and its applications. In: ASIACCS 2010 (2010)
19. Maji, H.K., Prabhakaran, M., Rosulek, M.: Attribute-based signatures. Cryptology ePrint Archive, Report 2010/595 (2010)
20. Microsoft.: U-prove community technology (2013)
21. Okamoto, T., Takashima, K.: Efficient attribute-based signatures for non-monotone predicates in the standard model. In: PKC 2011 (2011)
22. Shahandashti, S.F., Safavi-Naini, R.: Threshold attribute-based signatures and their application to anonymous credential systems. In: Preneel, B. (ed.) AFRICACRYPT 2009. LNCS, vol. 5580, pp. 198–216. Springer, Heidelberg (2009)
23. Zhang, Y., Feng, D.: Efficient attribute proofs in anonymous credential using attribute-based cryptography. In: Chim, T.W., Yuen, T.H. (eds.) ICICS 2012. LNCS, vol. 7618, pp. 408–415. Springer, Heidelberg (2012)

Privacy Preserving Computation in Cloud Using Noise-Free Fully Homomorphic Encryption (FHE) Schemes

Yongge Wang[1](✉) and Qutaibah M. Malluhi[2]

[1] Department of SIS, UNC Charlotte, Charlotte, USA
yonwang@uncc.edu
[2] KINDI Center, Qatar University, Doha, Qatar
qmalluhi@qu.edu.qa

Abstract. With the wide adoption of cloud computing paradigm, it is important to develop appropriate techniques to protect client data privacy in the cloud. Encryption is one of the major techniques that could be used to achieve this goal. However, data encryption at the rest alone is insufficient for secure cloud computation environments. There is also the need for efficient techniques to carry out computation over encrypted data. Fully homomorphic encryption (FHE) and garbled circuits are naturally used to process encrypted data without leaking any information about the data. However, existing FHE schemes are inefficient for processing large amount of data in cloud and garbled circuits are one time programs and cannot be reused. Based on quaternion/octonion algebra and Jordan algebra over finite rings $\mathbb{Z}_q$, this paper designs efficient fully homomorphic symmetric key encryption (FHE) schemes without bootstrapping (that is, noise-free FHE schemes) that are secure in the weak ciphertext-only security model assuming the hardness of solving multivariate quadratic equation systems and solving univariate high degree polynomial equation systems in $\mathbb{Z}_q$. The FHE scheme designed in this paper is sufficient for privacy preserving computation in cloud.

1 Introduction

Cloud computing techniques become pervasive and users begin to store their private data in cloud services. In order to take full advantage of the cloud computing paradigm, it is important to design efficient techniques to protect client data privacy in the cloud. From a first look, encryption at rest seems to be a feasible solution to address these challenges. But a truly optimal solution is still far from us since encryption is not a good or even an acceptable solution for cloud data storage. If encryption at rest is the only solution, then the functionality of cloud computing is limited to: encrypt data at the user's location, transmit encrypted data to the cloud, and then bring the data back to the user's location

---

The work reported in this paper is supported by Qatar Foundation Grants NPRP8-2158-1-423 and NPRP X-063-1-014.

I. Askoxylakis et al. (Eds.): ESORICS 2016, Part I, LNCS 9878, pp. 301–323, 2016.
DOI: 10.1007/978-3-319-45744-4_15

for decryption before being used locally. This is against one of the cloud computing paradigms "moving computation is cheaper than moving data". Indeed, in many scenarios, it becomes less expensive to store data locally than in the cloud. So using the cloud for data-storage without the capability of processing the data remotely may not be an economic approach.

This shows the importance of developing techniques for processing encrypted data at the cloud without downloading them to the local site. A natural solution is to use garbled computing techniques such as garbled circuits or fully homomorphic encryption schemes. That is, an adversary observing the computations of a garbled computation learns nothing about what it is doing, what data it is operating on (whether inputs or intermediate values), and the outputs it is producing. Yao [15] introduced the garbled circuit concept which allows computing a function f on an input x without leaking information about the input x or the circuit used for the computation of $f(x)$. Since then, garbled circuit based protocols have been used in numerous places and it has become one of the fundamental components of secure multi-party computation protocols. However, there are two disadvantages in Yao's approach. Firstly, Yao's garbled circuit is a one-time program that can not be reused. Secondly, using a garbled circuit to evaluate an algorithm on encrypted data takes the worst-case runtime of the algorithm on all inputs of the same length since Turing machines are simulated by circuits via unrolling loops to their worst-case runtime, and via considering all branches of a computation.

Gentry [6] proposed the first fully homomorphic encryption scheme (FHE) using two phases: the first phase designs a somewhat-homomorphic encryption scheme and the second phase uses bootstrapping techniques to convert it to a fully homomorphic encryption scheme. Since Gentry's initial FHE design, the performance of FHE schemes has improved a lot though it is still impractical for cloud garbled computation applications. For example, the most efficient implementation (until 2016) takes 4 min to carry out a garbled AES encryption on a 128 bit input.

The main performance bottleneck for Gentry's approach is the "noise" reduction process since the homomorphic operations increase the noise in ciphertexts. After a homomorphic operation (e.g., a circuit gate evaluation) is performed on the ciphertexts, Gentry's [6] bootstrapping technique is used to refresh the ciphertexts by homomorphically computing the decryption function and bringing the noise of the ciphertexts back to acceptable levels. The bootstrapping operation accounts for the major performance cost in FHE implementations. The performance of FHE schemes would be significantly improved if one could design noise-free FHE schemes. Using quaternion/octonion/Jordan algebra based coding techniques, this paper introduces noise-free fully homomorphic symmetric key encryption schemes. The proposed FHE schemes are secure in the weak ciphertext-only security model with the assumption that it is computationally infeasible to solve multivariate quadratic equation systems and it is computationally infeasible to solve univariate high degree polynomial equation systems in the underlying rings $\mathbb{Z}_q$. The hardness assumption for the security is reasonable for large enough $\mathbb{Z}_q$ (e.g., $|\mathbb{Z}_q| \geq 2^{1000}$) since it is known that finding square roots modulo a composite number is equivalent to factoring. This fact has been used in the literature to show the security of Rabin cryptosystem. The weak ciphertext-only security model for FHE is sufficient for garbled cloud computation applications (e.g., outsourcing of private algorithm implementations) mentioned in the preceding paragraphs.

We conclude this section by introducing some notations. The schemes in this paper will be based on finite rings $\mathbb{Z}_q = \mathbb{Z}/q\mathbb{Z}$ with $q = p_1^{r_1} \cdots p_m^{r_m}$ for some primes $p_1, \cdots, p_m$ and non-negative integers $r_1, \cdots, r_m$. Let $\mathbb{Z}_q^*$ denote of the set of invertible elements in $\mathbb{Z}_q$. Bold face letters such as $\mathbf{a}, \mathbf{b}, \mathbf{e}, \mathbf{f}, \mathbf{g}$ are used to denote row vectors over $\mathbb{Z}_q$. For a vector subset $V = \{\mathbf{a}_i : i \leq k - 1\} \subset \mathbb{Z}_q^n$, the span of V denoted by $\mathrm{span}(V)$ is defined as all linear combinations of vectors in V.

2   Linearly Decryptable Encryption Schemes

In the past few years, numerous works have been done to analyze the security and performance of FHE schemes (due to the space limit, we are unable to list these important works here). Brakerski [3] investigated the relationship between decryption circuit complexity and FHE scheme security. In particular, Brakerski showed that if a scheme can homomorphically evaluate the majority function, then its decryption cannot be weakly-learnable. A corollary of this result is that linearly decryptable FHE schemes cannot be secure in the CPA (chosen plaintext attacks) security model. In this paper, we show that linearly decryptable FHE schemes cannot be secure even in the ciphertext-only security model. With these impossibility results, one may wonder what kind of maximum security a FHE scheme with simple decryption circuit could achieve? By relaxing the definition of the ciphertext-only attacks to the weak ciphertext-only attacks, this paper is able to design efficient secure FHE schemes with linear decryption circuits.

Brakerski [3] called an encryption scheme to be linearly decryptable if the decryption circuit can be described as an inner product. We first formally define the Inner Product Encryption Scheme $\mathtt{IPE} = (\mathtt{IPE.Setup}, \mathtt{IPE.Enc}, \mathtt{IPE.Dec})$ over finite rings $\mathbb{Z}_q$. The definition remains the same for the $\mathtt{IPE}$ scheme over finite fields $\mathbb{F}_q$.

Setup $\mathtt{IPE.Setup}(n, \kappa)$: For the given security parameter κ and the dimension $n \geq 3$, choose a finite ring $\mathbb{Z}_q$ and a random $\mathbf{k} = [k_0, \cdots, k_{n-1}] \in \mathbb{Z}_q^n$ such that $k_i \in \mathbb{Z}_q^*$ for at least one $i < n$. Let $\mathbf{k}$ be the private key.

Encryption $\mathtt{IPE.Enc}$: For a message $m \in \mathbb{Z}_q$, select a random $\mathbf{c} \in \mathbb{Z}_q^n$ such that $m = \mathbf{ck}^T$ where $\mathbf{ck}^T$ is the inner product of $\mathbf{c}$ and $\mathbf{k}$. Let $\mathtt{IPE.Enc}(\mathbf{k}, m) = \mathbf{c}$.

Decryption $\mathtt{IPE.Dec}$: For a ciphertext $\mathbf{c}$, let $m = \mathtt{IPE.Dec}(\mathbf{k}, \mathbf{c}) = \mathbf{kc}^T$.

The definition of ciphertext-only security for an encryption scheme is closely related to the perfect secrecy definition for one-time pad encryption schemes. The commonly used security definition for one-time pad encryption scheme includes indistinguishability based $\mathtt{IND\text{-}onetime}$ and simulation based $\mathtt{SIM\text{-}onetime}$ security. We will use the indistinguishability based security definition for ciphertext-only security (COA).

Definition 1. *(COA model) Let* xx = (KeySetup, Enc, Dec) *be a symmetric key encryption scheme over a message space* $\mathcal{M}$. *For a pair of probabilistic polynomial time (PPT) algorithms* $A = (A_0, A_1)$, *define the following experiments:*

- A_0 *runs* key $\leftarrow$ xx.KeySetup(κ) *where* κ *is the security parameter.*
- A_0 *chooses* t *messages* $p_0, \cdots, p_{t-1}$ *according to the distribution of* $\mathcal{M}$ *and outputs* t *ciphertexts* $C_{p_0}, \cdots, C_{p_{t-1}}$ *by running* $C_{p_i} =$ xx.Enc(key, p_i).
- A_1 *selects* 2 *messages* $m_0, m_1 \in \mathcal{M}$ *and gives them to* A_0.
- A_0 *selects a random bit* $b \in \{0, 1\}$ *and outputs* $C_{m_b} =$ xx.Enc(key, m_b).
- A_1 *outputs a bit* b'.

The output of the above experiment is defined to be 1 if $b' = b$, *and 0 otherwise. We write* $\text{COA}^{(A_0, A_1)}(\kappa) = 1$ *if the output is 1 and in this case we say that* A_1 *succeeded. The encryption scheme* xx *is said to be* (t, ε)-*secure in the ciphertext-only attack (COA) security model for* $\varepsilon =$ negl(κ) *if for all PPT algorithms* $A = (A_0, A_1)$, *we have*

$$Prob[\text{COA}^{(A_0, A_1)}(\kappa) = 1] \le \frac{1}{2} + \varepsilon.$$

The following theorem shows that an IPE encryption scheme cannot be fully homomorphic and secure in the ciphertext-only security model at the same time.

Theorem 1. *Let* xx = (KeySetup, Enc, Dec) *be a fully homomorphic symmetric key encryption scheme over* $\mathbb{Z}_q$ *such that the decryption process* xx.Dec *is equivalent to* IPE.Dec *of dimension* n. *Then* xx *is not secure in the ciphertext-only security model.*

Proof. Let $\mathbf{k} \in \mathbb{Z}_q^n$ be the private key and xx.Dec($\mathbf{c}$) = $\mathbf{k}\mathbf{c}^T$ for ciphertexts $\mathbf{c} \in \mathbb{Z}_q^n$. Without loss of generality, we may assume that the messages selected by the PPT algorithm A_1 during the experiment is $m_0 = 0$ and $m_1 = 1$. Let $\mathbf{c}_b \in \mathbb{Z}_q^n$ be the ciphertext output by the algorithm A_0 during the experiment where $b = 0, 1$.

By using the multiplicative homomorphism property of xx, the algorithm A_1 can calculate ciphertexts $\mathbf{c}_{b,i} \in \mathbb{Z}_q^n$ of $b^i = b$ for $i \ge 1$. It is straightforward that, for $d = n + 1$, the ciphertexts $\mathbf{c}_{b,1}, \ldots, \mathbf{c}_{b,d}$ are linearly dependent. In other words, there exist $a_1, \cdots, a_d \in \mathbb{Z}_q$ such that $a_1\mathbf{c}_{b,1} + a_2\mathbf{c}_{b,2} + \cdots + a_d\mathbf{c}_{b,d} = 0$. This implies that

$$a_1 b + a_2 b^2 + \cdots + a_d b^d = 0 \tag{1}$$

If $a_1 + \cdots + a_d = 0$, the algorithm A_1 outputs $b' = 1$. Otherwise, it outputs $b' = 0$. The algorithm A_1 may repeat the above process for ciphertexts $\mathbf{c}_{b,i+1}, \ldots, \mathbf{c}_{b,i+d}$ with different $i > 1$ to get more accurate prediction b' of the value b. Thus it can be shown that $b' = b$ with a non-negligible probability. The theorem is proved. $\square$

One may wonder whether it is possible at all to design a linearly decryptable FHE scheme that is secure in some relaxed security model? Alternatively we may ask: what is the maximum security one can achieve with linearly decryptable FHE schemes? In next sections, we show that it is possible to design linearly decryptable FHE schemes that are secure in the following weak ciphertext-only security model (wCOA).s

Definition 2. *(wCOA model) Let* $\mathrm{xx} = (\mathsf{KeySetup}, \mathsf{Enc}, \mathsf{Dec})$ *be a symmetric key encryption scheme over a message space* $\mathcal{M}$*. For a pair of PPT algorithms* $A = (A_0, A_1)$*, define the following experiments:*

- A_0 *runs* $\mathrm{key} \leftarrow \mathrm{xx}.\mathsf{KeySetup}(\kappa)$ *where* κ *is the security parameter.*
- A_0 *chooses* t *messages* $p_0, \cdots, p_{t-1}$ *according to the distribution of* $\mathcal{M}$ *and outputs* t *ciphertexts* $C_{p_0}, \cdots, C_{p_{t-1}}$ *by running* $C_{p_i} = \mathrm{xx}.\mathsf{Enc}(\mathrm{key}, p_i)$*.*
- A_1 *outputs a message* $m' \in \mathcal{M}$*.*

The output of the experiment is 1 if $m' \in \{p_0, \cdots, p_{t-1}\}$*, and 0 otherwise. We write* $\mathrm{wCOA}^{(A_0, A_1)}(\kappa) = 1$ *if the output is 1 and in this case we say that* A_1 *succeeded. The scheme* xx *is said to be* (t, ε)*-secure in the weak ciphertext-only attack (wCOA) security model for* $\varepsilon = \mathtt{negl}(\kappa)$ *if for all PPT algorithms* $A = (A_0, A_1)$*, we have*

$$Prob[\mathrm{wCOA}^{(A_0, A_1)}(\kappa) = 1] \leq \varepsilon.$$

By the definition, wCOA model does not allow the adversary to ask the oracle to decrypt any ciphertext. In other words, the adversary sees a list of ciphertext and tries to guess a plaintext for one of these ciphertexts. On the other hand, in COA model, after seeing a list of ciphertexts, the adversary submits two messages (normally bit 0 and bit 1) to the oracle for encryption. The oracle encrypts one of the messages and returns the ciphertext. The adversary tries to guess which message the oracle has encrypted.

3   Octonions

Octonion (see, e.g., Baez [1]) is the largest among the four normed division algebras: real numbers $\mathbb{R}$, complex numbers $\mathbb{C}$, quaternions $\mathbb{H}$, and octonions $\mathbb{O}$. The real numbers have a complete order while the complex numbers are not ordered. The quaternions are not commutative and the octonions are neither commutative nor associative. Quaternions were invented by Hamilton in 1843. Octonions were invented by Graves (1844) and Cayley (1845) independently.

In mathematics, a vector space commonly refers to a finite dimensional module over the real number field $\mathbb{R}$. An algebra A refers to a vector space that is equipped with a multiplication map $\times : A^2 \to A$ and a nonzero unit $1 \in A$ such that $1 \times a = a \times 1 = a$. The multiplication $a \times b$ is usually abbreviated as $a \cdot b$ or ab. An algebra A is a division algebra if, for any $a, b \in A$, $ab = 0$ implies either $a = 0$ or $b = 0$. Equivalently, A is a division algebra if and only if the operations of left and right multiplication by any nonzero element are invertible. A normed division algebra is an algebra that is also a normed vector space with $\|ab\| = \|a\|\|b\|$.

An algebra is power-associative if the sub-algebra generated by any single element is associative and an algebra is alternative if the sub-algebra generated by any two elements is associative. It is straightforward to show that if the sub-algebra generated by any three elements is associative, then the algebra itself is associative. Artin's theorem states that an algebra is alternative if and only if for all $a, b \in A$, we have

$$(aa)b = a(ab), \qquad (ab)a = a(ba), \qquad (ba)a = b(aa).$$

It is well known that $\mathbb{R}$, $\mathbb{C}$, $\mathbb{H}$, $\mathbb{O}$ are the only normed division algebras and $\mathbb{O}$ is an alternative division algebra. It is also known that division algebras can only have dimension 1, 2, 4, or 8.

Using the same approach of interpreting a complex number $a + bi$ as a pair $[a, b]$ of real numbers, quaternions $\mathbb{H}$ (respectively, octonions $\mathbb{O}$) can be constructed from $\mathbb{C}$ (respectively, from $\mathbb{H}$) using the Cayley-Dickson construction formula $[a, b]$ where $a, b \in \mathbb{C}$ (respectively, $a, b \in \mathbb{H}$). The addition and multiplication are defined as follows.

$$[a, b] + [c, d] = [a + c, b + d], \quad [a, b][c, d] = [ac - db^*, a^*d + cb] \qquad (2)$$

where $a, b, c, d \in \mathbb{C}$ (respectively, $a, b, c, d \in \mathbb{H}$) and a^* is the conjugate of a. The conjugate of a real number a is defined as $a^* = a$ and the conjugate of a complex number or a quaternion number $[a, b]$ is defined by $[a, b]^* = [a^*, -b]$. Throughout paper, we will use the following notations for real and imaginary part of an octonion $\mathbf{a} \in \mathbb{O}$,

$$\mathrm{Re}(\mathbf{a}) = (\mathbf{a} + \mathbf{a}^*)/2 \in \mathbb{R}, \qquad \mathrm{Im}(\mathbf{a}) = (\mathbf{a} - \mathbf{a}^*)/2.$$

It is straightforward to check that for numbers in $\mathbb{R}$, $\mathbb{C}$, $\mathbb{H}$, $\mathbb{O}$, we have

$$[a, b][a, b]^* = [a, b]^*[a, b] = \|[a, b]\|^2[1, 0].$$

Thus all of $\mathbb{R}$, $\mathbb{C}$, $\mathbb{H}$, $\mathbb{O}$ are division algebras (that is, each non-zero element has a multiplicative inverse).

Each octonion is a vector $\mathbf{a} = [a_0, \cdots, a_7] \in \mathbb{R}^8$. The norm of an octonion $\mathbf{a} = [a_0, \cdots, a_7]$ is defined as $\|\mathbf{a}\| = \sqrt{a_0^2 + \cdots + a_7^2}$. By the inductive Cayley-Dickson construction, the conjugate of an octonion $\mathbf{a}$ is $\mathbf{a}^* = [a_0, -a_1, \cdots, -a_7]$ and the inverse is $\mathbf{a}^{-1} = \mathbf{a}^*/\|\mathbf{a}\|^2$. For each octonion number $\mathbf{a} = [a_0, \cdots, a_7]$, let $\alpha = [a_1, \cdots, a_7]$ and

$$B_{\mathbf{a}} = \begin{pmatrix} a_0 & a_4 & a_7 & -a_2 & a_6 & -a_5 & -a_3 \\ -a_4 & a_0 & a_5 & a_1 & -a_3 & a_7 & -a_6 \\ -a_7 & -a_5 & a_0 & a_6 & a_2 & -a_4 & a_1 \\ a_2 & -a_1 & -a_6 & a_0 & a_7 & a_3 & -a_5 \\ -a_6 & a_3 & -a_2 & -a_7 & a_0 & a_1 & a_4 \\ a_5 & -a_7 & a_4 & -a_3 & -a_1 & a_0 & a_2 \\ a_3 & a_6 & -a_1 & a_5 & -a_4 & -a_2 & a_0 \end{pmatrix}$$

Using the matrix $B_{\mathbf{a}}$, we can define two associated 8×8 matrices

$$A_{\mathbf{a}}^l = \begin{pmatrix} a_0 & \alpha \\ -\alpha^T & B_{\mathbf{a}} \end{pmatrix} \quad \text{and} \quad A_{\mathbf{a}}^r = \begin{pmatrix} a_0 & \alpha \\ -\alpha^T & B_{\mathbf{a}}^T \end{pmatrix} \tag{3}$$

Then for two octonions $\mathbf{a} = [a_0, \cdots, a_7]$ and $\mathbf{b} = [b_0, \cdots, b_7]$, we can add them as $\mathbf{a} + \mathbf{b} = [a_0 + b_0, \cdots, a_7 + b_7]$ and multiply them as $\mathbf{ab} = \mathbf{b}A_{\mathbf{a}}^l = \mathbf{a}A_{\mathbf{b}}^r$. We also note that

$$A_{\mathbf{a}^{-1}}^l = \frac{1}{\|\mathbf{a}\|^2} \begin{pmatrix} a_0 & -\alpha \\ \alpha^T & B_{\mathbf{a}}^T \end{pmatrix} \quad \text{and} \quad A_{\mathbf{a}^{-1}}^r = \frac{1}{\|\mathbf{a}\|^2} \begin{pmatrix} a_0 & -\alpha \\ \alpha^T & B_{\mathbf{a}} \end{pmatrix} \tag{4}$$

For any octonion $\mathbf{a} = [a_0, \cdots, a_7]$, it is straightforward to show that

$$\begin{aligned} B_{\mathbf{a}}\alpha^T &= B_{\mathbf{a}}^T \alpha^T = a_0 \alpha^T \\ B_{\mathbf{a}}B_{\mathbf{a}} &= \alpha^T \alpha - \|\mathbf{a}\|^2 \mathbf{I}_{7\times7} + 2a_0 B_{\mathbf{a}} \\ B_{\mathbf{a}}^T B_{\mathbf{a}}^T &= \alpha^T \alpha - \|\mathbf{a}\|^2 \mathbf{I}_{7\times7} + 2a_0 B_{\mathbf{a}}^T \\ B_{\mathbf{a}}B_{\mathbf{a}}^T &= -\alpha^T \alpha + \|\mathbf{a}\|^2 \mathbf{I}_{7\times7} \\ B_{\mathbf{a}}^T B_{\mathbf{a}} &= -\alpha^T \alpha + \|\mathbf{a}\|^2 \mathbf{I}_{7\times7} \end{aligned} \tag{5}$$

Thus we have

$$A_{\mathbf{a}}^l A_{\mathbf{a}}^r = A_{\mathbf{a}}^r A_{\mathbf{a}}^l = \begin{pmatrix} a_0^2 - \alpha\alpha^T & 2a_0\alpha \\ -2a_0\alpha^T & -\alpha^T\alpha + B_{\mathbf{a}}B_{\mathbf{a}}^T \end{pmatrix} \tag{6}$$

By substituting (5) into (6), we get

$$A_{\mathbf{a}}^l A_{\mathbf{a}}^r = A_{\mathbf{a}}^r A_{\mathbf{a}}^l = \begin{pmatrix} 2a_0^2 - \|\mathbf{a}\|^2 & 2a_0\alpha \\ -2a_0\alpha^T & -2\alpha^T\alpha + \|\mathbf{a}\|^2 \mathbf{I}_{7\times7} \end{pmatrix} \tag{7}$$

Similarly, we can get

$$\begin{aligned} A_{\mathbf{a}}^l A_{\mathbf{a}}^l &= 2a_0 A_{\mathbf{a}}^l - \|\mathbf{a}\|^2 \mathbf{I}_{8\times8} \\ A_{\mathbf{a}}^r A_{\mathbf{a}}^r &= 2a_0 A_{\mathbf{a}}^r - \|\mathbf{a}\|^2 \mathbf{I}_{8\times8} \end{aligned} \tag{8}$$

Finally, it is easy to check that $A_{\mathbf{a}}^l A_{\mathbf{a}^{-1}}^l = A_{\mathbf{a}^{-1}}^l A_{\mathbf{a}}^l = A_{\mathbf{a}}^r A_{\mathbf{a}^{-1}}^r = A_{\mathbf{a}^{-1}}^r A_{\mathbf{a}}^r = \mathbf{I}_{8\times8}$. But generally, we have $A_{\mathbf{a}}^l A_{\mathbf{a}^{-1}}^r \neq \mathbf{I}_{8\times8}$. We conclude this section with the following theorem that will be used frequently throughout this paper.

Theorem 2. *For $\mathbf{a} \in \mathbb{O}$, we have $\mathbf{a}^2 = 2\mathrm{Re}(\mathbf{a})\mathbf{a} - \|\mathbf{a}\|^2 \mathbf{1}$ where $\mathbf{1} = [1, 0, 0, 0, 0, 0, 0, 0]$.*

Proof. The identity $\mathbf{a}^* = 2\mathrm{Re}(\mathbf{a})\mathbf{1} - \mathbf{a}$ implies $\|\mathbf{a}\|^2 = \mathbf{a}\mathbf{a}^* = 2\mathrm{Re}(\mathbf{a})\mathbf{a} - \mathbf{a}^2$. $\quad\square$

Y. Wang and Q.M. Malluhi

Theorem 3. *For all* $\mathbf{a}, \mathbf{b} \in \mathbb{O}$, *we have* $(\mathbf{ab})^* = \mathbf{b}^*\mathbf{a}^*$.

Proof. By the fact that the octonion algebra is alternative, we have $(\mathbf{ab})(\mathbf{b}^*\mathbf{a}^*) = \mathbf{a}(\mathbf{bb}^*)\mathbf{a}^* = \|\mathbf{a}\|^2\|\mathbf{b}\|^2$. Thus $(\mathbf{ab})^{-1} = (\mathbf{b}^*\mathbf{a}^*)/(\|\mathbf{a}\|^2\|\mathbf{b}\|^2)$. The theorem follows from the fact that $(\mathbf{ab})^{-1} = (\mathbf{ab})^*/(\|\mathbf{ab}\|^2)$. $\qquad\square$

4 Octonions $\mathbb{O}(\mathbb{Z}_q)$ over $\mathbb{Z}_q$

In the preceding section, we briefly discussed the properties of octonions. Instead of using real numbers, one may also construct "octonions" over any field $\mathbb{F}_q$ with $q = p^m$ or over any ring $\mathbb{Z}_q$ with $q = p_1^{r_1} \cdots p_m^{r_m}$. In this section, we discuss octonions $\mathbb{O}(\mathbb{Z}_q)$ over $\mathbb{Z}_q$. Generally, all theorems except division-related results for octonions hold in $\mathbb{O}(\mathbb{Z}_q)$. It is straightforward to show that $\mathbb{O}(\mathbb{Z}_q)$ is a normed algebra. However, it is not a division algebra. In our FHE schemes, the division operation is not used.

An octonion $\mathbf{z} \in \mathbb{O}(\mathbb{Z}_q)$ is isotropic if $\|\mathbf{z}\| = 0$. By Theorem 6.26 in Lidl and Niederreiter [10, p. 282], there are $q^7 + q^4 - q^3 = (q^4 - 1)(q^3 + 1) + 1$ isotropic vectors in $\mathbb{F}_q^8$. A slightly modified proof of the Theorem 6.26 in [10] could be used to show that the number of isotropic vectors in $\mathbb{Z}_q^8$ is approximately in the same order of $q^7 + q^4 - q^3$ (the exact number is not important for our construction of the FHE scheme and the details are omitted here). A subspace V of $\mathbb{Z}_q^8$ is called totally singular or totally isotropic if all vectors in V are isotropic.

For an odd q and even n, the number of totally isotropic subspaces of dimension $k \leq n/2$ in $\mathbb{F}_q^n$ is given by the formula (see Pless [11] or Dembowski [5, p. 47])

$$\frac{(q^{n-k} - q^{n/2-k} + q^{n/2} - 1) \prod_{i=1}^{k-1}(q^{n-2i} - 1)}{\prod_{i=1}^{k}(q^i - 1)}, \tag{9}$$

and totally isotropic subspaces of dimension $k > n/2$ in $\mathbb{F}_q^n$ do not exist. It follows that the number of dimension 4 totally isotropic subspaces of $\mathbb{F}_q^8$ is given by

$$2(q + 1)(q^2 + 1)(q^3 + 1) \tag{10}$$

Similar results for the number of totally isotropic subspaces of dimension k over $\mathbb{Z}_q^n$ could be obtained and the details are omitted in this paper.

Let $\mathbf{a} \in \mathbb{O}(\mathbb{Z}_q)$ be a non-zero isotropic octonion. Then $\mathbf{aa}^* = \|\mathbf{a}\|^2 = 0$. That is, $\mathbf{a}$ has no multiplicative inverse. It follows that $\mathbb{O}(\mathbb{Z}_q)$ is not a division algebra. This also shows that $\mathbb{O}(\mathbb{Z}_q)$ is not nicely normed. Note that an algebra over $\mathbb{Z}_q$ is nicely normed if $\mathbf{a} + \mathbf{a}^* \in \mathbb{Z}_q$ and $\mathbf{aa}^* = \mathbf{a}^*\mathbf{a} > 0$ for all non zero $\mathbf{a} \in \mathbb{O}(\mathbb{Z}_q)$.

It is straightforward that Theorem 2 holds for $\mathbb{O}(\mathbb{Z}_q)$. We use an alternative proof to show that Theorem 3 holds for $\mathbb{O}(\mathbb{Z}_q)$ also. Note that the proof of Theorem 3 is not valid for $\mathbb{O}(\mathbb{Z}_q)$ since it uses octonion inverse properties.

Theorem 4. *For all* $\mathbf{a}, \mathbf{b} \in \mathbb{O}(\mathbb{Z}_q)$, *we have* $(\mathbf{ab})^* = \mathbf{b}^*\mathbf{a}^*$.

Proof. By the Definition in (3), we have $A_{\mathbf{a}*}^r = (A_{\mathbf{a}}^r)^T$. First, the identity $\mathbf{1b^*a^*} = \mathbf{1}(A_{\mathbf{b}}^r)^T(A_{\mathbf{a}}^r)^T = \mathbf{1}(A_{\mathbf{a}}^r A_{\mathbf{b}}^r)^T$ implies that $\mathbf{b^*a^*}$ is the first column of $A_{\mathbf{a}}^r A_{\mathbf{b}}^r$. Secondly, the identity $\mathbf{1ab} = \mathbf{1}(A_{\mathbf{a}}^r A_{\mathbf{b}}^r)$ implies that $(\mathbf{ab})^*$ is also the first column of $A_{\mathbf{a}}^r A_{\mathbf{b}}^r$. It follows that $(\mathbf{ab})^* = \mathbf{b^*a^*}$. $\qquad\square$

Finally, Theorem 2 implies the following result.

Theorem 5. *For an isotropic octonion* $\mathbf{a} \in \mathbb{O}(\mathbb{Z}_q)$, *we have* $\mathbf{a}^2 = 2\mathrm{Re}(\mathbf{a})\mathbf{a}$.

5 The Exceptional Lie Group G_2 and Its Finite Version $G_2(q)$

A Lie algebra $\mathfrak{g}$ over a field $\mathbb{F}$ is a vector space over $\mathbb{F}$ with a bilinear map (called a bracket or a commutator) $[\cdot,\cdot] : \mathfrak{g} \times \mathfrak{g} \to \mathfrak{g}$ with the following properties:

– Anti-commutativity: $[y,x] = -[x,y]$ for all $x, y \in \mathbb{F}$
– Jordan identity: $[[x,y],z] + [[y,z],x] + [[z,x],y] = 0$ for all $x, y, z \in \mathbb{F}$.

The classical example of Lie algebra is the special linear algebra $\mathfrak{sl}_n$ of $n \times n$ matrices of trace 0 with $[x,y] = xy - yx$. The Lie algebra $\mathfrak{sl}_n$ corresponds to the Lie group SL_n of determinant 1 matrices.

The automorphism group G_2 of octonions $\mathbb{O}$ (over $\mathbb{R}$) has dimension 14 and is the smallest among the ten families of exceptional Lie groups (G_2, F_4, E_6, E_7, E_8, $^2E_6$, $^3D_4$, $^2B_2$, $^2G_2$, and $^2F_4$). The corresponding Lie algebra $\mathfrak{g}_2$ for G_2 is the derivations $\mathfrak{Der}(\mathbb{O})$ of the octonions $\mathbb{O}$. We will use $G_2(q)$ to denote the finite automorphism group of octonions $\mathbb{O}(\mathbb{Z}_q)$. It should be noted that in the literature, the notation $G_2(q)$ is generally used to denote the finite automorphism group of octonions $\mathbb{O}(\mathbb{F}_q)$ over a finite field $\mathbb{F}_q$. However, for the finite automorphism group related results that we will use in this paper, they hold for $G_2(q)$ over $\mathbb{O}(\mathbb{Z}_q)$ as well as for $G_2(q)$ over $\mathbb{O}(\mathbb{F}_q)$.

A basic triple for octonions $\mathbb{O}(\mathbb{Z}_q)$ is three elements $\mathbf{e}_1, \mathbf{e}_2, \mathbf{e}_3$ of norm -1 such that

– $\mathbf{e}_1\mathbf{e}_2 = -\mathbf{e}_2\mathbf{e}_1$, $\mathbf{e}_2\mathbf{e}_3 = -\mathbf{e}_3\mathbf{e}_2$, and $\mathbf{e}_1\mathbf{e}_3 = -\mathbf{e}_3\mathbf{e}_1$.
– $(\mathbf{e}_1\mathbf{e}_2)\mathbf{e}_3 = -\mathbf{e}_3(\mathbf{e}_1\mathbf{e}_2)$.

It is straightforward to observe that $\mathbf{e}_1$ generates a sub-algebra of $\mathbb{O}(\mathbb{Z}_q)$ that is isomorphic to $\mathbb{C}(\mathbb{Z}_q)$, $(\mathbf{e}_1, \mathbf{e}_2)$ generates a sub-algebra of $\mathbb{O}(\mathbb{Z}_q)$ that is isomorphic to $\mathbb{H}(\mathbb{Z}_q)$, and $(\mathbf{e}_1, \mathbf{e}_2, \mathbf{e}_3)$ generates all $\mathbb{O}(\mathbb{Z}_q)$. In other words, given $(\mathbf{e}_1, \mathbf{e}_2, \mathbf{e}_3)$, there is a unique way to define the imaginary octonion units $i_1, \cdots, i_7$. It follows that given any two basic triples, there exists a unique automorphism in $G_2(q)$ that maps the first triple to the second triple. We can interpret this observation as follows to determine the size of $G_2(q)$. In order to construct an automorphism in $G_2(q)$, one first maps $\mathbf{e}_1$ to any point $\mathbf{e}_1'$ on the 6-sphere of unit imaginary octonions, then maps $\mathbf{e}_2$ to any point $\mathbf{e}_2'$ on the 5-sphere of unit imaginary octonions that are orthogonal to $\mathbf{e}_1'$, and finally maps $\mathbf{e}_3$ to any point $\mathbf{e}_3'$ on the 3-sphere of unit imaginary octonions that are orthogonal to $\mathbf{e}_1', \mathbf{e}_2'$, and $\mathbf{e}_1'\mathbf{e}_2'$. By counting the number of such kind of triples, one can show that $|G_2(q)| = q^6(q^6 - 1)(q^2 - 1)$.

6 Fully Homomorphic Encryption Scheme OctoM

In this section, we introduce an efficient noise-free symmetric key FHE scheme OctoM. It is shown in the next section that the scheme OctoM is secure in the weak ciphertext-only security model. A totally isotropic subspace $V \subset \mathbb{Z}_q^8$ is said to be closed under octonion multiplications if for any $\mathbf{r}_0, \mathbf{r}_1 \in V$, we have both $\mathbf{r}_0\mathbf{r}_1 \in V$ and $\mathbf{r}_1\mathbf{r}_0 \in V$ where $\mathbf{r}_0\mathbf{r}_1$ and $\mathbf{r}_1\mathbf{r}_0$ are the octonion multiplications (based on the definition, we may also call such kind of subspaces as "totally isotropic ideal subspaces"). By Theorem 5, for any isotropic vector $\mathbf{z} \in \mathbb{Z}_q^8$, we have $\mathbf{z}^2 = 2\mathrm{Re}(\mathbf{z})\mathbf{z}$. Thus for any nonzero isotropic vector $\mathbf{z} \in \mathbb{Z}_q^8$, span$\{\mathbf{z}\}$ is a dimension one totally isotropic subspace that is closed under octonion multiplications. The comment 2 in Sect. 7 will show that there exist dimension two totally isotropic subspaces that are closed under octonion multiplications. By formulas (9) and (10) in Sect. 4, there exist dimension 3 and 4 totally isotropic subspaces for octonions $\mathbb{Z}_q^8$. It is also known that there is no dimension $d \geq 5$ totally isotropic subspace for octonions $\mathbb{Z}_q^8$. It remains an open question whether there exist dimension 3 or 4 totally isotropic subspaces in $\mathbb{Z}_q^8$ that are closed under octonion multiplications.

It is noted that a totally isotropic subspace V of dimension d is uniquely determined by d isotropic octonions (that is, a basis of the subspace). For the construction of FHE scheme OctoM, it suffices to have a dimension one totally isotropic subspace that is closed under octonion multiplications. In the following, we present the FHE protocol using the parameter $q = p_1 p_2$. The protocol could be implemented over any finite rings $\mathbb{Z}_q$ with $q = p_1^{r_1} \cdots p_m^{r_m}$ and $m \geq 3$. In the following, we will use i to denote the octonion $[0, 1, 0, 0, 0, 0, 0, 0]$.

Key setup. Select $q = p_1 p_2$ according to the given security parameter κ. Select a totally isotropic subspace $V \subset \mathbb{Z}_q^8$ that is closed under octonion multiplications. Select a random $\phi \in G_2(q)$ and a random invertible 8×8 matrix $K \in \mathbb{Z}_q^{8 \times 8}$. The private key is (K, ϕ, V) and the system public parameter is $\mathbb{Z}_q$.

Encryption. For a message $m \in \mathbb{Z}_q$, choose random $r \in \mathbb{Z}_q$ and $\mathbf{z} \in V$ with the property that $|A_{\mathbf{m}'}^l| = 0$, where $\mathbf{m}' = \phi(mi + \mathbf{z})$ and $A_{\mathbf{m}'}^l$ is the associated matrix for the octonion number $\mathbf{m}'$. Note that such kind of r and $\mathbf{z}$ could be chosen in constant rounds since the probability for $|A_{\mathbf{m}'}^l| = 0$ converges to a uniform limit (see, e.g., [4]). Let the ciphertext $C_m = \texttt{OctoM.Enc}(\text{key}, m) = K^{-1} A_{\mathbf{m}'}^l K \in \mathbb{Z}_q^{8 \times 8}$.

Decryption. For a received ciphertext $C_{\mathbf{m}}$, decrypt the plaintext as

$$m = \texttt{OctoM.Dec}(\text{key}, C_m) = \phi^{-1}(\mathbf{1}(K C_m K^{-1})) \mod V$$

where $\mod V$ means to remove the components in the subspace V. It should be noted that $\mathbf{1}(K C_m K^{-1}) = \mathbf{1} A_{\mathbf{m}'} = \mathbf{m}'$. In order to carry out homomorphic operations on the ciphertext, the owner also needs to publish a ciphertext of -1. That is, let C_{-1} be the ciphertext of -1.

Ciphertext addition. The addition of ciphertexts C_{m_0} and C_{m_1} is defined as the regular component wise matrix addition $C_{m_0+m_1} = C_{m_0} + C_{m_1}$.

Ciphertext multiplication. The multiplication of ciphertexts C_{m_0} and C_{m_1} is defined as the regular matrix multiplication $C_{m_0 m_1} = C_{m_1} C_{m'_0} = K^{-1} A^l_{\mathbf{m}'_1} K K^{-1} A^l_{\mathbf{m}_0} K = K^{-1} A^l_{\mathbf{m}_1} A^l_{\mathbf{m}_0} K$.

It is straightforward to verify that the above encryption scheme is additive homomorphic. The multiplication homomorphic property follows from the following equations.

$$
\begin{aligned}
&\texttt{OctoM.Dec}(\texttt{key}, C_{m_0 m_1}) \\
&= \phi^{-1}(\mathbf{1}(A^l_{\mathbf{m}'_1} A^l_{\mathbf{m}'_0} A^l_{-1})) \mod V \\
&= \phi^{-1}(\mathbf{m}'_0(\mathbf{m}'_1 \cdot (-i + \mathbf{z}_2))) \mod V \\
&= \phi^{-1}(\phi(m_0 i + \mathbf{z}_0) \phi(m_1 i + \mathbf{z}_1) \phi(-i + \mathbf{z}_2)) \mod V \\
&= (m_0 i)(m_1 i)(-i) \\
&= m_0 m_1 i.
\end{aligned}
$$

We conclude this section by showing that the decryption process of $\texttt{OctoM}$ is equivalent to the decryption process $\texttt{IPE.Dec}$ of a dimension 64 IPE scheme of Sect. 2. Let $\texttt{key} = (K, \phi, V) = \texttt{OctoM.KeySetup}(\kappa)$ be the secret key of the encryption scheme $\texttt{OctoM}$. Let $\beta = [b_1, 1, b_2, \cdots, b_7] \in \mathbb{Z}_q^8$ be a vector that is orthogonal to $\phi(V)$. Then $\phi(mi + \mathbf{z})\beta^T = mi$. For a ciphertext C_m, let $\text{vec}(C_m) = [c_{0,0}, \cdots, c_{7,0}, \cdots, c_{7,7}]^T$ be the vectorization of C_m. The decryption process $\texttt{OctoM.Dec}(\texttt{key}, C_m)$ could be reformulated as

$$
\begin{aligned}
mi &= \phi(mi + \mathbf{z})\beta^T \\
&= (\mathbf{1} K C_m K^{-1})\beta^T \\
&= \left[\sum_{i,j=0}^{7} a_{0,i,j} c_{i,j}, \cdots, \sum_{i,j=0}^{7} a_{7,i,j} c_{i,j} \right] \beta^T \\
&= \sum_{i,j=0}^{7} k_{i,j} c_{i,j} \\
&= \mathbf{k} \cdot \text{vec}(C_m) \\
&= \texttt{IPE.Dec}(\mathbf{k}, \text{vec}(C_m))
\end{aligned}
\tag{11}
$$

for some $a_{0,i,j}, \cdots, a_{7,i,j} \in \mathbb{Z}_q$ and $\mathbf{k} = [k_{0,0}, \cdots, k_{0,7}, k_{1,0}, \cdots, k_{7,7}] \in \mathbb{Z}_q^{64}$.

7   Some Comments on the Design of OctoM

In this section, we present some comments on the design principles of $\texttt{OctoM}$. The first time reader may skip this section.

Comment 1: In the encryption scheme $\texttt{OctoM}$, the message m is encoded to $\mathbf{m}' = \phi(mi + \mathbf{z})$ with a randomly selected octonion $\mathbf{z}$ from a totally isotropic subspace that is closed under octonion multiplications. As a special case of the scheme, one can choose a random isotropic octonion $\mathbf{z}_0$ and let $V = \text{span}\{\mathbf{z}_0\}$. That is, each message m is encoded to $\mathbf{m}' = \phi(mi + r\mathbf{z}_0)$ for randomly selected $r \in \mathbb{Z}_q$.

Comment 2: In order to construct a dimension 2 totally isotropic subspace $V \subset \mathbb{Z}_q^8$, it suffices to choose linearly independent isotropic octonions $\mathbf{z}_0, \mathbf{z}_1$

(which forms a basis of V) in such a way that $r_0\mathbf{z}_0 + r_1\mathbf{z}_1$ is isotropic for all $r_0, r_1 \in \mathbb{Z}_q$. First we note that

$$
\begin{aligned}
\|r_0\mathbf{z}_0 + r_1\mathbf{z}_1\|^2 &= (r_0\mathbf{z}_0 + r_1\mathbf{z}_1)(r_0\mathbf{z}_0^* + r_1\mathbf{z}_1^*) \\
&= r_0 r_1 \mathbf{z}_0 \mathbf{z}_1^* + r_0 r_1 \mathbf{z}_1 \mathbf{z}_0^* \\
&= r_0 r_1 (\mathbf{z}_0 \mathbf{z}_1^* + (\mathbf{z}_0 \mathbf{z}_1^*)^*) \\
&= 2 r_0 r_1 \mathrm{Re}(\mathbf{z}_0 \mathbf{z}_1^*).
\end{aligned}
$$

Thus, for any nonzero octonions $\mathbf{z}_0, \mathbf{z}_1$ satisfying

$$
\|\mathbf{z}_0\| = \|\mathbf{z}_1\| = \mathrm{Re}(\mathbf{z}_0 \mathbf{z}_1^*) = 0, \tag{12}
$$

the subspace $\mathrm{span}(\mathbf{z}_0, \mathbf{z}_1)$ is a dimension 2 totally isotropic subspace of $\mathbb{Z}_q^8$. In order to construct a totally isotropic subspace V that is closed under octonion multiplications, it suffices to choose linearly independent isotropic octonions $\mathbf{z}_0, \mathbf{z}_1 \in \mathbb{Z}_q^8$ such that the identity (12) holds and there exist $r_0, r_1, r_2, r_3 \in \mathbb{Z}_q$ satisfying

$$
\begin{aligned}
\mathbf{z}_0\mathbf{z}_1 &= r_0\mathbf{z}_0 + r_1\mathbf{z}_1 \\
\mathbf{z}_1\mathbf{z}_0 &= r_2\mathbf{z}_0 + r_3\mathbf{z}_1
\end{aligned} \tag{13}
$$

Combing identities (12) and (13), we get 19 equations with 20 unknowns. Thus there exist dimension 2 totally isotropic subspaces $V \subset \mathbb{Z}_q^8$ that are closed under octonion multiplications. For $k \geq 3$, we conjecture that there exists no dimension k totally isotropic subspaces $V \subset \mathbb{Z}_q^8$ that are closed under octonion multiplication.

8   Proof of Security

The preceding section shows that the decryption process of the scheme OctoM is equivalent to the decryption process of the dimension 64 IPE. Thus the scheme OctoM is not secure against adversaries who have access to sufficiently many linearly independent ciphertexts with known plaintexts. Furthermore, by Theorem 1, OctoM is not secure in the ciphertext only attack (COA) security model. In this section, we show that OctoM is secure in the weak ciphertext-only (wCOA) security model.

We first show OctoM is secure in the wCOA model assuming that the only attack one could mount on OctoM is to guess the IPE decryption key via ciphertexts only without using the homomorphic properties and without using other algebraic attacks. Since the decryption process of OctoM is equivalent to IPE.Dec, it is sufficient for the adversary to recover the inner product decryption secret $\mathbf{k}$. Though we think that it is a folklore that the probability for one to recover the IPE.Dec secret $\mathbf{k}$ from IPE ciphertexts only is negligible (without limit on the number of ciphertexts), we did not find a literature reference for this. For completeness, we present a proof for this "folklore".

Theorem 6. *Let κ be the security parameter, $n \leq t \leq poly(\kappa)$, and assume that the plaintext messages are uniformly distributed over $\mathbb{Z}_q$. Given t ciphertexts $c_0, \cdots, c_{t-1} \in \mathbb{Z}_q^n$ of a dimension n encryption scheme IPE, the probability for one to guess the correct private key $\mathbf{k} \in \mathbb{Z}_q^n$ or for one to guess at least one correct plaintext for the given ciphertexts is at most $\frac{1}{q^n}$. In other words, the scheme IPE is secure in wCOA.*

Proof. For the given t ciphertexts, one can formulate t linear equations in $t + n$ variables $\mathbf{m} = [m_0, \cdots, m_{t-1}]$ and $\mathbf{k} = [k_0, \cdots, k_{n-1}]$:

$$\mathbf{k}[\mathbf{c}_0^T, \cdots, \mathbf{c}_{t-1}^T] = \mathbf{m}. \tag{14}$$

Assume that the ciphertexts $c_0, \cdots, c_{n-1}$ are linearly independent. Then for any fixed $m_0, \cdots, m_{n-1} \in \mathbb{Z}_q$, the equation system (14) has a unique solution. On the other hand, if no n ciphertexts are linearly independent, then for any fixed $m_0, \cdots, m_{n-1} \in \mathbb{Z}_q$, there are more than one solutions for the equation system (14). In a summary, the probability that the adversary recovers the private key is less than or equal to the probability that the adversary has a correct guess of the messages $m_0, \cdots, m_{n-1}$. This probability is at most $\frac{1}{q^n}$. Thus the Theorem is proved. $\qquad\square$

Before proving the main theorem, we first prove a Lemma. For a ciphertext C_m, we use C_m^0 to denote the identity matrix I.

Lemma 1. *Let $C_m = \texttt{OctoM.Enc}(\mathbf{key}, m)$ and $C_m^2, \cdots, C_m^8$ be ciphertexts of $m^2, \cdots, m^8$ respectively. Then $\text{vec}(C_m^0) = \text{vec}(\mathbf{I}), \text{vec}(C_m^1), \text{vec}(C_m^2)$ are linearly dependent.*

Proof. By (8), we know that for any octonion $\mathbf{a}$, we have $A_{\mathbf{a}}^l A_{\mathbf{a}}^l = 2a_0 A_{\mathbf{a}}^l - \|\mathbf{a}\|^2 \mathbf{I}_{8\times 8}$. It follows that $C_m^2 = K^{-1} A_{\mathbf{a}}^l A_{\mathbf{a}}^l K = 2a_0 C_m^1 - \|\mathbf{m}'\|^2 \mathbf{I}_{8\times 8}$. The Lemma is proved. $\qquad\square$

Theorem 7. *Assuming that it is computationally infeasible to solve multivariate/univariate quadratic equation systems in $\mathbb{Z}_q$, and the plaintext messages are uniformly distributed over $\mathbb{Z}_q$. Then the encryption scheme OctoM over $\mathbb{Z}_q$ is $(t, negl(\kappa))$-secure in the weak ciphertext-only security model for any $t \leq poly(\kappa)$.*

Proof. Let $C_{p_0}, \cdots, C_{p_{t-1}}$ be the ciphertext output by the PPT algorithm A_0. By Theorem 6, if the most efficient attack on OctoM in the weak ciphertext-only security model is to recover the IPE decryption key from ciphertexts without employing fully homomorphic or other algebraic properties, then the theorem follows from Theorem 6 already. Thus it is sufficient to show that it is computationally infeasible to use fully homomorphic properties and other algebraic attacks to recover the secret key or to recover secret messages for OctoM.

In the following, we established two claims to show that the problem of recovering OctoM's secret key (K, ϕ, V) from ciphertexts could be reduced to the problem of solving multivariate quadratic equation systems and the problem of recovering a secret message from OctoM's ciphertexts could be reduced to the problem of solving univariate high degree equation systems. By the hardness assumption of the theorem, these equation systems are computationally infeasible to be solved.

Claim 8. *Given t ciphertexts for the FHE scheme* OctoM, *the problem of finding the private key (K, ϕ, V) and corresponding private messages could be reduced to a multivariate quadratic equation system with $64t$ equations in $64 + 2t$ unknown variables.*

Proof. As a warming up exercise, we first show that, given t ciphertexts, one can obtain $64t$ equations in $64 + 8t$ or $64 + 8d + (d+1)t$ unknown variables where $d = \dim(V)$. For each ciphertext C_m, we have the identity $KC_m = A_{\mathbf{m}'}^l K$. If we assign 8 variables for $\mathbf{m}' = mi + \mathbf{r}$ and 64 variables for K. Then we get 64 equations in $64 + 8$ unknowns. For t ciphertexts, we obtain $64t$ equations in $64 + 8t$ unknowns. Alternatively, let d be the dimension of V (in our case, $d = 1$ or $d = 2$). Then we can assign $8d$ variables for a basis of V, d variables for $\mathbf{r}$ (note that $\mathbf{r}$ is uniquely determined by the d coordinates relative to the basis), and one variable for each message m. In other words, each ciphertext could be converted to 64 equations in $64 + 8d + d + 1$ unknowns and t ciphertext could be converted to $64t$ equations in $64 + 8d + (d+1)t$ unknowns.

We next reduce the number of unknown variables to $64 + 2t$ by using the homomorphic properties of OctoM. Let C_m be the ciphertext and $\mathbf{m}' = \phi(mi + \mathbf{r}) = [m_0, \cdots, m_7]$ where $\mathbf{r} \in V$. From the identity $KC_m = A_{\mathbf{m}'}^l K$ for the ciphertext C_m and by Lemma 1, we have

$$KC_m^2 = 2m_0 KC_m - \|\mathbf{m}'\|^2 K \tag{15}$$

If we consider $\|\mathbf{m}'\|^2$ as one variable, the identities (15) can be used to derive 64 multivariate quadratic equations in 66 variables (64 for K, one for m_0, and one for $\|\mathbf{m}'\|^2$). For t ciphertexts, one obtains $64t$ quadratic multivariate polynomial equation in $64 + 2t$ variables.   □

Claim 9. *Given one ciphertext C for the FHE scheme* OctoM, *the problem of finding the secret message m could be reduced to the problem of solving a univariate quadratic equation.*

Proof. Let $C_m = $ OctoM.Enc$(\mathbf{key}, m)$ be a ciphertext of m and $\mathbf{m}' = [m_0, \cdots, m_7] = [r_0, m + r_1, \cdots, r_7]$. By Lemma 1 and using the values of C_m and C_m^2, one learns the values of $\|\mathbf{m}'\|^2 = r_0^2 + (m + r_1)^2 + r_2^2 + \cdots + r_7^2$ and $m_1 = m + r_1$. Since $r_0^2 + \cdots + r_7^2 = 0$, one obtains $m^2 + 2mr_1 = \|\mathbf{m}'\|^2$. This completes the proof of the Claim.   □

By Claims 8 and 9, in order for one to recover the secret key or secret messages from the ciphertexts, one needs to solve a quadratic univariate polynomial equation in Claim 9 or to solve the multivariate equation system in Claim 8. By the assumption, it is computationally infeasible to solve univariate nonlinear polynomial equations over $\mathbb{Z}_q$ obtained in Claim 9. In the following, we show that it is computationally infeasible to solve the multivariate equation systems obtained in Claim 8.

For a system of $n(n + 1)/2$ homogeneous quadratic equations with n variables $x_0, \cdots, x_{n-1}$, the folklore linearization technique replaces each quadratic monomial $x_i x_j$ with a new variable y_{ij} and obtains $n(n + 1)/2$ linear equations with $n(n + 1)/2$ variables. The resulting equation system could be efficiently solved using Gauss elimination algorithm. The value of the original variable x_i can be recovered as one of the square roots of y_{ii}. Kipnis and Shamir [8] introduced a relinearization algorithm to solve quadratic equation systems with $l \geq 0.09175n^2$ linearly independent homogeneous quadratic equations in n variables. This is achieved by adding additional nonlinear equations. In the simplest form, we have $(x_{i_0} x_{i_1})(x_{i_2} x_{i_3}) = (x_{i_0} x_{i_2})(x_{i_1} x_{i_3}) = (x_{i_0} x_{i_3})(x_{i_1} x_{i_2})$. Thus we can add $y_{i_0 i_1} y_{i_2 i_3} = y_{i_0 i_2} y_{i_1 i_3} = y_{i_0 i_3} y_{i_1 i_2}$.

For the quadratic equation system obtained in Claim 8, there are $64t$ (not necessarily homogeneous) quadratic equations in $64 + 2t$ variables. Thus the relinearization algorithm in Kipnis and Shamir [8] might be applied to the equation system in Claim 8 only if $11 \leq t \leq 100$. Note that in order to apply the relinearization algorithm, these quadratic equations need to be converted to homogeneous quadratic equations first. Furthermore, the last step in the relinearization approach is to compute square roots in $\mathbb{Z}_q$. By the assumption of the theorem, this is computationally infeasible over $\mathbb{Z}_q$. For $t \leq 10$ and $t \geq 101$, the linearization and re-linearization approaches could not be applied to the equation systems constructed in Claim 8 since there is insufficient number of equations.

The most popular algorithm for solving multivariate polynomial equation systems over finite fields is Buchberger's Gröbner basis algorithm based on S-polynomials (see, e.g., [12]). The Gröbner basis algorithm is designed for polynomials over finite fields and the algorithm will not work in case any of the required inverses does not exist during the monomial elimination process. However, the algorithm could continue for polynomials over the ring $\mathbb{Z}_q$ in case all of the required inverses do exist. Indeed, we may assume that the algorithm can always continue since the probability for finding a non-invertible element is negligible (which is equivalent to finding a factor of q). However, it should also be noted that the last essential step for Gröbner basis algorithm family is to solve a univariate high degree polynomial equation which is computationally infeasible in $\mathbb{Z}_q$ by the theorem assumption. In summary, with the assumption of the theorem, it is computationally infeasible to solve the equation systems constructed in Claim 8. □

9   FHE over Other Algebras Such as Jordan Algebra

The preceding sections propose a fully homomorphic encryption scheme based on octonion algebra. One may wonder whether it is possible to use other normed finite algebras corresponding to $\mathbb{R}$, $\mathbb{C}$, $\mathbb{H}$, etc. to design FHE schemes. There is only one norm preserving automorphism (identity map) for $\mathbb{R}$. There are two norm preserving automorphisms (the identity map and the dual map) for $\mathbb{C}$. In addition to these two automorphisms for $\mathbb{C}$, there are infinitely many "wild" automorphisms for the complex number $\mathbb{C}$. For $\mathbb{H}$, the norm preserving automorphism is the group of real-linear transformations of $\text{Im}(\mathbb{H})$ preserving the cross product $a \times b = \frac{1}{2}(ab - ba)$. Thus the automorphism group for $\mathbb{H}$ is just the special orthogonal group $\text{SO}(3)$. That is, the group of 3×3 orthogonal matrices of determinant 1.

The corresponding finite algebras for the four division algebras are $\mathbb{F}_q$, $\mathbb{C}(\mathbb{F}_q)$, $\mathbb{H}(\mathbb{F}_q)$, and $\mathbb{O}(\mathbb{F}_q)$. For $\mathbb{F}_q$ with $q = p^m$, there are exactly m Frobenius automorphisms for $\mathbb{F}_q$ which are given by $\varphi^k : x \mapsto x^{p^k}$ for $0 \leq k < m$. It should be noted that all Frobenius automorphism fixes elements in $\mathbb{F}_q$. For $\mathbb{C}(\mathbb{F}_q)$, the automorphisms could be obtained by combining the Frobenius automorphism and the dual automorphism. The automorphism group for $\mathbb{H}(\mathbb{F}_q)$ could be obtained by combining the Frobenius automorphism and the special orthogonal group $\text{SO}(3, \mathbb{F}_q)$. Based on these facts, it is straightforward to check that it is insecure to use automorphism groups of $\mathbb{F}_q$ and $\mathbb{C}(\mathbb{F}_q)$ to design fully homomorphic encryption schemes.

In order to use the automorphism group for $\mathbb{H}(\mathbb{Z}_q)$ to design fully homomorphic encryption schemes, it is necessary to guarantee that the size of the automorphism group $\text{SO}(3)$ for $\mathbb{H}(\mathbb{Z}_q)$, the number of isotropic vectors in $\mathbb{Z}_q^4$, and the number of totally isotropic dimension 2 subspaces of $\mathbb{Z}_q^4$ are sufficiently large. By Theorem 6.26 of Lidl and Niederreiter [10, page 282], there are $q^3 + q(q-1)\eta(-1)$ isotropic vectors in $\mathbb{F}_q^4$, where η is the quadratic character of $\mathbb{F}_q$. That is, $\eta(-1) = 1$ if there is $x \in \mathbb{F}_q$ such that $x^2 = -1$. Otherwise, $\eta(-1) = -1$. By (9), the number of totally isotropic dimension 2 subspaces of $\mathbb{F}_q^4$ is $2(q + 1)$. These arguments could be revised to show that the number of isotropic vectors in $\mathbb{Z}_q^4$ and the number of totally isotropic dimension 2 subspaces of $\mathbb{Z}_q^4$ are large enough for the design of an FHE scheme QuatM over $\mathbb{H}(\mathbb{Z}_q)$ in the same way that OctoM is designed. The security analysis for QuatM is the same as that for OctoM. In particular, for t ciphertexts, the approach in Claim 8 could be used to construct a quadratic equation system of $16t$ equations in $16 + 2t$ unknown variables. Similarly, the security of QuatM depends on the hardness of solving multivariate quadratic equations in $\mathbb{Z}_q$ and the hardness of solving high degree univariate polynomial equations in $\mathbb{Z}_q$. Similar to the scheme OctoM, it can be shown that the scheme QuatM is weakly equivalent to the inner product encryption scheme IPE of dimension 16. Since quaternion multiplication is associative, for the design of QuatM, one may also choose the private matrix $K \in \mathbb{H}(\mathbb{Z}_q)^{4 \times 4}$. Thus the ciphertext is a matrix in $\mathbb{H}(\mathbb{Z}_q)^{4 \times 4}$ also. Consequently, the revised QuatM is weakly equivalent to the inner product encryption scheme IPE of dimension 64.

One may also use other Lie groups to design fully homomorphic encryption schemes. For example, one can use the second smallest exceptional Lie group F_4 which is the automorphism group for the exceptional Jordan algebra (or Alberta algebra) $\mathfrak{h}_3(\mathbb{O})$ over $\mathbb{R}$. Specifically, $\mathfrak{h}_3(\mathbb{O})$ consists of the following 3×3 Hermitian matrices (matrices that are equal to their own conjugate transposes):

$$(a, b, c, \mathbf{a}, \mathbf{b}, \mathbf{c}) = \begin{bmatrix} a & \mathbf{c} & \mathbf{b} \\ \mathbf{c}^* & b & \mathbf{a} \\ \mathbf{b}^* & \mathbf{a}^* & c \end{bmatrix}$$

where $a, b, c \in \mathbb{R}$ and $\mathbf{a}, \mathbf{b}, \mathbf{c} \in \mathbb{O}$ and the Jordan product $\circ$ is defined by $\alpha \circ \beta = \frac{1}{2}(\alpha\beta + \beta\alpha)$ for $\alpha, \beta \in \mathfrak{h}_3(\mathbb{O})$. It is straightforward that Jordan algebra is of 27-dimension over $\mathbb{R}$. The Lie algebra $\mathfrak{f}_4$ of F_4 is isomorphic to $\mathfrak{so}(\mathbb{O}) \oplus \mathbb{O}^3$.

For the finite exceptional Jordan algebra $\mathfrak{h}_3(\mathbb{O}(\mathbb{Z}_q))$, the 52-dimension $F_4(q) = \text{Aut}(\mathfrak{h}_3(\mathbb{O}(\mathbb{Z}_q)))$ is the automorphism group of algebra $\mathfrak{h}_3(\mathbb{O}(\mathbb{Z}_q))$ which is a collection of the Hermitian 3×3 matrices restricted to $\mathbb{O}(\mathbb{Z}_q)$. It can be shown that

$$|F_4(q)| = q^{24}(q^{12} - 1)(q^8 - 1)(q^6 - 1)(q^2 - 1))$$

and $G_2(q) \subset F_4(q)$.

The determinant of a matrix in $\mathfrak{h}_3(\mathbb{O}(\mathbb{Z}_q))$ is defined by

$$\det(a, b, c, \mathbf{a}, \mathbf{b}, \mathbf{c}) = abc - (a\|\mathbf{a}\|^2 + b\|\mathbf{b}\|^2 + c\|\mathbf{c}\|^2) + 2\text{Re}(\mathbf{a}\mathbf{b}\mathbf{c})$$

This can be expressed as $\det(x) = \frac{1}{3}\text{tr}(x^3) - \frac{1}{2}\text{tr}(x^2)\text{tr}(x) + \frac{1}{6}\text{tr}(x)^3$ for $x \in \mathfrak{h}_3(\mathbb{O}(\mathbb{Z}_q))$. Thus the determinant of a Jordan algebra matrix is invariant under all automorphism $F_4(q)$ of $\mathfrak{h}_3(\mathbb{O}(\mathbb{Z}_q))$. That is, for all $\phi \in F_4(q)$, we have $\det(x) = \det(\phi(x))$.

In the following, we first describe the protocol for the FHE scheme JordanM.
Key Setup. Select $q = p_1 p_2$ according to the given security parameter κ. Randomly select isotropic vectors $\mathbf{z}_1, \mathbf{z}_2, \mathbf{z}_3 \in \mathbb{O}(\mathbb{Z}_q)$ satisfying the following identity

$$\mathbf{z}_2 \mathbf{z}_1^* = \mathbf{z}_3 \quad \text{and} \quad \text{Re}(\mathbf{z}_1 \mathbf{z}_2 \mathbf{z}_3) \neq 0 \tag{16}$$

Note that such kind of $\mathbf{z}_1, \mathbf{z}_2, \mathbf{z}_3$ could be obtained by solving an equation system of 11 equations (eight obtained from (16) and three obtained from the identity $\|\mathbf{z}_1\| = \|\mathbf{z}_2\| = \|\mathbf{z}_3\| = 0$) in 24 variables. Let $\phi \in F_4(q)$ be a randomly selected automorphism and let $K \in \mathbb{Z}_q^{3 \times 3}$ be a randomly selected 3×3 nonsingular matrix. The private key is key $= (\phi, K, \mathbf{z}_1, \mathbf{z}_2, \mathbf{z}_3)$.

Encryption. For a message $m \in \mathbb{Z}_q$, choose random $r_1, r_2, r_3, r_4, r_5, r \in \mathbb{Z}_q$ such that $\det(E_m) \neq 0$, where E_m is the Hermitian matrix $E_m = (m, r_4, r_5, r_1\mathbf{z}_1, r_2\mathbf{z}_2, r_3\mathbf{z}_3)$. Let the ciphertext $C_m = $ JordanM.Enc(key, m) $= K^{-1}\phi(E_m)K$.

Decryption. For a received ciphertext C_m, decrypt the plaintext as

$$m = \text{JordanM.Dec(key}, C_m) = \mathbf{1}\phi^{-1}(KC_mK^{-1})\mathbf{1}^T.$$

Ciphertext addition. The addition of two ciphertexts C_{m_0} and C_{m_1} is defined as the regular component wise matrix addition $C_{m_0+m_1} = C_{m_0} + C_{m_1}$.

Ciphertext multiplication. The multiplication of two ciphertexts C_{m_0} and C_{m_1} is defined as the Jordan product $\circ$:

$$
\begin{aligned}
C_{m_0 m_1} &= C_{m_1} \circ C_{m_0} \\
&= (K^{-1}\phi(E_{m_0})\phi(E_{m_1})K + K^{-1}\phi(E_{m_1})\phi(E_{m_0})K)/2 \\
&= K^{-1}((\phi(E_{m_0})\phi(E_{m_1}) + \phi(E_{m_1})\phi(E_{m_0}))/2)K \\
&= K^{-1}\phi(E_{m_0} \circ E_{m_1})K.
\end{aligned}
$$

In the encryption process `JordanM.Enc`, the random numbers are chosen in such a way that $\det(E_m) \neq 0$ no matter whether $m = 0$ or not.

By the identity (16), we have $\mathbf{z}_2\mathbf{z}_1^* = \mathbf{z}_3$. This implies that $\mathbf{z}_3\mathbf{z}_1 = \mathbf{0}$ and $\mathbf{z}_3^*\mathbf{z}_2 = \mathbf{0}$. By these arguments and by the identity $(\mathbf{ab})^* = \mathbf{b}^*\mathbf{a}^*$ from Theorem 4, the multiplication homomorphism of `JordanM` could be verified straightforwardly and the details are omitted due to space limit.

Remark. In the key setup process `JordanM.KeySetup`, it is sufficient to use $\phi \in F_4(q)$ that are represented by the primitive idempotents $A \in \mathfrak{h}_3(\mathbb{O}(\mathbb{Z}_q))$ with $A \circ A = A$ and $\mathrm{tr}(A) = 1$. That is, ϕ is defined by

$$
\phi : B \mapsto B + 4\mathrm{tr}(A \circ B)A - 4B \circ A
$$

It is further noted that the primitive idempotents in the Jordan algebra are exactly the elements $(a, b, c, \mathbf{a}, \mathbf{b}, \mathbf{c})$ satisfying

$$
\begin{aligned}
a + b + c &= 1 \\
a^2 + \|\mathbf{b}\|^2 + \|\mathbf{c}\|^2 &= a \\
\mathbf{b}^*\mathbf{a} &= c\mathbf{c}^*
\end{aligned}
$$

and the equations obtained from these by cycling a, b, c and $\mathbf{a}, \mathbf{b}, \mathbf{c}$.

It should be noted that (see, e.g., Baez [1]), for any $(a, b, c, \mathbf{a}, \mathbf{b}, \mathbf{c}) \in \mathfrak{h}_3(\mathbb{O}(\mathbb{Z}_q))$, there exists $\phi \in F_4(q)$ such that $\phi((a, b, c, \mathbf{a}, \mathbf{b}, \mathbf{c}))$ is diagonalized. The security analysis for `JordanM` is similar to that of `OctoM` and we have the following theorem (proof is omitted due to space limit).

Theorem 10. *Assuming that it is computationally infeasible to solve univariate polynomial equation systems of degree larger than 2, it is computationally infeasible to solve multivariate/univariate quadratic equation systems in $\mathbb{Z}_q$, and the plaintext messages are uniformly distributed over $\mathbb{Z}_{q_0}$. Then the encryption scheme `JordanM` over $\mathbb{Z}_q$ is $(t, negl(\kappa))$-secure in the weak ciphertext-only security model for any $t \leq poly(\kappa)$.*

Remark. In the scheme `JordanM`, the private key K is chosen as a 3×3 matrix over $\mathbb{Z}_q$. If K were chosen as a 3×3 matrix over $\mathbb{O}(\mathbb{Z}_q)$, then the scheme would not be multiplicative homomorphic since octonion multiplication is not associative. However, one may use Jordan algebra restricted to quaternions $\mathbb{H}(\mathbb{Z}_q)$ to design an FHE scheme `JordanQuaterM`. Then one can use a 3×3 matrix $K \in \mathbb{H}(\mathbb{Z}_q)^{3 \times 3}$

as the private key since quaternion multiplication is associative. Furthermore, one may also use high dimension Hermitian matrices for the design of JordanM scheme. For example, one may use the n-dimension Hermitian matrices design JordanM.

10   Privacy Preserving Garbled Computation in Cloud

The efficient FHE schemes designed in this paper are expected to have a wide range of applications. In this section, we show its applications to privacy preserving garbled computation in cloud. Specifically, we consider the following special case of reusable privacy preserving software outsourcing problem:

> The owner has a software (e.g., with a slow but feasible secret algorithm to break RSA when powerful computing resources are available) and the cloud has a powerful computing resource. The software owner wants to run his software in the cloud but he does not want to leak his secret algorithm. The cloud provides computing resources to the software owner and it does not need to learn the software output. The actual protocol could work like this: the software owner uploads his re-usable obfuscated software to the cloud. Each time when the software owner wants to run the obfuscated software in the cloud, he provides obfuscated inputs to the cloud. The cloud runs the obfuscated software and the obfuscated software output is returned to the software owner. The software owner decrypts the obfuscated output and learns the actual output.

In the following paragraphs, we show how to use FHE schemes proposed in this paper to solve the above reusable privacy preserving software outsourcing problem.

10.1   Straight Line Programs, Arithmetic Circuits, and Universal Circuits

Arithmetic circuits have been used as a model for computing polynomials. An arithmetic circuit takes either variables or numbers as inputs. The only allowed gates in arithmetic circuits are additions and multiplications. For the Boolean circuit model, it uses AND, OR, and NOT gates. Since these gates could be redesigned using NAND gates, we assume that all circuits contain NAND gates only. Each NAND gate can be converted to two arithmetic gates using the formula "x NAND $y = 1 - xy$". Thus each Boolean circuit could be converted to an arithmetic circuit that computes the same function. By the above discussion, each Boolean circuit could be converted to a straight line program where a straight-line program is a sequence of operations that only uses additions and multiplications as follows.

Input: $x_0, \cdots, x_{n-1}$
$v_0 = w_{0,0}$ op $w_{0,1}$
$\cdots$

$v_{t-1} = w_{t-1,0}$ op $w_{t-1,1}$

where $v_0, \cdots, v_{t-1}$ are temporary variables. Each operator op is either $+$ or $\times$, and the variables $w_{i,0}, w_{i,1}$ are either constants within $\{1, -1\}$ or variables from the list $x_0, \cdots, x_{n-1}, v_0, \cdots, v_{i-1}$.

A universal straight line program U takes an input (C, x) where C is an encoded straight line program and $U(C, x) = C(x)$. The construction of universal Boolean circuits could be found in [9, 13]. When a universal straight line program U (alternatively, a universal arithmetic circuit or a universal circuit) is used, the structure of U is public knowledge and there is no need to protect the control flow within U. It is sufficient to protect the input privacy (that is, both C and x). It should be noted that this is also sufficient for the protection of keyed programs, where the obfuscation does not depend on hiding the entire structure of the obfuscated program from the adversary and it only hides a short secret key embedded in the program.

10.2   Protocol for Garbled Computation in Cloud

For the garbled computation in cloud that we have mentioned in the preceding paragraphs, the cloud does not need to know the software output. Thus an efficient FHE scheme together with a universal straight line program is sufficient for this kind of software obfuscation. In the proposed obfuscation approach, one only needs to homomorphically encrypt all input variables (that is, both C and x where C is the private circuit that the software owner wants to protect in order to evaluate $C(x)$). That is, each input variable x_i is homomorphically encrypted to $c_i = \text{FHE.Enc}(\text{key}, x_i)$. Each operator can then be evaluated homomorphically as $c = \text{FHE.Eval}(c_1, c_2; \text{op})$.

Let U be a universal straight line program and C be the straight line program that the software owner wants to obfuscate. Then the protocol proceeds as follows:

- The software owner constructs a reusable garbled software $\mathcal{C} = \text{FHE.Enc}(\text{key}, C)$ and uploads $\mathcal{C}$ to the cloud.
- For each evaluation, software owner provides an encrypted input $\text{FHE.Enc}(\text{key}, x)$ to the cloud.
- The cloud runs the universal straight line program U on $(\mathcal{C}, \text{FHE.Enc}(\text{key}, x))$ to obtain the encrypted output $\text{FHE.Enc}(\text{key}, C(x)) = \text{FHE.Eval}(\mathcal{C}, \text{FHE.Enc}(\text{key}, x); U)$
- The owner decrypts the actual output: $C(x) = \text{FHE.Dec}(\text{key}, \text{FHE.Enc}(\text{key}, C(x)))$.

11   Practical Considerations

The preceding sections show that the proposed FHE schemes OctoM, QuatM, JordanM are secure in the wCOA security mode. Furthermore, we also showed that known plaintext-ciphertext pairs of these FHE schemes could lead to the complete recovery of the private key. This gives the adversary the possibility of carrying out an exhaustive search based dictionary attacks in case that the guessable message space is small. As an example, assume that for given ciphertexts $c_1, \cdots, c_t$ of the scheme OctoM, one can obtain 64 independent ciphertext vectors from $c_1, \cdots, c_t$ using the fully homomorphic property. If the corresponding message $(m_1, \cdots, m_t) \in \mathcal{M}'$ for some $\mathcal{M}'$ with $|\mathcal{M}| \leq N$, then the adversary could do an exhaustive search of $\mathcal{M}'$ to obtain the candidate key space of size N. Furthermore, if the adversary can guess that some ciphertexts correspond to the same plaintext, then the adversary can use the additive homomorphism operations to obtain a valid ciphertext for the message 0. Based on these observations, an implementation of proposed FHE schemes should always take these factors into consideration. In particular, if possible, one should apply an appropriate message padding scheme before the FHE encryption process is used. These padding schemes should be compatible with the homomorphic operations.

The security of the FHE schemes OctoM, QuatM, JordanM depends on the hardness of solving multivariate quadratic equations and univariate high degree polynomial equations within $\mathbb{Z}_q$. The hardness of these problems are more or less related to the hardness of factoring q. For example, the problem of solving quadratic equations in $\mathbb{Z}_q$ is equivalent to the problem of factoring q. NIST SP 800-57 [2] recommends the security strength of $\mathbb{Z}_q$ for $q = p_1 p_2$. Wang [14] lists the security strength of $\mathbb{Z}_q$ when q is a multiplication of more than two primes. Following [2,14], we recommend the use of ring sizes for $\mathbb{Z}_q$ shown in Table 1.

Table 1. Bits of Security and $\mathbb{Z}_q$

Bits of Security	80	112	128	192	256
$q = p_1 p_2$ in bits [2]	1024	2048	3072	7680	15360
$q = p_1 p_2 p_3$ in bits [14]	1536	2335	3072	7680	15360
$q = p_1 p_2 p_3 p_4$ in bits [14]	2048	3072	4562	7680	15360

Table 2 lists the number of ring multiplications for the proposed FHE schemes. For performance comparison, we also include the number of ring multiplications needed for the RSA encryption scheme. In the table, we assume that the RSA public key is 3 and the private key size is the same as the modulus length. Furthermore, we assume that the RSA private key contains around 50 % ones and the "square-and-multiply" algorithm is used for the RSA decryption process. From the table, it is observed that both the schemes OctoM and QuatM are more efficient than the RSA decryption process for all parameters. For the scheme JordanM, if the automorphism ϕ is implemented as a regular Jordan product, then it requires 1734 multiplications at most. Thus the total number of multiplications for a JordanM.Enc or JordanM.Dec is 2127 and both JordanM encryption and decryption processes are more efficient than the RSA decryption process for the security strength of 128-bits or more. However, if special automorphism ϕ were chosen and ϕ were implemented more efficiently than the RSA decryption process, then both JordanM encryption and decryption processes are more efficient than the RSA decryption process for all parameters.

Table 2. Performance comparison in terms of field multiplications

	OctoM	QuatM	JordanM	RSA
Encryption	1026	130	393+1734 = 2127	3
Decryption	578	82	393+1734 = 2127	$1.5|q|$
Homo Multi.	512	64	3456	

We conclude this section by pointing out ciphertext expansion factors for schemes OctoM, QuatM, and JordanM. The ciphertext expansion factor for a scheme xx is defined as $\max\left\{\frac{|\mathbf{c}_m|}{|m|} : m \in \mathcal{M}\right\}$ where $\mathbf{c}_m = \mathrm{xx}(\mathbf{k}, m)$ is the ciphertext of m. For the scheme OctoM (respectively QuatM and JordanM), the ciphertext $\mathbf{c}_m$ for $m \in \mathbb{Z}_{q_0}$ is a collection of 64 elements (respectively, 16 and 72) from $\mathbb{Z}_q$. Thus the message expansion factors for the schemes OctoM, QuatM, and JordanM are 128, 32, and 144 respectively.

12   Conclusion

This paper introduces efficient noise-free FHE schemes in the weak ciphertext-only security model. The proposed schemes are used to solve the specific problem for privacy preserving garbled cloud computation. It is expected that there is a wide range of applications for the proposed FHE schemes. For an implementation of the proposed FHE schemes, if the message space in the application has a small guessable size and an appropriate padding scheme is not employed, then one may mount a dictionary attack on the implementation. It will be interesting to investigate FHE compatible "padding" techniques to defeat the potential dictionary attacks on these implementations.

Acknowledgments. The first author would like to thank Martin Strand for several comments on an early version of this paper and thank Craig Gentry for pointing out the reference [7].

References

1. Baez, J.: The octonions. Bullet. Am. Math. Soc. **39**(2), 145–205 (2002)
2. Barker, E., Barker, W., Burr, W., Polk, W., Smid, M.: NIST special publication 800–57. NIST Special Publication **800**(57), 1–142 (2007)
3. Brakerski, Z.: When homomorphism becomes a liability. In: Sahai, A. (ed.) TCC 2013. LNCS, vol. 7785, pp. 143–161. Springer, Heidelberg (2013)
4. Charlap, L.S., Rees, H.D., Robbins, D.P.: The asymptotic probability that a random biased matrix is invertible. Discrete Math. **82**(2), 153–163 (1990)
5. Dembowski, P.: Finite Geometries: Reprint of the 1968 Edition. Classics in Mathematics. Springer, Heidelberg (2012)
6. Gentry, C.: Fully homomorphic encryption using ideal lattices. STOC **9**, 169–178 (2009)
7. Kipnis, A., Hibshoosh, E.: Efficient methods for practical fully homomorphic symmetric-key encrypton, randomization and verification. IACR ePrint Archive 2012:637 (2012)
8. Kipnis, A., Shamir, A.: Cryptanalysis of the HFE public key cryptosystem. In: Proceeding Crypto (1999)
9. Kolesnikov, V., Schneider, T.: A practical universal circuit construction and secure evaluation of private functions. In: Tsudik, G. (ed.) FC 2008. LNCS, vol. 5143, pp. 83–97. Springer, Heidelberg (2008)
10. Lidl, R., Niederreiter, H.: Finite Fields, vol. 20. Cambridge University Press, Cambridge (1997)
11. Pless, V.: The number of isotropic subspaces in a finite geometry. (Italian summary). Atti Accad. Naz. Lincei Rend. Cl. Sci. Fis. Mat. Natur. (8) **39**, 418–421 (1965)
12. Sturmfels, B.: What is a Gröbner basis. Notices Amer. Math. Soc **52**(10), 1199–1200 (2005)
13. Valiant, L.: Universal circuits. In: Proceeding 8th ACM STOC, pp. 196–203. ACM (1976)
14. Wang, Y.: PKCS: public-key cryptography standards. In: Bidgoli, H. (ed.) Handbook of Information Security, pp. 966–978. Wiley, Hoboken (2006)
15. Yao, A.: How to generate and exchange secrets. In: Proceeding 27th IEEE FOCS, pp. 162–167. IEEE (1986)

Lightweight Delegatable Proofs of Storage

Jia Xu[1]([✉]), Anjia Yang[1,2]([✉]), Jianying Zhou[1], and Duncan S. Wong[3]

[1] Infocomm Security Department, Institute for Infocomm Research,
Singapore, Singapore
{xuj,jyzhou}@i2r.a-star.edu.sg
[2] City University of Hong Kong, Hong Kong, China
ayang3-c@my.cityu.edu.hk
[3] Hong Kong Applied Science and Technology Research Institute,
Hong Kong, China
duncanwong@astri.org

Abstract. Proofs of Storage (including Proofs of Retrievability and
Provable Data Possession) is a cryptographic tool, which enables data
owner or third party auditor to audit integrity of data stored remotely
in a cloud storage server, without keeping a local copy of data or downloading data back during auditing. We observe that all existing publicly
verifiable POS schemes suffer from a serious drawback: It is extremely
slow to compute authentication tags for all data blocks, due to many
expensive group exponentiation operations. Surprisingly, it is even much
slower than typical network uploading speed, and becomes the bottleneck of the setup phase of the POS scheme. We propose a new variant
formulation called "Delegatable Proofs of Storage". In this new relaxed
formulation, we are able to construct a POS scheme, which on one side
is as efficient as privately verifiable POS schemes, and on the other side
can support third party auditor and can efficiently switch auditors at
any time, close to the functionalities of publicly verifiable POS schemes.
Compared to traditional publicly verifiable POS schemes, we speed up
the tag generation process by at least several hundred times, without
sacrificing efficiency in any other aspect. Like many existing schemes, we
can also speed up our tag generation process by approximately N times
using N CPU cores in parallel, before I/O cost becomes the bottleneck.
We prove that our scheme is sound under Bilinear Strong Diffie-Hellman
Assumption in standard model.

Keywords: Proof of Storage · Proof of Retrievability · Third party
verifier · Lightweight homomorphic authentication tag · Applied
cryptography

---

(1) The full version [46] with all details of proof is available at http://eprint.iacr.
org/2014/395.

(2) A. Yang contributed to this work when he took his internship in Infocomm
Security Department, Institute for Infocomm Research, Singapore.

I. Askoxylakis et al. (Eds.): ESORICS 2016, Part I, LNCS 9878, pp. 324–343, 2016.
DOI: 10.1007/978-3-319-45744-4_16

1 Introduction

Since Proofs of Retrievability (POR [22]) and Provable Data Possession (PDP [4]) are proposed in 2007, a lot of effort of research community has been devoted to constructing proofs of storage schemes with more advanced features. The new features include, public key verifiability [30], supporting dynamic operations [10,16,35] (i.e. inserting/deleting/editing a data block), supporting multiple cloud servers [13], privacy-preserving against auditor [42], and supporting data sharing [37], etc.

1.1 Drawbacks of Publicly Verifiable Proofs of Storage

Expensive Setup Preprocessing. We look back into the very first feature—public verifiability, and observe that all existing publicly verifiable POS schemes suffer from serious drawbacks: (1) Merkle Hash Tree based method is not disk IO-efficient and not even a sub-linear memory authenticator [24]: Every bit of the file has to be accessed by the cloud storage server in each remote integrity auditing process. (2) By our knowledge, all other publicly verifiable POS schemes employ a lot of expensive operation (e.g. group exponentiation) to generate authentication tags for data blocks. As a result, it is prohibitively expensive to generate authentication tags for medium or large size data file. For example, Wang *et al.* [38] achieves throughput of data pre-processing (i.e. generating authentication tag) at speed 17.2 KB/s with an Intel Core 2 1.86 GHz workstation CPU, which means it will take about 17 h to generate authentication tags for a 1 GB file. Even if the user has a CPU with 8 cores, it still requires more than 2 h heavy computation. Such amount of heavy computation is not appropriate for a laptop, not to mention tablet computer (e.g. iPad) or smart phone. It might be weird to tell users that, *mobile device should be only used to verify or download data file stored in cloud storage server, and should not be used to upload (and thus pre-process) data file to cloud*. Unless a formal lower bound is proved and shows that existing study of POS has reach optimality, it is the responsibility of our researchers to make both pre-processing and verification of (third party verifiable) POS practically efficient, although the existing works have already reached good amortized complexity. In this paper, we make our effort towards this direction, improving pre-processing speed by several hundred times without sacrificing efficiency on other aspects.

In many publicly verifiable POS (POR/PDP) scheme (e.g. [4,30,38,42]), publicly verifiable authentication tag function, which is a variant of signing algorithm in a digital signature scheme, is applied directly over every block of a large user data. This is one of few application scenarios that a public key cryptography primitive is directly applied over large user data. In contrast, (1) public key encryption scheme is typically employed to encrypt a short symmetric cipher key, and the more efficient symmetric cipher (e.g. AES) will encrypt the user data; (2) digital signature scheme is typically applied over a short hash digest of large user data, where the hash function (e.g. SHA256) is much more efficient (in term of throughput) than digital signature signing algorithm.

Lack of Control on Auditing. The benefit of publicly verifiable POS schemes is that, anyone with the public key can audit the integrity of data in cloud storage, to relieve the burden from the data owner. However, one should not allow any third party to audit his/her data at their will, and delegation of auditing task should be in a controlled and organized manner. Otherwise, we cannot prevent extreme cases: (1) on one hand, some data file could attract too much attention from public, and are audited unnecessarily too frequently by the public, which might actually result in distributed denial of service attack against the cloud storage server; (2) on the other hand, some unpopular data file may be audited by the public too rarely, so that the possible data loss event might be detected and alerted to the data owner too late and no effective countermeasure can be done to reduce the damage at that time.

1.2   Existing Approaches to Mitigate Drawbacks

Outsourcing Expensive Operations. To reduce the computation burden on data owner for preprocessing in setup phase, the data owner could outsource expensive operations (e.g. group exponentiation) to some cloud computing server during authentication tag generation, by using existing techniques (e.g. [12,21]) as black-box, and verify the computation result.

However, this approach just shifts the computation burden from data owner to cloud storage server, instead of reducing the amount of expensive operations. Furthermore, considering the data owner and cloud computing server as a whole system, much more cost in network communication and computation will be incurred: (1) uploading (possibly transformed) data file, to the cloud computing server, and downloading computation results from the cloud computing server; (2) extra computation cost on both data owner side and cloud computing server side, in order to allow data owner to verify the computation result returned by the cloud computing server and maintain data privacy against cloud computing server.

One may argue that it could save much of the above cost, if the outsourcing of expensive operations and proofs of storage scheme are integrated together and letting cloud storage server takes the role of cloud computing server. But in this case, simple black-box combination of existing proofs of storage scheme and existing privacy-preserving and verifiable outsource scheme for expensive operations, may not work. Thus, a new sophisticated proofs of storage scheme is required to be constructed following this approach, which remains an open problem.

Dual Instantiations of Privately Verifiable Proof of Storage. The data owner could independently apply an existing privately verifiable POS scheme over an input file twice, in order to generate two key pairs and two authentication tags per each data block, where one key pair and authentication tag (per data block) will be utilized by data owner to perform data integrity check, and the other key pair and authentication tag (per data block) will be utilized by auditor to perform data integrity check, using the interactive proof algorithm in the privately verifiable POS scheme. The limitation of this approach is that, in order to add an extra auditor or switch the auditor, the data owner has to download the whole data file to refresh the key pair and authentication tags for auditor.

Recently, [2] gave an alternative solution. The data owner runs privately verifiable POS scheme (i.e. Shacham-Water's scheme [30] as in [2]) over a data file to get a key pair and authentication tag per each data block, and uploads the data file together with newly generated authentication tags to cloud storage server. Next, the auditor downloads the whole file from cloud storage server, and independently runs the same privately verifiable POS scheme over the downloaded file, to get another key pair and another set of authentication tags. The auditor uploads these authentication tags to cloud storage server. For each challenge query provided by the auditor, the cloud storage server will compute two responses, where one is upon data owner's authentication tags and the other is upon auditor's authentication tags. Then the auditor can verify the response generated upon his/her authentication tags, and keeps the other response available for data owner.

Since [2] aims to resolve possible framing attack among the data owner, cloud storage server and auditor, all communication messages are digitally signed by senders, and the auditor has to prove to the data owner that, his/her authentication tags are generated *correctly*, where this proof method is very expensive, and comparable to tag generation complexity of publicly verifiable POS scheme (e.g. [4, 30, 38, 42]). Furthermore, in this scheme, in the case of revoking or adding an auditor, the new auditor has to download the whole file, then compute authentication tags, and prove that these tags are correctly generated to the data owner.

We remark that our early version of this work appeared as a private internal technique report in early 2014, before [2] became available to public.

Program Obfuscation. Very recently, [19] proposed to construct publicly verifiable POR from privately verifiable POR using indistinguishability obfuscation technique [17]. This obfuscation technique is able to embed the data owner's secret key in a verifier program, in a way such that it is hard to recover the secret key from the obfuscated verifier program. Therefore, this obfuscated verifier program could be treated as public key and given to the auditor to perform data integrity check. However, both [17, 19] admit that indistinguishability obfuscation is currently impractical. Particularly, [1] implements the scheme of [17] and shows that, it requires about 9 h to obfuscate a simple function which contains just 15 AND gates, and resulted obfuscated program has size 31.1 GB. Furthermore, it requires around 3.3 h to evaluate the obfuscated program on a single input.

1.3   Our Approach

To address the issues of existing publicly verifiable POS schemes, we propose a *hybrid* POS scheme, which on one hand supports delegation of data auditing task and switching/adding/revoking an auditor, like publicly verifiable POS schemes, and on the other hand is as efficient as a privately verifiable POS scheme.

Unlike in publicly verifiable POS scheme, the data owner could delegate the auditing task to some semi-trusted third party auditor, and this auditor is responsible to audit the data stored in cloud storage on behalf of the data owner, in a controlled way and with proper frequency. We call such an exclusive auditor as *Owner-Delegated-Auditor* or ODA for short. In real world applications, ODA could be another server that provides free or paid auditing service to many cloud users.

Our bottom line is that, even if all auditors colluded with the dishonest cloud storage server, our formulation and scheme should guarantee that the data owner still retains the capability to perform POR auditing by herself.

Overview of Our Scheme. Our scheme generates two pairs of public/private keys: (pk, sk) and (vpk, vsk). The verification public/private key pair (vpk, vsk) is delegated to the ODA. Our scheme proposes a novel linear homomorphic authentication tag function [5], which is extremely lightweight, without any expensive operations (e.g. group exponentiation or bilinear map). Our tag function generates two tags (σ_i, t_i) for each data block, where tag σ_i is generated in a way similar to Shacham and Waters' privately verifiable POR scheme [30], and tag t_i is generated in a completely new way. Each of tag σ_i and tag t_i is of length equal to $1/m$-fraction of length of a data block, where the data block is treated as a vector of dimension m[1]. ODA is able to verify data integrity remotely by checking consistency among the data blocks and both tags $\{(\sigma_i, t_i)\}$ that are stored in the cloud storage server, using the verification secret key vsk. The data owner retains the capability to verify data integrity by checking consistency between the data blocks and tags $\{\sigma_i\}$, using the master secret key sk. When an ODA is revoked and replaced by a new ODA, data owner will update all authentication tags $\{t_i\}$ and the verification key pair (vpk, vsk) without downloading the data file from cloud, but keep tags $\{\sigma_i\}$ and master key pair (pk, sk) unchanged.

Furthermore, we customize the polynomial commitment scheme proposed by Kate *et al.* [23] and integrate it into our homomorphic authentication tag scheme, in order to reduce proof size from $O(m)$ to $O(1)$.

1.4   Contributions

Our main contributions can be summarized as below:

- We propose a new formulation called "Delegatable Proofs of Storage" (DPOS), as a relaxed variant of publicly verifiable POS. Our formulation allows data owner to delegate auditing task to a third party auditor, and meanwhile retains the capability to perform audit task by herself, even if the auditor colluded with the cloud storage server. Our formulation also supports revoking and switching auditors efficiently.
- We design a new scheme under this formulation. Our scheme is as efficient as privately verifiable POS: The tag generation throughput is slightly larger

---

[1] System parameter m can take any positive integer value and typical value is from a hundred to a thousand.

Table 1. Performance Comparison of Proofs of Storage (POR,PDP) Schemes. In this table, publicly verifiable POS schemes appear above our scheme, and privately verifiable POS schemes appear below our scheme.

Scheme	Computation Pre-process (Data)			Communication bits		Storage Over-head (Server)	Computation (Verifier)				Computation (Prover)			
	exp.	mul.	add.	Challenge	Response		exp.	mul.	pair.	add.	exp.	mul.	pair.	add.
[3,4]	$2\frac{|F|}{m\lambda}$	$\frac{|F|}{m\lambda}$	0	$\log\ell+2^\kappa$	2λ	$\frac{|F|}{m}$	ℓ	ℓ	0	0	ℓ	2ℓ	0	ℓ
[30,31]-pub.	$\frac{|F|}{\lambda}+\frac{|F|}{m\lambda}$	$\frac{|F|}{\lambda}$	0	$\ell\lambda+\ell\log(\frac{|F|}{m\lambda})$	$(m+1)\lambda$	$\frac{|F|}{m}$	$\ell+m$	$\ell+m$	2	0		$m\ell+\ell$	0	$m\ell$
[43,44]	$2\frac{|F|}{\lambda}$	$\frac{|F|}{\lambda}$	0	$\ell\lambda+\ell\log(\frac{|F|}{m\lambda})$	$(\ell+3)\lambda+\ell(\lceil\log(\frac{|F|}{m\lambda})\rceil-1)|h|$	$|F|$	ℓ	ℓ	4	0	ℓ	2ℓ	0	ℓ
[42]	$2\frac{|F|}{\lambda}$	$\frac{|F|}{\lambda}$	0	$\ell\lambda+\ell\log(\frac{|F|}{m\lambda})$	3λ	$|F|$	$\ell+m$	ℓ	2	0	ℓ	2ℓ	0	ℓ
[38][a]	$\frac{|F|}{\lambda}+\frac{|F|}{m\lambda}$	$\frac{|F|}{\lambda}$	0	$\ell\lambda+\ell\log(\frac{|F|}{m\lambda})$	$(2m+1)\lambda$	$\frac{|F|}{m}$	$\ell+m$	$\ell+2m$	2	0	$\ell+m$	$m\ell+\ell$	1	$m\ell$
[53]	$\frac{|F|}{m\lambda}+m$	$2\frac{|F|}{\lambda}+m$	$\frac{|F|}{\lambda}+m$	$\ell\lambda+\ell\log(\frac{|F|}{m\lambda})$	$(m+3)\lambda$	$\frac{|F|}{m}$	$\ell+m$	$\ell+m$	3	0	$\ell+m$	$m\ell+2\ell+2m$	1	$m\ell$
[20]	$\frac{|F|}{m\lambda}$	0	0	$\lambda+k$	λ	0^b	$\frac{|F|}{m\lambda}$	$\frac{|F|}{m\lambda}$	0	0	$\log(\frac{|F|}{m\lambda})+m$	$\frac{|F|}{m\lambda}$	0	$\frac{|F|}{m\lambda}$
[49]	$\frac{|F|}{\lambda}+\frac{|F|}{m\lambda}+m$	$\frac{|F|}{\lambda}$	0	$(\ell+1)\lambda+\ell\log(\frac{|F|}{m\lambda})$	2λ	$\frac{|F|}{m}$	ℓ	2ℓ	2	0	$\ell+m$	$m\ell+m+\ell$	2	$m\ell$
[50]	$\frac{|F|}{\lambda}+2\frac{|F|}{m\lambda}$	$\frac{|F|}{\lambda}$	0	$2\lambda+\ell\log(\frac{|F|}{m\lambda})$	3λ	$\frac{|F|}{m}$	ℓ	2ℓ	4	0	$\ell+m$	$m\ell+m+\ell$	0	$m\ell$
[34]	$2\frac{|F|}{m\lambda}$	$2\frac{|F|}{m\lambda}$	0	$\frac{|F|}{m}+2\lambda$	5λ	$\frac{2|F|}{m}$	$\frac{|F|}{m\lambda}+4$	$\frac{|F|}{m\lambda}+1$	5	0	$\frac{|F|}{m\lambda}+5$	$3\frac{|F|}{m\lambda}$	3	$2\frac{|F|}{m\lambda}$
Our Scheme	0	$\frac{2|F|}{\lambda}$	$\frac{2|F|}{\lambda}$	$3\lambda+280$	6λ	$\frac{2|F|}{m}$	6	ℓ	7	ℓ	$3m$	$m\ell+2\ell+6m$	0	$m\ell+2\ell+2m$
[30,31]-pri.[c]	0	$\frac{|F|}{\lambda}$	$\frac{|F|}{\lambda}$	$\ell\lambda+\ell\log(\frac{|F|}{m\lambda})$	$(m+1)\lambda$	$\frac{|F|}{m}$	0	$\ell+m$	0	$\ell+m$	0	$m\ell+\ell$	0	$m\ell+\ell$

[a] [38] is a journal version of [42], and the main scheme is almost the same as [42]. We now consider the one that divides each data block into m sectors.

[b] In Hao et al.'s paper [20], the authentication tags are stored at both the client and the verifier side, rather than the server side.

[c] The private key verifiable POR scheme of Shacham and Waters [30,31]. Notice that the public key verifiable POS scheme of [30,31] also appears in this table.

κ, k are system parameters, $|h|$ is the length of a hash output. $|F|$ is the data file size. λ is group element size. m is the number of sectors in each data block. ℓ is the sampling size.

than $10\,\mathrm{MB/s}$ per CPU core on a mobile CPU released in Year 2008. On the other side, our scheme allows delegation of auditing task to a semi-trusted third party auditor, and also supports switching and revoking an auditor at any time, like a publicly verifiable POS scheme. We compare the performance complexity of our scheme with the state of arts in Table 1, and experiment shows the tag generation speed of our scheme is more than hundred times faster than the state of art of publicly verifiable POS schemes.

- We prove that our scheme is sound (Theorems 1 and 2) under Bilinear Strong Diffie-Hellman Assumption in standard model.

2   Related Work

Recently, much growing attention has been paid to integrity check of data stored at untrusted servers [3–6,8,9,11,13–16,20,22,28–33,36–45,47–53]. In CCS'07, Ateniese *et al.* [4] defined the *provable data possession* (PDP) model and proposed the first publicly verifiable PDP scheme. Their scheme used RSA-based homomorphic authenticators and sampled a number of data blocks rather than the whole data file to audit the outsourced data, which can reduce the communication complexity significantly. However, in their scheme, a linear combination of sampled blocks are exposed to the third party auditor (TPA) at each auditing, which may leak the data information to the TPA. At the meantime, Juels and Kaliski [22] described a similar but stronger model: *proof of retrievability* (POR), which enables auditing of not only the integrity but also the retrievability of remote data files by employing spot-checking and error-correcting codes. Nevertheless, their proposed scheme allows for only a bounded number of auditing services and does not support public verification.

Shacham and Waters [30,31] proposed two POR schemes, where one is private key verifiable and the other is public key verifiable, and gave a rigorous proof of security under the POR model [22]. Similar to [4], their scheme utilized homomorphic authenticators built from BLS signatures [7]. Subsequently, Zeng *et al.* [51], Wang *et al.* [43,44] proposed some similar constructions for publicly verifiable remote data integrity check, which adopted the BLS based homomorphic authenticators. With the same reason as [4], these protocols do not support data privacy. In [38,42], Wang *et al.* extended their scheme to be privacy preserving. The idea is to mask the linear combination of sampled blocks in the server's response with some random value. With the similar masking technique, Zhu *et al.* [53] introduced another privacy-preserving public auditing scheme. Later, Hao *et al.* [20] and Yang *et al.* [49] proposed two privacy-preserving public auditing schemes without applying the masking technique. Yuan *et al.* [50] gave a POR scheme with public verifiability and constant communication cost. Ren [26] designed mutual verifiable public POS application.

However, by our knowledge, all of the publicly verifiable PDP/POR protocols require to do a large amount of computation of exponentiation on big numbers for generating the authentication tags upon preprocessing the data file. This makes these schemes impractical for file of medium or large size, especially limiting the usage on mobile devices.

Although delegable POS has been studied by [25, 27, 34], unfortunately these works have the same drawback with public POS, i.e., the cost of tag generation is extremely high.

3 Formulation

We propose a formulation called "Delegatable Proofs of Storage" scheme (DPOS for short), based on existing POR [22, 30] and PDP [4] formulations. We provide the system model in Sect. 3.1 and the trust model in Sect. 3.2. We will defer the security definition to Sect. 5, where the security analysis of our scheme will be provided.

3.1 System Model

Definition 1. *A* Delegatable Proofs of Storage *(DPOS) scheme consists of algorithms (*KeyGen, Tag, UpdVK, OwnerVerify*), and a pair of interactive algorithms* $\langle P, V \rangle$*, where each algorithm is described as below*

- KeyGen$(1^\lambda) \rightarrow (pk, sk, vpk, vsk)$: *Given a security parameter* 1^λ*, this randomized key generating algorithm generates a pair of public/private master keys* (pk, sk) *and a pair of public/private verification keys* (vpk, vsk)*.*
- Tag$(sk, vsk, F) \rightarrow (\mathtt{Param}_F, \{(\sigma_i, t_i)\})$: *Given the master secret key* sk*, the verification secret key* vsk*, and a data file* F *as input, the tag algorithm generates a file parameter* $\mathtt{Param}_F$ *and authentication tags* $\{(\sigma_i, t_i)\}$*, where a unique file identifier* $\mathtt{id}_F$ *is a part of* $\mathtt{Param}_F$*.*
- UpdVK$(vpk, vsk, \{t_i\}) \rightarrow (vpk', vsk', \{t_i'\})$: *Given the current verification key pair* (vpk, vsk) *and the current authentication tags* $\{t_i\}$*, this updating algorithm generates the new verification key pair* (vpk', vsk') *and the new authentication tags* $\{t_i'\}$*.*
- $\langle P(pk, vpk, \{(\vec{F}_i, \sigma_i, t_i)\}_i), V(vsk, vpk, pk, \mathtt{Param}_F) \rangle \rightarrow (b, \mathtt{Context}, \mathtt{Evidence})$: *The verifier algorithm* V *interacts with the prover algorithm* P *to output a decision bit* $b \in \{1, 0\}$*,* Context *and* Evidence*, where the input of* P *consists of the master public key* pk*, the verification public key* vpk*, and file blocks* $\{\vec{F}_i\}$ *and authentication tags* $\{\sigma_i, t_i\}$*, and the input of* V *consists of the verification secret key* vsk*, verification public key* vpk*, master public key* pk*, and file information* $\mathtt{Param}_F$*.*
- OwnerVerify$(sk, pk, \mathtt{Context}, \mathtt{Evidence}, \mathtt{Param}_F)) \rightarrow (b_0, b_1)$: *The owner verifier algorithm* OwnerVerify *takes as input the master key pair* (sk, pk) *and* Context *and* Evidence*, and outputs two decision bits* $b_0, b_1 \in \{0, 1\}$*, where* b_0 *indicates accepting or rejecting the storage server, and* b_1 *indicates accepting or rejecting the ODA.*

A DPOS system is described as below and illustrated in Fig. 1(a) and (b).

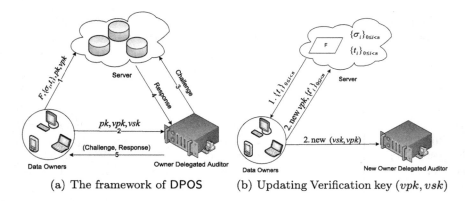

(a) The framework of DPOS   (b) Updating Verification key (vpk, vsk)

Fig. 1. Illustration of system model of DPOS.

Definition 2. *A* DPOS *system among three parties—data owner, cloud storage server and auditor, can be implemented by running a* DPOS *scheme (*KeyGen, Tag, UpdVK, $\langle$P, V$\rangle$, OwnerVerify*) in the following three phases, where the setup phase will execute at the very beginning, for only once (for one file); the proof phase and revoke phase can execute for multiple times and in any (interleaved) order.*

Setup phase. *The data owner runs the key generating algorithm* KeyGen(1^λ) *for only once across all files, to generate the per-user master key pair* (pk, sk) *and the verification key pair* (vpk, vsk). *For every input data file, the data owner runs the tag algorithm* Tag *over the (possibly erasure encoded) file, to generate authentication tags* $\{(\sigma_i, t_i)\}$ *and file parameter* Param$_F$. *At the end of setup phase, the data owner sends the file F, all authentication tags* $\{(\sigma_i, t_i)\}$, *file parameter* Param$_F$, *and public keys* (pk, vpk) *to the cloud storage server. The data owner also chooses an exclusive third party auditor, called* Owner-Delegated-Auditor *(*ODA, *for short), and delegates the verification key pair* (vpk, vsk) *and file parameter* Param$_F$ *to the* ODA. *After that, the data owner may keep only keys* (pk, sk, vpk, vsk) *and file parameter* Param$_F$ *in local storage, and delete everything else from local storage.*

Proof phase. *The proof phase consists of multiple proof sessions. In each proof session, the* ODA, *who runs algorithm* V, *interacts with the cloud storage server, who runs algorithm* P, *to audit the integrity of data owner's file, on behalf of the data owner. Therefore,* ODA *is also called* verifier *and cloud storage server is also called* prover. *ODA will also keep all outputs of algorithm* V, *i.e. tuples (b,* Context, Evidence*), and allow data owner to fetch and verify these tuples using algorithm* OwnerVerify *at any time.*

Revoke phase. *In the revoke phase, the data owner downloads all tags* $\{t_i\}$ *from cloud storage server, revokes the current verification key pair, and generates a fresh verification key pair and new tags* $\{t_i'\}$, *by running algorithm* UpdVK. *The data owner also chooses a new* ODA, *and delegates the new verification key pair* to this new ODA, and sends the updated tags $\{t'_i\}$ to the cloud storage server to replace the old tags $\{t_i\}$.

Definition 3 (Completeness). *A* DPOS *scheme (*KeyGen, Tag, UpdVK, $\langle$P, V$\rangle$, OwnerVerify*) is complete, if the following condition holds: For any keys* (pk, sk, vpk, vsk) *generated by* KeyGen, *for any file* F, *if all parties follow our scheme exactly and the data stored in cloud storage is intact, then interactive proof algorithms* $\langle$P, V$\rangle$ *will always output* $(1, \ldots)$ *and* OwnerVerify *algorithm will always output* $(1, 1)$.

3.2 Trust Model

In this paper, we aim to protect data integrity of data owner's file. The data owner is fully trusted, and the cloud storage server and ODA are semi-trusted in different sense: (1) The cloud storage server is trusted in maintaining service availability and is *not* trusted in maintaining data integrity (e.g. the server might delete some rarely accessed data for economic benefits, or hide the data corruption events caused by server failures or attacks to maintain reputation). (2) Before he/she is revoked, the ODA is trusted in performing the delegated auditing task and protecting his/her verification secret key securely. A revoked ODA could be potentially malicious and might surrender his/her verification secret key to the cloud storage server.

4 Our Proposed Scheme

4.1 Preliminaries

Let $\mathbb{G}$ and $\mathbb{G}_T$ be two multiplicative cyclic groups of prime order p. Let g be a randomly chosen generator of group $\mathbb{G}$. Let $e : \mathbb{G} \times \mathbb{G} \to \mathbb{G}_T$ be a non-degenerate and efficiently computable bilinear map. For vector $\vec{a} = (a_1, \ldots, a_m)$ and $\vec{b} = (b_1, \ldots, b_m)$, the notation $\langle \vec{a}, \vec{b} \rangle \overset{\text{def}}{=} \sum_{j=1}^{m} a_j b_j$ denotes the dot product (a.k.a inner product) of the two vectors $\vec{a}$ and $\vec{b}$. For vector $\vec{v} = (v_0, \ldots, v_{m-1})$ the notation $\mathsf{Poly}_{\vec{v}}(x) \overset{\text{def}}{=} \sum_{j=0}^{m-1} v_j x^j$ denotes the polynomial in variable x with $\vec{v}$ being the coefficient vector.

4.2 Construction of the Proposed DPOS Scheme

We define our DPOS scheme (KeyGen, Tag, UpdVK, $\langle$P, V$\rangle$, OwnerVerify) as below, and these algorithms will run in the way as specified in Definition 2. We remind that in the following description of algorithms, some equations have inline explanation highlighted in box, which is not a part of algorithm procedures but could be useful to understand the correctness of our algorithms.

KeyGen(1^λ) $\to (pk, sk, vpk, vsk)$ Choose at random a λ-bits prime p and a bilinear map $e : \mathbb{G} \times \mathbb{G} \to \mathbb{G}_T$, where $\mathbb{G}$ and $\mathbb{G}_T$ are both multiplicative cyclic groups of prime order p. Choose at random a generator $g \in \mathbb{G}$. Choose at random $\alpha, \gamma, \rho \in_R \mathbb{Z}_p^*$, and $(\beta_1, \beta_2, \ldots, \beta_m) \in_R (\mathbb{Z}_p)^m$. For each $j \in [1, m]$, define $\alpha_j := \alpha^j$ mod p, and compute $g_j := g^{\alpha_j}$, $h_j := g^{\rho \cdot \beta_j}$. Let $\alpha_0 := 1$, $\beta_0 := 1$, $g_0 = g^{\alpha^0} = g$, $h_0 = g^\rho$, vector $\vec{\alpha} := (\alpha_1, \alpha_2, \ldots, \alpha_m)$, and $\vec{\beta} := (\beta_1, \beta_2, \ldots, \beta_m)$. Choose two random seeds s_0, s_1 for pseudorandom function $\mathcal{PRF}_{\mathsf{seed}} : \{0,1\}^\lambda \times \mathbb{N} \to \mathbb{Z}_p$.

The secret key is $sk = (\alpha, \vec{\beta}, s_0)$ and the public key is $pk = (g_0, g_1, \ldots, g_m)$. The verification secret key is $vsk = (\rho, \gamma, s_1)$ and the verification public key is $vpk = (h_0, h_1, \ldots, h_m)$.

$\mathsf{Tag}(sk, vsk, F) \to (\mathsf{Param}_F, \{(\sigma_i, t_i)\})$ Split file[2] F into n blocks, where each block is treated as a vector of m elements from $\mathbb{Z}_p$: $\{\vec{F_i} = (F_{i,0}, \ldots, F_{i,m-1}) \in \mathbb{Z}_p^m\}_{i \in [0, n-1]}$. Choose a unique identifier $\mathsf{id}_F \in \{0,1\}^\lambda$ for file F. Define a customized[3] pseudorandom function w.r.t. the file F: $\mathcal{R}_s(i) = \mathcal{PRF}_s(\mathsf{id}_F, i)$.

For each block $\vec{F_i}$, $0 \le i \le n-1$, compute

$$\sigma_i := \left\langle \vec{\alpha}, \ \vec{F_i} \right\rangle + \mathcal{R}_{s_0}(i) \quad \boxed{= \alpha \cdot \mathsf{Poly}_{\vec{F_i}}(\alpha) + \mathcal{R}_{s_0}(i) \mod p} \tag{1}$$

$$t_i := \rho \left\langle \vec{\beta}, \ \vec{F_i} \right\rangle + \gamma \mathcal{R}_{s_0}(i) + \mathcal{R}_{s_1}(i) \mod p \tag{2}$$

The general information of F is $\mathsf{Param}_F := (\mathsf{id}_F, n)$.

$\mathsf{UpdVK}(vpk, vsk, \{t_i\}_{i \in [0, n-1]}) \to (vpk', vsk', \{t_i'\}_{i \in [0, n-1]})$ Parse vpk as $(h_0, \ldots, h_m)$ and vsk as (ρ, γ, s_1). Verify the integrity of all tags $\{t_i\}$ (*We will discuss how to do this verification later*), and abort if the verification fails. Choose at random $\gamma' \in_R \mathbb{Z}_p^*$ and choose a random seed s_1' for pseudorandom function $\mathcal{R}$. For each $j \in [0, m]$, compute $h_j' := h_j^{\gamma'} = g^{(\rho \cdot \gamma') \cdot \beta_j} \in \mathbb{G}$. For each $i \in [0, n-1]$, compute a new authentication tag

$$t_i' := \gamma'(t_i - \mathcal{R}_{s_1}(i)) + \mathcal{R}_{s_1'}(i) \mod p.$$

$$= \boxed{\gamma' \cdot \rho \left\langle \vec{\beta}, \ \vec{F_i} \right\rangle + (\gamma' \cdot \gamma) \mathcal{R}_{s_0}(i) + \mathcal{R}_{s_1'}(i) \mod p}$$

The new verification public key is $vpk' := (h_0', \ldots, h_m')$ and the new verification secret key is $vsk' := (\gamma' \cdot \rho, \ \gamma' \cdot \gamma, \ s_1')$.

$\langle \mathsf{P}(pk, vpk, \{\vec{F_i}, \sigma_i, t_i\}_{i \in [0, n-1]}), \mathsf{V}(vsk, vpk, pk, \mathsf{Param}_F) \rangle \to (b, \mathsf{Context}, \mathsf{Evidence})$

V1: Verifier parses Param_F as (id_F, n). Verifier chooses a random subset $\mathbf{C} = \{i_1, i_2, \ldots, i_c\} \subset [0, n-1]$ of size c, where $i_1 < i_2 < \ldots < i_c$. Choose at random $w, \xi \in_R \mathbb{Z}_p^*$, and compute $w_{i_\iota} := w^\iota \mod p$ for each $\iota \in [1, c]$. Verifier sends $(\mathsf{id}_F, \{(i, w_i) : i \in \mathbf{C}\}, \xi)$ to the prover to initiate a proof session.

---

[2] Possibly, the input has been encoded by the data owner using some error erasure code.

[3] With such a customized function $\mathcal{R}$, the input id_F will become *implicit* and this will make our expression short.

P1: Prover finds the file and tags $\{(\vec{F}_i, \sigma_i, t_i)\}_i$ corresponding to id_F. Prover computes $\vec{\mathcal{F}} \in \mathbb{Z}_p^m$, and $\bar{\sigma}, \bar{t} \in \mathbb{Z}_p$ as below.

$$\vec{\mathcal{F}} := \left(\sum_{i \in \mathbf{C}} w_i \vec{F}_i \right) \quad \bmod p; \tag{3}$$

$$\bar{\sigma} := \left(\sum_{i \in \mathbf{C}} w_i \sigma_i \right) \quad \bmod p; \tag{4}$$

$$\bar{t} := \left(\sum_{i \in \mathbf{C}} w_i t_i \right) \quad \bmod p. \tag{5}$$

Evaluate polynomial $\mathsf{Poly}_{\vec{\mathcal{F}}}(x)$ at point $x = \xi$ to obtain $z := \mathsf{Poly}_{\vec{\mathcal{F}}}(\xi)$ $\bmod p$. Divide the polynomial (in variable x) $\mathsf{Poly}_{\vec{\mathcal{F}}}(x) - \mathsf{Poly}_{\vec{\mathcal{F}}}(\xi)$ with $(x - \xi)$ using polynomial long division, and denote the coefficient vector of resulting quotient polynomial as $\vec{v} = (v_0, \dots v_{m-2})$, that is, $\mathsf{Poly}_{\vec{v}}(x) \equiv \frac{\mathsf{Poly}_{\vec{\mathcal{F}}}(x) - \mathsf{Poly}_{\vec{\mathcal{F}}}(\xi)}{x - \xi}$ $\bmod p$. (*Note*: $(x - \xi)$ *can divide polynomial* $\mathsf{Poly}_{\vec{\mathcal{F}}}(x) - \mathsf{Poly}_{\vec{\mathcal{F}}}(\xi)$ *perfectly, since the latter polynomial evaluates to 0 at point* $x = \xi$.)

Compute $(\psi_\alpha, \psi_\beta, \phi_\alpha) \in \mathbb{G}^3$ as below

$$\psi_\alpha := \prod_{j=0}^{m-1} g_j^{\vec{\mathcal{F}}[j]} \left| = \prod_{j=0}^{m-1} \left(g^{\alpha^j} \right)^{\vec{\mathcal{F}}[j]} = g^{\mathsf{Poly}_{\vec{\mathcal{F}}}(\alpha)}; \right. \tag{6}$$

$$\psi_\beta := \prod_{j=0}^{m-1} h_{j+1}^{\vec{\mathcal{F}}[j]} \left| = \prod_{j=0}^{m-1} \left(g^{\rho \cdot \beta_{j+1}} \right)^{\vec{\mathcal{F}}[j]} = g^{\rho \langle \vec{\beta}, \, \vec{\mathcal{F}} \rangle}; \right. \tag{7}$$

$$\phi_\alpha := \prod_{j=0}^{m-2} g_j^{v_j} \left| = \prod_{j=0}^{m-2} \left(g^{\alpha^j} \right)^{v_j} = g^{\mathsf{Poly}_{\vec{v}}(\alpha)}. \right. \tag{8}$$

Prover sends $(z, \phi_\alpha, \bar{\sigma}, \bar{t}, \psi_\alpha, \psi_\beta)$ to the verifier.

V2: Let $\mathtt{Context} := (\xi, \{(i, w_i) : i \in \mathbf{C}\})$ and $\mathtt{Evidence} := (z, \phi_\alpha, \bar{\sigma})$. Verifier sets $b := 1$ if the following equalities hold and sets $b := 0$ otherwise.

$$e(\psi_\alpha, g) \overset{?}{=} e(\phi_\alpha, \, g^\alpha / g^\xi) \cdot e(g, g)^z \tag{9}$$

$$\left(\frac{e(\psi_\alpha, \, g^\alpha)}{e(g, \, g^{\bar{\sigma}})} \right)^\gamma \overset{?}{=} \frac{e(\psi_\beta, \, g)}{e\left(g, \, g^{\bar{t}} \cdot g^{-\sum_{i \in \mathbf{C}} w_i \mathcal{R}_{s_1}(i)} \right)} \tag{10}$$

Output $(b, \mathtt{Context}, \mathtt{Evidence})$.

$\underline{\mathsf{OwnerVerify}(sk, pk, b, \mathtt{Context}, \mathtt{Evidence}, \mathtt{Param}_F)) \rightarrow (b_0, b_1)}$

Parse $\mathtt{Context}$ as $(\xi, \{(i, w_i) : i \in \mathbf{C}\})$ and parse $\mathtt{Evidence}$ as $(z, \phi_\alpha, \bar{\sigma})$. Verifier will set $b_0 := 1$ if the following equality hold; otherwise set $b_0 := 0$.

$$\left(e(\phi_\alpha, g^\alpha/g^\xi)e(g,g)^z\right)^\alpha \overset{?}{=} e(g,\ g^{\bar{\sigma}}) \cdot e(g,g)^{\left(-\sum\limits_{i \in \mathbf{C}} w_i \mathcal{R}_{s_0}(i)\right)} \tag{11}$$

If ODA's decision b equals to b_0, then set $b_1 := 1$; otherwise set $b_1 := 0$. Output (b_0, b_1).

The completeness of the above scheme is proved in the full paper [46].

4.3 Discussion

How to verify the integrity of all tag values $\{t_i\}$ in algorithm UpdVK*?* A straightforward method is that: The data owner keeps tack a hash (e.g. SHA256) value of $t_0 \| t_1 \ldots \| t_{n-1}$ in local storage, and updates this hash value when executing UpdVK.

How to reduce the size of challenge $\{(i, w_i) : i \in \mathbf{C}\}$*?* Dodis *et al.* [15]'s result can be used to represent a challenge $\{(i, w_i) : i \in \mathbf{C}\}$ compactly as below: Choose the subset $\mathbf{C}$ using Goldreich [18]'s (δ, ϵ)-hitter[4], where the subset $\mathbf{C}$ can be represented compactly with only $\log n + 3 \log(1/\epsilon)$ bits. Assume $n < 2^{40}$ (sufficient for practical file size) and let $\epsilon = 2^{-80}$. Then $\mathbf{C}$ can be represented with 280 bits. Recall that $\{w_i : i \in \mathbf{C}\}$ is derived from some single value $w \in \mathbb{Z}_p^*$.

4.4 Experiment Result

We implement a prototype of our scheme in C language and using GMP[5] and PBC[6] library. We run the prototype in a Laptop PC with a 2.5 GHz Intel Core 2 Duo mobile CPU (model T9300, released in 2008). Our test files are randomly generated and of size from 128 MB to 1 GB. We achieve a throughput of data preprocessing at speed slightly larger than 10 megabytes per second, with $\lambda = 1024$.

In contrast, Atenesis *et al.* [3,4] achieves throughput of data preprocessing at speed 0.05 megabytes per second with a 3.0 GHz desktop CPU [4]. Wang *et al.* [38] achieves throughput of data pre-processing at speed 9.0KB/s and 17.2KB/s with an Intel Core 2 1.86 GHz workstation CPU, when a data block is a vector of dimension $m = 1$ and $m = 10$, respectively. According to the pre-processing complexity of [38] shown in Table 1, the theoretical optimal throughput speed of [38] is twice of the speed for dimension $m = 1$, which can be approached only when m tends to $+\infty$.

Therefore, the data pre-processing in our scheme is 200 times faster than Atenesis et al. [3,4], and 500 times faster than Wang *et al.* [38], using a single

---

[4] Goldreich [18]'s (δ, ϵ)-hitter guarantees that, for any subset $W \subset [0, n-1]$ with size $|W| \geq (1-\delta)n$, $\Pr[\mathbf{C} \cap W \neq \emptyset] \geq 1 - \epsilon$. Readers may refer to [15] for more details.

[5] GNU Multiple Precision Arithmetic Library: https://gmplib.org/.

[6] The Pairing-Based Cryptography Library: http://crypto.stanford.edu/pbc/.

CPU core. We remark that, all of these schemes (ours and [3,4,38]) and some others can be speedup by N times using N CPU cores in parallel. However, typical cloud user who runs the data pre-processing task, might have CPU cores number ≤ 4.

5 Security Analysis

5.1 Security Formulation

We will define soundness security in two layers. Intuitively, if a cloud storage server can pass auditor's verification, then there exists an efficient extractor algorithm, which can output the challenged data blocks. Furthermore, if a cloud storage server with knowledge of verification secret key can pass data owner's verification, then there exists an efficient extractor algorithm, which can output the challenged data blocks. If the data file is erasure encoded in advance, the whole data file could be decoded from sufficiently amount of challenged data blocks.

5.1.1 Definition of Soundness w.r.t Verification of Auditor

Based on the existing Provable Data Possession formulation [4] and Proofs of Retrievability formulation [22,30], we define DPOS soundness security game $\mathsf{Game_{sound}}$ between a *probabilistic polynomial time* (PPT) adversary $\mathcal{A}$ (i.e. dishonest prover/cloud storage server) and a PPT challenger $\mathcal{C}$ w.r.t. a DPOS scheme $\mathcal{E} = (\mathsf{KeyGen}, \mathsf{Tag}, \mathsf{UpdVK}, \langle \mathsf{P}, \mathsf{V} \rangle, \mathsf{OwnerVerify})$ as below.

Setup: The challenger $\mathcal{C}$ runs the key generating algorithm $\mathsf{KeyGen}(1^\lambda)$ to obtain two pair of public-private keys (pk, sk) and (vpk, vsk). The challenger $\mathcal{C}$ gives the public key (pk, vpk) to the adversary $\mathcal{A}$ and keeps the private key (sk, vsk) securely.

Learning: The adversary $\mathcal{A}$ adaptively makes polynomially many queries, where each query is one of the following:

- STORE-QUERY(F): Given a data file F chosen by $\mathcal{A}$, the challenger $\mathcal{C}$ runs tagging algorithm $(\mathsf{Param}_F, \{(\sigma_i, t_i)\}) \leftarrow \mathsf{Tag}(sk, vsk, \mathsf{F})$, where $\mathsf{Param}_F = (\mathtt{id}_F, n)$, and sends the data file F, authentication tags $\{(\sigma_i, t_i)\}$, public keys (pk, vpk), and file parameter Param_F, to $\mathcal{A}$.
- VERIFY-QUERY($\mathtt{id}_F$): Given a file identifier $\mathtt{id}_F$ chosen by $\mathcal{A}$, if $\mathtt{id}_F$ is not the (partial) output of some previous STORE-QUERY that $\mathcal{A}$ has made, ignore this query. Otherwise, the challenger $\mathcal{C}$ initiates a proof session with $\mathcal{A}$ w.r.t. the data file F associated to the identifier $\mathtt{id}_F$ in this way: The adversary $\mathcal{C}$, who runs the verifier algorithm $\mathsf{V}(vsk, vpk, pk, \mathsf{Param}_F)$, interacts with the adversary $\mathcal{A}$, who replaces the prover algorithm P with any PPT algorithm of its choice, and obtains an output $(b, \mathtt{Context}, \mathtt{Evidence})$, where $b \in \{1, 0\}$. The challenger runs the algorithm $\mathsf{OwnerVerify}(b, \mathtt{Context}, \mathtt{Evidence})$ to obtain output $(b_0, b_1) \in \{0, 1\}^2$. The challenger sends the two decision bits (b, b_0) to the adversary as feedback.

- REVOKEVK-QUERY: To respond to this query, the challenger runs the verification key update algorithm to obtain a new pair of verification keys $(vpk', vsk', \{t_i'\}) := \mathsf{UpdVK}(vpk, vsk, \{t_i\})$, and sends the revoked verification secret key vsk and the new verification public key vpk' and new authentication tags $\{t_i'\}$ to the adversary $\mathcal{A}$, and keeps vsk' private.

Commit: Adversary $\mathcal{A}$ outputs and commits on $(\mathtt{id}^*, \mathtt{Memo}, \tilde{\mathsf{P}})$, where each of them is described as below:

- a file identifier $\mathtt{id}^*$ among all file identifiers it obtains from $\mathcal{C}$ by making STORE-QUERIES in **Learning** phase;
- a bit-string $\mathtt{Memo}$;
- a description of PPT prover algorithm $\tilde{\mathsf{P}}$ (e.g. an executable binary file).

Challenge: The challenger randomly chooses a subset $\mathbf{C}^* \subset [0, n_{F^*} - 1]$ of size $c < \lambda^{0.9}$, where F^* denotes the data file associated to identifier $\mathtt{id}^*$, and n_{F^*} is the number of blocks in file F^*.

Extract: Let $\mathcal{E}^{\tilde{\mathsf{P}}(\mathtt{Memo})}(vsk, vpk, pk, \mathtt{Param}_{F^*}, \mathtt{id}^*, \mathbf{C}^*)$ denote a knowledge-extractor algorithm with oracle access to prover algorithm $\tilde{\mathsf{P}}(\mathtt{Memo})$. More precisely, the extractor algorithm $\mathcal{E}$ will revoke the verifier algorithm $\mathsf{V}(vsk, vpk, pk, \mathtt{Param}_{F^*})$ to interact with $\tilde{\mathsf{P}}(\mathtt{Memo})$, and observes all communication between the prover and verifier. It is worthy pointing out that: (1) the extractor $\mathcal{E}$ can feed input (including random coins) to the verifier V, and cannot access the internal states (e.g. random coins) of the prover $\tilde{\mathsf{P}}(\mathtt{Memo})$, unless the prover $\tilde{\mathsf{P}}$ sends its internal states to verifier; (2) the extractor $\mathcal{E}$ can rewind the algorithm $\tilde{\mathsf{P}}$, as in formulation of Shacham and Waters [30,31]. The goal of this knowledge extractor is to output data blocks $\{(i, \mathsf{F}_i') : i \in \mathbf{C}^*\}$.

The adversary $\mathcal{A}$ wins this DPOS soundness security game $\mathsf{Game}_{\mathsf{Sound}}$, if the verifier algorithm $\mathsf{V}(vsk, vpk, pk, \mathtt{Param}_{F^*})$ accepts the prover algorithm $\tilde{\mathsf{P}}(\mathtt{Memo})$ with some noticeable probability $1/\lambda^\tau$ for some positive integer τ, where the sampling set is fixed as $\mathbf{C}^*$. More precisely,

$$\Pr\left[\langle \tilde{\mathsf{P}}(\mathtt{Memo}), \mathsf{V}(vsk, vpk, pk, \mathtt{Param}_{F^*}) \rangle = (1, \ldots) \,\middle|\, \begin{matrix} \texttt{Sampling} \\ \texttt{set is } \mathbf{C}^* \end{matrix} \right] \geq 1/\lambda^\tau. \quad (12)$$

The challenger $\mathcal{C}$ wins this game, if these exists PPT knowledge extractor algorithm $\mathcal{E}$ such that the extracted blocks $\{(i, \mathsf{F}_i') : i \in \mathbf{C}^*\}$ are identical to the original $\{(i, \mathsf{F}_i) : i \in \mathbf{C}^*\}$ with overwhelming high probability. That is,

$$\Pr\left[\mathcal{E}^{\tilde{\mathsf{P}}(\mathtt{Memo})}(vsk, vpk, pk, \mathtt{Param}_{F^*}, \mathtt{id}^*, \mathbf{C}^*) = \{(i, \mathsf{F}_i) : i \in \mathbf{C}^*\} \right] \geq 1 - negl(\lambda). \quad (13)$$

Definition 4 (Soundness-1). *A DPOS scheme is sound against dishonest cloud storage server w.r.t. auditor, if for any PPT adversary $\mathcal{A}$, $\mathcal{A}$ wins the above DPOS security game $\mathsf{Game}_{\mathsf{Sound}}$ implies that the challenger $\mathcal{C}$ wins the same security game.*

5.1.2   Definition of Soundness w.r.t Verification of Owner

We define $\text{Game2}_{\text{sound}}$ by modifying the DPOS soundness security game $\text{Game}_{\text{sound}}$ as below: (1) In the **Setup** phase, the verification private key vsk is given to the adversary $\mathcal{A}$; (2) in the **Extract** phase, the knowledge extractor has oracle access to $\text{OwnerVerify}(sk, \dots)$, additionally.

Definition 5 (Soundness-2). *A* DPOS *scheme is* sound *against dishonest cloud storage server w.r.t. owner, if for any PPT adversary $\mathcal{A}$, $\mathcal{A}$ wins the above* DPOS *security game* $\text{Game2}_{\text{sound}}$, *i.e.*

$$\Pr\left[\begin{array}{l} \text{OwnerVerify}(sk, pk, \langle \tilde{\text{P}}(\text{Memo}), \text{V}(vsk, vpk, pk, \text{Param}_{F^*}) \rangle) \\ = (1, \dots) \end{array} \middle| \begin{array}{l} Sampling \\ set\ is\ \mathbf{C}^* \end{array}\right]$$

$$\geq 1/\lambda^\tau, \quad for\ some\ positive\ integer\ constant\ \tau, \tag{14}$$

implies that the challenger $\mathcal{C}$ wins the same security game, i.e. there exists PPT knowledge extractor algorithm $\mathcal{E}$ such that

$$\Pr\left[\mathcal{E}^{\tilde{\text{P}}(\text{Memo}), \text{OwnerVerify}(sk, \dots)}(vsk, vpk, pk, \text{Param}_{F^*}, \text{id}^*, \mathbf{C}^*) = \{(i, \text{F}_i) : i \in \mathbf{C}^*\}\right]$$

$$\geq 1 - negl(\lambda) \tag{15}$$

Remarks

- The two events "adversary $\mathcal{A}$ wins" and "challenger $\mathcal{C}$ wins" are not *mutually exclusive*.
- The above knowledge extractor formulates the notion that "**data owner is *capable* to recover data file efficiently (i.e. in polynomial time) from the cloud storage server**", if the cloud storage sever can pass verification with noticeable probability and its behavior will not change any more. The knowledge extractor might also serve as the contingency plan[7] (or last resort) to recover data file, when downloaded file from cloud is always corrupt but the cloud server can always pass the verification with high probability.
- Unlike POR [30,31], our formulation separates "error correcting code" out from POS scheme, since error correcting code is orthogonal to our design of homomorphic authentication tag function. If required, error correcting code can be straightforwardly combined with our DPOS scheme, and the analysis of such combination is almost identical to previous works.

5.2   Security Claim

Definition 6. (m-Bilinear Strong Diffie-Hellman Assumption). *Let $e : \mathbb{G} \times \mathbb{G} \to \mathbb{G}_T$ be a bilinear map where $\mathbb{G}$ and $\mathbb{G}_T$ are both multiplicative cyclic groups of prime order p. Let g be a randomly chosen generator of group $\mathbb{G}$. Let $\varsigma \in_R \mathbb{Z}_p^*$ be chosen at random. Given as input a $(m+1)$-tuple*

---

[7] Cloud server's cooperation might be required.

$\mathbf{T} = (g, g^{\varsigma}, g^{\varsigma^2} \dots, g^{\varsigma^m}) \in \mathbb{G}^{m+1}$, *for any PPT adversary $\mathcal{A}$, the following probability is negligible*

$$\Pr\left[d = e(g,g)^{1/(\varsigma+c)} \text{ where } (c,d) = \mathcal{A}(\mathbf{T})\right] \leq negl(\log p).$$

Theorem 1. *Suppose m-BSDH Assumption hold, and* PRF *is a secure pseudorandom function. The* DPOS *scheme constructed in Sect. 4 is sound w.r.t. auditor, according to Definition 4 (Proof is given in the full paper [46]).*

Theorem 2. *Suppose m-BSDH Assumption hold, and* PRF *is a secure pseudorandom function. The* DPOS *scheme constructed in Sect. 4 is sound w.r.t. data owner, according to Definition 5 (Proof is given in the full paper [46]).*

6   Conclusion

We proposed a novel and efficient POS scheme. On one side, the proposed scheme is as efficient as privately verifiable POS scheme, especially very efficient in authentication tag generation. On the other side, the proposed scheme supports third party auditor and can revoke an auditor at any time, close to the functionality of publicly verifiable POS scheme. Compared to existing publicly verifiable POS scheme, our scheme improves the authentication tag generation speed by more than 100 times. How to prevent data leakage to ODA during proof process and how to enable dynamic operations (e.g. inserting/deleting a data block) in our scheme are in future work.

References

1. Apon, D., Huang, Y., Katz, J., Malozemoff, A.J.: Implementing cryptographic program obfuscation. Cryptology ePrint Archive, Report 2014/779 (2014). http://eprint.iacr.org/
2. Armknecht, F., Bohli, J.M., Karame, G.O., Liu, Z., Reuter, C.A.: Outsourced proofs of retrievability. In: Proceedings of the 2014 ACM SIGSAC Conference on Computer and Communications Security, CCS 2014, pp. 831–843 (2014)
3. Ateniese, G., Burns, R., Curtmola, R., Herring, J., Khan, O., Kissner, L., Peterson, Z., Song, D.: Remote data checking using provable data possession. ACM Tran. Inf. Sys. Sec. TISSEC 2011 14(1), 12:1–12:34 (2011)
4. Ateniese, G., Burns, R., Curtmola, R., Herring, J., Kissner, L., Peterson, Z., Song, D.: Provable data possession at untrusted stores. In: ACM CCS 2007, pp. 598–609. ACM (2007)
5. Ateniese, G., Kamara, S., Katz, J.: Proofs of storage from homomorphic identification protocols. In: Matsui, M. (ed.) ASIACRYPT 2009. LNCS, vol. 5912, pp. 319–333. Springer, Heidelberg (2009)
6. Ateniese, G., Pietro, R.D., Mancini, L.V., Tsudik, G.: Scalable and efficient provable data possession. In: SecureComm 2008, pp. 9:1–9:10. ACM (2008)
7. Boneh, D., Lynn, B., Shacham, H.: Short signatures from the weil pairing. J. Cryptology 17(4), 297–319 (2004)

8. Bowers, K.D., Juels, A., Oprea, A.: HAIL: A high-availability and integrity layer for cloud storage. In: ACM CCS 2009, pp. 187–198. ACM (2009)
9. Bowers, K.D., Juels, A., Oprea, A.: Proofs of retrievability: theory and implementation. In: CCSW 2009, pp. 43–54. ACM (2009)
10. Cash, D., Küpçü, A., Wichs, D.: Dynamic proofs of retrievability via oblivious RAM. In: Johansson, T., Nguyen, P.Q. (eds.) EUROCRYPT 2013. LNCS, vol. 7881, pp. 279–295. Springer, Heidelberg (2013)
11. Chang, E.-C., Xu, J.: Remote integrity check with dishonest storage server. In: Jajodia, S., Lopez, J. (eds.) ESORICS 2008. LNCS, vol. 5283, pp. 223–237. Springer, Heidelberg (2008)
12. Chen, X., Li, J., Ma, J., Tang, Q., Lou, W.: New algorithms for secure outsourcing of modular exponentiations. In: Foresti, S., Yung, M., Martinelli, F. (eds.) ESORICS 2012. LNCS, vol. 7459, pp. 541–556. Springer, Heidelberg (2012)
13. Curtmola, R., Khan, O., Burns, R., Ateniese, G.: MR-PDP: multiple-replica provable data possession. In: ICDCS 2008, pp. 411–420. IEEE (2008)
14. Deswarte, Y., Quisquater, J.J., Saïdane, A.: Remote integrity checking: how to trust files stored on untrusted servers. In: Jajodia, S., Strous, L. (eds.) IICIS 2003. IFIP, vol. 140, pp. 1–11. Springer, Heidelberg (2004)
15. Dodis, Y., Vadhan, S., Wichs, D.: Proofs of retrievability via hardness amplification. In: Reingold, O. (ed.) TCC 2009. LNCS, vol. 5444, pp. 109–127. Springer, Heidelberg (2009)
16. Erway, C., Küpçü, A., Papamanthou, C., Tamassia, R.: Dynamic provable data possession. In: ACM CCS 2009, pp. 213–222. ACM (2009)
17. Garg, S., Gentry, C., Halevi, S., Raykova, M., Sahai, A., Waters, B.: Candidate indistinguishability obfuscation and functional encryption for all circuits. In: Proceedings of the 2013 IEEE 54th Annual Symposium on Foundations of Computer Science, FOCS 2013, pp. 40–49 (2013)
18. Goldreich, O.: A sample of samplers: a computational perspective on sampling. In: Goldreich, O. (ed.) Studies in Complexity and Cryptography. LNCS, vol. 6650, pp. 302–332. Springer, Heidelberg (2011)
19. Guan, C., Ren, K., Zhang, F., Kerschbaum, F., Yu, J.: A symmetric-key based proofs of retrievability supporting public verification. In: Proceedings of 20th European Symposium on Research in Computer Security, ESORICS 2015, pp. 203–223 (2015). www.fkerschbaum.org/esorics15b.pdf
20. Hao, Z., Zhong, S., Yu, N.: A privacy-preserving remote data integrity checking protocol with data dynamics and public verifiability. In:TKDE 2011, vol. 23(9), pp. 1432–1437 (2011)
21. Hohenberger, S., Lysyanskaya, A.: How to securely outsource cryptographic computations. In: Kilian, J. (ed.) TCC 2005. LNCS, vol. 3378, pp. 264–282. Springer, Heidelberg (2005)
22. Juels, A., Kaliski, B.S.,J.: PORs: Proofs of retrievability for large files. In: ACM CCS 2007, pp. 584–597. ACM (2007)
23. Kate, A., Zaverucha, G.M., Goldberg, I.: Constant-size commitments to polynomials and their applications. In: ASIACRYPT 2010, pp. 177–194 (2010)
24. Naor, M., Rothblum, G.N.: The complexity of online memory checking. J. ACM, 56(1) (2009)
25. Ren, Y., Shen, J., Wang, J., Fang, L.: Outsourced data tagging via authority and delegable auditing for cloud storage. In: 49th Annual IEEE International Carnahan Conference on Security Technology, ICCST 2015, pp. 131–134. IEEE (2015)
26. Ren, Y., Shen, J., Wang, J., Han, J., Lee, S.: Mutual verifiable provable data auditing in public cloud storage. J. Internet Technol. 16(2), 317–324 (2015)

27. Ren, Y., Xu, J., Wang, J., Kim, J.U.: Designated-verifier provable data possession in public cloud storage. Int. J. Secur. Appl. **7**(6), 11–20 (2013)
28. Schwarz, T.J.E., Miller, E.L.: Store, forget, and check: using algebraic signatures to check remotely administered storage. In: ICDCS 2006. IEEE (2006)
29. Sebé, F., Domingo-Ferrer, J., Martínez-Ballesté, A., Deswarte, Y., Quisquater, J.J.: Efficient remote data possession checking in critical information infrastructures. In: TKDE 2008, vol. 20, no. 8, pp. 1034–1038 (2008)
30. Shacham, H., Waters, B.: Compact proofs of retrievability. In: Pieprzyk, J. (ed.) ASIACRYPT 2008. LNCS, vol. 5350, pp. 90–107. Springer, Heidelberg (2008)
31. Shacham, H., Waters, B.: Compact proofs of retrievability. J. Cryptology **26**(3), 442–483 (2013)
32. Shah, M.A., Baker, M., Mogul, J.C., Swaminathan, R.: Auditing to keep online storage services honest. In: HotOS 2007. USENIX Association (2007)
33. Shah, M.A., Swaminathan, R., Baker, M.: Privacy-preserving audit and extraction of digital contents. Cryptology ePrint Archive, Report 2008/186 (2008). http://eprint.iacr.org/2008/186
34. Shen, S.-T., Tzeng, W.-G.: Delegable provable data possession for remote data in the clouds. In: Qing, S., Susilo, W., Wang, G., Liu, D. (eds.) ICICS 2011. LNCS, vol. 7043, pp. 93–111. Springer, Heidelberg (2011)
35. Shi, E., Stefanov, E., Papamanthou, C.: Practical dynamic proofs of retrievability. In: ACM CCS 2013, pp. 325–336. ACM (2013)
36. Wang, B., Li, B., Li, H.: Oruta: Privacy-preserving public auditing for shared data in the cloud. In: IEEE Cloud 2012, pp. 295–302. IEEE (2012)
37. Wang, B., Li, B., Li, H.: Public auditing for shared data with efficient user revocation in the cloud. In: INFOCOM 2013, pp. 2904–2912. IEEE (2013)
38. Wang, C., Chow, S.S., Wang, Q., Ren, K., Lou, W.: Privacy-preserving public auditing for secure cloud storage. IEEE Trans. Comput. **62**(2), 362–375 (2013)
39. Wang, C., Ren, K., Lou, W., Li, J.: Toward publicly auditable secure cloud data storage services. IEEE Network Mag. **24**(4), 19–24 (2010)
40. Wang, C., Wang, Q., Ren, K., Cao, N., Lou, W.: Towards secure and dependable storate services in cloud computing. IEEE Trans. Serv. Comput. **5**(2), 220–232 (2012)
41. Wang, C., Wang, Q., Ren, K., Lou, W.: Ensuring data storage security in cloud computing. In: Proceedings of IWQoS 2009, pp. 1–9. IEEE (2009)
42. Wang, C., Wang, Q., Ren, K., Lou, W.: Privacy-preserving public auditing for data storage security in cloud computing. In: INFOCOM 2010, pp. 525–533. IEEE (2010)
43. Wang, Q., Wang, C., Li, J., Ren, K., Lou, W.: Enabling public verifiability and data dynamics for storage security in cloud computing. In: Backes, M., Ning, P. (eds.) ESORICS 2009. LNCS, vol. 5789, pp. 355–370. Springer, Heidelberg (2009)
44. Wang, Q., Wang, C., Ren, K., Lou, W., Li, J.: Enabling public auditability and data dynamics for storage security in cloud computing. TPDS **22**(5), 847–859 (2011)
45. Xu, J., Chang, E.C.: Towards efficient proofs of retrievability. In: ACM Symposium on Information, Computer and Communications Security, AsiaCCS 2012 (2012)
46. Xu, J., Yang, A., Zhou, J., Wong, D.S.: Lightweight and privacy-preserving delegatable proofs of storage. Cryptology ePrint Archive, Report 2014/395 (2014). http://eprint.iacr.org/2014/395
47. Xu, J., Zhou, J.: Leakage resilient proofs of ownership in cloud storage, revisited. In: Boureanu, I., Owesarski, P., Vaudenay, S. (eds.) ACNS 2014. LNCS, vol. 8479, pp. 97–115. Springer, Heidelberg (2014)

48. Yang, K., Jia, X.: Data storage auditing service in cloud computing: challenges, methods and opportunities. World Wide Web **15**(4), 409–428 (2012)
49. Yang, K., Jia, X.: An efficient and secure dynamic auditing protocol for data storage in cloud computing. TPDS **24**(9), 1717–1726 (2013)
50. Yuan, J., Yu, S.: Proofs of retrievability with public verifiability and constant communication cost in cloud. In: Proceedings of the 2013 International Workshop on Security in Cloud Computing, Cloud Computing 2013, pp. 19–26. ACM (2013)
51. Zeng, K.: Publicly verifiable remote data integrity. In: Chen, L., Ryan, M.D., Wang, G. (eds.) ICICS 2008. LNCS, vol. 5308, pp. 419–434. Springer, Heidelberg (2008)
52. Zhu, Y., Hu, H., Ahn, G.J., Yu, M.: Cooperative provable data possession for integrity verification in multicloud storage. TPDS **23**(12), 2231–2244 (2012)
53. Zhu, Y., Wang, H., Hu, Z., Ahn, G.J., Hu, H., Yau, S.S.: Dynamic audit services for integrity verification of outsourced storages in clouds. In: Proceedings of SAC 2011, pp. 1550–1557. ACM (2011)

Anonymous RAM

Michael Backes[1,2], Amir Herzberg[3], Aniket Kate[4], and Ivan Pryvalov[1(✉)]

[1] CISPA, Saarland University, Saarland Informatics Campus, Saarbrücken, Germany
pryvalov@cs.uni-saarland.de
[2] MPI-SWS, Saarland Informatics Campus, Saarbrücken, Germany
[3] Bar-Ilan University, Ramat Gan, Israel
[4] Purdue University, West Lafayette, USA

Abstract. We define the concept of and present provably secure constructions for *Anonymous RAM (AnonRAM)*, a novel multi-user storage primitive that offers strong privacy and integrity guarantees. AnonRAM combines privacy features of anonymous communication and oblivious RAM (ORAM) schemes, allowing it to protect, simultaneously, the *privacy of content, access patterns* and *user's identity*, from curious servers and from other (even adversarial) users. AnonRAM further protects *integrity*, i.e., it prevents malicious users from corrupting data of other users. We present two secure AnonRAM schemes, differing in design and time complexity. The first scheme has a simpler design; like efficient ORAM schemes, its time complexity is poly-logarithmic in the number of cells (per user); however, it is *linear* in the number of users. The second AnonRAM scheme reduces the overall complexity to poly-logarithmic in the total number of cells (of all users) at the cost of requiring two (non-colluding) servers.

Keywords: Anonymity · Access privacy · Oblivious RAM · Outsourced data · (Universal) Re-randomizable encryption · Oblivious PRF

1 Introduction

The advent of cloud-based outsourcing services has been accompanied by a growing interest in *security and privacy*, striving to prevent exposure and abuse of sensitive information by adversarial cloud service providers and users. This includes, in particular, the tasks of *data privacy*, i.e., hiding users' data from overly curious entities such as the provider, as well as *access privacy*, i.e., hiding information about data-access patterns such as *which* data element is being accessed and *how* (read/write?). The underlying rationale is that exposure of data access patterns may often lead to a deep exposure of *what* the user intends to do. An extensive line of research has produced impressive results and tools for achieving both data and access privacy. In particular, oblivious RAM (ORAM) schemes, first introduced by Goldreich and Ostrovsky [29], have been extensively investigated in the last few years, yielding a multitude of elegant and increasingly efficient results [11,22,26,27,30,34,36,38].

© Springer International Publishing Switzerland 2016
I. Askoxylakis et al. (Eds.): ESORICS 2016, Part I, LNCS 9878, pp. 344–362, 2016.
DOI: 10.1007/978-3-319-45744-4_17

Another important privacy goal is to hide *who* is accessing the data, i.e., conceal the *identity* of the user to ensure anonymity. This area spawned extensive research and multiple protocols and systems for anonymous communication [7,8,13,15]. The Tor network [37] currently constitutes the most widely used representative of these works.

We focus on the combination of these two goals: hiding content and access patterns as offered by ORAM schemes, but also concealing the user identities as offered by anonymous communication protocols. Experts in the relevant areas may not be completely surprised to find that designing this primitive is quite challenging. In particular, the privacy guarantees cannot be constructed by solely combining both approaches: the naïve idea to achieve these privacy properties simultaneously is to maintain separate ORAM data structures for each user and have users access the system using the anonymous communication protocol. However, this construction does not hide the access patterns, since the server can determine if the same data structure is accessed twice, and thereby trivially link two accesses made by the same anonymous user. Instead of multiple ORAMs, one could try to use a single ORAM as a black-box with data of all users contained in it. However, this does not work either, as inherently, the users have to share the same key, and the privacy properties immediately fail in presence of curious adversaries. (See Sect. 3 for more details.) Supporting multiple, potentially malicious (or even 'just curious') users is significantly harder than supporting multiple cooperating clients (e.g., devices of the same user), as in [17,23,28,39].

Furthermore, when considering an adversarial environment and, in particular, malicious users, *integrity*, i.e., preventing one user from corrupting data of other users, is also critical. Notice that the (popular) 'honest-but-curious' model is easier to justify for servers (e.g., running ORAM) than for clients; handling (also) malicious client is very important. Note also that ensuring integrity is fairly straightforward, when users can be identified securely; however, this conflicts with the goals of anonymity and, even more, with the desire for oblivious access, i.e., hiding even the pattern of access to data. As often happens in security, the mechanisms for the different goals do not seem to nicely combine, resulting in a rather challenging problem, to which we offer the first - but definitely not final - pair of solutions, albeit with significant limitations and room for improvement.

Our Contributions. We define *Anonymous RAM* (AnonRAM) schemes and present two constructions that are provably secure in the random oracle model. AnonRAM schemes support multiple users, each user owning multiple memory cells. AnonRAM schemes simultaneously hide data content, access patterns, and the users' identities against honest-but-curious servers and against malicious users of the same service while ensuring that data can only be modified by the legitimate owner (Sect. 2).

The first scheme, called AnonRAM$_{lin}$, realizes a conceptually simple transformation that turns any secure single-user ORAM scheme into a secure AnonRAM scheme (that supports multiple users). The key idea here is to convert every single-user ORAM cell to a multi-cell having a cell for each user, and to employ re-randomizable encryption such that a user can hide her identity by re-randomizing all other cells in a multi-cell while updating her own cell (Sect. 3). The drawback of $\mathsf{AnonRAM_{lin}}$, however, is that its complexity is linear in the number of users (although poly-logarithmic in the number of cells per users). This linear complexity stems from the requirement that a user has to touch one cell of each user when accessing her own cell.

The second scheme, called $\mathsf{AnonRAM_{polylog}}$, reduces the overall complexity to poly-logarithmic in the number of users (Sect. 4). This comes at the cost of requiring two non-colluding servers S and T. Server S maintains all user data in encrypted form using a *universal* re-encryption scheme, thereby disallowing S and other users to establish a mapping between a user and her data blocks. Essentially, $\mathsf{AnonRAM_{polylog}}$ constitutes an extension of hierarchical ORAM designs, e.g., by Goldreich-Ostrovski [19], where the reshuffle operation and mapping to 'dummy' blocks are performed by the dedicated server T. This prevents user deanonymization by the server S or by other users. Furthermore, mappings to specific buckets are achieved by means of a specific oblivious PRF.

For the sake of exposition, we first describe simplified variants of both schemes in the presence of honest-but-curious users. We subsequently show how to extend both constructions to handle malicious users as well. The extension mainly involves adding an integrity element to the employed (universal) re-encryption, such that any user can only re-encrypt data of other users, but not corrupt it.

Finally, we consider it an important contribution that we present a rigorous model and a definition for this challenging problem of AnonRAM, and show their suitability by providing provable security protocol instantiations.

Related Work. Several multi-*client* ORAM solutions have been proposed in literature. Goodrich et al. [23] observe that stateless ORAM schemes, in which no state is carried from one access action to another, are suitable for a group of trusted clients. [4,10] address the concurrent accesses by multiple client devices of the same user in the synchronous model, while [2,32,35,39] deal with asynchronous concurrent accesses.

Franz et al. [17] introduce the concept of delegatable ORAM, where a (trusted) database owner can delegate access rights to other users and periodically performs reshuffling to protect the privacy of their accesses. [28] allows a storage owner to share a server-side ORAM structure among a group of users, but assumes that all users share the same symmetric key which none of them is going to provide to the server. These works, however, do not protect privacy of a client from malicious or 'curious' clients.

AnonRAM schemes avoid the strong non-collusion assumption between the users and the storage server. In other words, we consider the problem of anonymously accessing the server by multiple users, where the server (cooperating with some users) should not be able to learn which honest user accessed which cell over the server. Notably, we achieve our stronger privacy guarantees against a stronger adversary without requiring any communication among the users.

The only other multi-*user* ORAM scheme has been proposed by Zhang et al. [25]. Their scheme uses a set of intermediate nodes to convert a user's query to an ORAM query to the server. Privacy of the scheme is, however, analyzed only for individual non-anonymous user accesses and not for multi-user anonymous access patterns. Furthermore, their scheme does not provide integrity protection against malicious users. Moreover, their work lacks both definitions and proofs; as the reader will see in our work, the definitions and proofs, we found necessary to claim security of our schemes, are non-trivial.

2   AnonRAM Definitions

We consider a set of N users $\mathcal{U} = \{U_1, \ldots, U_N\}$, a set of η servers $\mathcal{S} = \{S_1, \ldots, S_\eta\}$, a set Σ of messages, and we let M denote the number of data cells available to each user. All protocols are parametrized by the security parameter λ. Before defining the class of AnonRAM schemes, we provide the definitions of access requests and access patterns.

Definition 1 (Access Requests). *An* access request AR *is a tuple* $(j, \alpha, m) \in [1, M] \times \{\mathsf{Read}, \mathsf{Write}\} \times \Sigma$. *Here* j *is called the* (cell) index *of* AR, α *the* access type, *and* m *the* input message.

Intuitively, an access request (j, α, m) will denote that m should be written into cell j (if $\alpha = \mathsf{Write}$), or that the content of cell j should be read (if $\alpha = \mathsf{Read}$; in this case m is ignored and we often just write $(j, \alpha, *)$).

Definition 2 (Access Patterns). *An* access pattern *is a series of tuples* (i, AR_i) *where* $i \in [1, N]$ *is a user identifier and* AR_i *is an access request.*

For notational simplicity, we will write (i, j, α, m) instead of $(i, (j, \alpha, m))$ for the individual elements of access patterns.

We next define AnonRAM schemes. In this work, we consider sequential schemes where one participant is active at any point in time.

Definition 3 (AnonRAM Schemes). *An* AnonRAM *scheme is a tuple* $(\mathsf{Setup}, \mathsf{User}, \mathsf{Server}_1, \ldots, \mathsf{Server}_\eta)$ *of* $\eta + 2$ *PPT algorithms, where:*

- *The initialization algorithm* Setup *maps a security parameter* λ *and an identifier id, to an initial state, where* $id \in \{0, 1, \ldots, \eta\}$ *identifies one of the servers (for* $id > 0$*) or the user (for* $id = 0$*).*
- *The user algorithm* User *processes two kinds of inputs: (a) access requests (from the user) and (b) pairs* (l, m) *where* $l \in [1, \eta]$ *denotes a server and* m *a message from server* S_l. User *maps the current state and input to a new state and to either a response provided to the user or a pair* (l, m) *with* $l \in [1, \eta]$ *denoting a server and* m *being a message for* S_l.
- *The server algorithm* Server_l *for server* S_l *maps the current server state and input (message from user or from another server) to a new server state and a message either to the user or to another server.*

Adversarial Models and Protocol Execution. We consider two different adversarial models: (i) *honest-but-curious* (HbC) adversaries that learn the state of one server S^* and of a subset $\mathcal{U}^*$ of users, and (ii) *malicious users* (Mal_Users) adversaries that learn the state of one server (as before) and additionally control a subset $\mathcal{U}^*$ of users. In both models, the adversary can additionally eavesdrop on all messages sent on the network, i.e., between users and servers, and between two servers.

We now define the sequential execution $\mathsf{Exec}(\mathcal{AR}, \mathsf{Adv}, AP, \zeta)$ of an Anon-RAM scheme $\mathcal{AR}$ in the presence of an adversary Adv and a given access pattern AP assuming an adversarial model $\zeta \in \{\mathsf{HbC}, \mathsf{Mal\_Users}\}$.

Definition 4 (Execution). *Let $\mathcal{AR}$ be an AnonRAM scheme* (Setup, User, $\mathsf{Server}_1, \ldots, \mathsf{Server}_\eta$), Adv *be a PPT algorithm,* $\zeta \in \{\mathsf{HbC}, \mathsf{Mal\_Users}\}$ *and AP be an access pattern. The execution* $\mathsf{Exec}(\mathcal{AR}, \mathsf{Adv}, AP, \zeta)$ *is the following randomized process:*

1. *All parties are initialized using* Setup, *resulting in initial states σ_{U_i} for each user U_i, and σ_{S_l} for each server S_l.*
2. Adv *selects a server S^* and a strict subset $\mathcal{U}^* \subset \mathcal{U}$.*
3. *Let $(i, j, \alpha, m_{i,j})$ be the first element of AP; if AP is empty, terminate.*
4. *If $\mathsf{U}_i \in \mathcal{U}^*$ and $\zeta = \mathsf{Mal\_Users}$, then let (l, m) be the output of* Adv *on input $(i, j, \alpha, m_{i,j})$. Otherwise, let (l, m) be the output of* User *on input $(j, \alpha, m_{i,j})$, with state σ_{U_i}, and update σ_{U_i} accordingly.*
5. *Invoke S_l with (input) message m. The server S_l may call other servers (possibly recursively) and finally produces an (output) message m'.*
6. *If $\mathsf{U}_i \in \mathcal{U}^*$ and $\zeta = \mathsf{Mal\_Users}$, provide the message m' to* Adv. *Otherwise, provide m' to user U_i. U_i (Adv if $\mathsf{U}_i \in \mathcal{U}^*$ and $\zeta = \mathsf{Mal\_Users}$) may repeat sending messages to any servers. Eventually, U_i (Adv) terminates.*
7. *Repeat the loop (from step 3) with the next element of AP (until empty). Throughout the execution, the adversary learns the internal states of S^* and of all users in $\mathcal{U}^*$, as well as all messages sent on the network.*

A trace *is the random variable defined by an execution, using uniformly random coin-tosses for all parties. The trace includes the sequence of messages in the execution corresponding to access requests and the final state of the adversary. Let $\Theta(x)$ denote the trace of execution x.*

Privacy and Integrity of AnonRAM Schemes. To define privacy for Anon-RAM schemes, we consider an additional PPT adversary $\mathcal{D}$ called the distinguisher. $\mathcal{D}$ outputs two arbitrary access patterns of the same finite length, which differ only in inputs to unobserved users. We then randomly select and execute one of these two patterns. The distinguisher's goal is to identify which pattern was used. Since these two accesses may differ in user, cell, operation, or value, this definition encompasses all relevant privacy properties in this setting including anonymity (identity privacy), confidentiality (value privacy), and obliviousness (cell and operation privacy). We call an adversary Adv *compliant* with a pair of access patterns (AP_0, AP_1) if Adv only outputs sets $\mathcal{U}^*$ of users in Step (2) of

$\mathsf{Exec}(\mathcal{AR}, \mathsf{Adv}, AP_0, \zeta)$ and $\mathsf{Exec}(\mathcal{AR}, \mathsf{Adv}, AP_1, \zeta)$ such that AP_0 and AP_1 are identical when restricted to users in $\mathcal{U}^*$.

Definition 5 (Privacy of AnonRAM). *An AnonRAM scheme $\mathcal{AR}$ preserves privacy in adversarial model $\zeta \in \{\mathsf{HbC}, \mathsf{Mal\_Users}\}$; if for every pair of (same finite length) access patterns (AP_0, AP_1) and for every pair of PPT algorithms $(\mathsf{Adv}, \mathcal{D})$ s.t. Adv is compliant with (AP_0, AP_1), we have that*

$$\left| \Pr\left[b^* = b \colon b^* \leftarrow \mathcal{D}\left(\Theta\left(\mathsf{Exec}(\mathcal{AR}, \mathsf{Adv}, AP_b, \zeta)\right)\right)\right] - \frac{1}{2} \right|$$

is negligible in λ, where the probability is taken over uniform coin tosses by all parties, and $b \leftarrow_R \{0, 1\}$.

Note that when all-but-one (i.e., $N - 1$) users are observed and $\zeta = \mathsf{HbC}$, our privacy property corresponds to the standard ORAM access privacy definition [19]. ORAM is hence a special case of AnonRAM with a single user ($N = 1$).

AnonRAM should ensure *integrity* to prevent invalid executions caused by parties deviating from the protocol. Informally, a trace is invalid if a value read from a cell does not correspond to the most recently written value to the cell.

Definition 6 (Integrity of AnonRAM). *Let ϑ be a trace of execution with access pattern AP, and let $AR = (j, \mathsf{Read}, *)$ with $(i, AR_i) \in AP$ be a read request for cell j of user U_i, returning a value x. Let $AR' = (j, \mathsf{Write}, x')$ be the most recent previous write request to cell j of user U_i in AP, or $\perp$ if there was no such previous write request. If $x \neq x'$, we say that this read request is* invalid. *If any read request in the trace is invalid, then the trace is invalid.*

An AnonRAM scheme $\mathcal{AR}$ preserves integrity *if there is negligible (in λ) probability of invalid traces when the traces are constrained to the view of the honest users (all $\mathsf{U}_i \in \mathcal{U}$ in the HbC model, and all users $\mathsf{U}_i \in \mathcal{U}/\mathcal{U}^*$ in the $\mathsf{Mal\_Users}$ model) for any PPT adversary and any access pattern AP.*

3   Linear-Complexity AnonRAM

In this section, we present our first AnonRAM constructions and prove them secure in the underlying model. For the sake of exposition, we start with a few seemingly natural but flawed approaches to construct AnonRAM schemes.

Seemingly Natural but Flawed Approaches. A first natural idea to design an AnonRAM scheme is to maintain all the $M \cdot N$ cells in an encrypted form on the server and to only access them via an anonymous channel such as Tor [37]. However, this approach fails to achieve AnonRAM privacy, since the adversary can simply observe all memory accesses on the server and thereby determine how often the same cell j of a user is accessed. One may try to overcome this problem using a shared $(M \cdot N)$-cell *stateless* ORAM [23] containing M cells for each of N users and assuming that every user executes her ORAM requests via an anonymous channel. In this case, all users will have to use the *same* private key in the symmetric encryption scheme employed in the ORAM protocol to hide their cells from the server. However, this allows Eve, an HbC user, to break privacy of honest users, by observing the values in cells (allocated to honest users) which she downloads and decrypts as part of her legitimate ORAM requests.

Another natural design would be to use a separate ORAM for the M cells of each user and rely on anonymous access to hide user identities. This use would hide the users' individual access patterns, but the server can identify all accesses by the same user and thereby violate the AnonRAM privacy requirement.

The AnonRAM schemes presented in this paper overcome such problems by having users re-randomize cells belonging to other users as well whenever their own cells are being accessed in addition to encrypting the user's own cells.

3.1 AnonRAM$_{lin}$ and Its Security Against HbC Adversaries

We now present the AnonRAM$_{lin}$ construction and prove it secure in the HbC adversarial model. AnonRAM$_{lin}$ uses an anonymous communication channel [37] and the (single-user, single-server) Path ORAM [36] or other ORAM scheme satisfying a property identified below.

In Path ORAM, the user's cells are stored on the server RAM as a set of encrypted data *blocks* such that each block consists of a single ciphertext and all blocks are encrypted with the same key known to the user's ORAM client. A block encrypts either a user's cell, or auxiliary information used by the User algorithm. To access a cell, the ORAM client *reads* (and decrypts) a fixed number of blocks from the server, and *writes* encrypted values (cells or some special messages) in a fixed number of blocks. The server's duty is to execute these user's read and write requests.

AnonRAM$_{lin}$ employs N instances (one per user) of Path ORAM for M cells each while requiring a single server.[1] To encrypt data as required in the ORAM scheme, AnonRAM$_{lin}$ uses a semantically secure re-randomizable encryption (RE) scheme (E, R, D) (e.g., ElGamal encryption), where E, R, and D are respectively encryption, re-randomization, and decryption operations. The AnonRAM$_{lin}$ client of user U_i, has access to her private key sk_i and to the public keys $(pk_1, \ldots, pk_N)$ of all users. In AnonRAM$_{lin}$, the ORAM scheme uses this RE scheme (E, R, D) instead of the (symmetric) encryption scheme used in 'regular' Path ORAM.

Intuitively, an AnonRAM$_{lin}$ client internally runs an ORAM client and mediates its communication with the server. Whenever the ORAM client reads or writes a specific block, the AnonRAM$_{lin}$ client performs corresponding read or write operations *for all users*, without divulging the user identity to the server at the network level, as follows: Reading a block of another user can be trivially achieved, since the block is encrypted for the owner's key, but the contents are not used (our goal is only to create indistinguishable accesses for all users). Writing a block belonging to other user's ORAM must not corrupt the data inside and is hence achieved by re-randomizing the blocks of other users.

---

[1] AnonRAM$_{lin}$ can also use an ORAM scheme that uses multiple servers. In this case, AnonRAM$_{lin}$ will use the same number of servers.

The Setup and Server algorithms of AnonRAM$_{lin}$ are simply N instances of the corresponding algorithm of the underlying ORAM scheme (e.g., Path ORAM). Namely, the Setup initializes state for N copies of the ORAM (one per user) and the Server receives a 'user identifier' i together with each request, and runs the ORAM's Server algorithm using the ith state over the request. The Server algorithm for the AnonRAM$_{lin}$ scheme simply processes Read/Write requests sent by the users as in the ORAM scheme, e.g. the server returns the content of the requested block for Read requests or overrides the content of the requested block with the new value for Write requests.

We finally describe the User algorithm of AnonRAM$_{lin}$ using pseudocode in Fig. 1 to increase readability. It relies on an oracle $\mathcal{O}_c$ for the ORAM client, and an RE scheme (E, R, D). We write (E_i, R_i, D_i) for the corresponding encryption, re-encryption and decryption operations using the corresponding keys for user U_i. The pseudocode depicts which operations are performed for an individual access request (j, α, m) of user U_i. Its execution starts with invoking user U_i's local ORAM client $\mathcal{O}_c$ with the access request (j, α, m), and ends with a **Return** message to U_i. The process involves multiple instances of Read and Write requests from $\mathcal{O}_c$ for specified blocks kept by the server. These requests to Read and Write blocks kept by the server, should not be confused with access requests (j, α, m), where $\alpha \in \{Read, Write\}$ for ORAM cells.

---

upon access request (j, α, m) from user U_i :
    Invoke the ORAM client $\mathcal{O}_c$ with access request (j, α, m).

upon read request from $\mathcal{O}_c$ for block j' :
    for $k \in [1, N]$ **do** Let $B[j', k] \leftarrow$ Read block j' of user U_k kept by the server.
    Return $B[j', i]$ to $\mathcal{O}_c$.

upon write request from $\mathcal{O}_c$, for value (ciphertext) B in block j' :
    $B[j', i] \leftarrow B$
    for $k \in [1, N] | k \neq i$ **do** $B[j', k] \leftarrow R_k(B[j', k])$
    for $k \in [1, N]$ **do**
        Write block $B[j', k]$ to position j' of user U_k and release it from memory.

upon Receiving a result res from $\mathcal{O}_c$:
    Return res to U_i.

Fig. 1. User algorithm of AnonRAM$_{lin}$ with access request (j, α, m) for user U_i.

So far, we selected Path ORAM as a specific ORAM instantiation. However, any other ORAM scheme is equally applicable, provided that it exhibits an additional property: individual accesses have to be indistinguishable, i.e., the adversary observing just one access request from an access pattern should not be able to recognise how many accesses the honest user performed so far. We call this property *indistinguishability of individual accesses*, and it is trivially satisfied by

Path ORAM. Hierarchical ORAMs (e.g., [19,23,26,27]), however, do not achieve indistinguishability of individual accesses, as the runtime of individual accesses depends on the number of accesses performed so far; in particular, the client has to reshuffle periodically a variable amount of data.

Theorem 1. AnonRAM$_{lin}$ *preserves access privacy in the adversarial model* HbC, *when using a secure ORAM scheme* $\mathcal{O}$ *that satisfies indistinguishability of individual accesses, and a semantically secure re-randomizable encryption scheme* (E, R, D).

Proof. Assume to the contrary that some PPT HbC adversary $\mathcal{D}$ can efficiently distinguish, with a non-negligible advantage, between a pair of access-patterns $AP = \{(i_u, j_u, \alpha_u, m_u)\}, AP' = \{(i'_u, j'_u, \alpha'_u, m'_u)\}_{u \in [1,len]}$ of length *len*.

Let $AP_v = \{(i^*_u, j^*_u, \alpha^*_u, m^*_u)\}_{u \in [1,len]}$ be a 'hybrid' access pattern, where $(i^*_u, j^*_u, \alpha^*_u, m^*_u) = (i_u, j_u, \alpha_u, m_u)$ for $u \leq v$, and $(i^*_u, j^*_u, \alpha^*_u, m^*_u) = (i'_u, j'_u, \alpha'_u, m'_u)$ for $u > v$. In fact, let v be the smallest such value, where some adversary (say $\mathcal{D}$) can distinguish between AP_{v-1} and AP_v, and such $v > 0$ exists by the standard 'hybrid argument' as AP and AP' differ at least in one access.

If $i_v = i'_v$ (i.e., for the same user), the executions only differ in the ORAM client $\mathcal{O}_c$ Read/Write blocks for U_{i_v}; however, this immediately contradicts the privacy of the underlying ORAM scheme. Notice that a user does not decrypt or modify the other users' data during her accesses.

Therefore, assume $i_v \neq i'_v$. Since we expect our ORAM client $\mathcal{O}_c$ to satisfy indistinguishability of individual accesses, the difference between these two patterns is only between the encryption of the blocks output by $\mathcal{O}_c$ and the re-encryption of the blocks received anonymously by the ORAM server. However, ability to distinguish between these, contradicts the indistinguishability property of the semantically secure re-randomizable encryption scheme (E, R, D). □

Let c_S and c_B denote the amortized costs of client-side storage and communication complexity of the underlying ORAM protocol. Then, the respective amortized costs of AnonRAM$_{lin}$ are $N \cdot c_S$ and $N \cdot c_B$. For example, using Path ORAM, the client-side storage and communication complexity costs of AnonRAM$_{lin}$ become $O(N \log M)$ and $O(N \log^2 M)$.

3.2   AnonRAM$_{lin}^{M}$ and Its Security Against Malicious Users

When some users are malicious, we need to ensure that only a user knowing the private key associated with a block can update the value inside the block, while other users should only be able to re-randomize it. Leveraging the security of AnonRAM$_{lin}$ to the adversarial model of malicious users, we require a semantically secure encryption primitive such that a ciphertext C' can replace a ciphertext C if C' is a re-randomization of C or if the encryptor knows the encryption key for C. Whenever a block is written, the user attaches a zero-knowledge proof showing *either* that the ciphertext is re-encryption of the previous ciphertext *or* that the user has the (secret) encryption key. The server verifies the proof before updating the block in its RAM memory. This ensures indistinguishability of re-encryption from new encryptions, while ensuring that one user cannot corrupt or modify any value of another user. We denote the resulting scheme as $\mathsf{AnonRAM}_{\mathsf{lin}}^{\mathsf{M}}$.

The required ZK proofs are standard. For the re-randomizable CPA-secure ElGamal encryption scheme, this will involve a ZK proof of knowledge of discrete logarithm [33] and a ZK proof of equality of the discrete logarithm of two pairs of group elements [9] composed in such a way that a user proves validity of one of the statements, without releaving to the server which statement has been proven [12,14] (see also Example 3 of [5]). Following the formal notation from [24] and extending it for proving "one-out-of-several" statements, the required proof is

$$PoK\{x_i | pk_i = g^{x_i}\} \text{ or } P\{\exists r \text{ s.t. } (C_1', C_2') = (C_1^r, C_2^r)\},$$

where $P(PoK)$ stands for proof (of knowledge), g is a generator of a group of prime order q, $(pk_i, C = (C_1, C_2), C' = (C_1', C_2'))$ are group elements, and (x_i, r) are elements in $\mathbb{Z}_q$.

Theorem 2. $\mathsf{AnonRAM}_{\mathsf{lin}}^{\mathsf{M}}$ *based on a secure ORAM scheme $\mathcal{O}$ that satisfies indistinguishability of individual accesses, CPA-secure public-key encryption scheme (e.g., ElGamal), and a ZK proof defined above, preserves integrity and privacy in the adversarial model* $\mathsf{Mal\_Users}$.

Proof Sketch. The integrity argument is simple: use of the ZK proof for proving one-out-of-two statements ensures that the adversarial users cannot modify the cell of other honest users. The adversarial users also cannot change the order of cells in a sequence of cells as the server verifies correctness of one cell at a time. They can only re-randomize the cells of the honest users.

The privacy properties are also preserved similarly to $\mathsf{AnonRAM}_{\mathsf{lin}}$ as the disjunctive nature of the included ZK proof does not allow the server to determine which of N cells is modified by an honest user, while privacy of the accessed cell-index as well as the access type is maintained by the employed ORAM scheme.   □

4 Polylogarithmic-Complexity AnonRAM

The $\mathsf{AnonRAM}_{\mathsf{lin}}$ scheme exhibits acceptable performance for a small number of users, but linear overhead renders it prohibitively expensive as the number of users increases. In this section, we present $\mathsf{AnonRAM}_{\mathsf{polylog}}$, an AnonRAM scheme whose overhead is poly-logarithmic in the number of users.

$\mathsf{AnonRAM}_{\mathsf{polylog}}$ is conceptually based on the hierarchical Goldreich-Ostrovsky ORAM (GO-ORAM) construction [19], where a user periodically reshuffles her cells maintained over a *storage server* S. To reshuffle cells belonging to multiple users, we introduce in $\mathsf{AnonRAM}_{\mathsf{polylog}}$ an additional server, the so-called *tag server* T. The tag server reshuffles data on the users' behalf, without knowing the data elements, and thereby maintains a user privacy from the storage server S as well as from the other users. The tag server only requires constant-size storage to perform this reshuffling, and we show that, similarly to the storage server, it cannot violate (on its own or with colluding users) the privacy requirements of AnonRAM schemes.[2]

We first describe necessary cryptographic tools, and then the AnonRAM$_{\text{polylog}}$ construction. AnonRAM$_{\text{polylog}}$ is secure for honest-but-curious users. Due to space constraints, we only provide informal descriptions for parts of the construction; detailed descriptions of AnonRAM$_{\text{polylog}}$ and AnonRAM$_{\text{polylog}}^{\text{M}}$, an extension dealing with malicious users, and security analysis thereof are in the extended version [1]. AnonRAM$_{\text{polylog}}^{\text{M}}$ adds an integrity element to AnonRAM$_{\text{polylog}}$ which, in the end, boils down to constructing a ZK proof system based on techniques described in Sect. 3.2.

4.1 Cryptographic Building Blocks

Universally Re-randomizable Encryption. A universally re-randomizable encryption (UREnc) scheme [20,31] allows to re-randomize given ciphertexts without requiring access to the encryption key. We use the construction of Golle et al. [20]: for a generator g of a multiplicative group G_q of prime order q and a private/public key pair (x_i, g^{x_i}) for party i with $x_i \in \mathbb{Z}_q^*$, the encryption $C = \mathsf{E}_i^*(m)$ of a message m is computed as an El-Gamal encryption of m together with an El-Gamal encryption of the identity $1 \in G_q$; i.e., $C = (g^a, g^{ax_i} \cdot m, g^b, g^{bx_i} \cdot 1)$ for $a, b \in \mathbb{Z}_q^*$. The ciphertext C can be re-randomized, denoted $\mathsf{R}^*(C)$ by selecting $a', b' \leftarrow_R \mathbb{Z}_q^*$ and outputting $(g^a \cdot (g^b)^{a'}, g^{ax_i} \cdot m \cdot (g^{bx_i})^{a'}, (g^b)^{b'}, (g^{bx_i})^{b'})$ as the new ciphertext. Note that this scheme is also multiplicatively homomorphic.

We employ a distributed version of the UREnc scheme, where the private key is shared between two servers such that both have to be involved in decryption.

(Partially Key-Homomorphic) Oblivious PRF. An oblivious pseudo-random function (OPRF) [18,24] enables a party holding an input tag μ to obtain an output $f_s(\mu)$ of a PRF $f_s(\cdot)$ from another party holding the key s without the latter party learning any information about the input tag μ.

We use the Jarecki-Liu OPRF construction [24] as our starting point. Here, the underlying PRF $f_s(\cdot)$ is a variant of the Dodis-Yampolskiy PRF construction [16] such that $f_s(\mu) := g^{1/(s+\mu)}$ is defined over a composite-order group of order $n = p_1 p_2$ for safe primes p_1 and p_2. This function constitutes a PRF if factoring safe RSA moduli is hard and the Decisional q-Diffie-Hellman Inversion assumption holds on a suitable group family G_n [24].

To securely realize pre-tag randomization in our Reshuffle algorithm (explained later), we propose a modification of the Jarecki-Liu OPRF where a second key $\hat{s}$ is used to define a new PRF $f_{s,\hat{s}}(\mu) := g^{\hat{s}/(s+\mu)}$. We call such a PRF *partially key-homomorphic* as $(f_{s,\hat{s}}(\mu))^\delta = f_{s,(\hat{s}\cdot\delta)}(\mu)$ holds for it. For unlinkability of PRF values of the same input μ with updated δ, we expect the

---

[2] Adhering to our adversarial model from Sect. 2, we only consider the corruption of a single server, and hence assume non-colluding servers S and T.

Composite DDH assumption[3] [6] to hold in G_n. We denote our OPRF construction as $\mathsf{OPRF}^{\mathcal{A},\mathcal{B}}_{s,\hat{s}}(\mu)$, where $\mathcal{A}$ denotes a party with input μ, and $\mathcal{B}$ denotes a server possessing the keys s and $\hat{s}$. Our OPRF protocol makes only minor changes to the Jarecki-Liu OPRF, and we postpone its full description and security analysis to the extended version of the paper [1]

Multiplicatively Homomorphic Encryption. For appropriately computing on our OPRF outputs that are elements of a group of order n generated by g, we need a suitable multiplicatively homomorphic encryption scheme whose decryption is shared between our two servers. To this end, we employ a semantically-secure ElGamal encryption scheme, whose security relies on DDH assumption in the underlying group. Here, an encryption $\mathsf{E}^{+*}_{\mathsf{pk}}(m)$ denotes a message $m \in \mathsf{G}_n$ encrypted under a public key $\mathsf{pk} = \mathsf{g}^{\mathsf{sk}}$, where g is a generator of group G_n of size n, and the private key sk belongs to $\mathbb{Z}^*_{n/4}$.

On the one hand, ElGamal is a multiplicatively homomorphic encryption scheme; on the other hand, the message space matches the output space of our OPRF; therefore the scheme is additively homomorphic w.r.t. OPRF inputs: $\mathsf{E}^{+*}_{\mathsf{pk}}(m) \cdot \mathsf{E}^{+*}_{\mathsf{pk}}(m') = \mathsf{E}^{+*}_{\mathsf{pk}}(m \cdot m')$ for any $m, m' \in \mathsf{G}_n$, and $\mathsf{E}^{+*}_{\mathsf{pk}}(m)^\delta = \mathsf{E}^{+*}_{\mathsf{pk}}(m^\delta)$ for any $\delta \in \mathbb{Z}^*_n$. This scheme, moreover, allows shared decryption; i.e., given public/private key pairs $(\mathsf{pk}_{\mathcal{A}}, \mathsf{sk}_{\mathcal{A}})$ and $(\mathsf{pk}_{\mathcal{B}}, \mathsf{sk}_{\mathcal{B}})$ of parties $\mathcal{A}$ and $\mathcal{B}$ and the joint public key $\mathsf{pk} = \mathsf{pk}_{\mathcal{A}} \cdot \mathsf{pk}_{\mathcal{B}}$, parties $\mathcal{A}$ and $\mathcal{B}$ can jointly decrypt a ciphertext $\mathsf{E}^{+*}_{\mathsf{pk}}(m)$ for a receiver using their private keys $\mathsf{sk}_{\mathcal{A}}$ and $\mathsf{sk}_{\mathcal{B}}$. In our construction, given a ciphertext encrypted under the joint public key of servers S and T, they jointly decrypt the ciphertext such that the plaintext message is available to T.

Oblivious Sort. In oblivious sort (OSort), one party (in our case, S) holds an encrypted data array and the other party (T) operates on the data array such that the data array becomes sorted according to some comparison criteria, and S learns nothing about the array (therefore, the name "oblivious" sort). OSort can be instantiated by the recently introduced *randomized ShellSort* algorithm [21], which runs in $O(z \log(z))$ for z elements.

4.2 AnonRAM$_{\mathsf{polylog}}$ Data Structure

AnonRAM$_{\mathsf{polylog}}$ caters N independent users ($\mathsf{U}_1, \ldots, \mathsf{U}_N$) with their $M \cdot N$ cells (i.e., M cells per user) using a storage server S and a tag server T. Similarly to other hierarchical schemes [19,26,27,30], blocks are organized in $L = \lceil \log(M \cdot N) \rceil + 1$ levels, where each level $\ell \in [1, L]$ contents 2^ℓ buckets. Each bucket contains $\beta := \lceil c_\beta \log(M \cdot N) \rceil$ blocks, where c_β is a (small) constant.

Similarly to GO-ORAM, during each access, the user reads a pseudo-randomly chosen (entire) bucket from each level such that server S cannot learn anything by observing the bucket access patterns. AnonRAM$_{\mathsf{polylog}}$ adopts a recent improvement to GO-ORAM proposed in [26,27,30] to avoid duplicate user blocks in the server-side (RAM) storage at any point in time. To achieve this,

---

[3] Composite Decisional Diffie-Hellman assumption [6] is a variant of the standard DDH assumption [3], but defined over a composite order group.

on every access, the user has to write a 'dummy' block into the location where it finds the data such that S cannot distinguish between the added 'dummy' block and the 'real' data block. These user-added dummy blocks are periodically removed to avoid RAM memory expansion, and the rest of the blocks are periodically reshuffled to allow users to access the same cell multiple times.

In existing single-user single-server GO-ORAM designs [19, 26, 30], this reshuffling is performed by the user. In $\mathsf{AnonRAM}_{\mathsf{polylog}}$, reshuffling operations involve blocks of different users, and it cannot be performed by one or more users without interacting with all other users. As we want to avoid interaction among the users, reshuffling in $\mathsf{AnonRAM}_{\mathsf{polylog}}$ is jointly performed by two *non-colluding* servers (the storage-server S and the tag-server T) without exposing a user's data or access pattern to either server.

Block Types. Each block in $\mathsf{AnonRAM}_{\mathsf{polylog}}$ consists of two parts: a ElGamal-encrypted OPRF output called *pre-tag* part and a UREnc-encrypted *value* part. We consider three types of blocks: *real*, *empty*, and *dummy* blocks.

A *real* block is of the form $\langle \mathsf{E}_{\mathsf{TS}}^{+*}(\theta_i), \mathsf{E}_{\mathsf{U}_i}^*(j, m_{i,j}) \rangle$. Here, the value part contains the jth cell of user U_i with value $m_{i,j}$ encrypted with UREnc for U_i, while the pre-tag part contains a pre-tag θ_i computed using OPRF for some secret input of U_i and encrypted using ElGamal for a joint public key of T and S. The pre-tag θ_i is computed by U_i with help from the storage server S using OPRF and is used to map the block to a particular bucket on a given level. Given a pre-tag θ, for a level $\ell \in [1, L]$, the bucket index (or tag) is computed by applying a random oracle hash function, $h_\ell : \{0, 1\}^* \to \mathbb{Z}_{2^\ell}$. The mapping changes after 2^ℓ accesses, which we refer to as an *epoch*.

Empty blocks are padding blocks that are used to form buckets of the required size β on the storage server S. An empty block is of the form $\langle \mathsf{E}_{\mathsf{TS}}^{+*}(1), \mathsf{E}_{\mathsf{TS}}^*(\text{"}empty\text{"}) \rangle$, where "*empty*" is a constant in the UREnc message space. An empty block will be encrypted similarly to other types of blocks to ensure the privacy against the storage server S, and the server should not be able to determine whether a user fetched an empty block or a real block. The first part of the empty block is an encryption of unity 1, as it allows the tag server T to determine if a block is empty during the reshuffle.

Finally, similarly to most ORAM algorithms, we use *dummy* blocks to hide locations of the real blocks. Once a real block with a specific index is found at some level, it is moved to a new bucket at the first level and is replaced with a dummy block in its old location. A dummy block is of the form $\langle \mathsf{E}_{\mathsf{TS}}^{+*}(\theta_\mathcal{D}), \mathsf{E}_{\mathsf{TS}}^*(\text{"}dummy\text{"}) \rangle$, where the pre-tag $\theta_\mathcal{D}$ is computed using OPRF on the number (t) of accesses made by the users so far and a secret input $\mu_\mathcal{D}$ known only to server T, and "*dummy*" is a constant in the UREnc message space.

Note that different blocks are completely indistinguishable to non-colluding servers S and T individually. Nevertheless, during the reshuffle operations, when necessary, with help from server S, server T can determine the type of a block.

4.3   AnonRAM$_\mathsf{polylog}$ Protocol Overview

Initialization. We need to initialize UREnc, ElGamal, and OPRF. For the security parameter λ, we choose a multiplicative group G_q of an appropriate prime order q for UREnc, and a multiplicative group G_n of order equal to an appropriate safe RSA modulus n for ElGamal and OPRF. Let g and g be generators of groups G_q and G_n respectively.

Given this setup, every user generates her UREnc key from $\mathbb{Z}_q^*$. The two servers select their individual shared private keys for both UREnc and ElGamal and publish the corresponding combined public key for ElGamal; we do not need UREnc public key for two servers. We represent these encryptions as follows: $\mathsf{E}_{\mathsf{U}_i}^*(\cdot)$ represents a UREnc encryption for user U_i; $\mathsf{E}_{\mathsf{TS}}^*(\cdot)$ and $\mathsf{E}_{\mathsf{TS}}^{+*}(\cdot)$ respectively represent shared UREnc and ElGamal encryptions for the servers S and T. The servers make an encrypted empty block $\mathsf{E}_{\mathsf{TS}}^*(\textit{"empty"})$ and an encrypted dummy block $\mathsf{E}_{\mathsf{TS}}^*(\textit{"dummy"})$ public to all users.

Similarly to all existing hierarchical ORAM constructions, all levels in the AnonRAM$_\mathsf{polylog}$ data structure on S are initially empty. In particular, the complete first level is filled up with empty blocks, while the rest of the levels are not yet allocated. The users write $M \cdot N$ cells initialized to some default value, one by one, at the first level such that, at the end of the initialization procedure, $M \cdot N$ users' cells will be stored at level L and the remaining levels will be empty (w.l.o.g. we assume that $M \cdot N$ is power of 2). Let t denote the access counter, which is made available publicly by the servers. Each level ℓ has an epoch counter $\xi(t, \ell)$ that increments after every $2^{\ell-1}$ accesses. In other words, for level ℓ and t accesses, the epoch counter is $\xi(t, \ell) = \lfloor t/2^{\ell-1} \rfloor$.

Recall that our OPRF employs two keys. S generates the first (and fixed) OPRF key $s \leftarrow_R \mathbb{Z}_n^*$, and then a series of second OPRF keys $\hat{s}[\ell, \xi(t, \ell)] \leftarrow_R \mathbb{Z}_n^*$, for each level $\ell \in [1, L]$ and the current access t. A user U_i generates independently a secret PRF input $\mu_i \in \mathbb{Z}_n$ and computes a pre-tag θ for her block j using μ_i by performing OPRF with S. Similarly, the tag server T generates a secret input $\mu_\mathcal{D}$ for dummy blocks. To tag blocks, the construction uses a hash function family $\{h_\ell\}$ domain $[0, 2^\ell - 1]$, for each level $\ell \in [1, L]$. In particular, a tag (or bucket index) for a pre-tag θ is computed as $h_\ell(\xi(t, \ell)\|\theta)$, where $\|$ represents string concatenation.

Protocol Flow. Similarly to our constructions in Sect. 3, users have to communicate with the servers via anonymous channels. To access a cell j during the tth access, user U_i first computes the associated pre-tags for all levels θ_i using OPRF with S on her secret inputs μ_i and j. She also obtains $\theta_\mathcal{D}$ pre-tags from server T for all levels for the current value of access counter t. Here, T computes pre-tags for dummy blocks by interacting with S and sends those to the users, as the users cannot locally compute them. These pseudorandom pre-tag values depend on the level and the current epoch through the PRF keys used by S. Due to the oblivious nature of OPRF and secret inputs μ_i for U_i and $\mu_\mathcal{D}$ for T, server S does not learn the pre-tag values.

Once pre-tags are computed, the user maps each of those to a bucket index (or tag) in their level ℓ using h_ℓ. Now, she starts searching for her cell j from

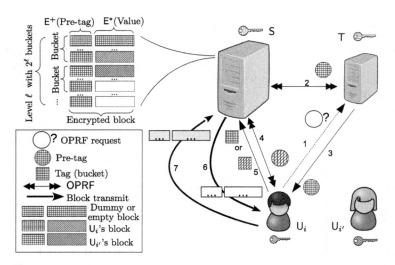

Fig. 2. Flow of User algorithm in AnonRAM$_{polylog}$ for user U_i, cell j, and level ℓ: (1) U_i asks the tag server T for a dummy pre-tag. (2) T runs an OPRF protocol with the storage server S such that T learns the dummy pre-tag and S learns nothing. (3) T sends the dummy pre-tag to U_i. (4) U_i runs OPRF with S to learn a pre-tag for her cell j obliviously. (5) Depending on whether cell j is found in the previous levels or not, U_i selects one of the two pre-tags to compute a tag and sends the tag to S. (6) S re-randomizes and sends the block(s) associated with the user's tag. (7) U_i re-randomizes or updates the block(s), and possibly learns the value of cell j. If $\ell = 1$, steps (4) and (5) are skipped, and in step (6) S sends all blocks from that level.

level 1 using tags computed using a pre-tag θ_i. Similarly to other hierarchical schemes, after obtaining her cell she searches for the remaining levels with tags computed using $\theta_{\mathcal{D}}$ values. The updated cell j is added back to the level 1. During this process, a pre-tag θ associated with the user's cell changes to another value θ' indistinguishable from random. Figure 2 shows the main sub-flow of User algorithm executed by U_i in cooperation with servers S and T. In User flow, this sub-flow is repeated once for each level. Finally, at the end of User, the user computes a new pre-tag for possibly updated cell j, and computes and stores a block with them at the first level.

Although dummy pre-tags and tags are computed by and known to T, it cannot learn a tag employed by a user while requesting blocks from S, as communication between the user and server S is encrypted. Neither can T learn this information based on the content of blocks of specific tags retrieved by observed users, since S *re-randomizes* blocks before sending them to users.

The main task of T is to reshuffle the blocks *without* involving the users. In the Reshuffle protocol, while reshuffling levels 1 to ℓ into level $\ell + 1$, server T copies, re-randomizes or changes blocks from levels 1 to ℓ, and then sorts them using oblivious-sorting (OSort) such that the users can obtain their required cells over level $\ell + 1$ by procuring the appropriate pre-tag values from server S. This step requires server S helping server T to decrypt the randomized version of pre-tags in blocks. Here, for every second access, T performs reshuffle of level 1 into level 2 on S to empty level 1. For every fourth access, all the real blocks at levels 1 and 2 will be moved to level 3, and so on.

The crucial property is that, while reshuffling, server T should not learn any information about user's data from pre-tags. To prevent T from identifying users' cells by pre-tags, S proactively shuffles all blocks that T will access during Reshuffle and updates the pre-tags associated with the blocks. Here, S utilizes homomorphic properties of OPRF: in particular, for some pre-tag $\theta = f_{s,\hat{s}}(\mu)$ for server S's OPRF keys $s, \hat{s}$, the server computes $\theta^\delta = f_{s,(\hat{s}\cdot\delta)}(\mu)$ for some random δ. Although pre-tags in the blocks are stored in the encrypted form and cannot be decrypted by S alone, the homomorphic properties of ElGamal allow S to apply the aforementioned trick to ciphertexts *without* knowing pre-tags in plain. Finally, S partially decrypts the pre-tags of the blocks that have to be reshuffled by T and moves these blocks to a temporary array.

After the pre-processing by server S, server T decrypts pre-tags of the blocks and reshuffles non-empty blocks to arrange them into buckets based on pre-tags. This process is essentially the same as the Oblivious-Hash step in GO-ORAM [19] except for de-duplication of blocks [30]. Specifically, while reshuffling blocks from levels 1 to ℓ into level $\ell + 1$, T first adds 2^ℓ *forward* dummy blocks that can potentially be accessed by a user in subsequent accesses. It then assigns tags to non-empty blocks using hash function $h_{\ell+1}$ and ensures that no tag gets assigned to more than β blocks. Finally, T pads the temporary array with the tagged empty blocks such that exactly β blocks have the same tag, replaces forward dummy blocks with empty ones, and moves all these blocks to level $\ell + 1$ on server S. Here, T cannot link the pre-tags seen in a current Reshuffle execution to those observed during previous reshuffles, as the value δ chosen by S is unknown to T.

Elaborate descriptions of the User and Reshuffle algorithms are available in the extended version of the paper [1].

Complexity Analysis. Computational and communication complexity of User is $O(\log^2(M \cdot N))$ since there are $L = O(\log(M \cdot N))$ levels, and for each level a user performs $\beta = O(\log(M \cdot N))$ encryptions, decryptions, and OPRF evaluations. Each of these operations requires $O(1)$ exponentiations.

Computational and communication complexity of Reshuffle depends on parameter t. Consider the state after Setup and the state after $M \cdot N$ subsequent accesses. They are identical, as all the real blocks are located at level L. Hence, it suffices to analyze the aforementioned interval. Let Reshuffle(ℓ) denote the reshuffle from levels 1 to ℓ into level $\ell + 1$, and let $\rho(\ell)$ denote the complexity thereof. In Reshuffle(ℓ), the number of blocks involved is $2^{\ell+1}\beta$, hence $\rho(\ell) = O(2^{\ell+1} \cdot \beta \cdot \log(2^{\ell+1} \cdot \beta))$ due to the cost of OSort. Then, within $M \cdot N$ accesses, there is one Reshuffle(L), none of Reshuffle($L - 1$) (since level L initially already contains $M \cdot N$ elements), one Reshuffle($L - 2$), two Reshuffle($L - 3$), four Reshuffle($L - 4$) etc. Thus, the total complexity of all reshuffles made within $M \cdot N$ accesses is $(\sum_{\ell=1}^{L-2} 2^{L-2-\ell} \cdot \rho(\ell)) + \rho(L)$

$$= (\textstyle\sum_{\ell=1}^{L-2} 2^{L-2-\ell} \cdot O(2^{\ell+1} \cdot \beta \cdot \log(2^{\ell+1} \cdot \beta))) + O(2^{L+1} \cdot \beta \cdot \log(2^{L+1} \cdot \beta))$$
$$= (2^{L-1} \cdot \beta \cdot \textstyle\sum_{\ell=1}^{L-2} O(\log(2^{\ell+1} \cdot \beta))) + O(M \cdot N \cdot \log(M \cdot N) \cdot \log(2^{L+1} \cdot \beta))$$
$$= O(M \cdot N) \cdot \beta \cdot O(L^2) + O(M \cdot N \cdot \log^2(M \cdot N)) = O(M \cdot N \cdot \log^3(M \cdot N)).$$

Hence, the amortized cost of Reshuffle is $\tilde{O}(\log^3(M \cdot N))$.

Theorem 3. AnonRAM$_{\text{polylog}}$ *preserves access privacy against HbC adversaries in the random oracle model, when instantiated with semantically secure universally re-randomizable encryption (UREnc) and multiplicatively homomorphic encryption schemes, and a secure (partially key-homomorphic) oblivious PRF scheme for appropriate compatible domains.*

The proof of Theorem 3 is available in the extended version of the paper [1].

5 Conclusion and Future Work

We have defined the concept of *Anonymous RAM (AnonRAM)* and presented two provably secure constructions. AnonRAM simultaneously provides privacy of content, access patterns and the user identities, while additionally ensuring the integrity of the user's data. It hence constitutes a natural extension of the concept of oblivious RAM (ORAM) to a domain with multiple, mutually distrusting users. Our first construction exhibits an access complexity linear in the number of users, while the second one improves the complexity to an amortized access cost that is poly-logarithmic in the total number of cells of all users, at the cost of requiring two non-colluding servers. Both constructions have a simpler version which assumes honest-but-curious users, but also a version secure against malicious users.

Several challenges still remain. In particular, it will be interesting to design a poly-logarithmic access complexity AnonRAM scheme using a single server. It will be also interesting to manage concurrent accesses to the server by the users.

Acknowledgements. We thank the anonymous reviewers for their valuable comments. This work was supported by the German Federal Ministry for Education and Research (BMBF) through funding for the Center for IT-Security, Privacy and Accountability (CISPA) and by a grant from the Israeli Ministry of Science and Technology.

References

1. Backes, M., Herzberg, A., Kate, A., Pryvalov, I.: Anonymous RAM (extended version). Cryptology ePrint Archive, Report 2016/678 (2016)
2. Bindschaedler, V., Naveed, M., Pan, X., Wang, X., Huang, Y.: Practicing oblivious access on cloud storage: the gap, the fallacy, and the new way forward. In: CCS, pp. 837–849 (2015)
3. Boneh, D.: The decision Diffie-Hellman problem. In: Buhler, J.P. (ed.) ANTS 1998. LNCS, vol. 1423, pp. 48–63. Springer, Heidelberg (1998)
4. Boyle, E., Chung, K.-M., Pass, R.: Oblivious parallel RAM and applications. In: Kushilevitz, E., Malkin, T. (eds.) TCC 2016-A. LNCS, vol. 9563, pp. 175–204. Springer, Heidelberg (2016). doi:10.1007/978-3-662-49099-0_7

5. Camenisch, J., Stadler, M.: Proof systems for general statements about discrete logarithms. Technical report, TR260. Dept. of Computer Science, ETH Zürich, March 1997

6. Catalano, D., Gennaro, R.: New efficient and secure protocols for verifiable signature sharing and other applications. In: Krawczyk, H. (ed.) CRYPTO 1998. LNCS, vol. 1462, pp. 105–120. Springer, Heidelberg (1998)

7. Chaum, D.: Untraceable electronic mail, return addresses, and digital pseudonyms. Commun. ACM **4**(2), 84–88 (1981)

8. Chaum, D.: The dining cryptographers problem: unconditional sender and recipient untraceability. J. Cryptology **1**(1), 65–75 (1988)

9. Chaum, D., Pedersen, T.P.: Wallet databases with observers. In: Brickell, E.F. (ed.) CRYPTO 1992. LNCS, vol. 740, pp. 89–105. Springer, Heidelberg (1993)

10. Chen, B., Lin, H., Tessaro, S.: Oblivious parallel RAM: improved efficiency and generic constructions. In: Kushilevitz, E., Malkin, T. (eds.) TCC 2016-A. LNCS, vol. 9563, pp. 205–234. Springer, Heidelberg (2016). doi:10.1007/978-3-662-49099-0_8

11. Chung, K.-M., Liu, Z., Pass, R.: Statistically-secure ORAM with $\tilde{O}(\log^2 n)$ overhead. In: Sarkar, P., Iwata, T. (eds.) ASIACRYPT 2014, Part II. LNCS, vol. 8874, pp. 62–81. Springer, Heidelberg (2014)

12. Cramer, R., Damgård, I.B., Schoenmakers, B.: Proof of partial knowledge and simplified design of witness hiding protocols. In: Desmedt, Y.G. (ed.) CRYPTO 1994. LNCS, vol. 839, pp. 174–187. Springer, Heidelberg (1994)

13. Danezis, G., Dingledine, R., Mathewson, N.: Mixminion: design of a type III anonymous remailer protocol. In: Security and Privacy (S&P), pp. 2–15 (2003)

14. De Santis, A., Di Crescenzo, G., Persiano, G., Yung, M.: On monotone formula closure of SZK. In: FOCS, pp. 454–465 (1994)

15. Dingledine, R., Mathewson, N., Syverson, P.: Tor: the second-generation onion router. In: Usenix Security, pp. 303–320 (2004)

16. Dodis, Y., Yampolskiy, A.: A verifiable random function with short proofs and keys. In: Vaudenay, S. (ed.) PKC 2005. LNCS, vol. 3386, pp. 416–431. Springer, Heidelberg (2005)

17. Franz, M., Williams, P., Carbunar, B., Katzenbeisser, S., Peter, A., Sion, R., Sotakova, M.: Oblivious outsourced storage with delegation. In: Danezis, G. (ed.) FC 2011. LNCS, vol. 7035, pp. 127–140. Springer, Heidelberg (2012)

18. Freedman, M.J., Ishai, Y., Pinkas, B., Reingold, O.: Keyword search and oblivious pseudorandom functions. In: Kilian, J. (ed.) TCC 2005. LNCS, vol. 3378, pp. 303–324. Springer, Heidelberg (2005)

19. Goldreich, O., Ostrovsky, R.: Software protection and simulation on oblivious RAMs. J. ACM (JACM) **43**(3), 431–473 (1996)

20. Golle, P., Jakobsson, M., Juels, A., Syverson, P.: Universal re-encryption for mixnets. In: Okamoto, T. (ed.) CT-RSA 2004. LNCS, vol. 2964, pp. 163–178. Springer, Heidelberg (2004)

21. Goodrich, M.T.: Randomized shellsort: a simple data-oblivious sorting algorithm. J. ACM (JACM) **58**(6), 27 (2011)

22. Goodrich, M.T., Mitzenmacher, M., Ohrimenko, O., Tamassia, R.: Oblivious RAM simulation with efficient worst-case access overhead. In: ACM CCSW, pp. 95–100 (2011)

23. Goodrich, M.T., Mitzenmacher, M., Ohrimenko, O., Tamassia, R.: Privacy-preserving group data access via stateless oblivious RAM simulation. In: SODA, pp. 157–167 (2012)

24. Jarecki, S., Liu, X.: Efficient oblivious pseudorandom function with applications to adaptive OT and secure computation of set intersection. In: Reingold, O. (ed.) TCC 2009. LNCS, vol. 5444, pp. 577–594. Springer, Heidelberg (2009)

25. Jinsheng, Z., Wensheng, Z., Qiao, D.: A Multi-user Oblivious RAM for outsourced data (2014). http://lib.dr.iastate.edu/cs_techreports/262/

26. Kushilevitz, E., Lu, S., Ostrovsky, R.: On the (in) security of hash-based oblivious RAM and a new balancing scheme. In: SODA, pp. 143–156 (2012)

27. Lu, S., Ostrovsky, R.: Distributed oblivious RAM for secure two-party computation. In: Sahai, A. (ed.) TCC 2013. LNCS, vol. 7785, pp. 377–396. Springer, Heidelberg (2013)

28. Maffei, M., Malavolta, G., Reinert, M., Schröder, D.: Privacy and access control for outsourced personal records. In: Security and Privacy (S&P), pp. 341–358 (2015)

29. Ostrovsky, R.: Efficient computation on oblivious RAMs. In: STOC, pp. 514–523 (1990)

30. Pinkas, B., Reinman, T.: Oblivious RAM revisited. In: Rabin, T. (ed.) CRYPTO 2010. LNCS, vol. 6223, pp. 502–519. Springer, Heidelberg (2010)

31. Prabhakaran, M., Rosulek, M.: Rerandomizable RCCA encryption. In: Menezes, A. (ed.) CRYPTO 2007. LNCS, vol. 4622, pp. 517–534. Springer, Heidelberg (2007)

32. Sahin, C., Zakhary, V., El Abbadi, A., Lin, H.R., Tessaro, S.: Taostore: Overcoming asynchronicity in oblivious data storage. In: Security and Privacy (S&P) (2016)

33. Schnorr, C.P.: Efficient signature generation by smart cards. J. Cryptology **4**(3), 161–174 (1991)

34. Shi, E., Chan, T.-H.H., Stefanov, E., Li, M.: Oblivious RAM with $O((\log N)^3)$ worst-case cost. In: Lee, D.H., Wang, X. (eds.) ASIACRYPT 2011. LNCS, vol. 7073, pp. 197–214. Springer, Heidelberg (2011)

35. Stefanov, E., Shi, E.: ObliviStore: High performance oblivious cloud storage. In: Security and Privacy (S&P), pp. 253–267 (2013)

36. Stefanov, E., Van Dijk, M., Shi, E., Fletcher, C., Ren, L., Yu, X., Devadas, S.: Path oram: an extremely simple oblivious ram protocol. In: CCS, pp. 299–310 (2013)

37. The Tor project (2003). https://www.torproject.org/. Accessed Feb 2016

38. Wang, X., Chan, T.H., Shi, E.: Circuit ORAM: on tightness of the goldreich-ostrovsky lower bound. In: CCS, pp. 850–861 (2015)

39. Williams, P., Sion, R., Tomescu, A.: PrivateFS: a parallel oblivious file system. In: CCS, pp. 977–988 (2012)

Efficient Sanitizable Signatures Without Random Oracles

Russell W.F. Lai[1], Tao Zhang[1], Sherman S.M. Chow[1(✉)],
and Dominique Schröder[2]

[1] Department of Information Engineering,
The Chinese University of Hong Kong, Sha Tin, N.T., Hong Kong
{wflai,zt112,sherman}@ie.cuhk.edu.hk
[2] Chair for Applied Cryptography,
Friedrich-Alexander University Erlangen-Nürnberg,
Erlangen and Nuremberg, Bavaria, Germany
schroeder@me.com

Abstract. Sanitizable signatures, introduced by Ateniese et al. (ESORICS '05), allow the signer to delegate the sanitization right of signed messages. The sanitizer can modify the message and update the signature accordingly, so that the sanitized part of the message is kept private. For stronger protection of sensitive information, it is desirable that no one can link sanitized message-signature pairs of the same document. This idea was formalized by Brzuska et al. (PKC '10) as unlinkability, which was followed up recently by Fleischhacker et al. (PKC '16). Unfortunately, these generic constructions of sanitizable signatures, unlinkable or not, are based on building blocks with specially crafted features which efficient (standard model) instantiations are absent. Basing on existing primitives or a conceptually simple primitive is more desirable.

In this work, we present two such generic constructions, leading to efficient instantiations in the standard model. The first one is based on rerandomizable tagging, a new primitive which may find independent interests. It captures the core accountability mechanism of sanitizable signatures. The second one is based on accountable ring signatures (CARDIS '04, ESORICS '15). As an intermediate result, we propose the first accountable ring signature scheme in the standard model.

1 Introduction

Regular signatures are non-malleable. It is infeasible to maul a valid message-signature pair (m, σ) into a modified pair (m', σ') that passes the verification. However, a controlled form of malleability can be desirable in many settings, such as research study on sanitized Internet traffic or anonymized medical data, commercial usages that replace advertisements in authenticated media streams, or updates of reliable routing information [2]. Sanitizable signatures, introduced by Ateniese *et al.* [2], support controlled malleability. The signer can specify parts of a (signed) message which a designated third party, called the sanitizer, is allowed to change and then adapt the signature accordingly. Brzuska *et al.* [10] formalized

© Springer International Publishing Switzerland 2016
I. Askoxylakis et al. (Eds.): ESORICS 2016, Part I, LNCS 9878, pp. 363–380, 2016.
DOI: 10.1007/978-3-319-45744-4_18

five security properties, including privacy which states that the sanitized part of the message cannot be recovered from a sanitized signature. A strictly stronger property, called unlinkability, was suggested one year later [11]. Unlinkability ensures that one cannot link sanitized message-signature pairs of the same document. It is particularly important in the motivating applications which sanitize data for privacy [2] as it prevents the attacker from combining information of several sanitized versions of a document for reconstructing (parts of) the original document. Such linkage is useful for de-anonymization.

Unlinkable sanitizable signatures was then constructed [11] from group signatures with an unusual property, that the keys of the signers can be computed independently even before seeing the keys of the group manager. In a typical application of group signature, the group is formed first and the signers join the group later. This order is even exploited for gaining efficiency in building group signature scheme via the notion of certified signatures [25]. In a very recent study of Fleischhacker *et al.* [23], in order to instantiate the generic construction of Brzuska *et al.* [11], they need to use an *inefficient* scheme based on the random oracle model (ROM) and generic group model (GGM) [24], or look into the details of the scheme [25] and perform the adaption accordingly to fit with the special requirement. This diminishes the benefits of a generic construction. Although the scheme [25] is proven in the standard model without random oracle, the proof requires the adversary to only perform group operations on the given elements (generic group model or GGM). No existing simple assumption supports the proof. Their study suggested that, to this date, no efficient group signature scheme *that has the required properties* is known, which also means that no efficient unlinkable sanitizable signature scheme is known. In response, they gave another generic construction from signatures with re-randomizable keys, which is very efficient when instantiated with Schnorr signature, yet with security argued with the ROM heuristics. Unfortunately, the re-randomizable keys property is also an unusual property, as showcased by the original authors [23] that two pairing-based short signature schemes cannot serve as a building block.

This leaves limited and unsatisfactory choices of schemes, (1) having a subset of the security properties [2,10], (2) relying on the ROM [23], or (3) secure without ROM, but building upon inefficient construction [11].

1.1   Our Contribution

Our main result is closing the research gap, presenting the first efficient (unlinkable) sanitizable signature schemes which are secure in the standard model. In fact, we propose two very different generic constructions which are both simple. Our study also gives several new results that are of independent interests.

Our first generic construction is based on *rerandomizable tagging* , a new notion which may find independent application. Indeed, it can be considered as a dual notion of double-trapdoor anonymous tag [1], a primitive proven to be useful for privacy-oriented authorship management mechanism. In particular, using it in a generic construction of traceable signature schemes allows the signer (or the group manager on behalf) to deny the authorship of a signature [1].

While both our tags and the public-keys expected by the signature scheme required in the previous generic construction [23] are "re-randomizable", we believe that our formulation captures the essential functionality to achieve accountability, for either creation or sanitization. This leads to our conceptually simple generic construction, in which the rerandomizable tagging scheme takes care of the accountability, a regular signature scheme for the signing functionality, a public-key encryption scheme for delegating signing power, and finally a pseudorandom function family for storing the randomness without maintaining local state. Using only basic primitives and our new rerandomizable tagging *without any zero-knowledge proof*, this construction is very efficient and achieves privacy, in the standard model and under only the relatively simpler static assumptions.

Our second generic construction, which achieves unlinkability, is based on *accountable ring signatures* [31]. In contrast to the existing generic construction from group signatures [11], where the latter is required to satisfy some special property, our construction relies on an existing notion which can be used as-is. One can immediately instantiate our construction by a recent scheme [7], which yields an efficient unlinkable sanitizable signature scheme in the ROM. As an extra feature, this generic construction naturally supports *multiple sanitizers* [16].

Aiming at constructing unlinkable sanitizable signatures in the standard model, we also construct the first accountable ring signature scheme in the standard model. The assumption required by this scheme is a q-type assumption due to the membership proof [8]. Our scheme inherits the constant signature size from non-accountable schemes in the literature [8]. Existing scheme [7] only relying on the (static) decisional Diffie-Hellman assumption requires a logarithmic size. Due to existing results [6,7], it also leads to a constant-size instantiation of a strong variant of fully dynamic group signatures, in which group manager not only can enroll, but also revoke group members.

1.2   Related Work

Ateniese *et al.* [2] informally describe the following properties of sanitizable signatures. *Unforgeability* says that signatures can only be created by honest signers and sanitizers. *Immutability* demands only designated parts of the message can be modified by the (malicious) sanitizer. *Transparency* ensures the indistinguishability of signatures computed by the signer and the sanitizer (or more precisely, they are indistinguishable to *public verifiers*, which means anyone other than the signer and the sanitizer themselves). *Accountability* means that neither the malicious signer nor the malicious sanitizer can deny authorship of the message. When need arises, the signer can generate a *proof of authorship*.

These requirements were formalized by Brzuska *et al.* [10]. Since then, many works formalize various other properties. Note that transparency ensures that any public verifier cannot even notice if the message has been sanitized. *Unlinkability*, introduced by Brzuska *et al.* [11], takes a step further in which a sanitized signature cannot be linked to its original version. This is crucial for privacy.

It is tricky to get a right balance of accountability and transparency. Canard *et al.* [17] addressed the lack of accountability in the seminal work [2], yet at the cost of transparency. On the other hand, unconditional transparency is often undesirable, which motivates the need of accountability. The original accountability notion [2,10] is interactive since it needs the participation of the signer. A non-interactive version was later proposed [12], which allows a third party to determine if a message originates from the signer or the sanitizer, without any help from the signer. Nevertheless, non-interactive accountability and transparency cannot be achieved simultaneously [23], so we focus on schemes that have (interactive) accountability and transparency.

Holding the sanitizer accountable is a measure after the fact. Another idea is to limit the allowable sanitization [15,28]. However, unlinkability in this setting is even more complicated. For instance, one may want to also conceal the sets of allowed modifications [13]. Yet, it appears to be difficult to construct such a scheme efficiently. Recently, Derler and Slamanig [22] suggested an intermediate notion (weaker than unlinkability but stronger than privacy) as a compromise for achieving efficient construction. We remark that Canard *et al.* [16] considered multiple signers and sanitizers, with construction based on group signatures.

Malleable signatures were considered in many variations, such as homomorphic signatures [18,27], which allows public evaluation of functions on more than one signed messages, or redactable signatures [9,27], which allows parts of the message to be removable. They aim to solve related but different problems, and are not directly applicable in our motivating scenarios as discussed [2,10,11,23].

Delegation of signing right is considered in proxy signatures [4]. Yet, the signatures produced by the proxy are often publicly distinguishable from signatures created by the designator, which violates the transparency property of sanitizable signatures. Recent advances such as (delegatable) functional signatures [3] associate the signing right with a policy specifying which messages can be signed, or even arbitrary functions to be applied on the key and the messages, such that the policy or the function remain hidden. These works show theoretical solutions, but are too slow for practical use.

2   Rerandomizable Tagging Schemes

In a high level, the core of a sanitizable signature is a cryptographic object which is computed by the signer with some secret information embedded, but can be rerandomized by the sanitizer many times in an indistinguishable way. In addition, when the sanitizer changes the object, it will no longer match with the embedded secret, indicating that the signature is sanitized.

To capture the above functionality, we introduce a new primitive called rerandomizable tagging. In a rerandomizable tagging scheme, the tag issuer generates a tag using its private key with respect to a user's public key. The user can then use its own private key to rerandomize the tag which looks indistinguishable from the one issued by the issuer. When necessary, however, the tag issuer can generate a proof to claim or deny the authorship of a (rerandomized) tag.

2.1 Definition of Rerandomizable Tagging Schemes

Definition 1. *A rerandomizable tagging scheme* $\mathcal{RT}$ = $(\mathsf{TGen_I}, \mathsf{TGen_U}, \mathsf{Tag},$ $\mathsf{ReTag}, \mathsf{TVer}, \mathsf{TProv}, \mathsf{TJud})$ *consists of seven efficient algorithms:*

KEY GENERATION. *The key generation algorithms for the issuer and the user respectively both create a pair of private and public key:* $(\mathsf{sk_I}, \mathsf{pk_I}) \leftarrow \mathsf{TGen_I}(1^\lambda)$, $(\mathsf{sk_U}, \mathsf{pk_U}) \leftarrow \mathsf{TGen_U}(1^\lambda)$.

TAGGING. *The tagging algorithm takes as input a message* $m \in \{0,1\}^*$, *an issuer's private key* $\mathsf{sk_I}$, *and a user public key* $\mathsf{pk_U}$. *It outputs a tag* $\tau \leftarrow \mathsf{Tag}(m, \mathsf{sk_I}, \mathsf{pk_U})$.

RE-TAGGING. *The re-tagging algorithm takes as input two messages* $m, m' \in \{0,1\}^*$, *the issuer's public key* $\mathsf{pk_I}$, *a user's private key* $\mathsf{sk_U}$, *and a tag* τ. *It outputs a new tag* $\tau' \leftarrow \mathsf{ReTag}(m, m', \mathsf{pk_I}, \mathsf{sk_U}, \tau)$.

VERIFICATION. *The verification algorithm takes as input a message* $m \in \{0,1\}^*$, *a tag* τ, *the issuer's public key* $\mathsf{pk_I}$, *a user's public key* $\mathsf{pk_U}$, *and outputs a bit* $b \leftarrow \mathsf{TVer}(m, \tau, \mathsf{pk_I}, \mathsf{pk_U})$.

PROOF. *The proof algorithm takes as input the issuer's private key* $\mathsf{sk_I}$, *a message* $m \in \{0,1\}^*$, *a user's public key* $\mathsf{pk_U}$, *and a tag* τ. *It outputs a proof* $\pi \leftarrow \mathsf{TProv}(\mathsf{sk_I}, m, \mathsf{pk_U}, \tau)$.

JUDGE. *The judge algorithm takes as input a message* $m \in \{0,1\}^*$, *issuer and user public keys* $\mathsf{pk_I}, \mathsf{pk_U}$, *a tag* τ, *and a proof* π. *It outputs a decision* $d \in \{\mathtt{I}, \mathtt{U}\}$ *indicating whether the tag was created by the issuer or the user:* $d \leftarrow \mathsf{TJud}(m, \mathsf{pk_I}, \mathsf{pk_U}, \tau, \pi)$.

A rerandomizable tagging scheme is correct if, for all parameters $\lambda \in \mathbb{N}$, for all keys generated from $(\mathsf{sk_I}, \mathsf{pk_I}) \leftarrow \mathsf{TGen_I}(1^\lambda)$ and $(\mathsf{sk_U}, \mathsf{pk_U}) \leftarrow \mathsf{TGen_U}(1^\lambda)$, for all tags generated from $\tau \leftarrow \mathsf{Tag}(m, \mathsf{sk_I}, \mathsf{pk_U})$ and $\tau' \leftarrow \mathsf{ReTag}(m, m', \mathsf{pk_I}, \mathsf{sk_U}, \tau)$, it holds that $\mathsf{TVer}(m, \tau, \mathsf{pk_I}, \mathsf{pk_U}) = 1$ and $\mathsf{TVer}(m', \tau', \mathsf{pk_I}, \mathsf{pk_U}) = 1$. Furthermore, for all $\pi \leftarrow \mathsf{TProv}(\mathsf{sk_I}, m, \mathsf{pk_U}, \tau)$ and $\pi' \leftarrow \mathsf{TProv}(\mathsf{sk_I}, m', \mathsf{pk_U}, \tau')$, it holds that $\mathsf{TJud}(m, \mathsf{pk_I}, \mathsf{pk_U}, \tau, \pi) = \mathtt{I}$ and $\mathsf{TJud}(m', \mathsf{pk_I}, \mathsf{pk_U}, \tau', \pi') = \mathtt{U}$.

2.2 Security of Rerandomizable Tagging Schemes

Rerandomizable tagging schemes abstract the core properties of sanitizable signatures. Therefore, their security properties, namely, privacy, accountability, and transparency, follow the corresponding property of sanitizable signatures [10].

Privacy. This property says that the rerandomized tag should be hiding. Note that information leakage through the new message itself can never be prevented.

Definition 2 (Privacy). *A rerandomizable tagging scheme* $\mathcal{RT}$ *is private if for all PPT adversaries* $\mathcal{A}$ *the probability that the experiment* $\mathsf{TPrivacy}_{\mathcal{A}}^{\mathcal{RT}}(\lambda)$ *evaluates to 1 is negligibly close to* $\frac{1}{2}$ *(in* λ), *where*

Experiment $\mathsf{TPrivacy}_{\mathcal{A}}^{\mathcal{RT}}(\lambda)$

$(\mathsf{sk_I}, \mathsf{pk_I}) \leftarrow \mathsf{TGen_I}(1^\lambda); \ (\mathsf{sk_U}, \mathsf{pk_U}) \leftarrow \mathsf{TGen_U}(1^\lambda); \ b \leftarrow \{0, 1\}$

$a \leftarrow \mathcal{A}^{\mathsf{Tag}(\cdot, \mathsf{sk_I}, \cdot), \mathsf{ReTag}(\cdot, \cdot, \cdot, \mathsf{sk_U}, \cdot), \mathsf{TProv}(\mathsf{sk_I}, \cdot, \cdot, \cdot), \mathsf{LoRReTag}(\cdot, \cdot, \mathsf{sk_I}, \mathsf{sk_U}, b)}(\mathsf{pk_I}, \mathsf{pk_U})$

    where oracle $\mathsf{LoRReTag}(\cdot, \cdot, \mathsf{sk_I}, \mathsf{sk_U}, b)$, *on input* $((m_{j,0}, m'_j), (m_{j,1}, m'_j))$

    computes $\tau_{j,b} \leftarrow \mathsf{Tag}(m_{j,b}, \mathsf{sk_I}, \mathsf{pk_U})$ *and returns*

    $\tau'_{j,b} \leftarrow \mathsf{ReTag}(m_{j,b}, m'_j, \mathsf{pk_I}, \mathsf{sk_U}, \tau_{j,b})$

if $a = b$ *then output* 1, *else output* 0.

Accountability. This property demands that the origin of a (possibly rerandomized) tag should be undeniable. We distinguish between *issuer-accountability* and *user-accountability*. The former says that, if a tag has not been rerandomized, then a malicious issuer cannot make the judge accuse the user. In the issuer-accountability game, a malicious issuer $\mathcal{A}_{\mathsf{Tag}}$ gets a user public key $\mathsf{pk_U}$ as input and has access to a re-tagging oracle, which takes as input tuples $(\mathsf{pk}_{\mathsf{I},i}, \tau_i)$ and returns τ'_i. Eventually, $\mathcal{A}_{\mathsf{Tag}}$ outputs a tuple $(\mathsf{pk}_{\mathsf{I}}^*, m^*, \tau^*, \pi^*)$ and wins the game if TJud accuses the user for the new key $\mathsf{pk}_{\mathsf{I}}^*$ with a valid tag τ^*.

Definition 3 (Issuer-Accountability). *A rerandomizable tagging scheme* $\mathcal{RT}$ *is* issuer-accountable *if for all PPT adversaries* $\mathcal{A}_{\mathsf{Tag}}$ *the probability that the experiment* $\mathsf{Iss\text{-}Acc}_{\mathcal{A}_{\mathsf{Tag}}}^{\mathcal{RT}}(\lambda)$ *outputs 1 is negligible (in* λ), *where*

Experiment $\mathsf{Iss\text{-}Acc}_{\mathcal{A}_{\mathsf{Tag}}}^{\mathcal{RT}}(\lambda)$

$(\mathsf{sk_U}, \mathsf{pk_U}) \leftarrow \mathsf{TGen_U}(1^\lambda); \ (\mathsf{pk}_{\mathsf{I}}^*, m^*, \tau^*, \pi^*) \leftarrow \mathcal{A}_{\mathsf{Tag}}^{\mathsf{ReTag}(\cdot, \cdot, \mathsf{sk_U}, \cdot)}(\mathsf{pk_U})$

    where $(\mathsf{pk}_{\mathsf{I},i}, m_i, m'_i, \tau_i)$ *and* τ'_i *denote the queries and answers to*

    and from oracle ReTag.

    Output 1 if for all i *the following holds:*

        $(\mathsf{pk}_{\mathsf{I}}^*, m^*) \neq (\mathsf{pk}_{\mathsf{I},i}, m'_i) \wedge \mathsf{TVer}(m^*, \tau^*, \mathsf{pk}_{\mathsf{I}}^*, \mathsf{pk_U}) = 1$

        $\wedge \mathsf{TJud}(m^*, \mathsf{pk}_{\mathsf{I}}^*, \mathsf{pk_U}, \tau^*, \pi^*) \neq \mathsf{I}$

    else output 0.

In the user-accountability game, $\mathcal{A}_{\mathsf{ReTag}}$ models a malicious user with access to Tag and TProv oracles. It succeeds if it outputs a message m^*, a tag τ^*, and a key $\mathsf{pk}_{\mathsf{U}}^*$ such that the output is different from $\mathsf{pk}_{\mathsf{U},i}$ previously queried to the Tag oracle. Moreover, it is required that the proof produced by the issuer via TProv still leads the judge to decide "I", *i.e.*, the tag was created by the issuer.

Definition 4 (User-Accountability). *A rerandomizable tagging scheme* $\mathcal{RT}$ *is* user-accountable *if for all PPT adversaries* $\mathcal{A}_{\mathsf{ReTag}}$ *the probability that the experiment* $\mathsf{Usr\text{-}Acc}_{\mathcal{A}_{\mathsf{ReTag}}}^{\mathcal{RT}}(\lambda)$ *evaluates to 1 is negligible (in* λ), *where*

Experiment $\mathsf{Usr\text{-}Acc}_{\mathcal{A}_{\mathsf{ReTag}}}^{\mathcal{RT}}(\lambda)$

$(\mathsf{sk_I}, \mathsf{pk_I}) \leftarrow \mathsf{TGen_I}(1^\lambda); \ (m^*, \mathsf{pk}_{\mathsf{U}}^*, \tau^*) \leftarrow \mathcal{A}_{\mathsf{ReTag}}^{\mathsf{Tag}(\cdot, \mathsf{sk_I}, \cdot), \mathsf{TProv}(\mathsf{sk_I}, \cdot, \cdot, \cdot)}(\mathsf{pk_I})$

    where $(m_i, \mathsf{pk}_{\mathsf{U},i})$ *and* τ_i *denote the queries and answers of oracle* Tag.

$\pi \leftarrow \mathsf{TProv}(\mathsf{sk_I}, m^*, \mathsf{pk}_{\mathsf{U}}^*, \tau^*)$

    Output 1 if for all i *the following holds:*

        $(\mathsf{pk}_{\mathsf{U}}^*, m^*) \neq (\mathsf{pk}_{\mathsf{U},i}, m_i) \wedge \mathsf{TVer}(m^*, \tau^*, \mathsf{pk_I}, \mathsf{pk}_{\mathsf{U}}^*) = 1$

        $\wedge \mathsf{TJud}(m^*, \mathsf{pk_I}, \mathsf{pk}_{\mathsf{U}}^*, \tau^*, \pi) \neq \mathsf{U}$

    else output 0.

Transparency. This property says that one cannot decide if a tag has been rerandomized or not. Formally, this is defined in a game where an adversary $\mathcal{A}$ has access to Tag, ReTag, and TProv oracles to create (rerandomized) tags and learn the proofs. In addition, $\mathcal{A}$ gets access to a Tag/ReTag$_b(\cdot, \cdot)$ oracle with a secret random bit $b \in \{0, 1\}$ embedded which, on input a messages m and m', behaves as follows:

- for $b = 0$ runs the tagging algorithm to create $\tau \leftarrow$ Tag$(m, \mathsf{sk_I}, \mathsf{pk_U})$, then runs the re-tagging algorithm $\tau' \leftarrow$ ReTag$(m, m', \mathsf{pk_I}, \mathsf{sk_U}, \tau)$ and returns the rerandomized tag τ',
- for $b = 1$ runs the tagging algorithm to create $\tau' \leftarrow$ Tag$(m', \mathsf{sk_I}, \mathsf{pk_U})$, then returns the tag τ'.

Adversary $\mathcal{A}$ eventually produces an output a as a guess for b. A rerandomizable tagging is *transparent* if for all efficient algorithms $\mathcal{A}$ the probability for a right guess $a = b$ in the above game is negligibly close to $\frac{1}{2}$. Below we also define a relaxed version called *proof-restricted transparency*.

Definition 5 ((Proof-Restricted) Transparency). *A rerandomizable tagging scheme $\mathcal{RT}$ is* proof-restrictedly transparent *if for all PPT adversaries $\mathcal{A}$ the probability that the experiment* Trans$_{\mathcal{A}}^{\mathcal{RT}}(\lambda)$ *returns 1 is negligibly close to $\frac{1}{2}$.*

Experiment Trans$_{\mathcal{A}}^{\mathcal{RT}}(\lambda)$
$(\mathsf{sk_I}, \mathsf{pk_I}) \leftarrow$ TGen$_\mathsf{I}(1^\lambda)$; $(\mathsf{sk_U}, \mathsf{pk_U}) \leftarrow$ TGen$_\mathsf{U}(1^\lambda)$; $b \leftarrow \{0, 1\}$
$a \leftarrow \mathcal{A}^{\mathsf{Tag}(\cdot, \mathsf{sk_I}, \cdot), \mathsf{ReTag}(\cdot, \cdot, \mathsf{sk_U}, \cdot), \mathsf{TProv}(\mathsf{sk_I}, \cdot, \cdot, \cdot), \mathsf{Tag/ReTag}_b(\cdot, \cdot)}(\mathsf{pk_I}, \mathsf{pk_U})$
Output 1 if $\left(a = b \wedge M_{\mathsf{Tag/ReTag}} \cap M_{\mathsf{TProv}} = \emptyset\right)$ else output 0
    where $M_{\mathsf{Tag/ReTag}}$ and M_{TProv} denote the sets of messages output from and queried to oracles Tag/ReTag *and* TProv *respectively.*

2.3   Construction of Rerandomizable Tagging Schemes

We describe a construction of rerandomizable tagging based on double-trapdoor chameleon hashing [19] and one-way functions. A double-trapdoor chameleon hash function is a chameleon hash function [29] for which there exists an efficient algorithm which takes as input a pair of collisions and outputs one of the trapdoors. Its formal definition can be found in the full version.

Informal Description. In our construction, the user public key is a public key of the double-trapdoor chameleon hashing scheme. A tag of a message m mainly consists of the randomness ρ used in computing a chameleon hash value of the message m. The pair (m, ρ) implicitly fixes the hash value μ. By the collision resistance of the chameleon hash, it is infeasible for the issuer to find another pair (m', ρ') which hashes to the same value μ, while the user can sample as many collisions as it wants, on arbitrary messages m'. Thus, to rerandomize a tag for a message m into a tag for another message m', the user simply replace ρ by ρ' such that the pairs (m, ρ) and (m', ρ') hash to the same value μ. To prove the authorship of this tag later, the issuer first obtains a random seed r

$\mathsf{TGen_I}(1^\lambda)$	$\mathsf{Tag}(m, \mathsf{sk_I}, \mathsf{pk_U})$	$\mathsf{TProv}(\mathsf{sk_I}, m, \mathsf{pk_U}, \tau)$
$K \leftarrow \{0,1\}^\lambda$	$q \leftarrow \{0,1\}^\lambda$	$r \leftarrow F(K, q)$
$(\mathsf{sk}_\Sigma, \mathsf{pk}_\Sigma) \leftarrow \mathsf{SGen}(1^\lambda)$	$r \leftarrow F(K, q)$	$\pi := (m, r)$
$\mathsf{sk_I} := (K, \mathsf{sk}_\Sigma)$	$\rho \leftarrow g(r)$	**return** π
$\mathsf{pk_I} := \mathsf{pk}_\Sigma$	$\mu \leftarrow \mathsf{CEval}(\mathsf{pk}_\mathcal{H}, m; \rho)$	
return $(\mathsf{sk_I}, \mathsf{pk_I})$	$\eta := (\mathsf{pk_U}, q, \mu)$	$\mathsf{TJud}(m, \mathsf{pk_I}, \mathsf{pk_U}, \tau, \pi)$
	$\sigma \leftarrow \mathsf{SSig}(\mathsf{sk}_\Sigma, \eta)$	$\rho' \leftarrow g(r')$
$\mathsf{TGen_U}(1^\lambda)$	$\tau := (\rho, q, \sigma)$	$\mu \leftarrow \mathsf{CEval}(\mathsf{pk}_\mathcal{H}, m; \rho)$
	return τ	$\mu' \leftarrow \mathsf{CEval}(\mathsf{pk}_\mathcal{H}, m'; \rho')$
$(\mathsf{sk}_{\mathcal{H},0}, \mathsf{sk}_{\mathcal{H},1}, \mathsf{pk}_\mathcal{H}) \leftarrow \mathsf{CGen}(1^\lambda)$		**if** $\mu = \mu' \wedge \rho \neq \rho'$ **then**
$\mathsf{sk_U} := \mathsf{sk}_{\mathcal{H},0}$	$\mathsf{Ver}(m, \tau, \mathsf{pk_I}, \mathsf{pk_U})$	**return** $d = \mathsf{U}$
$\mathsf{pk_U} := \mathsf{pk}_\mathcal{H}$	$\mu \leftarrow \mathsf{CEval}(\mathsf{pk}_\mathcal{H}, m; \rho)$	**else**
return $(\mathsf{sk_U}, \mathsf{pk_U})$	$\eta := (\mathsf{pk_U}, q, \mu)$	**return** $d = \mathsf{I}$
	$b \leftarrow \mathsf{SVer}(\eta, \sigma, \mathsf{pk}_\Sigma)$	**endif**
$\mathsf{ReTag}(m, m', \mathsf{pk_I}, \mathsf{sk_U}, \tau)$	**return** b	
$\rho' \leftarrow \mathsf{CInv}(\mathsf{sk}_{\mathcal{H},0}, m, \rho, m')$		
$\tau' := (\rho', q, \sigma)$		
return τ'		

Fig. 1. Our rerandomizable tagging scheme

by evaluating a pseudorandom function on a random input q, then applies a pseudorandom generator on r and uses it as the randomness ρ for the chameleon hash. It signs the random input q with the randomness ρ. In the case of dispute, the issuer can recover q and hence r from the signature, and uses r as the proof of (non-)authorship.

Formal Description. Let $F : \{0,1\}^\lambda \times \{0,1\}^* \rightarrow \{0,1\}^\lambda$ be a pseudorandom function. Let $g : \{0,1\}^\lambda \rightarrow \{0,1\}^{2\lambda}$ be a pseudorandom generator. Let $\mathcal{H} = (\mathsf{CGen}, \mathsf{TCGen}, \mathsf{CEval}, \mathsf{CInv})$ be a double-trapdoor chameleon hash which hashes messages $m \in \{0,1\}^*$ with randomness $\rho \in \{0,1\}^{2\lambda}$. Let $\Sigma = (\mathsf{SGen}, \mathsf{SSig}, \mathsf{SVer})$ be a signature scheme. We construct a rerandomizable tagging scheme $\mathcal{RT}$ as shown in Fig. 1. The correctness of $\mathcal{RT}$ follows those of $\mathcal{H}$ and Σ.

Theorem 1. *If $\mathcal{H}$ has uniform output distribution, then $\mathcal{RT}$ is private. If one-way function exists, then $\mathcal{RT}$ is user-accountable. If $\mathcal{H}$ is collision-resistant, then $\mathcal{RT}$ is issuer-accountable. If one-way function exists and $\mathcal{H}$ has uniform output distribution, then $\mathcal{RT}$ is proof-restrictedly transparent.*

Due to space constraint, detailed proofs can be found in the full version.

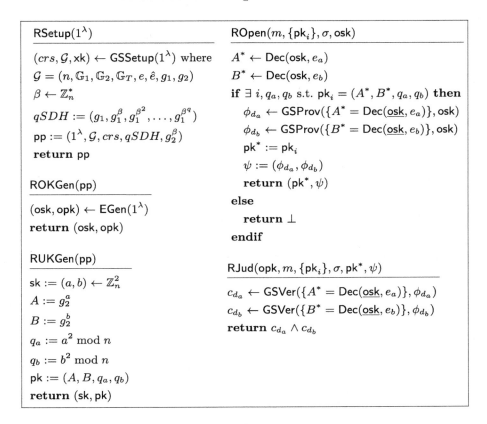

Fig. 2. Our accountable ring signature scheme - Part I

3 Accountable Ring Signatures

Accountable ring signatures, introduced by Xu and Yung [31] and recently formalized by Bootle $et\ al.$ [7], allows both spontaneous group formulation as ring signatures and designated opening of signer identity as group signatures. Bootle $et\ al.$ [7] gave a generic construction and an efficient instantiation in the random oracle model. We follow the the definitions of Bootle $et\ al.$ [7], which can be found in the full version.

We adopt the ring signature scheme of Bose $et\ al.$ [8] (referred to as BDR hereinafter), which in turn uses the Boneh-Boyen signature scheme [5] for signing hash values output by a collision-resistant hash function H : $\{0,1\}^* \rightarrow \mathbb{Z}_n$. We transform BDR into an accountable ring signature scheme $\mathcal{RS}$, described in Figs. 2 and 3, by using a structure-preserving encryption scheme $\mathcal{SPE} = (\mathsf{EGen}, \mathsf{Enc}, \mathsf{Dec})$ of Camenisch $et\ al.$ [14] which is secure against chosen-ciphertext attack (CCA). We use a collision-resistant hash function $H_2 : \mathbb{Z}_n \rightarrow \mathbb{G}_1$ to create a label for $\mathcal{SPE}$. Roughly, we encrypt the public key and prove using Groth-Sahai proof system [26] $\mathcal{GS} = (\mathsf{GSSetup}, \mathsf{GSProv}, \mathsf{GSVer})$

$$\text{RSig}(\text{opk}, m, (\text{pk}_1 = (q_{1,a}, q_{1,b}), \ldots, \text{pk}, \ldots, \text{pk}_k = (q_{k,a}, q_{k,b})), \text{sk})$$

$m' \leftarrow H(m \| \{\text{pk}_i\}); \rho \leftarrow \mathbb{Z}_n \setminus \{\frac{-a + m'}{b}\}; \Delta \leftarrow g_1^{\frac{1}{a + \rho b + m'}}$

$\mathcal{R}_a := (q_{1,a}, \ldots, q_{k,a}); \mathcal{R}_b := (q_{1,b}, \ldots, q_{k,b})$

$W_a \leftarrow \text{MemWit}(\text{pp}, q_a, \mathcal{R}_a); W_b \leftarrow \text{MemWit}(\text{pp}, q_b, \mathcal{R}_b)$

$\phi_{mem_a} \leftarrow \text{MemProv}(\text{pp}, \mathcal{R}_a, W_a); \phi_{mem_b} \leftarrow \text{MemProv}(\text{pp}, \mathcal{R}_b, W_b)$

$\phi_{q_a} \leftarrow \text{GSProv}(\{\underline{q_a} = \underline{a}^2\}, (q_a, a)); \phi_{q_b} \leftarrow \text{GSProv}(\{\underline{q_b} = \underline{b}^2\}, (q_b, b))$

$\phi_{\text{pk}_a} \leftarrow \text{GSProv}(\{\underline{A} = g_2^{\underline{a}}\}, (A, a)); \phi_{\text{pk}_b} \leftarrow \text{GSProv}(\{\underline{B} = g_2^{\underline{b}}\}, (B, b))$

$e_a \leftarrow \text{Enc}(\text{opk}, H_2(m'), A; r_a); e_b \leftarrow \text{Enc}(\text{opk}, H_2(m'), B; r_b)$

$\phi_{e_a} \leftarrow \text{GSProv}(\{e_a = \text{Enc}(\text{opk}, H_2(m'), \underline{A}; \underline{r_a})\}, (A, r_a))$

$\phi_{e_b} \leftarrow \text{GSProv}(\{e_b = \text{Enc}(\text{opk}, H_2(m'), \underline{B}; \underline{r_b})\}, (B, r_b))$

$\phi_{sig} \leftarrow \text{GSProv}(\{\underline{B}^\rho = \underline{B'} \wedge e(\underline{\Delta}, \underline{A})e(\underline{\Delta}, \underline{B'})e(\underline{\Delta}, g_2^{m'}) = e(g_1, g_2)\}, (\Delta, A, B, B'))$

$\textbf{return } \sigma := (\rho, e_a, e_b, \phi_{mem_a}, \phi_{mem_b}, \phi_{sig}, \phi_{q_a}, \phi_{q_b}, \phi_{\text{pk}_a}, \phi_{\text{pk}_b}, \phi_{e_a}, \phi_{e_b})$

$$\text{RVer}(\text{opk}, m, \{\text{pk}_i = (q_{i,a}, q_{i,b})\}_{i=1}^k, \sigma)$$

$m' \leftarrow H(m \| \{\text{pk}_i\}); \mathcal{R}_a := (q_{1,a}, \ldots, q_{k,a}); \mathcal{R}_b := (q_{1,b}, \ldots, q_{k,b})$

$c_{mem_a} \leftarrow \text{MemVer}(\text{pp}, \mathcal{R}_a, \phi_{mem_a}); c_{mem_b} \leftarrow \text{MemVer}(\text{pp}, \mathcal{R}_b, \phi_{mem_b})$

$c_{q_a} \leftarrow \text{GSVer}(\{\underline{q_a} = \underline{a}^2\}, \phi_{q_a}); c_{q_b} \leftarrow \text{GSVer}(\{\underline{q_b} = \underline{b}^2\}, \phi_{q_b})$

$c_{\text{pk}_A} \leftarrow \text{GSVer}(\{\underline{A} = g_2^{\underline{a}}\}, \phi_{\text{pk}_A}); c_{\text{pk}_B} \leftarrow \text{GSVer}(\{\underline{B} = g_2^{\underline{b}}\}, \phi_{\text{pk}_B})$

$c_{e_a} \leftarrow \text{GSVer}(\{e_a = \text{Enc}(\text{opk}, H_2(m'), \underline{A}; \underline{r_a})\}, \phi_{e_a})$

$c_{e_b} \leftarrow \text{GSVer}(\{e_b = \text{Enc}(\text{opk}, H_2(m'), \underline{B}; \underline{r_b})\}, \phi_{e_b})$

$c_{sig} \leftarrow \text{GSVer}(\{\underline{B}^\rho = \underline{B'} \wedge e(\underline{\Delta}, \underline{A})e(\underline{\Delta}, \underline{B'})e(\underline{\Delta}, g_2^{m'}) = e(g_1, g_2)\}, \phi_{sig})$

$\textbf{return } (c_{mem_a} \wedge c_{mem_b} \wedge c_{sig} \wedge c_{q_a} \wedge c_{q_b} \wedge c_{\text{pk}_A} \wedge c_{\text{pk}_B} \wedge c_{e_a} \wedge c_{e_b})$

Fig. 3. Our accountable ring signature scheme - Part II

that the encrypted key matches with the one for verifying the BDR signature. A tracing authority holding the decryption key can identify the real signer. BDR ring signature requires composite order group, so our accountable ring signature is also constructed in a composite order setting. Our scheme inherits the nice features of BDR, including constant signature size and security without random oracles. We underline the witness components in the statement to be proven by Groth-Sahai proof system. The details of $\mathcal{SPE}$ and Groth-Sahai proof system can be found in the full version.

Analysis. The correctness of $\mathcal{RS}$ follows those of BDR ring signatures and the proof on $\mathcal{SPE}$ ciphertexts. The efficiency of $\mathcal{RS}$ depends on the instantiation of the Groth-Sahai proof. Instantiating $\mathcal{SPE}$ and our accountable ring signature scheme with a composite order group, and the Groth-Sahai proof system with the symmetric external Diffie-Hellman (SXDH) assumption [26], there are 121 multiplications, 102 exponentiations (including the commitments for the proofs), and 10 pairings in the signing algorithm RSig().

Theorem 2. *If $\mathcal{GS}$ is sound and the underlying scheme [8] is unforgeable, $\mathcal{RS}$ is unforgeable. If $\mathcal{SPE}$ is CCA-secure, and $\mathcal{GS}$ is hiding, $\mathcal{RS}$ is CCA-anonymous under full key exposure. If $\mathcal{GS}$ is sound, $\mathcal{RS}$ is traceable and has tracing soundness.*

Due to space constraint, detailed proofs can be found in the full version.

4 Constructions of Sanitizable Signatures

Syntax. Sanitizable signature schemes allow the delegation of signing capabilities to a sanitizer. These capabilities are realized by letting the signer "attach" a description of the admissible modifications for a particular message and sanitizer. The sanitizers may then change the message according to some modification and update the signature. More formally, the signer uses its private key $\mathsf{sk_S}$ to sign a message m and the description of the admissible modifications α for some sanitizer $\mathsf{pk_Z}$. The sanitizer, having a matching private key $\mathsf{sk_Z}$, can update the message according to some modification δ and compute a new signature using $\mathsf{sk_Z}$. In case of a dispute about the origin of a message-signature pair, the signer can compute a proof π (using an algorithm Prov) from previously signed messages which proves that a signature has been created by the sanitizer. The verification of this proof is done by an algorithm Jud (that only decides the origin of a valid message-signature pair in question; for invalid pairs such decisions are in general impossible). We mostly follow the existing syntax [10,11] except that our key generation algorithms take as input a public parameter generated by a setup algorithm. For the formal syntax and security definitions of sanitizable signatures, readers can refer to the full version.

Sanitizable signatures should satisfy immutability, sanitizer- and signer-accountability, and proof-restricted transparency. In addition, they should satisfy privacy or, even stronger, unlinkability. It is known that full transparency or unlinkability both imply privacy separately [10,11], while proof-restricted transparency only implies a proof-restricted version of privacy [11].

To the best of our knowledge, there is no efficient instantiation of sanitizable signatures satisfying either privacy or unlinkability, and all other security properties simultaneously, without using random oracles. We thus fill this gap by describing two constructions. The first is more efficient while satisfying privacy based on the rerandomizable tagging. The second one uses the accountable ring signature scheme and can achieve unlinkability.

4.1 Privacy from Rerandomizable Tagging Scheme

Informal Description. Our first construction relies heavily on the rerandomizable tagging scheme (Sect. 2) which captures the accountability properties of sanitizable signatures. We complement it with pseudorandom functions, signatures,

Setup(1^λ)	KGen$_\mathsf{S}$(pp)	KGen$_\mathsf{Z}$(pp)
pp $= 1^\lambda$	$K_e \leftarrow \{0,1\}^\lambda$	$(\mathsf{sk}_e, \mathsf{pk}_e) \leftarrow \mathsf{EGen}(1^\lambda)$
return pp	$(\mathsf{sk}_f, \mathsf{pk}_f) \leftarrow \mathsf{SGen}(1^\lambda)$	$(\mathsf{sk}_U, \mathsf{pk}_U) \leftarrow \mathsf{TGen}_U(1^\lambda)$
	$(\mathsf{sk}_I, \mathsf{pk}_I) \leftarrow \mathsf{TGen}_I(1^\lambda)$	$\mathsf{sk}_z = (\mathsf{sk}_e, \mathsf{sk}_U)$
Prov($\mathsf{sk}_\mathsf{S}, m, \sigma, \mathsf{pk}_\mathsf{Z}$)	$\mathsf{sk}_\mathsf{S} = (K_e, \mathsf{sk}_f, \mathsf{sk}_I)$	$\mathsf{pk}_z = (\mathsf{pk}_e, \mathsf{pk}_U)$
$r_e \leftarrow F(K_e, q_e)$	$\mathsf{pk}_\mathsf{S} = (\mathsf{pk}_f, \mathsf{pk}_I)$	**return** ($\mathsf{sk}_z, \mathsf{pk}_z$)
$\pi := r_e$	**return** ($\mathsf{sk}_\mathsf{S}, \mathsf{pk}_\mathsf{S}$)	
return π		

Fig. 4. Our first sanitizable signature scheme - Part I

and extractable public key encryption to provide the functionality of delegating signing power of the signer to the sanitizers. The details of these primitives can be found in the full version.

To sign, the signer computes a tag τ of the message m using the rerandomizable tagging scheme. It generates a fresh key pair $(\hat{\mathsf{sk}}, \hat{\mathsf{pk}})$ of a signature scheme, and uses this newly generated $\hat{\mathsf{sk}}$ to sign m. The key pair $(\hat{\mathsf{sk}}, \hat{\mathsf{pk}})$ can be interpreted as the binding factor of the entire sanitizing chain. We assume there exists an efficient algorithm to check whether $\hat{\mathsf{sk}}$ and $\hat{\mathsf{pk}}$ forms a valid signing and verification key pair, denoted by $\hat{\mathsf{sk}} \sim \hat{\mathsf{pk}}$. To delegate the signing power to the sanitizer, the signer simply encrypts the fresh private key $\hat{\mathsf{sk}}$, together with some other identifying information, to the sanitizer. Finally, the signer uses its long term private key sk_S to sign the fixed part of the message $f_\alpha(m)$, the sanitizer's public key pk_Z, and the fresh public key $\hat{\mathsf{pk}}$, along with other information. This binds the sanitizer to the sanitizing chain identified by $\hat{\mathsf{pk}}$. The signature thus consists mainly of a signature σ_f of the fixed part, a signature $\hat{\sigma}$ signed by $\hat{\mathsf{sk}}$, the tag τ, the fresh public key $\hat{\mathsf{pk}}$, and the ciphertext c.

To sanitize, the sanitizer decrypts c to retrieve $\hat{\mathsf{sk}}$, and rerandomizes the tag with respect to the new message $m' = \delta(m)$ using the rerandomizable tagging scheme. It then uses $\hat{\mathsf{sk}}$ to sign m' and outputs it.

To extend the accountability of the rerandomizable tagging scheme to the sanitizable signature scheme, we use a similar technique as in the construction of the former: The signer generates the ciphertext using pseudorandomness generated from a random input, which is included in the sanitizable signature. The signer can later recover the pseudorandomness used for encryption by applying the pseudorandom function on this input. This pseudorandomness allows the judge to extract the identifying information from the ciphertext and verifies the authorship of the signature. The extractability of the encryption scheme relieves the signer of using any zero-knowledge proof in the proof algorithm.

Formal Description. Let $F : \{0,1\}^\lambda \times \{0,1\}^* \rightarrow \{0,1\}^\lambda$ be a pseudorandom function, $\Sigma = (\mathsf{SGen}, \mathsf{SSig}, \mathsf{SVer})$ be a digital signature scheme,

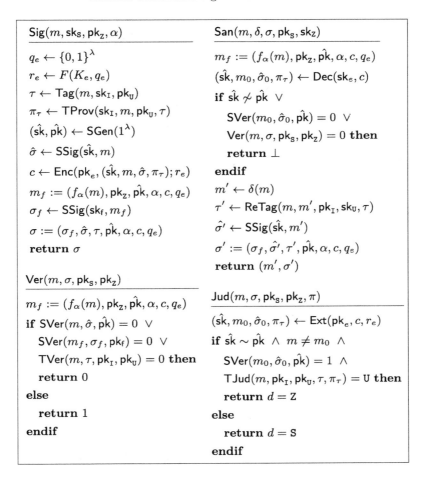

Fig. 5. Our first sanitizable signature scheme - Part II

$\mathcal{E} = (\mathsf{EGen}, \mathsf{Enc}, \mathsf{Dec}, \mathsf{Ext})$ be an extractable public key encryption scheme, and $\mathcal{RT} = (\mathsf{TGen_I}, \mathsf{TGen_U}, \mathsf{Tag}, \mathsf{ReTag}, \mathsf{TProv}, \mathsf{TJud})$ be a rerandomizable tagging scheme (Sect. 2). Figures 4 and 5 describe our first sanitizable signature scheme $\mathcal{SS}_1$. Its correctness follows directly from those of Σ, $\mathcal{E}$, and $\mathcal{RT}$.

Theorem 3. *If $\mathcal{RT}$ is private, then $\mathcal{SS}_1$ is private. If Σ is EUF-CMA secure, then $\mathcal{SS}_1$ is immutable. If Σ is EUF-CMA secure, $\mathcal{E}$ is correct, and $\mathcal{RT}$ is user-accountable, then $\mathcal{SS}_1$ is sanitizer-accountable. If $\mathcal{RT}$ is issuer-accountable, then $\mathcal{SS}_1$ is signer-accountable. If $\mathcal{RT}$ is proof-restrictedly transparent, then $\mathcal{SS}_1$ is proof-restrictedly transparent.*

Due to space constraint, detailed proofs can be found in the full version.

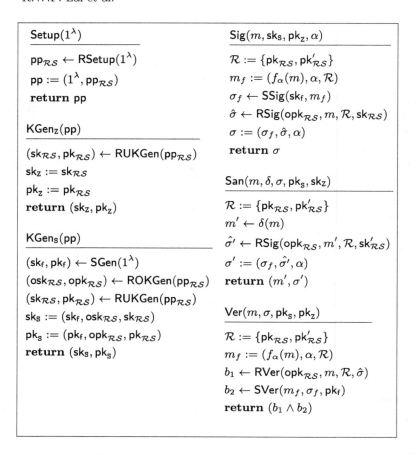

Setup(1^λ)	Sig($m, \mathsf{sk_s}, \mathsf{pk_z}, \alpha$)
$\mathsf{pp}_{\mathcal{RS}} \leftarrow \mathsf{RSetup}(1^\lambda)$	$\mathcal{R} := \{\mathsf{pk}_{\mathcal{RS}}, \mathsf{pk}'_{\mathcal{RS}}\}$
$\mathsf{pp} := (1^\lambda, \mathsf{pp}_{\mathcal{RS}})$	$m_f := (f_\alpha(m), \alpha, \mathcal{R})$
return pp	$\sigma_f \leftarrow \mathsf{SSig}(\mathsf{sk_f}, m_f)$
	$\hat{\sigma} \leftarrow \mathsf{RSig}(\mathsf{opk}_{\mathcal{RS}}, m, \mathcal{R}, \mathsf{sk}_{\mathcal{RS}})$
$\mathsf{KGen_z}(\mathsf{pp})$	$\sigma := (\sigma_f, \hat{\sigma}, \alpha)$
$(\mathsf{sk}_{\mathcal{RS}}, \mathsf{pk}_{\mathcal{RS}}) \leftarrow \mathsf{RUKGen}(\mathsf{pp}_{\mathcal{RS}})$	**return** σ
$\mathsf{sk_z} := \mathsf{sk}_{\mathcal{RS}}$	
$\mathsf{pk_z} := \mathsf{pk}_{\mathcal{RS}}$	San($m, \delta, \sigma, \mathsf{pk_s}, \mathsf{sk_z}$)
return $(\mathsf{sk_z}, \mathsf{pk_z})$	$\mathcal{R} := \{\mathsf{pk}_{\mathcal{RS}}, \mathsf{pk}'_{\mathcal{RS}}\}$
	$m' \leftarrow \delta(m)$
$\mathsf{KGen_s}(\mathsf{pp})$	$\hat{\sigma}' \leftarrow \mathsf{RSig}(\mathsf{opk}_{\mathcal{RS}}, m', \mathcal{R}, \mathsf{sk}'_{\mathcal{RS}})$
$(\mathsf{sk_f}, \mathsf{pk_f}) \leftarrow \mathsf{SGen}(1^\lambda)$	$\sigma' := (\sigma_f, \hat{\sigma}', \alpha)$
$(\mathsf{osk}_{\mathcal{RS}}, \mathsf{opk}_{\mathcal{RS}}) \leftarrow \mathsf{ROKGen}(\mathsf{pp}_{\mathcal{RS}})$	**return** (m', σ')
$(\mathsf{sk}_{\mathcal{RS}}, \mathsf{pk}_{\mathcal{RS}}) \leftarrow \mathsf{RUKGen}(\mathsf{pp}_{\mathcal{RS}})$	
$\mathsf{sk_s} := (\mathsf{sk_f}, \mathsf{osk}_{\mathcal{RS}}, \mathsf{sk}_{\mathcal{RS}})$	Ver($m, \sigma, \mathsf{pk_s}, \mathsf{pk_z}$)
$\mathsf{pk_s} := (\mathsf{pk_f}, \mathsf{opk}_{\mathcal{RS}}, \mathsf{pk}_{\mathcal{RS}})$	$\mathcal{R} := \{\mathsf{pk}_{\mathcal{RS}}, \mathsf{pk}'_{\mathcal{RS}}\}$
return $(\mathsf{sk_s}, \mathsf{pk_s})$	$m_f := (f_\alpha(m), \alpha, \mathcal{R})$
	$b_1 \leftarrow \mathsf{RVer}(\mathsf{opk}_{\mathcal{RS}}, m, \mathcal{R}, \hat{\sigma})$
	$b_2 \leftarrow \mathsf{SVer}(m_f, \sigma_f, \mathsf{pk_f})$
	return $(b_1 \wedge b_2)$

Fig. 6. Our second sanitizable signature scheme - Part I

4.2   Unlinkability from Accountable Ring Signatures

Our second construction is similar to the construction by Brzuska *et al.* [11] based on group signatures, except that we replace the special group signatures with accountable ring signatures reviewed in Sect. 3. This change has two interesting effects. First, the construction of sanitizable signatures becomes simpler: The signer does not need to create a new group for each sanitizable signature, which also eliminates the use of pseudorandom functions to generate the group [11]. Second, in contrast to the special group signatures, which the instantiations (with or without random oracle heuristics) are not efficient [23], our accountable ring signatures scheme in Sect. 3 is efficient and is secure without random oracles, though it requires composite order group.

Another route leading to our discovery is the observation that the fully dynamic group signatures constructed from accountable ring signatures [6,7] features the property that the user key generation does not depend on the group

$\mathsf{Prov}(\mathsf{sk_S}, m, \sigma, \mathsf{pk_Z})$	$\mathsf{Jud}(m, \sigma, \mathsf{pk_S}, \mathsf{pk_Z}, \pi)$
$\mathcal{R} := \{\mathsf{pk}_{\mathcal{RS}}, \mathsf{pk}'_{\mathcal{RS}}\}$	$\mathcal{R} := \{\mathsf{pk}_{\mathcal{RS}}, \mathsf{pk}'_{\mathcal{RS}}\}$
$(\mathsf{pk}^*_{\mathcal{RS}}, \psi) \leftarrow \mathsf{ROpen}(m, \mathcal{R}, \hat{\sigma}, \mathsf{osk}_{\mathcal{RS}})$	**if** $\mathsf{RJud}(\mathsf{opk}_{\mathcal{RS}}, m, \mathcal{R}, \hat{\sigma}, \mathsf{pk}^*_{\mathcal{RS}}, \psi) = 1$
$\pi := (\mathsf{pk}^*_{\mathcal{RS}}, \psi)$	$\wedge \ \mathsf{pk}^*_{\mathcal{RS}} = \mathsf{pk}'_{\mathcal{RS}}$ **then**
return π	**return** $d := \mathsf{Z}$
	else
	return $d := \mathsf{S}$
	endif

Fig. 7. Our second sanitizable signature scheme - Part II

key pair, which is the property required in the sanitizable signatures construction by Brzuska *et al.* [11].

Informal Description. We proceed directly to the signing and sanitizing procedures. To issue a signature, the signer forms a ring consisting of itself and the sanitizer, and ring-signs the message. It binds the sanitizer to this sanitizing chain by signing the fixed part of the message together with the sanitizer's public key using its private key. Sanitizing becomes computing a new accountable ring signature on the modified message.

Formal Description. Let $\mathcal{RS}$ = (RSetup, ROKGen, RUKGen, RSig, RVer, ROpen, RJud) be an accountable ring signature scheme (Sect. 3), and Σ = (SGen, SSig, SVer) be a digital signature scheme. Our unlinkable sanitizable signature scheme $\mathcal{SS}_2$ is constructed in Figs. 6 and 7. The correctness of $\mathcal{SS}_2$ follows those of $\mathcal{RS}$ and Σ.

Multiple Sanitizers. Ring signatures support rings containing more than two members, so we can extend $\mathcal{SS}_2$ easily to support more sanitizers: The signer can sign the public keys of a ring of multiple sanitizers when issuing a sanitizable signature. This grants partial signing power to each the sanitizers (possibly corresponding to different admissible modifications). Furthermore, since our accountable ring signatures have constant signature size with respect to the number of users in the ring, the multiple sanitizer scheme also features constant signature size with respect to the number of sanitizers.

Theorem 4. *If Σ is EUF-CMA secure, then $\mathcal{SS}_2$ is immutable and unlinkable. If $\mathcal{RS}$ is traceable and satisfies tracing soundness, then $\mathcal{SS}_2$ is sanitizer accountable. If $\mathcal{RS}$ is traceable and satisfies tracing soundness, then $\mathcal{SS}_2$ is signer accountable. If $\mathcal{RS}$ is anonymous, then $\mathcal{SS}_2$ is proof-restrictedly transparent.*

Due to space constraint, detailed proofs can be found in the full version.

Table 1. Comparison of different sanitizable signature schemes

	SS_1	SS_2	[23]	[11] using [25]	[11] using [24]
Security	Privacy	Unlinkability	Unlinkability	Unlinkability	Unlinkability
Model	Standard	Standard	ROM	Standard	ROM
Assumption	Static	q-type	Static	GGM	GGM
$KGen_S$	4E+2P	32E+1P	7E	1E	1E
$KGen_Z$	7E	2E	1E	1E	4E
Sig	15E+1P	103E+10P	15E	194E+2P	2813E
San	4E+12P	102E+10P	14E	186E+1P	2814E
Ver	2E+9P	2E+148P	17E	207E+62P	2011E
Prov	0E+0P	126E+152P	23E	14E+1P	18E
Jud	4E+3P	152P	6E	1E+2P	2E
pk_S, sk_S	$10 + 2|m|, 3$	26, 25	7, 14	1, 1	1, 1
pk_Z, sk_Z	5, 7	4, 2	1, 1	1, 1	5, 1
σ, π	$19 + |m|, 1$	120, 104	14, 4	69, 1	1620, 3

5   Concluding Remarks

We compare our two constructions with some recent results in Table 1, taking both their security and efficiency into consideration. To compare with SS_1 the signature scheme Σ is instantiated with Waters signature [30], the extractable public-key encryption scheme $\mathcal{E}$ is instantiated with Cramer-Shoup encryption [21], and the double-trapdoor chameleon hash is instantiated with the scheme by Chen et al. [20]. 'E' and 'P' denote the group exponentiation and pairing operation respectively. For SS_2, Σ is instantiated with full Boneh-Boyen signature [5]. For simplicity, we do not differentiate between elements from different groups in this comparison. A more detailed comparison can be found in the full version. We remark that SS_2 is instantiated with a composite order group. It shows that instantiating our generic construction leads to the first efficient unlinkable sanitizable signature schemes in the standard model.

Acknowledgments. We thank the anonymous reviewers for their comments on our manuscript.

Sherman Chow is supported by the Early Career Award and the Early Career Scheme (CUHK 439713), and General Research Funds (CUHK 14201914) of the Research Grants Council, University Grant Committee of Hong Kong.

Dominique Schröder is supported by the German Federal Ministry of Education and Research (BMBF) through funding for the project PROMISE and by the German research foundation (DFG) through funding for the collaborative research center 1223.

References

1. Abe, M., Chow, S.S.M., Haralambiev, K., Ohkubo, M.: Double-trapdoor anonymous tags for traceable signatures. Int. J. Inf. Sec. **12**(1), 19–31 (2013)
2. Ateniese, G., Chou, D.H., de Medeiros, B., Tsudik, G.: Sanitizable signatures. In: di Vimercati, S.C., Syverson, P.F., Gollmann, D. (eds.) ESORICS 2005. LNCS, vol. 3679, pp. 159–177. Springer, Heidelberg (2005)
3. Backes, M., Meiser, S., Schröder, D.: Delegatable functional signatures. In: Cheng, C.-M., et al. (eds.) PKC 2016. LNCS, vol. 9614, pp. 357–386. Springer, Heidelberg (2016). doi:10.1007/978-3-662-49384-7_14
4. Boldyreva, A., Palacio, A., Warinschi, B.: Secure proxy signature schemes for delegation of signing rights. J. Cryptology **25**(1), 57–115 (2012)
5. Boneh, D., Boyen, X.: Short signatures without random oracles. In: Cachin, C., Camenisch, J.L. (eds.) EUROCRYPT 2004. LNCS, vol. 3027, pp. 56–73. Springer, Heidelberg (2004)
6. Bootle, J., Cerulli, A., Chaidos, P., Ghadafi, E., Groth, J.: Foundations of fully dynamic group signatures. In: Manulis, M., Sadeghi, A.-R., Schneider, S. (eds.) ACNS 2016. LNCS, vol. 9696, pp. 117–136. Springer, Heidelberg (2016). doi:10.1007/978-3-319-39555-5_7
7. Bootle, J., Cerulli, A., Chaidos, P., Ghadafi, E., Groth, J., Petit, C.: Short accountable ring signatures based on DDH. In: Pernul, G., et al. (eds.) ESORICS. LNCS, vol. 9326, pp. 243–265. Springer, Heidelberg (2015). doi:10.1007/978-3-319-24174-6_13
8. Bose, P., Das, D., Rangan, C.P.: Constant size ring signature without random oracle. In: Foo, E., Stebila, D. (eds.) ACISP 2015. LNCS, vol. 9144, pp. 230–247. Springer, Heidelberg (2015)
9. Brzuska, C., et al.: Redactable signatures for tree-structured data: definitions and constructions. In: Zhou, J., Yung, M. (eds.) ACNS 2010. LNCS, vol. 6123, pp. 87–104. Springer, Heidelberg (2010)
10. Brzuska, C., Fischlin, M., Freudenreich, T., Lehmann, A., Page, M., Schelbert, J., Schröder, D., Volk, F.: Security of sanitizable signatures revisited. In: Jarecki, S., Tsudik, G. (eds.) PKC 2009. LNCS, vol. 5443, pp. 317–336. Springer, Heidelberg (2009)
11. Brzuska, C., Fischlin, M., Lehmann, A., Schröder, D.: Unlinkability of sanitizable signatures. In: Nguyen, P.Q., Pointcheval, D. (eds.) PKC 2010. LNCS, vol. 6056, pp. 444–461. Springer, Heidelberg (2010)
12. Brzuska, C., Pöhls, H.C., Samelin, K.: Non-interactive public accountability for sanitizable signatures. In: De Capitani di Vimercati, S., Mitchell, C. (eds.) EuroPKI 2012. LNCS, vol. 7868, pp. 178–193. Springer, Heidelberg (2013)
13. Brzuska, C., Pöhls, H.C., Samelin, K.: Efficient and perfectly unlinkable sanitizable signatures without group signatures. In: Katsikas, S., Agudo, I. (eds.) EuroMPI 2013. LNCS, vol. 8341, pp. 12–30. Springer, Heidelberg (2014)
14. Camenisch, J., Haralambiev, K., Kohlweiss, M., Lapon, J., Naessens, V.: Structure preserving CCA secure encryption and applications. In: Lee, D.H., Wang, X. (eds.) ASIACRYPT 2011. LNCS, vol. 7073, pp. 89–106. Springer, Heidelberg (2011)
15. Canard, S., Jambert, A.: On extended sanitizable signature schemes. In: Pieprzyk, J. (ed.) CT-RSA 2010. LNCS, vol. 5985, pp. 179–194. Springer, Heidelberg (2010)
16. Canard, S., Jambert, A., Lescuyer, R.: Sanitizable signatures with several signers and sanitizers. In: Mitrokotsa, A., Vaudenay, S. (eds.) AFRICACRYPT 2012. LNCS, vol. 7374, pp. 35–52. Springer, Heidelberg (2012)

17. Canard, S., Laguillaumie, F., Milhau, M.: *Trapdoor* sanitizable signatures and their application to content protection. In: Bellovin, S.M., Gennaro, R., Keromytis, A.D., Yung, M. (eds.) ACNS 2008. LNCS, vol. 5037, pp. 258–276. Springer, Heidelberg (2008)

18. Catalano, D.: Homomorphic signatures and message authentication codes. In: Abdalla, M., De Prisco, R. (eds.) SCN 2014. LNCS, vol. 8642, pp. 514–519. Springer, Heidelberg (2014)

19. Catalano, D., Di Raimondo, M., Fiore, D., Gennaro, R.: Off-line/on-line signatures: theoretical aspects and experimental results. In: Cramer, R. (ed.) PKC 2008. LNCS, vol. 4939, pp. 101–120. Springer, Heidelberg (2008)

20. Chen, X., Zhang, F., Tian, H., Wei, B., Susilo, W., Mu, Y., Lee, H., Kim, K.: Efficient generic on-line/off-line (threshold) signatures without key exposure. Inf. Sci. **178**(21), 4192–4203 (2008)

21. Cramer, R., Shoup, V.: A practical public key cryptosystem provably secure against adaptive chosen ciphertext attack. In: Krawczyk, H. (ed.) CRYPTO 1998. LNCS, vol. 1462, pp. 13–25. Springer, Heidelberg (1998)

22. Derler, D., Slamanig, D.: Rethinking privacy for extended sanitizable signatures and a black-box construction of strongly private schemes. In: Au, M.-H., et al. (eds.) ProvSec 2015. LNCS, vol. 9451, pp. 455–474. Springer, Heidelberg (2015). doi:10.1007/978-3-319-26059-4_25

23. Fleischhacker, N., Krupp, J., Malavolta, G., Schneider, J., Schröder, D., Simkin, M.: Efficient unlinkable sanitizable signatures from signatures with re-randomizable keys. In: Cheng, C.-M., et al. (eds.) PKC 2016. LNCS, vol. 9614, pp. 301–330. Springer, Heidelberg (2016). doi:10.1007/978-3-662-49384-7_12

24. Furukawa, J., Yonezawa, S.: Group signatures with separate and distributed authorities. In: Blundo, C., Cimato, S. (eds.) SCN 2004. LNCS, vol. 3352, pp. 77–90. Springer, Heidelberg (2005)

25. Groth, J.: Fully anonymous group signatures without random oracles. In: Kurosawa, K. (ed.) ASIACRYPT 2007. LNCS, vol. 4833, pp. 164–180. Springer, Heidelberg (2007)

26. Groth, J., Sahai, A.: Efficient non-interactive proof systems for bilinear groups. In: Smart, N.P. (ed.) EUROCRYPT 2008. LNCS, vol. 4965, pp. 415–432. Springer, Heidelberg (2008)

27. Johnson, R., Molnar, D., Song, D., Wagner, D.: Homomorphic signature schemes. In: Preneel, B. (ed.) CT-RSA 2002. LNCS, vol. 2271, pp. 244–262. Springer, Heidelberg (2002)

28. Klonowski, M., Lauks, A.: Extended sanitizable signatures. In: Rhee, M.S., Lee, B. (eds.) ICISC 2006. LNCS, vol. 4296, pp. 343–355. Springer, Heidelberg (2006)

29. Krawczyk, H., Rabin, T.: Chameleon signatures. In: NDSS 2000. The Internet Society, February 2000

30. Waters, B.: Efficient identity-based encryption without random oracles. In: Cramer, R. (ed.) EUROCRYPT 2005. LNCS, vol. 3494, pp. 114–127. Springer, Heidelberg (2005)

31. Xu, S., Yung, M.: Accountable ring signatures: a smart card approach. In: Quisquater, J.-J., Paradinas, P., Deswarte, Y., El Kalam, A.A. (eds.) Smart Card Research and Advanced Applications VI. IFIP, vol. 153, pp. 271–286. Springer, Heidelberg (2004)

Operating Systems Security

Intentio Ex Machina: Android Intent Access Control via an Extensible Application Hook

Carter Yagemann[✉] and Wenliang Du

Syracuse University, Syracuse, NY 13210, USA
{cmyagema,wedu}@syr.edu

Abstract. Android's intent framework serves as the primary method for interprocess communication (IPC) among apps. The increased volume of intent IPC present in Android devices, coupled with intent's ability to implicitly find valid receivers for IPC, bring about new security challenges. We propose *Intentio Ex Machina* (IEM), an access control solution for Android intent security. IEM separates the logic for performing access control from the point of interception by placing an interface in the Android framework. This allows the access control logic to be placed inside a normal application and reached via the interface. The app, called a "user firewall", can then receive intents as they enter the system and inspect them. Not only can the user firewall allow or block intents, but it can even modify them to a controlled extent. Since it runs as a user application, developers are able to create user firewalls that manufacturers can then integrate into their devices. In this way, IEM allows for a new genre of security application for Android systems offering a creative and interactive approach to active IPC defense.

1 Introduction

One of the constraints which has shaped the design of Android is the limited hardware resources of embedded devices. Due to small memory size, Android's creators wanted to design an architecture which encourages apps to leverage the functionalities and capabilities of apps already present on the device. This allows Android devices to conserve memory by avoiding overlapping code. From a security perspective, this increased utilization of frequently implicit interprocess communication (IPC) gives rise to interesting and unique security concerns.

First, since an app does not need to explicitly know a receiver in order to perform IPC, it can invoke any other app which has registered components. This is concerning for the receiving app because by registering components to handle external requests, the app is opening itself to every other app on the device. This includes apps that could be malicious or come from untrusted sources. If the receiving app's exposed components contain vulnerabilities, the attack surface for exploitation immediately becomes systemwide. Attacks related to this problem have already been observed in the wild and are categorized as component hijacking [21].

© Springer International Publishing Switzerland 2016
I. Askoxylakis et al. (Eds.): ESORICS 2016, Part I, LNCS 9878, pp. 383–400, 2016.
DOI: 10.1007/978-3-319-45744-4_19

Second, since any app can register components, senders do not have full control over where their data will end up. If a malicious app registers itself to handle a wide variety of requests, apps using intents could find their data being exfiltrated into the hands of devious actors. This kind of attack has been categorized in other works as intent spoofing [1,10].

These problems have motivated both researchers and developers to seek solutions. Our proposal for intent IPC access control is an architecture which leverages the system-centric and standardized nature of intent IPC. *Intentio Ex Machina*[1] (IEM) is motivated by the insight that while every firewall intercepts packets and takes actions based on a decision engine, these two pieces do not have to reside near each other. More specifically, IEM replaces the intent firewall's engine with an interface that can bind to a user app. This "user firewall" can then act as the system's intent firewall. By placing the decision engine in an app, rather than in the framework like the current intent firewall, developers can easily design engines to utilize all the capabilities of a user app including pushed updates that do not require rebooting or flashing, rich graphically enhanced user interaction, and simplified access to system resources such as GPS and networking.

We have made a virtual machine image containing IEM and a proof-of-concept user firewall available for download[2].

2   Background

2.1   Intent

Intents are a framework level abstraction of Linux binder IPC. They provide a simplified and standardized object for communicating with other apps and system services.

The Android system server maintains a binder of handles to create a mapping between sources and destinations. Whenever a system or user app is created, it is assigned a binder handle, which allows the app to send messages to the system server. Upon startup, every app uses its binder handle to the system server to register itself as an active app on the Android device. This registration establishes a network of paths for intents to take, all centered around the system server. Apps can also register intent filters to define the kinds of external intents that their components are willing to receive.

Upon receiving an intent, the system server has to resolve which component should be the receiver. If a target is explicitly specified in the intent, the system server checks it against the receiver's intent filter and confirms that they match before delivering it. Otherwise, the system server will search its list of intent filters to find eligible receivers.

---

[1] Latin for *intent of the machine*. *Ex Machina* is an acronym meaning *Extensible Mandatory Access Control Hook Integrating Normal Applications*.
[2] http://jupiter.syr.edu/iem.amp.html.

Once the receiver[3] has been resolved, the intent is then passed to the intent firewall. The firewall compares it against its policies to decide whether it should be blocked or not.

Finally, the receiver processes the intent and if a result is needed, it gives this to the system server to forward to the original sender. The overall transaction occurs asynchronously since it involves communicating across several processes.

2.2 Activity Manager Service

The system server in Android is a privileged process running in user space. Apps communicate with it via binder messages and intents. The system server itself can be further divided into a collection of services, each of which is designed to manage a particular functionality of the system.

Activity Manager Service (AMS) is responsible for handling intents. It has a collection of public methods that apps can invoke; it communicates with all the other services to make sure that intents are resolved, permissions are checked, and receivers are running and ready to receive.

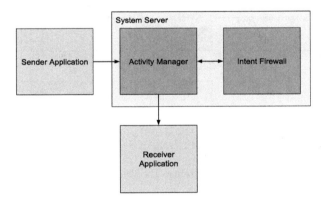

Fig. 1. Android intent firewall.

2.3 Intent Firewall

The intent firewall is an access control mechanism originally introduced in Android 4.3 and is present in all production devices. SEAndroid[4] configuration files support intent firewall policies, but few devices utilize it [29]. The main purpose of the intent firewall is to stall major malware outbreaks by allowing device manufacturers to push policies that will explicitly block the malware's components. Since such outbreaks are extremely rare, the intent firewall has

---

[3] There can also be multiple receivers in the case of broadcast intents.

[4] Security Enhancements for Android. Facilities device hardening via a bundle of policies.

almost never been used [22]. Figure 1 shows how the intent firewall fits into the framework.

AMS checks intents against the intent firewall near the end of the process. As a consequence, even though intents can be created with implicit or explicit destinations, they are all resolved to a receiver by the time they enter the firewall. Also, all three types of intents[5] are checked by the intent firewall before reaching the receiver. In other words, every intent type goes through the firewall before delivery. No intents can bypass it.

3   Design

In this section, we formulate the main architectural goal of IEM and assess the challenges in trying to achieve it. Figure 2 contains a high-level overview of the design, which will be explained in the following subsections.

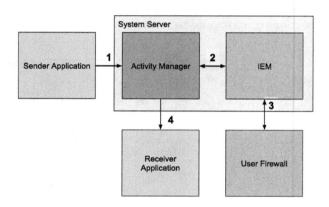

Fig. 2. Intentio Ex Machina.

3.1   Architectural Goal

All firewalls contain three critical pieces: the interceptor, the decision engine, and the policy. The interceptor captures the data packets and delivers them to the decision engine, which then decides if the packets should be allowed or denied based on the configuration defined in the policy. From this model, we can make some insightful observations. First, there is little flexibility in where an interceptor can be placed since it has to be somewhere along the original path of the packets. On the other hand, the decision engine can be placed anywhere so long as the interceptor can reach it. Second, while the policy is easy to reconfigure, it is restricted by the logic of the decision engine. A policy can only refer to attributes which the engine recognizes.

---

[5] AMS differentiates via distinct API intents targeting activities, services, and broadcast receivers.

With these two observations in mind, reconsider the intent firewall in Fig. 1. In this case, the interceptor and the decision engine both reside in the framework. This is the only possible placement for the interceptor, but what about the engine? Since it too resides in the framework, modifications require an OS patch, which requires the device to shutdown for several minutes. What would happen if the engine was placed inside a user app instead? It could then be installed, updated, and maintained with the ease of any other app. Now the policy is less restricted by the engine because it can easily be changed.

With this in mind, the goal of IEM is to provide a hook in the intent flow to allow for an app to serve in place of the intent firewall. As previously stated, doing this makes changing the firewall's enforcement logic easier, which in turn allows for more flexibility. Making the firewall an app empowers the device manufacturer to deploy the solution that fits the needs of the customer. One manufacturer might deploy a user firewall which monitors location and allows the user to restrict which apps run while in the office. Another user firewall might allow a user to prevent apps from getting her location while she's driving. A parent might use a user firewall on her child's device to prevent him from playing video games before dinner, or maybe he can text message his friends only after he finishes his math homework. These are all apps an Android developer can program, so these are all apps which IEM can empower.

Figure 2 shows IEM and how it interfaces with the rest of the framework and user apps. From here on, "IEM" specifically refers to the hook which resides in the framework while "user firewall" refers to any app which utilizes IEM. Intents first enter the system server through the public API at edge 1. This is where AMS resolves the receiver. The intent then enters IEM via edge 2. The intent is delivered to the user firewall and a decision is returned via edge 3. If the user firewall decides to allow the intent, the activity manager is alerted via edge 2 and the intent is delivered via edge 4.

In the next subsection, we identify and address the key challenges in trying to achieve this architecture.

3.2 Design Challenges

Figure 3 shows the three new pieces introduced into the framework by IEM. This subsection considers each piece in turn and addresses the challenges caused by their addition.

Intent Interceptor. The first new piece an intent reaches is IEM's interceptor. The challenge here is deciding which intents are appropriate to intercept. This problem is nontrivial because we cannot assume that the user firewall will always be responsive since it is a user app. Like any other app, it can crash or freeze. This is different from the original intent firewall, which can simply intercept all intents because it is self-contained.

Since the system server uses intents to start components, if the interceptor intercepts everything and the user firewall crashes, the system will no longer be able to start components. The device will end up in an unrecoverable state.

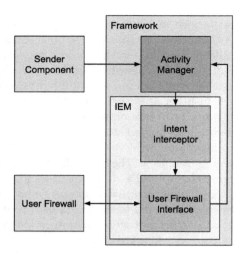

Fig. 3. The flow of intents through IEM.

For this reason, intents created by the system server are exempt from being intercepted. All other intents can be safely intercepted because failing to deliver them will not impact stability.

User Firewall Interface. After the interceptor, the intent next reaches the user firewall interface. In order for this interface to work, it has to be able to send intents to an app (the user firewall) and get responses containing decisions.

How can the interface forward an intent to an app and get a response? The answer to this challenge can be derived from a feature that already exists in Android: the extensible framework. This design pattern works by having a system service bind to an app service chosen by the user in the device settings. Once bound, the two services can directly exchange messages though binder IPC to communicate. This allows the user to install third party apps to serve as the keyboard, the settings administrator, the "daydream" screen when the device is docked, and more.

IEM mimics this architecture and consequently satisfies the same security guarantees. Once the device manufacturer explicitly enables a user firewall, IEM will bind to that app's user firewall service at startup. Once bound, the intercepted intents will be sent to the user firewall via the binding. The messages include a "reply to" handle, which the user firewall can use to return a response. Note that this is a direct bidirectional binder IPC channel. The messages traversing the channel are *not* intents.

There is another challenge regarding the design of the user firewall interface. In the original architecture, intents are resolved entirely inside the framework using additional stateful information being held in AMS. Consequently, while the intent flow as a whole is asynchronous, it is necessary that the portion that occurs inside AMS never block so resource exhaustion cannot occur. Since IEM inserts a binder IPC exchange into the middle of this resolution logic, avoiding blocks can no longer be taken for granted.

As mentioned earlier, the user firewall app could crash or freeze. If this happens, the app will cease to respond to the interface. This will cause resource exhaustion inside AMS. Even if a timeout mechanism is implemented to prevent buildup, the resulting design will be weakened because now an artificial time limit has been imposed on the user firewall for making access control decisions. If this timeout is short, it no longer becomes possible for the user firewall to involve the user in critical decision making processes. This reduces the flexibility of the firewall logic, which weakens the goal our architecture strives to achieve. Alternatively if the timeout is long, the device will become unresponsive, which is unacceptable. There is no middle ground. Either choice is detrimental to the goal of designing a platform that is flexible. For this reason, there cannot be any timeouts. The interface must be completely stateless so no blocking occurs. This distinguishes IEM from many other hook designs.

Since IEM has to maintain statelessness and never be waiting on the user firewall, the messages it sends have to contain all the information necessary to reconstruct the state. To address this challenge, we introduce the concept of intent wrapper. The wrapper is a bundle containing the original intent along with everything necessary to duplicate its state. This includes sender information, which is something the original intent firewall does not consider. By wrapping these additional variables together along with the intent, not only does the user firewall now receive a complete picture of sender, receiver, and interaction being performed, but the interface no longer has to remember the intent's state because that information will be returned by the user firewall in the response. However, this state information has to be protected from being modified by the user firewall; a challenge which will be addressed next.

User Firewall. The intent wrapper now reaches the user firewall. What should it be allowed to modify? It could, for example, perform data sanitization or redirect the intent to a different receiver. However, allowing the user firewall to modify all the fields of the wrapper would give it the power to send any intent to any app on behalf of any other app. There is value in allowing for modification, but having no restrictions breaks the principal of least privilege. We introduce the intent token to address this concern.

Inspiration for the intent token comes from SYN cookies, which prevents SYN flooding by making TCP handshakes stateless [5]. Similarly, the intent token allows IEM to remain stateless while still restricting the user firewall's power. Tokens are generated inside IEM by hashing a secret created at startup with the parts of the state that should not be modified. Randomized salts are used to ensure that tokens are unique. As long as the secret is kept confidential, the user firewall will be unable to create valid tokens and consequently cannot arbitrarily modify an intent's state. Intents are also numbered sequentially and checked against a sliding window inside IEM to prevent replay. While the window could be considered stateful, its fixed size makes it not prone to resource exhaustion and therefore acceptable for the IEM design. In this way, the user firewall is a privileged app, but only to the extent essential for performing its role as an intent firewall.

More challenging, however, is deciding which parts of the state should be included in the token to prevent modification. This answer can be determined by grouping the contents of the intent wrapper into the three mutually exclusive categories: sender, intent, and receiver. The variables pertaining to the sender's identity stand out from those of the intent and receiver because the sender is the creator of the intent. If the user firewall changes who created the intent, all integrity is lost. On the other hand, the sender already expects that the system will resolve the receiver. For this reason, the user firewall is allowed to modify the action to be performed and who will carry it out, but it cannot change who sent it.

While this subsection has provided an overview of the security mechanisms inside IEM, the following subsection explains in detail how these mechanisms mitigate threats at each surface.

3.3 Threat Model

Figure 3 shows that the boundaries between IEM, framework, and app are crossed in four places. This subsection addresses the security of these crossings in the order that intents reach them.

The threat model for IEM assumes that the framework is secure and trustworthy. This includes AMS since it is a part of the framework. This assumption is made because IEM is designed solely to enforce intent security, so any compromise of other framework components is out of scope. The model also assumes that the secret created by IEM for generating tokens is kept secret. This is a safe assumption because IEM never needs to share this secret with any other component.

The first boundary crossing is from the sending app to AMS. The intents enter AMS through an API that is unmodified by IEM. Therefore, IEM assumes that this boundary is secure.

The next boundary is between IEM and AMS. Since the threat model already assumes that AMS is trustworthy, the boundary is between two trusted parties. This makes the boundary secure.

After entering IEM, the intent next reaches the boundary between the interface and the user firewall in user space. This surface can be attacked by a malicious app, but the previously mentioned security mechanisms prevent the attacker from having any success.

Three actions occur over this boundary. First, the interface binds to the app. Second, the interface sends the app intents to inspect. Third, the interface receives intents from the app. Attacking the first action requires the attacker to bind to either the interface or the user firewall. The interface protects against this by disallowing apps from initiating the binding process. Instead, it is always the interface that initiates the binding and since it gets its target from the device settings, it will bind with the correct service. Since the interface is a part of the system, the user firewall can differentiate the attacker from the interface by checking the UID of the bind request. This action can also be protected using the permissions mechanism already present in Android. To attack the second action, the adversary will have to sniff and spoof binder messages. Since the binder is part of the Linux kernel, this is only doable by either gaining root privileges or by compromising the kernel. In either case, the integrity of the entire system is compromised, which is beyond the scope of IEM. Finally, an attacker targeting the third action would have to spoof a user firewall response, but as stated earlier, this is prevented by the intent token.

This completes the threat model for IEM. As a side note, we would like to mention that there are also multiple challenges pertaining to the implementation of IEM in Android, but due to length constraints we cannot go into the necessary detail to explain them in this publication.

Listing 1.1. UFW service handler template.

```
@Override
public void handleMessage(Message msg) {
  Bundle data = msg.getData();
  Bundle res = checkIntent(data);
  if (res != null) { //allow
    Message r = Message.obtain(null, 1);
    r.setData(res);
    try {
      msg.replyTo.send(r);
    } catch (RemoteException e) {}
  } //blocked intents require no action
}
```

4 Applications

The generic nature of IEM allows developers to create many different kinds of user firewalls to serve a variety of purposes. All the user firewalls presented in this section could be implemented by modifying the original intent firewall, but doing so would be vastly impractical. Developers would need to have Android framework expertise to access resources without using an SDK and each firewall would have to be tested extensively since implementation modifies the operating system. Some of the examples are designed to address very specific needs, so it would be very challenging to anticipate and generalize these firewalls to a degree which justifies implementing them directly into the Android framework.

The developer of a user firewall only needs to implement a service component. Listing 1.1 is a template for the handler. This architecture gives the user firewall developer the flexibility to design the internal logic of his app however he desires to provide whatever services and features his end-users require.

In this section, we describe a few examples of user firewalls made possible by IEM. We have chosen just a small sample from the infinite number of possible

392 C. Yagemann and W. Du

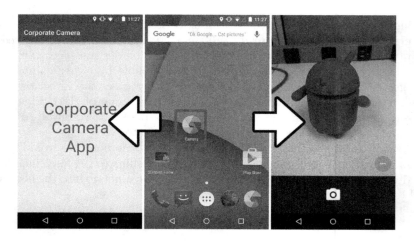

Fig. 4. Redirecting intents.

user firewalls, which we believe are sufficient to demonstrate the flexibility of the IEM architecture.

4.1 Redirecting Intents

Unlike traditional firewalls, user firewalls are not restricted to binary allow or deny access control. It is also possible for user firewalls to allow an intent, but modify some of its contents. This allows for some interesting use cases such as intent redirection.

Consider a corporation that is concerned about employees taking pictures using their phone while in the office. Banking institutions are an example since there may be sensitive information in documents and on computer monitors that could be captured when the photo is taken. Suppose that the corporation has created a camera app for their employees, which is designed to only take "safe" photos. However, since this app is very restrictive, employees do not want to have to use the corporate camera app when they are not at work. A user firewall can control which camera app is launched based on GPS location using intent redirection.

Figure 4 demonstrates this case. When the user wants to launch the normal camera app, the user firewall will check the user's current location. If they are not in the office, the intent will be allowed. If they are in the office, the intent will be redirect to the corporate camera app and it will appear instead.

4.2 Preventing Intent Denial of Service

When we implemented the intent token, we intentionally created a new field for it inside the intent because attempting to read or write to any part of the extras bundle of an intent will raise an unmarshaling exception if any object in the

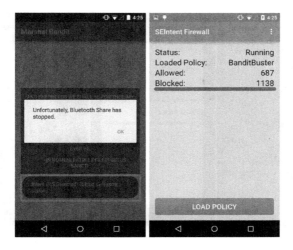

Fig. 5. Intent DoS detection.

extras is a custom class and the receiver does not have a definition for it. We discovered that most apps do not handle the unmarshaling exception and will crash. The Gmail app is one such example. This is a known vulnerability that Google has acknowledged [27].

To demonstrate the potential damage of this vulnerability, we created a malicious app called Marshal Bandit. Upon boot, Marshal Bandit queries AMS for all the running services and spams them with intents containing a custom object in the extras bundle. This causes services on the device to repeatedly crash and overwhelms the system's worker threads. The result is a denial of service, which causes the device to become unresponsive and eventually reboot. Since the user cannot access the Settings app while the attack is underway, the device is crippled. Even if the user knows how to boot the device into the recovery mode, she will not know which app to uninstall. Marshal Bandit is a normal app with no granted permissions.

This type of attack cannot be stopped in current Android devices, but it can be stopped by a user firewall thanks to IEM. In Fig. 5, we demonstrate a user firewall that can detect the sudden flood of intents coming from our malicious app. Upon detection, the user firewall will inform the user which app is performing the attack while stopping background processes, halting the spam of intents. The user can then regain control of the device and uninstall the malicious app. This user firewall is a normal app using only the "stop background processes" permission and IEM. The successful thwarting of this recently discovered denial of service attack demonstrates the flexibility and capability of IEM. Implementation logic of this complexity at the framework level would be challenging compared to the narrow scope of attacks it addresses. With IEM, a user firewall that addresses this vulnerability can be developed by a single developer in one work day.

Fig. 6. Data sanitization.

4.3 Sanitizing Intent Data

Since user firewalls can modify the contents of the intent itself, they can perform data sanitization. This is applicable to trends such as *bring your own device* for the corporate environment.

If an Android app wants to share data with another app, most ways of doing so require an intent. The intent will either contain the data itself, a URI pointing to a file containing the data, or the intent will be for a service binding that will then be used to share data back and forth. In all three cases, a user firewall can either block or alter the data by dropping or modifying the initial intent. Figure 6 demonstrates this functionality. In this example, when the user tries to open a malicious image file, the user firewall modifies the intent so a benign image is opened instead. This same technique can just as easily be applied to other types of data to either prevent data leakage or to protect apps from exploitation. This functionality is similar to the web application firewall (WAF) concept [26].

This is not a complete solution to controlling data flow, but IEM can allow user firewalls to address some flow concerns while being easy to develop, deploy, and maintain.

4.4 Determining Caller Chains

One potential shortcoming with the Android permissions architecture is it only considers the immediate sender of an intent. It does not account for the case where a chain of apps are invoked via intents. If an attacker invokes an app with slightly greater permissions and that in turn invokes another app with still greater permissions, the final receiver could be excessively more privileged than the original sender. This pattern can lead to privilege escalation [6,7,12,14,19, 28]. Multiple works have identified this problem and implemented caller chains

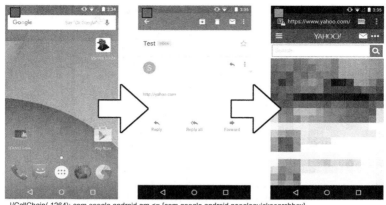

I/CallChain(1264): com.google.android.gm <= {com.google.android.googlequicksearchbox}
I/CallChain(1264): com.android.browser <= {com.google.android.gm, com.google.android.googlequicksearchbox}

Fig. 7. Caller chain.

to resolve it [3]. However, all these solutions are relatively complex and require modification of the Android operating system.

Using IEM, it is easy to implement a user firewall which can track call chains. Figure 7 demonstrates a user firewall which a single developer programmed in under an hour. When an intent enters this user firewall, it records the sender and receiver as a pair. The user firewall can then use these pairs to recursively determine all the callers associated with a particular receiving app. The user firewall can then analyze the callers to determine if the permissions of the receiver greatly exceed those of the sender.

5   Evaluation

In addition to evaluating IEM in terms of what useful user firewalls it allows developers to create, we also formally evaluate it based on two additional criteria. First, how does IEM impact the stability of currently existing Android apps; both when allowing and blocking intents. Second, how does IEM impact the time it takes to route intents?

5.1   Application Stability

We tested IEM using the standard Google apps which come on Nexus devices as well as the top 50 free third-party apps from the Google Play Store. We explicitly included the Google apps in our evaluation because we found that they communicate with each other heavily using a wide variety of intent types.

During our tests of IEM, we did not find any cases where blocking an intent would cause an app to crash or become unresponsive. When blocking access to the Google Play Services, we did find apps that would refuse to start, prompting the user that Play Services needs to be installed. In either case, the apps behaved well even while the user firewall is blocking intents.

Table 1. Milliseconds to route intents, averaged over 5000 trials.

	No UFW	Allow All	Call Chain
Activity	346.9	348.2	352.1
Service	14.0	14.9	16.8
Broadcast	7.6	11.8	12.2

5.2 Performance

To test the intent routing performance of IEM, we created two simple apps to send and receive activity, service, and broadcast intents.

Table 1 shows the milliseconds needed to send the intent across apps. Each value shown is the average of 5000 trials. Our test device was a Nexus 5 running our modified version of Android 5.0.2 with IEM.

For our first set of trials, we configured IEM to not use a user firewall. This serves as our baseline as the logic in this configuration is identical to the original intent firewall. We then tested the intents using two user firewall policies. The "allow all" policy accepts any intent and serves to measure the overhead added by the round trip between the interface and the user firewall. The "call chain" policy inspects, stores, and logs every intent's sender and receiver and then recursively constructs chains. This is the most performance intensive example from our applications section.

Our results in Table 1 show that the user firewall interface adds some overhead, but the difference in routing time remains well below what a human user can perceive.

6 Related Works

This section discusses the IPC security mechanisms already present in Android as well as proposed designs from related research. These security architectures can be categorized into two general categories: access control and virtualization.

6.1 Access Control

In the access control category, we first find the sender permissions mechanism currently implemented in Android. This security feature allows receivers to require of the sender a particular permission. This mechanism improves security by allowing for some restriction in which senders can invoke the receiver's exposed components, but it has its limitations [12]. First, the receiver can only specify a single permission which the sender must have. Since it is common for Android apps to have multiple permissions, this means that the receiver's exposed components can be invoked by apps of lesser privilege. Second, even in the case of requester apps of equal or greater privilege, privilege and trustworthiness are not strongly correlated [13,15]. Applications coming from a variety of sources can request any combination of permissions and these permissions are granted upon approval by the user during installation. This makes it possible for a malicious app to have as many, if not more, permissions than the receiving app it is trying to exploit. These problems have been the motivation for works such as XmanDroid [6], Saint [25], CRePE [11], and others [9,16,18,23,24]. Even if the developer of the receiving app wants to explicitly check who the sender of the intent is, his app can only see the last app to send the intent. Chain-Droid [31] and Scippa [3] both demonstrate situations where this is inadequate for enforcing access control.

The other IPC access control mechanism present in Android is the intent firewall. Unfortunately, this firewall also has major shortcomings in the robustness of its rule set which is why very few production Android devices have intent firewall policies despite the firewall being present and enabled [22].

Other works, such as Boxify [4], use runtime sandboxing to force untrusted apps to send their system transactions through additional access control mechanisms. These solutions can also restrict binder IPC, but implementing them requires expert knowledge of Linux IPC and syscalls. Since they work at the native level, the context of the transaction is obscured. IEM user firewalls use concepts the average app developer is already familiar with.

Our work is conceptually similar to Android Security Modules [17], but differentiates itself in two key aspects. First, while ASM only facilitates the monitoring of resources, our work enables modification for the purposes of redirection and data sanitization. Second, ASM uses callback timeouts; a limitation our work avoids by being stateless.

6.2 Virtualization

On the virtualization side of Android security, solutions attempt to achieve isolation between processes by virtualizing different portions of the Android device. One solution, Cells [2], achieves this isolation by creating virtual devices that run on top of the host device. Another solution, Airbag [30], also achieves process isolation, but rather than creating full virtual devices, this solution creates virtual system servers which prevents processes from different containers from communicating. There are also other works which implement isolation, such as Trust-Droid [8].

We chose an access control design for IEM because we want to leverage the unique nature of intent IPC. Specifically, we want to leverage the fact that all intents must travel through the framework using a standardized message format which the system can understand. A virtualization solution would not leverage the semantic understanding the system server has of intent messages.

7   Conclusion

Android is the most popular operating system for embedded mobile devices. It is designed to encourage apps to leverage IPC with a greater frequency than seen in operating systems which target traditional computers. This, coupled with the unique properties of intent IPC, makes the study a worthy endeavor. The current Android system includes a firewall which can perform access control on intent IPC. However, it is very limited and its poor usability means it has almost never been utilized in practice. We propose IEM to separate the interceptor of the firewall from its decision engine using a novel stateless interface. This allows a normal application, called a user firewall, to become the engine for intent access control. By doing so, IEM makes it easy to develop and modify the firewall's logic, allowing for easy implementation of interesting new access control.

Acknowledgments. This project was supported in part by the NSF grant 1318814.

References

1. Aafer, Y., Zhang, N., Zhang, Z., Zhang, X., Chen, K., Wang, X., Zhou, X., Wenliang, D., Grace, M.: Hare hunting in the wild android: a study on the threat of hanging attribute references. In: Proceedings of the 22nd ACM SIGSAC Conference on Computer and Communications Security, CCS 2015, pp. 1248–1259. ACM, New York (2015)
2. Andrus, J., Dall, C., Van't Hof, A., Laadan, O., Nieh, J.: Cells: a virtual mobile smartphone architecture. In: Proceedings of the Twenty-Third ACM Symposium on Operating Systems Principles, SOSP 2011, pp. 173–187. ACM, New York (2011)
3. Backes, M., Bugiel, S., Gerling, S., Scippa: system-centric IPC provenance on android. In: Proceedings of the 30th Annual Computer Security Applications Conference, ACSAC 2014, pp. 36–45. ACM, New York (2014)
4. Backes, M., Bugiel, S., Hammer, C., Schranz, O., von Styp-Rekowsky, P.: Boxify: full-fledged app sandboxing for stock android. In: 24th USENIX Security Symposium (USENIX Security 2015), pp. 691–706. USENIX Association, Washington, D.C., August 2015
5. Bernstein, D.J.: Syn cookies. http://cr.yp.to/syncookies.html. Accessed 20 Nov 2015
6. Bugiel, S., Davi, L., Dmitrienko, A., Fischer, T., Sadeghi, A.-R.: Xmandroid: a new android evolution to mitigate privilege escalation attacks. Technical report TR-2011-04, Technische Universität Darmstadt, April 2011
7. Bugiel, S., Davi, L., Dmitrienko, A., Fischer, T., Sadeghi, A.-R., Shastry, B.: Towards taming privilege-escalation attacks on android. In: NDSS (2012)
8. Bugiel, S., Davi, L., Dmitrienko, A., Heuser, S., Sadeghi, A.-R., Shastry, B.: Practical and lightweight domain isolation on android. In: Proceedings of the 1st ACM Workshop on Security and Privacy in Smartphones and Mobile Devices, SPSM 2011, pp. 51–62. ACM, New York (2011)
9. Bugiel, S., Heuser, S., Sadeghi, A.-R.: Flexible and fine-grained mandatory access control on android for diverse security and privacy policies. In: Presented as Part of the 22nd USENIX Security Symposium (USENIX Security 2013), pp. 131–146. USENIX, Washington, D.C. (2013)
10. Chin, E., Felt, A.P., Greenwood, K., Wagner, D.: Analyzing inter-application communication in android. In: Proceedings of the 9th International Conference on Mobile Systems, Applications, and Services, MobiSys 2011, pp. 239–252. ACM, New York (2011)

11. Conti, M., Nguyen, V.T.N., Crispo, B.: CRePE: context-related policy enforcement for android. In: Burmester, M., Tsudik, G., Magliveras, S., Ilić, I. (eds.) ISC 2010. LNCS, vol. 6531, pp. 331–345. Springer, Heidelberg (2011)

12. Davi, L., Dmitrienko, A., Sadeghi, A.-R., Winandy, M.: Privilege escalation attacks on android. In: Burmester, M., Tsudik, G., Magliveras, S., Ilić, I. (eds.) ISC 2010. LNCS, vol. 6531, pp. 346–360. Springer, Heidelberg (2011)

13. Elish, K.O., Yao, D.D., Ryder, B.G.: On the need of precise inter-app ICC classification for detecting android malware collusions. In: Proceedings of IEEE Mobile Security Technologies (MoST), in Conjunction with the IEEE Symposium on Security and Privacy (2015)

14. Enck, W., Ongtang, M., Mcdaniel, P.: Mitigating android software misuse before it happens (2008)

15. Felt, A.P., Hanna, S., Chin, E., Wang, H.J., Moshchuk, E.: Permission redelegation: attacks and defenses. In: 20th Usenix Security Symposium (2011)

16. Hay, R., Tripp, O., Pistoia, M.: Dynamic detection of inter-application communication vulnerabilities in android. In: Proceedings of the 2015 International Symposium on Software Testing and Analysis, ISSTA 2015, pp. 118–128. ACM, New York (2015)

17. Heuser, S., Nadkarni, A., Enck, W., Sadeghi, A.-R.: ASM: a programmable interface for extending android security. In: 23rd USENIX Security Symposium (USENIX Security 2014), pp. 1005–1019. USENIX Association, San Diego, August 2014

18. Kantola, D., Chin, E., He, W., Wagner, D.: Reducing attack surfaces for intra-application communication in android. Technical report UCB/EECS-2012-182, EECS Department, University of California, Berkeley, July 2012

19. Lineberry, A., Richardson, D.L., Wyatt, T.: These arent the permissions you are looking for. In: DefCon, vol. 18 (2010)

20. Linux-PAM. A linux-pam page. http://www.linux-pam.org/. Accessed 02 Dec 2015

21. Long, L., Li, Z., Zhenyu, W., Lee, W., Jiang, G., Chex: statically vetting android apps for component hijacking vulnerabilities. In: Proceedings of the 2012 ACM Conference on Computer and Communications Security, CCS 2012, pp. 229–240. ACM, New York (2012)

22. Ludwig, A.: Android security state of the union. In: Black Hat USA (2015)

23. Maji, A.K., Arshad, F.A., Bagchi, S., Rellermeyer, J.S.: An empirical study of the robustness of inter-component communication in android. In: Proceedings of the 2012 42nd Annual IEEE/IFIP International Conference on Dependable Systems and Networks (DSN), DSN 2012, pp. 1–12. IEEE Computer Society, Washington, D.C. (2012)

24. Nadkarni, A., Enck, W.: Preventing accidental data disclosure in modern operating systems. In: Proceedings of the 2013 ACM SIGSAC Conference on Computer & Communications Security, CCS 2013, pp. 1029–1042. ACM, New York (2013)

25. Ongtang, M., McLaughlin, S., Enck, W., McDaniel, P.: Semantically rich application-centric security in android. In: Computer Security Applications Conference, ACSAC 2009, Annual, pp. 340–349, December 2009

26. OWASP. Web application firewall. http://tinyurl.com/3cakwty. Accessed 4 Dec 2015

27. Android Open Source Project. Android open source project - issue tracker - issue 177223: Intent/bundle security issue. https://code.google.com/p/android/issues/detail?id=177223. Accessed 20 Nov 2015

28. Schlegel, R., Zhang, K., Zhou, X., Intwala, M., Kapadia, A., Wang, X.F.: Sound-comber: a stealthy and context-aware sound trojan for smartphones. NDSS **11**, 17–33 (2011)
29. Smalley, S., Craig, R.: Security enhanced (se) android: bringing flexible MAC to android. NDSS **310**, 20–38 (2013)
30. Chiachih, W., Zhou, Y., Patel, K., Liang, Z., Jiang, X., Airbag: boosting smart-phone resistance to malware infection. In: Proceedings of the Network and Distrib-uted System Security Symposium (2014)
31. Zhou, Q., Wang, D., Zhang, Y., Qin, B., Aimin, Y., Zhao, B.: Chaindroid: safe and flexible access to protected android resources based on call chain. In: 2013 12th IEEE International Conference on Trust, Security and Privacy in Computing and Communications (TrustCom), pp. 156–162, July 2013

Hey, You, Get Off of My Image: Detecting Data Residue in Android Images

Xiao Zhang$^{(\boxtimes)}$, Yousra Aafer, Kailiang Ying, and Wenliang Du

Department of Electrical Engineering and Computer Science,
Syracuse University, Syracuse, NY, USA
{xzhang35,yaafer,kying,wedu}@syr.edu

Abstract. Android's data cleanup mechanism has been called into question with the recently discovered data residue vulnerability. However, the existing study only focuses on one particular Android version and demands heavy human involvement. In this project, we aim to fill the gap by providing a comprehensive understanding of the data residue situation across the entire Android ecosystem. To this end, we propose ANRED(ANRED is a former French public institution for the recovery and disposal of waste.), an ANdroid REsidue Detector that performs static analysis on Android framework bytecode and automatically quantifies the risk for each identified data residue instance within collected system services. The design of ANRED has overcome several challenges imposed by the special characteristic of Android framework and data residue vulnerability. We have implemented ANRED in WALA and further evaluated it against 606 Android images. The analysis results have demonstrated the effectiveness, efficiency and reliability of ANRED. In particular, we have confirmed the effect of vendor customization and version upgrade on data residue vulnerability. We have also identified five new data residue instances that have been overlooked in the previous study, leading to data leakage and privilege escalation attacks.

1 Introduction

The prosperity of Android ecosystem contrasts sharply with the short lifespan of applications (apps, in short) on devices. Seemingly harmless, a recent study [40] has uncovered the data residue vulnerability arising from the app uninstallation process on the Android platform. In particular, when an app is uninstalled from the device, its data may be still scattered stealthily around privileged system services within Android framework. More surprisingly, the protection on these data leftover is problematic, empowering unauthorized adversaries to access users' sensitive information, such as credentials, emails and bank statements. As a pioneer that sheds lights on the data residue vulnerability, the above-mentioned study limits its scope to AOSP version 5.0.1 with the requirement of source code and significant manual effort. However, the extensive customization on Android devices from different vendors and the high fragmentation of Android operating system demand an automatic, scalable and source code independent framework for data residue detection.

© Springer International Publishing Switzerland 2016
I. Askoxylakis et al. (Eds.): ESORICS 2016, Part I, LNCS 9878, pp. 401–421, 2016.
DOI: 10.1007/978-3-319-45744-4_20

To this end, we propose ANRED, an ANdroid REsidue Detector that takes an Android device image as input and automatically quantifies the risk for each identified data residue instance within collected system services. The design of ANRED has overcome several challenges. First, we have employed several novel techniques to generically preprocess Android images from different vendors, accurately pinpoint all system services within the given image, identify entry points for each system service and connect the broken links on the call graph resulting from the event-driven nature of Android system. Second, we have inferred data residue instances from mismatches between the deleting data set and the saving data set. To retrieve those two data sets, we have divided the original call graph into two subgraphs originating from the saving and deleting entry points. While the saving entry points capture all interactions with the apps, deleting entry points are functions that handle app uninstallation. Further complicating the detection process is when the data removal operation is present in Android framework, but the underlying logic is flawed. In these cases, we have taken the complexity of the deleting logic into consideration and quantified the possibility of each detected data residue instance.

We have evaluated ANRED against 606 Android images from several major vendors, such as Google, Samsung, Xiaomi and CyanogenMod, covering all platform versions from Gingerbread to the newest Marshmallow. ANRED detects 191 likely data residue instances on average for each image, of which 106 (55.5 %) are missing data deletion logic upon app uninstallation. We have confirmed that, vendor customization is indeed a major factor in introducing new data residue instances, while the effect of version upgrade varies from vendor to vendor. To evaluate its effectiveness, we compare the analysis result from ANRED with that from the previous study [40] for the same image. Totally, 253 likely data residue instances are identified on this image by ANRED, with 205 (%81) of them labelled as highly risky. We have manually validated all 205 risky instances and uncovered 15 data residue vulnerabilities. The other 190 instances are neither app specific nor security relevant. Among those 15 identified vulnerabilities, 10 of them have been captured in the previous study, while the other 5 vulnerabilities are newly discovered, leading to data leakage and privilege escalation attacks.

Contributions. The contribution of our work is three-fold:

- *New Framework*: we have designed and implemented ANRED as an automatic, scalable and source code independent framework for data residue detection on Android.
- *New Understanding*: we have evaluated ANRED against 606 images and presented an accurate and comprehensive understanding of the data residue situation across the entire Android ecosystem.
- *New Findings*: we have identified a large amount of risky data residue instances and further confirmed 5 new vulnerabilities with severe real-world damage.

Roadmap. The rest of this paper is organized as follows: Sect. 2 explains the necessary background knowledge and presents a motivating example to drive our framework design. Section 3 breaks down the design details of each building block in ANRED. Section 4 further explains the technical details. Section 5 breaks down the evaluation results of ANRED on 606 images. Finally, Sect. 6 describes the related work and Sect. 7 makes conclusions.

2 Background

In this section, we present necessary background knowledge to facilitate the design of ANRED.

Android System Services. In Android, system services provide privileged operations that can be requested by apps via permission declaration in their AndroidManifest files. Android system services execute in the System_Server process, and expose their functionalities through APIs defined in corresponding interfaces. Figure 1 demonstrates this process with a manually crafted system service AbcService based on real instances (DreamManagerService and SpellCheckerService). During system booting up, the SystemServer class adds the AbcService to the system service list (Fig. 1(a)). By doing so, it triggers the lifecycle event onStart() in the AbcService implementation (Fig. 1(c)). Upon starting, AbcService exposes its functionalities via an IBinder object that implements the APIs defined in the IAbc interface (Fig. 1(b)). An interface essentially defines the protocol between two communication endpoints across the process boundary. In this case, an app can use the exposed IBinder object to invoke the setComponent() API in the System_Server process by complying with the protocol defined in the AbcService interface. All functions defined in

```
1  final  Class  SystemServer{
2     public  SystemServer(){
3        ...
4        // starting the AbcService
5        ServiceManager.addService
6          ("Abc",  new  AbcService());
7        ...
8     }
9  }
```

(a) Service Start-up

```
1  /* @hide */
2  interface  IAbc{
3     ...
4     // one of the exposed APIs
5     void  setComponent(String  s);
6     ...
7  }
```

(b) Service Interface

```
1   Class  AbcService  extends  SystemService
2      extends  BroadcastReceiver{
3   @Override
4   onStart(){
5      publishBinderService(
6         new  BinderService());
7   }
8   Class  BinderService  extends  IAbc.Stub{
9      Public  void  setComponent(String  s){
10        new  MyHandler().sendEmptyMessage();
11     }
12  }
13  Class  MyHandler  extends  Handler{
14     @Override
15     public  void  handleMessage(Message  m){
16        db.putStringForUser("Abc",s);
17     }
18  }
19  @Override
20  onReceive(){
21     prepare();
22     removeData();
23  }
24  }
```

(c) Service Implementation

Fig. 1. A motivating example that shows the working flow of Android system services and origin of data residue instances.

the interface are entry points for outside apps to trigger the saving operations within this privileged system service.

Android App Uninstallation. When an app is uninstalled from the Android system, the `PackageManagerService` will remove any resources stored in the app's private directories. Then, it sends out a broadcast event to awake the uninstallation handling logic in other parts of the system. In Fig. 1(c), the `AbcService` will receive such a broadcast event in its `onReceive()` function, and responds by removing related data after preparation. Apart from the generic `BroadcastReceiver` approach in Fig. 1(c), there exist three other ways to get notified upon app uninstallation, including `PackageMonitor`, `DeathRecipient` and `RegisteredServicesCacheListener`. All of them are entry points for triggering data deleting logic within system services upon app uninstallation.

Android Data Residue Vulnerability. Data residue exist on Android due to the mismatch between saved data and deleted data within a system service upon app uninstallation. This process usually involves four steps, as illustrated in Fig. 2. It starts with the installation of a normal app (step 1). Upon user interaction, the data related to this app will be saved by certain system services within Android framework (step 2). For instance, the implementation of `AbcService` shown in Fig. 1(c) asynchronizely handles the IPC invocation of `setComponent()` by saving user configuration into a database with `Abc` as the entry key. Files, databases and well-marked data structures (e.g. `Hashmap`) are normally used to store app-specific data. Later on, when the app is uninstalled, Android will try to delete related data from memory and persistent storage (step 3). In this step, the above-mentioned `Abc` entry will become residue if the app uninstallation handling logic is not in place or flawed. Having data leftover does not necessarily lead to security breaches, as long as the protection is sound. Otherwise, sensitive information will be leaked out to adversaries (step 4).

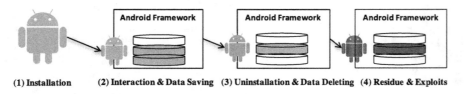

(1) Installation   (2) Interaction & Data Saving   (3) Uninstallation & Data Deleting   (4) Residue & Exploits

Fig. 2. Flow of data residue generation and exploits on Android

3   Design

The high-level flow of ANRED is depicted in Fig. 3. To mitigate the absence of framework source code and limitation of hardware resources, ANRED depends on static analysis to directly work on Java bytecode. In this process, ANRED takes the entire Android image as input, extracts the framework's and preloaded

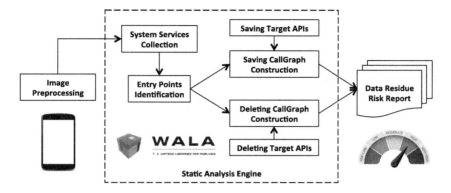

Fig. 3. Overview of ANRED design

apps' bytecode, and collects candidate system services. As the data residue vulnerability occurs at the level of system services, ANRED's static analysis logic also resides at the same level. For each system service, we are interested in two types of operations inside: saving operation and deleting operation. Mixing both operations on the same call graph will make them indistinguishable at the end. Thus, ANRED generates two call graphs for each system service: a saving graph and a deleting graph. The saving graph captures the data that will be saved inside the system service, while the deleting graph indicates what data will be removed when handling app uninstallation. Based on that, data residue instances are inferred from mismatches between the deleting data set and the saving data set. To cover instances that are caused by flawed deleting logic, ANRED also takes into consideration the complexity of the deleting logic to quantify the underlying risks. We explain the design challenges of each block in following sections.

3.1   Image Preprocessing

Given an Android image, ANRED extracts the Android framework code and its preloaded apps. Since different vendors or different versions of Android pack the code in different formats (i.e., `apk`, `dex`, `odex` to `oat`), ANRED employs several utilities to handle each format gracefully. We employ `dex2jar` utility to convert `dex` and `apk` files into `jar`s, suitable for standard static analysis platforms. Additionally, we use `apktool` to retrieve the `AndroidManifest` configuration file from each app. We use `baksmali` and `smali` to convert `odex` code to `dex` files. Images that contain `oat` files or target Android Lollipop require special handling with `dextra` [7] and `deodex-lollipop` [13].

3.2   System Service Collection

To detect data residue instances, we need to identify all system services from a compiled image. Such list is challenging to obtain, as the registration place of each system service varies greatly among images. Our key observation is that system services registration APIs are more stable across Android customization and version upgrade. The service example shown in Fig. 1 demonstrates the two most representative APIs, addService() and publishBinderService(), for publishing a system service. Thus, to retrieve the system service list, ANRED first collects functions that invoke addService() or publishBinderService() and marks them as entry points. For each entry, ANRED constructs a call graph. By traversing through the call graph, not only can we pinpoint the places where system services are registered, but also resolve the service class and exposed interface class. For system services that are within preloaded apps, the above process is simplified by directly searching the AndroidManifest file for services that are accessible from the outside world. In both cases, we further filter out unnecessary jars and generate input specifications for the static analysis platform.

3.3   Entry Point Identification

Static analysis on Android platform demands the construction of a precise call graph. For that purpose, an accurate and complete list of entry point functions needs to be provided. In normal Java programs, the entry point is the main function. However, the widely adopted callback mechanism in Android framework complicates this task. In ANRED, we consider entry points as asynchronized invocations where their callees are present in the analysis scope, but their callers are not. As shown in Fig. 1(b), the AbcService specifies a list of exposed APIs in the interface file, namely AIDL, for apps to interact with. Naturally, all public AIDL functions become entry points. However, a great amount of other asynchronized invocation patterns are present within different system services. One representative example is the onClick function inside the onClickListener interface. In this case, the system service provides the implementation of onClick function (callee), while the caller (user event) triggers the invocation. Clearly, the caller does not exist in the analysis scope, and thus, ANRED considers the callee function, onClick, as an entry point.

To collect all entry points, we take a similar approach as in EdgeMiner [22] by searching all internal classes within each system service for interfaces and abstract classes. The reason behind is that, both interfaces and abstract classes rely on other parties to provide the actual implementation, indicating the absence of a caller. Different from EdgeMiner, we exclude functions within Handler, Thread, AsyncTask and ServiceConnection classes, since they are asynchronized invocations where the caller and callee are both present in the analysis scope, as illustrated in Fig. 4(a). Such cases lead to broken links in the constructed call graph, which we will handle differently in Sect. 3.4. After identifying all entry points, we further divide them into saving entry points and deleting entry points for the construction of the saving call graph and the deleting call graph, respectively. We consider all the APIs that handle app uninstallation as deleting entry points, and the rest as saving entry points. Specifically, ANRED includes the following four classes as the source for deleting entry points: `PackageMonitor`, `BroadcastReceiver`, `DeathRecipient` and `RegisteredServicesCacheListener`.

3.4   Call Graph Construction

We choose WALA [16] as the static analysis platform for call graph construction, due to its popularity and strength in data flow analysis, which is our main concern in the data residue detection process. The analysis stays at the Android framework level, but inherits all challenges (i.e., broken links) from the app level. Take `MyHandler` class in Fig. 1(c) as an example. Its execution is conducted with the help of a `Message` queue. The caller side (`setComponent()`) puts a message on the queue, and waits until it is consumed by the callee side (`handleMessage()`). Even though both the caller and callee are present in the analysis scope, the connection is missing. Those broken links greatly affect the code coverage in static analysis, and thus, hinder ANRED's performance. Existing solutions [17,33,35] model the behavior of caller and callee functions, and add edges in the constructed call graph to connect them. Such bridges mitigate the reachability issues (control flow) on the call graph, but do not explicitly catenate the data flow.

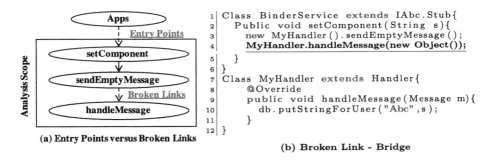

(a) Entry Points versus Broken Links

(b) Broken Link - Bridge

Fig. 4. Connecting broken links in ANRED via bytecode rewriting

To this end, we would like to connect broken links at the bytecode level, independent from the static analysis platform. The output will be a fixed `jar` file with all broken links connected. Benefit from this, researchers can apply it directly for different purposes with their own choices of static analysis platforms. More specifically, we propose to rewrite the bytecode of collected system services to connect the broken links. ANRED performs bytecode rewriting using the `shrike` utility in WALA, which is capable of looping through all instructions from the given bytecode. Ideally, once the invocation that causes broken links is found, we rewrite the instruction to bridge the connection. The real challenges lie in patching a diversity of invocations with a generic scheme. We use the `MyHandler` example in Fig. 1(b) to explain the details.

First of all, there are various functions for delivering messages with different arguments. In Java, replacing the current invocation to `handleMessage()` requires loading the correct handler instance and constructing the proper arguments. An easier and more stable approach is to add instructions at the end, instead of replacing existing ones. In the `MyHandler` case, ANRED adds the invocation to `handleMessage()` at the end of `setComponent()` function, as demonstrated in Fig. 4(b). However, adding the instruction still requires the creation of corresponding handler instance and argument instances. To be more specific, in order to invoke `handleMessage()`, an instance of the `MyHandler` class is needed, as well as a `Messsage` instance if the argument is not empty. It is quite challenging to statically accommodate all situations. Our design choice is to invoke the `handleMessage()` API as a static function and provide generic objects as necessary arguments. Although the generated `jar` may not execute properly, it is not an issue since static analysis does not check for conflicting method descriptors. To handle the case where the handler class type is inherited, ANRED locates the outermost class, and searches all internal classes for the ones that extend the base handler class or implement the callback interface. Theoretically, such approach will generate false mappings when multiple handler classes are present within the same outer class, however, our observation is that, inside each Android system service, there is usually only one handler class in use. Eventually, the bridge will be connected as in Fig. 4(b).

3.5   Target APIs Harvest

To detect mismatches between storage operations and cleanup logic, a complete list of saving and deleting API pairs is necessary. For instance, the `AbcService` shown in Fig. 1 uses `db.putStringForUser()` to save entries into a database. To check the existence of data residue, we would like to know the usage of corresponding deleting API (in this case, identical to the saving API) in handling app uninstallation. The manual identification of such API pairs is a tedious work, and lacks the guarantee on code coverage. Instead, ANRED applies heuristics generalized from manual inspection to harvest API pairs automatically. In particular, we categorize all saving/deleting API pairs into `SQLiteDatabase`, `SharedPreference`, `Settings`, `Java_Util` and `XML`. For each category, we then generalize heuristics at the level of package, class and function. At the top level, each category corresponds to a Java package, and all classes in it will be the source of API pairs. At the second level, we exclude classes that are irrelevant to storage operations. To illustrate, although thousands of classes exist in the `Java_Util` category, we can safely remove those related to `Exception`, `Concurrency` or `Thread`. At the last stage, both saving and deleting APIs follow strict naming schemes, like `put*()`/`remove*()` in `Java_Util` classes and `create*()`/`delete*()` in `File` classes. Such naming schemes allow a further filtering on the API descriptors directly. With these three levels of heuristics, ANRED is able to reliably exclude 95 % of total API candidates.

3.6 Risk Evaluation

Following the steps above, ANRED constructs two call graphs, i.e., saving graph and deleting graph, for each collected system service. Guided by the storage API pairs, we can further gather all saving and deleting operations via traversing through corresponding call graphs. Ideally, only the mismatches indicate data residue instances. However, as shown in Fig. 1 and previous work [40], the data cleanup logic may be flawed. As a result, ANRED quantifies the likelihood of each data residue instance with respect to the complexity of data deleting logic. A variant [11] of the standard Cyclomatic complexity [5] is used in ANRED against each deleting function. When the deleting logic is missing, we assign the largest complexity value, indicating the highest risk for this instance to be a real data residue vulnerability. At the image level, ANRED further aggregates all data residue instances together into a well-formatted XML report as shown in Fig. 5.

```
<image carrier="" manufacturer="" model="" name="" region="" version="">
  ......
  <service category="java_util" finished="" ibinder="" name=""
     output_time_cost="" size="" type="">
     ......
     <residue complexity="1000" deletingInstructions="" name=""
        savingInstructions=""/>
     ......
  </service>
  ......
  <serviceDetectionCost></serviceDetectionCost>
  <rewritingCost></rewritingCost>
  <residueDetectionCost></residueDetectionCost>
</image>
```

Fig. 5. ANRED final report template

4 Implementation

The implementation of ANRED consists of around 7,500 **L**ines **O**f Java **C**ode (LOC) and 5,000 lines of Python code with comments included. We further break down the entire code base into four modules: `Jar` extraction, `Jar` decompilation, residue detection and result analysis. The code composition and library dependency for individual module is shown in Table 1. To handle different situations, our code base contains functions with small deviations. For instance, we have slightly different Python scripts to extract `jars` from Nexus images and Samsung images. We emphasize that, those functions are counted twice in the presented statistics, i.e., the count of effective LOC will be smaller. The code base of ANRED, as well as our image collection and evaluation results from Sect. 5, are publicly available on [2].

4.1 Bridging Broken Links

ANRED leverages WALA's `shrike` utility to bridge broken links caused by the `Handler`, `Thread`, `AsyncTask` and `ServiceConnection` classes in Android. We fit `jar` files into `shrike` individually, and traverse through each embedded class, functions in each class and bytecode instructions in each function. For each instruction, we check it against the candidate invocations that can cause broken links. In the `Handler` case, such invocations include `send*Message()` and `sendToTarget()` APIs, while in the `AsyncTask` case, `execute*()` typed APIs will be our candidates. For functions that do not contain candidate invocations, they stay untouched in the fixed `jar` file.

For each target instruction identified, ANRED records its position within the method body and inserts a static invocation to the callee function. Such a function invocation requires totally four types of instructions. `NewInstructions` are used to create generic java objects to be fed as function arguments, followed by `StoreInstructions` and `LoadInstructions`, which store and load the generated variables, respectively. Eventually, an `InvocationInstruction` initiates the function call. In `shrike`, each `InvocationInstruction` consists of four segments: function descriptor, object type, function name and dispatch mode. As explained in Sect. 3.4, ANRED dispatches this instruction as a static invocation, and searches from the outermost class for the object type. While function name is self-explanatory, an accurate function descriptor could be challenging to obtain. In most cases, we can manually craft the descriptor string according to the Android documentation. However, in the `AsyncTask` case, all callee functions contain `Params...`, known as Java Varargs [12] that takes an arbitrary number of values with arbitrary types upon invocation. ANRED overcomes the challenge by directly resolving the function descriptor from the object class implementation. Specifically, we search the entire class hierarchy for the class that implements the object type, and then obtain descriptor for each function inside.

Table 1. ANRED code base breakdown

Module	#LOC	Language	Dependency
Jar Extraction	1438	Python	`ext4utils` [8]
Jar Decompilation	2638	Python	`dex2jar` [6], `apktool` [3], `dextra` [7]
			`deodex-lollipop` [13], `baksmali/smali` [15]
Residue Detection	7568	Java	WALA [16]
Result Analysis	857	Python	-

4.2 Building Class Hierarchy and Call Graph

ANRED totally constructs three call graphs: one for system service collection, one for the saving logic analysis and the last one for the deleting logic analysis. Since these three graphs serve for different purposes, they demand different level of precision. In particular, we use RTA [18,19] algorithm in constructing the call graph for system service collection, as it is relatively simple and fast. All we need from this call graph is the identification of certain APIs. In contrast, we employ 0-CFA [32,36] algorithm to construct call graphs for the saving and deleting logic analysis, since they both require an accurate control flow and data flow dependency.

4.3   Discussion

There are a few limitations resulting from ANRED's implementation. First of all, WALA can only perform static analysis on Java bytecode, excluding native Android system services from our study. From the previous study [40], the percentage of native services is relatively small. Secondly, the complexity of static analysis has long been a concern. In the data residue detection process, we make the best effort to guarantee the code coverage, but there will be inaccuracy introduced in various stages, such as in the code decompilation and broken link reconnection. At last, human effort is still needed to validate possible data residue instances reported by ANRED. However, as we show in Sect. 5.2, the manual involvement has been greatly reduced with the help of ANRED, yet more data residue instances are captured (Fig. 6).

5   Evaluation

We have collected a total of 606 Android images from various sources [1, 4, 9, 10, 14]. Figure 5 depicts the distribution of our image collection with respect to the diversity of vendors as well as coverage of Android versions. In particular, we have covered all major vendors, such as Samsung, HTC, CyanogenMod (CM, in short), Google, Xiaomi, etc., and all major Android versions from Gingerbread up to the newest Marshmallow. Throughout the experiment, we consider the OS provider, instead of the device manufacturer, as the real vendor of the image. For instance, we have labeled Google as the vendor for all Nexus images. CM provides Android OS for various device models from different manufacturers, and thus, it becomes the vendor for all of them. We have conducted our experiments on Dell PowerEdge T620 with Intel Xeon CPU E5-2660 v2 @ 2.20 GHz running Ubuntu 14.04.1 LTS. The Jar extraction and decompilation stages took around one week to finish for all images, and the processing outputs are available on [2]. After that, we ran ANRED against each image with 16G heap memory size allocated for the Java Virtual Machine (JVM) and with the default timeout value (60 s) for each system service.

5.1   Panorama of Android Data Residue

Overview. On average, we have identified 191 likely data residue instances on each image, with 106 (55.5 %) of them being labeled as missing data removal logic. Not all of them will necessarily lead to the data residue vulnerability,

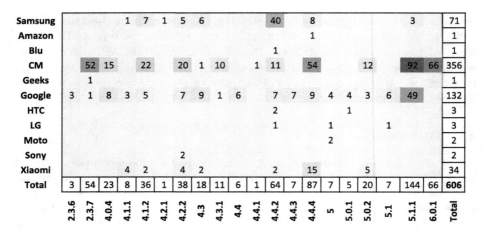

Fig. 6. Distribution of collected android images for ANRED evaluation

depending on whether the data leftover is security-critical and exploitable by adversaries. To separate the data residue instances introduced by vendor customization and the ones inherited from the AOSP code base, we consider Google images as the reference. Given one data residue instance on a vendor image, we label it as AOSP instance if such instance has also been identified on Google images with the same version number. Otherwise, we consider it as vendor introduced instance. For images that do not have a corresponding Google image in our collection, we exclude them from our data analysis. In following sections, we further break down the data residue situation on Android from four perspectives: vendor, version, service category and residue type.

Vendor-wise View. In our image collection, the version distribution varies greatly from vendor to vendor. Thus, a direct comparison of the average residue count for each vendor will not accurately reflect the effect of vendor customization on the data residue vulnerability. To remove the version bias, we compare the percentage of vendor introduced data residue instances instead. The result is shown in Fig. 7(a). We have observed that, vendor customization is indeed a big factor contributing to the data residue vulnerability. In particular, vendors like Samsung, Amazon, HTC, and Sony are responsible for more than 65 % of data residue instances identified on their images. One extreme case is the Amazon image running 4.4.4. Our analysis result indicates that, 95 % of data residue instances identified on this image are due to the heavy customization. Even for vendors like Moto, LG and Xiaomi, the percentage of vendor introduced data residue instances is higher than 40 %. In comparison, Blu, Geeks and CM make fewer changes to the Android OS, and thus, only introduce a small portion of data residue instances to their images.

Version-wise View. Apart from vendor customization, we would like to further evaluate the effect of Android's frequent version upgrade on the data residue vul-

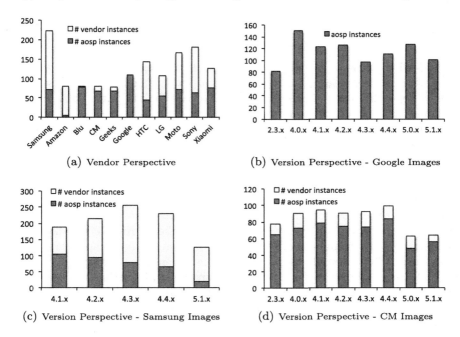

(a) Vendor Perspective

(b) Version Perspective - Google Images

(c) Version Perspective - Samsung Images

(d) Version Perspective - CM Images

Fig. 7. Effect of vendor customization and version upgrade on data residue

nerability. The data residue trend across different Android versions is meaningful only if all selected images are belonging to the same vendor. We have chosen three vendors, i.e., Google, Samsung and CM, since our image collection contains different versions of these vendors. The results are depicted in Fig. 7(b), (c) and (d), respectively. As Fig. 7(b) shows, the average count of AOSP data residue instances fluctuates around 100 across version upgrade. We have observed that, there is always an increment when new Android branches, like Ice Cream Sandwich (4.0.x) and Lollipop (5.0.x), are released. We suspect that, new branches tend to come with new features, and thus, introduce new system services with possible data residue instances.

The version trends on Samsung images and CM images have quite different characteristics, as shown in Fig. 7(c) and (d). For Samsung, as the version increases, we have observed a steady decrease of data residue instances inherited from AOSP code base. In comparison, the percentage of vendor introduced ones rises from 44 % to 84 %. The result indicates that, Samsung's customization on Android OS has grown heavier as Android evolves, resulting in fewer similarities with AOSP images. Thus, the data residue situation on upcoming Samsung images will be mostly determined by the level of its own customization. On the other hand, the count of data residue instances introduced by CM remains the same at around 15 from Gingerbread to Lollipop. Clearly, the customization performed by CM is quite consistent across version upgrade. In this case, the data residue situation on upcoming CM images depends highly on the corresponding AOSP version release.

Service-wise View. ANRED has considered two categories of system services in the static analysis stage, i.e., preloaded app services and framework services. We have separated their effects and concluded that the majority (65 %) of identified data residue instances are from framework services. This is consistent with the manual analysis result from previous work [40], where only 2 (download and print) out of 12 instances are within preloaded apps. However, we argue that, the framework developers and preloaded app developers should work together to remove all the data residue instances.

Residue-wise View. As mentioned in Sect. 3.5, we have included five types of data residue instances in our analysis, i.e., SQLiteDatabase, SharedPreference, Settings, Java_Util and XML. With a total of 116 K data residue instances identified on all images from our collection, 73 % of them are in memory data structures (Java_Util) and configuration entries (Settings). In comparison, previous work [40] has also identified 8 (2 capability instances, 5 Settings instances and 1 permission instance) out of 12 instances belonging to those two types. It is worth mentioning that, among all data residue instances, 1,629 (1.4 %) unique ones are found. In this process, we have used a combination of service name, residue type and entry name as the key to remove duplicates. Moreover, only 312 (19 %) of the unique ones are from AOSP images, while the rest (81 %) are all introduced by vendor customization.

Risk Quantification. In our analysis, we have identified an average of 85 instances on each image that have data deletion operations in place upon app uninstallation. However, the complexity of each one's deleting logic varies greatly. We further calculate the average count of data residue instances for each complexity value. The overall distribution is shown in Fig. 8. A total of 42 (50 %) instances have deleting complexity value less than 10, and thus, should be considered as safe. However, the deleting logic of the other half is overcomplicated and may lead to security flaws. To understand how bad the situation is, we zoom in to the region with complexity value between 11 and 200, as shown in Fig. 8. Surprisingly, a significant portion of functions that handle data removal upon app uninstallation even have a complexity value larger than 30. Based on our analysis, we suggest system service developers to follow clear guidelines to remove app data upon its uninstallation.

5.2   ANRED Effectiveness

To demonstrate the effectiveness of ANRED, we have evaluated it against AOSP 5.0.1 image, which was manually examined in previous work [40]. We use their results as the basis for comparison. The analysis takes 11 min in ANRED with the default 60 s timeout value, and covers a total of 133 system services. Among them, 123 (%92.5) services are finished within timeout limit. Totally, 253 likely data residue instances are identified on this image. More importantly, 205 (%81)

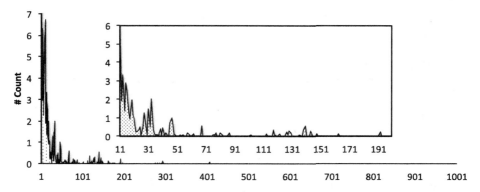

Fig. 8. Data residue instance distribution based on the complexity of deleting logic

of them have a complexity value larger than 10, which are considered as highly risky [11]. We have further validated all 205 risky instances manually. This process was completed by one single Android security analyst within a day, in comparison with 6 person-month in the previous work [40]. It is made possible because of ANRED's detailed report, which not only presents each likely data residue instance, but also pinpoints its saving instruction and risky deleting instruction. We envision that, Android vendors will utilize ANRED in a similar manner to detect and remove data residue instances from their images before the final release.

In addition to the significantly reduced human involvement, we are able to capture 10 out of 12 real data residue instances presented in [40]. The only two missing instances are Keystore and Download, which have been resolved on Android Lollipop. The previous work reproduces the vulnerability on KitKat and prior versions. One representative data residue vulnerability is on Android printing framework. ANRED actually identifies two related instances: one from the XML category corresponding to the print record residue and the other one from the File category mapping to the print content residue. Other than that, ANRED has detected five new data residue instances. Three of them are actually exploitable, leading to data leakage and privilege escalation attacks. We have further measured the frequency of those three vulnerabilities within our image collection. As summarized in Table 2, these vulnerabilities are pervasive, with a total of 571 (%94) unique images containing at least one of them.

Backup Mis-transport. Android backup framework helps to copy a user's persistent app data to remote cloud storage. Internally, there is a system service called BackupManagerService, which forwards all requests from registered client apps to the current enabled backup service. Android backup service serves as a backup transport between the device and the remote storage. Once enabled, the package name and service name will be jointly saved into Android Settings with entry name backup_transport. However, this configuration entry will remain effective even after the referring app has been uninstalled. As a result, an adver-

Table 2. New data residue instances identified by ANRED on AOSP 5.0.1

Instances	Category	Damage	Frequency
backup_transport	Settings	data leakage	359 (%59)
app restrictions	XML	privilege escalation	396 (%65)
notification_policy	XML	privilege escalation	200 (%33)
app-ops	XML	-	-
media_store	Content Provider	-	-

sary can impersonate the uninstalled app and mis-transport the user's private data to malicious servers. This is not a big concern right now, as only vendor issued backup services can be installed on the device. But in the future, if Android decides to open this feature to 3rd-party apps, such a residue instance demands great attention.

App No-restrictions. The multi-user feature on Android has been a viable approach for creating another restricted environment on the same device. On tablet devices, the restricted profile feature has been used mainly for parental control, while on Android phones, such restricted environment, namely managed profile, is favored by enterprise companies to control the environment where company-specific apps and data are running. In both cases, an administrator app is responsible for specifying the restrictions of individual apps. Such configurations will be saved into user_id.xml by a system service, UserManagerService, with attribute restrictions. However, these access control policies will not be removed, even after the targeted app has been uninstalled. In return, an adversary can inherit all privilege from the uninstalled app.

Notification Flooding. Android supports three levels of notification restrictions on each app, i.e., allow, block and priority. By default, any notifications from the app will be allowed. However, a user can flip the configuration from the Settings app or choose to show priority ones only. The corresponding specifications will be saved in notification_policy.xml by a system service, namely NotificationManagerService, with attribute notification-policy. We have found that, when an app is removed from the device, its notification policy configured by the user will be left over. Thus, an adversary can impersonate this app and flood the user with annoying notifications.

Two Harmless Residue Instances. Another two data residue instances have been found in our manual verification, but with limited implications. For instance, Android system service, AppOpsService, saves restrictions on app operations into appops.xml, but fails to immediately clean them up upon app uninstallation. Actually, the cleanup task is scheduled periodically for every 30 min. The second instance is related to the mediastore provider on Android, which contains meta data for all available media on both internal and external storage. An app can send a request to MediaScannerService for adding a media file into the `mediastore`. When the app is uninstalled, although the file is deleted from the file system, its meta data remains in the `mediastore` until Android scans the system for new media, which typically happens when the system first boots up or can be called explicitly from apps. Noting that the meta data includes a URI referring to the actual file, we further evaluated it against the capability intruding attack as in the Clipboard residue case [40]. However, as it turns out, URIs saved in `mediastore` do not possess any capabilities and immune from this attack. In both residue cases, although the attacking time window is quite small, we argue that, a timely data cleanup approach, like `BroadcastReceiver`, should be employed to provide better security guarantee.

5.3   ANRED Performance

Time Consumption. On average, it takes ANRED 43.5 min to analyze one image, with 1.6 min (3.6 %) on system service extraction, 6.5 min (15 %) on `jar` patching and 35.4 min (81.4 %) on static analysis.

System Service Analysis - Success Rate. With an average of 205 system services being analyzed for each image in ANRED, 82.67 % of them are finished in our experiment. In particular, framework services (86.53 %) have a higher success rate than preloaded app services (80.63 %). A closer look at the `jar` decompilation results reveals that, certain preloaded apps have applied code obfuscation techniques in the final packaging process. Another factor affecting the success rate is the timeout value. In our experiment, we have used the default 60 s timeout value. With more time allowed for each service, the success rate of ANRED's system service analysis can be improved.

Broken Link Patching Stats. In our experiment, ANRED totally patched around 3 million broken links. In particular, `Thread` and `Handler` are the two most commonly used classes in Android framework and preloaded apps. They account for a total of 92 % of the overall patched broken links. As mentioned in Sect. 3.4, ANRED patches broken links with static invocations inserted at the end, while the object type is resolved based on a heuristic. We have further measured the accurate connection rate of ANRED for different categories of broken links. The result demonstrates the reliability of ANRED with 86 % accurate connection rate on average. The patching accuracy for `AsyncTask` and `ServiceConnection` is slightly lower, indicating that multiple implementations of them may coexist in certain system services. Even for those cases, ANRED is still able to patch broken links conservatively without causing any exceptions.

6   Related Work

Android Vulnerability Exploration. Earlier and recent research work have identified several worrisome security vulnerabilities in the Android apps. Prominent examples include the re-delegation problem [28], content providers leak and pollution [31], crypto-misuse in Android apps [25] and vulnerabilities in the Android's WebView component [34]. Other studies revealed security risks in the Android system itself. PileUp [37] uncovers a flaw in the `PackagemMangerService` that targets system update and allows a malicious app installed on a lower version Android and claiming specific capabilities to actually acquire these capabilities after system update. Two other works [27,39] reveal exploits on the `ClipboardService` that enables an unprivileged attacker to gain access to important private data. Our work aims to automatically detect the data residue vulnerability [40] scattering through a wider range of system services.

Static Analysis. Several systems have been accordingly proposed to mitigate these discovered vulnerabilities. A great deal of previous studies aims to mitigate the confused deputy problem and permission leaks by either checking IPC call chains or by monitoring the communication between apps at run time [20,21, 24,28,29]. To better understand the scope of the attacks discovered, several other static analysis frameworks have been proposed, including ComDroid [23], CHEX [33], FlowDroid [17], DroidSafe [30], Epicc [35], etc. These tools, however, analyze Android apps and cannot handle framework-level code, thus, cannot be adopted to automatically discover the data residue vulnerability in system services within the Android framework. Our efforts in this work aim to fill this gap by introducing ANRED, which automatically examines each system service's bytecode to accurately uncover any data residue instances.

Dynamic Analysis. Few Other dynamic approaches have been proposed to detect and defeat the discovered vulnerabilities. A prominent example in the literature is TaintDroid [26], a framework that allows to perform taint analysis on Android to track data flow across apps and the OS. Another prominent tool is DroidScope [38], which runs the whole Android platform on an emulator to reconstruct both Dalvik and OS level semantics. Dynamic solutions could possibly enable us to uncover data residue vulnerabilities at app uninstallation time. However, the triggering conditions leading to the data residue problem (such as device reboot, app installation and uninstallation) are difficult to fully emulate using dynamic approaches. Besides, even if taint tracking might look like a possible solution for detecting the data residue problem, the process is quite complicated because the data creation points might not necessarily appear in apps. ANRED aims to overcome these challenges that cannot be solved through a dynamic solution, through a purely static solution that performs the detection of data residue problems automatically and efficiently.

7   Conclusion

In this project, we propose ANRED to automatically detect data residue instances on a large scale of Android images with minimal human involvement. The evaluation results against 606 images have again brought questions over the extensive vendor customization and frequent version upgrade on Android.

We hope that, vendors can use ANRED to check their images against the data residue vulnerability before shipping with new devices. More importantly, Google should take the lead to provide a clear guideline in reacting to the event of app uninstallation. Additional efforts are also required from the research committee to propose a runtime solution to eliminate the data residue vulnerability.

Acknowledgment. We greatly appreciate the insightful comments and constructive feedback from the anonymous reviewers. This project was supported in part by the NSF grant 1318814. Any opinions, findings and conclusions or recommendations expressed in this material are those of the authors and do not necessarily reflect the views of the National Science Foundation.

References

1. Android Revolution. http://goo.gl/MVigfq
2. ANRED: Android Residue Detection Framework. https://goo.gl/Q0d5qH
3. Apktool: A tool for reverse engineering Android apk files. http://goo.gl/LdB4V7
4. Cyanogenmod Downloads. http://download.cyanogenmod.org/
5. Cyclomatic complexity. https://goo.gl/1VqYUj
6. dex2jar. https://goo.gl/5fzsd5
7. dextra - A tool for DEX and OAT dumping, decompilation, and fuzzing. http://goo.gl/NPG0Kz
8. ext4_utils. https://goo.gl/1nyYfM
9. Factory Images for Nexus Devices. https://goo.gl/i0RJnN
10. Huawei ROMs. http://goo.gl/dYPTE5
11. Java: Computing Cyclomatic Complexity. http://goo.gl/tduqlP
12. Java Varargs. http://goo.gl/TEMrjk
13. Lollipop deodexing. https://goo.gl/uw2KmR
14. Official Oxygen OS ROMs and OTA updates. https://goo.gl/cBTF1w
15. smali and baksmali. https://goo.gl/JS7Mgw
16. WALA. http://wala.sourceforge.net/
17. Arzt, S., Rasthofer, S., Fritz, C., Bodden, E., Bartel, A., Klein, J., Le Traon, Y., Octeau, D., McDaniel, P.: Flowdroid: Precise context, flow, field, object-sensitive and lifecycle-aware taint analysis for android apps. In: Proceedings of the 35th ACM SIGPLAN Conference on Programming Language Design and Implementation, PLDI 2014, New York, NY, USA (2014)
18. Bacon, D.F.: Fast and effective optimization of statically typed object-oriented. Technical report, Berkeley, CA, USA (1998)
19. Bacon, D.F., Sweeney, P.F.: Fast static analysis of c++ virtual function calls. In: Proceedings of the 11th ACM SIGPLAN Conference on Object-oriented Programming, Systems, Languages, and Applications, OOPSLA 1996, pp. 324–341. ACM, New York, NY, USA (1996)
20. Bugiel, S., Davi, L., Dmitrienko, A., Fischer, T., Sadeghi, A.-R.: Xmandroid: A new android evolution to mitigate privilege escalation attacks. Technical report, Technische Universität Darmstadt, Technical Report TR-2011-04 (2011)
21. Bugiel, S., Davi, L., Dmitrienko, A., Fischer, T., Sadeghi, A.-R., Shastry, B.: Towards taming privilege-escalation attacks on android. NDSS (2012)

22. Cao, Y., Fratantonio, Y., Bianchi, A., Egele, M., Kruegel, C., Vigna, G., Chen, Y.: EdgeMiner: automatically detecting implicit control flow transitions through the android framework. In: Proceedings of the ISOC Network and Distributed System Security Symposium (NDSS) (2015)

23. Chin, E., Felt, A.P., Greenwood, K., Wagner, D.: Analyzing inter-application communication in android. In: Proceedings of the 9th International Conference on Mobile Systems, Applications, and Services, MobiSys 2011. ACM, New York, NY, USA (2011)

24. Dietz, M., Shekhar, S., Pisetsky, Y., Shu, A., Wallach, D.S.: Quire: lightweight provenance for smart phone operating systems. In: 20th USENIX Security Symposium, San Francisco, CA, August 2011

25. Egele, M., Brumley, D., Fratantonio, Y., Kruegel, C.: An empirical study of cryptographic misuse in android applications. In: Proceedings of the 2013 ACM SIGSAC Conference on Computer and Communications security. ACM (2013)

26. Enck, W., Gilbert, P., Chun, B.-G., Cox, L.P., Jung, J., McDaniel, P., Sheth, A.N.: Taintdroid: an information-flow tracking system for realtime privacy monitoring on smartphones. In: Proceedings of the 9th USENIX Conference on Operating Systems Design and Implementation, OSDI 2010, pp. 1–6. USENIX Association, Berkeley, CA, USA (2010)

27. Fahl, S., Harbach, M., Oltrogge, M., Muders, T., Smith, M.: Hey, you, get off of my clipboard. In: Sadeghi, A.-R. (ed.) FC 2013. LNCS, vol. 7859, pp. 144–161. Springer, Heidelberg (2013)

28. Felt, A.P., Wang, H.J., Moshchuk, A., Hanna, S., Chin, E.: Permission redelegation: Attacks and defenses. In: Proceedings of the 20th USENIX Security Symposium, pp. 22–37 (2011)

29. Fragkaki, E., Bauer, L., Jia, L., Swasey, D.: Modeling and enhancing androids permission system. In: 17th European Symposium on Research in Computer Security (2012)

30. Gordon, M.I., Kim, D., Perkins, J.H., Gilham, L., Nguyen, N., Rinard, M.C.: Information-flow analysis of android applications in droidsafe. In: NDSS (2015)

31. Grace, M., Zhou, Y., Wang, Z., Jiang, X.: Systematic detection of capability leaks in stock Android smartphones. In: Proceedings of the 19th Network and Distributed System Security Symposium (NDSS), February 2012

32. Grove, D., DeFouw, G., Dean, J., Chambers, C.: Call graph construction in object-oriented languages. In: Proceedings of the 12th ACM SIGPLAN Conference on Object-oriented Programming, Systems, Languages, and Applications, OOPSLA 1997, pp. 108–124. ACM, New York, NY, USA, (1997)

33. Lu, L., Li, Z., Wu, Z., Lee, W., Jiang, G.: Chex: statically vetting android apps for component hijacking vulnerabilities. In: Proceedings of the 2012 ACM Conference on Computer and Communications Security, CCS 2012, pp. 229–240. ACM, New York, NY, USA (2012)

34. Luo, T., Hao, H., Du, W., Wang, Y., Yin, H.: Attacks on webview in the android system. In: ACSAC (2011)

35. Octeau, D., McDaniel, P., Jha, S., Bartel, A., Bodden, E., Klein, J., Le Traon, Y.: Effective inter-component communication mapping in android with epicc: an essential step towards holistic security analysis. In: Proceedings of the 22nd USENIX Conference on Security, SEC 2013, pp. 543–558. USENIX Association, Berkeley, CA, USA (2013)

36. Shivers, O.G.: Control-flow Analysis of Higher-order Languages of Taming Lambda. Ph.D. thesis, Pittsburgh, PA, USA (1991). UMI Order No. GAX91-26964

37. Xing, L., Pan, X., Wang, R., Yuan, K., Wang, X.: Upgrading your android, elevating my malware: privilege escalation through mobile os updating. In: Proceedings of the 2014 IEEE Symposium on Security and Privacy, SP 2014, pp. 393–408. IEEE Computer Society, Washington, DC, USA (2014)
38. Yan, L.K., Yin, H.: Droidscope: seamlessly reconstructing the os and dalvik semantic views for dynamic android malware analysis. In: Proceedings of the 21st USENIX Conference on Security Symposium, Security 2012, p. 29. USENIX Association, Berkeley, CA, USA (2012)
39. Zhang, X., Du, W.: Attacks on android clipboard. In: Dietrich, S. (ed.) DIMVA 2014. LNCS, vol. 8550, pp. 72–91. Springer, Heidelberg (2014)
40. Zhang, X., Ying, K., Aafer, Y., Qiu, Z., Du, W.: Life after app. uninstallation: are the data still alive? data residue attacks on android. In: Proceedings of the ISOC Network and Distributed System Security Symposium (NDSS) (2016)

NaClDroid: Native Code Isolation
for Android Applications

Elias Athanasopoulos[1]([✉]), Vasileios P. Kemerlis[2], Georgios Portokalidis[3],
and Angelos D. Keromytis[4]

[1] Vrije Universiteit Amsterdam, Amsterdam, The Netherlands
i.a.athanasopoulos@vu.nl
[2] Brown University, Providence, RI, USA
vpk@cs.brown.edu
[3] Stevens Institute of Technology, Hoboken, NJ, USA
gportoka@stevens.edu
[4] Columbia University, New York, NY, USA
angelos@cs.columbia.edu

Abstract. Android apps frequently incorporate third-party libraries
that contain native code; this not only facilitates rapid application development and distribution, but also provides new ways to generate revenue.
As a matter of fact, one in two apps in Google Play are linked with a
library providing ad network services. However, linking applications with
third-party code can have severe security implications: malicious libraries
written in native code can exfiltrate sensitive information from a running
app, or completely modify the execution runtime, since all native code is
mapped inside the same address space with the execution environment,
namely the Dalvik/ART VM. We propose NaClDroid, a framework that
addresses these problems, while still allowing apps to include third-party
code. NaClDroidprevents malicious native-code libraries from hijacking
Android applications using Software Fault Isolation. More specifically,
we place all native code in a Native Client sandbox that prevents uncon-
strained reads, or writes, inside the process address space. NaClDroidhas little overhead; for native code running inside the NaCl sandbox the
slowdown is less than 10 % on average.

Keywords: SFI · NaCl · Android

1 Introduction

Android is undoubtedly the most rapidly growing platform for mobile devices,
with estimates predicting one billion Android-based smartphones shipping in
2017 [12]. App developers have great incentives to release their software without
delays, ahead of their competitors; for that reason, they frequently decide to
incorporate already available third-party code, typically included in the form of
native-code libraries, loaded at run time. For example, ∼50 % of apps are linked

I. Askoxylakis et al. (Eds.): ESORICS 2016, Part I, LNCS 9878, pp. 422–439, 2016.
DOI: 10.1007/978-3-319-45744-4_21

with a library providing ad services [25]. Moreover, native libraries are heavily used among the most popular applications [32].

Including untrusted, third-party code in an application has severe security consequences, affecting both the developers and the users of apps. *Lookout*, a smartphone-centric security firm, recently identified 32, otherwise legitimate, apps in Google Play that were linked with a malicious ad library [7]. They estimated the number of affected users to be in the range of 2–9 million, and their advice was the following: *"Developers need to pay very close attention to any third-party libraries they include in their applications. Unsafe libraries can put their users and reputation at risk"* [7].

The current design of the Android runtime allows a malicious *native* library, included in an otherwise legitimate app, to: (a) exfiltrate private information from the app; or (b) change the functionality of the app. To address the above, we propose NaClDroid: a framework that provides strong confidentiality and integrity guarantees to the Android execution environment. NaClDroidintroduces a sandbox for running native third-party code that has been packaged with an app. This enables us to retain support for native code, while concurrently preventing it from arbitrarily reading process memory, tampering with the Dalvik runtime[1], or directly accessing operating system (OS) interfaces, like system calls. We employ Software Fault Isolation [33] (SFI) and sandbox all native library code using Google's Native Client (NaCl) [27,37]. Therefore, we separate the runtime, Dalvik VM, from the native part of the app, while at the same time permitting the use of native code through JNI. Note that this architectural model is already used by Google Chrome for running untrusted browser extensions [5]; in this work, we extend it to the mobile setting.

We briefly explain how NaClDroidprotects Android apps from a malicious library. Consider, a legitimate instant messaging (IM) application; it is written in Java and provided for free. To compensate, it includes a third-party, native-code library to display advertisements that generate revenue for its authors. The third-party library is mapped to the same address space with the rest of the VM executing the app, and can access all app information just by reading memory (e.g., sensitive information like user passwords and discussions). Notice, that whether encryption is used to transmit data is inconsequential, since the information is available in plaintext in process memory. NaClDroid's sandbox confines the library, so that is can only access its own memory region(s) and data exchanged with the app through JNI, thereby making it impossible to exfiltrate sensitive information.

As a second example, we can look at Facebook's Android application, which updated itself without going through the app store [9], avoiding verification and analysis of the updated app. Google eventually banned Facebook's official app from its app store [3], and the ban was accompanied with a change in the store terms of service that forbids developers from independently updating their apps.

---

[1] Dalvik has evolved to ART, which supports ahead-of-time compilation. The system we present here works with both Dalvik and ART. Since many Android OSes still support Dalvik, we use the term Dalvik to refer to both systems.

However, this policy update is *not* enforced by the platform. NaClDroidprevents the introduction of new functionality outside the app store, since dangerous system calls that load new code and modify the VM are no longer possible. Additionally, attacks that attempt to hijack the control flow for activating hidden functionality [34] are also prevented, as NaCl only allows code that has been compiled in a certain way (i.e., unvetted control flows are not possible).

Isolating code, using SFI, in Java-based runtime environments has been demonstrated in the past [28,29]. For Android, in particular, there is Native-Guard [30], which performs isolation without heavily modifying the runtime. In this paper, we present NaClDroidfor completeness, as an additional purely SFI-based solution for isolating native code in Android. First, we begin with the underlying principles of NaClDroid. Next, we implement, and evaluate, a Dalvik VM, which is fully equipped with loading and running NaCl-compiled libraries.

Other approaches focus on Android's permission model, which is fundamental to the security of the platform [16,17,24,35]. An app is only allowed to perform actions (e.g., calling or texting) based on the permissions it holds, and these permissions are enforced by the OS. However, applications frequently request a broad set of permissions, users are not sufficiently attentive, and applications can collude with each other. As a result, we are increasingly relying on the analysis of apps to determine whether they are malicious. As these methodologies keep improving, ensuring the integrity of the verified code and the execution environment, under the presence of untrusted native third-party code, becomes even more important, because the modification of the execution *after* review will eventually become the sole avenue for malware authors [7]. NaClDroidis orthogonal to such proposals.

Previous approaches, unlike NaClDroid, do not attempt to provide developers with the means to isolate their apps from third-party code (or control how they interact with it). Furthermore, even though we do not aim to detect or protect from malware, through NaClDroidwe confine native code, preventing the abuse of system call interfaces. For example, the DroidKungFu and DroidDream malware use a native library to execute exploits against the OS kernel [36]. These would fail under NaClDroid, since all native code is running under the constraints of a NaCl sandbox.

1.1 Contributions

To summarize, this paper makes the following contributions:

- We experimentally demonstrate the various ways third-party code can tamper with an app and its execution environment.
- We design and implement NaClDroid: an SFI-based framework that ensures the integrity and confidentiality of Android's execution environment. We embed Google's NaCl in Android's runtime to safely allow the use native code; with NaClDroidin place malicious libraries cannot leak information from, or subvert the control flow of, running apps.
- We thoroughly evaluate the proposed framework. Running native code through NaClDroidimposes a moderate slowdown of less than 10 % on average.

- In contrast to similar approaches based on a strict review process, completely disallowing third-party code, or relying on code signing, this paper presents a series of challenges and systematic solutions for confining native third-party code linked with apps running in a highly open platform.

1.2   Organization

The rest of the paper is organized as follows. In Sect. 2, we present background information regarding the Android platform, and through detailed examples we discuss how malicious libraries can leak information from, or subvert control flow of, legitimate apps. Additionally, we discuss the threat model we consider in this paper. We present the architecture of NaClDroidand provide implementation details in Sect. 3. We analyze the security guarantees offered by NaClDroid, possible attacks against it, and additional hardening in Sect. 4. We evaluate the performance of our solution in Sect. 5. Related work is in Sect. 6, and conclusions in Sect. 7.

2   Malicious Third-Party Code

Android apps are written in Java, and, once compiled, the produced Java bytecode is transformed to a bytecode variant called Dalvik, which can be executed by the Dalvik VM [11]. Dalvik supports standard Java technologies, such as the Java Native Interface (JNI) [20], and hence all Android apps can attach native code to their bytecode. Native code was originally allowed to enable apps to quickly and efficiently perform computationally intensive tasks, such as cryptographic operations, image recognition, etc.

Android applications may include multiple third-party components, implemented either in native code or in Java, to complement their functionality; this is typical of many apps because it facilitates rapid development and code reuse. For example, it has been estimated that one in two Android applications is linked to an ad library [25]. Linking code in an application is not an unusual practice, and it is the *modus operandi* in many platforms—from desktop to mobile. However, linking code has major security implications in the case of Android. The openness of the platform allows adversaries to craft malicious libraries and implicitly attack a bigger user base than making malware popular. This has been recently demonstrated by researchers who identified malicious libraries that infected more than 32 legitimate applications in Google Play [7].

In the rest of this section, we investigate how malicious, native third-party code can break the integrity and confidentiality of legitimate apps that link to it. We look into how malicious libraries of native code can arbitrarily corrupt the virtual runtime, which executes the app, by re-writing the process virtual address space or exfiltrate sensitive information by reading the process memory. This technique can be used by any malicious third-party code for transforming a legitimate application to a malicious application [7].

2.1   Altering the Execution Environment

Native code resides inside the same virtual address space with the Dalvik VM. Therefore, it has direct access to all of the process memory, and can directly read or write anywhere in the process, easily tampering-with the Android runtime in arbitrary ways.

First, native code can *read* process memory, as it is mapped in the same virtual address space; this can break the confidentiality of the execution environment. Sensitive information that is stored in process memory can be easily exfiltrated by scanning the (virtual) memory footprint of the process. Consider, the example we presented in the introduction: an instant messaging application that uses a native-code library to serve advertisements to its users. The native library can easily scan the process image for sensitive data, like the user's password or message content exchanged with other users. Notice that even if the developer of the instant messenger is careful enough to encrypt all conversations exchanged, the library can still gain access to the unencrypted content, since it can read data before reaching the encryption code. Therefore, *all* data manipulated by the app are exposed to the library's code.

Second, native code can *write* the process image, as it is mapped in the same virtual address space; this can break the integrity of the execution environment. Native code can directly modify the bytecode or the virtual runtime itself. To better illustrate this, in Fig. 1, we show a code sample of a JNI function (`nativeInjection()`, lines 22–31) that scans the app to locate a specific bytecode pattern and replace it with a different one; we have omitted some parts and simplified the code for brevity. The JNI function initially performs a `getpid()` system call (line 24) to retrieve the process ID. It then opens and scans the `/proc/[pid]/maps` file (lines 26–28) to obtain the memory layout of the current process. Function `patch_file()` is responsible for finding where the `.dex` file (i.e., the path indicated by `MAP` in line 1) is mapped in memory, and, finally, calling function `patch_bytecode()`, which replaces the targeted opcode. To do so, it first uses `mprotect` to make the particular region writable and then scans the region to find and replace the respective opcode. In this example, we change the first byte from `0x90`, which is the Dalvik opcode for addition, to `0x91`, which is the opcode for subtraction.

A real-world incident of such behavior is the Facebook app that altered the Dalvik VM to increase the size of one of its internal buffers [9], before it was banned from the Google Play store [3]. Facebook did this to overcome some internal constraints imposed by the Dalvik architecture, but it is evident that the same technique(s) can be used by malicious libraries against legitimate apps.

2.2   Threat Model

NaClDroidprotects applications from malicious third-party code, contained in shared libraries of native code. Although, in general, malicious third-party code can be implemented in Java as well, as we showed in this section, native code that plugs in with the rest of the code has superior capabilities. First, native

```
1    #define MAP "/path/program@classes.dex"
2    char bytecode[4] = {0x90, 0x02, 0x00, 0x01};
3
4    void patch_bytecode(...) {
5        ...
6        mprotect((const void*)p, len, PROT_WRITE);
7        while (...) {
8            if (bytecode_found(p)) {
9                *p = 0x91;
10               break;
11           }
12       }
13   }
14
15   void patch_file(FILE *fp) {
16       ...
17       if (file_found(MAP)) {
18          patch_bytecode(start_address, length);
19       }
20   }
21
22   void nativeInjection(...) {
23       char process_path[16]; FILE *fp;
24       pid_t pid = getpid();
25
26       sprintf(process_path, "/proc/%d/maps", pid);
27
28       fp = fopen(process_path, "r");
29
30       patch_file(fp);
31   }
```

Fig. 1. Native injection. First, the `pid` of the running process is resolved (line 24). Next, the file `/proc/[pid]/maps` is opened (line 28) and scanned for finding the memory area where the Dalvik bytecode has been mapped (lines 15–20). Once found, the area is scanned for a particular opcode sequence, and, once located, the opcode `0x90` (integer addition) is changed to `0x91` (integer subtraction) (line 9).

code can read or write to the rest of the process image, and, second, it can implement this malicious functionality, silently. More importantly, analysis of the semantics of native code can be substantially harder (when compared to Java bytecode). Therefore, NaClDroidprotects only from malicious native code that directly interferes with the process image. Additionally, NaClDroidassumes that the main app is legitimate and trusted. The app may expose interfaces to the third-party code, but it is assumed that the correct use of such interfaces (either through Java or native code) does not compromise the functionality of the application. However, since native code can interact with the rest of the app in unforeseen ways, not through APIs but by directly accessing the process image, NaClDroidconfines all native code in an isolated sandbox.

3   NaClDroid

In this section we present in detail the NaClDroidimplementation. We first describe how SFI works and how the sandbox of native code is implemented.

```
1   void *_r__dlopen(const char *filename, int flag) {
2
3       uint32_t saved_esp = knatp->user.stack_ptr;
4
5       void * addr = (void *) setjmp(kbuf);
6       if (addr == 0) {
7           uint32_t esp = NaClUserToSys(knatp->nap,
8                              knatp->user.stack_ptr);
9           /* Prepare stack (fname, *fname, flag). */
10          __prepare_stack(...);
11
12          /* Call dlopen(). */
13          __call_fcn(knatp, ...);
14      }
15      /* longjmp continues from here. */
16      /* Restore esp. */
17      knatp->user.stack_ptr = saved_esp;
18      /* Return result (i.e., pointer from dlopen()). */
19      return handle_return(addr);
20  }
21  int32_t
22  __syscall_handler(struct NaClAppThread *natp) {
23      struct __trampoline *rt;
24      ...
25      rt = __parse_args(natp);
26      ...
27      if (rt->rtf == rt_FunctionReturn) {
28              longjmp(kbuf, rt->ret);
29      }
30      ...
31      return 1;
32  }
```

Fig. 2. Example of a NaClDroidcall. First, we store the current stack pointer of the NaCl thread (line 3). We then use `setjmp()` for saving the current state (line 5) and prepare the stack with the parameters required for calling `dlopen()` (line 10). Once the stack is prepared, we jump to the address of NaCl `dlopen()` (line 13). Once that happens, a custom handler is called for serving the system call (lines 22–32). The handler parses the arguments of the system call (line 25) and if the system call refers to a function return, the return value is taken and passed to a `longjmp()` call, which will resume back to line 17. Finally, we restore the saved stack and return the value taken from `longjmp()` (the handle of the shared library just loaded using `dlopen()`) back to Dalvik.

We then discuss how the new trust domains operate in an Android application. Finally, we comment on architecture specific issues.

3.1 Software Fault Isolation

Android apps can host native code, which is mapped on the same virtual address-space occupied by the Dalvik process. Therefore native code can read process memory, leak sensitive data, modify existing bytecode, or change the semantics of the execution environment by directly patching its code [9]. In order to prevent this, NaClDroidisolates all native code, using SFI, in a NaCl [37] sandbox. To achieve this all native code is compiled with the NaCl toolchain, so upon execution, although it is mapped on the same address space with the running process, it can no longer read or write on memory areas outside of the sandbox boundaries. Many dangerous system calls (like mprotect) are also prohibited. We further refer to all native code built with the NaCl toolchain as NaCl modules to be consistent with current NaCl terminology.

Dalvik uses the dynamic loader API, namely functions dlopen(), dlsym(), and friends, for loading external native code. Since, all native code is now compiled as NaCl modules, we need to use the NaCl versions of dlopen() and friends, which can handle the modifications performed by the NaCl toolchain. NaClDroidincludes a NaCl program, the NaClDroidbridge, which can dynamically load and call code hosted in a NaCl module. Thus, when Dalvik invokes dlopen() to load a native library, NaClDroidtakes over and passes control to the NaClDroidbridge, which redirects the call to the correct dlopen(), for loading a NaCl module. The NaClDroidbridge runs in a separated thread, which we will further refer to as the NaCl thread.

When Dalvik invokes the NaCL-compliant dlopen() to load NaCl modules, it expects a pointer to the loaded object to be returned. However, code compiled with NaCl, and thus using NaClDroidbridge, is isolated from the rest of the process. Returning the pointer practically involves escaping the sandbox, so we need a way to communicate the pointer back to Dalvik. This is achieved using a NaCl system call, that is, special trampoline code, hosted in a different section, that can transfer data from NaCl modules to the rest of the process.

Based on the above, we now describe in detail the steps taken during a dlopen() call, using the example code illustrated in Fig. 2. The code has been simplified for readability. Once _r__dlopen() is called, which is the dlopen() implemented by NaClDroid, the following things take place. First, we store the current stack pointer of the NaCl thread (line 3), the thread running the NaClDroidbridge. Next, we use setjmp() for saving the current state (line 5); once the actual dlopen() is called, we are not going to return to the main thread normally, but using a special NaCl system call. We then prepare the stack with the parameters required for calling dlopen() (line 10). Notice, that we need to jump directly to the address where the NaCl dlopen() is implemented, and, thus, we need to prepare the appropriate stack manually. The address of NaCl dlopen() has been communicated to the main thread during initialization the same way to the one we describe now. Once the stack is prepared, we directly jump to NaCl's dlopen() (line 13).

At this point, execution has been transferred to the NaCl thread. As we have already stated, execution can be resumed to the main thread only using a NaCl system call. Once that happens, a custom handler is called for serving it (lines 22–32). The handler parses the arguments of the system call (line 25) and if the system call refers to a function return, the return value is taken and passed to a longjmp() call, which will resume back to line 17. We then restore the saved stack and return the value taken from longjmp() (i.e., the handle of the shared library just loaded) back to Dalvik, which initially called dlopen(), This technique is carried out for loading, resolving functions (using dlsym()),

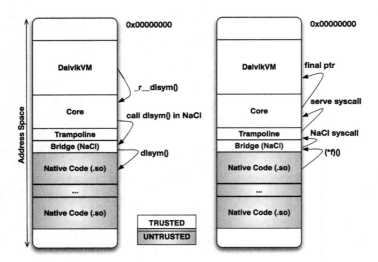

Fig. 3. Implementation of `dlsym()` in NaClDroid. Dalvik VM has been modified and `dlsym()` has been replaced with a wrapper that calls the NaCl compatible `dlsym()` implemented in NaClDroid **bridge**. The wrapper resolves the symbol inside the untrusted sandboxed library, and by using a NaCl system call the address of the symbol is returned back to the VM.

and calling functions in native code. We present a graph of the control flow we follow for calling `dlsym()` in Fig. 3.

3.2 Native-to-Java Communication

Native code can interact with the Java program. All native functions loaded through JNI take as a parameter a pointer to a structure, named JNIEnv. This structure, essentially, encapsulates all available functionality provided from the Java environment to native code. For example, a Java string object can be created in native code by simply calling the following code:

```
jstring s = (*env)->NewStringUTF(env,"jni");
```

The implementation of `NewStringUTF` lies in the trusted domain, which means that it cannot be directly reached by code inside the sandbox. We could follow a similar technique with the one we outlined for `dlopen` earlier in this section. However, notice, that in this case the code for the string creation is called by the developer, who is unaware of the existence of the sandbox. This is in contrast with `dlopen`, which is called by the VM under our control.

To allow native code access the API provided by Java we proceed as follows. First, we clone the environment structure, JNIenv, and make all function pointers, like the one for `NewStringUTF`, point at placeholder implementations located in NaClDroidbridge. Each native call receives a copy of the structure, and when a call takes place, the placeholder implementation located in the bridge

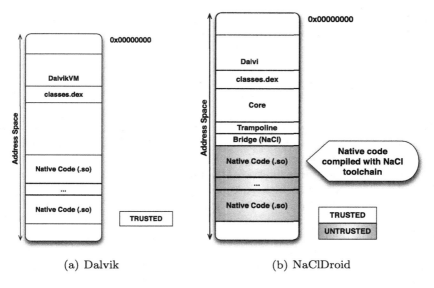

(a) Dalvik   (b) NaClDroid

Fig. 4. NaClDroidarchitecture compared to the original Dalvik system. All dark grey boxes are considered untrusted. We consider the environment, which executes the bytecode as trusted. The bytecode, by itself, cannot modify the trusted VM. Native code can modify it and thus all supplied native code is considered untrusted. For ensuring that untrusted code cannot modify the trusted execution, we isolate it in a NaCl sandbox.

is invoked, instead of the actual function located in the Dalvik VM. The placeholder serves the call by parsing all arguments and preparing a NaCl system call, which is the only way to communicate information to the trusted domain. Finally, NaClDroidserves the incoming system call by calling the actual function, getting the result, and communicating it back to the untrusted part. Recall, that the trusted domain can return to the sandbox normally, without following a particular procedure.

3.3   Trust Domains

NaClDroidseparates Android applications in two parts, one considered trusted and one untrusted. We depict this separation in Fig. 4, where NaClDroidis compared with the original Dalvik architecture. All dark gray boxes are considered untrusted. More precisely, we treat all Dalvik bytecode as untrusted, since it can potentially *change* at run-time. However, we consider the VM, which executes the bytecode as trusted. The bytecode, by itself, cannot modify the trusted VM; however, native code can modify it. User supplied (native) code is considered untrusted. Dalvik, NaClDroid, and the bridge, are all trusted. For ensuring that untrusted code cannot modify the trusted execution, we isolate it in a NaCl sandbox. This guarantees that native code cannot read/write outside its mapped memory, and cannot invoke OS system calls. NaClDroidintroduces trust relationships in Android software, for the first time.

3.4   Architecture Issues

Dalvik targets x86-32 and ARM architectures. NaCl is also available for both x86-32, using the segmentation unit, and ARM, using pure SFI. The Dalvik interface for loading native code is based on dynamic linking. Dynamic linking can be provided by the GNU C Library (`glibc`) [22] or Android's `bionic` [1]. The latter is an extended version of Newlib [19], which is designed for embedded systems (i.e., it is much more lightweight compared to `glibc`). The NaCl port for ARM is based on Newlib, which does not support dynamic linking. Hopefully, there are thoughts about porting `glibc` [8] or `bionic` [2] to NaCl for ARM. The design of NaClDroid, as outlined in this paper, is based on Dalvik for x86-32, and NaCl supporting dynamic linking through the NaCl port of `glibc` for x86-32. If `glibc` or `bionic` is ported to NaCl for ARM, then NaClDroidcan be used *as is*, since it is based on an abstract interface for dynamic linking, like `dlopen()`, `dlsym()`, etc.

4   Security Evaluation

In this section we discuss potential avenues of attacking NaClDroidand how it tackles each one. In all cases we assume a legitimate Android app which includes malicious third-party code, contained in a native library.

4.1   Running External Binaries

Android apps are allowed to launch external binaries to access system utilities and third-party programs. This is possible both through native code using one of the `execve` family of system calls, and through the Java `Runtime.exec()` API call. Allowing an app to invoke arbitrary binaries, essentially enables it to download any binary from the Internet and execute it, if permission for network access has been granted. It is apparent that allowing arbitrary execution of binaries is overly permissive. A malicious app could use such a binary to launch exploits against the kernel and essentially break the guarantees offered by NaClDroid.

Blocking the execution of binaries is not straightforward. Applications can write in their own directory under `/data`, which permits execution. Preventing execution from `/data` is currently not possible because it also holds the native libraries included with apps. As a result, disallowing execution from the partition (e.g., by setting the `noexec` flag during mounting) will also prevent loading of any shared library using `dlopen`. An app can also execute a binary indirectly by simply invoking the shell (`/system/bin/sh -c [my_command]`) or use a shell script that will invoke its binary.

To address these issues we propose permitting the execution of stock binaries alone, such as the binaries located under `/system`, with the exception of the shell command that can be used to launch other commands. Executing binaries through native code is not allowed under NaClDroid, since native code now executes in a NaCl sandbox that blocks system calls. We tackle binary execution from Java code by modifying the `Runtime.exec()` call to disallow applications outside whitelisted directories. For also blocking the shell command Android fortunately provides us with the means to easily block access to it. The stock shell of Android is owned by `root` and belongs to group `shell`. We can prevent most apps from executing it by removing their user ids (`uid`) from the `shell` group in Android, and removing the executable bit from non-group members.

4.2 Malicious Apps

NaClDroidis not meant for detecting or identifying Android malware, but for protecting legitimate apps from malicious libraries. However, traditional malware can be also substantially confined if running under NaClDroid. By examining a popular malware dataset [38] we identified that over 53 % of the malicious applications contain native code, such as native libraries or known exploits (e.g., `rageagainstthecage`) in their `assets` folder. This percentage is one order of magnitude higher than the one expected for Android markets, which is reported to be only about 4.52 % (8272 out of the 204,040 studied) [39]. Therefore, we see a trend in malware towards hosting native code, potentially for exploiting and rooting the victim's device. NaClDroidprevents *all* these exploits, since it prohibits external programs from running, unless they are part of the system tools, and all native code is constrained in a NaCl sandbox.

4.3 JVM Type Safety

Native code can modify data structures hosted in the Java domain through JNI. This can be used for modifying the state of the JVM, by assigning a pointer to a non-compatible type, something often identified with the term *type-confusion attack* [23]. Type safety is orthogonal to bytecode integrity and confidentiality, and, therefore, *NaClDroidis orthogonal to existing frameworks that ensure type safety of heterogeneous programs that contain Java and C components* [21,31].

4.4 Memory Corruption

Bugs in native code can corrupt memory. These bugs are usually due to memory writes outside the bounds of buffers or careless dereferences of pointers. An attacker able to trigger such a bug can change the original control flow of the buggy program and run his own code. There are many bugs that can lead to memory corruption, such as buffer overflows, null-pointer dereferences, integer overflows, etc. In the context of our threat model, there is a critical difference. Memory corruption bugs may be *intentionally* implanted in the malicious application. [34] The attacker can trigger the bug at a later time, hijacking his own program, and modifying the app's behavior with new, malicious code.

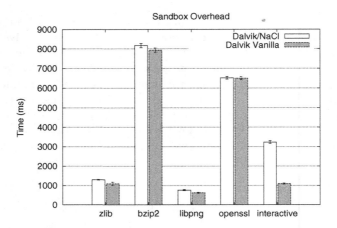

Fig. 5. Evaluation of NaClDroid's NaCl sandbox using popular packages ported on NaCl [4], such as `zlib`, `bzip2`, `libpng`, and OpenSSL. We also use a worse-case scenario, handcrafted test, which involves communicating large amounts of data between Java and native code, labeled as `interactive`.

NaClDroidcannot prevent memory corruption, but can significantly confine it in the memory region where the vulnerable native module has been mapped. As a result, an attacker can only redirect control within the module. This, combined with the fact that there are no memory pages both writable and executable in the module, prevents code-injection attacks. The attacker could still employ code-reuse techniques to alter the functionality of the binary, but remember that system calls cannot be executed. Consequently, even if the native library part of the app is compromised, it cannot escape the sandbox.

5   Performance Evaluation

In this section we experimentally evaluate the performance overhead for sand-boxing all native code. We show that, as expected, the overhead of NaClDroidis acceptable and similar to that of similar work [37].

To evaluate the overhead imposed by sandboxing, we use custom Android applications linked with popular packages that have been ported to NaCl [4], such as `zlib`, `bzip2`, `libpng`, and OpenSSL. We also created a custom test, which involves communicating a large number of data objects between Java and native code, which we call `interactive`. Notice that this test is artificially made and does not follow correctly the paradigm of using native code with Java. Native code is meant to be used for performing heavy computation and return results back to Java and not for heavy exchanging of data structures between the native and the Java part.

We run each Android application linked with a native library over NaClDroid and over the standard run-time. Workloads for all applications are part of the test programs of each particular package. We depict our results in Fig. 5. Notice that in all cases, except `interactive`, the run time overhead is moderate; the NaCl sandbox imposes a slowdown of less than 10 % on average, similarly to reports found in literature [37]. However, the overhead becomes significant in the `interactive` test, since this test represents a worst-case scenario, where no computation is actually performed by the library and large amounts of data are copied over JNI. The increased overhead is primarily due to switching between the trusted thread of execution and the untrusted thread, which runs inside the sandbox. Recall that trust domain switching is a complicated process for guaranteeing that execution will leave the sandbox only in a very precise and confined way (see Sect. 3). Most Android applications do not use native code in that way (i.e., intensively exchanging data, back and forth, between Java and native code), but rather outsource computationally intensive tasks to the native part, and only receive back the final result; `interactive` serves as a micro-benchmark for measuring the overhead of merely switching trust domains.

6 Related Work

Mobile and Android security has received a lot of attention by the research community. In this section, we review related work in various fields of mobile security research.

6.1 Malware

An initial study of mobile threats for Android, iOS, and Symbian, was carried out by Felt et al. [18]. Shortly after, larger studies of Android malware were carried out [38,39]. NaClDroidoperates orthogonally to detection methods applied on app stores and focuses solely on prevention at the end-host level. NaClDroid guarantees that legitimate applications cannot be hijacked by malicious libraries. However, NaClDroid can also implicitly protect the system from traditional malware that aims at rooting the device. Lately we see a trend in malware towards hosting native code, potentially for exploiting and rooting the victim's device. NaClDroidprevents *all* these exploits, since it prohibits external programs from running, unless they are part of the system tools, and all native code is constrained in a NaCl sandbox.

6.2 Analysis

The research community has developed various techniques, employing static and dynamic analysis, as well as symbolic execution, that can assist in the reviewing of mobile apps. Ded [15] decompiles Dalvik programs to Java, which can then be analyzed using numerous, already available static analysis tools. With the assistance of Ded, researchers managed to study more than 21 million lines of source code. ComDroid [13] also uses static analysis to infer malicious inter-application communication performed through message passing. Paranoid Android [26] is a system based on dynamic analysis of Android applications. In the same fashion, AASandbox [10] combines both static and dynamic analysis for identifying Android malware, while SymDroid [6] is a symbolic execution framework for Dalvik. Finally, TaintDroid [14] uses tainting for the analyzing apps.

The above are some representative works in the field of static analysis, dynamic analysis, and symbolic execution, for mobile software. NaClDroid complements these systems in the following way. Assuming that applications are thoroughly reviewed before distribution using such analysis systems, we argue that malware writers will utilize more advanced techniques for modifying legitimate applications at run-time [9] using malicious third-party code [7]. NaClDroid guarantees that an app cleared during reviewing will not deviate by altering the semantics of the underlying execution environment.

6.3   Permission Model

Researchers have also focused in enhancing and optimizing the Android's permission model, which is crucial for the security of the platform. Kirin [16] attempts to resolve dangerous combinations of permissions at install time and warn the user. The authors also provide an implementation of a service performing application certification based on Kirin. Stowaway [17] can statically analyze Android apps to identify unnecessary permissions. This can drastically reduce the the capabilities of over-privileged applications. Saint [24] enhances Android's permission model with policies, which are more powerful than static permissions enforced at installation time. Saint policies can assist in trusted communication between applications and components. Aurasium [35] enforces policies through user-level sandboxing. The authors automatically repackage Android applications with custom code, which is able to resolve offensive actions (e.g., calling or texting premium numbers). The great advantage of Aurasium is that it needs no system modifications, since apps are automatically extended to support the framework.

All these frameworks can be easily integrated with NaClDroid, since we make no assumptions about Android's permission and software model. Applications running over NaClDroid are only confined in terms of code integrity and code confidentiality; we do not focus on abuses of the permission model. NaClDroid operates transparently and does not affect, or interfere in any way, with the currently deployed permission model.

7   Conclusion

We presented how malicious third-party code can hijack legitimate applications and break their integrity and confidentiality. We showed that native code, included in Android apps in the form of a library, can steal sensitive information from the app or even change its control flow; a capability that has already been taken advantage by apps distributed through Google Play.

To address this issue, in this paper we designed, implemented, and evaluated NaClDroid, a framework that leverages Software Fault Isolation and embeds Native Client in Android's runtime to allow apps to safely use native code, while at the same time ensuring that the code cannot exfiltrate sensitive data from the app's memory, extend itself, or tamper with the Dalvik VM. Confining untrusted native code using SFI has been also adopted by successful projects such as Chrome. We this work, we argue that stricter isolation is also crucial for the Android platform to safely support native code in apps. We showed that NaClDroidhas moderate overhead; our SFI-based implementation imposes a slowdown of less than 10 % on average.

Acknowledgements. This work was supported by the European Commission through project H2020 ICT-32-2014 "SHARCS" under Grant Agreement No. 644571 and the U.S. Office of Naval Research under award number N00014-16-1-2261. Any opinions, findings, conclusions and recommendations expressed herein are those of the authors and do not necessarily reflect the views of the US Government, or the ONR.

References

1. Bionic c library. https://android.googlesource.com/platform/bionic/+/android-4.2.2_r1/libc/README. Accessed Jan 2013
2. Dynamic linking in native client. http://code.google.com/p/nativeclient/wiki/DynamicLinkingPlan. Accessed Jan 2013
3. Google bans self-updating Android apps, possibly including Facebook's, May 2013. http://arstechnica.com/information-technology/2013/04/google-bans-self-updating-android-apps-possibly-including-facebooks/
4. NaCl ports. http://code.google.com/p/naclports/
5. Native client in Google Chrome. https://support.google.com/chrome/answer/1647344?hl=en
6. SymDroid: symbolic execution for Dalvik bytecode (Not yet published). http://www.cs.umd.edu/~jfoster/papers/symdroid.pdf
7. The bearer of badnews. https://blog.lookout.com/blog/2013/04/19/the-bearer-of-badnews-malware-google-play/
8. Thoughts about porting glibc to NaCl for ARM native-client-discussion list. Private communication, December 2012
9. Under the hood: Dalvik patch for Facebook for Android. https://www.facebook.com/notes/facebook-engineering/under-the-hood-dalvik-patch-for-facebook-for-android/10151345597798920
10. Bläsing, T., Schmidt, A.D., Batyuk, L., Camtepe, S.A., Albayrak, S.: An android application sandbox system for suspicious software detection. In: 5th International Conference on Malicious and Unwanted Software (Malware: MALWARE 2010), Nancy, France (2010)
11. Bornstein, D.: Dalvik VM internals. In: Google I/O Developer Conference, vol. 23, pp. 17–30 (2008)
12. Canalys: over 1 billion android-based smart phones to ship in 2017. http://www.canalys.com/newsroom/over-1-billion-android-based-smart-phones-ship-2017. Accessed Oct 2013

13. Chin, E., Felt, A.P., Greenwood, K., Wagner, D.: Analyzing inter-application communication in android. In: Proceedings of the 9th International Conference on Mobile Systems, Applications, and Services (MobiSys 2011), NY, USA, pp. 239–252 (2011). http://doi.acm.org/10.1145/1999995.2000018

14. Enck, W., Gilbert, P., Chun, B.G., Cox, L.P., Jung, J., McDaniel, P., Sheth, A.N.: Taintdroid: an information-flow tracking system for realtime privacy monitoring on smartphones. In: Proceedings of the 9th USENIX Conference on Operating Systems Design and Implementation (OSDI 2010), pp. 1–6. USENIX Association, Berkeley (2010). http://dl.acm.org/citation.cfm?id=1924943.1924971

15. Enck, W., Octeau, D., McDaniel, P., Chaudhuri, S.: A study of android application security. In: Proceedings of the 20th USENIX Conference on Security (SEC 2011), p. 21. USENIX Association, Berkeley(2011). http://dl.acm.org/citation.cfm?id=2028067.2028088

16. Enck, W., Ongtang, M., McDaniel, P.: On lightweight mobile phone application certification. In: Proceedings of the 16th ACM Conference on Computer and Communications Security (CCS 2009), NY, USA, pp. 235–245 (2009). http://doi.acm.org/10.1145/1653662.1653691

17. Felt, A.P., Chin, E., Hanna, S., Song, D., Wagner, D.: Android permissions demystified. In: Proceedings of the 18th ACM Conference on Computer and Communications Security (CCS 2011), NY, USA, pp. 627–638 (2011). http://doi.acm.org/10.1145/2046707.2046779

18. Felt, A.P., Finifter, M., Chin, E., Hanna, S., Wagner, D.: A survey of mobile malware in the wild. In: Proceedings of the 1st ACM Workshop on Security and Privacy in Smartphones and Mobile Devices (SPSM 2011), NY, USA, pp. 3–14 (2011). http://doi.acm.org/10.1145/2046614.2046618

19. Gatliff, B.: Embedding with GNU: Newlib. Embed. Syst. Program. 15(1), 12–17 (2002)

20. Gordon, R.: Essential JNI: Java Native Interface. Prentice-Hall, Inc., Upper Saddle River (1998)

21. Lee, B., Wiedermann, B., Hirzel, M., Grimm, R., McKinley, K.S.: Jinn: synthesizing dynamic bug detectors for foreign language interfaces. In: Zorn, B.G., Aiken, A. (eds.) Proceedings of the 2010 ACM SIGPLAN Conference on Programming Language Design and Implementation (PLDI 2010), 5–10 June 2010, Toronto, Ontario, Canada, pp. 36–49. ACM (2010)

22. Loosemore, S., Stallman, R.M., McGrath, R., Oram, A., Drepper, U.: The GNU C Library Reference Manual. Free Software Foundation, Boston (2001)

23. McGraw, G., Felten, E.W.: Securing Java: Getting Down to Business with Mobile Code. Wiley, New York (1999)

24. Ongtang, M., McLaughlin, S.E., Enck, W., McDaniel, P.: Semantically rich application-centric security in android. Secur. Commun. Netw. 5(6), 658–673 (2012)

25. Pearce, P., Felt, A.P., Nunez, G., Wagner, D.: AdDroid: privilege separation for applications and advertisers in android. In: Proceedings of the 7th ACM Symposium on Information, Computer and Communications Security (ASIACCS 2012), NY, USA, pp. 71–72 (2012). http://doi.acm.org/10.1145/2414456.2414498

26. Portokalidis, G., Homburg, P., Anagnostakis, K., Bos, H.: Paranoid android: versatile protection for smartphones. In: ACSAC, pp. 347–356 (2010)

27. Sehr, D., Muth, R., Biffle, C., Khimenko, V., Pasko, E., Schimpf, K., Yee, B., Chen, B.: Adapting software fault isolation to contemporary CPU architectures. In: Proceedings of the 19th USENIX Conference on Security (USENIX Security 2010), p. 1. USENIX Association, Berkeley (2010). http://dl.acm.org/citation.cfm?id=1929820.1929822

28. Siefers, J., Tan, G., Morrisett, G.: Robusta: taming the native beast of the JVM. In: Al-Shaer, E., Keromytis, A.D., Shmatikov, V. (eds.) Proceedings of the 17th ACM Conference on Computer and Communications Security (CCS 2010), 4–8 October 2010, Chicago, Illinois, USA, pp. 201–211. ACM (2010)

29. Sun, M., Tan, G.: JVM-portable sandboxing of java's native libraries. In: Foresti, S., Yung, M., Martinelli, F. (eds.) ESORICS 2012. LNCS, vol. 7459, pp. 842–858. Springer, Heidelberg (2012)

30. Sun, M., Tan, G.: Nativeguard: protecting android applications from third-party native libraries. In: Proceedings of the 2014 ACM Conference on Security and Privacy in Wireless and Mobile Networks (WiSec 2014), NY, USA, pp. 165–176 (2014). http://doi.acm.org/10.1145/2627393.2627396

31. Tan, G., Appel, A.W., Chakradhar, S., Raghunathan, A., Ravi, S., Wang, D.: Safe java native interface. In: IEEE International Symposium on Secure Software Engineering, March 2006

32. Viennot, N., Garcia, E., Nieh, J.: A measurement study of google play. In: The 2014 ACM International Conference on Measurement and Modeling of Computer Systems (SIGMETRICS 2014), NY, USA, pp. 221–233 (2014). http://doi.acm.org/10.1145/2591971.2592003

33. Wahbe, R., Lucco, S., Anderson, T.E., Graham, S.L.: Efficient software-based fault isolation. In: Proceedings of the Fourteenth ACM Symposium on Operating Systems Principles (SOSP 1993), NY, USA, pp. 203–216 (1993). http://doi.acm.org/10.1145/168619.168635

34. Wang, T., Lu, K., Lu, L., Chung, S., Lee, W.: Jekyll on IOS: when benign apps become evil. In: Proceedings of the 22nd USENIX Conference on Security. USENIX Association (2013)

35. Xu, R., Saidi, H., Anderson, R.: Aurasium: practical policy enforcement for android application. In: Proceedings of the 21st USENIX Conference on Security. USENIX Association (2012)

36. Yan, L.K., Yin, H.: Droidscope: seamlessly reconstructing the OS and Dalvik semantic views for dynamic android malware analysis. In: Proceedings of the 21st USENIX Conference on Security Symposium (Security 2012), p. 29. USENIX Association, Berkeley, CA, USA (2012). http://dl.acm.org/citation.cfm?id=2362793.2362822

37. Yee, B., Sehr, D., Dardyk, G., Chen, J.B., Muth, R., Orm, T., Okasaka, S., Narula, N., Fullagar, N., Inc, G.: Native client: a sandbox for portable, untrusted x86 native code. In: Proceedings of the 2007 IEEE Symposium on Security and Privacy (2009)

38. Zhou, Y., Jiang, X.: Dissecting android malware: characterization and evolution. In: IEEE Symposium on Security and Privacy, pp. 95–109 (2012)

39. Zhou, Y., Wang, Z., Zhou, W., Jiang, X.: Hey, you, get off of my market: detecting malicious apps in official and alternative Android markets. In: Proceedings of the 19th Annual Network & Distributed System Security Symposium, February 2012

AsyncShock: Exploiting Synchronisation Bugs in Intel SGX Enclaves

Nico Weichbrodt[1]([✉]), Anil Kurmus[2], Peter Pietzuch[3], and Rüdiger Kapitza[1]

[1] TU Braunschweig, Braunschweig, Germany
{weichbr,kapitza}@ibr.cs.tu-bs.de
[2] IBM Research Zurich, Zürich, Switzerland
kur@zurich.ibm.com
[3] Imperial College London, London, UK
prp@imperial.ac.uk

Abstract. Intel's Software Guard Extensions (SGX) provide a new hardware-based trusted execution environment on Intel CPUs using *secure enclaves* that are resilient to accesses by privileged code and physical attackers. Originally designed for securing small services, SGX bears promise to protect complex, possibly cloud-hosted, legacy applications. In this paper, we show that previously considered harmless synchronisation bugs can turn into severe security vulnerabilities when using SGX. By exploiting use-after-free and time-of-check-to-time-of-use (TOCTTOU) bugs in enclave code, an attacker can hijack its control flow or bypass access control.

We present *AsyncShock*, a tool for exploiting synchronisation bugs of multithreaded code running under SGX. AsyncShock achieves this by only manipulating the scheduling of threads that are used to execute enclave code. It allows an attacker to interrupt threads by forcing segmentation faults on enclave pages. Our evaluation using two types of Intel Skylake CPUs shows that AsyncShock can reliably exploit use-after-free and TOCTTOU bugs.

Keywords: Intel Software Guard Extensions (SGX) · Threading · Synchronisation · Vulnerability

1 Introduction

Recently, Intel's Software Guard Extensions (SGX), a new hardware-supported trusted execution environment for CPUs, has reached the mass market[1]. Similarly to previous trusted execution environments such as ARM TrustZone [1], SGX allows the execution of applications inside *secure enclaves*, without trusting other applications, the operating system (OS) or the boot process. Unlike previous solutions, SGX supports hardware multithreading, which is a fundamental requirement for modern performant applications.

---

[1] https://qdms.intel.com/dm/i.aspx/5A160770-FC47-47A0-BF8A-062540456F0A/PCN114074-00.pdf.

© Springer International Publishing Switzerland 2016
I. Askoxylakis et al. (Eds.): ESORICS 2016, Part I, LNCS 9878, pp. 440–457, 2016.
DOI: 10.1007/978-3-319-45744-4_22

Secure enclaves reduce the overall trusted computing base (TCB) to essentially the TCB of the enclave. SGX by itself, however, cannot prevent vulnerable enclave applications from being exploited. Although it was initially assumed that only small tailored applications would be executed inside enclaves [11], a recent trend is to consider enclaves as a generic isolation environment for arbitrary applications: VC3 [21] uses enclaves to secure computation for the Hadoop map/reduce framework; Haven [2] places a library OS inside an enclave for running unmodified Windows server applications.

This trend towards more complex, multi-threaded applications inside enclaves opens up new attacks. In particular, existing applications are designed to protect against a threat model that is not the same as the one for enclave code—traditional applications assume that the OS is trusted. As recent work has shown, an untrusted OS enables powerful side channel [28] and Iago [5] attacks.

In this paper, we explore a new angle for mounting attacks against SGX enclaves. We show that *synchronisation bugs* that are unlikely to be exploitable outside of SGX become reliably exploitable by carefully scheduling enclave threads. We achieve this by manipulating the page access permissions of enclave pages to force segmentation faults that interrupt enclave execution. Through this method, we are able to widen the traditionally small attack window of synchronisation bugs and increase the chances of a successful exploit.

Typically, the impact of such *concurrency attacks* [29] is to prevent or slow down certain activities in favour of others, create inconsistencies, extract data, bypass access control, or hijack the control flow of the attacked program (e.g., CVE-2009-1837, CVE-2010-5298, CVE-2013-6444). In the case of SGX, the impact of controlling code execution within an enclave is higher. At the time of writing, Intel only licenses the creation of SGX production enclaves after examination of the software development practices of the licensee[2]. Controlling enclave code execution would be a way to circumvent this practice, similarly to how "jailbroken" iPhones can execute non-Apple approved applications.

The contributions of the paper are:

- we show that synchronisation bugs are easier to exploit within SGX enclaves than in traditional applications. This is partly because, by design, the attacker can control thread scheduling of enclaves in the SGX attacker model;
- we describe AsyncShock, a tool that facilitates the reliable and semi-automated exploitation of synchronisation bugs in SGX enclaves. AsyncShock leverages the ability of the untrusted OS to arbitrarily interrupt and re-schedule enclave threads. AsyncShock is designed to target enclaves built with the official SGX Software Development Kit (SDK) for Linux[3];
- we explain how to track enclave execution near critical sections by removing permissions from pages, which triggers notifications when enclave execution has reached a particular point;

---

[2] https://software.intel.com/en-us/articles/intel-sgx-product-licensing.
[3] https://software.intel.com/en-us/blogs/2016/04/11/intel-software-guard-extensions
-sdk-for-linux-availability-update.

- we show how use-after-free and TOCTTOU [3] bugs can be exploited by AsyncShock; and
- we provide evaluation results of attack success rates by AsyncShock on current Intel Skylake CPUs, exploring a variety of different implementations of the attack.

The paper is structured as follows: Sect. 2 provides background on SGX, the assumed attacker model and the impact of synchronisation bugs when using SGX; Sect. 3 describes our forced segmentation fault approach and the Async-Shock tool; Sect. 4 gives evaluation results and discusses protective measures; Sect. 5 surveys related work on SGX and similar attacks; and Sect. 6 concludes the paper.

2   Background

First, we give a brief introduction to trusted execution as implemented by SGX. After that, we present an attacker model that is tailored towards typical usage scenarios of SGX. Finally, we discuss the impact of synchronisation bugs.

2.1   SGX in a Nutshell

SGX allows developers to create an isolated context inside their applications, called a secure *enclave* [13,18]. Enclaves feature multiple properties: (i) enclaves are isolated from other untrusted applications (including higher-privileged ones) through memory access control mechanisms enforced by the CPU; (ii) memory encryption is used to defend against physical attacks and to secure swapped out enclave pages; and (iii) enclaves support remote attestation at the level of enclave instances.

Programming Model. A typical workflow for using SGX with the support of the SGX SDK [12] starts with creating an enclave as part of an application. The necessary instructions for creating an enclave are only callable from kernel mode (ring 0) and thus require kernel support. Once successfully performed, the application can issue `Ecalls` ① to enter an enclave as seen in Fig. 1. Inside the enclave, input parameters passed with the call can be processed, and enclave code is executed. Developers specify the enclave interface and the direction of data with a SDK-specific file written in the Enclave Description Language (EDL) [12]. The SDK handles data movement across the enclave boundary by performing the necessary memory copy operations. However, this is only supported for primitive data types and flat structures. Data structures with pointers are not deep-copied and therefore expose the enclave to TOCTTOU attacks.

`Ocalls` ② may be performed to leave the enclave and execute untrusted application code before an `Ecall` returns ③ to the enclave. While the enclave has access to inside and outside memory, the untrusted application is not allowed to access memory inside the enclave: any attempt to read enclave data results in abort page semantics, i.e. reading `0xFF`; write attempts are simply ignored.

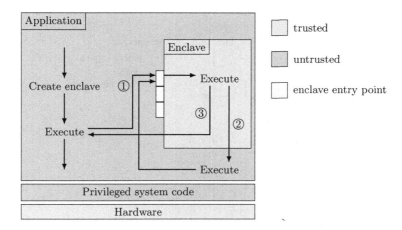

Fig. 1. Basic enclave interaction showing an `Ecall` ① into an enclave, an `Ocall` ② and the return ③ to the untrusted application. (The enclave entry points are shown in yellow.) (Color figure online)

Memory Management. Enclave creation and its memory layout are handled by an SGX kernel module. During enclave creation, the enclave code and data are copied page-by-page into the Enclave Page Cache (EPC), which is protected system memory. Mapped pages and their permissions are saved in the Enclave Page Cache Map (EPCM). Enclave page permissions are thus managed twice, once through the OS page table and once through the EPCM. Accessing an enclave page also leads to two permissions checks: once by the Memory Management Unit (MMU) reading the permissions from the page table, and once by SGX reading them from the EPCM. While it is possible to restrict page table permissions further using `mprotect`, it is not possible to extend them because the EPCM cannot be modified. The possibility of removing page permissions is important for AsyncShock—it means that an attacker can mark pages and get notified when they are used.

Support for Multithreading and Synchronisation Mechanisms. Each enclave must have at least one entry point that defines an address at which the enclave may be entered. The SDK implements a trampoline to allow multiple `Ecalls` through a single entry point. Multithreading is supported by having multiple entry points and permitting multiple threads to enter them concurrently. Similar to regular applications, interrupts may occur during enclave execution and must be handled. SGX achieves this by performing an Asynchronous Enclave Exit (AEX), which saves the current processor state into enclave memory, leaves the enclave and jumps to the Interrupt Service Routine (ISR). Enclave execution is resumed after the ISR finishes, restoring the saved processor state.

The SGX SDK offers synchronisation primitives such as mutexes and condition variables. These primitives do not operate exclusively inside the enclave: for instance, thread blocking requires a system call that is unavailable inside enclaves.

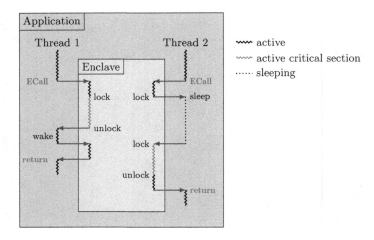

Fig. 2. Mutex lock/unlock operations provided by the SGX SDK may exit the enclave.

Furthermore, managing a lock variable outside of the enclave is not advised because an attacker could change it. A hybrid approach has been adopted by Intel in which the lock variables are maintained inside the enclave whereas system calls are issued outside. Therefore, using synchronisation primitives may result in enclave exits. Figure 2 shows this behaviour for a mutex lock operation.

2.2 Attacker Model

We consider a typical attacker model for SGX enclaves: an attacker has full control over the environment that starts and stops SGX enclaves. They have full control of the OS and all code invoked prior to the transfer of control, using Ecalls, to the SGX enclave, and also when an enclave calls outside code via Ocalls. More specifically, the attacker can interrupt and resume SGX threads (see Sect. 2.1), which is the main attack vector exploited in this paper.

The attacker's goal is to compromise the confidentiality or integrity of the SGX enclave. For example, they may want to gain the ability to execute arbitrary code within the enclave. Note that we ignore availability threats, such as crashing an enclave: the untrusted OS can simply stop SGX threads.

2.3 Synchronisation Bugs in Software

Synchronisation bugs are caused by the improper synchronised access of shared data by multiple threads, and previous studies have shown that they are a widespread issue [15,27]. A large number of tools were proposed to help developers find different kinds of synchronisation bugs, such as *atomicity violations* [6,8,16], *order violations* [9,17,32] and *data races* [20,31]. These studies, however, do not explore the security implications of discovered bugs—in most cases, the discovered bugs lead to memory corruption or crashes. Although such bugs may seem benign and unlikely to occur, synchronisation bugs are likely to lead to exploitable security vulnerabilities [7,23,26].

Unlike traditional applications, in the context of SGX, enclave code is trusted both by its developer and Intel to run untampered on untrusted machines (e.g., hosted at an untrusted cloud service provider). Memory corruption inside an enclave may therefore be used to hijack execution of the enclave, potentially leading to the disclosure of enclave cryptographic keys. In addition, such vulnerabilities may be used by malicious attackers, e.g., botnet herders, to bypass Intel's vetting process and design rootkits that run inside the enclave and are undetectable by security software running in the OS: by design, the OS cannot introspect an enclave running in production mode. Therefore, vulnerabilities in enclaves are worrisome to enclave developers, enclave hosters, and Intel.

In the following, we show that synchronisation bugs are a real security threat to enclave developers by exploiting two examples of the common atomicity-violation bugs: a use-after-free bug as well as a TOCTTOU bug.

3   Exploiting Synchronisation Bugs with Scheduler Control

Exploiting synchronisation bugs inside an SGX enclave can be broken down into: (i) finding an exploitable synchronisation bug; (ii) providing a way to interrupt and schedule enclave threads; and (iii) determining experimentally *when* to interrupt and schedule enclave threads. Next we describe each of these steps through the example of a use-after-free bug. In addition, we describe the AsyncShock tool, which generalises this approach and allow the easy adaptation of these steps to other vulnerabilities. We explain how AsyncShock exploits a TOCTTOU bug.

3.1   Exploiting Synchronisation Bugs Inside an Enclave

We focus on the atomicity-violation class of bugs and show how such a bug can be exploited. Figure 3 shows an example of an atomicity violation. A possible use-after-free bug occurs if the first thread is interrupted directly after the `free` but before the assignment. The second thread performs a `NULL` check during this time, which succeeds even though the pointer has been freed. The call to `free` and the assignment were intended to be an atomic block by developer, but this is not reflected in the implementation.

During execution, such an interruption is a scheduling decision by the OS, and the probability that the interruption occurs at the right point is low. Furthermore, the thread itself is not paused but is scheduled again later while the second thread is still executing. The second thread may thus be interrupted during its execution before the freed pointer can be used.

As shown in the litterature [25,29], the attack window for memory races is small in practice. In some cases, the attacker may only have a single chance to

```
1   ...                                      1   ...
2   free(pointer);                           2   ...
3   // thread is not active                  3   if (pointer != NULL) {
4   // between those two                     4       // use pointer
5   // statements                            5   }
6   pointer = NULL;                          6   ...
7   ...                                      7   ...
```

Thread 1   Thread 2

Fig. 3. Simple use-after-free. Thread one frees `pointer` but is not able to set it to `NULL` because thread two is scheduled in.

exploit the vulnerability. Even if an attacker can execute the application many times, it may still take a long time until the interruption occurs at precisely the correct time. Being able to increase the attack window would thus help exploit such bugs more effectively. The AsyncShock tool aims to help exploit synchronisation bugs that are present inside an enclave by pausing and resuming threads during execution, which is possible when threads are inside an SGX enclave. We explore two techniques for interrupting threads, as described in the following sections.

3.2 Interrupting Threads via Linux Signals

One approach to interrupt threads is to leverage the Linux signal subsystem. Handling a signal interrupts the thread and redirects control to the signal handler. We therefore register a signal handler for the `SIGUSR1` and `SIGUSR2` signals. We use the `SIGUSR1` signal to pause a thread and the `SIGUSR2` signal to resume it again. A control thread sends these signals to specific threads based on a configurable delay. Elapsed time since the application start is measured and compared to the delay in a loop. When the delay is reached, a signal is issued. The signal is sent by the `pthread_kill` function provided by `pthreads`.

Pausing the thread is performed by using a condition variable to wait inside the signal handler that suspends the thread. Sending the resume signal causes a second signal handler invocation, which in turn uses a condition variable signal to resolve the wait in the first signal handler's invocation. Each thread has its own condition variable, facilitating the pausing and resuming of multiple threads.

While this approach works, it is unreliable and depends on the specifics of the Linux task scheduler. We experimented with different delays for the same exploit but observed the same success rate regardless of the delay. We suspect that the signal dispatching is too slow, leading to inaccurate interruptions. Furthermore, this approach requires a deterministic runtime of the program because the delay is fixed—non-deterministic execution inside the enclave defeats this approach.

3.3 Interrupting Threads via Forced Segmentation Faults

We explore another approach based on interrupting threads to force segmentation faults. Using `mprotect`, we remove the "read" and "execute" permissions from

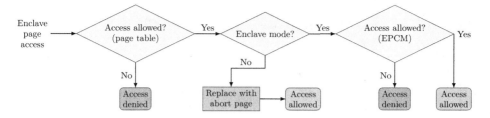

Fig. 4. Memory access permission checks on an enclave page. Permissions are checked and managed twice: once by the MMU (page table) and once by SGX (EPCM).

enclave pages, i.e. *marking* the page. As soon as an enclave page with stripped permissions is accessed, a `SIGSEGV` signal is dispatched by the kernel as a response to the fault generated by the MMU, notifying the attacker of the page access.

This approach exploits the fact that memory access checks with SGX are performed twice, as shown in Fig. 4. The call to `mprotect` changes the permissions inside the page table, but not inside the EPCM. Therefore the access fails at the page table check, even though the real permissions are unchanged.

We install our own signal handler, as described in Sect. 3.2, but this time for `SIGSEGV`. Inside the handler, we can restore the page permissions, start a timer with a configurable delay and resume execution. If a timer is started, it can remove the permissions upon expiration. This leads to another `SIGSEGV`, which again invokes our handler. We can now employ the same thread stopping mechanism described for the signal approach using condition variables. The `mprotect` approach is more reliable than the signal approach because page permissions are changed instantaneously.

3.4   AsyncShock Tool

AsyncShock incorporates the described approaches into an easy-to-use tool. It is implemented as a shared library, which is preloaded using the `LD_PRELOAD` mechanism of the dynamic linker. To interact with the target application, AsyncShock provides its own implementation of certain functions that shadow their real implementations. An example is `pthread_create`, which is normally provided by the C standard library. AsyncShock provides its own implementation that observes thread creation and takes actions upon the creation of specific threads.

To use AsyncShock, an attacker must know how the scheduling needs to be influenced to successfully trigger an exploit. They then must transform the attack into a series of actions in reaction to certain events. Possible events include thread creation, segmentation faults and timer expirations; possible actions include pausing or resuming a thread, starting a timer or changing page permissions. We call this series of actions the attack *playbook*. AsyncShock enforces that the targeted application behaves according to the playbook while also manipulating the environment.

```
1   on thread creation"thread1":
2       remove read,exec on enclave+0x5000
3
4   on thread creation"thread2":
5       pause thread this
6
7   on segfault 1:
8       set read,exec on enclave+0x5000
9       remove read,exec on enclave+0x1000
10
11  on segfault 2:
12      set read,exec on enclave+0x1000
13      resume thread thread2
14      pause thread this
```

Listing 1.1. Example playbook for the use-after-free bug from Fig. 3.

A textual representation of a playbook for the use-after-free bug from Fig. 3 is given in Listing 1.1. It includes the definition of four reactions to events: on thread creation of the first thread, an enclave page (enclave base address + 0x5000) is stripped of its read and execute permissions. By using objdump, we find that the free function is located on this code page, and we mark it to get notified when it is called. As soon as a thread calls the free function, a segmentation fault occurs, which is handled by the signal handler registered by AsyncShock. It reapplies the removed permissions and removes the permissions at another page. The marked page contains the calling function that we mark to get notified when free finishes.

The resulting segmentation fault is again handled by AsyncShock. This time, the faulting thread is paused, and the second thread is allowed to continue. As a result, the attack window has been widened for the second thread to exploit the bug.

3.5   AsyncShock in Action

We use AsyncShock to successfully exploit a use-after-free bug inside an enclave and take control of the instruction pointer. Listing 1.2 shows the exploited enclave code.

The code contains two Ecalls, one set-up Ecall only executed once and another Ecall. While the enclave contains no threads, the second Ecall is used by two untrusted threads to enter the enclave simultaneously. However, a synchronisation bug exists between lines 26 and 27 if multiple threads execute the Ecall function in line 19. glob_str_ptr is a shared variable between all executions that is freed inside the Ecall and set to NULL. The bug triggers if a thread has just executed the free but not yet the assignment, while a second thread enters the Ecall function. Due to the nature of the memory allocator provided by the SDK, the malloc call (line 20) provides the old glob_str_ptr address, which leads to glob_str_ptr and my_func_ptr pointing to the same memory. The second thread passes the NULL check and copies the user provided input to glob_str_ptr, which sets my_func_ptr. The function call in line 25 now receives

```
1   char *glob_str_ptr;
2
3   int other_functions(const char *c) { /* do other things */ }
4
5   int puts(const char * c) {
6       printf("%s", c);
7       return 0;
8   }
9
10  struct my_func_ptr {
11      int (*my_puts) (const char *);
12      char desc[8];
13  } my_func_ptr;
14
15  void ecall_setup() {
16      glob_str_ptr = malloc(sizeof(struct my_func_ptr));
17  }
18
19  void ecall_print_and_save_arg_once(void *str) {
20      struct my_func_ptr *mfp = malloc(sizeof(struct my_func_ptr));
21      mfp->my_puts = puts;
22      if (glob_str_ptr != NULL) {
23          memcpy(glob_str_ptr, (char *)str, sizeof(glob_str_ptr));
24          glob_str_ptr[sizeof(glob_str_ptr)] ='\0';
25          mfp->my_puts(glob_str_ptr);
26          free(glob_str_ptr);
27          glob_str_ptr = NULL;
28      }
29      free(mfp);
30  }
```

Listing 1.2. Example enclave containing a user-after-free bug.

its address from the user-provided input and can be given the address of another enclave function, thus hijacking the control flow inside the enclave.

We use AsyncShock with a playbook similar to the one shown in Listing 1.1 to exploit the bug. Figure 5 shows how AsyncShock exploits the bug in detail. AsyncShock lies dormant until one of its overwritten functions are called. The application first creates a thread that is paused immediately by AsyncShock ①. A second thread is created that is allowed to execute ②. At this point, the "read" and "execute" permissions are removed from the code page containing the `free` function. The second thread enters the enclave and begins execution. When it calls `free` ③, an access violation occurs, resulting in an AEX and a segmentation fault caught by AsyncShock ④. The permissions are restored for this page, but removed for another before the thread is allowed to continue.

When the next marked page is hit ⑤, resulting in another AEX and segmentation fault ⑥, we know that `free` has returned. In the signal handler, the permissions are restored again. We stop the thread and signal the sleeping thread to execute ⑦. This concludes the successful exploit.

3.6 AsyncShock and a TOCTTOU Bug

To show how AsyncShock can be adapted to a different type of bug, we exploit a TOCTTOU bug. Listing 1.3 shows an enclave with three **Ecalls**: two threads

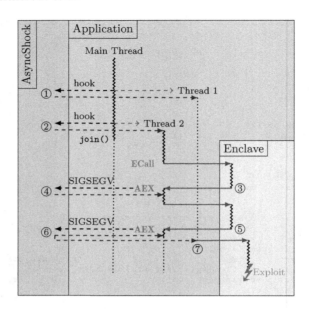

Fig. 5. AsyncShock exploiting the synchronisation bug from Listing 1.2

enter the enclave, the first through the `ecall_writer_thread` and the second through the `ecall_checker_thread` Ecall. The second thread checks (line 20) if the shared variable `data` contains the string `"bad data"` and, if so, does not access it. Other content leads to a successful check and results in the second use of the variable. The first thread writes to the shared variable after executing a non-deterministic amount of time.

A TOCTTOU bug exists in lines 18 (check) and 19 (use). AsyncShock exploits this bug by delaying the writer thread, interrupting enclave execution after the check and then letting the writer thread proceed with the write to the shared variable. Interrupting between the check and the use in this example is challenging because the code pages containing `strncmp` and `memcpy` also contain some frequently called methods of the SDK. We therefore opt to start a timer right before entering the enclave, which expires between the check and the use. The timer has a configurable delay that postpones its execution. The correct delay must be determined empirically by observing the behaviour of the application with different delays. In our example, we observe the most successful exploits by choosing delays between 80000 and 120000 cycles, as described in Sect. 4.3.

4   Evaluation

To show the effectiveness of AsyncShock, we evaluate it by exploiting two atomicity violation bugs. First, we describe our evaluation set-up. After that, we present the results of exploiting a use-after-free bug and a TOCTTOU bug inside an enclave. We finish with a discussion of possible defenses.

```
1   static char data[] = {'g','o','o','d',' ','d','a','t','a','\0'};
2   static int random_wait = 0;
3
4   void ecall_setup() {
5       random_wait = get_random_int();
6   }
7
8   void ecall_writer_thread() {
9   //This function has a constant delay >> check + use plus a random delay
10  //to simulate complex execution that takes a non-deterministic amount of
        time
11      for (int i = 0; i < 100000; ++i);
12      for (int j = 0; j < random_wait; ++j);
13      snprintf(data, 10,"bad data");
14  }
15
16  int ecall_checker_thread() {
17      char *str = calloc(1, 10);
18      if (strncmp("bad data", data, 9) != 0) {
19          memcpy(str, data, 10);
20          printf("Access ok: %s\n", str);
21          free(str);
22          return 0;
23      } else {
24          printf("Sorry, no access!\n");
25          return -1;
26      }
27  }
```

Listing 1.3. Example enclave containing a TOCTTOU bug.

4.1 Experimental Set-Up

We evaluate the effectiveness of AsyncShock by exploiting a use-after-free bug, as well as a TOCTTOU bug, on real SGX hardware. We used a Dell Optiplex 7040 with an i7-6700 Intel CPU and 24 GB of memory. We also evaluate AsyncShock on a white-box server with an Intel E3-1230v5 CPU and 32 GB of memory. Both CPUs have four cores and are capable of hyper-threading, doubling the possible active threads. For our evaluation, hyper-threading has not been disabled. The desktop machine runs Ubuntu Linux 14.04.3 Desktop with kernel version 3.19.0-49; the server machine runs Ubuntu Linux 14.04.4 Server with kernel version 3.13.0-85. The server machine has a lower base load because fewer processes exist due to the missing desktop environment. All evaluations use a pre-release version of the SGX SDK which Intel provided to us.

4.2 Exploiting a Use-After-Free Bug

First, we establish a baseline by running the application without AsyncShock. We execute the application with its enclave one million times without observing a single successful exploit. We conclude that the attack window is too small to be exploitable just through controlled input.

We exploit the bug shown in Listing 1.2. Given the playbook from Listing 1.1, we can reliably exploit the use-after-free bug. We also modify the playbook to change the function arguments for the second thread so that the use-after-free results in a control flow modification, i.e. a call to `other_function`, which is otherwise not called. We execute the exploit 100000 times on both machines and observe a 100 % success rate.

4.3 Exploiting a TOCTOU Bug

To put the high rate chance of exploiting the use-after-free bug into perspective, we also consider a more difficult bug to exploit reliably: a TOCTTOU bug inside an enclave. Here we exploit the enclave code shown in Listing 1.3. We also establish a baseline by executing the application without AsyncShock. As with the use-after-free bug, we also do not see a single exploit occurring by chance. The non-deterministic delay in the writer thread is long enough so that the other thread can always perform the check and the use on the same data.

Next, we try to exploit the bug with AsyncShock. We evaluate a wide range of delays for the timer, as described in Sect. 3.6. Each delay is executed 10000 times. We record the successful exploits every 100 executions, obtaining 100 result sets per delay. We report the mean success rate for a given delay, with error bars representing a 95 % confidence interval.

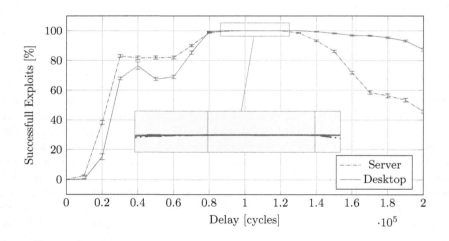

Fig. 6. Graph showing the success rate of AsyncShock exploiting the TOCTTOU bug at different timer delays.

Figure 6 shows the results for the TOCTTOU exploit. As can be seen, the success rate varies not only with timer delay, but also differs for both machines with the same delay. We attribute this behaviour to the differences in base load and active processes on both machines. We are able to achieve near 100 % success rates with timer delays of 80,000 cycles to 120,000 cycles. (As explained in Sect. 3.3, the delay is the time until AsyncShock removes the "execute" permissions from an enclave page, effectively forcing a stop to execution.) Our goal

Table 1. Detailed success rates for selected delays.

Delay (cycles)	Success rate	
	Server	Desktop
80,000	98.57 % ± 0.27	99.40 % ± 0.17
90,000	99.81 % ± 0.08	99.93 % ± 0.05
100,000	99.99 % ± 0.02	99.99 % ± 0.03
110,000	99.98 % ± 0.03	99.99 % ± 0.02
120,000	99.98 % ± 0.03	99.98 % ± 0.03

is to stop the enclave between the check and the use, which we achieve almost always with the correct delay.

Table 1 shows the results in more detail for selected delays. With a delay of 100,000, AsyncShock can almost always exploit the TOCTTOU bug with a low deviation. In conclusion, AsyncShock can be used to reliably exploit atomicity violation bugs with a high success rate.

4.4   Protective Measures Against AsyncShock

Our experimental results show that synchronisation bugs can lead to viable attacks against SGX enclaves. However, there already exist defense mechanisms for protecting from these attacks.

A first defence against the use-after-free bug is the sanitisation of user input as AsyncShock changes the `Ecall` parameters to direct the control flow. In general, sanitisation is advisable when unexpected input can be abused in a similar way to Iago attacks [5]. Enclave code should always check outside input for validity as an attacker may change the result from `Ocalls` or the parameters to `Ecalls` when using the SDK. In addition, enclave developers should not rely on the SDK's ability to defend against simple TOCTTOU attacks. While the SDK does copy `Ecall` parameters into enclave memory before passing them to enclave functions, it does not deep-copy data structures. Pointers in data structures are not followed and may lead to an enclave accessed outside memory. This type of vulnerability has often been exploited in OS kernels (e.g., [14] for Windows, and in general in filesystems [25]).

Another defense against the use-after-free bug presented here is possible because the bug relies on the in-enclave implementation of `malloc` to return recently freed memory. The attack can be mitigated by heap hardening methods, such as the one recently implemented in Internet Explorer through delayed free [10], or even with tools such as AddressSanitizer [22] that delay the reuse of recently freed memory or by changing the behaviour of the in-enclave memory allocator.

Protection from all synchronisation bugs can be achieved by prohibiting threading altogether—if only a single thread can enter the enclave at any time, no inconsistencies are possible due to serial execution. Such a solution, however, negatively impacts performance. If parallelism is needed, one can also adapt other techniques to work inside enclaves such as Stable Multithreading [30] or use tools such as ThreadSanitizer [23] during development in order to find and eliminate synchronisation bugs.

While many hardening techniques are applicable to enclave code, some traditional techniques do not work in the context of SGX. For example, the use of address space layout randomisation (ASLR) [19] is not directly applicable inside enclaves because any changes of the enclave memory would change the enclave measurement and therefore fail the signature check.

5   Related Work

Because SGX is a new technology with limited production use, only few use cases have been described so far. Haven [2] executes unmodified Windows applications inside an enclave. To achieve this, the combination of a shield module and a library OS provides the necessary execution support. The shield module manages synchronisation primitives and ensures their correct behaviour, similar to the SGX SDK. Furthermore, Haven tries to defend against Iago attacks be sanitising and checking the parameters of `Ecalls` and results of `Ocalls`. Haven also proposes a decoupling of enclave threads and host threads via user-level scheduling to hinder the exploitation of synchronisation bugs. However, AsyncShock should still be effective as it marks pages in close proximity to the synchronisation bugs to force an AEX. Thus, it does not necessarily need to observe the enclave-internal thread scheduling.

Fine-grained page tracking can be used for powerful side channel attacks [28]. For example, a JPEG image generated inside an enclave could be reconstructed outside: by paging out enclave pages to repeatedly induce page faults, memory accesses could be related to certain code paths. In contrast, AsyncShock is geared towards the exploitation of synchronisation bugs, albeit it can also be used to extract information from an enclave. However, for synchronisation bugs, AsyncShock only needs a small number of marker pages to track the enclave execution close to the critical section.

Yang et al. [29] identify concurrency attacks as a risk to real-world systems. They classify different types of attacks based on memory access patterns, and identify the attack window as an important factor for exploitability. Memory races usually have a small attack window at the level of nanoseconds. Async-Shock widens the attack window by stopping threads when a critical state is reached, steering other activities to allow reliable exploitation of memory-based concurrency bugs.

Synchronisation bugs have also been studied for their security implications. For instance, TOCTTOU races often affect filesystem-related code, typically when performing access control decisions. Dean and Hu [7] propose a countermeasure to alleviate those risks. Borisov et al. [4] show that this probabilistic countermeasure can be reliably defeated with filesystem mazes. Tsafrir et al. [25] propose another way to instrument those access checks to make the exploitation of those races significantly more difficult even against filesystem mazes.

Twiz and Sgrakkyu [26] extensively treat techniques for the exploitation of logical bugs in OS kernels. Jurczyk and Coldwind [14] describe how to exploit race conditions via memory access patterns in the Windows kernel. The Windows kernel copies the arguments to system calls from user to kernel space. However, the kernel does not copy pointer-referenced data in some cases. The authors exploit this by using the Bochs CPU emulator to interrupt the kernel, similar to how AsyncShock swaps out the data between two reads by the kernel—a classical TOCTTOU attack. However, in contrast, AsyncShock attacks an SGX enclave and not the kernel, in a setting where the attacker controls the scheduler and has reliable side channels on a thread's progress.

Moat [24] makes a first step towards the verification of SGX enclaves. The authors propose an approach to verify that enclave code is unable to disclose secrets. They employ static analysis on the x86 machine code, introducing "ghost variables" to track the secrecy of data in a manner similar to taint tracking. With this method, they are able to find occurrences of possible sensitive data disclosure. While their approach is promising for detecting data disclosure, they, unlike AsyncShock, do not consider multi-threaded code in enclaves.

6   Conclusion

This paper analyses the impact of synchronisation bugs inside SGX enclaves. We have shown that the impact of synchronisation bugs is greater within SGX enclaves than in traditional applications, because their exploitation becomes highly reliable through attacker-controlled scheduling. We described Async-Shock, a tool for thread manipulation, and showed how it can be used to exploit synchronisation bugs by widening the attack window through controlled thread pausing and resuming. AsyncShock operates as a preloaded library without modifications of the target application or host OS. We demonstrated that synchronisation bugs can be exploited inside SGX enclaves using AsyncShock for control flow hijacking or bypassing access checks.

Acknowledgements. We would like to thank the anonymous reviewers for their input. This project has received funding from the European Union's Horizon 2020 Research and Innovation Programme under Grant Agreement No. 645011 and No. 644412.

References

1. ARM   TrustZone.   http://www.arm.com/products/processors/technologies/trust zone/index.php
2. Baumann, A., Peinado, M., Hunt, G.: Shielding applications from an untrusted cloud with haven. In: Proceedings of the 11th USENIX Conference on Operating Systems Design and Implementation, OSDI 2014, pp. 267–283 (2014)
3. Bishop, M., Dilger, M.: Checking for race conditions in file accesses. Comput. Syst. **2**(2), 131–152 (1996)

4. Borisov, N., Johnson, R., Sastry, N., Wagner, D.: Fixing races for fun and profit: how to abuse atime. In: Proceedings of the 14th Conference on USENIX Security Symposium, SSYM 2005, vol. 14, p. 20 (2005)
5. Checkoway, S., Shacham, H.: Iago attacks: why the system call API is a bad untrusted RPC interface. In: Proceedings of the Eighteenth International Conference on Architectural Support for Programming Languages and Operating Systems, ASPLOS 2013, pp. 253–264 (2013)
6. Chew, L., Lie, D.: Kivati: fast detection and prevention of atomicity violations. In: Proceedings of the 5th European Conference on Computer Systems, EuroSys 2010, pp. 307–320 (2010)
7. Dean, D., Hu, A.J.: Fixing races for fun and profit: how to use access(2). In: Proceedings of the 13th Conference on USENIX Security Symposium, SSYM 2004, vol. 13, p. 14 (2004)
8. Flanagan, C., Freund, S.N.: Atomizer: a dynamic atomicity checker for multithreaded programs. SIGPLAN Not. **39**(1), 256–267 (2004)
9. Gao, Q., Zhang, W., Chen, Z., Zheng, M., Qin, F.: 2ndStrike: toward manifesting hidden concurrency typestate bugs. In: Proceedings of the Sixteenth International Conference on Architectural Support for Programming Languages and Operating Systems, ASPLOS XVI, pp. 239–250 (2011)
10. Hariri, A.-A., Zuckerbraun, S., Gorenc, B.: Abusing silent mitigations. In: BlackHat USA (2015)
11. Hoekstra, M., Lal, R., Pappachan, P., Phegade, V., Del Cuvillo, J.: Using innovative instructions to create trustworthy software solutions. In: Proceedings of the 2nd International Workshop on Hardware and Architectural Support for Security and Privacy, HASP 2013, p. 11: 1 (2013)
12. Intel: Intel® Software Guard Extensions SDK for Linux* OS, Revision 1.5. https://01.org/intel-software-guard-extensions/documentation/intel-sgx-sdkdeveloper-reference
13. Intel: Intel(R) Software Guard Extensions Programming Reference, Revision 2. https://software.intel.com/sites/default/files/managed/48/88/329298-002.pdf
14. Jurczyk, M., Coldwind, G.: Identifying and exploiting windows kernel race conditions via memory access patterns. In: Bochspwn: Exploiting Kernel Race Conditions Found via Memory Access Patterns, p. 69 (2013)
15. Lu, S., Park, S., Seo, E., Zhou, Y.: Learning from mistakes: a comprehensive study on real world concurrency bug characteristics. In: Proceedings of the 13th International Conference on Architectural Support for Programming Languages and Operating Systems, ASPLOS XIII, pp. 329–339 (2008)
16. Lu, S., Tucek, J., Qin, F., Zhou, Y.: AVIO: detecting atomicity violations via access interleaving invariants. In: Proceedings of the 12th International Conference on Architectural Support for Programming Languages and Operating Systems, ASPLOS XII, pp. 37–48 (2006)
17. Lucia, B., Ceze, L.: Finding concurrency bugs with context-aware communication graphs. In: Proceedings of the 42nd Annual IEEE/ACM International Symposium on Microarchitecture, MICRO 42, pp. 553–563 (2009)
18. McKeen, F., Alexandrovich, I., Berenzon, A., Rozas, C.V., Shafi, H., Shanbhogue, V., Savagaonkar, U.R.: Innovative instructions and software model for isolated execution. In: Proceedings of the 2nd International Workshop on Hardware and Architectural Support for Security and Privacy, HASP 2013, p. 10: 1 (2013)
19. PaX, PaX address space layout randomization (ASLR) (2003)

20. Savage, S., Burrows, M., Nelson, G., Sobalvarro, P., Anderson, T.: Eraser: a dynamic data race detector for multithreaded programs. ACM Trans. Comput. Syst. **15**(4), 391–411 (1997)
21. Schuster, F., Costa, M., Fournet, C., Gkantsidis, C., Peinado, M., Mainar-Ruiz, G., Russinovich, M.: VC3: trustworthy data analytics in the cloud using SGX. In: 2015 IEEE Symposium on Security and Privacy (SP), pp. 38–54 (2015)
22. Serebryany, K., Bruening, D., Potapenko, A., Vyukov, D.: AddressSanitizer: a fast address sanity checker. In: Proceedings of the 2012 USENIX Annual Technical Conference (USENIX ATC 2012), pp. 309–318 (2012)
23. Serebryany, K., Iskhodzhanov, T.: ThreadSanitizer: data race detection in practice. In: Proceedings of the Workshop on Binary Instrumentation and Applications, pp. 62–71 (2009)
24. Sinha, R., Rajamani, S., Seshia, S., Vaswani, K.: Moat: verifying confidentiality of enclave programs. In: Proceedings of the 22nd ACM SIGSAC Conference on Computer and Communications Security, CCS 2015, pp. 1169–1184 (2015)
25. Tsafrir, D., Hertz, T., Wagner, D., Da Silva, D.: Portably solving file TOCTTOU races with hardness amplification. In: FAST 2008, pp. 1–18 (2008)
26. Twiz, S.: Attacking the Core: Kernel Exploitation Notes. Phrack 64 file 6
27. Xiong, W., Park, S., Zhang, J., Zhou, Y., Ma, Z.: Ad hoc synchronization considered harmful. In: OSDI, pp. 163–176 (2010)
28. Xu, Y., Cui, W., Peinado, M.: Controlled-channel attacks: deterministic side channels for untrusted operating systems. In: 2015 IEEE Symposium on Security and Privacy (SP), pp. 640–656 (2015)
29. Yang, J., Cui, A., Stolfo, S., Sethumadhavan, S.: Concurrency attacks. In: Presented as Part of the 4th USENIX Workshop on Hot Topics in Parallelism (2012)
30. Yang, J., Cui, H., Wu, J., Tang, Y., Hu, G.: Making parallel programs reliable with stable multithreading. Commun. ACM **57**(3), 58–69 (2014)
31. Yu, Y., Rodeheffer, T., Chen, W.: RaceTrack: efficient detection of data race conditions via adaptive tracking. In: Proceedings of the Twentieth ACM Symposium on Operating Systems Principles, SOSP 2005, pp. 221–234 (2005)
32. Zhang, W., Sun, C., Lu, S.: ConMem: detecting severe concurrency bugs through an effect-oriented approach. In: Proceedings of the Fifteenth Edition of ASPLOS on Architectural Support for Programming Languages and Operating Systems, ASPLOS XV, pp. 179–192 (2010)

Stay in Your Cage! A Sound Sandbox for Third-Party Libraries on Android

Fabo Wang[1,2], Yuqing Zhang[1,2(✉)], Kai Wang[2], Peng Liu[3], and Wenjie Wang[2,4]

[1] State Key Laboratory of Integrated Services Networks, Xidian University, Xi'an, China
fbwang@stu.xidian.edu.cn
[2] National Computer Network Intrusion Protection Center, University of Chinese Academy of Sciences, Beijing, China
{zhangyq,wangk}@nipc.org.cn
[3] College of Information Sciences and Technology, Pennsylvania State University, University Park, PA, USA
[4] State Key Laboratory of Information Security, Institute of Information Engineering, Chinese Academy of Sciences, Beijing, China

Abstract. Third-party libraries are widely used in Android application development. While they extend functionality, third-party libraries are likely to pose a threat to users. Firstly, third-party libraries enjoy the same permissions as the applications; therefore libraries are over-privileged. Secondly, third-party libraries and applications share the same internal file space, so that applications' files are exposed to third-party libraries. To solve these problems, a considerable amount of effort has been made. Unfortunately, the requirement for a modified Android framework makes their methods impractical.

In this paper, a developer-friendly tool called LibCage is proposed, to prohibit permission abuse of third-party libraries and protect user privacy without modifying the Android framework or libraries' bytecode. At its core, LibCage builds a sandbox for each third-party library in order to ensure that each library is subject to a separate permission set assigned by developers. Moreover, each library is allocated an isolated file space and has no access to other space. Importantly, LibCage works on Java reflection as well as dynamic code execution, and can defeat several possible attacks. We test on real-world third-party libraries, and the results show that LibCage is capable of enforcing a flexible policy on third-party libraries at run time with a modest performance overhead.

1 Introduction

Android application developers are becoming increasingly dependent on third-party libraries, to simplify and speed up development or improve performance. However, when developers import third-party libraries, they often pay most attention to what abilities third-party libraries provide, regardless of their risks.

© Springer International Publishing Switzerland 2016
I. Askoxylakis et al. (Eds.): ESORICS 2016, Part I, LNCS 9878, pp. 458–476, 2016.
DOI: 10.1007/978-3-319-45744-4_23

Third-party libraries differ from system libraries in that it is difficult to guarantee their security.

Third-party libraries may pose a threat to users. First, as the permission system of Android is application-level, when an application is installed, both the host application and third-party libraries in it share the same permissions [1,2]. What's worse, some libraries may request more permissions than they need to complete their jobs [3]. This obviously violates the *Principle of Least Privilege* [4,5], which suggests that every program (module) should run with the least set of privileges necessary to complete a specific job. As a result, third-party libraries may abuse some permissions to collect user data [6,7]. Second, the host application and third-party libraries share the same internal storage, meaning that third-party libraries can operate the application's internal files, which may lead to a privacy leak.

Several approaches have been proposed to separate third-party libraries' permissions from the host application's permissions. Based on process isolation, some approaches [1,8–13] achieve permission separation by isolating the untrusted third-party library into another process. Compac [2] proposes an approach that enforces component-level access control on applications, while enabling developers to assign different permissions to each third-party library. FLEXDROID [14] provides in-app privilege separation for applications, with which developers can grant permissions to third-party libraries and also specify how to change their behavior after detecting a privacy violation. However, these pervious approaches require modifications to the Android framework or the applications (or libraries), which determines that they cannot be adopted widely. Aside from this, some of them are unable to solve the problem of libraries having the ability to steal the application's internal files.

Some work [15–17] has presented a sandbox based on application virtualization, to enforce a fine-grained permission control on applications at run time. However, these approaches cannot be applied to the case of third-party libraries since they target the whole application, and make no distinction between the host application and third-party libraries.

In this paper, we present LibCage, a friendly tool to help developers isolate third-party libraries from the host application in terms of permission and file space. Within the context of the host application, LibCage builds a sandbox for each library. First, each sandbox is assigned to a permission set by developers, so its library cannot perform privileged operations beyond these permissions. Our prototype focuses primarily on the dangerous permissions, which may carry a risk to user data. In fact, LibCage can be extended to support all permissions. Second, each sandbox has its own file space, and its library cannot operate files beyond this space. LibCage doesn't modify the Android framework or libraries, and thus it can be deployed widely. It also works on some unusual situations, such as dynamic loading or Java reflection. It doesn't require developers to modify the existing code or change the way in which they use third-party libraries. All they need to do is integrate LibCage into their projects, create some configurations and initialize LibCage. To the best of our knowledge, LibCage is the first solution to introduce a fine-grained sandbox on third-party libraries.

The contributions of this paper can be summarized as follows:

1. We present a novel approach to isolating each third-party library in an independent sandbox, ensuring that each library has a separate permission set and an isolated file space. Our approach covers Java and native libraries while eliminating the necessity of modifying the Android framework or libraries' bytecode.
2. We implement the prototype named LibCage, using which developers can assign a different permission set to each third-party library, and allocate each library an isolated internal file space.
3. We systematically evaluate the generality, effectiveness and performance overhead of LibCage. Results show that LibCage can effectively enforce a flexible security policy on any third-party libraries while introducing an acceptable performance overhead.

2   Android Security and Related Work

2.1   Android Security

Android provides several mechanisms to ensure the security of user data and device resources. We describe several main mechanisms as follows.

Application Sandboxing. Android adopts the Linux sandbox mechanism. When an application is installed, Android will give it an unique Linux user ID (UID). Each application runs in its own isolated process and doesn't have the privilege to interact with other processes directly (as can happen through IPC mechanism).

Permission System. By default, an application doesn't have any permissions to do privileged things, e.g., getting the location information. In order to be privileged, an application must explicitly declare the related permissions. On devices running Android 5.1 or lower, an application asks for users' approval at installation. Users either grant all the permissions to it or cancel the installation. Once an application is installed, it can use the permissions at any time and users can not revoke any permissions unless they uninstall it, which is called All-or-Nothing. To remedy this situation, Android 6.0 introduces dynamic permission assignment, which demands that an application should request permissions at run time and allows users to revoke any permissions at any time.

File Access Control. Android devices have two file storage areas, i.e., internal and external storage. External storage is world-readable, which means that all applications have access to files in this storage. By contrast, internal storage is private. When an application is installed, the system will assign an internal storage to it and this internal storage is accessible only by this application.

Operating files in the external storage requires the permission READ_EXTERNAL_S-TORAGE or WRITE_EXTERNAL_STORAGE, while operating files in the internal storage requires no permissions.

It is worth mentioning that under the current permission model, permissions are assigned at the application level, so the incorporated libraries and the host application have exactly the same permissions. It is impossible to grant permissions to only part of an application. Moreover, the libraries and the host application share the same internal file space, and libraries' access to internal files is out of the system's control.

2.2 Related Work

In this section, we describe related work in two categories: permission separation for third-party libraries and fine-grained sandboxing for applications.

Permission Separation for Third-Party Libraries. To separate the permissions of third-party libraries from the host application's permissions, several approaches have been proposed. AdSplit [8] and AFrame [9] isolate an advertisement library into another Activity (also in a different process) by extending the Android framework. In order to display both the advertisement and the host application, AdSplit allows two activities to share the screen, while AFrame supports embedded activities. Leveraging bytecode rewriting, Dr. Android and Mr. Hide [10] moves the untrusted code from the host application into another application. Targeting advertisement libraries, AdDroid [1] integrates advertisement libraries into the Android framework, introducing new advertising API and corresponding permissions. SanAdBox [12] diverts advertisement libraries into standalone applications with separated permissions.

Focusing on native libraries, NativeGuard [11] automatically repackages the target application and divides it in two: the client application, which holds the Java code and the resource; and the service application, which takes the native libraries. NativeProtector [13] isolates native libraries in a similar way to Native-Guard, and further performs fine-grained control of native libraries by instrumenting them and intercepting their calls.

These approaches achieve permission separation based on process isolation. They also provide storage isolation, ensuring the isolation of third-party libraries' file space. By contrast, Compac [2] enforces component-level access control on applications by extending Android's permission model. Developers and users can use it to assign different permissions to each component (e.g., third-party library). Based on hardware fault isolation, FLEXDROID [14] extends Android's permission system to provide in-app privilege separation for applications. With FLEXDROID, developers can grant permissions to third-party libraries and also can specify how to control their behavior after detecting a privacy violation. However, Compac and FLEXDROID don't provide storage isolation. Additionally, these work (a comparison can be seen in Table 1) require either modifications to the Android framework or the applications' (or libraries') bytecode, and thus they cannot be employed widely.

Table 1. A comparison of some related work

	Target	No framework modification	No bytecode rewriting	Permission separation	Storage isolation
AdSplit	Ad lib	✗	✓	✓	✓
AFrame	Ad lib	✗	✓	✓	✓
Dr. Android and Mr. Hide	All libs	✓	✗	✓	✓
AdDroid	Ad lib	✗	✓	✓	✓
SanAdBox	Ad lib	✓	✗	✓	✓
NativeGuard	Native lib	✓	✗	✓	✓
NativeProtector	Native lib	✓	✗	✓	✓
Compac	Java lib	✗	✓	✓	✗
FLEXDROID	All libs	✗	✓	✓	✗
LibCage	All libs	✓	✓	✓	✓

Fine-Grained Sandboxing for Applications. Several work has proposed a fine-grained sandbox to constrain the run-time permissions or behaviors of applications without modifications to the Android framework. Based on application virtualization and process-based privilege separation, Boxify [15] runs untrusted applications in a de-privileged, isolated process (leveraging the isolatedProcess[1] feature). AppCage [16] confines the run-time behaviors of applications by interposing and regulating an application's access to sensitive APIs. Specifically, AppCage builds a dex sandbox by hooking into the application's instance of Dalvik Virtual Machine to confine the access to sensitive framework APIs, and native sandbox leveraging software fault isolation (SFI) [19] to ensure that native libraries cannot escape the sandbox. NJAS [17] loads and executes the code of a given application within the context of a monitoring application and achieves sandbox by means of system call interposition (using ptrace mechanism).

However, these sandboxes cannot be applied to confining the permissions of third-party libraries, because they target the entire application without making any distinction between behaviors of the host application and of third-party libraries. Apart from this, they are unable to control file access.

3   Design

3.1   Objectives

Third-party libraries are not sufficiently trustworthy, though they enable some features and abilities developers desire. In this paper, we focus on the following threats introduced by untrusted third-party libraries:

---

[1] IsolatedProcess is an attribute of a service. If set to true, the service will run under a special process that is isolated from the rest of the system and has no permissions [18].

T1. Permission Sharing. As discussed in Sect. 2.1, at run time, the incorporated third-party libraries and the host application share the exact same permissions. If a library is malicious, then it may abuse the permissions, and steal private information. Some surveys [14] have shown that even benign libraries may use the host application's permissions without documenting them.

T2. File Exposure. Third-party libraries and the host application occupy the same internal file space, so that all the internal files are exposed to third-party libraries. This may result in untrusted libraries grabbing the application's files, which store the user data.

In this paper, we aim to provide a tool for helping developers eliminate the threats above. We identify the following objectives:

O1. Permission Separation. Developers can assign permissions to each third-party library, so that the library will not enjoy all of the host application's permissions.

O2. File Space Isolation. Each library is allocated an isolated internal file space and has no access to other file space (e.g., the host application's internal space).

O3. No Framework or Library Modification. For greater usability, our approach does not rely on any modifications to the Android framework or third-party libraries.

O4. Least Manual Effort for Developers. Our approach only requires minimal manual effort on the part of developers, such as permission configuration.

3.2   Approach

We isolate each third-party library by creating a sandbox for it within the host application's context (depicted in Fig. 1). The key insight is that we add a permission checker in an application, whose job is to validate a library's permissions when this library tries to perform a sensitive operation (sensitive operations are those related to collecting user privacy, such as accessing the contact data). In addition, checker is responsible for judging whether a library's access to a file is legal. If we detect that a library tries to perform an over-privileged operation (i.e., an operation beyond its permissions) or access files not belonging to it, we will block this operation. And thus we can confine the libraries' run-time permissions and control their file access.

The main challenge is *how to monitor third-party libraries' behaviors*. Based on system call interception, we interpose their invocations to sensitive methods or functions (In this paper, methods mean the framework APIs and functions refer to the system C native functions) and redirect these invocations to our monitoring proxies. In this way, we can monitor all sensitive invocations of libraries. Since the host application, libraries and our tool are in the same process, interception doesn't rely on modification to the Android framework or the code of these libraries (O3: ✓).

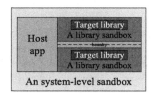

Fig. 1. Our library sandbox

The next challenge we encounter is *how to safely block an operation of a third-party library*. In fact, blocking an illegal operation directly will cause unexpected results (e.g., crash of the library, or even the entire application). In our system, we block an illegal operation in the following way. We first classify all sensitive methods and functions into two categories by the return type (void or not). For those methods or functions without a return result, the proxies simply return, so that the original invocations cannot proceed. For those methods or functions with a return result, the proxies return a mock value to avoid a crash. A mock value will not result in a privacy leak. Thus we can prohibit a permission by blocking the corresponding operation (O1: ✓).

Since external file access is controlled by permissions related to file operations, we only consider the internal file access here. In order to isolate third-party libraries' internal file space, we allocate each library an internal space under the path of the application's internal space. If this library tries to create a new file in the application's internal space, we will change the file's path to its own space. Therefore all files that belong to a library reside in this library's internal space. If the library attempts to access files beyond its space, we deny the attempt (O2: ✓).

Having described our idea, we now present the architecture of our tool named LibCage at a high level (depicted in Fig. 2). LibCage is composed of four entities: Interceptor, Controller, Checker and `Policy.xml` file.

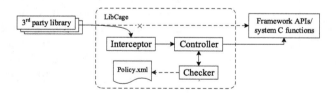

Fig. 2. The architecture of LibCage

Interceptor is responsible for intercepting the calls to the Android framework APIs or system C functions and redirecting them to Controller. For greater efficiency, the interception will be done automatically once an application starts. Controller handles the redirected calls and acts as a mandatory proxy between third-party libraries and the framework APIs or system C functions. Controller queries Checker as to whether a call is legal. If a call is permitted, Controller will call back the original method or function. Otherwise, Controller blocks this call.

Checker's job is to judge whether a third-party library has the permission to perform related operations according to the `Policy.xml` file. To do this, it maintains a mapping between methods or functions and permissions required by these methods or functions. It also determines whether an internal file access is legal.

`Policy.xml` is a configuration file under the assets folder, describing the dangerous permissions an application declares and the permissions assigned to each third-party library. Developers can set flexible security policies on third-party libraries by configuring this file.

Libcage doesn't require much manual effort; all developers need to do is incorporate LibCage into their projects, configure the `Policy.xml`, and add some code to initialize LibCage. When an application starts, LibCage will automatically sandbox each library used in this application (O4: ✓).

In reality, a third-party library may contain Java code and native code (i.e., using JNI). In fact, LibCage works on this library as well because regardless of how Java code interacts with native code, both of them are under the control of LibCage (They cannot directly call the framework APIs or system C functions). If a library consists of Java code and native code, we assign the same permissions to them, and allocate them the same internal file space.

3.3 Policy

LibCage ensures that a third-party library runs in an independent sandbox with only the permissions developers grant, while other over-privileged operations are denied. We are interested primarily in the dangerous permissions [20] (listed in Table 3 in the Appendix), since they may carry a risk to user data. For example, the `READ_CONTACTS` permission allows an application to read contacts, which could be abused by a malicious third-party library, resulting in a leak of user privacy. In fact, our approach can be easily extended to support all permissions; it simply requires more engineering effort.

As described above, LibCage relies on system call interception, including calls to Java methods and native functions. We intercept all methods or functions related to the dangerous permissions. Similar to [21], we identify the Java methods and the permissions required by these methods. For example, the method `getDeviceId()` requires the permission `READ_PHONE_STATE`. We also dig out the native methods related to the dangerous permissions, such as functions used to operate files[2] and *ioctl* function, through which an IPC is sent [22].

LibCage can be used to enforce a flexible policy on third-party libraries. When using LibCage, developers need to list the dangerous permissions, specify the information of third-party libraries, and assign a separate permission set to

---

[2] Technically, operating an internal file doesn't require any permissions. According to the file path, LibCage distinguishes whether the file being operated is internal.

```
<LibCage>
   <!--the dangerous permissions declared by your application -->
   <permission name="READ_CONTACTS" />
   <permission name="ACCESS_COARSE_LOCATION" />
   <!--for each library used, create a tag lib-->
   <lib>
      <!--specify the library information-->
      <pkgname="lib.package.name"/>
      <soname="nativelib.so"/>
      <!--the dangerous permission assigned to this library-->
      <permission name="ACCESS_COARSE_LOCATION" />
   </lib>
</LibCage>
```

Fig. 3. An example of configuring the `Policy.xml` file

each library. This is done by configuring the `Policy.xml` file[3]. Figure 3 illustrates the process.

In this example, the application has the `READ_CONTACTS` and `ACCESS_COAR-SE_LOCATION` permissions. We want to use a third-party library, which consists of a Java library[4] whose package name is `lib.pacakge.name` and a native library whose name is `nativelib.so`. We have assigned the `ACCESS_COARSE_LOCATION` permission to this library. At run time, this library (both the Java part and native part) can access the location information, but won't be able to read users' contact data. Moreover, an isolated internal file space is allocated to this library, and the library only has access to that space.

4   Implementation

4.1   Interceptor

Interceptor's job is to interpose third-party libraries' calls to target methods or functions and dispatch them to Controller. This takes place once an application starts (before any third-party libraries call target methods or functions). We implement the interception on both the Java library and native library.

Java Library. Interception is implemented by manipulating the internal data structures of target methods. At present, the Android system has two different runtimes: Dalvik on previous versions and Android Runtime (ART) which is introduced in Android 4.4 and set default after 5.0 [23]. Since the implementation on ART and Dalvik is similar, here we only describe the implementation on ART. ART maintains a data structure called `Class` (a C++ data struct) and a structure called `ArtMethod` for each method declared in this class. When a method is called, ART searches for the `Class` related to the class in which

---

[3] In our system, a permission name is shortened by removing the prefix. For example, the full name of `READ_SMS` is `android.permission.READ_SMS`.

[4] A Java library may include several packages or native libraries; for a package or native library, developers should add a tag.

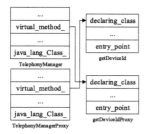
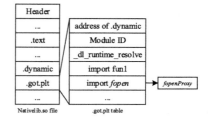

Fig. 4. Intercepting `getDeviceId()` method on ART

Fig. 5. Intercepting *fopen* function on the native library

this method is declared, and then the corresponding `ArtMethod`, which will be executed. By manipulating the data structure of a target method, LibCage interposes all calls to this method and redirects them to Controller.

Figure 4 shows an example of intercepting the `getDeviceId()` method, which provides access to the unique device ID (which can be used to identify a user). To interpose this method, Interceptor obtains the pointer of the related `ArtMethod` in the `Class` of `TelephonyManager` class and replaces it with the pointer of `getDeviceIdProxy()` method. As a result, when a library tries to call `getDeviceId()` method, this invocation is actually redirected to `getDeviceIdProxy()` method.

Once we manipulate a target method, all calls to this method in the same process will be interposed, which means that the interception is once for all (we don't need to deal with the libraries one by one). Since that Java code can't directly modify the process memory, we implement the interposition in C++ code and compile them to a native library.

Native Library. Similar to the traditional Linux model, Android native libraries are relocatable ELF (Executable and Linkable Format) files, which will be mapped into the process's address when loaded [22]. For the sake of memory and code size, these libraries adopt the dynamic linking mechanism. If a library imports an external function, the .got.plt table will contain a respective stub. This imported function will be resolved when the library is loaded and its address will be saved in its stub in the .got.plt table. When an imported function is called, the system first retrieves its address from its stub in the .got.plt table and then executes the code. This indirection can be exploited to implement interception neatly. It's sufficient to replace the stub of an external function in the .got.plt table with the pointer to our monitoring function [24], so that calls to this function will be intercepted and redirected to our function.

Figure 5 shows an example of intercepting *fopen* function, which is used to open a file. To intercept the calls to *fopen* function, LibCage replaces its address in .got.plt table with the address of *fopenProxy* function, a proxy function defined in Controller. As a consequence, when Nativelib.so tries to call *fopen* function, this invocation is actually redirected to the *fopenProxy* function.

Modifying the .got.plt table of one native library differs from interception on Java libraries in that it will not affect other native libraries. In order to interpose all untrusted native libraries' sensitive calls, LibCage manipulates their .got.plt tables one by one.

4.2   Controller

Controller is responsible for taking over the redirected calls and handling the results of these calls. Thanks to Interceptor, all sensitive calls are forwarded to Controller, which is a mandatory layer between third-party libraries and framework APIs or system C functions. To correctly handle the redirected call from Interceptor, Controller contains a proxy method or function for each target method or function.

Java Library. Usually, one Java method call carries two important pieces of information: the receiver object, representing which object calls this method (except for the `static` method), and the passed parameters. After obtaining this information from a redirected call, Controller queries Checker whether this call should be permitted or denied. If this call is permitted, Controller calls back the original method with the receiver object and the passed parameters. Otherwise, Controller blocks this call.

As previously mentioned, all libraries' calls to a target method are intercepted. We first identify the caller by analyzing the stack trace. If it is the host application, Controller calls back the original method immediately. Otherwise, it's a third-party Java library. Controller gets this library's package name and further queries Checker what to do next.

Native Library. Similar to how Controller works on Java libraries, Controller first gets the passed parameters of the redirected calls (native functions don't have the concept of receiver object). Then it identifies who the caller is by analyzing the back trace. If it's the host application, Controller calls back the original function immediately. Otherwise, it's a native library, and Controller decides whether to call back the original function or to block this call by asking Checker.

4.3   Checker

Checker judges whether a call from a third-party library to a method or function is legal or not based on the permissions assigned to this library by developers. Developers grant permissions to each third-party library by configuring the `Policy.xml` file in the assets folder (A demonstration can be seen in Fig. 3).

Checker maintains a Java HashMap, of which the key is the name of a method or function, and the value is the permission required by the method or function. For example, `getDeviceId()` method maps to the READ_PHONE_STATE permission. When Controller queries whether a call is legal, Checker searches for the permission set assigned to this library by parsing the `Policy.xml` file, and judges whether the permission the call requires is contained in the permission set. If it is, the operation is defined as legal.

When Checker decides whether a file access is permitted, it first identifies whether the file being operated is in internal storage, according to the file path. If this file is located in external storage, Checker judges whether the library is assigned the right permission. If so, this file operation is legal. If the file is located in internal storage, Checker judges whether it is in the isolated file space allocated to the library. If so, this file operation is legal.

5 Evaluation

In this section, we describe how we evaluate LibCage in terms of generality, effectiveness, and the performance overhead it brings. These experiments are performed on Samsung Galaxy Note 5, running 5.1.1, and MI 3, running 4.4.4.

5.1 Generality

First, we tested the generality of LibCage on various Android versions. Different Android versions may have different DVM or ART internal data structure. For example, the `ArtMethod` structure in Android 5.1 differs from that in Android 5.0. To adapt to the changes of DVM (or ART) in different versions, LibCage maintains different data structures for different versions. We tested on 4.0, 4.1, 4.2, 4.3, 4.4, 5.0, 5.1, 6.0, and the results showed that LibCage works well on these versions.

Second, we assert that LibCage can be applied to an arbitrary library. LibCage covers both Java libraries and native libraries. However, there are thousands of libraries in the real world, some of which may be programmed in an unusual way, such as dynamic loading or Java reflection. We describe how LibCage deals with these situations.

Dynamic Loading. Some Java libraries may use dynamic loading to execute external DEX (Dalvik executable format) files at run time. LibCage works in this situation too, because the loaded code still needs to call the sensitive APIs which are interposed by LibCage.

Java Reflection. Some Java libraries may use Java reflection to hide the actual API they are calling. To deal with this situation, LibCage intercepts the key method `invoke`, which is used in reflection to call a method. By analyzing the redirected call to `invoke` method, LibCage obtains the actual calling method. If LibCage determines that this call is over-privileged, it will block the call.

We have tested these unusual situations, and the results were successful.

5.2 Effectiveness

In order to evaluate the effectiveness of our prototype, we developed several libraries, including Java libraries and native libraries, performing some sensitive operations related to the dangerous permissions (listed in Table 3 in the

Appendix) and some file operations. The test application also declared all the permissions needed to perform these operations. We then defined a set of security policies and used LibCage to enforce these policies on the test libraries. Results showed that LibCage can limit the run-time permissions of third-party libraries and also showed that LibCage can forbid a library's attempt to access files beyond its file space.

To better demonstrate the results, we tested LibCage on third-party libraries from real world. First, we downloaded 250 applications from the "Top free in Android Apps" chart in Google Play [25], regardless of their categories. We then decoded these APK files and collected the top 10 third-party libraries (depicted in Fig. 6). The detailed permissions they require are listed in Table 4 in the Appendix. Some of these libraries require two levels of permissions: mandatory permissions (developers must list these) and optional permissions (used to provide more functionality; developers can list these optionally).

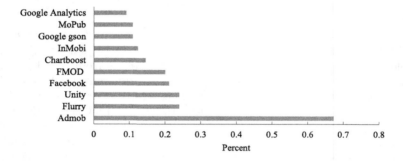

Fig. 6. Popularity of the top 10 libraries in our dataset

We developed a test application with these libraries and execute it manually. First, we enforced a normal policy on each library, that is, we granted all the required permissions to these libraries while the application's other permissions are prohibited. The results were exciting. LibCage forces these libraries to run with only their own permissions, without rendering them dysfunctional.

Second, we enforced a more rigid policy on the libraries. Note that some of them require optional permissions. For example, Flurry and InMobi require the ACCESS_FINE_LOCATION permission, which can be used to track a user. We tested these libraries without granting them optional permissions, though the host application still listed those permissions (If the host application doesn't list these optional permissions, these libraries obviously cannot use them. In this test, we checked whether LibCage could cut off the libraries' optional permissions even when they were available), and the results also showed that these libraries worked well.

These tests showed that LibCage can confine the run-time permissions of third-party libraries and can also cut off unnecessary permissions.

5.3   Performance Overhead

We also evaluated the run-time performance overhead introduce by LibCage. We measured the time required to complete a method or function invocation with and without LibCage. For Java libraries, we tested on these operations in relation to the dangerous permissions (see Table 3 in the Appendix), including querying contacts, getting location, and getting device ID. For native libraries, we tested on some functions used to operate files. The results are shown in Table 2.

Table 2. Overhead introduced by LibCage

	Operation	Without LibCage	With LibCage	Overhead
Java method	Read SMS (100 runs)	2539 ms	2720 ms	7.14 %
	Get location (1 k runs)	949 ms	981 ms	3.40 %
	Get device ID (1 k runs)	397 ms	423 ms	6.59 %
	Query contacts (100 runs)	2885 ms	3076 ms	6.63 %
	Delete a file (1 k runs)	2539 ms	2720 ms	7.29 %
	Open camera (10 runs)	1292 ms	1332 ms	3.11 %
	Record an audio (10 runs)	2374 ms	2395 ms	0.88 %
Native function	Open a file (10 runs)	1333 ms	1383 ms	3.75 %
	Edit a file (200 runs)	119 ms	125 ms	5.33 %
	Read a file (10 runs)	103 ms	110 ms	7.13 %

Intercepting calls to Java method or native function imposes an overhead less than 10 %, among which the highest is 7.15 % and the lowest is 0.88 %. For a single method or function invocation, the overhead is less than 4 ms, which is so negligible that users can't perceive it. We believe that this overhead is acceptable.

5.4   Security Analysis

In this section, we explore some possible attacks to bypass or subvert LibCage and describe how we defend against them.

Manual Resolution. A native library can link the system C libs manually, get the pointer of the target function, and call the function through this pointer. In this case, the .got.plt table of the library doesn't contain the stub of this function, so LibCage becomes invalid. To remedy this situation, LibCage interposes the *dlsym* function, which is used to resolve (get the address of) a function. Then LibCage can know which function is being resolved. LibCage will return the address of the proxy function if this function is sensitive, and thus the call to this function is interposed. Then the operation can continue as usual.

Privilege Escalation. LibCage judges whether a library's behavior is over-privileged according to the `Policy.xml` file. One concern is that a library may tamper with this file, and then its privilege can be escalated up to the application's privilege (that is, it may access all permissions). In fact, the `Policy.xml` file cannot be modified by any libraries at run time, meaning that no libraries can bypass the permission check, since files in the assets folder are read-only.

Modify Mapped Bytecode. A library may change the loaded code by writing the mapped bytecode. LibCage foils this attack, since the functions used to manipulate memory (e.g., *mmap* function, used to map files into memory and *mprotect* function, used to specify the protection level for a memory page) are interposed and this attempt is denied.

6 Discussions

In our work, we focus on dangerous permissions, since our goal is to protect user privacy. In fact, LibCage can be easily extended to support all permissions. It's just a matter of engineering efforts. Our approach can limit the run-time permissions of third-party libraries and cut off their additional permissions which are unnecessary to complete their jobs. However, developers still need to list all permissions required by a third-party library in the Manifest file. Our next objective is to eliminate this need.

Moreover, the crash of a third-party library will result in the breakdown of the entire application, which is undesirable for both developers and users. [19] proposed software fault isolation (SFI) to make sure that faults in one module cannot render a software system unreliable. Based on SFI, several work [26,27] has been done to sandbox untrusted native libraries. In our future work, we will adopt the idea of software fault isolation to ensure that crashes of third-party libraries cannot influence the availability of the host application.

7 Conclusion

The security of third-party libraries has attracted much attention because of their prevalence in recent years. In this paper, we proposed a novel sandbox for third-party libraries, which ensures that each library runs in a respective sandbox. Each sandbox is assigned to a separate permission set by developers and its library cannot carry out privileges beyond this permission set. In particular, developers can cut off the unnecessary permissions of a third-party library. Further, each sandbox is allocated an isolated file space while its library has no access to any other space. We have implemented this approach in a tool called LibCage and evaluate it in terms of generality, effectiveness and performance. The results show that LibCage can be adopted to any library, its effectiveness is remarkable, and the performance overhead it introduces is negligible.

Acknowledgments. This work is supported in part by the National Natural Science Foundation of China (61272481, 61572460), the National Key Research and Development Project (2016YFB0800703), the National Information Security Special Projects of National Development, the Reform Commission of China [(2012)1424], and the Open Project Program of the State Key Laboratory of Information Security (2015-MS-06) and China 111 Project (No. B16037). Peng Liu is supported by NSF SBE-1422215, ARO W911NF-13-1-0421 (MURI), and ARO W911NF-15-1-0576.

A   Appendix

A.1   The Dangerous Permissions

Table 3 lists the dangerous permissions and the corresponding descriptions.

Table 3. Dangerous permissions LibCage enforces

Permission group	Permission	Description
CALENDAR	READ_CALENDAR	Read calendar data
	WRITE_CALENDAR	Edit calendar data
CONTACTS	READ_CONTACTS	Read a contact
	WRITE_CONTACTS	Edit or delete a contact
LOCATION	ACCESS_FINE_LOCATION	Get fine location
	ACCESS_COARSE_LOCATION	Get coarse location
PHONE	READ_PHONE_STATE	Read phone state
	CALL_PHONE	Make a phone call
	READ_CALL_LOG	Read call logs
	WRITE_CALL_LOG	Edit or delete call logs
SMS	SEND_SMS	Send a SMS
	READ_SMS	Read a SMS
	RECEIVE_SMS	Receive a SMS
STROGE	READ_EXTERNAL_STORAGE	Read a file
	WRITE_EXTERNAL_STORAGE	Edit or delete a file
CAMERA	CAMERA	Take a picture or video
MICROPHONE	RECORD_AUDIO	Record an audio

A.2   Interception on DVM

Different from Android Runtime (ART), Dalvik Virtual Machine (DVM) maintains a data structure called ClassObject (a C data struct) for each Java class and a structure (called Method) for each method declared in this class. When a method is called, DVM searches for the ClassObject related to the class in which this method is declared, and then the corresponding Method, which will be executed. Similar to the implementation on ART, we manipulate the data structure of a target method, and replace its pointer with the pointer of data structure of the proxy method.

A.3   The Details of Test Third-Party Libraries

Table 4 lists the details of permissions required by third-party libraries we tested on (✓: mandatory permission, O: optional permission, ×: not required).

Table 4. The details of permissions required by third-party libraries in our dataset

Library	INTERNET	ACCESS_NETWORK_STATE	ACCESS_COARSE_LOCATION	ACCESS_FINE_LOCATION	WRITE_EXTERNAL_STORAGE	NFC	ACCESS_WIFI_STATE	BLUETOOTH	VIBRATE	WRITE_CALENDAR	RECORD_AUDIO	READ_PHONE_STATE	READ_CALENDAR	GET_TASKS	CHANGE_WIFI_STATE
AdMob	✓	✓	×	×	×	×	×	×	×	×	×	×	×	×	×
Flurry	✓	O	×	O	×	×	×	×	×	×	×	×	×	×	×
Unity	×	×	×	×	×	×	×	×	×	×	×	×	×	×	×
Facebook	✓	×	×	×	×	×	×	×	×	×	×	×	×	×	×
Fmod	✓	×	×	×	✓	×	×	×	×	×	×	×	×	×	×
Chartboost	✓	✓	×	×	O	×	✓	×	×	×	×	O	×	×	×
InMobi	✓	✓	O	O	×	×	×	×	×	×	×	×	O	O	O
Google Gson	✓	×	×	×	×	×	×	×	×	×	×	×	×	×	×
MoPub	✓	✓	✓	O	O	O	O	O	O	O	O	×	×	×	×
Google Analytics	✓	✓	×	×	×	×	×	×	×	×	×	×	×	×	×

References

1. Pearce, P., Felt, A.P., Nunez, G., Wagner, D.: Addroid: privilege separation for applications and advertisers in android. In: Proceedings of the 7th ACM Symposium on Information, Computer and Communications Security, pp. 71–72. ACM (2012)

2. Wang, Y., Hariharan, S., Zhao, C., Liu, J., Du, W.: Compac: enforce component-level access control in android. In: Proceedings of the 4th ACM Conference on Data and Application Security and Privacy, pp. 25–36. ACM (2014)

3. Stevens, R., Gibler, C., Crussell, J., Erickson, J., Chen, H.: Investigating user privacy in android ad libraries. In: Workshop on Mobile Security Technologies (MoST). Citeseer (2012)

4. Saltzer, J.H., Schroeder, M.D.: The protection of information in computer systems. Proc. IEEE **63**(9), 1278–1308 (1975)

5. Gries, D., Schneider, F.B.: Monographs in computer science (2008)
6. Zhou, Y., Jiang, X.: Dissecting android malware: characterization and evolution. In: 2012 IEEE Symposium on Security and Privacy (SP), pp. 95–109. IEEE (2012)
7. Grace, M.C., Zhou, W., Jiang, X., Sadeghi, A.-R.: Unsafe exposure analysis of mobile in-app. advertisements. In: Proceedings of the Fifth ACM Conference on Security and Privacy in Wireless and Mobile Networks, pp. 101–112. ACM
8. Shekhar, S., Dietz, M., Wallach, D.S.: Adsplit: separating smartphone advertising from applications. In: USENIX Security Symposium, pp. 553–567 (2012)
9. Zhang, X., Ahlawat, A., Du, W.: Aframe: isolating advertisements from mobile applications in android. In: Proceedings of the 29th Annual Computer Security Applications Conference, pp. 9–18. ACM (2013)
10. Jeon, J., Micinski, K.K., Vaughan, J.A., Fogel, A., Reddy, N., Foster, J.S., Millstein, T.: Dr. android and mr. hide: fine-grained permissions in android applications. In: Proceedings of the Second ACM Workshop on Security and Privacy in Smartphones and Mobile Devices, pp. 3–14. ACM (2012)
11. Sun, M., Tan, G.: Nativeguard: protecting android applications from third-party native libraries. In: Proceedings of the 2014 ACM Conference on Security and Privacy in Wireless & Mobile Networks, pp. 165–176. ACM (2014)
12. Kawabata, H., Isohara, T., Takemori, K., Kubota, A., Kani, J.-I., Agematsu, H., Nishigaki, M.: Sanadbox: sandboxing third party advertising libraries in a mobile application. In: 2013 IEEE International Conference on Communications (ICC), pp. 2150–2154. IEEE (2013)
13. Hong, Y.-Y., Wang, Y.-P., Yin, J.: NativeProtector: protecting android applications by isolating and intercepting third-party native libraries. In: Hoepman, J.-H., Katzenbeisser, S. (eds.) SEC 2016. IFIP AICT, vol. 471, pp. 337–351. Springer, Heidelberg (2016). doi:10.1007/978-3-319-33630-5_23
14. Seo, J., Kim, D., Cho, D., Kim, T., Shin, I.: Flexdroid: enforcing in-app. privilege separation in android (2016)
15. Backes, M., Bugiel, S., Hammer, C., Schranz, O., von Styp-Rekowsky, P.: Boxify: full-fledged app. sandboxing for stock android. In: 24th USENIX Security Symposium (USENIX Security 15) (2015)
16. Zhou, Y., Patel, K., Wu, L., Wang, Z., Jiang, X.: Hybrid user-level sandboxing of third-party android apps. Memory **2200**(0500), 0e00 (2015)
17. Bianchi, A., Fratantonio, Y., Kruegel, C., Vigna, G.: Njas: sandboxing unmodified applications in non-rooted devices running stock android. In: Proceedings of the 5th Annual ACM CCS Workshop on Security and Privacy in Smartphones and Mobile Devices, pp. 27–38. ACM (2015)
18. Android service element (2016). http://developer.android.com/intl/zh-cn/guide/topics/manifest/service-element.html
19. Wahbe, R., Lucco, S., Anderson, T.E., Graham, S.L.: Efficient software-based fault isolation. In: ACM SIGOPS Operating Systems Review, vol. 27, pp. 203–216. ACM (1994)
20. System permissions (2016). http://developer.android.com/intl/zh-cn/guide/topics/security/permissions.html#normal-dangerous
21. Au, K.W.Y., Zhou, Y.F., Huang, Z., Lie, D.: Pscout: analyzing the android permission specification. In: Proceedings of the 2012 ACM Conference on Computer and Communications Security, pp. 217–228 (2012)
22. Rubin, X., Saldi, H., Anderson, R.: Aurasium: practical policy enforcement for android applications. In: USENIX Security Symposium, pp. 539–552 (2012)
23. Android 5.0 behavior changes (2016). http://developer.android.com/intl/zh-cn/about/versions/android-5.0-changes.html

24. Redirecting functions in shared elf libraries (2016). http://www.codeproject.com/Articles/70302/Redirecting-functions-in-shared-ELF-libraries#_Toc257815978
25. Top free in android apps (2016). https://play.google.com/store/apps/top
26. Wu, Y., Sathyanarayan, S., Yap, R.H.C., Liang, Z.: Codejail: application-transparent isolation of libraries with tight program interactions. In: Foresti, S., Yung, M., Martinelli, F. (eds.) ESORICS 2012. LNCS, vol. 7459, pp. 859–876. Springer, Heidelberg (2012)
27. Yee, B., Sehr, D., Dardyk, G., Chen Bradley, J., Muth, R., Ormandy, T., Okasaka, S., Narula, N., Fullagar, N.: Native client: a sandbox for portable, untrusted x86 native code. In: 2009 30th IEEE Symposium on Security and Privacy, pp. 79–93. IEEE (2009)

Android Permission Recommendation
Using Transitive Bayesian Inference Model

Bahman Rashidi[1(✉)], Carol Fung[1], Anh Nguyen[2], and Tam Vu[2]

[1] Virginia Commonwealth University, Richmond, VA 23284, USA
{rashidib,cfung}@vcu.edu
[2] University of Colorado Denver, Denver, CO 80202, USA
{anh.t4.nguyen,tam.vu}@ucdenver.edu

Abstract. In current Android architecture, users have to decide whether an app is safe to use or not. Technical-savvy users can make correct decisions to avoid unnecessary privacy breach. However, most users may have difficulty to make correct decisions. DroidNet is an Android permission recommendation framework based on crowdsourcing. In this framework, DroidNet runs new apps under probation mode without granting their permission requests up-front. It provides recommendations on whether to accept or reject the permission requests based on decisions from peer expert users. To seek expert users, we propose an expertise rating algorithm using transitional Bayesian inference model. The recommendation is based on the aggregated expert responses and its confidence level. Our evaluation results demonstrate that given sufficient number of experts in the network, DroidNet can provide accurate recommendations and cover majority of app requests given a small coverage from a small set of initial experts.

1 Introduction

As the population of smartphone users continues to grow, smartphones have brought significant impact to businesses, social, and lifestyle. With the expectation of over 10 billion mobile Internet devices by 2016, the mobile application industry is putting forward tremendous effort to match the demand and keep up with the ever-evolving technologies [17]. On the other hand, the number of mobile apps has been growing exponentially in the past few years. According to the report by Android Google Play Store, the number of apps in the store has reached 1.8 billion in 2015, surpassing its major competitor Apple App Store [22].

Unlike iOS, Android device owners do not have to root or "jailbreak" their devices to install apps from "unknown sources". This gives Android users broad capability to install pirated, corrupted or banned apps from Google Play simply by changing a systems setting. This provides further incentive for the users to install third-party applications from various (potentially untrusted) app markets [2], but exposes their privacy to significant security risks [3].

In the current Android architecture (6.0), users decide what resources are given to an app by responding to permission requests from apps. Users can also

© Springer International Publishing Switzerland 2016
I. Askoxylakis et al. (Eds.): ESORICS 2016, Part I, LNCS 9878, pp. 477–497, 2016.
DOI: 10.1007/978-3-319-45744-4_24

manually manage any app's permissions after installation. However, this permission control mechanism has been proven to be ineffective to protect users from malicious apps. Study shows that more than 70 % of smartphone apps request to collect data irrelevant to the main functionality of the app [1]. In addition, study shows that only a very small portion (3 %) of users pay attention and make correct decisions to the resource being requested at installation time, since they tend to rush through to get to use the application. The current Android permission pop-ups (Android 6) still depends on users for security and privacy decisions, which is not reliable since inexperienced users may not be able to or care to make correct decisions.

As pointed out in [11,12], the reasons for the ineffectiveness of the current permission control system include: (1) inexperienced users do not realize resource requests are irrelevant and could compromise their privacy, (2) users have the urge to use the app and may be obliged to exchange their privacy for using the app. To address these problems, we propose DroidNet, a framework to assist mobile users to control their resource usage and privacy through crowdsourcing-based permission control recommendations. First, the framework allows users to use apps without granting all permissions. Second, DroidNet allows receiving help from expert users when permission requests appear. Specifically, DroidNet allows users to install untrusted apps under a *"probation"* mode, while the trusted ones are installed in normal *"trusted"* mode. In probation mode, users make real-time resource granting decisions when apps are running. The framework facilitates a user-help-user environment, where expert users are identified and their decisions are recommended to inexperienced users.

The key challenge is to expand the expert user base so that their expertise can cover all applications on the market. More importantly, these expert users should be selected so that their responses and recommendation to their peer of high quality. DroidNet starts from a small set of trusted expert users and propagates the expert evaluation using a transitional Bayesian learning model. We evaluate the effectiveness of the model through a set of experiments. The major contributions of this paper include: (1) A comprehensive Android permission control framework to facilitate a user-help-user environment in terms of permission control. (2) A novel *transitive Bayesian inference model* to propagate expertise rating of users through pairwise similarity among users. (3) A low-risk recommendation algorithm which can help inexperienced users with permission control decision making. (4) A prototype implementation of the system and evaluation on the reliability of the system.

The rest of the paper is organized as following. We first discuss the existing literature in resource management and permission controls in the next section. We then discuss the DroidNet's system view in Sect. 3, followed by the presentation of our algorithms in Sect. 4. Sections 5 and 6 present our implementation and evaluation results respectively. Section 6 shows our evaluation results brought about by our real experiments. We conclude this paper by a discussion and conclusion of our work.

2   Related Work

Due to its inherent constraints in resources, much effort has been done towards the principles and practices to manage resource usage and privacy protection [8,13] of mobile applications. However, the most common practice for resource access management today is Mandatory Access Control (MAC) mechanism [10,21], which is found in API from major mobile players such as iPhone, Android, and Windows Phone. In such paradigm, resource access from apps needs to be granted by users. In Android, this is done through its *Static Permission Model* [14] where users need to grant all requested permissions on installation.

Kathy Wain Yee et al. proposed PScout and studied the design implications of this model and performed an analysis to extract the permission specification from the Android OS [6]. The large number of permissions and APIs in Android suggests that the permission specification for Android is complicated. They also found out that documented and undocumented APIs are heavily interconnected.

Studies [11,12] have shown that such permission control paradigms are not efficient since users are either not paying attention to permissions being requested or not aware of the permissions' implications.

Revising the current Android framework and/or runtime to provide *fine-grained permission controls*, AppFence [15], MockDroid [9], and TISSA [25] avoid giving out sensitive data by granting fake permissions. While such approaches reduce the risk of leaking private information and critical resources, it requires users to make decisions on *every resource request*, which is difficult for inexperienced users and time consuming. Alternatively, AppGuards [7], Aurasium [23], and FireDroid [20] allow users to define security policies on Android apps in which the policies are enforced through their framework. In FireDroid, an application monitor is created to track all processes spawned in Android and allow/deny them based on human managed policies. This approach requires *rooting* the device and extracting the Android booting partition, which is not practical for most users. In addition, the policy file editing and management are also difficult for most inexperienced users. Therefore, FireDroid targets on corporation phone users where the FireDroid can be pre-installed and policies are managed by administrators. Similarly, AppGuards and Aurasium require users to define security policies which is not practical for inexperienced users. In contrast DroidNet is designed for inexperienced users since it does not require users to have prior knowledge or be technical savvy to use it.

Exploring user perceptions of privacy on smartphones using crowdsourcing has been studied in the literature. Agarwal et al. propose PMP [4] which collects users' privacy protection decisions and analyses them to recommend them to other iOS users. However, their recommendations are based on simple *majority opinion* condition which causes high false recommendation rate. In contrast, we propose an expertise ranking algorithm to evaluate the expertise level of users for a higher quality recommendation. Ismail et al. propose a crowdsourcing solution to find a minimal set of permissions that will preserve the usability of the app for diverse users [16]. Their proposed work has a few shortcomings. Repackaging apps for all possible permission combinations is not plausible in reality. Also their indifference among inexperienced and malicious users makes their recommendations with limited quality. Yang et al. [24] propose a system to allow users to share their permission reviews with each other. Users leave comments on permissions and the system ranks reviews and recommends top quality reviews to users. Android 4.3 (App Ops [5]) and 6's permission control mechanisms allow users to selectively disable permissions for apps on their phones.

In our previous work RecDroid [18,19], we proposed to utilize experts users' decisions to help inexperienced users on Android permission control using a simple expert rating and recommendation algorithm. However, only users who have direct overlap with seed experts will be rated, which largely limits its coverage in a large network. In this paper, we developed a network-based expert seeking and a decision recommendation algorithm based on *transitive Bayesian inference theory*, with which more users can be rated through the transition model. Furthermore, we implemented the system on Android platform and conducted a set of comprehensive experiments to evaluate the performance and reliability of the system.

3   System Design

DroidNet has four functional processes, of which two are on mobile clients and the other two are on remote servers. In particular, DroidNet (1) collects users permission-request responses, (2) analyses the responses to eliminate untruthful and biased responses, (3) suggests other users with low-risk responses to permission requests, and (4) ranks apps based on their security and privacy risk level inferred from users' responses. Figure 1 shows an overview of DroidNet architecture, which is composed of a *thin OS patch* allowing mobile clients to automatically report users' responses to and receive permission request response suggestions from a *DroidNet* service. The differentiating factor of DroidNet is the ability to seek expert user base on a small set of seed users (Sect. 4). In the rest of this section, we describe four key features of the DroidNet system.

Permission handling. When installing an app, package installer needs to request permission to access resources on the device. Instead of sending requests to the Android system's legacy permission handler (e.g. Package Manager Service), DroidNet handles the permission requests through the logistics illustrated in Fig. 2. At the installation process of apps, DroidNet allows users to install the apps on one of the two modes: *Probation* mode and *Trusted* mode. On *Probation* mode, DroidNet closely monitors the requests to access a list of user-defined critical permissions, such as location access, contact list access, and camera access, during the application execution. When those resources are requested, a dialog box will pop up to guide users to make customized decision on whether the access to those critical resources should be granted to the app or not. Otherwise, on *Trusted* mode, all requested permissions are permanently granted to the app.

In order to capture the realtime interaction between the system and users, we designed a *Permission Control Portal* on the mobile devices to intercept

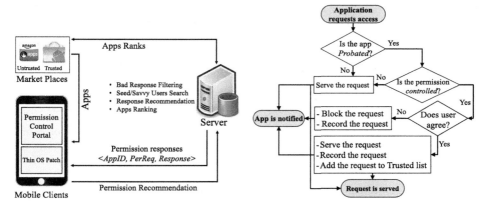

Fig. 1. DroidNet service overview

Fig. 2. Permission request flow in DroidNet

apps' permission requests, record the requests, and collect users' response to the requests. Since intercepting permission requests requires OS level access, we created a small software patch to modify client's operating system. We investigated different potential approaches to perform OS modification and designed a solution that causes minimum impact to legacy apps and applicable to a broad range of OS versions, hardware platforms, and permission access models.

Permission recommendation. To help inexperienced users with their decisions, DroidNet also provides recommended response to the users (Fig. 5 (c)). If a user chooses to deny a request, a dummy data or *void* will be returned to the application. For example, a denied GPS location request could be responded with a random location. The user decisions are recorded by the DroidNet client and sent to the DroidNet server for further analysis. After that, the requests are forwarded to legacy permission handler for book keeping and minimizing DroidNet's unexpected impact on legacy apps. In DroidNet, users make decisions twice:(1) selecting the installation mode ("probation", "trusted"), (2) responding to the permission requests (once for every selected permissions by user). In a later phase when sufficient data is collected, and a security ranking of the app is available, DroidNet server can decide whether to pop up permission requests to users or automatically respond them based on prior knowledge. Therefore, DroidNet manages to achieve a balance between the fine-grained control and the usability of the system.

4   Expert Users Seeking

In DroidNet users' responses to permission requests are recorded by a central server and the responses from expert users are used to generate recommendation to help inexperienced users make low-risk decisions. However, an effective

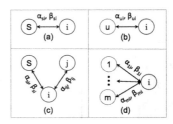

Table 1. Notations

Notation	Description
$\mathcal{U}$	$\{U_1, ..., U_n\}$: Set of n DroidNet users in the system
s	The seed user set
$\mathcal{R}_i$	The set of requests responded by user i in the past
p_i	The true expertise level of user i
R_i, C_i	The expertise rating and confidence of user i
$(\alpha_{ij}, \beta_{ij})$	The similarity tuple between user i and j
(α_i, β_i)	The expertise level distribution parameters for user

Fig. 3. The illustration of four cases of DroidNet graphs. (a) a user is connected directly to a seed user; (b) a user is connected to a non-seed user; (c) a multi-hop rating propagation case; (d) a multi-path rating aggregation case.

method to find expert users in the network is the key. DroidNet starts from a small set of trusted seed expert users, and propagate the expertise evaluation based on similarity among users using a transitive Bayesian inference model. This section describes the model in more detail.

4.1 Assumptions and Notations

The DroidNet can be seen as a network $\mathcal{G} = \{s \cup \mathcal{U}, \mathcal{E}\}$, which consists of a *seed expert* s, a set of n regular users $\mathcal{U} = \{U_1, U_2, ..., U_n\}$, and a set of edges $\mathcal{E} = \{e_{ij} | \mathcal{R}_i \cap \mathcal{R}_j \neq \emptyset, \forall i, j\}$ denoting users i and j have installed apps in common. Where $\mathcal{R}_i$ denotes the set of permission requests responded by user i.

The *seed expert* (SE) is one or a set of trusted expert users who might be employed by a DroidNet facilitator to provide accurate responses to permission requests. We assume seed experts are fully trusted and always provide correct response to permission requests of the apps they cover. However, due to the high cost of human labor, the seed expert can only cover limited number of applications. Therefore, identifying expert users from regular users can expand the coverage of apps that can benefit from DroidNet recommendation.

It is noteworthy that to make seeds' responses context-independent, they follow the principle of least privilege, which is finding a minimal set of permissions that are necessary for apps' legitimate purposes. This way, the seeds' responses are not depend on preference or context.

Let $\mathcal{R}_s$ denote the set of requests covered by seed experts. Then the common set of requests responded by both the seed user and user i can be written as $\mathcal{R}_{si} = \mathcal{R}_s \cap \mathcal{R}_i$. In general, the common set of requests responded by any two users i, j can be written as $\mathcal{R}_{ij} = \mathcal{R}_i \cap \mathcal{R}_j$. Table 1 lists the notations we use in this paper.

4.2   The Users Expertise Rating Problem

The key challenge of DroidNet is to seek experts from the regular users in the DroidNet so that the system can make low-risk recommendations based on the responses from those expert users. The *expertise level* of a user i, denoted by $p_i \in [0, 1]$, is the likelihood that the user makes correct permission granting decisions. Given the set of responses that user i has given to permission requests and their corresponding ground truth, a Bayesian inference model can be used to estimate p_i.

Definition 1. (*Expertise Rating and Rating Confidence*) Assume the likelihood that a user i makes correct decision (p_i) satisfies a distribution Y_i with pdf $f_i(x)$. Then we define the expected expertise level of the user to be:

$$R_i = \mathbb{E}[Y_i] = \int_{x=0}^{1} x f_i(x) dx,$$

the confidence level of the estimation is:

$$C_i = 1 - \theta \delta[Y_i] = 1 - \theta \Big(\int_{x=0}^{1} (x - R_i)^2 f_i(x) dx \Big)^{1/2}$$

where θ is the normalization factor. Therefore, the expertise seeking problem can be described as follows:

Problem 2. (*Expertise Rating Problem*) Given a seed user s and a set of users $\mathcal{U} = \{U_1, \ldots, U_n\}$, a DroidNet graph is denoted as $\mathcal{G} = \{\mathcal{U} \cup s, \mathcal{E}\}$. Where $\mathcal{E} = \{e_{ij} | \mathcal{R}_i \cap \mathcal{R}_j \neq \emptyset, \forall i, j\}$ is a set of edges between users where they have overlap on responded requests. The expertise rating problem is to find the posterior distributions of all p_i, given their past history of responding to permission requests.

To present the solution of Problem 2, we first define the concept of similarity between a pair of users and then the computation method on expertise levels.

Definition 3. (*Similarity of Two Users*) Suppose user i and user j have responded to a common set of permission requests $\mathcal{R}_{ij}$, then we define the similarity between these two users using a *similarity tuple* $(\alpha_{ij}, \beta_{ij})$, denoting the accumulated number of consistent responses and inconsistent responses to those common requests, respectively.

Let $\{x_k \in \{0, 1\} | 1 \leq k \leq n\}$ denote a sequence of n observations in history, where $x_k = 1$ means the two users provided consistent responses at the kth overlapped request, and vice versa. The similarity tuple can be computed as follows:

$$\alpha_{ij}^{(n)} = \sum_{k=1}^{n} q^{n-k} x_k + q^n C_0 \qquad (1)$$

$$= x_n + q x_{n-1} + \ldots + q^{n-1} x_1 + q^n C_0$$

$$\beta_{ij}^{(n)} = \sum_{k=1}^{n} q^{n-k}(1 - x_k) + q^n C_0 \tag{2}$$
$$= (1 - x_n) + q(1 - x_{n-1}) + \dots + q^{n-1}(1 - x_1) + q^n C_0$$

Where C_0 is a constant weighting the initial belief; $q \in [0, 1]$ is the remembering factor which is used to discount the influence from past experience and therefore emphasize the importance of more recent observations.

4.3 Users Connected to the Seed Expert

We start with the case that a user i who has a common set of responded requests with the seed expert (see Fig. 3(a)). In such case, our approach is to compute the similarity tuple $(\alpha_{si}, \beta_{si})$ between the user and the seed, and then the distribution of p_i based on the observations.

We have the following Lemma:

Lemma 1. *Let i be a user i that has only one seed expert neighbor in the Droid-Net graph. Let $(\alpha_{si}, \beta_{si})$ be the similarity tuple of i and the seed expert. Then the rating of the user can be estimated as follows:*

$$R_i = \frac{\alpha_{si}}{\alpha_{si} + \beta_{si}} \tag{3}$$

$$C_i = 1 - \sqrt{\frac{12\alpha_{si}\beta_{si}}{(\alpha_{si} + \beta_{si})^2(\alpha_{si} + \beta_{si} + 1)}} \tag{4}$$

Proof. Since the seed expert's advise is assumed correct, α and β are indeed the number of correct and incorrect responses that the user answered in the past. Let a random variable $X \in \{0, 1\}$ denote whether a user answers the permission requests correctly or not. $X = 1$ indicates that user responds to a request correctly, vice versa. Therefore, we have $p = \mathbb{P}(X = 1)$. Given a sequence of observations on X, a beta distribution can be used to model the distribution of p.

In Bayesian inference theory, posterior probabilities of Bernoulli variable given a sequence of observed outcomes of the random event can be represented by a Beta distributions. The Beta-family of probability density functions is a continuous family of functions indexed by the two parameters α and β, where they represent the accumulative observation of occurrence of outcome 1 and outcome 0, respectively. The beta PDF distribution can be written as:

$$f(p|\alpha, \beta) = \frac{\Gamma(\alpha + \beta)}{\Gamma(\alpha)\Gamma(\beta)} p^{\alpha-1}(1 - p)^{\beta-1} \tag{5}$$

The above can also be written as,

$$p \sim \frac{\Gamma(\alpha + \beta)}{\Gamma(\alpha)\Gamma(\beta)} y^{\alpha-1}(1-y)^{\beta-1} \tag{6}$$

According to Definition 1, we have Eqs. (3) and (4). □

4.4   Users Connected to a Regular User

Due to the limited coverage of the seed user, there may be many users who do not have direct overlap with the seed user (see Fig. 3(b)). To rate users who are connected only to a regular user with known expert rating, we can use the following theorem:

Theorem 4. *Let i be a user connected to a user u with known expertise level $p_u > \frac{1}{2}$ in the DroidNet graph; let $(\alpha_{ui}, \beta_{ui})$ be the similarity tuple of i and u, where $\alpha_{ui} \geq \beta_{ui}$. Then p_i satisfies a Beta distribution: $p_i \sim Beta(\alpha_i, \beta_i)$, where*

$$\alpha_i = \frac{\alpha_{ui}p_u + \beta_{ui}(p_u - 1)}{2p_u - 1} \tag{7}$$

$$\beta_i = \frac{\alpha_{ui}(p_u - 1) + \beta_{ui}p_u}{2p_u - 1} \tag{8}$$

Proof. Let random variables $X_i \in \{0, 1\}$ and $X_u \in \{0, 1\}$ denote a random event that user i and u respond to permission requests correctly or not. $X_i(X_u) = 1$ means that user $i(u)$ responds to a permission request correctly. Therefore, we have $p_i = \mathbb{P}(X_i = 1)$ and $p_u = \mathbb{P}(X_u = 1)$.

Using Bayes theory, the probability that a consistent response being a correct response is formulated as follows:

$$
\begin{aligned}
&\mathbb{P}(X_i = 1 | X_i = X_u) \\
&= \frac{\mathbb{P}(X_i = X_u | X_i = 1)\mathbb{P}(X_i = 1)}{\mathbb{P}(X_i = X_u)} \\
&= \frac{\mathbb{P}(X_u = 1 | X_i = 1)\mathbb{P}(X_i = 1)}{\mathbb{P}(X_i = 1, X_u = 1) + \mathbb{P}(X_i = 0, X_u = 0)} \\
&= \frac{\mathbb{P}(X_u = 1)\mathbb{P}(X_i = 1)}{\mathbb{P}(X_i = 1)\mathbb{P}(X_u = 1) + \mathbb{P}(X_i = 0)\mathbb{P}(X_u = 0)} \\
&= \frac{p_i p_u}{p_i p_u + (1 - p_i)(1 - p_u)}
\end{aligned}
\tag{9}
$$

Similarly, the probability that an inconsistent response being a correct response is formulated as follows:

$$\mathbb{P}(X_i = 1 | X_i \neq X_u)$$
$$= \frac{\mathbb{P}(X_i = X_u | X_i \neq 1)\mathbb{P}(X_i = 1)}{\mathbb{P}(X_i \neq X_u)}$$
$$= \frac{p_i(1 - p_u)}{p_i(1 - p_u) + (1 - p_i)p_u} \tag{10}$$

Note that α_i and β_i denote the cumulative observations that user i responds correctly. Then α_i and β_i can be obtained indirectly from α_{ui} and β_{ui} from the formula below,

$$\alpha_i = \alpha_{ui}\mathbb{P}(X_i = 1 | X_i = X_u) + \beta_{ui}\mathbb{P}(X_i = 1 | X_i \neq X_u)$$
$$\beta_i = \alpha_{ui}\mathbb{P}(X_i = 0 | X_i = X_u) + \beta_{ui}\mathbb{P}(X_i = 0 | X_i \neq X_u)$$

The above equation set can be transformed into:

$$\alpha_i = \frac{\alpha_{ui}p_i p_u}{p_i p_u + (1 - p_i)(1 - p_u)} + \frac{\beta_{ui}p_i(1 - p_u)}{p_i(1 - p_u) + (1 - p_i)p_u} \tag{11}$$

$$\beta_i = \frac{\alpha_{ui}(1 - p_i)(1 - p_u)}{p_i p_u + (1 - p_i)(1 - p_u)} + \frac{\beta_{ui}p_u(1 - p_i)}{p_i(1 - p_u) + (1 - p_i)p_u} \tag{12}$$

Note that the estimated expertise level of user i can be written as $R_i = \alpha_i/(\alpha_i + \beta_i)$. However, the actual expertise level p_i of user i is unknown. An iterative method can be used to iteratively update Eqs. (11) and (12) starting from $R_i^{(0)} = \frac{1}{2}$ and at each round t replaces p_i with the last round expertise level $R_i^{(t-1)}$. The process stops when $R_i^{(t)}$ converges.

Alternatively we can solve Equation set (11) and (12) by replacing p_i with $\alpha_i/(\alpha_i + \beta_i)$. Then we get (5) and (6). $\qquad\square$

4.5   Multi-hop User Rating Propagation

Since not all users are connected to the seed user, a rating propagation model is called upon to rate users who are indirectly connected to the seed. As shown in Fig. 3(c), user i has overlap with the seed user, so it can be ranked through our Bayesian ranking algorithm described in Lemma 1. User j only has overlap with user i, so it can be ranked based on its similarity to user i. However, Theorem 4 only works when the expertise of user i is known. Therefore, here we use an iterative method to update the rating of all regular users in DroidNet.

Corollary 1. *Let i be a regular user directly connected to a set of users $\mathcal{N}_i$. The ratings of the neighbors at round t are (α_i^t, β_i^t), then the rating tuple $(\alpha_i^{(t+1)}, \beta_i^{(t+1)})$ of user i at time $t + 1$, can be computed as follows:*

$$\alpha_i^{(0)} = \beta_i^{(0)} = 1, \forall i, s.t. U_i \in \mathcal{U}$$

$$\alpha_i^{(t+1)} = \sum_{k \in \mathcal{N}_i} \left(\frac{\alpha_{ik} \alpha_i^{(t)} \alpha_k^{(t)}}{\alpha_i^{(t)} \alpha_k^{(t)} + \beta_i^{(t)} \beta_k^{(t)}} + \frac{\beta_{ik} \alpha_i^{(t)} \beta_k^{(t)}}{\alpha_i^{(t)} \beta_k^{(t)} + \alpha_k^{(t)} \beta_i^{(t)}} \right)$$

$$\beta_i^{(t+1)} = \sum_{k \in \mathcal{N}_i} \left(\frac{\alpha_{ik} \beta_i^{(t)} \beta_k^{(t)}}{\alpha_i^{(t)} \alpha_k^{(t)} + \beta_i^{(t)} \beta_k^{(t)}} + \frac{\beta_{ik} \alpha_k^{(t)} \beta_i^{(t)}}{\alpha_i^{(t)} \beta_k^{(t)} + \alpha_k^{(t)} \beta_i^{(t)}} \right) \qquad (13)$$

Proof. From Eqs. (11) and (12) we learn that the rating of a node can be computed using the similarity with a source of known rating. We use (α_i^k, β_i^k) denote the transformed observation on user i passed by user k, then we have:

$$\alpha_i^k = \frac{\alpha_{ki} p_i p_k}{p_i p_k + (1 - p_i)(1 - p_k)} + \frac{\beta_{ki} p_i (1 - p_k)}{p_i(1 - p_k) + (1 - p_i) p_k}$$

$$\beta_i^k = \frac{\alpha_{ki}(1 - p_i)(1 - p_k)}{p_i p_k + (1 - p_i)(1 - p_k)} + \frac{\beta_{ki} p_k (1 - p_i)}{p_i(1 - p_k) + (1 - p_i) p_k}$$

By replacing p_i with $\frac{\alpha_i}{\alpha_i + \beta_i}$ and p_k with $\frac{\alpha_k}{\alpha_k + \beta_k}$, we have:

$$\alpha_i^k = \alpha_{ki} \frac{\alpha_k \alpha_i}{\alpha_k \alpha_i + \beta_k \beta_i} + \beta_{ki} \frac{\beta_k \alpha_i}{\beta_k \alpha_i + \alpha_k \beta_i}, \forall k \in \{1, 2, ..., m\}$$

$$\beta_i^k = \alpha_{ki} \frac{\beta_k \beta_i}{\alpha_k \alpha_i + \beta_k \beta_i} + \beta_{ki} \frac{\alpha_k \beta_i}{\beta_k \alpha_i + \alpha_k \beta_i}, \forall k \in \{1, 2, ..., m\}$$

In Bayesian inference theory, the observations on one variable can be cumulated through simple summation on all observations, given that they are observed independently. In this case the rating of a user can be represented by the total number of positive and negative observations observed by connected users on different paths. Given that α_i and β_i represent the cumulative positive/negative observations on user i, we have:

$$\alpha_i = \alpha_i^1 + ... + \alpha_i^m = \sum_{k=1}^{m} \alpha_i^k$$

$$\beta_i = \beta_i^1 + ... + \beta_i^m = \sum_{k=1}^{m} \beta_i^k \qquad (14)$$

$\square$

4.6   Multi-path User Rating Aggregation

A user may have overlap with multiple other users. As shown in Fig. 3(d), user i is connected to m other users. The overlap with multiple users can be seen as observations from multiple sources and those observations can be aggregated to generate a more accurate ranking of user i.

Corollary 2. *Let i be a user who has overlap with a set of users $\mathcal{M} = \{U_1, U_2, ..., U_m\}$ with corresponding similarity tuples $\mathcal{S} = \{(\alpha_{1i}, \beta_{1i}), ..., (\alpha_{mi}, \beta_{mi})\}$. Then we have:*

$$\alpha_i = \alpha_i^1 + ... + \alpha_i^m = \sum_{k=1}^{m} \alpha_i^k$$

$$\beta_i = \beta_i^1 + ... + \beta_i^m = \sum_{k=1}^{m} \beta_i^k \tag{15}$$

where,

$$\alpha_i^k = \alpha_{ki} \frac{\alpha_k \alpha_i}{\alpha_k \alpha_i + \beta_k \beta_i} + \beta_{ki} \frac{\beta_k \alpha_i}{\beta_k \alpha_i + \alpha_k \beta_i}, \forall k \in \{1, 2, ..., m\}$$

$$\beta_i^k = \alpha_{ki} \frac{\beta_k \beta_i}{\alpha_k \alpha_i + \beta_k \beta_i} + \beta_{ki} \frac{\alpha_k \beta_i}{\beta_k \alpha_i + \alpha_k \beta_i}, \forall i \in \{1, 2, ..., m\}$$

Proof. This results is derived from Corollary 1 by iteratively computing α_i and β_i on node i in a graph starting from initial setting $\alpha_i^{(0)} = 1$ and $\beta_i^{(0)} = 1$. □

Our approach to define the order of user rating is to start from the direct neighbors of the seed expert, and then we expand the list by looking for the next hop users, and so on. An iterative algorithm is described in Algorithm 1 which rates all regular users in DroidNet. The iteration stops when the difference between two rounds of ratings are sufficiently close.

4.7   Recommendation Algorithm

After rating users in the network, the next step is to generate recommendations based on responses from expert users. We propose a weighted voting method to handle the decision making. The voting process is divided into three steps: qualification, voting, and decision. The algorithm is described in Algorithm 2.

In the qualification step, only responses from qualified users are included into the voting process. Initially the ballot count for reception and rejection decisions are equally initialized to D_0. For each qualified voter, the weight of the cast ballot is the ranking score of the voter. After the voting process finishes, the average ballot score is used to make a final decision. If the average ballot score exceeds a decision threshold, then corresponding recommendations are made. Otherwise, no recommendation is made.

5   Implementation

To prove the concept of feasibility, we implemented a prototype of DroidNet. We modified the permission management component of the Android operating system. We also provide users with an Android application to monitor and

Algorithm 1. Rate All Regular Users

```
1: Compute expertise rating of all reg-
   ular users in DroidNet
2: Notations:
3: R(𝒰): the current rating of all users
4: R̂(𝒰): the last round rating of all
   users
5: s: the seed expert
6: 𝒰ᵢ: the iₜₕ user
7: 𝒢 = (V, E): the generated graph of
   users and overlaps
8: RU: the set of rated users
9: QU: the queue of users to be rated
10: //parameters initialization
11: set R(s) = 1 and R(U) = 0.5
12: while (Distance(R(𝒰), R̂(𝒰)) > ε)
    do
13:     RU ← s
14:     QU ← findNeighbors(s)
15:     R̂(𝒰) ← R(𝒰)
16:     while (u ← remove(QU) is not
        null) do
17:         //Users rating using Corollary
            5.2
18:         R(u) ← computeRating(u)
19:         RU ← RU ∪ u
20:         𝒩 =
            findNeighborsNotInRUorQU(u, 𝒢)
21:         push(𝒩, QU)
22:     end while
23: end while
```

Algorithm 2. Vote for Recommendation

```
1: Notations :
2: R(u), C(u) :the rating score and confi-
   dence of user u
3: x(u) :the response to permission request
   from user u
4: τₑ, τc :the minimum rating score and rat-
   ing confidence to be considered as an
   expert user
5: τd :the recommendation threshold
6: a, b :the cumulative ballots for yes or no
   decision
7: D₀ :the initial ballot count for both deci-
   sions
8: a = b = D₀
9: //Users filtering and ballots casting
10: for each user u who responded to the
    request do
11:     if R(u) > τₑ and C(u) > τc then
12:         if x(u) = 1 then
13:             a+ = R(u)
14:         else
15:             b+ = R(u)
16:         end if
17:     end if
18: end for
19: //decision making based on final ballots
    count
20: if a/(a+b) > τd then
21:     Recommend to accept the request
        with confidence a/(a+b) − τd
22: else if a/(a+b) < 1 − τd then
23:     Recommend to reject the request with
        confidence 1 − a/(a+b) − τd
24: else
25:     No recommendation
26: end if
```

manage resource access permissions at fine-grain level. Figure 4 illustrates Droid-Net's implementation architecture. DroidNet is installed by applying a software patch which includes some modification on the Android operating system and a pre-installed app `DroidNet.apk` on the application level.

5.1 Permission Control User Interaction

The users of DroidNet have an option to install apps under a *probation mode*. We use the app "Telegram" (a popular messaging application) as an example. The first screenshot (Fig. 5(a)) displays two options when installing the app on the smartphone. They can be either *probation mode* or *trusted mode*.

For each installed app, users can use the pre-installed DroidNet application to view a list of apps which are under the probation mode. If the user clicks on an app in the list, a set of requested resources is displayed (see Fig. 5(b)) where checked resources are monitored. By default all sensitive resources are monitored, and can be changed by users. If an app is installed under the probation mode, whenever the app requests to access to a resource under monitoring, the user is informed by a pop-up (Fig. 5(c)).

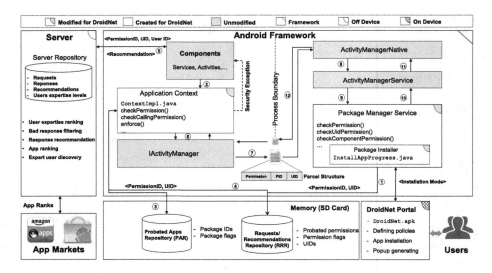

Fig. 4. DroidNet implementation architecture overview

5.2   Android OS Modification

To implement a real-time resource permission control, DroidNet monitors all resource access requests (system calls) at runtime. We modified a few components and methods in Android OS version 4.3 to meet our goal.

App Installation Mode: To allow users to have the option to install under probation or trusted mode, we modified the *Package Manager Service*, which plays the main role in the installation of apps and their requested permissions management. Installation is managed by the *PackageInstaller* activity and when an application installation is completed, a notification is sent to `InstallAppProgress.java`, which is the place we added a post install prompt to ask users if they would like to put application on probation mode.

If a user selects trusted mode installation then app would not be managed by DroidNet, and no information will be recorded about the application. If the user selects probation mode, DroidNet records app's UID and the set of requested permissions by probated app within the *Probated Apps Repository* (PAR) and *Request/Recommendation Repository* (RRR) repositories. Note that communication is obtained through using these repositories that all layers (framework and application) read and write from.

System Calls monitoring and Permission Enforcement: Our implementation is designed to be extensible and generic. While our implementation requires multiple changes in one place, it doesn't require modifications on every permission request handler, as it was the case on some previous works, such as in MockDroid [9]. The modification is presented in the form of an OS patch, which can be executed from a user's space, making this technique easier to adopt.

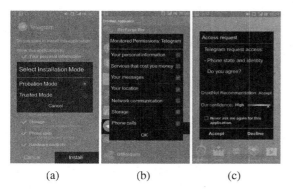

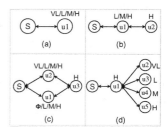

Fig. 5. An example of Line app: (a) probation and trusted installation modes; (b) users pick which critical resources to be monitored; (c) pop-up for permission granting with suggestion from DroidNet and its confidence.

Fig. 6. The four user profiles designed for evaluation: (a) a user is connected directly to a seed user; (b) a user is away from seed by 1 hop; (c) a multi-path rating propagation case; (d) a multi-path rating case, designed for α and β calculation convergence.

In order to design an extensible and central permission enforcing point, we modified the `ContextImpl.java` class of the *context* component of the Android. This is called whenever an application seeks to use some permissions that are not hardware related. When this method is called, it is passed a UID and a permission name. We first check to see if the UID is a system call. If yes then we check the repository to see if the UID is present, and if it is, what value the flag associated with the passed in permission has.

5.3   DroidNet Recommendation Server

Recording the users' responses and providing decision recommendations to users are essential to DroidNet. For this purpose we maintain a remote server to record the responses on an online server and also compute recommendations according to the recorded responses from users. The DroidNet clients request recommendations from the server when needed.

6   Performance Evaluation

In this section we use simulation to evaluate the performance of the expert rating and recommendation algorithms. We also conduct a set of experiments to evaluate the reliability of the system.

6.1   Simulation Setup

As a proof of concept, we created a set of DroidNet user profiles consisting of four different types of expertise levels. The expertise level we refer here is the probability that a user responds to permission requests correctly (a.k.a. consistent with the correct responses). User profiles consist of users with a high (H) expertise (0.9), medium (M) expertise (0.7), low (L) expertise (0.5), and the remaining are users with a very low (VL) expertise (0.1). Note that VL is considered to be malicious since their responses are misleading most of the time. In order to measure the effectiveness of the DroidNet expertise rating, we use a few study cases of multi-hop and multi-path propagation. Our simulation environment is Visual Studio C++ on a Windows machine with 3.6 Ghz Intel Core i7 and 16 GB RAM. All results are based on an average of 500 repeated runs with different random generator seeds.

6.2   Expertise Rating and Confidence Level

To evaluate the effectiveness of the rating and recommendation model, we start from 4 study cases on a set of nodes with designed configuration. The average number of permission requests per app is set to 5 and the maximum number of requests is 500. Figure 6 shows the four study cases and their configurations.

We start from a simple case study that a user is connected to a seed expert only (Fig. 6(a)), and study the expertise ratings and rating confidence when the user is initialized with H, M, L and VL expertise ratings respectively. Figure 7(a) shows the estimated expertise rating for all four types of user's expertise. We can see that when the number of overlapped requests increases, the estimated expertise ratings approach to their true expertise levels. Figure 7(b) shows the corresponding confidence levels of estimation. The confidence level also increases with the number of overlapped apps. From these results, we can see that Droid-Net can have high quality users' expertise rating when the user has sufficient requests overlap with the seed expert.

In the second study case (Fig. 6(b)), we investigate the influence of intermediate users on the expertise rating propagation. We set user 1 with L, M and H expertise and user 2 with H expertise. Figure 7(c) shows that the expertise rating of user 2 is influenced by the expertise level of user 1. The higher expertise of the intermediate node, the closer user 2's is rated to its actual expertise level. We call a high expertise node has a *high rating conductivity*. We also conclude that through multi-hop rating propagation, we can find expert users who do not have direct overlap with the seed expert.

In the third study case (Fig. 6(c)), user 3 connects to the seed expert with two intermediate users. We vary the type of user 1 to be ∅ (non-exist), H, M, and L and vary the type of user 2 to be H, M, L, and VL. Figure 7(d) shows the *conductivity rule* of rating: high expert rating is propagable through expert intermediate nodes (conductive nodes).

Figure 7(e) shows the expertise rating of five users (with expertise 0.1, 0.5, 0.7, and 0.9) for study case shown in Fig. 6(d). As we described in Algorithm 1, we con-

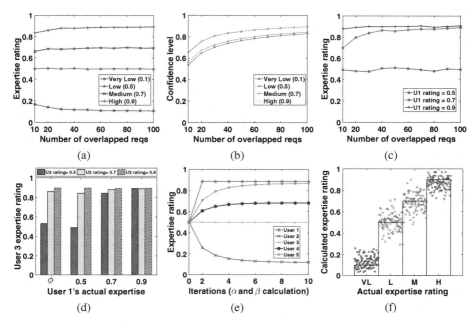

Fig. 7. User expertise and confidence level: (a) expertise level of user with different initial expertise level; (b) computed confidence level of user with different initial expertise level; (c) expertise rating of a user with only one user in its locality and different expertise ratings; (d) expertise rating of a user with two users in its locality and different expertise levels; (e) expertise rating of users for different number of α and β calculation iterations; (f) expertise rating distribution after rating users with different actual expertise rating.

tinue updating the expertise rating parameters (α and β) of a user until they converge to a stable value. In this experiment, we show the convergence speed of different types of users through iterating α and β calculation process 10 times start from 1 iteration to 10 iterations. From this figure we can see that after 10 iterations of computing the all ratings converge to stable values, while the user directly connected to the seed expert achieves stableness after one computation cycle.

In the next experiment we test on a medium size network with 400 users and 250 apps in total. We set up 100 user for each type (VL, L, M and H). Users choose to install 20 apps out of 250 apps randomly. Figure 7(f) shows the distribution of the final expertise ratings for all 400 users. We can see that the estimated expertise ratings are clustered around their actual expertise levels and false positive and false negative exists.

To find the relationship between the seed expert coverage and false positive on user classification, we repeated the last experiment under 10 different coverage rate from seed experts, while remaining the same configuration otherwise. As shown in Fig. 8(a), the number of users assigned to high rating group increases when the seed expert coverage increases.

6.3   Quality of DroidNet Recommendation

We evaluate the quality of DroidNet recommendations using two metrics: *coverage* and *accuracy*. Coverage is the percentage of the requests that DroidNet can offer low-risk recommendation to users, while accuracy is the percentage of correct recommendation that DroidNet makes. Note that if a request is covered by a seed expert, DroidNet always recommend the response from the seed expert.

Our network setting consists of 250 apps with 5 requests per app (total 1250 requests). 400 users with four different types of users (100 users each type), and each user installed and responded to 20 apps (100 requests). Among the 250 apps, 20 of them are covered by the seed expert.

Figure 8(b) shows the coverage and accuracy of DroidNet under different τ_e and τ_d settings. We can see that with higher τ_d (Algorithm 2), the coverage increases while the accuracy decreases. This shows the trade-off between the coverage and accuracy. We also notice that the accuracy increases with experts filtering threshold τ_e. However, with very low or very high τ_e, the coverage is low. This is because when all users are included in the decision process, the conflict

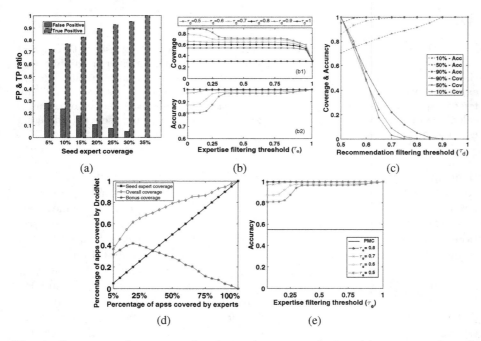

Fig. 8. Coverage and accuracy of rating and recommendation: (a) accuracy of rated users (high rating) and seed expert coverage relation; (b) percentage of requests that DroidNet makes recommendation; (c) percentage correct recommendations that Droid-Net makes; (d) coverage of overall requests vs. coverage of seed experts; (e) PMP accuracy comparison.

of responses among users leads to low voting score and therefore DroidNet is less likely to make recommendations.

To study the impact from the number of expert users ($\tau_e = 0.9$) to DroidNet performance, we vary the percentage of expert users in the network (10 %, 50 % and 90 %). Figure 8(c) shows the results for the coverage and accuracy. We can see that DroidNet achieves higher coverage and accuracy with more expert users in the system.

Next we study the impact from seed expert coverage. As shown in Fig. 8(d), the overall DroidNet recommendation rate increases with coverage rate from the seed expert. The linear line represents the coverage rate from the seed user. The difference between the overall coverage and seed expert coverage is called the *bonus coverage*. Higher bonus coverage represents a higher utilization of DroidNet. From the economic point of view, if the coverage of seed expert brings cost to the coordinator (since the seed expert is hired), then the bonus coverage brings down cost to the coordinator. The decision makers can choose the optimal seed coverage based on its optimal profit.

In the last experiment, we compare the performance of DroidNet and the PMP system [4]. Figure 8(e) shows that the PMP achieves the accuracy of 0.47, whereas DroidNet's accuracy is higher than 0.8.

7   Discussion and Conclusion

While the major challenges for DroidNet have been discussed, many other ones still remain. In this section we address some potential issues in DroidNet and our solutions to those issues.

False Responses: One of the main threats to the system is the injection of false responses to mislead the recommendation system. We investigated this potential threat and developed a multi-agent game theory model to study the gain and loss of malicious user and the DroidNet defense system. We derived a system configuration to discourage rational attackers to launch such attacks. Furthermore, we also consider enhancing DroidNet in which recommendations are adapted according to each user's different security and privacy needs.

Users' Privacy: As a crowdsourcing based solution, DroidNet collects permission responses from all participating users. To protect the privacy of users, we have designed a privacy-aware data collection mechanism that uses *hashing and salting* method to protect the true identity of the users. The salt is randomly generated upon installation. The solution provides *double-blind* protection, which means attacker who successfully attacked the database will not be able to reverse the function to find out the real phone ID or even verify whether an given phone ID is in the database. Therefore, the identity of the users are well-protected, and the mechanism does not compromise the usability of the collected data.

In summary DroidNet is an Android permission control and recommendation system which serves the goal of helping users perform low-risk resource accessing control on untrusted apps to protect their privacy and potentially improve efficiency of resource usages. The framework allows users to install apps in probation mode where users are prompted with resource accessing requests and make decisions on whether to grant the permissions or not. To assist inexperienced users to make low-risk decisions, DroidNet provides recommendations on permission granting based on the responses from expert users in the system. In order to do so, DroidNet uses crowdsourcing techniques to search for expert users using a transitive Bayesian inference model. Our evaluation results demonstrate that DroidNet can effectively locate expert users in the system through a small set of seed experts. The recommending algorithm can achieve high accuracy and good coverage when parameters are carefully selected. We implemented our system on Android phones and demonstrate that the system is feasible and effective through real user experiments.

References

1. What is the price of free. http://www.cam.ac.uk/research/news/what-is-the-price-of-free
2. F-droid - free and open source android app repository. https://f-droid.org/. Accessed August 2015
3. Bit9 report: pausing google play: more than 100,000 android apps may pose security risks. https://www.bit9.com/files/1/Pausing-Google-Play-October2012.pdf. Accessed May 2015
4. Agarwal, Y., Hall, M.: Protectmyprivacy: detecting and mitigating privacy leaks on IOS devices using crowdsourcing. In: Proceeding of the 11th Annual International Conference on Mobile Systems, Applications, and Services (MobiSys 2013), New York, NY, USA, pp. 97–110. ACM (2013)
5. Amadeo, R.: App Ops: Android 4.3's hidden app permission manager, control permissions for individual apps! http://www.androidpolice.com/2013/07/25/app-ops-android-4-3s-hidden-app-permission-manager-control-permissions-for-individual-apps/
6. Au, K.W.Y., Zhou, Y.F., Huang, Z., Lie, D. Pscout: analyzing the android permission specification. In: Proceedings of the ACM Conference on Computer and Communications Security (CCS 2012), New York, NY, USA, pp. 217–228. ACM (2012)
7. Backes, M., Gerling, S., Hammer, C., Maffei, M., von Styp-Rekowsky, P.: App-Guard – enforcing user requirements on android apps. In: Piterman, N., Smolka, S.A. (eds.) TACAS 2013 (ETAPS 2013). LNCS, vol. 7795, pp. 543–548. Springer, Heidelberg (2013)
8. Barrera, D., Clark, J., McCarney, D., van Oorschot, P.C.: Understanding and improving app installation security mechanisms through empirical analysis of android. In: SPSMD (SPSM 2012), New York, NY, USA, pp. 81–92. ACM (2012)
9. Beresford, A.R., Rice, A., Skehin, N., Sohan, R.: Mockdroid: trading privacy for application functionality on smartphones. In: HotMobile 2011, pp. 49–54 (2011)
10. Enck, W., Ongtang, M., McDaniel, P.D., et al.: Understanding android security. IEEE Secur. Priv. 7(1), 50–57 (2009)
11. Felt, A.P., Chin, E., Hanna, S., Song, D., Wagner, D.: Android permissions demystified. In: 18th CCS, pp. 627–638. ACM (2011)

12. Felt, A.P., Ha, E., Egelman, S., Haney, A., Chin, E., Wagner, D.: Android permissions : user attention, comprehension, and behavior. In: SOUPS 2012, New York, NY, USA, pp. 3:1–3:14. ACM (2012)
13. Guha, S., Jain, M., Padmanabhan, V.N.: Koi: a location-privacy platform for smartphone apps. In: NSDI, NSDI 2012, p. 14. USENIX Association (2012)
14. Hildenbrand, J.: Android app permissions - how google gets it right. http://www.windowsphone.com/
15. Hornyack, P., Han, S., Jung, J., Schechter, S., Wetherall, D.: These aren't the droids you're looking for: retrofitting android to protect data from imperious applications. In: CCS (2011)
16. Ismail, Q., Ahmed, T., Kapadia, A., Reiter, M.K.: Crowdsourced exploration of security configurations. In: Proceedings of the 33rd Annual ACM Conference on Human Factors in Computing Systems (CHI 2015), pp. 467–476, New York, NY, USA. ACM (2015)
17. University of Alabama at Birmingham Online. The future of mobile application. http://businessdegrees.uab.edu/resources/infographics/the-future-of-mobile-application/
18. Rashidi, B., Fung, C., Dude, T.: Ask the experts! android resource access permission recommendation with recDroid. In: 2015 IFIP/IEEE International Symposium on Integrated Network Management (IM), pp. 296–304, May 2015
19. Rashidi, B., Fung, C., Vu, T.: Android fine-grained permission control system with real-time expert recommendations. Pervasive Mob. Comput. (2016)
20. Russello, G., Jimenez, A.B., Naderi, H., van der Mark, W.: Firedroid: hardening security in almost-stock android. In: ACSAC 2013, New York, NY, USA, pp. 319–328. ACM (2013)
21. Shabtai, A., Fledel, Y., Kanonov, U., Elovici, Y., Dolev, S., Glezer, C.: Google android: a comprehensive security assessment. IEEE Secur. Priv. 8(2), 35–44 (2010)
22. Victor, H.: Android's google play beats app store with over 1 million apps, now officially largest. http://www.phonearena.com/news/Androids-Google-Play-beats-App-Store-with-over-1-million-apps-now-officially-largest_id45680
23. Xu, R., Sadi, H., Anderson, R.: Aurasium: practical policy enforcement for android applications. In: 21st CSS, Security 2012, p. 27. USENIX Association (2012)
24. Yang, L., Boushehrinejadmoradi, N., Roy, P., Ganapathy, V., Iftode, L.: Short paper : enhancing users' comprehension of android permissions. In: Proceedings of the Second ACM Workshop on Security and Privacy in Smartphones and Mobile Devices (SPSM 2012), New York, NY, USA, pp. 21–26. ACM (2012)
25. Zhou, Y., Zhang, X., Jiang, X., Freeh, V.W.: Taming information-stealing smartphone applications (on android). In: McCune, J.M., Balacheff, B., Perrig, A., Sadeghi, A.-R., Sasse, A., Beres, Y. (eds.) Trust 2011. LNCS, vol. 6740, pp. 93–107. Springer, Heidelberg (2011)

Information Flow

Spot the Difference: Secure Multi-execution and Multiple Facets

Nataliia Bielova$^{(\boxtimes)}$ and Tamara Rezk

Université Côte d'Azur, Inria, Sophia Antipolis, France
{nataliia.bielova,tamara.rezk}@inria.fr

Abstract. We propose a rigorous comparison of two widely known dynamic information flow mechanisms: Secure Multi-Execution (SME) and Multiple Facets (MF). Informally, it is believed that MF simulates SME while providing better performance. Formally, it is well known that SME has stronger soundness guarantees than MF.

Surprisingly, we discover that even if we approach them to enforce the same soundness guarantees, they are still different. While modeling them in the same language, we are able to precisely identify the features of the semantics that lead to their differences. In the process of comparing them, we also discovered four new mechanisms that share features of MF and SME. We prove that one of them simulates SME, which was falsely believed to be true for MF.

1 Introduction

Information flow security [22] is an important guarantee for computer systems. A common security guarantee, called *noninterference*, requires that the secret inputs to the program do not influence (*flow into*) public outputs. In recent years, with the growing impact of highly dynamic languages such as JavaScript, a significant number of dynamic mechanisms [2–4,12,15,19,24] were proposed for information flow control and enforcement of noninterference.

A dynamic information flow mechanism is *sound* if it ensures equal observable outputs when executions start in equal observable inputs. In other words, a sound dynamic mechanism must detect all insecure executions and enforce noninterference by modifying the insecure executions. An important property of dynamic mechanisms is transparency [6,13]. A dynamic mechanism is *transparent* if it does not modify the executions of the program that are already secure. In other words, a transparent mechanism does not have any "false positives" when it comes to detecting secure executions.

Secure Multi Execution (SME) [12] and Multiple Facets (MF) [4] are two dynamic sound mechanisms to enforce noninterference. For brevity, we call these mechanisms SME monitor and MF monitor.

The main idea behind SME is to execute a program multiple times, one for each security level. Each execution receives only input visible to its level, and a default value for inputs that should not be visible. In this way, executions cannot depend on non observable inputs. Moreover, SME uses a low priority scheduler

© Springer International Publishing Switzerland 2016
I. Askoxylakis et al. (Eds.): ESORICS 2016, Part I, LNCS 9878, pp. 501–519, 2016.
DOI: 10.1007/978-3-319-45744-4_25

so that non-termination does not depend on high inputs. This allows SME to prevent information leaks due to program non-termination.

The main idea behind MF is to execute a program using faceted values, one facet for each security level. When a facet possesses nothing to be observed, there is a special value to signal this. Moreover, based on the Fenton strategy [14], MF also skips assignment to public variables in a context that depends on a secret to prevent implicit information flows.

By appropriately manipulating the faceted values, a single execution of MF is claimed to *simulate* the multiple executions of SME with the primary benefit of being more performant [1,4,25]:

> "Faceted evaluation is a technique for *simulating secure multi-execution* with a single process" – from [25, p. 4]
> "Austin and Flanagan [6] show how secure multi-execution can be *optimized* by executing a single program on faceted values" – from [15, p.15]

One of the two formally studied differences between SME and MF before this work is their soundness guarantee. SME enforces the soundness guarantee of *Termination-Sensitive Noninterference* (TSNI), by preventing information flows when a program has a different termination behaviour based on a secret input. However, MF is only proven to enforce *Termination-Insensitive Noninterference (TINI)*, a weaker information flow policy [22] that does not prevent leaks due to program non-termination. For transparency, SME has been proved to be TSNI precise [12,27], a flavour of monitor transparency which means that SME outputs without changes any execution of a noninterferent program. In contrast, MF is recently demonstrated not to be TINI precise [9].

In this work, we investigate if the generalized belief on the equivalence of SME and MF can be formally supported by appropriate hypotheses. Hence, we raised the following questions:

- Are these monitors essentially different or do they become semantically equivalent when adapted to the same soundness guarantees?
- Can SME and MF actually be adapted to other soundness guarantees?

Our contributions are the following:

- A formal demonstration of the differences between SME and MF in a simple programming language. We underline their different guarantees in Sect. 4.
- A comparison of different SME-based and MF-based monitors with respect to soundness and transparency. We have discovered four new monitors:
  - SME-TINI monitor, based on SME, which enforces a weaker termination-insensitive noninterference policy than SME.
  - MFd monitor, based on MF, which is semantically equivalent to SME-TINI (Sect. 5).
  - MFd-TSNI monitor, based on MFd, semantically equivalent to the original SME (Sect. 6).

- MF-TSNI monitor, based on MF, which enforces a stronger termination-sensitive noninterference policy than original MF.

The comparison of the guarantees of all the monitors described in this paper is summarized in Fig. 8 (Sect. 8). The companion technical report [8] includes all the proofs as well as more details and a formalization of the MFd-TSNI monitor in a language with input and output channels as the one of [12].

2   Soundness and Transparency

The syntax of the language to demonstrate our technical results is:

(programs) $P ::= \mathtt{skip} \mid x := e \mid P_1; P_2 \mid \mathtt{if}\ x\ \mathtt{then}\ P_1\ \mathtt{else}\ P_2 \mid \mathtt{while}\ x\ \mathtt{do}\ P$

(expressions) $e ::= v \mid x \mid e_1 \oplus e_2$

The language's expressions include constants or values (v), variables (x) and operators ($\oplus$) to combine them. We present the standard big-step deterministic semantics denoted by $(P, \mu) \Downarrow \mu'$, where P is the program, and μ is a memory mapping variables to values (Fig. 1).

$$\text{SKIP}\ \frac{}{(\mathtt{skip}, \mu) \Downarrow \mu} \qquad \text{ASSIGN}\ \frac{}{(x := e, \mu) \Downarrow \mu[x \mapsto [\![e]\!]_\mu]} \qquad \text{SEQ}\ \frac{(P_1, \mu) \Downarrow \mu' \qquad (P_2, \mu') \Downarrow \mu''}{(P_1; P_2, \mu) \Downarrow \mu''}$$

$$\text{IF}\ \frac{[\![x]\!]_\mu = \alpha \qquad (P_\alpha, \mu) \Downarrow \mu'}{(\mathtt{if}\ x\ \mathtt{then}\ P_{true}\ \mathtt{else}\ P_{false}, \mu) \Downarrow \mu'} \qquad \text{WHILE}\ \frac{(\mathtt{if}\ x\ \mathtt{then}\ P; \mathtt{while}\ x\ \mathtt{do}\ P\ \mathtt{else}\ \mathtt{skip}, \mu) \Downarrow \mu'}{(\mathtt{while}\ x\ \mathtt{do}\ P, \mu) \Downarrow \mu'}$$

where $[\![x]\!]_\mu = \mu(x)$, $[\![v]\!]_\mu = v$ and $[\![e_1 \oplus e_2]\!]_\mu = [\![e_1]\!]_\mu \oplus [\![e_2]\!]_\mu$

Fig. 1. Language semantics

Noninterference. We assume a two-element security lattice with $L \sqsubseteq H$ and a security environment Γ that maps program variables to security levels. By μ_L we denote the projection of the memory μ on low variables, according to an implicitly parameterized security environment Γ. We first define noninterferent executions, following [9].

Definition 1 (Termination-Sensitive Noninterference for μ_L). *Given a semantics relation $\Downarrow$, program P is termination-sensitive noninterferent for an initial low memory μ_L, written $TSNI_\Downarrow(P, \mu_L)$, if and only if for all memories μ^1 and μ^2, such that $\mu_L^1 = \mu_L^2 = \mu_L$ we have $\exists \mu'.(P, \mu^1) \Downarrow \mu' \Rightarrow \exists \mu''.(P, \mu^2) \Downarrow \mu'' \wedge \mu_L' = \mu_L''$.*

Program P is *termination-sensitive noninterferent*, written $TSNI_\Downarrow(P)$, if all its executions are TSNI, that is, for all μ_L, $TSNI_\Downarrow(P, \mu_L)$ holds.

Example 1. Consider Program 1, where variable h can take only two possible values: 0 and 1.

₁ l = 1; if h = 1 then (while true do skip)	**Program 1**

If an attacker observes that l=1, she learns that h was 0, and if she doesn't see any program output (divergence), then she learns that h was 1. TSNI captures this kind of information leakage, hence TSNI doesn't hold.

A weaker security condition, called *termination-insensitive noninterference* (*TINI*), allows information leakage through program divergence.

Definition 2 (Termination-Insensitive Noninterference for μ_L). *Given a semantics relation* $\Downarrow$, *program P is* termination-insensitive noninterferent *for an initial low memory* μ_L, *written* $TINI_{\Downarrow}(P, \mu_L)$, *if and only if for all* μ^1 *and* μ^2, *such that* $\mu_L^1 = \mu_L^2 = \mu_L$, *we have* $\exists \mu'.(P, \mu^1) \Downarrow \mu' \wedge \exists \mu''.(P, \mu^2) \Downarrow \mu'' \Rightarrow \mu_L' = \mu_L''$.

Program P is *termination-insensitive noninterferent*, written $TINI_{\Downarrow}(P)$, if all its executions are TINI, that is, for all μ_L, $TINI_{\Downarrow}(P, \mu_L)$ holds[1].

Termination-insensitive noninterference is a strictly weaker property than termination-sensitive noninterference [22]. For example, Program 1 is insecure with respect to TSNI, however it is secure with respect to TINI since whenever a program execution terminates, it always finishes in a memory with l=1.

Monitor Soundness and Transparency. To define a *sound monitor* for termination-sensitive (resp., -insensitive) noninterference, we only substitute the semantics relation $\Downarrow$ with the monitor semantics relation $\Downarrow_M$ in the definitions of TINI and TSNI. Instead of using a subscript $\Downarrow_M$ (e.g., in $TINI_{\Downarrow_M}$) for a semantics of a monitor M, we will use a subscript M (e.g., $TINI_M$).

Definition 3 (Soundness). *Monitor M is* termination-sensitive (resp., -insensitive) sound *if for all programs P, $TSNI_M(P)$ (resp., $TINI_M(P)$).*

A number of works on dynamic information flow monitors try to analyse transparency of monitors. Intuitively, transparency describes how often a monitor accepts (doesn't block or modify) secure program executions without changing the original semantics. Different approaches have been taken to compare transparency of monitors (see [9] for a survey): in this work, we adhere to the standard meaning [6,13] of "transparency" as the capability of a monitor to accept secure executions and use the term "precision" as the capability to accept all executions of secure programs. To formally define transparency, we first define a predicate $\mathcal{A}(P, \mu, M)$ (where $\mathcal{A}$ stands for "accepted") that holds if:

– whenever a program P terminates for an initial memory μ, then the monitor M will also terminate on μ, producing the same final memory as the original program: $\exists \mu'. (P, \mu) \Downarrow \mu' \Rightarrow (P, \mu) \Downarrow_M \mu'$, and

---

[1] In the following, we don't write the semantics relation $\Downarrow$ when we mean the original program semantics and the semantics is clear from the context.

– whenever a program P does not terminate for an initial memory μ (denoted by $\perp$), then the monitor does not terminate for μ: $(P, \mu) \Downarrow \perp \Rightarrow (P, \mu) \Downarrow_M \perp$.

The notion of *transparency* for TSNI (TINI) requires a monitor to accept all the TSNI (TINI) executions of a program. Our choice of transparency definition is based on the original literature on runtime monitors [6, 13], which requires that if a program execution is secure (noninterferent), then the monitor must accept this execution without modifications. Our definition is similar to the one of [21], which considers both terminating and nonterminating executions, however it differs because we don't require the set of executions accepted by a monitor and the set of noninterferent executions to be equal.

Definition 4 (Transparency). *Monitor M is* TSNI *(resp., TINI) transparent if for any program P, and any memory μ, $TINI(P, \mu_L) \Rightarrow \mathcal{A}(P, \mu, M)$ (resp., $TSNI(P, \mu_L) \Rightarrow \mathcal{A}(P, \mu, M)$).*

3   SME and MF Original Semantics

In order to compare SME and MF, we first model them in the same language defined in Sect. 2. The semantics relation of a command P is denoted by $\Gamma \vdash (P, \mu) \Downarrow_M \mu'$ where Γ is a security environment, and M is the name of the monitor and $\Downarrow_M$ relates a program configuration and a memory. Both SME and MF monitors have deterministic semantics.

Secure Multi-execution (SME). Devriese and Piessens proposed secure multi-execution (SME) [12]. The idea of SME is to execute the program multiple times: one for each security level. SME has two mechanisms to enforce noninterference:

– Each execution receives only inputs visible to its security level and a fixed default value for each input that should not be visible to the execution. This default value predefines a so-called "default" execution, so that under SME all the interferent executions would behave like a "default" execution.
– A low priority scheduler ensures that lower executions do not depend on the termination of higher executions. Therefore, the low priority scheduler ensures that the program termination based on a secret input does not influence a public output, and hence enforces TSNI.

The SME adaptation for the while language, taken from [9], is given in Fig. 2, with executions for levels L and H. The $\mu|_\Gamma$ function substitutes the values of all the high variables in μ with the default value def_H, such that all the insecure program executions will behave as an execution predefined by def_H.

Example 2 (SME imitates "default" executions). Consider the following program and assume that the SME's default value is $\text{def}_H = 0$.

```
1 l = 1; if h = 0 then l = 0                                    Program 2
```

$$\text{SME} \; \dfrac{(P, \mu|_\Gamma) \Downarrow \mu_2 \qquad \mu_1 = \begin{cases} \mu' & \text{if } \exists \mu'.(P, \mu) \Downarrow \mu' \\ \bot & \text{otherwise} \end{cases}}{\Gamma \vdash (P, \mu) \Downarrow_{\text{SME}} \mu_1 \odot_\Gamma \mu_2}$$

where

$$\mu|_\Gamma(x) = \begin{cases} \text{def}_H & \Gamma(x) = H \\ \mu(x) & \Gamma(x) = L \end{cases} \qquad \mu_1 \odot_\Gamma \mu_2(x) = \begin{cases} \mu_1(x) & \Gamma(x) = H \\ \mu_2(x) & \Gamma(x) = L \end{cases}$$

Fig. 2. Secure Multi-execution semantics (SME)

A "default" execution would take def_H value instead of a real high value and compute the final memory with $\mathtt{l}{=}0$. This program is not TINI, and therefore all its executions will terminate under SME with the memory where $\mathtt{l}{=}0$.

In our SME semantics, the special runtime value $\bot$ represents the idea that no value can be observed (notice that original programs use only standard values). We overload the symbol to also denote a memory that maps every variable to $\bot$. Using memory $\bot$ we simulate the low priority scheduler of SME in our setting: *if the high execution does not terminate*, the low observer will still see the low part of the memory in the SME semantics. In this case all the high variables, whose values should correspond to values obtained in the normal execution of the program, are given value $\bot$. We model the final memory by a merging function $\odot_\Gamma$ that combines high and low parts of two final memories from high and low executions. Notice that even though the semantics becomes non computable, this model allows us to prove the same results as for the original SME and further use it for comparison with MF.

Example 3 (SME prevents leakage through non-termination). Consider Program 3:

```
1 if l = 0 then (while h=0 do skip)                  Program 3
2 else (while h=1 do skip)
```

This program is TINI but not TSNI. Assume $\mu = [\mathtt{h}{=}0,\ \mathtt{l}{=}1]$ and that the default high value used by SME is $\text{def}_H{=}1$. The program terminates on memory μ, producing $\mathtt{l}{=}0$, however there exists a memory $\mu' = [\mathtt{h}{=}0,\ \mathtt{l}{=}1]$, low-equal to μ, on which the original program doesn't terminate, thus leaking secret information through non-termination. SME prevents such leakage, because SME terminates on both memories μ and μ' producing $\mathtt{l}{=}0$.

Multiple Facets (MF). Austin and Flanagan [4] proposed multiple facets (MF). In MF, each variable is mapped to several values or facets, one for each security level: each value corresponds to the view of the variable The main mechanisms used by MF are the following:

– MF uses a special value $\bot$ to signal that a variable contains no information to be observed at a given security level.

– MF uses the Fenton strategy [14] that skips *sensitive upgrades*. A sensitive upgrade is an assignment to a low variable in a high security context that may cause an implicit information flow. If there is a sensitive upgrade, MF semantics does not update the observable facet. Otherwise, if there is no sensitive upgrade, MF semantics updates it according to the original semantics.

$$\text{MF} \quad \boxed{\dfrac{(P, \mu \uparrow_\Gamma) \downarrow_{MF} \hat{\mu}}{\Gamma \vdash (P, \mu) \Downarrow_{\mathbf{MF}} \hat{\mu} \downarrow_\Gamma}} \qquad\qquad \text{SKIP} \ \dfrac{}{(\mathsf{skip}, \hat{\mu}) \downarrow_{MF} \hat{\mu}}$$

$$\text{ASSIGN} \ \dfrac{}{(x := e, \hat{\mu}) \downarrow_{MF} \hat{\mu}[x \mapsto [e]_{\hat{\mu}}]} \qquad \text{SEQ} \ \dfrac{(P_1, \hat{\mu}) \downarrow_{MF} \hat{\mu}' \qquad (P_2, \hat{\mu}') \downarrow_{MF} \hat{\mu}''}{(P_1; P_2, \hat{\mu}) \downarrow_{MF} \hat{\mu}''}$$

$$\text{IF-BOT} \ \dfrac{[x]_{\hat{\mu}} = \langle \alpha : \perp \rangle \qquad (P_\alpha, \hat{\mu}) \downarrow_{MF} \hat{\mu}'}{(\mathsf{if}\ x\ \mathsf{then}\ P_{true}\ \mathsf{else}\ P_{false}, \hat{\mu}) \downarrow_{MF} \hat{\mu}' \otimes \hat{\mu}}$$

$$\text{IF-VAL} \ \dfrac{[x]_{\hat{\mu}} = \langle \alpha_1 : \alpha_2 \rangle \qquad \alpha_2 \neq \perp \qquad (P_{\alpha_1}, \hat{\mu}) \downarrow_{MF} \hat{\mu}_1 \qquad (P_{\alpha_2}, \hat{\mu}) \downarrow_{MF} \hat{\mu}_2}{(\mathsf{if}\ x\ \mathsf{then}\ P_{true}\ \mathsf{else}\ P_{false}, \hat{\mu}) \downarrow_{MF} \hat{\mu}_1 \otimes \hat{\mu}_2}$$

$$\text{WHILE} \ \dfrac{(\mathsf{if}\ x\ \mathsf{then}\ P; \mathsf{while}\ x\ \mathsf{do}\ P\ \mathsf{else}\ \mathsf{skip}, \hat{\mu}) \downarrow_{MF} \hat{\mu}'}{(\mathsf{while}\ x\ \mathsf{do}\ P, \hat{\mu}) \downarrow_{MF} \hat{\mu}'}$$

where

$$\mu \uparrow_\Gamma (x) = \begin{cases} \langle \mu(x) : \perp \rangle & \text{if } \Gamma(x) = H \\ \langle \mu(x) : \mu(x) \rangle & \text{if } \Gamma(x) = L \end{cases} \qquad \hat{\mu} \downarrow_\Gamma (x) = \begin{cases} \hat{\mu}(x)_1 & \text{if } \Gamma(x) = H \\ \hat{\mu}(x)_2 & \text{if } \Gamma(x) = L \end{cases}$$

and $\hat{\mu}_1 \otimes \hat{\mu}_2 (x) = \langle \hat{\mu}_1(x)_1 : \hat{\mu}_2(x)_2 \rangle$

Fig. 3. Multiple Facets semantics (MF)

Our adaptation of MF semantics is given in Fig. 3, where we use the following notation: a faceted value, denoted $\hat{v} = \langle v_1 : v_2 \rangle$, is a pair of values v_1 and v_2. The first value presents the view of an observer at level H and the second value the view of an observer at level L. In the syntax, we interpret a constant v as the faceted value $\langle v : v \rangle$. The evaluation of faceted expressions is strict in $\perp$ – if an expression contains $\perp$ then it evaluates to $\perp$ – and it is defined as follows:

$$[\hat{v}]_{\hat{\mu}} = \hat{v} \qquad [x]_{\hat{\mu}} = \hat{\mu}(x) \qquad [e_1 \oplus e_2]_{\hat{\mu}} = [e_1]_{\hat{\mu}} \oplus [e_2]_{\hat{\mu}}$$

where $\langle v_1 : v_1' \rangle \oplus \langle v_2 : v_2' \rangle = \langle v_1 \oplus v_2 : v_1' \oplus v_2' \rangle$.

Faceted memories, ranged over by $\hat{\mu}$, are mappings from variables to faceted values. A function $\mu \uparrow_\Gamma$ creates a faceted memory from a memory μ using the labelling function Γ, and function $\hat{\mu} \downarrow_\Gamma$ erases facets from the faceted memory $\hat{\mu}$ and returns a normal memory μ. We use the notation $\hat{\mu}(x)_i$ ($i \in \{1, 2\}$) for the first or second projection of a faceted value stored in x. Similar to the formalisation of SME, the special runtime value $\perp$ represents the idea that no value can be observed (program syntax only uses standard values). Moreover, MF skips any operation that depends on a value $\perp$ (see rule IF-BOT in Fig. 3).

Example 4 (MF uses $\bot$ to signal "no information"). Consider the following program, that copies the secret from h to low variable 1 : 1 = h. Given an initial environment $\mu=$ [h=0, 1=1], the function $\mu \uparrow_\Gamma$ creates a faceted memory $\hat{\mu}$, where h = $\langle 1 : \bot \rangle$. After assignment, the variable 1 will contain the faceted value of h, that will be projected to the $\bot$ value using the function $\hat{\mu} \downarrow_\Gamma$ to erase facets in the end of the execution.

Example 5 (MF "skips" sensitive upgrades). Consider Program 4.

₁ 1 = 0; if h = 1 then 1 = 1 else 1 = 2   **Program 4**

In MF, the L facet of variable 1 will be the initial value of variable 1 since MF will not update a low variable in a high context. Therefore, all the executions of Program 4 are modified by MF, producing the final memory with 1=0.

4   Differences Between SME and MF

Even though MF is claimed to simulate SME, the example below demonstrates that even in a simple language, SME and MF semantics are different.

Example 6 (SME and MF semantics are different) Consider Program 5 and an initial memory [h=0, 1=0].

₁ 1 = 0;   **Program 5**
₂ if h = 0 then 1 = 1;
₃ if 1 = 1 then 1 = 2 else 1 = 3

This program terminates in MF with the final memory where 1=3 because the value of 1 is not updated due to a sensitive upgrade. In contrast, under SME with $\text{def}_H = 0$, the program terminates with the final memory where 1=2.

Projection Theorem of MF. For MF semantics, a Projection Theorem [4, Theorem 1] states that a computation over a 2-faceted memory simulates 2 non-faceted computations, one per each security level. The theorem uses a projection of a faceted memory into a normal memory using the following functions (simplified for our setting), where Lev represents either a high viewer H or a low viewer L, so that $H(\langle v_1 : v_2 \rangle) = v_1, L(\langle v_1 : v_2 \rangle) = v_2, Lev(\hat{\mu}) = \lambda x.Lev(\hat{\mu}(x))$

The Projection Theorem states that whenever the monitor terminates[2] for some memory $\hat{\mu}$, $\Gamma \vdash (P, \hat{\mu}) \downarrow_{MF} \hat{\mu}'$, then for any viewer Lev,

$$(P, Lev(\hat{\mu})) \Downarrow Lev(\hat{\mu}').$$

The Projection Theorem may resemble to an equivalence between SME and MF semantics, however, as we have shown above, MF is not equivalent to SME.

---

[2] Notice that the original program semantics in [4] already contains rules that deal with special $\bot$ values, that skip any operation that involves a $\bot$ value.

Example 7 (Projection Theorem of MF doesn't imply equivalence to SME). Consider Program 6 and an initial memory μ=[h=1, l=1]. This program is TINI and TSNI and SME would terminate in the memory $\mu' = $ [h=1, l=0].

```
1 if h = 0 then l = 0 else l = 0                                          Program 6
```

The Projection theorem is based on the assumption that MF terminates on a given initial faceted memory. We use the function $\mu \uparrow_\Gamma$ that creates a faceted memory from a normal memory μ given a security labelling Γ. The obtained memory is $\hat{\mu} = $ [h = $\langle 1 : \bot \rangle$, l = $\langle 1 : 1 \rangle$]. Upon a faceted execution of the program, the final faceted memory is $\hat{\mu}' = $ [h = $\langle 1 : \bot \rangle$, l = $\langle 0 : 1 \rangle$].

For a viewer at level H, the initial projected memory is $H(\hat{\mu})$ =[h=1, l=1], and the final projected memory is $H(\hat{\mu}')$=[h=1, l=0], which corresponds to the original final memory μ'. However, only a viewer a level H is able to see this memory, while a viewer at level L will see a different memory.

For a viewer at level L, the projected initial memory is $L(\hat{\mu})$ =[h = $\bot$, l = 1], and the final projected memory is also $L(\hat{\mu}')$ =[h = $\bot$, l = 1], since the mechanism of MF skips the sensitive upgrades and the value of l is not changed. It means that a viewer at level L will see l=1 in MF, however will see l=0 in SME.

Soundness. Monitors that enforce TSNI and TINI are comparable with respect to soundness thanks to the fact that TSNI is a stronger guarantee than TINI [22]. SME was previously proven TSNI sound [12], and therefore SME is also TINI sound. Example 3 demonstrated how SME enforces TSNI and hence TINI soundness. In contrast, MF was previously proven TINI sound [4], however it is unable to enforce TSNI.

Example 8 (MF is not TSNI sound). Consider Program 1. When h=1, the MF semantics will diverge because the faceted value of h is $\langle 1 : \bot \rangle$ and the premises of the IF-BOT rule are not satisfied (the program diverges on line 3). However when h=0, the MF semantics will terminate with final memory where l=1.

Transparency. Devriese and Piessens [12, Theorem 2] have proven that SME is TSNI precise, meaning that for TSNI secure programs, all their executions are not modified by SME.

Theorem 1 ([12, Thm. 12]). *SME is TSNI precise, meaning that for any program P, the following holds: $TSNI(P) \Rightarrow \forall \mu. \mathcal{A}(P, \mu, SME)$.*

In this paper, we prove a more fine-grained guarantee for SME, which is TSNI transparency. Notice that TSNI transparency is stronger than TSNI precision because it requires that the monitor not only does not modify any executions of secure programs, but also secure executions of insecure programs.

Theorem 2. *SME is TSNI transparent.*

Example 9. Consider Program 7.This program is not TSNI, however there are TSNI-secure executions of this program when initially l=1. For an initial memory where l=1, and for any default high value $\mathtt{def}_H$, SME will terminate in a final memory, where l=1, like the original program.

₁ **if l=0 then (while h=0 do skip)**   **Program 7**

Example 10 (MF is not TSNI and not TINI transparent). Consider Program 6, which is TSNI secure, and an initial memory [h=1, l=1]. The MF semantics will modify this execution. Since the test depends on a high variable h, the IF-BOT rule will be used to evaluate the conditional, and only the high facet of the value in l will be updated, getting the value 0, while the low facet will not be updated, hence the new faceted value of l is $\langle 0 : 1 \rangle$. Following the definition of the $\downarrow_\Gamma$ function, the final memory will contain l=1 because $\Gamma(\mathtt{l}) = L$, while the original program would terminate in the memory where l=0. Hence, this is a counter example for TSNI and TINI transparency of MF.

5   SME vs MF by Downgrading SME to TINI

The first reason for SME and MF to be incomparable is that SME enforces termination-sensitive noninterference (TSNI), whereas MF enforces a weaker version of noninterference called termination-insensitive noninterference (TINI). To formally compare SME and MF, we modify SME semantics in order for SME to enforce the same version of noninterference as MF, which is TINI.

SME that Enforces TINI (SME-TINI). We propose a version of SME, that we call SME-TINI and present its semantics in Fig. 4. SME-TINI runs the program multiple times like SME, but it does not have a low priority scheduler and hence is not sensitive to termination leaks.

$$\text{SME-TINI} \quad \frac{(P, \mu|_\Gamma) \Downarrow \mu_2 \qquad (P, \mu) \Downarrow \mu_1}{\Gamma \vdash (P, \mu) \Downarrow_{\text{SMETINI}} \mu_1 \odot_\Gamma \mu_2}$$

Fig. 4. SME semantics for TINI (SME-TINI)

Example 11 (SME-TINI does not enforce TSNI). Consider Program 1 and a default value for SME is $\mathtt{def}_H = 0$. In an initial memory where h=1, the program will diverge in the SME-TINI semantics whereas it will terminate with the memory l=1 in the SME semantics. In an initial memory where h=0, the program will terminate with l=1 in both SME-TINI and SME semantics. This example shows that, in contrast to SME, SME-TINI does not enforce TSNI.

Theorem 3. *SME-TINI is TINI sound.*

Example 12 (SME-TINI is TINI sound). Consider Program 4 and an initial memory [h=1,l=0]. SME-TINI with $\text{def}_H = 0$ enforces TINI by always terminating in a final memory where l=2.

However, differently from original SME, SME-TINI does not provide transparency guarantee.

Example 13 (SME-TINI is not TINI transparent). Consider Program 3, an initial memory μ=[h=0, l=1] and def_H=1. The original program terminates on memory μ= [h=0, l=1]. Though program is TINI, SME-TINI does not terminate on μ because its low execution does not terminate since def_H=1.

Surprisingly, we find out that even if we downgrade SME to only enforce TINI, and SME-TINI and MF now have the same soundness guarantees, still SME-TINI and MF semantics are different.

Example 14 (SME-TINI and MF semantics are different). Consider again Program 4 and an initial memory [h=1, l=0]. SME-TINI with $\text{def}_H = 0$ enforces TINI by always producing an output 2, however MF does not execute an alternative else-branch, and keeps an initial value of 1, terminating with the final memory where l=0.

The main reason for a different semantics now is the way in which SME-TINI and MF treat insecure executions: while SME forces all insecure executions to behave like the "default" executions, MF uses the Fenton strategy to skip sensitive upgrades.

Multiple Facets with Default (MFd). To propose a version of MF that has the same semantics as SME-TINI, we replace the $\bot$ value of MF with def_H as the default high value (this is exactly as the default of SME). In fact, there is a maybe different default high value for each high variable, so in fact def_H is a vector of variables but for simplicity of presentation (and without loss of generality), we call it a default value and use only one high variable in our examples.

The new version of MF, that we call MFd, uses the semantics rules of MF, and instead of a $\mu \uparrow_\Gamma$ function that creates a faceted memory in the MF rule, it uses a $\mu \uparrow_\Gamma^{\text{def}}$ function, that is defined as follows:

$$\mu \uparrow_\Gamma^{\text{def}} (x) = \begin{cases} \langle \mu(x) : \mu(x) \rangle & \text{if } \Gamma(x) = L \\ \langle \mu(x) : \text{def}_H \rangle & \text{if } \Gamma(x) = H \end{cases}$$

Therefore, the MFd semantics is presented with only one rule shown in Fig. 5. Since the MFd semantics never introduces a runtime value $\bot$, the MFd rules do not include the rule IF-BOT of the original MF semantics (Fig. 3). Notice that, the fact that the rule IF-BOT is not included implies that one of the bases of original MF, which is to skip sensitive upgrades as originally proposed by Fenton [14], is made obsolete.

$$\text{MFd} \quad \frac{(P, \mu \uparrow_{\Gamma}^{\text{def}}) \downarrow_{MF} \hat{\mu}}{\Gamma \vdash (P, \mu) \Downarrow_{\text{MFd}} \hat{\mu} \downarrow_{\Gamma}}$$

Fig. 5. Multiple Facets with default (MFd).

Theorem 4. *MFd is TINI sound.*

To prove that MFd is equivalent to SME-TINI, we first propose the following definition of an equivalence relation on two monitor semantics.

Definition 5. *A monitor A is semantically equivalent to a monitor B, written $A \approx B$, if and only if for all programs P, all memories μ and μ', and all labelling functions Γ, the following holds:*

$$\Gamma \vdash (P, \mu) \Downarrow_A \mu' \iff \Gamma \vdash (P, \mu) \Downarrow_B \mu'.$$

Theorem 5. *MFd $\approx$ SME-TINI.*

Example 15 (MFd and SME-TINI semantics are equivalent). Consider Program 4 and an initial memory [h=1, l=0]. SME-TINI with $\text{def}_H = 0$ always terminates in a final memory where l=2. MFd also terminates in a final memory with l=2, because differently from original MF, it does not skip the sensitive upgrades but rather uses the results of the "default" execution, like SME.

6   SME vs MF by Upgrading MFd to TSNI

By analysing SME and MF semantics, we concluded that they are different for two reasons. First, SME enforces TSNI, while MF enforces TINI. In the previous section we have downgraded SME to enforce a weaker property TINI, however the resulting SME-TINI monitor was not semantically equivalent to MF. Therefore, we have found the second reason for their difference: while SME is using a default value for high variables in the low execution, MF uses special runtime values $\perp$, allowing the execution of some branches to be skipped.

In the previous section we proposed a new version of MF, called MFd, that solves the second difference of SME and MF, but does not solve the first one: MFd does not have the same strong soundness guarantee, TSNI, that original SME has. Therefore, we propose modifications to the MFd semantics in order for MFd to enforce TSNI.

We propose a new monitor, that we call MFd-TSNI, and present its semantics in Fig. 6. The main difference between MFd and MFd-TSNI is the embedding of a low priority scheduler to schedule with priority the low facet in the execution. This can be observed in the rules IF-VAL and IF-BOT-VAL. The rule IF-VAL simulates the idea behind the low priority scheduler from original SME. The symbol $\perp$ is overloaded to denote a memory that maps every variable to $\perp$ when the high execution does not terminate. We illustrate the efficiency of MFd-TSNI in enforcing TSNI in the following example.

Example 16. Consider Program 8 which is not TSNI and initial memory $\mu=$ [h=1, l=1], the default value used to create a faceted memory is $\mathtt{def}_H = 0$.

```
1 if h=1 then (while true skip);                    Program 8
2 if h=0 then l=0
```

An initial value of h in the new faceted memory $\hat{\mu}$ is h=$\langle 1 : 0 \rangle$, while l $= \langle 1 : 1 \rangle$. Upon the first test, the IF-VAL rule is applied. This rule first requires that the execution corresponding to the low facet terminates, which is the case and the final faceted memory after the first test is $\hat{\mu}_2 = \hat{\mu}$. However, the program does not terminate if we use the high facet of h, therefore all the program variables get assigned to $\bot$ in a memory $\hat{\mu}_1$. After the combination of memories, we get the final memory after the first test, which is $\hat{\mu}_1 \otimes \hat{\mu}_2$, where h $= \langle \bot : 0 \rangle$ and l $= \langle \bot : 1 \rangle$.

Upon the second test, the IF-BOT-VAL rule is applied since the high facet of variable h is now $\bot$. Therefore, MFd-TSNI executes only one branch where h=0 and computes the final memory where l $= \langle 0 : 0 \rangle$.

$$\text{MFD-TSNI} \quad \boxed{\dfrac{(P, \mu \uparrow_\Gamma^{def}) \downarrow_{MFT} \hat{\mu}}{\Gamma \vdash (P, \mu) \Downarrow_{\mathbf{MFdT}} \hat{\mu} \downarrow_\Gamma}} \qquad \text{SKIP} \dfrac{}{(\mathsf{skip}, \hat{\mu}) \downarrow_{MFT} \hat{\mu}}$$

$$\text{ASSIGN} \dfrac{}{(x := e, \hat{\mu}) \downarrow_{MFT} (\hat{\mu}[x \mapsto [e]_{\hat{\mu}}])} \qquad \text{SEQ} \dfrac{(P_1, \hat{\mu}) \downarrow_{MFT} \hat{\mu}' \qquad (P_2, \hat{\mu}') \downarrow_{MFT} \hat{\mu}''}{(P_1; P_2, \hat{\mu}) \downarrow_{MFT} \hat{\mu}''}$$

$$\text{IF-BOT-VAL} \dfrac{[x]_{\hat{\mu}} = \langle \bot : \alpha \rangle \qquad \alpha \neq \bot \qquad (P_\alpha, \hat{\mu}) \downarrow_{MFT} \hat{\mu}'}{(\text{if } x \text{ then } P_{true} \text{ else } P_{false}, \hat{\mu}) \downarrow_{MFT} \bot \otimes \hat{\mu}'}$$

$$\text{IF-VAL} \dfrac{\begin{array}{c} [x]_{\hat{\mu}} = \langle \alpha_1 : \alpha_2 \rangle \qquad \alpha_1 \neq \bot \\ \alpha_2 \neq \bot \quad (P_{\alpha_2}, \hat{\mu}) \downarrow_{MFT} \hat{\mu}_2 \qquad \hat{\mu}_1 = \begin{cases} \hat{\mu}' & \text{if } \exists \hat{\mu}'.(P_{\alpha_1}, \hat{\mu}) \downarrow_{MFT} \hat{\mu}' \\ \bot & \text{otherwise} \end{cases} \end{array}}{(\text{if } x \text{ then } P_{true} \text{ else } P_{false}, \hat{\mu}) \downarrow_{MFT} \hat{\mu}_1 \otimes \hat{\mu}_2}$$

$$\text{WHILE} \dfrac{(\text{if } x \text{ then } P; \text{while } x \text{ do } P \text{ else } \mathsf{skip}, \hat{\mu}) \downarrow_{MFT} \hat{\mu}'}{(\text{while } x \text{ do } P, \hat{\mu}) \downarrow_{MFT} \hat{\mu}'}$$

Fig. 6. Multiple Facets semantics with default for TSNI (MFd-TSNI)

We prove that the new monitor MFd-TSNI is semantically equivalent to original SME.

Theorem 6. *MFd-TSNI ≈ SME.*

As a direct consequence of the semantical equivalence to SME, MFd-TSNI is TSNI sound and TSNI transparent. Notice that MFd was not transparent.

Theorem 7. *MFd-TSNI is TSNI sound and TSNI transparent.*

Example 17. (MFd-TSNI is TINI sound and TSNI sound). Consider Program 4 and $\mathsf{def}_H = 0$. For any initial memory, MFd-TSNI always terminates in final memory where l=2, thus enforcing TINI and TSNI.

Example 18. (MFd-TSNI is TSNI transparent). Consider again Program 7. For the initial memory where l=1, and for any default high value def_H, MFd-TSNI will terminate in a final memory, where l=1, like the original program.

MF that enforces TSNI. Given the technique we used to upgrade MFd to MFd-TSNI to enforce termination-sensitive noninterference, in this section we show how to upgrade the original MF in order to enforce TSNI using the same low priority scheduler.

The new monitor, that we call MF-TSNI, uses the $\uparrow_\Gamma$ function from MF to create a faceted memory, and uses all the rules of MFd-TSNI, with additional two rules to incorporate the possibility of having a special $\bot$ value in the low facet of the faceted value. We present these additional rules in Fig. 7.

$$
\text{MF-TSNI} \quad \frac{(P, \mu \uparrow_\Gamma) \downarrow_{MFT} \hat{\mu}}{\Gamma \vdash (P, \mu) \Downarrow_{\mathbf{MFT}} \hat{\mu} \downarrow_\Gamma}
$$

$$
\text{IF-BOT} \quad \frac{[x]_{\hat{\mu}} = \langle \alpha : \bot \rangle \qquad \alpha \neq \bot \qquad \hat{\mu}_1 = \begin{cases} \hat{\mu}' & \text{if } \exists \hat{\mu}'.(P_\alpha, \hat{\mu}) \downarrow_{MFT} \hat{\mu}' \\ \bot & \text{otherwise} \end{cases}}{(\text{if } x \text{ then } P_{true} \text{ else } P_{false}, \hat{\mu}) \downarrow_{MFT} \hat{\mu}_1 \otimes \hat{\mu}}
$$

$$
\text{IF-BOT-BOT} \quad \frac{[x]_{\hat{\mu}} = \langle \bot : \bot \rangle}{(\text{if } x \text{ then } P_{true} \text{ else } P_{false}, \hat{\mu}) \downarrow_{MFT} \hat{\mu}}
$$

Fig. 7. Additional rules for the Multiple Facet semantics for TSNI (MF-TSNI)

We now prove that the new MF-TSNI monitor indeed enforces termination-sensitive noninterference.

Theorem 8. *MF-TSNI is TSNI sound.*

Example 19 (MF-TSNI is TSNI sound and TINI sound). Consider Program 1. When h=1, the IF-BOT rule of MF-TSNI (Fig. 7) will construct a memory $\hat{\mu}_1$, where all the variables are assigned to $\bot$ value since the high facet execution does not terminate. Therefore, MF-TSNI will terminate with the final memory where $l = \langle \bot : 1 \rangle$. When h=0, the MF-TSNI will terminate in the final memory where $l = \langle 1 : 1 \rangle$, thus enforcing TINI and TSNI.

MF-TSNI is not TSNI transparent for the same reason that MF is not TSNI transparent: the Fenton strategy of skipping sensitive upgrades prevents a mechanism from being transparent.

Example 20 (MF-TSNI is not TSNI transparent). Consider again Program 6, which is TSNI and TINI. For an initial memory where l=1, MF-TSNI will terminate in a final memory, where l=1, thus being not transparent.

7 Related Work

We present only SME and MF closely related work. We refer to [22, 23] for a wider overview on information flow properties, to [6, 13, 18] for a wider overview on transparency properties of monitors, and to [9, 17] for a wider overview on information flow monitors.

Originally, Secure Multi-execution is presented in a while language featuring input/output commands and channels [12]. An output command produces a value that is queued in the output channel. An input command reads a value that is read from the input channel. We model SME as in [9], in a while language without channels. Instead of channels, we use memories mapping variables to values. To simulate an input (resp. output) command, our language reads (resp. writes) a variable from memory. In the original SME semantics [12], a configuration contains a pool of threads, one thread for each level. Then, a scheduler selects to execute first all steps of the lower level threads. Hence, all outputs of a low execution appear first in the output channel in the original SME semantics. The low priority scheduler is simulated in our model by the only rule of Fig. 2. In this rule, the low thread executes to the end to obtain the low part of the final memory and, *if the high thread does not terminate*, the high part of the final memory is ⊥. Hence, the semantics becomes non computable. With the current model we can at least prove the same results as in the original SME monitor, and further use it for comparison with MF. Notice that, at the cost of simplicity we could have used the original SME language and semantics in order to have computability (we have modelled the MFd-TSNI monitor in the original SME language as a proof of concept in the companion technical report [8]).

SME is proved to be TSNI sound in Theorem 1 of [12]. Kashyap *et al.* [16] investigate different strategies for SME to also enforce several flavours of time-sensitive noninterference. Intuitively, time-sensitive noninterference is stronger than termination-sensitive noninterference because it requires that two executions starting in low-equal memories must terminate within the same number of program execution steps. Other works [10, 20, 26] have proposed other information flow properties, declassification properties, for modified SME monitors. We do not study in this work SME-based monitors for declassification. SME is proved to be TSNI precise in Theorem 2 of [12]. Notice that TSNI precision is a weaker property than transparency since a program which is not secure may still have some secure executions.

TSNI transparency does not hold for original SME because the low priority scheduler may reorder outputs compared to the original program semantics, letting outputs of low executions appear first in the output channel.

Zanarini et al. [27] propose a modification to SME in order to prove a version of TSNI transparency (In fact, they prove a property called CP precision in Theorem 23 of [27], which is a weaker notion that TSNI transparency because it recognizes as secure a program that silently diverges on one branch, and terminates without producing any outputs on the other branch). In contrast, we can prove TSNI transparency in our SME model (and also CP precision) without need of the SME modifications proposed in Zanarini et al. because reordering is not visible in our model due to the lack of output channels, and intermediate outputs.

Zanarini et al. [27] also prove a version of TINI transparency for their TSNI sound SME-based monitor (Theorem 22 of [27]). Using our notations, their notion of TINI transparency is different from ours since if an execution is secure, if the original program terminates in a final memory μ and *if the monitor terminates* in final memory μ', then μ and μ' should be low equal (in fact, they prove a property called ID-transparency in Theorem 22 of [27], which recognizes as transparent a monitor that always diverges).

SME is also shown TSNI sound and TSNI precise for a language featuring dynamic code evaluation [5] and adapted to reactive systems [7]. SME is implemented in a real browser called FlowFox [11], and SME guarantees via program transformations are implemented in JavaScript and Python [5].

Originally, Multiple Facets is presented in a lambda calculus with mutable reference cells and reactive input/output [4]. In contrast, we model MF in an imperative while language without mutable references. Moreover, since our language features memories that map variables to values, we use security environments as a means to create faceted values in our MF model. As we do, the original MF semantics [4] uses the special value $\bot$ in order to model the Fenton strategy [14], which roughly means to skip sensitive upgrades [2,28] to prevent implicit flows.

MF is also modelled in [9] using an imperative while language as ours. The semantics in [9] uses security environments and program counters in order to implement the Fenton strategy. Our formalisation is simpler since we use facets and $\bot$ to do this, as in [4]. MF is proved to be TINI sound in Theorem 2 of [4] and also is extended to declassification and proved sound in Theorem 6 of [4].

Transparency guarantees of MF are studied in [9]. It was first shown that MF is not TINI transparent (more precisely, TINI transparency is called true transparency in [9]). Using a notion of false transparency, it is then shown that MF can accept more insecure executions than any other information flow monitor with the exception of SME (Table 1 of [9]). Moreover, Theorems 3 and 4 of [4] prove that MF generalizes no-sensitive upgrade monitor (NSU) [2,28] and permissive-upgrade monitor (PU) [3]. These theorems imply that MF is relatively more transparent than NSU and PU [9].

MF has been implemented in JavaScript as a Firefox browser extension [4] and also as a Haskell Library using monads [25].

8 Conclusion

We have formally compared SME, MF, and other mechanisms derived from them. We present a summary of the comparison in Fig. 8 We have first downgraded SME to enforce only TINI, and proposed a new version of MF, called MFd, which is indeed semantically equivalent to a TINI version of SME. We then upgraded the

	Soundness		Transparency	
	TINI	TSNI	TINI	TSNI
SME	✓	✓	✗	✓
MF	✓	✗	✗	✗
SME-TINI	✓	✗	✗	✗
MFd	✓	✗	✗	✗
MFd-TSNI	✓	✓	✗	✓
MF-TSNI	✓	✓	✗	✗

Fig. 8. Summary of our results

MFd monitor to enforce TSNI and proposed a new monitor that we call MFd-TSNI. We have proven that MFd-TSNI is semantically equivalent to SME, and therefore enjoys the same TSNI soundness and TSNI transparency guarantees as SME. Finally, we propose to upgrade MF semantics so that it can also enforce termination-sensitive noninterference (TSNI). The new monitor, that we call MF-TSNI, is not semantically equivalent to MFd-TSNI, and is not TSNI transparent. Both SME [10,20,26], and MF [4] have been extended to handle declassification, a security property more versatile than noninterference. It is left as future work to understand if our results generalize to declassification properties in order to compare SME and MF.

Acknowledgment. We would like to thank Frank Piessens on valuable feedback on earlier versions of this paper and anonymous reviewers who helped us to improve the paper. This work has been partially supported by the ANR project AJACS ANR-14-CE28-0008.

References

1. Austin, T., Knowles, K., Flanagan, C.: Typed faceted values for secure information flow in haskell. Technical report UCSC-SOE-14-07, University of California, Santa Cruz (2014)
2. Austin, T.H., Flanagan, C.: Efficient purely-dynamic information flow analysis. In: PLAS 2009, pp. 113–124 (2009)
3. Austin, T.H., Flanagan, C.: Permissive dynamic information flow analysis. In: PLAS 2010, pp. 3:1–3:12. ACM (2010)
4. Austin, T.H., Flanagan, C.: Multiple facets for dynamic information flow. In: Proceeding of the 39th Symposium of Principles of Programming Languages. ACM (2012)
5. Barthe, G., Crespo, J.M., Devriese, D., Piessens, F., Rivas, E.: Secure multi-execution through static program transformation. In: Giese, H., Rosu, G. (eds.) FORTE 2012 and FMOODS 2012. LNCS, vol. 7273, pp. 186–202. Springer, Heidelberg (2012)

6. Bauer, L., Ligatti, J., Walker, D.: Edit automata: enforcement mechanisms for run-time security policies. Int. J. Inf. Secur. **4**(1–2), 2–16 (2005)
7. Bielova, N., Devriese, D., Massacci, F., Piessens, F.: Reactive non-interference for a browser model. In: Proceeding of the 5th International Conference on Network and System Security (NSS), pp. 97–104. IEEE (2011)
8. Bielova, N., Rezk, T. Spot the difference: secure multi-execution and multiple facets technical report. https://goo.gl/b7yoQ9
9. Bielova, N., Rezk, T.: A taxonomy of information flow monitors. In: Piessens, F., Viganò, L. (eds.) POST 2016. LNCS, vol. 9635, pp. 46–67. Springer, Heidelberg (2016). doi:10.1007/978-3-662-49635-0_3
10. Bolosteanu, I., Garg, D.: Asymmetric secure multi-execution with declassification. In: Piessens, F., Viganò, L. (eds.) POST 2016. LNCS, vol. 9635, pp. 24–45. Springer, Heidelberg (2016). doi:10.1007/978-3-662-49635-0_2
11. Groef, W., Devriese, D., Nikiforakis, N., Piessens, F.: FlowFox: a web browser with flexible and precise information flow control. In: Proceeding of the 19th ACM Conference on Communications and Computer Security, pp. 748–759 (2012)
12. Devriese, D., Piessens, F.: Non-interference through secure multi-execution. In: Proceeding of the Symposium on Security and Privacy, pp. 109–124. IEEE (2010)
13. Erlingsson, U.: The inlined reference monitor approach to security policy enforcement. Ph.D. thesis, Cornell University (2003)
14. Fenton, J.S.: Memoryless subsystems. Comput. J. **17**(2), 143–147 (1974)
15. Hedin, D., Bello, L., Sabelfeld, A.: Value-sensitive hybrid information flow control for a Javascript-like language. In: IEEE 28th Computer Security Foundations Symposium, CSF (2015)
16. Kashyap, V., Wiedermann, B., Hardekopf, B.: Timing-and termination-sensitive secure information flow: Exploring a new approach. In: IEEE Symposium on Security and Privacy (SP), pp. 413–428 (2011)
17. Le Guernic, G.: Confidentiality enforcement using dynamic information flow analyses. Ph.D. thesis, Kansas State University and University of Rennes 1 (2007)
18. Ligatti, J., Bauer, L., Walker, D.W.: Enforcing non-safety security policies with program monitors. In: Vimercati, S.C., Syverson, P.F., Gollmann, D. (eds.) ESORICS 2005. LNCS, vol. 3679, pp. 355–373. Springer, Heidelberg (2005)
19. Almeida-Matos, A., Fragoso Santos, J., Rezk, T.: An information flow monitor for a core of DOM. In: Maffei, M., Tuosto, E. (eds.) TGC 2014. LNCS, vol. 8902, pp. 1–16. Springer, Heidelberg (2014)
20. Rafnsson, W., Sabelfeld, A.: Secure multi-execution: fine-grained, declassification-aware, and transparent. In: IEEE 26th Computer Security Foundations Symposium (2013)
21. Rafnsson, W., Sabelfeld, A.: Secure multi-execution: fine-grained, declassification-aware, and transparent. J. Comput. Secur. **24**(1), 39–90 (2016)
22. Sabelfeld, A., Myers, A.C.: Language-based information-flow security. IEEE J. Sel. Areas Commun. **21**(1), 5–19 (2003)
23. Sabelfeld, A., Sands, D.: Declassification: dimensions and principles. J. Comput. Secur. **17**(5), 517–548 (2009)
24. Santos, J.F., Rezk, T.: An information flow monitor-inlining compiler forsecuring a core of Javascript. In: 29th IFIP TC 11 International Conference on ICT Systems Security and Privacy Protection, SEC 2014 (2014)
25. Schmitz, T., Rhodes, D., Austin, T.H., Knowles, K., Flanagan, C.: Faceted dynamic information flow via control and data monads. In: Piessens, F., Viganò, L. (eds.) POST 2016. LNCS, vol. 9635, pp. 3–23. Springer, Heidelberg (2016). doi:10.1007/978-3-662-49635-0_1

26. Vanhoef, M., Groef, W.D., Devriese, D., Piessens, F., Rezk, T.: Stateful declassification policies for event-driven programs. In: IEEE 27th Computer Security Foundations Symposium, CSF, pp. 293–307 (2014)
27. Zanarini, D., Jaskelioff, M., Russo, A.: Precise enforcement of confidentiality for reactive systems. In: IEEE 26th Computer Security Foundations Symposium, pp. 18–32 (2013)
28. Zdancewic, S.A.: Programming languages for information security. Ph.D. thesis, Cornell University (2002)

On Reductions from Multi-Domain Noninterference to the Two-Level Case

Oliver Woizekowski[1]([⊠]) and Ron van der Meyden[2]

[1] Department of Computer Science, Kiel University, Kiel, Germany
oliver.woizekowski@email.uni-kiel.de
[2] School of Computer Science and Engineering, UNSW Australia, Sydney, Australia
meyden@cse.unsw.edu.au

Abstract. The literature on information flow security with respect to
transitive policies has been concentrated largely on the case of policies
with two security domains, High and Low, because of a presumption
that more general policies can be reduced to this two-domain case. The
details of the reduction have not been the subject of careful study, however. Many works in the literature use a reduction based on a quantification over "Low-down" partitionings of domains into those below and
those not below a given domain in the information flow order. A few
use "High-up" partitionings of domains into those above and those not
above a given domain. Our paper argues that more general "cut" partitionings are also appropriate, and studies the relationships between the
resulting multi-domain notions of security when the basic notion for the
two-domain case to which we reduce is either Nondeducibility on Inputs
or Generalized Noninterference. The Low-down reduction is shown to be
weaker than the others, and while the High-up reduction is sometimes
equivalent to the cut reduction, both it and the Low-down reduction
may have an undesirable property of non-monotonicity with respect to
a natural ordering on policies. These results suggest that the cut-based
partitioning yields a more robust general approach for reduction to the
two-domain case.

Keywords: Noninterference · Nondeterminism · Information flow ·
Covert channels · Policies

1 Introduction

Information flow security is concerned with finding, preventing and understanding the unwanted flow of information within a system implementation. One of its
applications is the detection of covert channels, which might arise due to hard-
to-foresee side-effects in the combination of smaller components, or even have
been deliberately planted in the implementation by a rogue systems designer.

In order to reason about information flow, one needs to decompose the system into information *domains*. Domains are thought of as active components
(users, processes, pieces of hardware, organisational units, etc.) and change the

© Springer International Publishing Switzerland 2016
I. Askoxylakis et al. (Eds.): ESORICS 2016, Part I, LNCS 9878, pp. 520–537, 2016.
DOI: 10.1007/978-3-319-45744-4_26

system state by performing actions. Domains may also make observations of the
system state. One way for information to flow from one domain to another is
for the actions of the first to change the observations of the second. To describe
the allowed flows of information in the system, one can specify for each pair of
domains in which directions a flow of information is permissible. This specification is called a *policy* and usually represented as a directed graph: two examples
are depicted in Fig. 1. Policies are generally taken to be reflexive relations, since
nothing can prevent a domain from obtaining information about itself. Moreover, they are often assumed to be transitive, (i.e., if $A \mapsto B$ and $B \mapsto C$ then
we must also have $A \mapsto C$) since if B may obtain information about A, and B
may pass this information to C, then there is nothing to prevent C receiving
information about A.[1]

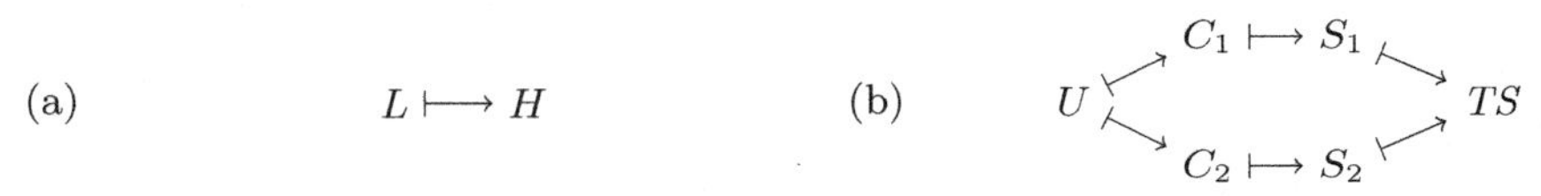

(a) $L \longmapsto H$ (b) $U \begin{array}{c} \nearrow C_1 \mapsto S_1 \searrow \\ \searrow C_2 \mapsto S_2 \nearrow \end{array} TS$

Fig. 1. The two-level policy $H \not\mapsto L$ and a transitive MLS-style policy.

Policy (a) in Fig. 1, which we call $H \not\mapsto L$, is the simplest and most-studied
case. Here we have two domains H and L, where H is thought to possess high
and L low level clearance in the system, and information flow is permitted from L
to H, but prohibited in the other direction. In practice, a larger set of domains
is used to represent different security classifications, such as Unclassified (U),
Confidential (C), Secret (S) and Top Secret (TS), and each security level may
moreover be partitioned into compartments representing different types of information relevant to 'need to know' restrictions. This leads to policies such as the
transitive policy whose Hasse diagram is depicted in Fig. 1(b). Here the Confidential classification has two independent compartment domains (C_1, C_2), as
does the Secret classification (S_1, S_2).

Informally, the statement $u \mapsto v$ can be read as "u's behaviour may influence
v's observations" or "v may deduce something about u's behaviour". A first formal definition for this intuition, called *noninterference* was given by Goguen and
Meseguer [4], in the context of a *deterministic* automaton-based model. A generalization to nondeterministic systems is desirable so one can extend information
flow analysis to, for example, the use of unreliable components, randomness or
underspecification. Several works (e.g., [5–11]) extended the theory to nondeterministic systems and richer semantic models such as process algebras, resulting
in a multitude of security definitions for several kinds of models, and with different intentions in mind.

Much of this subsequent literature has confined itself to the two-domain
policy $H \not\mapsto L$, because there has been a view that more complex policies can be

---

[1] We confine our attention in this paper to the transitive case. Works that have investigated intransitive information flow theory include [1–3].

treated by reduction to this case. One obvious way to do so, that we may call the *pointwise* approach, is to apply a two-domain notion of noninterference for each pair of domains u, v in the policy with $u \not\mapsto v$. However, even in the case of deterministic systems, this can be shown to fail to detect situations where a domain may have disjunctive knowledge about a pair of other domains, neither of which may interfere with it individually (we present an example of this in Sect. 4). Goguen and Meseguer [4] already address this deficiency by what we may call a *setwise* approach, which requires that for each domain u, the set of domains v with $v \not\mapsto u$ does not collectively interfere with u.

However, while the setwise definition deals with what an individual domain may learn about a group of other domains, it does not deal with what groups may learn about individuals, or other groups. Subsequent work in the literature has taken this issue of *collusion* into account in reducing to the two-domain case. For example, a survey by Ryan [11] states:

> It might seem that we have lost generality by assuming that the alphabet of the system is partitioned into High and Low. In fact we can deal with more general MLS-style policy with a lattice of classifications by a set of non-interference constraints corresponding to the various lattice points. For each lattice point l we define High to be the union of the interfaces of agents whose clearance dominates that of l. Low will be the complement, i.e., the union of the interfaces of all agents whose clearance does not dominate that of l. Notice also that we are assuming that we can clump all the high-level users together and similarly all the low-level users. There is nothing to stop all the low users from colluding. Similarly any high-level user potentially has access to the inputs of all other high users. We are thus again making a worst-case assumption.

We call the kind of groupings that Ryan describes *High-up coalitions*, and interpret his comments as the suggestion to extend existing, already understood security definitions for $H \not\mapsto L$ to the multi-domain case by generating multiple instances of $H \not\mapsto L$ formed from the policy in question using High-up coalitions. Ryan's High-up approach is used in some works (e.g., [12]), but many others (e.g., [13–16]) use instead a dual notion of *Low-down coalitions*, where for some domain l, the group L is taken to be the set of domains u with $u \mapsto l$ and H is taken to be the complement of this set.

Yet other groupings exist that are neither High-up nor Low-down coalitions. For example, in Fig. 1(b), the grouping $L = \{U, C_1, C_2\}$ and $H = \{S_1, S_2, TS\}$, corresponds to neither a High-up nor a Low-down coalition. It seems no less reasonable to consider L to be a colluding group that is seeking to obtain H level information. Note that this grouping is a *cut* in the sense that there is no $u \in H$ and $v \in L$ such that $u \mapsto v$. Since in such a cut, domains in L cannot individually obtain information about domains in H, it is reasonable to expect that they should not be able to get such information collectively. This motivates a reduction to the two-domain case that quantifies over all cuts.

Our contribution in this paper is to consider this range of alternative reductions from multi-domain policies to the two-domain case, and to develop an understanding of how these definitions are related and which are reasonable. Reductions must start with an existing notion of security for the two-domain case. We work with two basic security definitions: Generalized Noninterference, which was introduced in [17], and Nondeducibility on Inputs, first presented in [5]. Our analysis shows that the relationships between the resulting notions of security are subtle, and the adequacy of a reduction approach may depend on the base notion for the two-domain policy. Amongst other results, we show that:

1. When the basic notion for the two-domain case is Generalized Noninterference, High-up coalitions yield a notion that is strictly stronger than the notion based on Low-down coalitions, which in turn is stronger than the pointwise generalization. For Nondeducibility on Inputs, however, High-up coalitions and Low-down coalitions give independent notions of security. Low-down coalitions imply the setwise definition in this case, but High-up coalitions imply only the weaker pointwise version.
2. For Generalized Noninterference, High-up coalitions are 'complete' in the sense of being equivalent to a reduction quantifying over all cuts. However, this completeness result does not hold for Nondeducibility on Inputs, where cuts yield a stronger notion of security.
3. Not all the resulting notions of security have an expected property of monotonicity with respect to a natural restrictiveness order on policies. (Security of a system should be preserved when one relaxes policy constraints.) In particular, High-up coalitions with respect to Nondeducibility on Inputs does not have this property, and Low-down coalitions do not have this property for either Generalized Noninterference or Nondeducibility on Inputs.

These conclusions indicate that while Ryan's proposal to use High-up coalitions is sometimes adequate, a reduction that quantifies over the larger set of all cut coalitions seems to yield the most generally robust approach for reducing multi-domain policies to the two-domain case.

The structure of the paper is as follows. In Sect. 2, we introduce our model and show how systems and policies are described. Our reductions will use two basic security definitions for two-domain policies that are recalled and generalized to their obvious pointwise versions for the multi-domain case in Sect. 3. Section 4 gives some examples showing why the pointwise versions are still weaker than required, and it is necessary to consider reductions using groupings of domains. The range of reductions we consider are defined in Sect. 5. Our main results are stated in Sect. 6, and an outline of the proof technique involved to prove these results is presented in Sect. 7. Finally, we conclude and motivate further research in Sect. 8.

2   Background: Systems and Policy Model

Notational conventions. Sequences are represented as xyz, or $x \cdot y \cdot z$ if it helps readability. The set of finite sequences over a set A is denoted A^*, and the empty sequence is denoted ε. We write $\alpha(i)$ to denote the element with index i of a sequence α, where $i \in \mathbb{N}$, and the first element of α is $\alpha(0)$. We let $\mathrm{last}(\alpha)$ be the last element of α if α is non-empty, and let it be undefined if α is empty. If $X \subseteq A$ and $\alpha \in A^*$ then let $\alpha|_X$ be the subsequence of α with only elements from X retained. The set of total functions from A to B is denoted B^A.

Systems. We use an automaton-based model similar to the original Goguen-Meseguer one from [4]. A *system* is a structure $(S, A, O, D, \Delta, \mathrm{obs}, \mathrm{dom}, s_I)$ with S a set of *states*, A a finite set of *actions*, D a finite set of domains with at least two members, O a finite set of *observations* such that A and O are disjoint, $\Delta \subseteq S \times A \times S$ a (nondeterministic) transition relation, obs: $D \times S \to O$ an observation function, dom: $A \to D$ an assignment of actions to domains, and s_I the initial state. We write $\mathrm{obs}_u(s)$ for $\mathrm{obs}(u, s)$. The value $\mathrm{obs}_u(s)$ represents the observation the domain u makes when the system is in state s. Observations can also be interpreted as outputs from the system. For an action a, the domain $\mathrm{dom}(a)$ is the domain from which a originates. The relation Δ is called *deterministic* if for all $s, s', s'' \in S$, $a \in A$: if $(s, a, s') \in \Delta$ and $(s, a, s'') \in \Delta$ then $s' = s''$. We assume systems to be *input-enabled*, i.e. that for every $s \in S$ and $a \in A$ there is $s' \in S$ with $(s, a, s') \in \Delta$. The assumption of input-enabledness is made to guarantee that the domains' reasoning is based on their actions and observations only and cannot use system blocking behaviour as a source of information.

A *run* of a system is a sequence $s_0 a_1 s_1 \ldots a_n s_n \in S(AS)^*$ such that for $i < n$, we have $(s_i, a_i, s_{i+1}) \in \Delta$. It is *initial* if $s_0 = s_I$. If not explicitly mentioned otherwise, we always assume initial runs. The set of initial runs of a system $\mathcal{M}$ will be denoted $\mathrm{Runs}(\mathcal{M})$. For a run r, the subsequence of actions of r is denoted $\mathrm{act}(r)$ and the subsequence of actions performed by a domain u is denoted $\mathrm{act}_u(r)$.

Notational and diagrammatic conventions for systems. If u is a domain and A the action set of a system, we write A_u for the set of actions a with $\mathrm{dom}(a) = u$. Similarly, for X a set of domains we write A_X for the set of actions a with $\mathrm{dom}(a) \in X$. Systems are depicted as directed graphs, where the vertices contain the state names. Domain observations are written near the vertices that represent the states. Edges are labelled with action names and represent transitions from one state to another. The initial state is marked with an arrow that points to it. Self-looping edges are omitted when possible to reduce clutter: thus, the lack of an edge labelled by action a from state s (as would be required by input-enabledness) implies the existence of edge (s, a, s).

Modelling information by views. We will be interested in an asynchronous semantics for information, and capture asynchrony by treating sequences that differ only by stuttering observations as indistinguishable. This can also be described as no domain having access to a global clock. Intuitively, systems can be imagined as distributed and domains as representing network hosts. From this intuition it follows, for a given domain u, that local state changes within domains distinct from u that do not provide a new observation to u must not generate a copy of u's current observation. To this end, we use an 'absorptive concatenation' operator $\hat{\circ}$ on sequences. For all sequences α and $b_0 \ldots b_n$ we let $\alpha \,\hat{\circ}\, \varepsilon = \alpha$ and

$$\alpha \,\hat{\circ}\, b_0 \ldots b_n = \begin{cases} \alpha \,\hat{\circ}\, b_1 \ldots b_n & \text{if } \alpha \neq \varepsilon \text{ and } \text{last}(\alpha) = b_0 \\ (\alpha \cdot b_0) \,\hat{\circ}\, b_1 \ldots b_n & \text{otherwise.} \end{cases}$$

One can imagine $\alpha \,\hat{\circ}\, \beta$ as $\alpha \cdot \beta$ with stuttering at the point of connection removed. The information a domain acquires over the course of a run is modelled by the notion of *view*. Considering systems as networks suggests that, during a run, a domain can only directly see the actions performed by itself. This is reflected in our definition of view by eliminating actions performed by all other domains. For a domain u the operator $\text{view}_u \colon \text{Runs}(\mathcal{M}) \to (A \cup O)^*$ is defined inductively: for the base case $r = s_I$ let $\text{view}_u(r) = \text{obs}_u(s_I)$. For all $r \in \text{Runs}(\mathcal{M})$ of the form $r = r'as$, where $r' \in \text{Runs}(\mathcal{M})$, $a \in A$ and $s \in S$, let

$$\text{view}_u(r) = \begin{cases} \text{view}_u(r') \cdot a \cdot \text{obs}_u(s) & \text{if } \text{dom}(a) = u \\ \text{view}_u(r') \,\hat{\circ}\, \text{obs}_u(s) & \text{otherwise.} \end{cases}$$

An element $\text{view}_u(r)$ is called a u *view*. The set of all u views in system $\mathcal{M}$ is denoted $\text{Views}_u(\mathcal{M})$.

For an example of a view, see the system in Fig. 2 (recall that we elide self-loops) and consider the run $r = s_I a s_1 b s_2 b s_2 a s_3$; the domains are given by the set $\{A, B\}$, the domain assignment is given by $\text{dom}(a) = A$ and $\text{dom}(b) = B$, and the observations made by domain B are depicted near the state names. We have $\text{view}_B(r) = \bot b1b12$.

Note that B does not notice the first transition in r because we have $\text{obs}_B(s_I) = \text{obs}_B(s_1)$. Domain B does, however, learn about the last transition in r due to $\text{obs}_B(s_2) \neq \text{obs}_B(s_3)$. With the network analogy mentioned above, the last transition might model a communication from A to B.

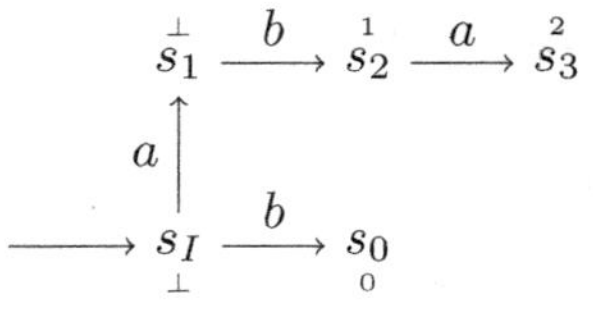

Fig. 2. System example.

Policies. A *policy* is a reflexive binary relation $\mapsto$ over a set of domains D. We require $\mapsto$ to be reflexive because we assume that domains are aware of their own behaviour at all times. We assume also that policies are transitive, to avoid additional complexities associated with the semantics of intransitive policies. Transitive policies arise naturally from lattices of security levels. The policy that has received the most attention in the literature is over the set $D = \{H, L\}$, consisting of a domain H (or *High*), representing a high security domain whose activity needs to be protected, and a domain L (or *Low*), representing a low security attacker who aims to learn High secrets. We refer to this policy as $H \not\mapsto L$; it is given by the relation $\mapsto = \{(H, H), (L, L), (L, H)\}$.

If $\mapsto$ is a policy over some domain set D, we write $u^\mapsto$ for the set $\{v \in D : u \mapsto v\}$, and $^\mapsto u$ for the set $\{v \in D : v \mapsto u\}$. Similarly, the expression $^{\not\mapsto}u$ shall denote the set $\{v \in D : v \not\mapsto u\}$.

Further notational conventions for policies. Policies are depicted as directed graphs and their vertices carry domain names. Edges due to reflexivity or transitivity are omitted.

Policy abstractions and cuts. A set of domains can be abstracted by grouping its elements into sets. Such groupings can be motivated in a number of ways. One is simply that we wish to take a coarser view of the system, and reduce the number of domains by treating several domains as one. Groupings may also arise from several domains deciding to collude in an attack on the security of the system. Abstractions of a set of domains lead to associated abstractions of policies and systems.

An *abstraction* of a set of domains D is a set $\mathcal{D}$ of subsets of D with $D = \bigcup_{F \in \mathcal{D}} F$ and $F \cap G \neq \emptyset$ implies $F = G$ for all $F, G \in \mathcal{D}$. Associated with each abstraction $\mathcal{D}$ of D is a function $f_{\mathcal{D}} \colon D \to \mathcal{D}$ defined by taking $f_{\mathcal{D}}(u)$ to be the unique $F \in \mathcal{D}$ with $u \in F$. For a policy $\mapsto$ over D we let $\mapsto^{\mathcal{D}}$ be the policy over $\mathcal{D}$ defined by $F \mapsto^{\mathcal{D}} G$ if and only if there are $x \in F$ and $x' \in G$ with $x \mapsto x'$.

In order to formalize the idea of a reduction to $H \not\mapsto L$, we use abstractions that group all domains into two sets that correspond to the High and Low domains. A *cut* of a set of domains D with respect to a policy $\mapsto$ is a tuple $\mathcal{C} = (\mathcal{H}, \mathcal{L})$ such that $\{\mathcal{H}, \mathcal{L}\}$ is an abstraction of D and there does not exist $u \in \mathcal{H}$ and $v \in \mathcal{L}$ with $u \mapsto v$. When forming policies, we identify cuts with their underlying abstractions, and write $\mapsto^{\mathcal{C}}$ for $\mapsto^{\{\mathcal{H},\mathcal{L}\}}$, so the last requirement can also be formulated as $\mathcal{H} \not\mapsto^{\mathcal{C}} \mathcal{L}$. We mainly deal with abstractions that are given by cuts in this paper. See Fig. 3 for an illustration of how policy (b) in Fig. 1 is abstracted using $\mathcal{C} := (\mathcal{H}, \mathcal{L}) = (\{S_1, S_2, TS\}, \{U, C_1, C_2\})$, where we get $\mathcal{L} \mapsto^{\mathcal{C}} \mathcal{H}$ due to $C_1 \mapsto S_1$ or $C_2 \mapsto S_2$ and $\mathcal{H} \not\mapsto^{\mathcal{C}} \mathcal{L}$ as required for a cut.

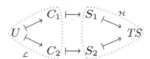

Fig. 3. Illustration of a policy abstraction.

Systems and abstractions. Systems can be viewed from the perspective of an abstraction. Intuitively, the actions of an abstract domain F are all the actions of any of its subdomains $u \in F$. It observes the collection of all observations made by the members of F and thus their observations are functions from F to O. Let $\mathcal{M} = (S, A, O, D, \Delta, \mathrm{obs}, \mathrm{dom}, s_I)$ be a system and $\mathcal{D}$ be an abstraction of D. Then $\mathcal{M}^{\mathcal{D}}$ is the system $(S, A, O', \mathcal{D}, \Delta, \mathrm{obs}^{\mathcal{D}}, \mathrm{dom}^{\mathcal{D}}, s_I)$, where O' is the union of O^F for all $F \in \mathcal{D}$, its set of domains is $\mathcal{D}$, for a state $s \in S$, the observation $\mathrm{obs}^{\mathcal{D}}_F(s)$ is the function with domain $F \in \mathcal{D}$ that sends each $x \in F$ to $\mathrm{obs}_x(s)$, and $\mathrm{dom}^{\mathcal{D}}(a) = f_{\mathcal{D}}(\mathrm{dom}(a))$ for all $a \in A$. Intuitively, $\mathrm{obs}^{\mathcal{D}}_F(s)$ records the observations made in each domain in F at s. Again, if $\mathcal{C} = (\mathcal{H}, \mathcal{L})$ is a cut we write $\mathcal{M}^{\mathcal{C}}$ for $\mathcal{M}^{\{\mathcal{H},\mathcal{L}\}}$.

Monotonicity with respect to restrictiveness. In [18] the notion of *monotonicity with respect to restrictiveness* is discussed, which holds for a given notion of security X if, for all systems $\mathcal{M}$ and policies $\mapsto$ over the domain set of $\mathcal{M}$, the following statement holds: if $\mathcal{M}$ is X-secure with respect to $\mapsto$ then $\mathcal{M}$ is X-secure with respect to every policy $\mapsto'$ with $\mapsto \subseteq \mapsto'$. If a notion of security satisfies this property, we will say that it is *monotonic*. Intuitively, adding edges to a policy reduces the set of information flow restrictions $u \not\mapsto v$ implied by the policy, making the policy easier to satisfy, so one would expect every sensible notion of security to be monotonic. However, we will show that some notions of security obtained by a sensible construction based on cuts do not support this intuition.

3   Basic Notions of Noninterference

In this section we recall two security definitions which have been proposed in the literature for nondeterministic, asynchronous automaton-based models. We use these as the basic definitions of security for $H \not\mapsto L$ in the reductions that we study. For purposes of comparison, we state the definitions using the most obvious pointwise generalization from the usual two-domain case to the general multi-domain case.

3.1   Nondeducibility on Inputs

Goguen and Meseguer's definition of noninterference [19] was for deterministic systems only. Historically, Sutherland [5] was the first to consider information flow in nondeterministic systems. He presented a general scheme to instantiate notions of *Nondeducibility*, i.e., epistemic definitions of absence of information flows. The notion of Nondeducibility on Inputs is one instance of this general scheme.

Let $u, v \in D$. We say that $\alpha \in A_u{}^*$ and $\beta \in \text{Views}_v(\mathcal{M})$ are v *compatible* if there is $r \in \text{Runs}(\mathcal{M})$ with $\text{act}_u(r) = \alpha$ and $\text{view}_v(r) = \beta$. We write $u \rightsquigarrow_I v$ if there are $\alpha \in A_u{}^*$ and $\beta \in \text{Views}_v(\mathcal{M})$ which are not v compatible. In that case v gains information about u's behaviour in the following sense: if β is observed by v then v can deduce that u did not perform α. Nondeducibility $u \not\rightsquigarrow_I v$ therefore says that v is unable to make any nontrivial deductions about u behaviour. Applying this idea pointwise, we get the following definition of security:

Definition 1. *A system is* NDI_{pw}*-secure for a policy* $\mapsto$ *over domains* D *when for all* $u, v \in D$*: if* $u \not\mapsto v$ *then* $u \not\rightsquigarrow_I v$.

In the case of the policy $H \not\mapsto L$ with just two domains, NDI_{pw} is the notion *Nondeducibility on Inputs* as it is usually defined. We denote it as just NDI in this case. The definition above generalizes this notion in one possible way to the multi-domain case. We discuss several others below.

3.2   Generalized Noninterference

The nondeducibility relation $H \not\rightarrow L$ states that L considers all sequences of actions of H possible, but allows that L has some information about how these actions, if any, are interleaved with L's actions. See Fig. 4 for a system that is NDI-secure but can be argued to leak information about how H's actions are interleaved into a run. The observations made by L are written near the state names.

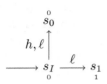

Fig. 4. System demonstrating a weakness of NDI.

This system is NDI-secure because every L view is compatible with every possible sequence of h actions performed by H. However, note that if the view $0\ell1$ is observed by L then it obtains the knowledge that it was the very first domain to act. The stronger notion of *Generalized Noninterference* introduced by McCullough [17] says that L does not have even this weaker form of knowledge. The original formulation is for a two-domain policy and is based on a model that uses sets of event sequences. We present a straightforward multi-domain variant (that is similar to Mantel's combination BSI+BSD [8]).

Definition 2. *A system $\mathcal{M}$ is GN_{pw}-secure for $\mapsto$ if for all $u, v \in D$ with $u \not\rightarrow v$, the properties*

- $GN^+(u,v)$: *for all $r \in \mathrm{Runs}(\mathcal{M})$, for all $\alpha_0, \alpha_1 \in A^*$ with $\mathrm{act}(r) = \alpha_0\alpha_1$, and all $a \in A_u$ with there is $r' \in \mathrm{Runs}(\mathcal{M})$ with $\mathrm{act}(r') = \alpha_0 a \alpha_1$ and $\mathrm{view}_v(r') = \mathrm{view}_v(r)$, and*
- $GN^-(u,v)$: *for all $r \in \mathrm{Runs}(\mathcal{M})$, all $\alpha_0, \alpha_1 \in A^*$ and all $a \in A_u$, with $\mathrm{act}(r) = \alpha_0 a \alpha_1$, there is $r' \in \mathrm{Runs}(\mathcal{M})$ with $\mathrm{act}(r') = \alpha_0\alpha_1$ and $\mathrm{view}_v(r') = \mathrm{view}_v(r)$.*

are satisfied.

Intuitively, this definition says that actions of domains u with $u \not\rightarrow v$ can be arbitrarily inserted and deleted, without changing the set of possible views that v can obtain. In the case of the two-domain policy $H \not\rightarrow L$, the notion GN_{pw} is equivalent to the definition of Generalized Noninterference given in [20], and we denote this case by GN. Note that the system in Fig. 4 is not GN-secure, because performing h as first action in a run makes it impossible for L to observe the view $0\ell1$.

In *deterministic* systems, for the two-domain policy $H \not\rightarrow L$, the notions NDI_{pw} and GN_{pw}, and Goguen and Meseguer's orginal notion of Noninterference are known to be equivalent. Thus, both NDI_{pw} and GN_{pw} are reasonable candidates for the generalization of Noninterference to nondeterministic systems.

4   Motivation for Abstraction

The definitions NDI_{pw} and GN_{pw} have generalized the corresponding definitions NDI and GN usually given for the two-domain policy $H \not\rightarrow L$ in a *pointwise* fashion, stating in different ways that there should not be a flow of information from domain u to domain v when $u \not\mapsto v$. We now present some examples that suggest that these pointwise definitions may be weaker than required in the case of policies with more than two domains.

We first present an example which demonstrates that NDI_{pw}-security is flawed with respect to combined behaviour of multiple domains. (Interestingly, this can already be shown in a deterministic system.)

Fig. 5. A system and policy showing a weakness of NDI_{pw}.

Example 1. Consider the system and policy depicted in Fig. 5. The domain assignment is given by $\mathrm{dom}(l) = L$, $\mathrm{dom}(h_1) = H_1$ and $\mathrm{dom}(h_2) = H_2$. We have $H_1 \not\mapsto L$ and $H_2 \not\mapsto L$ and show that $H_1 \not\leadsto_I L$ and $H_2 \not\leadsto_I L$ hold. Let $\alpha = h_1{}^a$ for $a \geq 0$ and β be an L view, then β must have the form $0(\ell 0)^b(\ell 1)^c$, where $b, c \geq 0$. Consider the run $r = s_I(\ell s_I)^b h_2 s_0(h_1 s_0)^a(\ell s_1)^c$, which satisfies $\mathrm{view}_L(r) = 0(\ell 0)^b(\ell 1)^c = \beta$ and $\mathrm{act}_{H_1}(r) = h_1{}^a$, and thus α and β are L compatible. Due to symmetry, we also get $H_2 \not\leadsto_I L$ with the same argument. The system therefore is NDI_{pw}-secure for the policy. However, if L observes the view $0\ell 1$ then H_1 or H_2 must have performed h_1 or h_2, respectively. □

In the example, domain L cannot know which of H_1 or H_2 was active upon observing the view $0\ell 1$, but L can tell that at least one of them was active nonetheless. It can be argued that this is a flow of information that is not permitted by the depicted policy. The example would turn formally insecure if we changed the policy to $H \not\mapsto L$ and set $\mathrm{dom}(h_1) = \mathrm{dom}(h_2) = H$. The problem arises as soon as more than one domain must be noninterfering with L.

One way to address this weakness of NDI_{pw} is to revise the definition so that it deals with what a domain can learn about the actions of a set of domains collectively, rather than about these domains individually. We may extend the relation $\leadsto_I$ to sets of domains as follows: for $X \subseteq D$, $X \neq \emptyset$ and $u \in D$, write $X \leadsto_I u$ if there are $\alpha \in A_X{}^*$ and $\beta \in \mathrm{Views}_u(\mathcal{M})$ such that no $r \in \mathrm{Runs}(\mathcal{M})$ satisfies both $\mathrm{act}_X(r) = \alpha$ and $\mathrm{view}_u(r) = \beta$. Applying this with the set $X = \not\mapsto u$ consisting of all domains that may not interfere with domain u, we obtain the following setwise version of Nondeducibility on Inputs:

Definition 3. *A system is NDI_{sw}-secure for $\mapsto$ if for all $u \in D$, we have that $\not\mapsto u \not\leadsto_I u$.*

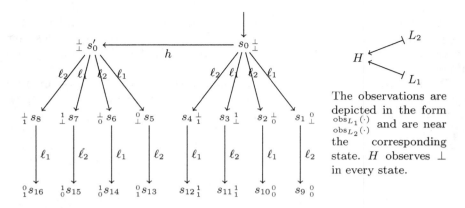

Fig. 6. System and policy illustrating a collusion attack.

This gives a notion that is intermediate between the pointwise versions of Generalized Noninterference and Nondeducibility on Inputs:

Proposition 1. GN_{pw} *is strictly contained in* NDI_{sw}, *and* NDI_{sw} *is strictly contained in* NDI_{pw}. *A system is* NDI_{sw}*-secure for* $H \not\rightarrow L$ *if and only if it is* NDI_{pw}*-secure for* $H \not\rightarrow L$.

We remark that there is not a need to give a similar setwise definition of Generalized Noninterference, because the definition of GN_{pw} already allows the set of actions in a run to be modified, without change to the view of u, by arbitrary insertions and deletions of actions with domains v in $\not\rightarrow u$, through a sequence of applications of $GN^+(v, u)$ and $GN^-(v, u)$.

Despite NDI_{sw} and GN_{pw} being suitable for the multi-domain case and the latter notion being quite strict, one can argue that neither of them can handle collusion, where multiple domains join forces in order to attack the system as a team. The system depicted in Fig. 6, a variant of Example 3 and Fig. 4 from [21], can be shown to satisfy GN_{pw}-security, hence is secure in the strongest sense introduced so far. However, if L_1 and L_2 collude, they can infer from the parity of their observations that H performed h at the beginning of the run. This motivates the introduction of stronger *coalition-aware* notions of security.

5   Reduction-Based Notions of Noninterference for Multi-Domain Policies

The examples of the previous section indicate that in nondeterministic settings, it is necessary to deal with groups of agents both on the side of the attackers and the side of the domains being attacked. Policy cuts provide types of groupings and enable a reduction to a basic notion of security for two-domain policies. The question that then remains is what types of cut we should use, and which basic notion of security. In this section, we define three types of cut and the resulting notions of security when GN and NDI are taken to be the basic notion of security.

Let D be a set of domains. For $u \in D$ we define the following two special cuts $\mathrm{Hu}(u)$ and $\mathrm{Ld}(u)$.

$$\mathrm{Hu}(u) := (u^{\mapsto}, \ D \setminus u^{\mapsto}) \text{ and } \mathrm{Ld}(u) := (D \setminus {}^{\mapsto}u, \ {}^{\mapsto}u)$$

The term $\mathrm{Hu}(u)$ stands for the cut that forms a High-up coalition starting at domain u, while $\mathrm{Ld}(u)$ stands for the cut that forms a Low-down coalition with respect to u. Figure 7 depicts an example of each on the same policy.

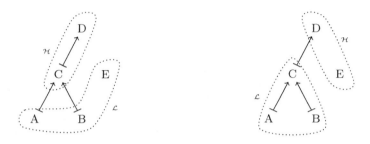

Fig. 7. Cuts $\mathrm{Hu}(C)$ and $\mathrm{Ld}(C)$ visualized.

Abstractions of type $\mathrm{Hu}(\cdot)$ are suggested by Ryan (as discussed in the introduction), while the type $\mathrm{Ld}(\cdot)$ is what we referred to as its dual. As already noted in the introduction, there are additional 'cut' abstractions that are neither High-up nor Low-down. In a systematic way, we can now obtain new notions of security based on cuts as follows.

Definition 4. *Let $\mathcal{M}$ be a system with domain set D and $\mapsto$ be a policy over D. For $X \in \{GN, NDI\}$, we say $\mathcal{M}$ is*

- *Cut X-secure (C-X-secure) for $\mapsto$, if $\mathcal{M}^C$ is X-secure for $\mapsto^C$ for all cuts C of D,*
- *High-up X-secure (H-X-secure) for $\mapsto$, if $\mathcal{M}^{\mathrm{Hu}(u)}$ is X-secure for $\mapsto^{\mathrm{Hu}(u)}$ for all $u \in D$,*
- *Low-down X-secure (L-X-secure) for $\mapsto$, if $\mathcal{M}^{\mathrm{Ld}(u)}$ is X-secure for $\mapsto^{\mathrm{Ld}(u)}$ for all $u \in D$.*

There is a straightforward relationship between these notions of GN and their NDI-counterparts.

Proposition 2. *For all $X \in \{C, H, L\}$: the notion X-GN is strictly contained in X-NDI.*

This follows directly from Definition 4, the fact that GN implies NDI due to Proposition 1, and that the system depicted in Fig. 4 provides separation for each case. Also, one would expect that reasonable extensions of GN and NDI agree if applied to $H \not\mapsto L$, and this is exactly what we find, since we can identify singleton coalitions with their only member.

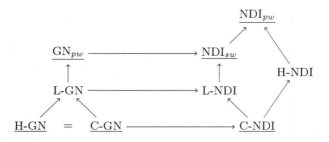

Fig. 8. Implications between our notions of security.

6   Main Result

We now state the main result of the paper. We have a set of definitions of security that address the need to consider groupings of attackers and defenders in multi-domain policies, based on two basic notions of security NDI and GN for the two-domain case. We are now interested in understanding the relationships between these definitions. Additionally, we are interested in understanding which definitions satisfy the desirable property of monotonicity.

Theorem 1. *The notions of GN_{pw}, L-GN, H-GN, C-GN, NDI_{pw}, NDI_{sw}, L-NDI, H-NDI and C-NDI-security are ordered by implication as depicted in Fig. 8. The containment relations are strict; arrows due to reflexivity or transitivity are omitted. The name of a notion is underlined if and only if it is monotonic.*

In particular, we find for the GN-variants that Ryan's proposal to use reductions based on High-up coalitions is complete, in the sense that it yields the same notion of security as a quantification over all cuts. This notion is moreover adequate in the sense of being monotonic. Somewhat surprisingly, the dual notion based on Low-down coalitions is strictly weaker, and also fails to be monotonic.

The situation is different for the basic notion of NDI. In this case, we see that Ryan's proposal is not complete with respect to quantification over all cuts. Indeed, the resulting notion H-NDI does not even imply the more adequate setwise version of NDI, although it does imply the pointwise version. The Low-down version of NDI does imply the setwise version, and is independent of H-NDI. However, neither H-NDI nor L-NDI is monotonic. This leaves the (monotonic) cut based variant as the most satisfactory notion in this case.

7   Technical Details

This section provides an overview of how to show some relationships claimed by Theorem 1. First, the concept of a *vulnerability* of a system is introduced for GN_{pw} and NDI_{sw}. A vulnerability of a system is a witness of a security violation for the respective notion of security. The proofs to compare the different variants of GN and NDI are done by contraposition and show how, for given cuts $\mathcal{C}_0$ and $\mathcal{C}_1$, a vulnerability of $\mathcal{M}^{\mathcal{C}_0}$ can be translated into a vulnerability of $\mathcal{M}^{\mathcal{C}_1}$. This shows that security for all cuts of type $\mathcal{C}_1$ implies security for all cuts of type $\mathcal{C}_0$. We use technical lemmas, one for GN_{pw} and one for NDI_{sw}, that give sufficient conditions in order to facilitate this translation. Separation of two notions is done by giving a concrete example that exhibits the one, but not the other, security property.

Due to space constraints, we only present proofs for some relationships between GN variants. Proofs for all results in this section can be found in [22].

GN vulnerabilities. A of a system $\mathcal{M}$ is a tuple $(u, \alpha_0, a, \alpha_1, \beta, \mapsto)$, where $\mapsto$ is a policy over the domain set of $\mathcal{M}$, u is a domain in $\mathcal{M}$, $\alpha_0, \alpha_1 \in A^*$, $a \in A$ with $\text{dom}(a) \not\mapsto u$ and $\beta \in \text{Views}_u(\mathcal{M})$ such that there is a run r that satisfies $\text{view}_u(r) = \beta$ and at least one of

- $\text{act}(r) = \alpha_0 \alpha_1$ and no run r' with $\text{act}(r') = \alpha_0 a \alpha_1$ satisfies $\text{view}_u(r') = \beta$,
- $\text{act}(r) = \alpha_0 a \alpha_1$ and no run r' with $\text{act}(r') = \alpha_0 \alpha_1$ satisfies $\text{view}_u(r') = \beta$.

We evidently have a vulnerability of a system if and only if $\text{GN}^+(\text{dom}(a), u)$ or $\text{GN}^-(\text{dom}(a), u)$ does not hold. Without loss of generality we always assume a violation of $\text{GN}^+(\text{dom}(a), u)$ if there is a vulnerability, since the case of a $\text{GN}^-(\text{dom}(a), u)$ violation is similar.

7.1 Translating GN Vulnerabilities

The next definition formalizes the idea that the view of an attacking coalition, e.g. the Low domain of a cut, has at least as much information as the view of a sub-coalition. We will need this to argue that if a coalition possesses enough information to successfully launch an attack on a system (i.e. it can violate GN^+) then, a fortiori, a bigger coalition possesses enough information for an attack.

Definition 5. *Let $\mathcal{M}$ be a system with action set A and observation set O, let $\mathcal{D}_0$ and $\mathcal{D}_1$ be abstractions of its domain set, and $F \in \mathcal{D}_0$, $G \in \mathcal{D}_1$ such that $F \subseteq G$. Then the operator*

$$\text{pr}^G_F \colon A \cup O^G \cup \text{Views}_G(\mathcal{M}^{\mathcal{D}_1}) \to \text{Views}_F(\mathcal{M}^{\mathcal{D}_0})$$

is defined as follows:

- *if $a \in A$ then $\text{pr}^G_F(a) = a|_F$, where a is considered to be a sequence of length one. The result is its subsequence of actions that F can perform, i.e. it is either a or ε,*
- *if $o \in O^G$ then $\text{pr}^G_F(o) = o|_F$, that is observations made by G are restricted such that the result is the observation made by F,*
- *if α is a G view and $\beta \in O^G \cup A_G \cdot O^G$ such that $\alpha\beta$ is a G view, then*

$$\text{pr}^G_F(\alpha\beta) = \text{pr}^G_F(\alpha) \mathbin{\hat{\circ}} \text{pr}^G_F(\beta).$$

For all other cases let the result be undefined. The symbol $\mathrm{pr}_F^G(\cdot)$ *is chosen to support the intuition that G views are 'projected down' to F views.*

That the previous definition is reasonable is established by a correctness lemma which makes the restriction aspect of the operator clear.

Lemma 1. *Let* $\mathcal{M}$ *be a system, let* $\mathcal{D}_0$ *and* $\mathcal{D}_1$ *be abstractions of its domain set, and* $F \in \mathcal{D}_0$, $G \in \mathcal{D}_1$ *such that* $F \subseteq G$. *Then for all* $r \in \mathrm{Runs}(\mathcal{M})$ *we have* $\mathrm{pr}_F^G(\mathrm{view}_G(r)) = \mathrm{view}_F(r)$.

Conditions under which the translation of a vulnerability is possible are established by the following result: the attacking coalition may not shrink and the translation must respect the status of being the attacker's victim.

Lemma 2. *Let* $\mathcal{M}$ *be a system and* $\mapsto$ *be a policy, and* $\mathcal{C}_0 = (\mathcal{H}_0, \mathcal{L}_0)$ *be a cut of the domain set of* $\mathcal{M}$ *with respect to* $\mapsto$. *Let* $(F, \alpha_0, a, \alpha_1, \beta, \mapsto^{\mathcal{C}_0})$ *be a vulnerability of* $\mathcal{M}^{\mathcal{C}_0}$. *Let* $\mathcal{C}_1 = (\mathcal{H}_1, \mathcal{L}_1)$ *be a cut such that there is* $G \in \{\mathcal{H}_1, \mathcal{L}_1\}$ *with* $\mathrm{dom}^{\mathcal{C}_1}(a) \not\mapsto^{\mathcal{C}_1} G$ *and* $F \subseteq G$. *Then there is* $\beta' \in \mathrm{Views}_G(\mathcal{M}^{\mathcal{C}_1})$ *such that a vulnerability of* $\mathcal{M}^{\mathcal{C}_1}$ *is given by* $(G, \alpha_0, a, \alpha_1, \beta', \mapsto^{\mathcal{C}_1})$.

That High-up GN implies Cut GN, and therefore these notions are equivalent, might not be apparent, but can be explained by the fact that the Low component $\mathcal{L}$ of a cut is the intersection of the Low components $\mathcal{L}_0, ..., \mathcal{L}_{n-1}$ of n High-up cuts and thus can obtain no more information about High behaviour than each $\mathcal{L}_i$ individually. If we can prevent each $\mathcal{L}_i$ from obtaining any information about how High actions are interleaved into runs then the same must apply to $\mathcal{L}$ as well.

Theorem 2. *The notions C-GN and H-GN are equivalent.*

Proof. Because C-GN implies H-GN it suffices to show that H-GN implies C-GN. The proof is done by contraposition and translates a vulnerability with respect to an arbitrary cut into a vulnerability with respect to a $\mathrm{Hu}(\cdot)$-style cut.

Let $\mathcal{M}$ be a system with domain set D, $\mapsto$ a policy over D and $\mathcal{C}_0$ a cut of D. Furthermore, let $(F, \alpha_0, a, \alpha_1, \beta, \mapsto^{\mathcal{C}_0})$ be a GN vulnerability of $\mathcal{M}^{\mathcal{C}_0}$. Set $\mathcal{C}_1 := \mathrm{Hu}(\mathrm{dom}(a))$, $\mathcal{H} := \mathrm{dom}(a)^{\mapsto}$ and $\mathcal{L} := D \setminus \mathrm{dom}(a)^{\mapsto}$. Then we have $\mathcal{C}_1 = (\mathcal{H}, \mathcal{L})$. We show that the prerequisites for Lemma 2 are satisfied, which gives us a vulnerability of $\mathcal{M}^{\mathcal{C}_1}$.

First, we demonstrate that $\mathrm{dom}^{\mathcal{C}_1}(a) = \mathcal{H} \not\mapsto^{\mathcal{C}_1} \mathcal{L}$. Let $u \in \mathcal{H}$ and $v \in \mathcal{L}$, we must show that $u \not\mapsto v$. Assume $u \mapsto v$, then by choice of $\mathcal{C}_1$ we have $\mathrm{dom}(a) \mapsto u$, which implies $\mathrm{dom}(a) \mapsto u \mapsto v$ and $\mathrm{dom}(a) \mapsto v$ by transitivity. Therefore $v \in \mathcal{H}$, which contradicts $v \in \mathcal{L}$, and hence we have $u \not\mapsto v$. It remains to prove that $F \subseteq \mathcal{L}$. Let $u \in F$, then due to vulnerability we have $\mathrm{dom}^{\mathcal{C}_0}(a) \not\mapsto^{\mathcal{C}_0} F$, i.e. $\mathrm{dom}(a) \not\mapsto u$. By choice of $\mathcal{C}_1$ we get $u \notin \mathcal{H}$, which is equivalent to $u \in \mathcal{L}$. Now application of Lemma 2 yields a vulnerability of $\mathcal{M}^{\mathcal{C}_1}$. □

7.2 Separation of the GN Variants

The result obtained by Theorem 2 shows completeness of Ryan's technique for GN. From this follows that the High-up variant of GN implies the Low-down variant. There is also an example that demonstrates that these notions are distinct, and thus the High-up variant is stricter.

Theorem 3. *H-GN is strictly contained in L-GN.*

Proof. Containment follows from the facts that H-GN = C-GN and that C-GN implies L-GN. For separation, we recall Fig. 6, and modify it slightly to suit our needs. This system can be verified to be GN-secure for the separation policy (i.e., the identity relation) on $\{H, L_1, L_2\}$; add the edges (L_1, H) and (L_2, H) to it and call it $\mapsto$.

With respect to $\mapsto$, the domain set has two Low-down cuts, which are $\mathrm{Ld}(L_1)$ and $\mathrm{Ld}(L_2)$. The systems $\mathcal{M}^{\mathrm{Ld}(L_1)}$ and $\mathcal{M}^{\mathrm{Ld}(L_2)}$ can be shown to be GN-secure for $\mapsto^{\mathrm{Ld}(L_1)}$ and $\mapsto^{\mathrm{Ld}(L_2)}$, respectively, and therefore $\mathcal{M}$ is L-GN-secure for $\mapsto$. However, for the High-up cut $\mathrm{Hu}(H)$, one can see that $\mathcal{M}^{\mathrm{Hu}(H)}$ fails to be GN-secure for $\mapsto^{\mathrm{Hu}(H)}$. Consider the run $r := s_0 h s_0' \ell_1 s_5 \ell_2 s_{13}$. We have $\mathrm{view}_L(r) = {}^{\perp}_{\perp} \ell_1 {}^{0}_{\perp} \ell_2 {}^{0}_{1}$, where L observations are written in the form $\genfrac{}{}{0pt}{}{\mathrm{obs}_{L_1}(\cdot)}{\mathrm{obs}_{L_2}(\cdot)}$. By the parity of their final observations after performing r, domains L_1 and L_2 together can determine that H performed h at the very beginning of the run. Thus, $\mathcal{M}^{\mathrm{Hu}(H)}$ doesn't satisfy the property $\mathrm{GN}^-(\{H\}, \{L_1, L_2\})$ for $\mapsto^{\mathrm{Hu}(H)}$, which means that $\mathcal{M}$ is not H-GN-secure for $\mapsto$. □

The weakness of Low-down GN is that it assumes a somewhat restricted attacker that never groups domains into Low that may not interfere with each other according to the policy. (For example, for the policy in Fig. 6, the coalition $\{L_1, L_2\}$ is not covered.) But nevertheless such coalitions are possible, which provides an argument against Low-down GN if coalitions are a risk. However, as one would expect, Low-down GN turns out to be stricter than GN_{pw}.

Theorem 4. *L-GN is strictly contained in GN_{pw}.*

Proof. Containment is shown by contraposition. Let $\mathcal{M}$ be a system with domain set D and $\mapsto$ a policy over D. Assume that $\mathcal{M}$ is not GN_{pw}-secure for $\mapsto$ and has a vulnerability $(u, \alpha_0, a, \alpha_1, \beta, \mapsto)$.

Set $\mathcal{C} := \mathrm{Ld}(u)$, $\mathcal{L} := {}^{\vdash}u$ and $\mathcal{H} := D \setminus {}^{\vdash}u$. We show, using Lemma 1, that there is β' so that $(\mathcal{L}, \alpha_0, a, \alpha_1, \beta', \mapsto^{\mathcal{C}})$ is a vulnerability in $\mathcal{M}^{\mathcal{C}}$. First, we have $\mathrm{dom}^{\mathcal{C}}(a) = \mathcal{H}$, due to $\mathrm{dom}(a) \not\mapsto u$, which implies $\mathrm{dom}^{\mathcal{C}}(a) \not\mapsto^{\mathcal{C}} \mathcal{L}$. Next, we demonstrate existence of a suitable β'. We identify observations made by v with observations made by the singleton coalition $\{v\}$, and consider the trivial abstraction of D, which is $\{\{w\} : w \in D\}$. Then we clearly have $\{v\} \subseteq \mathcal{L}$ and can apply Lemma 1. Due to vulnerability, there is a run on $\alpha_0 \alpha_1$ which has a $\{u\}$ view of β such that no run on $\alpha_0 a \alpha_1$ has a $\{u\}$ view of β. Let β' be the $\mathcal{L}$ view of this run. If there were a run r on $\alpha_0 a \alpha_1$ with $\mathcal{L}$ view of β', then $\mathrm{view}_u(r) = \mathrm{pr}^{\mathcal{L}}_{\{u\}}(\mathrm{view}_{\mathcal{L}}(r)) = \mathrm{pr}^{\mathcal{L}}_{\{u\}}(\beta') = \beta$ by identification of u and $\{u\}$ and

Lemma 1, contradicting the violation of $GN^+(u,v)$ in $\mathcal{M}$. Therefore, no such run can exist and $(\mathcal{L}, \alpha_0, a, \alpha_1, \beta', \mapsto^{\mathcal{C}})$ is a vulnerability of $\mathcal{M}^{\mathcal{C}}$.

For separation, take the example from Theorem 3 and add the additional edge (L_1, L_2) to $\mapsto$. The system is still GN_{pw}-secure for $\mapsto$ as GN_{pw} is monotonic, but since we have $\{H\} \not\mapsto^{\mathrm{Ld}(L_2)} \{L_1, L_2\}$, the system $\mathcal{M}^{\mathrm{Ld}(L_2)}$ is not GN-secure by the argument in the proof of Theorem 3.   □

8 Conclusion

In this work we have discussed several variants of Generalized Noninterference and Nondeducibility on Inputs for multi-domain policies that use reductions to the two-level case, including a technique proposed by Ryan. We have found that this technique leads to a stricter notion in the case of Generalized Noninterference, but behaves counter-intuitively in the case of Nondeducibility on Inputs, where it yields a notion that is incomparable to a natural variant for multi-domain policies. We have found evidence that seems to suggest that considering all cuts is a more robust choice as a reduction technique. Some notions we obtained break our intuitions in the sense that they are not preserved under removing noninterference constraints.

These results have left open a question about how to handle the general case of collusion, as reductions to $H \not\mapsto L$ are a special case of collusion where two coalitions are operating, while general abstractions can model an arbitrary number of coalitions. It seems natural to extend the theory such that it can handle general abstractions, but then we leave the area of transitive noninterference. For example, consider the transitive policy $\mapsto$ that contains the relations $A \mapsto B$ and $C \mapsto D$ only, and the abstraction $\mathcal{D}$ that forms the coalitions $\{A\}$, $\{B, C\}$ and $\{D\}$. The resulting policy $\mapsto^{\mathcal{D}}$ is intransitive, as it has edges $\{A\} \mapsto^{\mathcal{D}} \{B, C\}$ and $\{B, C\} \mapsto^{\mathcal{D}} \{D\}$, but lacks the edge $\{A\} \mapsto^{\mathcal{D}} \{D\}$. In this case, it seems reasonable to say that information may get from A to D, as domains B and C collude and share their observations, but it needs intermediate behaviour by them in order to forward the information. Adding the edge $\{A\} \mapsto^{\mathcal{D}} \{D\}$ clashes with this reasoning, as it would express that A may *directly* communicate with D. This suggests that dealing with general abstractions requires techniques from the theory of intransitive noninterference. Semantics for intransitive noninterference that build in types of collusion have been considered in a few works [21,23], but the relationship of these definitions to abstractions remains to be studied.

References

1. Haigh, J.T., Young, W.D.: Extending the noninterference version of MLS for SAT. IEEE Trans. Softw. Eng. **13**(2), 141 (1987)
2. Rushby, J.: Noninterference, transitivity, and channel-control security policies. Technical report, SRI international, December 1992
3. van der Meyden, R.: What, indeed, is intransitive noninterference? J. Comput. Secur. **23**(2), 197–228 (2015). Extended version of a paper in ESORICS 2007. http://dx.doi.org/10.3233/JCS-140516

4. Goguen, J.A., Meseguer, J.: Security policies and security models. In: 1982 IEEE Symposium on Security and Privacy, Oakland, CA, USA, 26–28 April, pp. 11–20 (1982)
5. Sutherland, D.: A model of information. In: Proceedings of the 9th National Computer Security Conference, DTIC Document, pp. 175–183 (1986)
6. McCullough, D.: Foundations of Ulysses: The theory of security. Technical report, DTIC Document (1988)
7. McLean, J.: A general theory of composition for trace sets closed under selective interleaving functions. In: Proceedings of the 1994 IEEE Computer Society Symposium on Research in Security and Privacy, pp. 79–93. IEEE (1994)
8. Mantel, H.: Possibilistic definitions of security - an assembly kit. In: Proceedings of the 13th IEEE Computer Security Foundations Workshopp, CSFW-13, pp. 185–199. IEEE (2000)
9. Focardi, R., Gorrieri, R.: Classification of security properties. In: Focardi, R., Gorrieri, R. (eds.) FOSAD 2000. LNCS, vol. 2171, p. 331. Springer, Heidelberg (2001)
10. Roscoe, A.W.: CSP and determinism in security modelling. In: Proceedings of the IEEE Symposium on Security and Privacy, pp. 114–221 (1995)
11. Ryan, P.Y.A.: Mathematical models of computer security. In: Focardi, R., Gorrieri, R. (eds.) FOSAD 2000. LNCS, vol. 2171, pp. 1–62. Springer, Heidelberg (2001)
12. Forster, R.: Non-interference properties for nondeterministic processes. Ph.D. thesis, Dissertation for transfer to D.Phil status, Oxford University Computing Laboratory (1997)
13. Mantel, H.: A uniform framework for the formal specification and verification of information flow security. Ph.D. thesis, Universität des Saarlandes (2003)
14. Millen, J.K.: Unwinding forward correctability. In: Proceedings of the IEEE Computer Security Foundations Workshop, pp. 2–10 (1994)
15. Roscoe, A.W., Woodcock, J., Wulf, L.: Non-interference through determinism. J. Comput. Secur. 4(1), 27–54 (1996)
16. Sutherland, D.: A model of information. In: Proceedings of the National Computer Security Conference, pp. 175–183 (1986)
17. McCullough, D.: Noninterference and the composability of security properties. In: Proceedings of the 1988 IEEE Symposium on Security and Privacy, Oakland, California, USA, 18–21 April, pp. 177–186 (1988)
18. Eggert, S., van der Meyden, R.: Dynamic intransitive noninterference revisited. CoRR (2016) arXiv:1601.05187 [cs.CR]
19. Goguen, J.A., Meseguer, J.: Unwinding and inference control. In: Proceedings of the 1984 IEEE Symposium on Security and Privacy, Oakland, California, USA, 29 April–2 May, pp. 75–87 (1984)
20. van der Meyden, R., Zhang, C.: Algorithmic verification of noninterference properties. Electr. Notes Theor. Comput. Sci. 168, 61–75 (2007)
21. Engelhardt, K., van der Meyden, R., Zhang, C.: Intransitive noninterference in nondeterministic systems. In: Proceedings of the 2012 ACM Conference on Computer and Communications Security, pp. 869–880. ACM (2012)
22. Woizekowski, O., van der Meyden, R.: On reductions from multi-domain noninterference to the two-level case. CoRR (2016). arXiv:1605.00474
23. Backes, M., Pfitzmann, B.: Intransitive non-interference for cryptographic purposes. In: IEEE Symposium on Security and Privacy, pp. 140–152 (2003)

Flexible Manipulation of Labeled Values for Information-Flow Control Libraries

Marco Vassena[1]($\boxtimes$), Pablo Buiras[1], Lucas Waye[2], and Alejandro Russo[1]

[1] Chalmers University of Technology, Gothenburg, Sweden
{vassena,buiras,russo}@chalmers.se
[2] Harvard University, Cambridge, USA
lwaye@seas.harvard.edu

Abstract. The programming language Haskell plays a unique, privileged role in Information-Flow Control (IFC) research: *it is able to enforce information security via libraries*. Many state-of-the-art libraries (e.g., **LIO**, **HLIO**, and **MAC**) allow computations to manipulate data with different security labels by introducing the notion of *labeled values*, which protect values with explicit labels by means of an abstract data type. While computations have an underlying algebraic structure in such libraries (i.e. monads), there is no research on structures for labeled values and their impact on the programming model. In this paper, we add the *functor* structure to labeled values, which allows programmers to conveniently and securely perform computations without side-effects on such values, and an *applicative* operator, which extends this feature to work on multiple labeled values combined by a multi-parameter function. This functionality simplifies code, as it does not force programmers to spawn threads to manipulate sensitive data with side-effect free operations. Additionally, we present a *relabel* primitive which securely modifies the label of labeled values. This operation also helps to simplify code when aggregating data with heterogeneous labels, as it does not require spawning threads to do so. We provide mechanized proofs of the soundness our contributions for the security library **MAC**, although we remark that our ideas apply to **LIO** and **HLIO** as well.

1 Introduction

Nowadays, many applications (apps) manipulate users' private data. Such apps *could have been written by anyone* and users who wish to benefit from their functionality are forced to grant them access to their data—something that most users will do without a second thought [21]. Once apps collect users' information, there are no guarantees about how they handle it, thus leaving room for data theft and data breach by malicious apps. The key to guaranteeing security without sacrificing functionality is not granting or denying access to sensitive data, but rather ensuring that *information only flows into appropriate places*.

Information-flow control (IFC) [32] is a promising programming language-based approach to enforcing security. IFC scrutinizes how data of different sensitivity levels (e.g., public or private) flows within a program, and raises alarms

© Springer International Publishing Switzerland 2016
I. Askoxylakis et al. (Eds.): ESORICS 2016, Part I, LNCS 9878, pp. 538–557, 2016.
DOI: 10.1007/978-3-319-45744-4_27

when there is an unsafe flow of information. Most IFC tools require the design of new languages, compilers, interpreters, or modifications to the runtime, e.g., [4, 24, 26, 29]. In this scenario, the functional programming language Haskell plays a unique privileged role: *it is able to enforce security via libraries* [18] by using an embedded domain-specific language.

Many of the state-of-the-art Haskell security libraries, namely **LIO** [37], **HLIO** [6], and **MAC** [31], bring ideas from Mandatory Access Control [3] into a language-based setting. Every computation in such libraries has a *current label* which is used to (i) approximate the sensitivity level of all the data in scope and (ii) restrict subsequent side-

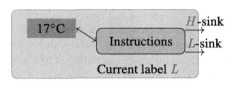

Fig. 1. Public computation

effects which might compromise security. From now on, we simply use the term libraries when referring to **LIO**, **HLIO**, and **MAC**.

IFC uses labels to model the sensitivity of data, which are then organized in a security lattice [7] specifying the allowed flows of information, i.e., $\ell_1 \sqsubseteq \ell_2$ means that data with label ℓ_1 can flow into entities labeled with ℓ_2. Although these libraries are parameterized on the security lattice, for simplicity we focus on the classic two-point lat-

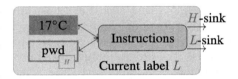

Fig. 2. Labeled values

tice with labels H and L to respectively denote secret (high) and public (low) data, and where $H \not\sqsubseteq L$ is the only disallowed flow. Figure 1 shows a graphical representation of a public computation in these libraries, i.e. a computation with current label L. The computation can read or write data in scope, which is considered public (e.g., average temperature of 17°C in the Swedish summer), and it can write to public (L-) or secret (H-) sinks. By contrast, a secret computation, i.e. a computation with current label H, can also read and write data in its scope, which is considered sensitive, but in order to prevent information leaks it can *only* write to sensitive/secret sinks. Structuring computations in this manner ensures that sensitive data does not flow into public entities, a policy known as noninterference [10]. While secure, programming in this model can be overly restrictive for users who want to manipulate differently-labeled values.

To address this shortcoming, libraries introduce the notion of a *labeled value* as an abstract data type which protects values with explicit labels, in addition to the current label. Figure 2 shows a public computation with access to both public and sensitive pieces of information, such as a password (pwd). Public computations can freely manipulate sensitive labeled values provided that they are treated as black boxes, i.e. they can be stored, retrieved, and passed around as long as its content is not inspected. Libraries **LIO** and **HLIO** even allow public computations to inspect the contents of sensitive labeled values, raising the current label to H to keep track of the fact that a secret is in scope—this variant is known as a *floating-label* system.

Reading sensitive data usually amounts to "tainting" the entire context or ensuring the context is as sensitive as the data being observed. As a result, the system is susceptible to an issue known as *label creep*: reading too many secrets may cause the current label to be so high in the lattice that the computation can no longer perform any useful side effects. To address this problem, libraries provide a primitive which enables public computations to spawn sub-computations that access sensitive labeled values without tainting the parent. In a sequential setting, such sub-computations are implemented by special function calls. In the presence of concurrency, however, they must be executed in a different thread to avoid compromising security through *internal timing* and *termination covert channels* [36].

Practical programs need to manipulate sensitive labeled values by transforming them. It is quite common for these operations to be naturally free of I/O or other side effects, e.g., arithmetical or algebraic operations, especially in applications like image processing, cryptography, or data aggregation for statistical purposes. Writing such functions, known as *pure* functions, is the bread and butter of functional programming style, and is known to improve programmer productivity, encourage code reuse, and reduce the likelihood of bugs [14]. Nevertheless, the programming model involving sub-computations that manipulate secrets forces an imperative style, whereby computations must be structured into separate compartments that must communicate explicitly. While side-effecting instructions have an underlying structure (called monad [22]), research literature has neglected studying structures for labeled values and their consequences for the programming model. To empower programmers with the simpler, functional style, we propose additional operations that allow pure functions to securely manipulate labeled values, specifically by means of a structure similar to *applicative functors* [20]. In particular, this structure is useful in concurrent settings where it is no longer necessary to spawn threads to manipulate sensitive data, thus making the code less imperative (i.e., side-effect free). Interestingly, the evaluation strategy of the host language (i.e. call-by-value or call-by-name) affects the validity of our security guarantees. Specifically, call-by-name turns out to naturally enforce progress-sensitive non-interference in a concurrent setting.

Additionally, practical programs often aggregate information from heterogeneous sources. For that, programs needs to upgrade labeled values to an upper bound of the labels being involved before data can be combined. In previous incarnations of the libraries, such relabelings require to spawn threads just for that purpose. As before, the reason for that is libraries decoupling every computation which manipulate sensitive data—even those for simply relabeling—so that the internal timing and termination covert channels imposed no threats. In this light, we introduce a primitive to securely relabel labeled values, which can be applied irrespective of the computation's current label and does not require spawning threads.

We provide a mechanized security proof for the security library **MAC** and claim our results also apply to **LIO** and **HLIO**. **MAC** has fewer lines of code and leverages types to enforce confidentiality, thus making it ideal to model its semantics in a dependently-typed language like Agda. The contributions of this paper are: (i) we introduce a *functor* structure equipped with an *applicative* operator that enables users to conveniently manipulate and combine labeled values using pure functions, encouraging a more functional (side-effect free) programming style; (ii) we introduce a relabeling primitive that securely modifies the label of labeled values, bypassing the need to spawn threads when aggregating heterogeneous data; (iii) we identify and discuss the impact of the evaluation strategy of the host language on the security of the applicative operators in **MAC** with respect to the internal timing and termination covert channels; (iv) we implement a prototype of our ideas in the **MAC** library[1]; and (v) we formalize **MAC** with secure applicative operators as a λ-calculus, providing a mechanized proof in Agda of progress-insensitive (PINI) and progress-sensitive noninterference (PSNI) [1] for the sequential and (respectively) concurrent setting.

This paper is organized as follows. Section 2 describes the core aspects of **MAC**. Sections 3 and 4 present functors, applicative, and relabeling operations. Section 5 gives formal guarantees. Section 6 gives related work and Sect. 7 concludes.

2   Background

In **MAC**, each label is represented as an abstract data type. Figure 3 shows the core part of **MAC**'s API. Abstract data type *Labeled ℓ a* classifies data of type *a* with a security label *ℓ*. For instance, *creditCard* :: *Labeled H Int* is a sensitive integer, while *weather* :: *Labeled L String* is a public string. (Symbol :: is used to describe the type of terms in Haskell.) Abstract data type *MAC ℓ a* denotes a (possibly) side-effectful secure computation which handles information at sensitivity

```
-- Abstract data types
data Labeled ℓ a
data MAC ℓ a

-- Monadic structure for computations
instance Monad (MAC ℓ)

-- Core operations
label  :: ℓ_L ⊑ ℓ_H ⇒
          a → MAC ℓ_L (Labeled ℓ_H a)
unlabel :: ℓ_L ⊑ ℓ_H ⇒
           Labeled ℓ_L a → MAC ℓ_H a

-- Only for sequential programs
join^MAC :: ℓ_L ⊑ ℓ_H ⇒
            MAC ℓ_H a → MAC ℓ_L (Labeled ℓ_H a)

-- Only for concurrent programs
fork^MAC :: ℓ_L ⊑ ℓ_H ⇒
            MAC ℓ_H () → MAC ℓ_L ()
```

Fig. 3. Simplified API for **MAC**

level ℓ and yields a value of type a as a result. A *MAC ℓ a* computation enjoys a monadic structure, i.e. it is built using the fundamental operations

---

[1] https://hackage.haskell.org/package/mac.

$return :: a \rightarrow MAC\ \ell\ a$ and $(\ggg) :: MAC\ \ell\ a \rightarrow (a \rightarrow MAC\ \ell\ b) \rightarrow MAC\ \ell\ b$ (read as "bind"). The operation $return\ x$ produces a computation that returns the value denoted by x and produces no side-effects. The function $(\ggg)$ is used to *sequence* computations and their corresponding side-effects. Specifically, $m \ggg f$ takes a computation m and function f which will be applied to the *result* produced by running m and yields the resulting computation. We sometimes use Haskell's do-notation to write such monadic computations. For example, the program $m \ggg \lambda x \rightarrow return\ (x + 1)$, which adds 1 to the value produced by m, can be written as shown in Fig. 4.

Secure flows of information. Generally speaking, side-effects in a $MAC\ \ell\ a$ computation can be seen as actions which either read or write data. Such actions, however, need to be conceived in a manner that respects the sensitivity of the computations' results as well as the sensitivity

```
do x ← m
   return (x + 1)
```

Fig. 4. do-notation

of sources and sinks of information modeled as labeled values. The functions *label* and *unlabel* allow $MAC\ \ell\ a$ computations to securely interact with labeled values. To help readers, we indicate the relationship between type variables in their subindexes, i.e. we use ℓ_L and ℓ_H to attest that $\ell_L \sqsubseteq \ell_H$. If a $MAC\ \ell_L$ computation writes data into a sink, the computation should have at most the sensitivity of the sink itself. This restriction, known as *no write-down* [3], respects the sensitivity of the data sink, e.g., the sink never receives data more sensitive than its label. In the case of function *label*, it creates a fresh labeled value, which from the security point of view can be seen as allocating a fresh location in memory and immediately writing a value into it—thus, it applies the no write-down principle. In the type signature of *label*, what appears on the left-hand side of the symbol $\Rightarrow$ are *type constraints*. They represent properties that must be statically fulfilled about the types appearing on the right-hand side of $\Rightarrow$. Type constraint $\ell_L \sqsubseteq \ell_H$ ensures that when calling *label* x (for some x in scope), the computation creates a labeled value only if ℓ_L, i.e. the current label of the computation, is no more confidential than ℓ_H, i.e. the sensitivity of the created labeled value. In contrast, a computation $MAC\ \ell_H\ a$ is only allowed to read labeled values at most as sensitive as ℓ_H—observe the type constraint $\ell_L \sqsubseteq \ell_H$ in the type signature of *unlabel*. This restriction, known as *no read-up* [3], protects the confidentiality degree of the result produced by $MAC\ \ell_H\ a$, i.e. the result might only involve data ℓ_L which is, at most, as sensitive as ℓ_H.

```
impl :: Labeled H Bool →
         MAC H (Labeled L Bool)
impl secret = do
  bool ← unlabel secret
  -- H ⋢ L
  if bool then label True
          else  label False
```

Fig. 5. Implicit flows are ill-typed.

The interaction between the current label of a computation and the no write-down restriction makes implicit flow ill-typed, as shown in Fig. 5. In order to branch on sensitive data, a program needs first to unlabel it, thus requiring the computation to be of type $MAC\ H\ a$ (for some type a). From that point, the computation cannot write to public data regardless of the taken branch. As **MAC** provides additional primitives responsible for producing useful side-effects like exception handling, network communication, references, and synchronization primitives—we refer the interested reader to [31] for further details.

Handling data with different sensitivity. Programs handling data with heterogeneous labels necessarily involve *nested MAC ℓ a* computations in its return type. For instance, consider a piece of code *m* with type *MAC L (String, MAC H Int)* which handles both public and secret information. Note that the type indicates that it returns a public string and a sensitive computation *MAC H Int*. While somehow manageable for a two-point lattice, it becomes intractable for general cases. In a *sequential setting*, **MAC** presents the primitive *join*^{MAC} to safely *integrate* more sensitive computations into less sensitive ones—see Fig. 3. Operationally, function *join*^{MAC} runs the computation of type *MAC* ℓ_{H} *a* and wraps the result into a labeled expression to protect its sensitivity. As we will show in Sect. 5, Haskell programs written using the monadic API, *label*, *unlabel*, and *join*^{MAC} satisfy PINI, where leaks due to non-termination of programs are ignored. This design decision is similar to that taken by mainstream IFC compilers (e.g., [11,25,34]), where the most effective manner to exploit termination takes exponential time in the size (of bits) of the secret [1].

Concurrency. The mere possibility to run (conceptually) simultaneous *MAC ℓ* computations provides attackers with new tools to bypass security checks. In particular, the presence of threads introduce the internal timing covert channel, a channel that gets exploited when, depending on secrets, the timing behavior of threads affect the order of events per-

```
-- Publish a number in a blog
publish :: Int → MAC L ()

-- Attack
leak :: Int → Labeled H Secret → MAC L ()
leak n secret = do
   joinMAC (do bits ← unlabel secret
               when (bits !! n) loop
               return True)
   publish n
```

Fig. 6. Termination leak

formed on public-shared resources [35]. Furthermore, concurrency magnifies the bandwidth of the termination covert channel to be linear in the size (of bits) of secrets [36]. Since the same countermeasure closes both covert channels, we focus on the latter. What constitutes a termination leak is the fact that a non-terminating *MAC* ℓ_{H}-computation can suppress the execution of subsequently *MAC* ℓ_{L}-events. To illustrate this point, we present the attack in Fig. 6. We assume that there exists a function *publish* which sends an integer to a public blog. Observe how function *leak* may suppress subsequent public events with infinite loops. If a thread runs *leak* 0 *secret*, the code publishes 0 *only if* the first bit of *secret* is 0; otherwise it loops (see function *loop*) and it does not produce any public effect. Similarly, a thread running *leak* 1 *secret* will leak the second bit of *secret*, while a thread running *leak* 2 *secret* will leak the third bit of it and so on. To securely support concurrency, **MAC** forces programmers to decouple computations which depend on sensitive data from those performing public side-effects. As a result, non-terminating loops based on secrets cannot affect the outcome of public events. To achieve this behavior, **MAC** replaces $join^{\mathsf{MAC}}$ by $fork^{\mathsf{MAC}}$ as defined in Fig. 3. It is secure to spawn sensitive computations ($MAC\ \ell_{\mathrm{H}}$) from non-sensitive ones ($MAC\ \ell_{\mathrm{L}}$) because that decision depends on data at level ℓ_{L}.

Example 1. To show how to program using **MAC**, we present a simple scenario where Alice writes an API that helps users prepare and file their taxes. Alice models a tax declaration as values of type *TaxDecl*, which is obtained based on users' personal information—modeled as values of type *Data*. She releases the first version of the API:

```
    -- API
declareTaxes :: Data → IO ()
declareTaxes user = send (fillTaxes user)

    -- Internal operations (not exported)
fillTaxes :: Data      → TaxDecl
send      :: TaxDecl → IO ()
```

We remark that, although we focus on this API for simplicity, Alice is using the concurrent version of **MAC**. Function *declareTaxes* does two things: it fills out the tax forms (function *fillTaxes*) and sends them to the corresponding government agency (function *send*). Due to the use of *send*, function *declareTaxes* returns a computation in the *IO*-monad—a special data type which permits arbitrary I/O effects in Haskell. Function *send* generates a valid PDF for tax declarations and sends it to the corresponding authorities. However, there is nothing stopping this function from leaking tax information to unauthorized entities over the network. Alice's customers notice this problem and are concerned about how their sensitive data gets handled by the API.

Alice then decides to adapt the API to use **MAC**. For simplicity, we assume that **MAC** also includes a secure operation to send data over the network:

$$send^{\mathsf{MAC}} :: \ell_{\mathrm{L}} \sqsubseteq \ell_{\mathrm{H}} \Rightarrow Labeled\ \ell_{\mathrm{H}}\ URL \to Labeled\ \ell_{\mathrm{H}}\ a \to MAC\ \ell_{\mathrm{L}}\ ()$$

This primitive sends a labeled value of type a to the URL given as an argument, e.g., via HTTP-request or other network protocol. Using **MAC**'s concurrent API and primitive $send^{\mathsf{MAC}}$, Alice rewrites her API to adhere to the following interface.

```
declareTaxes :: Labeled H URL → Labeled H Data → MAC L ()
declareTaxes url user = forkMAC (do info ← unlabel user
                                     tax ← label (fillTaxes info)
                                     sendMAC url tax

    -- Internal operations
fillTaxes :: Data → TaxDecl
```

Observe that Alice's API needs to spawn a secure computation of type $MAC\ H\ ()$ in order to unlabel and access user's data (*user*). Once user's data is accessible, a pure function gets applied to it (*fillTaxes info*), the result is relabeled (*tax*) again and a side-effectful action takes place ($send^{\mathsf{MAC}}$). In the next section we extend **MAC**'s API so that it is possible to manipulate labeled values with pure functions, like *fillTaxes*, and perform side-effectful actions, like *send*^{MAC}, without the need to spawn threads.

3   Functors for Labeled Values

In this section, we show how labeled values can be manipulated using *functors*.

$$fmap :: (a \to b) \to Labeled \; \ell \; a \to Labeled \; \ell \; b$$

Fig. 7. Functor structure for labeled values

Intuitively, a functor is a container-like data structure which provides a method called *fmap* that applies (maps) a function over its content, while preserving its structure. Lists are the most canonical example of a functor data-structure. In this case, *fmap* corresponds to the function *map*, which applies a function to each element of a list, e.g. *fmap* $(+1)$ $[1, 2, 3] \equiv [2, 3, 4]$. A functor structure for labeled values allows to manipulate sensitive data without the need to explicitly extract it—see Fig. 7. For instance, *fmap* $(+1)$ d, where $d :: Labeled \; H \; Int$ stores the number 42, produces the number 43 as a sensitive labeled value. Observe that sensitive data gets manipulated without the need to use *label* and *unlabel*, thus avoiding their overhead (no security checks are performed). Despite what intuition might suggest, it is possible to securely apply *fmap* in any *MAC* ℓ-computation to any labeled value *irrespectively of its security level*. A secure implementation of *fmap* then allows manipulation of data without forking threads in a concurrent setting—thus, introducing flexibility when data is processed by pure (side-effect free) functions. However, obtaining a secure implementation of *fmap* requires a careful analysis of its security implications.

Interestingly, the evaluation strategy of the programming language and the sequential or concurrent setting determine different security guarantees in the presence of *fmap*. Figure 9 shows our findings. In a sequential setting with *call-by-value* semantics, *fmap* can be

	Sequential	Concurrent
call-by-value	**PINI**	**✗**
call-by-name	**PINI**	**PSNI**

Fig. 9. Security guarantees

exploited to create a termination covert channel in a similar manner as it is done with *join*^{MAC}. To illustrate this point, we rephrase the attack in Fig. 6 to use *fmap* rather than *join*^{MAC}—see Fig. 8. Under a *call-by-value* evaluation strategy, function *loopOn* passed to *fmap* is eagerly applied to the secret, which might introduce a loop depending on the value of the n-th bit of the secret—a termination leak. Under a *call-by-name* evaluation strategy, however, function

$leak :: Int \to Labeled \; H \; Secret \to MAC \; L \; ()$
$leak \; n \; secret = \textbf{let} \; result = fmap \; loopOn \; secret \; \textbf{in} \; publish \; n$
   $\textbf{where} \; loopOn = \lambda bits \to \textbf{if} \; (bits \; !! \; n) \; \textbf{then} \; loop \; \textbf{else} \; bits$

Fig. 8. Termination leak under call-by-value evaluation

loopOn does not get immediately evaluated since *result* is not needed for computing *publish n*. Therefore, *publish n* gets executed independently of the value of the secret, i.e. no termination leaks are introduced. Instead, *loopOn* gets evaluated when "unlabeling" *result* and inspecting its value in a computation of type *MAC H a* (for some *a*), which is secure to do so. Although *functors* can be used to exploit non-termination of programs, they impose no new risks for sequential programs (**MAC** already ignores termination leaks in such setting).

Unfortunately, a call-by-value concurrent semantics magnifies the bandwidth of the attack in Fig. 8 to the point where confidentiality can be systematically and efficiently broken—see Fig. 10. Assuming a secret of 100-bits, the magni-

$$magnify :: Labeled\ H\ Secret \rightarrow MAC\ L\ ()$$
$$magnify\ secret =$$
$$for\ [0 \mathbin{.\,.} 99]$$
$$(\lambda n \rightarrow fork^{\mathsf{MAC}}\ (leak\ n\ secret))$$

Fig. 10. Attack magnification

fication consists on leaking the whole secret by spawning a sufficient number of threads—each of them leaking a different bit. Since *leak* cannot exploit the termination channel under a *call-by-name* evaluation strategy, the magnification attack becomes vacuous under such semantics. More precisely, the attack can only trigger the execution of *leak* by first unlabeling *result*, an operation impossible to perform in a public computation—recall there is no *join*^{MAC} primitive for concurrent programs. As the table suggests, call-by-name gives the strongest security guarantees when extending **MAC** with functors. We remark that it is possible to close this termination channel under a call-by-value semantics by defining *Labeled* with an explicit suspension, e.g. **data** *Labeled ℓ a = Labeled (() → a)*, and corresponding forcing operation, so that *fmap* behaves lazily as desired.

Example 2. Alice's realizes that she could spare her API from forking threads by exploiting the *functorial* structure of labeled values.

```
declareTaxes :: Labeled H URL → Labeled H Data → MAC L ()
declareTaxes url user = send^MAC url (fmap fillTaxes user)

    -- Internal operations
fillTaxes :: Data → TaxDecl
```

The construct *fmap* applies the function *fillTaxes* without requiring use of *unlabel*, while keeping the result securely encapsulated in a labeled value. Observe how the code is much less imperative, since there is no need to fork a thread to unlabel sensitive data just to apply a pure function to it.

While functors help to make the code more functional, there are still other programming patterns which draw developers to fork threads due to security reasons rather than the need for multi-threading. Specifically, when aggregating data from sources with incomparable

$$H$$
$$\nearrow \quad \nwarrow$$
$$L \qquad\quad TP$$

Fig. 11. Lattice.

labels, computations are forced to spawn a thread with a sufficiently high label. To illustrate this point, we present the following example.

Example 3. Alice knows that there is a third-party API which provides financial planning and she would gladly incorporate its functionality into her API. However, Alice wants to keep the third-party code isolated from hers, while still providing functionality to the user. To do so, she incorporates a new label into the system, namely TP and modifies the lattice as shown in Fig. 11. The lattice reflects the mistrust that Alice has over the third-party code by making L and TP incomparable elements.

Alice's API is extended with the third-party code as follows.

$declare\,Taxes :: Labeled\ H\ URL \rightarrow Labeled\ H\ Data \rightarrow MAC\ L\ ()$
$reportPlan\ \ :: Labeled\ H\ URL \rightarrow Labeled\ H\ Data \rightarrow MAC\ L\ ()$
   -- Internal operations
$fillTaxes :: Data \rightarrow TaxDecl$
$financialPlan :: Labeled\ TP\ (Data \rightarrow FinancePlan)$

Function *reportPlan* needs to fork a thread in order to unlabel the third-party code (*financialPlan*).

$reportPlan :: Labeled\ H\ URL \rightarrow Labeled\ H\ Data \rightarrow MAC\ L\ ()$
$reportPlan\ url\ user = \mathbf{do}$
$\quad fork^{\text{MAC}}\ (\mathbf{do}\ user \qquad\qquad \leftarrow unlabel\ user$
$\qquad\qquad\ financialPlan' \leftarrow unlabel\ financialPlan$
$\qquad\qquad\ plan \qquad\qquad \leftarrow label\ (financialPlan'\ user)$
$\qquad\qquad\ send^{\text{MAC}}\ url\ plan)$

In the next section, we show how to avoid forking threads for this kind of scenarios.

4   Applicative Operator and Relabeling

To aggregate sensitivity-heterogeneous data without forking, we further extend the API with the primitives shown in Fig. 12. Primitive *relabel* copies, and possibly upgrades, a labeled value. This primitive is useful to "lift" data to an upper bound of all the data involved in a computation prior to combining them. Operator $(\langle * \rangle)$ supports function application within a labeled value, i.e. it allows to feed functions wrapped in a labeled value (*Labeled* $\ell\ (a \rightarrow b)$) with arguments also wrapped (*Labeled* $\ell\ a$), where aggregated results get wrapped as well (*Labeled* $\ell\ b$). We demonstrate the utility of *relabel* and $(\langle * \rangle)$ by rewriting Example 3.

$relabel :: \ell_{\text{L}} \sqsubseteq \ell_{\text{H}} \Rightarrow$
$\qquad\qquad Labeled\ \ell_{\text{L}}\ a \rightarrow Labeled\ \ell_{\text{H}}\ a$
$(\langle * \rangle)\ \ :: Labeled\ \ell\ (a \rightarrow b) \rightarrow$
$\qquad\qquad Labeled\ \ell\ a \rightarrow Labeled\ \ell\ b$

Fig. 12. Extended API for labeled values

Example 4. Alice easily modifies *reportPlan* as follows:

> *reportPlan url user* = **do**
>   **let** *financialPlan'* = *relabel financialPlan*
>   **in** *send*^MAC *url* (*financialPlan'* ⟨∗⟩ *user*)

The third-party function (*financialPlan*) is relabeled to H, which is justified since $TP \sqsubseteq H$, and then applied to the user data (*financialPlan'* ⟨∗⟩ *user*) using the applicative (functor) operator. Note that the result is still labeled with H.

Discussion. In function programming, operator (⟨∗⟩) is part of the *applicative functors* [20] interface, which in combinations with *fmap*, is used to map functions over functors. Note that if labeled values fully enjoyed the applicative functor structure, our API would include also the primitive *pure* :: $a \rightarrow Labeled\ \ell\ a$. This primitive brings arbitrary values into labeled values, which might break the security principles enforced by **MAC**. Instead of *pure*, **MAC** centralizes the creation of labeled values in the primitive *label*. Observe that, by using *pure*, a programmer could write a computation $m :: MAC\ H\ (Labeled\ L\ a)$ where the *created* labeled information is sensitive rather than public. We argue that this situation ignores the no-write down principle, which might bring confusion among developers. More importantly, freely creating labeled values is not compatible with the security notion of *cleareance*, where secure computations have an upper bound on the kind of sensitive data the they can observe and generate. This notion becomes useful to address certain covert channels [40] as well as poison-pill attacks [13]. While **MAC** does not yet currently support cleareance, we state this research direction as future work.

5   Security Guarantees

This section presents the core part of our formalization of **MAC** as a simply typed call-by-name λ-calculus extended with booleans, unit values, and monadic operations. Note that our mechanized proofs, available online[2], cover the full calculus which also includes references, synchronization variables, and exceptions. Given the number of advanced features in the calculus we remark that a proof assistant has proved to be an invaluable tool to verify the correctness of our proofs. Figure 13 shows the formal syntax. Meta variables τ, v and t denote types, values, and terms, respectively. Most of these syntactic categories are self-explanatory with the exception of a few cases that we proceed to clarify. We note that, even though labels are actual types in **MAC**, we use a separate syntactic category ℓ for clarity in this calculus. Furthermore, we assume that labels form a lattice $(\mathscr{L}, \sqsubseteq)$. Constructors MAC and Res represent a secure computation and a labeled resource, respectively. The latter is an established technique to lift arbitrary resources such as references and synchronization variables into

---

[2] https://bitbucket.org/MarcoVassena/mac-agda.

Label: ℓ
Types: $\tau ::= Bool \mid () \mid \tau_1 \rightarrow \tau_2 \mid MAC\ \ell\ \tau \mid Id\ \tau \mid Res\ \ell\ \tau$
Values: $v ::= True \mid False \mid () \mid \lambda x.t \mid Id\ t \mid MAC\ t \mid Res\ t$
Terms: $t ::= v \mid t_1\ t_2 \mid \textbf{if } t_1 \textbf{ then } t_2 \textbf{ else } t_3 \mid return\ t \mid t_1 \ggg t_2$
$\qquad \mid relabel\ t \mid label\ t \mid unlabel\ t \mid join\ t \mid \langle * \rangle$
$\qquad \mid fork\ t \mid \langle * \rangle_\bullet \mid relabel_\bullet \mid \bullet$

Fig. 13. Formal syntax for types, values, and terms.

(HOLE)

$\bullet \rightsquigarrow \bullet$

(LABELED$\langle * \rangle$)

$(Res\ t_1)\ \langle * \rangle\ (Res\ t_2) \rightsquigarrow Res\ (t_1\ \langle * \rangle\ t_2)$

(ID $\langle * \rangle$)

$Id\ (\lambda x.t_1)\ \langle * \rangle\ Id\ t_2 \rightsquigarrow Id\ ([x\ /\ t_2]\ t_1)$

(RELABEL)

$relabel\ (Res\ t) \rightsquigarrow Res\ t$

(UNLABEL)

$unlabel\ (Res\ (Id\ t)) \rightsquigarrow return\ t$

Fig. 14. Semantics for non-standard constructs.

MAC [31]. *MAC* and *Res* are **MAC**'s internals constructors, therefore they are not available to users of the library and are not part of the surface syntax. Data type $Id\ \tau$ denotes an expression of type τ and $Res\ (Id\ t)$ represents a labeled expression t, which we abbreviate as *Labeled t*. Similarly we write *Labeled $\ell\ \tau$* for the type $Res\ \ell\ (Id\ \tau)$. Node $\langle * \rangle$ corresponds to the applicative (functor) operator and is overloaded for *Labeled $\ell\ t$* and $Id\ \tau$. Every applicative functor is also a functor [20], hence *fmap f x* is simply defined as $(Labeled\ f)\ \langle * \rangle\ x$. The special syntax nodes $\bullet$, $\langle * \rangle_\bullet$, and *relabel$_\bullet$* represent *erased terms* and are used by our proof technique to examine the security guarantees of the calculus.

Types. The typing judgment $\Gamma \vdash t : \tau$ denotes that term t has type τ assuming the typing environment Γ. All the typing rules are standard and thus omitted, except for $\bullet$ which can assume any type, i.e. $\Gamma \vdash \bullet : \tau$.

Semantics. The small-step semantics of the calculus is represented by the relation $t_1 \rightsquigarrow t_2$, which denotes that t_1 reduces to t_2 in one step. Most of the rules are standard and hence omitted; the rules for interesting constructs are shown in Fig. 14. Term $\bullet$ merely reduces to itself according to rule [HOLE.] Rule [LABELED$\langle * \rangle$] describes the semantics of operator $\langle * \rangle$, which applies a labeled function to a labeled value. Terms t_1 and t_2 are wrapped in Id so they cannot be combined by plain function application. As rule [ID$\langle * \rangle$] shows, Id is also an applicative operator and therefore $\langle * \rangle$ is used instead. Observe that symbol $\langle * \rangle$ is overloaded, where the type of its argument determines which rule to apply, i.e. either [LABELED$\langle * \rangle$] or [ID$\langle * \rangle$]. Rule [ID$\langle * \rangle$] requires a function to be in weak-head normal form $((\lambda x.t_1)\ t_2)$ where *beta reduction* occurs right away. (As usual, we write $[t_1\ /\ x]\ t_2$ for the capture-avoiding substitution of every occurrence of x with t_1 in t_2). This manner to write the rule is unusual since it would be expected that $Id\ f\ \langle * \rangle\ Id\ t \rightsquigarrow Id\ (f\ t)$. Nevertheless, the eagerness of $\langle * \rangle$ in its first argument is needed for technical reasons in order to guarantee non-interference. Rule [RELABELu]pgrades the label of a labeled value. Since relabeling occurs at the level of types, the reduction rules simply create another labeled term. Finally rule [UNLABELe]xtracts the labeled value and returns it in a computation at the appropriate security level. We omit the two context rules that first reduce the labeled value to weak-head normal form and then the expression itself.

5.1   Sequential Calculus

In this section, we prove progress-insensitive non-interference for our calculus. Similar to other work [19,30,37], we employ the *term erasure* proof technique. To that end, we introduce an erasure function which rewrites sensitive information, i.e. data above the security level of the attacker, to term $\bullet$. Since security levels are at the type-level, the erasure function is type-driven.

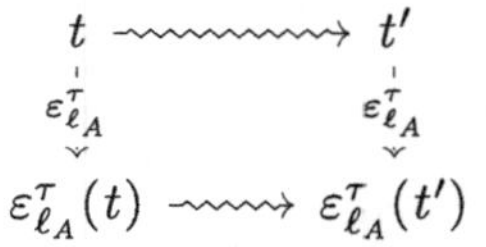

Fig. 15. Commutative diagram

We write $\varepsilon^{\tau}_{\ell_A}(t)$ for the erasure of term t with type τ of data above the security of the attacker ℓ_A. We omit the type superscript when it is either irrelevant or clear from the context. Figure 15 highlights the intuition behind the used proof technique: *showing that the drawn diagram commutes.* More precisely, we show that erasing sensitive data from a term t and then taking a step (lower part of the diagram) is the same as firstly taking a step (upper part of the diagram) and then erasing sensitive data. If term t leaks data which sensitivity label is above ℓ_A, then erasing all sensitive data and taking a step might not be the same as taking a step and then erasing secret values—the leaked sensitive data in t' might remain in $\varepsilon^{\tau}_{\ell_A}(t')$.

$$\varepsilon_{\ell_A}(\bullet) = \bullet \qquad \varepsilon^{Res\ \ell\ \tau}_{\ell_A}(Res\ t) = \begin{cases} Res\ \varepsilon_{\ell_A}(t), & \text{if } \ell \sqsubseteq \ell_A \\ Res\ \bullet, & \text{otherwise} \end{cases}$$

$$\varepsilon^{Labeled\ \ell\ \tau}_{\ell_A}(t_1\ \langle * \rangle\ t_2) = \begin{cases} \varepsilon_{\ell_A}(t_1)\ \langle * \rangle\ \varepsilon_{\ell_A}(t_2) & \text{if } \ell \sqsubseteq \ell_A \\ \varepsilon_{\ell_A}(t_1)\ \langle * \rangle_\bullet\ \varepsilon_{\ell_A}(t_2) & \text{otherwise} \end{cases}$$

$$\varepsilon^{Labeled\ \ell\ \tau}_{\ell_A}(t_1\ \langle * \rangle_\bullet\ t_2) = \varepsilon_{\ell_A}(t_1)\ \langle * \rangle_\bullet\ \varepsilon_{\ell_A}(t_2)$$

$$\varepsilon^{Labeled\ \ell\ \tau}_{\ell_A}(relabel\ t) = \begin{cases} relabel\ \varepsilon_{\ell_A}(t) & \text{if } \ell \sqsubseteq \ell_A \\ relabel_\bullet\ \varepsilon_{\ell_A}(t) & \text{otherwise} \end{cases}$$

$$\varepsilon^{Labeled\ \ell\ \tau}_{\ell_A}(relabel_\bullet\ t) = relabel_\bullet\ \varepsilon_{\ell_A}(t) \qquad \varepsilon^{MAC\ \ell\ \tau}_{\ell_A}(t) = \bullet, \text{ if } \ell \not\sqsubseteq \ell_A$$

Fig. 16. Erasure function.

(LABELED⟨∗⟩•)   (RELABEL•)

$(Res\ t_1)\ ⟨∗⟩•\ (Res\ t_2) \rightsquigarrow Res\ •$ $relabel•\ (Res\ t) \rightsquigarrow Res\ •$

Fig. 17. Reduction rules for $⟨∗⟩•$ and $relabel•$.

Figure 16 shows the definition of the erasure functions for the interesting cases. Before explaining them, we remark that ground values (e.g., *True*) are unaffected by the erasure function and that, for most of the terms, the function is homomorphically applied, e.g., $\varepsilon_\ell^{()}(\textbf{if}\ t_1\ \textbf{then}\ t_2\ \textbf{else}\ t_3) =$ **if** $\varepsilon_\ell^{Bool}(t_1)$ **then** $\varepsilon_\ell^{()}(t_2)$ **else** $\varepsilon_\ell^{()}(t_3)$. Labeled resources are erased according to the label found in their type ($Res\ \ell\ \tau$). If the attacker can observe the term ($\ell \sqsubseteq \ell_A$), the erasure function is homomorphically applied; otherwise, it is replaced with •. In principle, one might be tempted to apply the erasure function homomorphically for $⟨∗⟩$ and *relabel*, but such approach unfortunately breaks the commutativity of Fig. 15. To illustrate this point, consider the term $(Res\ f)\ ⟨∗⟩\ (Res\ x)$ of type *Labeled H Int*, which reduces to $Res\ (f\ ⟨∗⟩\ x)$ according to rule [LABELED⟨∗⟩]. By applying the erasure function homomorphically, we get $\varepsilon_L(Res\ f)\ ⟨∗⟩\ \varepsilon_L(Res\ x)$, that is $(Res\ •)\ ⟨∗⟩\ (Res\ •)$ which reduces to $Res\ (•\ ⟨∗⟩\ •) \not\equiv Res\ •$. Operator *relabel* raises a similar problem. Consider for example the term *relabel* (*Labeled* 42) :: *Labeled H Int*, where *Labeled* 42::*Labeled L Int*. If the erasure function were applied homomorphically, i.e. consider $relabel\ \varepsilon_L^{Labeled\ L\ Int}(Labeled\ 42)$, it means that *sensitive data produced by relabel remains after erasure*—thus, breaking commutativity. Instead, we perform erasure in *two-steps*—a novel technique if compared with previous papers (e.g., [37]). Rather than being a pure syntactic procedure, erasure is also performed by additional evaluation rules, triggered by special constructs introduced by the erasure function. Specifically, the erasure function replaces $⟨∗⟩$ with $⟨∗⟩•$ and erasure is then performed by means of rule [LABELED⟨∗⟩•]—see Fig. 17. Following the same scheme, the erasure function replaces *relabel* with *relabel•* and rule [RELABEL•] performs the erasure. $⟨∗⟩•$ and *relabel•* and their semantics rules are introduced due to mere technical reasons (as explained above) and they do not impact the performance of **MAC** since they are not part of its implementation. Finally, *terms* of type *MAC* $\ell\ \tau$ are replaced by • when the computation is more sensitive than the attacker level ($\ell \not\sqsubseteq \ell_A$); otherwise, the erasure function is homomorphically applied.

Progress-Insensitive Non-interference. The non-interference proof relies on two fundamental properties of our calclulus: *determinism* and *distributivity*.

Proposition 1 (Sequential determinancy and distributivity)

- *If $t_1 \rightsquigarrow t_2$ and $t_1 \rightsquigarrow t_3$ then $t_2 = t_3$.*
- *If $t_1 \rightsquigarrow t_2$ then $\varepsilon_{\ell_A}(t_1) \rightsquigarrow \varepsilon_{\ell_A}(t_2)$.*

In Proposition 1, we show the auxiliary property that erasure distributes over substitution, i.e. $\varepsilon_{\ell_A}([x \,/\, t_1] \, t_2) = [x \,/\, \varepsilon_{\ell_A}(t_1)] \, \varepsilon_{\ell_A}(t_2)$. Note, however, that the erasure function does not always distribute over function application, i.e. $\varepsilon_{\ell_A}^\tau(t_1 \, t_2) \not\equiv \varepsilon_{\ell_A}(t_1) \, \varepsilon_{\ell_A}(t_2)$ when $\tau = MAC \; h \; \tau'$ and $h \not\sqsubseteq \ell_A$. It is precisely for this reason that rule $[\textsc{Id}\langle * \rangle]$ performs substitution rather than function application. Before stating non-interference, we formally define ℓ_A-equivalence.

Definition 1 *(ℓ_A-equivalence). Two terms are indistinguishable from an attacker at security level ℓ_A, written $x \approx_{\ell_A} y$, if and only if $\varepsilon_{\ell_A}(x) = \varepsilon_{\ell_A}(y)$.*

Using Proposition 1, we show that our semantics preserves ℓ_A-equivalence.

Proposition 2 *(ℓ_A-equivalence preservation). If $t_1 \approx_{\ell_A} t_2$, $t_1 \rightsquigarrow t_1'$, and $t_2 \rightsquigarrow t_2'$, then $t_1' \approx_{\ell_A} t_2'$.*

We finally prove progress-insensitive non-interference for the sequential calculus. We employ *big-step* semantics, denoted by $t \Downarrow v$, which reduces term t to value v in a finite number of steps.

Theorem 1 (PINI). *If $t_1 \approx_{\ell_A} t_2$, $t_1 \Downarrow v_1'$, and $t_2 \Downarrow v_2'$, then $v_1' \approx_{\ell_A} v_2'$.*

5.2   Concurrent Calculus

Figure 18 extends the calculus from Sect. 5 with concurrency. It introduces *global configurations* of the form $\langle s, \Phi \rangle$ composed by an abstract scheduler state s and a thread pool Φ. Threads are secure computa-

Scheduler state: s
Thread pool : $\Phi ::= (\ell : Label) \rightarrow (Pool \; \ell)$
Pool ℓ: $t_s ::= [\,] \mid t : t_s \mid \bullet$
Configuration: $c ::= \langle s, \Phi \rangle$

Fig. 18. Syntax for concurrent calclulus.

tions of type $MAC \; \ell \; ()$ which get organized in isolated thread pools according to their security label. A pool t_s in the category *Pool ℓ* contains exclusively threads at security level ℓ. We use the standard list interface $[\,]$, $t : t_s$, and $t_s[n]$ for the empty list, the insertion of a term into an existing list, and accessing the nth-element, respectively. We write $\Phi[\ell][n] = t$ to retrieve the nth-thread in the ℓ-thread pool—it is a syntax sugar for $\Phi(\ell) = t_s$ and $t_s[n] = t$. The notation $\Phi[\ell][n] := t$ denotes the thread pool obtained by performing the update $\Phi(\ell)[n \mapsto t]$. Reading from an erased thread pool results in an erased thread, i.e. $\bullet[n] = \bullet$ and updating it has no effect, i.e. $\bullet[n \mapsto t] = \bullet$.

Semantics. The relation $\hookrightarrow_{(\ell,n)}$ represents an evaluation step for global configurations, where the thread identified by (ℓ, n) gets scheduled. Figure 19 shows the scheme rule for $\hookrightarrow_{(\ell,n)}$. The

$$\frac{\Phi[\ell][n] = t_1 \qquad t_1 \rightsquigarrow_e t_2 \qquad s_1 \xrightarrow{(\ell,n,e)} s_2}{\langle s_1, \Phi \rangle \hookrightarrow_{(\ell,n)} \langle s_2, \Phi[\ell][n] := t_2 \rangle}$$

Fig. 19. Scheme rule for concurrent semantics.

scheduled thread is retrieved from the configuration ($\Phi[\ell][n] = t_1$) and executed ($t_1 \rightsquigarrow_e t_2$). We decorate the sequential semantics with events e, which provides to the scheduler information about the effects produced by the scheduled instruction, for example $\bullet \rightsquigarrow_\bullet \bullet$. Events inform the scheduler about the evolution of the global configuration, so that it can realize concrete scheduling policies. The relation $s_1 \xrightarrow{(\ell,n,e)} s_2$ represents a transition in the scheduler, that depending on the initial state s_1, decides to run thread identified by (ℓ, n) and updates its state according to the event e. Lastly, the thread pool is updated with the final state of the thread ($\Phi[\ell][n] := t_2$).

Progress-Sensitive Non-interference. Our concurrent calculus satisfies progress sensitive non-interference—a security condition often enforced by IFC techniques for π-calculus [12, 27]. A *global configurations* is erased by erasing its components, that is $\varepsilon_{\ell_A}(\langle s, \Phi \rangle) = \langle \varepsilon_{\ell_A}(s), \varepsilon_{\ell_A}(\Phi) \rangle$. The thread pool Φ is erased point-wise, pools are either completely collapsed if not visible from the attacker, i.e. $\varepsilon_{\ell_A}^{Pool\ \ell}(t_s) = \bullet$ if $\ell \not\sqsubseteq \ell_A$, or the erasure function is homomorphically applied to their content. The erasure of the scheduler state s is scheduler specific. To obtain a parametric proof of non-interference, we assume certain properties about the scheduler. Specifically, our proof is valid for deterministic schedulers which fulfill progress and non-interference themselves, i.e. schedulers cannot leverage sensitive information in threads to determine what to schedule next As for the sequential calculus, we rely on determinancy and distributivity of the concurrent semantics.

Proposition 3 (Concurrent determinancy and distributivity)

- If $c_1 \hookrightarrow_{(\ell,n)} c_2$ and $c_1 \hookrightarrow_{(\ell,n)} c_3$, then $c_2 = c_3$.
- If $c_1 \hookrightarrow_{(\ell,n,e)} c_2$, then it holds that $\varepsilon_{\ell_A}(c_1) \hookrightarrow_{(\ell,n,\varepsilon_{\ell_A}(e))} \varepsilon_{\ell_A}(c_2)$.

In the non-interference theorem, we write as usual $\hookrightarrow^*$ for the reflexive transitive closure of $\hookrightarrow$ and we generalize $\approx_{\ell_A}$ to denote ℓ_A-equivalence between configurations.

Theorem 2 (Progress-sensitive non-interference). *Given the global configurations c_1, c_1', c_2, and assuming a deterministic and non-interfering scheduler that makes progress, if $c_1 \approx_{\ell_A} c_2$ and $c_1 \hookrightarrow_{(\ell,n)} c_1'$, then there exists c_2' such that $c_2 \hookrightarrow^* c_2'$ and $c_2 \approx_{\ell_A} c_2'$.*

6   Related Work

Security Libraries. Li and Zdancewic's seminal work [18] shows how the structure *arrows* can provide IFC as a library in Haskell. Tsai et al. [39] extend that work to support concurrency and data with heterogeneous labels. Russo et al. [30] implement the security library **SecLib** using a simpler structure than arrows, i.e. monads—rather than labeled values, this work introduces a monad which statically label side-effect free values. The security library **LIO** [36,37] dynamically enforces IFC for both sequential and concurrent settings. **LIO** presents operations similar to *fmap* and ⟨∗⟩ for labeled values with differences in the returning type due to **LIO**'s checks for clearence—this work provides a foundation to analyze the security implications of such primitives. Mechanized proofs for **LIO** are given only for its core sequential calculus [37]. Inspired by **SecLib** and **LIO**'s designs, **MAC** leverages Haskell's type system to enforce IFC [31]—this work does not contain formal guarantees and relies on its simplicity to convince the reader about its correctness. **HLIO** uses advanced Haskell's type-system features to provide a hybrid approach: IFC is statically enforce while allowing the programmers to defer selected security checks to be done at runtime [6]. Our work studies the security implications of extending **LIO**, **MAC**, and **HLIO** with a rich structure for labeled values. Devriese and Piessens provide a monad transformer to extend imperative-like APIs with support for IFC in Haskell [8]. Jaskelioff and Russo implements a library which dynamically enforces IFC using secure multi-execution (SME) [15]—a technique that runs programs multiple times. Rather than running multiple copies of a program, Schmitz et al. [33] provide a library with *faceted values*, where values present different behavior according to the privilege of the observer. Different from the work above, we present a fully-fledged mechanized proof for our sequential and concurrent calculus which includes references, synchronization variables, and exceptions.

IFC tools. IFC research has produced compilers capable of preserving confidentiality of data: Jif [25] and Paragon [4] (based on Java), and FlowCaml [34] (based on Caml). The SPARK language presents a IFC analysis which has been extended to guarantee progress-sensitive non-inference [28]. JSFlow [11] is one of the state-of-the-art IFC system for the web (based on JavaScript). These tools preserve confidentiality in a fine-grained fashion where every piece of data is explicitly label. Specifically, there is no abstract data type to label data, so our results cannot directly apply to them.

Operating systems research. MAC systems [3] assign a label with an entire OS process—settling a single policy for all the data handled by it. While proposed in the 70s, there are modern manifestations of this idea (e.g., [17,23,40]) applied to diverse scenarios like the web (e.g., [2,38]) and mobile devices (e.g., [5,16]). In principle, it would be possible to extend such MAC-like systems to include a notion of labeled values with the functor structure as well as the relabeling primitive proposed by this work. For instance, COWL [38] presents the notion of *labeled blob* and *labeled XHR* which is isomorphic to the notion of labeled values, thus making possible to apply our results. Furthermore, because many MAC-like system often ignore termination leaks (e.g., [9,40]), there is no need to use call-by-name evaluation to obtain security guarantees.

7   Conclusions

We present an extension of **MAC** that provides labeled values with an applicative functor-like structure and a relabeling operation, enabling convenient and expressive manipulation of labeled values using side effect-free code and saving programmers from introducing unnecessary sub-computations (e.g., in the form of threads). We have proved this extension secure both in sequential and concurrent settings, exposing an interesting connection between evaluation strategy and progress-sensitive non-interference. This work bridges the gap between existing IFC libraries (which focus on side-effecting code) and the usual Haskell programming model (which favors pure code), with a view to making IFC in Haskell more practical.

Acknowledgement. This work was supported in part by the Swedish research agencies VR and STINT, The Sloan Foundation, and by NSF grant 1421770.

References

1. Askarov, A., Hunt, S., Sabelfeld, A., Sands, D.: Termination-Insensitive noninterference leaks more than just a bit. In: Jajodia, S., Lopez, J. (eds.) ESORICS 2008. LNCS, vol. 5283, pp. 333–348. Springer, Heidelberg (2008)
2. Bauer, L., Cai, S., Jia, L., Passaro, T., Stroucken, M., Tian, Y.: Run-time monitoring and formal analysis of information flows in Chromium. In: Annual Network & Distributed System Security Symposium. Internet Society (2015)
3. Bell, D.E., La Padula, L.: Secure computer system: unified exposition and multics interpretation. Technical report MTR-2997, Rev. 1, MITRE Corporation, Bedford, MA (1976)
4. Broberg, N., van Delft, B., Sands, D.: Paragon for practical programming with information-flow control. In: Shan, C. (ed.) APLAS 2013. LNCS, vol. 8301, pp. 217–232. Springer, Heidelberg (2013)
5. Bugiel, S., Heuser, S., Sadeghi, A.R.: Flexible and fine-grained mandatory access control on android for diverse security and privacy policies. In: USENIX Conference on Security, SEC. USENIX Association (2013)
6. Buiras, P., Vytiniotis, D., Russo, A.: HLIO: Mixing static and dynamic typing for information-flow control in Haskell. In: ACM SIGPLAN International Conference on Functional Programming. ACM (2015)
7. Denning, D.E., Denning, P.J.: Certification of programs for secure information flow. Commun. ACM **20**(7), 504–513 (1977)
8. Devriese, D., Piessens, F.: Information flow enforcement in monadic libraries. In: ACM SIGPLAN Workshop on Types in Language Design and Implementation. ACM (2011)

9. Efstathopoulos, P., Krohn, M., VanDeBogart, S., Frey, C., Ziegler, D., Kohler, E., Mazières, D., Kaashoek, F., Morris, R.: Labels and event processes in the asbestos operating system. In: ACM Symposium on Operating Systems Principles, SOSP. ACM (2005)

10. Goguen, J., Meseguer, J.: Security policies and security models. In: IEEE Symposium on Security and Privacy. IEEE Computer Society (1982)

11. Hedin, D., Birgisson, A., Bello, L., Sabelfeld, A.: JSFlow: Tracking information flow in JavaScript and its APIs. In: ACM Symposium on Applied Computing. ACM (2014)

12. Honda, K., Vasconcelos, V.T., Yoshida, N.: Secure information flow as typed process behaviour. In: Smolka, G. (ed.) ESOP 2000. LNCS, vol. 1782, pp. 180–199. Springer, Heidelberg (2000)

13. Hritcu, C., Greenberg, M., Karel, B., Peirce, B.C., Morrisett, G.: All your IFCexception are belong to us. In: IEEE Symposium on Security and Privacy. IEEE Computer Society (2013)

14. Hughes, J.: Why functional programming matters. Comput. J. **32**, 98–107 (1984)

15. Jaskelioff, M., Russo, A.: Secure multi-execution in Haskell. In: Clarke, E., Virbitskaite, I., Voronkov, A. (eds.) PSI 2011. LNCS, vol. 7162, pp. 170–178. Springer, Heidelberg (2012)

16. Jia, L., Aljuraidan, J., Fragkaki, E., Bauer, L., Stroucken, M., Fukushima, K., Kiyomoto, S., Miyake, Y.: Run-time enforcement of information-flow properties on android (extended abstract). In: Crampton, J., Jajodia, S., Mayes, K. (eds.) ESORICS 2013. LNCS, vol. 8134, pp. 775–792. Springer, Heidelberg (2013)

17. Krohn, M., Yip, A., Brodsky, M., Cliffer, N., Kaashoek, M.F., Kohler, E., Morris, R.: Information flow control for standard OS abstractions. In: ACM SIGOPS Symposium on Operating Systems Principles, SOSP. ACM (2007)

18. Li, P., Zdancewic, S.: Encoding information flow in Haskell. In: IEEE Workshop on Computer Security Foundations. IEEE Computer Society (2006)

19. Li, P., Zdancewic, S.: Arrows for secure information flow. Theoret. Comput. Sci. **411**(19), 1974–1994 (2010)

20. Mcbride, C., Paterson, R.: Applicative programming with effects. J. Funct. Program. **18**(1), 1–13 (2008)

21. Meurer, S., Wismüller, R.: APEFS: an infrastructure for permission-based filtering of android apps. In: Schmidt, A.U., Russello, G., Krontiris, I., Lian, S. (eds.) MobiSec 2012. LNICST, vol. 107, pp. 1–11. Springer, Heidelberg (2012)

22. Moggi, E.: Notions of computation and monads. Inf. Comput. **93**(1), 55–92 (1991)

23. Murray, T., Matichuk, D., Brassil, M., Gammie, P., Bourke, T., Seefried, S., Lewis, C., Gao, X., Klein, G.: sel4: from general purpose to a proof of information flow enforcement. In: 2012 IEEE Symposium on Security and Privacy (2013)

24. Myers, A.C.: JFlow: practical mostly-static information flow control. In: ACM Symposium on Principles of Programming Languages, pp. 228–241 (1999)

25. Myers, A.C., Zheng, L., Zdancewic, S., Chong, S., Nystrom, N.: Jif: Java information flow (2001). http://www.cs.cornell.edu/jif

26. Pottier, F., Simonet, V.: Information flow inference for ML. In: ACM Symposium on Principles of Programming Languages, pp. 319–330 (2002)

27. Pottier, F.: A simple view of type-secure information flow in the π-calculus. In: IEEE Computer Security Foundations Workshop, pp. 320–330 (2002)

28. Rafnsson, W., Garg, D., Sabelfeld, A.: Progress-sensitive security for SPARK. In: Caballero, J., Bodden, E., Athanasopoulos, E. (eds.) ESSoS 2016. LNCS, vol. 9639, pp. 20–37. Springer, Heidelberg (2016). doi:10.1007/978-3-319-30806-7_2

29. Roy, I., Porter, D.E., Bond, M.D., McKinley, K.S., Witchel, E.: Laminar: practical fine-grained decentralized information flow control. In: ACM SIGPLAN Conference on Programming Language Design and Implementation, PLDI. ACM (2009)

30. Russo, A., Claessen, K., Hughes, J.: A library for light-weight information-flow security in Haskell. In: ACM SIGPLAN Symposium on Haskell. ACM (2008)

31. Russo, A.: Functional pearl: two can keep a secret, if one of them uses Haskell. In: ACM SIGPLAN International Conference on Functional Programming, ICFP. ACM (2015)

32. Sabelfeld, A., Myers, A.C.: Language-based information-flow security. IEEE J. Sel. Areas Commun. **21**(1), 5–19 (2003)

33. Schmitz, T., Rhodes, D., Austin, T.H., Knowles, K., Flanagan, C.: Faceted dynamic information flow via control and data monads. In: Piessens, F., Viganò, L. (eds.) POST 2016. LNCS, vol. 9635, pp. 3–23. Springer, Heidelberg (2016). doi:10.1007/978-3-662-49635-0_1

34. Simonet, V.: The Flow Caml system (2003), software release at http://cristal.inria.fr/~simonet/soft/flowcaml/

35. Smith, G., Volpano, D.: Secure information flow in a multi-threaded imperative language. In: ACM symposium on Principles of Programming Languages (1998)

36. Stefan, D., Russo, A., Buiras, P., Levy, A., Mitchell, J.C., Maziéres, D.: Addressing covert termination and timing channels in concurrent information flow systems. In: ACM SIGPLAN International Conference on Functional Programming. ACM (2012)

37. Stefan, D., Russo, A., Mitchell, J.C., Mazières, D.: Flexible dynamic information flow control in Haskell. In: ACM SIGPLAN Haskell Symposium (2011)

38. Stefan, D., Yang, E.Z., Marchenko, P., Russo, A., Herman, D., Karp, B., Mazières, D.: Protecting users by confining JavaScript with COWL. In: USENIX Symposium on Operating Systems Design and Implementation. USENIX Association (2014)

39. Tsai, T.C., Russo, A., Hughes, J.: A library for secure multi-threaded information flow in Haskell. In: IEEE Computer Security Foundations Symposium (2007)

40. Zeldovich, N., Boyd-Wickizer, S., Kohler, E., Mazières, D.: Making information flow explicit in HiStar. In: USENIX Symposium on Operating Systems Design and Implementation. USENIX (2006)

Software Security

Let's Face It: Faceted Values for Taint Tracking

Daniel Schoepe[1(✉)], Musard Balliu[1], Frank Piessens[2], and Andrei Sabelfeld[1]

[1] Chalmers University of Technology, Gothenburg, Sweden
daniel@schoepe.org
[2] iMinds-DistriNet, KU Leuven, Leuven, Belgium

Abstract. Taint tracking has been successfully deployed in a range of security applications to track data dependencies in hardware and machine-, binary-, and high-level code. Precision of taint tracking is key for its success in practice: being a vulnerability analysis, false positives must be low for the analysis to be practical. This paper presents an approach to taint tracking, which does not involve tracking taints throughout computation. Instead, we include shadow memories in the execution context, so that a single run of a program has the effect of computing on both tainted and untainted data. This mechanism is inspired by the technique of secure multi-execution, while in contrast to the latter it does not require running the entire program multiple times. We present a general framework and establish its soundness with respect to explicit secrecy, a policy for preventing insecure data leaks, and its precision showing that runs of secure programs are never modified. We show that the technique can be used for attack detection with no false positives. To evaluate the mechanism in practice, we implement DroidFace, a source-to-source transform for an intermediate Java-like language and benchmark its precision and performance with respect to representative static and dynamic taint trackers for Android. The results indicate that the performance penalty is tolerable while achieving both soundness and no false positives on the tested benchmarks.

1 Introduction

Taint tracking has been successfully deployed in a range of security applications to track data dependencies in hardware [14,35] and binary [13,34] code, as well as high-level code, with popular usage in mobile [1,10,19,21,22,40] and web [26,28,36] applications.

Background. Taint tracking is about tracking direct data dependencies, or *explicit flows* [16], when data is passed directly from one data container to another. Taint tracking typically ignores *implicit flows* [16], when the information flows through the control structure of the program, as in, e.g., branching on a secret and assigning to different publicly observable variables in the branches.

What makes taint tracking a popular security mechanism? Missing out on implicit flows is clearly a disadvantage from the security point of view. This makes taint tracking a vulnerability finding mechanism rather than a mechanism

© Springer International Publishing Switzerland 2016
I. Askoxylakis et al. (Eds.): ESORICS 2016, Part I, LNCS 9878, pp. 561–580, 2016.
DOI: 10.1007/978-3-319-45744-4_28

that provides comprehensive security assurance. This brings us to an important observation: *precision* of taint tracking is key for its success in practice: being a vulnerability analysis, false positives must be low for the analysis to be practical.

This observation is echoed by the state of the art on taint tracking for Android applications (detailed in Sect. 5). Static taint trackers (such as FlowDroid [1], Amandroid [40], DroidSafe [21], and HornDroid [10]) and dynamic taint trackers (such as TaintDroid [19] and AppFence [22]) incorporate increasingly sophisticated features to catch data leaks while reducing the false positives.

Problem. Motivated by the above, we seek to devise a general technique for tracking data leaks with high precision. Our goal is to formally establish the soundness and precision as well as demonstrate them in practice, with taint tracking in Android applications as a target for case studies.

The general setting is a program that operates in an environment with information *sources* and *sinks*. The goal of taint tracking is to prevent information from sensitive sources to directly affect the information sent to insensitive sinks. For confidentiality, this corresponds to not directly propagating information from secret sources to public sinks. This is often a desirable goal in the context of Android apps, as in e.g. allowing an app to access the file system to choose an image for a user profile but ensuring that no other files are leaked. In the examples throughout the paper, we will stick to confidentiality policies, noting that taint tracking has also been used successfully for integrity checks, e.g., [13,14,34,35].

Facelifted values. This paper presents an approach to taint tracking, which, somewhat surprisingly, does not involve tracking taints throughout computation. Instead, we include shadow memories in the execution context, so that a single run of a program has the effect of computing on both sensitive and non-sensitive data. We refer to such values that carry both secret data as well as a public shadow value as *facelifted values*, in reference to the *faceted value* approach [2] by Austin and Flanagan.

Consider a simple example program:

$$h \leftarrow \mathbf{in}(\mathbf{H}); l := h; \mathbf{out}(\mathbf{L}, l) \tag{1}$$

Secret, or *high* (**H**), input is stored in a variable h and is explicitly leaked into the variable l, which in turn is output on a public, or *low* (**L**), channel. In essence, our approach has the effect of running the program:

$h \leftarrow \mathbf{in}(\mathbf{H})$; $h' := d$; // secret input and shadow input with default value d
$l := h$; $l' := h'$;   // original assignment and shadow assignment
$\mathbf{out}(l', \mathbf{L})$ // public output from shadow memory

The shadow memory is represented by the shadow variables h' and l'. This represents the public view of the system. On a secret input, a default value d is stored in the shadow variable h'. On a public output, the value is retrieved from the shadow memory.

Soundness and precision. This mechanism is inspired by the technique of *secure multi-execution* (SME) [11,17], where programs are executed as many times as there are security levels, with outputs at each level computed by the respective runs. SME addresses both explicit and implicit flows, enforcing the policy of *noninterference* [15,20] that prescribes no leaks from sensitive inputs to insensitive outputs.

In contrast to SME, our mechanism does not re-run the entire program, focusing on secure-multi execution of the individual side-effectful commands that cause explicit flows. Moreover, it is independent of the choice of scheduling strategy for different runs. As such, this technique is similar to Austin and Flanagan's *faceted values* [2]. Re-purposing faceted values to track explicit flows results in a powerful mechanism for a policy that the original faceted values were not intended for: *explicit secrecy* [33], a policy that captures what it means to leak information explicitly. Further, facelifted values are different in that: (i) Faceted values face challenges with tracking implicit flows, which results in propagating context labels through the computation. (ii) Facelifted values are sound and precise for explicit secrecy, while faceted values are sound and *not* precise for noninterference [6]. (iii) Facelifted values only require a single path through the program, while faceted values may execute both branches of a conditional [2]. (iv) As a consequence, facelifted values can be implemented by means of a relatively simple program transformation whereas faceted values require modification of the runtime or explicit use of a library [32].

We present a general framework and establish its soundness with respect to explicit secrecy. Our results guarantee that the attacker learns nothing about secrets via explicit flows.

Similarly to SME, our mechanism may "repair" programs, i.e. force their security by modifying their original behavior. Yet, we show that the mechanism is precise in the sense that runs of secure programs are never modified. An example where classical taint trackers (e.g. [19]) are conservative is related to the handling of arrays. Modify the assignment in the simple example program above to be:

$$\mathbf{int}[]\ a := [0,0];\ a[h\%2] := h;\ l := a[1 - h\%2]$$

This is a secure program as the value assigned to the secretly-indexed element is never used. However, a typical taint tracker would taint the entire array and raise an alarm. In contrast, our approach will accept runs of this program.

Attack detection. Further, our technique can be used for attack detection. We detect attacks by matching the outcomes of the insensitive outputs from the sensitive and insensitive runs. If the values mismatch it means that there is an influence from the sensitive data to insensitive data in the original run.

In the example above, assume the default value is 0 and the secret input is 1. The detection mechanism will compare l and l' before outputting on the public sink to find out that they mismatch, being 1 and 0, respectively.

Implementation. Our technique can be deployed either by extending the runtime system with shadow memories or by a source-to-source inlining transformation that injects computation on shadow memories in the original code.

We implement the approach by a source-to-source transformation for an intermediate Java-like language and benchmark its precision and performance with respect to static and dynamic taint tracking. Noteworthy, language constructs such as exceptions and multithreading require no special treatment. The practical evaluation of soundness and precision uses the DroidBench [18] test suite. The results demonstrate that performance penalty is tolerable while achieving both soundness and no false positives on the tested benchmarks.

Contributions. The paper comprises these contributions: (i) We present a framework of facelifted values. We illustrate the concepts for a simple imperative language with pointers and I/O (Sect. 2.1). (ii) We establish precision results showing that runs of secure programs are never modified by the enforcement framework (Sect. 2.2). (iii) We give a general, language-independent, view of the framework and show that our approach guarantees soundness with respect to explicit secrecy (Sect. 2.5). (iv) We leverage our approach to build an attack detection mechanism that is free of false positives: whenever an execution is flagged by the enforcement, there is an actual attack detected (Sect. 2.3). (v) We present DroidFace, a tool that implements our approach as a source-to-source transformation for a core of Java (Sect. 3). (vi) We evaluate the precision and performance of DroidFace with respect to the state-of-the-art static and dynamic tools for Android applications (Sect. 4).

2   Facelifted Values for Taint Tracking

We present the facelifted values technique and show that it enforces explicit secrecy. To illustrate the essence of facelifted values, we introduce a simple imperative language with pointers and I/O. We briefly review explicit secrecy and show that facelifted executions enforce the property. We elaborate on the use of the enforcement technique to detect potential attacks. Lastly, we present a source-to-source transformation for statically inlining facelifted values. The proofs for lemmas and theorems can be found in the full version of the paper [5].

2.1   Language with Facelifted Values

At the heart of our mechanism is the intuition that every computation that is not related to control flow is executed multiple times, once for each security level, using default values for data from higher security levels. Consider a simple imperative language with pointers and I/O primitives:

$$e ::= x \mid n \mid e_1 \oplus e_2 \mid \&x \mid *e$$
$$c ::= \textbf{skip} \mid c_1; c_2 \mid x \leftarrow \textbf{alloc} \mid x := e \mid *e_1 := e_2$$
$$\mid x \leftarrow \textbf{in}(\ell) \mid \textbf{out}(\ell, e) \mid \textbf{if } e \textbf{ then } c_1 \textbf{ else } c_2 \mid \textbf{while } e \textbf{ do } c$$

The language expressions consist of global variables $x \in Var$, built-in values $n \in Val$, binary operators $\oplus$, variable references $\&x$ and dereferences $*e$. $Addr$ is the set of memory addresses and, for simplicity, $Addr \subseteq Val$. The language constructs contain assignment, conditional, loops, input and output. In addition, the language includes dynamic memory allocation $x \leftarrow$ **alloc** and pointer assignment $*e_1 := e_2$. We use **nil** as a way to represent uninitialized memory.

We assume a bounded lattice of security levels $(\mathcal{L}, \sqsubseteq, \sqcup, \sqcap)$. We write $\top$ and $\bot$ to denote the top and the bottom element of the lattice, respectively (actually a partially ordered set suffices). Each I/O channel is annotated with a fixed security label $\ell \in \mathcal{L}$. In the examples, we use a two-level security lattice consisting of **H** for variables containing confidential information and **L** for variables containing public information and $\mathbf{L} \sqsubseteq \mathbf{H}$. Input to programs is modeled by environments mapping channels to streams of inputs values; we denote the set of environments by Env. Without loss of generality, we consider one stream for each level $\ell \in \mathcal{L}$. An environment $\mathcal{E} : \mathcal{L} \rightarrow Val^{\mathbb{N}}$ maps levels to infinite sequences of values. A facelifted value $v \in Val^{\mathcal{L}}$ maps levels to values; to distinguish streams and facelifted values from other functions, we write A^B for the function space $B \rightarrow A$.

We define equivalence at security level $\ell \in \mathcal{L}$ for environments, facelifted memories and traces. Intuitively, two environments, memories or traces are equivalent at level ℓ iff they look the same to an observer at level ℓ, i.e. one that can observe events at any level $\ell' \sqsubseteq \ell$, as defined by the lattice $\mathcal{L}$.

Definition 1. *Two environments $\mathcal{E}_1$ and $\mathcal{E}_2$ are ℓ-equivalent, written $\mathcal{E}_1 \approx_\ell \mathcal{E}_2$, iff $\forall \ell'. \ell' \sqsubseteq \ell \Rightarrow \mathcal{E}_1(\ell') = \mathcal{E}_2(\ell')$.*

A facelifted memory $m : Addr \rightarrow Val^{\mathcal{L}}$ maps addresses to facelifted values, i.e. to functions mapping levels to values. We globally fix a mapping $A(\cdot) : Var \rightarrow Addr$ from variables to addresses. Note that environments are the only source of inputs. Programs start executing with the fixed memory m_0 where $m_0(a)(\ell) = $ **nil** for all $a \in Addr$ and $\ell \in \mathcal{L}$. To support pointers, we assume that $Addr \subseteq Val$. We write $m(\cdot)(\ell)$ to denote the facelifted memory projected at level ℓ, i.e. the function $a \mapsto m(a)(\ell)$. In the following, this is called ℓ-facelifted memory or non-facelifted memory (whenever the level ℓ is unimportant). We use $m, m_1, \ldots$ to range over facelifted memories and $\widetilde{m}, \widetilde{m_1}, \ldots$ to range over non-facelifted memories.

Definition 2. *Two facelifted memories m_1 and m_2 are ℓ-equivalent, written $m_1 \approx_\ell m_2$, iff $\forall \ell'. \ell' \sqsubseteq \ell \Rightarrow m_1(\cdot)(\ell') = m_2(\cdot)(\ell')$.*

An observation is a pair of a value and a security level, i.e. $Obs = Val \times \mathcal{L}$, or empty. We write π_1 (resp. π_2) for the first (resp. second) projection of a tuple. A trace τ is a finite sequence of observations. We write ε for the empty trace/observation. We write $\tau \upharpoonright_\ell$ for the projection of trace τ at security level ℓ.

Definition 3. *Two traces τ_1 and τ_2 are ℓ-equivalent, written $\tau_1 \approx_\ell \tau_2$, iff $\forall \ell'. \ell' \sqsubseteq \ell \Rightarrow \tau_1 \upharpoonright_{\ell'} = \tau_2 \upharpoonright_{\ell'}$.*

We now present the semantics of the language in terms of facelifted memories and environments. We evaluate expressions in the context of a facelifted memory and, for each security level, use the memory facet of that level.

Definition 4. *The evaluation of an expression e in a facelifted memory m, written $[\![e]\!]_m \in Val^{\mathcal{L}}$, is defined by:*

$$[\![x]\!]_m(\ell) = m(A(x))(\ell)$$
$$[\![n]\!]_m(\ell) = n$$
$$[\![e_1 \oplus e_2]\!]_m(\ell) = f_\oplus([\![e_1]\!]_m(\ell), [\![e_2]\!]_m(\ell))$$
$$[\![\&x]\!]_m(\ell) = A(x)$$
$$[\![* e]\!]_m(\ell) = m([\![e]\!]_m(\ell))(\ell)$$

where $f_\oplus$ denotes the semantics of the operator $\oplus$.

Figure 1 gives the operational semantics of facelifted evaluation. A state $(\mathcal{E}, m)$ is a pair of an environment $\mathcal{E}$ and a memory m. A configuration $\mathcal{E} \vdash \langle c, m \rangle$ consists of an environment $\mathcal{E}$, a command c and a memory m. We write $\mathcal{E} \vdash \langle c, m \rangle \xrightarrow{\tau} \mathcal{E}' \vdash \langle c', m' \rangle$ to denote that a configuration $\mathcal{E} \vdash \langle c, m \rangle$ evaluates in one step to configuration $\mathcal{E}' \vdash \langle c', m' \rangle$, producing observations $\tau \in Obs^*$. We use ε and $\frac{1}{2}$ to denote normal and abnormal termination of a program, respectively.

F-ASSIGN

$$\overline{\mathcal{E} \vdash \langle x := e, m \rangle \twoheadrightarrow \mathcal{E} \vdash \langle \varepsilon, m[A(x) \mapsto [\![e]\!]_m] \rangle}$$

F-IFTRUE
$$\frac{[\![e]\!]_m(\top) = \mathbf{tt}}{\mathcal{E} \vdash \langle \mathbf{if}\ e\ \mathbf{then}\ c_1\ \mathbf{else}\ c_2, m \rangle \twoheadrightarrow \mathcal{E} \vdash \langle c_1, m \rangle}$$

F-OUT

$$\overline{\mathcal{E} \vdash \langle \mathbf{out}(\ell, e), m \rangle \xrightarrow{[([\![e]\!]_m(\ell),\ell)]} \mathcal{E} \vdash \langle \varepsilon, m \rangle}$$

F-ASSIGNPTR
$$\frac{[\![e_1]\!]_m = l \quad l \in Addr^{\mathcal{L}} \quad m' = update(m, l, e_2)}{\mathcal{E} \vdash \langle *e_1 := e_2, m \rangle \twoheadrightarrow \mathcal{E} \vdash \langle \varepsilon, m' \rangle}$$

F-IN
$$\frac{\mathcal{E}' = \mathcal{E}[\ell \mapsto n \mapsto \mathcal{E}(\ell)(n+1)] \quad m' = m[A(x) \mapsto \ell' \mapsto \mathcal{F}_{in}(\mathcal{E}, \ell, \ell')]}{\mathcal{E} \vdash \langle x \leftarrow \mathbf{in}(\ell), m \rangle \twoheadrightarrow \mathcal{E}' \vdash \langle \varepsilon, m' \rangle}$$

F-ALLOC
$$\frac{m' = m[A(x) \mapsto \ell \mapsto a, a \mapsto \ell \mapsto 0] \quad a = \min\{a | a \notin rng(A) \wedge \forall \ell.\ m(a)(\ell) = \mathbf{nil}\}}{\mathcal{E} \vdash \langle x \leftarrow \mathbf{alloc}, m \rangle \twoheadrightarrow \mathcal{E} \vdash \langle \varepsilon, m' \rangle}$$

$$\mathcal{F}_{in}(\mathcal{E}, \ell, \ell') = \begin{cases} \mathcal{E}(\ell)(0) & \ell \sqsubseteq \ell' \\ d & \ell \not\sqsubseteq \ell' \end{cases} \qquad update(m, l, e)(a')(\ell) = \begin{cases} [\![e]\!]_m(\ell) & a' = l(\ell) \\ m(a')(\ell) & \text{otherwise} \end{cases}$$

Fig. 1. Excerpt of operational semantics of facelifted evaluation

We comment on some of the interesting rules in Fig. 1. The full table of rules can be found in the full version. Rule F-ASSIGN evaluates an expression e in the context of a facelifted memory m, as in Definition 4, and yields a new facelifted memory m' where variable x is mapped to the resulting facelifted value. Similarly, rule F-ASSIGNPTR evaluates expressions e_1 and e_2 to obtain a facelifted address and a facelifted value, respectively, and uses the function *update* to assign the latter to the former. Rule F-ALLOC allocates a fresh global variable, assigns the address to x, and initializes all its facets with the default value 0. Rule F-IN reads the next (non-facelifted) input value from the environment stream $\mathcal{E}$ at security level ℓ and uses the function $\mathcal{F}_{in}$ to create a facelifted value which is then assigned to global variable x. Rule F-OUT evaluates an expression e in the context of the ℓ-facelifted memory and outputs the resulting (ℓ-facelifted) value to an observer at security level ℓ. Rule F-IFTRUE evaluates the branch condition e *only* in the context of the $\top$-facelifted memory and executes the command in the true branch. We denote the standard evaluation relation with non-facelifted memories by $\rightarrow$; associated functions are defined analogously and reported in the full version [5].

To illustrate the facelifted semantics, consider program 1 from the introduction. Assume the domain of variables l and h is $\{0, 1\}$ and the default value d is 0. The program starts executing with facelifted memory m_0 such that $m_0(A(l))(\ell) = m_0(A(h))(\ell) = \mathbf{nil}$ for all $\ell \in \mathcal{L}$. If the secret input is 1, the facelifted semantics will apply the rules F-IN, F-ASSIGN and F-OUT, and output the default value 0 on the low channel. Similarly, if the secret input is 0, the output will again be 0, thus closing the leak of the insecure program. On the other hand, if we replace the output instruction in program 1 with $\mathbf{out}(\mathbf{H}, l)$, the program is secure. In fact, the variable l will be evaluated in the context of the $\mathbf{H}$-facelifted memory and yield the correct result for an observer with high security level.

Note that declassification policies can be naturally enforced by pumping high values into low memories since the runtime has access to both during the execution (cf. Fig. 1).

2.2   Explicit Secrecy

Explicit secrecy [33] is a knowledge-based security condition that formalizes the idea of "security with respect to explicit flows only". To achieve this, explicit secrecy distinguishes between changes to the state of the program and changes to the control flow, and demands security of information flows for the state part only. Concretely, it leverages the (small-step) operational semantics to extract a function that captures the state modification and the possible output for each execution step.

Definition 5. *Whenever $\mathcal{E} \vdash \langle c, m \rangle \xrightarrow{\alpha} \mathcal{E}' \vdash \langle c', m' \rangle$, we define a function $f : Env \times Mem \rightarrow ((Env \times Mem) \times Obs)$ associated with the step. For every $\mathcal{E} \in Env$ and $m \in Mem$, we define $f((\mathcal{E}, m)) = ((\mathcal{E}', m'), \alpha)$ where $\mathcal{E}'$, m' and α are unique and $\mathcal{E} \vdash \langle c, m \rangle \xrightarrow{\alpha} \mathcal{E}' \vdash \langle c', m' \rangle$. We write $\mathcal{E} \vdash \langle c, m \rangle \xrightarrow[f]{\alpha} \mathcal{E}' \vdash \langle c', m' \rangle$*

to denote this function.

Intuitively, for each step $\mathcal{E} \vdash \langle c, m \rangle \xrightarrow{\alpha} \mathcal{E}' \vdash \langle c', m' \rangle$, $f((\mathcal{E}_1, m_1))$ simulates how the input state $(\mathcal{E}_1, m_1)$ would change by executing the same step that $\mathcal{E} \vdash \langle c, m \rangle$ performs. In general, it is the language designer who defines which parts of a configuration hold state and which hold the control flow of a program. We extend the construction of state transformers to multiple steps by composing the state modifications and concatenating the output.

Example 1. Given a state $(\mathcal{E}, m)$ and command c, the state transformer for our language (cf. Definition 5) is $f((\mathcal{E}, m))$:

$$
\begin{array}{ll}
((\mathcal{E}, m[A(x) \mapsto [\![e]\!]_m]), \varepsilon) & \text{if } c = x := e \\
((\mathcal{E}, update(m, [\![e_1]\!]_m, e_2)), \varepsilon) & \text{if } c = *e_1 := e_2 \\
((\mathcal{E}, m[A(x) \mapsto \ell \mapsto a]), \varepsilon) & \text{if } c = x \leftarrow \mathbf{alloc} \\
\quad \text{where } a \notin \text{rng}(A) \wedge \forall \ell.\ m(a)(\ell) = \mathbf{nil} \\
((\mathcal{E}, m), [([\![e]\!]_m(\ell), \ell)]) & \text{if } c = \mathbf{out}(\ell, e) \\
((\mathcal{E}', m[A(x) \mapsto \ell' \mapsto \mathcal{F}_{in}(\mathcal{E}, \ell, \ell')]), \varepsilon) & \text{if } c = x \leftarrow \mathbf{in}(\ell) \\
\quad \text{and } \mathcal{E}' = \mathcal{E}[\ell \mapsto n \mapsto \mathcal{E}(\ell)(n+1)] \\
((\mathcal{E}, m), \varepsilon) & \text{otherwise}
\end{array}
$$

The state transformer f acts on the memory part of the configuration (assignments, memory allocation, input and output), and leaves the control-flow statements unchanged.

We can now define the knowledge an attacker at security level ℓ obtains from observing only outputs from a sequence of changes to the state. We capture this by the set of initial environments that the attacker considers possible based on their observations. Concretely, for a given initial state $(\mathcal{E}_0, m_0)$ and a state transformer f, an environment $\mathcal{E}$ is considered possible if $\mathcal{E}_0 \approx_\ell \mathcal{E}$ and it matches the trace produced by $f((\mathcal{E}_0, m_0))$, i.e. $\pi_2(f((\mathcal{E}_0, m_0))) \approx_\ell \pi_2(f((\mathcal{E}, m_0)))$.

Definition 6 (Explicit knowledge). *The explicit knowledge at level ℓ for an environment $\mathcal{E}_0$, memory m_0 and function f, written $k_e(\ell, \mathcal{E}_0, f) \subseteq Env$, is defined by $k_e(\ell, \mathcal{E}_0, f) = \{\mathcal{E} | \mathcal{E}_0 \approx_\ell \mathcal{E} \wedge (\pi_2 \circ f)((\mathcal{E}_0, m_0)) \approx_\ell (\pi_2 \circ f)((\mathcal{E}, m_0))\}$.*

Intuitively, the attacker considers as possible all environments $\mathcal{E}$ from the set $k_e(\ell, \mathcal{E}_0, f)$. Then, given an initial state $(\mathcal{E}, m_0)$, a program satisfies explicit secrecy iff no indistinguishable initial states can be ruled out from observing the output generated by the extracted state transformer f. We define $\text{id}(s) = (s, [])$.

Definition 7 (Explicit secrecy). *A program c satisfies explicit secrecy for security level ℓ and evaluation relation $\hookrightarrow$, written $ES(\hookrightarrow, \ell) \vDash c$, iff whenever $\mathcal{E} \vdash \langle c, m_0 \rangle \underset{f}{\hookrightarrow}^* \mathcal{E}' \vdash \langle c', m' \rangle$, then $\forall \mathcal{E}_0.\ k_e(\ell, \mathcal{E}_0, f) = k_e(\ell, \mathcal{E}_0, \text{id})$. We write $ES(\hookrightarrow) \vDash c$ iff $\forall \ell.\ ES(\hookrightarrow, \ell) \vDash c$.*

Let us consider again program 1 with the initial conditions defined as above. The program satisfies explicit secrecy for the facelifted semantics in Fig. 1, i.e. $ES(\twoheadrightarrow, \ell) \vDash c_1$. Following Example 1 and Definition 5, we sequentially compose the state transformers for the input, assignment and output statements and obtain the state transformer $f((\mathcal{E}, m_0)) = ((\mathcal{E}', m'), [(0, \mathbf{L})])$, for some $\mathcal{E}'$ and m' such that $\mathcal{E} \vdash \langle c_1, m_0 \rangle \twoheadrightarrow^* \mathcal{E}' \vdash \langle \varepsilon, m' \rangle$. Independently of the initial environment, f will always produce the output trace 0 for an observer at level $\mathbf{L}$. Therefore, $\forall \mathcal{E}_0.\ k_e(\mathbf{L}, \mathcal{E}_0, f) = k_e(\mathbf{L}, \mathcal{E}_0, \text{id})$.

Program 1 does not satisfy explicit secrecy with respect to the standard evaluation relation. In this case, the state transformer is extracted as $f((\mathcal{E}, m_0)) = ((\mathcal{E}', m'), [(\mathcal{E}(\mathbf{H})(0), \mathbf{L})])$, capturing that the program explicitly sends the input from a high channel to a low one, thus increasing the knowledge of the observer.

The following theorems prove that facelifted execution ensures soundness and precision for any program.

Theorem 1 (Soundness). *For any program c, $ES(\twoheadrightarrow) \models c$.*

Theorem 2 (Precision). *If $ES(\rightarrow) \models c$, then $\mathcal{E} \vdash \langle c, \widetilde{m}_0 \rangle \xrightarrow{\tau}{}^{*}$ if and only if $\mathcal{E} \vdash \langle c, m_0 \rangle \xrightarrow{\tau}\twoheadrightarrow^{*}$.*

Explicit secrecy assumes totality on the transition relation and on the corresponding state transformers. As a result, it does not account for information leaks due to abnormal termination of a program, e.g. by applying a partial function such as division by zero. Arguably, we can consider the program $h \leftarrow \mathbf{in}(\mathbf{H}); x := 1/h; \mathbf{out}(\mathbf{L}, 1)$ insecure since it may or may not execute the output statement depending on the input value of h, and thus leak information. We call this *crash-sensitive* explicit secrecy. Crash sensitivity can be captured by making abnormal termination visible to a low observer, e.g. by adding a special observation $\frac{1}{2}$. On the other hand, leaks due to program crashes generally trigger exceptions, which can be seen as control flows, hence the program above should then be secure. We call this *crash-insensitive* explicit secrecy. Crash insensitivity can be formalized by constructing partial state transformers.

The proposed enforcement mechanism is fully precise with respect to crash-sensitive explicit secrecy, however, it may lose precision when enforcing the crash-insensitive version. We further discuss these issues in the full version [5].

2.3 Attack Detection

Theorem 2 shows that if a program is already secure, the facelifted execution produces the same outputs as the standard execution. Otherwise, the standard semantics is intentionally changed for the sake of security. Thus, a user can not tell whether or not the outcome of the computation is correct, let alone decide whether an unexpected result is due to a software bug or a security attack.

We show that facelifted semantics can be extended to detect changes to the standard program semantics and thus unveil potential attacks. Concretely, attack detection can be performed by using the following rules for output statements:

F-OutT
$$\frac{[\![e]\!]_m(\ell) = [\![e]\!]_m(\top)}{\mathcal{E} \vdash \langle \mathbf{out}(\ell, e), m \rangle \xrightarrow{[([\![e]\!]_m(\ell), \ell)]} \mathcal{E} \vdash \langle \varepsilon, m \rangle}$$

F-OutFail
$$\frac{[\![e]\!]_m(\ell) \neq [\![e]\!]_m(\top)}{\mathcal{E} \vdash \langle \mathbf{out}(\ell, e), m \rangle \twoheadrightarrow \frac{1}{2}}$$

For each output statement at some security level ℓ, we evaluate the output expression both in the context of the ℓ-facelifted memory and in the context of the

$\top$-facelifted memory, and compare the results. Since the $\top$-facelifted memory is never affected by the default values, it will always contain the result of evaluation under the standard semantics. Therefore, if the two values differ, we have detected an attack and thus terminate the execution abnormally. The following theorem shows that the abnormal termination implies real attacks (only true positives).

Theorem 3 (Attack Detection). *If* $\mathcal{E} \vdash \langle c, m_0 \rangle \twoheadrightarrow^* \, \maltese$, *then* $ES(\to) \not\vdash c$.

Like SME [17] and faceted execution [2], the mechanism can fail to detect insecurities, i.e. $ES(\to) \not\vdash c \not\Rightarrow (\forall \mathcal{E}.\ \mathcal{E} \vdash \langle c, m_0 \rangle \twoheadrightarrow^* \, \maltese)$. This happens if the the chosen default values produce the same outputs as the real execution, for example if the default values are equal to the real inputs. Even if the program is run with multiple different default values, this may not be detected (consider, for example the program $h \leftarrow \mathbf{in}(\mathbf{H}); \mathbf{out}(\mathbf{L}, (h - d_1) \times (h - d_2))$ where d_1 and d_2 are possible default values. For an environment $\mathcal{E}$ where $\mathcal{E}(\mathbf{H})(0) \in \{d_1, d_2\}$, the above detection will never see the attack, despite the program being insecure. More generally, trying to detect an attack using a finite set $\mathcal{D}$ of default values will yield a false negative if the high input matches any of the default values; then the following program will hide an insecurity: $h \leftarrow \mathbf{in}(\mathbf{H})$; $\mathbf{out}(\mathbf{L}, \Pi_{d \in \mathcal{D}}(h - d))$. In practice, random defaults or multiple defaults for a single location take us a long way. We obtain no false negatives on the DroidBench suite, as reported in Sect. 4.

This also entails that despite the precision and soundness results, this mechanism does not give rise to a decision procedure for (per-run) explicit secrecy.

2.4 Inlining Facelifted Values Through Static Program Transformation

Facelifted evaluation enforces explicit secrecy dynamically by means of unconventional semantics, as described in Fig. 1. This requires modification of the underlying language runtime which makes it difficult to deploy for many settings. We present a program transformation that statically inlines facelifted values into the source code and uses standard semantics to achieve the same result as facelifted evaluation. We transform a program $c \in Com$ by applying a transformation function $\mathcal{T}(\cdot) : Com \to Com$. For each security level $\ell \in \mathcal{L}$ and for each variable x, we introduce a shadow variable x_ℓ to carry the ℓ-facelifted value for an observer at level ℓ. We write $[e]_\ell$ to denote the renaming of all variables x in e with x_ℓ and $; S$ to denote the sequential composition of commands from a set S.

$$
\begin{aligned}
\mathcal{T}(\mathbf{skip}) &= \mathbf{skip} \\
\mathcal{T}(x \leftarrow \mathbf{alloc}) &= ; \{[x]_\ell \leftarrow \mathbf{alloc} \mid \ell \in \mathcal{L}\} \\
\mathcal{T}(x := e) &= ; \{x_\ell := [e]_\ell \mid \ell \in \mathcal{L}\} \\
\mathcal{T}(*e_1 := e_2) &= ; \{*[e_1]_\ell := [e_2]_\ell \mid \ell \in \mathcal{L}\} \\
\mathcal{T}(\mathbf{out}(\ell, e)) &= \mathbf{out}(\ell, [e]_\ell) \\
\mathcal{T}(x \leftarrow \mathbf{in}(\ell)) &= x_\ell \leftarrow \mathbf{in}(\ell); \ ; \{\mathcal{T}_{in}(\ell, \ell') \mid \ell' \in \mathcal{L} \text{ and } \ell \neq \ell'\} \\
\mathcal{T}(c_1 \ ; c_2) &= \mathcal{T}(c_1) \ ; \mathcal{T}(c_2) \\
\mathcal{T}(\mathbf{if}\ e\ \mathbf{then}\ c_1\ \mathbf{else}\ c_2) &= \mathbf{if}\ [e]_\top\ \mathbf{then}\ \mathcal{T}(c_1)\ \mathbf{else}\ \mathcal{T}(c_2) \\
\mathcal{T}(\mathbf{while}\ e\ \mathbf{do}\ c) &= \mathbf{while}\ [e]_\top\ \mathbf{do}\ \mathcal{T}(c)
\end{aligned}
$$

where $\mathcal{T}_{in}(\ell, \ell')$ equals $x_{\ell'} := x_\ell$ if $\ell \sqsubseteq \ell'$, otherwise $x_{\ell'} := d$.

Note that faceted values and SME can not be implemented as easily with a program transformation [4]. We then show the correctness of the transformation.

Theorem 4 (Correctness). $\mathcal{E} \vdash \langle c, m_0 \rangle \xrightarrow{\tau}^* iff \mathcal{E} \vdash \langle \mathcal{T}(c), \tilde{m}_0 \rangle \xrightarrow{\tau}^*$.

Corollary 1 (Soundness and Precision). $\mathcal{T}(c)$ *is sound and precise.*

2.5   General Framework

The presented approach is not specific to a concrete language. presents a general version of this technique applicable to a wide range of languages under fairly unrestrictive assumptions: The number and level of outputs performed by an evaluation step may not depend on the memory; moreover, the semantics is assumed to be total and deterministic. Under these assumptions, satisfied by many realistic languages, the framework provides soundness and precision guarantees. Moreover, we also sketch an approach to lift the totality assumption on the semantics.

3   Implementation

This section presents DroidFace, a dynamic analysis tool for taint tracking in Android applications, based on the facelifted values from Sect. 2. The tool is a prototype built on top of the *Soot* framework [37]. DroidFace leverages an intermediate bytecode language, *Jimple* [37], to implement the static source-to-source transformation for facelifted evaluation. As a result, the implementation works with both ordinary Java *class* files as well as *APK* files for the Android platform. We further discuss Jimple in the full version of the paper [5].

DroidFace. We give a general overview of the architecture, features and limitations of DroidFace. We emphasize that the main contribution is the development of a fundamentally new approach to taint tracking applicable in many settings. Our main goal is to demonstrate feasibility of our approach in terms of precision, performance and flexibility, *not* to fully cover the Android platform.

DroidFace takes as input an Android APK file (a compressed archive) and uses Soot to convert it to a set of Jimple programs. Next, it applies the source-to-source transformation (as outlined in Sect. 2.4) to inline facelifted values and therefore produce a secure version of the input program. Finally, DroidFace converts the program back to an APK file that can be run on the Android platform. The source code of DroidFace is available online [5].

DroidFace is implemented in *Scala* [29] and supports an arbitrary lattice, represented as a Scala class. Noteworthy, many language constructs such as exceptions and multithreading require no special treatment and are transformed correctly by DroidFace. Control-flow statements like **if** e **goto** pc are transformed to refer to the variable copies at level $\top$. Similarly, method invocations with

virtualinvoke may select an object based on secret data, resulting in a control-flow leak; as an example, consider a program allocating two objects of type A and calling a method that sends the first constructor argument:

$A[]\ x = [\textbf{new}\ A(1), \textbf{new}\ A(2)]; x[h\%2].send()$

This is a leak through the program's control-flow (execution jumps to a different object's method depending on h), hence we use the values at level $\top$.

Since secret input usually consists of primitive data, such as numbers or strings, the transformation only replicates variables and fields of primitive types. Moreover, this is needed to avoid duplicating calls to constructors and other methods, as they may have side effects that should only be performed once. Since bodies of built-in methods are not affected by the program transformation, such calls need to be handled specially. Calls to side-effect free methods, e.g. `java.lang.Math.sin()`, can be duplicated for each level. However, other methods, e.g. sending data over the network, must only be performed once. A whitelist is used to determine which methods are side-effect free.

The implementation makes a number of simplifications. For example, file access is not handled in a precise way: While an implementation could duplicate file contents to maintain both soundness and precision, doing so in an efficient manner would require deduplication to manage the storage space overhead. As a result, the implementation writes either the *low* or *high* data to a file, depending on a configuration parameter. Inter-application communication (IAC) has not been modified to propagate facelifted values. However, the approach extends naturally to IAC by adding data for all levels to objects passed between apps.

Facelifted values are passed between methods by creating objects that contain one field for each level in the lattice. These objects are constructed for each primitive argument at a call site and returned by each non-entry method with a primitive return type. This creates additional overhead due to object creation; however, this can be avoided if facelifted values are implemented by modifying the runtime. More details on the performance impact can be found in Sect. 4.

Since source and sink detection is covered in related work [1,21], we use an incomplete set of known sources and sinks for the purposes of this evaluation.

Alternative strategies. While implementing facelifted values via program transformation as presented here provides a reasonable proof-of-concept implementation, there are a number of alternative techniques that can be explored. A minor optimization is to avoid creating a new object when passing facelifted values to methods; however, this is still necessary when passing facelifted return values. One possible approach is to simply run the program twice, once with real values while recording control-flow decisions and once with default values making use of the recorded control flow. However, this requires careful suppression of publicly observable side effects and outputs in the run with real values and vice versa. Moreover, this technique requires synchronization of the two runs of the program, leading to similar issues as SME [17].

4   Benchmarks

This section evaluates our prototype. Soundness and precision are evaluated using the *DroidBench* [1] benchmark suite. DroidBench is a set of small Android apps to evaluate static analysis tools for the Android platform. The main goal is to test sensitivity of a static analysis with respect to complex language features. To obtain better coverage for dynamic analysis, we have developed additional micro-applications that exercise other features such as path sensitivity and complex expression evaluation. As described in Sect. 3, the implementation does not support the full range of Android features; as a result we only provide partial benchmark results. However, the current results indicate that the presented approach prevents information leaks while not producing false positives. For performance evaluation, we use the *CaffeineMark* [8] benchmark suite to compare our implementation to both, unmodified Android, as well as *TaintDroid* [19].

Precision. We run DroidFace on a number of examples from DroidBench. Due to constraints outlined in Sect. 3, not all examples are used for this evaluation. Moreover, a number of examples, such as emulator detection, are not relevant to a dynamic enforcement technique. Furthermore, some examples produced errors (e.g. missing permissions) when executed and could not be tested.

For the tested examples, DroidFace remains both sound and precise. A more detailed comparison to other taint-tracking systems can be found in the full version. Note that TaintDroid also maintains soundness and precision for all tested APKs (with the exception of `PublicAPIField1.apk` for which TaintDroid is unsound). However, TaintDroid does not remain fully precise in the presence of arrays. Consider the following secure program similar to the example from Sect. 1:

$$\mathbf{int}[]\ a := [0, 0];\ a[h\%2] \leftarrow \mathbf{in}(\mathbf{H});\ \mathbf{out}(\mathbf{L}, a[1 - h\%2])$$

Since a secret value h is assigned to a position in an array that depends on a secret, TaintDroid taints the entire array a and hence yields a false positive. DroidFace, however, produces the unmodified trace.

Performance. We compare the performance of DroidFace to TaintDroid and unmodified Android using the CaffeineMark benchmark suite. For running the benchmark on Android, we used a CaffeineMark app [9] from Google Play. Figure 2 shows a comparative performance evaluation using an ARM-based Android emulator running Android 4.3. The emulator was run on a Dell Latitude E7440 laptop with a i7-4600U CPU. Performance benchmarks on an emulator are indicative at best, but we did find that the results reported by CaffeineMark stabilize after running the benchmarks a few times to allow for startup effects to die out. The figure shows the scores of the fifth run of the benchmark.

CaffeineMark reports a custom score value useful for relative comparison only. The scores for individual categories are proportional to the number of times a test is run divided by the average time of a test execution. The *Overall* score is the geometric mean of the scores in the individual categories. A description of the individual categories can be found in the full version.

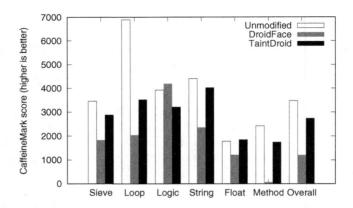

Fig. 2. Performance comparison using *CaffeineMark*.

The performance overhead is not prohibitively high given that DroidFace, being a proof-of-concept, produces unoptimized code. Note that due to different experimental setup and different versions of TaintDroid and CaffeineMark, our measurements for TaintDroid differ from the previously reported results [19]. Also note that many popular applications are not bound by CPU performance, but by user interaction [19]; hence, the real-world impact of these performance results may be negligible. The increase in code size is minor, as the bytecode itself is probably much smaller than other resources that ship with Android application. A more detailed comparison can be found in the full version. Similarly, preliminary experiments show the increase in memory usage to be insignificant as well, as the memory required for duplicates of primitive values is overshadowed by other resources loaded by the application.

5   Related Work

This section compares our work with closely related works for Android security. Table 1 gives a comparative overview of the state-of-the-art (static and dynamic) approaches to enforcing confidentiality for Android apps. We elaborate on the data from Table 1 (on a scale from ✗, 1, 2 to ✓) and other related work.

Reasoning about taint tracking. Taint tracking has been widely adopted as an ad-hoc technique in many security settings both for confidentiality and integrity. As a result, the majority of existing works either propose taint tracking as a bug-finding tool or justify its correctness using informal and custom-tailored soundness criteria [1,10,12,19,21,26]. Recently, Schoepe et al. [33] have proposed *explicit secrecy*, a semantic characterization of policies for taint tracking that captures the intuition of tracking direct data dependencies and generalizes Volpano's *weak secrecy* [39].

Our work presents a general technique for precise enforcement of explicit secrecy through facelifted execution and establishes soundness and precision.

Table 1. Comparison of state-of-the-art taint trackers

Tool	Value	Flow	Context	Object	Path	Arrays	Native	Enforcement	Sound	Precise
FlowDroid	✗	✓	✓	✓	✗	✗	1	Static	✗	✗
Amandroid	✓	✓	✓	✓	✗	✗	1	Static	✗	✗
DroidSafe	✗	✗	✓	✓	✗	✗	1	Static	✗	✗
HornDroid	✓	1	✓	✓	✗	1	1	Static	1	✗
TaintDroid	✓	✓	✓	✓	✓	1	1	Dynamic	✗	✗
AppFence	✓	✓	✓	✓	✓	✗	1	Dynamic	✗	✗
DroidFace	✓	✓	✓	✓	✓	✓	2	Dynamic	✓	✓

As reported in Table 1 (SOUND), the majority of existing approaches use taint-tracking in an ad-hoc manner without providing formal security justifications (✗). It is noteworthy that HornDroid [10] presents a correctness proof for their abstract data-flow analysis with respect to an instrumented semantics of Android activities. Instrumented semantics allow to approximate non-safety security properties such as explicit secrecy in terms of safety properties, thus not capturing the precise semantics of taint tracking. Chaudhuri et al. [12] and Livshits and Chong [26] propose similar conditions. Our enforcement is the first fully precise mechanism with respect to explicit secrecy (no false positives). As discussed before, existing approaches differ in precision, yet none of them is fully precise.

Static taint analysis. Static analysis has been proposed to tracking explicit flows in the Android domain. As shown in Table 1, static approaches differ on the features of analysis they implement. The complexity of the Android stack makes static analysis cumbersome and often leads to unsoundness or false positives [21].

Bodden et al. [1] present FlowDroid, a static taint analysis tool for Android applications. The analysis is path- and value- insensitive and it overapproximates arrays in a coarse manner. Due to event-driven nature of Android apps (multiple entry point, asynchronous components, callbacks, · · ·), flow sensitivity often leads to incompleteness and false negatives [21]. Li et al. [25] present IccTA, an extension of FlowDroid analysis with inter-component communication. Gordon et al. present DroidSafe [21], a static taint analysis tool that offers a high degree of precision and soundness. DroidSafe is a significant engineering effort to model the Android runtime behavior for non-Java code (native methods, event callbacks, component lifecycle, hidden state) using analysis stubs. The analysis is flow insensitive since interactions between apps and the Android environment are mediated by asynchronous callbacks, hence all event orderings are to be considered. Points-to and information flow analysis are also flow insensitive, which improves scalability at the expense of losing precision. DroidSafe may raise false positives due to the coarse modeling of arrays, maps, lists, flow insensitivity or event ordering. It is worth noting that although DroidSafe is more precise than FlowDroid, yet the number of false positives is too high for unknown applications. Wei et al. [40] present Amandroid, a general framework for determining points-to information for all objects in Android apps in a flow and context-sensitive way across Android apps components.

Amandroid can be specialized to solve security problems including taint tracking with high precision.

Calzavara et al. [10] present HornDroid, an approach that uses Horn clauses for soundly abstracting the semantics of Android applications. HornDroid expresses security properties as a set of proof obligations that are automatically discharged by an off-the-shelf SMT solver. The analysis is value- and context-sensitive. The authors argue that these features in combination are important. The analysis is flow sensitive on registers and flow insensitive on heap locations and callback methods, which increases precision without compromising soundness. Moreover, the static analysis is field-insensitive on arrays, although, being value-sensitive, HornDroid supports a more precise treatment of array indexes.

Static analysis approaches have the advantage of no-runtime overhead, however, especially for Android, they are fated to be imprecise. This is not only due to the complexity of the language and the execution lifecycle, but also to theoretical and practical limitations of current verification technologies. For instance, DroidSafe uses analysis stubs for native methods to approximate the data flow, object instantiation and aliasing of the missing native code. As recognized by the authors, this approach is not always sound. DroidFace faces the same problems with respect to native code with side effects, yet being fully precise for side-effect free native code. On the downside, DroidFace introduces runtime overhead which may deteriorate the performance.

Dynamic taint analysis. Dynamic taint analysis has been proposed for tracking privacy leaks at runtime in Android applications. Enck et al. present Taint-Droid [19] a system-wide integration of dynamic taint tracking into Android. Taint-Droid simultaneously tracks sensitive data from multiple sources by extending and modifying the Android environment with taint tags. Tracking is done at different levels: (i) variable-level: by instrumenting the Dalvik VM; (ii) message-level for IPC communication: by assigning one taint per serialized object (parcel); (iii) method-level: by providing method summaries for native methods; (iv) file-level: by assigning one taint per file. TaintDroid has different sources of false positives: for instance, by assigning one taint per file or one taint per parcel. Surprisingly, we found out that although the paper claims to assign one taint per array [19], the TaintDroid tool appears to assign one taint per array cell in our experiments. Native methods take the union of arguments' taints as resulting taint for the method return, which may cause false negatives due to possible side effects. TaintDroid requires modification of the JIT compiler in order to implement the taint propagation logic for applications using JIT. By contrast, our source-to source transformation requires no modification of the Android runtime and it is more precise. Hornyack et al. present AppFence [22], an extension of TaintDroid with shadow data for sensitive information that a user does not want to share. As for TaintDroid, AppFence implements modifications at the Android OS level. In addition to the precision issues inherited by TaintDroid, AppFence modifies the semantics of secure apps that never leak sensitive information.

Beyond taint tracking. DroidFace does not prevent insecure information flows through *covert channels*. For instance, applications can still leak sensitive information through implicit flows [16], where the information may flow through the control structure of the program. Information flow control [31] comprises methods and techniques that, in addition to explicit flows, also prevent implicit flows. Soundness is typically shown with respect to the semantic property of noninterference [20]. Information flow security has been explored in the context of Android apps by, e.g., Lortz et al. [27] and Jia et al. [23].

Our work draws inspiration from SME [17]. SME provides a precise enforcement of noninterference by running a program in a controlled manner, once for each security level. Kashyap et al. [24] study different scheduling strategies for SME and address the subtleties of timing- and termination-sensitive noninterference. Rafnsson and Sabelfeld [30], and Zanarini et al. [42] explore scheduling strategies with the goal to leverage SME for attack detection. By contrast to SME, our enforcement does not require scheduling different program copies.

Austin and Flanagan [2,32] enforce noninterference by runtime manipulation of faceted values. A challenging aspect for this line of work is dealing with non-local control flow and I/O, as the facets must record what can happen when the program takes different control-flow paths. Having explicit secrecy as the goal, our approach is free of these challenges because under our enforcement the program takes the same control-flow path as the original run. Section 1 offers further points of contrast to facelifted values.

Barthe et al. [4] implement SME for noninterference through static program transformation. This approach inherits the scheduling issues from SME and requires the buffering of inputs from lower security levels so that these inputs can be reused by executions running at higher security levels. These issues are not present in our work at the expense of enforcing the more liberal security policy.

Jeeves [41] is a programming language that uses symbolic evaluation and constraint-solving for enforcing information-flow policies. Austin et al. [3] show how to extend Jeeves with faceted values to propagate multiple views of sensitive information in a single faceted execution.

Boloşteanu and Garg propose asymmetric SME with declassification [7], focusing on robustness of SME wrt. modified inputs. This is achieved by producing a *low slice*, a program to compute the public results of the original program.

6   Conclusion

We have presented a dynamic mechanism for taint tracking. Its distinguishing feature is that it does not track taint propagation. Instead, it duplicates the state, representing its tainted and untainted views. We have showed that the mechanism is sound with respect to the policy of explicit secrecy and that it is precise in the sense that runs of secure programs are never modified. Further, we have leveraged the mechanism to detect attacks with zero false positives: whenever a mismatch between tainted and untainted views is detected, it must be due to an attack. Finally, we have implemented DroidFace, a source-to-source transformation for an intermediate Java-like language and benchmarked its precision and performance with respect to typical static and dynamic taint trackers for Android apps. The results show that performance penalty is tolerable while achieving both soundness and no false positives on the tested benchmarks.

Future work includes support for declassification policies. Recent progress on declassification for SME [2,7,30,38] gives us an encouraging start. Exploring facelifted values for machine code integrity is another promising line of future work. We are also interested in extending and optimizing the DroidFace tool as to make it suitable for a large-scale study of Android apps from Google Play. Finally, we will also explore memory optimizations in cases of large numbers of security levels, avoiding duplication.

Acknowledgments. This work was funded by the European Community under the ProSecuToR project and the Swedish research agencies SSF and VR.

References

1. Arzt, S., Rasthofer, S., Fritz, C., Bodden, E., Bartel, A., Klein, J., Traon, Y.L., Octeau, D., McDaniel, P.: Flowdroid: precise context, flow, field, object-sensitive and lifecycle-aware taint analysis for android apps. In: PLDI (2014)
2. Austin, T.H., Flanagan, C.: Multiple facets for dynamic information flow. In: POPL (2012)
3. Austin, T.H., Yang, J., Flanagan, C., Solar-Lezama, A.: Faceted execution of policy-agnostic programs. In: PLAS (2013)
4. Barthe, G., Crespo, J.M., Devriese, D., Piessens, F., Rivas, E.: Secure multi-execution through static program transformation. In: Giese, H., Rosu, G. (eds.) FORTE 2012 and FMOODS 2012. LNCS, vol. 7273, pp. 186–202. Springer, Heidelberg (2012)
5. Let's face it: faceted values for taint tracking. Full version and implementation. http://www.cse.chalmers.se/research/group/security/facets
6. Bielova, N., Rezk, T.: A taxonomy of information flow monitors. In: Piessens, F., Viganò, L. (eds.) POST 2016. LNCS, vol. 9635, pp. 46–67. Springer, Heidelberg (2016). doi:10.1007/978-3-662-49635-0_3
7. Bolosteanu, I., Garg, D.: Asymmetric secure multi-execution with declassification. In: Piessens, F., Viganò, L. (eds.) POST 2016. LNCS, vol. 9635, pp. 24–45. Springer, Heidelberg (2016). doi:10.1007/978-3-662-49635-0_2
8. Caffeinemark. http://www.benchmarkhq.ru/cm30/
9. Caffeinemark for android. https://play.google.com/store/apps/details?id=com.android.cm3
10. Calzavara, S., Grishchenko, I., Maffei, M.: Horndroid: practical and sound security static analysis of android applications by smt solving. In: EuroS&P (2016)
11. Capizzi, R., Longo, A., Venkatakrishnan, V.N., Sistla, A.P.: Preventing information leaks through shadow executions. In: ACSAC (2008)
12. Chaudhuri, A., Naldurg, P., Rajamani, S.K.: A type system for data-flow integrity on windows vista. In: PLAS (2008)
13. Cheng, W., Zhao, Q., Yu, B., Hiroshige, S.: TaintTrace: efficient flow tracing with dynamic binary rewriting. In: ISCC (2006)

14. Chow, J., Pfaff, B., Garfinkel, T., Christopher, K., Rosenblum, M.: Understanding data lifetime via whole system simulation. In: USENIX Security Symposium (2004)
15. Cohen, E.S.: Information transmission in sequential programs. In: FSC. Academic Press (1978)
16. Denning, D.E., Denning, P.J.: Certification of programs for secure information flow. Commun. ACM **20**(7), 504–513 (1977)
17. Devriese, D., Piessens, F.: Noninterference through secure multi-execution. In: S&P (2010)
18. Droidbench: a micro-benchmark suite to assess the stability of taint-analysis tools for android. https://github.com/secure-software-engineering/DroidBench
19. Enck, W., Gilbert, P., Han, S., Tendulkar, V., Chun, B.-G., Cox, L.P., Jung, J., McDaniel, P., Sheth, A.N.: Taintdroid: an information-flow tracking system for realtime privacy monitoring on smartphones. ACM Trans. Comput. Syst. **32**(2), 5:1–5:29 (2014). http://doi.acm.org/10.1145/2619091
20. Goguen, J.A., Meseguer, J.: Security policies and security models. In: S&P (1982)
21. Gordon, M.I., Kim, D., Perkins, J.H., Gilham, L., Nguyen, N., Rinard, M.C.: Information flow analysis of android applications in droidsafe. In: NDSS (2015)
22. Hornyack, P., Han, S., Jung, J., Schechter, S., Wetherall, D.: These aren't the droids you're looking for: retrofitting android to protect data from imperious applications. In: CCS (2011)
23. Jia, L., Aljuraidan, J., Fragkaki, E., Bauer, L., Stroucken, M., Fukushima, K., Kiyomoto, S., Miyake, Y.: Run-time enforcement of information-flow properties on android. In: Crampton, J., Jajodia, S., Mayes, K. (eds.) ESORICS 2013. LNCS, vol. 8134, pp. 775–792. Springer, Heidelberg (2013)
24. Kashyap, V., Wiedermann, B., Hardekopf, B.: Timing- and termination-sensitive secure information flow: exploring a new approach. In: S&P (2011)
25. Li, L., Bartel, A., Bissyandé, T.F., Klein, J., Traon, Y.L., Arzt, S., Rasthofer, S., Bodden, E., Octeau, D., McDaniel, P.: Iccta: detecting inter-component privacy leaks in android apps. In: ICSE, vol. 1 (2015)
26. Livshits, B., Chong, S.: Towards fully automatic placement of security sanitizers and declassifiers. In: POPL (2013)
27. Lortz, S., Mantel, H., Starostin, A., Bähr, T., Schneider, D., Weber, A.: Cassandra: towards a Certifying App. Store for Android. In: SPSM (2014)
28. Netscape: using data tainting for security (2006). http://www.aisystech.com/resources/advtopic.htm
29. Odersky, M., Rompf, T.: Unifying functional and object-oriented programming with scala. Commun. ACM **57**(4), 76–86 (2014)
30. Rafnsson, W., Sabelfeld, A.: Secure multi-execution: fine-grained, declassification-aware, and transparent. In: CSF (2013)
31. Sabelfeld, A., Myers, A.C.: Language-based information-flow security. JSAC **21**(1), 5–19 (2003)
32. Schmitz, T., Rhodes, D., Austin, T.H., Knowles, K., Flanagan, C.: Faceted dynamic information flow via control and data monads. In: Piessens, F., Viganò, L. (eds.) POST 2016. LNCS, vol. 9635, pp. 3–23. Springer, Heidelberg (2016). doi:10.1007/978-3-662-49635-0_1
33. Schoepe, D., Balliu, M., Pierce, B.C., Sabelfeld, A.: Explicit secrecy: a policy for taint tracking. In: EuroS&P (2016)
34. Schwartz, E.J., Avgerinos, T., Brumley, D.: All you ever wanted to know about dynamic taint analysis and forward symbolic execution (but might have been afraid to ask). In: S&P 2010 (2010)

35. Song, D., et al.: BitBlaze: a new approach to computer security via binary analysis. In: Sekar, R., Pujari, A.K. (eds.) ICISS 2008. LNCS, vol. 5352, pp. 1–25. Springer, Heidelberg (2008)

36. Tripp, O., Pistoia, M., Fink, S.J., Sridharan, M., Weisman, O.: Taj: effective taint analysis of web applications. In: PLDI (2009)

37. Vallée-Rai, R., Co, P., Gagnon, E., Hendren, L.J., Lam, P., Sundaresan, V.: Soot - a java bytecode optimization framework. In: CASCON (1999)

38. Vanhoef, M., De Groef, W., Devriese, D., Piessens, F., Rezk, T.: Stateful declassification policies for event-driven programs. In: CSF (2014)

39. Volpano, D.: Safety versus secrecy. In: Cortesi, A., Filé, G. (eds.) SAS 1999. LNCS, vol. 1694, p. 303. Springer, Heidelberg (1999)

40. Wei, F., Roy, S., Ou, X., Robby: Amandroid: a precise and general inter-component data flow analysis framework for security vetting of android apps. In: CCS (2014)

41. Yang, J., Yessenov, K., Solar-Lezama, A.: A language for automatically enforcing privacy policies. In: POPL (2012)

42. Zanarini, D., Jaskelioff, M., Russo, A.: Precise enforcement of confidentiality for reactive systems. In: CSF (2013)

IFuzzer: An Evolutionary Interpreter Fuzzer Using Genetic Programming

Spandan Veggalam[1($\boxtimes$)], Sanjay Rawat[2,3], Istvan Haller[2,3], and Herbert Bos[2,3]

[1] International Institute of Information Technology, Hyderabad, India
`veggalam.s@research.iiit.ac.in`
[2] Computer Science Institute,
Vrije Universiteit Amsterdam, Amsterdam, The Netherlands
`s.rawat@vu.nl, i.haller@student.vu.nl, herbertb@cs.vu.nl`
[3] Department of Informatics,
Vrije Universiteit Amsterdam, Amsterdam, The Netherlands

Abstract. We present an automated *evolutionary fuzzing* technique to find bugs in JavaScript interpreters. Fuzzing is an automated black box testing technique used for finding security vulnerabilities in the software by providing random data as input. However, in the case of an interpreter, fuzzing is challenging because the inputs are piece of codes that should be syntactically/semantically valid to pass the interpreter's elementary checks. On the other hand, the fuzzed input should also be *uncommon enough* to trigger exceptional behavior in the interpreter, such as crashes, memory leaks and failing assertions. In our approach, we use evolutionary computing techniques, specifically *genetic programming*, to guide the fuzzer in generating uncommon input code fragments that may trigger exceptional behavior in the interpreter. We implement a prototype named **IFuzzer** to evaluate our technique on real-world examples. IFuzzer uses the language grammar to generate valid inputs. We applied IFuzzer first on an older version of the JavaScript interpreter of Mozilla (to allow for a fair comparison to existing work) and found 40 bugs, of which 12 were exploitable. On subsequently targeting the latest builds of the interpreter, IFuzzer found 17 bugs, of which four were security bugs.

Keywords: Fuzzing · System security · Vulnerability · Genetic programming · Evolutionary computing

1 Introduction

Browsers have become the main interface to almost all online content for almost all users. As a result, they have also become extremely sophisticated. A modern browser renders content using a wide variety of interconnected components with interpreters for a growing set of languages such as JavaScript, Flash, Java, and XSLT. Small wonder that browsers have turned into prime targets for attackers who routinely exploit the embedded interpreters to launch sophisticated

© Springer International Publishing Switzerland 2016
I. Askoxylakis et al. (Eds.): ESORICS 2016, Part I, LNCS 9878, pp. 581–601, 2016.
DOI: 10.1007/978-3-319-45744-4_29

attacks [1]. For instance, the JavaScript interpreter in modern browsers (e.g., SpiderMonkey in Firefox) is a widely used interpreter that is responsible for many high-impact vulnerabilities [2]. Unfortunately, the nature and complexity of these interpreters is currently well beyond state-of-the-art bug finding techniques, and therefore, further research is necessary [3]. In this paper, we propose a novel evolutionary fuzzing technique that explicitly targets interpreters.

Fuzz testing is a common approach for finding vulnerabilities in software [4–8]. Many fuzzers exist and range from a simple random input generator to highly sophisticated testing tools. For instance, in this paper, we build on evolutionary fuzzing which has proven particularly effective in improving fuzzing efficiency [5, 9,10] and makes use of evolutionary computing to generate inputs that exhibit vulnerabilities. While fuzzing is an efficient testing tool in general, applying it to interpreters brings its own challenges. Below, we list a few of the issues that we observed in our investigations:

1. Traditionally, fuzzing is about mutating *input* that is manipulated by a software. In the case of the interpreter, the input is *program (code)*, which needs to be mutated.
2. Interpreter fuzzers must generate syntactically valid inputs, otherwise, inputs will not pass the elementary interpreter checks (mainly the parsing phase) and testing will be restricted to the input checking part of the interpreter. Therefore, the input grammar is a key consideration for this scenario. For instance, if the JavaScript interpreter is the target, the fuzzed input *must* follow the syntax specifications of the JavaScript language, lest the inputs be discarded early in the parsing phase.
3. An interpreter may use a somewhat different (or evolved) version of the grammar than the one publicly known. These small variations are important to consider when attempting fuzzing the interpreter fully.

Genetic Programming is a variant of evolutionary algorithms, inspired by biological evolution and brings transparency in making decisions. It follows Darwin's theory of evolution and generates new individuals in the eco-system by recombining the current characteristics from individuals with the highest fitness. Fitness is a value computed by an objective function that directs the evolution process. Genetic Programming exploits the modularity and re-usability of solution fragments within the problem space to improve the fitness of individuals. This approach has been shown to be very appropriate for generating code fragments [11–13], but hasn't been used for fuzz-testing in general as program inputs are typically unstructured and highly inter-dependent. However, our key insight is that, as described before, interpreter fuzzing is a special case. Using code as input, Genetic Programming seems like a natural fit!

par In this paper, we introduce a framework called *IFuzzer*, which generates code fragments using Genetic Programming [14]—allowing us to test interpreters by following a black-box fuzzing technique and mainly looks for vulnerabilities like memory corruptions. IFuzzer takes a language's context-free grammar as input for test generation. It uses the grammar to generate parse trees and to extract code fragments from a given test-suite. For instance, IFuzzer can take the

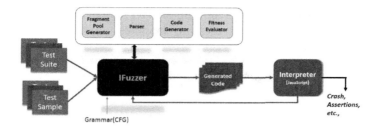

Fig. 1. Overview of IFuzzer approach

JavaScript grammar and the test-suite of the SpiderMonkey interpreter as input and generate parse trees and relevant code fragments for in-depth testing. IFuzzer leverages the fitness improvement mechanism within Genetic Programming to improve the quality of the generated code fragments.

Figure 1 describes the overview of IFuzzer. The fuzzer takes as input a test suite, a language grammar and sample codes. The parser module uses the language grammar to parse the program and generates an abstract syntax tree. The fragment pool extractor generates a pool of code fragments extracted from a set of sample code inputs for different nodes (Non-Terminals) in the grammar. The code generator generates new code fragments by performing genetic operations on the test suite. The interpreter executes all the generated code fragments. Based on the feedback from the interpreter, the fragments are evaluated by the fitness evaluator and accordingly used (or discarded) for future generations of inputs. We evaluated IFuzzer on two versions of Mozilla JavaScript interpreter. Initially, we configured it to target SpiderMonkey 1.8.5 in order to have a comparison with LangFuzz [3], a state-of-art mutation fuzzer for interpreter testing. In another experiment, we configured IFuzzer to target the latest builds of SpiderMonkey. Apart from finding several bugs that were also found by LangFuzz, IFuzzer found *new exploitable* bugs in these versions.

In summary, this paper makes the following contributions:

1. We introduce a fully automated and systematic approach for code generation for interpreter testing by *mapping the problem of interpreter fuzz testing onto the space of evolutionary computing for code generation*. By doing so, we establish a path for applying advancements made in evolutionary approaches to the field of interpreter fuzzing.
2. We show that Genetic Programming techniques for code generation result in a diverse range of code fragments, making it a very suitable approach for interpreter fuzzing. We attribute this to inherent randomness in Genetic Programming.
3. We propose a *fitness function* (objective function) by analyzing and identifying different code parameters, which guide the fuzzer to generate inputs which can trigger uncommon behavior within interpreters.

4. We implement these techniques in a full-fledged (to be) open sourced fuzzing tool called *IFuzzer* that can target any language interpreter with minimal configuration changes.
5. We show the effectiveness of IFuzzer empirically by finding new bugs in Mozilla's JavaScript engine SpiderMonkey—including several exploitable security vulnerabilities.

The rest of the paper is organized as follows. Section 2 presents the motivation for choosing Genetic Programming for code generation. We explain the implementation of IFuzzer in Sect. 3. Section 4 discusses the experimental set-up and evaluation step of IFuzzer and Sect. 7 concludes the work with comments on possible future work.

2   Genetic Programming

Evolutionary algorithms build up a search space for finding solutions to optimization problems, by evolving a population of individuals. An *objective function* evaluates the fitness of these individuals and provides feedback for next generations of individuals. These algorithms build on the Darwinian principle of natural selection and biologically inspired genetic operations. In prior work, Genetic Algorithms proved successful in the generation of test cases [13,15].

Genetic programming (GP) [14,16] achieves the goal of generating a population by following a similar process as that of most genetic algorithms, but it represents the individuals it manipulates as tree structures. Out of the many variants of GP in the literature, we follow Grammar-based Genetic Programming (GGP). In GGP, we consider programs, that are generated based on the rules formulated in the grammar (context free), as the individuals and represent them by parse trees. This procedure is a natural fit for the interpreters. All the individuals in a new generation are the result of applying the genetic operators—crossover and mutation—on the parse tree structures.

Search Space: The search space is the set of all feasible solutions. Each point in the space represents a solution defined by the fitness values or some other values related to an individual. Based on fitness constraints, the individual with highest fitness is considered the best feasible solution.

Bloating: Bloating [16] is a phenomenon that adversely affects input generation in evolutionary computing. There are two types of bloating: structural and functional bloating.

- *Structural Bloating*: While iterating over generations, after a certain number of generations, the average size of individuals (i.e. the code) grows rapidly due to uncontrolled growth [17]. This results in inefficient code, while the growth hardly contributes to the improvement of fitness. Moreover, large programs require more computation to process.

– *Functional Bloating*: In functional bloating [18], a range of fitness values become narrow and thereby reduces the search space. However, it is common to have different individuals with the same fitness, because after some time bloating makes everything look linear. As a result, it becomes hard to distinguish individuals.

As the process of fuzzing may run for a very long period, neglecting or failing to handle the bloating problem may lead to very unproductive results.

2.1 Representation of the Individuals

We consider input code to be the individuals manipulated by GP. Each individual is represented by its parse tree, generated using the corresponding language grammar. IFuzzer performs all its genetic operations on these parse trees and generates new individuals (input code)from the resulting parse trees. Figure 2 illustrates an example of valid program for the simple language grammar (Listing 1.1) and the corresponding parse tree derived.

⟨*statement*⟩ ::= ⟨*variable Statement*⟩*
⟨*variable Statement*⟩ ::= **var** ⟨*identifier*⟩ ⟨*initializer*⟩?
⟨*initializer*⟩ ::= **=** ⟨*numLiteral*⟩ | ⟨*identifier*⟩
⟨*identifier*⟩ ::= [a-zA-Z0-9]*
⟨*numLiteral*⟩ ::= [0-9]*

Listing 1.1. Example of a simple language grammar

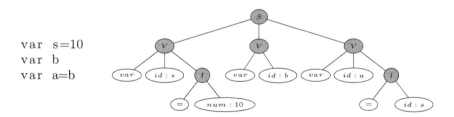

Fig. 2. Example of a syntactically valid program and its derived parse tree

2.2 Fragment Pool

The fragment pool is a collection of code fragments for each non-terminal in the grammar specification. We can tag each possible code fragment in a program with a non-terminal in the grammar specification. Using the parser, IFuzzer parses all the input files in the test suite and extracts the corresponding code fragments for different non-terminals. With a sufficient number of input files, we can generate code fragments for all non-terminals in the language grammar. It stores these code fragments in tree representations with the corresponding non-terminal as root. At a later stage, it uses these code fragments for mutation and code generation. The same process of generating parse trees is followed in the crossover operation for identifying code fragments for selected common non-terminal between the participating individuals. An example of a fragment pool for the derived parse tree, summarized in Fig. 2, is shown in the box below.

```
(S) <statement> = { var  s=10, var  b, var  a=s }
(V) <variableStatement>
    = { var  s=10, var  b , var  a=s }
(I) <initializer> = {=  10,=s }
terminals = { id : s , id : a , id : b ,num:10 , var ,=}
```

3   Implementation

We implement IFuzzer as a proof-of-concept based on the methods discussed in the previous sections. It works as described in the overview diagram of Fig. 1 and in the following, we elaborate on IFuzzer's individual components.

3.1   Code Generation

In this section, we explain various genetic operators that IFuzzer uses for input generation. After each genetic operation, the objective function, discussed in Sect. 3.3, evaluates the fitness of the offspring.

IFuzzer uses the ANTLR parser for the target language and generates the parser using the ANTLR parser generator framework [19] with the language grammar as input. The initial population, the fragment pool generation (discussed in Sect. 2), and the crossover and mutation operations all make use of parse tree returned by the parser.

Initial Population. The initial population of individuals consists of random selection of programs, equal to the population size, from the input test samples. This forms the first generation. After each generation, individuals from the parent set undergo genetic operations and thereby evolve into offspring.

Mutation. During mutation, IFuzzer selects random code fragments of the input code for replacement. It performs replacement by selecting a random member of the fragment pool which corresponds to the same non-terminal, or by generating a new fragment using an expansion algorithm. Our expansion algorithm assumes that all the production rules have equal and fixed probabilities for selection. We use the following expansion algorithm:

1. Select the non-terminal n from the parse tree to expand.
2. From the production rules of the grammar, select a production for n and replace it with n.
3. Repeat the following steps up to *num* iterations.

(a) Identify a random set N of non-terminals in the resulting incomplete parse tree.

(b) Extract a set of production rules P_n, for the selected non-terminal n, from the production rules P (i.e., $P_n \subseteq P$) listed in the grammar specification.

(c) Select a production $P_{selected}$ randomly for each identified non-terminal $\in N$.

(d) Replace the non-terminals occurrence with $P_{selected}$.

4. After expansion, replace all remaining occurrences of non-terminals with corresponding code fragments, selected randomly from the fragment pool. Note that steps 3 & 4 also solve the problem of non-termination in the presence of mutually recursive production rules.

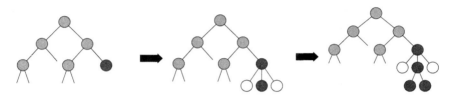

Fig. 3. Example of stepwise expansion on the parse tree: all the dark nodes represent non-terminals and white nodes represent terminals. A particular node is selected and expanded as shown.

Figure 3 illustrates an example of the expansion algorithm. Dark nodes in the parse tree represent the non-terminals and white nodes represent the terminals. A dark node from the parse tree is selected during the mutation process and is expanded to the certain depth (num) as discussed above. This algorithm does not yield a valid expansion with more iterations. After expansion, we may still have unexpanded non-terminals. IFuzzer handles this by choosing *code fragments* from the fragment pool and replaces remaining non-terminals by such code fragments, which are represented by the same non-terminals. In this way, the tree converges with terminals and results in a valid parse tree.

Crossover. During crossover, for a given pair of individuals (parents), IFuzzer selects a common non-terminal n from parse trees of the individuals and extracts random fragments, originating from n, from both the individuals. These selected fragments from one individual are exchanged with fragments of another individual, thereby generating two new parse trees. Using these trees, IFuzzzer generates two new offsprings.

Replacement. During the process of offspring generation, it is important to retain the features of the best individuals (parents) participating in evolution. Therefore, IFuzzer adopts the common technique of *fitness elitism* to retain the best individuals among the parents in the next generation. IFuzzer generates the remaining population in the next generation by crossover and mutation. Elitism prevents losing the best configurations in the process.

Reusing Literals. The code generation operations may result in semantically invalid fragments or a loss of context. For instance, after a modification a statement in the program may use an identifier a which is not declared in this program. Introducing language semantics will tie IFuzzer to a language specification and we therefore perform generic semantic improvements at the syntactic level. Specifically, IFuzzer reduces the errors due to undeclared identifiers by renaming the identifiers around the modification points to the ones declared elsewhere in the program. Since it knows the grammar rules that contain them, IFuzzer can easily extract such identifiers from the parse tree automatically. In our example of the undeclared variable a, it will mapped it to another identifier b declared elsewhere and replace all occurrences of a with b.

3.2   Bloat Control

Bloat control pertains to different levels [20] and IFuzzer uses it during the fitness evaluation and breeding stages:

Stage 1: Fitness Evaluation. Applying bloat control at the level of fitness evaluation is a common technique. In IFuzzer, we use *parsimony pressure* [21,22] to alter the selection probability of individuals by penalizing larger ones.

   Calculating Parsimony Coefficient: The parsimony co-efficient $c(t)$ at each generation t is given by the following correlation coefficient [23].

$$c(t) = \frac{Covariance(f,l)}{Variance(l)} = \frac{\sum_{i=0}^{n}(f_i - \bar{f})(l_i - \bar{l})}{n-1} \times \frac{n-1}{\sum_{i=0}^{n}(l_i - \bar{l})^2} \qquad (1)$$

where $\bar{l}$ and $\bar{f}$ are the mean fitness and length of all individuals in the population, and f_i and l_i are the original fitness and length of an individual i. $Covariance(f,l)$ calculates the co-variance between an individual's fitness and length, while $Variance(l)$ gives the variance in the length of the individuals. In Sect. 3.3, we will see that IFuzzer uses the parsimony coefficient to add penalty to the fitness value.

Stage 2: We also apply bloat control at the breeding level by means of fair size generation techniques [16]. *Fair Size Generation* limits the growth of the offspring's program size. In our approach, we restrict the percentage of increase in program size to a biased value:

$$length_{generated\_code}/length_{original\_code} < bias_{threshold}$$

   where $length_x$ gives information about the number of non-terminals in the parse tree x and $bias_{threshold}$ is the threshold value for fair size generation.

This restricts the size of code and if the generated program fails to meet this constraint, IFuzzer discards as invalid. In that case, it re-generates the program using the same GA operator with which it started. After a certain number of failed attempts, it discards the individual completely and excludes it from further consideration for offspring generation.

Finally, we use *Delta debugging* algorithm [24, 25] to determine the code fragments that are relevant for failure production and to filter out irrelevant code fragments from the test cases, further reduces the size of test case. This essentially results in part of the test case that is relevant to the failure [26]. The same algorithm reduces the number of lines of code executed and results in suitably possible valid small test case.

3.3   Fitness Evaluation

The evolutionary process is an objective driven process and the fitness function that defines the objective of the process plays a vital role in the code generation process. After crossover and mutation phases, the generated code fragments are evaluated for fitness.

As IFuzzer aims to generate uncommon code structures to trigger exceptional behavior, we consider both *structural* aspects and interpreter *feedback* of the generated program as inputs to the objective function. The interpreter feedback includes warnings, execution timeouts, errors, crashes, etc.—in other words, the goal itself. Moreover, during the fitness evaluation, we calculate structural metrics such as the cyclomatic complexity for the program. The cyclomatic complexity [27] gives information about the structural complexity of the code. For instance, nested (or complex) structure has a tendency to create uncommon behavior [28], so such structures have higher scores than less complex programs.

At its core, IFuzzer calculates the base fitness value $f_b(x)$ of an individual x as the sum of its structural score ($score_{structure}$) and its feedback score ($score_{feedback}$).

$$f_b(x) = score_{structure} + score_{feedback}$$

Finally, as discussed in Sect. 3.2, IFuzzer's bloat control re-calculates the fitness with a penalty determined by the product of its parsimony co-efficient c and the length of the individual l:

$$f_{final}(x) = f_b(x) - c * (l(x))$$

where $f_{final}(x)$ is the updated fitness value of an individual x.

Parameters. IFuzzer contains many adjustable GP and fitness parameters, including the mutation rate, crossover rates, population size, and the number of generations. In order to arrive at a set of optimal values, we ran application (to be tested) with various combinations of these parameters and observed for properties like input diversity, structural properties etc. We adhere to the policy that higher the values of such properties, better is the combination of parameters. In the experiments, we use the best combination based on observations, made during a fixed profiling period. We, however, note that it should be possible to fine tune all these parameters further for optimal results.

4   Experimentation

In this section, we evaluate the effectiveness of IFuzzer by performing experimentation on real-world applications. IFuzzer is a cross platform tool, which runs on UNIX and Windows operating systems. All the experiments were performed on a standalone machine with a configuration of Quad-Core 1.6 Ghz Intel i5-4200 CPU and 8 GB RAM. The outcome of our experiments aims to answer the following questions:

1. Does IFuzzer perform better than the known state-of-art tools? What is the effectiveness of IFuzzer?
2. What are the benefits of using GP? What drives GP to reach its objective?
3. Does our defined objective function encourage the generation of uncommon code?
4. How important is it that IFuzzer generates uncommon code? How is this related to having high coverage of the interpreter?

In order to answer the questions mentioned above, we performed two experiments. In the first experiment, we evaluate IFuzzer and compare it against the state-of-the-art LangFuzz using the same test software [3]. In the second experiment, we run IFuzzer against the latest build of SpiderMonkey. We have also run IFuzzer with different configurations in order to evaluate the effect of separate code generation strategies. Results of these experiments are in the Appendix.

We also ran IFuzzer on Chrome JavaScript engine V8 and reported few bugs. However, our reported-bugs do not appear to be *security bugs* (as per Chrome V8 team) and therefore, we do not report them in detail in this paper. In order to establish the usability of IFuzzer to other interpreters, we could configure IFuzzer for Java by using Java Grammar Specifications, available at [29]. However, we have not tested this environment to its full extent. The main intention of performing this action is to show the flexibility of IFuzzer to other grammars.

4.1   Testing Environment

In our experiments, we used the Mozilla development test suite as the initial input set. The test suite consists of 3000 programs chosen from a target version. We used the same test suite for fragment pool generation and program generation. Fragment Pool generation is a one-time process, which reads all programs at the start of the fuzzing process and extracts fragments for different non-terminals. We assume that the test suite involves inputs (i.e. code fragments) that have been used in testing in the past and resulted in triggering bugs. We choose *SpiderMonkey* as the target interpreter for JavaScript. We write input grammar specification from the ECMAScipt standard specification and grammar rules from the ECMAScript 262 specification [30].

4.2   IFuzzer vs. LangFuzz

Our first experiment evaluated IFuzzer by running it against interpreters with the aim of finding exploitable bugs and compare our results to those of LangFuzz. We compare in terms of time taken in finding bugs and the extent of the overlap in bugs found by both the fuzzers. Since we do not have access to the LangFuzz code, we base our comparison on the results reported in [3]. For a meaningful comparison with LangFuzz, we chose SpiderMonkey 1.8.5 as the interpreter as this was the version of SpiderMonkey that was current when LangFuzz was introduced in [3].

During the experiment on SpiderMonkey 1.8.5 version, IFuzzer found 40 bugs in a time span of one month, while Langfuzz found 51 bugs in 3 months. More importantly, when comparing the bugs found by the two fuzzers, the overlap is "only" 24 bugs. In other, a large fraction of the bugs found by IFuzzer is unique.

With roughly 36 % overlap in the bugs (Fig. 4), IFuzzer clearly finds different bugs–bugs that were missed by today's state-of-the-art interpreter fuzzer—in comparable time frames.

We speculate that IFuzzer will find even more bugs if we further fine-tune its parameters and run it for a longer period. We also notice that there are many build configurations possible for SpiderMonkey, and Langfuzz tries to run on all such possible build configurations. In contrast, due to resource constraints, we configured IFuzzer to run only on two such different configurations (with and without enabling debugging). Trying more configurations may well uncover more bugs [31].

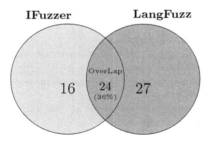

Fig. 4. Number of defects found by IFuzzer (40) and LangFuzz (51) in SpiderMonkey version 1.8.5

In order to determine the severity of the bugs, we investigated them manually with gdb-exploitable [32]–a widely used tool for classifying a given application crash file (core dump) as *exploitable* or non-exploitable. Out of IFuzzer's 40 bugs, gdb-exploitable classified no fewer than 12 as *exploitable*.

Example of a Defect Triggered by IFuzzer: Listing 1.2 shows an example of a generated program triggering an assertion violation in SpiderMonkey 1.8.5.

The JavaScript engine crashes at line 6, as it fails to build an argument array for the given argument value `abcd*&^%$$`. Instead, one would expect an exception or error stating that the argument as invalid.

```
1  if (typeof options =="function")
2  { var opts = options();
3  if (!/\bstrict\b/.test(opts))
4      options("strict");
5  if (!/\bwerror\b/.test(opts))
6      options('abcd*&^%$$');
7  }
```

Listing 1.2. A test Case generated by IFuzzer, which crashes the SpiderMonkey JavaScript engine with an internal assertion upon executing line 6

```
1  function test(code) {
2  f = eval("(function(){"
3      + code + "})")
4      f()
5  }
6  test("x=7");
7  test("\"use strict\"";
8  for(d in [x=arguments]){}");
9  test("for(v in((Object.seal)(x)));
10 x.length=Function")
```

Listing 1.3. Test Case generated by IFuzzer, that crashes the SpiderMonkey JavaScript engine 1.8.5.

Another example (shown in Listing 1.3) exposes security issues in SpiderMonkey 1.8.5, which is related to strict mode changes to the JavaScript semantics [33].

Table 1. Bugs found in the latest version of Mozilla's SpiderMonkey

Bug ID	Description
1131986	Segmentation fault
1133247	OOM error is not reported in the browser console
1141969*	Crash[@js::SCInput::SCInput] or assertion failure: (nbytes & 7) == 0 at StructuredClone.cpp:463
1192381*	Crash due to Assertion failure: input()-> isRecoveredOnBailout() == mustBeRecovered_ (assertRecoveredOnBailout failed during compilation), at js/src/jit/Recover.cpp:1465
1192379	input()->isRecoveredOnBailout()
1192401 (CVE-2015-4507)	Crash due to Assertion failure: getSlotRef(EVAL).isUndefined(), at js/src/vm/GlobalObject.h:147
1193307	evaluate() method results in "Error: compartment cannot save singleton anymore"
1205603	crash due to uncaught exception: out of memory
1205605	InternalError: too much recursion
1234323	AddressSanitizer failed to allocate 0x001000000000 bytes. AddressSanitizer's allocator is terminating the process instead of returning 0
1248188*	Crash due to Assertion Failure : Could not allocate ObjectGroup in EnsureTrackPropertyTyp
1234979	Segmentation fault at js/src/jsobj.h:122
1235122	AddressSanitizer failed to allocate 0x400002000 (17179877376) bytes of LargeMmapAllocator
1235160	crash due to Assertion failure: index < length_, at js/src/jit/FixedList.h:84
1247231*	Segmentation fault at js/src/vm/NativeObject.h:86
1248321*	Crash due to Assertion failure: JSScript::argumentsOptimizationFailed, at js/src/jscntxt.cpp:12
1258189	Crash due to Assertion failure: isLive(), at js/src/build1/dist/include/js/HashTable.h:774

Line 8 enables the strict mode which makes changes to the way, SpiderMonkey executes the code. On execution, the JavaScript engine crashes due to an access violation and results in a stack overflow.

4.3 Spidermonkey Version 38

We also ran an instance of IFuzzer to target SpiderMonkey 38 (latest version at the time of experimentation). Table 1 shows the results of running IFuzzer on latest build. IFuzzer detected 17 bugs and out of these, 4 were confirmed to be exploitable. Five of the crashes (marked with *) are due to assertion failures (which may be fixed in subsequent versions), unhandled out of memory crashes, or spurious crashes that we could not reproduce. The remaining ones are significant bugs in the interpreter itself.

For instance, the following code looks to be an infinite loop, except that one of the interconnected components may fail to handle the memory management and, hence the JavaScript engine keeps consuming the heap memory, creating a denial of service by crashing the machine in few seconds. The code fragment responsible for the crash is shown in Listing 1.4.

```
1   try {
2     a = new Array() ;
3     while(1)
4       a = new Array(a) ;
5   }
6   catch (e) { }
```

Listing 1.4. Test Case generated by IFuzzer, crashing the latest version XXX of SpiderMonkey JavaScript engine. JavaScript engine fails to handle the situation, leading to a memory leak

Also, in this case, our contribution and efforts were rewarded by the Mozilla's bounty program for one of the bugs detected by IFuzzer. The bug received an advisory from mozilla [34] and CVE Number CVE-2015-4507 and concerns a crash due to a `getSlotRef` assertion failure and application exit in the `SavedStacks` class in the JavaScript implementation. Mozilla classified its security severeness as "moderate".

The results discussed so far establishes that the evolutionary approach followed by *IFuzzer* tool is capable of generating programs with a given objective and trigger significant bugs in real-world applications.

Other Interpreters. When evaluating our work on the Chrome JavaScript engine V8, IFuzzer worked out of the box and reported few bugs that resulted in crash (see Table 2). As far as we can tell, these bugs do not appear to be security bugs and require further scrutiny.

```
 1  function f() {
 2      var s ="switch (x) {";
 3      for (var i = 8000; i < 16400; g++) {
 4          s += "case" + i + ": return" + i + "; break;";
 5      }
 6      s += "case 8005: return -1; break;";
 7      s += "}";
 8      var g = Func.tion("x", s);
 9      assertEq(g(8005), 8005);
10  }
11  f();
```

Listing 1.5. Test Case generated by IFuzzer, crashing the latest version XXX of Chrome V8 JavaScript engine. JavaScript engine fails to handle the situation crashes with an illegal instruction error.

Table 2. IFuzzer crashes found on Chrome V8 [4.7.0]

1 -	2 crashes with Fatal error in CALL_AND_RETRY_LAST # Allocation failed - process out of memory
2 -	few crashes due to NULL pointer exception

In order to establish the usability of IFuzzer to other languages, we could further configure IFuzzer for Java by using Java Grammar Specifications, available at [29]. However, we have not fully tested this environment to its full extent.

5   Remarks on IFuzzer's Design Decisions

Recall that IFuzzer uses an evolutionary approach for code generation by guiding the evolution process to generate uncommon code fragments. As stated earlier, there are several parameters available to fine-tune IFuzzer for better performance. For example, the choice of using a subset (of cardinality equal to the size of population) of the initial test suite, rather than the whole suite, as the first generation is to make an effective use of resources available. The remaining inputs from test suite can be used in later generation when IFuzzer gets stuck at some *local minima*, which is a known obstacle in evolutionary algorithms.

The generation in which a bug is identified depends on different factors, including the size of the input test sample, the size of the fragment considered for genetic operation and the size of new fragment induced etc. As discussed, the higher the complexity of inputs, the higher the probability of finding a bug. Bloat control and the time taken by the parser to process the generated programs (one of the fitness parameters) will restrict larger programs from making it into the next generations. IFuzzer does not completely discard larger programs, but deprioritizes them.

We also observed that almost all the bugs in SpiderMonkey 1.8.5 are triggered in the range of 3–120 generations with an average range of 35–40 generations.

With the increase in complexity and number of language features added to the interpreter, the latest version requires more uncommonness to trigger the bugs, which implies more time to evolve inputs. As an example, all the bugs in the latest version are found on average after 90–95 generations.

While there are some similarities between LangFuzz and IFuzzer, the differences are significant. It is difficult to make a fair comparison on all aspects. IFuzzer's GP-based approach is a guided evolutionary approach with the help of a fitness function, whereas LangFuzz follows a pure mutation-based approach by changing the input and testing. IFuzzer's main strength is its feedback loop and the *evolution* of inputs as dictated by its new fitness function makes the design of IFuzzer very different from that of LangFuzz.

Both IFuzzer and LangFuzz are generative fuzzers that use grammars in order to be language independent but differ in their code generation processes. LangFuzz uses code mutation whereas IFuzzer uses GP for code generation. The use of GP provides IFuzzer the flexibility of tuning various parameters for efficient code generation.

Intuitively, the fitness function (objective function) is constructed to use the structural information about the program along with interpreter feedback information to calculate the fitness. Structural metrics, along with the interpreter feedback information, are also considered in the fitness calculation. Structural information is used to measure the singularity and complexity of the code generated. The chances of introducing errors are higher with larger and more complex code. Hence, the inputs that triggered bugs are not entirely new inputs but have evolved through generations starting from the initial test cases. We observed this evolutionary manifestation repeatedly during our experimentation.

In a nutshell, we observed that the *uncommonness* characteristic of the input code (like the structural complexity or the presence of type casting and type conversions) relates well with the possibility of finding exceptional behavior of the interpreter. Throughout this work, the driving intuition has been that most tests during development of the interpreter focused on the common cases. Therefore, testing the interpreter on uncommon ("weird") test cases should be promising as generating such test cases manually may not be straightforward and thereby some failure cases are missed.

6   Related Work

Fuzz testing was transformed from a small research project for testing UNIX system utilities [35] to an important and widely-adopted technique.

Researchers started fuzzers as brute forcing tools [36] for discovering flaws, after which they would analyze for the possibility of security exploitation. Later, the community realized that such simple approaches have many limitations in discovering complex flaws. Smart Fuzzer, overcame some of these limitations and proved more effective [37].

In 2001, Kaksonen et al. [38] used an approach known as *mini-simulation*, a simplified description of protocols and syntax, to generate inputs that nearly match with the protocol used. This approach is generally known as a grammar-based approach. It provides the fuzzer with sufficient information to understand protocol specifications. Kaksonen's *mini-simulation* ensures that the protocol checksums are always valid and systematically checks which rules are broken. In contrast, IFuzzer uses the grammar *specification* to generate valid inputs.

Yang et al. [39] presented their work on CSmith, a random "C program" generator. It uses grammar for producing programs with different features, thereby performing testing and analyzing C compilers. This process is a language independent fuzzer and uses semantic information during the generation process.

In the area of security, Zalewski presented ref_fuzz [40] and crossfuzz [41] aiming at the DOM component in browsers. JsFunFuzz [42] is a language-dependent generative tool written by Ruddersman in 2007, which targets JavaScript interpreters in web browsers, and has led to the discovery of more than 1800 bugs in SpiderMonkey. It is considered as one of the most relevant work in the field of web interpreters. LangFuzz, a language independent tool presented by Holler *et al.* [3] uses language grammar and code mutation approaches for test generation. In contrast, IFuzzer uses grammar specification and code generation. Proprietary fuzzers include Google's ClusterFuzz [43] which tests a variety of functionalities in Chrome. It is tuned to generate almost 5 million tests in a day and has detected several unique vulnerabilities in chrome components.

However, all these approaches may deviate the process of code generation from generating the required test data, thereby degenerating into random search, and providing low code coverage. Feedback fuzzers, on the other hand, adjust and generate dynamic inputs based on information from the target system.

An example of feedback-based fuzzing is an *evolutionary fuzzer*. Evolutionary fuzzing uses evolutionary algorithms to create the required search space of data and operates based on an objective function that controls the test input generation. One of the first published evolutionary fuzzers is by DeMott et al. in 2007 [10]. This is a grey-box technique that generates new inputs with better code coverage to find bugs by measuring code block coverage.

Search-based test generation using metaheuristic search techniques and evolutionary computation has been explored earlier for generating test data [44,45]. In the context of generating inputs using GP for code generation (as also adopted by IFuzzer), recent work by Kifetew *et al.* [46] combines stochastic grammar with GP to evolve test suites for system-level *branch coverage* in the system under test.

Our approach differs from existing work in many aspects. First, our approach uses GP with a uniquely designed guiding objective function, directed towards generating uncommon code combinations—making it more suitable for fuzzing. In order to be syntactically correct but still *uncommon*, we apply several heuristics when applying mutation and crossover operations. Our approach is implemented as a language independent black box fuzzer. To the best of our knowledge, IFuzzer is the first prototype to use GP for interpreter fuzzing with very encouraging results on real-world application.

7   Conclusion and Future Work

In this paper, we elaborate on the difficulties of efficiently fuzzing an interpreter as well as our ideas to mitigate them. The main challenge comes from the fact that we need to generate *code* that is able to fuzz the interpreter to reveal bugs buried deep inside the interpreter implementation. Several of these bugs are found to be security bugs, which are exploitable, which makes an interpreter a very attractive target for future attacks.

In this work, we proposed an effective, fully automated, and systematic approach for interpreter fuzzing and evaluated a prototype, IFuzzer, on real-world applications. IFuzzer uses an evolutionary code generation strategy that applies to any computer language of which we have the appropriate grammar specifications and a set of test cases for the code generation process. IFuzzer introduces a novel objective function that helps the fuzzer to reach its goal of generating valid but uncommon code fragments in an efficient way. In our evaluation, we show that IFuzzer is fast at discovering bugs when compared with a state-of-the-art fuzzer of its class. IFuzzer found several security bugs in the SpiderMonkey JavaScript interpreter that is used in Mozilla browser. The approach used in this paper is generic enough for automated code generation for the purpose of testing any targeted language interpreters and compilers, for which a grammar specification is available and serves as a *framework* for generating fuzzers for any interpreted language and corresponding interpreters.

IFuzzer is still *evolving* and we envision avenues for further improvements. We plan to investigate more code (property) parameters to be considered for the fitness evaluation. In our experiments, we observed that the parameters for the genetic operations (mutation and crossover) should be tuned further to improve the evolutionary process. Another improvement can be to keep track of more information during program execution, which helps to guide the fuzzer in a more fine-grained manner. For example through dynamic program analysis we can gather information about the program paths traversed, which gives coverage information as well as correlation between program paths and the bugs they lead to. This information could be used to refine the fitness function, thus improving the quality of code generation.

Acknowledgments. This work was partially supported by Netherlands Organisation for Scientific Research through the NWO 639.023.309 VICI "Dowsing" project.

We would like to thank Mozilla Security Team and conference reviewers for their useful suggestions to improve the paper.

Appendix

Comparing Code Generation Approaches

The aim of this experiment is to compare GP based code generative approach against code mutation, employed by [3] and pure generative approach. This experiment should clarify how these approaches accounts for good results. To measure the impact of these approaches, we need three independent runs of IFuzzer.

Genetic Programming Approach. First run is with a default configuration that follows the GP approach by performing genetic operations on the individuals, making a semantic adjustment, and using extracted code fragments for replacements.

Code Mutation Approach. In the Second run, IFuzzer is set to perform code mutation and to use parsed fragments in replacement process, which is similar to LangFuzz approach. This process is performed by disabling crossover and replacement functionality of the IFuzzer. Objective function has no role in this process, and we do not calculate the fitness of the individuals.

Generative Approach. The third run perform code generation using the generative approach, the configuration should produce a random code generation without using mutation or genetic operators. This falls back to pure generative approach and does not use extracted fragments for replacement. In this approach, we start with a *start terminal* in the language grammar and generate the code by randomly selecting the production rules for a non-terminal that appears in this process. This process will be terminated after reaching terminals and in case of recursive grammar rules sometimes it may result in an infinite loop.

Code Mutation and GP approaches can bring diversity among the generated code, thereby resulting in the higher chance to introduce errors. The generative approach, by definition, should have been easier to construct valid programs, but this leads to incomparable results, as there is no consistent environment.

In order to compare these approaches, we initially ran all three independent configurations on SpiderMonkey 1.8.5 for 2–3 days. All these processes are driven by randomization and therefore it is difficult to compare the results. The main intuition of our experiment was to observe the divergence of the code generation and the performance. It was observed that generative approach required more semantic knowledge without which it generated very large code fragments and its performance is based on the structure of grammar. We continued for multiple instances with the first and second configurations for five more days and observed that IFuzzer is fast enough to find bugs with the first configuration. Even with a greater overlap ratio, the number of bugs found was slightly higher with a GP approach when compared with the pure code mutation approach.

Figure 5 shows the results of comparison experiments between IFuzzer's GP and code mutation approaches. By considering the fact that both runs are independent and results are very hard to compare as the entire process runs on randomization, it appears that GP directs the program to generate required output and improves the performance of the program.

To measure the impact of code mutation and GP approach, we recorded the code evolution process. In code mutation and GP approaches code generation is performed with or without expanding. In either approach, extracted fragments

Genetic Programming   **Code Mutation**

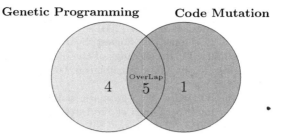

Fig. 5. Defects found with code mutation and genetic programming approaches

are used for replacements. Both the approaches brought divergence, but without evolutionary computing divergence was achieved at a slower rate.

The IFuzzer's GP based approach is a guided evolutionary approach with the help of fitness function, whereas LangFuzz follows a pure mutation-based approach by changing the input and testing. There is no evolutionary process involved in LangFuzz by using a fitness function. The inputs that triggered bugs are not entirely new inputs but have evolved through generations starting from the initial test cases. We repeated this experiment and observed such findings.

References

1. Anupam, V., Mayer, A.J.: Security of web browser scripting languages: vulnerabilities, attacks, and remedies. In: Proceedings of the 7th USENIX Security Symposium, San Antonio, TX, USA, 26–29 January (1998)
2. Hallaraker, O., Vigna, G.: Detecting malicious javascript code in mozilla. In: Proceedings of the 10th IEEE International Conference on Engineering of Complex Computer Systems (ICECCS 2005), pp. 85–94 (2005)
3. Holler, C., Herzig, K., Zeller, A.: Fuzzing with code fragments. In: Proceedings of the 21th USENIX Security Symposium, pp. 445–458, August 2012
4. Guang-Hong, L., Gang, W., Tao, Z., Jian-Mei, S., Zhuo-Chun, T.: Vulnerability analysis for x86 executables using genetic algorithm and fuzzing. In: Third International Conference on Convergence and Hybrid Information Technology (ICCIT 2008), pp. 491–497, November 2008
5. Rawat, S., Mounier, L.: An evolutionary computing approach for hunting buffer overflow vulnerabilities: a case of aiming in dim light. In: Proceedings of the European Conference on Computer Network Defense (EC2ND 2010), pp. 37–45 (2010)
6. Sparks, S., Embleton, S., Cunningham, R., Zou, C.: Automated vulnerability analysis: leveraging control flow for evolutionary input crafting. In: Twenty-Third Annual Computer Security Applications Conference (ACSAC), pp. 477–486 (2007)
7. DelGrosso, C., Antoniol, G., Merlo, E., Galinier, P.: Detecting buffer overflow via automatic test input data generation. Comput. Oper. Res. **35**, 3125–3143 (2008)
8. Alba, E., Chicano, J.F.: Software testing with evolutionary strategies. In: Guelfi, N., Savidis, A. (eds.) RISE 2005. LNCS, vol. 3943, pp. 50–65. Springer, Heidelberg (2006)
9. Zalewski, M.: American fuzzy lop. http://lcamtuf.coredump.cx/afl/

10. DeMott, J., Enbody, R., Punch, W.F.: Revolutionizing the field of grey-box attack surface testing with evolutionary fuzzing (2007)
11. Weimer, W., Nguyen, T., LeGoues, C., Forrest, S.: Automatically finding patches using genetic programming. In: Proceedings of the 31st International Conference on Software Engineering (ICSE 2009), Washington, DC, USA, pp. 364–374. IEEE Computer Society (2009)
12. Kim, D., Nam, J., Song, J., Kim, S.: Automatic patch generation learned from human-written patches. In: Proceedings of the International Conference on Software Engineering (ICSE 2013), Piscataway, NJ, USA, pp. 802–811. IEEE Press (2013)
13. Fraser, G., Arcuri, A.: Whole test suite generation. IEEE Trans. Softw. Eng. **39**(2), 276–291 (2013)
14. McKay, R.I., Hoai, N.X., Whigham, P.A., Shan, Y., O'Neill, M.: Grammar-based genetic programming: a survey. Genet. Program Evolvable Mach. **11**, 365–396 (2010)
15. Pargas, R.P., Harrold, M.J., Peck, R.R.: Test-data generation using genetic algorithms. Softw. Test. Verification Reliab. **9**(4), 263–282 (1999)
16. Poli, R., Langdon, W.B., McPhee, N.F., Koza, J.R.: A Field Guide to Genetic Programming (2008)
17. Soule, T., Foster, J.A., Dickinson, J.: Code growth in genetic programming. In: Proceedings of the First Annual Conference Genetic Programming, pp. 215–223, May 1996
18. Langdon, W.B., Poli, R.: Fitness causes bloat: mutation. In: Banzhaf, W., Poli, R., Schoenauer, M., Fogarty, T.C. (eds.) EuroGP 1998. LNCS, vol. 1391, p. 37. Springer, Heidelberg (1998)
19. Parr, T.: The Definitive ANTLR 4 Reference, 2nd edn. Pragmatic Bookshelf, Dallas (2013)
20. Luke, S., Panait, L.: A comparison of bloat control methods for genetic programming. Evol. Comput. **14**, 309–344 (2006)
21. Soule, T., Foster, J.A.: Effects of code growth and parsimony pressure on populations in genetic programming. Evol. Comput. **6**, 293–309 (1998)
22. Zhang, B.-T., Mhlenbein, H.: Balancing accuracy and parsimony in genetic programming. Evol. Comput. **3**(1), 17–38 (1995)
23. Poli, R., McPhee, N.F.: Covariant Parsimony Pressure in Genetic Programming. Citeseer (2008)
24. McPeak, S., Wilkerson, D.S.: The delta tool. http://delta.tigris.org
25. Javascript delta tool. https://github.com/wala/jsdelta
26. Zeller, A., Hildebrandt, R.: Simplifying and isolating failure-inducing input. IEEE Trans. Software Eng. **28**(2), 183–200 (2002)
27. McCabe, T.: A complexity measure. IEEE Trans. Softw. Eng. **SE-2**, 308–320 (1976)
28. Mitchell, R.J.: Managing complexity in software engineering. No.17 in IEE Computing series, P. Peregrinus Ltd. on behalf of the Institution of Electrical Engineers (1990)
29. Gosling, J., Joy, B., Steele, G., Bracha, G., Buckley, A.: The Java Language Specification: Java SE 8 Edition
30. ECMA International, Standard ECMA-262 - ECMAScript Language Specification. 5.1st edn., June 2011
31. https://bugzilla.mozilla.org/show_bug.cgi?id=676763
32. Gdb 'exploitable' plugin. http://www.cert.org/vulnerability-analysis/tools/triage.cfm

33. https://developer.mozilla.org/en/docs/Web/JavaScript/Reference/Strict_mode
34. https://www.mozilla.org/en-US/security/advisories/mfsa2015-102/
35. Miller, B.P., Fredriksen, L., So, B.: An empirical study of the reliability of UNIX utilities. Commun. ACM **33**, 32–44 (1990)
36. Clarke, T.: Fuzzing for software vulnerability discovery. Department of Mathematic, Royal Holloway, University of London, Technical report RHUL-MA-2009-4 (2009)
37. Miller, C.: How smart is intelligent fuzzing-or-how stupid is dumb fuzzing, August 2007
38. Kaksonen, R., Laakso, M., Takanen, A.: Software security assessment through specification mutations and fault injection. In: Steinmetz, R., Dittman, J., Steinebach, M. (eds.) Communications and Multimedia Security Issues of the New Century. IFIP—the International Federation for Information Processing, vol. 64, pp. 173–183. Springer, New York (2001)
39. Yang, X., Chen, Y., Eide, E., Regehr, J.: Finding and understanding bugs in C compilers. In: Proceedings of the 32nd ACM SIGPLAN Conference on Programming Language Design and Implementation, pp. 283–294, June 2011
40. Zalewski, M.: Announcing ref_fuzz a 2 year old fuzzer. http://lcamtuf.blogspot. in/2010/06/announcing-reffuzz-2yo-fuzzer.html
41. Zalewski, M.: Announcing cross_fuzz a potential 0-day in circulation and more. http://lcamtuf.blogspot.in/2011/01/announcing-crossfuzz-potential-0-day-in. html
42. Rudersman, J.: Introducing jsfunfuzz. http://www.squarefree.com/2007/08/02/ introducing-jsfunfuzz
43. Arya, A., Neckar, C.: Fuzzing for security. http://blog.chromium.org/2012/04/ fuzzing-for-security.html
44. Afzal, W., Torkar, R., Feldt, R.: A systematic review of search-based testing for non-functional system properties. Inf. Softw. Technol. **51**(6), 957–976 (2009)
45. McMinn, P.: Search-based software test data generation: a survey. Softw. Test. Verification Reliab. **14**(2), 105–156 (2004)
46. Kifetew, F.M., Tiella, R., Tonella, P.: Combining stochastic grammars and genetic programming for coverage testing at the system level. In: Goues, C., Yoo, S. (eds.) SSBSE 2014. LNCS, vol. 8636, pp. 138–152. Springer, Heidelberg (2014)

Automated Multi-architectural Discovery of CFI-Resistant Code Gadgets

Patrick Wollgast, Robert Gawlik$^{(\boxtimes)}$, Behrad Garmany, Benjamin Kollenda, and Thorsten Holz

Horst Görtz Institute for IT-Security (HGI), Ruhr-Universität Bochum, Bochum, Germany
robert.gawlik@rub.de

Abstract. Memory corruption vulnerabilities are still a severe threat for software systems. To thwart the exploitation of such vulnerabilities, many different kinds of defenses have been proposed in the past. Most prominently, *Control-Flow Integrity* (CFI) has received a lot of attention recently. Several proposals were published that apply coarse-grained policies with a low performance overhead. However, their security remains questionable as recent attacks have shown.

To ease the assessment of a given CFI implementation, we introduce a framework to discover code gadgets for code-reuse attacks that conform to coarse-grained CFI policies. For this purpose, binary code is extracted and transformed to a symbolic representation in an architecture-independent manner. Additionally, code gadgets are verified to provide the needed functionality for a security researcher. We show that our framework finds more CFI-compatible gadgets compared to other code gadget discovery tools. Furthermore, we demonstrate that code gadgets needed to bypass CFI solutions on the ARM architecture can be discovered by our framework as well.

1 Introduction

Memory corruption vulnerabilities have threatened software systems for decades. The deployment of various defense mechanisms, such as *data execution prevention* (DEP) [15], *stack smashing protection* (SSP) [10], and *address space layout randomization* (ASLR) [30] have raised the bar for reliable memory corruption exploitation significantly. Nevertheless, a dedicated attacker is still able to achieve code execution [24,31]. *Information leaks* are utilized to counter ASLR and reveal the layout of the address space, or to harvest code to build a payload just-in-time [31,41]. To circumvent DEP, attackers have added code-reuse attacks to their repertoire, such as *return-oriented programming* (ROP) [5,25,37], *jump-oriented programming* (JOP) [3,8,13], and *call-oriented programming* (COP) [7]. Code-reuse attacks do not inject new code but chain together small chunks of existing code, called *gadgets*, to achieve arbitrary code execution.

In response to this success, the defensive research was driven to find protection methods against code-reuse attacks. Some results of this research

© Springer International Publishing Switzerland 2016
I. Askoxylakis et al. (Eds.): ESORICS 2016, Part I, LNCS 9878, pp. 602–620, 2016.
DOI: 10.1007/978-3-319-45744-4_30

are *kBouncer* [29], *ROPecker* [9], *EMET* [17] including *ROPGuard* [18], *BinCFI* [45], and *CCFIR* [44]. These defenses incorporate two main ideas. The first is to enforce *control-flow integrity* (CFI) [1,2]. With perfect CFI, the control-flow can neither be hijacked by code-injection nor by code-reuse [20]. However, the overhead of perfect CFI is too high to be practical. Therefore, the proposed defense methods try to strike a balance between security and tolerable overhead. The second idea is to detect code-reuse attacks by known characteristics of an attack like a certain amount of gadgets chained together. All of those schemes defend attacks on the x86/x86-64 architecture. For other architectures the research is lacking behind [12,32]. Several generic attack vectors have been published by the offensive side to highlight the limitations of the proposed defense methods. Although single implementations can be bypassed with common code-reuse attacks by exploiting a vulnerability in the implementation [4,11], generic circumventions rely on longer and more complex gadgets [7,14,20,21,35] or complete functions [34]. Since the gadgets loose their simplicity by becoming longer, it also becomes harder to find specific gadgets and chain them together. To the best of our knowledge there is no gadget discovery framework available to search for CFI resistant gadgets. To be able to assess a CFI solution, it is necessary to discover code gadgets which could execute within the boundaries of the solution's CFI policies or detection heuristics. We provide a framework which is able to discover CFI resistant code gadgets or complete functions across different architectures, an increasingly important property as CFI starts to evolve on non-x86 systems as well. Notably, no search for CFI resistant code gadgets has been performed for ARM, while defenses for this architecture have already been developed [12,32]. The information provided by our framework helps security researchers to quickly prototype exploit examples to test a given CFI solution.

We opted to use an *intermediate language* (IL) for the analysis of extracted code to support different architectures without the effort to adjust the algorithms to new architectures. Because of the high architecture coverage, *VEX* is our choice for the IL. VEX is part of *Valgrind*, an instrumentation framework intended for dynamic use [42]. We harness VEX in static analysis manner [38,40] and utilize the SMT solver *Z3* [27] to translate code gadgets into a symbolic representation to enable symbolic execution and path constraint analysis. Our evaluations shows that our framework discovers 1.2 to 154.3 times more CFI-resistant gadgets across different architectures and operating systems than other gadget discovery tools. Additionally, we show that CFI-resistant gadgets are available in binary code for the ARM architecture as well, which should be taken into account by future CFI solutions.

In summary, we make the following contributions:

- We develop a framework to discover CFI and heuristic-check resistant gadgets in an architecture-independent, offline search.
- Our framework delivers semantic definitions of extracted code gadgets and classifies them based on these definitions for convenient search and utilization by a security researcher.

– To the best of our knowledge, we are the first to provide a code gadget discovery framework which reveals CFI resistant gadgets across different processor architectures, and show that CFI-compatible gadgets are also prevalent on the ARM architecture.

2   Technical Background

We begin by briefly describing code-reuse attacks, CFI approaches, and heuristic techniques proposed by recent research to defend against runtime attacks. It is important to understand the concept of CFI and the heuristic checks, as we focus on gadgets that are resistant against these approaches. Architecture independence is another issue that is tackled by our framework.

2.1   Code-Reuse Attacks

The introduction of *data execution prevention* (DEP) [15] on modern operating systems provided a useful protection against the injection of new code. To bypass DEP, attackers often resort to reusing code already provided by the vulnerable executable itself (or one of its libraries). Vulnerabilities suitable for code-reuse attacks are memory corruptions such as stack, heap or integer overflows, or a dangling pointer. The technique most commonly applied to reuse existing code is *return-oriented programming* (ROP) [5,37]. The concept behind ROP is to combine small sequences of code, called *gadgets*, that end with a return instruction. All combined gadgets of an exploit are often referred to as a *gadget chain*. To be able to combine these gadgets, either a sequence of return addresses has to be placed on the stack where each address points to the next gadget, or the stack pointer has to be redirected to a buffer containing these addresses. The process of redirecting the stack pointer is called *stack pivoting*.

For architectures with variable opcode length like x86/x86-64, the instructions used for the gadgets do not have to be aligned as intended by the compiler. Previous work has shown that enough gadgets for arbitrary computations can be located [5,13,25] even without those unintended instructions. This is an interesting observation that especially concerns architectures with fixed opcode length. Automated tools that search for gadgets and chain them together have also been developed by past research [22,28].

Over the years, research on code-reuse attacks has proposed different variations of ROP such as *jump-oriented programming* (JOP) [3,8,13] and *call-oriented programming* (COP) [7]. JOP uses jumps instead of returns to direct the control-flow to the next gadget, and COP uses calls. Due to their complexity, code-reuse attacks are typically used to make injected code executable thus defeating protections like DEP and redirect the control-flow to the injected code [24,31].

2.2   Control-Flow Integrity (CFI)

The concept of CFI was first introduced by Abadi et al. [1,2]. A program maintains the CFI property, if the control flow remains in a predefined *control-flow graph* (CFG). This predefined CFG contains all intended execution paths of the program. If an attacker redirects the control flow via code injection or code-reuse attacks to an unintended execution path, the CFI property is violated and the attack is detected. In an ideal CFG, every indirect transfer has a list of valid unique identifiers (IDs) and every transfer target has an ID assigned to it [20]. These IDs are checked before indirect transfers occur to ensure that the target is valid.

If CFI is applied to proprietary software, it becomes problematic to generate such a detailed CFG. To construct the CFG, the program has to be disassembled and a pointer analysis performed. Every error made during this process may lead to false positives during runtime of the protected program. Another issue with the classical CFI approach as proposed by Abadi et al. is performance. Therefore, implemented CFI solutions—also called coarse-grained approaches—typically reduce the number of IDs by assigning the same ID to the same category of targets. Examples of coarse-grained approaches are BinCFI [45] and CCFIR [44]. BinCFI uses two IDs to ensure the integrity of the CFG. The first ID defines rules for targets of *return* (RET) instructions and *indirect jumps* (IJ). The second ID combines rules for indirect control-transfers from the *procedure linkage table* (PLT) and indirect calls (ICs). Each ID has its own routine which resides inside the protected binary. Every indirect transfer is instrumented to jump to one of the two verification routines. Similar to BinCFI, CCFIR is also a coarse-grained CFI approach applied to binaries without source code. Each indirect transfer is redirected through a *Springboard*. The Springboard contains all valid control-flow targets and thereby prevents that the flow is redirected to invalid targets. An initial permutation of the Springboard at program startup additionally raises the bar for attackers.

2.3   Heuristic Approaches

In 2013 Pappas et al. [29] introduced kBouncer, an heuristic-aided approach that leverages modern hardware features to prevent code-reuse attacks. To perform CFI checks, kBouncer utilizes the *Last Branch Record* (LBR). LBR is a feature of contemporary Intel and AMD processors which can only be enabled and disabled in kernel mode. Therefore, kBouncer consists of a user and kernel mode component. Like the name suggests, LBR records the last taken branches or a subset of the last branches. Each entry in the LBR contains the source and destination address of the taken branch. By fetching some bytes just before the destination address, kBouncer can examine and enforce that every return address is preceded by a call instruction. Otherwise kBouncer reports a CFI violation. Besides the CFI enforcement, a heuristic check is performed by inspecting the last 8 indirect branches. If all entries match kBouncers gadget definition, an attack is reported. A gadget is considered as an entry if it contains up to 20 instructions and ends in an indirect control flow. The checks are invoked whenever one out of 52 critical WinAPI functions such as *VirtualProtect* or *WinExec* is called. The user-mode component hooks these critical functions and triggers the checks in the kernel mode component.

Another heuristic-aided approach is ROPecker by Cheng et al. [9], which also utilizes the LBR stack to look for gadgets in the past control flow. Additionally, the future control flow is also examined. To check for gadgets in the future control flow, ROPecker combines online emulation of the flow, stack inspection, and an offline gadget search. Since gadgets are already searched offline and stored to a database, ROPecker has also the possibility to detect unaligned gadgets. To detect gadgets, ROPecker does not apply CFI enforcements, but merely relies on heuristics. A gadget in the context of ROPecker is a sequence of up to 6 instructions ending with an indirect control-flow transfer. Sequences containing direct branch instructions are excluded from the definition. ROPecker inspects the past control flow first by utilizing the LBR to record indirect branch instructions. The first non-gadget encountered while walking the LBR backwards terminates the search for gadgets in the past control flow. Afterwards, the future control flow is inspected for gadgets. If the combined number of encountered gadgets from the past and future control flow is above a predefined threshold, an attack is reported. The research of Cheng et al. suggests that a threshold between 11 and 16 gadgets is a suitable number.

2.4   Defeating the Countermeasures

All presented defenses against code-reuse attacks have been bypassed in recent years. While some attacks exploit vulnerabilities in a specific implementation to disable the checks [4,11], we focus on generic bypasses to defeat the protections. We divide the defense policies in two categories, CFI policies posing limitations on indirect branch instructions and heuristic policies looking for typical characteristics of code-reuse attack vectors.

Attacks focusing on kBouncer, ROPecker, and EMET/ROPGuard [7,21,35] just have to bypass the call site (CS) checks. However, attacks against BinCFI and CCFIR [14,20] also have to take into account that ICs and IJs are limited to certain control-flow targets like function entry points (EPs). Göktaş et al. [20] categorize the gadgets by their prefix (CS or EP), their payload (IC, *fixed function call* (F), other instructions), and their suffix (RET, IC, IJ). This categorization results in 18 $(2 \cdot 3 \cdot 3)$ different gadget types. They even use gadgets containing conditional jumps. With these gadget categories, they are able to bypass CCFIR, which they consider stricter than BinCFI. Another interesting gadget type is the *i-loop-gadget* [35]. In their work, Schuster et al. use a loop containing an IC to chain gadgets and invoke security sensitive functions.

The heuristic policies explained in Sect. 2.3 check for chains of short instruction sequences. To evade these checks, long gadgets with minimal side effects were proposed [7,21]. If the heuristic check encounters a long instruction sequence, the evaluation is terminated and the chain is classified as benign. Another elegant method is to invoke a function call to an unsuspicious function like *lstrcmpiW* [35].

If the unsuspicious function does not alter the global state of the program and takes enough indirect branches, the attack cannot be discovered by the heuristic checks.

3   Design and Implementation

The process of discovering suitable code gadgets which fulfill certain CFI policies consist of broadly two phases: first, appropriate code has to be discovered and extracted. Second, it is translated into the symbolic representation and can then be classified according to semantic definitions.

3.1   Gadget Discovery

Before we can describe the process of the gadget discovery, we have to define the gadgets' properties first. The definition of the gadgets is important as they define the bounds and specify the content of the gadgets. After the definition of the gadgets is given, we introduce the algorithms to locate all points of interest for the gadget discovery and the algorithm to discover the gadgets themselves.

Gadget Categories. Except minor modifications, our gadgets conform to the specifications defined by by Göktaş et al. [20] and Schuster et al. [35] as explained in Sect. 2.4. Their definitions provide sufficient properties to, for example, find complete functions for code-reuse and other CFI resistant gadgets. We used their definitions to restrict the gadget discovery, but definitions can be extended and added in modular fashion to our framework to support additional gadget types. The bounds of our gadgets have to conform to legitimate control-flow targets. Thus, they have to start at an EP or at a CS and end with an IC, IJ, or RET. The content of a gadget is defined as either an IC, a *fixed function call* (F), or other arbitrary instructions. We opted to drop IC as gadget content definition, because we can connect a gadget ending with an IC with the gadget it follows starting at the CS. Fixed function calls are beneficial in two ways. Instead of reading the address of the function from the *import address table* (IAT) and preparing the call, one can simply use the gadget with the fixed function call. However, this just works if all parameters of the function can be set to the desired values. Furthermore, defenses preventing calls to security sensitive functions [44] can be circumvented by using gadgets containing a legitimate call to the function. As we show in Sect. 4.1, many hardcoded function calls inside of gadgets exist.

Another useful gadget is the loop gadget. Loops can be used as a *dispatch gadget* [3,35] to invoke other gadgets. Figure 1 shows a gadget proposed by Schuster et al. During the first iteration of the loop, RBX points to the beginning of a list with the addresses of the to-be dispatched gadgets. RDI points to the end of this list during all iterations of the loop. If the end of the loop is reached the gadget returns. The difference between the proposed gadget and the gadget defined for our search is that just the gray basic blocks in Fig. 1 belong to our loop gadget definition. For simplicity, loop gadgets end with an IC and start either at the CS of its IC or at an EP. Hence, the basic block beginning with the label *@skip* and

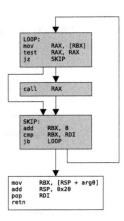

Fig. 1. Instructions of an example loop gadget. Just the gray basic blocks belong to a loop gadget by our definition.

Table 1. Gadget types supported by our framework.

Prefix	Content	Suffix
EP	Arbitrary instructions	IC
EP	Arbitrary instructions	IJ
EP	Arbitrary instructions	RET
EP	F	IC
EP	F	IJ
EP	F	RET
CS	Arbitrary instructions	IC
CS	Arbitrary instructions	IJ
CS	Arbitrary instructions	RET
CS	F	IC
CS	F	IJ
CS	F	RET
CS	Loop	IC

the last basic block comprise a separate, overlapping CS-RET gadget. This has the advantage that also loop gadgets in big functions without a tailing gadget (CS-RET) are found. Additionally, one can query if another gadget starts at the end of the loop gadget. This way, when searching for *tailless* loop gadgets, we can query if code which overlaps, comprises a gadget containing another suffix than RET. All supported gadget definitions are summarized in Table 1. These definitions allow us to extract code with conditional jumps such that each single code path represents a single gadget in a path-insensitive way. As each of them is verified with symbolic execution later on, path-sensitive code gadgets arise and path-insensitive gadgets are dropped (see Sect. 3.2).

Discovering Points of Interest. To locate gadgets, our search algorithm follows the paths of the CFG. The starting points for the search algorithm are IC, IJ, and RET instructions. The algorithm to locate these points of interest works in two phases. In the first phase, addresses of all calls to fixed functions in all modules of a program of interest are extracted and kept. The set of fixed functions comprises critical imported functions which handle memory management, process and thread creation, and file I/O. These are typically very valuable for an attacker. During the second phase, the algorithm iterates over every instruction belonging to a function. If an instruction is a RET, IC, IJ, or a call, the address of the instruction is added to the corresponding list of starting points.

Gadget Extraction with Depth-First Search. To retrieve the gadgets shown in Table 1, we have to traverse the CFG of every function in the binary. As we limit gadgets to single paths at first and can merge them into conditional gadgets later on in Sect. 3.2, we walk *each* path separately. We start our traversal from the discovered gadget endpoints, namely ICs, IJs, and RETs. We walk every possible path backwards until we discover a gadget starting point (EP and CS), or until we exceed an adjustable maximum instruction length of the gadgets. The algorithms we use are a modification of depth-first search (DFS).

First, the basic block is located containing the gadget endpoint. Afterwards, we check if there are any calls or fixed function calls between the endpoint and the basic block's beginning. If we encounter a call, a CS gadget is created and the path traversal stops. Before a gadget is added to the gadget list, we check if a gadget with the same opcode sequence is already in that list to optionally discard or keep it for later analysis. If a fixed function call is encountered, we store the information of the fixed function call and split the current basic block. The resulting first block starts at the beginning of the original basic block and ends at the fixed function call. The resulting second block starts at the CS of the fixed function call and ends with the gadget endpoint. Thus, a CS prefixed gadget is created. Path traversal continues and on a hit of a call, the traversal stops. We check if the current basic block contains the EP. In that case, we create a EP prefixed gadget. To traverse all possible paths backwards, we keep path information and iterate over all direct preceding basic blocks.

Then, for each block, we check if the basic block has been visited before. If that is the case, a loop gadget is only added, if the traversed path starts at a CS and ends at a IC. In any case, the traversal returns if the basic block has already been visited. Afterwards, the checks for a call, fixed function call, and EP are repeated. Finally, the instruction length of the gadget is checked and updated.

3.2 Gadget Analysis

Two objectives are accomplished with the gadget analysis: first, we sort out gadgets with unsatisfiable path constraints, and second, gadgets are matched to semantic definitions and classified accordingly. This simplifies the utilization by a security researcher to find wanted functionality. To make a simplified search possible, code gadgets are transformed to a symbolic representation, executed symbolically to determine its execution contexts and clustered into semantics due to their execution effects.

Lifting Code Gadgets with Zex3 *to Raw Symbolic Representations.* Code gadgets are first translated to instructions of the VEX IL. These are mapped to Z3 expression as evaluable strings and stored offline. Thereby, most architecture-dependent peculiarities, such as stack and flags usage, are abstracted away and implicit execution effects are made explicit. The goal of this part of the framework, which we named *Zex3*, is to gather raw symbolic expression which are closely related to the structure of VEX IL instructions. Thus, registers and memory accesses are still architecture dependent.

Unification of Raw Symbolics with Zolver3. Unification of architecture-dependent registers and memory handling is done by a developed Z3 wrapper which we named *Zolver3*. The goal is to gather symbolic expressions for each gadget to be symbolically evaluable by *one* component only, namely Z3. Therefore, symbolic equations created by Zex3 are transformed into a generic format, such that register usage, memory reads and writes are adjusted. This produces a single base usable to separate symbolic representations into semantic bins and to verify satisfiability of each code gadget. As mentioned in Sect. 3.1, each gadget is a single path. Thus, symbolic execution of overlapping gadgets can yield conditional gadgets as well.

Symbolic Analysis of Code Gadgets. It is necessary for a security researcher during exploit development to rule out code gadgets which do not fulfill a desired functionality. We illustrate what we name *unsatisfiability* on a gadget with a fixed function call: at the time of compilation, it is unknown if a function call during runtime will succeed. Therefore, checks for the return value are normally inserted in the calling function by the developer. Depending on the return value, a different path in the control flow is taken. We might encounter such checks in gadgets containing a fixed function call. During exploitation we expect the fixed function call to succeed, hence, a gadget depending on a failed fixed function call poses unsatisfiable path constraints.

With the current level of information, a researcher is only able to search through the discovered gadgets based on their boundaries. There is no knowledge about the gadget's effects on the state of the to-be-exploited process during runtime. This makes an efficient search to chain gadgets cumbersome. Therefore, the second objective is to match every register output and every memory effect of the symbolic representation to a semantic definition. Zolver3 provides the state of every register and every memory effect based on the symbolic variables and input values of the registers and memory. We do not have to trace every instruction of the gadget ourself, but we can treat the gadget as a black box. We send symbolic input values in and get all modifications to the global state of the process by the gadget based on these symbolic input values. This means that all register and memory store output values are symbolic expressions of the input values. We can use these expressions to apply our semantic definitions to the gadgets. The process of applying the semantic definitions to the output equations is explained as follows.

Semantic Definitions. In the following, we present our semantic definitions. These definitions allow the researcher, combined with the search presented in Sect. 3.3, to search gadgets with specific operations performed on a specific register or memory address. One or more definitions are assigned to each gadget, based on the operations the gadget performs. When a security researcher develops a code-reuse attack, the defined gadget types are the available instruction set. Therefore, the gadget definitions must cover all necessary instructions to perform arbitrary computations. The following gadget types are necessary to accomplish this:

- MovReg: A gadget to move the content of one register to another.
- LoadReg: A gadget to load a specific content into a register.

- Arithmetic: A gadget to perform arithmetic operations between registers.
- LoadMem: A gadget to load the content of a specified memory area into a register.
- StoreMem: A gadget to store the content of a register to a specified memory area.

We add following four semantic definitions, because they represent operations which are commonly found in gadgets. Alternatives to extend the gadget definitions are discussed in Sect. 6.

- ArithmeticLoad: A gadget that loads the value from a specified memory address, performs an arithmetic operation on it, and stores the result to the destination register.
- ArithmeticStore: A gadget that extends a StoreMem gadget with an arithmetic operation
- NOP - No Operation: A gadget that keeps certain registers untouched. This is very useful during a gadget search, because untouched registers can be marked as static.
- Undefined: If none of the previous semantic definitions match the equation of the register, the register gets marked as undefined.

These gadget types are enough to create functionality containing jumps and conditional jumps. ROP uses the stack pointer to load the next instruction. Hence, an addition to or subtraction from the stack pointer changes the next instruction. This way, the developer can jump through her ROP chain. JOP and COP often use a dispatcher gadget, like the loop gadget, to invoke the gadgets of the chain. During the loop iteration one register holds a pointer into the buffer containing subsequent gadgets. Instead of the stack pointer (like in ROP), the register holding the pointer to the buffer has to be modified for jumps. Conditional jumps, however, are more complicated as they have to be accomplished by chaining several arithmetic operations [14]. But a study of exploits [31] reveals that jumping by manipulating the stack pointer is rarely used. Normally the chains just set the shellcode to executable and redirect the control flow to the beginning of the shellcode. Snow et al. [41] come to a similar conclusion regarding the gadget definitions in their research.

Applying the Definitions. At the end of the symbolic execution, we have an output equation for every register and memory write. These equations consists of Z3 *expression trees*, which represent the AST of Z3 expressions. Our definitions are stored as Z3 expression trees as well. Thus, we can match each symbolic operation a gadget performs against our definition and tag the gadget with one or more definitions.

   We take the approach to apply our definitions to every register and get as many operations for every gadget, as the architecture has registers. To apply the definitions to every register, we loop over all equations belonging to classifiable registers and perform checks if the definitions match. Classifiable registers are the general purpose registers of the architecture and the instruction pointer. These are the registers that are usually accessible. We try to match every memory write to definitions recursively, because memory accesses can be nested and every new memory store adds a new layer consisting of Z3 store operations.

3.3 Semantic Search

In the previous steps, the gadgets have been discovered by their bounds and we have analyzed every effect the gadgets may have on the global state of a running process. As we want the search for the gadgets to be flexible, we perform the search on a register and memory write basis. One can specify the type of a single register or the types, operations, and operands of many registers. Naturally, a search with just the type of a single register yields a lot of potential gadget candidates. In the following section, we explain methods to order the gadget candidates and to eliminate unsatisfiable gadgets.

Complexity Ordering. We have to present the simplest gadgets first upon a search to speed up the process of the gadget chaining. To provide the gadgets in a decreasing complexity order, we apply four criteria. The first criteria is that the gadgets with the lowest instruction count are presented first. Gadgets with a low instruction count are usually simple, as they typically do not perform many operations. The second criterion is to sort by the least amount of memory writes. For every unnecessary memory write, it has to be ensured that the write address is inside a writable memory area. Then the priority comes to contain the least amount of memory reads in the gadgets. The reason is the same as for the memory writes. However, readable memory areas are typically encountered more often and therefore easier to set up. Our last ordering criterion requires as many registers as possible to contain NOP definitions, as this limits unwanted side-effects such as overwriting a register which is set up by a previous gadget.

Gadget Verification. Our gadgets support paths containing conditional branches. The exact analysis of the conditions can be tricky. For example, a gadget is needed to load the value 0x12345678 from a specific memory address into a register. The complexity ordering algorithm may return a gadget list with a LoadMem gadget ranked first that contains a conditional jump. The pitfall is that the jump is only taken, if the LoadMem operation loads a NULL value. This renders the gadget useless to load the value 0x12345678. Therefore, invalid gadgets similar to the one described above have to be sorted out. We automatically check the constraints of the gadget list with Zolver3 until a satisfiable gadget is encountered. A search query is specified by a researcher in the language *Python*. Thereby the start/end type and the content definition of the gadget is normally specified, as well as the semantics and operations which the gadget has to fulfill.

4   Evaluation

In the following, we evaluate our prototype. More specifically, we analyze the distribution of the different gadget types across different processor architectures,

Table 2. Number of available gadgets listed by gadget start and end type, and their corresponding discovery and analysis runtime.

	ieframe.dll	mshtml.dll	ieframe.dll	mshtml.dll	libc-2.19.so
Architecture	x86	x86	AMD64	AMD64	ARM
EP-IC	4255	4245	4354	3947	261
EP-IJ	59	370	172	1009	79
EP-RET	11521	16723	10950	16517	2615
CS-IC	36300	55225	38679	68791	1226
CS-IJ	67	28	76	1365	240
CS-RET	39382	71104	40831	72198	6029
Loops	348	443	335	464	55
Runtime (s)	12925.2	29058.7	16309.4	51259.8	4079.0

demonstrate that we can discover enough gadgets for successful exploitation, and compare our framework to existing tools. We conducted all tests for our evaluation on a 64 bit Linux system running on an Intel Xeon processor E3 with 3.3 GHz. For CFG and disassembly creation, we use IDA Pro, and VEX of Valgrind 3.9.0 is used for Zex3's translation process. Furthermore, we use pyvex's latest commit at the time of testing [39].

4.1 Gadget Type Distribution

For our evaluation, we analyzed the x86/AMD64 version of *ieframe.dll* and *mshtml.dll* of Microsoft's Internet Explorer (IE) 8.0.7601.17514. We selected these libraries as they are often used during exploitation of IE [31]. To evaluate our gadget finder on ARM, we analyzed Debian's (little-endian) libc-2.19.so, because we expect *libc* to always be loaded during exploitation of a Linux system on ARM. All gadgets residing in libc-2.19.so are in ARM mode. The gadget numbers presented in this section are the total number of gadgets, including gadgets with and without conditional branches.

Table 2 summarizes the gadget start and end type distribution. Note that the combination with the highest number of gadgets is CS-RET. With CS-RET gadgets, one can execute common ROP exploits without triggering CFI checks. Due to the high proportion of CS-RET gadgets, the highest possibility to find suitable gadgets for a gadget chain is searching for a ROP chain. Our loop counts, also presented in Table 2, are based on our loop definition. This means that all listed loops end with an IC and start at the CS of the IC. The number of discovered loops can still be further increased by implementing loops for JOP or allowing relaxed loop definitions.

It is worth noting that all functions typically used by attackers for malicious behavior are available, such as *VirtualProtect* to set memory to executable or writable, *LoadLibrary* to load a library into the address space, and *CreateProcess* to create a process. Gadgets containing fixed function calls are not restricted to some gadget start and end types, but are interspersed throughout all start and end type combinations. For the x86 and AMD64 DLLs mentioned in Table 2, we found 982 gadgets with hardcoded calls to functions which allocate memory, change memory permissions, load DLLs, or perform file I/O operations.

4.2   Exploiting ARM with One CFI-Resistant Gadget

To evaluate our gadget finder on ARM, we exploit an artificial use-after-free vulnerability. The instruction initiating our chain is an IC in ARM mode and the first argument, stored in R0, contains a pointer to our prepared buffer. The protection in place is similar to CCFIR. This means, IC and IJ can just transfer the control flow to EPs, and RETs are only allowed to return to legitimate CS. We assume that an information leak is available, which is usually the case for real-world exploits. Our gadget pool is derived from Debian's libc-2.19.so. All discovered gadgets are in ARM mode. The goal of the exploit is to execute `system("/bin/sh")`. On ARM, the first argument to a function is not passed on the stack, but in the register R0. Therefore, to execute `system("/bin/sh")` we have to load the address of a string containing `"/bin/sh"` into R0. We do not have to write the string to memory ourselves, as it is already present in libc-2.19.so. We use the information leak to get the base address of libc-2.19.so. The address of libc-2.19.so is also required to get the address of `system()`. But at first, we have to find the gadgets to load the address of `system()` and the string `"/bin/sh"` from the buffer and call the `system()` function. These addresses are placed later on in our buffer. A pointer to the buffer is passed to our gadgets in R0. Due to the protection scheme in place, the gadget has to start at an EP. The end of the gadget is not defined, yet. An automatically discovered gadget that exhibits the required actions is displayed in Fig. 2. First, it loads the address of `"/bin/sh"` from our buffer to R0 via `LDR R0, [R0,#0x1C]`. And second, it loads the address of `system()` to R12 and calls R12 at the end. This way,

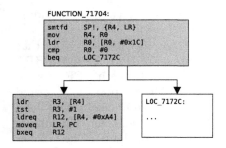

Fig. 2. An ARM gadget which loads the address of `"/bin/sh"` from the supplied buffer in R0, loads the address of `system()` from the buffer to R12, and ends with an IC of R12.

Fig. 3. Buffer exploit data. Only addresses at the offsets `0x1C` and `0xA4`, the address for the initial control-flow transfer (`0x71704`), and `0x1` at offset `0x00` have to be set.

the objective to execute `system("/bin/sh")` is achieved with a single gadget. The buffer that we use during the exploit is shown in Fig. 3. At offset `0x00` the buffer must contain `0x1` to satisfy `TST R3,#1`. Just if this check is valid, the address of `system()` gets loaded and called.

4.3   Comparison to Other Gadget Discovery Tools

To investigate how our framework performs compared to other tools, we used ROPgadget [33], XROP [43], and IDA sploiter [23] to search for unique gadgets in *mshtml.dll*, *ieframe.dll*, and *libc-2.19.so*. ROPgadget performs a semantic search based on the disassembly of Capstone [6], while XROP and IDA sploiter perform a standard instruction search. Thereby, IDA sploiter uses IDA Pro. Hence, we can compare our framework to a tool which uses the same disassembly as input. We searched gadgets with a length of max. 30 instructions with ROPgadget and IDA sploiter, and with a max. length of five instructions in XROP, because the length cannot be adjusted. Then we dropped unaligned gadgets which these tools

Table 3. Number of unique EP and CS gadgets found by other tools in comparison to our framework. Improvement factor states the factor of more gadgets found by our tool.

Tool		CFI-resistant gadgets	Improvement factor
IDA sploiter:	libc (ARM):	0	ARM not supported
	ieframe.dll (x86):	11721	7.8
	mshtml.dll (x86):	14762	10.0
	ieframe.dll (x86_64):	14192	6.7
	mshtml.dll (x86_64):	19984	8.2
ROPgadget:	libc (ARM):	8677	1.2
	ieframe.dll (x86):	28747	3.2
	mshtml.dll (x86):	30631	4.8
	ieframe.dll (x86_64):	10479	9.1
	mshtml.dll (x86_64):	14283	11.5
XROP:	libc (ARM):	1107	9.4
	ieframe.dll (x86):	660	138.8
	mshtml.dll (x86):	957	154.3
	ieframe.dll (x86_64):	1531	62.1
	mshtml.dll (x86_64):	2479	66.1
Our framework:	libc (ARM):	10450	-
	ieframe.dll (x86):	91584	-
	mshtml.dll (x86):	147695	-
	ieframe.dll (x86_64):	95062	-
	mshtml.dll (x86_64):	163827	-

delivered, as well as non CFI-resistant gadgets. Overall, it is shown in Table 3 that our tool found 1.2 times to 154.3 times more gadgets than other tools.

5   Related Work

Code-reuse attacks have evolved from a simple *return-into-libc* [16] into a highly sophisticated attack vector. In times of DEP, Krahmer was the first to propose a method called *borrowed code chunks* technique [26]. By chaining code snippets together that end with return instructions, Krahmer showed how to perform specific operations and as a consequence bypass DEP. His work was extended by Shacham in 2007 [37], who showed that Turing-completeness can be achieved by reusing instruction sequences that end in return opcodes, thus leading to the name *Return-Oriented-Programming*. He called those sequences *gadgets*. Large code bases typically provide enough gadgets to achieve Turing-completeness.

While the first attacks targeted the x86 architecture, the concepts have been shown to be applicable on ARM [25] or SPARC [5] systems as well. ASLR [30] has been successful in stopping static ROP chains. However, its ineffectiveness has also been shown in the presence of *information leaks*. Even fine-grained re-randomization can be circumvented by the means of *just-in-time ROP* as demonstrated by Snow et al. [41]. During the attack, they harvest gadgets based on the *Galileo* algorithm introduced by Shacham et al [37]. The algorithm starts at *return* instructions and iterates backwards over a code section to retrieve gadgets that end with the return instruction. A table lookup matches their gadgets against semantic definitions. This differs from our approach as we lift only CFI-permitted code paths to an intermediate representation (VEX) having a high ISA coverage, and symbolically evaluate the gadgets to achieve a semantic binning. Schwartz et al. developed a gadget search and compiler framework to automatically generate ROP chains. They apply program verification techniques to categorize gadgets into semantic definitions [36]. However, they do not take CFI policies into account.

To aid in both the development of ROP attacks and CFI defenses, toolkits to locate suitable gadgets have emerged. Frameworks such as the one introduced by Kornau [25] or ROPgadget [33] utilize an intermediate language to abstract the underlying architecture. However, these do not locate gadgets conforming to the constraints introduced by CFI solutions. Our framework fills this gap and enables researchers to test their CFI policies on multiple architectures with only one toolkit. Closely related to our work is research which tries to measure the *gadget quality* by introducing several metrics [19]. However, these metrics are bound to an architecture, while our approach is architecture independent.

6   Discussion

The core property of our framework is the ability to quickly test CFI policies on multiple architectures. With the possibility to locate gadgets conforming to the same constraints in multiple environments, we enable researches to gain a fast overview on the security of policies. This is applicable not only to one architecture, but to all systems supported by our toolkit. As such, it speeds up evaluation allowing more time to be invested into the design of the policies. The multi-platform approach also enables to determine differences between architectures, each of which have an impact on the availability of certain gadget classes. One specific gadget class can commonly occur on one architecture, while it is nearly non-existent on another architecture, consequently not posing a risk. Allowing researchers to focus on the most relevant gadget classes for each architecture may lead to defenses that fit more to the environment. While there are other toolkits that are able to locate gadgets on ARM, our framework differs in that it allows to apply the same CFI policies to different architectures.

Limitations. At the current state, we did not include a compiler that is able to generate complete chains from the found gadgets. While we simplify the task by providing a query interface, the last step is still manual. The simplest approach would be to blindly combine chains of gadgets until one of them satisfies the constraints. However, a better solution is to combine gadgets based on a logic that translates an intermediate language written by a developer to a series of gadgets. However, this is no easy task as avoding CFI detections requires longer and more complex gadgets, which are not side-effect free. The compiler would need to account for both, the intended effects and the compensation of any side effect of the gadget. Due to the modular design, we can support additional gadget types and architectures. For instance, it is possible to extend the discovery phase to locate unintended instructions or whole virtual functions needed for a COOP-attack [34]. Another option is extending the definitions by a limit of targets for an IC of a gadget. This allows assessing fine-grained CFI defenses.

7 Conclusion

We presented a framework that not only discovers code-reuse gadgets across multiple architectures, but also locates gadgets that can be used with deployed CFI defenses. While our framework can be used in an offensive way, we deem its value for defensive research to be higher. By quickly testing CFI constraints on multiple architectures, it is possible to focus on the most relevant attack vectors and improve both the defensive capabilities and the performance. In this process, we also showed that it is possible to locate CFI-compatible gadgets not only on x86, but also on ARM. CFI research is lacking behind on mobile platform and we hope that by providing an effective evaluation tool, further work on this topic can be simplified.

Acknowledgment. This work was supported by ERC Starting Grant No. 640110 (BASTION).

References

1. Abadi, M., Budiu, M., Erlingsson, U., Ligatti, J.: Control-flow integrity. In: ACM Conference on Computer and Communications Security (CCS) (2005)
2. Abadi, M., Budiu, M., Erlingsson, U., Ligatti, J.: Control-flow integrity principles, implementations, and applications. ACM Trans. Inform. Syst. Secur. (TISSEC) (2009)
3. Bletsch, T., Jiang, X., Freeh, V.W., Liang, Z.: Jump-oriented programming: a new class of code-reuse attack. In: ACM Symposium on Information, Computer and Communications Security (ASIACCS) (2011)
4. Bypassing Microsoft EMET 5.1 - Yet Again. http://blog.sec-consult.com/2014/11/bypassing-microsoft-emet-51-yet-again.html
5. Buchanan, E., Roemer, R., Shacham, H., Savage, S.: When good instructions go bad: generalizing return-oriented programming to RISC. In: ACM Conference on Computer and Communications Security (CCS) (2008)
6. Capstone - The Ultimate Disassembly Framework. http://www.capstone-engine.org/
7. Carlini, N., Wagner, D.: ROP is still dangerous: breaking modern defenses. In: USENIX Security Symposium (2014)
8. Checkoway, S., Davi, L., Dmitrienko, A., Sadeghi, A.-R., Shacham, H., Winandy, M.: Return-oriented programming without returns. In: ACM Conference on Computer and Communications Security (CCS) (2010)
9. Cheng, Y., Zhou, Z., Yu, M., Ding, X., Deng, R.H.: ROPecker: a generic and practical approach for defending against ROP attacks. In: Symposium on Network and Distributed System Security (NDSS) (2014)
10. Cowan, C., Pu, C., Maier, D., Hintony, H., Walpole, J., Bakke, P., Beattie, S., Grier, A., Wagle, P., Zhang, Q.: StackGuard: automatic adaptive detection and prevention of buffer-overflow attacks. In: USENIX Security Symposium (1998)
11. Disarming and Bypassing EMET 5.1. https://www.offensive-security.com/vulndev/disarming-and-bypassing-emet-5-1/
12. Davi, L., Dmitrienko, A., Egele, M., Fischer, T., Holz, T., Hund, R., Nürnberger, S., Sadeghi, A.: MoCFI: a framework to mitigate control-flow attacks on smartphones. In: Symposium on Network and Distributed System Security (NDSS) (2012)
13. Davi, L., Dmitrienko, A., Sadeghi, A.-R., Winandy, M.: Return-oriented programming without returns on ARM. Technical report, HGI-TR-2010-002, Ruhr-University Bochum (2010)
14. Davi, L., Lehmann, D., Sadeghi, A.-R., Monrose, F.: Stitching the gadgets: on the ineffectiveness of coarse-grained control-flow integrity protection. In: USENIX Security Symposium (2014)
15. Changes to Functionality in Microsoft Windows XP Service Pack 2. https://technet.microsoft.com/en-us/library/bb457151.aspx
16. Designer, S.: Return-to-Libc. Attack (1997)
17. Enhanced Mitigation Experience Toolkit - EMET - TechNet Security. https://technet.microsoft.com/en-us/security/jj653751
18. Microsoft Security Toolkit Delivers New BlueHat Prize Defensive Technology — News Center. http://news.microsoft.com/2012/07/25/microsoft-security-toolkit-delivers-new-bluehat-prize-defensive-technology/
19. Follner, A., Bartel, A., Bodden, E.: Analyzing the gadgets. In: Caballero, J., Bodden, E., Athanasopoulos, E. (eds.) ESSoS 2016. LNCS, vol. 9639, pp. 155–172. Springer, Heidelberg (2016). doi:10.1007/978-3-319-30806-7_10

20. Göktaş, E., Athanasopoulos, E., Bos, H., Portokalidis, G.: Out of control: overcoming control-flow integrity. In: IEEE Symposium on Security and Privacy (2014)
21. Göktaş, E., Athanasopoulos, E., Polychronakis, M., Bos, H., Portokalidis, G.: Size does matter: why using gadget-chain length to prevent code-reuse attacks is hard. In: USENIX Security Symposium (2014)
22. Hund, R., Holz, T., Freiling, F.C.: Return-oriented rootkits: bypassing kernel code integrity protection mechanisms. In: USENIX Security Symposium (2009)
23. IDA Sploiter. https://thesprawl.org/projects/ida-sploiter/
24. Joly, N.: Criminals are getting smarter: analysis of the adobe acrobat/reader 0-day exploit, September 2009. http://web.archive.org/web/20141018060115/, http://www.vupen.com/blog/20100909.Adobe_Acrobat_Reader_0_Day_Exploit_CVE-2010-2883_Technical_Analysis.php
25. Kornau, T.: Return-oriented programming for the ARM architecture (2009). http://www.zynamics.com/downloads/kornau-tim-diplomarbeit-rop.pdf
26. Krahmer, S.: x86-64 buffer overflow exploits and the borrowed code chunks exploitation technique (2005). http://users.suse.com/~krahmer/no-nx.pdf
27. Microsoft-Research. Z3: Theorem Prover (2014). http://z3.codeplex.com/
28. Pakt. ROPC - A Turing Complete ROP Compiler. https://github.com/pakt/ropc
29. Pappas, V., Polychronakis, M., Keromytis, A.D.: Transparent ROP exploit mitigation using indirect branch tracing. In: USENIX Security Symposium (2013)
30. PaX Team. Address Space Layout Randomization (2001). https://pax.grsecurity.net/docs/aslr.txt
31. Pelletier, A.: Advanced Exploitation of Internet Explorer Heap Overflow (Pwn2Own 2012 Exploit), July 2012. http://web.archive.org/web/20141005134545/, http://www.vupen.com/blog/20120710.Advanced_Exploitation_of_Internet_Explorer_HeapOv_CVE-2012-1876.php
32. Pewny, J., Holz, T.: Control-flow restrictor: compiler-based CFI for iOS. In: Annual Computer Security Applications Conference (ACSAC) (2013)
33. ROPgadget - Gadgets finder and auto-roper. http://shell-storm.org/project/ROPgadget/
34. Schuster, F., Tendyck, T., Liebchen, C., Davi, L., Sadeghi, A.-R., Holz, T.: Counterfeit object-oriented programming: on the difficulty of preventing code-reuse attacks in C++ applications. In: IEEE Symposium on Security and Privacy (2015)
35. Schuster, F., Tendyck, T., Pewny, J., Maaß, A., Steegmanns, M., Contag, M., Holz, T.: Evaluating the effectiveness of current Anti-ROP defenses. In: Stavrou, A., Bos, H., Portokalidis, G. (eds.) RAID 2014. LNCS, vol. 8688, pp. 88–108. Springer, Heidelberg (2014)
36. Schwartz, E.J., Avgerinos, T., Brumley, D.: Q: exploit hardening made easy. In: USENIX Security Symposium (2011)
37. Shacham, H.: The geometry of innocent flesh on the bone: return-into-libc without function calls (on the x86). In: ACM Conference on Computer and Communications Security (CCS) (2007)
38. Shoshitaishvili, Y.: Pyvex - GitHub. https://github.com/zardus/pyvex
39. Shoshitaishvili, Y.: Pyvex@d81bfe0 - GitHub. https://github.com/zardus/pyvex/commit/d81bfe0ee7583d599bdd6d6c8cc091a61a42e01e
40. Shoshitaishvili, Y., Wang, R., Hauser, C., Kruegel, C., Vigna, G.: Firmalice - automatic detection of authentication bypass vulnerabilities in binary firmware. In: Symposium on Network and Distributed System Security (NDSS) (2015)
41. Snow, K.Z., Monrose, F., Davi, L., Dmitrienko, A., Liebchen, C., Sadeghi, A.-R.: Just-in-time code reuse: on the effectiveness of fine-grained address space layout randomization. In: IEEE Symposium on Security and Privacy (2013)

42. Valgrind Home. http://valgrind.org/
43. XROP - Tool to generate ROP gadgets for ARM, x86, MIPS and PPC. https://github.com/acama/xrop
44. Zhang, C., Wei, T., Chen, Z., Duan, L., Szekeres, L., McCamant, S., Song, D., Zou, W.: Practical control-flow integrity and randomization for binary executables. In: IEEE Symposium on Security and Privacy (2013)
45. Zhang, M., Sekar, R.: Control-flow integrity for COTS binaries. In: USENIX Security Symposium (2013)

Author Index